Com… …ries

Engli…
Italian…

Peter F. Ross BSc

Pan Books London and Sydney

Trademarks

The symbol ® designates entered words that we have reason to believe constitute trademarks. However, neither the presence or absence of such designation should be regarded as affecting the legal status of any trademark.

Marchi di fabbrica depositati

Il simbolo ® viene usato per indicare le voci che crediamo costituiscono marchi di fabbrica depositati. Comunque si voglia notare che nè tale indicazione nè l'assenza di esso in alcun modo incidono sulla validità legale del marchio stesso.

First published 1982 by Pan Books Ltd.
Cavaye Place, London SW10 9PG

ISBN 0 330 26651 9
Printed and bound in Great Britain by Hunt Barnard Printing Ltd., Aylesbury, Bucks.

Abbreviations/Abbreviazioni

adj adjective
admin administration
adv adverb
aero aeronautics
agg aggettivo
agric agriculture, agricoltura
anat anatomy, anatomia
arch architecture, architettura
art article, articolo
astrol astrology, astrologia
astron astronomy, astronomia
auto automobilismo
aux auxiliary
avv avverbio
biol biology, biologia
bot botany, botanica
chem chemistry
chim chimica
coll colloquial
comm commerce, commercio
cong congiunzione
conj conjunction
derog derogatory
dir diritto
econ economics, economia
elec electricity
elett elettricità
f feminine, femminile
fam familiar, familiare
ferr ferrovia
fig figurato
filos filosofia
fis fisica
foto fotografia
gastr gastronomia
geog geography, geografia
geol geology, geologia
geom geometry, geometria
gramm grammar, grammatica
impol impolite
inter interiezione
interj interjection
invar invariable, invariabile
m masculine, maschile
mar marina
mat matematica
math mathematics
mec mechanical, meccanica
med medicine, medicina
mil military, militare
n noun
naut nautical
phone telephone
phot photography
pl plural, plurale
pol politics, politica
prep preposition, preposizione
pron pronoun, pronome
psic psicologia, psichiatria
psych psychology, psychiatry
rail railways
rel religion, religione
s sostantivo
sing singular, singolare
spreg spregiativo
tec tecnologia
tech technical
TV television, televisione
v verb, verbo
V vide (see, vedi)
volg volgare
zool zoology, zoologia

Italian pronunciation

As wide variations exist between pronunciations in different parts of Italy, we have favoured the standard accepted in the north as this is rapidly gaining general acceptance.

a sano ['sano]
ɛ bene ['bɛne]
e festa ['festa]
i tinto ['tinto]
ɔ brodo ['brɔdo]
o mondo ['mondo]
u fune ['fune]
b bene ['bɛne]
d dito ['dito]
f fine ['fine]
g gallo ['gallo]
j lezione [le'tsjone]
k capo ['kapo]
l legge ['leddʒe]
m mago ['mago]
n nitido ['nitido]
p pulce ['pultʃe]
r rete ['rete]
s sabbia ['sabbja]
t tanto ['tanto]
v via ['via]
w quando ['kwando]
z viso ['vizo]
dz zucchero ['dzukkero]
ts anzi ['antsi]
ʃ sciame ['ʃame]
tʃ cibo ['tʃibo]
dʒ gentile [dʒen'tile]
ʎ figlio ['fiʎo]
ɲ ragno ['raɲo]
ŋ smoking ['zmɔkiŋ]

The symbol ' indicates that the following syllable should be stressed.

Pronuncia inglese

a hat [hat]
e bell [bell]
i big [big]
o dot [dot]
ʌ bun [bʌn]
u book [buk]
ə alone [ə'loun]
a: card [ka:d]
ə: word [wə:d]
i: team [ti:m]
o: torn [to:n]
u: spoon [spu:n]
ai die [dai]
ei ray [rei]
oi toy [toi]
au how [hau]
ou road [roud]
eə lair [leə]
iə fear [fiə]
uə poor [puə]
b back [bak]
d dull [dʌl]
f find [faind]
g gaze [geiz]
h hop [hop]
j yell [jel]
k cat [kat]
l life [laif]
m mouse [maus]
n night [nait]
p pick [pik]
r rose [rouz]
s sit [sit]
t toe [tou]
v vest [vest]
w week [wi:k]
z zoo [zu:]
θ think [θiŋk]
ð those [ðouz]
ʃ shoe [ʃu:]
ʒ treasure ['treʒə]
tʃ chalk [tʃo:k]
dʒ jump [dʒʌmp]
ŋ sing [siŋ]

Il simbolo ' precede la sillaba che ha l'accento tonico principale.
Il simbolo ˌ precede la sillaba che ha l'accento tonico secondario.

Guide to the dictionary

Irregular plural forms are shown at the headword and in the text. The following categories of Italian plural forms are considered regular:

alber**o**	alber**i**
vial**e**	vial**i**
chies**a**	chies**e**
ami**ca**	ami**che**
lun**ga**	lun**ghe**
città	città
tesi	tesi

In addition, masculine Italian words ending in **-a** are considered regular if they form their plural in **-i**. Masculine words ending in **-co** and **-go** form their plurals in **-chi** and **-ghi** unless the word is of more than two syllables and the **-co** or **-go** preceded by a vowel, in which case the plural is formed in **-ci** and **-gi**. Exceptions to this rule are considered irregular.

Irregular verbs listed in the verb tables are marked with an asterisk in the headword list. Compounds are not listed in the verb tables.

Adverbs are shown only if their formation is irregular. English adverbs are considered regular if they are formed by adding *-ly* or *-ally* to the adjective. Italian adverbs are considered regular if they are formed by adding *-mente* to the feminine form of the adjective.

Guida all'uso del vocabolario

I plurali irregolari dei sostantivi sono indicati sia sotto la voce di partenza sia nel testo stesso. Le seguenti categorie vengono considerate di formazione regolare in inglese:

cat	cats
glass	glasses
fly	flies
half	halves
wife	wives

I verbi irregolari nell'apposita tavola sono contraddistinti con un asterisco nella lista delle voci di partenza. Non sono compresi nella tavola i verbi composti.

Gli avverbi sono indicati con voci proprie solo quando si tratta di formazioni irregolari. Vengono considerati regolari in inglese gli avverbi formati con l'aggiunta di *-ly* o di *-ally* all'aggettivo. Vengono considerati regolari in italiano gli avverbi formati mediante l'aggiunta di *-mente* al femminile dell'aggettivo.

Italian irregular verbs

Infinitive	Present	Past Absolute	Future	Past Participle
addurre	adduco	addussi	addurrò	addotto
affiggere	affiggo	affissi	affiggerò	affisso
affliggere	affliggo	afflissi	affliggerò	afflitto
alludere	alludo	allusi	alluderò	alluso
andare	vado	andai	andrò	andato
annettere	annetto	annessi	annetterò	annesso
apparire	appaio	apparvi	apparirò	apparso
appendere	appendo	appesi	appenderò	appeso
aprire	apro	aprii	aprirò	aperto
ardere	ardo	arsi	ardirò	arso
assistere	assisto	assistetti	assisterò	assistito
assolvere	assolvo	assolsi	assolverò	assolto
assumere	assumo	assunsi	assumerò	assunto
avere	ho	ebbi	avrò	avuto
bere	bevo	bevvi	berrò	bevuto
cadere	cado	caddi	cadrò	caduto
cogliere	colgo	colsi	coglierò	colto
comprimere	comprimo	compressi	comprimerò	compresso
concedere	concedo	concedetti	concederò	concesso
conoscere	conosco	conobbi	conoscerò	conosciuto
correre	corro	corsi	correrò	corso
crescere	cresco	crebbi	crescerò	cresciuto
cuocere	cuocio	cossi	cuocerò	cotto
dare	do	diedi	darò	dato
dire	dico	dissi	dirò	detto
dirigere	dirigo	diressi	dirigerò	diretto
discutere	discuto	discussi	discuterò	discusso
dissuadere	dissuado	dissuasi	dissuaderò	dissuaso
distinguere	distinguo	distinsi	distinguerò	distinto
dolere	dolgo	dolsi	dorrò	doluto
dovere	debbo	dovetti	dovrò	dovuto
emergere	emergo	emersi	emergerò	emerso
erigere	erigo	eressi	erigerò	eretto
esigere	esigo	esigetti	esigerò	esatto
espellere	espello	espulsi	espellerò	espulso
esplodere	esplodo	esplosi	esploderò	esploso
essere	sono	fui	sarò	stato

Infinitive	Present	Past Absolute	Future	Past Participle
estinguere	estinguo	estinsi	estinguerò	estinto
evadere	evado	evasi	evaderò	evaso
fare	faccio	feci	farò	fatto
flettere	fletto	flessi	fletterò	flesso
fondere	fondo	fusi	fonderò	fuso
friggere	friggo	frissi	friggerò	fritto
giacere	giaccio	giacqui	giacerò	giaciuto
godere	godo	godetti	godrò	goduto
incutere	incuto	incussi	incuterò	incusso
infliggere	infliggo	inflissi	infliggerò	inflitto
invadere	invado	invasi	invaderò	invaso
leggere	leggo	lessi	leggerò	letto
mettere	metto	misi	metterò	messo
mordere	mordo	morsi	morderò	morso
morire	muoio	morii	morirò	morto
muovere	muovo	mossi	muoverò	mosso
nascere	nasco	nacqui	nascerò	nato
nascondere	nascondo	nascosi	nasconderò	nascosto
nuocere	nuoccio	nocqui	nuocerò	nociuto
offrire	offro	offersi	offrirò	offerto
parere	paio	parvi	parrò	parso
perdere	perdo	perdetti	perderò	perso
persuadere	persuado	persuasi	persuaderò	persuaso
piacere	piaccio	piacque	piacerò	piaciuto
porgere	porgo	porsi	porgerò	porto
porre	pongo	posi	porrò	posto
potere	posso	potei	potrò	potuto
proteggere	proteggo	protessi	proteggerò	protetto
redimere	redimo	redensi	redimerò	redento
redigere	redigo	redassi	redigerò	redatto
reggere	reggo	ressi	reggerò	retto
rifulgere	rifulgo	rifulsi	rifulgerò	rifulso
rimanere	rimango	rimasi	rimarrò	rimasto
rispondere	rispondo	risposi	risponderò	risposto
rodere	rodo	rosi	roderò	roso
rompere	rompo	ruppi	romperò	rotto
sapere	so	seppi	saprò	saputo
scegliere	scelgo	scelsi	sceglierò	scelto
scindere	scindo	scissi	scinderò	scisso

Infinitive	Present	Past Absolute	Future	Past Participle
sciogliere	sciolgo	sciolsi	scioglierò	sciolto
scoprire	scopro	scoprii	scoprirò	scoperto
scorgere	scorgo	scorsi	scorgerò	scorto
scrivere	scrivo	scrissi	scriverò	scritto
scuotere	scuoto	scossi	scuoterò	scosso
sedere	siedo	sedetti	sederò	seduto
solere	soglio	solei	solerò	solito
sommergere	sommergo	sommersi	sommergerò	sommerso
sorgere	sorgo	sorsi	sorgerò	sorto
spandere	spando	spansi	spanderò	spanto
spargere	spargo	sparsi	spargerò	sparso
spegnere	spengo	spensi	spegnerò	spento
stare	sto	stetti	starò	stato
stringere	stringo	strinsi	stringerò	stretto
struggere	struggo	strussi	struggerò	strutto
svellere	svello	svelsi	svellerò	svelto
tacere	taccio	tacqui	tacerò	taciuto
tenere	tengo	tenni	terrò	tenuto
togliere	tolgo	tolsi	toglierò	tolto
torcere	torco	torsi	torcerò	torto
trarre	traggo	trassi	trarrò	tratto
udire	odo	udii	udirò	udito
ungere	ungo	unsi	ungerò	unto
uscire	esco	uscii	uscirò	uscito
valere	valgo	valsi	varrò	valso
vedere	vedo	vidi	vedrò	visto
venire	vengo	venni	verrò	venuto
vincere	vinco	vinsi	vincerò	vinto
vivere	vivo	vissi	vivrò	vissuto
volere	voglio	volli	vorrò	voluto
volgere	volgo	volsi	volgerò	volto

For verbs ending in:

-cedere see **concedere**
-durre see **addurre**
-endere see **appendere**
-figgere see **affiggere**
-idere or **-udere** see **alludere**
-nettere see **annettere**
-ngere (except **stringere**) see **ungere**
-parire see **apparire**
-primere see **comprimere**
-sistere see **assistere**

Verbi inglesi irregolari

Infinito	Preterito	Participo Passato	Infinito	Preterito	Participo Passato
abide	abode	abode	**deal**	dealt	dealt
arise	arose	arisen	**dig**	dug	dug
awake	awoke	awoken	**do**	did	done
be	was	been	**draw**	drew	drawn
bear	bore	borne *or* born	**dream**	dreamed *or* dreamt	dreamed *or* dreamt
beat	beat	beaten	**drink**	drank	drunk
become	became	become	**drive**	drove	driven
begin	began	begun	**dwell**	dwelt	dwelt
behold	beheld	beheld	**eat**	ate	eaten
bend	bent	bent	**fall**	fell	fallen
bet	bet	bet	**feed**	fed	fed
beware			**feel**	felt	felt
bid	bid	bidden *or* bid	**fight**	fought	fought
			find	found	found
bind	bound	bound	**flee**	fled	fled
bite	bit	bitten	**fling**	flung	flung
bleed	bled	bled	**fly**	flew	flown
blow	blew	blown	**forbid**	forbade	forbidden
break	broke	broken	**forget**	forgot	forgotten
breed	bred	bred	**forgive**	forgave	forgiven
bring	brought	brought	**forsake**	forsook	forsaken
build	built	built	**freeze**	froze	frozen
burn	burnt *or* burned	burnt *or* burned	**get**	got	got
			give	gave	given
burst	burst	burst	**go**	went	gone
buy	bought	bought	**grind**	ground	ground
can	could		**grow**	grew	grown
cast	cast	cast	**hang**	hung *or* hanged	hung *or* hanged
catch	caught	caught			
choose	chose	chosen	**have**	had	had
cling	clung	clung	**hear**	heard	heard
come	came	come	**hide**	hid	hidden
cost	cost	cost	**hit**	hit	hit
creep	crept	crept	**hold**	held	held
cut	cut	cut	**hurt**	hurt	hurt

Infinito	Preterito	Participo Passato	Infinito	Preterito	Participo Passato
keep	kept	kept	**say**	said	said
kneel	knelt	knelt	**see**	saw	seen
knit	knitted	knitted	**seek**	sought	sought
	or knit	*or* knit	**sell**	sold	sold
know	knew	known	**send**	sent	sent
lay	laid	laid	**set**	set	set
lead	led	led	**sew**	sewed	sewn
lean	leant	leant			*or* sewed
	or leaned	*or* leaned	**shake**	shook	shaken
leap	leapt	leapt	**shear**	sheared	sheared
	or leaped	*or* leaped			*or* shorn
learn	learnt	learnt	**shed**	shed	shed
	or learned	*or* learned	**shine**	shone	shone
leave	left	left	**shoe**	shod	shod
lend	lent	lent	**shoot**	shot	shot
let	let	let	**show**	showed	shown
lie	lay	lain	**shrink**	shrank	shrunk
light	lit	lit	**shut**	shut	shut
	or lighted	*or* lighted	**sing**	sang	sung
lose	lost	lost	**sink**	sank	sunk
make	made	made	**sit**	sat	sat
may	might		**sleep**	slept	slept
mean	meant	meant	**slide**	slid	slid
meet	met	met	**sling**	slung	slung
mow	mowed	mown	**slink**	slunk	slunk
must			**slit**	slit	slit
ought			**smell**	smelt	smelt
pay	paid	paid		*or* smelled	*or* smelled
put	put	put	**sow**	sowed	sown
quit	quitted	quitted			*or* sowed
	or quit	*or* quit	**speak**	spoke	spoken
read	read	read	**speed**	sped	sped
rid	rid	rid		*or* speeded	*or* speeded
ride	rode	ridden	**spell**	spelt	spelt
ring	rang	rung		*or* spelled	*or* spelled
rise	rose	risen	**spend**	spent	spent
run	ran	run	**spill**	spilt	spilt
saw	sawed	sawn		*or* spilled	*or* spilled
		or sawed	**spin**	spun	spun

Infinito	Preterito	Participo Passato	Infinito	Preterito	Participo Passato
spit	spat	spat	**swim**	swam	swum
split	split	split	**swing**	swung	swung
spread	spread	spread	**take**	took	taken
spring	sprang	sprung	**teach**	taught	taught
stand	stood	stood	**tear**	tore	torn
steal	stole	stolen	**tell**	told	told
stick	stuck	stuck	**think**	thought	thought
sting	stung	stung	**throw**	threw	thrown
stink	stank	stunk	**thrust**	thrust	thrust
	or stunk		**tread**	trod	trodden
stride	strode	stridden	**wake**	woke	woken
strike	struck	struck	**wear**	wore	worn
string	strung	strung	**weave**	wove	woven
strive	strove	striven	**weep**	wept	wept
swear	swore	sworn	**win**	won	won
sweep	swept	swept	**wind**	wound	wound
swell	swelled	swollen	**wring**	wrung	wrung
		or swelled	**write**	wrote	written

English–Italiano

A

a, an [ə, ən] *art* un, uno *m*; una *f*.
aback [ə'bak] *adv* **be taken aback** essere colto di sorpresa.
abandon [ə'bandən] *v* abbandonare. *n* abbandono *m*.
abashed [ə'baʃt] *adj* confuso.
abate [ə'beit] *v* diminuire. **abatement** *n* diminuzione *f*.
abattoir ['abətwaː] *n* macello *m*.
abbey ['abi] *n* abbazia *f*. **abbess** *n* badessa *f*. **abbot** *n* abate *m*.
abbreviate [ə'briːvieit] *v* abbreviare. **abbreviation** *n* abbreviazione *f*.
abdicate ['abdikeit] *v* abdicare. **abdication** *n* abdicazione *f*.
abdomen ['abdəmən] *n* addome *m*. **abdominal** *adj* addominale.
abduct [əb'dʌkt] *v* rapire. **abduction** *n* rapimento *m*.
aberration [abə'reiʃən] *n* aberrazione *f*. **aberrant** *adj* aberrante.
abet [ə'bet] *v* favoreggiare. **aid and abet** farsi complice di.
abeyance [ə'beiəns] *n* sospensione *f*. **in abeyance** in sospeso.
abhor [əb'hoː] *v* aborrire. **abhorrence** *n* aborrimento *m*. **abhorrent** *adj* aborrevole, odioso.
***abide** [ə'baid] *v* (*wait*) aspettare; (*tolerate*) soffrire. **abide by** sostenere, restar fedele a.
ability [ə'biləti] *n* abilità *f*. **to the best of one's ability** come meglio potrà.
abject [ˌabdʒekt] *adj* abietto.
ablaze [ə'bleiz] *adj* in fiamme, risplendente.
able ['eibl] *adj* capace; (*talented*) abile. **able-bodied** *adj* robusto. **be able** potere, essere in grado di.
abnormal [ab'noːml] *adj* anormale. **abnormality** *n* anormalità *f*.
aboard [ə'boːd] *adv*, *prep* a bordo (di). **all aboard!** tutti a bordo! **go aboard** imbarcarsi.
abode [ə'boud] *V* **abide**. *n* dimora *f*.
abolish [ə'boliʃ] *v* abolire. **abolition** *n* abolizione *f*.
abominable [ə'bominəbl] *adj* abominevole. **abominate** *v* detestare. **abomination** *n* abominazione *f*.
aborigine [abə'ridʒini] *n* indigeno *m*.
abortion [ə'boːʃən] *n* aborto *m*. **abort** *v* abortire.
abound [ə'baund] *v* abbondare.
about [ə'baut] *adv* (*around*) intorno; (*nearly*) verso, presso; circa; (*concerning*) su. *prep* di, su; intorno a. **be about to** stare per.
above [ə'bʌv] *adv* in alto, di sopra. *prep* sopra, al di sopra di; (*number*) più di; (*rank*) superiore a. **above all** sopratutto. **above-mentioned** *adj* suddetto. **from above** dall'alto.
abrasion [ə'breiʒən] *n* abrasione *f*. **abrasive** *adj* abrasivo.
abreast [ə'brest] *adv* **keep abreast of** *or* **with** tenersi al corrente di. **two abreast** due per due.
abridge [ə'bridʒ] *v* abbreviare. **abridgement** *n* abbreviazione *f*.
abroad [ə'broːd] *adv* all'estero.
abrupt [ə'brʌpt] *adj* brusco.
abscess ['abses] *n* ascesso *m*.
abscond [əb'skond] *v* rendersi latitante.
absent ['absənt] *adj* assente. **absent-minded** *adj* distratto. *v* **absent oneself** assentarsi. **absence** *n* assenza *f*. **absentee** *n* assente *m*. **absenteeism** *n* assenteismo *m*.
absolute ['absəluːt] *adj* assoluto. **absolutely** *adv* assolutamente, perfettamente. **absolutism** *n* assolutismo *m*.

absolve [əb'zolv] *v* assolvere. **absolution** *n* assoluzione *f*.
absorb [əb'zoːb] *v* assorbire. **be absorbed in** essere concentrato in. **absorbent** *adj* assorbente. **absorbing** *adj* (*coll*) molto interessante. **absorption** *n* assorbimento *m*.
abstain [əb'stein] *v* astenersi. **abstention** *n* astensione *f*.
abstemious [əb'stiːmiəs] *adj* astemio.
abstinence ['abstinəns] *n* astinenza *f*.
abstract ['abstrakt; *v* ab'strakt] *adj* astratto. *v* astrarre. **abstractedly** *adv* distrattamente. **abstraction** *n* astrazione *f*.
absurd [əb'səːd] *adj* assurdo, ridicolo. **absurdity** *n* assurdità *f*.
abundance [ə'bʌndəns] *n* abbondanza *f*. **abundant** *adj* abbondante.
abuse [ə'bjuːs; *v* ə'bjuːz] *n* abuso *m*; insulto *m*. *v* abusare di, maltrattare; insultare, oltraggiare. **abusive** *adj* offensivo; abusivo.
abyss [ə'bis] *n* abisso *m*. **abysmal** *adj* abissale; profondo.
academy [ə'kadəmi] *n* accademia *f*. **academic** *n*, *adj* accademico, -a.
accede [ak'siːd] *v* accedere.
accelerate [ək'seləreit] *v* accelerare. **acceleration** *n* accelerazione *f*. **accelerator** *n* acceleratore *m*.
accent ['aksənt] *n* accento *m*. *v* accentuare; (*gramm*) accentare.
accept [ək'sept] *v* accettare, accogliere. **acceptable** *adj* (*agreeable*) gradevole; accettabile. **acceptance** *n* accettazione *f*.
access ['akses] *n* accesso *m*. **accessible** *adj* accessibile.
accessory [ək'sesəri] *n* accessorio *m*; (*law*) complice *m*, *f*. *adj* accessorio.
accident ['aksidənt] *n* accidente *m*, infortunio *m*. **by accident** per caso. **accidental** *adj* fortuito.
acclaim [ə'kleim] *v* acclamare. *n also* **acclamation** acclamazione *f*.
acclimatize [ə'klaimətaiz] *v* acclimatare.
accolade ['akəleid] *n* abbraccio *m*.
accommodate [ə'komədeit] *v* accomodare; (*lodge*) ospitare; (*provide*) provvedere (di). **accommodating** *adj* cortese, conciliante. **accommodation** *n* (*housing*) alloggio *m*; (*hotel*) posto *m*.
accompany [ə'kʌmpəni] *v* accompagnare. **accompaniment** *n* accompagnamento *m*. **accompanist** *n* accompagnatore, -trice *m*, *f*.
accomplice [ə'kʌmplis] *n* complice *m*, *f*.
accomplish [ə'kʌmpliʃ] *v* compiere, realizzare. **accomplished** *adj* (*talented*) compito. **accomplishment** *n* effettuazione *f*; talento *m*.
accord [ə'koːd] *v* concedere, accordare. *n* accordo *m*. **of one's own accord** spontaneamente. **in accordance with** in conformità con. **accordingly** *adv* pertanto, quindi, di conseguenza. **according to** secondo.
accordion [ə'koːdiən] *n* fisarmonica *f*.
accost [ə'kost] *v* rivolgersi a.
account [ə'kaunt] *n* (*report*) relazione *f*, versione *f*; (*status*) importanza *f*; (*bank*) conto *m*. **by all accounts** a quanto si dice. **on no account** a nessuna condizione. **on one's own account** per propria iniziativa. *v* **account for** spiegare la ragione di, giustificare. **accountant** *n* contabile *m*, *f*, ragioniere *m*.
accrue [ə'kruː] *v* accrescere.
accumulate [ə'kjuːmjuleit] *v* accumulare. **accumulation** *n* ammasso *m*, accumulamento *m*.
accurate ['akjurət] *adj* accurato, preciso. **accuracy** *n* accuratezza *f*, precisione *f*.
accuse [ə'kjuːz] *v* accusare, incolpare. **the accused** *n* l'imputato, -a *m*, *f*. **accusation** *n* accusa *f*.
accustom [ə'kʌstəm] *v* abituare.
ace [eis] *n* asso *m*. **within an ace of** a un dito di.
ache [eik] *n* dolore *m*. *v* far male, dolere.
achieve [ə'tʃiːv] *v* concludere, ottenere, compiere. **achievement** *n* compimento *m*, successo *m*.
acid ['asid] *nm*, *adj* acido.
acknowledge [ək'nolidʒ] *v* riconoscere, ammettere. **acknowledge receipt of** accusare ricevuta di. **acknowledgement** *n* riconoscimento *m*; ricevuta *f*.
acne ['akni] *n* acne *m*.
acorn ['eikoːn] *n* ghianda *f*.
acoustic [ə'kuːstik] *adj* acustico. **acoustics** *pl n* acustica *f sing*.
acquaint [ə'kweint] *v* avvertire, mettere al corrente. **acquaintance** *n* (*knowledge*) conoscenza *f*; (*person*) conoscente *m*, *f*. **become acquainted with** (*person*) fare la conoscenza di; (*thing*) informarsi su.
acquiesce [akwi'es] *v* acconsentire tacitamente. **acquiescence** *n* acquiescenza *f*. **acquiescent** *adj* acquiescente.

acquire [ə'kwaiə] *v* acquisire, acquistare.
acquisition [akwi'ziʃən] *n* acquisto *m*; acquisizione *f*. **acquisitive** *adj* avido di guadagno.
acquit [ə'kwit] *v* esonerare. **acquit oneself** comportarsi. **acquittal** *n* (*law*) assoluzione *f*.
acrid ['akrid] *adj* acre, pungente.
acrimony ['akriməni] *n* acrimonia *f*. **acrimonious** *adj* acrimonioso, astioso.
acrobat ['akrəbat] *n* acrobata *m*, *f*. **acrobatic** *adj* acrobatico. **acrobatics** *pl n* acrobazie *f pl*.
across [ə'kros] *adv* per traverso; (*crossword*) orizzontali. *prep* al di là di, attraverso.
acrylic [ə'krilik] *adj* acrilico.
act [akt] *v* agire; (*theatre*) recitare; (*behave*) comportarsi. **act as** fungere da. **act for** agire per conto di. *n* (*deed*) azione *f*; (*theatre*) atto *m*; (*law*) decreto *m*. **actor** *n* attore *m*. **actress** *n* attrice *f*.
action ['akʃən] *n* azione *f*; (*law*) processo *m*; (*mil*) combattimento *m*. **out of action** fuori uso.
active ['aktiv] *adj* attivo, energico. **activate** *v* attivare. **activist** *n* attivista *m*. **activity** *n* attività *f*.
actual ['aktʃuəl] *adj* effettivo, reale. **actually** *adv* effettivamente.
actuate ['aktjueit] *v* mettere in atto *or* moto.
acupuncture ['akjupʌŋktʃə] *n* acupuntura *f*.
acute [ə'kjuːt] *adj* acuto, perspicace.
adamant ['adəmənt] *adj* inflessibile.
Adam's apple [adəm'zapl] *n* pomo d'Adamo *m*.
adapt [ə'dapt] *v* adattare, modificare. **adaptability** *n* adattibilità *f*. **adaptable** *adj* adattabile. **adaptation** *n* adattamento *m*. **adapter** *n* (*theatre*) riduttore *m*; (*elec*) raccordo *m*.
add [ad] *v* aggiungere. **add to** aumentare. **add up** fare la somma di, sommare. **addition** *n* addizione *f*. **additional** *adj* supplementare.
addendum [ə'dendəm] *n* aggiunta *f*.
adder ['adə] *n* vipera *f*.
addict ['adikt; *v* ə'dikt] *n* (*drug*) drogato, -a *m*, *f*, tossicomane *m*, *f*. **be addicted to** essere abituato *or* dedito a. **addiction** *n* dedizione *f*; tossicomania *f*.
additive ['aditiv] *n* aggiunta *f*.
address [ə'dres] *v* (*letter*) indirizzare; (*meeting, etc.*) rivolgere la parola a, fare un discorso a. **address oneself to** mettersi a. *n* (*speech*) discorso *m*; (*letter*) indirizzo *m*, recapito *m*. **addressee** *n* destinatario *m*.
adenoids ['adənoidz] *pl n* adenoidi *f pl*.
adept [ə'dept] *nm*, *adj* esperto.
adequate ['adikwət] *adj* sufficiente, adeguato.
adhere [əd'hiə] *v* aderire, attaccarsi. **adhesion** *n* adesione *f*. **adhesive** *nm*, *adj* adesivo.
adherent [əd'hiərənt] *n* partigiano *m*, seguace *m*.
adjacent [ə'dʒeisənt] *adj* adiacente, contiguo.
adjective ['adʒiktiv] *n* aggettivo *m*.
adjoin [ə'dʒoin] *v* confinare (con). **adjoining** *adj* adiacente.
adjourn [ə'dʒəːn] *v* aggiornare, rinviare. **adjournment** *n* rinvio *m*.
adjudicate [ə'dʒuːdikeit] *v* aggiudicare. **adjudicator** *n* arbitro *m*.
adjust [ə'dʒʌst] *v* regolare, mettere a punto. **adjustment** *n* adattamento *m*, rettifica *f*.
ad-lib ['ad'lib] *v* improvvisare.
administer [əd'ministə] *v* amministrare; (*med*) somministrare. **administration** *n* amministrazione *f*. **administrative** *adj* amministrativo. **administrator** *n* amministratore, -trice *m*, *f*.
admiral ['admərəl] *n* ammiraglio *m*.
admire [əd'maiə] *v* ammirare. **admirable** *adj* ammirevole. **admiration** *n* ammirazione *f*. **admiringly** *adv* con meraviglia.
admit [əd'mit] *v* ammettere; concedere; confessare. **admissible** *adj* ammissibile. **admission** *n* ammissione *f*. **admittance** *n* ingresso *m*, entrata *f*.
adolescence [adə'lesns] *n* adolescenza *f*. **adolescent** *n*(*m*+*f*), *adj* adolescente.
adopt [ə'dopt] *v* adottare. **adopted** *adj* (*child*) adottivo. **adoption** *n* adozione *f*.
adore [ə'doː] *v* adorare. **adoration** *n* adorazione *f*.
adorn [ə'doːn] *v* abbellire, guarnire. **adornment** *n* ornamento *m*.
adrenaline [ə'drenəlin] *n* adrenalina *f*.
adrift [ə'drift] *adv* alla deriva.
adroit [ə'droit] *adj* abile, destro.
adulation [adju'leiʃən] *n* adulazione *f*.
adult ['adʌlt] *n*, *adj* adulto, -a.

adulterate [ə'dʌltəreit] *v* adulterare; (*wine*) sofisticare.
adultery [ə'dʌltəri] *n* adulterio *m*. **adulterer** *n* adultero, -a *m*, *f*.
advance [əd'vaːns] *v* avanzare, progredire, anticipare. *n* avanzamento *m*; (*mil*) marcia in avanti *f*; (*cash*) anticipo *m*. **book in advance** prenotare.
advantage [əd'vaːntidʒ] *n* vantaggio *m*, beneficio *m*. **take advantage of** approfittare di. **advantageous** *adj* vantaggioso.
advent ['advənt] *n* avvento *m*.
adventure [əd'ventʃə] *n* avventura *f*, impresa rischiosa *f*. **adventurer** *n* avventuriero *m*. **adventurous** *adj* avventuroso.
adverb ['advəːb] *n* avverbio *m*.
adversary ['advəsəri] *n* avversario, -a *m*, *f*.
adverse ['advəːs] *adj* avverso. **adversity** *n* avversità *f*.
advertise ['advətaiz] *v* annunziare, fare pubblicità a. **advertisement** *n* annunzio *m*, inserzione *f*. **advertising** *n* pubblicità *f*.
advise [əd'vaiz] *v* consigliare, raccomandare. **ill-advised** *adj* imprudente, inopportuno. **well-advised** *adj* saggio. **advice** *n* consiglio *m*, suggerimento *m*. **advisable** *adj* opportuno, consigliabile. **adviser** *n* consulente *m*, *f*. **advisory** *adj* consultivo.
advocate ['advəkeit] *v* sostenere.
aerial ['eəriəl] *adj* aereo. *n* antenna *f*.
aerodynamics [eərədai'namiks] *n* aerodinamica *f*.
aeronautics [eərə'noːtiks] *n* aeronautica *f*.
aeroplane ['eərəplein] *n* aereo *m*.
aerosol ['eərəsol] *n* aerosol *m*.
aesthetic [iːs'θetik] *adj* estetico. **aesthetics** *n* estetica *f*.
affair [ə'feə] *n* affare *m*. **have an affair** avere una relazione intima.
affect[1] [ə'fekt] *v* (*influence*) colpire, toccare.
affect[2] [ə'fekt] *v* (*pretend*) fingere, simulare.
affection [ə'fekʃən] *n* affetto *m*, affezione *f*. **affectionate** *adj* affezionato.
affiliate [ə'filieit] *v* affiliare. **affiliation** *n* affiliazione *f*.
affinity [ə'finəti] *n* affinità *f*.
affirm [ə'fəːm] *v* affermare, confermare. **affirmation** *n* affermazione *f*, conferma *f*. **affirmative** *adj* affermativo.
affix [ə'fiks] *v* affiggere.
afflict [ə'flikt] *v* affliggere, angosciare. **affliction** *n* afflissione *f*, dolore *m*.
affluent ['afluənt] *adj* ricco, opulento. **affluence** *n* affluenza *f*, ricchezza *f*.
afford [ə'foːd] *v* avere i mezzi per; (*produce*) dare, offrire; (*allow oneself to*) permettersi di.
affront [ə'frʌnt] *n* affronto *m*, offesa *f*. *v* insultare, offendere.
afloat [ə'flout] *adv* a galla.
afoot [ə'fut] *adv* a piedi; (*fig*) in atto.
aforesaid [ə'foːsed] *adj* suddetto, soprannominato.
afraid [ə'freid] *adj* impaurito, pauroso, spaventato. **be afraid of** temere, aver paura di.
afresh [ə'freʃ] *adv* da capo, nuovamente.
Africa ['afrikə] *n* Africa *f*. **African** *n*, *adj* africano, -a.
aft [aːft] *adv* a poppa.
after ['aːftə] *prep* dopo, in seguito a. *adv* dopo, poi. *conj* dopo che. **after all** dopo tutto, insomma. **afterwards** *adv* dopo, poi.
afternoon [ˌaːftə'nuːn] *n* pomeriggio *m*, dopo pranzo *m*. **good afternoon!** buona sera!
aftershave ['aːftəʃeiv] *n* dopobarba *m invar*.
again [ə'gen] *adv* di nuovo, ancora. **again and again** ripetutamente. **never again** mai più.
against [ə'genst] *prep* contro, in opposizione a.
age [eidʒ] *n* età *f*; era *f*. **of age** maggiorenne. **old age** vecchiaia *f*. **under age** minorenne. *v* invecchiare. **aged** *adj* vecchio; (*seasoned*) invecchiato.
agency ['eidʒənsi] *n* agenzia *f*, rappresentanza *f*.
agenda [ə'dʒendə] *n* ordine del giorno *m*.
agent ['eidʒənt] *n* agente *m*, *f*; rappresentante *m*, *f*.
aggravate ['agrəveit] *v* aggravare; (*coll*) irritare. **aggravation** *n* aggravamento *m*; (*coll*) irritazione *f*.
aggregate ['agrigət] *nm*, *adj* aggregato.
aggression [ə'greʃən] *n* aggressione *f*. **aggressive** *adj* aggressivo. **aggressor** *n* aggressore *m*.
aghast [ə'gaːst] *adj* stupefatto, atterrito.
agile ['adʒail] *adj* agile. **agility** *n* agilità *f*.
agitate ['adʒiteit] *v* agitare, turbare. **agitation** *n* agitazione *f*. **agitator** *n* agitatore, -trice *m*, *f*.

agnostic [ag'nostik] *n, adj* agnostico, -a. **agnosticism** *n* agnosticismo *m.*

ago [ə'gou] *adv* fa.

agog [ə'gog] *adj* bramoso.

agony ['agəni] *n* agonia *f,* angoscia *f.* **be in agony** soffrire dolori atroci.

agree [ə'griː] *v* essere *or* andare d'accordo, convenire, accordarsi. **agreeable** *adj* piacevole, simpatico. **agreement** *n* accordo *m,* patto *m,* contratto *m.*

agriculture ['agrikʌltʃə] *n* agricoltura *f.* **agricultural** *adj* agricolo.

aground [ə'graund] *adv* arenato. **run aground** incagliarsi.

ahead [ə'hed] *adv* (in) avanti.

aid [eid] *v* aiutare, sovvenire, soccorrere. *n* aiuto *m,* sussidio *m.* **first aid** pronto soccorso *m.* **in aid of** a favore di.

aim [eim] *v* puntare, prendere di mira; aspirare. *n* mira *f;* (*purpose*) scopo *m,* proposito *m.*

air [eə] *n* aria *f;* (*bearing*) aspetto *m,* contegno *m. v* ventilare.

airbed ['eəbed] *n* materassimo pneumatico *m.*

airborne ['eəbɔːn] *adj* aerotrasportato.

air-conditioned *adj* ad aria condizionata.

aircraft ['eəkraːft] *n* aereo *m.* **aircraft-carrier** *n* portaerei *m invar.*

airfield ['eəfiːld] *n* campo d'aviazione *m.*

air force *n* aviazione *f.*

air-hostess *n* assistente di volo *f,* hostess *f invar.*

air lift *n* ponte aereo *m.*

airline ['eəlain] *n* linea aerea *f.*

airmail ['eəmeil] *n* posta aerea *f.*

airport ['eəpɔːt] *n* aeroporto *m.*

air-raid *n* incursione aerea *f.* **air-raid shelter** rifugio contraereo *m.*

airtight ['eətait] *adj* ermetico, impenetrabile all'aria.

airy ['eəri] *adj* arioso, ben ventilato.

aisle [ail] *n* navata *f.*

ajar [ə'dʒaː] *adj* socchiuso.

akin [ə'kin] *adj* simile, parente.

alabaster ['aləbaːstə] *n* alabastro *m.*

alarm [ə'laːm] *n* allarme *m.* **alarm clock** sveglia *f. v* allarmare.

alas [ə'las] *interj* purtroppo!

Albania [al'beinjə] *n* Albania *f.* **Albanian** *n(m+f), adj* albanese.

albatross ['albətros] *n* albatro *m.*

albino [al'biːnou] *n, adj* albino -a.

album ['albəm] *n* album *m.*

alchemy ['alkəmi] *n* alchimia *f.* **alchemist** *n* alchimista *m, f.*

alcohol ['alkəhol] *n* alcool *m.*

alcoholic [alkə'holik] *adj* alcoolico. *n* alcoolizzato, -a *m, f.* **alcoholism** *n* alcoolismo *m.*

alcove ['alkouv] *n* nicchia *f.*

alderman ['oːldəmən] *n* assessore municipale *m.*

ale [eil] *n* birra *f.*

alert [ə'ləːt] *adj* vigilante. *v* avvertire. **be on the alert** stare all'erta.

algebra ['aldʒibrə] *n* algebra *f.*

alias ['eiliəs] *adv* altrimenti detto.

alibi ['alibai] *n* alibi *m invar.*

alien ['eiliən] *n, adj* straniero, -a, forestiero, -a. **alienate** *v* alienare. **alienation** *n* alienazione *f.*

alight[1] [ə'lait] *v* scendere, smontare.

alight[2] [ə'lait] *adj* acceso, illuminato.

align [ə'lain] *v* allineare.

alike [ə'laik] *adj* simile, somigliante. *adv* ugualmente. **be alike** assomigliarsi.

alimentary canal [ali'mentəri] *adj* alimentare.

alimony ['aliməni] *n* alimenti *m pl.*

alive [ə'laiv] *adj* vivo, vivente. **alive to** sensibile a.

alkaline ['alkəlain] *adj* alcalino.

all [oːl] *adj* tutto. *adv* completamente. *n* tutti *m pl,* tutte *f pl.* **all right!** va bene! **All Saints' Day** Ognissanti *m.* **All Souls' Day** giorno dei morti *m.* **all the same** con tutto ciò. **not at all** niente affatto.

allay [ə'lei] *v* calmare.

allege [ə'ledʒ] *v* allegare, asserire. **alleged** *adj* sedicente.

allegiance [ə'liːdʒəns] *n* obbedienza *f,* fedeltà *f.*

allegory ['aligəri] *n* allegoria *f.*

allergy ['alədʒi] *n* allergia *f.* **allergic** *adj* allergico.

alleviate [ə'liːvieit] *v* alleviare, attenuare.

alley ['ali] *n* vicolo *m.*

alliance [ə'laiəns] *n* alleanza *f,* patto *m.*

alligator ['aligeitə] *n* alligatore *m.*

alliteration [əlitə'reiʃən] *n* allitterazione *f.*

allocate ['aləkeit] *v* assegnare, collocare. **allocation** *n* assegnamento *m.*

allot [ə'lot] *v* assegnare. **allotment** *n* (*land*) lotto *m,* pezzo di terreno *m;* (*portion*) parte assegnata *f.*

allow [ə'lau] *v* permettere, concedere. **allow for** tener conto di. **allow me!**

permetta! **allowance** *n* (*grant*) assegno *m*; (*reduction*) sconto *m*.
alloy ['aloi; *v* ə'loi] *n* lega *f*. *v* legare, amalgamare.
allude [ə'luːd] *v* riferirsi (a), alludere (a). **allusion** *n* allusione *f*, riferimento *m*.
allure [ə'ljuə] *n* fascino *m*. *v* affascinare. **alluring** *adj* seducente.
ally ['alai; *v* ə'lai] *n* alleato, -a *m, f*. *v* alleare.
almanac ['oːlmənak] *n* almanacco *m*.
almighty [oːl'maiti] *adj* onnipotente. **the Almighty** *n* il Padreterno *m*.
almond ['aːmənd] *n* (*nut*) mandorla *f*; (*tree*) mandorlo *m*.
almost ['oːlmoust] *adv* quasi.
alms [aːmz] *pl n* elemosina *f sing*. **give alms** fare l'elemosina. **almshouse** *n* ospizio dei poveri *m*.
aloft [ə'loft] *adv* in alto.
alone [ə'loun] *adj* solo. *adv* solo, da solo; (*only*) solamente. **leave alone** lasciar stare.
along [ə'loŋ] *prep* lungo. **along with** insieme a. **come along!** su! avanti! **alongside** *prep* accanto a.
aloof [ə'luːf] *adj* riservato, freddo. *adv* a distanza.
aloud [ə'laud] *adv* ad alta voce.
alphabet ['alfəbit] *n* alfabeto *m*.
Alps [alps] *pl n* **the Alps** le Alpi *f pl*. **alpine** *adj* alpino.
already [oːl'redi] *adv* già.
also ['oːlsou] *adv* anche, pure, inoltre.
altar ['oːltə] *n* altare *m*. **altarpiece** *n* pala d'altare *f*. **high altar** altare maggiore *m*.
alter ['oːltə] *v* alterare, cambiare, alterarsi. **alteration** *n* cambiamento *m*, mutamento *m*.
alternate ['oːltəneit; *adj* oːl'təːnət] *v* alternare, alternarsi, succedersi. *adj* alterno. **alternation** *n* alternazione *f*, successione reciproca *f*.
alternative [oːl'təːnətiv] *adj* alternativo. *n* alternativa *f*.
although [oːl'ðou] *conj* sebbene, benché.
altitude ['altitjuːd] *n* altezza *f*, altitudine *f*; (*aircraft*) quota *f*.
altogether [oːltə'geðə] *adv* complessivamente, nell'insieme.
altruistic [altru'istik] *adj* altruistico. **altruism** *n* altruismo *m*. **altruist** *n* altruista *m, f*.
aluminium [alju'miniəm] *n* alluminio *m*.
always ['oːlweiz] *adv* sempre.
am [am] *V* **be**.
amalgamate [ə'malgəmeit] *v* amalgamare. **amalgam** *n* amalgama *m*.
amass [ə'mas] *v* accumulare.
amateur ['amətə] *n* dilettante *m, f*. **amateurish** *adj* da dilettante.
amaze [ə'meiz] *v* stupire, meravigliare. **amazement** *n* stupore *m*, meraviglia *f*. **amazing** *adj* straordinario, stupendo.
ambassador [am'basədə] *n* ambasciatore, -trice *m, f*.
amber ['ambə] *n* ambra *f*.
ambidextrous [ambi'dekstrəs] *adj* ambidestro.
ambiguous [am'bigjuəs] *adj* ambiguo.
ambition [am'biʃən] *n* ambizione *f*. **ambitious** *adj* ambizioso.
ambivalent [am'bivələnt] *adj* ambivalente.
amble ['ambl] *v* camminare lentamente.
ambulance ['ambjuləns] *n* ambulanza *f*.
ambush ['ambuʃ] *n* imboscata *f*, agguato *m*. *v* tendere un agguato.
ameliorate [ə'miːliəreit] *v* migliorare.
amenable [ə'miːnəbl] *adj* trattabile, suscettibile.
amend [ə'mend] *v* emendare, correggere. **amendment** *n* emendamento *m*, correzione *f*. **make amends** fare ammenda.
amenity [ə'miːnəti] *n* amenità *f*. **amenities** *pl n* comodità *f pl*.
America [ə'merikə] *n* America *f*. **American** *n, adj* americano, -a.
amethyst ['aməθist] *n* ametista *f*.
amiable ['eimiəbl] *adj* gentile, amabile.
amicable ['amikəbl] *adj* amichevole.
amid [ə'mid] *prep* fra, tra, in mezzo a.
amiss [ə'mis] *adv* **take amiss** aversene a male.
ammonia [ə'mouniə] *n* ammoniaca *f*.
ammunition [amju'niʃən] *n* munizioni *f pl*.
amnesia [am'niːziə] *n* amnesia *f*.
amnesty ['amnəsti] *n* amnistia *f*.
amoeba [ə'miːbə] *n* ameba *f*.
among [ə'mʌŋ] *prep* fra, tra, in mezzo a.
amoral [ei'morəl] *adj* amorale.
amorous ['amərəs] *adj* amoroso.
amorphous [ə'moːfəs] *adj* amorfo.
amount [ə'maunt] *n* quantità *f*, importo *m*, somma *f*. *v* ammontare, equivalere.
ampere ['ampeə] *n* ampere *m invar*.
amphetamine [am'fetəmiːn] *n* amfetamina *f*, anfetamina *f*.

amphibian [am'fibiən] *nm, adj* anfibio.
amphitheatre ['amfiθiətə] *n* anfiteatro *m.*
ample ['ampl] *adj* ampio, abbondante.
amplify ['amplifai] *v* amplificare, ampliare. **amplification** *n* amplificazione *f.* **amplifier** *n* amplificatore *m.*
amputate ['ampjuteit] *v* amputare. **amputation** *n* amputazione *f.*
amuse [ə'mjuːz] *v* divertire, dilettare. **amusement** *n* divertimento *m,* svago *m.* **amusing** *adj* divertente, buffo.
anachronism [ə'nakrənizəm] *n* anacronismo *m.*
anaemia [ə'niːmiə] *n* anemia *f.* **anaemic** *adj* anemico.
anaesthetic [anəs'θetik] *nm, adj* anestetico. **anaesthesia** *n* anestesia *f.* **anaesthetist** *n* anestesista *m, f.* **anaesthetize** *v* anestetizzare.
anagram ['anəgram] *n* anagramma *m.*
anal ['einl] *adj* anale.
analogy [ə'nalədʒi] *n* analogia *f.* **analogous** *adj* analogo (*m pl* -ghi).
analysis [ən'aləsis] *n, pl* **-ses** analisi *f.* **analyse** *v* analizzare. **analyst** *n* analista *m, f.* **analytical** *adj* analitico.
anarchy ['anəki] *n* anarchia *f.* **anarchic** *adj* anarchico. **anarchist** *n* anarchico, -a *m, f.*
anathema [ə'naθəmə] *n* anatema *f.*
anatomy [ə'natəmi] *n* anatomia *f.* **anatomical** *adj* anatomico. **anatomist** *n* anatomista *m, f.*
ancestor ['ansestə] *n* antenato *m.* **ancestral** *adj* avito. **ancestry** *n* stirpe *f,* lignaggio *m.*
anchor ['aŋkə] *n* ancora *f.* *v* ancorare.
anchovy ['antʃəvi] *n* acciuga *f.*
ancient ['einʃənt] *adj* antico (*m pl* -chi), anziano.
ancillary [an'siləri] *adj* ausiliario, sussidiario.
and [and] *conj* e, ed.
anecdote ['anikdout] *n* aneddoto *m.*
anemone [ə'neməni] *n* anemone *m.*
anew [ə'njuː] *adv* da capo, di nuovo.
angel ['eindʒəl] *n* angelo *m.* **angelic** *adj* angelico.
anger ['aŋgə] *n* rabbia *f,* stizza *f,* ira *f.* *v* far arrabbiare.
angina [an'dʒainə] *n* (*med*) angina *f.*
angle ['aŋgl] *n* (*corner*) angolo *m*; (*viewpoint*) punto di vista *m.*
angling ['aŋgliŋ] *n* pesca all'amo *f.* **angler** *n* pescatore *m.*
angry ['aŋgri] *adj* arrabbiato, stizzito.
anguish ['aŋgwiʃ] *n* angoscia *f,* tormento *m.* *v* angosciare, tormentare.
angular ['aŋgjulə] *adj* angolare.
animal ['animəl] *n* animale *m,* bestia *f.* *adj* animale.
animate ['animət; *v* 'animeit] *adj* animato, vivente. *v* animare. **animated** *adj* vivace. **animation** *n* animazione *f.*
animosity [ani'mosəti] *n* animosità *f.*
aniseed ['anisiːd] *n* anice *m.*
ankle ['aŋkl] *n* caviglia *f.*
annals ['anlz] *pl n* annali *m pl.*
annex [ə'neks; *n* 'aneks] *v* annettere. *n* annesso *m*; (*hotel*) dipendenza *f.* **annexation** *n* annessione *f.*
annihilate [ə'naiəleit] *v* annientare. **annihilation** *n* annientamento *m.*
anniversary [ˌani'vəːsəri] *nm, adj* anniversario.
annotate ['anəteit] *v* annotare.
announce [ə'nauns] *v* annunciare, rendere noto. **announcement** *n* annuncio *m.* **announcer** *n* annunciatore, -trice *m, f.*
annoy [ə'noi] *v* dar noia a, disturbare, seccare. **annoyance** *n* fastidio *m,* noia *f.* **annoying** *adj* seccante, fastidioso.
annual ['anjuəl] *adj* annuale, annuo. *n* (*book*) annuario *m*; (*plant*) pianta annuale *f.* **annually** *adv* annualmente.
annuity [ə'njuːəti] *n* annualità *f.* **life annuity** *n* vitalizio *m.*
annul [ə'nʌl] *v* annullare. **annulment** *n* annullamento *m.*
•**Annunciation** [əˌnʌnsi'eiʃn] *n* (*rel*) Annunziazione *f.*
anode ['anoud] *n* anodo *m.*
anomaly [ə'noməli] *n* anomalia *f.* **anomalous** *adj* anomalo, irregolare.
anonymous [ə'noniməs] *adj* anonimo.
anorak ['anərak] *n* giacca a vento *f.*
another [ə'nʌðə] *adj, pron* un altro. **one another** l'un l'altro.
answer ['aːnsə] *v* rispondere (a). **answer for** rispondere di. *n* risposta *f.*
ant [ant] *n* formica *f.* **ant-hill** *n* formicaio *m.*
antagonize [an'tagənaiz] *v* provocare l'ostilità (di). **antagonism** *n* antagonismo *m.* **antagonist** *n* antagonista *m, f.*
antecedent [anti'siːdənt] *adj* antecedente. **antecedents** *pl n* precedenti *m pl*; (*forbears*) antenati *m pl.*

antelope ['antəloup] *n* antilope *f*.
antenatal [anti'neitl] *adj* prenatale.
antenna [an'tenə] *n* antenna *f*.
anthem ['anθəm] *n* inno *m*.
anthology [an'θolədʒi] *n* antologia *f*.
anthropology [anθrə'polədʒi] *n* antropologia *f*. **anthropologist** *n* antropologo, -a *m, f*.
anti-aircraft [anti'eəkraːft] *adj* contraereo.
antibiotic [antibai'otik] *nm, adj* antibiotico.
antibody ['anti,bodi] *n* anticorpo *m*.
anticipate [an'tisipeit] *v* anticipare, prevenire. **in anticipation** in anticipo.
anticlimax [anti'klaimaks] *n* conclusione banale *f*.
anticlockwise [anti'klokwaiz] *adj, adv* in senso antiorario.
antics ['antiks] *pl n* buffoneria *f sing*.
anticyclone [anti'saikloun] *n* anticiclone *m*.
antidote ['antidout] *n* antidoto *m*.
antifreeze ['antifriːz] *n* antigelo *m*.
antipathy [an'tipəθi] *n* antipatia *f*.
antique [an'tiːk] *adj* antico (*m pl* -chi). *n* oggetto antico *m*. **antique dealer** *n* antiquario *m*. **antiquity** *n* antichità *f*.
anti-Semitic [antisə'mitik] *n* antisemita *m, f*. **anti-Semitism** *n* antisemitismo *m*.
antiseptic [anti'septik] *nm, adj* antisettico.
antisocial [anti'souʃəl] *adj* antisociale.
anti-tank [anti'taŋk] *adj* anticarro.
antithesis [an'tiθəsis] *n, pl* **-ses** antitesi *f*.
antler ['antlə] *n* corno *m*.
antonym ['antənim] *n* antonimo *m*.
anus ['einəs] *n* ano *m*.
anvil ['anvil] *n* incudine *f*.
anxious ['aŋkʃəs] *adj* ansioso, preoccupato. **anxiety** *n* ansia *f*, ansietà *f*.
any ['eni] *adj* del, della, etc.; qualche *invar*; alcuno. *pron* alcuno, nessuno, ne. **anybody** *or* **anyone** *pron* qualcuno, alcuno; chiunque. **anyhow** *or* **anyway** *adv* in ogni caso, tuttavia; ad ogni modo. **anything** *pron* qualcosa, qualche cosa; (*everything*) qualunque cosa. **anywhere** *adv* in qualunque luogo, in alcun luogo; (*everywhere*) dovunque.
apart [ə'paːt] *adv* a parte, in disparte. **come apart** disfarsi. **tell apart** distinguere l'uno dall'altro.
apartment [ə'paːtmənt] *n* appartamento *m*, alloggio *m*.
apathy ['apəθi] *n* apatia *f*. **apathetic** *adj* apatico.
ape [eip] *n* scimmia *f*. *v* scimmiottare, imitare.
aperitif [əperi'tiːf] *n* aperitivo *m*.
aperture ['apətjuə] *n* apertura *f*.
apex ['eipeks] *n* vertice *m*, apice *m*.
aphid ['eifid] *n* afide *m*.
aphrodisiac [afrə'diziak] *n* afrodisiaco *m*.
apiece [ə'piːs] *adv* a testa, per ciascuno, per uno.
apology [ə'polədʒi] *n* scusa *f*, giustificazione *f*. **apologetic** *adj* apologetico. **apologize** *v* chiedere scusa, scusarsi.
apoplexy ['apəpleksi] *n* apoplessia *f*. **apoplectic** *adj* apoplettico. **apoplectic fit** colpo apoplettico *m*.
apostle [ə'posl] *n* apostolo *m*.
apostrophe [ə'postrəfi] *n* (*punctuation*) apostrofo *m*; (*speech*) apostrofe *f*.
appal [ə'poːl] *v* inorridire, sgomentare. **appalling** *adj* terribile, spaventoso.
apparatus [apə'reitəs] *n* apparecchio *m*, apparato *m*.
apparent [ə'parənt] *adj* apparente, evidente, manifesto.
apparition [apə'riʃən] *n* visione *f*, fantasma *m*.
appeal [ə'piːl] *n* appello *m*. *v* appellarsi, fare appello; (*law*) ricorrere in appello. **appealing** *adj* attraente, commovente.
appear [ə'piə] *v* apparire, sembrare, parere. **appearance** *n* apparenza *f*, aspetto *m*. **put in an appearance** fare atto di presenza.
appease [ə'piːz] *v* calmare, pacificare. **appeasement** *n* pacificazione *f*.
appendix [ə'pendiks] *n* appendice *m*. **appendicitis** *n* appendicite *f*.
appetite ['apitait] *n* appetito *m*. **appetizing** *adj* gustoso, succolento.
applaud [ə'ploːd] *v* applaudire. **applause** *n* applauso *m*.
apple ['apl] *n* (*fruit*) mela *f*; (*tree*) melo *m*.
apply [ə'plai] *v* rivolgersi, fare domanda; (*refer*) riferirsi; (*use*) applicare. **apply oneself to** dedicarsi a. **appliance** *n* apparecchio *m*, strumento *m*. **applicable** *adj* applicabile, idoneo. **applicant** *n* candidato *m*. **application** *n* domanda *f*, richiesta *f*. **application form** modulo di richiesta *m*.
appoint [ə'point] *v* nominare; (*arrange*) fissare. **appointment** *n* (*engagement*) appuntamento *m*; (*post*) nomina *f*.

apportion [ə'pɔːʃən] *v* distribuire.
appraisal [ə'preizl] *n* valutazione *f*. **appraise** *v* stimare, valutare.
appreciate [ə'priːʃieit] *v* (*esteem*) apprezzare, stimare; (*be aware of*) rendersi conto di; (*increase in value*) aumentare di valore. **appreciable** *adj* apprezzabile, sensibile. **appreciation** *n* apprezzamento *m*, stima *f*.
apprehend [apri'hend] *v* cogliere, arrestare. **apprehension** *n* arresto *m*; (*worry*) timore *m*. **apprehensive** *adj* timoroso, preoccupato.
apprentice [ə'prentis] *n* apprendista *m, f*. **apprenticeship** *n* tirocinio *m*, apprendistato *m*.
approach [ə'proutʃ] *v* avvicinare; (*come near*) avvicinarsi (a). *n* avvicinamento *m*, accesso *m*.
appropriate [ə'proupriət; *v* ə'prouprieit] *adj* adatto, opportuno. *v* impadronirsi di.
approve [ə'pruːv] *v* approvare, dare il benestare. **approval** *n* approvazione *f*, benestare *m*. **on approval** in visione, in esame. **approved** *adj* approvato, convalidato, riconosciuto.
approximate [ə'proksimeit; *adj* ə'proksimət] *v* approssimare. *adj* approssimativo. **approximately** *adv* approssimativamente, all'incirca, su per giù.
apricot ['eiprikot] *n* (*fruit*) albicocca *f*; (*tree*) albicocco *m*.
April ['eiprəl] *n* aprile *m*.
apron ['eiprən] *n* grembiule *m*, grembiale *m*.
apt [apt] *adj* atto, adatto.
aptitude ['aptitjuːd] *n* abilità *f*, attitudine *f*.
aqualung ['akwəlʌŋ] *n* autorespiratore *m*.
aquarium [ə'kweəriəm] *n* acquario *m*.
Aquarius [ə'kweəriəs] *n* Acquario *m*.
aquatic [ə'kwatik] *adj* acquatico.
aqueduct ['akwidʌkt] *n* acquedotto *m*.
Arab ['arəb] *n, adj* arabo, -a. **Arabia** *n* Arabia *f*. **Arabic** *n* (*language*) arabo *m*.
arable ['arəbl] *adj* arabile.
arbitrary ['aːbitrəri] *adj* arbitrario.
arbitrate ['aːbitreit] *v* arbitrare. **arbitration** *n* arbitraggio *m*.
arc [aːk] *n* arco *m*. **arc lamp** lampada ad arco *f*.
arcade [aː'keid] *n* portico *m*, galleria *f*.
arch[1] [aːtʃ] *n* arco *m*, volta *f*. *v* curvare, arcuare.
arch[2] [aːtʃ] *adj* (*chief*) arci-.
archaeology [aːki'olədʒi] *n* archeologia *f*. **archaeologist** *n* archeologo, -a *m, f*.
archaic [aː'keiik] *adj* arcaico.
archbishop [aːtʃ'biʃəp] *n* arcivescovo *m*.
archduke [aːtʃ'djuːk] *n* arciduca *m*.
archery ['aːtʃəri] *n* tiro all'arco *m*. **archer** *n* arciere *m*.
archetype ['aːkitaip] *n* archetipo *m*.
archipelago [aːki'peləgou] *n* arcipelago (*pl* -ghi) *m*.
architect ['aːkitekt] *n* architetto, -a *m, f*. **architecture** *n* architettura *f*.
archives ['aːkaivz] *pl n* archivio *m sing*.
arctic ['aːktik] *adj* artico.
ardent ['aːdənt] *adj* ardente, appassionato.
ardour ['aːdə] *n* ardore *m*, fervore *m*.
arduous ['aːdjuəs] *adj* arduo, difficile.
are [aː] *V* **be**.
area ['eəriə] *n* area *f*, superficie *f*, zona *f*.
arena [ə'riːnə] *n* arena *f*.
argue ['aːgjuː] *v* argomentare, discutere, disputare. **arguable** *adj* discutibile. **argument** *n* argomento *m*, discussione *f*. **argumentative** *adj* polemico.
arid ['arid] *adj* arido.
Aries ['eəriːz] *n* Ariete *m*.
***arise** [ə'raiz] *v* alzarsi, sorgere.
arisen [ə'rizn] *V* **arise**.
aristocracy [ari'stokrəsi] *n* aristocrazia *f*. **aristocrat** *n* aristocratico, -a *m, f*. **aristocratic** *adj* aristocratico.
arithmetic [ə'riθmətik] *n* aritmetica *f*.
ark [aːk] *n* arca *f*. **Noah's Ark** arca di Noè *f*.
arm[1] [aːm] *n* (*limb*) braccio *m* (*pl* -a *f*). **armchair** *n* poltrona *f*. **arm in arm** a braccetto. **armpit** *n* ascella *f*. **within arm's reach** a portata di mano.
arm[2] [aːm] *n* (*weapon*) arma (*pl* -i) *f*. **bear arms** essere sotto le armi. **be up in arms against** essere in rivolta contro. **coat of arms** stemma *m*. *v* armare.
armistice ['aːmistis] *n* armistizio *m*.
armour ['aːmə] *n* armatura *f*, corazza *f*. **armourer** *n* armiere *m*. **armour-plated** *adj* corazzato. **armoury** *n* arsenale *m*.
army ['aːmi] *n* esercito *m*, armata *f*.
aroma [ə'roumə] *n* aroma *m*.
arose [ə'rouz] *V* **arise**.
around [ə'raund] *prep* attorno a, intorno a. *adv* intorno. **all around** tutto intorno.
arouse [ə'rauz] *v* destare, eccitare.

arrange [ə'reindʒ] *v* accomodare, ordinare; (*music*) adattare; (*meeting, etc.*) organizzare; (*put in order*) sistemare. **arrangement** *n* combinazione *f*; accomodamento *m*; adattamento *m*. **come to an arrangement** mettersi d'accordo.
array [ə'rei] *n* schieramento *m*; mostra imponente *f*. *v* ornare, schierare.
arrears [ə'riəz] *pl n* arretrati *m pl*. **be in arrears** avere degli arretrati.
arrest [ə'rest] *n* arresto. **under arrest** in stato d'arresto. *v* arrestare, sospendere.
arrive [ə'raiv] *v* arrivare, giungere. **arrival** *n* arrivo *m*; (*person*) arrivato, -a *m, f*.
arrogant ['arəgənt] *adj* arrogante. **arrogance** *n* arroganza *f*.
arrow ['arou] *n* freccia *f*.
arse [aːs] *n* (*vulgar*) culo *m*.
arsenal ['aːsənl] *n* arsenale *m*.
arsenic ['aːsnik] *n* arsenico *m*.
arson ['aːsn] *n* incendio doloso *m*.
art [aːt] *n* arte *f*. **art gallery** galleria d'arte *f*, pinacoteca *f*. **artful** *adj* astuto.
artefact ['aːtifakt] *n* artefatto *m*.
artery ['aːtəri] *n* arteria *f*.
arthritis [aː'θraitis] *n* artrite *f*.
artichoke ['aːtitʃouk] *n* carciofo *m*.
article ['aːtikl] *n* articolo *m*; oggetto *m*.
articulate [aː'tikjuleit; *adj* aː'tikjulət] *v* articolare. *adj* articolato, distinto.
artifice ['aːtifis] *n* artifizio *m*, astuzia *f*.
artificial [aːti'fiʃəl] *adj* artificiale, finto. **artificiality** *n* artificiosità *f*.
artillery [aː'tiləri] *n* artiglieria *f*.
artisan [aːti'zan] *n* artigiano, -a *m, f*.
artist ['aːtist] *n* artista *m, f*. **artistic** *adj* artistico.
as [az] *adv* come, quanto. *conj* come; (*while*) mentre; (*because*) poiché, siccome. **as ... as** cosi ... come, tanto ... quanto. *prep* da. **as far as** (*distance*) sino a. **as for** *or* **to** per quanto riguarda. **as if** come se. **as long as** finché, purché. **as much** altrettanto. **as soon as** (non) appena. **as well** anche. **as well as** (*in addition to*) oltre a.
asbestos [az'bestos] *n* asbesto *m*, amianto *m*.
ascend [ə'send] *v* salire, ascendere. **ascendancy** *n* ascendente *m*. **ascension** *n* ascensione *f*. **ascent** *n* ascesa *f*, salita *f*.
ascertain [asə'tein] *v* accertarsi di, verificare.
ascetic [ə'setik] *adj* ascetico. *n* asceta *m, f*.
ash[1] [aʃ] *n* (*cinder*) cenere *f*. **ashen** *adj* cinereo. **ashtray** *n* portacenere *m*.
ash[2] [aʃ] *n* (*tree*) frassino *m*.
ashamed [ə'ʃeimd] *adj* vergognoso. **be ashamed of** vergognarsi di.
ashore [ə'ʃoː] *adv* a terra, sulla riva.
Ash Wednesday *n* mercoledì delle Ceneri *m*.
Asia ['eiʃə] *n* Asia *f*. **Asian** *n, adj* asiatico, -a.
aside [ə'said] *adv* da parte, a parte, in disparte. *n* (*theatre*) parole dette a parte *f pl*.
ask [aːsk] *v* domandare, chiedere. **ask about** informarsi di *or* su. **ask after** chiedere notizie di.
askew [ə'skjuː] *adv* di traverso.
asleep [ə'sliːp] *adj* addormentato. **fall asleep** addormentarsi.
asparagus [ə'sparəgəs] *n* asparago *m*.
aspect ['aspekt] *n* aspetto *m*, apparenza *f*.
asphalt ['asfalt] *n* asfalto *m*.
asphyxiate [əs'fiksieit]
aspire [ə'spaiə] *v* ambire. **aspiration** *n* ambizione *f*.
aspirin ['aspərin] *n* aspirina *f*.
ass [as] *n* asino *m*, somaro *m*.
assail [ə'seil] *v* assalire, aggredire. **assailant** *n* aggressore *m*.
assassinate [ə'sasineit] *v* assassinare. **assassin** *n* assassino, -a *m, f*. **assassination** *n* assassinio *m*.
assault [ə'soːlt] *n* assalto *m*, attacco *m*. *v* assalire, attaccare.
assemble [ə'sembl] *v* riunire, riunirsi; (*put together*) montare. **assembly** *n* assemblea *f*, riunione *f*. **assembly line** catena di montaggio *f*.
assent [ə'sent] *v* assentire, approvare. *n* assenso *m*, consenso *m*.
assert [ə'səːt] *v* asserire, sostenere. **assert oneself** farsi valere, imporsi. **assertion** *n* asserzione *f*, rivendicazione *f*.
assess [ə'ses] *v* valutare, stimare. **assessment** *n* valutazione *f*, imposizione di tassa *f*. **assessor** *n* assessore *m*, agente del fisco *m*.
asset ['aset] *n* bene *m*. **assets** *pl n* attività *f pl*.
assiduous [ə'sidjuəs] *adj* assiduo.
assign [ə'sain] *v* assegnare; (*law*) delegare. **assignee** *n* mandatario *m*. **assignment** *n* assegnazione *f*, attribuzione *f*.

assimilate [ə'simileit] *v* assimilare. **assimilation** *n* assimilazione *f*.
assist [ə'sist] *v* assistere, aiutare. **assistance** *n* assistenza *f*, soccorso *m*. **assistant** *n* assistente *m*, *f*, aiutante *m*, *f*; (*shop*) commesso, -a *m*, *f*.
associate [ə'sousieit; *n* ə'sousiət] *v* associare, associarsi. **associate with** frequentare. *n* socio, -a *m*, *f*, collega *m*, *f*. **association** *n* associazione *f*, società *f*; (*club*) circolo *m*.
assorted [ə'soːtid] *adj* assortito. **assortment** *n* assortimento *m*.
assume [ə'sjuːm] *v* assumere; presumere. **assumption** *n* assunzione *f*, supposizione *f*. **assuming that** supposto che.
assure [ə'ʃuə] *v* assicurare. **assurance** *n* assicurazione *f*, certezza *f*, promessa *f*.
asterisk ['astərisk] *n* asterisco *m*.
asthma ['asmə] *n* asma *m*.
astonish [ə'stoniʃ] *v* stupire, meravigliare. **astonishing** *adj* sbalorditivo, sorprendente. **astonishment** *n* sorpresa *f*, stupore *m*.
astound [ə'staund] *v* stupefare, stupire. **astounding** *adj* stupefacente, sbalorditivo.
astray [ə'strei] *adv* fuori strada. **go astray** smarrirsi. **lead astray** sviare, traviare.
astride [ə'straid] *adv* a cavalcioni.
astringent [ə'strindʒənt] *adj* astringente.
astrology [ə'strolədʒi] *n* astrologia *f*. **astrologer** *n* astrologo, -a *m*, *f*.
astronaut ['astrənoːt] *n* astronauta *m*, *f*.
astronomy [ə'stronəmi] *n* astronomia *f*. **astronomer** *n* astronomo, -a *m*, *f*. **astronomic(al)** *adj* astronomico.
astute [ə'stjuːt] *adj* astuto, furbo.
asunder [ə'sʌndə] *adv* a pezzi.
asylum [ə'sailəm] *n* ricovero *m*, rifugio *m*; (*for the insane*) manicomio *m*.
at [at] *prep* a, in, da.
ate [et] *V* **eat**.
atheism ['eiθiizəm] *n* ateismo *m*. **atheist** *n* ateo, -a *m*, *f*.
Athens ['aθinz] *n* Atene *f*. **Athenian** *n*(*m*+*f*), *adj* ateniese.
athlete ['aθliːt] *n* atleta *m*, *f*. **athletic** *adj* atletico. **athletics** *n* atletica *f*.
Atlantic [ət'lantik] *nm*, *adj* atlantico.
atlas ['atləs] *n* atlante *m*.
atmosphere ['atməsfiə] *n* atmosfera *f*; ambiente *m*. **atmospheric** *adj* atmosferico. **atmospherics** *pl n* disturbi atmosferici *m pl*.
atom ['atəm] *n* atomo *m*. **atomic** *adj* atomico.
atone [ə'toun] *v* espiare, fare ammenda. **atonement** *n* espiazione *f*.
atrocious [ə'trouʃəs] *adj* atroce, terribile. **atrocity** *n* atrocità *f*.
attach [ə'tatʃ] *v* attaccare, attribuire. **become attached to** affezionarsi a. **attachment** *n* (*friendship*) affezione *f*; (*law*) sequestro *m*; (*tech*) accessorio *m*.
attaché [ə'taʃei] *n* addetto *m*. **attaché case** *n* valigetta rigida *f*, borsa per documenti *f*.
attack [ə'tak] *v* attaccare, assalire. *n* attacco *m*; offensiva *f*; (*med*) accesso. **attacker** *n* aggressore *m*.
attain [ə'tein] *v* ottenere, raggiungere. **attainment** *n* raggiungimento *m*, conseguimento *m*. **attainments** *pl n* coltura *f sing*.
attempt [ə'tempt] *v* tentare, provare. *n* tentativo *m*, prova *f*; (*crime*) attentato *m*.
attend [ə'tend] *v* (*wait on*) servire, accompagnare; (*listen*) prestar attenzione; (*be present at*) assistere. **attendance** *n* presenza *f*; servizio *m*. **attendant** *n* inserviente *m*, *f*; sorvegliante *m*, *f*, assistente *m*, *f*.
attention [ə'tenʃən] *n* attenzione *f*, cura *f*. **pay attention** far attenzione, stare attento. **attentive** *adj* attento, sollecito, premuroso.
attic ['atik] *n* attico *m*, soffitta *f*.
attire [ə'taiə] *n* abbigliamento *m*. *v* vestire.
attitude ['atitjuːd] *n* atteggiamento *m*, posa *f*.
attorney [ə'təːni] *n* procuratore *m*. **power of attorney** procura *f*.
attract [ə'trakt] *v* attrarre, attirare; affascinare. **attraction** *n* attrazione *f*; fascino *m*. **attractive** *adj* attraente; affascinante.
attribute ['atribjuːt; *v* ə'tribjuːt] *n* attributo *m*, qualità *f*. *v* attribuire, ascrivere. **attribution** *n* attribuzione *f*.
attrition [ə'triʃən] *n* attrito *m*.
atypical [ei'tipikl] *adj* atipico.
aubergine ['oubəʒiːn] *n* melanzana *f*.
auburn ['oːbən] *adj invar* color rame.
auction ['oːkʃən] *n* asta. *v* vendere all'asta. **auctioneer** *n* venditore all'asta *m*, banditore *m*.
audacious [oː'deiʃəs] *adj* audace, intrepido. **audacity** *n* temerità *f*.

audible ['oːdəbl] *adj* udibile. **audibility** *n* udibilità *f.*
audience ['oːdjəns] *n* pubblico *m*; (*assembly of spectators*) uditorio *m*; (*formal interview*) udienza *f.*
audiovisual [oːdiou'viʒuəl] *adj* audiovisivo.
audit ['oːdit] *n* controllo *m*, verifica dei conti *f*, revisione *f*. *v* rivedere, verificare i conti. **auditor** *n* revisore di conti *m*; sindaco *m*.
audition [oː'diʃən] *n* audizione *f*. *v* ascoltare in audizione.
auditorium [oːdi'toːriəm] *n* sala per concerti *f*, auditorio *m*.
augment [oːg'ment] *v* aumentare, crescere.
August ['oːgəst] *n* agosto *m*.
aunt [aːnt] *n* zia *f*.
au pair [ou 'peə] *n* ragazza alla pari *f*.
aura ['oːrə] *n* aura *f*.
auspicious [oː'spiʃəs] *adj* propizio, di buon augurio.
austere [oː'stiə] *adj* austero. **austerity** *n* austerità *f*.
Australia [o'streiljə] *n* Australia *f*. **Australian** *n*, *adj* australiano, -a.
Austria ['ostriə] *n* Austria *f*. **Austrian** *n*, *adj* austriaco, -a.
authentic [oː'θentik] *adj* autentico. **authenticate** *v* convalidare. **authenticity** *n* autenticità *f*.
author ['oːθə] *n* autore, -trice *m*, *f*.
authority [oː'θorəti] *n* autorità *f*; (*influence*) ascendente *m*; (*accepted source*) fonte autorevole *f*. **on good authority** da fonte autorevole. **authoritative** *adj* autorevole. **authoritarian** *adj* autoritario.
authorize ['oːθəraiz] *v* autorizzare. **authorization** *n* autorizzazione *f*.
autobiography [oːtoubai'ogrəfi] *n* autobiografia *f*. **autobiographical** *adj* autobiografico.
autocratic [oːtou'kratik] *adj* autocratico.
autograph ['oːtəgraːf] *n* autografo *m*. *v* autografare.
automatic [oːtə'matik] *adj* automatico. **automation** *n* automazione *f*.
automobile ['oːtəməbiːl] *n* automobile *f*; (*fam*) macchina *f*.
autonomous [oː'tonəməs] *adj* autonomo.
autopsy ['oːtopsi] *n* autopsia *f*.
autumn ['oːtəm] *n* autunno *m*. **autumnal** *adj* autunnale.

auxiliary [oːg'ziljəri] *n*, *adj* ausiliario, -a.
avail [ə'veil] *v* servire, giovare a. **avail oneself of** servirsi di. *n* vantaggio *m*. **be of no avail** non servire a nulla.
available [ə'veiləbl] *adj* disponibile, libero; (*to hand*) sotto mano. **availability** *n* disponibilità *f*.
avalanche ['avəlaːnʃ] *n* valanga *f*.
avarice ['avəris] *n* avarizia *f*. **avaricious** *adj* avaro.
avenge [ə'vendʒ] *v* vendicare, vendicarsi. **avenger** *n* vendicatore, -trice *m*, *f*.
avenue ['avinjuː] *n* viale *m*.
average ['avəridʒ] *n* media *f*. **on average** in media. *adj* medio. *v* fare la media.
aversion [ə'vəːʃən] *n* avversione *f*, antipatia *f*. **not be averse to** non aver nulla in contrario a.
avert [ə'vəːt] *n* (*turn away*) distogliere; (*ward off*) allontanare; (*prevent*) prevenire.
aviary ['eiviəri] *n* uccelliera *f*.
aviation [eivi'eiʃən] *n* aviazione *f*.
avid ['avid] *adj* avido.
avocado [avə'kaːdou] *n* pera avocado *f*.
avoid [ə'void] *v* evitare, schivare. **avoidance** *n* fuga *f*; l'evitare *m*.
await [ə'weit] *v* aspettare, attendere.
***awake** [ə'weik] *adj* sveglio. *v* svegliare, svegliarsi. **awaken** *v* risvegliare, risvegliarsi. **awakening** *n* risveglio *m*.
award [ə'woːd] *n* premio *m*; (*honour*) onorificenza *f*. *v* aggiudicare, premiare, conferire.
aware [ə'weə] *adj* consapevole, conscio. **be aware of** sapere, rendersi conto di. **awareness** *n* consapevolezza *f*, sensibilità *f*.
away [ə'wei] *adv* lontano, via; (*absent*) fuori.
awe [oː] *n* timore reverenziale *m*. **awestruck** *adj* in preda a timore. **awe-inspiring** *adj* che incute rispetto.
awful ['oːful] *adj* terribile, spaventoso. **awfully** *adv* terribilimente; (*coll*) molto.
awkward ['oːkwəd] *adj* goffo, sgraziato.
awl [oːl] *n* lesina *f*.
awning ['oːniŋ] *n* tenda *f*.
awoke [ə'wouk] *V* **awake**.
awoken [ə'woukn] *V* **awake**.
axe [aks] *n* ascia *f*, scure *f*.
axiom ['aksiəm] *n* assioma *m*.
axis ['aksis] *n* asse *m*.
axle ['aksl] *n* asse *m*; perno *m*.

B

babble ['babl] *v* balbettare, ciarlare. *n* balbettio *m*.
baby ['beibi] *n* bimbo, -a *m, f*, bebè *m*. **babysitter** *n* babysitter *m, f invar*. **babyish** *adj* bambinesco.
bachelor ['batʃələ] *n* scapolo *m*. **Bachelor of Arts/Science** *n* laureato, -a in lettere/scienze *m, f*.
back [bak] *n* (*anat*) dorso *m*, schiena *f*; (*chair*) schienale *m*; (*reverse*) rovescio *m*. **back to front** a rovescio. *adv* dietro, indietro, di ritorno. *v* appoggiare, sostenere; (*bet on*) scommettere su, puntare su. **back out** ritirarsi.
***backbite** ['bakbait] *v* calunniare, sparlare di.
backbone ['bakboun] *n* spina dorsale *f*.
backdate [ˌbak'deit] *v* retrodatare.
backfire [ˌbak'faiə] *v* far ritorno di fiamma; (*coll*) andare all'aria.
background ['bakgraund] *n* sfondo *m*; (*milieu*) ambiente *m*.
backhand ['bakhand] *n* rovescio *m*.
backlash ['baklaʃ] *n* contraccolpo *m*.
backlog ['baklog] *n* arretrati *m pl*.
back pay *n* arretrati di paga *m pl*.
backside ['baksaid] *n* sedere *m*.
***backslide** ['bakslaid] *v* ricadere nell'errore.
backstage ['baksteidʒ] *adv* dietro le quinte.
backstroke ['bakstrouk] *n* nuoto sul dorso *m*.
backward ['bakwəd] *adj* tardivo, arretrato.
backwards ['bakwədz] *adv* indietro, all'indietro.
backwater ['bakwoːtə] *n* (*pool*) acqua stagnante *f*; (*place*) posto dove non succede mai nulla *m*.
bacon ['beikən] *n* pancetta *f*.
bacteria [bak'tiəriə] *pl n* batteri *m pl*.
bad [bad] *adj* cattivo, malvagio, dannoso, brutto; (*serious*) grave. **bad language** parolacce *f pl*. **feel bad** sentirsi male. **go bad** andare a male. **badly** *adv* male, malamente; (*seriously*) gravemente.
badge [badʒ] *n* distintivo *m*, emblema *m*.
badger ['badʒə] *n* tasso *m*. *v* molestare.
baffle ['bafl] *v* sconcertare, confondere. **baffling** *adj* sconcertante.
bag [bag] *n* sacco *m*, borsa *f*, borsetta *f*. *v* insaccare; (*coll*) impadronirsi di, prendere.
bail¹ [beil] *n* (*law*) cauzione *f*, garanzia *f*. **grant bail** concedere libertà provvisoria (su cauzione). **stand bail for** rendersi garante per. *v* dar garanzia per, prestar cauzione a. **bail out** ottenere libertà provvisoria (su cauzione) per.
bail² *or* **bale** [beil] *v* **bail out** (*flooded boat*) aggottare; (*from aircraft*) lanciarsi.
bailiff ['beilif] *n* (*law*) funzionario incaricato a fare sequestri *m*; (*of estate*) fattore *m*.
bait [beit] *n* (*fishing*) esca *f*; (*lure*) lusinga *f*. *v* adescare; (*annoy*) tormentare.
bake [beik] *v* cuocere al forno. **baker** *n* fornaio panettiere *m*. **bakery** *n* panificio *m*. **baking powder** lievito minerale *m*, bicarbonato *m*. **baking tin** teglia *f*.
balance ['baləns] *n* equilibrio *m*, armonia *f*; (*scales*) bilancia *f*; (*comm*) bilancio *m*. **balance of payments** bilancia dei pagamenti *f*. *v* bilanciare, equilibrare; (*comm*) fare il bilancio.
balcony ['balkəni] *n* balcone *m*; (*theatre*) balconata *f*.
bald [boːld] *adj* calvo; (*naked*) nudo, disadorno. **baldness** *n* calvizie *f invar*.
bale¹ [beil] *n* balla *f*. *v* imballare.
bale² *V* **bail²**.
baleful ['beilful] *adj* maligno, distruttivo.
ball¹ [boːl] *n* palla *f*; (*inflatable*) pallone *m*; (*sphere*) sfera *f*. **ball-bearings** *pl n* cuscinetti a sfere *m pl*. **ball-point pen** penna a sfera *f*.
ball² [boːl] *n* (*dance*) ballo *m*. **ballroom** *n* sala da ballo *f*.
ballad ['baləd] *n* ballata *f*; (*music*) canzone popolare *f*.
ballast ['baləst] *n* zavorra *f*. *v* zavorrare.
ballet ['balei] *n* balletto *m*. **ballet dancer** ballerino, -a *m, f*.
ballistic [bə'listik] *adj* balistico. **ballistic missile** proiettile balistico *m*.
balloon [bə'luːn] *n* pallone *m*, aerostato *m*; (*toy*) palloncino *m*. **balloonist** *n* aeronauta *m*.
ballot ['balət] *n* votazione *f*, scrutinio *m*; (*paper*) scheda *f*. *v* ballottare, votare segretamente. **ballot-box** *n* urna elettorale *f*.

bamboo [bam'buː] *n* bambù *m*.
ban [ban] *n* proibizione *f*, bando *m*, interdizione *f*. *v* proibire, interdire.
banal [bə'naːl] *adj* banale.
banana [bə'naːnə] *n* (*fruit*) banana *f*; (*tree*) banano *m*.
band[1] [band] *n* (*troop*) banda *f*, schiera *f*; (*music*) banda *f*, orchestrina *f*. **bandstand** *n* palco per banda *m*. *v* **band together** legare insieme.
band[2] [band] *n* (*strip*) striscia *f*, fascia *f*.
bandage ['bandidʒ] *n* benda *f*, fascia *f*. *v* bendare, fasciare.
bandit ['bandit] *n* bandito *m*.
bandy ['bandi] *adj* storto, curvo. **bandy-legged** *adj* a gambe storte. *v* **bandy words** scambiare parole.
bang [baŋ] *n* colpo *m*, botta *f*. *v* sbattere.
bangle ['baŋgl] *n* braccialetto *m*.
banish ['baniʃ] *v* bandire, esiliare. **banishment** *n* bando *m*, esilio *m*.
banister ['banistə] *n* ringhiera *f*.
banjo ['bandʒou] *n* banjo *m invar*.
bank[1] [baŋk] *n* (*edge*) sponda *f*; (*river*) riva *f*. *v* arginare.
bank[2] [baŋk] *n* banca *f*, banco *m*. **bank account** conto in banca *m*. **bank holiday** festa legale *f*. **bank manager** direttore di banca *m*. *v* depositare in banca. **bank on** contare su.
bankrupt ['baŋkrʌpt] *adj* fallito. *v* far fallire. **bankruptcy** *n* fallimento *m*.
banner ['banə] *n* stendardo *m*, insegna *f*.
banquet ['baŋkwit] *n* banchetto *m*.
banter ['bantə] *v* canzonare, prendere in giro. *n* presa in giro *f*.
baptize [bap'taiz] *v* battezzare. **baptism** *n* battesimo *m*. **baptismal** *adj* battesimale. **Baptist** *n* battista *m*.
bar [baː] *n* (*metal*) sbarra *f*, stanga *f*; (*line*) striscia *f*; (*chocolate*) tavoletta *f*; (*law*) ordine degli avvocati *m*; barriera *f*; (*drinks*) bar *m invar*; (*music*) battuta *f*. **barmaid** *n* cameriera al banco *f*, barista *f*. **barman** *n* barista *m*. *v* proibire, impedire, escludere. *prep* eccetto, tranne.
barbarian [baː'beəriən] *n*, *adj* barbaro, -a.
barbecue ['baːbikjuː] *n* arrosto all'aperto *m*. *v* arrostire all'aperto.
barb [baːb] *n* spina *f*. **barbed** *adj* pungente. **barbed wire** filo spinato *m*.
barber ['baːbə] *n* barbiere *m*, parrucchiere *m*.
barbiturate [baː'bitjurət] *n* barbiturato *m*.
bare [beə] *adj* (*without covering*) scoperto; (*simple*) semplice; (*naked, unadorned*) nudo; (*just sufficient*) appena sufficiente. *v* denudare, rivelare. **barefoot** *adj*, *adv* scalzo, a piedi scalzi. **barely** *adv* appena.
bargain ['baːgin] *n* (*transaction*) affare *m*; (*offer*) occasione *f*. **into the bargain** per giunta, in più. *v* contrattare, mercanteggiare.
barge [baːdʒ] *n* barcone *m*, chiatta *f*. *v* **barge in** intervenire a sproposito, irrompere. **barge into** imbattersi per caso.
baritone ['baritoun] *n* baritono *m*.
bark[1] [baːk] *n* (*dog*) latrato *m*. *v* abbaiare, latrare.
bark[2] [baːk] *n* (*tree*) scorza *f*, corteccia *f*.
barley ['baːli] *n* orzo *m*. **barley sugar** zucchero d'orzo *m*. **barley water** tisana d'orzo *f*.
barn [baːn] *n* granaio *m*.
barometer [bə'romitə] *n* barometro *m*.
baron ['barən] *n* barone *m*. **baroness** *n* baronessa *f*. **baronet** *n* baronetto *m*.
baroque [bə'rok] *nm*, *adj* barocco.
barracks ['barəks] *pl n* caserma *f sing*.
barrage ['baraːʒ] *n* sbarramento *m*.
barrel ['barəl] *n* (*cask*) barile *m*, botte *f*; (*gun, etc.*) canna *f*. **barrel organ** organetto *m*.
barren ['barən] *adj* sterile, infecondo.
barricade [bari'keid] *n* barricata *f*. *v* barricare.
barrier ['bariə] *n* barriera *f*.
barrister ['baristə] *n* avvocato *m*.
barrow ['barou] *n* carretta *f*; (*archaeol*) tumulo *m*.
barter ['baːtə] *v* barattare. *n* baratto *m*.
base[1] [beis] *v* fondare, basare. *n* base *f*, fondamento *m*. **baseless** *adj* infondato.
base[2] [beis] *adj* vile, basso. **baseness** *n* bassezza *f*.
basement ['beismənt] *n* sottosuolo *m*.
bash [baʃ] *n* colpo violento *m*. *v* colpire violentemente.
bashful ['baʃful] *adj* timido, vergognoso.
basic ['beisik] *adj* fondamentale; (*chem*) basico.
basil ['bazl] *n* basilico *m*.
basin ['beisin] *n* bacino *m*, catino *m*; (*wash-basin*) lavabo *m*.
basis ['beisis] *n*, *pl* **-ses** base *f*, fondamento *m*.
bask [bask] *v* crogiolarsi.

basket ['baːskit] *n* cesto *m*, paniere *m*. **basketball** *n* pallacanestro *f*.

Basle [baːl] *n* Basilea *f*.

bas-relief ['basri,liːf] *n* bassorilievo *m*.

bass[1] [beis] *n* basso *m*.

bass[2] [bas] *n* (*sea*) branzino *m*, spigola *f*; (*freshwater*) pesce persico *m*.

bassoon [bə'suːn] *n* fagotto *m*.

bastard ['baːstəd] *n*, *adj* bastardo, -a.

baste [beist] *v* (*cookery*) arrosolare; (*sewing*) imbastire; (*beat*) bastonare.

bastion ['bastjən] *n* bastione *m*.

bat[1] [bat] *n* (*cricket, baseball*) mazza *f*; (*table tennis*) racchetta *f*. *v* battere.

bat[2] [bat] *n* (*zool*) pipistrello *m*. **blind as a bat** cieco come una talpa.

batch [batʃ] *n* lotto *m*, partita *f*; (*bread*) infornata *f*.

bath [baːθ] *n* bagno *m*. *v* fare un bagno; lavare. **bathchair** *n* carrozzella per invalidi *f*. **bathmat** *n* stuoia da bagno *f*. **bathrobe** *n* accappatoio *m*. **bathroom** *n* stanza da bagno *f*.

bathe [beið] *v* bagnare, fare un *or* il bagno. **bather** *n* bagnante *m, f*. **bathing cap** cuffia da bagno *f*. **bathing costume** costume da bagno *m*. **bathing trunks** calzoncini da bagno *m pl*.

baton ['batn] *n* (*mil*) bastone *m*; (*music*) bacchetta *f*.

battalion [bə'taljən] *n* battaglione *m*.

batter[1] ['batə] *v* percuotere, colpire con violenza. **battering ram** (*mil*) ariete *m*.

batter[2] ['batə] *n* (*cookery*) pastella *f*.

battery ['batəri] *n* batteria *f*, pila *f*.

battle ['batl] *n* battaglia *f*, combattimento *m*. **battlefield** *n* campo di battaglia *m*. **battleship** *n* nave da battaglia *f*. *v* combattere, lottare.

bawdy ['boːdi] *adj* licenzioso.

bawl [boːl] *v* urlare, gridare.

bay[1] [bei] *n* (*geog*) baia *f*, golfo *m*, insenatura *f*.

bay[2] [bei] *v* (*cry*) abbaiare. *n* latrato *m*. **at bay** a bada.

bay[3] [bei] *n* (*tree*) lauro *m*.

bayonet ['beiənit] *n* baionetta *f*.

bay window *n* finestra sporgente *f*.

***be** [biː] *v* essere, esistere; (*remain*) stare.

beach [biːtʃ] *n* spiaggia *f*, lido *m*.

beacon ['biːkən] *n* faro *m*; (*fire*) falò *m*.

bead [biːd] *n* grano *m*; (*liquid*) goccia *f*.

beagle ['biːgl] *n* cane da caccia *m*.

beak [biːk] *n* becco *m*, rostro *m*.

beaker ['biːkə] *n* coppa *f*.

beam [biːm] *n* (*wood*) trave *f*; (*light*) raggio *m*; (*radio*) segnale *m*; (*smile*) sorriso *m*. *v* irradiare; (*smile*) sorridere.

bean [biːn] *n* fava *f*, fagiolo *m*; (*coffee*) chicco *m*. **French bean** fagiolino *m*. **full of beans** energico.

***bear**[1] [beə] *v* (*carry*) portare; (*support weight*) reggere; (*tolerate*) soffrire, sopportare; (*give birth to*) dare alla luce. **bear oneself** comportarsi. **bear with** aver pazienza con. **bearable** *adj* sopportabile. **bearer** *n* portatore, -trice *m, f*.

bear[2] [beə] *n* orso, -a *m, f*.

beard [biəd] *n* barba *f*. *v* sfidare. **bearded** *adj* barbuto. **beardless** *adj* imberbe.

bearing ['beəriŋ] *n* condotta *f*, contegno *m*; (*aircraft*) rilevamento *m*; (*mech*) cuscinetto *m*. **bearings** *pl n* orientamento *m sing*, senso di direzione *m sing*. **lose one's bearings** disorientarsi.

beast [biːst] *n* bestia *f*, animale *m*. **beastly** *adj* bestiale; (*coll*) veramente cattivo.

***beat** [biːt] *v* battere; (*hit*) bastonare; (*heart*) palpitare; (*defeat*) sconfiggere; (*eggs, etc.*) sbattere. *n* battito *m*, palpito *m*; (*music*) battuta *f*; (*police*) ronda *f*. **beating** *n* bastonata *f*, sconfitta *f*.

beaten ['biːtn] *V* **beat**.

beauty ['bjuːti] *n* bellezza *f*. **beautiful** *adj* bello. **beautify** *v* abbellire.

beaver ['biːvə] *n* castoro *m*.

became [bi'keim] *V* **become**.

because [bi'koz] *conj* perché, poiché. **because of** a causa di.

beckon ['bekən] *v* chiamare con un cenno.

***become** [bi'kʌm] *v* diventare, divenire. **becoming** *adj* che sta bene; (*suitable*) conveniente.

bed [bed] *n* letto *m*; (*sea*) fondo *m*; (*coal*) giacimento *m*; (*flowers*) aiuola *f*. **bedbug** *n* cimice *m*. **bedroom** *n* camera da letto *f*. **bedside** *n* capezzale *m*. **bedsitter** *n* camera studio *f*. **bedspread** *n* copriletto *m*. **double bed** letto matrimoniale *m*. **go to bed** andare a letto. **twin beds** letti gemelli *m pl*. **bedding** *n* (*sheets*) lenzuola *f pl*; (*covers*) coperte *f pl*.

bedevil [bi'devl] *v* vessare.

bedlam ['bedləm] *n* confusione *f*.

bedraggled [bi'dragld] *adj* fradicio, inzaccherato.

bee [biː] *n* ape *f*. **beehive** *n* alveare *m*. **bee-keeper** *n* apicoltore *m*.

beech [biːtʃ] *n* faggio *m*.
beef [biːf] *n* manzo *m*. **beefsteak** *n* bistecca *f*.
been [biːn] *V* **be**.
beer [biə] *n* birra *f*.
beetle ['biːtl] *n* scarabeo *m*. **black beetle** scarafaggio *m*.
beetroot ['biːtruːt] *n* barbabietola *f*.
before [bi'foː] *adv* prima, già. *prep* prima di, davanti a. *conj* prima che. **beforehand** *adv* in anticipo.
befriend [bi'frend] *v* sostenere, mostrarsi amico a.
beg [beg] *v* implorare, pregare; (*for alms*) chiedere l'elemosina. **beggar** *n* mendicante *m, f*.
began [bi'gan] *V* **begin**.
***begin** [bi'gin] *v* cominciare, iniziare. **to begin with** anzitutto. **beginner** *n* principiante *m, f*. **beginning** *n* principio *m*, inizio *m*.
begrudge [bi'grʌdʒ] *v* invidiare.
begun [bi'gʌn] *V* **begin**.
behalf [bi'haːf] *n* **on behalf of** a nome di.
behave [bi'heiv] *v* comportarsi. **behaviour** *n* condotta *f*, comportamento *m*.
behead [bi'hed] *v* decapitare.
beheld [bi'held] *V* **behold**.
behind [bi'haind] *adv* dietro, indietro; (*late*) in ritardo. *prep* dietro a *or* di, dopo. **behindhand** *adv* in arretrato, in ritardo. *n* (*coll*) sedere *m*.
***behold** [bi'hould] *v* vedere. **beholder** *n* osservatore, -trice *m, f*.
beige [beiʒ] *adj* beige *invar*.
being ['biːiŋ] *n* essere *m*, creatura *f*. **for the time being** per il momento.
belated [bi'leitid] *adj* tardivo.
belch [beltʃ] *v* ruttare. *n* rutto *m*.
belfry ['belfri] *n* campanile *m*.
Belgium ['beldʒəm] *n* Belgio *m*. **Belgian** *n*(*m*+*f*), *adj* belga (*m pl* -gi).
believe [bi'liːv] *v* credere, pensare, aver fede in. **make believe** *v* far finta. **belief** *n*, *pl* -s fede *f*, credenza *f*, opinione *f*. **believable** *adj* credibile. **believer** *n* credente *m, f*, fedele *m, f*.
bell [bel] *n* campana *f*; (*door*) campanello *m*. **bellringer** *n* campanaro *m*. **bell-tower** *n* campanile *m*.
belligerent [bi'lidʒərənt] *adj* belligerente.
bellow ['belou] *v* urlare, muggire.
bellows ['belouz] *pl n* soffietto *m sing*, mantice *m sing*.
belly ['beli] *n* pancia *f*, ventre *m*.
belong [bi'loŋ] *v* appartenere, spettare, far parte (di). **belongings** *pl n* roba *f sing*, effetti personali *m pl*.
beloved [bi'lʌvid] *n*, *adj* amato, -a.
below [bi'lou] *adv* sotto, di sotto, giù. *prep* sotto, al di sotto di, inferiore a.
belt [belt] *n* cintura *f*; (*mech*) cinghia *f*; (*zone*) fascia *f*. *v* (*coll*: *hit*) picchiare; (*coll*: *rush*) precipitarsi.
bench [bentʃ] *n* (*workshop*) banco *m*; (*long seat*) panchina *f*, panca *f*; (*law*) magistratura *f*.
***bend** [bend] *v* piegare, curvare. *n* curva *f*, svolta *f*.
beneath [bi'niːθ] *adv* giù, abbasso. *prep* sotto, al di sotto di.
benefactor ['benəfaktə] *n* benefattore, -trice *m, f*. **benefaction** *n* beneficenza *f*.
benefit ['benəfit] *n* beneficio *m*, vantaggio *m*, utilità *f*. *v* giovare a, far bene a, approfittare. **beneficial** *adj* vantaggioso, utile. **beneficiary** *n*, *adj* beneficiario, -a.
benevolent [bi'nevələnt] *adj* benevolo, caritatevole. **benevolence** *n* benevolenza *f*.
benign [bi'nain] *adj* benevolo; (*med*) benigno.
bent [bent] *V* **bend**. *adj* curvato; (*determined*) risoluto; (*dishonest*) corrotto. *n* tendenza *f*.
bequeath [bi'kwiːð] *v* lasciare per testamento. **bequest** *n* lascito *m*.
bereaved [bi'riːvd] **be bereaved** essere in lutto. **bereavement** *n* lutto *m*.
beret ['berei] *n* beretto *m*.
berry ['beri] *n* bacca *f*, chicco *m*.
berserk [bə'səːk] *adv* **go berserk** montare su tutte le furie.
berth [bəːθ] *n* (*sleeping*) cuccetta *f*; (*naut*) posto d'ormeggio *m*. **give a wide berth to** evitare. *v* ancorare.
beside [bi'said] *prep* accanto a, presso, vicino a. **be beside oneself** essere fuori di sè. **besides** *adv* d'altronde, inoltre, per di più.
besiege [bi'siːdʒ] *v* assediare.
best [best] *adj* il migliore. *adv* meglio. **as best one can** come meglio si può, il meglio possibile. **come off best** avere la meglio. **do one's best** fare del proprio meglio. **the best** il meglio. **to the best of my knowledge** per quanto ne sappia.
bestial ['bestjəl] *adj* bestiale.

bestow [bi'stou] *v* conferire, dare.
bet [bet] *n* scommessa *f*. *v* scommettere.
betray [bi'trei] *v* tradire, svelare. **betrayal** *n* tradimento *m*.
better ['betə] *adj* meglio, migliore. *adv* meglio, in modo migliore. *v* migliorare. **all the better** tanto meglio. **be** *or* **feel better** star meglio. **get the better of** aver la meglio su.
between [bi'twiːn] *adv* in mezzo. *prep* tra, fra, in mezzo a.
beverage ['bevəridʒ] *n* bevanda *f*, bibita *f*.
***beware** [bi'weə] *v* guardarsi da, stare attento a. **beware of the dog!** attenti al cane!
bewilder [bi'wildə] *v* sconcertare, confondere. **bewildered** *adj* sconcertato, perplesso. **bewildering** *adj* sconcertante. **bewilderment** *n* disorientamento *m*.
beyond [bi'jond] *adv* oltre, più in là. *prep* oltre, al di là di.
bias ['baiəs] *n* inclinazione *f*, pregiudizio *m*, preconcetto *m*. **on the bias** (*tailoring*) per sbieco. **biased** *adj* prevenuto.
bib [bib] *n* bavaglino *m*.
Bible ['baibl] *n* bibbia *f*. **biblical** *adj* biblico.
bibliography [bibli'ogrəfi] *n* bibliografia *f*. **bibliographer** *n* bibliografo, -a *m*, *f*. **bibliographical** *adj* bibliografico.
biceps ['baiseps] *n* bicipite *m*.
bicker ['bikə] *v* litigare, bisticciare. **bickering** *n* bisticciarsi *m invar*.
bicycle ['baisikl] *n* bicicletta *f*.
***bid** [bid] *n* offerta *f*; (*cards*) dichiarazione *f*. *v* (*order*) comandare; (*auction*) offrire; (*cards*) dichiarare. **bidder** *n* offerente *m*, *f*; dichiaratore, -trice *m*, *f*. **bidding** *n* ordine *m*; dichiarazione *f*.
bide [baid] *v* **bide one's time** aspettare il momento propizio.
bidet ['biːdei] *n* bidè *m*.
biennial [bai'eniəl] *adj* biennale.
bifocals [bai'foukəlz] *pl n* lenti bifocali *f pl*.
big [big] *adj* grande, grosso, importante.
bigamy ['bigəmi] *n* bigamia *f*. **bigamist** *n* bigamo *m*. **bigamous** *adj* bigamo.
bigot ['bigət] *n* bigotto *m*, fanatico, -a *m*, *f*. **bigoted** *adj* bigotto, fanatico. **bigotry** *n* bigotteria *f*, fanatismo *m*.
bikini [bi'kiːni] *n* bikini *m invar*.
bilateral [bai'latərəl] *adj* bilaterale.
bilingual [bai'liŋgwəl] *adj* bilingue.
bilious ['biljəs] *adj* (*med*) biliare; (*irritable*) collerico; (*sickly*) nauseante. **bile** *n* bile *f*. **biliousness** *n* travaso di bile *m*.
bill[1] [bil] *n* (*hotel*, *restaurant*) conto *m*; (*shop*, *invoice*) fattura *f*; (*pol*) progetto di legge *m*, atto *m*; (*poster*) affisso *m*; (*theatre*) cartellone *m*. **bill of fare** menù *m*. *v* fatturare; (*poster*) affiggere; (*theatre*) mettere in programma.
bill[2] [bil] *n* (*beak*) becco *m*, rostro *m*.
billiards ['biljədz] *n* biliardo *m*.
billion ['biljən] *n* (10^{12}) bilione *m*, mille miliardi *m pl*; (10^9) miliardo *m*.
billow ['bilou] *n* onda *f*; (*smoke*) ondata *f*. *v* (*sail*) gonfiarsi; (*smoke*) emanare.
bin [bin] *n* recipiente *m*; (*dustbin*) pattumiera *f*.
binary ['bainəri] *adj* binario.
***bind** [baind] *v* legare, attaccare; (*book*) rilegare; (*force*) costringere. *n* (*slang*) scocciatura *f*.
binding ['baindiŋ] *n* legatura *f*, legame *m*; (*book*) rilegatura *f*. *adj* impegnativo, obbligatorio.
binoculars [bi'nokjuləz] *pl n* binocolo *m sing*.
biography [bai'ogrəfi] *n* biografia *f*. **biographer** *n* biografo, -a *m*, *f*. **biographical** *adj* biografico.
biology [bai'olədʒi] *n* biologia *f*. **biological** *adj* biologico. **biologist** *n* biologo, -a *m*, *f*.
birch [bəːtʃ] *n* betulla *f*.
bird [bəːd] *n* uccello *m*. **bird's-eye view** veduta a volo d'uccello *f*.
birth [bəːθ] *n* nascita *f*; origine *f*; discendenza *f*. **birth certificate** atto di nascita *m*. **birth control** controllo delle nascite *m*. **birthday** *n* compleanno *m*. **birthmark** *n* voglia *f*. **birthplace** *n* luogo di nascita *m*. **birth rate** natalità *f*, indice demografico *m*. **give birth to** mettere al mondo, dare alla luce.
biscuit ['biskit] *n* biscotto *m*.
bishop ['biʃəp] *n* (*church*) vescovo *m*; (*chess*) alfiere *m*.
bison ['baisən] *n* bisonte *m*.
bit[1] [bit] *V* **bite**. *n* (*horse*) morso *m*; (*drill*) punta *f*, morsa *f*.
bit[2] [bit] *n* (*morsel*) boccone *m*; (*small piece*) pezzo *m*, pezzetto *m*. **bit by bit** poco a poco. **do one's bit** fare la propria parte. **wait a bit!** aspetta un po'!
bitch [bitʃ] *n* cagna *f*; (*slang*) antipatica *f*. **bitchy** *adj* malvagio.

***bite** [bait] *n* morso *m*; (*insect*) puntura *f*; (*fish*) l'abboccare *m*; (*food*) boccone *m*. *v* mordere, addentare. **biting** *adj* pungente, mordente.
bitten ['bitn] *V* **bite**.
bitter ['bitə] *adj* amaro, aspro, accanito. **bitter-sweet** *adj* agrodolce. **to the bitter end** ad oltranza. **bitterness** *n* amarezza *f*, rancore *m*.
bizarre [bi'zaː] *adj* bizzarro, strano.
black ['blak] *adj* nero. **things look black** le cose si mettono male. *n* (*colour*) nero *m*; (*person*) negro, -a *m*, *f*. **blacken** *v* annerire.
blackberry ['blakbəri] *n* (*fruit*) mora *f*; (*bush*) rovo *m*.
blackbird ['blakbəːd] *n* merlo *m*.
blackboard ['blakboːd] *n* lavagna *f*.
blackcurrant [ˌblak'kʌrənt] *n* ribes nero *m invar*.
blackhead ['blakhed] *n* comedone *m*.
blackleg ['blakleg] *n* crumiro *m*.
blackmail ['blakmeil] *n* ricatto *m*. *v* ricattare. **blackmailer** *n* ricattatore, -trice *m*, *f*.
black market *n* borsa nera *f*.
blackout ['blakaut] *n* oscuramento *m*; (*med*) svenimento *m*.
blacksmith ['blaksmiθ] *n* fabbro *m*.
blackshirt ['blakʃəːt] *n* camicia nera *f*.
bladder ['bladə] *n* vescica *f*.
blade [bleid] *n* lama *f*; (*oar*, *propeller*) pala *f*; (*grass*) filo d'erba *m*.
blame [bleim] *n* biasimo *m*, responsabilità *f*. *v* biasimare, incolpare, rimproverare. **blameless** *adj* innocente.
blanch [blaːntʃ] *v* (*cookery*) sbollentare; (*go pale*) impallidire.
bland [bland] *adj* blando.
blank [blaŋk] *adj* vuoto, in bianco; (*puzzled*) perplesso. *n* spazio vuoto *m*; (*cartridge*) cartuccia a salve *f*. **point blank** a bruciapelo.
blanket ['blaŋkit] *n* coperta *f*. *v* ricoprire.
blare [bleə] *v* squillare, sonare con tutta forza. *n* (*trumpet*) squillo *m*; (*loud noise*) chiasso *m*.
blaspheme [blas'fiːm] *v* bestemmiare. **blasphemous** *adj* blasfemo, empio. **blasphemy** *n* bestemmia *f*.
blast [blaːst] *n* (*wind*) raffica *f*; esplosione *f*. *v* far esplodere, far saltare. **blast-furnace** *n* altoforno (*pl* altiforni) *m*.
blatant ['bleitənt] *adj* vistoso, evidente.
blaze [bleiz] *n* (*flame*) fiamma *f*; (*sudden outburst of fire*) vampata *f*. *v* ardere, divampare. **blazer** *n* giacca sportiva *f*.
bleach [bliːtʃ] *v* scolorire, candeggiare. *n* candeggina *f*.
bleak [bliːk] *adj* (*desolate*) triste; (*dreary*) squallido; (*depressing*) deprimente.
bleat [bliːt] *v* belare.
bled [bled] *V* **bleed**.
***bleed** [bliːd] *v* sanguinare, perder sangue. **bleeding** *n* emoraggia *f*, perdita di sangue *f*.
blemish ['blemiʃ] *n* difetto *m*, imperfezione *f*. *v* sfigurare, macchiare.
blend [blend] *v* mescolare, combinare. *n* miscela intima *f*.
bless [bles] *v* benedire. **be blessed with** godere di, essere dotato di. **bless you!** salute! **blessing** *n* benedizione *f*.
blew [bluː] *V* **blow²**.
blind [blaind] *adj* cieco. **blind drunk** ubriaco fradicio. **blind spot** punto cieco *m*. **turn a blind eye to** chiudere gli occhi davanti a. **blindness** *n* cecità *f*. *v* accecare, ingannare. *n* (*window*) tendina *f*, persiana *f*; (*pretence*) finzione *f*.
blindfold ['blaindfould] *n* benda (agli occhi) *f*. *v* bendare gli occhi.
blink [bliŋk] *v* battere le palpebre; (*wink*) ammiccare.
bliss [blis] *n* beatitudine *f*. **blissful** *adj* beato.
blister ['blistə] *n* bolla *f*, vescica *f*. *v* far venire vesciche; coprirsi di vesciche.
blizzard ['blizəd] *n* tormenta *f*, bufera *f*.
blob [blob] *n* macchia *f*.
bloc [blok] *n* blocco *m*.
block [blok] *v* bloccare, sbarrare. *n* blocco *m*, ceppo *m*; (*large building*) palazzo *m*; (*obstacle*) ostacolo *m*. **block letter** stampatello *m*; (*capital*) maiuscola *f*.
blockade [blo'keid] *n* blocco *m*, assedio *m*. *v* bloccare.
bloke [blouk] *n* (*coll*) tipo *m*.
blond [blond] *adj* biondo. **blonde** *n* bionda *f*.
blood [blʌd] *n* sangue *m*; (*descent*) stirpe *f*. **blood clot** coagulo di sangue *m*. **blood-curdling** *adj* raccapricciante. **blood group** gruppo sanguigno *m*. **bloodhound** *n* segugio *m*. **blood poisoning** setticemia *f*. **blood pressure** pressione sanguigna *f*. **bloodshed** *n* carneficina *f*. **bloodshot** *adj* arrossato. **bloodthirsty** *adj* assetato di sangue. **bloody** *adj* macchiato di sangue; (*slang*) maledetto.

bloom [bluːm] *v* fiorire. *n* fiore *m*, fioritura *f*.
blot [blot] *n* macchia *f*, sgorbio *m*. *v* macchiare. **blot out** cancellare. **blotting paper** carta assorbente *f*.
blouse [blauz] *n* blusa *f*, camicetta *f*.
blow[1] [blou] *n* colpo *m*; (*fist*) pugno *m*; (*stick*) bastonata *f*. **come to blows** venire alle mani.
***blow**[2] [blou] *v* soffiare; (*trumpet, etc.*) suonare. **blow away** spazzar via. **blow one's nose** soffiarsi il naso. **blow out** spegnere. **blow up** (*explode*) far saltare; (*inflate*) gonfiare.
blown [bloun] *V* **blow**[2].
blubber ['blʌbə] *n* (*whale*) grasso di balene *m*. *v* (*weep*) piangere singhiozzando.
blue [bluː] *nm, adj* azzurro; (*pale*) celeste; (*dark*) blu. **bluebell** *n* giacinto selvatico *m*. **blueprint** *n* progetto *m*.
bluff [blʌf] *v* ingannare; (*cards*) bluffare. *n* vanteria infondata *f*; (*poker*) bluff *m invar*.
blunder [blʌndə] *n* errore *m*, papera *f*. *v* commettere un errore.
blunt [blʌnt] *adj* (*not sharp*) ottuso, spuntato; (*frank*) brusco. *v* smussare, ottundere.
blur [bləː] *v* rendere confuso, oscurare. *n* offuscamento *m*, macchia *f*.
blush [blʌʃ] *v* arrossire. *n* rossore *m*.
boar [boː] *n* cinghiale *m*.
board [boːd] *v* (*ship, etc.*) abbordare, imbarcarsi. *n* (*wood*) asse *m*, tavola *f*; (*food*) vitto *m*; (*examiners*) commissione *f*. **board of directors** consiglio d'amministrazione *m*. **full board** pensione completa *f*. **half board** mezza pensione *f*. **on board** a bordo. **boarding house** pensione *f*. **boarding school** collegio *m*.
boast [boust] *n* vanto *m*. *v* vantare. **boastful** *adj* millantatore, vanaglorioso.
boat [bout] *n* barca *f*, battello *m*. **boat race** gara di canottaggio *f*. **boating** *n* canottaggio *m*.
bob [bob] *v* **bob up** (*come to surface*) venire a galla. **bob up and down** muoversi in su e in giù.
bobbin ['bobin] *n* bobina *f*.
bodice ['bodis] *n* busto *m*, liseuse *f*.
body ['bodi] *n* corpo *m*; entità *f*; gruppo *m*; (*corpse*) cadavere *m*; (*organization*) ente *m*. **bodyguard** *n* guardia del corpo *f*.
bog [bog] *n* palude *f*, pantano *m*.
bogus ['bougəs] *adj* falso.
bohemian [bə'hiːmiən] *adj* da artista.
boil[1] [boil] *v* bollire, far bollire, lessare. **boiler** *n* caldaia *f*. **boiler suit** tuta *f*. **boiling point** punto d'ebollizione *m*.
boil[2] [boil] *n* (*swelling*) foruncolo *m*.
boisterous ['boistərəs] *adj* chiassoso, impetuoso.
bold [bould] *adj* audace, ardito, sfacciato. **boldness** *n* audacia *f*, coraggio *m*.
bolster ['boulstə] *n* capezzale *m*, cuscino *m*. *v* **bolster up** sostenere.
bolt [boult] *n* (*for nut*) bullone *m*; (*door*) catenaccio *m*; (*arrow*) freccia *f*. *v* (*bar*) sprangare; (*run away*) scappare. **a bolt from the blue** un fulmine a ciel sereno. **bolt upright** diritto come un fuso.
bomb [bom] *n* bomba *f*. *v* bombardare. **bombing** *n* bombardamento *m*.
bond [bond] *n* (*tie*) legame *m*, vincolo *m*; (*agreement*) impegno *m*; (*comm*) titolo *m*; (*law*) cauzione *f*. **bonded warehouse** magazzino doganale *m*. **bondage** *n* schiavitù *f*.
bone [boun] *n* osso *m* (*pl* -a *f*). *v* disossare. **bony** *adj* ossuto.
bonfire ['bonfaiə] *n* falò *m*.
bonnet ['bonit] *n* (*hat*) cappellino *m*; (*car*) cofano *m*.
bonus ['bounəs] *n* gratifica *f*, premio *m*.
booby trap ['buːbi] *n* mina nascosta *f*, trappola esplosiva *f*; (*pitfall*) trabocchetto *m*.
book [buk] *n* libro *m*. *v* (*reserve*) prenotare.
bookcase ['bukkeis] *n* scaffale *m*.
booking ['bukiŋ] *n* prenotazione *f*.
bookkeeping ['bukˌkiːpiŋ] *n* contabilità *f*. **bookkeeper** *n* contabile *m, f*.
booklet ['buklit] *n* opuscolo *m*.
bookmaker ['bukmeikə] *n* bookmaker *m invar*, allibratore *m*.
bookmark ['bukmaːk] *n* segnalibro *m*.
bookseller ['bukselə] *n* libraio *m*.
bookshop ['bukʃop] *n* libreria *f*.
bookstall ['bukstoːl] *n* edicola *f*.
boom [buːm] *v* (*noise*) rimbombare, tuonare; (*econ*) essere in gran voga. *n* rimbombo *m*, tuono *m*; (*econ*) boom *m invar*.
boorish ['buəriʃ] *adj* grossolano.
boost [buːst] *n* pressione *f*, spinta *f*. *v* aumentare, spingere.

boot [buːt] *n* (*shoe*) stivale *m*; (*car*) portabagagli *m*.
booth [buːð] *n* baracca *f*, cabina *f*.
booze [buːz] (*coll*) *n* bevanda alcoolica *f*. *v* ubriacarsi, sbronzarsi.
border ['boːdə] *n* orlo *m*, limite *m*, frontiera *f*. *v* (*embroidery*) orlare; (*geog*) confinare (con). **borderline case** caso limite *m*.
bore[1] [boː] *n* (*hole*) buco *m*, foro *m*; (*gun*) calibro *m*. *v* forare, trapanare; (*mech*) alesare.
bore[2] [boː] *v* (*weary*) seccare, annoiare. *n* (*person*) seccatore, -trice *m*, *f*; (*matter*) seccatura *f*; noia *f*.
bore[3] [boː] *V* **bear**[1].
born [boːn] *adj* nato. **be born** nascere.
borne [boːn] *V* **bear**[1].
borough ['bʌrə] *n* comune *m*, borgo *m*.
borrow ['borou] *v* prendere a prestito, farsi prestare.
bosom ['buzəm] *n* petto *m*, seno *m*.
boss [bos] *n* capo *m*, direttore *m*. *v* comandare. **bossy** *adj* prepotente.
botany ['botəni] *n* botanica *f*. **botanical** *adj* botanico. **botanist** *n* botanico, -a *m*, *f*.
both [bouθ] *adj*, *pron* ambedue, entrambi, tutti e due.
bother ['boðə] *n* seccatura *f*, noia *f*. *v* seccare, preoccuparsi.
bottle ['botl] *n* bottiglia *f*. *v* imbottigliare. **bottleneck** *n* ingorgo *m*. **bottle-opener** *n* apribottiglie *m invar*.
bottom ['botəm] *n* fondo *m*. *adj* ultimo, inferiore. **bottomless** *adj* senza fondo.
bough [bau] *n* ramo *m*.
bought [boːt] *V* **buy**.
boulder ['bouldə] *n* macigno *m*, masso roccioso *m*.
bounce [bauns] *v* (far) rimbalzare. *n* balzo *m*, rimbalzo *m*.
bound[1] [baund] *v* saltare, rimbalzare. *n* salto *m*, balzo *m*. **by leaps and bounds** a passi da gigante.
bound[2] [baund] *n* confine *m*, restrizione *f*. *v* porre limiti a, confinare. **boundary** *n* limite *m*, frontiera *f*. **boundless** *adj* illimitato.
bound[3] [baund] *adj* **bound for** diretto per, con destinazione per.
bound[4] [baund] *V* **bind**.
bouquet [buːkei] *n* mazzo *m*.
bourgeois ['buəʒwaː] *n*(*m*+*f*), *adj* borghese.
bout [baut] *n* periodo d'attività *m*; (*illness*) attacco *m*; (*match*) ripresa *f*.
bow[1] [bau] *n* (*greeting*) saluto *m*; (*bend*) inchino *m*. *v* inchinarsi, salutare, chinare.
bow[2] [bou] *n* (*archery*) arco *m*; (*violin, etc.*) archetto *m*; (*ribbon*) fiocco *m*. **bow-legged** *adj* dalle gambe storte. **bow-tie** *n* cravatta a farfalla *f*.
bow[3] [bau] *n* (*naut*) prua *f*, prora *f*.
bowels ['bauəlz] *pl n* viscere *f pl*.
bowl[1] [boul] *n* (*basin*) scodella *f*, bacino *m*.
bowl[2] [boul] *n* (*ball*) boccia *f*. *v* far rotolare, servire la palla. **bowls** *n* gioco delle bocce *m*. **bowler** *n* (*hat*) bombetta *f*.
box[1] [boks] *n* scatola *f*, cassetta *f*; (*theatre*) palco *m*. **box number** casella postale *f*. **box office** botteghino *m*.
box[2] [boks] *v* fare a pugni, fare del pugilato, fare la boxe. **boxing** *n* pugilato *m*, boxe *f*.
Boxing Day *n* giorno di San Stefano *m*.
boy [boi] *n* ragazzo *m*. **boyhood** *n* fanciullezza *f*. **boyish** *adj* da ragazzo.
boycott ['boikot] *n* boicottaggio *m*. *v* boicottare.
bra [braː] *n* reggipetto *m*, reggiseno *m*.
brace [breis] *v* fortificare, rinvigorire. *n* sostegno; (*tool*) trapano *m*; (*pair*) coppia *f*. **braces** *pl n* bretelle *f pl*.
bracelet ['breislit] *n* braccialetto *m*.
bracken ['brakən] *n* felce *f*.
bracket ['brakit] *n* mensola *f*, braccio *m*; (*printing*) parentesi *f invar*. **put in brackets** mettere fra parentesi. **bracket together** accoppiare.
brag [brag] *v* vantarsi. **braggart** *n* fanfarone *m*.
brain [brein] *n* cervello *m*. **brainwashing** *n* lavaggio del cervello *m*. **brainwave** *n* idea geniale *f*. **brainy** *adj* intelligente.
braise [breiz] *v* brasare, cuocere a stufato.
brake [breik] *n* freno *m*. *v* frenare, serrare il freno.
bramble ['brambl] *n* (*bush*) rovo *m*; (*fruit*) mora *f*.
bran [bran] *n* crusca *f*.
branch [braːntʃ] *n* ramo *m*; (*office*) succursale *f*. **branch off** biforcarsi. **branch out** estendersi.
brand [brand] *n* (*trademark*) marchio *m*; (*grade, make*) marca *f*; (*marking*) marchio *m*, stigma *m*; (*burning wood*) tizzone *m*. **brand-new** *adj* nuovo di zecca,

nuovo fiammante. *v* marchiare, stigmatizzare.

brandish ['brandiʃ] *v* brandire.

brandy ['brandi] *n* cognac *m*, acquavite *f*.

brass [braːs] *n* ottone *m*. **brassy** *adj* d'ottone; (*impudent*) sfacciato.

brassiere ['brasiə] *V* **bra**.

brave [breiv] *adj* prode, coraggioso, ardito. *v* sfidare, affrontare. **bravery** *n* audacia *f*, coraggio *m*.

brawl [broːl] *n* rissa *f*, zuffa *f*. *v* rissare, azzuffarsi.

brawn [broːn] *n* (*strength*) forza muscolare *f*; (*meat*) testina *f*.

brazen ['breizn] *adj* sfacciato, impudente; (*brass*) di ottone.

breach [briːtʃ] *n* violazione *f*, rottura *f*; (*mil*) breccia *f*. *v* far una breccia in, rompere.

bread [bred] *n* pane *m*. **breadcrumbs** *pl n* briciole di pane *f pl*.

breadth [bredθ] *n* larghezza *f*, ampiezza *f*; (*cloth*) altezza *f*.

***break** [breik] *n* rottura *f*, frattura *f*; interruzione *f*, pausa *f*; (*chance*) opportunità *f*. *v* rompere, spezzare, infrangere; (*record*) battere. **at breakneck speed** a rompicollo. **break away** fuggire, distaccarsi. **break off** mandare a monte. **break out** (*war*) scoppiare. **breakthrough** *n* scoperta *f*, innovazione *f*. **breakable** *adj* fragile. **breakage** *n* rottura *f*.

breakdown ['breikdaun] *n* crollo *m*; (*car*) panna *f*; (*nerves*) esaurimento nervoso *m*. *v* **break down** demolire; analizzare; (*car*) avere una panna; (*nerves*) avere un esaurimento nervoso.

breakfast ['brekfəst] *n* prima colazione *f*.

breast [brest] *n* petto *m*, seno *m*. **breastbone** *n* sterno *m*. **breast-stroke** *n* nuoto a rana *m*.

breath [breθ] *n* respiro *m*, fiato *m*, soffio *m*. **breathless** *adj* ansimante. **breathtaking** *adj* sorprendente.

breathalyser ['breθəlaizə] *n* analizzatore del fiato *m*.

breathe [briːð] *v* respirare, prender fiato; (*sigh*) sospirare. **breathing** *n* respirazione *f*.

bred [bred] *V* **breed**.

***breed** [briːd] *v* generare, allevare. *n* razza *f*, stirpe *f*. **breeding** *n* (*animals*) allevamento *m*; (*manners*) educazione *f*.

breeze [briːz] *n* brezza *f*. **breezily** *adj* con disinvoltura.

brew [bruː] *v* (*beer*) far fermentare; (*tea*) preparare; (*storm*) essere nell'aria. *n* miscela *f*. **brewer** *n* birraio *m*. **brewery** *n* birreria *f*.

bribe [braib] *v* corrompere, allettare. *n* dono a scopo di corruzione *m*; (*coll*) bustarella *f*. **bribery** *n* corruzione *f*.

brick [brik] *n* mattone *m*. **bricklayer** *n* muratore *m*. **drop a brick** fare una gaffe.

bride [braid] *n* sposa *f*, sposina *f*. **bridal** *adj* nuziale. **bridegroom** *n* sposo *m*. **bridesmaid** *n* damigella d'onore della sposa *f*.

bridge[1] [bridʒ] *n* ponte *m*. *v* congiungere. **bridge a gap** colmare una lacuna.

bridge[2] [bridʒ] *n* (*cards*) bridge *m*.

bridle ['braidl] *n* briglia *f*, freno *m*. *v* risentirsi. **bridle-path** *n* sentiero percorribile a cavallo *m*.

brief [briːf] *adj* breve. *n* riassunto *m*; istruzioni *m pl*; lettera *f*. *v* riassumere per sommi capi; (*law*) affidare una causa. **brief-case** *n* borsa *f*.

brigade [bri'geid] *n* brigata *f*.

bright [brait] *adj* lucido, risplendente; (*lively*) vivace; (*clever*) intelligente. **brighten** *v* rendere più brillante, illuminare. **brightness** *n* luminosità *f*, splendore *m*.

brilliant ['briljənt] *adj* brillante.

brim [brim] *n* orlo *m*, bordo *m*; (*hat*) falda *f*. **brimful** *adj* colmo.

brine [brain] *n* acqua salata *f*.

***bring** [briŋ] *v* portare, condurre. **bring about** causare. **bring back** riportare; restituire. **bring up** educare; vomitare.

brink [briŋk] *n* orlo *m*.

brisk [brisk] *adj* vivace, arzillo.

bristle ['brisl] *n* (*human*) pelo duro *m*; (*animal*) setola *f*. *v* rizzarsi.

Britain ['britn] *n* Gran Bretagna *f*. **British** *adj* britannico. **Briton** *n* britannico, -a *m*, *f*.

brittle ['britl] *adj* fragile.

broach [broutʃ] *v* (*subject*) intavolare un discorso su.

broad [broːd] *adj* (*wide*) largo, ampio; (*overall*) generale. **broad bean** fava *f*. **broad-minded** *adj* di larghe vedute. **broaden** *v* allargare.

***broadcast** ['broːdkaːst] *v* trasmettere alla radio. *adj* radiodiffuso. *n* trasmissione radio *f*.

broccoli ['brokəli] *n* broccolo *m*.
brochure ['brouʃuə] *n* opuscolo *m*.
broke [brouk] *V* **break**. *adj* (*coll*) al verde, rovinato.
broken ['broukn] *V* **break**.
broker ['broukə] *n* agente *m*, commissionario *m*, sensale *m*.
bronchitis [broŋ'kaitis] *n* bronchite *f*.
bronze [bronz] *n* bronzo *m*. *v* abbronzare.
brooch [broutʃ] *n* spilla *f*.
brood [bruːd] *n* covata *f*, figliolanza *f*. *v* covare; (*think*) meditare.
brook [bruk] *n* ruscello *m*. *v* ammettere.
broom [bruːm] *n* (*brush*) scopa *f*; (*plant*) ginestra *f*.
broth [broθ] *n* brodo *m*.
brothel ['broθl] *n* bordello *m*.
brother ['brʌðə] *n* fratello *m*. **brother-in-law** *n* cognato *m*. **brotherhood** *n* fratellanza *f*, fraternità *f*. **brotherly** *adj* fraterno.
brought [broːt] *V* **bring**.
brow [brau] *n* fronte *f*; (*hill*) cima *f*. **browbeat** *v* intimidire.
brown [braun] *nm*, *adj* bruno, marrone, castano. *v* abbrunire, abbronzare; (*cooking*) rosolare.
browse [brauz] *v* brucare, scartabellare.
bruise [bruːz] *v* ammaccare, intaccare. *n* livido *m*, contusione *f*. **bruised** *adj* (*person*) contuso; (*fruit*) ammaccato.
brunette [bruː'net] *nf*, *adj* bruna, brunetta.
brush [brʌʃ] *n* spazzola *f*; spazzolino *m*; (*paint*) pennello *m*; (*encounter*) scontro *m*. *v* spazzolare. **brush against** sfiorare. **brush aside** ignorare. **brush up** (*revise*) ripassare.
brusque [brusk] *adj* brusco.
Brussels ['brʌsəlz] *n* Brusselle *f*. **Brussels sprouts** cavoli di Brusselle *m pl*.
brute [bruːt] *nm*, *adj* bruto. **brutal** *adj* brutale.
bubble ['bʌbl] *n* bolla *f*. *v* formar bolle, gorgogliare.
buck [bʌk] *n* maschio *m*; (*deer*) daino *m*. **buck-tooth** *n* dente sporgente *m*. **pass the buck** scaricare la responsabilità. *v* **buck up** (*rear up*) impennarsi; (*coll: cheer up*) rallegrarsi.
bucket ['bʌkit] *n* secchio *m*, secchia *f*.
buckle ['bʌkl] *n* fibbia *f*, fermaglio *m*. *v* affibbiare.
bud [bʌd] *n* bocciolo *m*, gemma *f*. *v* germogliare, sbocciare. **nip in the bud** troncare sul nascere.
budge [bʌdʒ] *v* scostarsi.
budget ['bʌdʒit] *n* bilancio preventivo *m*. *v* fare un bilancio preventivo.
buffalo ['bʌfəlou] *n* bufalo, -a *m*, *f*.
buffer ['bʌfə] *n* (*trains*) respingente *m*. **buffer state** stato cuscinetto *m*.
buffet[1] ['bʌfit] *v* (*hit*) schiaffeggiare. *n* schiaffo *m*.
buffet[2] ['bufei] *n* (*cafeteria*) buffet *m*, caffè ristoratore *m*; (*sideboard*) credenza *f*. **cold buffet** cibi freddi *m pl*.
bug [bʌg] *n* cimice *f*; (*coll*) piccolo insetto *m*.
bugger ['bʌgə] (*impol*) *n* sodomita *m*; (*fellow*) tizio *m*; (*derog*) brutto ceffo *m*. *v* inculare. **bugger off** *v* svignarsela. **bugger off!** va a quel paese! va al diavolo! **buggery** *n* sodomia *f*, pederastia *f*.
bugle ['bjuːgl] *n* tromba *f*.
***build** [bild] *v* costruire, fabbricare. *n* corporatura *f*. **building** *n* edificio *m*, costruzione *f*. **building society** *n* società immobiliare *f*, credito edilizio *m*.
built [bilt] *V* **build**.
bulb [bʌlb] *n* (*plant*) bulbo *m*; (*light*) lampadina *f*.
Bulgaria [bʌl'geəriə] *n* Bulgaria *f*. **Bulgarian** *n*, *adj* bulgaro, -a.
bulge [bʌldʒ] *n* protuberanza *f*, gonfiore *m*. *v* gonfiarsi, sporgere.
bulk [bʌlk] *n* massa *f*, volume *m*. **the bulk** la maggior parte *f*. **bulky** *adj* massiccio, voluminoso.
bull [bul] *n* toro *m*; (*papal*) bolla *f*. **bulldog** *n* mastino *m*. **bulldozer** *n* livellatrice *f*. **bullfight** *n* corrida *f*. **bull's eye** centro (del bersaglio) *m*.
bullet ['bulit] *n* pallottola *f*. **bullet-proof** *adj* blindato, corazzato.
bulletin ['bulətin] *n* bollettino *m*.
bullion ['buliən] *n* lingotto (di metallo prezioso) *m*.
bully ['buli] *n* prepotente *m*. *v* tiranneggiare, maltrattare.
bum [bʌm] (*coll*) *n* sedere *m*. *adj* scadente. *v* **bum around** vagabondare.
bump [bʌmp] *v* urtare. *n* protuberanza *f*, bernoccolo *m*. **bump into** (*collide*) andare a sbattere contro; (*meet*) incontrare per caso. **bumpy** *adj* irregolare.
bumper ['bʌmpə] *n* (*mot*) paraurti *m*. *adj* abbondante.

bun [bʌn] *n* (*cake*) focaccia *f*; (*hair*) crocchia *f*.
bunch [bʌntʃ] *n* fascio *m*, mazzo *m*, gruppo *m*; (*grapes*) grappolo d'uva *m*. *v* riunire, raggruppare.
bundle ['bʌndl] *n* fagotto *m*, involto *m*. *v* mettere insieme alla rinfusa, fare un involto di, affastellare.
bungalow ['bʌŋgəlou] *n* bungalow *m*, villino ad un piano *m*.
bungle ['bʌŋgl] *v* sciupare, lavorar male. *n* lavoro malfatto *m*. **bungler** *n* confusionario *m*, guastamestieri *m*.
bunion ['bʌnjən] *n* protuberanza callosa *f*.
bunk [bʌŋk] *n* cuccetta *f*.
bunker ['bʌŋkə] *n* (*coal*) carbonaia *f*; (*mil*) ricovero militare seminterrato *m*; (*golf*) ostacolo *m*.
buoy [boi] *n* gavitello *m*, boa *f*. **buoyancy** *n* galleggiabilità *f*. **buoyant** *adj* galleggiante.
burden ['bəːdn] *n* peso *m*, onere *m*. *v* caricare, tassare.
bureau ['bjuərou] *n* (*desk*) scrittoio *m*; (*office*) ufficio *m*.
bureaucracy [bju'rokrəsi] *n* burocrazia *f*. **bureaucrat** *n* burocrate *m*, *f*. **bureaucratic** *adj* burocratico.
burglar ['bəːglə] *n* scassinatore *m*, ladro *m*. **burgle** *v* scassinare, svaligiare.
***burn** [bəːn] *v* bruciare, scottare, risplendere. **burn down** incendiare. *n* ustione *f*, scottatura *f*. **burner** *n* bruciatore *m*, becco a gas *m*.
burnt [bəːnt] *V* **burn**.
burrow ['bʌrou] *n* tana *f*, covo *m*. *v* farsi una tana, scavare.
***burst** [bəːst] *n* scoppio *m*, raffica *f*. *v* scoppiare, esplodere.
bury ['beri] *v* seppellire, sotterrare. **burial** *n* sepoltura *f*.
bus [bʌs] *n* autobus *m invar*. **bus station** capolinea (*pl* capilinea) *m*. **bus stop** fermata dell'autobus *f*.
bush [buʃ] *n* (*shrub*) cespuglio *m*; (*woodland*) macchia *f*. **bushy** *adj* folto.
business ['biznis] *n* affare *m*, mestiere *m*. **business-like** *adj* metodico. **businessman** *n* uomo d'affari *m*.
bust[1] [bʌst] *n* (*anat*) busto *m*, petto *m*.
bust[2] [bʌst] *adj* (*coll*: *bankrupt*) rovinato. *v* rovinare.
bustle ['bʌsl] *n* trambusto *m*, agitazione *f*. *v* agitarsi, affacendarsi.
busy ['bizi] *adj* occupato, attivo, indaffarato. **busybody** *n* ficcanaso *m*. *v* **busy oneself with** occuparsi di.
but [bʌt] *conj* ma. *adv* (*only*) solo, soltanto. *prep* (*except*) eccetto, tranne.
butane ['bjuːtein] *n* butano *m*.
butcher [butʃə] *n* macellaio *m*. **butcher's shop** macelleria *f*. *v* macellare, massacrare. **butchery** *n* strage *f*, massacro *m*.
butler ['bʌtlə] *n* maggiordomo *m*.
butt[1] [bʌt] *n* (*gun*) calcio *m*, impugnatura *f*; (*cigarette*) mozzicone *m*.
butt[2] [bʌt] *n* (*laughing-stock*) bersaglio *m*, zimbello *m*.
butt[3] [bʌt] *n* (*hit*) cornata *f*, cozzo *m*. *v* cozzare, urtare con la testa. **butt in** interrompere, intromettersi.
butter ['bʌtə] *n* burro *m*. *v* imburrare.
buttercup ['bʌtəkʌp] *n* ranuncolo *m*.
butterfly ['bʌtəflai] *n* farfalla *f*.
buttocks ['bʌtəks] *pl n* natiche *f pl*.
button ['bʌtn] *n* bottone *m*. **buttonhole** *n* occhiello *m*, asola *f*. *v* attaccare un bottone. **button up** abbottonare.
buttress ['bʌtris] *n* sostegno *m*, sperone *m*. *v* sostenere.
***buy** [bai] *v* acquistare, comprare. *n* acquisto *m*. **buyer** *n* compratore *m*.
buzz [bʌz] *n* ronzio *m*; (*phone*) telefonata *f*. *v* ronzare; telefonare.
by [bai] *adv* vicino. *prep* da, con, a, di, per, entro. **by and large** generalmente parlando. **by the way** a proposito. **by-law** *n* legge locale *f*. **bypass** *n* circonvallazione *f*; deviazione stradale *f*. **by-product** *n* prodotto secondario *m*. **bystander** *n* astante *m*, *f*. **byword** *n* detto *m*.

C

cab [kab] *n* tassì *m*.
cabaret ['kabərei] *n* caffè concerto *m*, cabaret *m invar*.
cabbage ['kabidʒ] *n* cavolo *m*.
cabin ['kabin] *n* cabina *f*, capanna *f*.
cabinet ['kabinit] *n* (*furniture*) armadietto *m*; (*pol*) gabinetto *m*; (*cocktails*) bar *m invar*. **cabinet-maker** *n* ebanista *m*.
cable ['keibl] *n* cavo *m*; telegramma *m*. *v* telegrafare. **cable-car** *n* funivia *f*.
cackle ['kakl] *v* (*hens*) schiamazzare; (*people*) chiacchierare. *n* schiamazzo *m*, chiacchiera *f*.

cactus ['kaktəs] *n* cactus *m*.
caddie ['kadi] *n* (*golf*) caddie *m*.
cadence ['keidəns] *n* cadenza *f*.
cadet [kə'det] *n* cadetto *m*.
café ['kafei] *n* caffè *m*.
cafeteria [kafə'tiəriə] *n* bar-ristorante *m*.
caffeine ['kafiːn] *n* caffeina *f*.
cage [keidʒ] *n* gabbia *f*. *v* ingabbiare. **cagey** *adj* cauto.
cake [keik] *n* (*sweet*) torta *f*, focaccia *f*, dolce *m*; (*soap*) saponetta *f*, pezzo di sapone *m*. *v* incrostarsi.
calamine ['kaləmain] *n* calamina *f*.
calamity [kə'laməti] *n* calamità *f*, disgrazia *f*.
calcium ['kalsiəm] *n* calcio *m*.
calculate ['kalkjuleit] *v* calcolare. **calculation** *n* calcolo *m*. **calculator** *n* calcolatore *m*, macchina calcolatrice *f*.
calendar ['kaləndə] *n* calendario *m*.
calf[1] [kaːf] *n* (*animal*) vitello, -a *m*, *f*.
calf[2] [kaːf] *n* (*leg*) polpaccio *m*.
calibre ['kalibə] *n* calibro *m*, qualità *f*.
call [koːl] *n* chiamata *f*, appello *m*, grido *m*, visita *f*. **call-box** *n* cabina telefonica *f*. **call-girl** *n* ragazza squillo *f*. *v* chiamare. **call off** annullare. **call on** visitare. **call up** telefonare; (*mil*) richiamare sotto le armi. **calling** *n* vocazione *f*.
callous ['kaləs] *adj* insensibile. *n* insensibilità *f*.
calm [kaːm] *adj* calmo. *v* calmare. **calm down** calmarsi. *n* calma *f*.
calorie ['kaləri] *n* caloria *f*.
came [keim] *V* **come**.
camel ['kaməl] *n* cammello *m*.
camera ['kamərə] *n* macchina fotografica *f*. **(film/television) cameraman** *n* operatore (cinematografico/televisivo) *m*.
camouflage ['kaməflaːʒ] *v* mimetizzazione *f*, mascheramento *m*. *v* mimetizzare, mascherare.
camp [kamp] *n* campo *m*, accampamento *m*. **camp-bed** *n* branda *f*. **campsite** *n* campeggio *m*. *v* accamparsi, campeggiare.
campaign [kam'pein] *n* campagna *f*. *v* fare una campagna.
campus ['kampəs] *n* campo universitario *m*.
camshaft ['kamʃaːft] *n* albero a camme *or* eccentrici *m*.
***can**[1] [kan] *v* (*be able*) potere, essere in grado di; (*know how*) sapere.
can[2] [kan] *n* scatola *f*, recipiente *m*. **can-opener** *n* apriscatole *m invar*. *v* mettere in scatola.
Canada ['kanədə] *n* Canadà *m*. **Canadian** *n*(*m*+*f*), *adj* canadese.
canal [kə'nal] *n* canale *m*.
canary [kə'neəri] *n* canarino *m*.
cancel ['kansəl] *v* annullare, disdire. **cancellation** *n* annullamento *m*.
cancer ['kansə] *n* cancro *m*. **Cancer** *n* Cancro *m*.
candid ['kandid] *adj* candido, sincero.
candidate ['kandidət] *n* candidato, -a *m*, *f*.
candle ['kandl] *n* candela *f*; (*church*) cero *m*. **candlelight** *n* lume di candela *m*. **candlestick** *n* candeliere *m*.
candour ['kandə] *n* franchezza *f*.
candy ['kandi] *n* (*US*) caramella *f*. **candied** *adj* candito.
cane [kein] *n* canna *f*, bastone *m*; (*school*) verga *f*. *v* bastonare.
canine ['keinain] *adj* canino.
canister ['kanistə] *n* latta *f*.
cannabis ['kanəbis] *n* hascisc *m*.
cannibal ['kanibəl] *n* cannibale *m*. **cannibalism** *n* cannibalismo *m*.
cannon ['kanən] *n* cannone *m*. **cannonball** *n* palla di cannone *f*.
canoe [kə'nuː] *n* canoa *f*.
canon ['kanən] *n* canone *m*, criterio *m*; (*church dignitary*) canonico *m*. **canonical** *adj* canonico. **canonize** *v* canonizzare.
canopy ['kanəpi] *n* baldacchino *m*.
canteen [kan'tiːn] *n* (*dining place*) mensa *f*; (*cutlery*) posateria *f*.
canter ['kantə] *n* piccolo galoppo *m*. *v* andare al piccolo galoppo.
canvas ['kanvəs] *n* tela *f*; (*sails*) velatura *f*.
canvass ['kanvəs] *v* (*orders*, *votes*) sollecitare. **canvasser** *n* sollecitatore, -trice *m*, *f*.
canyon ['kanjən] *n* burrone *m*.
cap [kap] *n* (*hat*) berretto *m*; (*bathing*) cuffia *f*; (*mech*) coperchio *m*, cappello *m*. *v* coprire; sorpassare.
capable ['keipəbl] *adj* capace. **capability** *n* capacità *f*.
capacity [kə'pasəti] *n* capacità *f*, abilità *f*. **in the capacity of** nella qualità di.
cape[1] [keip] *n* (*cloak*) mantellina *f*.
cape[2] [keip] *n* (*geog*) capo *m*, promontorio *m*.

caper[1] ['keipə] *n* (*bot*) cappero *m*.
caper[2] ['keipə] *n* capriola *f*.
capillary [kə'piləri] *adj* capillare. *n* vaso capillare *m*.
capital ['kapitl] *n* capitale *f*; (*arch*) capitello *m*; (*letter*) maiuscola *f*. *adj* capitale. **capitalism** *n* capitalismo *m*. **capitalist** *n*(*m*+*f*), *adj* capitalista. **capitalize** *v* capitalizzare.
Capitol ['kapitl] *n* Campidoglio *m*.
capitulate [kə'pitjuleit] *v* capitolare. **capitulation** *n* resa *f*.
capricious [kə'priʃəs] *adj* capriccioso.
Capricorn ['kaprikoːn] *n* Capricorno *m*.
capsicum ['kapsikəm] *n* peperone *m*.
capsize [kap'saiz] *v* capovolgere, capovolgersi.
capsule ['kapsjuːl] *n* capsula *f*.
captain ['kaptin] *n* (*chief*) capo *m*; (*army, team*) capitano *m*; (*navy*) capitano di vascello *m*; comandante *m*. *v* comandare.
caption ['kapʃən] *n* didascalia *f*.
captive ['kaptiv] *n*, *adj* prigioniero, -a; schiavo, -a. **captivate** *v* cattivare. **captivity** *n* cattività *f*, prigionia *f*.
capture ['kaptʃə] *v* catturare. *n* cattura *f*. **captor** *n* catturatore *m*.
car [kaː] *n* macchina *f*, automobile *f*. **car park** parcheggio *m*. **go by car** andare in macchina.
carafe [kə'raf] *n* caraffa *f*.
carat ['karət] *n* carato *m*.
caravan ['karəvan] *n* (*vehicle*) roulotte (*pl* -s) *f*; (*travelling group*) carovana *f*.
caraway ['karəwei] *n* cumino *m*.
carbohydrate [kaːbə'haidreit] *n* carboidrato *m*.
carbon ['kaːbən] *n* carbonio *m*. **carbon paper** carta carbone *f*.
carbuncle ['kaːbʌŋkl] *n* carbonchio *m*, pustola *f*.
carburettor ['kaːbjuretə] *n* carburatore *m*.
carcass ['kaːkəs] *n* carcassa *f*.
card [kaːd] *n* carta *f*; (*greetings, etc.*) cartolina *f*; (*playing*) carta da gioco; (*visiting*) biglietto da visita *m*; (*index*) scheda *f*.
cardboard ['kaːdboːd] *n* cartone *m*, cartoncino *m*.
cardiac ['kaːdiak] *adj* cardiaco. **cardiac arrest** arresto cardiaco *m*.
cardigan ['kaːdigən] *n* golf *m*, giacca *f*.
cardinal ['kaːdənl] *nm*, *adj* cardinale.
care [keə] *v* curare; preoccuparsi; interessarsi. *n* cura *f*, premura *f*; ansietà *f*; responsabilità *f*. **carefree** *adj* spensierato. **care of** presso. **caretaker** *n* custode *m*, *f*. **care-worn** *adj* preoccupato. **careful** *adj* attento; (*thorough*) curato. **careless** *adj* disattento, trascurato. **carelessness** *n* trascuratezza *f*.
career [kə'riə] *n* carriera *f*.
caress [kə'res] *n* carezza *f*. *v* accarezzare.
cargo ['kaːgou] *n* carico (*pl* -chi) *m*.
caricature ['karikətjuə] *n* caricatura *f*. *v* mettere in caricatura. **caricaturist** *n* caricaturista *m*, *f*.
carnage ['kaːnidʒ] *n* strage *f*.
carnal ['kaːnl] *adj* carnale, sensuale.
carnation [kaː'neiʃən] *n* garofano *m*.
carnival ['kaːnivəl] *n* carnevale *m*.
carnivorous [kaː'nivərəs] *adj* carnivoro. **carnivore** *n* carnivoro *m*.
carol ['karəl] *n* cantico *m*. **Christmas carol** cantico di Natale *m*.
carpenter ['kaːpəntə] *n* falegname *m*. **carpentry** *n* falegnameria *f*, ebanisteria *f*.
carpet ['kaːpit] *n* tappeto *m*, moquette *f*.
carriage ['karidʒ] *n* (*vehicle*) carrozza *f*, vettura *f*; (*bearing*) portamento *m*; (*railway*) vagone *m*.
carrier ['kariə] *n* portatore, -trice *m*, *f*; (*comm*) trasportatore *m*; (*med*) vettore *m*. **carrier bag** sacchetto per acquisti *m*. **carrier pigeon** piccione viaggiatore *m*.
carrot ['karət] *n* carota *f*.
carry ['kari] *v* portare, trasportare. **carrycot** *n* culla portabile *f*. **carry on** proseguire, gestire. **carry out** eseguire, realizzare. **carry over** riportare.
cart [kaːt] *n* carro *m*, carretta *f*. **cartload** *n* carrettata *f*. **turn cartwheels** fare la ruota. *v* **cart off** portar via.
cartilage ['kaːtəlidʒ] *n* cartilagine *f*.
cartography [kaː'togrəfi] *n* cartografia *f*. **cartographer** *n* cartografo, -a *m*, *f*.
carton ['kaːtən] *n* scatola di cartone *f*; (*cigarettes*) stecca *f*.
cartoon [kaː'tuːn] *n* (*drawing*) cartone *m*; (*film*) cartone animato *m*; caricatura *f*. **cartoonist** *n* disegnatore, -trice *m*, *f*; caricaturista *m*, *f*.
cartridge ['kaːtridʒ] *n* cartuccia *f*.
carve [kaːv] *v* (*meat*) tagliare, trinciare; (*art*) scolpire, intagliare. **carving** *n* intaglio *m*. **carving knife** trinciante *m*.
cascade [kas'keid] *n* cascata *f*. *v* scrosciare.

case[1] [keis] *n* (*matter*) caso *m*, fatto *m*, questione *f*; cosa *f*; (*law*) causa *f*, processo *m*. **in any case** ad ogni modo. **in case** qualora. **in most cases** in genere. **in that case** allora.
case[2] [keis] *n* (*box*) scatola *f*; (*luggage*) valigia *f*; (*glasses, pens*) astuccio *f*.
cash [kaʃ] *v* incassare, riscuotere. *n* denaro *m*; contanti *m pl*. **cash desk** cassa *f*. **cash payment** pagamento in contanti *m*. **petty cash** spese varie *f pl*.
cashier[1] [ka'ʃiə] *n* cassiere, -a *m, f*.
cashier[2] [ka'ʃiə] *v* destituire.
cashmere [kaʃ'miə] *n* cachemire *m invar*.
casing ['keisiŋ] *n* copertura *f*, rivestimento *m*.
casino [kə'siːnou] *n* casinò *m*.
casket ['kaːskit] *n* cofanetto *m*; (*coffin*) cassa da morto *f*.
casserole ['kasəroul] *n* casseruola *f*. *v* cucinare in umido.
cassette [kə'set] *n* cassetta *f*.
cassock ['kasək] *n* tonaca *f*.
***cast** [kaːst] *n* (*throw*) lancio *m*, getto *m*; (*mould*) forma *f*, calco *m*; (*metal*) fusione *f*; (*theatre*) complesso *m*, insieme degli attori *m*; (*plaster*) ingessatura *f*. *v* lanciare, gettare; (*metal*) fondere; (*theatre*) dare la parte. **cast away** gettar via. **cast iron** ghisa *f*. **cast-off** *adj* abbandonato.
caste [kaːst] *n* casta *f*.
castle ['kaːsl] *n* castello *m*.
castor ['kaːstə] *n* (*furniture*) rotella al piede di mobili *f*; (*condiments*) ampolliera *f*. **castor oil** olio di ricino *m*. **castor sugar** zucchero semolato *m*.
castrate [kə'streit] *v* castrare. **castration** *n* castratura *f*.
casual ['kaʒuəl] *adj* casuale, fortuito, disinvolto.
casualty ['kaʒuəlti] *n* vittima *f*; (*accident*) incidente *m*; (*hospital*) pronto soccorso *m*.
cat [kat] *n* gatto, -a *m, f*. **cat's eye** catarifrangente *m*. **catty** *adj* malevolo.
catalogue ['katəlog] *n* catalogo (*pl* -ghi) *m*, elenco *m*. *v* elencare.
catalyst ['katəlist] *n* catalizzatore *m*. **catalysis** *n*, *pl* **-ses** catalisi *f*.
catamaran [katəmə'ran] *n* catamarano *m*.
catapult ['katəpʌlt] *n* catapulta *f*, fionda *f*. *v* scagliare.
cataract ['katərakt] *n* cateratta *f*.
catarrh [kə'taː] *n* catarro *m*.
catastrophe [kə'tastrəfi] *n* catastrofe *f*. **catastrophic** *adj* catastrofico.
***catch** [katʃ] *n* preda *f*, cattura *f*; (*door*) spranga *f*; (*fish*) retata *f*. *v* prendere, acchiappare; (*fish*) pescare. **catch-phrase** *n* frase fatta *f*. **catch up with** raggiungere. **catchword** *n* slogan *m*. **catching** *adj* (*med*) contagioso, infettivo.
category ['katəgəri] *n* categoria *f*. **categorical** *adj* categorico.
cater ['keitə] *v* provvedere cibo. **cater for** provvedere a. **caterer** *n* approvvigionatore, -trice *m, f*. **catering** *n* approvvigionamento *m*.
caterpillar ['katəpilə] *n* bruco *m*.
cathedral [kə'θiːdrəl] *n* cattedrale *f*.
catheter ['kaθətə] *n* catetere *m*.
cathode ['kaθoud] *n* catodo *m*.
catholic ['kaθəlik] *n*, *adj* cattolico, -a. **catholicism** *n* cattolicesimo *m*.
catkin ['katkin] *n* gattino *m*.
cattle ['katl] *n* bestiame *m*.
caught [koːt] *V* **catch**.
cauliflower ['koliflauə] *n* cavolfiore *m*.
cause [koːz] *n* causa *f*, ragione *f*, motivo *m*. *v* causare, provocare, suscitare.
causeway ['koːzwei] *n* strada rialzata *f*; (*main highway*) strada maestra *f*.
caustic ['koːstik] *adj* caustico.
caution ['koːʃən] *n* cautela *f*, circospezione *f*; (*law*) diffida *f*, ammonimento *m*. *v* ammonire, mettere in guardia. **cautious** *adj* cauto, prudente.
cavalry ['kavəlri] *n* cavalleria *f*.
cave [keiv] *n* caverna *f*, grotta *f*.
caviar ['kaviaː] *n* caviale *m*.
cavity ['kavəti] *n* cavità *f*, buco *m*.
cease [siːs] *v* cessare, smettere. **cease-fire** *n* tregua *f*, cessate il fuoco *m invar*. **ceaseless** *adj* continuo, incessante.
cedar ['siːdə] *n* cedro *m*.
ceiling ['siːliŋ] *n* soffitto *m*.
celebrate ['seləbreit] *v* celebrare, festeggiare, far festa. **celebration** *n* festa *f*, commemorazione *f*. **celebrity** *n* celebrità *f*.
celery ['seləri] *n* sedano *m*.
celestial [sə'lestiəl] *adj* celestiale, celeste.
celibate ['selibət] *n*, *adj* celibe *m*. **celibacy** *n* celibato *m*.
cell [sel] *n* (*room*) cella *f*; (*biol*) cellula *f*; (*elec*) pila *f*.
cellar ['selə] *n* cantina *f*, sottosuolo *m*.

cello ['tʃelou] *n* violoncello *m*. **cellist** *n* violoncellista *m*, *f*.
cellular ['seljulə] *adj* cellulare.
cement [sə'ment] *n* cemento *m*. *v* cementare, consolidare.
cemetery ['semətri] *n* cimitero *m*, camposanto *m*.
censor ['sensə] *n* censore *m*. *v* censurare. **censorious** *adj* ipercritico. **censorship** *n* censura *f*.
censure ['senʃə] *n* censura *f*.
census ['sensəs] *n* censimento *m*.
cent [sent] *n* centesimo *m*, soldo *m*.
centenary [sen'tiːnəri] *nm*, *adj* centenario.
centigrade ['sentigreid] *adj* centigrado.
centimetre ['sentimiːtə] *n* centimetro *m*.
centipede ['sentipiːd] *n* millepiedi *m invar*.
centre ['sentə] *n* centro *m*. *v* centrare, accentrare. **central** *adj* centrale. **central heating** riscaldamento centrale *m*. **centralization** *n* centralizzazione *f*. **centralize** *v* centralizzare.
centrifugal [sen'trifjugəl] *adj* centrifugo (*m pl* -ghi). **centrifuge** *n* centrifuga *f*.
century ['sentʃuri] *n* secolo *m*.
ceramic [sə'ramik] *adj* ceramico. **ceramics** *n* ceramica *f*.
cereal ['siəriəl] *nm*, *adj* cereale.
cerebral ['serəbrəl] *adj* cerebrale.
ceremony ['serəməni] *n* cerimonia *f*, funzione *f*. **stand on ceremony** far complimenti. **ceremonial** *adj* solenne, rituale. **ceremonious** *adj* formalista, cerimonioso.
certain ['səːtn] *adj* certo, sicuro. **certainly** *adv* certo, certamente, senza dubbio. **certainty** *n* certezza *f*, sicurezza *f*.
certificate [sə'tifikət] *n* certificato *m*, atto *m*, diploma *m*. **certify** *v* certificare, attestare, vidimare; (*declare insane*) classificare come pazzo.
cervix ['səːviks] *n* cervice *f*.
cesspool ['sespuːl] *n* cloaca *f*.
chafe [tʃeif] *v* irritarsi.
chaffinch ['tʃafintʃ] *n* fringuello *m*.
chain [tʃein] *n* catena *f*. **chain-smoke** *v* fumare ininterrottamente. **chain store** magazzino a catena *m*. *v* incatenare.
chair [tʃeə] *n* sedia *f*, seggio *m*; (*university*) cattedra *f*. **chairlift** *n* seggiovia *f*. **chairman** *n* presidente *m*. *v* presiedere.
chalk [tʃoːk] *n* gesso *m*. **chalky** *adj* gessoso; pallido.
challenge ['tʃalindʒ] *n* sfida *f*, provocazione *f*. *v* sfidare, opporsi a, provocare. **challenging** *adj* stimolante, provocatorio.
chamber ['tʃeimbə] *n* camera *f*. **chambermaid** *n* cameriera *f*. **chamber music** musica da camera *f*.
chameleon [kəmiːliən] *n* camaleonte *m*.
chamois ['ʃamwaː] *n* camoscio *m*; (*leather*) pelle di camoscio *f*.
champagne [ʃam'pein] *n* champagne *m*.
champion ['tʃampiən] *n* campione, -essa *m*, *f*. **championship** *n* campionato *m*. *v* difendere, sostenere.
chance [tʃaːns] *n* caso *m*, fortuna *f*, opportunità *f*, rischio *m*. **by chance** per caso. *v* (*risk*) arrischiare; (*happen*) capitare. *adj* fortuito.
chancellor [tʃaːnsələ] *n* cancelliere *m*; (*university*) rettore titolare *m*.
chandelier [ʃandə'liə] *n* lampadario *m*.
change [tʃeindʒ] *n* cambio *m*, mutamento *m*; (*money*) resto *m*, spiccioli *m pl*. *v* cambiare, mutare, cambiarsi. **changeable** *adj* variabile, mutevole. **changeability** *n* variabilità *f*. **changeless** *adj* immutevole, costante.
channel ['tʃanl] *n* canale *m*. **English Channel** Manica *f*. *v* incanalare.
chant [tʃaːnt] *n* canto *m*, salmodia *f*. *v* cantare, salmodiare.
chaos ['keios] *n* caos *m*.
chap[1] [tʃap] *v* screpolare, screpolarsi. *n* fessura *f*.
chap[2] [tʃap] *n* (*fellow*) tipo *m*, tizio *m*.
chapel ['tʃapəl] *n* cappella *f*.
chaperon ['ʃapəroun] *n* chaperon *m*. *v* accompagnare.
chaplain ['tʃaplin] *n* cappellano *m*.
chapter ['tʃaptə] *n* capitolo *m*.
char[1] [tʃaː] *v* carbonizzare, bruciare.
char[2] [tʃaː] *v* fare i lavori di casa. **charwoman** *n* donna di servizio *f*, donna a mezzo servizio *f*.
character ['karəktə] *n* carattere *m*, indole *f*, qualità *f*; (*acting*) personaggio *m*. **characterization** *n* caratterizzazione *f*. **characterize** *v* caratterizzare.
characteristic [ˌkarəktə'ristik] *adj* caratteristico. *n* caratteristica *f*.
charcoal ['tʃaːkoul] *n* carbone di legna *m*.
charge [tʃaːdʒ] *n* spesa *f*, costo *m*; cura *f*, custodia *f*; (*law*) accusa *f*; (*mil*) carica *f*. **free of charge** gratis, gratuito. **in charge**

addetto, incaricato. **take charge of** incaricarsi di. *v* addebitare; caricare. **chargeable** *adj* addebitabile.

charity ['tʃarəti] *n* carità *f*, elemosina *f*. **charitable** *adj* caritatevole.

charm [tʃaːm] *n* fascino *m*, incantesimo *m*; (*trinket*) portafortuna *m invar*. *v* affascinare, incantare. **charming** *adj* incantevole, affascinante.

chart [tʃaːt] *n* mappa *f*, diagramma *m*, grafico *m*, quadro *m*. *v* tracciare un diagramma *or* grafico di.

charter ['tʃaːtə] *n* carta *f*, documento *m*; (*flight*) volo charter *m*. *v* (*document*) istituire; (*hire*) noleggiare. **chartered accountant** ragioniere diplomato *m*.

chase [tʃeis] *n* caccia *f*, inseguimento *m*. *v* cacciare, inseguire; (*jewellery*) incastonare; (*metal*) cesellare.

chasm ['kazəm] *n* abisso *m*.

chassis ['ʃasi] *n* telaio *m*.

chaste [tʃeist] *adj* casto, austero. **chastity** *n* castità *f*, purezza *f*.

chastise [tʃas'taiz] *v* castigare, punire. **chastisement** *n* castigo (*pl* -ghi) *m*, punizione *f*.

chat [tʃat] *n* chiacchiera *f*, chiacchierata *f*. *v* chiacchierare.

chatter ['tʃatə] *v* chiacchierare; (*teeth*) battere. *n* chiacchiera *f*.

chauffeur ['ʃoufə] *n* autista *m*, *f*.

chauvinism ['ʃouvinizəm] *n* sciovinismo *m*. **chauvinist** *n*(*m*+*f*), *adj* sciovinista.

cheap [tʃiːp] *adj* economico, a buon mercato, poco caro; (*derog*) spregevole. **cheapen** *v* abbassare il prezzo di, screditare.

cheat [tʃiːt] *n* imbroglione, -a *m*, *f*, truffatore, -trice *m*, *f*; (*cards*) baro, -a *m*, *f*. *v* imbrogliare, truffare; barare. **cheating** *n* imbroglio *m*, truffa *f*.

check [tʃek] *n* controllo *m*, pausa *f*, ostacolo *m*; (*chess*) scacco *m*. *v* controllare, verificare, fermare; (*chess*) dare scacco. **check in** registrare all'arrivo. **check up on** informarsi su.

cheek [tʃiːk] *n* guancia *f*; (*insolence*) faccia tosta *f*. **cheeky** *adj* sfacciato, sfrontato.

cheer [tʃiə] *n* (*shout*) applauso *m*; (*mood*) allegria *f*, buonumore *m*. **cheerio!** *interj* ciao! arrivederci! *v* applaudire. **cheer up** rallegrare, rallegrarsi. **cheerful** *adj* allegro, di buonumore. **cheerless** *adj* triste.

cheese [tʃiːz] *n* formaggio *m*. **cheesecloth** *n* garza *f*. **cheese-paring** *adj* tirchio.

chef [ʃef] *n* capocuoco (*pl* -chi) *m*.

chemical ['kemikl] *n* prodotto chimico *m*. *adj* chimico.

chemistry ['kemistri] *n* chimica *f*. **chemist** *n* chimico, -a *m*, *f*, farmacista *m*, *f*. **chemist's shop** farmacia *f*.

cheque *or US* **check** [tʃek] *n* assegno *m*. **cheque-book** *n* libretto d'assegni *m*.

cherish ['tʃeriʃ] *v* tener caro, nutrire, amare.

cherry ['tʃeri] *n* (*fruit*) ciliegia *f*; (*tree*) ciliegio *m*.

chess [tʃes] *n* scacchi *m pl*. **chessboard** *n* scacchiera *f*.

chest [tʃest] *n* cassa *f*; (*anat*) petto *m*, torace *m*. **chest of drawers** cassettone *m*.

chestnut ['tʃesnʌt] *n* (*fruit*) castagna *f*; (*tree*) castagno *m*. *adj* castano.

chew [tʃuː] *v* masticare. **chew over** meditare. **chewing-gum** *n* chewing gum *m invar*, gomma da masticare *f*.

chicken ['tʃikin] *n* pollo *m*; (*chick*) pulcino *m*. **chicken-coop** *n* pollaio *m*. **chicken-pox** *n* varicella *f*.

chicory ['tʃikəri] *n* cicoria *f*, indivia *f*.

chick-pea ['tʃik,piː] *n* cece *m*.

chide [tʃaid] *v* sgridare.

chief [tʃiːf] *nm*, *pl* -s, *adj* capo, principale.

chilblain ['tʃilblein] *n* gelone *m*.

child [tʃaild] *n*, *pl* **children** bambino, -a *m*, *f*; ragazzo, -a *m*, *f*; (*offspring*) figlio, -a *m*, *f*. **childbirth** *n* parto *m*. **childhood** *n* infanzia *f*. **childish** *adj* puerile, infantile. **childlike** *adj* da bambino, semplice, innocente.

chill [tʃil] *v* raffreddare, agghiacciare. *adj* freddo, gelido. *n* freddo *m*, brivido *m*; (*illness*) raffreddore *m*. **catch a chill** buscarsi un raffreddore. **take the chill off** intiepidire. **chilly** *adj* freddo, fresco, freddoloso.

chilli ['tʃili] *n* peperone *m*, pepe rosso *m*.

chime [tʃaim] *v* suonare, scampanare. *n* scampanio *m*, rintocco *m*.

chimney ['tʃimni] *n* camino *m*, caminetto *m*. **chimney-pot** *n* ciminiera *f*, fumaiolo *m*. **chimney-sweep** *n* spazzacamino *m*.

chimpanzee [tʃimpən'ziː] *n* scimpanzè *m*.

chin [tʃin] *n* mento *m*. **chin-strap** *n* sottogola *m invar*.

china ['tʃainə] *n* porcellana *f*, ceramica *f*. **china clay** caolino *m*.

China ['tʃainə] *n* Cina *f*. **Chinese** *n*(*m*+*f*), *adj* cinese.
chink[1] [tʃiŋk] *n* (*fissure*) fessura *f*, crepa *f*.
chink[2] [tʃiŋk] *n* (*sound*) tintinnio *m*. *v* tintinnare.
chip [tʃip] *n* scheggia *f*, frammento *m*, truciolo *m*; (*gambling*) cip (*pl* -s) *m*, gettone *m*. **chips** *pl n* (*cookery*) patatine fritte *f pl*. *v* scheggiare. **chip in** intervenire; (*contribute money*) contribuire.
chiropodist [ki'ropədist] *n* pedicure *m*, *f invar*.
chirp [tʃəːp] *v* cinguettare, pigolare. *n* cinguettio *m*, pigolio *m*. **chirpy** *adj* allegro.
chisel ['tʃizl] *n* cesello *m*, bulino *m*. *v* cesellare.
chivalry ['ʃivəlri] *n* galanteria *f*. **chivalrous** *adj* galante.
chive [tʃaiv] *n* erba cipollina *f*.
chlorine ['kloːriːn] *n* cloro *m*.
chlorophyll ['klorəfil] *n* clorofilla *f*.
chocolate ['tʃokələt] *n* cioccolato *m*, cioccolatino *m*; (*drink*) cioccolata *f*. *adj* cioccolato *invar*.
choice [tʃois] *n* scelta *f*, assortimento *m*. *adj* scelto, di prima qualità.
choir ['kwaiə] *n* coro *m*.
choke [tʃouk] *v* soffocare, strozzare. *n* (*motor*) valvola dell'aria *f*, diffusore *m*.
cholera ['kolərə] *n* colera *m*.
***choose** [tʃuːz] *v* scegliere, eleggere, preferire.
chop[1] [tʃop] *n* (*meat*) braciola *f*; (*blow*) colpo *m*. *v* (*split*) spaccare; (*mince*) tagliuzzare, tritare. **chop down** abbattere. **chopper** *n* accetta *f*. **chopping-block** *n* tagliere *m*. **choppy sea** maretta *f*.
chop[2] [tʃop] *v* **chop and change** fare e disfare. **chop logic** cavillare.
chops [tʃops] *pl n* mascelle *f pl*. **lick one's chops** leccarsi i baffi.
chord [koːd] *n* corda *f*, accordo *m*.
chore [tʃoː] *n* (*task*) lavoro *m*, compito *m*. **household chores** lavori domestici *m pl*.
choreography [kori'ogrəfi] *n* coreografia *f*. **choreographer** *n* coreografo, -a *m*, *f*.
chorus ['koːrəs] *n* coro *m*. **choral** *adj* corale. **chorister** *n* corista *m*, *f*.
chose [tʃouz] *V* **choose**.
chosen ['tʃouzn] *V* **choose**.
Christ [kraist] *n* Cristo *m*.
christen ['krisn] *v* battezzare; (*name*) chiamare. **christening** *n* battesimo *m*.
Christian ['kristʃən] *n*, *adj* cristiano, -a. **Christian Democrat** democriziano, -a *m*, *f*. **Christian name** nome di battesimo *m*. **Christendom** *n* cristianesimo *m*. **Christianity** *n* cristianità *f*.
Christmas ['krisməs] *n* Natale *m*. *adj* di Natale; natalizio.
chromatic [krə'matik] *adj* cromatico.
chromium ['kroumiəm] *n* cromo *m*. **chromium-plate** *v* cromare. **chromium-plating** *n* cromatura *f*.
chromosome ['krouməsoum] *n* cromosoma *m*.
chronic ['kronik] *adj* cronico.
chronicle ['kronikl] *n* cronaca *f*. *v* narrare, fare la cronaca di.
chronological [kronə'lodʒikəl] *adj* cronologico.
chrysalis ['krisəlis] *n* crisalide *f*.
chrysanthemum [kri'sanθəməm] *n* crisantemo *m*.
chubby ['tʃʌbi] *adj* paffuto, grassoccio.
chuck [tʃʌk] *v* gettare, buttare. **chuck out** buttar fuori.
chuckle ['tʃʌkl] *v* ridacchiare, ridere di soppiatto.
chunk [tʃʌŋk] *n* grosso pezzo *m*; (*food*) fetta *f*.
church [tʃəːtʃ] *n* chiesa *f*. **church-goer** *n* praticante *m*, *f*. **churchyard** *n* cimitero *m*, camposanto *m*.
churlish ['tʃəːliʃ] *adj* burbero.
churn [tʃəːn] *n* zangola *f*. *v* agitare, sbattere.
chute [ʃuːt] *n* (*slide*) scivolo *m*; (*waterfall*) cascata *f*.
cider ['saidə] *n* sidro *m*.
cigar [si'gaː] *n* sigaro *m*.
cigarette [sigə'ret] *n* sigaretta *f*. **cigarette-end** *n* mozzicone *m*. **cigarette-lighter** *n* accendino *m*.
cinder ['sində] *n* tizzone *m*, cenere *f*. **burnt to a cinder** carbonizzato.
cine camera ['sini] *n* macchina da presa *f*.
cinema ['sinəmə] *n* cinema *m*.
cinnamon ['sinəmən] *n* cannella *f*.
circle ['səːkl] *n* cerchio *m*, circolo *m*; (*theatre*) galleria *f*; (*environment*) cerchia *f*, ambiente *m*. *v* girare attorno a, accerchiare; (*aeroplane*) volteggiare. **circular** *adj* circolare. *n* volantino *m*. **circulate** *v* circolare, mettere in circolazione, girare. **circulation** *n* (*movement*) circolazione *f*; (*distribution*) tiratura *f*.

circuit ['sɔːkit] *n* circuito *m*, giro *m*.
circumcise ['sɔːkəmsaiz] *v* circoncidere. **circumcision** *n* circoncisione *f*.
circumference [sɔr'kʌmfərəns] *n* circonferenza *f*.
circumscribe ['sɔːkəmskraib] *v* circoscrivere.
circumstance ['sɔːkəmstans] *n* circostanza *f*, condizione *f*. **circumstantial** *adj* particolareggiato. **circumstantial evidence** prove indiziarie indirette *f pl*.
circus ['sɔːkəs] *n* circo *m*; (*convergence of streets*) largo *m*.
cistern ['sistən] *n* cisterna *f*, serbatoio *m*.
cite [sait] *v* citare. **citation** *n* citazione *f*; (*mil*) encomio *m*.
citizen ['sitizn] *n* cittadino, -a *m*, *f*. **citizenship** *n* cittadinanza *f*.
citrus fruits ['sitrəs] *pl n* agrumi *m pl*.
city ['siti] *n* città *f*; (*business centre*) centro degli affari *m*. **city hall** municipio *m*.
civic ['sivik] *adj* civico, municipale.
civil ['sivl] *adj* civile; (*polite*) cortese, educato. **civil engineer** ingegnere civile *m*. **civil engineering** ingegneria civile *f*. **civil servant** funzionario, -a statale *m*, *f*. **Civil Service** amministrazione dello Stato *f*. **civil war** guerra civile *f*.
civilian [sə'viljən] *n*(*m*+*f*), *adj* civile, borghese. **in civilian clothes** in borghese.
civilization [ˌsivilai'zeiʃən] *n* civiltà *f*, civilizzazione *f*. **civilize** *v* civilizzare, incivilire. **civilized** *adj* civilizzato.
clad [klad] *adj* vestito.
claim [kleim] *n* (*right*) diritto *m*; (*title*) titolo *m*; (*complaint*) reclamo *m*; (*insurance*) rivendicazione *f*; asserzione *f*. *v* chiedere, esigere; rivendicare; asserire.
clairvoyant [kleə'voiənt] *n* chiaroveggente *m*, *f*.
clam [klam] *n* vongola *f*.
clamber ['klambə] *v* arrampicarsi.
clammy ['klami] *adj* viscido.
clamour ['klamə] *n* clamore *m*, schiamazzo *m*. *v* strepitare, vociferare. **clamorous** *adj* clamoroso, strepitoso.
clamp [klamp] *n* morsa *f*, morsetto *m*. *v* tener fermo, stringere. **clamp down on** far smettere.
clan [klan] *n* tribù *f*, famiglia *f*. **clannish** *adj* imbevuto di spirito di parte.
clandestine [klan'destin] *adj* clandestino.
clang [klaŋ] *n* suono metallico *m*, strepito *m*. *v* strepitare.
clap [klap] *n* (*blow*, *noise*) colpo *m*, scoppio *m*; applauso *m*, battimano *m*. *v* applaudire. **clap hands** battere le mani. **clap into prison** sbattere in prigione. **clapper** *n* (*bell*) battaglio *m*. **claptrap** *n* sproloquio *m*.
claret ['klarət] *n* chiaretto *m*.
clarify ['klarəfai] *v* chiarire, raffinare.
clarinet [klarə'net] *n* clarinetto *m*. **clarinettist** *n* clarinettista *m*, *f*.
clash [klaʃ] *n* (*noise*) strepito *m*; (*collision*) urto *m*; (*conflict*) scontro *m*, contrasto *m*; (*colours*, *sounds*) stonatura *f*. *v* urtare, urtarsi; scontrarsi; stonare.
clasp [klaːsp] *n* (*device*) fermaglio *m*; (*grasp*) stretta *f*; (*embrace*) abbraccio *m*. **clasp-knife** *n* coltello a serramanico *m*. *v* agganciare, stringere, abbracciare.
class [klaːs] *n* classe *f*, categoria *f*, qualità *f*. **class-mate** *n* compagno, -a di classe *m*, *f*. **classroom** *n* aula *f*. *v also* **classify** classificare. **classy** *adj* di classe.
classic ['klasik] *nm*, *adj* classico.
clatter ['klatə] *n* fracasso *m*. *v* far fracasso.
clause [kloːz] *n* clausola *f*, proposizione *f*, articolo *m*.
claustrophobia [kloːstrə'foubiə] *n* claustrofobia *f*. **claustrophobic** *adj* claustrofobico.
claw [kloː] *n* artiglio *m*; (*tool*) raffio *m*. *v* (*seize*) aggraffare; (*scratch*) graffiare.
clay [klei] *n* argilla *f*, creta *f*.
clean [kliːn] *adj* pulito, nitido. **clean-shaven** *adj* sbarbato. **make a clean breast** confessare tutto. *v* pulire; (*remove stains*) smacchiare. **cleanliness** *n* pulizia *f*, nettezza *f*.
cleanse [klenz] *v* pulire, depurare.
clear [kliə] *adj* chiaro, limpido; ovvio; libero. **keep clear of** tenersi lontano da. *v* chiarire, chiarificare; (*empty*) vuotare; (*overcome*) superare; (*law*) assolvere; (*comm*) sdoganare. **clear away** portar via; (*table*) sparecchiare. **clear off** andarsene. **clear up** chiarire, mettere in chiaro; (*weather*) rasserenarsi; (*tidy*) rassettare. **clearance** *n* (*customs*) sdoganamento *m*; (*sale*) liquidazione *f*; (*distance*) gioco *m*. **clearing** *n* (*land*) radura *f*; (*bank*) clearing *m*; (*emptying*) sgombro *m*.
clef [klef] *n* chiave *f*.
clench [klentʃ] *v* stringere. **with clenched fists** a pugni stretti.

clergy ['klə:dʒi] *n* clero *m*. **clergyman** *n* ecclesiastico *m*, pastore *m*, prete *m*.
clerical ['klerikəl] *adj* (*church*) clericale; (*office*) d'ufficio, impiegatizio. **clerical error** *n* errore materiale *m*, errore di trascrizione *m*.
clerk [klaːk] *n* impiegato, -a *m, f*; commesso, -a *m, f*.
clever ['klevə] *adj* abile, ingegnoso, bravo. **cleverness** *n* abilità *f*, ingegnosità *f*, intelligenza *f*.
cliché ['kliːʃei] *n* espressione stereotipata *f*, frase fatta *f*.
click [klik] *n* scatto *m*, schiocco *m*. *v* scattare, schioccare.
client ['klaiənt] *n* cliente *m, f*.
cliff [klif] *n* scoglio *m*.
climate ['klaimət] *n* clima *m*.
climax ['klaimaks] *n* apice *m*, apogeo *m*.
climb [klaim] *v* scalare, salire, arrampicarsi. *n* scalata *f*, salita *f*. **climb down** scendere; (*withdraw*) tirarsi indietro. **climb over** scavalcare.
***cling** [kliŋ] *v* aggrapparsi, aderire.
clinic ['klinik] *n* clinica *f*, ambulatorio *m*. **clinical** *adj* clinico.
clip[1] [klip] *n* (*cut*) taglio *m*; (*slap*) scappellotto *m*. *v* tagliare, tosare. **clip the wings of** tarpare le ali a.
clip[2] [klip] *n* (*fastener*) fermaglio *m*, graffa *f*.
clipper ['klipə] *n* (*boat*) clipper *m*, goletta *f*.
clitoris ['klitəris] *n* clitoride *f*.
cloak [klouk] *n* (*garment*) mantello *m*, cappa *f*; (*mask*) maschera *f*; (*pretext*) pretesto *m*, scusa *f*. *v* (*conceal*) celare. **cloak and dagger** cappa e spada. **cloakroom** *n* guardaroba *m*.
clock [klok] *n* orologio *m*. **clockmaker** *n* orologiaio *m*. **clockwork** *n* meccanismo d'orologeria *m*. **clockwise** *adv* in senso orario.
clog [klog] *n* (*shoe*) zoccolo *m*. *v* intasare.
cloister ['kloistə] *n* chiostro *m*. *v* rinchiudere in convento.
close[1] [klouz] *v* chiudere, concludere. **close down** (*shop*) chiudere bottega. **close ranks** serrare le file. *n* (*end*) fine *f*.
close[2] [klous] *n* (*place*) recinto *m*. *adj* vicino, stretto; intimo. **close by** vicino.
closet ['klozit] *n* gabinetto *m*, studio *m*. *v* rinchiudere.
clot [klot] *n* grumo *m*, coagulo *m*; (*coll*) scemo, -a *m, f*. *v* raggrumare, coagulare, coagularsi, rapprendersi. **clotted cream** panna rappresa *f*.
cloth [kloθ] *n* panno *m*, stoffa *f*, tessuto *m*; (*for dishes*) strofinaccio *m*.
clothe [klouð] *v* vestire, abbigliare; (*dress*) vestirsi. **clothes** *pl n* vestiti *m pl*, abiti *m pl*, indumenti *m pl*. **clothes line** corda per il bucato *f*. **clothes peg** molletta *f*. **clothing** *n* vestiario *m*, abbigliamento *m*.
cloud [klaud] *n* nuvola *f*. **cloudburst** *n* acquazzone *m*. *v* annuvolare; (*obscure*) offuscare. **cloud over** annuvolarsi. **cloudy** *adj* nuvoloso; (*liquid*) torbido.
clove[1] [klouv] *n* (*plant*) garofano *m*; (*spice*) chiodo di garofano *m*.
clove[2] [klouv] *n* (*part of bulb*) spicchio *m*.
clover ['klouvə] *n* trifoglio *m*.
clown [klaun] *n* pagliaccio *m*, buffone, -a *m, f*. *v* fare il pagliaccio. **clownery** *n* pagliacciata *f*. **clownish** *adj* pagliaccesco.
club [klʌb] *n* (*stick*) mazza *f*, randello *m*; (*golf*) bastone da golf *m*; (*social*) circolo *m*, club *m*; (*cards*) fiore *m*. *v* picchiare, bastonare. **club together** associarsi, riunirsi.
clue [kluː] *n* indizio *m*, chiave *f*.
clump [klʌmp] *n* gruppo *m*, cespo *m*.
clumsy ['klʌmzi] *adj* maldestro, goffo. **clumsiness** *n* goffaggine *f*, malaccortezza *f*.
clung [klʌŋ] *V* **cling**.
cluster ['klʌstə] *n* gruppo *m*; (*bunch*) grappolo *m*.
clutch [klʌtʃ] *n* presa *f*; (*mot*) frizione *f*. **fall into the clutches of** cadere nelle grinfie di. *v* afferrare, aggrapparsi a.
clutter ['klʌtə] *n* ingombro *m*, confusione *f*. *v* ingombrare.
coach [koutʃ] *n* carrozza *f*; (*bus*) corriera *f*, torpedone *m*; (*tutor*) ripetitore, -trice *m, f*; (*sport*) allenatore, -trice *m, f*. **coachbuilder** *n* carrozziere *m*. **coachwork** *n* carrozzeria *f*. *v* (*teach*) dare lezioni private; (*sport*) allenare.
coagulate [kou'agjuleit] *v* coagulare, coagularsi, accagliarsi. **coagulant** *n* coagulante *m*.
coal [koul] *n* carbone *m*. **coal-tar** *n* catrame *m*. **coalmine** *n* miniera di carbone *f*.
coalition [kouə'liʃən] *n* coalizione *f*.
coarse [koːs] *adj* (*rude*) grossolano, rozzo; (*rough*) ruvido. **coarseness** *n* volgarità *f*, ruvidezza *f*.

coast [koust] *n* costa *f*, litorale *m*. *v* (*cycling*) scendere a ruota libera; (*motoring*) andare in folle. **coastal** *adj* costiero.

coat [kout] *n* soprabito *m*, cappotto *m*; (*jacket*) giacca *f*; (*animal*) pelame *m*, pelliccia *f*; (*paint*) mano *f*. **coat-hanger** *n* attaccapanni *m*. **coat-of-arms** *n* stemma *m*. **coating** *n* rivestimento *m*. *v* coprire, rivestire.

coax [kouks] *v* blandire, lusingare.

cobbler ['koblə] *n* ciabattino *m*, calzolaio *m*.

cobra ['koubrə] *n* cobra *m*.

cobweb ['kobweb] *n* ragnatela *f*.

cocaine [kə'kein] *n* cocaina *f*.

cock[1] [kok] *n* (*male bird*) uccello maschio *m*; (*chicken*) gallo *m*; (*tap*) rubinetto *m*; (*gun*) cane *m*; (*vulgar*) cazzo *m*. **cocky** *adj* impertinente, pieno di sè.

cock[2] [kok] *v* (*gun*) armare; (*ears*) drizzare. **cock a snook** fare marameo.

cockle ['kokl] *n* cardio *m*. **cockle-shell** *n* conchiglia *f*.

cockpit ['kokpit] *n* (*plane*) carlinga *f*, cabina di guida *f*; (*naval*) cassero *m*.

cockroach ['kokroutʃ] *n* scarafaggio *m*.

cocktail ['kokteil] *n* cocktail *m*.

cocoa ['koukou] *n* cacao *m*.

coconut ['koukənʌt] *n* noce di cocco *f*.

cocoon [kə'kuːn] *n* bozzolo *m*.

cod [kod] *n* merluzzo *m*. **cod-liver oil** olio di fegato di merluzzo *m*.

code [koud] *n* cifrario *m*, codice *m*.

codeine ['koudiːn] *n* codeina *f*.

coeducation [kouedju'keiʃən] *n* scuola mista *f*.

coerce [kou'əːs] *v* costringere, forzare.

coexist [kouig'zist] *v* coesistere. **coexistence** *n* coesistenza *f*.

coffee ['kofi] *n* caffè *m*. **coffee bean** chicco di caffè *m*. **coffee pot** caffettiera *f*.

coffin ['kofin] *n* cassa da morto *f*, bara *f*, feretro *m*.

cog [kog] *n* dente *m*.

cohabit [kou'habit] *v* coabitare.

coherent [kou'hiərənt] *adj* coerente. **cohesion** *n* coesione *f*.

coil [koil] *n* rotolo *m*, bobina *f*. *v* avvolgere, attorcigliare, ravvolgere.

coin [koin] *n* moneta *f*.

coincide [kouin'said] *v* coincidere. **coincidence** *n* coincidenza *f*.

colander ['koləndə] *n* colabrodo *m*, colino *m*.

cold [kould] *adj* freddo, gelido; (*unfriendly*) riservato. **be cold** (*person*) aver freddo; (*weather*) far freddo. *n* freddo *m*; (*illness*) raffreddore *m*. **catch a cold** prendere un raffreddore, raffreddarsi. **have a cold** essere raffreddato.

colic ['kolik] *n* colica *f*.

collaborate [kə'labəreit] *v* collaborare. **collaboration** *n* collaborazione *f*. **collaborator** *n* collaboratore, -trice *m*, *f*.

collapse [kə'laps] *v* crollare, afflosciarsi. *n* crollo *m*, collasso *m*, rovina *f*.

collar ['kolə] *n* colletto *m*, bavero *m*; (*animal*) collare *m*; (*mech*) manicotto *m*. *v* afferrare per il collo; (*take possession*) appropriarsi di.

colleague ['koliːg] *n* collega (*m pl* -ghi) *m*, *f*.

collect [kə'lekt] *v* raccogliere, riunire; (*take delivery*) prendere in consegna, ricuperare; (*make collection of*) far collezione di; (*meet*) radunarsi. **collect call** *n* (*US*) chiamata rovesciata *f*. **collected** *adj* calmo, padrone di sè. **collection** *n* collezione *f*, raccolta *f*; (*charity*) colletta *f*. **collective** *adj* collettivo. **collector** *n* collezionista *m*, *f*.

college ['kolidʒ] *n* collegio *m*, istituto *m*, università *f*.

collide [kə'laid] *v* scontrarsi, investire. **collision** *n* urto *m*, scontro *m*, investimento *m*.

colloid ['koloid] *n* colloide *m*.

colloquial [kə'loukwiəl] *adj* familiare. **colloquialism** *n* espressione familiare *f*.

colon ['koulon] *n* (*biol*) colon *m invar*; (*gramm*) due punti.

colonel ['kəːnl] *n* colonnello *m*.

colonnade [kolə'neid] *n* colonnata *f*, portico *m*.

colony ['koləni] *n* colonia *f*. **colonial** *n*, *adj* coloniale. **colonize** *v* colonizzare.

colossal [kə'losəl] *adj* colossale, enorme.

colour ['kʌlə] *n* colore *m*, tinta *f*. **colour bar** discriminazione razziale *f*. **colour-blind** *adj* daltonico. *v* colorare, tingere, colorire. **coloured** *adj* colorato, colorito, a colori; (*person*) di colore. **colourful** *adj* pittoresco, a tinte vivaci. **colouring** *n* colorito *m*.

colt [koult] *n* puledro *m*.

column ['koləm] *n* colonna *f*; (*newspaper*) rubrica *f*, cronaca *f*. **columnist** *n* cronista *m*, *f*, giornalista *m*, *f*.

coma ['koumə] *n* coma *m invar.*
comb [koum] *n* pettine *m*; (*horse*) striglia *f*; (*birds*) cresta *f*. *v* pettinare, strigliare. **comb one's hair** pettinarsi.
combat ['kombat] *n* combattimento *m*, lotta *f*. *v* combattere, lottare. **combatant** *n* combattente *m, f*.
combine [kəm'bain; *n* 'kombain] *v* combinare, unire, abbinare, combinarsi. *n* associazione *f*, consorzio *m*. **combine-harvester** *n* mietitrebbiatrice *f*. **combination** *n* combinazione *f*.
combustion [kəm'bʌstʃən] *n* combustione *f*. **internal combustion engine** motore a combustione interna *m*.
***come** [kʌm] *v* venire, arrivare, giungere. **come about** accadere. **come across** incontrare per caso, trovare per caso. **come in** entrare. **come into force** entrare in vigore. **come off** (*succeed*) riuscire. **come to blows** venire alle mani. **come to light** venire alla luce. **come up** salire; (*to the surface*) venire a galla.
comedy ['komədi] *n* commedia *f*. **comedian** *n* commediante *m, f*, comico, -a *m, f*.
comet ['komit] *n* cometa *f*.
comfort ['kʌmfət] *n* agio *m*, conforto *m*, consolazione *f*, agiatezza *f*. *v* consolare, confortare.
comic ['komik] *n* comico, -a *m, f*; (*periodical*) giornaletto a fumetti *m*. *adj* comico. **comic opera** opera buffa *f*. **comic strip** fumetto *m*. **comical** *adj* comico.
comma ['komə] *n* virgola *f*. **in inverted commas** fra virgolette.
command [kə'maːnd] *n* comando *m*, ordine *m*. *v* comandare; (*mil*) ordinare, avere il comando di. **commander** *n* comandante *m*, capo *m*. **commanding position** posizione dominante *f*. **commandment** *n* comandamento *m*, precetto *m*.
commandeer [komən'diə] *v* requisire.
commando [kə'maːndou] *n* truppe d'assalto *f pl*, commando *m invar.*
commemorate [kə'meməreit] *v* commemorare. **commemoration** *n* commemorazione *f*.
commence [kə'mens] *v* cominciare, iniziare. **commencement** *n* inizio *m*, principio *m*.
commend [kə'mend] *v* raccomandare, lodare. **commendable** *adj* lodevole, encomiabile. **commendation** *n* lode *f*, encomio *m*.
comment ['koment] *n* commento *m*, osservazione *f*, rilievo *m*. *v* commentare, fare delle osservazioni. **commentary** *n* commentario *m*, cronaca *f*. **commentator** *n* commentatore, -trice *m, f*; cronista *m, f*; radiocronista *m, f*.
commerce ['koməːs] *n* commercio *m*, scambi *m pl*. **commercial** *adj* commerciale.
commiserate [kə'mizəreit] *v* commiserare, compiangere.
commission [kə'miʃən] *n* commissione *f*, delegazione *f*; (*authority*) incarico *m*; (*comm*) provvigione *f*; (*mil*) brevetto da ufficiale *m*. *v* incaricare, dare una carica; nominare ufficiale; (*ship*) armare. **commissionaire** *n* portiere *m*. **commissioned officer** ufficiale *m*. **non-commissioned officer** sottufficiale *m*. **commissioner** *n* commissario *m*.
commit [kə'mit] *v* commettere; affidare, rimettere. **commit oneself** impegnarsi. **commit to memory** imparare a memoria. **commitment** *n* impegno *m*. **committed** *adj* impegnato.
committee [kə'miti] *n* comitato *m*, commissione *f*.
commodity [kə'modəti] *n* merce *f*, derrata *f*.
common ['komən] *adj* comune, ordinario, volgare. *n* parco demaniale *m*. **commonplace** *adj* ordinario, banale. **common sense** buonsenso *m*.
commotion [kə'mouʃən] *n* agitazione *f*, confusione *f*.
commune[1] [kə'mjuːn] *v* intrattenersi, discutere.
commune[2] ['komjuːn] *n* comune *m*, comunità *f*. **communal** *adj* comunale, in comune.
communicate [kə'mjuːnikeit] *v* comunicare, informare, trasmettere. **communicate with** essere in comunicazione con. **communication** *n* comunicazione *f*, informazione *f*, rapporto *m*.
communion [kə'mjuːnjən] *n* comunione *f*.
communism ['komjunizəm] *n* comunismo *m*. **communist** *n*(*m*+*f*), *adj* comunista.
community [kə'mjuːnəti] *n* comunità *f*.
commute [kə'mjuːt] *v* commutare; (*travel*) fare il pendolare. **commuter** *n* pendolare *m, f*.
compact[1] [kəm'pakt; *n* 'kompakt] *adj* compatto, serrato. *n* (*powder*) portacipria *m invar.*

compact² ['kompakt] *n* (*agreement*) patto *m*, accordo *m*.
companion [kəm'panjən] *n* compagno, -a *m*, *f*. **companionship** *n* compagnia *f*, cameratismo *m*, amicizia *f*.
company ['kʌmpəni] *n* compagnia *f*, comitiva *f*; (*comm*) ditta *f*, società *f*; (*ship*) equipaggio *m*. **in the company of** accompagnato da. **part company with** separarsi da.
compare [kəm'peə] *v* paragonare, confrontare, essere paragonabile a. **comparable** *adj* paragonabile, comparabile. **comparative** *adj* comparativo, relativo. **compared with** rispetto a, di fronte a. **comparison** *n* confronto *m*, paragone *m*.
compartment [kəm'paːtmənt] *n* compartimento *m*, casella *f*; (*railway*) scompartimento *m*.
compass ['kʌmpəs] *n* bussola *f*. **compasses** *pl n* compasso *m sing*. *v* cingere, circondare.
compassion [kəm'paʃən] *n* compassione *f*, pietà *f*, misericordia *f*. **compassionate** *adj* misericordioso, pieno di compassione.
compatible [kəm'patəbl] *adj* compatibile. **compatibility** *n* compatibilità *f*.
compel [kəm'pel] *v* costringere, obbligare, forzare. **compel respect** farsi rispettare. **compelling** *adj* irresistibile.
compensate ['kompənseit] *v* compensare, ricompensare, indennizzare. **compensation** *n* compenso *m*, ricompensa *f*; (*comm*) compensazione *f*.
compete [kəm'piːt] *v* concorrere, fare concorrenza a, gareggiare. **competition** *n* (*contest*) gara *f*; (*rivalry*) concorrenza *f*; (*exam*) concorso *m*. **competitive** *adj* competitivo. **competitor** *n* concorrente *m*, *f*; rivale *m*, *f*.
competent ['kompətənt] *adj* competente, capace. **competence** *n* competenza *f*, capacità *f*.
compile [kəm'pail] *v* compilare. **compilation** *n* compilazione *f*.
complacent [kəm'pleisnt] *adj* soddisfatto di sè.
complain [kəm'plein] *v* lamentarsi, lagnarsi. **complaint** *n* (*discontent*) lamentela *f*; (*merchandise*) reclamo *m*; (*illness*) malattia *f*.
complement ['kompləmənt] *n* complemento *m*. *v* completare, fare da complemento a. **complementary** *adj* complementare.
complete [kəm'pliːt] *adj* completo, intero. *v* completare, finire. **completion** *n* fine *f*, compimento *m*.
complex ['kompleks] *nm*, *adj* complesso.
complexion [kəm'plekʃən] *n* (*skin*) colorito *m*; (*nature*) aspetto *m*.
complicate ['komplikeit] *v* complicare. **complicated** *adj* complicato, complesso. **complication** *n* difficoltà *f*.
complicity [kəm'plisəti] *n* complicità *f*.
compliment ['kompləmənt] *n* complimento *m*. *v* congratularsi con. **complimentary** *adj* (*flattering*) lusinghiero; (*free*) di favore.
comply [kəm'plai] *v* ubbidire, acconsentire. **in compliance with** conforme a.
component [kəm'pounənt] *nm*, *adj* componente.
compose [kəm'pouz] *v* comporre. **composed** *adj* calmo. **composer** *n* compositore, -trice *m*, *f*. **composite** *adj* composto, misto. **composition** *n* composizione *f*.
compost ['kompost] *n* concime *m*.
composure [kəm'pouʒə] *n* compostezza *f*, calma *f*.
compound¹ [kəm'paund; *n* 'kompaund] *v* (*compose*) comporre; (*mix*) mescolare; (*settle*) regolare. *n* composto *m*, miscela *f*. *adj* composto.
compound² ['kompaund] *n* (*enclosure*) campo *m*, accampamento *m*.
comprehend [kompri'hend] *v* comprendere, capire. **comprehensible** *adj* comprensibile. **comprehension** *n* comprensione *f*. **comprehensive** *adj* comprensivo, esauriente.
compress [kəm'pres; *n* 'kompres] *v* comprimere. *n* compressa *f*. **compression** *n* compressione *f*.
comprise [kəm'praiz] *v* includere.
compromise ['komprəmaiz] *n* compromesso *m*. *v* giungere a un compromesso; (*endanger*) compromettere. **compromising** *adj* compromettente, imbarazzante.
compulsion [kəm'pʌlʃən] *n* costrizione *f*, obbligo *m*. **compulsive** *adj* coercitivo. **compulsory** *adj* obbligatorio.
compunction [kəm'pʌŋkʃən] *n* rimorso *m*.
computer [kəm'pjuːtə] *n* computer (*pl* -s) *m*, elaboratore elettronico *m*.
comrade ['komrid] *n* compagno, -a *m*, *f*; camerata *m*, *f*. **comradeship** *n* cameratismo *m*.

concave [kon'keiv] *adj* concavo.
conceal [kən'siːl] *v* celare, nascondere.
concede [kən'siːd] *v* concedere, ammettere, riconoscere.
conceit [kən'siːt] *n* vanità *f*, presunzione *f*. **conceited** *adj* vanitoso, presuntuoso.
conceive [kən'siːv] *v* concepire; immaginare. **conceivable** *adj* concepibile, immaginabile.
concentrate ['konsəntreit] *v* concentrare. *n* concentrato *m*. **concentration** *n* concentrazione *f*. **concentration camp** campo di concentramento *m*.
concentric [kən'sentrik] *adj* concentrico.
concept ['konsept] *n* concetto *m*, nozione *f*.
conception [kən'sepʃən] *n* concezione *f*, idea *f*.
concern [kən'səːn] *n* (*care*) sollecitudine *f*, preoccupazione *f*; (*business*) affare *m*, faccenda *f*; interesse *m*; (*firm*) azienda *f*, ditta *f*. *v* riguardare, toccare. **concerned** *adj* in questione; (*anxious*) preoccupato. **concerning** *prep* riguardo a, in merito a, inerente a.
concert ['konsət] *n* concerto *m*. **concerted** *adj* predisposto, stabilito d'accordo con altri.
concertina [konsə'tiːnə] *n* fisarmonica *f*.
concerto [kən'tʃəːtou] *n* concerto *m*.
concession [kən'seʃən] *n* concessione *f*.
conciliate [kən'silieit] *v* conciliare. **conciliation** *n* conciliazione *f*. **conciliatory** *adj* conciliatorio.
concise [kən'sais] *adj* conciso, breve.
conclude [kən'kluːd] *v* concludere, dedurre. **conclusion** *n* conclusione *f*, fine *f*. **in conclusion** *adv* in fine, insomma. **conclusive** *adj* conclusivo.
concoct [kən'kokt] *v* (*contrive*) inventare. **concoction** *n* intruglio *m*, pasticcio *m*.
concrete ['koŋkriːt] *adj* concreto. *n* calcestruzzo *m*, cemento *m*. **concrete mixer** betoniera *f*. **reinforced concrete** cemento armato *m*. *v* cementare, rivestire di calcestruzzo.
concussion [kən'kʌʃən] *n* commozione cerebrale *f*.
condemn [kən'dem] *v* condannare. **condemnation** *n* condanna *f*.
condense [kən'dens] *v* condensare. **condensation** *n* condensazione *f*.
condescend [kondi'send] *v* degnarsi. **condescending** *adj* condiscendente. **condescension** *n* condiscendenza *f*.
condition [kən'diʃən] *n* condizione *f*. *v* condizionare. **conditional** *adj* condizionale.
condolence [kən'douləns] *n* condoglianza *f*. **express condolences** fare le condoglianze.
condom ['kondom] *n* preservativo *m*.
condone [kən'doun] *v* perdonare.
conducive [kən'djuːsiv] *adj* contribuente.
conduct [kən'dʌkt; *n* 'kondʌkt] *v* condurre; (*music*) dirigere. **conduct oneself** comportarsi. *n* condotta *f*, comportamento *m*.
conductor [kən'dʌktə] *n* (*transport*) bigliettario, -a *m*, *f*; (*music*) direttore d'orchestra *m*; (*physics*) conduttore *m*.
cone [koun] *n* cono *m*; (*fir*) pigna *f*.
confectioner [kən'fekʃənə] *n* pasticciere, -a *m*, *f*. **confectioner's shop** *n* pasticceria *f*.
confederate [kən'fedərət] *adj* confederato, alleato. *v* confederarsi, allearsi.
confer [kən'fəː] *v* conferire, consultarsi. **conference** *n* conferenza *f*. **conferment** *n* conferimento *m*.
confess [kən'fes] *v* confessare, ammettere; (*rel*) confessarsi. **confession** *n* confessione *f*, professione *f*. **confessor** *n* confessore *m*.
confetti [kən'feti] *n* coriandoli *m pl*.
confide [kən'faid] *v* confidare. **confidant, -e** *n* confidente *m*, *f*. **confidence** *n* fiducia *f*; sicurezza di sè *f*. **have confidence in** aver fiducia in. **in confidence** in confidenza. **confident** *adj* fiducioso, sicuro. **confidential** *adj* riservato.
confine [kən'fain] *n* confine *m*. *v* relegare; (*to barracks*) consegnare. **be confined** (*childbirth*) partorire. **confinement** *n* imprigionamento *m*, segregazione *f*; (*childbirth*) parto *m*.
confirm [kən'fəːm] *v* confermare; (*statement*) ribadire; (*rel*) cresimare; (*law*) omologare. **confirmation** *n* conferma *f*; (*law*) ratifica *f*; (*rel*) confermazione *f*, cresima *f*. **confirmed** *adj* confermato; (*belief*) convinto, impenitente.
confiscate ['konfiskeit] *v* confiscare.
conflict ['konflikt; *v* kən'flikt] *n* conflitto *m*, lotta *f*, contrasto *m*. *v* **conflict with** essere in disaccordo *or* contrasto con. **conflicting** *adj* (*evidence*) contradditorio; (*interests*) contrastante.

conform [kən'fɔːm] *v* conformare, adattarsi. **conformist** *n* conformista *m, f.* **conformity** *n* conformità *f.* **in conformity with** conforme a, conformemente a.
confound [kən'faund] *v* sconcertare, sconvolgere.
confront [kən'frʌnt] *v* affrontare; (*law*) mettere a confronto. **confrontation** *n* confronto *m.*
confuse [kən'fjuːz] *v* confondere, sconcertare, disorientare, scambiare. **confusing** *adj* sconcertante, che rende perplesso. **confusion** *n* confusione *f,* disordine *m.*
congeal [kən'dʒiːl] *v* (*freeze*) congelare, congelarsi; coagulare, coagularsi.
congenial [kən'dʒiːniəl] *adj* congeniale.
congenital [kən'dʒenitl] *adj* congenito, innato.
congested [kən'dʒestid] *adj* congestionato. **congestion** *n* congestione *f.*
conglomeration [kənˌglomə'reiʃən] *n* conglomerazione *f.*
congratulate [kən'gratjuleit] *v* congratularsi con, felicitare, felicitarsi con. **congratulation** *n* felicitazione *f.* **congratulations!** *interj* auguri!
congregate ['koŋgrigeit] *v* congregare, riunirsi. **congregation** *n* (*rel*) comunità *f,* adunanza dei fedeli *f.*
congress ['koŋgres] *n* congresso *m.*
conical ['konikəl] *adj* conico.
conifer ['konifə] *n* conifera *f.*
conjecture [kən'dʒektʃə] *v* supporre. *n* supposizione *f.*
conjugal ['kondʒugəl] *adj* coniugale.
conjugate ['kondʒugeit] *v* coniugare. **conjugation** *n* coniugazione *f.*
conjunction [kən'dʒʌŋkʃən] *n* congiunzione *f.*
conjunctivitis [kənˌdʒʌŋkti'vaitis] *n* congiuntivite *f.*
conjure ['kʌndʒə; (*invoke*) kən'dʒuə] *v* fare giochi di prestigio; (*invoke*) scongiurare. **conjure up** evocare. **conjurer** *n* prestigiatore, -trice *m, f.* **conjuring trick** gioco di prestigio *m.*
connect [kə'nekt] *v* connettere, congiungere; associare; (*trains*) far coincidenza. **connection** *n* connessione *f,* rapporto *m*; coincidenza *f.* **in connection with** in merito a.
connoisseur [konə'səː] *n* intenditore, -trice *m, f.*
connotation [konə'teiʃən] *n* significato implicito *m.*
conquer ['koŋkə] *v* conquistare, vincere. **conqueror** *n* conquistatore, -trice *m, f*; vincitore, -trice *m, f.* **conquest** *n* conquista *f,* vittoria *f.*
conscience ['konʃəns] *n* coscienza *f.*
conscientious [konʃi'enʃəs] *adj* coscienzioso, diligente. **conscientious objector** obiettore di coscienza *m.*
conscious ['konʃəs] *adj* conscio, cosciente; (*deliberate*) intenzionale. **consciousness** *n* coscienza *f.*
conscript ['konskript] *v* chiamare alle armi, arruolare. *n* soldato di leva *m.* **conscription** *n* leva *f.*
consecrate ['konsikreit] *v* consacrare. **consecration** *n* consacrazione *f.*
consecutive [kən'sekjutiv] *adj* consecutivo.
consensus [kən'sensəs] *n* consenso *m,* assenso *m.*
consent [kən'sent] *v* consentire, acconsentire. *n* consenso *m,* benestare *m,* accordo *m.*
consequence ['konsikwəns] *n* conseguenza *f,* effetto *m,* importanza *f.* **consequently** *adv* di conseguenza, quindi, perciò.
conserve [kən'səːv] *v* conservare, preservare. *n* conserva *f.* **conservation** *n* preservazione *f.* **conservative** *adj* conservativo, cauto; (*pol*) conservatore. **conservatoire** *n* (*music*) conservatorio *m.* **conservatory** *n* serra *f.*
consider [kən'sidə] *v* considerare, giudicare, ritenere, pensare. **considerable** *adj* notevole. **considerate** *adj* sollecito, riguardoso. **consideration** *n* considerazione *f,* riflessione *f*; (*feeling, regard*) riguardo *m,* sollecitudine *f,* delicatezza *f.*
consign [kən'sain] *v* consegnare, affidare. **consignee** *n* destinatario, -a *m, f.* **consignor** *n* mittente *m, f.* **consignment** *n* spedizione *f,* invio *m*; (*goods*) partita di merce *f.*
consist [kən'sist] *v* consistere (in), essere composto. **consistency** *n* consistenza *f.* **consistent** *adj* regolare, costante, coerente.
console[1] [kən'soul] *v* confortare. **consolation** *n* consolazione *f,* conforto *m.*
console[2] ['konsoul] *n* (*arch*) mensola *f*; (*furniture*) mobile *m*; (*tech*) quadro di comando *m.*

consolidate [kən'solideit] *v* consolidare. **consolidation** *n* consolidazione *f.*
consommé [kən'somei] *n* brodo *m.*
consonant ['konsənənt] *n* consonante *f.*
consortium [kən'soːtiəm] *n* consorzio *m.*
conspicuous [kən'spikjuəs] *adj* cospicuo, evidente.
conspire [kən'spaiə] *v* complottare. **conspiracy** *n* complotto *m,* congiura *f.*
constable ['kʌnstəbl] *n* vigile *m,* poliziotto *m.*
constant ['konstənt] *adj* costante, invariabile. *n* costante *f.*
constellation [konstə'leiʃən] *n* costellazione *f.*
constipation [konsti'peiʃən] *n* stitichezza *f.* **constipated** *adj* stitico.
constitute ['konstitjuːt] *v* costituire, creare. **constituent** *nf, adj* costituente. **constituency** *n* collegio elettorale *m.* **constitution** *n* costituzione *f*; statuto *m*; (*health*) salute *f.*
constraint [kən'streint] *n* (*restriction*) costrizione *f*; (*embarrassment*) imbarazzo *m.*
constrict [kən'strikt] *v* stringere, restringere, comprimere. **constriction** *n* restringimento *m*; (*tight feeling*) oppressione *f.*
construct [kən'strʌkt] *v* costruire. **construction** *n* costruzione *f*; (*building*) edificio *m*; (*meaning*) senso *m.* **constructive** *adj* costruttivo, positivo.
consul ['konsəl] *n* console. **consulate** *n* consolato *m.*
consult [kən'sʌlt] *v* consultare; (*consider*) tener conto di. **consultant** *n* consulente *m, f,* esperto, -a *m, f.* **consultation** *n* consultazione *f*; (*med*) consulta *f.* **consulting room** (*med*) studio *m.*
consume [kən'sjuːm] *v* consumare. **consumer** *n* consumatore, -trice *m, f.* **consumer goods** generi di consumo *m pl.*
contact ['kontakt] *n* contatto *m*; (*acquaintance*) conoscenza *f.* *v* mettere in contatto con, mettersi in contatto. **contact lens** *n* lente a contatto *f.*
contagious [kən'teidʒəs] *adj* contagioso.
contain [kən'tein] *v* contenere, includere. **container** *n* recipiente *m.*
contaminate [kən'tamәneit] *v* contaminare, inquinare. **contamination** *n* contaminazione *f,* inquinamento *m.*
contemplate ['kontəmpleit] *v* contemplare, meditare; (*intend to*) proporsi, aver intenzione di. **contemplation** *n* contemplazione *f.*
contemporary [kən'tempərəri] *n, adj* contemporaneo, -a; coetaneo, -a.
contempt [kən'tempt] *n* disprezzo *m.* **contempt of court** oltraggio alla corte *m.* **contemptible** *adj* spregevole. **contemptuous** *adj* sprezzante, altezzoso.
contend [kən'tend] *v* contendere, sostenere, affermare. **bone of contention** pomo della discordia *m.*
content[1] ['kontent] *n* contenuto *m.*
content[2] [kən'tent] *adj* contento, soddisfatto. *v* accontentare.
contest ['kontest; *v* kən'test] *n* gara *f,* lotta *f.* *v* contestare, impugnare.
context ['kontekst] *n* contesto *m.*
continent ['kontinənt] *nm, adj* continente. **continental** *adj* continentale.
contingency [kən'tindʒənsi] *n* contingenza *f.*
continue [kən'tinjuː] *v* continuare, proseguire. **continual** *or* **continuous** *adj* continuo, ininterrotto. **continuation** *n* seguito *m.* **continuity** *n* continuità *f*; (*film*) sceneggiatura *f.*
contort [kən'toːt] *v* contorcere. **contortion** *n* contorcimento *m.* **contortionist** *n* contorsionista *m, f.*
contour ['kontuə] *n* contorno *m.* **contour map/line** carta/curva ipsometrica *f.*
contraband ['kontrəband] *n* contrabbando *m.*
contraception [kontrə'sepʃən] *n* pratiche antifecondative *f pl.* **contraceptive** *nm, adj* anticoncezionale, anticoncettivo, antifecondativo.
contract ['kontrakt; *v* kən'trakt] *n* patto *m,* accordo *m,* contratto *m.* *v* (*draw together*) contrarre, restringere; (*acquire, take on*) contrarre; (*enter into*) contrattare. **contraction** *n* contrazione *f.*
contradict [kontrə'dikt] *v* contraddire, smentire. **contradiction** *n* contraddizione *f,* smentita *f.*
contralto [kən'traltou] *n* contralto *m.*
contraption [kən'trapʃən] *n* congegno *m,* aggeggio *m.*
contrary ['kontrəri] *nm, adj* contrario, opposto. **contrary to** contrariamente a. **on the contrary** al contrario, anzi.
contrast ['kontraːst; *v* kən'traːst] *n* contrasto *m,* antitesi *f invar.* *v* contrastare, confrontare, mettere in contrasto.

contravene [kontrə'viːn] *v* contravvenire a.

contribute [kən'tribjut] *v* contribuire. **contributor** *n* contributore, -trice *m, f*; (*writer*) collaboratore, -trice *m, f*. **contribution** *n* contributo *m*; (*writing*) articolo *m*.

contrive [kən'traiv] *v* riuscire a, escogitare.

control [kən'troul] *v* controllare, dominare. *n* controllo *m*, autorità *f*. **controls** *pl n* comandi *m pl*. **remote control** controllo a distanza *m*, telecontrollo *m*.

controversy [kən'trovəsi] *n* controversia *f*. **controversial** *adj* controverso.

convalesce [konvə'les] *v* rimettersi in salute. **convalescence** *n* convalescenza *f*. **convalescent home** convalescenziario *m*.

convector [kən'vektə] *nm, adj* convettore.

convenience [kən'viːnjəns] *n* comodo *m*, comodità *f*, convenienza *f*. **at the earliest convenience** alla prima occasione. **public convenience** gabinetto pubblico *m*. **convenient** *adj* conveniente, comodo.

convent ['konvənt] *n* convento *m*.

convention [kən'venʃən] *n* convenzione *f*; (*meeting*) adunata *f*; (*agreement*) accordo *m*. **convene** *v* convocare, adunare. **conventional** *adj* convenzionale.

converge [kən'vəːdʒ] *v* convergere.

converse [kən'vəːs; *n, adj* 'konvəːs] *v* conversare. *nm, adj* contrario, opposto. **conversation** *n* conversazione *f*.

convert [kən'vəːt; *n* 'konvəːt] *v* convertire, trasformare. *n* convertito, -a *m, f*. **convertible** *n* (*car*) auto decapottabile *f*.

convex ['konveks] *adj* convesso.

convey [kən'vei] *v* trasportare; (*impart*) esprimere. **conveyance** *n* mezzo di trasporto *m*; (*law*) atto di cessione *m*. **conveyor belt** nastro trasportatore *m*.

convict [kən'vikt; *n* 'konvikt] *v* condannare. *n* carcerato, -a *m, f*; prigioniero, -a *m, f*.

conviction [kən'vikʃən] *n* (*sentence*) condanna *f*; persuasione *f*, convinzione *f*.

convince [kən'vins] *v* convincere, persuadere.

convivial [kən'viviəl] *adj* allegro.

convoy ['konvoi] *n* convoglio *m*, scorta *f*. *v* convogliare, scortare.

convulsion [kən'vʌlʃən] *n* convulsione *f*. *v* **be convulsed (with laughter)** contorcersi (dalle risa).

cook [kuk] *n* cuoco, -a *m, f*. *v* cuocere, cucinare, far la cucina. **cook the books** falsificare i registri. **cooker** *n* fornello *m*. **cookery** *or* **cooking** *n* cucina *f*, arte culinaria *f*.

cool [kuːl] *adj* fresco, calmo. *v* rinfrescare, raffreddare. **cooler** *n* refrigerante *m*; (*slang*) gattabuia *f*.

coop [kuːp] *n* stia *f*. *v* **coop up** stipare, pigiarsi.

cooperate [kou'opəreit] *v* cooperare. **cooperation** *n* cooperazione *f*, collaborazione *f*. **cooperative** *adj* cooperativo. **cooperator** *n* collaboratore, -trice *m, f*.

coordinate [kou'oːdineit] *v* coordinare. *n* coordinata *f*. *adj* coordinato. **coordination** *n* coordinazione *f*.

cop [kop] *n* (*slang*) poliziotto *m*. *v* pescare. **cop it** prenderle.

cope[1] [koup] *v* riuscire. **cope with** far fronte a.

cope[2] [koup] *n* cappa *f*.

Copenhagen [koupən'heigən] *n* Copenhagen *f*.

copious ['koupiəs] *adj* abbondante.

copper[1] ['kopə] *n* rame *m*. *adj* color rame.

copper[2] ['kopə] *n* (*slang*) poliziotto *m*.

copulate ['kopjuːleit] *v* accoppiarsi. **copulation** *n* accoppiamento *m*, copulazione *f*.

copy ['kopi] *v* copiare; ricopiare, riprodurre; imitare. *n* copia *f*, trascrizione *f*, imitazione *f*; (*book*) esemplare *m*. **copyright** *n* diritti d'autore *m pl*.

coral ['korəl] *n* corallo *m*.

cord [koːd] *n* corda *f*; (*string*) spago *m*; (*elec*) filo *m*, cavo *m*.

cordial ['koːdiəl] *adj* cordiale, caloroso.

cordon ['koːdn] *n* cordone *m*. **cordon off** fare cordone intorno a, isolare.

corduroy ['koːdəroi] *n* fustagno *m*.

core [koː] *n* centro *m*; (*fruit*) torsolo *m*; (*mech*) anima *f*.

cork [koːk] *n* (*bark*) sughero *m*; (*stopper*) tappo *m*, turacciolo *m*. **corkscrew** *n* cavatappi *m invar*. *v* turare. **corked** *adj* (*wine*) che sa di turacciolo.

corn[1] [koːn] *n* (*grain*) grano *m*; (*wheat*) frumento *m*; (*maize*) mais *m invar*, granturco *m*. **cornflour** *n* farina finissima di granturco *f*. **corny** *adj* banale.

corn[2] [koːn] *n* (*toe*) callo *m*.

corner ['koːnə] *n* angolo *m*; (*football*) corner *m invar*, calcio d'angolo *m*. *v* (*prevent escape*) mettere alle strette; (*stock*) accaparrare; (*drive*) fare una curva.

cornet ['kɔːnit] *n* (*music*) cornetta *f*; (*ice-cream*) cono *m*.
coronary ['korənəri] *adj* coronario. **coronary thrombosis** trombosi coronaria *f*.
coronation [korə'neiʃən] *n* incoronazione *f*.
corporal[1] ['kɔːpərəl] *adj* (*bodily*) corporale; (*material*) corporeo.
corporal[2] ['kɔːpərəl] *n* caporale, -a *m, f*.
corporation [ˌkɔːpə'reiʃən] *n* corporazione *f*, ente *m*.
corps [kɔː] *n* corpo *m*.
corpse [kɔːps] *n* cadavere *m*.
correct [kə'rekt] *v* correggere. *adj* corretto, giusto, esatto. **correction** *n* correzione *f*, rettifica *f*.
correlate ['korəleit] *v* mettere in correlazione. **correlated** *adj* correlativo. **correlation** *n* correlazione *f*.
correspond [korə'spond] *v* corrispondere, equivalere; (*letters*) essere in corrispondenza, scambiare lettere. **correspondence** *n* corrispondenza *f*, scambio di lettere *m*. **correspondent** *n* corrispondente *m, f*. **corresponding** *adj* corrispondente.
corridor ['koridoː] *n* corridoio *m*.
corrode [kə'roud] *v* corrodere, corrodersi. **corrosion** *n* corrosione *f*. **corrosive** *adj* corrosivo.
corrupt [kə'rʌpt] *v* corrompere. *adj* corrotto. **corruption** *n* corruzione *f*.
corset ['kɔːsit] *n* busto *m*; (*orthopaedic*) corsetto *m*.
Corsica ['kɔːsikə] *n* Corsica *f*. **Corsican** *n*, *adj* corso, -a.
cosh [koʃ] *n* randello *m*.
cosmetic [koz'metik] *nm*, *adj* cosmetico. **cosmetics** *pl n* prodotti di bellezza *m pl*.
cosmic ['kozmik] *adj* cosmico. **cosmonaut** *n* cosmonauta *m, f*.
cosmopolitan [kozmə'politən] *nm*, *adj* cosmopolitano.
***cost** [kost] *n* costo *m*, prezzo *m*. *v* costare. **costly** *adj* costoso, caro.
costume ['kostjuːm] *n* costume *m*, abito *m*; (*suit*) tailleur *m*.
cosy ['kouzi] *adj* comodo, intimo, accogliente.
cot [kot] *n* lettino *m*, culla *f*.
cottage ['kotidʒ] *n* villino *m*, casetta *f*.
cotton ['kotn] *n* cotone *m*. **cotton-wool** *n* bambagia *f*, ovatta *f*; (*med*) cotone idrofilo *m*.
couch [kautʃ] *n* divano *m*, canapè *m*.
cough [kof] *n* tosse *f*. **cough mixture** sciroppo per la tosse *m*. *v* tossire.
could [kud] *V* **can**[1]
council ['kaunsəl] *n* consiglio *m*; (*rel*) concilio *m*. **councillor** *n* consigliere *m*, membro del consiglio *m*.
counsel ['kaunsəl] *n* (*advice*) consiglio *m*; (*lawyer*) avvocato *m*. *v* raccomandare, consigliare. **counsellor** *n* consigliere, -a *m, f*; (*consultant*) consulente *m, f*.
count[1] [kaunt] *v* contare, includere. **count on** contare su, fare affidamento su. *n* conto *m*, calcolo *m*; (*law*) capo d'accusa *m*.
count[2] [kaunt] *n* conte *m*. **countess** *n* contessa *f*.
countenance ['kauntinəns] *n* espressione *f*. *v* tollerare.
counter[1] ['kauntə] *n* (*token*) gettone *m*; (*table top*) banco *m*; (*device*) calcolatore *m*.
counter[2] ['kauntə] *v* opporsi a, controbattere. *adj* contrario, opposto.
counteract [kauntə'rakt] *v* neutralizzare, invalidare, mandare a vuoto.
counter-attack *n* contrattacco *m*. *v* contrattaccare.
counterfeit ['kauntəfit] *adj* falsificato, falso. *v* falsificare.
counterfoil ['kauntəˌfoil] *n* matrice *f*, figlia *f*.
counterpart ['kauntəˌpaːt] *n* contropartita *f*, complemento *m*.
country ['kʌntri] *n* (*countryside*) campagna *f*; (*state*) paese *m*; (*homeland*) patria *f*.
county ['kaunti] *n* provincia *f*, regione *f*.
coup [kuː] *n* **coup de grace** colpo di grazia *m*. **coup d'état** colpo di stato *m*.
couple ['kʌpl] *n* coppia *f*, paio *m* (*pl* -a *f*). *v* accoppiare, abbinare.
coupon ['kuːpon] *n* tagliando *m*, scontrino *m*.
courage ['kʌridʒ] *n* coraggio *m*. **courageous** *adj* coraggioso.
courgette [kuə'ʒet] *n* zucchina *f*, zucchino *m*.
courier ['kuriə] *n* accompagnatore, -trice *m, f*; messaggero, -a *m, f*.
course [kɔːs] *n* corso *m*, percorso *m*, linea *f*; (*food*) piatto *m*; (*aircraft*) rotta *f*. **in due course** a tempo debito. **in the course of** durante, nel corso di. **of course** naturalmente, beninteso.

court [koːt] *n* corte *f*; (*law*) tribunale *m*; (*tennis*) campo *m*. **court-martial** *n* corte marziale *f*. **courtyard** *n* cortile *m*. *v* corteggiare, far la corte a.
courteous ['kəːtiəs] *adj* cortese, gentile. **courtesy** *n* cortesia *f*, gentilezza *f*.
cousin ['kʌzn] *n* cugino, -a *m*, *f*.
cove [kouv] *n* insenatura *f*.
cover ['kʌvə] *n* coperta *f*, copertura *f*; (*shelter*) riparo *m*; (*book*) copertina *f*. *v* coprire, ricoprire; (*travel*) percorrere; (*journalism*) riferire. **covering** *n* copertura *f*. **covering letter** lettera d'accompagnamento *f*.
cow [kau] *n* vacca *f*, mucca *f*. *v* intimidire.
coward ['kauəd] *n* vigliacco, -a *m*, *f*; vile *m*, *f*. **cowardly** *adj* vigliacco, vile. **cowardice** *n* vigliaccheria *f*.
cower ['kauə] *v* accovacciarsi, rannicchiarsi.
cowl [kaul] *n* (*chimney*) comignolo *m*; (*hood*) cappa *f*; (*car*) cofano *m*.
coy [koi] *adj* ritroso, timido.
crab [krab] *n* granchio *m*.
crack [krak] *n* (*opening*) screpolatura *f*, fessura *f*; (*whip*) schiocco *m*; (*rifle*) scoppio *m*; (*noise*) schianto *m*. **have a crack at** provare a fare. *v* spaccare, schioccare, screpolare.
cracker ['krakə] *n* (*biscuit*) cracker (*pl* -s) *m*, gallettina *f*; (*firework*) mortaretto *m*.
crackle ['krakl] *v* crepitare, scricchiolare. *n* crepitio *m*, scricchiolio *m*.
cradle ['kreidl] *n* culla *f*. *v* cullare.
craft [kraːft] *n* mestiere *m*, professione *f*; (*cunning*) astuzia *f*; (*boat*) imbarcazione *f*. **crafty** *adj* astuto.
cram [kram] *v* ficcare, cacciare.
cramp [kramp] *n* (*med*) crampo *m*. *v* paralizzare, bloccare.
cranberry ['kranbəri] *n* mirtillo rosso *m*.
crane [krein] *n* gru *f invar*. *v* **crane one's neck** allungare il collo.
crank [kraŋk] *n* (*mech*) gomito *m*, manovella *f*; eccentrico, -a *m*, *f*. *v* **crank up** avviare.
crap [krap] *n* (*vulgar*) merda *f*; (*impol: nonsense*) scemenze *f pl*, stupidaggini *f pl*. *v* (*vulgar*) cacare.
crash [kraʃ] *n* (*collision*) scontro *m*; (*noise*) fracasso *m*; (*collapse*) crollo *m*; (*aircraft*) caduta *f*. **crash-helmet** *n* casco paraurti *m*. **crash-landing** *n* atterraggio di fortuna *m*. *v* (*clash*) scontrarsi; fracassare; crollare; precipitare.
crate [kreit] *n* cassa *f*. *v* imballare.
crater ['kreitə] *n* cratere *m*.
crave [kreiv] *v* ambire, bramare. **craving** *n* smania *f*, brama *f*.
crawl [kroːl] *v* trascinarsi, strisciare. *n* (*swimming*) crawl *m invar*.
crayfish ['kreifiʃ] *n* gambero (di fiume) *m*.
crayon ['kreiən] *n* pastello *m*, matita colorata *f*.
craze [kreiz] *n* mania *f*, pazzia *f*. **crazy** *adj* pazzo, matto. **drive crazy** far impazzire.
creak [kriːk] *v* cigolare, scricchiolare. *n* cigolio *m*, scricchiolio *m*.
cream [kriːm] *n* panna *f*, crema *f*. *v* scremare. **creamy** *adj* cremoso; (*soft*) morbido.
crease [kriːs] *n* piega *f*, grinza *f*. *v* sgualcirsi, raggrinzarsi. **creased** *adj* raggrinzato; (*clothes*) sgualcito.
create [kri'eit] *v* creare, provocare. **creation** *n* creazione *f*. **creative** *adj* creativo, originale. **creativity** *n* potenza creativa *f*, originalità *f*. **creator** *n* creatore, -trice *m*, *f*. **creature** *n* creatura *f*.
credentials [kri'denʃəlz] *pl n* credenziali *f pl*.
credible ['kredəbl] *adj* credibile. **credibility** *n* credibilità *f*.
credit ['kredit] *n* credito *m*; (*trustworthyness*) fiducia *f*; considerazione *f*; (*bank*) attivo *m*. **credit balance** saldo attivo *m*. **credit card** carta di credito *f*. *v* (*comm*) accreditare; (*have faith in*) credere, prestar fede a; (*ascribe*) attribuire. **creditable** *adj* degno di lode, che fa onore. **creditor** *n* creditore, -trice *m*, *f*.
credulous ['kredjuləs] *adj* credulo, ingenuo.
creed [kriːd] *n* credo *m*, professione di fede *f*.
***creep** [kriːp] *v* strisciare, insinuarsi; (*plants*) arrampicarsi. **creeper** *n* (*plant*) pianta rampicante *f*. **creepy** *adj* che dà i brividi.
cremate [kri'meit] *v* cremare. **cremation** *n* cremazione *f*. **crematorium** *n* crematorio *m*.
crept [krept] *V* **creep**.
crescent ['kresnt] *n* mezzaluna *f*.
cress [kres] *n* crescione *m*. **mustard and cress** crescione inglese *m*, agretto *m*. **watercress** *n* crescione d'acqua *m*.

crest [krest] *n* cresta *f*, ciuffo *m*; (*heraldry, helmet*) cimiero *m*. **crestfallen** *adj* mortificato.
crevice ['krevis] *n* crepa *f*, fessura *f*.
crew [kruː] *n* equipaggio *m*, squadra *f*.
crib [krib] *n* (*rel*) presepio *m*; (*bed*) lettino *m*; (*manger*) mangiatoia *f*; (*coll*) bigino *m*. *v* plagiare.
cricket¹ ['krikit] *n* (*insect*) grillo *m*.
cricket² ['krikit] *n* (*sport*) cricket *m*.
crime [kraim] *n* delitto *m*, reato *m*. **criminal** *n*(*m*+*f*), *adj* criminale.
crimson ['krimzn] *adj* cremisi.
cringe [krindʒ] *v* comportarsi in modo servile.
crinkle ['kriŋkl] *n* grinza *f*. *v* raggrinzare.
cripple ['kripl] *n* storpio, -a *m*, *f*; invalido, -a *m*, *f*. *v* storpiare, mutilare, paralizzare.
crisis ['kraisis] *n*, *pl* **-ses** crisi *f invar*.
crisp [krisp] *adj* (*lively*) nitido; (*bracing*) invigorante; (*firm, fresh*) fresco; (*brittle*) croccante; (*crinkled*) crespo. **crisps** *pl n* patatine fritte croccanti *f pl*.
criterion [krai'tiəriən] *n*, *pl* **-ria** criterio *m*.
criticize ['kriti,saiz] *v* criticare, esprimere un giudizio su. **critic** *n* critico *m*. **critical** *adj* critico. **criticism** *n* critica *f*; (*philosophy*) criticismo *m*. **critique** *n* saggio critico *m*.
croak [krouk] *v* gracchiare, gracidare; (*grumble*) brontolare. *n* gracchiare *m*, gracchio *m*, gracidio *m*.
crochet ['krouʃei] *v* lavorare all'uncinetto.
crockery ['krokəri] *n* vasellame *m*, stoviglie *f pl*.
crocodile ['krokə,dail] *n* coccodrillo *m*.
crocus ['kroukəs] *n* croco *m*.
crook [kruk] *n* (*hook*) uncino *m*; (*bishop's*) pastorale *m*; (*shepherd's*) bastone da pastore *m*; (*criminal*) truffatore, -trice *m*, *f*. *v* piegare, curvare.
crooked ['krukid] *adj* (*bent*) piegato, storto; disonesto.
crop [krop] *n* (*produce*) raccolto *m*; (*riding*) frusta *f*; (*gullet*) gozzo *m*. *v* (*clip hair*) tagliar corto; (*trees*) mozzare; (*cut grain, etc.*) mietere. **come a cropper** far fiasco.
croquet ['kroukei] *n* croquet *m invar*.
cross [kros] *n* croce *f*. *adj* arrabbiato. **be cross** arrabbiarsi. *v* incrociare; (*street, etc.*) attraversare; (*threshold*) varcare; (*cheque*) sbarrare; (*annoy*) ostacolare. **cross oneself** segnarsi. **cross one's mind** venire in mente a uno. **cross out** cancellare. **cross-examine** *v* sottoporre a interrogatorio. **cross-examination** *n* interrogatorio *m*. **cross-eyed** *adj* strabico. **crossfire** *n* fuoco incrociato *m* **cross-legged** *adj* a gambe accavallate. **cross-reference** *n* richiamo *m*. **crossroads** *n* crocevia *m*, incrocio *m*. **crossword** *n* cruciverba *m invar*, parole incrociate *f pl*. **crossing** *n* traversata *f*.
crotchet ['krotʃit] *n* (*music*) semiminima *f*; (*hook*) uncinetto *m*. **crotchety** *adj* irritabile.
crouch [krautʃ] *v* ranicchiarsi.
crow¹ [krou] *n* (*bird*) corvo *m*, cornacchia *f*. **as the crow flies** in linea diretta. **crow's nest** coffa *f*. **crow's foot** ruga *f*, zampa di gallina *f*.
crow² [krou] *v* cantare, esultare; (*boast*) vantarsi, trionfare.
crowd [kraud] *n* folla *f*, massa *f*, compagnia *f*. *v* affollare, ammassare. **crowded** *adj* affollato, stipato, pieno zeppo.
crown [kraun] *n* corona *f*; (*hat*) cocuzzolo *m*; (*head*) calotta *f*; (*road*) colmo *m*. **crown-prince** *n* principe ereditario *m*. *v* incoronare; (*reward*) ricompensare; (*tooth*) mettere una corona a. **to crown it all** come se non bastasse.
crucial ['kruːʃəl] *adj* decisivo, critico.
crucify ['kruːsi,fai] *v* crocifiggere, mettere in croce; tormentare, mortificare. **crucifix** *n* crocifisso *m*. **crucifixion** *n* crocifissione *f*.
crude [kruːd] *adj* (*rough, vulgar*) grossolano, rozzo, volgare; (*unrefined*) grezzo.
cruel ['kruːəl] *adj* crudele. **be cruel to** maltrattare. **cruelty** *n* crudeltà *f*.
cruise [kruːz] *n* crociera *f*. **go on a cruise** fare una crociera.
crumb [krʌm] *n* briciola *f*.
crumble ['krʌmbl] *v* sgretolare; (*collapse*) crollare. **crumbly** *adj* friabile.
crumple ['krʌmpl] *v* sgualcire, sgualcirsi; (*collapse*) sfasciarsi, accasciarsi.
crunch [krʌntʃ] *v* sgretolare, sgranocchiare. *n* scricchiolio *m*; (*critical point*) momento di crisi *m*.
crusade [kruː'seid] *n* crociata *f*. **crusader** *n* crociato *m*.
crush [krʌʃ] *v* schiacciare, frantumare; (*destroy*) annientare. *n* calca *f*, ressa *f*. **have a crush on** prendersi una cotta per. **crusher** *n* frantoio *m*.

crust [krʌst] *n* crosta *f*, corteccia *f*. **crusty** *adj* crostoso; (*surly*) burbero.
crutch [krʌtʃ] *n* gruccia *f*, stampella *f*.
crux [krʌks] *n* **the crux of the matter** il nodo della questione *m*.
cry [krai] *n* urlo *m*, strillo *m*, lamento *m*. *v* urlare, gridare; (*weep*) piangere.
crypt [kript] *n* cripta *f*. **cryptic** *adj* ambiguo, misterioso.
crystal ['kristl] *n* cristallo *m*. **crystallization** *n* cristallizzazione *f*. **crystallize** *v* cristallizzare.
cub [kʌb] *n* cucciolo *m*.
cube [kjuːb] *n* cubo *m*. *v* elevare al cubo. **cubic** *adj* cubico.
cubicle ['kjuːbikl] *n* stanzino *m*; (*changing-room*) spogliatoio *m*.
cuckold ['kʌkould] *n* cornuto *m*. *v* fare le corna a.
cuckoo ['kukuː] *n* cuculo *m*, cucù *m*.
cucumber [kju'kʌmbə] *n* cetriolo *m*.
cuddle ['kʌdl] *v* coccolare, abbracciare teneramente. *n* abbraccio tenero *m*.
cue[1] [kjuː] *n* (*theatre*) battuta d'entrata *f*; (*hint*) spunto *m*.
cue[2] [kjuː] *n* (*billiards*) stecca *f*.
cuff[1] [kʌf] *n* (*shirt*) polsino *m*. **cuff-links** *pl n* gemelli *m pl*.
cuff[2] [kʌf] *n* (*hit*) schiaffo *m*, sberla *f*. *v* schiaffeggiare.
culinary ['kʌlinəri] *adj* culinario, gastronomico.
culminate ['kʌlmiˌneit] *v* concludersi. **culmination** *n* culmine *m*.
culprit ['kʌlprit] *n* colpevole *m, f*.
cult [kʌlt] *n* culto *m*.
cultivate ['kʌltiˌveit] *v* coltivare. **cultivation** *n* coltivazione *f*, coltura *f*.
culture ['kʌltʃə] *n* cultura *f*; (*land, plants*) coltura *f*. **cultural** *adj* culturale. **cultured** *adj* colto.
cumbersome ['kʌmbəsəm] *adj* ingombrante.
cunning ['kʌniŋ] *adj* scaltro, astuto. *n* astuzia *f*, scaltrezza *f*.
cup [kʌp] *n* tazza *f*; (*sport*) coppa *f*.
cupboard ['kʌbəd] *n* armadio *m*, credenza *f*. **cupboard love** amore interessato *m*.
curate ['kjuərət] *n* curato *m*, parroco *m*.
curator [kjuə'reitə] *n* direttore, -trice di museo *m, f*; curatore, -trice *m, f*.
curb [kəːb] *v* frenare.
curdle ['kəːdl] *v* cagliare, cagliarsi; (*blood*) gelare.
cure [kjuə] *n* cura *f*, rimedio *m*. *v* sanare, guarire; (*food*) conservare; (*salt*) salare; (*smoke*) affumicare.
curfew ['kəːfjuː] *n* coprifuoco *m*.
curious ['kjuəriəs] *adj* (*odd*) strano, curioso, insolito; (*inquisitive*) curioso.
curl [kəːl] *n* ricciolo *m*. *v* arricciare, arrotolare; (*lip*) torcere. **curl up** rannicchiarsi; (*animal*) accucciarsi. **curler** *n* bigodino *m*.
currant ['kʌrənt] *n* ribes *m invar*; (*dried*) uva passa *f*, uvetta *f*.
currency ['kʌrənsi] *n* decorrenza *f*; (*money*) valuta *f*, moneta legale *f*.
current ['kʌrənt] *n* corrente *f*. *adj* corrente, comune.
curry ['kʌri] *n* curry *m invar*. *v* **curry favour** ingraziarsi.
curse [kəːs] *n* (*oath*) bestemmia *f*; (*evil*) maledizione *f*. *v* bestemmiare, maledire. **be cursed with** essere afflitto da.
curt [kəːt] *adj* brusco.
curtail [kəː'teil] *v* limitare, ridurre.
curtain ['kəːtn] *n* cortina *f*; (*cloth*) tenda *f*, tendina *f*; (*theatre*) sipario *m*.
curtsy ['kəːtsi] *n* inchino *m*. *v* inchinarsi.
curve [kəːv] *n* curva *f*, svolta *f*. *v* curvare, svoltare.
cushion ['kuʃən] *n* cuscino *m*; (*billiards*) sponda *f*. *v* smorzare, assorbire.
custody ['kʌstədi] *n* custodia *f*, guardia *f*. **take into custody** arrestare. **custodian** *n* guardiano *m*, custode *m, f*.
custom ['kʌstəm] *n* costume *m*, usanza *f*, abitudine *f*. **customs** *n* dogana *f*. **customs officer** doganiere, -a *m, f*. **customary** *adj* abituale, solito. **customer** *n* cliente *m, f*.
***cut** [kʌt] *n* taglio *m*, incisione *f*; (*wound*) ferita *f*. *v* tagliare, incidere; (*wound*) ferire; (*cards*) alzare le carte. **cut down** ridurre; (*fell*) abbattere. **cut off** tagliar via; (*suspend*) sospendere. **cut out** ritagliare; omettere; (*elec*) interrompere. **cut it out!** piantala! **cut price** prezzo ridotto *m*. **cut-throat** *adj* spietato.
cute [kjuːt] *adj* grazioso, ingegnoso.
cutlery ['kʌtləri] *n* posate *f pl*, posateria *f*; (*knives*) coltelleria *f*.
cutlet ['kʌtlit] *n* costoletta *f*, cotoletta *f*.
cutting ['kʌtiŋ] *adj* tagliente. *n* (*newspaper*) ritaglio *m*; (*plant*) margotta *f*; (*railway*) trincea *f*.
cycle ['saikl] *n* ciclo *m*, periodo *m*; (*bicycle*) bicicletta *f*. *v* andare in bicicletta. **cyclic** *adj* ciclico. **cycling** *n* ciclismo *m*. **cyclist** *n* ciclista *m, f*.

cyclone ['saikloun] *n* ciclone *m*.
cylinder ['silində] *n* cilindro *m*; (*revolver*) tamburo *m*; (*printing*) rullo *m*; (*gas*) bombola *f*.
cymbal ['simbəl] *n* cembalo *m*.
cynic ['sinik] *n* cinico, -a *m, f*. **cynical** *adj* cinico. **cynicism** *n* cinismo *m*.
cypress ['saiprəs] *n* cipresso *m*.
Cyprus ['saiprəs] *n* Cipro *m*. **Cypriot** *n*(*m*+*f*), *adj* cipriota.
cyst [sist] *n* cisti *f*.
Czechoslovakia [ˌtʃekəslə'vakiə] *n* Cecoslovacchia *f*. **Czech** *n*, *adj* ceco, -a, cecoslovacco, -a.

D

dab [dab] *v* toccare leggermente; applicare. *n* (*small quantity*) tocco *m*; (*light blow*) colpetto *m*.
dabble ['dabl] *v* (*dip, paddle*) guazzare. **dabble in** dilettarsi a; fare da dilettante.
dad [dad] *n* babbo *m*, papà *m*.
daffodil ['dafədil] *n* narciso *m*.
daft [daːft] *adj* scemo, sciocco.
dagger ['dagə] *n* pugnale *m*, stiletto *m*. **be at daggers drawn** essere ai ferri corti.
daily ['deili] *adj* giornaliero, quotidiano. *n* giornale *m*; (*maid*) domestica a giornata *f*. *adv* ogni giorno, quotidianamente.
dainty ['deinti] *adj* delicato, squisito.
dairy ['deəri] *n* latteria *f*. **dairy produce** latticini *m pl*.
daisy ['deizi] *n* margherita *f*.
dam [dam] *n* diga *f*, argine *m*. *v* sbarrare, arginare.
damage ['damidʒ] *n* danno *m*, guasto *m*; (*law*) indennizzo *m*. *v* danneggiare, guastare, nuocere. **damaging** *adj* dannoso.
damn [dam] *v* dannare, maledire. *interj* maledizione! *n* (*negligible amount*) bel niente *m*.
damp [damp] *adj* umido, madido. *n* umido *m*. *v also* **dampen** (*moisten*) inumidire; (*dull*) smorzare, deprimere. **damper** *n* (*furnace*) valvola di tiraggio *f*; (*elec*) smorzatore *m*; (*music*) sordina *f*.
damson ['damzən] *n* (*fruit*) susina selvatica *f*; (*tree*) susino selvatico *m*.
dance [daːns] *n* danza *f*, ballo *m*. *v* danzare, ballare. **dancer** *n* danzatore, -trice *m, f*; ballerino, -a *m, f*.
dandelion ['dandiˌlaiən] *n* dente di leone *m*.
dandruff ['dandrəf] *n* forfora *f*.
danger ['deindʒə] *n* pericolo *m*. **dangerous** *adj* pericoloso.
dangle ['daŋgl] *v* (far) ciondolare *or* dondolare.
Danish ['deiniʃ] *nm*, *adj* danese. **Dane** *n* danese *m, f*.
dare [deə] *v* (*be bold*) osare; (*challenge*) sfidare. **I dare say** suppongo; probabilmente; (*not deny*) non nego.
daring ['deəriŋ] *adj* audace. *n* audacia *f*.
dark [daːk] *n also* **darkness** buio *m*, oscurità *f*. *adj* buio, oscuro, cupo. **darken** *v* scurire, offuscare, rabbuiarsi.
darling ['daːliŋ] *n* tesoro *m*, gioia *f*, favorito, -a *m, f*. *adj* carissimo, amatissimo.
darn [daːn] *v* rammendare. *n* rammendo *m*, rammendatura *f*.
dart [daːt] *n* dardo *m*, freccia *f*. *v* (*move swiftly*) balzare, slanciarsi, precipitarsi; (*throw*) lanciare.
dash [daʃ] *v* buttare, urtare; (*spoil*) frustrare; (*rush*) scappare. *n* spruzzo *m*; (*rush*) slancio *m*; (*drink*) goccio *m*; (*pinch*) pizzico *m*; (*printing*) lineetta *f*. **dashboard** *n* cruscotto *m*.
data ['deitə] *pl n* dati *m pl*, elementi *m pl*. **data processing** elaborazione di dati *f*.
date[1] [deit] *n* (*calendar*) data *f*; (*appointment*) appuntamento *m*. *v* datare, fare appuntamento con. **date from** risalire a. **out of date** fuori moda, antiquato. **up to date** aggiornato.
date[2] [deit] *n* (*fruit*) dattero *m*.
daughter ['doːtə] *n* figlia *f*, figliola *f*. **daughter-in-law** *n* nuora *f*.
daunt [doːnt] *v* intimidire.
dawdle ['doːdl] *v* sprecar tempo, bighellonare. **dawdler** *n* fannullone, -a *m, f*; bighellone, -a *m, f*.
dawn [doːn] *n* alba *f*, aurora *f*; (*beginning*) inizio *m*. *v* albeggiare; (*appear*) apparire, manifestarsi.
day [dei] *n* giorno *m*, giornata *f*. **by day** di giorno. **daybreak** *n* alba *f*, spuntar del giorno *m*. **daylight** *n* luce del giorno *f*. **every other day** un giorno si e uno no. **the day before yesterday** ieri l'altro. **the day after tomorrow** dopodomani.
daydream ['deidriːm] *v* sognare ad occhi aperti; fantasticare. *n* sogno ad occhi aperti *m*, fantasticheria *f*.

daze [deiz] *v* stordire, sbalordire. *n* stupore *m.*
dazzle ['dazl] *v* abbagliare.
dead [ded] *adj* morto, defunto; (*coll: absolute*) assoluto, completo. **dead drunk** ubriaco fradicio. **deadline** *n* scadenza *f.* **deadlock** *n* punto morto *m*; incaglio *m.* **dead slow** a passo d'uomo. **deaden** *v* attutire. **deadly** *adj* mortale.
deaf [def] *adj* sordo. **turn a deaf ear** fare orecchi da mercante. **deaf-mute** *n* sordomuto, -a *m, f.* **deafen** *v* rendere sordo, intontire. **deafness** *n* sordità *f.*
***deal** [diːl] *v* (*cards*) dare le carte. **deal in** commerciare in. **deal with** occuparsi di; (*things*) trattare di; (*people*) avere rapporti con. *n* (*business*) affare *m*; (*agreement*) accordo *m*; (*amount*) quantità *f.* **dealer** *n* commerciante *m, f*; (*retail*) dettagliante *m, f*; (*wholesale*) grossista *m, f.*
dealt [delt] *V* **deal**.
dean [diːn] *n* (*university*) preside di facoltà *m, f*; (*rel*) decano *m.*
dear [diə] *adj* caro. **oh dear!** ahimè! Dio mio!
death [deθ] *n* morte *f.* **death certificate** certificato di morte *m.* **death duties** tassa di successione *f sing.* **death warrant** sentenza di morte *f.* **deathly** *adj, adv* mortale; cadaverico.
debase [di'beis] *v* degradare, svalutare.
debate [di'beit] *v* dibattere, discutere. *n* dibattito *m*, discussione *f.*
debit ['debit] *n* debito *m*; (*accounts*) dare *m.* *v* addebitare.
debris ['deibriː] *n* detrito *m*, macerie *f pl.*
debt [det] *n* debito *m*; (*obligation*) obbligo *m.* **debt collector** *n* esattore, -trice *m, f.* **debtor** *n* debitore, -trice *m, f.*
decade ['dekeid] *n* decennio *m.*
decadent ['dekədənt] *adj* decadente.
decant [di'kant] *v* travasare. **decanter** *n* caraffa *f.*
decay [di'kei] *v* deperire, putrefare, putrefarsi, andare in rovina; (*teeth*) cariare. *n* sfacelo *m*, rovina *f*, deperimento *m.*
deceased [di'siːst] *n, adj* defunto, -a. **decease** *n* decesso *m.*
deceit [di'siːt] *n* inganno *m*, truffa *f.* **deceitful** *adj* falso, perfido.
deceive [di'siːv] *v* ingannare, imbrogliare, illudersi.
December [di'sembə] *n* dicembre *m.*
decent ['diːsənt] *adj* (*proper*) decente; (*fitting*) decoroso; (*fair*) discreto; (*respectable*) bravo. **decency** *n* decenza *f*, decoro *m.*
deceptive [di'septiv] *adj* ingannevole, illusorio. **deception** *n* inganno *m*, imbroglio *m.*
decibel ['desiˌbel] *n* decibel *m invar.*
decentralization [diːˌsentrəlai'zeiʃn] *n* decentramento *m.*
decide [di'said] *v* decidere, decidersi. **decided** *adj* deciso, risoluto.
deciduous [di'sidjuəs] *adj* deciduo.
decimal ['desiməl] *nm, adj* decimale.
decipher [di'saifə] *v* decifrare.
decision [di'siʒən] *n* decisione *f.* **decisive** *adj* decisivo.
deck [dek] *n* (*naut*) ponte *m*, coperta *f*; (*cards*) mazzo *m.* *v* ornare. **deck-chair** *n* sedia a sdraio *f.*
declare [di'kleə] *v* dichiarare, proclamare. **declaration** *n* dichiarazione *f*, proclama *m.*
decline [di'klain] *v* (*refuse*) rifiutare; (*gramm*) declinare; (*deteriorate*) deperire. *n* (*gradual loss*) declino *m*; deterioramento *m*; decadenza *f.*
decompose [ˌdiːkəm'pouz] *v* decomporre. **decomposition** *n* decomposizione *f*, putrefazione *f.*
decorate ['dekəˌreit] *v* decorare, ornare; (*house*) verniciare. **decoration** *n* decorazione *f*, ornamento *m.* **decorator** *n* (*interior*) arredatore, -trice *m, f*; (*building*) decoratore, -trice *m, f*, pittore, -trice *m, f.* **decorous** *adj* decoroso. **decorum** *n* decoro *m.*
decoy ['diːkoi] *n* richiamo *m*, uccello da richiamo *m*, esca *f*; (*person*) adescatore, -trice *m, f.*
decrease [di'kriːs] *n* diminuire. *n* diminuzione *f*, ribasso *m.*
decree [di'kriː] *n* decreto *m*, ordinanza *f.* *v* decretare.
decrepit [di'krepit] *adj* decrepito.
dedicate ['dediˌkeit] *v* dedicare. **dedication** *n* dedicazione *f*; (*book*) dedica *f.*
deduce [di'djuːs] *v* dedurre, inferire. **deduction** *n* (*inference*) deduzione *f.*
deduct [di'dʌkt] *v* dedurre, sottrarre. **deduction** *n* (*subtraction*) sottrazione *f.*
deed [diːd] *n* fatto *m*, azione *f*; (*law*) atto notarile *m*, strumento *m*; (*undertaking*) impresa *f.* **good deed** buona azione *f.*

deep [diːp] *adj* profondo, alto; (*colour*) scuro, cupo. **deep-rooted** *or* **deep-seated** *adj* radicato. **deepen** *v* approfondire.
deep-freeze *v* surgelare. *n* congelatore *m*, freezer *m invar*.
deer [diə] *n* (*roe*) capriolo *m*; (*fallow*) daino *m*.
deface [di'feis] *v* sfregiare, mutilare.
defamatory [di'famətəri] *adj* diffamatorio. **defamation** *n* diffamazione *f*, calunnia *f*.
default [di'foːlt] *v* rendersi contumace. *n* **by default** in contumacia. **in default of** in difetto di.
defeat [di'fiːt] *n* sconfitta *f*, disfatta *f*. *v* sconfiggere. **defeatism** *n* disfattismo *m*. **defeatist** *n* disfattista *m*, *f*.
defect[1] ['diːfekt] *n* difetto *m*, mancanza *f*. **defective** *adj* difettoso, imperfetto; (*gramm*) difettivo.
defect[2] [di'fekt] *v* disertare. **defection** *n* diserzione *f*, defezione *f*.
defend [di'fend] *v* difendere, proteggere. **defence** *n* difesa *f*. **defenceless** *adj* indifeso, senza difesa. **defendant** *n* imputato, -a *m*, *f*. **defender** *n* difensore *m*.
defensive [di'fensiv] *adj* difensivo. *n* difensiva *f*. **be on the defensive** stare sulla difesa.
defer[1] [di'fəː] *v* (*put off*) rimandare, rinviare.
defer[2] [di'fəː] *v* (*yield to*) sottoporsi. **deferential** *adj* rispettoso, deferente.
deficient [di'fiʃənt] *adj* deficiente, incompleto, insufficiente. **deficiency** *n* deficienza *f*, mancanza *f*, carenza *f*.
deficit ['defisit] *n* deficit *m invar*, disavanzo *m*.
define [di'fain] *v* definire, precisare. **definition** *n* definizione *f*.
definite ['definit] *adj* definito, determinato, preciso.
deflate [di'fleit] *v* sgonfiare; (*comm*) deflazionare. **deflation** *n* sgonfiamento *m*, deflazione *f*.
deflect [di'flekt] *v* deviare. **deflection** *n* deviazione *f*.
deform [di'foːm] *v* deformare. **deformity** *or* **deformation** *n* deformazione *f*.
defraud [di'froːd] *v* frodare, defraudare.
defray [di'frei] *v* **defray expenses** rimborsare le spese.
defrost [diː'frost] *v* scongelare.
deft [deft] *adj* destro, lesto. **deftness** *n* destrezza *f*, agilità *f*.
defunct [di'fʌŋkt] *adj* defunto.
defy [di'fai] *v* sfidare, provocare. **defiance** *n* (*resistance*) sfida *f*; dispetto *m*. **in defiance of** a dispetto di. **defiant** *adj* ribelle, ricalcitrante.
degenerate [di'dʒenərit; *v* di'dʒenəreit] *adj* degenerato, perverso. *v* degenerare. **degeneracy** *or* **degeneration** *n* degenerazione *f*.
degrade [di'greid] *v* degradare. **degrading** *adj* degradante.
degree [di'griː] *n* grado *m*; (*diploma*) titolo di studio *m*, laurea *f*.
dehydrate [diː'haidreit] *v* disidratare. **dehydration** *n* disidratazione *f*.
de-icer [diː'aisə] *n* dispositivo antighiaccio *m*.
deign [dein] *v* degnarsi.
deity ['diːəti] *n* divinità *f*, deità *f*.
dejected [di'dʒektid] *adj* avvilito, abbattuto.
delay [di'lei] *n* ritardo *m*, indugio *m*. *v* ritardare, differire.
delegate ['deləgit; *v* 'deləgeit] *n* delegato, -a *m*, *f*. *v* delegare, autorizzare. **delegation** *n* delegazione *f*.
delete [di'liːt] *v* espungere. **deletion** *n* cancellatura *f*, espunzione *f*.
deliberate [di'libərət; *v* di'libəreit] *adj* (*intentional*) voluto; (*unhurried*) misurato; (*carefully considered*) ponderato. *v* deliberare, riflettere. **deliberation** *n* riflessione *f*, deliberazione *f*.
delicate ['delikət] *adj* delicato, fine; (*sensitive*) sensibile. **delicacy** *n* delicatezza *f*; sensibilità *f*; (*food*) leccornia *f*.
delicious [di'liʃəs] *adj* delizioso; (*food*) squisito.
delight [di'lait] *n* delizia *f*, diletto *m*. *v* dilettare. **delight in** rallegrarsi di. **delighted** *adj* ben lieto. **delightful** *adj* delizioso, incantevole, simpaticissimo.
delinquency [di'liŋkwənsi] *n* delinquenza *f*. **delinquent** *n*(*m*+*f*), *adj* delinquente.
delirious [di'liriəs] *adj* (*feverish*) delirante; (*wildly excited*) ebbro.
deliver [di'livə] *v* (*hand over*) recapitare, consegnare; (*set free*) liberare; (*save*) salvare; (*speech*) pronunciare. **deliverance** *n* liberazione *f*. **delivery** *n* consegna *f*; (*birth*) parto *m*; (*diction*) dizione *f*.
delta ['deltə] *n* delta *m*.
delude [di'luːd] *v* deludere, deludersi. **delusion** *n* delusione *f*.

deluge ['deljuːdʒ] *n* diluvio *m*. *v* diluviare.
delve [delv] *v* (*dig*) scavare; (*research*) far ricerche.
demand [di'maːnd] *v* esigere, pretendere. *n* pretesa *f*, richiesta *f*. **in demand** ricercato. **on demand** su richiesta. **demanding** *adj* esigente.
demented [di'mentid] *adj* demente, impazzito.
democracy [di'mokrəsi] *n* democrazia *f*. **democrat** *n* democratico, -a *m, f*. **democratic** *adj* democratico.
demolish [di'moliʃ] *v* demolire, abbattere. **demolition** *n* demolizione *f*.
demon ['diːmən] *n* demonio *m*, diavolo *m*.
demonstrate ['demənˌstreit] *v* dimostrare. **demonstrable** *adj* dimostrabile. **demonstration** *n* dimostrazione *f*; (*proof*) prova *f*; (*meeting*) manifestazione *f*. **demonstrative** *adj* dimostrativo; (*feeling*) espansivo.
demoralize [di'morəˌlaiz] *v* demoralizzare, scoraggiare.
demure [di'mjuə] *adj* modesto, schivo.
den [den] *n* tana *f*.
denial [di'naiəl] *n* (*contradiction*) smentita *f*; (*negation*) diniego *m*; (*refusal*) rifiuto *m*.
denim ['denim] *n* tela pesante *f*.
Denmark ['denmaːk] *n* Danimarca *f*.
denomination [diˌnomi'neiʃən] *n* denominazione *f*; (*belief*) setta *f*, religione *f*; (*money*) taglio *m*. **denominator** *n* denominatore *m*.
denote [di'nout] *v* denotare, indicare.
denounce [di'nauns] *v* denunciare; (*openly accuse*) inveire contro.
dense [dens] *adj* denso, fitto. **density** *n* densità *f*.
dent [dent] *n* tacca *f*, ammaccatura *f*. *v* intaccare, ammaccare.
dental ['dentl] *adj* dentale; (*of dentistry*) dentistico.
dentist ['dentist] *n* dentista *m, f*. **dentistry** *n* odontoiatria *f*.
denture ['dentʃə] *n* dentiera *f*.
denude [di'njuːd] *v* denudare, privare.
denunciation [dinʌnsi'eiʃən] *n* denuncia *f*.
deny [di'nai] *v* negare, smentire. **deny oneself** privarsi di, fare a meno di.
deodorant [diː'oudərənt] *nm, adj* deodorante.
depart [di'paːt] *v* (*leave*) partire; (*diverge*) deviare. **departure** *n* partenza *f*, deviazione *f*.
department [di'paːtmənt] *n* reparto *m*. **department store** grande magazzino *m*.
depend [di'pend] *v* dipendere, fare assegnamento. **depend on** dipendere da, fare assegnamento su. **dependable** *adj* fidato. **dependence** *n* dipendenza *f*. **dependent** *n*(*m*+*f*), *adj* dipendente.
depict [di'pikt] *v* rappresentare, descrivere.
deplete [di'pliːt] *v* esaurire, vuotare.
deplore [di'ploː] *v* biasimare, disapprovare. **deplorable** *adj* riprensibile, biasimevole.
deport [di'poːt] *v* deportare, espellere. **deportation** *n* deportazione *f*, espulsione *f*.
depose [di'pouz] *v* (*dismiss*) deporre; (*witness*) testimoniare. **deposition** *n* deposizione *f*, testimonianza *f*.
deposit [di'pozit] *v* depositare, posare. *n* deposito *m*; (*security*) cauzione *f*, pegno *m*. **deposit account** conto vincolato *m*.
depot ['depou] *n* deposito *m*, magazzino *m*, parco *m*.
deprave [di'preiv] *v* corrompere, depravare.
depreciate [di'priːʃiˌeit] *v* deprezzare; (*money*) svalutare; (*belittle*) screditare, denigrare. **depreciation** *n* deprezzamento *m*, svalutazione *f*; discredito *m*, denigrazione *f*.
depress [di'pres] *v* deprimere. **depressed** *adj* depresso, abbattuto; (*market*) basso. **depressing** *adj* deprimente, triste. **depression** *n* depressione *f*; (*comm*) crisi *f invar*.
deprive [di'praiv] *v* privare. **deprivation** *n* privazione *f*.
depth [depθ] *n* profondità *f*, altezza *f*. **be out of one's depth** non essere all'altezza.
deputy ['depjuti] *n* delegato *m*, deputato *m*. **deputation** *n* deputazione *f*.
derail [di'reil] *v* uscire dalle rotaie, deragliare. **derailment** *n* deragliamento *m*.
derelict ['derilikt] *adj* derelitto, abbandonato.
deride [di'raid] *v* deridere, schernire. **derision** *n* derisione *f*, scherno *m*. **derisive** *or* **derisory** *adj* irrisorio, derisivo.
derive [di'raiv] *v* derivare, provenire. **derivation** *n* derivazione *f*, provenienza *f*, origine *f*.
derogatory [di'rogətəri] *adj* sprezzante, diffamante.

descend [di'send] *v* scendere; (*come from*) derivare, discendere. **descent** *n* discesa *f*; (*ancestry*) discendenza *f*, lignaggio *m*. **descendant** *n* discendente *m*, *f*.
describe [di'skraib] *v* descrivere. **description** *n* descrizione *f*.
desert[1] ['dezət] *n* deserto *m*.
desert[2] [di'zəːt] *v* disertare, abbandonare. **deserter** *n* disertore *m*. **desertion** *n* diserzione *f*, abbandono *m*.
desert[3] [di'zəːt] *n* **get one's just deserts** ricevere quel che si merita.
deserve [di'zəːv] *v* meritare, essere degno di.
design [di'zain] *v* (*plan*) progettare; (*intend*) destinare. *n* disegno *m*, progetto *m*; (*intention*) proposito *m*. **have designs on** avere delle mire su. **designer** *n* progettista *m*, *f*, modellista *m*, *f*.
designate ['dezigˌneit] *v* designare. *adj* designato.
desire [di'zaiə] *v* desiderare, bramare. *n* (*wish*) desiderio *m*; (*craving*) brama *f*; passione *f*. **desirable** *adj* desiderabile.
desk [desk] *n* scrivania *f*; (*school*) banco *m*; (*cash*) cassa *f*.
desolate ['desələt] *adj* desolato; (*barren*) deserto; (*lonely*) solitario; (*sad*) afflitto, rattristato.
despair [di'speə] *n* disperazione *f*. *v* disperare.
desperate ['despərət] *adj* disperato; (*hopeless*) senza speranza. **desperation** *n* disperazione *f*.
despise [di'spaiz] *v* disprezzare.
despite [di'spait] *prep* malgrado.
despondent [di'spondənt] *adj* accasciato, depresso.
despot ['despot] *n* despota *m*, *f*.
dessert [di'zəːt] *n* dessert *m invar*.
destine ['destin] *v* destinare. **destination** *n* destinazione *f*, recapito *m*. **destiny** *n* destino *m*, sorte *f*.
destitute ['destitjuːt] *adj* indigente.
destroy [di'stroi] *v* distruggere. **destruction** *n* distruzione *f*.
detach [di'tatʃ] *v* staccare, distaccare. **detached** *adj* staccato; (*house*) isolato; (*aloof*) distaccato; (*objective*) obiettivo. **detachment** *n* distacco *m*; (*army*) distaccamento *m*; indifferenza *f*; obiettività *f*.
detail ['diːteil] *n* particolare *m*, dettaglio *m*. *v* dettagliare, descrivere minutamente.
detain [di'tein] *v* detenere; (*delay*) trattenere. **detainee** *n* detenuto, -a *m*, *f*; carcerato, -a *m*, *f*.
detect [di'tekt] *v* scoprire, individuare. **detection** *n* scoperta *f*. **detective** *n* detective *m invar*, investigatore, -trice *m*, *f*. **detective novel** romanzo poliziesco *m*, romanzo giallo *m*.
détente [dei'tãːnt] *n* distensione *f*.
detention [di'tenʃən] *n* detenzione *f*.
deter [di'təː] *v* dissuadere, scoraggiare. **deterrent** *n* deterrente *m*.
detergent [di'təːdʒənt] *nm*, *adj* detergente, detersivo.
deteriorate [di'tiəriəˌreit] *v* deteriorare, peggiorare. **deterioration** *n* deterioramento *m*, peggioramento *m*.
determine [di'təːmin] *v* determinare, stabilire; decidere. **determination** *n* determinazione *f*, risolutezza *f*. **determined** *adj* determinato, risoluto.
detest [di'test] *v* detestare, odiare. **detestable** *adj* detestabile, odioso.
detonate ['detəˌneit] *v* detonare, esplodere. **detonation** *n* detonazione *f*, esplosione *f*. **detonator** *n* detonatore *m*.
detour ['diːtuə] *n* deviazione *f*.
detract [di'trakt] *v* detrarre.
detriment ['detrimənt] *n* **to the detriment of** a scapito di.
deuce [djuːs] *n* (*cards*) due *m*; (*tennis*) quaranta pari.
devalue [diː'valjuː] *v* svalutare. **devaluation** *n* svalutazione *f*.
devastate ['devəˌsteit] *v* devastare, rovinare. **devastating** *adj* devastatore; (*highly effective*) schiacciante.
develop [di'veləp] *v* sviluppare; elaborare; (*land*) usare come terreno da costruzione. **develop into** diventare. **developer** *n* (*phot*) sviluppatore *m*; (*land*) persona che apporta migliorie *f*. **development** *n* sviluppo *m*; evoluzione *f*; (*land*) valorizzazione di terreno *f*.
deviate ['diːviˌeit] *v* deviare. **deviation** *n* deviazione *f*.
device [di'vais] *n* (*contrivance*) congegno *m*; (*crafty scheme*) schema *m*, espediente *m*; (*heraldry*) motto *m*, divisa *f*.
devil ['devl] *n* diavolo *m*, demonio *m*. **devilish** *adj* diabolico, infernale.
devious ['diːviəs] *adj* indiretto, tortuoso.
devise [di'vaiz] *v* escogitare, progettare.
devoid [di'void] *adj* privo.
devolution [ˌdiːvə'luːʃən] *n* devoluzione *f*.

devote [di'vout] *v* dedicare, consacrare. **devoted** *adj* devoto, affezionato. **devotion** *n* devozione *f*; (*prayer*) preghiere *f pl*.
devour [di'vauə] *v* divorare.
devout [di'vaut] *adj* devoto, pio, fervente.
dew [djuː] *n* rugiada *f*.
dextrous ['dekstrəs] *adj* destro, abile. **dexterity** *n* destrezza *f*.
diabetes [ˌdaiə'biːtiːz] *n* diabete *m*. **diabetic** *nm*, *adj* diabetico.
diagnose [ˌdaiəg'nouz] *v* fare la diagnosi. **diagnosis** *n*, *pl* **-ses** diagnosi *f*. **diagnostic** *adj* diagnostico.
diagonal [dai'agənəl] *nf*, *adj* diagonale.
diagram ['daiəˌgram] *n* diagramma *m*.
dial ['daiəl] *n* (*watch*) quadrante *m*; (*telephone*) disco combinatore *m*. *v* (*number*) comporre.
dialect ['daiəlekt] *n* dialetto *m*.
dialogue ['daiəlog] *n* dialogo (*pl* -ghi) *m*.
diameter [dai'amitə] *n* diametro *m*.
diamond ['daiəmənd] *n* diamante *m*. **diamonds** *pl n* (*cards*) quadri *m pl*.
diaper ['daiəpə] *n* (*US*) pannolino (per neonati) *m*.
diaphragm ['daiəˌfram] *n* diaframma *m*.
diarrhoea [ˌdaiə'riə] *n* diarrea *f*.
diary ['daiəri] *n* diario *m*, agenda *f*.
dice [dais] *n* dado *m*.
dictate [dik'teit] *v* dettare, imporre. *n* (*order*) comando *m*; (*rule*) regola *f*. **dictation** *n* dettato *m*. **dictator** *n* dittatore *m*. **dictatorial** *adj* dittatorio, dittatoriale. **dictatorship** *n* dittatura *f*.
dictionary ['dikʃənəri] *n* dizionario *m*, vocabolario *m*.
did [did] *V* **do**.
die [dai] *v* morire. **die away** scomparire. **die down** spegnersi lentamente.
diehard ['daihaːd] *n*(*m*+*f*), *adj* tradizionalista, intransigente.
diesel ['diːzəl] *n* **diesel engine** motore diesel *m*. **diesel oil** gasolio *m*, nafta *f*.
diet ['daiət] *n* dieta *f*; (*food*) alimentazione *f*, vitto *m*. **be on a diet** stare a dieta, stare *or* essere a regime. **dietary** *adj* dietetico.
differ ['difə] *v* essere diverso, differire; (*disagree*) dissentire. **difference** *n* differenza *f*. **different** *adj* differente, diverso.
difficult ['difikəlt] *adj* difficile; (*troublesome*, *tricky*) difficoltoso. **difficulty** *n* difficoltà *f*.
diffident ['difidənt] *adj* timido.
***dig** [dig] *v* scavare; (*agric*) vangare. *n* (*archaeol*) scavi *m pl*.
digest [dai'dʒest; *n* 'daidʒest] *v* digerire, assimilare. *n* sommario *m*, selezione *f*. **digestible** *adj* digeribile. **digestion** *n* digestione *f*.
digit ['didʒit] *n* (*figure*) numero semplice *m*, cifra *f*; (*finger*, *toe*) dito *m*. **digital** *adj* digitale.
dignified ['digniˌfaid] *adj* dignitoso, nobile.
dignity ['dignəti] *n* dignità *f*.
digress [dai'gres] *v* digredire, deviare. **digression** *n* digressione *f*.
digs [digz] *pl n* alloggio *m sing*.
dilapidated [di'lapiˌdeitid] *adj* decrepito.
dilate [dai'leit] *v* dilatare.
dilemma [di'lemə] *n* dilemma *m*.
diligent ['dilidʒent] *adj* diligente, assiduo.
dilute [dai'luːt] *v* diluire, allungare. *adj* diluito.
dim [dim] *v* attenuare, affievolire. *adj* fioco, tenue; (*stupid*) poco intelligente.
dimension [di'menʃən] *n* dimensione *f*.
diminish [di'miniʃ] *v* diminuire, ridurre.
diminutive [di'minjutiv] *adj* diminutivo, minuscolo.
dimple ['dimpl] *n* fossetta *f*.
din [din] *n* fracasso *m*, baccano *m*.
dine [dain] *v* pranzare. **dining car** vagone ristorante *m*. **dining room** sala da pranzo *f*.
dinghy ['diŋgi] *n* barca *f*.
dingy ['dindʒi] *adj* squallido.
dinner ['dinə] *n* pranzo *m*, cena *f*.
dinosaur ['dainəˌsoː] *n* dinosauro *m*.
diocese ['daiəsis] *n* diocesi *f invar*.
dip [dip] *v* abbassare, tuffare, immergere. *n* immersione *f*; (*swim*) nuotata *f*; inclinazione *f*.
diphthong ['difθoŋ] *n* dittongo *m*.
diploma [di'ploumə] *n* diploma *m*.
diplomacy [di'ploumәsi] *n* diplomazia *f*. **diplomat** *n* diplomatico *m*. **diplomatic** *adj* diplomatico.
dipstick ['dipstik] *n* asta di livello *f*.
dire [daiə] *adj* **dire need** bisogno urgente *m*. **dire straits** miseria squallida *f sing*.
direct [di'rekt] *adj* diretto, immediato; sincero. *v* dirigere, amministrare. **direction** *n* direzione *f*; (*management*) amministrazione; (*address*) indirizzo *m*; (*stage*) didascalia *f*. **director** *n* (*comm*) amministratore, -trice *m*, *f*; (*theatre*)

regista *m, f.* **directory** *n* annuario *m*, guida *f*; (*phone*) elenco telefonico *m*.
dirt [dəːt] *n* sporcizia *f*. **dirty** *adj* sporco, sudicio. **dirty word** parolaccia *f*.
disability [disəˈbiləti] *n* incapacità *f*, inabilità *f*. **disabled** *nm, adj* invalido, mutilato.
disadvantage [ˌdisədˈvaːntidʒ] *n* svantaggio *m*.
disagree [ˌdisəˈgriː] *v* non andar d'accordo, non essere d'accordo. **disagree with** (*food*) far male a. **disagreeable** *adj* sgradevole, antipatico. **disagreement** *n* disaccordo *m*, dissenso *m*.
disappear [ˌdisəˈpiə] *v* sparire, scomparire. **disappearance** *n* scomparsa *f*.
disappoint [ˌdisəˈpoint] *v* deludere. **disappointed** *adj* deluso, scontento. **disappointment** *n* delusione *f*.
disapprove [ˌdisəˈpruːv] *v* disapprovare, riprovare. **disapproval** *n* disapprovazione *f*.
disarm [disˈaːm] *v* disarmare. **disarmament** *n* disarmo *m*.
disaster [diˈzaːstə] *n* disastro *m*, disgrazia *f*; calamità *f*. **disastrous** *adj* disastroso.
disband [disˈband] *v* sbandare, sciogliere, congedare.
disc *or* *US* **disk** [disk] *n* disco *m*.
discard [disˈkaːd] *v* scartare.
discern [diˈsəːn] *v* discernere, scorgere. **discerning** *adj* avveduto, accorto. **discernment** *n* discernimento *m*, giudizio *m*.
discharge [disˈtʃaːdʒ] *v* scaricare; (*dismiss*) licenziare; (*law*) assolvere; (*radiation*) emettere; (*med*) suppurare; (*a duty*) adempiere; (*a debt*) saldare. *n* scarico *m*; licenziamento *m*; assoluzione *f*; emissione *f*; suppurazione *f*; (*elec*) scarica *f*.
disciple [diˈsaipl] *n* discepolo, -a *m, f*.
discipline [ˈdisiplin] *n* disciplina *f*. *v* disciplinare. **disciplinary** *adj* disciplinare.
disclaim [disˈkleim] *v* ripudiare, sconfessare, smentire. **disclaimer** *n* ripudio *m*, smentita *f*; denunzia di un contratto *f*.
disclose [disˈklouz] *v* svelare, rivelare. **disclosure** *n* rivelazione *f*.
discolour [disˈkʌlə] *v* scolorire, sbiadire.
discomfort [disˈkʌmfət] *n* disagio *m*. *v* mettere a disagio.
disconcert [diskənˈsəːt] *v* sconcertare. **disconcerting** *adj* sconcertante.
disconnect [diskəˈnekt] *v* sconnettere; (*mech*) disinnestare.
disconsolate [disˈkonsələt] *adj* sconsolato, desolato.
discontinue [diskənˈtinjuː] *v* sospendere, interrompere, terminare.
discord [ˈdiskoːd] *n* discordia *f*, dissenso *m*; (*music*) dissonanza *f*, disarmonia *f*. **discordant** *adj* discorde; (*noise*) discordante; dissonante.
discotheque [ˈdiskətek] *n* discoteca *f*.
discount [ˈdiskaunt] *v* (*disregard*) non badare a. *n* sconto *m*, ribasso *m*.
discourage [disˈkʌridʒ] *v* scoraggiare. **discouragement** *n* scoraggiamento *m*. **discouraging** *adj* scoraggiante.
discover [disˈkʌvə] *v* scoprire. **discovery** *n* scoperta *f*.
discredit [disˈkredit] *v* screditare, mettere in dubbio.
discreet [diˈskriːt] *adj* discreto, riservato. **discretion** *n* discrezione *f*; prudenza *f*; (*judgment*) giudizio *m*. **discretionary** *adj* discrezionale.
discrepancy [diˈskrepənsi] *n* divario *m*, disaccordo *m*.
discrete [diˈskriːt] *adj* separato, distinto, discreto.
discriminate [diˈskrimiˌneit] *v* discriminare, differenziare. **discriminating** *adj* penetrante, giudizioso. **discrimination** *n* discriminazione *f*, distinzione *f*.
discus [ˈdiskəs] *n* disco *m*.
discuss [diˈskʌs] *v* discutere, dibattere. **discussion** *n* discussione *f*, dibattimento *m*.
disease [diˈziːz] *n* malattia *f*. **diseased** *adj* malato, ammalato.
disembark [disimˈbaːk] *v* sbarcare.
disengage [disinˈgeidʒ] *v* disimpegnare, liberare; (*mech*) disinnestare. **disengaged** *adj* libero.
disfigure [disˈfigə] *v* sfigurare, deturpare.
disgrace [disˈgreis] *n* disonore *m*, vergogna *f*, scandalo *m*, ignominia *f*. *v* disonorare, screditare. **disgraceful** *adj* vergognoso.
disgruntled [disˈgrʌntld] *adj* di cattivo umore, scontento.
disguise [disˈgaiz] *v* camuffare, mascherare. *n* maschera *f*, travestimento *m*.
disgust [disˈgʌust] *n* disgusto *m*, ribrezzo *m*, schifo *m*. *v* disgustare, far schifo, nauseare. **disgusting** *adj* disgustoso, schifoso.
dish [diʃ] *n* piatto *m*. **dishcloth** *n*

strofinaccio per i piatti *m*. **dishwasher** *n* lavapiatti *m*.
dishearten [dis'haːtn] *v* scoraggiare.
dishevelled [di'ʃevəld] *adj* scapigliato, arruffato.
dishonest [dis'onist] *adj* disonesto. **dishonesty** *n* disonestà *f*.
dishonour [dis'onə] *v* disonorare. *n* disonore *m*, infamia *f*. **dishonourable** *adj* disonorevole.
disillusion [disi'luːʒən] *v* disilludere, disingannare. *n* disillusione *f*, disinganno *m*.
disinfect [disin'fekt] *v* disinfettare. **disinfectant** *nm*, *adj* disinfettante.
disinherit [disin'herit] *v* diseredare.
disintegrate [dis'intiˌgreit] *v* disintegrare, disgregare, disfare, disfarsi. **disintegration** *n* disfacimento *m*, sfacelo *m*, disintegrazione *f*.
disinterested [dis'intristid] *adj* disinteressato.
disjointed [dis'dʒointid] *adj* sconnesso, incoerente.
dislike [dis'laik] *v* detestare, sentire antipatia per. *n* antipatia *f*, avversione *f*.
dislocate ['disləˌkeit] *v* dislocare; (*joint*) lussare. **dislocation** *n* dislocazione *f*; lussazione *f*.
dislodge [dis'lodʒ] *v* sloggiare, scacciare.
disloyal [dis'loiəl] *adj* sleale, infedele. **disloyalty** *n* slealtà *f*, infedeltà *f*.
dismal ['dizməl] *adj* triste, lugubre, malinconico.
dismantle [dis'mantl] *v* smantellare.
dismay [dis'mei] *v* costernare, sgomentare. *n* costernazione *f*, sgomento *m*.
dismiss [dis'mis] *v* (*send away*) respingere; (*discard*) scartare; (*discharge*) licenziare. **dismissal** *n* licenziamento *m*.
dismount [dis'maunt] *v* smontare.
disobey [disə'bei] *v* disubbidire, disobbedire. **disobedience** *n* disubbidienza *f*. **disobedient** *adj* disubbidiente.
disorder [dis'oːdə] *n* disordine *m*, confusione *f*; (*med*) disturbo *m*. **disorderly** *adj* disordinato.
disorganized [dis'oːgənaizd] *adj* disorganizzato. **disorganization** *n* disorganizzazione *f*.
disown [dis'oun] *v* ripudiare, rinnegare.
disparage [di'sparidʒ] *v* denigrare, screditare.
disparity [dis'pariti] *n* disparità *f*.
dispassionate [dis'paʃənit] *adj* spassionato, obiettivo.
dispatch [di'spatʃ] *v* spedire, inviare; (*settle*) sbrigare; (*kill*) spacciare. *n* spedizione *f*; (*mil*) dispaccio *m*; (*speed*) prontezza *f*, sollecitudine *f*.
dispel [di'spel] *v* dissipare, scacciare.
dispense [di'spens] *v* dispensare, distribuire; (*justice*) amministrare. **dispense with** fare a meno di. **dispensary** *n* dispensario *m*, farmacia *f*.
disperse [di'spəːs] *v* disperdere, sparpagliare, dileguarsi. **dispersion** *n* dispersione *f*, diffusione *f*.
displace [dis'pleis] *v* spostare; (*take place of*) soppiantare. **displaced person** profugo (*pl* -ghi) *m*, -a *f*. **displacement** *n* spostamento *m*.
display [di'splei] *v* mostrare, esibire, ostentare, manifestare. *n* mostra *f*, manifestazione *f*, esposizione *f*.
displease [dis'pliːz] *v* spiacere, dispiacere, scontentare. **displeasure** *n* dispiacere *m*, ira *f*.
dispose [di'spouz] *v* disporre, sistemare. **dispose of** sbarazzarsi di, eliminare. **disposal** *n* (*control*) disposizione *f*; (*act of disposing*) sistemazione *f*. **disposed** *adj* disposto, intenzionato. **disposition** *n* disposizione *f*, tendenza *f*; (*character*) indole *f*.
disprove [dis'pruːv] *v* confutare.
dispute [di'spjuːt] *n* disputa *f*, vertenza *f*; (*quarrel*) lite *f*. *v* contestare.
disqualify [dis'kwoliˌfai] *v* (*sport*) squalificare; (*render unfit*) incapacitare; (*law*) interdire. **disqualification** *n* squalifica *f*, incapacità *f*, interdizione *f*.
disregard [disrə'gaːd] *v* non far caso a, ignorare. *n* noncuranza *f*, inosservanza *f*.
disreputable [dis'repjutəbl] *adj* malfamato, vergognoso.
disrespect [disrə'spekt] *n* mancanza di rispetto *f*, irreverenza *f*. **disrespectful** *adj* poco rispettoso, che non mostra rispetto.
disrupt [dis'rʌpt] *v* scompigliare, mettere in confusione. **disruption** *n* scompiglio *m*.
dissatisfy [di'satisfai] *v* scontentare. **dissatisfaction** *n* insoddisfazione *f*.
dissect [di'sekt] *v* sezionare; (*corpse*) dissecare; (*analyse*) analizzare. **dissection** *n* sezionamento *m*; dissezione *f*; analisi *f*.
dissent [di'sent] *n* dissenso *m*. *v* dissentire.
dissident ['disidənt] *n*(*m*+*f*), *adj* dissidente.

dissimilar [di'similə] *adj* dissimile.
dissipated ['disipeitid] *adj* dissoluto.
dissociate [di'sousieit] *v* dissociare, sdoppiare. **dissociation** *n* dissociazione *f*, sdoppiamento *m*.
dissolve [di'zolv] *v* sciogliere, sciogliersi, dissolvere. **dissolute** *adj* dissoluto, licenzioso.
dissuade [di'sweid] *v* dissuadere, distogliere. **dissuasion** *n* dissuasione *f*, distoglimento *m*.
distance ['distəns] *n* distanza *f*, lontananza *f*; (*reserve*) riserbo *m*. **distant** *adj* distante, lontano, remoto; riservato.
distaste [dis'teist] *n* avversione *f*. **distasteful** *adj* sgradevole.
distemper [di'stempə] *n* (*paint*) intonaco *m*; (*canine*) cimurro *m*. *v* intonacare.
distended [di'stendid] *adj* dilatato.
distil [di'stil] *v* distillare. **distillation** *n* distillazione *f*. **distillery** *n* distilleria *f*.
distinct [di'stiŋkt] *adj* differente, diverso; distinto; (*clear*) chiaro. **distinction** *n* distinzione *f*; differenza *f*. **distinctive** *adj* caratteristico, distintivo.
distinguish [di'stiŋgwiʃ] *v* distinguere, differenziare, individuare. **distinguish oneself** farsi notare. **distinguishable** *adj* distinguibile. **distinguished** *adj* distinto, insigne.
distort [di'stoːt] *v* deformare, alterare. **distortion** *n* deformazione *f*, alterazione *f*.
distract [di'strakt] *v* distrarre; (*disturb*) turbare. **distraction** *n* distrazione *f*.
distraught [di'stroːt] *adj* turbato.
distress [di'stres] *n* (*anxiety*) angoscia *f*; (*poverty*) miseria *f*; (*ship*) pericolo *m*; (*worry*) preoccupazione *f*. *v* angosciare, affliggere, preoccupare. **distressed** *adj* dolente, angosciato. **distressing** *adj* penoso, doloroso.
distribute [di'stribjut] *v* distribuire. **distribution** *n* distribuzione *f*. **distributor** *n* distributore *m*.
district ['distrikt] *n* distretto *m*, quartiere *m*, zona *f*.
distrust [dis'trʌst] *v* diffidare di, sospettare, non aver fiducia in. *n* sospetto *m*, sfiducia *f*, diffidenza *f*.
disturb [di'stəːb] *v* disturbare, incomodare. **disturbance** *n* disturbo *m*; (*breach of peace*) sommossa *f*.
ditch [ditʃ] *n* fossa *f*, fossato *m*. *v* (*abandon*) piantare.
ditto ['ditou] *adv* idem.
divan [di'van] *n* divano *m*.
dive [daiv] *v* tuffarsi, fare un tuffo, sommergersi. *n* (*plunge*) tuffo *m*; (*coll*) taverna *f*, bettola *f*. **diver** *n* palombaro *m*. **diving board** trampolino *m*. **diving suit** scafandro *m*.
diverge [dai'vəːdʒ] *v* divergere.
diversify [dai'vəːsifai] *v* diversificare, differenziare.
divert [dai'vəːt] *v* deviare; distrarre; (*amuse*) divertire. **diversion** *n* (*distraction*) diversivo *m*, distrazione *f*; (*mil*) diversione *f*; deviazione *f*.
divide [di'vaid] *v* dividere, separare. **divided** *adj* diviso. **dividers** *pl n* compasso *m sing*. **division** *n* divisione *f*.
dividend ['dividend] *n* dividendo *m*.
divine [di'vain] *adj* divino, sacro. *n* teologo *m*, sacerdote *m*. *v* scoprire, indovinare; (*prophesy*) pronosticare. **diviner** *n* (*soothsayer*) indovino, -a *m*, *f*; (*user of divining rod*) rabdomante *m*. **divinity** *n* divinità *f*.
divorce [di'voːs] *n* divorzio *m*. *v* divorziare, divorziarsi.
divulge [dai'vʌldʒ] *v* divulgare, diffondere.
dizzy ['dizi] *adj* vertiginoso. **feel dizzy** avere il capogiro; sentirsi girare la testa. **dizziness** *n* capogiro *m*, vertigine *f*.
***do** [duː] *v* fare; (*suffice*) bastare; (*achieve*) compiere; (*carry out*) eseguire. **do away with** abolire; (*kill*) uccidere. **do-it-yourself** *adj* da fare da soli. **do out of** deprivare di. **do up** (*clothes, etc.*) abbottonare. **do without** fare a meno di. **how do you do?** come sta? (*polite*) come stai? **make do** arrangiarsi.
docile ['dousail] *adj* docile, mansueto.
dock[1] [dok] *n* (*wharf*) banchina *f*; (*waterway*) bacino *m*; (*port area*) zona portuale *f*. *v* attraccare. **docker** *n* portuale *m*. **dockyard** *n* cantiere navale *m*.
dock[2] [dok] *v* mozzare, troncare.
dock[3] [dok] *n* (*law*) banco degli imputati *m*.
docket ['dokit] *n* bolletta *f*.
doctor ['doktə] *n* dottore, -essa *m*, *f*; (*med*) medico, -chessa *m*, *f*. **doctorate** *n* dottorato *m*.
doctrine ['doktrin] *n* dottrina *f*. **doctrinal** *adj* dottrinale.
document ['dokjumənt] *n* documento *m*. *v* documentare. **documentary** *n* documentario *m*. **documentation** *n* documentazione *f*.

dodge [dodʒ] *v* schivare, scansare. *n* sotterfugio *m*, stratagemma *f*.
doe [dou] *n* selvaggina femmina *f*; (*deer*) daina *f*; (*rabbit*) femmina del coniglio *f*; (*hare*) lepre femmina *f*.
dog [dog] *n* cane *m*. **dog-eared** *adj* (*page*) accartocciato, con le orecchie. **dogrose** *n* rosa canina *f*. **dog-tired** *adj* stanco morto. **dogtooth** *n* dente canino *m*. *v* pedinare. **be dogged by** essere perseguitato da. **dogged** *adj* ostinato, accanito.
doge [doudʒ] *n* doge *m*.
dogma ['dogmə] *n* dogma *m*. **dogmatic** *adj* dogmatico.
dole [doul] *n* sussidio di disoccupazione *m*. *v* **dole out** distribuire.
doll [dol] *n* bambola *f*, pupa *f*. *v* **doll up** agghindarsi, abbellirsi.
dollar ['dolə] *n* dollaro *m*.
dolphin ['dolfin] *n* delfino *m*.
domain [də'mein] *n* (*land*) proprietà *f*; (*law*) demanio *m*; (*control, sphere of activity*) dominio *m*.
dome [doum] *n* cupola *f*.
domestic [də'mestik] *adj* domestico; (*not foreign*) nazionale. *n* domestico, -a *m*, *f*. **domesticate** *v* addomesticare. **domesticity** *n* domesticità *f*.
domicile ['domisail] *n* domicilio *m*.
dominate ['domi,neit] *v* dominare. **dominant** *adj* dominante.
domineer [domi'niə] *v* signoreggiare. **domineering** *adj* imperioso; (*overbearing*) prepotente.
dominion [də'minjən] *n* dominio *m*; autorità *f*.
domino ['dominou] *n* domino *m*.
don[1] [don] *v* vestire, indossare.
don[2] [don] *n* (*Spanish title*) don *m invar*; (*scholar*) docente universitario, -a *m*, *f*.
donate [də'neit] *v* donare. **donation** *n* dono *m*, donazione *f*. **donor** *n* donatore, -trice *m*, *f*.
done [dʌn] *V* **do**.
donkey ['doŋki] *n* asino, -a *m*, *f*; somaro, -a *m*, *f*.
doom [duːm] *n* destino *m*, sorte *f*; (*ruin*) rovina *f*. *v* destinare, condannare. **doomed** *adj* condannato. **doomsday** *n* giorno del giudizio *m*.
door [doː] *n* porta *f*, uscio *m*. **doorbell** *n* campanello *m*. **door-handle** *n* maniglia *f*. **door-keeper** *n* portiere, -a *m*, *f*, portinaio, -a *m*, *f*. **door-knocker** *n* battiporta *m*, batacchio *m*. **doormat** *n* zerbino *m*, stoino *m*. **doorstep** *n* soglia *f*. **doorway** *n* entrata *f*, portone *m*.
dope [doup] *n* (*slang: drug*) stupefacente *m*, droga *f*; (*slang: information*) notizie *f pl*. *v* drogare. **dopey** *adj* inebetito.
dormant ['doːmənt] *adj* addormentato, latente.
dormitory ['doːmitəri] *n* dormitorio *m*.
dormouse ['doː,maus] *n* ghiro *m*.
dose [dous] *n* dose *f*. *v* dosare.
dot [dot] *n* punto *m*. *v* punteggiare. **on the dot** in orario. **dotty** *adj* (*coll*) picchiatello.
dote [dout] *v* **dote on** essere infatuato di.
double ['dʌbl] *v* raddoppiare. **double up** piegare *or* piegarsi in due; contorcersi. *adj* doppio. *n* doppio *m*; (*person*) sosia *m invar*. **at the double** a passo di corsa. **double-barrelled** *adj* a doppia canna. **double bass** contrabbasso *m*. **double bed** letto matrimoniale *m*. **double-breasted** *adj* a doppio petto. **double-cross** *v* fare il doppio gioco, tradire.
doubt [daut] *n* dubbio *m*, incertezza *f*. *v* dubitare, mettere in dubbio. **doubtful** *adj* dubbio, incerto, problematico. **doubtless** *adv* senza dubbio.
dough [dou] *n* pasta *f*; (*slang*) quattrini *m pl*. **doughnut** *n* ciambella *f*, krapfen *m invar*.
dove [dʌv] *n* colomba *f*. **dovecot** *n* colombaia *f*. **dovetail** *v* (*carpentry*) incastrare a coda di rondine; (*fit exactly*) combaciare, far combaciare.
dowdy ['daudi] *adj* sciatto, trasandato.
down[1] [daun] *adv* giù, di sotto, per terra. *adj* depresso, abbattuto. **down and out** ridotto in miseria. *v* **down tools** abbandonare il lavoro.
down[2] [daun] *n* (*plumage*) piumino *m*, lanugine *f*; (*soft hair*) peluria *f*.
downcast ['daun,kaːst] *adj* abbattuto, depresso.
downfall ['daun,foːl] *n* rovina *f*, caduta *f*.
downhearted [,daun'haːtid] *adj* depresso, scoraggiato.
downhill [,daun'hil] *adv* in discesa.
downpour ['daun,poː] *n* acquazzone *m*.
downright ['daun,rait] *adv* categoricamente, nettamente.
downstairs [,daun'steəz] *adv* da basso, al piano inferiore. **go downstairs** scendere le scale.

downstream [ˌdaun'striːm] *adv* a valle, seguendo la corrente.
downtrodden ['daunˌtrodn] *adj* oppresso.
downward ['daunwəd] *adj* discendente.
downwards ['daunwədz] *adv* in giù, verso il basso.
dowry ['dauəri] *n* dote *f*.
doze [douz] *v* sonnecchiare, fare un pisolino. **doze off** assopirsi. **dozy** *adj* sonnolento.
dozen ['dʌzn] *n* dozzina *f*.
drab [drab] *adj* squallido, scialbo.
draft [draːft] *n* (*sketch*) abbozzo *m*; (*preliminary copy*) brutta copia *f*; (*conscription*) leva *f*; (*written order*) tratta *f*, cambiale *f*; (*bank*) assegno circolare *m*. *v* abbozzare, delineare; (*conscript*) chiamare sotto le armi, arruolare.
drag [drag] *v* trascinare; (*search*) dragare; (*extract*) strappare. *n* trazione *f*. **in drag** vestito da donna.
dragon ['dragən] *n* drago *m*; (*woman*) megera *f*. **dragon-fly** *n* libellula *f*.
drain [drein] *n* fogna *f*, tubo di scarico *m*. *v* (*draw off*) scolare, prosciugare; (*med*) drenare; (*exhaust*) esaurire; (*drink up*) bere fino all'ultimo. **drainage** *n* scarico *m*, fognatura *f*, drenaggio *m*. **draining board** scolatoio *m*. **drainpipe** *n* grondaia *f*.
drama ['draːmə] *n* dramma *m*. **dramatic** *adj* drammatico, impressionante. **dramatist** *n* drammaturgo, -a *m*, *f*. **dramatize** *v* drammatizzare.
drank [draŋk] *V* **drink**.
drape [dreip] *v* drapeggiare.
draper ['dreipə] *n* negoziante di tessuti *m*, *f*. **drapery** *n* tessuti *m pl*; tendaggio *m*.
drastic ['drastik] *adj* drastico.
draught *or US* **draft** [draːft] *n* (*air current*) corrente d'aria *f*; (*drink*) sorso *m*; (*pull*) tiro *m*; (*fishing*) retata *f*. **draughts** *n* gioco della dama *m*. **draughtsman** *n* disegnatore, -trice *m*, *f*, progettista *m*, *f*; (*of documents*) compilatore, -trice *m*, *f*. **it's draughty** c'è una corrente d'aria.
***draw** [droː] *v* (*pull*) tirare; (*attract*) attirare, attrarre; (*picture*) disegnare; (*sport*) pareggiare; (*extract*) estrarre. **draw back** ritirarsi. **drawback** *n* inconveniente *m*. **drawbridge** *n* ponte levatoio *m*. **draw near** avvicinarsi. **draw on** (*funds*) attingere (a). *n* (*sport*) pareggio *m*. **drawing** *n* disegno *m*. **drawing-board** *n* tavola da disegno *f*. **drawing-pin** *n* puntina da disegno *f*. **drawing-room** *n* salotto *m*.
drawer ['droːə] *n* cassetto *m*. **chest of drawers** cassettone *m*. **drawers** *pl n* (*underclothes*) mutandine *f pl*.
drawl [droːl] *v* strascicare le parole.
drawn [droːn] *V* **draw**.
dread [dred] *v* aver paura di. *n* timore *m*, paura *f*, fobia *f*. **dreadful** *adj* spaventoso.
***dream** [driːm] *n* sogno *m*; visione *f*. *v* sognare; immaginare. **dreamer** *n* sognatore, -trice *m*, *f*; visionario, -a *m*, *f*. **dreamy** *adj* (*vague*) vago.
dreamt [dremt] *V* **dream**.
dreary ['driəri] *adj* triste; (*boring*) noioso. **dreariness** *n* tristezza *f*.
dredge [dredʒ] *v* dragare.
dregs [dregz] *pl n* feccia *f sing*; (*coffee*) fondo *m sing*.
drench [drentʃ] *v* inzuppare, bagnare.
dress [dres] *v* (*clothe*) vestire; (*salad, etc.*) condire; (*wounds*) bendare. *n* abito *m*, vestito *m*. **dress circle** prima galleria *f*. **dressmaker** *n* sarta *f*. **dressmaking** *n* confezione di abiti da donna *f*. **dress rehearsal** prova generale *f*. **dressing** *n* condimento *m*; benda *f*. **dressing down** rimprovero *m*. **dressing-gown** *n* vestaglia *f*. **dressing-room** *n* camerino *m*. **dressing-table** *n* toilette (*pl* -s) *f*.
dresser[1] ['dresə] *n* (*furniture*) credenza *f*.
dresser[2] ['dresə] *n* (*theatre*) vestiarista *m*, *f*; (*med*) assistente medico, -a *m*, *f*.
drew [druː] *V* **draw**.
dribble ['dribl] *v* sbavare; (*trickle*) gocciolare; (*ball*) palleggiare. *n* bava *f*; gocciolamento *m*; palleggio *m*.
drier ['draiə] *n* (*clothes*) asciugatrice *f*; (*hair*) asciugacapelli *m*.
drift [drift] *v* andare alla deriva; (*wander aimlessly*) lasciarsi andare. **drift apart** perdersi di vista. *n* tendenza *f*, direzione *f*; (*movement*) deriva *f*; (*current*) corrente *f*.
drill[1] [dril] *n* trivella *f*, sonda *f*, trapano *m*. *v* trapanare, sondare.
drill[2] [dril] *n* esercitazioni *f pl*, addestramento *m*. *v* esercitare, fare esercitazioni, addestrare.
***drink** [driŋk] *v* bere. *n* bibita *f*, bevanda *f*. **drinkable** *adj* bevibile, potabile. **drinking fountain** fontanella *f*. **drinking water** acqua potabile *f*.
drip [drip] *v* gocciolare. *n* gocciolio *m*, gocciolatura *f*; (*slang*) persona insulsa *f*.

dripping *n* stillicidio *m*; (*fat*) grasso colato *m*.
***drive** [draiv] *v* condurre; (*car*) guidare; (*push*) spingere. **drive away** scacciare. *n* (*road*) viale *m*; (*trip*) corsa *f*, giro *m*; energia *f*, iniziativa *f*; (*golf*) colpo forte *m*. **driver** *n* guidatore, -trice *m, f*. **driving-licence** *n* patente di guida *f*. **driving-test** *n* esame di guida *m*.
drivel ['drivl] *n* (*nonsense*) sciocchezze *f pl*. *v* dir sciocchezze.
driven ['drivn] *V* **drive**.
drizzle ['drizl] *v* piovigginare. *n* pioggerella *f*.
drone [droun] *n* (*bee*) fuco *m*, pecchione *m*; (*idler*) fannullone *m*; (*hum*) ronzio *m*. *v* (*hum*) ronzare. **droning** *adj* ronzante, monotono.
droop [druːp] *v* afflosciarsi, accasciarsi. *n* accasciamento *m*. **drooping** *adj* piegato in giù, floscio.
drop [drop] *n* goccia *f*; (*fall*) caduta *f*. *v* (*fall*) cadere; (*let fall*) far cadere; (*lower*) calare; diminuire, abbassarsi. **dropper** *n* contagocce *m*. **droppings** *pl n* sterco *m sing*.
dropout ['dropaut] *n* emarginato, -a *m, f*. *v* **drop out** ritirarsi, rinunciare.
drought [draut] *n* siccità *f*.
drove [drouv] *V* **drive**.
drown [draun] *v* annegare, affogare.
drowsy ['drauzi] *adj* sonnolento, assopito.
drudge [drʌdʒ] *v* sfacchinare, sgobbare. *n* sgobbone, -a *m, f*. **drudgery** *n* sfacchinata *f*.
drug [drʌg] *n* medicinale *m*, droga *f*, stupefacente *m*. **drug-addict** *n* drogato, -a *m, f*, tossicomane *m, f*. *v* narcotizzare, drogare.
drum [drʌm] *n* tamburo *m*, timpano *m*; (*cylinder*) cilindro *m*, rullo *m*. **drumstick** *n* bacchetta da tamburo *f*; (*chicken*) coscia di pollo *f*. *v* suonare il tamburo; (*beat*) tamburellare. **drummer** *n* tamburo *m*.
drunk [drʌŋk] *V* **drink**. *adj* ubriaco (*m pl* -chi), sbronzo. **get drunk** ubriacarsi. **drunkard** *n* ubriacone, -a *m, f*; sbronzo, -a *m, f*. **drunkenness** *n* ubriachezza *f*.
dry [drai] *adj* asciutto, secco; (*uninteresting*) monotono; (*caustic*) mordace. *v* asciugare, seccare. **dry-clean** *v* lavare a secco. **dry-cleaning** *n* lavaggio a secco *m*. **dry rot** carie del legno *f*.
dual ['djuəl] *adj* doppio, duplice.
dubbed ['dʌbd] *adj* (*film*) doppiato; (*name*) qualificato.
dubious ['djuːbiəs] *adj* dubbio, equivoco, incerto. **dubiousness** *n* incertezza *f*.
duchess ['dʌtʃis] *n* duchessa *f*.
duck[1] [dʌk] *n* (*zool*) anitra *f*. **duckling** *n* anatroccolo *m*.
duck[2] [dʌk] *v* (*plunge*) tuffare, immergere; (*dodge*) schivare; (*lower the head*) chinarsi di colpo.
dud [dʌd] *adj* inutile. *n* (*explosive*) proiettile che non esplode *m*.
due [djuː] *adj* (*owing*) da pagarsi; (*rightful, proper*) debito; (*attributable*) dovuto; (*expected*) atteso, in arrivo. *adv* direttamente. **due to** a causa di. **dues** *pl n* dazio *m sing*, diritti *m pl*.
duel ['djuəl] *n* duello *m*, lotta *f*.
duet [dju'et] *n* duetto *m*.
duffel bag ['dʌfəl] *n* sacca da viaggio *f*.
duffel coat ['dʌfəl] *n* montgomery *m invar*.
dug [dʌg] *V* **dig**.
duke [djuːk] *n* duca *m*.
dull [dʌl] *adj* (*unintelligent*) ottuso; (*boring*) noioso; (*slow*) lento; monotono; (*not sharp*) non tagliente; (*weather*) grigio. *v* attutire, attenuare, intorpidire. **dullness** *n* lentezza *f*; noia *f*.
duly ['djuːli] *adv* debitamente.
dumb [dʌm] *adj* muto, reticente; (*slang: foolish*) scemo. **dumbfound** *v* sbalordire, stupire.
dummy ['dʌmi] *adj* falso, finto. *n* (*man of straw*) uomo di paglia *m*; (*cards*) morto *m*; (*baby's*) biberon *m invar*, poppatoio *m*; (*model*) manichino *m*.
dump [dʌmp] *n* (*tip*) luogo di scarico *m*; (*coll*) posto triste *m*. *v* (*get rid of*) scartare, disfarsi di; (*unload*) scaricare.
dunce [dʌns] *n* ignorante *m, f*.
dune [djuːn] *n* duna *f*.
dung [dʌŋ] *n* letame *m*, sterco *m*.
dungarees [ˌdʌŋgə'riːz] *pl n* (*overalls*) tuta *f sing*.
dungeon ['dʌndʒən] *n* segreta *f*, cella sotterranea *f*.
duplicate ['djuːplikət; *v* 'djuːplikeit] *adj* duplice, doppio. *n* duplicato *m*, duplice copia *f*, doppione *m*. *v* duplicare.
durable ['djuərəbl] *adj* durevole, duraturo.
duration [dju'reiʃən] *n* durata *f*.

during ['djuriŋ] *prep* durante, nel corso di.
dusk [dʌsk] *n* crepuscolo *m*.
dust [dʌst] *n* polvere *f*. *v* (*clean*) spolverare; (*sprinkle*) cospargere. **dustbin** *n* pattumiera *f*. **dustman** *n* spazzino *m*. **dustpan** *n* paletta per la spazzatura *f*. **duster** *n* spolverino *m*, strofinaccio *m*. **dusty** *adj* polveroso.
Dutch [dʌtʃ] *adj* olandese. **Dutch person** olandese *m*, *f*. **go Dutch** fare *or* pagare alla romana.
duty ['djuːti] *n* dovere *m*; (*customs*) dogana *f*.
duvet ['duːvei] *n* piumino *m*.
dwarf [dwoːf] *n* nano *m*. *v* (*make appear small*) far sembrar piccolo; (*render insignificant*) sminuire.
***dwell** [dwel] *v* (*reside*) dimorare. **dwell on** soffermarsi su. **dwelling** *n* dimora *f*, abitazione *f*.
dwelt [dwelt] *V* **dwell.**
dwindle ['dwindl] *v* diminuire; (*decline*) deperire.
dye [dai] *n* colorante *m*, tintura *f*. *v* colorare, tingere. **dyed in the wool** inveterato, radicato. **dyer** *n* tintore *m*.
dyke [daik] *n* diga *f*, argine *m*.
dynamic [dai'namik] *adj* dinamico. **dynamics** *n* dinamica *f*.
dynamite ['dainəˌmait] *n* dinamite *f*.
dynamo ['dainəˌmou] *n* dinamo *f invar*.
dynasty ['dinəsti] *n* dinastia *f*.
dysentery ['disəntri] *n* dissenteria *f*.
dyslexia [dis'leksiə] *n* dislessia *f*.
dyspepsia [dis'pepsiə] *n* dispepsia *f*.

E

each [iːtʃ] *adj* ogni, ciascuno. *pron* ognuno. *adv* (*apiece*) l'uno, l'una. **each other** l'un l'altro.
eager ['iːgə] *adj* avido, premuroso; impaziente. **eagerness** *n* impazienza *f*; zelo *m*; brama *f*.
eagle ['iːgl] *n* aquila *f*.
ear[1] [iə] *n* orecchio *m*. **be up to one's ears in . . .** aver . . . fin sopra i capelli. **earache** *n* mal d'orecchi *m*. **eardrum** *n* timpano *m*. **earmark** *v* contrassegnare; (*set aside*) mettere da parte; (*money*) stanziare. **ear-plug** *n* tappo per orecchi *m*. **ear-ring** *n* orecchino *m*. **ear-splitting** *adj* assordante. **within earshot** a portata d'orecchio.
ear[2] [iə] *n* spiga *f*.
earl [əːl] *n* conte *m*.
early ['əːli] *adv* presto, di buon'ora. *adj* primo; (*morning*) mattiniero, mattutino; (*before time*) prematuro; (*ancient*) antico (*m pl* -chi).
earn [əːn] *v* guadagnare, meritare. **earnings** *pl n* guadagni *m pl*, stipendio *m*.
earnest ['əːnist] *adj* serio, coscienzioso. **be in earnest** fare sul serio. **earnestness** *n* serietà *f*.
earth [əːθ] *n* terra *f*; (*world*) mondo *m*; (*soil*) terreno *m*. **earthquake** *n* terremoto *m*. *v* (*elec*) mettere a terra. **earthenware** *n* terraglia *f*. **earthly** *adj* terrestre. **earthy** *adj* (*coarse*) grossolano; robusto.
earwig ['iəwig] *n* forbicina *f*.
ease [iːz] *n* agio *m*, comodo *m*. **at ease** tranquillo. **ill at ease** a disagio. *v* agevolare, alleggerire.
easel ['iːzl] *n* cavalletto *m*.
east [iːst] *adj* orientale, dell'est. *n* oriente *m*, est *m*. **Middle/Near/Far East** medio/prossimo/estremo oriente *m*. **eastward** *adv*, *adj* verso est, ad est, verso oriente.
Easter ['iːstə] *n* Pasqua *f*.
easy ['iːzi] *adj* facile, semplice; (*informal*) disinvolto; (*compliant*) accomodante. **easy chair** poltrona *f*. **easy-going** *adj* (*placid*) bonaccione, pacione; indolente; tollerante.
***eat** [iːt] *v* mangiare. **eatable** *adj* mangiabile, mangereccio.
eaten ['iːtn] *V* **eat.**
eavesdrop ['iːvzdrop] *v* origliare.
ebb [eb] *n* riflusso *m*; declino *m*. *v* rifluire; declinare.
eccentric [ik'sentrik] *nm*, *adj* eccentrico. **eccentricity** *n* eccentricità *f*.
ecclesiastical [iklizi'astikl] *adj* ecclesiastico.
echo ['ekou] *v* echeggiare, far eco a. *n* eco *f*, *m* (*pl* -i *m*).
eclair [ei'kleə] *n* bignè *m invar*.
eclipse [i'klips] *n* eclissi *f*. *v* eclissare.
ecology [i'kolədʒi] *n* ecologia *f*.
economy [i'konəmi] *n* economia *f*. **economical** *or* **economic** *adj* economico, a buon prezzo; (*thrifty*) frugale. **economics** *n* economia *f*, scienze economiche *f pl*. **economist** *n* economista *m*, *f*. **economize** *v* economizzare, fare economia.

ecstasy ['ekstəsi] *n* estasi *f*. **ecstatic** *adj* estatico.
eczema ['eksimə] *n* eczema *m*.
edge [edʒ] *n* orlo *m*, margine *m*; (*blade*) filo *m*; (*road*) ciglio *m*; (*river*) sponda *f*. **be on edge** avere i nervi. *v* orlare.
edible ['edəbl] *adj* mangereccio, mangiabile.
Edinburgh ['edinbərə] *n* Edimburgo *f*.
edit ['edit] *v* curare, redigere, dirigere. **editor** *n* redattore, -trice *m*, *f*; (*newspaper*) direttore, -trice *m*, *f*. **editorial** *n* articolo di fondo *m*. **edition** *n* edizione *f*.
educate ['edju,keit] *v* educare, istruire. **educated** *adj* colto, istruito. **education** *n* educazione *f*, istruzione *f*; (*teaching*) insegnamento *m*, pedagogia *f*.
eel [iːl] *n* anguilla *f*.
eerie ['iəri] *adj* (*strange*) misterioso; (*causing fear*) pauroso.
effect [i'fekt] *n* effetto *m*; conseguenza *f*, risultato *m*; impressione *f*. **take effect** entrare in vigore. **with effect from** a partire da. *v* effettuare, realizzare. **effective** *adj* efficace, efficiente.
effeminate [i'feminət] *adj* effeminato.
effervescent [,efə'vesənt] *adj* effervescente.
efficient [i'fiʃənt] *adj* efficiente, capace. **efficiency** *n* efficienza *f*, capacità *f*; (*machine*) rendimento *m*.
effigy ['efidʒi] *n* effigie *f*.
effort ['efət] *n* sforzo *m*, fatica *f*. **make an effort** sforzarsi, fare di tutto. **effortless** *adj* senza sforzo.
egg [eg] *n* uovo *m* (*pl* -a *f*). **egg-cup** *n* portauovo *m*. **egg-shaped** *adj* ovale. **egg-shell** *n* guscio d'uovo *m*. **egg-whisk** *n* frullino *m*. *v* **egg on** aizzare.
ego ['iːgou] *n* ego *m*. **egocentric** *adj* egocentrico. **egoism** *n* egoismo *m*. **egoist** *n* egoista *m*, *f*. **egoistic(al)** *adj* egoista, egoistico. **egotism** *n* egotismo *m*. **egotist** *n* egotista *m*, *f*. **egotistic(al)** *adj* egotista.
Egypt ['iːdʒipt] *n* Egitto *m*. **Egyptian** *n*, *adj* egiziano, -a; (*ancient*) egizio, -a.
eiderdown ['aidədaun] *n* piumino *m*.
eight [eit] *nm*, *adj* otto. **eighth** *nm*, *adj* ottavo.
eighteen [ei'tiːn] *nm*, *adj* diciotto. **eighteenth** *nm*, *adj* diciottesimo.
eighty ['eiti] *nm*, *adj* ottanta. **eightieth** *nm*, *adj* ottantesimo.
either ['aiðə] *pron*, *adj* l'uno o l'altro; (*each*) ciascuno dei due, tutti e due. *adv* nemmeno, neppure, neanche. *conj* **either ... or ...** o ... o ..., sia ... che ..., sia ... sia ....
ejaculate [i'dʒakjuleit] *v* eiaculare; esclamare. **ejaculation** *n* eiaculazione *f*, esclamazione *f*.
eject [i'dʒekt] *v* espellere, gettar fuori. **ejector seat** sedile eiettabile *m*.
eke [iːk] *v* **eke out** supplire. **eke out a living** sbarcare il lunario.
elaborate [i'labəreit; *adj* i'labərət] *v* elaborare, sviluppare. *adj* elaborato, minuzioso.
elapse [i'laps] *v* passare, decorrere.
elastic [i'lastik] *nm*, *adj* elastico.
elated [i'leitid] *adj* giubilante, euforico.
elbow ['elbou] *n* gomito *m*. **elbow-room** *n* libertà di movimento *f*. *v* (*jostle*) dar gomitate.
elder[1] ['eldə] *adj* più vecchio, maggiore. *n* anziano, -a *m*, *f*. **elderly** *adj* di una certa età, anziano.
elder[2] ['eldə] *n* sambuco (*pl* -chi) *m*. **elderberry** *n* bacca di sambuco *f*.
eldest ['eldist] *adj* più vecchio, maggiore, primogenito.
elect [i'lekt] *v* eleggere, scegliere. *adj* eletto, scelto. **election** *n* elezione *f*. **electioneering** *n* campagna elettorale *f*. **electorate** *n* elettorato *m*. **elector** *n* elettore, -trice *m*, *f*.
electricity [elek'trisəti] *n* elettricità *f*. **electric** *adj* elettrico. **electric appliances** elettrodomestici *m pl*. **electrician** *n* elettricista *m*. **electrify** *v* elettrificare. **electrocution** *n* elettroesecuzione *f*. **electrode** *n* elettrodo *m*. **electrolysis** *n* elettrolisi *f*. **electron** *n* elettrone *m*. **electronic** *adj* elettronico. **electronics** *n* elettronica *f*.
elegant ['eligənt] *adj* elegante, fine. **elegance** *n* eleganza *f*, finezza *f*.
elegy ['elidʒi] *n* elegia *f*. **elegiac** *adj* elegiaco.
element ['eləmənt] *n* elemento *m*, fattore *m*. **elemental** *adj* fondamentale. **elementary** *adj* elementare.
elephant ['elifənt] *n* elefante *m*. **elephantine** *adj* elefantesco.
elevate ['eliveit] *v* elevare, innalzare; (*exalt*) esaltare. **elevated** *adj* elevato, eminente. **elevation** *n* (*altitude*) altezza *f*; (*drawing*) proiezione ortogonale *f*; (*grandeur*) elevatezza *f*. **elevator** *n* (*lift*) ascensore *m*.

eleven [i'levn] *nm, adj* undici. **eleventh** *nm, adj* undicesimo.
elf [elf] *n* elfo *m*, folletto *m*.
eligible ['elidʒəbl] *adj* eleggibile; desiderabile.
eliminate [i'limineit] *v* eliminare, scartare. **elimination** *n* eliminazione *f*.
elite [ei'liːt] *n* élite (*pl* -s) *f*, fior fiore *m invar*.
ellipse [i'lips] *n* ellisse *f*.
elm [elm] *n* olmo *m*.
elocution [elə'kjuːʃən] *n* elocuzione *f*.
elope [i'loup] *v* fuggire. **elopement** *n* fuga *f*.
eloquent ['eləkwənt] *adj* eloquente, rettorico. **eloquence** *n* eloquenza *f*, rettorica *f*.
else [els] *adv, pron* altro, altrimenti. **elsewhere** *adv* altrove.
elucidate [i'luːsideit] *v* chiarire, spiegare.
elude [i'luːd] *v* eludere, evitare. **elusive** *adj* evasivo, elusivo.
emaciated [i'meisieitid] *adj* scarno, emaciato.
emanate ['eməneit] *v* emanare, emettere, scaturire. **emanation** *n* emanazione *f*, emissione *f*.
emancipate [i'mansipeit] *v* emancipare. **emancipation** *n* emancipazione *f*.
embalm [im'baːm] *v* imbalsamare.
embankment [im'baŋkmənt] *n* argine *m*, lungofiume *m*.
embargo [im'baːgou] *n* embargo *m*, sanzioni *f pl*, proibizione *f*.
embark [im'baːk] *v* imbarcare. **embark on** intraprendere.
embarrass [im'barəs] *v* mettere in imbarazzo. **embarrassment** *n* imbarazzo *m*.
embassy ['embəsi] *n* ambasciata *f*.
embellish [im'beliʃ] *v* abbellire, ornare. **embellishment** *n* abbellimento *m*.
ember ['embə] *n* tizzone *m*. **embers** *pl n* brace *f pl*.
embezzle [im'bezl] *v* appropriarsi indebitamente. **embezzlement** *n* appropriazione indebita *f*, malversazione *f*. **embezzler** *n* malversatore, -trice *m, f*.
embitter [im'bitə] *v* rendere amaro, amareggiare.
emblem ['embləm] *n* emblema m, simbolo *m*.
embody [im'bodi] *v* incorporare; (*comprise*) comprendere; incarnare; concretare.
emboss [im'bos] *v* sbalzare, fare in rilievo, scolpire in rilievo.
embrace [im'breis] *v* abbracciare. *n* abbraccio *m*.
embroider [im'broidə] *v* ricamare; (*embellish*) abbellire. **embroidery** *n* ricamo *m*.
embryo ['embriou] *n* embrione *m*. **embryonic** *adj* embrionale.
emerald ['emərəld] *n* smeraldo *m*.
emerge [i'məːdʒ] *v* emergere.
emergency [i'məːdʒənsi] *n* emergenza *f*, caso imprevisto *m*. **emergency exit** uscita di sicurezza *f*. **in case of emergency** in caso di urgenza.
emigrate ['emigreit] *v* emigrare. **emigration** *n* emigrazione *f*.
eminent ['eminənt] *adj* eminente, distinto.
emit [i'mit] *v* emettere, emanare. **emission** *n* emissione *f*.
emotion [i'mouʃən] *n* emozione *f*, sentimento *m*, commozione *f*. **emotional** emotivo; impressionabile.
empathy ['empəθi] *n* empatia *f*, immedesimazione *f*.
emphasis ['emfəsis] *n, pl* **-ses** enfasi *f*, veemenza *f*, rilievo *m*. **emphasize** *v* dare rilievo a, mettere in evidenza. **emphatic** *adj* enfatico, risoluto, intenso.
empire ['empaiə] *n* impero *m*. **emperor** *n* imperatore *m*. **empress** *n* imperatrice *f*.
empirical [im'pirikəl] *adj* empirico.
employ [im'ploi] *v* impiegare; (*use*) adoperare, usare. **employee** *n* impiegato, -a *m, f*. **employer** *n* padrone, -a *m, f*; datore, -trice di lavoro *m, f*. **employment** *n* impiego (*pl* -ghi) *m*, lavoro *m*. **employment agency** ufficio di collocamento *m*.
empower [im'pauə] *v* autorizzare.
empty ['empti] *adj* vuoto. *v* vuotare, scaricare. **empty-handed** *adj* a mani vuote.
emulate ['emjuːleit] *v* emulare. **emulation** *n* emulazione *f*.
emulsion [i'mʌlʃən] *n* emulsione *f*.
enable [i'neibl] *v* mettere in grado di, permettere; (*law*) abilitare.
enact [i'nakt] *v* (*ordain*) ordinare; (*decree*) decretare; (*put into operation*) promulgare; (*theatre*) recitare.
enamel [i'naməl] *n* smalto *m*. *v* smaltare.
enamoured [i'naməd] *adj* innamorato.
enchant [in'tʃaːnt] *v* incantare, affascinare, ammaliare. **enchanting** *adj* incantevole. **enchantment** *n* incanto *m*, incantesimo *m*, fascino *m*.

encircle [in'səːkl] *v* cingere, accerchiare. **encirclement** *n* accerchiamento *m*.
enclose [in'klouz] *v* rinchiudere; (*letter*) allegare. **enclosure** *n* recinto *m*; (*letter*) allegato *m*; (*rel*) clausura *f*.
encore ['oŋkoː] *nm*, *interj* bis.
encounter [in'kauntə] *v* incontrare, affrontare. *n* incontro *m*; (*battle*) lotta *f*.
encourage [in'kʌridʒ] *v* incoraggiare, favorire, stimolare. **encouragement** *n* incitamento *m*, stimolo *m*.
encroach [in'kroutʃ] *v* **encroach on** abusare di; (*intrude on*) invadere.
encumber [in'kʌmbə] *v* ingombrare, impacciare; (*burden*) sopraffare. **encumbrance** *n* (*hindrance*) impaccio *m*; (*burden*) carico (*pl* -chi) *m*.
encyclopedia [insaiklə'piːdiə] *n* enciclopedia *f*.
end [end] *n* fine *f*, termine *m*; (*purpose*) scopo *m*; (*result*) conclusione *f*. **in the end** infine. **make ends meet** sbarcare il lunario. *v* finire, concludere, terminare. **endless** *adj* interminabile, senza fine.
endanger [in'deindʒə] *v* mettere in pericolo, compromettere.
endear [in'diə] *v* rendere caro. **endearing** *adj* simpatico, amabile.
endeavour [in'devə] *v* cercare, tentare. *n* sforzo *m*, tentativo *m*.
endemic [en'demik] *n* endemico.
endive ['endiv] *n* indivia *f*, cicoria *f*.
endorse [in'doːs] *v* approvare; (*sign*) vistare; (*cheque*) girare; (*record infringement*) annotare le infrazioni commesse. **endorsement** *n* visto *m*, girata *f*, annotazione delle infrazioni commesse *f*.
endow [in'dau] *v* dotare, fornire. **endowment** *n* dotazione *f*, donazione *f*.
endure [in'djuə] *v* tollerare, sopportare; (*last*) durare; resistere. **endurance** *n* resistenza *f*.
enema ['enəmə] *n* clistere *m*, enteroclisma *m*.
enemy ['enəmi] *n* nemico, -a *m*, *f*; avversario, -a *m*, *f*.
energy ['enədʒi] *n* energia *f*. **energetic** *adj* energico.
enfold [in'fould] *v* avvolgere.
enforce [in'foːs] *v* imporre, far valere, far rispettare. **enforced** *adj* obbligatorio, imposto. **enforcement** *n* imposizione *f*, applicazione *f*.
engage [in'geidʒ] *v* (*employ*) assumere, impiegare; (*occupy*) impegnare, occupare; (*mil*) attaccare; (*interlock*) ingranare, innestare; (*reserve*) prenotare. **engaged** *adj* (*busy*) occupato; (*betrothed*) fidanzato. **get engaged** fidanzarsi. **engagement** *n* fidanzamento *m*; (*employment*) impiego (*pl* -ghi) *m*; (*obligation*) impegno *m*; (*appointment*) appuntamento *m*.
engine ['endʒin] *n* motore *m*, macchina *f*; (*rail*) locomotiva *f*.
engineer [endʒi'niə] *n* ingegnere, -a *m*, *f*; meccanico, -a *m*, *f*; tecnico, -a *m*, *f*; (*mil*) geniere *m*. *v* (*construct*) costruire; (*contrive*) macchinare, tramare. **engineering** *n* costruzione *f*; (*study*, *science*) ingegneria *f*.
England ['iŋglənd] *n* Inghilterra *f*. **English** *n*(*m*+*f*), *adj* inglese.
engrave [in'greiv] *v* incidere, intagliare; (*printing*) imprimere. **engraver** *n* incisore *m*. **engraving** *n* incisione *f*.
engrossed [in'groust] *adj* preso (da), immerso.
engulf [in'gʌlf] *v* ingolfare.
enhance [in'haːns] *v* intensificare, aumentare, migliorare.
enigma [i'nigmə] *n* enigma *m*. **enigmatic** *adj* enigmatico, misterioso.
enjoy [in'dʒoi] *v* godere, apprezzare. **enjoy oneself** divertirsi. **enjoyable** *adj* divertente, piacevole. **enjoyment** *n* piacere *m*, godimento *m*, gioia *f*, divertimento *m*.
enlarge [in'laːdʒ] *v* ingrandire. **enlarge on** dilungarsi su. **enlargement** *n* ingrandimento *m*; (*med*) ipertrofia *f*.
enlighten [in'laitn] *v* illuminare, chiarire. **enlightenment** *n* schiarimento *m*, delucidazione *f*; (*history*) illuminismo *m*.
enlist [in'list] *v* arruolare; (*obtain*) ottenere. **enlistment** *n* arruolamento *m*.
enliven [in'laivn] *v* animare, ravvivare.
enmity ['enməti] *n* ostilità *f*.
enormous [i'noːməs] *adj* enorme, immenso.
enough [i'nʌf] *adv* abbastanza, sufficientemente. *adj* sufficiente, abbastanza, bastante. **be enough** bastare. *interj* basta!
enquire [in'kwaiə] *V* **inquire**.
enrage [in'reidʒ] *v* far arrabbiare. **enraged** *adj* arrabbiato, furioso.
enrich [in'ritʃ] *v* arricchire, abbellire.
enrol [in'roul] *v* (*mil*) arruolare; (*college*, *etc.*) iscrivere. **enrolment** *n* arruolamento *m*; iscrizione *f*.

enslave [in'sleiv] *v* far schiavo, assoggettare. **enslavement** *n* schiavitù *f*.
ensue [in'sjuː] *v* seguire, risultare.
ensure [in'ʃuə] *v* assicurare, garantire.
entail [in'teil] *v* comportare, implicare.
entangle [in'taŋgl] *v* impigliare, aggrovigliare; (*involve*) coinvolgere. **entanglement** *n* impiccio *m*, imbroglio *m*.
enter ['entə] *v* entrare (in); penetrare; (*join*) iscriversi a; (*record*) notare.
enterprise ['entəˌpraiz] *n* impresa *f*, iniziativa *f*. **enterprising** *adj* intraprendente, pieno d'iniziativa.
entertain [ˌentə'tein] *v* (*amuse*) divertire; (*receive guests*) ricevere ospitare; (*consider*) concepire, prendere in considerazione. **entertainer** *n* (*actor*) attore, -trice *m, f*; (*singer*) cantante *m, f*. **entertaining** *adj* divertente, piacevole. **entertainment** *n* divertimento *m*, spettacolo *m*.
enthral [in'θroːl] *v* affascinare.
enthusiasm [in'θuːziˌazəm] *n* entusiasmo *m*. **enthusiast** *n* entusiasta *m, f*; (*fam*) tifoso, -a *m, f*. **enthusiastic** *adj* entusiastico, appassionato.
entice [in'tais] *v* sedurre, allettare. **enticement** *n* seduzione *f*, allettamento *m*.
entire [in'taiə] *adj* intero, completo, assoluto. **in its entirety** nel suo insieme.
entitle [in'taitl] *v* dar diritto a, qualificare, autorizzare; (*name*) intitolare. **entitlement** *n* diritto *m*, titolo *m*.
entity ['entəti] *n* entità *f*.
entrails ['entreilz] *pl n* viscere *f pl*.
entrance[1] ['entrəns] *n* entrata *f*, ingresso *m*, ammissione *f*.
entrance[2] [in'traːns] *v* incantare, estasiare.
entrant ['entrənt] *n* candidato, -a *m, f*; concorrente *m, f*.
entreat [in'triːt] *v* supplicare, implorare. **entreaty** *n* supplica *f*, preghiera *f*.
entrée ['ontrei] *n* (*main course*) piatto principale *m*, secondo piatto *m*; (*first course*) primo piatto *m*.
entrench [in'trentʃ] *v* trincerare, rafforzare. **entrenched** *adj* (*set*) radicato.
entrepreneur [ˌontrəprə'nəː] *n* imprenditore, -trice *m, f*.
entrust [in'trʌst] *v* affidare.
entry ['entri] *n* entrata *f*; (*book-keeping*) partita *f*; annotazione *f*.
entwine [in'twain] *v* intrecciare.
enumerate [i'njuːməreit] *v* annoverare, elencare.
enunciate [i'nʌnsiˌeit] *v* enunciare; articolare.
envelop [in'veləp] *v* avvolgere.
envelope ['envəˌloup] *n* busta *f*.
environment [in'vaiərənmənt] *n* ambiente *m*.
envisage [in'vizidʒ] *v* contemplare, immaginare.
envoy ['envoi] *n* inviato, -a *m, f*.
envy ['envi] *n* invidia *f*. *v* invidiare. **envious** *adj* invidioso.
enzyme ['enzaim] *n* enzima *m*.
ephemeral [i'femərəl] *adj* effimero, passeggero.
epic ['epik] *adj* epico. *n* epopea *f*.
epicure ['epikjuə] *n* epicureo *m*; (*gourmet*) buongustaio, -a *m, f*.
epidemic [epi'demik] *n* epidemia *f*. *adj* epidemico.
epilepsy ['epilepsi] *n* epilessi *f*. **epileptic** *nm, adj* epilettico.
epilogue ['epilog] *n* epilogo (*pl* -ghi) *m*.
Epiphany [i'pifəni] *n* Epifania *f*.
episcopal [i'piskəpəl] *adj* vescovile.
episode ['episoud] *n* episodio *m*, incidente *m*.
epitaph ['epiˌtaːf] *n* epitaffio *m*.
epitome [i'pitəmi] *n* epitome *f*, compendio *m*.
epoch ['iːpok] *n* epoca *f*.
equable ['ekwəbl] *adj* equanime, sereno, uniforme.
equal ['iːkwəl] *adj* eguale, uguale, pari. *v* uguagliare; (*in calculations*) fare. **equality** *n* uguaglianza *f*, parità *f*. **equalize** *v* ragguagliare; (*sport*) pareggiare.
equanimity [ekwə'niməti] *n* equanimità *f*, serenità *f*.
equate [i'kweit] *v* uguagliare, paragonare. **equation** *n* equazione *f*.
equator [i'kweitə] *n* equatore *m*.
equestrian [i'kwestriən] *adj* equestre.
equilateral [ˌiːkwi'latərəl] *adj* equilatero.
equilibrium [ˌiːkwi'libriəm] *n* equilibrio *m*. **equilibrate** *v* equilibrare, bilanciare.
equinox ['ekwinoks] *n* equinozio *m*.
equip [i'kwip] *v* (*array*) allestire; (*furnish*) attrezzare, fornire (di), dotare (di). **equipment** *n* equipaggiamento *m*, attrezzatura *f*.
equity ['ekwəti] *n* giustizia *f*; imparzialità *f*; (*property*) valore netto *m*; (*securities*) azioni ordinarie *f pl*.
equivalent [i'kwivələnt] *nm, adj* equivalente.

era ['iərə] *n* era *f*, epoca *f*.
eradicate [i'radi,keit] *v* sradicare, estirpare.
erase [i'reiz] *v* cancellare.
erect [i'rekt] *v* erigere, costruire. *adj* eretto, dritto. **erection** *n* erezione *f*.
ermine ['əːmin] *n* ermellino *m*.
erode [i'roud] *v* erodere. **erosion** *n* erosione *f*.
erotic [i'rotik] *adj* erotico.
err [əː] *v* errare; (*make mistakes*) sbagliare; (*sin*) peccare.
errand ['erənd] *n* commissione *f*. **errand-boy** *n* fattorino *m*.
erratic [i'ratik] *adj* erratico.
error ['erə] *n* errore *m*, sbaglio *m*, torto *m*. **erroneous** *adj* erroneo.
erudite ['erudait] *adj* erudito, dotto. **erudition** *n* erudizione *f*.
erupt [i'rupt] *v* (*volcano*) eruttare; (*burst out*) erompere. **eruption** *n* eruzione *f*.
escalate ['eskə,leit] *v* intensificare. **escalation** *n* intensificazione *f*. **escalator** *n* scala mobile *f*.
escalope ['eskə,lop] *n* scaloppina *f*.
escape [is'keip] *v* fuggire, sfuggire; (*avoid*) evitare. *n* fuga *f*, evasione *f*. **escapism** *n* evasione dalla realtà *f*.
escort ['eskoːt; *v* i'skoːt] *n* scorta *f*. *v* scortare.
esoteric [esə'terik] *adj* esoterico.
especial [i'speʃəl] *adj* notevole, particolare. **especially** *adv* specie, specialmente.
espionage ['espiə,naːʒ] *n* spionaggio *m*.
esplanade [,esplə'neid] *n* spianata *f*; lungomare *m*.
essay ['esei] *n* saggio *m*, tema *m*.
essence ['esns] *n* essenza *f*; (*gist*) nocciolo *m*.
essential [i'senʃəl] *adj* essenziale, indispensabile.
establish [i'stabliʃ] *v* stabilire, fondare; (*ascertain*) constatare; (*set up*) istituire, instaurare; (*fix*) determinare. **established** *adj* (*set*) radicato; (*beyond question*) indubbio. **establishment** *n* costituzione *f*, fondazione *f*; (*house*) casa *f*; (*organization*) personale effettivo *m*.
estate [i'steit] *n* (*property*) tenuta *f*; (*possessions*) beni *m pl*, patrimonio *m*. **estate agent** agente immobiliare *m*. **estate car** giardinietta *f*. **housing estate** quartiere residenziale *m*.
esteem [i'stiːm] *n* stima *f*, considerazione *f*. *v* stimare, apprezzare.
estimate ['esti,meit; *n* 'estimət] *v* (*value*) valutare; (*judge*) stimare; (*assess cost*) preventivare. *n* preventivo *m*; valutazione *f*. **estimation** *n* valutazione *f*; considerazione *f*.
estrange [i'streindʒ] *v* alienare. **estrangement** *n* alienazione *f*; allontanamento *m*.
estuary ['estjuəri] *n* estuario *m*.
eternal [i'təːnl] *adj* eterno. **eternity** *n* eternità *f*.
ether ['iːθə] *n* etere *m*.
ethereal [i'θiəriəl] *adj* etereo, evanescente.
ethical ['eθikl] *adj* etico, morale. **ethics** *pl n* etica *f sing*, morale *f sing*.
ethnic ['eθnik] *adj* etnico. **ethnology** *n* etnologia *f*.
etiquette ['eti,ket] *n* etichetta *f*, comportamento *m*, cerimoniale *m*.
etymology [,eti'molədʒi] *n* etimologia *f*. **etymological** *adj* etimologico.
Eucharist ['juːkərist] *n* eucaristia *f*.
eunuch ['juːnək] *n* eunuco (*pl* -chi) *m*.
euphemism ['juːfə,mizəm] *n* eufemismo *m*. **euphemistic** *adj* eufemistico.
euphoria [ju'foːriə] *n* euforia *f*. **euphoric** *adj* euforico.
Europe ['juərəp] *n* Europa *f*. **European** *n*, *adj* europeo, -a. **European Economic Community** Comunità Economica Europea *f*.
euthanasia [,juːθə'neiziə] *n* eutanasia *f*.
evacuate [i'vakju,eit] *v* evacuare, sfollare. **evacuation** *n* evacuazione *f*, sfollamento *m*.
evade [i'veid] *v* evadere, evitare, eludere. **evasion** *n* evasione *f*. **evasive** *adj* evasivo, elusivo.
evaluate [i'valju,eit] *v* valutare. **evaluation** *n* valutazione *f*.
evangelical [,iːvan'dʒelikəl] *adj* evangelico. **evangelist** *n* evangelista *m*.
evaporate [i'vapə,reit] *v* evaporare, far evaporare. **evaporation** *n* evaporazione *f*.
eve [iːv] *n* vigilia *f*.
even ['iːvən] *adj* (*flat*) piano, piatto; (*regular*) uniforme, regolare; (*not odd*) pari. *adv* (*still*) ancora; (*indeed*) perfino. **even if** benchè, sebbene, quantunque. *v* livellare, uguagliare.
evening ['iːvniŋ] *n* sera *f*, serata *f*. **evening class** classe *or* scuola serale *f*. **evening dress** abito da sera *m*.
evensong ['iːvən,soŋ] *n* vespro *m*.

event [i'vent] *n* avvenimento *m*, evento *m*; (*outcome*) eventualità *f*; (*sport*) gara *f*. **eventful** *adj* ricco di vicende, memorabile. **eventual** *adj* finale, contingente. **eventually** *adv* alla fine, ultimamente.

ever ['evə] *adv* sempre, mai. **ever since** da quando, da allora. **evergreen** *nm, adj* sempreverde. **everlasting** *adj* eterno, perpetuo, perenne. **hardly ever** quasi mai.

every ['evri] *adj* ogni, ognuno, ciascuno. **everybody** *or* **everyone** *pron* ognuno, tutti *pl*. **everyday** *adj* quotidiano, normale. **every now and then** di tanto in tanto. **every other day** un giorno si un giorno no. **everything** *pron* tutto, ogni cosa. **everywhere** *adv* dovunque, dappertutto.

evict [i'vikt] *v* sfrattare. **eviction** *n* sfratto *m*.

evidence ['evidəns] *n* prova *f*, evidenza *f*; (*law*) testimonianza *f*, deposizione *f*. **give evidence** (*law*) deporre, testimoniare. **evident** *adj* evidente, manifesto, ovvio.

evil ['iːvl] *adj* cattivo, malvagio. *n* male *m*, peccato *m*. **evil-doer** malfattore, -trice *m, f*. **evil eye** malocchio *m*. **evil-looking** *adj* losco. **evil-minded** *adj* malintenzionato.

evoke [i'vouk] *v* evocare.

evolve [i'volv] *v* evolvere, sviluppare. **evolution** *n* evoluzione *f*.

ewe [juː] *n* pecora (femmina) *f*.

exacerbate [ig'zasəˌbeit] *v* esacerbare, inasprire, irritare.

exact [ig'zakt] *adj* esatto, preciso. *v* esigere, richiedere. **exacting** *adj* esigente, impegnativo. **exactitude** *n* esattezza *f*, precisione *f*.

exaggerate [ig'zadʒəˌreit] *v* esagerare. **exaggeration** *n* esagerazione *f*.

exalt [ig'zolt] *v* esaltare; (*praise*) vantare, lodare. **exaltation** *n* esaltazione *f*.

examine [ig'zamin] *v* esaminare; verificare; (*med*) visitare; (*law*) interrogare. **examination** *n* esame *m*; verifica *f*; visita medica *f*; (*law*) interrogatorio *m*. **examiner** *n* ispettore, -trice *m, f*.

example [ig'zaːmpl] *n* esempio *m*; (*specimen*) esemplare *m*. **for example** per esempio.

exasperate [ig'zaːspəˌreit] *v* esasperare; esacerbare; irritare. **exasperating** *adj* esasperante. **exasperation** *n* esasperazione *f*.

excavate ['ekskəˌveit] *v* scavare. **excavation** *n* scavo *m*.

exceed [ik'siːd] *v* eccedere, superare. **exceedingly** *adv* estremamente.

excel [ik'sel] *v* eccellere.

excellent ['eksələnt] *adj* eccellente, ottimo. **excellence** *n* eccellenza *f*, superiorità *f*. **Excellency** *n* Eccellenza *f*.

except [ik'sept] *prep* eccetto, salvo, tranne, all'infuori di. *v* escludere, eccettuare.

excerpt ['eksəːpt] *n* estratto *m*, brano *m*.

excess [ik'ses] *n* eccesso *m*, sovrabbondanza *f*. **excess baggage** eccedenza di bagaglio *f*. **excess weight** soprappeso *m*. **excessive** *adj* eccessivo, smoderato.

exchange [iks'tʃeindʒ] *n* cambio *m*, scambio *m*; (*phone*) centralino *m*. **rate of exchange** cambio *m*. *v* cambiare, scambiare.

exchequer [iks'tʃekə] *n* tesoro *m*, erario *m*.

excise ['eksaiz] *n* imposta di consumo *f*. *v* recidere, tagliar via.

excite [ik'sait] *v* eccitare, stimolare, provocare. **excitable** *adj* eccitabile, impressionabile. **excitement** *n* eccitamento *m*, agitazione *f*, emozione *f*.

exclaim [ik'skleim] *v* esclamare. **exclamation** *n* esclamazione *f*. **exclamation mark** punto esclamativo *m*.

exclude [ik'skluːd] *v* escludere. **excluding** *prep* escluso, eccetto. **exclusion** *n* esclusione *f*. **exclusive** *adj* esclusivo. **exclusivity** *n* esclusiva *f*.

excommunicate [ekskə'mjuːniˌkeit] *v* scomunicare. **excommunication** *n* scomunica *f*.

excrement ['ekskrəmənt] *n* sterco *m*, feci *f pl*. **excrete** *v* defecare. **excretion** *n* escrezione *f*.

excruciating [ik'skruːʃieitiŋ] *adj* atroce.

excursion [ik'skəːʃən] *n* escursione *f*, gita *f*.

excuse [ik'skjuːz] *n* scusa *f*, pretesto *m*. **make excuses** scusarsi. *v* scusare, perdonare; giustificare. **excuse from** esentare da. **excuse me!** scusi!

execute ['eksiˌkjuːt] *v* eseguire, mettere in esecuzione, effettuare; (*kill*) giustiziare. **execution** *n* esecuzione *f*; (*death*) esecuzione capitale *f*. **executioner** *n* boia *m invar*.

executive [ig'zekjutiv] *adj* esecutivo. *n* (*body*) esecutivo *m*; (*person*) funzionario,

-a *m, f.* **executor** *n* esecutore, -trice *m, f.* testamentario, -a *m, f.*
exemplify [ig'zempliˌfai] *v* esemplificare, illustrare.
exempt [ig'zempt] *v* esentare, esonerare. *adj* esente. **exemption** *n* esenzione *f*, dispensa *f.*
exercise ['eksəˌsaiz] *n* esercizio *m*, uso *m*; (*task*) compito *m*; (*mil*) manovra *f.* *v* esercitare, usare. **exercise-book** *n* quaderno *m.*
exert [ig'zəːt] *v* esercitare. **exert oneself** sforzarsi. **exertion** *n* sforzo *m.*
exhale [eks'heil] *v* emanare; (*breathe out*) esalare.
exhaust [ig'zoːst] *v* stancare, esaurire, estenuare. *n* scarico (*pl* -chi) *m*, scappamento *m.* **exhausted** *adj* sfinito, esausto. **exhausting** *adj* faticoso, estenuante. **exhaustion** *n* esaurimento *m.*
exhibit [ig'zibit] *v* esibire, esporre. *n* oggetto per mostra *m*; (*law*) oggetto di appoggio *m.* **exhibition** *n* mostra *f*, esposizione *f.* **exhibitionism** *n* esibizionismo *m.* **exhibitionist** *n* esibizionista *m, f.* **exhibitor** *n* esibitore, -trice *m, f.*
exhilarating [ig'ziləreitiŋ] *adj* esilarante, rallegrante.
exigency [ig'zidʒənsi] *n* esigenza *f*, necessità *f.*
exile ['eksail] *n* (*expulsion*) esilio *m*; (*person*) esule *m, f*, esiliato, -a *m, f.* *v* esiliare, mettere al bando.
exist [ig'zist] *v* esistere, vivere. **existence** *n* esistenza *f*, vita *f.* **existentialism** *n* esistenzialismo *m.* **existing** *adj* esistente, attuale.
exit ['egzit] *n* uscita *f.* *v* uscire.
exodus ['eksədəs] *n* esodo *m.*
exonerate [ig'zonəˌreit] *v* esonerare, assolvere.
exorbitant [ig'zoːbitənt] *adj* esorbitante, esagerato.
exorcize ['eksoːsaiz] *v* esorcizzare. **exorcism** *n* esorcismo *m.* **exorcist** *n* esorcista *m, f.*
exotic [ig'zotik] *adj* esotico; (*strange*) strano.
expand [ik'spand] *v* espandere, estendere. **expansion** *n* espansione *f.*
expanse [ik'spans] *n* spazio *m*, distesa *f.*
expatriate [eks'peitrieit; *n, adj* eks'peitriət] *v* espatriare, emigrare. *n, adj* espatriato, -a.
expect [ik'spekt] *v* (*await*) aspettare; anticipare; (*believe*) credere. **expectant** *adj* in attesa. **expectation** *n* aspettativa *f*, attesa *f*, prospettiva *f.*
expedient [ik'spiːdiənt] *n* espediente *m*, accorgimento *m.* *adj* opportuno, conveniente.
expedition [ˌekspi'diʃən] *n* spedizione *f.* **expeditious** *adj* sbrigativo.
expel [ik'spel] *v* espellere, scacciare.
expenditure [ik'spenditʃə] *n* spesa *f*, consumo *m.*
expense [ik'spens] *n* spesa *f.* **expense account** conto spese *m.* **expensive** *adj* caro, costoso.
experience [ik'spiəriəns] *v* provare, subire. *n* esperienza *f*; incidente *m*, avventura *f.*
experiment [ik'sperimənt] *n* esperimento *m*, prova *f.* *v* sperimentare, provare, fare esperimenti. **experimental** *adj* sperimentale.
expert ['ekspəːt] *adj* esperto, perito, competente. *n* esperto, -a *m, f*, perito, -a *m, f*; conoscitore, -trice *m, f.*
expertise [ˌekspəː'tiːz] *n* perizia *f*, maestria *f.*
expire [ik'spaiə] *v* scadere, terminare; (*die*) morire. **expiry** *n* termine *m*, scadenza *f.*
explain [ik'splein] *v* spiegare, chiarire. **explanation** *n* spiegazione *f*, chiarimento *m.* **explanatory** *adj* esplicativo.
expletive [ek'spliːtiv] *n* (*profanity*) bestemmia *f.*
explicit [ik'splisit] *adj* esplicito, chiaro.
explode [ik'sploud] *v* esplodere, far saltare, scoppiare; (*discredit*) screditare. **explosion** *n* esplosione *f.*
exploit[1] ['eksploit] *n* impresa *f.* **exploits** *pl n* gesta *f pl.*
exploit[2] [ik'sploit] *v* sfruttare, valorizzare. **exploitation** *n* sfruttamento *m*, valorizzazione *f.*
explore [ik'sploː] *v* esplorare; studiare. **exploration** *n* esplorazione *f*; studio *m.* **exploratory** *adj* esploratorio.
exponent [ik'spounənt] *n* esponente *m, f*; (*representative*) interprete *m, f*, rappresentante *m, f.* **exponential** *adj* esponenziale.
export ['ekspoːt; *v* ik'spoːt] *n* esportazione *f.* *v* esportare.
expose [ik'spouz] *v* esporre, mostrare; (*reveal*) svelare; (*unmask*) smascherare. **exposition** *n* spiegazione *f*; mostra *f.*

exposure *n* esposizione *f*; smascheramento *m*; rivelazione *f*; (*phot*) posa *f*.
express [ik'spres] *adj* espresso, esplicito. **express train** direttissimo *m*, rapido *m*. *v* esprimere. **expression** *n* espressione *f*; manifestazione *f*; (*phrase*) modo di dire *m*. **expressionless** *adj* impassibile. **expressive** *adj* espressivo.
expulsion [ik'spʌlʃən] *n* espulsione *f*.
expurgate ['ekspəgeit] *v* espurgare.
exquisite ['ekswizit] *adj* squisito; (*intense*) vivo, acuto.
extend [ik'stend] *v* estendere, prolungare. **extension** *n* estensione *f*; (*time*) proroga *f*; (*phone*) telefono interno *m*. **extensive** *adj* esteso, vasto.
extent [ik'stent] *n* estensione *f*; limite *m*.
extenuating [ik'stenjueitiŋ] *adj* attenuante.
exterior [ik'stiəriə] *nm*, *adj* esterno.
exterminate [ik'stəːmiˌneit] *v* sterminare, annientare. **extermination** *n* sterminio *m*, annientamento *m*.
external [ik'stəːnl] *adj* esterno.
extinct [ik'stiŋkt] *adj* estinto.
extinguish [ik'stiŋgwiʃ] *v* estinguere, spegnere. **fire extinguisher** estintore *m*.
extol [ik'stoul] *v* esaltare, lodare.
extort [ik'stoːt] *v* estorcere, strappare. **extortion** *n* estorsione *f*. **extortionate** *adj* esorbitante, esagerato.
extra ['ekstrə] *adj* extra *invar*, straordinario, supplementare, in più. *n* (*theatre*) comparsa *f*; (*additional charge*) spesa extra *f*. *adv* in più.
extract [ik'strakt] *v* estrarre; (*tooth*) cavare. **extraction** *n* estrazione *f*; origine *f*.
extradite ['ekstrəˌdait] *v* estradare. **extraditable** *adj* passibile di estradizione. **extradition** *n* estradizione *f*.
extramural [ˌekstrə'mjuərəl] *adj* fuori le mura; (*university*) al di fuori dell'università. **extramural course** corso libero *m*.
extraneous [ik'streiniəs] *adj* estraneo.
extraordinary [ik'stroːdənəri] *adj* straordinario, eccezionale, fenomenale.
extravagant [ik'stravəgənt] *adj* stravagante; (*wasteful*) prodigo, spendereccio; (*exaggerated*) esagerato. **extravagance** *n* stravaganza *f*, prodigalità *f*.
extreme [ik'striːm] *adj* estremo, ultimo. *n* estremo *m*. **extremist** *n* estremista *m*, *f*. **extremity** *n* estremità *f*.
extricate ['ekstriˌkeit] *v* **extricate oneself** districarsi, tirarsi d'impaccio, liberarsi.
extrovert ['ekstrəvəːt] *nm*, *adj* estroverso.
exuberant [ig'zjuːbərənt] *adj* esuberante. **exuberance** *n* esuberanza *f*.
exude [ig'zjuːd] *v* emanare.
exult [ig'zʌlt] *v* esultare. **exultant** *adj* esultante, trionfante. **exultation** *n* esultazione *f*, trionfo *m*.
eye [ai] *n* occhio *m*; (*needle*) cruna *f*. **see eye to eye (with)** vederla allo stesso modo (di). *v* adocchiare, osservare.
eyeball ['aiboːl] *n* bulbo oculare *m*.
eyebrow ['aibrau] *n* sopracciglio *m*.
eyelash ['ailaʃ] *n* ciglio *m* (*pl* -a *f*).
eyelet ['ailit] *n* occhiello *m*.
eyelid ['ailid] *n* palpebra *f*.
eye-opener *n* fatto rivelatore *m*.
eye shadow *n* bistro *m*, ombretto *m*.
eyesight ['aisait] *n* vista *f*, visione *f*.
eyesore ['aisoː] *n* pugno in un occhio *m*.
eyewitness ['aiˌwitnis] *n* testimonio oculare *m*.

F

fable ['feibl] *n* favola *f*.
fabric ['fabrik] *n* (*cloth*) tessuto m, stoffa *f*; (*structure*) struttura *f*.
fabricate ['fabrikeit] *v* (*make up*) inventare; (*fake*) falsificare; (*construct*) fabbricare. **fabrication** *n* costruzione *f*, invenzione *f*.
fabulous ['fabjuləs] *adj* favoloso.
façade [fə'saːd] *n* facciata *f*.
face [feis] *n* faccia *f*, volto *m*, viso *m*; (*clcck*) quadrante *m*; (*type*) carattere *m*. *v* (*look towards*) fronteggiare; (*confront*) affrontare; (*cover*) rivestire. **face-cloth** *n* pezzuola per lavarsi *f*. **face-lift** *n* plastica facciale *f*; (*restyling*) restauro *m*. **face-pack** *n* maschera di bellezza *f*. **face value** valore nominale *m*. **lose face** perdere prestigio.
facet ['fasit] *n* (*small plane*) faccetta *f*; (*aspect*) aspetto *m*.
facetious [fə'siːʃəs] *adj* arguto, spiritoso.
facial ['feiʃəl] *adj* facciale.
facile ['fasail] *adj* (*glib*) superficiale, pronto; (*easy*) facile.
facilitate [fə'siliˌteit] *v* facilitare, agevolare.

facility [fə'siləti] *n* facilità *f*; (*help*) facilitazione *f*, agevolazione *f*; opportunità *f*. **facilities** *pl n* servizi *m pl*.
facing ['feisiŋ] *n* (*covering*) rivestimento *m*; (*dress*) risvolto *m*.
facsimile [fak'siməli] *n* facsimile *m invar*.
fact [fakt] *n* fatto *m*, verità *f*. **as a matter of fact** in effetti. **fact-finding** *adj* di inchiesta. **in fact** infatti. **factual** *adj* effettivo.
faction ['fakʃən] *n* fazione *f*, dissenso *m*. **factious** *adj* fazioso, partigiano.
factor ['faktə] *n* fattore *m*; agente *m*, *f*.
factory ['faktəri] *n* fabbrica *f*, stabilimento *m*.
faculty ['fakəlti] *n* facoltà *f*.
fad [fad] *n* capriccio *m*; (*fashion*) moda *f*.
fade [feid] *v* (*colour*) sbiadire; (*lose freshness*) appassire; (*disappear*) svanire. **fade away** affievolirsi.
fag [fag] *v* sfacchinare. *n* (*hard work*) sgobbata *f*; (*slang*) sigaretta *f*. **fag-end** *n* cicca *f*. **fagged out** stanco morto.
fail [feil] *v* fallire; (*fall short*) mancare; (*not pass*) bocciare, essere respinto. **without fail** senza fallo. **failure** *n* insuccesso *m*, mancanza *f*.
failing ['feiliŋ] *n* debole *m*, difetto *m*. *adj* debile. *prep* salvo.
faint [feint] *v* svenire. *adj* fiacco, tenue, appena percettibile. **feel faint** sentirsi venir meno. **not have the faintest idea** non avere la più pallida idea.
fair[1] [feə] *adj* (*colouring*) biondo, chiaro; (*unbiased*) giusto, imparziale; (*moderately good*) discreto. **fair copy** bella copia *f*. **fair play** comportamento leale *m*. *adv* secondo le regole. **fairly** *adv* (*moderately*) abbastanza; (*properly*) giustamente. **in all fairness** in tutta franchezza.
fair[2] [feə] *n* fiera *f*, mercato *m*.
fairy ['feəri] *n* fata *f*. **fairy-tale** *n* fiaba *f*.
faith [feiθ] *n* (*belief*) fede *f*; (*confidence*) fiducia *f*. **faith-healer** *n* guaritore, -trice per suggestione *m*, *f*. **faithful** *adj* fedele. **faithless** *adj* che non ha fede, sleale.
fake [feik] *v* contraffare, fingere. *n* (*object*) contraffazione; (*person*) impostore, -a *m*, *f*.
falcon ['foːlkən] *n* falco *m*, falcone *m*.
***fall** [foːl] *v* cadere, cascare; (*collapse*) crollare; (*lower*) abbassarsi. **fall asleep** addormentarsi. **fall back on** riccorrere a. **fall behind** rimanere indietro; (*fig*) essere in arretrato. **fall ill** ammalarsi. **fall-out** *n* pioggia radioattiva *f*. **fall through** fallire. *n* caduta *f*; crollo *m*, rovina *f*; abbassamento *m*; (*autumn*) autunno *m*.
fallacy ['faləsi] *n* falsità *f*. **fallacious** *adj* fallace, falso.
fallen ['foːlən] *V* **fall**.
fallible ['faləbl] *adj* fallibile. **fallibility** *n* fallibilità *f*.
fallow ['falou] *adj* a maggese.
false [foːls] *adj* falso, artificiale, finto. **false alarm** falso allarme *m*. **false pretences** (*law*) millantato credito *m*. **false teeth** denti artificiali *m pl*. **falsehood** *n* menzogna *f*. **falseness** *n* perfidia *f*. **falsify** *v* falsificare.
falsetto [foːl'setou] *n* falsetto *m*.
falter ['foːltə] *v* (*waver*) vacillare, titubare; (*speak hesitatingly*) balbettare. **faltering** *adj* titubante.
fame [feim] *n* fama *f*, rinomanza *f*. **famed** *adj* rinomato.
familiar [fə'miljə] *adj* familiare; intimo; (*impudent*) sfacciato; (*well-known*) noto. **be on familiar terms with** aver dimestichezza con. **familiarity** *n* familiarità *f*; intimità *f*; (*impertinence*) sfacciataggine *f*.
family ['faməli] *n* famiglia *f*. **family allowance** assegni familiari *m pl*. **family tree** albero genealogico *m*.
famine ['famin] *n* carestia *f*.
famished ['famiʃt] *adj* affamato.
famous ['feiməs] *adj* famoso, celebre.
fan[1] [fan] *n* ventaglio *m*; (*mechanical*) ventilatore *m*. **fan-belt** *n* cinghia per ventilatore *f*. *v* (*flames*) soffiare su; (*excite*) aizzare. **fan oneself** farsi vento.
fan[2] [fan] *n* (*admirer*) tifoso, -a *m*, *f*.
fanatic [fə'natik] *n*, *adj* fanatico, -a; (*sport*) tifoso, -a. **fanaticism** *n* fanatismo *m*; tifo *m*.
fancy ['fansi] *adj* elaborato, raffinato, di fantasia. **fancy-dress** *n* costume *m*. **fancy-dress ball** ballo in maschera *m*. *n* immaginazione *f*, fantasia *f*, capriccio *m*. *v* desiderare, immaginare. **fanciful** *adj* fantasioso, capriccioso.
fanfare ['fanfeə] *n* fanfara *f*.
fang [faŋ] *n* zanna *f*.
fantastic [fan'tastik] *adj* fantastico, strano.
fantasy ['fantəsi] *n* fantasia *f*, capriccio *m*.
far [faː] *adv*, *adj* lontano, distante; (*much*) molto. **as far as** (*place*) fino a. **as far as I know** a quanto sappia. **far-fetched** *adj* improbabile, forzato. **far-reaching** *adj* di

gran portata. **far-sighted** *adj* (*prudent*) previdente. **so far** (*up to this point*) fin qui.

farce [faːs] *n* farsa *f*.

fare [feə] *n* tariffa *f*, prezzo del biglietto *m*; (*person*) viaggiatore, -trice *m*, *f*; (*food*) vitto *m*. *v* vivere, trovarsi.

farewell [feə'wel] *n* addio *m*, congedo *m*. *interj* addio!

farm [faːm] *n* fattoria *f*, podere *m*. **farmhouse** *n* casa colonica *f*. *v* coltivare, fare l'agricoltore. **farm out** dare in appalto. **farmer** *n* agricoltore *m*, contadino, -a *m*, *f*. **farming** *n* agricoltura *f*, coltivazione *f*.

fart [faːt] (*vulgar*) *n* scoreggia *f*. *v* fare scoregge.

farther ['faːðə] *adj*, *adv* più lontano; ulteriore. **farthest** *adj* il più lontano.

fascinate ['fasi,neit] *v* affascinare, incantare. **fascinating** *adj* affascinante, avvincente. **fascination** *n* fascino *m*, attrattiva *f*.

fascism ['faʃizəm] *n* fascismo *m*. **fascist** *n*(*m*+*f*), *adj* fascista.

fashion ['faʃən] *n* (*manner*) modo *m*, maniera *f*; (*dress*) moda *f*; (*style*) stile *m*; (*vogue*) voga *f*. **after a fashion** in un certo modo. **in fashion** alla moda. **out of fashion** fuori moda. *v* foggiare, modellare. **fashionable** *adj* elegante, di moda.

fast[1] [faːst] *adj* rapido, veloce; (*firmly held*) fisso, saldo; (*colour*) solido. *adv* presto, rapidamente. **the clock is ... fast** l'orologio va avanti di ... .

fast[2] [faːst] *n* digiuno *m*. *v* digiunare.

fasten ['faːsn] *v* legare, fissare, agganciare, attaccare. **fastener** *or* **fastening** *n* chiusura *f*, fermaglio *m*.

fastidious [fa'stidiəs] *adj* meticoloso, schifiltoso.

fat [fat] *adj*, *nm* grasso. **fatten** *v* ingrassare. **fatty** *adj* grasso, untuoso.

fatal ['feitl] *adj* fatale, ineluttabile. **fatalism** *n* fatalismo. **fatalist** *n* fatalista *m*, *f*. **fatality** *n* fatalità *f*.

fate [feit] *n* fato *m*, destino *m*. **fated** *adj* destinato. **fateful** *adj* decisivo.

father ['faːðə] *n* padre *m*; (*coll*) babbo *m*. *v* procreare, originare. **fatherhood** *n* paternità *f*. **father-in-law** *n* suocero *m*. **fatherland** *n* patria *f*. **fatherly** *adj* paterno.

fathom ['faðəm] *v* (*understand*) indovinare, penetrare; (*depth*) sondare. *n* braccio *m*.

fatigue [fə'tiːg] *n* stanchezza *f*, esaurimento *m*. *v* stancare.

fatuous ['fatjuəs] *adj* fatuo, frivolo, vuoto.

fault [foːlt] *n* (*flaw*) difetto *m*, imperfezione *f*; errore *m*; (*cause for blame*) colpa *f*; (*geol*) faglia *f*; (*tennis*) fallo *m*. **be at fault** essere colpevole. **find fault with** criticare, biasimare. **faultless** *adj* senza colpa. **faulty** *adj* difettoso.

favour ['feivə] *n* favore *m*, piacere *m*. *v* favorire, favoreggiare, preferire. **favourable** *adj* favorevole, vantaggioso.

favourite ['feivrit] *adj* preferito. *n* favorito, -a *m*, *f*.

fawn[1] [foːn] *n* (*zool*) daino *m*, cerbiatto *m*. *adj* (*colour*) fulvo.

fawn[2] [foːn] *v* **fawn on** adulare.

fear [fiə] *v* temere, aver paura di. *n* timore *m*, paura *f*. **fearful** *adj* terribile, spaventoso. **fearless** *adj* intrepido.

feasible ['fiːzəbl] *adj* fattibile, realizzabile. **feasibility** *n* praticabilità *f*.

feast [fiːst] *n* festa *f*, banchetto *m*.

feat [fiːt] *n* impresa *f*, azione *f*.

feather ['feðə] *n* penna *f*, piuma *f*. **feather-bed** *n* letto di piume *m*. **feathered** *adj* pennuto.

feature ['fiːtʃə] *n* caratteristica *f*, tratto distintivo *m*; (*newspaper*) elzeviro *m*; (*geog*) configurazione *f*. **features** *pl n* (*anat*) lineamenti *m pl*. *v* dar rilievo a; (*theatre*) presentare. **featureless** *adj* scialbo.

February ['februəri] *n* febbraio *m*.

fed [fed] *V* **feed**.

federal ['fedərəl] *adj* federale. **federation** *n* federazione *f*.

fee [fiː] *n* onorario *m*, parcella *f*; (*school*) retta *f*; (*entrance fee*) tassa d'iscrizione *f*.

feeble ['fiːbl] *adj* debole, fiacco. **feeble-minded** *adj* cretino, debole di mente. **feebleness** *n* debolezza *f*.

***feed** [fiːd] *v* nutrire; (*supply*) alimentare; (*eat*) mangiare, nutrirsi. *n* mangime *m*, nutrimento *m*; (*baby*) poppata *f*. **feedback** *n* retroreazione *f*, feedback *m invar*; (*response*) reazione. **fed up** (*coll*) stufo.

***feel** [fiːl] *v* (*touch*) tastare, toccare; (*emotion*) sentire. **feel like** sentirsi disposto a. **feeler** *n* tentacolo *m*; (*proposal*) sondaggio *m*. **feeling** *n* (*physical*) senso *m*, sensazione *f*; (*emotion*) sensibilità *f*, suscettibilità *f*; (*affection*) affetto *m*.

feet [fiːt] *V* **foot.**
feign [fein] *v* fingere, simulare, far finta.
feline ['fiːlain] *adj* felino.
fell[1] [fel] *V* **fall.**
fell[2] [fel] *v* (*cut down*) abbattere; (*strike down*) atterrare.
fellow ['felou] *n* individuo *m*, tipo *m*; (*companion*) compagno *m*, collega *m*, *f*; (*member*) membro *m*, socio *m*. **fellow-countryman** *n* compatriota *m*, *f*. **fellowship** *n* (*companionship*) cameratismo *m*; (*rel*) comunità *f*; (*allowance*) borsa di studio *f*.
felony ['feləni] *n* crimine *m*. **felon** *n* delinquente *m*, *f*.
felt[1] [felt] *V* **feel.**
felt[2] [felt] *n* feltro *m*.
female ['fiːmeil] *n* femmina *f*. *adj also* **feminine** femminile.
feminism ['feminizəm] *n* femminismo *m*. **feminist** *n* femminista *m*, *f*.
fence [fens] *n* (*barrier*) steccato *m*, palizzata *f*; (*receiver of stolen goods*) ricettatore, -trice *m*, *f*. *v* (*sport*) tirar di scherma. **fence in** recintare. **fencing** *n* recinto *m*; (*sport*) scherma *f*.
fend [fend] *v* **fend for oneself** provvedere a sè stesso, arrangiarsi. **fend off** parare, schivare.
fender ['fendə] *n* paracenere *m invar*; (*US*) paraurti *m*.
fennel ['fenl] *n* finocchio *m*.
ferment ['fəːment; *v* fə'ment] *n* fermento *m*. *v* fermentare. **fermentation** *n* fermentazione *f*.
fern [fəːn] *n* felce *f*.
ferocious [fə'rouʃəs] *adj* feroce. **ferocity** *n* ferocia *f*.
ferret ['ferit] *n* furetto *m*. *v* **ferret out** scovare.
ferry ['feri] *n* traghetto *m*. *v* traghettare.
fertile ['fəːtail] *adj* fertile, fecondo. **fertility** *n* fertilità *f*, fecondità *f*. **fertilize** *v* (*enrich*) fertilizzare; fecondare. **fertilizer** *n* fertilizzante *m*, concime *m*.
fervent ['fəːvənt] *adj* fervente, fervido. **fervour** *n* fervore *m*, ardore *m*.
fester ['festə] *v* suppurare; (*rankle*) bruciare.
festival ['festəvəl] *n* festival *m invar*, festa *f*.
festoon [fə'stuːn] *v* decorare con festoni. *n* festone *m*.
fetch [fetʃ] *v* andare a prendere; (*call*) chiamare; (*a price*) realizzare. **fetching** *adj* attraente.
fête [feit] *n* festa *f*. *v* festeggiare.
fetid ['fiːtid] *adj* fetido, puzzolente.
fetish ['fetiʃ] *n* feticcio *m*, idolo *m*.
fetter ['fetə] *n* catena *f*. *v* incatenare.
feud [fjuːd] *n* lite *f*. *v* essere in lotta.
feudal ['fjuːdl] *adj* feudale. **feudalism** *n* feudalesimo *m*.
fever ['fiːvə] *n* febbre *f*. **feverish** *adj* febbricitante; (*restless*) febbrile.
few [fjuː] *pron*, *adj* pochi, -e. **a few** alcuni, -e. **quite a few** parecchi, parecchie. **fewer** *adj* meno *invar*. **fewest** *adj* meno *invar*.
fiancé [fi'onsei] *n* fidanzato *m*. **fiancée** *n* fidanzata *f*.
fiasco [fi'askou] *n* fiasco *m*.
fib [fib] (*coll*) *n* frottola *f*. *v* raccontar frottole.
fibre ['faibə] *n* fibra *f*. **fibreglass** *n* fibra di vetro *f*. **fibrous** *adj* fibroso.
fickle ['fikl] *adj* volubile. **fickleness** *n* volubilità *f*.
fiction ['fikʃən] *n* (*invention*) finzione *f*; (*novels, etc.*) novellistica *f*, narrativa *f*. **fictional** *or* **fictitious** *adj* fittizio, immaginario.
fiddle ['fidl] *n* violino *m*; (*coll*: *fraud*) imbroglio *m*, truffa *f*. *v* suonare il violino; (*coll*: *cheat*) truffare, imbrogliare. **fit as a fiddle** sano come un pesce.
fidelity [fi'deləti] *n* fedeltà *f*.
fidget ['fidʒit] *v* muoversi irrequietamente, dimenarsi. **fidgety** *adj* irrequieto, nervoso.
field [fiːld] *n* campo *m*; (*of knowledge, etc.*) settore *m*. **field glasses** binoccolo *m sing*. **field marshal** maresciallo *m*.
fiend [fiːnd] *n* demonio *m*. **fiendish** *adj* infernale, diabolico.
fierce [fiəs] *adj* feroce, intenso.
fiery ['faiəri] *adj* focoso, ardente.
fifteen [fif'tiːn] *nm*, *adj* quindici. **fifteenth** *nm*, *adj* quindicesimo.
fifth [fifθ] *nm*, *adj* quinto.
fifty ['fifti] *nm*, *adj* cinquanta. **fiftieth** *nm*, *adj* cinquantesimo.
fig [fig] *n* fico *m*.
***fight** [fait] *v* lottare, combattere. *n* lotta *f*, combattimento *m*; (*scuffle*) zuffa *f*.
figment ['figmənt] *n* **figment of the imagination** finzione *f*.
figure ['figə] *n* (*numeral*) cifra *f*; (*shape*) forma *f*; (*pictorial*) figura *f*; (*character*) personaggio *m*; (*bodily form*) linea *f*.

figurehead *n* (*naut*) polena *f*; (*derog*) uomo di paglia *m*. **figure of speech** modo di dire *m*. *v* (*appear*) apparire. **figure out** **calcolare.**

filament ['filəmənt] *n* filamento *m*.

file[1] [fail] *n* (*dossier*) pratica *f*; archivio *m*; (*for papers*) cartella *f*; (*card with details*) scheda *f*; (*row*) fila *f*. *v* archiviare, mettere in ordine, registrare. **filing** *n* schedare *m*. **filing cabinet** schedario *m*. **single file** fila indiana *f*.

file[2] [fail] *n* (*tool*) lima *f*. *v* limare, levigare.

filial ['filiəl] *adj* filiale.

fill [fil] *v* riempire; (*tooth*) otturare. **fill in** completare, inserire. **fill up** (*mot*) fare il pieno. **filling** *n* (*cookery*) ripieno *m*; (*tooth*) otturazione *f*. **filling station** stazione di rifornimento *f*.

fillet ['filit] *n* (*meat*) filetto *m*. *v* disossare.

film [film] *n* pellicola *f*; (*phot*, *cinema*) film *m invar*. **film star** divo, -a del cinema *m*, *f*. *v* girare un film.

filter ['filtə] *n* filtro *m*. **filter-tip** *n* filtro *m*. *v* filtrare.

filth [filθ] *n* sudiciume *m*, sporcizia *f*; oscenità *f*. **filthy** *adj* sudicio, sporco; lurido, osceno.

fin [fin] *n* pinna *f*.

final ['fainl] *adj* finale, ultimo. *n* finale *f*. **finalist** *n* finalista *m*, *f*. **finally** *adv* infine.

finance [fai'nans] *n* finanza *f*. *v* finanziare. **financial** *adj* finanziario. **financier** *n* finanziere *m*, finanziatore *m*.

finch [fintʃ] *n* fringuello *m*.

***find** [faind] *v* scoprire, trovare. **find out** scoprire.

fine[1] [fain] *adj* (*high quality*) pregiato, raffinato; (*minute*) fine; (*accomplished*) bravo; (*beautiful*) bello. *adv* bene.

fine[2] [fain] *n* (*penalty*) multa *f*. *v* multare.

finesse [fi'nes] *n* finezza *f*.

finger ['fiŋgə] *n* dito *m* (*pl* dita *f*). **cross one's fingers** toccar ferro. **finger bowl** lavadita *m invar*. **finger-mark** *n* ditata *f*. **fingernail** *n* unghia *f*. **fingerprint** *n* impronta digitale *f*. **fingertip** *n* punta delle dita *f*. *v* (*touch*) palpare.

finish ['finiʃ] *v* finire, concludere. *n* fine *f*, conclusione *f*; (*surface*) finitura *f*; (*textile*) appretto *m*.

finite ['fainait] *adj* limitato, circoscritto; (*math*) finito.

Finland ['finlənd] *n* Finlandia *f*. **Finn** *n* finlandese *m*, *f*. **Finnish** *nm*, *adj* finlandese.

fir [fəː] *n* abete *m*.

fire ['faiə] *n* fuoco *m*; (*conflagration*) incendio *m*; (*heater*) stufa *f*. **catch fire** prender fuoco. **hang fire** indugiare. **set fire to** appiccare il fuoco a, incendiare. *v* (*shoot*) sparare; (*dismiss*) licenziare, silurare; (*inflame*) eccitare, infiammare; (*inspire*) ispirare.

fire alarm *n* allarme d'incendio *m*.

firearm ['faiəˌaːm] *n* arma da fuoco *f*.

fire brigade *n* corpo dei vigili del fuoco *m*.

fire door *n* esercitazione antincendio *f*.

fire drill *n* pompa antincendio *f*.

fire engine *n* uscita di sicurezza *f*.

fire escape *n* uscita di sicurezza *f*.

fire extinguisher *n* estintore *m*.

firefly ['faiəflai] *n* lucciola *f*.

fire-guard *n* parafuoco *m*, paracenere *m invar*.

fireman ['faiəmən] *n* pompiere *m*, vigile del fuoco *m*.

fireplace ['faiəˌpleis] *n* focolare *m*, camino *m*, caminetto *m*.

fireproof ['faiəˌpruːf] *adj* incombustibile, resistente al fuoco.

fireside ['faiəˌsaid] *n* focolare *m*.

fire station *n* caserma dei pompieri *f*.

firewood ['faiəˌwud] *n* legna da ardere *f*.

fireworks ['faiəˌwəːks] *pl n* fuochi d'artifizio *m pl*.

firing squad *n* plotone d'esecuzione *m*.

firm[1] [fəːm] *adj* fermo; (*steady*) saldo; (*steadfast*) risoluto; solido; stabile. **stand firm** tener duro. **firmness** *n* fermezza *f*; saldezza *f*; risolutezza *f*.

firm[2] [fəːm] *n* (*comm*) ditta *f*, azienda *f*.

first [fəːst] *adj* primo. *adv* prima; in primo luogo; anzitutto. **first aid** pronto soccorso *m*. **first-class** *adj* ottimo, di prima qualità, eccellente; (*rail*, *etc*.) di prima classe. **first floor** primo piano *m*. **first-hand** *adj*, *adv* di prima mano. **first name** nome di battesimo *m*.

fiscal ['fiskəl] *adj* fiscale.

fish [fiʃ] *n* pesce *m*. *v* pescare. **fishy** *adj* (*coll*) losco.

fishbone ['fiʃˌboun] *n* lisca *f*.

fisherman ['fiʃəmən] *n* pescatore *m*.

fish fingers *pl n* bastoncini di pesce *m pl*.

fishing ['fiʃiŋ] *n* pesca *f*. **fishing boat** peschereccio *m*. **fishing rod** canna da pesca *f*.

fishmonger ['fiʃ,mʌŋgə] *n* pescivendolo, -a *m, f.*
fishpond ['fiʃ,pond] *n* vivaio *m.*
fission ['fiʃən] *n* fissione *f.*
fissure ['fiʃə] *n* fessura *f.*
fist [fist] *n* pugno *m.*
fit[1] [fit] *adj* (*suitable*) adatto; competente; (*healthy*) sano. **keep fit** mantenersi sano, mantenersi in forma. *n* misura *f.* *v* (*clothes, etc.*) star bene; (*suit*) adeguare, convenire. **fit in** incastrare. **fitting** *adj* conveniente, adatto. **fittings** *pl n* suppellettili *m pl,* arredi *m pl.*
fit[2] [fit] *n* accesso *m,* attacco *m.* **fitful** *adj* intermittente.
five [faiv] *nm, adj* cinque.
fix [fiks] *v* fissare, stabilire. **fix up** sistemare, mettere a posto. *n* (*coll*) difficoltà *f,* guaio *m.* **fixation** *n* fissazione *f.* **fixed** *adj* fisso, stabile. **fixture** *n* (*accessory*) attrezzatura *f;* (*sport*) avvenimento sportivo *m.*
fizz [fiz] *v* frizzare. *n* spumante *m.* **fizzy** *adj* effervescente, frizzante.
fizzle ['fizl] *v* **fizzle out** far cilecca.
flabbergast ['flabəgaːst] *v* sbalordire.
flabby ['flabi] *adj* floscio, flaccido.
flag[1] [flag] *n* (*banner*) bandiera *f.* **flag-pole** *n* asta di bandiera *f.* **flagship** n nave ammiraglia *f.* *v* **flag down** intimare di fermarsi.
flag[2] [flag] *v* (*tire*) indebolirsi, accasciarsi.
flag[3] [flag] *n* (*stone*) lastra (di pietra) *f.*
flagon ['flagən] *n* bottiglione *m.*
flagrant ['fleigrənt] *adj* flagrante.
flair [fleə] *n* intuito *m,* inclinazione *f.*
flake [fleik] *v* sfaldare, sfaldarsi. *n* falda *f,* scaglia *f.* **flaky** *adj* a scaglie. **flaky pastry** sfoglia *f.*
flamboyant [flam'boiənt] *adj* sgargiante.
flame [fleim] *n* fiamma *f.* *v* fiammeggiare, risplendere. **burst into flames** divampare. **flaming** *adj* fiammeggiante, violento.
flamingo [flə'miŋgou] *n* fiammingo *m.*
flan [flan] *n* sformato *m,* torta *f.*
flank [flaŋk] *v* fiancheggiere. *n* fianco *m,* lato *m.*
flannel ['flanl] *n* (*fabric*) flanella *f;* (*face-cloth*) pezzuola per lavarsi *f.* *v* (*slang*) abbindolare con le chiacchiere.
flap [flap] *v* agitare; (*wings*) battere; (*coll*) agitarsi. *n* lembo *m;* (*wings*) colpo *m;* panico *m.*
flare [fleə] *n* fiammata *f,* bagliore *m;* (*rocket*) razzo *m.* *v* brillare; (*clothes*) svasare. **flare up** divampare; (*anger, etc.*) arrabbiarsi.
flash [flaʃ] *n* baleno *m,* lampo *m.* *v* balenare. **flashback** *n* scena retrospettiva *f,* flashback *m invar.* **flash bulb** lampadina flash *f.* **flashlight** *n* fotolampo *m,* flash *m invar.*
flask [flaːsk] *n* flacone *m,* borraccia *f.*
flat[1] [flat] *adj* piatto, piano; (*tyre*) a terra; (*net*) netto; (*stale*) svanito, insipido. *n* (*music*) bemolle *m.* **flat-footed** *adj* con i piedi piatti. **flat out** a briglia sciolta. *n* (*music*) bemolle *m.* **flatten** *v* appiattire, livellare.
flat[2] [flat] *n* appartamento *m.*
flatter ['flatə] *v* adulare, lusingare. **flatterer** *n* adulatore, -trice *m, f.* **flattering** *adj* lusinghiero. **flattery** *n* lusinghe *f pl,* adulazione *f.*
flatulence ['flatjuləns] *n* flatulenza *f.* **flatulent** *adj* flatulento.
flaunt [floːnt] *v* ostentare, pavoneggiarsi.
flautist ['floːtist] *n* flautista *m, f.*
flavour ['fleivə] *n* sapore *m,* gusto *m.* *v* condire. **flavouring** *n* condimento *m.*
flaw [floː] *n* tacca *f,* difetto *m.* **flawed** *adj* difettoso. **flawless** *adj* perfetto.
flax [flaks] *n* lino *m.* **flaxen** *adj* di lino; (*colour*) biondissimo.
flea [fliː] *n* pulce *f.*
fleck [flek] *n* chiazza *f,* macchia *f.* *v* chiazzare, macchiare.
fled [fled] *V* **flee.**
***flee** [fliː] *v* fuggire, scappare.
fleece [fliːs] *n* vello *m.* *v* (*coll*) pelare, derubare.
fleet [fliːt] *n* flotta *f;* (*of cars*) parco *m.*
fleeting ['fliːtiŋ] *adj* fugace, transitorio.
Flemish ['flemiʃ] *nm, adj* fiammingo.
flesh [fleʃ] *n* carne *f;* (*fruit*) polpa *f.*
flew [fluː] *V* **fly**[1].
flex [fleks] *v* flettere. *n* filo *or* cavo elettrico *m.* **flexible** *adj* flessibile. **flexibility** *n* flessibilità *f.*
flick [flik] *n* colpetto *m.* *v* dare un colpetto a.
flicker ['flikə] *v* tremolare. *n* tremolio *m.*
flight[1] [flait] *n* (*flying*) volo *m;* (*steps*) rampa *f.* **flighty** *adj* frivolo.
flight[2] [flait] *n* (*fleeing*) fuga *f.*
flimsy ['flimzi] *adj* tenue, fragile; (*inadequate*) insufficiente.
flinch [flintʃ] *v* (*wince*) sussultare; (*shrink from*) sottrarsi a. **without flinching** senza batter ciglio.

***fling** [fliŋ] *v* lanciare, scagliare, buttare. *n* **have one's fling** godersela.

flint [flint] *n* selce *f*; (*lighter*) pietrina *f*.

flip [flip] *n* colpetto *m*. *v* dare un colpetto a. **flip a coin** fare testa e croce. **flip through** sfogliare, dare una scorsa a.

flippant ['flipənt] *adj* poco serio, frivolo. **flippancy** *n* mancanza di serietà *f*.

flirt [fləːt] *v* flirtare. *n* dongiovanni *m*; civetta *f*.

flit [flit] *v* svolazzare; (*disappear*) squagliarsela.

float [flout] *v* galleggiare, stare a galla. *n* galleggiante *m*; (*angling*) sughero *m*; (*procession*) carro *m*.

flock[1] [flok] *n* (*animals*) branco *m*; (*birds*) stormo *m*; (*sheep*) gregge *m*; (*crowd*) folla *f*. *v* accorrere in massa, affluire. **flock together** radunarsi.

flock[2] [flok] *n* fiocco *m*; (*mattress filling*) borra *f*.

flog [flog] *v* bastonare, frustare; (*sell*) spacciare.

flood [flʌd] *v* inondare, allagare. *n* inondazione *f*, alluvione *f*, diluvio *m*; (*outpouring*) torrente *m*, ondata *f*. **floodlight** *n* riflettore *m*. **floodlit** *adj* illuminato a giorno.

floor [floː] *n* pavimento *m*; (*storey*) piano *m*. **floorboard** *n* tavola di pavimento *f*. **take the floor** (*speak*) prendere la parola; (*dance*) ballare. *v* pavimentare; (*knock down*) atterrare.

flop [flop] *n* tonfo *m*; (*coll*) fiasco *m*. *v* cader di schianto; (*coll*) fallire.

Florence ['florəns] *n* Firenze *f*. **Florentine** *n*, *adj* fiorentino, -a.

florist ['florist] *n* fioraio, -a *m*, *f*; fiorista *m*, *f*.

flotsam ['flotsəm] *n* relitti *m pl*. **flotsam and jetsam** (*people*) relitti umani *m pl*.

flounce[1] [flauns] *v* dimenare.

flounce[2] [flauns] *n* balza *f*.

flounder ['flaundə] *v* dibattersi, dimenarsi; (*speech*) impappinarsi. *n* passera di mare *f*.

flour ['flauə] *n* farina *f*. **floury** *adj* farinoso.

flourish ['flʌriʃ] *v* (*prosper*) fiorire; (*brandish*) brandire. *n* (*fanfare*) squillo di tromba *m*; (*writing*) ghirigoro *m*; (*speech*) fiorettatura *f*; (*gesture*) largo gesto *m*.

flout [flaut] *v* sprezzare, schernire.

flow [flou] *n* corrente *f*, flusso *m*. *v* scorrere, circolare.

flower ['flauə] *n* fiore *m*. **flower-bed** *n* aiuola *f*. **flower-pot** *n* vaso da fiori *m*. *v* fiorire, essere in fiore. **flowering** *adj* in fiore. **flowery** *adj* fiorito.

flown [floun] *V* **fly**[1].

flu [fluː] *n* influenza *f*.

fluctuate ['flʌktjuˌeit] *v* fluttuare. **fluctuation** *n* fluttuazione *f*.

flue [fluː] *n* gola del camino *f*.

fluent ['fluənt] *adj* corrente, scorrevole. **speak fluently** parlare correntemente.

fluff [flʌf] *n* lanugine *f*, peluria *f*.

fluid ['fluid] *nm*, *adj* fluido, liquido.

fluke [fluːk] *n* (*lucky chance*) colpo fortunato *m*.

flung [flʌŋ] *V* **fling**.

fluorescent [fluə'resnt] *adj* fluorescente.

fluoride ['fluəraid] *n* fluoruro *m*. **fluoridation** *n* fluorizzazione *f*.

flush[1] [flʌʃ] *n* (*colouring*) rossore *m*; (*rush of liquid*) flusso *m*; (*blushing*) vampa *f*; (*poker*) flush *m invar*. *v* (*wash out*) pulire con un getto d'acqua; (*lavatory*) vuotare; (*redden*) arrossire, avvampare.

flush[2] [flʌʃ] *adj* (*level*) a livello, rasente; (*slang*: *rich*) ben fornito.

fluster ['flʌstə] *v* turbare, confondere.

flute [fluːt] *n* flauto *m*.

flutter ['flʌtə] *v* battere; agitare, confondere; (*fly*) svolazzare. *n* battito *m*, agitazione *f*; (*bet*) scommessa *f*.

flux [flʌks] *n* flusso *m*.

***fly**[1] [flai] *v* volare; (*flutter*) svolazzare; (*flag*) sventolare; (*flee*) fuggire, scappare. **fly away** *or* **off** volar via. **flyleaf** *n* risguardo *m*. **flyover** *n* cavalcavia *m invar*. **flysheet** *n* volantino *m*. **flywheel** *n* volano *m*. **flying squad** squadra mobile *f*.

fly[2] [flai] *n* (*insect*) mosca *f*.

foal [foul] *n* puledro *m*.

foam [foum] *n* schiuma *f*. **foam rubber** gomma piuma *f*. *v* spumeggiare.

focus ['foukəs] *n* fuoco *m*, centro *m*. *v* concentrare; (*bring into focus*) mettere a fuoco. **focal** *adj* focale.

fodder ['fodə] *n* mangime *m*, foraggio *m*.

foe [fou] *n* nemico, -a *m*, *f*; avversario, -a *m*, *f*.

foetus ['fiːtəs] *n* feto *m*.

fog [fog] *n* nebbia *f*. **fog-bound** *adj* fermo per la nebbia. **fog-horn** *n* sirena da nebbia *f*. **foggy** *adj* nebbioso.

foible ['foibl] *n* debole *m*.
foil[1] [foil] *v* frustrare, sventare.
foil[2] [foil] *n* lamina (di metallo) *f*; (*tinfoil*) stagnolo *m*; (*contrast*) contrappeso *m*.
foist [foist] *v* rifilare, affibbiare.
fold[1] [fould] *v* piegare; (*envelop*) avvolgere. **fold one's arms** incrociare le braccia. **fold (up)** (*collapse*) chiudere, cessare l'esercizio. *n* piega *f*, ripiegatura *f*. **folder** *n* cartella *f*. **folding** *adj* pieghevole.
fold[2] [fould] *n* (*enclosure*) ovile *m*.
foliage ['fouliidʒ] *n* fogliame *m*.
folk [fouk] *n* gente *f*, popolo *m*. **folk dance** danza rustica *f*. **folklore** *n* folclore *m*. **folk song** canto popolare *m*.
follicle ['folikl] *n* follicolo *m*.
follow ['folou] *v* seguire, succedere; (*understand*) capire; (*result*) risultare, conseguire. **follower** *n* seguace *m*, *f*. **following** *adj* seguente, successivo.
folly ['foli] *n* follia *f*.
fond [fond] *adj* affettuoso, affezionato. **become fond of** affezionarsi a. **be fond of** voler bene a; (*person*) amare.
fondle ['fondl] *v* accarezzare, coccolare.
font [font] *n* fonte battesimale *f*.
food [fuːd] *n* cibo *m*, vitto *m*; (*foodstuffs*) generi alimentari *m pl*.
fool [fuːl] *n* sciocco, -a *m*, *f*; cretino, -a *m*, *f*; (*jester*) buffone, -a *m*, *f*, pagliaccio *m*. **foolhardy** *adj* temerario. **foolproof** *adj* sicurissimo. *v* (*deceive*) ingannare. **foolish** *adj* sciocco, insensato. **foolishness** *n* sciocchezza *f*.
foolscap ['fuːlskap] *n* carta protocollo *f*.
foot [fut] *n*, *pl* **feet** piede *m*; (*birds, animals*) zampa *f*. *v* **foot the bill** saldare il conto. **on foot** a piedi. **put one's foot down** farsi valere. **put one's foot in it** fare una gaffe.
football ['fut,boːl] *n* football *m invar*, pallone *m*. **footballer** *n* calciatore *m*.
foot-bridge ['fut,bridʒ] *n* passerella *f*.
foothold ['fut,hould] *n* punto d'appoggio *m*.
footing ['futiŋ] *n* (*foundation*) base *f*; (*mutual standing*) relazioni *f pl*.
footlights ['fut,laits] *pl n* luci della ribalta *f pl*.
footnote ['fut,nout] *n* postilla *f*, nota in calce *f*.
footpath ['fut,paːθ] *n* sentiero *m*.
footprint ['fut,print] *n* orma *f*.
footstep ['fut,step] *n* passo *m*.
footwear ['fut,weə] *n* calzatura *f*.
for [foː] *prep* per, a favore di, a, di, da. *conj* poiché.
forage ['foridʒ] *v* foraggiare. *n* foraggio *m*.
forbade [foː'bad] *V* **forbid**.
***forbear** [foː'beə] *v* astenersi da, pazientare.
***forbid** [foː'bid] *v* proibire, vietare. **forbidding** *adj* austero, formidabile.
forbidden [foː'bidn] *V* **forbid**.
force [foːs] *n* forza *f*. **in force** in vigore. *v* forzare; (*compel*) costringere. **forceful** *adj* energico.
forceps ['foːseps] *pl n* forcipe *m sing*.
ford [foːd] *n* guado *m*. *v* guadare.
fore [foː] *adj* anteriore. **come to the fore** venire alla ribalta.
forearm ['foːraːm] *n* avambraccio *m*.
forebear ['foːbeə] *n* antenato, -a *m*, *f*.
foreboding [foː'boudiŋ] *n* presagio *m*.
***forecast** ['foːkaːst] *n* previsione *f*, pronostico *m*. *v* prevedere.
forecourt ['foːkoːt] *n* cortile *m*.
forefather ['foːfaːðə] *n* antenato *m*, avo *m*.
forefinger ['foːfiŋgə] *n* indice *m*.
forefront ['foːfrʌnt] *n* prima linea *f*.
foreground ['foːgraund] *n* primo piano *m*.
forehand ['foːhand] *nm*, *adj* (*tennis*) diritto.
forehead ['forid] *n* fronte *f*.
foreign ['forən] *adj* straniero, forestiero; (*trade, etc.*) estero; (*not belonging*) estraneo. **foreigner** *n* straniero, -a *m*, *f*; forestiero, -a *m*, *f*.
foreleg ['foːleg] *n* zampa anteriore *f*.
foreman ['foːmən] *n* caposquadra (*pl* capisquadra) *m*, capo operaio *m*; (*jury*) presidente *m*.
foremost ['foːmoust] *adj* principale, primo. *adv* in primo luogo. **first and foremost** anzitutto.
forename ['foːneim] *n* nome di battesimo *m*.
forensic [fə'rensik] *adj* forense. **forensic medicine** medicina legale *f*.
forerunner ['foːrʌnə] *n* precursore *m*.
***foresee** [foː'siː] *v* prevedere. **foreseeable** *adj* prevedibile.
foreshadow [foː'ʃadou] *v* adombrare.
foreshorten [foː'ʃoːtn] *v* scorciare. **foreshortened** *adj* di scorcio.
foresight ['foːsait] *n* (*prevision*) preveggenza *f*; (*care for future*) previdenza *f*.

foreskin ['foːskin] *n* prepuzio *m*.
forest ['forist] *n* foresta *f*. **forester** *n* guardia forestale *f*. **forestry** *n* selvicoltura *f*.
forestall [foː'stoːl] *v* anticipare, prevenire.
foretaste ['foːteist] *n* pregustazione *f*.
***foretell** [foː'tel] *v* predire, pronosticare.
forethought ['foːθoːt] *n* premeditazione *f*, previdenza *f*.
forever [foː'evə] *adv* per sempre.
foreword ['foːwəːd] *n* prefazione *f*.
forfeit ['foːfit] *n* (*pawn*) pegno *m*; (*fine*) multa *f*. *v* (*give up*) dover abbandonare; pagare il fio.
forgave [fə'geiv] *V* **forgive**.
forge[1] [foːdʒ] *v* (*counterfeit*) falsificare, contraffare; (*metal*) forgiare. *n* fucina *f*. **forger** *n* falsario, -a *m*, *f*. **forgery** *n* contraffazione *f*, falso *m*.
forge[2] [foːdʒ] *v* avanzare. **forge ahead** farsi strada; (*take lead*) distanziarsi, staccarsi.
***forget** [fə'get] *v* dimenticare, scordare, non ricordarsi di. **forget-me-not** *n* nontiscordardimè *m*. **forget oneself** lasciarsi andare. **forgetful** *adj* smemorato.
***forgive** [fə'giv] *v* perdonare, rimettere. **forgiveness** *n* perdono *m*, indulgenza *f*. **forgiving** *adj* clemente, indulgente.
forgiven [fə'givn] *V* **forgive**.
***forgo** [foː'gou] *v* rinunciare a.
forgot [fə'got] *V* **forget**.
forgotten [fə'gotn] *V* **forget**.
fork [foːk] *n* (*cutlery*) forchetta *f*; (*agriculture*) forca *f*, forcone *m*; (*road*) bivio *m*; (*branching*) biforcazione *f*. *v* forcare; biforcarsi. **fork out** (*slang*: *pay*) metter mano alla borsa.
forlorn [fə'loːn] *adj* disperato, desolato.
form [foːm] *n* forma *f*; (*document*) modulo *m*; (*bench*) banco *m*; (*school*) classe *f*. *v* formare. **formation** *n* formazione *f*. **formative** *adj* formativo.
formal ['foːməl] *adj* formale, esplicito. **formality** *n* formalità *f*, cerimonia *f*.
format ['foːmat] *n* formato *m*.
former ['foːmə] *adj* precedente, anteriore. **the former** il primo. **formerly** *adv* in passato, già, in altri tempi.
formidable ['foːmidəbl] *adj* formidabile, spaventoso, terribile.
formula ['foːmjulə] *n*, *pl* **-ae** formula *f*.
formulate ['foːmjuˌleit] *v* formulare. **formulation** *n* formulazione *f*.
***forsake** [fə'seik] *v* abbandonare.
forsaken [fə'seikn] *V* **forsake**.
forsook [fə'suk] *V* **forsake**.
fort [foːt] *n* fortezza *f*, forte *m*.
forth [foːθ] *adv* avanti; (*out of concealment*) fuori. **and so forth** e cosi via. **forthcoming** *adj* imminente, prossimo. **forthright** *adj* franco, schietto. **forthwith** *adv* immediatamente.
fortify ['foːtiˌfai] *v* fortificare, rafforzare, dar forza a; (*wine*) alcolizzare. **fortification** *n* fortificazione *f*.
fortitude ['foːtiˌtjuːd] *n* forza d'animo *f*; (*virtue*) fortezza *f*.
fortnight ['foːtnait] *n* quindicina *f*, due settimane *f pl*. **fortnightly** *nm*, *adj* quindicinale, bimensile.
fortress ['foːtris] *n* fortezza *f*.
fortuitous [foː'tjuːitəs] *adj* fortuito.
fortune ['foːtʃən] *n* fortuna *f*; (*riches*) ricchezza *f*; futuro *m*. **fortune-teller** *n* chiromante *m*, *f*. **fortune-telling** *n* chiromanzia *f*. **fortunate** *adj* fortunato.
forty ['foːti] *nm*, *adj* quaranta. **fortieth** *nm*, *adj* quarantesimo.
forum ['foːrəm] *n* foro *m*; (*court*) tribuna *f*.
forward ['foːwəd] *adj* avanzato; presuntuoso. *adv also* **forwards** avanti, in avanti. **look forward to** anticipare con piacere. **put forward** proporre. *v* spedire, inoltrare; (*mail*) rispedire.
fossil ['fosl] *n* fossile *m*. **fossilized** *adj* fossilizzato.
foster ['fostə] *v* (*child*) allevare; incoraggiare; nutrire, alimentare. **foster-child** *n* figlio adottivo *m*. **foster-parents** *pl n* genitori adottivi *m pl*.
fought [foːt] *V* **fight**.
foul [faul] *adj* lurido, schifoso; (*weather*) pessimo. **foul play** (*crime*) delitto *m*; (*sport*) gioco falloso *m*.
found[1] [faund] *V* **find**.
found[2] [faund] *v* fondare, istituire, basare. **foundation** *n* fondazione *f*; istituto *m*; (*base*) fondamento *m*, base *f*. **founder** *n* fondatore, -trice *m*, *f*.
founder ['faundə] *v* (*sink*) colare a picco.
foundry ['faundri] *n* fonderia *f*.
fountain ['fauntin] *n* fontana *f*. **fountain pen** penna stilografica *f*.
four [foː] *nm*, *adj* quattro. **foursome** *n* quattro *m*. **on all fours** (a) carponi. **fourth** *nm*, *adj* quarto.

fourteen [fo:'ti:n] *nm, adj* quattordici. **fourteenth** *nm, adj* quattordicesimo.

fowl [faul] *n* pollame *m*; (*chicken*) pollo *m*.

fox [foks] *n* volpe *f*; (*sly person*) furbacchione *m*, furbo, -a *m, f*. **foxglove** *n* digitale *f*. **fox-hound** *n* bracco *m*. *v* (*coll*) ingannare. **foxed** *adj* perplesso.

foyer ['foiei] *n* ridotto *m*.

fraction ['frakʃən] *n* frazione *f*.

fracture ['fraktʃə] *n* frattura *f*, rottura *f*. *v* rompere, fratturare.

fragile ['fradʒail] *adj* fragile; (*delicate*) gracile.

fragment ['fragmənt] *n* frammento *m*.

fragrant ['freigrənt] *adj* fragrante, profumato. **fragrance** *n* profumo *m*.

frail [freil] *adj* fragile, gracile.

frame [freim] *n* struttura *f*; (*skeleton*) ossatura *f*; (*picture*) cornice *f*; (*machine*) telaio *m*. **frame of mind** disposizione d'animo *f*, umore *m*. **framework** *n* (*mech*) intelaiatura *f*; (*outline*) abbozzo *m*. *v* incorniciare, costruire; (*compose*) redigere; (*fabricate evidence*) calunniare.

France [fra:ns] *n* Francia *f*.

franchise ['frantʃaiz] *n* (*privilege*) franchigia *f*; (*comm*) concessione *f*.

frank [fraŋk] *adj* sincero, schietto. **frankness** *n* sincerità *f*, schiettezza *f*.

frantic ['frantik] *adj* frenetico.

fraternal [frə'tə:nl] *adj* fraterno. **fraternity** *n* fratellanza *f*; (*friendship*) fraternità *f*. **fraternize** *v* fraternizzare.

fraud [fro:d] *n* (*deceit*) frode *f*, inganno *m*; (*deceiver*) impostore, -a *m, f*, truffatore, -trice *m, f*. **fraudulent** *adj* fraudolento, doloso.

fraught [fro:t] *adj* (*tense*) nervoso. **fraught with** pieno *or* denso di.

fray[1] [frei] *v* (*unravel*) logorare, consumare. **frayed** *adj* (*clothes, etc.*) logoro dall'uso, liso. **frayed nerves** nervi scoperti *m pl*.

fray[2] [frei] *n* (*brawl*) mischia *f*.

freak [fri:k] *n* fenomeno *m*; figura grottesca *f*, mostro *m*.

freckle ['frekl] *n* lentiggine *f*. **freckled** *adj* lentigginoso.

free [fri:] *adj* libero; (*without payment*) gratis, gratuito; (*unconstrained*) disinvolto, sciolto; (*lavish*) generoso. **free from** esente da. **freehold** *n* proprietà fondiaria assoluta *f*. **freelance** *adj* indipendente. **Freemason** *n* massone *m*. **free speech** libertà di parola *f*. **free trade** libero scambio *m*. **free will** libero arbitrio *m*. *v* liberare. **freedom** *n* libertà *f*.

freesia ['fri:ziə] *n* fresia *f*.

***freeze** [fri:z] *v* gelare, congelare; (*block*) bloccare. *n* gelo *m*. **freezer** *n* congelatore *m*, freezer *m invar*. **freezing** *adj* gelido. **below freezing** sotto zero. **freezing point** punto di congelamento *m*.

freight [freit] *n* (*cargo*) carico *m*; (*charge*) nolo *m*; (*conveyance*) trasporto *m*. **freight train** treno merci *m*. *v* trasportare. **freighter** *n* nave da carico *f*.

French [frentʃ] *nm, adj* francese. **French bean** *n* fagiolino verde *m*, cornetto *m*. **French horn** corno (a pistoni) *m*. **Frenchman/woman** *n* francese *m, f*. **French window** portafinestra *f*.

frenzy ['frenzi] *n* frenesia *f*. **frenzied** *adj* frenetico.

frequent ['fri:kwənt; *v* fri'kwent] *adj* frequente. *v* frequentare. **frequency** *n* frequenza *f*.

fresco ['freskou] *n* affresco *f*.

fresh [freʃ] *adj* fresco; (*water*) dolce; (*brisk*) vigoroso; (*cheeky*) insolente. **fresh from** appena venuto da. **freshman** *n* matricola *f*. **freshen** *v* rinfrescare, rinnovare. **freshness** *n* freschezza *f*, vigore *m*.

fret[1] [fret] *v* inquietarsi. **fretful** *adj* irritabile.

fret[2] [fret] *n* (*pattern*) fregio *m*. *v* ornare con fregi, traforare. **fretwork** *n* lavoro di traforo *m*.

friar ['fraiə] *n* frate *m*. **friary** *n* convento di frati *m*.

friction ['frikʃən] *n* attrito *m*; (*conflict*) dissenso *m*.

Friday ['fraidei] *n* venerdì *m*.

fridge [fridʒ] *n* (*coll*) frigorifero *m*.

fried [fraid] *adj* fritto.

friend [frend] *n* amico, -a *m, f*. **make friends** fare amicizia. **friendless** *adj* senza amici. **friendliness** *n* amichevolezza *f*, cordialità *f*. **friendly** *adj* amichevole, cordiale, gentile. **be friendly with** essere amico di. **friendship** *n* amicizia *f*.

frieze [fri:z] *n* fregio *m*.

frigate ['frigit] *n* fregata *f*.

fright [frait] *n* spavento *m*. **frighten** *v* spaventare, allarmare. **be frightened** aver paura. **frightening** *adj* spaventevole, terribile. **frightful** *adj* terribile.

frigid ['fridʒid] *adj* freddo; (*woman*) frigido. **frigidity** *n* freddezza *f*; frigidità *f*.
frill [fril] *n* fronzolo *m*. **frilly** *adj* carico di fronzoli.
fringe [frindʒ] *n* (*border*) orlo *m*; limite *m*; (*ornamental border, hair*) frangia *f*; periferia *f*. *v* ornare di frange.
frisk [frisk] *v* saltellare; (*search*) perquisire. **frisky** *adj* vivace.
fritter[1] ['fritə] *v* **fritter away** sprecare.
fritter[2] ['fritə] *n* (*cookery*) frittella *f*.
frivolity [fri'voliti] *n* frivolezza *f*. **frivolous** *adj* superficiale, frivolo.
frizz [friz] *v* arricciare. *n* ricciolo *m*. **frizzy** *adj* ricciuto.
fro [frou] *adv* **to and fro** avanti e indietro.
frock [frok] *n* vestito *m*.
frog [frog] *n* rana *f*. **frogman** *n* uomo rana *m*.
frolic ['frolik] *v* trastullarsi, scherzare. *n* scherzo *m*.
from [from] *prep* da, per, da parte di.
front [frʌnt] *n* parte anteriore *f*; (*mil, pol*) fronte *m*; (*arch*) facciata *f*; (*seaside*) lungomare *m*. *adj* primo, anteriore. **front door** portone *m*. **in front of** davanti a.
frontier ['frʌntiə] *n* frontiera *f*, confine *m*.
frost [frost] *n* gelo *m*. **frost-bite** *n* gelone *m*. *v* brinare; (*cookery*) glassare. **frosted glass** vetro smerigliato *m*. **frosty** *adj* (*weather*) gelido; (*manner*) freddo.
froth [froθ] *n* schiuma *f*. *v* spumare, schiumare.
frown [fraun] *v* aggrottare le ciglia, corrugare la fronte. **frown at** guardare in cagnesco. *n* cipiglio *m*, viso arcigno *m*.
froze [frouz] *V* **freeze**.
frozen ['frouzn] *V* **freeze**. *adj* gelato, congelato; bloccato.
frugal ['fruːgəl] *adj* frugale, sobrio.
fruit [fruːt] *n* frutto *m*; (*collectively*) frutta *f*; (*result*) risultato *m*. **fruit salad** macedonia di frutta *f*. *v* (*bear fruit*) fruttare. **fruiterer** *n* fruttivendolo, -a *m, f*. **fruitful** *adj* fecondo; (*profitable*) redditizio. **fruition** *n* realizzazione *f*. **fruitless** *adj* infruttuoso; inutile. **fruity** *adj* saporito; di frutta; (*wine*) dal gusto d'uva.
frustrate [frʌ'streit] *v* frustrare. **frustration** *n* frustrazione *f*.
fry [frai] *v* friggere. **frying pan** padella *f*.
fuchsia ['fjuːʃə] *n* fucsia *f*.
fuck [fʌk] *v* (*vulgar*) fottere, chiavare.
fuel ['fjuəl] *n* combustibile *m*; (*mot*) carburante *m*. **fuel oil** gasolio *m*, nafta *f*. *v* alimentare.
fugitive ['fjuːdʒitiv] *adj* (*runaway*) fuggitivo, fuggiasco; (*fleeting*) effimero, fugace. *n* fuggiasco, -a *m, f*; profugo, -a *m, f*.
fugue [fjuːg] *n* fuga *f*.
fulcrum ['fulkrəm] *n* fulcro *m*.
fulfil [ful'fil] *v* adempiere, compiere, soddisfare. **fulfilment** *n* adempimento *m*, realizzazione *f*.
full [ful] *adj* pieno; completo; intero. **full-length** *adj* di lunghezza normale; (*portrait*) in piedi. **full moon** luna piena *f*. **full-sized** *adj* di grandezza naturale. **full stop** punto *m*. **full-time** *adj, adv* a tempo intero, a orario completo. **fully** *adv* completamente.
fumble ['fʌmbl] *v* brancolare.
fume [fjuːm] *v* emettere fumo; (*coll: rage*) arrabbiarsi, imperversare. *n* fumo *m*, esalazione *f*.
fumigate ['fjuːmigeit] *v* suffumicare.
fun [fʌn] *n* spasso *m*, divertimento *m*, scherzo *m*. **funfair** *n* luna park *m invar*. **in fun** per ridere. **make fun of** prendere in giro.
function ['fʌŋkʃən] *n* funzione *f*; (*purpose*) scopo *m*; (*duty*) mansione *f*; (*ceremony*) cerimonia *f*. *v* funzionare. **functional** *adj* funzionale.
fund [fʌnd] *n* fondo *m*, riserva *f*, capitale *m*. **funds** *pl n* soldi *m pl*.
fundamental [fʌndə'mentl] *adj* fondamentale, basilare.
funeral ['fjuːnərəl] *n* funerale *m*. *adj* funebre. **funereal** *adj* funereo.
fungus ['fʌŋgəs] *n, pl* **-gi** fungo *m*. **fungicide** *n* anticrittogamico *m*.
funnel ['fʌnl] *n* imbuto *m*; (*ship*) ciminiera *f*.
funny ['fʌni] *adj* divertente, comico; (*odd*) strano. **funny story** barzelletta *f*. **the funny thing is** il bello è.
fur [fəː] *n* (*skin*) pelo *m*; pelliccia *f*. *v* incrostarsi. **furrier** *n* pellicciaio *m*. **furry** *adj* peloso.
furious ['fjuəriəs] *adj* furibondo, arrabbiatissimo.
furnace ['fəːnis] *n* fornace *f*.
furnish ['fəːniʃ] *v* (*supply*) fornire, dotare; (*house, etc.*) arredare, ammobiliare.
furniture ['fəːnitʃə] *n* mobilio *m*, mobili *m pl*; (*fittings*) attrezzatura *f*.

furrow ['fʌrou] *n* solco *m*; (*brow*) ruga *f*, grinza *f*.
further ['fəːðə] *adj* ulteriore, più lontano. *adv* più lontano, oltre. **furthermore** *adv* inoltre. **further on** più avanti. **further up** più in su. *v* favorire, promuovere.
furthest ['fəːðist] *adj* in più lontano, estremo.
furtive ['fəːtiv] *adj* furtivo, di soppiatto.
fury ['fjuəri] *n* furia *f*.
fuse[1] [fjuːz] *n* (*elec*) valvola *f*, fusibile *m*. **blow a fuse** saltare la corrente. *v* (*melt*) fondere; (*blend*) amalgamare, unire. **fusion** *n* fusione *f*.
fuse[2] [fjuːz] *n* (*bomb*) detonatore *m*.
fuselage ['fjuːzəˌlaːʒ] *n* fusoliera *f*.
fuss [fʌs] *v* lamentarsi, agitarsi. **fuss over** affaccendarsi attorno a. *n* scalpore *m*, trambusto *m*. **make a fuss** fare un gran chiasso. **fussy** *adj* pignolo, meticoloso.
futile ['fjuːtail] *adj* vano, inutile. **futility** *n* inutilità *f*.
future ['fjuːtʃə] *n* futuro *m*, avvenire *m*. *adj* futuro.
fuzz [fʌz] *n* lanugine *f*, peluria *f*. **fuzzy** *adj* peloso; (*unclear*) sfocato.

G

gabble ['gabl] *v* borbottare. *n* borbottio *m*.
gaberdine [gabə'diːn] *n* gabardina *f*.
gable ['geibl] *n* pigna *f*, frontone *m*.
gadget ['gadʒit] *n* congegno *m*, dispositivo *m*.
gag[1] [gag] *n* bavaglio *m*. *v* imbavagliare.
gag[2] [gag] *n* (*joke*) battuta *f*.
gaiety ['geiəti] *n* allegria *f*.
gaily ['geili] *adv* allegramente.
gain [gein] *n* guadagno *m*, profitto *m*. *v* guadagnare; (*obtain*) ottenere.
gait [geit] *n* andatura *f*, passo *m*.
gala ['gaːlə] *n* festa *f*.
galaxy ['galəksi] *n* galassia *f*.
gale [geil] *n* bufera *f*, burrasca *f*.
gallant ['galənt] *adj* (*courageous*) prode; (*courtly*) galante. *n* cavaliere *m*. **gallantry** *n* valore *m*, coraggio *m*; galanteria *f*.
gall-bladder ['goːlˌbladə] *n* cistifellea *f*, vescica biliare *f*.
galleon ['galiən] *n* galeone *m*.
gallery ['galəri] *n* galleria *f*; (*theatre*) loggione *m*.
galley ['gali] *n* (*naut*) galea *f*; (*kitchen*) cambusa *f*.
gallop ['galəp] *n* galoppo *m*; galoppata *f*. *v* galoppare, andare al galoppo.
gallows ['galouz] *n* patibolo *m*.
gallstone ['goːlstoun] *n* calcolo biliare *m*.
galore [gə'loː] *adv* in quantità.
galvanize ['galvənaiz] *v* galvanizzare. **galvanometer** *n* galvanometro *m*.
gambit ['gambit] *n* gambetto *m*.
gamble ['gambl] *v* (*risk*) rischiare, arrischiare; (*game*) giocare. *n* impresa rischiosa *f*, speculazione *f*. **gambler** *n* giocatore, -trice *m*, *f*. **gambling** *n* gioco d'azzardo *m*.
game [geim] *n* gioco *m*; (*match*) partita *f*; (*hunting*) selvaggina *f*. **gamekeeper** *n* guardacaccia *m*. *adj* (*plucky*) che ha del fegato.
gammon ['gamən] *n* prosciutto *m*.
gander ['gandə] *n* papero *m*.
gang [gaŋ] *n* squadra *f*, gruppo *m*; (*youths*, *thieves*, *etc.*) banda *f*. *v* **gang up** allearsi. **gangster** *n* gangster *m invar*, bandito *m*.
gangling ['gaŋgliŋ] *adj* allampanato.
gangrene ['gaŋgriːn] *n* cancrena *f*.
gangway ['gaŋwei] *n* passaggio *m*, corsia *f*; (*naut*) barcarizzo *m*.
gaol *V* **jail**.
gap [gap] *n* (*breach*) breccia *f*; (*opening*) apertura *f*; (*hole*) buco *m*; (*vacant space*) vuoto *m*; intervallo *m*; (*divergence*) distacco *m*.
gape [geip] *v* stare a bocca aperta; (*open wide*) spalancare.
garage ['garaːdʒ] *n* garage *m invar*; (*repairs*) autorimessa *f*.
garbage ['gaːbidʒ] (*US*) *n* rifiuti *m pl*. **garbage can** bidone della spazzatura *m*.
garble ['gaːbl] *v* mutilare.
garden ['gaːdn] *n* giardino *m*. *v* fare del giardinaggio. **gardener** *n* giardiniere, -a *m*, *f*. **gardening** *n* giardinaggio *m*.
gargle ['gaːgl] *v* gargarizzare. *n* gargarismo *m*.
garish ['geəriʃ] *adj* vistoso.
garland ['gaːlənd] *n* ghirlanda *f*. *v* inghirlandare.
garlic ['gaːlik] *n* aglio *m*.
garment ['ga:mənt] *n* indumento *m*, capo di vestiario *m*.
garnish ['gaːniʃ] *v* guarnire, adornare. *n* ornamento *m*, guarnizione *f*.

garret ['garət] *n* soffitta *f*.
garrison ['garisn] *n* guarnigione *f*, presidio *m*. *v* presidiare.
garrulous ['garələs] *adj* loquace.
garter ['gaːtə] *n* giarrettiera *f*.
gas [gas] *n* gas *m invar*; (*US*: *petrol*) benzina *f*. **gas cooker** fornello a gas *m*. **gas fire** stufa a gas *f*. **gas mask** maschera antigas *f*. *v* asfissiare.
gash [gaʃ] *n* sfregio *m*, squarcio *m*. *v* sfregiare, squarciare.
gasket ['gaskit] *n* guarnizione *f*.
gasoline ['gasəˌliːn] *n* (*US*) benzina *f*.
gasp [gaːsp] *v* boccheggiare, ansimare. *n* rantolo *m*.
gastric ['gastrik] *adj* gastrico.
gastronomy [ga'stronəmi] *n* gastronomia *f*. **gastronomic** *adj* gastronomico.
gate [geit] *n* cancello *m*, porta *f*. **gatecrash** *v* fare il portoghese, entrare senza invito *or* pagare. **gatepost** *n* montante del cancello *m*. **gateway** *n* entrata *f*, portone *m*.
gateau ['gatou] *n* pasticcino *m*, gateau *m*.
gather ['gaðə] *v* cogliere; (*bring together*) raccogliere; (*infer*) dedurre; (*assemble*) radunarsi. **gathering** *n* riunione *f*, adunata *f*.
gaudy ['goːdi] *adj* vistoso.
gauge [geidʒ] *n* (*measure*) misura *f*; (*instrument*) calibro *m*; (*rail*) scartamento *m*. *v* misurare, calibrare.
gaunt [goːnt] *adj* emaciato, desolato.
gauze [goːz] *n* garza *f*.
gave [geiv] *V* **give**.
gay [gei] *adj* vivace, allegro; (*slang*) omosessuale.
gaze [geiz] *v* mirare, guardare fissamente. **gaze at** fissare. *n* sguardo fisso *m*.
gazelle [gə'zel] *n* gazzella *f*.
gazette [gə'zet] *n* gazzetta ufficiale *f*.
gazetteer [gazə'tiə] *n* dizionario geografico *m*.
gear [giə] *n* (*mot*) marcia *f*, velocità *f*; (*equipment*, *tools*) arnesi *m pl*, attrezzatura *f*; (*belongings*) roba *f*. **change gear** cambiare velocità. **gearbox** *n* scatola del cambio *f*. **gear lever** leva del cambio *f*. *v* preparare, adattare.
gelatine ['dʒeləˌtiːn] *n* gelatina *f*.
gelignite ['dʒeligˌnait] *n* gelatina esplosiva *f*.
gem [dʒem] *n* gemma *f*.
Gemini ['dʒemini] *n* Gemelli *m pl*.
gender ['dʒendə] *n* genere *m*, sesso *m*.
gene [dʒiːn] *n* gene *m*.
genealogy [dʒiːniˌalədʒi] *n* genealogia *f*. **genealogical** *adj* genealogico.
general ['dʒenərəl] *nm*, *adj* generale. **general practitioner** medico generico *m*. **generalization** *n* generalizzazione *f*. **generalize** *v* generalizzare.
generate ['dʒenəreit] *v* generare, produrre. **generation** *n* generazione *f*. **generator** *n* generatore *m*.
generic [dʒi'nerik] *adj* generico.
generous ['dʒenərəs] *adj* generoso. **generosity** *n* generosità *f*.
genetic [dʒi'netik] *adj* genetico. **geneticist** *n* genetista *m*, *f*. **genetics** *n* genetica *f*.
Geneva [dʒi'niːvə] *n* Ginevra *f*.
genial ['dʒiːniəl] *adj* gioviale, simpatico.
genital ['dʒenitl] *adj* genitale. **genitals** *pl n* organi genitali *m pl*.
genius ['dʒiːnjəs] *n* genio *m*.
Genoa ['dʒenouə] *n* Genova *f*. **Genoese** *n*(*m*+*f*), *adj* genovese.
genteel [dʒen'tiːl] *adj* signorile. **gentility** *n* signorilità *f*.
gentle ['dʒentl] *adj* tenero; (*mild*) mite; (*not steep*) dolce. **gentleman** *n* signore *m*; (*of good breeding*, *etc.*) gentiluomo *m*. **gentlemanly** *adj* signorile. **gentleness** *n* dolcezza *f*. **gently** *adv* dolcemente; adagio, piano.
gentry ['dʒentri] *n* piccola nobiltà *f*.
gents [dʒents] *n* (*sign*) uomini, signori.
genuine ['dʒenjuin] *adj* genuino, autentico; sincero. **genuinely** *adv* (*really*) veramente.
genus ['dʒiːnəs] *n* genere *m*.
geography [dʒi'ogrəfi] *n* geografia *f*. **geographer** *n* geografo, -a *m*, *f*. **geographical** *adj* geografico.
geology [dʒi'olədʒi] *n* geologia *f*. **geological** *adj* geologico. **geologist** *n* geologo, -a *m*, *f*.
geometry [dʒi'omətri] *n* geometria *f*. **geometric** *adj* geometrico.
geranium [dʒə'reiniəm] *n* geranio *m*.
geriatric [dʒeri'atrik] *adj* geriatrico. **geriatrics** *n* geriatria *f*.
germ [dʒəːm] *n* germe *m*.
Germany ['dʒəːməni] *n* Germania *f*. **German** *n*, *adj* tedesco, -a. **German measles** rosolia *f*, rubeola *f*.
germinate ['dʒəːmineit] *v* germinare. **germination** *n* germinazione *f*.

gerund ['dʒerənd] *n* gerundio *m*.
gesticulate [dʒe'stikju,leit] *v* gesticolare. **gesticulation** *n* gesticolazione *f*.
gesture ['dʒestʃə] *n* gesto *m*. *v* gesticolare, fare gesti.
***get** [get] *v* (*obtain*) ottenere, procurare; (*fetch*) andare a prendere; (*receive*) ricevere; (*understand*) capire; (*become*) diventare; (*reach*) arrivare. **get across** attraversare; (*make understand*) far capire. **get along with** andare d'accordo con. **get at** (*reach*) raggiungere; (*hint*) alludere. **getaway** *n* fuga *f*. **get off** scendere. **get out** uscire. **get up** alzarsi.
geyser ['giːzə] *n* (*geog*) geyser *m*; (*water-heater*) scaldabagno *m*.
ghastly ['gaːstli] *adj* orrendo; (*pale*) spettrale.
gherkin ['gəːkin] *n* cetriolino *m*.
ghetto ['getou] *n* ghetto *m*.
ghost [goust] *n* fantasma *m*, spettro *m*. **ghostly** *adj* spettrale.
giant ['dʒaiənt] *n* gigante, -essa *m, f*. *adj* gigantesco, gigante.
gibberish ['dʒibəriʃ] *n* discorso incomprensibile *m*.
gibe [dʒaib] *n* beffa *f*; scherno *m*. *v* **gibe at** beffarsi di, beffare.
giblets ['dʒiblits] *pl n* rigaglie *f pl*, frattaglie *f pl*.
giddy ['gidi] *adj* (*flighty*) incostante, volubile; (*dizzy*) preso da vertigini; (*height*) vertiginoso. **feel giddy** avere il capogiro. **giddiness** *n* capogiro *m*, vertigini *f pl*.
gift [gift] *n* dono *m*, regalo *m*. **gifted** *adj* dotato.
gigantic [dʒai'gantik] *adj* gigantesco.
giggle ['gigl] *v* ridere scioccamente. *n* risatina sciocca *f*. **have the giggles** avere la ridarella.
gill [gil] *n* (*fish*) branchia *f*; (*mushroom*) lamella *f*.
gilt [gilt] *n* doratura *f*. *adj* dorato.
gimmick ['gimik] *n* (*coll*: *device*) congegno *m*; stratagemma *m*.
gin [dʒin] *n* gin *m invar*.
ginger ['dʒindʒə] *n* zenzero *m*. *adj* fulvo.
gingerly ['dʒindʒəli] *adj* cauto.
gipsy ['dʒipsi] *n* zingaro, -a *m, f*.
giraffe [dʒi'raːf] *n* giraffa *f*.
girder ['gəːdə] *n* trave maestra *f*, putrella *f*.
girdle ['gəːdl] *n* busto *m*, cintura *f*. *v* cingere.
girl [gəːl] *n* ragazza *f*. **girlfriend** *n* amica *f*. **girlish** *adj* da ragazza.
giro ['dʒairou] *n* giroconto *m*, postagiro *m*.
girth [gəːθ] *n* circonferenza *f*.
gist [dʒist] *n* nocciolo *m*.
***give** [giv] *v* dare; (*present*) regalare; (*relinquish*) cedere. **give away** regalare; (*betray*) tradire; (*secret*) rivelare. **give back** restituire. **give in** cedere. **give oneself up** costituirsi. **give out** distribuire. **give rise to** risultare in. **give up** abbandonare; (*cease*) smettere. *n* elasticità *f*.
given ['givn] *V* **give**.
glacier ['glasiə] *n* ghiacciaio *m*.
glad [glad] *adj* lieto, contento. **gladden** *v* rallegrare. **gladly** *adv* con piacere.
glamour [glamə] *n* fascino *m*. **glamorous** *adj* affascinante.
glance [glaːns] *n* sguardo *m*. **at a glance** a prima vista. *v* dare un'occhiata.
gland [gland] *n* ghiandola *f*. **glandular** *adj* ghiandolare.
glare [gleə] *n* (*light*) bagliore *m*; (*fierce look*) sguardo torvo *m*. *v* **glare at** guardare con cipiglio, guardare con occhio torvo.
glass [glaːs] *n* vetro *m*; (*container*) bicchiere *m*. **glasses** *pl n* occhiali *m pl*. **glassy** *adj* vitreo.
glaze [gleiz] *n* smalto *m*, patina *f*. *v* smaltare, verniciare; (*fit with glass*) fornire di vetri.
gleam [gliːm] *v* luccicare. *n* barlume *m*, luccichio *m*.
glean [gliːn] *v* racimolare.
glee [gliː] *n* gioia *f*. **gleeful** *adj* pieno di gioia.
glib [glib] *adj* facondo.
glide [glaid] *v* scivolare, scorrere; (*aero*) planare. **glider** *n* aliante *m*. **gliding** *n* volo a vela *m*.
glimmer ['glimə] *v* luccicare; (*of dawn*) albeggiare. *n* barlume *m*, luccichio *m*.
glimpse [glimps] *n* occhiata *f*, visione *f*. *v* intravedere.
glint [glint] *n* luccichio *m*. *v* luccicare, scintillare.
glisten ['glisn] *v* luccicare, brillare.
glitter ['glitə] *v* brillare, scintillare. *n* lucentezza *f*.
gloat [glout] *v* gongolare (malignamente).

globe [gloub] *n* globo *m*. **global** *adj* globale.
gloom [gluːm] *n* (*darkness*) oscurità *f*; (*depression*) malinconia *f*, tristezza *f*. **gloomy** *adj* malinconico, triste.
glory ['gloːri] *n* gloria *f*, splendore *m*. **glorify** *v* glorificare. **glorious** *adj* illustre, splendido.
gloss[1] [glos] *n* (*lustre*) lucentezza *f*; (*appearance*) apparenza *f*. **glossy** *adj* lucido.
gloss[2] [glos] *n* (*explanation*) chiosa *f*. *v* chiosare, commentare.
glossary ['glosəri] *n* lessico *m*.
glove [glʌv] *n* guanto *m*.
glow [glou] *v* risplendere; ardere. *n* rossore *m*; (*colour*) luminosità *f*. **glowing** *adj* acceso, ardente; fervente.
glucose ['gluːkous] *n* glucosio *m*.
glue [gluː] *n* colla *f*. *v* incollare.
glum [glʌm] *adj* tetro, cupo.
glut [glʌt] *n* sovrabbondanza *f*. *v* saturare.
glutton ['glʌtən] *n* ghiottone, -a *m*, *f*; goloso, -a *m*, *f*. **gluttonous** *adj* ghiotto, goloso. **gluttony** *n* golosità *f*.
gnarled [naːld] *adj* nodoso.
gnash [naʃ] *v* **gnash one's teeth** digrignare i denti.
gnat [nat] *n* zanzara *f*.
gnaw [noː] *v* rodere, rosicchiare. **gnawing** *adj* rosicante.
gnome [noum] *n* gnomo *m*.
***go** [gou] *v* andare; (*become*) diventare. **go away** andarsene. **go back** ritornare. **go-between** *n* intermediario *m*. **go by** passare; (*be guided by*) regolarsi su. **go down** scendere; (*sink*) affondare. **go in** entrare. **go off** esplodere; (*spoil*) guastarsi; (*leave*) andarsene. **go on** continuare. **go out** uscire. **go up** salire. **go without** fare a meno di. *n* energia *f*; (*try*) colpo *m*. **on the go** molto attivo.
goad [goud] *n* pungolo *m*. *v* incitare.
goal [goul] *n* (*aim*) meta *f*; (*sport*) porta *f*, rete *f*. **goalkeeper** *n* portiere *m*. **goal-post** *n* palo della porta *m*.
goat [gout] *n* capra *f*.
gobble ['gobl] *v* inghiottire.
goblin ['goblin] *n* folletto *m*.
god [god] *n* dio (*pl* dei) *m*. **goddaughter** *n* figlioccia *f*. **godfather** *n* padrino *m*. **godmother** *n* madrina *f*. **godson** *n* figlioccio *m*. **goddess** *n* dea *f*.
goggles ['goglz] *pl n* occhiali di protezione *m pl*.
gold [gould] *n* oro *m*. **goldfinch** *n* cardellino *m*. **goldfish** *n* pesce dorato *or* rosso *m*. **gold mine** miniera d'oro *f*. **goldsmith** *n* orefice *m*. **golden** *adj* d'oro; (*colour*) aureo. **golden rule** regola d'oro *f*.
golf [golf] *n* golf *m*. **golf course** campo di golf *m*. **golfer** *n* giocatore, -trice di golf *m*, *f*.
gondola ['gondələ] *n* gondola *f*.
gone [gon] *V* **go**.
gong [goŋ] *n* gong *m invar*.
gonorrhoea [ˌgonə'riə] *n* gonorrea *f*.
good [gud] *adj* buono; valido; (*well-behaved, clever*) bravo. **good afternoon** buon giorno; (*later*) buona sera. **goodbye** *interj* addio; arrivederci; (*coll*) ciao. **good-for-nothing** *n* buono a nulla *m*. **good-looking** *adj* bello. **good morning** buon giorno. **goodnight** *interj* buona notte. **goodwill** *n* benevolenza *f*; (*comm*) avviamento *m*. *n* bene *m*, vantaggio *m*. **be no good** non servire. **for good** per sempre. **goodness** *n* bontà *f*, gentilezza *f*, virtù *f*.
Good Friday *n* Venerdi Santo *m*.
goods [gudz] *pl n* merce *f pl*, beni *m pl*. **goods train** treno merci *m*.
goose [guːs] *n*, *pl* **geese** oca *f*.
gooseberry ['guzbəri] *n* uva spina *f*.
gore [goː] *v* trafiggere.
gorge [goːdʒ] *n* (*geol*) gola *f*. *v* rimpinzarsi (di).
gorgeous ['goːdʒəs] *adj* splendido.
gorilla [gə'rilə] *n* gorilla *m invar*.
gorse [goːs] *n* ginestrone *m*.
gory [goːri] *adj* cruento.
gosling ['gozliŋ] *n* papero, -a *m*, *f*.
gospel ['gospəl] *n* vangelo *m*; (*coll*: *truth*) verità implicita *f*.
gossip ['gosip] *n* ciarla *f*, pettegolezzo *m*; (*person*) ciarlone, -a *m*, *f*, chiacchierone, -a *m*, *f*. *v* ciarlare, chiacchierare.
got [got] *V* **get**.
Gothic ['goθik] *adj* gotico.
gourd [guəd] *n* zucca *f*.
gourmet ['guəmei] *n* buongustaio, -a *m*, *f*.
gout [gaut] *n* gotta *f*.
govern ['gʌvən] *v* governare *f*; (*gramm*) reggere. **governess** *n* governante *f*. **government** *n* governo *m*. **governor** *n* governatore *m*; (*coll*: *boss*) capo *m*.
gown [gaun] *n* (*dress*) veste *f*; (*robe*) toga *f*.

grab [grab] *v* arraffare. *n* strappo *m*.
grace [greis] *n* grazia *f*, eleganza *f*. *v* adornare. **graceful** *adj* grazioso. **gracious** *adj* benigno.
grade [greid] *n* grado *m*; (*level*) livello *m*; classe *f*. *v* classificare.
gradient ['greidiənt] *n* gradiente *m*; (*slope*) pendio *m*.
gradual ['gradjuəl] *adj* graduale. **gradually** *adv* poco a poco.
graduate ['gradjuət; *v* 'gradjueit] *n* laureato, -a *m*, *f*. *v* laurearsi.
graft[1] [graːft] *n* (*bot*) innesto *m*; (*med*) trapianto *m*; (*hard work*) sgobbata *f*. *v* innestare; trapiantare; sgobbare.
graft[2] [graːft] *n* (*bribery*) corruzione *f*. *v* corrompere.
grain [grein] *n* (*seed*) chicco *m*, granello *m*; (*wheat*) grano *m*; (*wood*) venatura *f*; (*leather*) grana *f*. **against the grain** contro pelo.
gram [gram] *n* grammo *m*.
grammar ['gramə] *n* grammatica *f*. **grammatical** *adj* grammaticale.
gramophone ['graməfoun] *n* grammofono *m*.
granary ['granəri] *n* granaio *m*.
grand [grand] *adj* (*imposing*) grandioso; (*first rate*) splendido. **grandchild** *n* nipote *m*, *f*; nipotino, -a *m*, *f*. **grandfather** *n* nonno *m*. **grandmother** *n* nonna *f*. **grand piano** pianoforte a coda *m*. **grandstand** *n* tribuna coperta *f*. **grand total** somma *f*. **grandeur** *n* grandiosità *f*.
granite ['granit] *n* granito *m*.
grant [graːnt] *v* (*confer*) concedere, accordare; (*give*) dare; (*admit*) ammettere. **take for granted** ritenere per certo. *n* (*student*) borsa di studio *f*; concessione *f*.
granule ['granjuːl] *n* granello *m*.
grape [greip] *n* acino *m*, chicco d'uva *m*. **grapes** *pl n* uva *f sing*. **grapevine** *n* vite *f*; (*coll*) canali confidenziali *m pl*.
grapefruit ['greipfruːt] *n* pompelmo *m*.
graph [graf] *n* (*math*) grafico *m*; diagramma *m*. **graphic** *adj* grafico. **graph paper** carta millimetrata *f*.
grapple ['grapl] *v* **grapple with** venire alle prese con.
grasp [graːsp] *v* afferrare; (*understand*) capire. *n* stretta *f*. **grasping** *adj* avaro.
grass [graːs] *n* erba *f*; (*lawn*) prato *m*. **grasshopper** *n* cavalletta *f*. **grassy** *adj* erboso.
grate[1] [greit] *n* graticola *f*. **grating** *n* inferriata *f*.
grate[2] [greit] *v* grattugiare; (*sound harshly*) stridere; (*irritate*) dare sui nervi.
grateful ['greitful] *adj* riconoscente, grato.
gratify ['grati͵fai] *v* appagare.
gratitude ['gratitjuːd] *n* gratitudine *f*.
gratuitous [grə'tjuitəs] *adj* (*free*) gratuito; (*without cause*) ingiustificato.
gratuity [grə'tjuəti] *n* (*tip*) mancia *f*; (*unsolicited gift*) gratifica *f*.
grave[1] [greiv] *n* tomba *f*, sepolcro *m*. **gravedigger** *n* becchino *m*. **gravestone** *n* lapide funeraria *f*. **graveyard** *n* cimitero *m*.
grave[2] [greiv] *adj* grave.
gravel ['gravəl] *n* ghiaia *f*.
gravity ['gravəti] *n* gravità *f*. **gravitate** *v* gravitare.
gravy ['greivi] *n* sugo di carne *m*; salsa *f*.
graze[1] [greiz] *v* (*touch*) sfiorare; (*scrape*) scalfire. *n* scalfitura *f*, lesione superficiale *f*.
graze[2] [greiz] *v* (*animal*) pascolare.
grease [griːs] *n* grasso *m*, unto *m*. **greaseproof paper** carta oleata *f*. *v* ungere, ingrassare. **greasy** *adj* grasso, unto; (*slippery*) scivoloso.
great [greit] *adj* grande; (*very good*) magnifico; (*very large*) grandissimo. **Great Britain** Gran Bretagna *f*. **greatly** *adv* molto. **greatness** *n* grandezza *f*.
Greece [griːs] *n* Grecia *f*. **Greek** *n*, *adj* greco (*pl* -ci), -a.
greed [griːd] *n* ingordigia *f*. **greedy** *adj* ingordo.
green [griːn] *adj* verde. *n* verde *m*; (*land*) prato *m*; (*golf*) green *m*. **greenfly** *n* afide *m*. **greengage** *n* prugna verde *f*. **greengrocer** *n* erbivendolo, -a *m*, *f*, fruttivendolo, -a *m*, *f*. **greenhouse** *n* serra *f*. **green light** luce verde *f*. **greens** *pl n* verdura *f sing*.
Greenland ['griːnlənd] *n* Groenlandia *f*. **Greenlander** *n* groenlandese *m*, *f*.
greet [griːt] *v* salutare. **greeting** *n* saluto *m*.
gregarious [gri'geə͵riəs] *adj* gregario, socievole.
grenade [grə'neid] *n* granata *f*.
grew [gruː] *V* **grow**.
grey [grei] *adj* grigio.
grid [grid] *n* (*network*) rete *f*; (*map*) reticolo *m*; (*grating*) grata *f*.

grief [griːf] *n* dolore *m*, afflizione *f*. **come to grief** far fiasco *or* cilecca.
grieve [griːv] *v* (*upset*) affliggere, addolorare; (*sorrow*) affliggersi. **grievance** *n* (*injustice*) ingiustizia *f*; (*complaint*) lamentela *f*. **grievous** *adj* doloroso, atroce.
grill [gril] *n* (*cookery*) graticola *f*, gratella *f*; (*grilled meat*) carne ai ferri *f*. *v* (*cookery*) cucinare ai ferri; (*question severely*) sottoporre a un interrogatorio severo.
grille [gril] *n* inferriata *f*, grata *f*.
grim [grim] *adj* (*unrelenting*) inesorabile; (*fierce*) feroce; (*forbidding*) arcigno. **grimly** *adv* con severità.
grimace [gri'meis] *n* smorfia *f*. *v* fare smorfie.
grime [graim] *n* sudiciume *m*. **grimy** *adj* sudicio.
grin [grin] *v* fare un largo sorriso. *n* largo sorriso *m*.
***grind** [graind] *v* (*pulverize*) macinare; (*sharpen*) affilare; (*teeth*) digrignare. *n* (*coll*: *hard work*) sgobbata *f*.
grip [grip] *v* stringere; (*hold interest*) avvincere; (*take firm hold*) far presa. *n* presa *f*, stretta *f*; (*control*) padronanza *f*. **come to grips with** venire alle prese con.
gripe [graip] *n* colica *f*. *v* (*coll*) lagnarsi.
grisly ['grizli] *adj* orribile, macabro.
gristle ['grisl] *n* cartilagine *f*. **gristly** *adj* cartilaginoso.
grit [grit] *n* (*sand*) sabbia *f*; (*mech*) graniglia *f*; (*coll*: *courage*) fegato *m*. *v* (*teeth*) digrignare. **gritty** *adj* sabbioso.
groan [groun] *n* gemito *m*, lamento *m*. *v* gemere, lamentarsi.
grocer ['grousə] *n* droghiere, -a *m*, *f*. **grocer's** *n* (*shop*) drogheria *f*. **groceries** *pl n* generi coloniali *m pl*.
groin [groin] *n* inguine *m*.
groom [gruːm] *n* stalliere *m*; (*bridegroom*) sposo *m*. *v* preparare; (*horse*) strigliare.
groove [gruːv] *n* solco *m*. *v* scanalare.
grope [group] *v* brancolare. **grope for** cercare a tentoni, brancolare in cerca di.
gross [grous] *adj* grossolano, volgare; (*not net*) lordo. *v* (*income*) avere un introito lordo di. *n* grossa *f*.
grotesque [grə'tesk] *adj* fantastico; (*incongruous*) grottesco.
grotto ['grotou] *n* grotta *f*.
ground[1] [graund] *V* **grind**.
ground[2] [graund] *n* (*soil*) terreno *m*; (*earth, floor*) terra *f*; (*sport*) campo *m*; (*reason*) motivo *m*; (*bottom*) fondo *m*. **ground floor** pianterreno *m*. **grounds** *pl n* (*sediment*) deposito *m sing*; (*dregs*) fondi *m pl*. *v* (*base*) fondare; (*teach*) insegnare i primi elementi; (*aircraft*) impedire di volare. **grounding** *n* base *f*. **groundless** *adj* infondato.
group [gruːp] *n* gruppo *m*. *v* raggruppare, disporre.
grouse[1] [graus] *n* (*bird*) urogallo *m*.
grouse[2] [graus] (*coll*) *v* brontolare, lamentarsi. *n* lagnanza *f*.
grove [grouv] *n* boschetto *m*.
grovel ['grovl] *v* umiliarsi; (*cringe*) strisciare.
***grow** [grou] *v* crescere; (*thrive*) prosperare; (*become*) diventare. **grown-up** *n*, *adj* adulto, -a. **grow on** piacere sempre più. **grow up** crescere, sorgere. **grower** *n* coltivatore, -trice *m*, *f*. **growth** *n* crescita *f*, progresso *m*; (*med*) escrescenza *f*, tumore *m*.
growl [graul] *v* ringhiare; (*rumble*) brontolare. *n* ringhio *m*; brontolio *m*.
grown [groun] *V* **grow**.
grub [grʌb] *n* (*insect*) larva *f*, bruco *m*; (*coll*) roba da mangiare *f*. *v* ripulire; (*uproot*) sradicare.
grubby ['grʌbi] *adj* (*dirty*) sudicio; (*contemptible*) abietto.
grudge [grʌdʒ] *n* rancore *m*. **bear a grudge against** nutrire rancore verso. *v* (*give reluctantly*) dare malvolentieri; (*resent*) invidiare. **grudgingly** *adv* malvolentieri.
gruelling ['gruəliŋ] *adj* faticoso.
gruesome ['gruːsəm] *adj* raccapricciante.
gruff [grʌf] *adj* (*surly*) burbero; (*hoarse*) rauco; (*harsh*) aspro.
grumble ['grʌmbl] *v* (*complain*) lagnarsi; (*growl*) brontolare. *n* lagnanza *f*, brontolio *m*.
grumpy ['grʌmpi] *adj* scontroso.
grunt [grʌnt] *v* grugnire. *n* grugnito *m*.
guarantee [garən'tiː] *v* garantire, rispondere di. *n* garanzia *f*.
guard [gaːd] *v* (*keep safe*) custodire; (*watch over*) sorvegliare; (*keep watch*) stare in guardia. **guard against** badare a. *n* guardia *m*, *f*; (*appliance*) protezione *f*; (*railway*) capotreno *m*. **guarded** *adj* cauto. **guardian** *n* custode *m*; (*legal*) tutore *m*.

guerrilla [gə'rilə] *n* guerrigliero *m*. **guerrilla warfare** guerriglia *f*.
guess [ges] *n* congettura *f*, supposizione *f*. **at a rough guess** a occhio e croce. *v* indovinare.
guest [gest] *n* ospite *m*, *f*; (*of hotel*) cliente *m*, *f*. **guest-house** *n* pensione *f*.
guide [gaid] *n* guida *f*; (*of tourists*) cicerone *m*. **guidebook** *n* guida *f*. *v* guidare; (*advise*) consigliare; (*direct*) dirigere. **be guided by** seguire il consiglio di. **guidance** *n* (*leadership*) guida *f*; (*instruction*) norma *f*.
guild [gild] *n* corporazione *f*.
guile [gail] *n* astuzia *f*. **guileless** *adj* ingenuo.
guillotine ['gilətiːn] *n* ghigliottina *f*.
guilt [gilt] *n* colpa *f*. **guiltless** *adj* innocente. **guilty** *adj* colpevole. **have a guilty conscience** avere la coscienza sporca *or* cattiva.
guinea-pig ['ginipig] *n* cavia *f*.
guitar [gi'taː] *n* chitarra *f*. **guitarist** *n* chitarrista *m*, *f*.
gulf [gʌlf] *n* (*geog*) golfo *m*; (*wide separation*) abisso *m*.
gull [gʌl] *n* gabbiano *m*.
gullet ['gʌlit] *n* (*throat*) gola *f*; (*oesophagus*) esofago *m*.
gullible ['gʌləbl] *adj* credulo. **gullibility** *n* credulità *f*.
gully ['gʌli] *n* (*canyon*) burrone *m*; (*ditch*) cunetta *f*.
gulp [gʌlp] *n* (*food*) boccone *m*; (*drink*) sorso *m*. *v* (*food*) ingoiare; (*drink*) tracannare; (*choke*) soffocare.
gum[1] [gʌm] *n* (*secretion*) gomma *f*; (*glue*) colla *f*. *v* ingommare; incollare.
gum[2] [gʌm] *n* (*mouth*) gengiva *f*.
gun [gʌn] *n* fucile *m*; cannone *m*. **gunfire** *n* sparatoria *f*. **gunman** *n* bandito armato *m*. **gunner** *n* artigliere *m*. **gunpowder** *n* polvere da sparo *f*. **gunshot** *n* colpo di fucile *m*.
gurgle ['gəːgl] *v* gorgogliare. *n* gorgoglio *m*.
gush [gʌʃ] *n* sgorgo *m*; (*language*) torrente *m*. *v* (*liquid*) scaturire; (*speech*) parlare con effusione.
gust [gʌst] *n* raffica *f*.
gusto ['gʌstou] *n* fervore *m*.
gut [gʌt] *n* budello *m* (*pl* -a *f*). **guts** *pl n* (*coll*) fegato *m sing*. *v* sbudellare.
gutter ['gʌtə] *n* (*house*) grondaia *f*; (*street*) cunetta *f*; (*conduit*) condotto *m*. **guttersnipe** *n* scugnizzo *m*.
guy[1] [gai] *n* tipo *m*, individuo *m*.
guy[2] [gai] *n* (*rope*) tirante *m*.
gymnasium [dʒim'neiziəm] *n* palestra *f*. **gymnast** *n* ginnasta *m*, *f*. **gymnastics** *n* ginnastica *f*.
gynaecology [gainə'kolədʒi] *n* ginecologia *f*. **gynaecological** *adj* ginecologico. **gynaecologist** *n* ginecologo, -a *m*, *f*.
gypsum ['dʒipsəm] *n* gesso *m*.
gyrate [ˌdʒai'reit] *v* girare, roteare.
gyroscope ['dʒairəˌskoup] *n* giroscopio *m*.

H

haberdasher ['habədaʃə] *n* merciaio, -a *m*, *f*. **haberdashery** *n* merceria *f*.
habit ['habit] *n* abitudine *f*; (*dress*) tonaca *f*. **habitual** *adj* abituale. **habitually** *adv* di solito.
habitable ['habitəbl] *adj* abitabile.
habitat ['habitat] *n* ambiente *m*.
hack[1] [hak] *v* tagliare, troncare. **hacksaw** *n* seghetto *m*.
hack[2] [hak] *n* (*horse*) ronzino *m*; (*writer*) scribacchino *m*.
hackneyed ['haknid] *adj* trito, comune.
had [had] *V* **have**.
haddock ['hadək] *n* eglefino *m*.
haemorrhage ['hemərid ʒ] *n* emorragia *f*.
haemorrhoids ['hemərоidz] *pl n* emorroidi *f pl*.
hag [hag] *n* vecchiaccia *f*, strega *f*.
haggard ['hagəd] *adj* smunto, scarno.
haggle ['hagl] *v* mercanteggiare.
Hague [heig] *n* l'Aia *f*.
hail[1] [heil] *n* grandine *f*. **hailstone** *n* chicco di grandine *m*. *v* grandinare.
hail[2] [heil] *v* salutare; (*call*) chiamare. **hail from** essere oriundo di. *interj* salve! *n* saluto *m*.
hair [heə] *n* capelli *m pl*; (*single strand*) capello *m*; (*of animals*) pelo *m*. **split hairs** cercare il pelo nell'uovo. **hairy** *adj* capelluto; peloso.
hairbrush ['heəbrʌʃ] *n* spazzola per capelli *f*.
haircut ['heəkʌt] *n* taglio dei capelli *m*. **have a haircut** farsi tagliare i capelli.
hairdresser ['heəˌdresə] *n* parrucchiere, -a *m*, *f*.

hair-dryer ['heəˌdraiə] *n* asciugacapelli *m invar.*
hairpin ['heəpin] *n* forcina *f.*
hair-raising ['heəˌreiziŋ] *adj* raccapricciante.
hake [heik] *n* nasello *m.*
half [haːf] *adj* mezzo. *n* mezzo *m*, metà *f*; (*sport: period*) tempo *m*. **in half** in due.
half-and-half *adj, adv* metà e metà.
half-back ['haːfbak] *n* mediano *m.*
half-baked [ˌhaːf'beikt] *adj* (*coll*) inesperto, immaturo.
half-breed ['haːfbriːd] *nm, adj* ibrido.
half-brother ['haːfbrʌðə] *n* fratellastro *m.*
half-hearted [ˌhaːf'haːtid] *adj* esitante, poco entusiasta.
half-hour [ˌhaːf'auə] *n* mezz'ora *f.*
half-mast [ˌhaːf'maːst] *n* **at half-mast** a mezz'asta.
half-moon [ˌhaːf'muːn] *n* mezzaluna *f.*
half-sister ['haːfsistə] *n* sorellastra *f.*
half-time [ˌhaːf'taim] *n* intervallo *m.*
half-tone ['haːftoun] *n* mezzatinta *f*, fotoriproduzione *f.*
halfway [ˌhaːf'wei] *adj, adv* a metà strada. **meet halfway** giungere a un compromesso.
half-witted [ˌhaːf'witid] *adj* scemo, deficiente.
halibut ['halibət] *n* halibut *m invar*, ippoglosso *m.*
hall [hoːl] *n* (*entrance*) entrata *f*; (*room*) sala *f*, salone *m*; (*building*) villa *f*, casa signorile *f.*
hallmark ['hoːlmaːk] *n* marchio d'autenticità *m*; elemento caratteristico *m*. *v* marcare.
hallowed ['haloud] *adj* venerato.
hallucination [həˌluːsi'neiʃən] *n* allucinazione *f.*
halo ['heilou] *n* aureola *f*; (*astron*) alone *m.*
halt [hoːlt] *n* fermata *f*; (*temporary*) sosta *f*. *v* sostare, fermare, fermarsi. *interj* alt!
halter ['hoːltə] *n* capestro *m*; cavezza *f.*
halve [haːv] *v* dimezzare, ridurre della *or* alla metà.
ham [ham] *n* prosciutto *m.*
hamburger ['hambəːgə] *n* hamburger *m invar.*
hammer ['hamə] *n* martello *m*. *v* martellare.
hammock ['hamək] *n* amaca *f.*
hamper[1] ['hampə] *v* intralciare, ostacolare.
hamper[2] ['hampə] *n* paniere *m.*
hamster ['hamstə] *n* criceto *m.*
hand [hand] *n* mano (*pl* -i) *f*; (*clock*) lancetta *f*; (*worker*) operaio, -a *m, f*. **at hand** a portata di mano. **by hand** a mano. **hands down** completamente, con facilità. **hands off!** via le mani! **hands up!** alto le mani! **in hand** (*under control*) sotto controllo; (*available*) a disposizione; (*being dealt with*) in corso. **on hand** presente; (*available*) disponibile. **on the other hand** d'altra parte. *v* (*give*) dare, porgere. **hand down** trasmettere, tramandare. **hand in** *or* **over** consegnare. **hand out** distribuire. **handful** *n* manata *f*; piccolo gruppo *m.*
handbag ['handbag] *n* borsetta *f.*
handbill ['handbil] *n* volantino *m.*
handbook ['handbuk] *n* manuale *m.*
handbrake ['handbreik] *n* freno a mano *m.*
handcuff ['handkʌf] *n* manetta *f*. *v* ammanettare.
handicap ['handikap] *n* svantaggio *m*, impedimento *m*; (*sport*) handicap *m invar*. *v* impedire.
handicraft ['handikraːft] *n* artigianato *m*; (*trade*) mestiere *m.*
handiwork ['handiwəːk] *n* (*personal work*) opera *f.*
handkerchief ['haŋkətʃif] *n* fazzoletto *m.*
handle ['handl] *n* manico *m*; (*door*) maniglia *f*; (*crank*) manovella *f*. *v* (*manipulate*) maneggiare; (*deal with*) trattare. **handlebar** *n* manubrio *m.*
handmade [ˌhand'meid] *adj* fatto a mano.
hand-out ['handaut] *n* comunicato *m*, campione pubblicitario *m.*
hand-pick [hand'pik] *v* scegliere a mano.
handrail ['handreil] *n* ringhiera *f.*
handshake ['handʃeik] *n* stretta di mano *f.*
handsome ['hansəm] *adj* bello; generoso, considerevole.
handstand ['handˌstand] *n* posata verticale sulle mani *f.*
hand-towel ['handˌtauəl] *n* asciugamano *m.*
handwriting ['handˌraitiŋ] *n* calligrafia *f.*
handy ['handi] *adj* (*accessible*) a portata di mano; (*deft*) destro, abile; (*convenient*) comodo.
***hang** [haŋ] *v* pendere, appendere, sospendere; (*execute*) impiccare. **hang around** bazzicare. **hanger** *n* (*clothes*)

attaccapanni *m invar.* **hanger-on** *n* scroccone *m.* **hangman** *n* boia *m invar.* **hang on** persistere, indugiare; (*phone*) restare in linea. **hangover** *n* postumi di una sbornia *m pl.*

hangar ['haŋə] *n* hangar *m invar*; aviorimessa *f.*

hanker ['haŋkə] *v* **hanker after** bramare. **hankering** *n* forte desiderio *m*, brama *f.*

haphazard [ˌhap'hazəd] *adj* casuale.

happen ['hapən] *v* (*take place*) accadere, succedere. **as it happens** per caso. **happening** *n* avvenimento *m.*

happy ['hapi:] *adj* felice, contento, lieto; (*in greetings*) buono. **happy-go-lucky** *adj* spensierato. **happiness** *n* felicità *f*, contentezza *f.*

harass ['harəs] *v* molestare, tormentare, irritare. **harassment** *n* tormento *m*, molestia *f.*

harbour ['haːbə] *n* porto *m.* *v* (*shelter*) dare asilo a.

hard [haːd] *adj* duro; difficile; severo. *adv* molto; (*solidly*) sodo. **hard and fast** immutabile. **hard-boiled** *adj* (*egg*) sodo; (*person*) duro. **hard core** nucleo *m.* **hard-headed** *adj* accorto, pratico. **hard-hearted** *adj* insensibile. **hard up** al corto di quattrini. **hardware** *n* ferramenta *f pl*; (*computer*) meccanismo *m.* **hard-wearing** *adj* duraturo, durevole. **hard work** lavoro faticoso *m.* **try hard** provare assiduamente. **work hard** lavorar sodo. **hardness** *n* durezza *f.* **hardship** *n* privazione *f.*

hardly ['haːdli] *adv* (*not quite*) non esattamente; (*barely, almost not*) quasi, appena; (*with difficulty*) a stento.

hardy ['haːdi] *adj* robusto, resistente; (*courageous*) coraggioso.

hare [heə] lepre *f.* **hare-brained** *adj* scervellato.

harm [haːm] *n* male *m*, danno *m.* *v* nuocere a, far male a. **harmful** *adj* nocivo, dannoso. **harmless** *adj* innocuo, inoffensivo.

harmony ['haːməni] *n* armonia *f*, accordo *m.* **harmonic** *adj* armonico, armonioso. **harmonize** *v* armonizzare.

harness ['haːnis] *n* briglia *f.* *v* imbrigliare.

harp [haːp] *n* arpa *f.* **harpist** *n* arpista *m*, *f.*

harpoon [haː'puːn] *n* rampone *m.* *v* ramponare.

harpsichord ['haːpsiˌkoːd] *n* clavicembalo *m.*

harrowing ['harouiŋ] *adj* straziante.

harsh [haːʃ] *adj* aspro, duro. **harshness** *n* asprezza *f*, durezza *f.*

harvest ['haːvist] *n* raccolto *m.* *v* raccogliere, mietere.

has [haz] *V* **have.**

hash [haʃ] *n* carne tritata *f*; (*coll*: *mess*) confusione *f*, pasticcio *m.* **make a hash of** sciupare, mandare a rotoli.

hashish ['haʃiːʃ] *n* (h)ascisc *m invar.*

haste [heist] *n* fretta *f.* **hasten** *v* precipitare, affrettarsi. **hasty** *adj* frettoloso.

hat [hat] *n* cappello *m.*

hatch[1] [hatʃ] *v* (*bring forth*) covare; (*contrive*) tramare.

hatch[2] [hatʃ] *n* (*naut*) boccaporto *m*; (*opening*) portello *m*, sportello *m.*

hatchet ['hatʃit] *n* accetta *f.*

hate [heit] *v* odiare. *n also* **hatred** odio *m.* **hateful** *adj* odioso.

haughty ['hoːti] *adj* altezzoso, arrogante.

haul [hoːl] *n* tiro *m*; (*fish*) retata *f*; (*coll*: *booty*) bottino *m.* *v* tirare.

haunch [hoːntʃ] *n* anca *f.*

haunt [hoːnt] *v* perseguitare, ossessionare. *n* ritrovo *m.* **haunting** *adj* ossessionante.

***have** [hav] *v* avere. **have to** avere da, dovere. **have it in for** avercela con. **have on** (*wear*) portare; (*have planned*) aver intenzione di fare, aver da fare; (*coll*: *tease*) prendere in giro.

haven ['heivn] *n* (*harbour*) porto *m*; (*shelter*) rifugio *m.*

haversack ['havəsak] *n* bisaccia *f.*

havoc ['havək] *n* **play havoc with** rovinare, far strage di.

hawk[1] [hoːk] *n* falco *m*, falcone *m.*

hawk[2] [hoːk] *v* spacciare; fare il venditore ambulante.

hawthorn ['hoːθoːn] *n* biancospino *m.*

hay [hei] *n* fieno *m.* **go haywire** perdere le staffe. **hay fever** raffreddore del fieno *m.* **haystack** *n* fienile *m.*

hazard ['hazəd] *n* (*danger*) pericolo *m*; (*risk*) rischio *m.* *v* azzardare. **hazardous** *adj* pericoloso, rischioso.

haze [heiz] *n* foschia *f.* **hazy** *adj* nebuloso, indistinto.

hazel ['heizl] *n* (*tree*) nocciolo *m.* **hazelnut** *n* nocciola *f.* *adj* color nocciola *invar.*

he [hiː] *pron* egli, lui. **he who** colui che.

head [hed] *n* testa *f*; (*leader*) capo *m.* *v* (*lead*) essere a capo di; (*direct*) dirigere.

headache ['hedeik] *n* mal di testa *m*; (*coll*) preoccupazione *f*.
headdress ['heddres] *n* copricapo *m*.
heading *n* (*title*) intestazione *f*; (*topic*) voce *f*.
headlamp ['hedlamp] *n* *also* **headlight** (*mot*) faro *m*, fanale *m*.
headland ['hedlənd] *n* promontorio *m*.
headline ['hedlain] *n* titolo *m*. **headlines** *pl n* (*news*) sommario *m sing*.
headlong ['hedloŋ] *adv* a capofitto.
headmaster [ˌhed'maɪstə] *n* preside *m*.
headphones ['hedfounz] *pl n* cuffia *f sing*.
headquarters [ˌhed'kwoɪtəz] *n* (*mil*) quartiere generale *m*; (*office*) sede *f*, direzione *f*.
headrest ['hedrest] *n* appoggiatesta *m invar*.
headscarf ['hedskaɪf] *n* foulard *m invar*.
headstrong ['hedstroŋ] *adj* testardo, cocciuto.
headway ['hedwei] *n* progresso *m*. **make headway** fare strada.
heady ['hedi] *adj* impetuoso; (*intoxicating*) che dà alla testa.
heal [hiɪl] *v* guarire, sanare.
health [helθ] *n* salute *f*. **healthy** *adj* (*person*) sano; (*climate, etc.*) salubre.
heap [hiɪp] *n* mucchio *m*. *v* ammucchiare.
***hear** [hiə] *v* udire, sentire; (*be informed of*) venire a sapere. **hear about** aver notizie di. **hear from** aver notizie da. **hearing** *n* udito *m*; (*audience*) udienza *f*. **hearsay** *n* voce *f*.
heard [həɪd] *V* **hear**.
hearse [həɪs] *n* carro funebre *m*.
heart [haɪt] *n* cuore *m*; (*feeling*) animo *m*; (*essential part*) parte centrale *f*, centro *m*. **by heart** a memoria. **hearts** *pl n* (*cards*) cuori *m pl*. **take to heart** prendersi a cuore.
heart attack *n* attacco cardiaco *m*.
heartbeat ['haɪtbiɪt] *n* battito del cuore *m*.
heart-breaking ['haɪtbreikiŋ] *adj* straziante. **heart-broken** *adj* accorato, affranto.
heartburn ['haɪtbəɪn] *n* bruciore di stomaco *m*.
heartening ['haɪtniŋ] *adj* incoraggiante.
heartfelt ['haɪtfelt] *adj* sincero.
hearth [haɪθ] *n* focolare *m*.
heartless ['haɪtləs] *adj* spietato, insensibile.
hearty ['haɪti] *adj* (*warm-hearted*) caloroso; sincero; vigoroso.

heat [hiɪt] *n* calore *m*, caldo *m*; (*sport*) batteria *f*; (*oestrum*) estro *m*. **heat wave** calura *f*. *v* scaldare, riscaldare. **heated** *adj* animato. **heater** *n* riscaldatore *m*; stufa elettrica *f*. **heating** *n* riscaldamento *m*.
heath [hiɪθ] *n* brughiera *f*.
heathen ['hiɪðn] *n*, *adj* pagano, -a.
heather ['heðə] *n* erica *f*.
heave [hiɪv] *v* sollevare; (*retch*) avere i conati di vomito. **heave a sigh** tirare un sospiro. *n* sollevamento *m*.
heaven ['hevn] *n* cielo *m*, paradiso *m*. **for heaven's sake!** per l'amor del cielo! **good heavens!** santo cielo! **heavenly** *adj* divino, delizioso.
heavy ['hevi] *adj* pesante, forte. **heavyweight** *n* peso massimo *m*.
Hebrew ['hiɪbruɪ] *n* (*language*) ebraico *m*; (*person*) ebreo, -a *m*, *f*. *adj* ebraico; ebreo.
heckle ['hekl] *v* interrompere con domande imbarazzanti.
hectare ['hektaɪ] *n* ettaro *m*.
hectic ['hektik] *adj* febbrile.
hedge [hedʒ] *n* siepe *f*; (*bet*) copertura *f*. *v* (*bet*) coprire dai rischi. **as a hedge against** per mettersi al riparo contro.
hedgehog ['hedʒhog] *n* riccio *m*.
heed [hiɪd] *v* badare a, dar retta a. **heedless** *adj* noncurante.
heel [hiɪl] *n* (*anat*) calcagno *m*; (*shoe*) tacco *m*. **Achilles' heel** tallone d'Achille *m*.
hefty ['hefti] *adj* robusto.
heifer ['hefə] *n* giovenca *f*.
height [hait] *n* altezza *f*; (*hill*) collina *f*; (*highest degree*) colmo *m*; (*highest point*) culmine *m*. **heighten** *v* intensificare.
heir [eə] *n* erede *m*, *f*.
held [held] *V* **hold**[1].
helicopter ['helikoptə] *n* elicottero *m*.
hell [hel] *n* inferno *m*. **hellish** *adj* infernale.
hello [hə'lou] *interj* (*on meeting*) ciao! (*phone*) pronto!
helm [helm] *n* timone *m*.
helmet ['helmit] *n* elmo *m*, elmetto *m*; (*motorcyclist, airman*) casco *m*.
help [help] *n* aiuto *m*, assistenza *f*; (*remedy*) rimedio *m*. *v* aiutare, assistere. **helpful** *adj* utile, vantaggioso. **helping** *n* porzione *f*. **helpless** *adj* impotente, indifeso.
hem [hem] *n* orlo *m*. *v* orlare. **hem in** rinchiudere, accerchiare.
hemisphere ['hemiˌsfiə] *n* emisfera *f*.

hemp [hemp] *n* canapa *f*.
hen [hen] *n* gallina *f*.
hence [hens] *adv* quindi.
henna ['henə] *n* tintura di henna *f*.
her [həː] *pron* (*direct object*) la; (*indirect object*) le; (*after prep*) lei. *adj* (il) suo, (la) sua; (*pl*) (i) suoi, (le) sue.
herald ['herəld] *n* araldo *m*, messaggero *m*.
heraldry ['herəldri] *n* araldica *f*.
herbs [həːbz] *pl n* erbe aromatiche *f pl*.
herd [həːd] *n* gregge *m*, mandria *f*; (*people*) massa *f*. **herd together** raggruppare, radunare.
here [hiə] *adv* qui, qua; (*emphasizing*) ecco. **here I am!** eccomi qua!
hereabouts ['hiərəˌbauts] *adv* qui vicino.
hereafter [ˌhiər'aːftə] *adv* d'ora innanzi, in futuro. *n* **the hereafter** l'al di là *m*.
hereby [ˌhiə'bai] *adv* così, con questo.
hereditary [hi'reditri] *adj* ereditario.
heredity [hi'redəti] *n* eredità *f*.
heresy ['herəsi] *n* eresia *f*. **heretic** *n* eretico, -a *m, f*. **heretical** *adj* eretico.
herewith [ˌhiə'wið] *adv* con questo; (*correspondence*) con la presente.
heritage ['heritidʒ] *n* patrimonio *m*.
hermit ['həːmit] *n* eremita *m*.
hernia ['həːniə] *n* ernia *f*.
hero ['hiərou] *n* eroe *m*; (*principal character*) protagonista *m*. **heroic** *adj* eroico. **heroine** *n* eroina *f*; protagonista *f*.
heroin ['herouin] *n* eroina *f*.
heron ['herən] *n* airone *m*.
herring ['heriŋ] *n* aringa *f*. **herring-bone** *adj* a lisca di pesce.
hers [həːz] *pron* il suo, la sua; (*pl*) i suoi, le sue.
herself [həː'self] *pron* lei stessa; (*after prep*) sè (stessa); (*reflexive*) si; (*emphatic*) proprio lei.
hesitate ['heziteit] *v* esitare. **hesitant** *adj* esitante. **hesitation** *n* esitazione *f*. **without hesitation** decisamente.
heterogeneous [hetərə'dʒiːmiəs] *adj* eterogeneo.
heterosexual [hetərə'sekʃuəl] *adj* eterosessuale.
hexagon ['heksəgən] *n* esagono *m*. **hexagonal** *adj* esagonale.
heyday ['heidei] *n* (*prime*) fiore *m*; più bel periodo *m*; (*splendour*) fulgore *m*.
hiatus [hai'eitəs] *n* interruzione *f*; (*med*) iato *m*.
hibernate ['haibəneit] *v* svernare; (*of animals*) ibernare.
hiccup ['hikʌp] *n* singhiozzo *m*. *v* singhiozzare. **have hiccups** avere il singhiozzo.
hid [hid] *V* **hide**[1].
hidden ['hidn] *V* **hide**[1].
***hide**[1] [haid] *v* nascondere, nascondersi. **hide-out** *n* nascondiglio *m*.
hide[2] [haid] *n* (*raw*) pelle *f*; (*dressed*) cuoio *m*. **hidebound** *adj* gretto, di mentalità ristretta.
hideous ['hidiəs] *adj* orrendo, ripugnante.
hiding[1] ['haidiŋ] *n* **be in hiding** essere *or* tenersi nascosto. **go into hiding** nascondersi, darsi alla macchia.
hiding[2] ['haidiŋ] *n* (*beating*) batosta *f*.
hierarchy ['haiəraːki] *n* gerarchia *f*.
high [hai] *adj* alto, elevato; (*of meat*) andato a male. **it's high time** è ora. **leave high and dry** piantare in asso. *adv* in alto. *n* culmine *f*; (*weather*) anticiclone *m*. **highness** *n* altezza *f*.
highbrow ['haibrau] *n*(*m*+*f*), *adj* intellettuale.
high chair *n* seggiolina *f*.
high-fidelity *adj* ad alta fedeltà.
high frequency *adj* ad alta frequenza.
high jump *n* salto in alto *m*.
highlight ['hailait] *v* mettere in rilievo. *n* clou *m invar*, culmine *m*.
high-pitched [ˌhai'pitʃd] *adj* acuto.
high point *n* culmine *m*.
high-powered *adj* potente, dinamico.
high pressure *n* alta pressione *f*. **high-pressure** *adj* ad alta pressione; (*coll*) aggressivo.
high-rise block *adj* a molti piani.
high-spirited [ˌhai'spiritid] *adj* vivace. **high spirits** *pl n* buonumore *m sing*.
high street *n* corso *m*.
highway ['haiwei] *n* strada maestra *f*. **highway code** codice della strada *m*.
hijack ['haidʒak] *v* (*goods*) rubare in transito; (*aero*) dirottare. **hijacker** *n* dirottatore *m*, pirata dell'aria *m*. **hijacking** *n* dirottamento *m*.
hike [haik] *n* gita a piedi *f*. *v* fare una gita *or* escursione a piedi.
hilarious [hi'leəriəs] *adj* divertente, allegro.
hill [hil] *n* colle *m*, collina *f*; (*slope*) salita *f*.
him [him] *pron* (*direct object*) lo; (*indirect object*) gli; (*after prep*) lui.

himself [him'self] *pron* lui stesso; (*after prep*) sè (stesso); (*reflexive*) si; (*emphatic*) proprio lui.
hinder ['hində] *v* (*make difficult*) intralciare; (*make impossible*) impedire.
Hindu [hin'duː] *n*(*m*+*f*), *adj* indù *invar*. **Hinduism** *n* induismo *m*.
hinge [hindʒ] *n* cardine *m*, perno *m*. *v* (*depend*) dipendere (da).
hint [hint] *n* cenno *m*, allusione *f*; (*clue*) suggerimento *m*; (*slight amount*) traccia *f*. *v* far capire, accennare, alludere.
hip [hip] *n* fianco *m*, anca *f*.
hippopotamus [hipə'potəməs] *n* ippopotamo *m*.
hire [haiə] *v* prendere a nolo, noleggiare. **hire out** dare a nolo, noleggiare. *n* nolo *m*, noleggio *m*. **hire purchase** vendita a rate *f*.
his [hiz] *adj* (il) suo, (la) sua; (*pl*) (i) suoi, (le) sue. *pron* il suo, la sua; (*pl*) i suoi, le sue.
hiss [his] *v* sibilare. *n* sibilo *m*. **hissing** *adj* sibilante.
history ['histəri] *n* storia *f*; (*past*) passato *m*. **historian** *n* storico *m*. **historic** *adj* storico; memorabile.
***hit** [hit] *n* colpo *m*, botta *f*; successo *m*. *v* colpire, bàttere. **hit on** scoprire. **hit-or-miss** *adv* alla buona.
hitch [hitʃ] *v* attaccare. **hitch-hike** *v* fare l'autostop. **hitch up** tirar su. *n* (*obstacle*) intoppo *m*; (*knot*) nodo *m*.
hitherto [ˌhiðə'tuː] *adv* finora.
hive [haiv] *n* alveare *m*.
hoard [hoːd] *n* scorta *f*, mucchio *m*. *v* ammucchiare.
hoarding ['hoːdiŋ] *n* (*billboard*) tabellone *m*.
hoarse [hoːs] *adj* rauco. **hoarseness** *n* raucedine *f*.
hoax [houks] *n* beffa *f*.
hobble ['hobl] *v* zoppicare.
hobby ['hobi] *n* passatempo *m*, hobby *m invar*.
hock[1] [hok] *n* (*joint*) garretto *m*.
hock[2] [hok] *n* (*wine*) vino bianco del Reno *m*.
hockey ['hoki] *n* hockey *m invar*.
hoe [hou] *n* zappa *f*. *v* zappare.
hog [hog] *n* maiale *m*, porco *m*. *v* (*coll*) monopolizzare.
hoist [hoist] *n* montacarichi *m invar*. *v* sollevare.
***hold**[1] [hould] *n* presa *f*, stretta *f*; (*dominating influence*) ascendente *m*. **get hold of** (*grasp*) afferrare; (*obtain*) ottenere. *v* tenere; contenere; esser valido. **hold back** trattenere. **hold out** resistere. **hold up** (*delay*) ostacolare; (*stop by force*) fermare per derubare; (*exhibit*) esibire. **hold-up** *n* intoppo *m*; (*robbery*) rapina a mano armata *f*. **holder** *n* supporto *m*; detentore *m*. **holding** *n* (*land*) tenuta *f*; (*shares*) pacchetto (di azioni) *m*.
hold[2] [hould] *n* (*naut*) stiva *f*.
hole [houl] *n* buco *m*; (*in the ground*) buca *f*; (*burrow*) tana *f*; (*predicament*) guaio *m*.
holiday ['holədi] *n* (*day*) giorno festivo *m*, festa *f*; (*period*) vacanza *f*. **go on holiday** andare in vacanza *or* villeggiatura. **holiday-maker** *n* villeggiante *m*, *f*.
Holland ['holənd] *n* Olanda *f*.
hollow ['holou] *adj* cavo; concavo; (*not solid*) vuoto; (*of sound*) cupo; falso. *n* buca *f*, cavità *f*; (*anat*) cavo *m*.
holly ['holi] *n* agrifoglio *m*.
holster ['houlstə] *n* fondina *f*.
holy ['houli] *adj* santo, sacro.
homage ['homidʒ] *n* omaggio *m*. **pay homage to** rendere omaggio a.
home [houm] *n* (*house*) casa *f*, domicilio *m*; (*land*) patria *f*; (*institution*) ricovero *m*, rifugio *m*; (*habitat*) ambiente naturale *m*. **at home** a casa. **feel at home** sentirsi a proprio agio. **leave home** lasciare la casa paterna. *adj* domestico, casalingo. *adv* a casa; in patria; (*all the way*) a fondo. **strike home** colpire nel vivo.
homecoming ['houmˌkʌmiŋ] *n* ritorno in casa *or* patria *m*.
home-grown [houm'groun] *adj* nostrano.
homeless ['houmləs] *adj* senza tetto.
homely ['houmli] *adj* semplice, senza pretese; (*unattractive*) brutto.
home-made [ˌhoum'meid] *adj* fatto in casa.
homesick ['houmsik] *adj* nostalgico.
homework ['houmwəːk] *n* compiti di casa *m pl*.
homicide ['homisaid] *n* (*crime*) omicidio *m*; (*murderer*) omicida *m*, *f*. **homicidal** *adj* micidiale.
homogeneous [homə'dʒiːniəs] *adj* omogeneo.
homosexual [homə'sekʃuəl] *n*(*m*+*f*), *adj* omosessuale.

honest ['onist] *adj* onesto. **honestly!** *interj* davvero! **honesty** *n* onestà *f*.
honey ['hʌni] *n* miele *m*. **honeycomb** *n* favo *m*. **honeymoon** *n* luna di miele *f*.
honeysuckle ['hʌnisʌkl] *n* caprifoglio *m*.
honour ['onə] *n* onore *m*; (*respect*) stima *f*. *v* onorare; (*comm*) far onore a. **honours** *pl n* (*titles*) onorificenza *f sing*. **honorary** *adj* onorario. **honourable** *adj* onorevole, stimato, probo.
hood [hud] *n* cappuccio *m*; (*mot*) cappotta *f*.
hoof [huːf] *n* zoccolo *m*.
hook [huk] *n* gancio *m*; (*fishing*) amo *m*. *v* agganciare.
hooligan ['huːligən] *n* teppista *m*.
hoop [huːp] *n* cerchio *m*.
hoot [huːt] *v* (*car*) suonare il clacson; (*shriek*) stridere; (*hiss*) fischiare. **hooter** *n* sirena *f*; (*car*) clacson *m invar*.
hop[1] [hop] *v* salterellare. *n* salterello *m*.
hop[2] [hop] *n* (*bot*) luppolo *m*.
hope [houp] *n* speranza *f*. *v* sperare. **hopeful** *adj* pieno di speranza, fiducioso; (*promising*) promettente. **hopeless** *adj* senza speranza, disperato; (*not resolvable*) irrimediabile.
horde [hoːd] *n* banda *f*.
horizon [hə'raizn] *n* orizzonte *m*. **horizontal** *adj* orizzontale.
hormone ['hoːmoun] *n* ormone *m*.
horn [hoːn] *n* corno (*pl* -a) *m*; (*mot*) clacson *m invar*.
hornet ['hoːnit] *n* calabrone *m*.
horoscope ['horəskoup] *n* oroscopo *m*.
horrible ['horibl] *adj also* **horrid** orribile, orrendo.
horrify ['horifai] *v* inorridire, raccapricciare. **horrifying** *adj* raccapricciante.
horror ['horə] *n* orrore *m*, spavento *m*.
hors d'oeuvre [oː'dəːvr] *n* antipasto *m*.
horse [hoːs] *n* cavallo *m*.
horseback ['hoːsbak] *n* **on horseback** a cavallo.
horse-chestnut *n* ippocastano *m*.
horse-fly *n* tafano *m*.
horseman ['hoːsmən] *n* cavaliere *m*.
horsepower ['hoːsˌpauə] *n* cavallo vapore *m*.
horse-race *n* corsa ippica *f*.
horseradish ['hoːsˌradiʃ] *n* cren *m invar*; (*plant*) barbaforte *m*.
horseshoe ['hoːʃʃuː] *n* ferro di cavallo *m*.
horsewoman ['hoːsˌwumən] *n* cavallerizza *f*.
horticulture ['hoːtikʌltʃə] *n* orticultura *f*.
hose [houz] *n* (*stocking*) calza *f*, calzino *m*; (*pipe*) tubo flessibile *m*, manichetta *f*. *v* **hose (down)** dare una lavata a, annaffiare.
hosiery ['houziəri] *n* calzetteria *f*.
hospitable [ho'spitəbl] *adj* ospitale.
hospital ['hospitl] *n* ospedale *m*. **hospitalize** far ricoverare in ospedale.
hospitality [ˌhospi'taliti] *n* ospitalità *f*.
host[1] [houst] *n* oste *m*, ospite *m*. **hostess** *n* ospite *f*, ostessa *f*.
host[2] [houst] *n* moltitudine *f*, gran numero *m*.
host[3] [houst] *n* (*rel*) ostia *f*.
hostage ['hostidʒ] *n* ostaggio *m*.
hostel ['hostəl] *n* ostello *m*, alloggio *m*.
hostile ['hostail] *adj* ostile. **hostility** *n* antagonismo *m*. **hostilities** *pl n* ostilità *f pl*.
hot [hot] *adj* caldo; ardente, impetuoso; (*pungent, peppery*) forte, piccante. **be hot** aver caldo. **hot-blooded** *adj* dal sangue caldo. **hot-headed** *adj* impetuoso. **hothouse** *n* serra *f*. **hotplate** *n* scaldavivande *m invar*; (*hob*) fornello *m*. **hot-tempered** *adj* irascibile.
hotel [hou'tel] *n* albergo *m*. **hotel-keeper** *n* albergatore, -trice *m, f*.
hound [haund] *n* bracco *m*.
hour ['auə] *n* ora *f*. **hours** *pl n* (*time spent*) orario *m sing*. **kilometres/miles per hour** chilometri/miglia all'ora.
hourly ['auəli] *adj* orario. *adv* (*every hour*) ogni ora; (*hour by hour*) d'ora in ora, continuamente.
house [haus; *v* hauz] *n* casa *f*; (*theatre attendance*) sala *f*; (*audience*) pubblico *m*; (*dynasty*) dinastia *f*, famiglia *f*; (*comm*) ditta *f*. *v* (*shelter*) alloggiare; (*put in safe place*) mettere al sicuro.
houseboat ['hausbout] *n* casa galleggiante *f*, houseboat *f invar*.
housebound ['hausbaund] *adj* costretto a stare a casa.
housebreaking ['hausˌbreikiŋ] *n* scasso *m*.
household ['haushould] *n* famiglia *f*, casa *f*. *adj* casalingo, domestico.
housekeeper ['hausˌkiːpə] *n* massaia *f*, governante *f*. **housekeeping** *n* economia domestica *f*.
housemaid ['hausmeid] *n* domestica *f*, cameriera *f*.

house-to-house *adj* di porta in porta.
housewife ['hauswaif] *n* massaia *f*, casalinga *f*.
housework ['hauswəːk] *n* lavori di casa *m pl*.
housing ['hauziŋ] *n* alloggio *m*. **housing estate** quartiere residenziale *m*.
hovel ['hovəl] *n* tugurio *m*.
hover ['hovə] *v* librarsi. **hovercraft** *n* hovercraft *m invar*.
how [hau] *adv* come, in che modo; (*to what extent*) quanto. **how are you?** come sta? **how do you do** (*after introduction*) piacere; buon giorno. **how much** quanto. **how many** quanti. **how often** quante volte. *conj* che.
however [hau'evə] *adv* comunque, tuttavia. *conj* nonostante, tuttavia.
howl [haul] *v* ululare, lamentarsi. *n* ululato *m*, lamento *m*.
hub [hʌb] *n* parte centrale *f*; (*of wheel*) mozzo *m*. **hub cap** coppa *f*.
hubbub ['hʌbʌb] *n* baccano *m*.
huddle ['hʌdl] *v* **huddle together** affollarsi, accalcarsi.
hue [hjuː] *n* colore *m*, tinta *f*.
huff [hʌf] *n* stizza *f*, risentimento *m*. **in a huff** offeso.
hug [hʌg] *v* abbracciare. *n* abbraccio *m*.
huge [hjuːdʒ] *adj* enorme, immenso.
hulk [hʌlk] *n* carcassa *f*. **hulking** *adj* goffo.
hull [hʌl] *n* (*shell*) guscio *m*; (*husk*) buccia *f*; (*of nuts*) mallo *m*; (*pod*) baccello *m*; (*naut*) scafo *m*.
hum [hʌm] *v* ronzare; cantare a bocca chiusa, canterellare. *n* ronzio *m*.
human ['hjuːmən] *adj* umano. **human being** essere umano *m*.
humane [hjuː'mein] *adj* umanitario, umano, compassionevole.
humanism ['hjuːmənizəm] *n* umanesimo *m*. **humanist** *n* umanista *m*, *f*.
humanitarian [hjuːˌmani'teəriən] *adj* filantropico. *n* filantropo, -a *m*, *f*.
humanity [hjuː'manəti] *n* umanità *f*; compassione *f*.
humble ['hʌmbl] *adj* umile, modesto. *v* umiliare.
humdrum ['hʌmdrʌm] *adj* monotono, noioso.
humid ['hjuːmid] *adj* umido. **humidity** *n* umidità *f*.
humiliate [hjuː'milieit] *v* umiliare.
humility [hjuː'miləti] *n* umiltà *f*.
humour ['hjuːmə] *n* (*mood*) umore *m*; stato d'animo *m*, disposizione *f*; (*comic quality*) comicità *f*. *v* compiacere, accontentare. **humorist** *n* umorista *m*, *f*. **humorous** *adj* divertente, spiritoso.
hump [hʌmp] *n* gobba *f*; (*hill*) cresta *f*.
hunch [hʌntʃ] *n* gobba *f*. **have a hunch** (*coll*) avere un sospetto. **hunchback** *n* gobbo *m*. **hunchbacked** *adj* gobbo.
hundred ['hʌndrəd] *nm*, *adj* cento. **hundredth** *nm*, *adj* centesimo.
hung [hʌŋ] *V* **hang**.
Hungary ['hʌŋgəri] *n* Ungheria *f*. **Hungarian** *n*(*m*+*f*), *adj* ungherese.
hunger ['hʌŋgə] *n* fame *f*, appetito *m*. **hungry** *adj* affamato. **be hungry** aver fame.
hunt [hʌnt] *n* caccia *f*; (*pursuit*) inseguimento *m*; (*search*) ricerca affannosa *f*. *v* andare a caccia di; inseguire; cercare affannosamente. **hunter** *n* cacciatore *m*.
hurdle ['həːdl] *n* ostacolo *m*. *v* fare la corsa a ostacoli.
hurl [həːl] *v* scagliare, scaraventare.
hurrah [hu'raː] *interj* evviva!
hurricane ['hʌrikən] *n* uragano *m*. **hurricane lamp** lanterna controvento *f*.
hurry ['hʌri] *n* fretta *f*. **be in a hurry** aver fretta. *v* affrettare. **hurry up** sbrigarsi.
***hurt** [həːt] *v* far male a, nuocere a; (*wound*) ferire; (*feel painful*) dolere. *n* dolore *m*, male *m*; ferita *f*; offesa *f*. **feel hurt** rimanere offeso.
husband ['hʌzbənd] *n* marito *m*.
hush [hʌʃ] *n* silenzio *m*. *interj* zitto! *v* far tacere. **hush-hush** *adj* (*coll*) segretissimo. **hush up** nascondere, dissimulare; (*suppress*) soffocare.
husk [hʌsk] *n* guscio *m*, baccello *m*.
husky ['hʌski] *adj* (*of voice*) rauco, fioco; (*burly*) grande e grosso.
hustle ['hʌsl] *n* spintone *m*. *v* spingere, sbrigarsi.
hut [hʌt] *n* capanna *f*, baracca *f*.
hutch [hʌtʃ] *n* conigliera *f*.
hyacinth ['haiəsinθ] *n* giacinto *m*.
hybrid ['haibrid] *nm*, *adj* ibrido.
hydrant ['haidrənt] *n* idrante *m*.
hydraulic [hai'droːlik] *adj* idraulico.
hydrocarbon [ˌhaidrou'kaːbən] *n* idrocarburo *m*.
hydro-electric [ˌhaidrouiˈlektrik] *adj* idroelettrico.
hydrofoil ['haidroufoil] *n* aliscafo *m*.

hydrogen ['haidrədʒən] *n* idrogeno *m*.
hyena [hai'iːnə] *n* iena *f*.
hygiene ['haidʒiːn] *n* igiene *f*. **hygienic** *adj* igienico.
hymn [him] *n* inno *m*, canto sacro *m*.
hyphen ['haifən] *n* lineetta *f*.
hypnosis [hip'nousis] *n* ipnosi *f*. **hypnotic** *adj* ipnotico. **hypnotism** *n* ipnotismo *m*, ipnosi *f*. **hypnotist** *n* ipnotizzatore, -trice *m*, *f*.
hypochondria [haipə'kondriə] *n* ipocondria *f*. **hypochondriac** *n*, *adj* ipocondriaco, -a.
hypocrisy [hi'pokrəsi] *n* ipocrisia *f*. **hypocrite** *n* ipocrita *m*, *f*. **hypocritical** *adj* ipocrita.
hypodermic [haipə'dəːmik] *adj* ipodermico.
hypotenuse [hai'potənjuːz] *n* ipotenusa *f*.
hypothesis [hai'poθəsis] *n*, *pl* **-ses** ipotesi *f*. **hypothetical** *adj* ipotetico.
hysterectomy [histə'rektəmi] *n* isterectomia *f*.
hysteria [his'tiəriə] *n* isterismo *m*. **hysterical** *adj* isterico. **hysterics** *pl n* crisi isterica *f sing*.

I

I [ai] *pron* io.
ice [ais] *n* ghiaccio *m*. **iceberg** *n* iceberg *m invar*. **ice-cold** *adj* freddo come il ghiaccio, glaciale, gelido. **ice cream** gelato *m*. **ice lolly** ghiacciolo *m*. **ice rink** pista di pattinaggio *f*. *v* (*cookery*) glassare; (*cover with ice*) ghiacciare. **icing** *n* glassa *f*. **icy** *adj* glaciale, gelido.
Iceland ['aislənd] *n* Islanda *f*. **Icelander** *n* islandese *m*, *f*. **Icelandic** *adj* islandese.
icicle ['aisikl] *n* ghiacciolo *m*.
icon ['aikon] *n* icona *f*. **iconoclast** *n* iconoclasta *m*, *f*.
idea [ai'diə] *n* idea *f*, concetto *m*, impressione *f*.
ideal [ai'diəl] *nm*, *adj* ideale. **idealist** *n* idealista *m*, *f*. **idealistic** *adj* idealistico. **idealize** *v* idealizzare.
identical [ai'dentikəl] *adj* identico.
identify [ai'dentifai] *n* identificare. **identification** *n* identificazione *f*.
identity [ai'dentiti] *n* identità *f*. **identity card** carta d'identità *f*. **identity parade** confronto all'americana *m*. **mistaken identity** errore di persona *m*.
ideology [aidi'olədʒi] *n* ideologia *f*. **ideological** *adj* ideologico.
idiom ['idiəm] *n* (*expression*) frase idiomatica *f*; (*language*) idioma *m*.
idiosyncrasy [ˌidiə'siŋkrəsi] *n* idiosincrasia *f*.
idiot ['idiət] *n* idiota *m*, *f*; cretino, -a *m*, *f*. **idiotic** *adj* idiota, cretino, imbecille.
idle ['aidl] *adj* (*lazy*) pigro; (*doing nothing*) disoccupato; (*machine*) fermo; (*worthless*) vano. *v* stare senza far nulla; (*machine*) girare a folle. **idler** *n* fannullone, -a *m*, *f*.
idol ['aidl] *n* idolo *m*. **idolatry** *n* idolatria *f*. **idolize** *v* idoleggiare.
idyllic [i'dilik] *adj* idillico.
if [if] *conj* se. **as if** come se. **if not** se no. **if you please** per piacere.
ignite [ig'nait] *v* accendere, dar fuoco a; (*catch fire*) prender fuoco.
ignition [ig'niʃən] *n* accensione *f*. **ignition key** interruttore dell'accensione *m*.
ignorant ['ignərənt] *adj* ignorante. **be ignorant of** ignorare. **ignorance** *n* ignoranza *f*.
ignore [ig'noː] *v* (*disregard*) non badare a, trascurare; (*refrain from seeing/recognizing/hearing*) fingere di non vedere/riconoscere/sentire.
ill [il] *adj* (*sick*) malato; (*bad*) cattivo. *nm*, *adv* male. **ill-advised** *adj* malavveduto. **ill-bred** *or* **ill-mannered** *adj* maleducato. **ill-treat** *v* maltrattare. **illness** *n* malattia *f*.
illegal [i'liːgəl] *adj* illegale.
illegible [i'ledʒəbl] *adj* illeggibile.
illegitimate [ˌili'dʒitimit] *adj* illegittimo.
illicit [i'lisit] *adj* illecito.
illiterate [i'litərit] *n*(*m*+*f*), *adj* analfabeta.
illogical [i'lodʒikəl] *adj* illogico.
illuminate [i'luːmiˌneit] *v* illuminare, rischiarare. **illuminating** *adj* illuminante. **illumination** *n* illuminazione *f*.
illusion [i'luːʒən] *n* illusione *f*.
illustrate ['iləˌstreit] *v* illustrare. **illustration** *n* illustrazione *f*.
illustrious [i'lʌstriəs] *adj* illustre, celebre.
image ['imidʒ] *n* immagine *f*, ritratto *m*. **imagery** *n* immagini *f pl*.
imagine [i'madʒin] *v* farsi un'idea di, immaginarsi; (*suppose*) supporre; (*believe*) credere. **imaginary** *adj* immaginario. **imagination** *n* immaginazione *f*, fantasia *f*.

imbalance [im'baləns] *n* squilibrio *m*.
imbecile ['imbə,siːl] *n*(*m*+*f*), *adj* imbecille.
imitate ['imi,teit] *v* imitare, contraffare. **imitation** *n* imitazione *f*, copia *f*, contraffattura *f*.
immaculate [i'makjulit] *adj* immacolato.
immaterial [,imə'tiəriəl] *adj* (*unimportant*) di nessuna importanza.
immature [,imə'tjuə] *adj* immaturo. **immaturity** *n* immaturità *f*.
immediate [i'miːdiət] *adj* immediato. **immediately** *adv* immediatamente, subito.
immense [i'mens] *adj* immenso.
immerse [i'məːs] *v* immergere. **immersion** *n* immersione *f*. **immersion heater** riscaldatore a immersione *m*.
immigrate ['imi,greit] *v* immigrare. **immigrant** *n*(*m*+*f*), *adj* immigrante. **immigration** *n* immigrazione *f*.
imminent ['iminənt] *adj* imminente.
immobile [i'moubail] *adj* immobile, fermo. **immobilize** *v* immobilizzare.
immoral [i'morəl] *adj* immorale. **immorality** *n* immoralità *f*.
immortal [i'moːtl] *adj* immortale. **immortality** *n* immortalità *f*. **immortalize** *v* immortalare.
immovable [i'muːvəbl] *adj* inamovibile, fisso.
immune [i'mjuːn] *adj* immune. **immunity** *n* immunità *f*. **immunization** *n* immunizzazione *f*. **immunize** *v* immunizzare.
imp [imp] *n* folletto *m*.
impact ['impakt] *n* urto *m*, scontro *m*; (*effect*) impressione *f*.
impair [im'peə] *v* danneggiare, menomare.
impale [im'peil] *v* impalare.
impart [im'paːt] *v* impartire.
impartial [im'paːʃəl] *adj* imparziale. **impartiality** *n* imparzialità *f*.
impasse [am'paːs] *n* impasse *m*, intoppo *m*.
impatient [im'peiʃənt] *adj* impaziente. **get impatient** impazientirsi. **impatience** *n* impazienza *f*.
impeach [im'piːtʃ] *v* accusare; (*call in question*) mettere in dubbio, imputare.
impeccable [im'pekəbl] *adj* impeccabile.
impede [im'piːd] *v* ostacolare, impedire.
impediment [im'pedimənt] *n* impedimento *m*, ostacolo *m*. **speech impediment** difetto *or* impedimento di lingua *m*.
impel [im'pel] *v* spingere, impellere.
impending [im'pendiŋ] *adj* imminente.
imperative [im'perətiv] *nm*, *adj* imperativo.
imperfect [im'pəːfikt] *nm*, *adj* imperfetto.
imperial [im'piəriəl] *adj* imperiale. **imperialism** *n* imperialismo *m*.
imperil [im'perəl] *v* mettere in pericolo, compromettere.
impersonal [im'pəːsənl] *adj* impersonale, comune.
impersonate [im'pəːsə,neit] *v* impersonare; (*theatre*) interpretare.
impertinent [im'pəːtinənt] *adj* impertinente. **impertinence** *n* impertinenza *f*.
impervious [im'pəːviəs] *adj* impervio; impermeabile; (*fig*) sordo.
impetuous [im'petjuəs] *adj* impetuoso.
impetus ['impətəs] *n* impeto *m*, slancio *m*.
impinge [im'pindʒ] *v* **impinge on** colpire.
implement ['implimənt; *v* 'impliment] *n* attrezzo *m*, utensile *m*. *v* adempire. **implementation** *n* adempimento *m*.
implicate ['implikeit] *v* implicare, coinvolgere. **implication** *n* implicazione *f*.
implicit [im'plisit] *adj* implicito.
implore [im'ploː] *v* supplicare.
imply [im'plai] *v* (*mean*) significare; (*suggest*) far pensare a.
impolite [impə'lait] *adj* scortese, sgarbato.
import [im'poːt] *v* importare. *n* (*comm*) importazione *f*; importanza *f*. **importer** *n* importatore *m*.
importance [im'poːtəns] *n* importanza *f*. **important** *adj* importante.
impose [im'pouz] *v* imporre. **impose on** abusare di. **imposing** *adj* imponente. **imposition** *n* imposizione *f*.
impossible [im'posəbl] *adj* impossibile. **impossibility** *n* impossibilità *f*.
impostor [im'postə] *n* impostore *m*.
impotent ['impətənt] *adj* impotente. **impotence** *n* impotenza *f*.
impound [im'paund] *v* confiscare.
impoverish [im'povəriʃ] *v* impoverire.
impractical [im'praktikəl] *adj* (*person*) privo di senso pratico; (*thing*) inservibile, non pratico.
impregnate ['impreg,neit] *v* impregnare. **impregnation** *n* impregnazione *f*.
impress [im'pres] *v* colpire, fare impressione su; (*urge*) raccomandare; (*print*) imprimere, stampare. **impression** *n* impressione *f*; (*print*) stampa *f*, ristampa *f*. **impressive** *adj* impressionante.

imprint ['imprint] *n* impronta *f*.
imprison [im'prizn] *v* carcerare. **imprisonment** *n* carcerazione *f*.
improbable [im'probəbl] *adj* improbabile. **improbability** *n* improbabilità *f*.
impromptu [im'promptjuː] *adj* improvvisato. *adv* all'improvviso.
improper [im'propə] *adj* (*inappropriate*) improprio; (*unseemly*) indecente, indecoroso.
improve [im'pruːv] *v* migliorare; (*increase value*) valorizzare; (*get better*) star meglio. **improve on** perfezionare. **improvement** *n* miglioramento *m*; (*making more valuable*) miglioria *f*.
improvise ['imprəˌvaiz] *v* improvvisare. **improvisation** *n* improvvisazione *f*.
impudent ['impjudənt] *adj* sfacciato. **impudence** *n* sfacciataggine *f*.
impulse ['impʌls] *n* impulso *m*, stimolo *m*. **impulsive** *adj* impulsivo.
impure [im'pjuə] *adj* impuro. **impurity** *n* impurità *f*.
in [in] *prep* in; (*within*) tra, entro. *adv* dentro, a casa, in sede.
inability [ˌinə'biləti] *n* incapacità *f*.
inaccessible [ˌinak'sesəbl] *adj* inaccessibile.
inaccurate [in'akjurit] *adj* inesatto. **inaccuracy** *n* inesattezza *f*.
inactive [in'aktiv] *adj* inattivo, passivo.
inadequate [in'adikwit] *adj* inadeguato, insufficiente, inetto. **inadequacy** *n* inadeguatezza *f*.
inadmissible [inəd'misəbl] *adj* inammissibile.
inadvertent [ˌinəd'vəːtənt] *adj* involontario.
inane [in'ein] *adj* insensato, futile.
inanimate [in'animit] *adj* (*not animate*) inanimato; (*lifeless*) esanime.
inarticulate [ˌinaː'tikjulit] *adj* (*person*) che non sa esprimersi; inarticolato.
inasmuch [ˌinəz'mʌtʃ] *conj* dacchè, poichè.
inaudible [in'oːdəbl] *adj* inaudibile.
inaugurate [i'noːgjuˌreit] *v* inaugurare. **inaugural** *adj* inaugurale. **inauguration** *n* inaugurazione *f*.
inauspicious [inoː'spiʃəs] *adj* infausto.
inbred [ˌin'bred] *adj* (*inborn*) innato; (*resulting from inbreeding*) endogamo. **inbreeding** *n* endogamia *f*.
incalculable [in'kalkjuləbl] *adj* incalcolabile, imprevedibile.
incapable [in'keipəbl] *adj* incapace, inetto.
incendiary [in'sendiəri] *adj* incendiario.
incense[1] ['insens] *n* incenso *m*.
incense[2] [in'sens] *v* irritare, provocare.
incentive [in'sentiv] *n* incentivo *m*.
incessant [in'sesənt] *adj* continuo.
incest ['insest] *n* incesto *m*. **incestuous** *adj* incestuoso.
inch [intʃ] *n* pollice *m*. **inch by inch** gradatamente. *v* **inch forward** avanzare poco alla volta.
incident ['insidənt] *n* caso *m*, episodio *m*; (*event with serious consequences*) incidente *f*. **incidental** *adj* incidentale. **incidentally** *adv* tra parentesi, a proposito.
incinerator [in'sinəˌreitə] *n* inceneritore *m*. **incinerate** *v* incenerire.
incisive [in'saisiv] *adj* acuto.
incite [in'sait] *v* incitare, spronare. **incitement** *n* incitamento *m*.
incline [in'klain] *v* inclinare, chinare. **be inclined to** essere propenso *or* disposto a. *n* piano inclinato *m*, pendio *m*. **inclination** *n* inclinazione *f*; propensione *f*.
include [in'kluːd] *v* includere. **inclusion** *n* inclusione *f*. **inclusive** *adj* compreso.
incoherent [ˌinkə'hiərənt] *adj* incoerente.
income ['inkʌm] *n* entrata *f*, reddito *m*. **income tax** imposta sull'entrata *f*. **incoming** *adj* in arrivo.
incompatible [inkəm'patəbl] *adj* incompatibile. **incompatibility** *n* incompatibilità *f*.
incompetent [in'kompitənt] *adj* incompetente. **incompetence** *n* incompetenza *f*.
incomplete [ˌinkəm'pliːt] *adj* incompleto.
incomprehensible [inˌkompri'hensəbl] *adj* incomprensibile.
inconceivable [inkən'siːvəbl] *adj* inconcepibile.
inconclusive [inkən'kluːsiv] *adj* inconcludente.
incongruous [in'koŋgruəs] *adj* incongruo.
inconsiderate [ˌinkən'sidərit] *adj* sconsiderato; (*person*) che manca di riguardo.
inconsistent [ˌinkən'sistənt] *adj* inconsistente. **inconsistency** *n* inconsistenza *f*.
incontinence [in'kontinəns] *n* incontinenza *f*. **incontinent** *adj* incontinente.
inconvenience [inkən'viːnjəns] *n* sconvenienza *f*. *v* sconvenire, disturbare. **inconvenient** *adj* sconveniente, scomodo.

incorporate [in'koːpəˌreit] *v* incorporare.
incorrect [inkə'rekt] *adj* scorretto.
increase [in'kriːs] *v* aumentare, ingrandirsi, crescere. *n* aumento *m*. **increasingly** *adv* sempre più.
incredible [in'kredəbl] *adj* incredibile.
incredulous [in'kredjuləs] *adj* incredulo.
increment ['iŋkrəmənt] *n* incremento *m*, aumento *m*.
incriminate [in'krimineit] *v* incolpare.
incubate ['iŋkjuˌbeit] *v* incubare. **incubation** *n* incubazione *f*. **incubator** *n* incubatrice *f*.
incumbent [in'kʌmbənt] *adj* **be incumbent on** spettare a.
incur [in'kəː] *v* incorrere in.
incurable [in'kjuərəbl] *adj* incurabile.
indebted [in'detid] *adj* (*owing money*) indebitato; (*under obligation*) riconoscente.
indecent [in'diːsnt] *adj* indecente. **indecency** *n* indecenza *f*; (*law*) oltraggio al pudore *m*.
indeed [in'diːd] *adv* infatti, effettivamente, proprio. *interj* davvero!
indefatigable [indi'fatigəbl] *adj* indefesso.
indefinite [in'definit] *adj* indefinito, vago, illimitato.
indelible [in'deləbl] *adj* indelebile; (*memory*) indimenticabile.
indemnity [in'demnəti] *n* indennità *f*; (*sum paid*) indennizzo *m*. **indemnify** *v* indennizzare.
indent [in'dent] *v* (*notch*) dentellare; (*make recess*) incavare. **indentation** *n* incavo *m*, dentellatura *f*, rientranza *f*; (*printing*) capoverso *m*.
independent [ˌindi'pendənt] *adj* indipendente. **independence** *n* indipendenza *f*.
index ['indeks] *n* indice *m*. **index card** scheda *f*. **index finger** indice *m*.
India ['indjə] *n* India *f*. **India rubber** gomma *f*. **Indian** *n*, *adj* indiano, -a. **Indian ink** inchiostro di china *m*.
indicate ['indikeit] *v* indicare.
indict [in'dait] *v* accusare. **indictment** *n* accusa *f*; (*law*) atto d'accusa *m*.
indifferent [in'difrənt] *adj* indifferente. **indifference** *n* indifferenza *f*.
indigenous [in'didʒinəs] *adj* indigeno.
indigestion [ˌindi'dʒestʃən] *n* indigestione *f*.
indignant [in'dignənt] *adj* sdegnato. **feel indignant** indignarsi, sdegnarsi (contro).
indignity [in'dignəti] *n* indegnità *f*.
indirect [ˌindi'rekt] *adj* indiretto.
indiscreet [ˌindi'skriːt] *adj* indiscreto. **indiscretion** *n* indiscrezione *f*.
indiscriminate [ˌindi'skriminit] *adj* indiscriminato.
indispensable [ˌindi'spensəbl] *adj* indispensabile.
indisposed [ˌindi'spouzd] *adj* indisposto.
individual [ˌindi'vidjuəl] *n* individuo *m*. *adj* individuale, particolare.
indoctrinate [in'doktriˌneit] *v* indottrinare. **indoctrination** *n* indottrinamento *m*.
indolent ['indələnt] *adj* indolente. **indolence** *n* indolenza *f*.
indoor ['indoː] *adj* di *or* da casa. **indoors** *adv* in casa, all'interno, dentro.
induce [in'djuːs] *v* indurre.
indulge [in'dʌldʒ] *v* (*gratify*) appagare, soddisfare; essere indulgente verso. **indulge in** abbandonarsi a, dedicarsi a. **indulgence** *n* indulgenza *f*. **indulgent** *adj* indulgente.
industry ['indəstri] *n* industria *f*; diligenza *f*, zelo *m*. **industrial** *adj* industriale. **industrialize** *v* industrializzare. **industrious** *adj* diligente, operoso.
inebriated [i'niːbrieitid] *adj* ubriaco.
inedible [in'edibl] *adj* immangiabile.
inefficient [ˌini'fiʃnt] *adj* inefficiente. **inefficiency** *n* inefficienza *f*.
inept [i'nept] *adj* inetto, incapace.
inequality [ˌini'kwoləti] *n* ineguaglianza *f*.
inert [i'nəːt] *adj* inerte. **inertia** *n* inerzia *f*.
inevitable [in'evitəbl] *adj* inevitabile.
inexcusable [inik'skjuːzəbl] *adj* imperdonabile, ingiustificabile.
inexhaustible [inig'zoːstəbl] *adj* inesauribile.
inexpensive [ˌinik'spensiv] *adj* a buon mercato, poco caro.
inexperienced [ˌinik'spiəriənst] *adj* inesperto.
inexplicable [inik'splikəbl] *adj* inspiegabile.
infallible [in'faləbl] *adj* infallibile. **infallibility** *n* infallibilità *f*.
infamous ['infəməs] *adj* infame. **infamy** *n* infamia *f*.
infancy ['infənsi] *n* infanzia *f*.
infant ['infənt] *n* infante *m*, bambino, -a *m*, *f*. **infantile** *adj* infantile, puerile. **infant prodigy** bambino prodigio *m*.

infantry ['infəntri] *n* fanteria *f.*
infatuated [in'fatjueitid] *adj* infatuato. **be infatuated** prendere una cotta.
infect [in'fekt] *v* infettare. **infection** *n* infezione *f.* **infectious** *adj* infettivo.
infer [in'fəː] *v* dedurre, desumere. **inferable** *adj* deducibile. **inference** *n* inferenza *f,* deduzione *f.*
inferior [in'fiəriə] *n(m+f), adj* inferiore. **inferiority** *n* inferiorità *f.*
infernal [in'fəːnl] *adj* infernale.
infest [in'fest] *v* infestare.
infidelity [ˌinfi'deliti] *n* infedeltà *f.*
infiltrate [in'filˌtreit] *v* infiltrare. **infiltration** *n* infiltrazione *f.*
infinite ['infinit] *nm, adj* infinito. **infinity** *n* infinità *f,* infinito *m.*
infinitive [in'finitiv] *nm, adj* infinito.
infirm [in'fəːm] *adj* infermo. **infirmity** *n* infermità *f.*
inflame [in'fleim] *v* infiammare. **inflammable** *adj* infiammabile. **inflammation** *n* infiammazione *f.*
inflate [in'fleit] *v* gonfiare. **inflation** *n* inflazione *f.*
inflection [in'flekʃən] *n* inflessione *f.*
inflexible [in'fleksəbl] *adj* inflessibile.
inflict [in'flikt] *v* infliggere.
influence ['influəns] *n* influenza *f,* ascendente *m. v* influire su, influenzare. **influential** *adj* autorevole, importante.
influenza [ˌinflu'enzə] *n* influenza *f.*
influx ['inflʌks] *n* afflusso *m,* affluenza *f.*
inform [in'foːm] *v* informare, far sapere a. **inform against** *or* **on** (*denounce*) denunziare. **informant** *n* informatore, -trice *m, f.* **informer** *n* spia *f,* delatore, -trice *m, f.*
informal [in'foːml] *adj* alla buona, senza cerimonia, non ufficiale. **informality** *n* mancanza di formalità *f.*
information [ˌinfə'meiʃən] *n* informazioni *f pl,* notizie *f pl.* **for your information** a titolo d'informazione.
infra-red [ˌinfrə'red] *adj* infrarosso.
infrequent [in'friːkwənt] *adj* raro.
infringe [in'frindʒ] *v* violare, trasgredire. **infringement** *n* violazione *f.*
infuriate [in'fjuəriˌeit] *v* fare arrabbiare. **be infuriated** essere furibondo *or* arrabbiatissimo.
ingenious [in'dʒiːnjəs] *adj* ingegnoso. **ingenuity** *n* ingegnosità *f.*
ingot ['iŋgət] *n* lingotto *m.*
ingredient [in'griːdjənt] *n* ingrediente *m.*
inhabit [in'habit] *v* abitare, vivere, dimorare. **inhabitant** *n* abitante *m, f.*
inhale [in'heil] *v* inalare.
inherent [in'hiərənt] *adj* inerente.
inherit [in'herit] *v* ereditare. **inheritance** *n* eredità *f.*
inhibit [in'hibit] *v* inibire. **inhibition** *n* inibizione *f.*
inhuman [in'hjuːmən] *adj* inumano. **inhumanity** *n* inumanità *f.*
iniquity [i'nikwəti] *n* iniquità *f.* **iniquitous** *adj* iniquo.
initial [i'niʃl] *nf, adj* iniziale. *v* siglare.
initiate [i'niʃiˌeit] *v* iniziare, istituire. **initiation** *n* iniziazione *f,* inizio *m.*
initiative [i'niʃiətiv] *n* iniziativa *f.*
inject [in'dʒekt] *v* iniettare; (*introduce*) immettere. **injection** *n* iniezione *f.*
injure ['indʒə] *v* (*damage*) danneggiare; (*hurt*) far male a; (*wound*) ferire; (*law*) ledere. **injurious** *adj* dannoso, nocivo. **injury** *n* male *m*; danno *m*; torto *m*; ferita *f.*
injustice [in'dʒʌstis] *n* ingiustizia *f.*
ink [iŋk] *n* inchiostro *m.* **ink-well** *n* calamaio *m.*
inkling ['iŋkliŋ] *n* sospetto *m,* sentore *m.*
inland ['inlənd; *adv* in'land] *adj* interno. *adv* all' *or* nell'interno.
in-laws ['inˌloːs] *pl n* (*coll*) parenti acquisiti *m pl.*
***inlay** ['inlei] *v* intarsiare. *n* intarsio *m.*
inlet ['inlet] *n* (*geog*) insenatura *f.*
inmate ['inmeit] *n* (*of hospital, etc.*) ricoverato, -a *m, f*; (*of prison*) carcerato, -a *m, f.*
inn [in] *n* locanda *f,* osteria *f,* albergo *m.* **innkeeper** *n* locandiere, -a *m, f*; oste, -essa *m, f*; albergatore, -trice *m, f.*
innate [ˌi'neit] *adj* innato.
inner ['inə] *adj* interno, interiore; (*thoughts, etc.*) intimo. **inner tube** camera d'aria *f.*
innocent ['inəsnt] *n(m+f), adj* innocente. **innocence** *n* innocenza *f.*
innocuous [i'nokjuəs] *adj* innocuo.
innovation [inə'veiʃən] *n* innovazione *f,* novità *f.* **innovate** *v* innovare. **innovator** *n* innovatore, -trice *m, f.*
innuendo [ˌinju'endou] *n* insinuazione *f.*
innumerable [i'njuːmərəbl] *adj* innumerevole.
inoculate [i'nokjuˌleit] *v* inoculare. **inoculation** *n* inoculazione *f.*

inorganic [ˌinoːˈganik] *adj* inorganico.
input [ˈinput] *n* (*elec*) alimentazione *f*; (*computer*) input *m invar*.
inquest [ˈinkwest] *n* inchiesta *f*, istruttoria *f*.
inquire [inˈkwaiə] *v* chiedere, domandare. **inquiry** *n* domanda *f*, informazione *f*, inchiesta *f*.
inquisition [ˌinkwiˈziʃən] *n* inquisizione *f*, inchiesta *f*.
inquisitive [inˈkwizətiv] *adj* curioso.
insane [inˈsein] *adj* pazzo, matto. **insanity** *n* pazzia *f*, follia *f*.
insatiable [inˈseiʃəbl] *adj* insaziabile.
inscribe [inˈskraib] *v* (*enrol*) inscrivere; (*engrave*) incidere. **inscription** *n* iscrizione *f*, dedica *f*.
insect [ˈinsekt] *n* insetto *m*. **insecticide** *n* insetticida *m*.
insecure [ˌinsiˈkjuə] *adj* malsicuro, instabile. **insecurity** *n* incertezza *f*, instabilità *f*.
inseminate [inˈsemineit] *v* inseminare. **insemination** *n* inseminazione *f*.
insensible [inˈsensəbl] *adj* insensibile; (*unconscious*) privo di sensi.
insensitive [inˈsensətiv] *adj* insensibile, indifferente.
inseparable [inˈsepərəbl] *adj* inseparabile.
insert [inˈsəːt; *n* ˈinsəːt] *v* inserire. *n also* **insertion** inserzione *f*.
inshore [ˌinˈʃoː] *adj* costiero. *adv* verso la riva.
inside [ˌinˈsaid] *adv* dentro, internamente. *prep* dentro, all'interno. *adj* interno, interiore; (*confidential*) riservato. *n* interno *m*; (*soccer*) mezzala *f*. **inside out** a rovescio.
insidious [inˈsidiəs] *adj* insidioso, perfido.
insight [ˈinsait] *n* discernimento *m*, intuito *m*.
insignificant [ˌinsigˈnifikənt] *adj* insignificante.
insincere [ˌinsinˈsiə] *adj* insincero.
insinuate [inˈsinjueit] *v* insinuare, dare ad intendere. **insinuation** *n* insinuazione *f*.
insipid [inˈsipid] *adj* insipido.
insist [inˈsist] *v* insistere. **insistence** *n* insistenza *f*. **insistent** *adj* insistente.
insolent [ˈinsələnt] *adj* impertinente. **insolence** *n* impertinenza *f*.
insoluble [inˈsoljubl] *adj* insolubile; (*not solvable*) insolvibile.
insomnia [inˈsomniə] *n* insonnia *f*. **insomniac** *n* insonne *m, f*.
inspect [inˈspekt] *v* ispezionare, verificare; (*troops*) passare in rivista. **inspection** *n* ispezione *f*, verifica *f*; rivista *f*. **inspector** *n* ispettore, -trice *m, f*; (*bus, train*) controllore, -a *m, f*; (*police*) commissario *m*.
inspire [inˈspaiə] *v* ispirare, infondere. **inspiration** *n* ispirazione *f*.
instability [ˌinstəˈbiləti] *n* instabilità *f*.
install [inˈstoːl] *v* installare. **installation** *n* installazione *f*.
instalment [inˈstoːlmənt] *n* (*comm*) rata *f*; (*serial*) puntata *f*.
instance [ˈinstəns] *n* esempio *m*. **for instance** per esempio.
instant [ˈinstənt] *adj* immediato; urgente; (*comm*) corrente; (*of food*) istantaneo. *n* istante *m*, momento *m*. **instantaneous** *adj* istantaneo.
instead [inˈsted] *adv* invece.
instep [ˈinstep] *n* (*anat*) collo del piede *m*; (*shoe*) collo della scarpa *m*.
instigate [ˈinstigeit] *v* istigare. **instigation** *n* istigazione *f*.
instil [inˈstil] *v* instillare, infondere.
instinct [ˈinstiŋkt] *n* istinto *m*. **instinctive** *adj* istintivo.
institute [ˈinstitjuːt] *n* istituto *m*. *v* istituire, iniziare. **institution** *n* istituzione *f*.
instruct [inˈstrʌkt] *v* (*teach*) istruire; (*direct*) dare istruzioni *or* disposizioni a. **instruction** *n* istruzione *f*, disposizioni *f pl*. **instructive** *adj* istruttivo. **instructor** *n* istruttore, -trice *m, f*, insegnante *m, f*.
instrument [ˈinstrəmənt] *n* strumento *m*; (*tool*) arnese *m*; (*law*) titolo *m*, atto *m*. **instrumental** *adj* strumentale. **be instrumental in** essere utile a.
insubordinate [ˌinsəˈboːdənət] *adj* insubordinato. **insubordination** *n* insubordinazione *f*.
insufficient [ˌinsəˈfiʃənt] *adj* insufficiente.
insular [ˈinsjulə] *adj* insulare; (*outlook*) gretto.
insulate [ˈinsjuleit] *v* isolare. **insulating tape** nastro isolante *m*. **insulation** *n* isolamento *m*.
insulin [ˈinsjulin] *n* insulina *f*.
insult [inˈsʌlt; *n* ˈinsʌlt] *v* insultare, offendere. *n* insulto *m*, offesa *f*.
insure [inˈʃuə] *v* assicurare. **insurance** *n* assicurazione *f*.
intact [inˈtakt] *adj* intatto.

intake ['inteik] *n* (*consumption*) consumo *m*; (*employment*) assunzione *f*; (*people newly taken on*) reclute *f pl*.
intangible [in'tandʒəbl] *adj* intangibile.
integral ['intigrəl] *adj* integrale.
integrate ['intigreit] *v* integrare. **integration** *n* integrazione *f*.
integrity [in'tegrəti] *n* integrità *f*.
intellect ['intilekt] *n* intelletto *m*. **intellectual** *n*(*m*+*f*), *adj* intellettuale.
intelligent [in'telidʒənt] *adj* intelligente. **intelligence** *n* intelligenza *f*; informazioni *f pl*. **intelligentsia** *n* intellighenzia *f*.
intelligible [in'telidʒəbl] *adj* intelligibile.
intend [in'tend] *v* intendere, aver l'intenzione di. **intended** *adj* premeditato, voluto.
intense [in'tens] *adj* intenso, profondo.
intent[1] [in'tent] *n* intento *m*, proposito *m*, intenzione *f*. **to all intents and purposes** a tutti gli effetti.
intent[2] [in'tent] *adj* intento, assorto. **intent on** deciso a.
intention [in'tenʃən] *n* intenzione *f*, proposito *m*. **intentional** *adj* intenzionale.
inter [in'təː] *v* seppellire. **interment** *n* sepoltura *f*.
interact [ˌintər'akt] *v* esercitare un'azione reciproca, interagire. **interaction** *n* azione reciproca *f*.
intercede [ˌintə'siːd] *v* intercedere.
intercept [ˌintə'sept] *v* intercettare. **interception** *n* intercettazione *f*.
interchange [ˌintə'tʃeindʒ] *v* scambiare. **interchangeable** *adj* intercambiabile, scambievole.
intercom ['intəˌkom] *n* citofono *m*.
intercourse ['intəkoːs] *n* rapporti *m pl*.
interest ['intrist] *v* interessare. **be interested in** interessarsi di. *n* interesse *m*. **interesting** *adj* interessante.
interfere [ˌintə'fiə] *v* interferire, immischiarsi. **interference** *n* interferenza *f*.
interim ['intərim] *n* interim *m*. *adj* provvisorio, temporaneo.
interior [in'tiəriə] *nm*, *adj* interno. **interior decorator** arredatore, -trice *m*, *f*.
interjection [ˌintə'dʒekʃən] *n* interiezione *f*.
interlude ['intəluːd] *n* interludio *m*.
intermediary [intə'miːdiəri] *n* intermediario *m*.
intermediate [ˌintə'miːdiət] *adj* intermedio.
interminable [in'təːminəbl] *adj* senza fine.
intermission [ˌintə'miʃən] *n* interruzione *f*.
intermittent [ˌintə'mitənt] *adj* intermittente.
intern [in'təːn] *v* internare. **internment** *n* internamento *m*.
internal [in'təːnl] *adj* interno, interiore.
international [ˌintə'naʃənl] *adj* internazionale.
interpose [ˌintə'pouz] *v* frapporre.
interpret [in'təːprit] *v* interpretare. **interpretation** *n* interpretazione *f*. **interpreter** *n* interprete *m*, *f*.
interrogate [in'terəgeit] *v* interrogare. **interrogation** *n* interrogazione *f*. **interrogative** *adj*, *nm* interrogativo.
interrupt [ˌintə'rʌpt] *v* interrompere. **interruption** *n* interruzione *f*.
intersect [ˌintə'sekt] *v* intersecare. **intersection** *n* intersezione *f*.
intersperse [ˌintə'spəːs] *v* cospargere.
interval ['intəvəl] *n* intervallo *m*.
intervene [ˌintə'viːn] *v* intervenire. **intervention** *n* intervento *m*.
interview ['intəvjuː] *n* intervista *f*, colloquio *m*. *v* intervistare.
intestine [in'testin] *n* intestino *m*. **intestinal** *adj* intestinale.
intimate[1] ['intimət] *adj* intimo, familiare. **intimacy** *n* intimità *f*.
intimate[2] ['intimeit] *v* intimare, suggerire. **intimation** *n* intimazione *f*.
intimidate [in'timideit] *v* intimidire, intimorire. **intimidation** *n* intimidazione *f*.
into ['intu] *prep* in, dentro.
intolerable [in'tolərəbl] *adj* insopportabile, intollerabile.
intolerant [in'tolərənt] *adj* intollerante. **intolerance** *n* intolleranza *f*.
intonation [ˌintə'neiʃən] *n* intonazione *f*.
intoxicate [in'toksikeit] *v* intossicare; (*with drink*) ubriacare; (*excite*) esaltare. **intoxicated** *adj* ubriaco, eccitato.
intransigent [in'transidʒənt] *adj* intransigente.
intransitive [in'transitiv] *adj* intransitivo.
intravenous [ˌintrə'viːnəs] *adj* endovenoso.
intrepid [in'trepid] *adj* intrepido.
intricate ['intriket] *adj* complicato, complesso. **intricacy** *n* complicazione *f*.
intrigue ['intriːg; *v* in'triːg] *n* intrigo (*pl*

-ghi) *m.* *v* (*plot*) intrigare; (*excite curiosity*) incuriosire. **intriguing** *adj* interessante, affascinante.
intrinsic [in'trinsik] *adj* intrinseco.
introduce [ˌintrə'djuːs] *v* introdurre; (*people*) presentare. **introduction** *n* introduzione *f*, presentazione *f*. **introductory** *adj* introduttorio, introduttivo.
introspective [ˌintrə'spektiv] *adj* introspettivo. **introspection** *n* introspezione *f*.
introvert ['intrəˌvəːt] *adj*, *n* introverso, -a.
intrude [in'truːd] *v* intrudere. **intrusion** *n* intrusione *f*.
intuition [ˌintjuː'iʃən] *n* intuito *m*; (*psychol, etc.*) intuizione *f*. **intuitive** *adj* intuitivo.
inundate ['inʌndeit] *v* inondare, allagare. **inundation** *n* allagamento *m*.
invade [in'veid] *v* invadere. **invader** *n* invasore *m*. **invasion** *n* invasione *f*.
invalid[1] ['invəlid] *n*, *adj* invalido, -a; malato, -a.
invalid[2] [in'valid] *adj* (*not valid*) invalido, senza validità, nullo. **invalidate** *v* invalidare, annullare.
invaluable [in'valjuəbl] *adj* inestimabile, incalcolabile.
invariable [in'veəriəbl] *adj* invariabile, costante.
invective [in'vektiv] *n* invettiva *f*.
invent [in'vent] *v* inventare. **invention** *n* invenzione *f*.
inventory ['invəntri] *n* inventario *m*.
invert [in'vəːt] *v* invertire; (*inside out*) rovesciare; (*upside down*) capovolgere. **inverted commas** virgolette *f pl*. **inversion** *n* inversione *f*, rovesciamento *m*.
invertebrate [in'vəːtibrət] *nm*, *adj* invertebrato.
invest [in'vest] *v* investire. **investment** *n* investimento *m*.
investigate [in'vestigeit] *v* investigare, svolgere indagini. **investigation** *n* indagine *f*.
invigorating [in'vigəreitiŋ] *adj* che invigorisce, fortificante.
invincible [in'vinsəbl] *adj* invincibile.
invisible [in'vizəbl] *adj* invisibile. **invisibility** *n* invisibilità *f*.
invite [in'vait] *v* invitare; provocare; (*lay oneself open to*) esporsi a. **invitation** *n* invito *m*. **inviting** *adj* attraente, seducente.
invoice ['invois] *n* fattura *f*. *v* fatturare.
invoke [in'vouk] *v* invocare. **invocation** *n* invocazione *f*.
involuntary [in'voləntəri] *adj* involontario.
involve [in'volv] *v* (*imply*) implicare; (*implicate*) coinvolgere; (*entail*) comportare. **involvement** *n* implicazione *f*.
inward ['inwəd] *adj* interno, intimo. **inwardly** *adv* interiormente. **inwards** *adv* verso il centro.
iodine ['aiədiːn] *n* iodio *m*.
ion ['aiən] *n* ione *m*.
irate [ai'reit] *adj* arrabbiato.
Ireland ['aiələnd] *n* Irlanda *f*. **Irish** *n*(*m*+*f*), *adj* irlandese.
iris ['aiəris] *n* (*anat*) iride *f*; (*bot*) giaggiolo *m*.
irk [əːk] *v* infastidire, dar noia a. **irksome** *adj* seccante, noioso.
iron ['aiən] *n* ferro *m*; (*for pressing*) ferro da stiro *m*. **iron curtain** cortina di ferro *f*. **ironmonger's** *n* ferramenta *f*. *v* stirare. **ironing board** tavola da stiro *f*.
irony ['aiərəni] *n* ironia *f*. **ironic** *adj* ironico.
irrational [i'raʃənl] *adj* irrazionale.
irregular [i'regjulə] *adj* irregolare. **irregularity** *n* irregolarità *f*.
irrelevant [i'reləvənt] *adj* non pertinente.
irreparable [i'repərəbl] *adj* irreparabile.
irresistible [ˌiri'zistəbl] *adj* irresistibile.
irrespective [ˌiri'spektiv] *adj* **irrespective of** senza riguardo a, senza tener conto di.
irresponsible [ˌiri'sponsəbl] *adj* irresponsabile. **irresponsibility** *n* irresponsabilità *f*.
irrevocable [i'revəkəbl] *adj* irrevocabile.
irrigate ['irigeit] *v* irrigare. **irrigation** *n* irrigazione *f*.
irritate ['iriteit] *v* irritare. **irritating** *adj* irritante. **irritation** *n* irritazione *f*.
Islam ['izlaːm] *n* Islam *m*. **Islamic** *adj* islamico.
island ['ailənd] *n* isola *f*.
isolate ['aisəleit] *v* isolare. **isolation** *n* isolamento *m*.
issue ['iʃuː] *n* questione *f*, problema *m*; (*outcome*) conclusione *f*; edizione *f*; (*shares, etc.*) emissione *f*. *v* pubblicare; emettere; uscire.
isthmus ['isməs] *n* istmo *m*.
it [it] *pron* (*subject*) esso, -a; (*direct object*) lo, la; (*indirect object*) gli, le.
italic [i'talik] *adj* (*handwriting*) italico;

(*printing*) corsivo. **in italics** in (carattere) corsivo.
Italy ['itəli] *n* Italia *f*. **Italian** *n, adj* italiano, -a; (*language*) italiano *m*.
itch [itʃ] *n* (*sensation*) prurito *m*; (*desire*) gran voglia *f*. *v* sentire prurito.
item ['aitəm] *n* voce *f*, capo *m*, pezzo *m*.
itinerary [ai'tinərəri] *n* itinerario *m*.
its [its] *adj* (il) suo, (la) sua; (*pl*) (i) suoi, (le) sue.
itself [it'self] *pron* (*reflexive*) si; (*after prep*) sè; (*emphatic*) se esso, -a, se stesso, -a.
ivory ['aivəri] *n* avorio *m*.
ivy ['aivi] *n* edera *f*.

J

jab [dʒab] *n* puntura *f*. *v* pungere, punzecchiare.
jack [dʒak] *n* (*car*) cricco *m*; (*cards*) fante *m*; (*bowls*) boccino *m*. *v* **jack up** alzare.
jackdaw ['dʒakdoː] *n* taccola *f*.
jacket ['dʒakit] *n* giacca *f*; (*of book*) copertina *f*; (*boiler, etc*.) rivestimento *m*. **jacket potato** patata in camicia *f*.
jack-knife ['dʒaknaif] *n* coltello a serramanico *m*.
jackpot ['dʒakpot] *n* posta intera *f*, monte premi *m*. **hit the jackpot** avere un colpo di fortuna.
jade [dʒeid] *n* giada *f*.
jaded ['dʒeidid] *adj* stracco, spossato.
jagged ['dʒagid] *adj* scabro, intaccato, dentellato.
jaguar ['dʒagjuə] *n* giaguaro *m*.
jail *or* **gaol** [dʒeil] *n* prigione *f*, carcere *m*. *v* incarcerare, mettere in prigione.
jam[1] [dʒam] *v* (*block*) bloccare; (*cause to stop functioning*) intralciare; (*squeeze*) pigiare; (*radio*) disturbare; (*traffic*) intasare. **jam on the brakes** bloccare i freni. *n* (*traffic*) intasamento *m*. **get into a jam** mettersi nei pasticci.
jam[2] [dʒam] *n* marmellata *f*, conserva di frutta *f*.
janitor ['dʒanitə] *n* portinaio, -a *m, f*.
January ['dʒanjuəri] *n* gennaio *m*.
Japan [dʒə'pan] *n* Giappone *m*. **Japanese** *n*(*m*+*f*), *adj* giapponese.
jar[1] [dʒaː] *n* (*vessel*) brocca *f*; (*usually with lid*) barattolo *m*.
jar[2] [dʒaː] *v* vibrare; produrre un suono aspro. **jarring** *adj* discorde.
jargon ['dʒaːgən] *n* gergo *m*.
jasmine ['dʒazmin] *n* gelsomino *m*.
jaundice ['dʒoːndis] *n* itterizia *f*. **jaundiced** *adj* distorto, invelenito.
jaunt [dʒoːnt] *n* gita *f*.
jaunty ['dʒoːnti] *adj* vivace, disinvolto.
javelin ['dʒavəlin] *n* giavellotto *m*.
jaw [dʒoː] *n* (*upper*) mascella *f*; (*lower*) mandibola *f*.
jay [dʒei] *n* ghiandaia *f*.
jazz [dʒaz] *n* jazz *m invar*.
jealous ['dʒeləs] *adj* geloso. **become jealous** ingelosirsi. **make jealous** ingelosire. **jealousy** *n* gelosia *f*.
jeans [dʒiːns] *pl n* jeans *m pl*.
jeep [dʒiːp] *n* jeep *f invar*.
jeer [dʒiə] *v* schernire, canzonare. *n* derisione *f*, scherno *m*.
jelly ['dʒeli] *n* gelatina *f*, budino di gelatina *m*.
jeopardize ['dʒepədaiz] *v* mettere a repentaglio, arrischiare. **jeopardy** *n* repentaglio *m*.
jerk [dʒəːk] *n* (*shock*) scossa *f*; (*pull*) strappo *m*; (*sudden start*) scatto *m*. *v* scuotere; dare uno strappoa; scattare.
jersey ['dʒəːzi] *n* (*fabric*) jersey *m invar*; (*garment*) maglione *m*.
jest [dʒest] *n* scherzo *m*, burla *f*. *v* scherzare. **jester** *n* buffone *m*.
Jesuit ['dʒezjuit] *adj, nm* gesuita. **Jesuitical** *adj* gesuitico.
Jesus ['dʒiːzəs] *n* Gesù *m*. **Jesus Christ** Gesù Cristo.
jet [dʒet] *n* getto *m*, zampillo *m*; (*spout*) becco *m*; (*aero*) aviogetto *m*, aeroplano a reazione *m*. **jet-black** *adj* (nero) ebano *invar*. **jet engine** motore a reazione *m*.
jettison ['dʒetisn] *v* buttar via, disfarsi di.
jetty ['dʒeti] *n* molo *m*, banchina *f*.
Jew [dʒuː] *n* ebreo, -a *m, f*. **Jewish** *adj* (*person*) ebreo; (*thing*) ebraico.
jewel ['dʒuːəl] *n* gioiello *m*; (*watch*) rubino *m*; (*treasure*) tesoro *m*. **jeweller** *n* gioielliere *m*. **jewellery** *n* gioielleria *f*.
jib[1] [dʒib] *n* (*sail*) fiocco *m*; (*crane*) braccio *m*.
jib[2] [dʒib] *v* **jib at** essere restio *or* ritroso a.
jig[1] [dʒig] *n* (*machine tool*) maschera di montaggio *f*. *v* lavorare con maschere.
jig[2] *n* (*dance*) giga *f*. *v* ballare la giga. **jig up and down** salterellare su e giù.

jiggle ['dʒigl] *v* dondolare, muoversi in qua e in là.
jigsaw ['dʒigsoː] *n* sega da traforo *f*. **jigsaw puzzle** puzzle *m*.
jilt [dʒilt] *v* piantare in asso.
jingle ['dʒiŋgl] *n* (*sound*) tintinnio *m*; (*song*) ritornello *m*, cantilena *f*. *v* tintinnare.
jinx [dʒiŋks] *n* malocchio *m*.
job [dʒob] *n* impiego (*pl* -ghi) *m*, lavoro *m*; (*coll*) affare *m*, mestiere *m*.
jockey ['dʒoki] *n* fantino *m*. *v* maneggiare.
jocular ['dʒokjulə] *adj* faceto.
jodhpurs ['dʒodpəz] *pl n* calzoni da equitazione *m pl*.
jog [dʒog] *v* (*sport*) fare il footing; (*horse*) andare al piccolo trotto. **jog the memory** richiamare alla memoria. *n* (*push*) spinta *f*; (*nudge*) colpetto *m*; (*elbowing*) gomitata *f*; (*trot*) piccolo trotto *m*.
join [dʒoin] *n* giuntura *f*. *v* unire, congiungere, unirsi a; (*become member*) iscriversi a, entrare. **join in** entrare a far parte di.
joiner ['dʒoinə] *n* falegname *m*.
joint [dʒoint] *n* (*join*) giuntura *f*; articolazione *f*; (*plant*) nodo *m*; (*meat*) taglio (di carne) *m*; (*coll*: *bar*, *etc*.) bettola *f*. *adj* comune, collettivo.
joist [dʒoist] *n* trave *f*, travicello *m*.
joke [dʒouk] *n* scherzo *m*, barzelletta *f*. **no joke** un affare serio *m*. *v* scherzare. **joker** *n* burlone *m*; (*cards*) jolly *m invar*, matta *f*.
jolly ['dʒoli] *adj* divertente, ameno, gaio. *adv* molto.
jolt [dʒoult] *v* scuotere, far sobbalzare. *n* scossa *f*, sobbalzo *m*.
jostle ['dʒosl] *n* (*push*) spinta *f*; (*elbowing*) gomitata *f*. *v* fare a gomitate, spingersi avanti.
journal ['dʒəːnl] *n* periodico *m*; (*daily record*) diario *m*, giornale *m*; (*day-book*) brogliaccio *m*. **journalism** *n* giornalismo *m*. **journalist** *n* giornalista *m*, *f*.
journey ['dʒəːni] *n* viaggio *m*. *v* viaggiare. **go on a journey** andare *or* mettersi in viaggio.
jovial ['dʒouviəl] *adj* gioviale, lieto.
jowl [dʒaul] *n* (*jaw*) mascella *f*; (*flesh*) gota *f*.
joy [dʒoi] *n* gioia *f*, allegrezza *f*, allegria *f*. **joyful** *or* **joyous** *adj* gioioso.
jubilant ['dʒuːbilənt] *adj* giubilante.
jubilee ['dʒuːbiliː] *n* giubileo *m*.
Judaism ['dʒuːdei,izəm] *n* giudaismo *m*.
judge [dʒʌdʒ] *n* giudice *m*; (*of competition*) arbitro *m*; (*expert*) intenditore, -trice *m*, *f*. *v* giudicare, considerare. **judgment** *n* giudizio *m*; (*law*) sentenza *f*; (*opinion*) parere *m*. **Last Judgment** giudizio universale *m*.
judicial [dʒuːˈdiʃəl] *adj* giudiziario; legale.
judiciary [dʒuˈdiʃiəri] *n* magistratura *f*.
judicious [dʒuːˈdiʃəs] *adj* giudizioso, prudente.
judo ['dʒuːdou] *n* judo *m invar*, giudò *m*.
jug [dʒʌg] *n* brocca *f*, caraffa *f*.
juggernaut ['dʒʌgənoːt] *n* (*lorry*) grosso autotreno *m*.
juggle ['dʒʌgl] *v* giocolare, prestigiare; (*trick*) truffare. **juggle with** svisare, travisare. **juggler** *n* giocoliere, -a *m*, *f*; prestigiatore, -trice *m*, *f*.
jugular ['dʒʌgjulə] *adj* giugulare.
juice [dʒuːs] *n* succo *m*, sugo *m*. **juicy** *adj* sugoso, succolento.
jukebox ['dʒuːkboks] *n* jukebox *m invar*.
July [dʒuˈlai] *n* luglio *m*.
jumble ['dʒʌmbl] *n* miscuglio *m*, confusione *f*. **jumble sale** bazar di beneficenza *m invar*.
jump [dʒʌmp] *n* salto *m*; (*sudden rise*) balzo *m*; (*nervous*) sussulto *m*. **long/high jump** salto in lungo/alto *m*. *v* saltare, fare un salto; sussultare; (*of prices*) rincarare. **jump at** accettare con entusiasmo. **jump off** lanciarsi da. **jump over** scavalcare.
jumper ['dʒʌmpə] *n* (*pullover*) maglione *m*, pullover *m invar*; (*jacket*) casacca *f*; (*person*) saltatore, -trice *m*, *f*.
junction ['dʒʌŋktʃən] *n* congiunzione *f*; (*rail*) nodo ferroviario *m*.
juncture ['dʒʌŋkʃə] *n* frangente *m*, momento (critico) *m*.
June [dʒuːn] *n* giugno *m*.
jungle ['dʒʌŋgl] *n* giungla *f*.
junior ['dʒuːnjə] *adj* minore, più giovane.
juniper ['dʒuːnipə] *n* ginepro *m*.
junk[1] [dʒʌŋk] *n* (*rubbish*) roba vecchia *f*, robaccia *f*, rifiuti *m pl*.
junk[2] [dʒʌŋk] *n* (*boat*) giunca *f*.
junta ['dʒʌntə] *n* giunta *f*.
jurisdiction [dʒuərisˈdikʃən] *n* giurisdizione *f*.
jury ['dʒuəri] *n* giuria *f*. **juror** *n* giurato, -a *m*, *f*.

just [dʒʌst] *adj* giusto, preciso. *adv* giusto, per l'appunto, proprio; (*barely*) appena; (*not more than*) soltanto.
justice ['dʒʌstis] *n* giustizia *f*; (*judge*) giudice *m*, magistrato *m*. **do justice to** (*show appreciation*) far onore a; (*concede what is due*) apprezzare, stimare.
justify ['dʒʌstifai] *v* giustificare, scusare. **justifiable** *adj* giustificabile, scusabile, legittimo. **justification** *n* giustificazione *f*, scusa *f*.
jut [dʒʌt] *v* sporgere, protendere (in fuori).
jute [dʒuːt] *n* giuta *f*.
juvenile ['dʒuːvənail] *adj* giovanile, per ragazzi, minorenne.
juxtapose [ˌdʒʌkstə'pouz] *v* giustapporre. **juxtaposition** *n* giustapposizione *f*.

K

kaleidoscope [kə'laidəskoup] *n* caleidoscopio *m*.
kangaroo [kaŋgə'ruː] *n* canguro *m*.
karate [kə'raːti] *n* karatè *m invar*.
keel [kiːl] *n* chiglia *f*. *v* **keel over** capovolgersi.
keen [kiːn] *adj* (*cutting*) tagliente; (*sharp*) aguzzo; (*perceptive*) vivo, perspicace; (*biting*) mordace; (*eager*) appassionato, entusiasta. **keenness** *n* passione *f*, entusiasmo *m*, intensità *f*; (*eagerness*) ardore *m*.
***keep** [kiːp] *v* tenere; mantenere; conservare; (*hold in custody*) custodire; (*manage*) gestire; (*observe*) osservare, rispettare. **keep at** persistere, continuare a fare. **keep back** (*stay behind*) stare indietro; (*withhold*) trattenere. **keep down** reprimere. **keep good time** (*watch*) funzionare bene. **keep in with** mantenersi in buoni rapporti con. **keep on** continuare. **keep out** non lasciar entrare; restar fuori. **keep to** aderire a. *n* **earn one's keep** mantenersi. **for keeps** per sempre.
keeper ['kiːpə] *n* guardiano, -a *m*, *f*; custode *m*, *f*.
keeping ['kiːpiŋ] *n* custodia *f*. **in keeping with** conforme *or* consono a.
keepsake ['kiːpseik] *n* ricordo *m*.
keg [keg] *n* barilotto *m*.
kennel ['kenl] *n* canile *m*.
kept [kept] *V* **keep**.
kerb [kəːb] *n* banchina *f*.
kernel ['kəːnl] *n* nocciolo *m*, nucleo *m*.
kerosene ['kerəsiːn] *n* cherosene *m*.
kettle ['ketl] *n* bollitore *m*, pentola *f*.
kettledrum ['ketldrʌm] *n* timpano *m*.
key [kiː] *n* chiave *f*; (*part of keyboard*) tasto *m*. **keyboard** *n* tastiera *f*. **keyhole** *n* buco della chiave *m*. **keynote** *n* nota determinante *f*.
khaki ['kaːki] *adj* cachi.
kick [kik] *v* dare un calcio a, dare una pedata a; protestare. **kick off** iniziare. **kick out** buttar fuori. **kick up** scatenare, provocare. *n* calcio *m*, pedata *f*; (*force*) forza *f*.
kid[1] [kid] *n* (*child*) bimbo, -a *m*, *f*; (*goat*) capretto *m*. **handle with kid gloves** trattare coi guanti.
kid[2] [kid] *v* (*coll*) prendere in giro.
kidnap ['kidnap] *v* rapire. **kidnapper** *n* rapitore, -trice *m*, *f*.
kidney ['kidni] *n* (*organ*) rene *m*; (*food*) rognone *f*. **kidney bean** fagiolo *m*.
kill [kil] *v* uccidere, ammazzare. **killer** *n* assassino, -a *m*, *f*.
kiln [kiln] *n* forno *m*.
kilo ['kiːlou] *n* chilo *m*. **kilogram** *n* chilogrammo *m*.
kilometre ['kiləmiːtə] *n* chilometro *m*.
kilt [kilt] *n* gonnellino scozzese *m*.
kin [kin] *n* parenti *m pl*; (*kinship*) parentela *f*. **kinsman** *n* parente *m*. **next of kin** parente prossimo *m*.
kind[1] [kaind] *adj* gentile, cortese, buono; (*well-meant*) cordiale. **kind-hearted** *adj* benevolo. **kindly** *adv* gentilmente; (*please*) per cortesia, per favore. **kindness** *n* gentilezza *f*, cortesia *f*.
kind[2] [kaind] *n* genere *m*, specie *f*, razza *f*.
kindergarten ['kindəgaːtn] *n* giardino d'infanzia *m*, asilo (infantile) *m*.
kindle ['kindl] *v* accendere; (*excite*) eccitare.
kindred ['kindrid] *n* parentela *f*. *adj* affine, simile. **kindred spirit** anima gemella *f*.
kinetic [kin'etik] *adj* chinetico.
king [kiŋ] *n* re *m invar*. **kingdom** *n* regno *m*.
kingfisher ['kiŋˌfiʃə] *n* martin pescatore *m*.
kink [kiŋk] *n* attorcigliamento *m*, piega *f*; (*whim*) ghiribizzo *m*. **kinky** *adj* (*odd*) strambo; (*coll*) pervertito.

kiosk ['kiːosk] *n* chiosco *m*; (*newsagent*) edicola *f*.
kipper ['kipə] *n* aringa affumicata *f*.
kiss [kis] *n* bacio *m*. *v* baciare.
kit [kit] *n* (*tools*) attrezzi *m pl*, utensili *m pl*; (*outfit*) corredo *m*. *v* attrezzare. **kit out** equipaggiare.
kitchen ['kitʃin] *n* cucina *f*.
kite [kait] *n* aquilone *m*; (*bird*) nibbio *m*.
kitten ['kitn] *n* micio *m*, gattino *m*.
kitty ['kiti] *n* (*joint pool*) fondo comune *m*; (*cards*) posta *f*.
kleptomania [kleptə'meiniə] *n* cleptomania *f*. **kleptomaniac** *n* cleptomane *m*, *f*.
knack [nak] *n* desterità *f*, bernoccolo *m*.
knapsack ['napsak] *n* zaino *m*.
knave [neiv] *n* furfante *m*; (*cards*) fante *m*.
knead [niːd] *v* impastare.
knee [niː] *n* ginocchio *m* (*pl* -a *f*). **kneecap** *n* rotula *f*, patella *f*. **knee-deep** *adj* che arriva fino al ginocchio; (*submerged*) sommerso.
***kneel** [niːl] *v* inginocchiarsi, mettersi in ginocchio.
knelt [nelt] *V* **kneel**.
knew [njuː] *V* **know**.
knickers ['nikəz] *pl n* mutandine *f pl*.
knife [naif] *n* coltello *m*. *v* accoltellare.
knight [nait] *n* cavaliere *m*.
***knit** [nit] *v* lavorare a maglia, fare la calza; (*join together*) unire. **knit one's brows** aggrottare le ciglia. **knitting needle** ferro da calza *m*. **knitwear** *n* maglieria *f*.
knob [nob] *n* pomo *m*, manopola *f*; (*protuberance*) bitorzolo *m*. **knobbly** *adj* bitorzoluto, nodoso.
knock [nok] *v* (*at door*) bussare; (*hit*) colpire, battere; (*of motor engine*) battere in testa. **knock about** (*mistreat*) malmenare; (*wander aimlessly*) fare vita randagia. **knock down** (*strike*) abbattere; demolire; (*lower*) abbassare. **knock-kneed** *adj* dalle gambe a X. **knock off** (*stop work*) tralasciare, smettere; (*deduct*) dedurre; (*coll*: *steal*) far man bassa, portar via; (*complete hurriedly*) buttar giù. **knock out** (*stun*) far perdere i sensi a; (*put out of action*) mettere fuori combattimento. **knock together** (*make hurriedly*) acciabattare. **knock up** (*wake*) svegliare; (*tennis*) fare del palleggio. *n* colpo *m*; bussata *f*; (*blow*) batosta *f*. **knocker** *n* battiporta *m invar*, picchiotto *m*.
knot [not] *n* nodo *m*. *v* annodare. **knotted** *adj* nodoso, annodato, pieno di nodi. **knotty** *adj* pieno di nodi; difficile, complesso.
***know** [nou] *v* (*facts*) sapere; (*be acquainted with*) conoscere; (*understand*) capire; (*recognize*) riconoscere. **as far as is known** per quanto si sappia. **know about** essere informato su, essere al corrente di. **know how to** sapere. *n* **in the know** (*coll*) al corrente. **knowing** *adj* accorto, intelligente. **known** *adj* noto, conosciuto. **make known** far sapere *or* conoscere, divulgare, render noto.
knowledge ['nolidʒ] *n* cognizione *f*, conoscenze *f pl*.
known [noun] *V* **know**.
knuckle ['nʌkl] *n* nocca *f*. **knuckle down** applicarsi. **knuckle under** sottomettersi, piegarsi.
kosher ['kouʃə] *adj* kasher, cascer.

L

label ['leibl] *n* etichetta *f*; (*strip of paper*) cartellino *m*; definizione *f*. *v* etichettare, qualificare.
laboratory [lə'borətəri] *n* laboratorio *m*.
labour ['leibə] *n* (*toil*) lavoro *m*; (*hard work, task*) fatica *f*; (*effort*) sforzo *m*; (*workforce*) manodopera *f*; (*childbirth*) doglie del parto *f pl*, travaglio del parto *m*. **Labour Party** partito laburista *m*. **labour-saving** *adj* che risparmia fatica. *v* faticare, lavorare. **labour under** essere vittima di. **laborious** *adj* laborioso, faticoso.
laburnum [lə'bəːnəm] *n* laburno *m*.
labyrinth ['labərinθ] *n* labirinto *m*.
lace [leis] *n* pizzo *m*, merletto *m*, brina *f*; (*string, cord*) laccio *m*; (*braid*) gallone *m*. *v* (*fasten*) allacciare; (*trim with lace*) ornare di pizzi; (*add to drink*) correggere. **lacemaker** *n* trinaia *f*.
lacerate ['lasəreit] *v* lacerare.
lack [lak] *n* mancanza *f*, insufficienza *f*. *v* mancare (di).
lackadaisical [ˌlakə'deizikəl] *adj* svogliato, infingardo.
lacquer ['lakə] *n* lacca *f*. *v* laccare.
lad [lad] *n* ragazzo *m*, giovanotto *m*.

ladder ['ladə] *n* scala *f*; (*stocking*) smagliatura *f*. *v* smagliarsi. **ladder-proof** *adj* indemagliabile.
laden ['leidn] *adj* carico (*m pl* -chi).
ladle ['leidl] *n* (*dish-shaped*) mestolo *m*; (*cup-shaped*) ramaiuolo *m*, cucchiaione *m*. *v* scodellare.
lady ['leidi] *n* signora *f*. **lady of the house** padrona di casa *f*.
ladybird ['leidibəːd] *n* coccinella *f*.
lag[1] [lag] *v* avanzare lentamente. **lag behind** rimanere indietro. *n* ritardo *m*, intervallo *m*.
lag[2] [lag] *v* (*cover*) rivestire di materiale isolante, isolare. **lagging** *n* rivestimento isolante *m*.
lager ['laːgə] *n* birra (chiara) *f*.
lagoon [lə'guːn] *n* laguna *f*.
laid [leid] *V* **lay**[1].
lain [lein] *V* **lie**[1].
lair [leə] *n* tana *f*.
laity ['leiəti] *n* **the laity** i laici *m pl*.
lake [leik] *n* lago *m*.
lamb [lam] *n* agnello *m*.
lame [leim] *adj* zoppo, storpio; (*poor*) debole, insufficiente. **lame duck** fallito *m*.
lament [lə'ment] *n* lamento *m*. *v* lamentare, compiangere. **lamented** *adj* compianto.
laminate ['lamineit] *v* laminare.
lamp [lamp] *n* lampada *f*, lume *m*; (*of car, ship*) fanale *m*. **lamp-holder** *n* portalampada *m*. **lamp-post** *n* lampione *m*. **lampshade** *n* paralume *m*.
lance [laːns] *n* lancia *f*. *v* incidere col bisturi. **lancet** *n* bisturi *m invar*.
land [land] *n* terra *f*; (*country*) paese *m*; (*agricultural area*) campagna *f*; (*site, soil*) terreno *m*. *v* (*put on shore*) sbarcare, approdare; (*from the air*) atterrare; (*obtain*) ottenere. **landing** *n* sbarco *m*; atterraggio *m*; (*of stairs*) pianerottolo *m*.
landlady ['landleidi] *n* padrona di casa *f*, proprietaria *f*.
landlord ['landloːd] *n* padrone di casa *m*, proprietario *m*; (*of inn*) oste *m*.
landmark ['landmaːk] *n* punto di riferimento *m*.
landscape ['landskeip] *n* paesaggio *m*.
landslide ['landslaid] *n* frana *f*.
lane [lein] *n* (*between houses*) vicolo *m*; (*track*) sentiero *m*; (*part of road, sports track*) corsia *f*.
language ['laŋgwidʒ] *n* (*of a nation*) lingua *f*; (*means of expression*) linguaggio *m*.
languish ['laŋgwiʃ] *v* languire.
lanky ['laŋki] *adj* alto e magro.
lantern ['lantən] *n* lanterna *f*.
lap[1] [lap] *n* (*anat*) grembo *m*; (*loose fold*) falda *f*, piega *f*; (*circuit*) giro *m*; (*part of journey*) tappa *f*.
lap[2] [lap] *v* lambire. **lap up** lappare; (*coll*) ascoltare *or* accettare con avidità.
lapel [lə'pel] *n* risvolto *m*.
Lapland ['lapland] *n* Lapponia *f*. **Lapp** *n*(*m*+*f*), *adj* lappone.
lapse [laps] *n* svista *f*, errore *m*; (*time*) corso *m*, periodo *m*; (*law*) scadenza *f*; decadenza *f*. *v* (*become void*) scadere; (*decline*) decadere; (*time*) trascorrere. **lapsed** *adj* (*law*) decaduto; (*rel*) apostata.
larceny ['laːsəni] *n* furto *m*.
larch [laːtʃ] *n* larice *m*.
lard [laːd] *n* strutto *m*.
larder ['laːdə] *n* dispensa *f*.
large [laːdʒ] *adj* grande, ampio. **at large** in libertà; (*in general*) in complesso.
lark[1] [laːk] *n* (*bird*) allodola *f*.
lark[2] [laːk] (*coll*) *n* burla *f*. *v* **lark about** divertirsi.
larva ['laːvə] *n*, *pl* **larvae** larva *f*.
larynx ['lariŋks] *n* laringe *f*. **laryngitis** *n* laringite *f*.
laser ['leizə] *n* laser *m invar*.
lash [laʃ] *n* sferzata *f*; (*eye*) ciglio *m* (*pl* -a *f*). *v* (*whip*) sferzare; (*tie*) legare. **lash out** menar colpi; (*coll: money*) non badare a spese. **lash out at** inveire contro.
lass [las] *n* fanciulla *f*, giovane *f*.
lassitude ['lasitjuːd] *n* stanchezza *f*.
lasso [la'suː] *n* lasso *m*, laccio *m*. *v* catturare al lasso *or* laccio.
last[1] [laːst] *adj* finale, ultimo; (*past*) scorso, passato. **last but one** penultimo. **last night** ieri sera. *adv* (*after all others*) per ultimo; (*most recently*) l'ultima volta; finalmente. **at last** alla fine, finalmente.
last[2] [laːst] *v* durare. **lasting** *adj* durevole.
latch [latʃ] *n* saliscendi *m invar*, chiavistello *m*. *v* chiudere con saliscendi. **latch on to** afferrare.
late [leit] *adj* tardo; recente; (*former*) precedente; (*dead*) defunto, fu. *adv* (*not on time*) in ritardo; (*not early*) tardi. **lately** *adv* recentemente. **lateness** *n* ritardo

m. **later** *adv* più tardi, dopo. **see you later!** a più tardi! **latest** *adj* ultimo; recentissimo. **at the latest** al più tardi.
latent ['leitənt] *adj* latente.
lateral ['latərəl] *adj* laterale.
lathe [leið] *n* tornio *m*.
lather ['laːðə] *n* schiuma *f*. *v* (*of soap*) far schiuma.
Latin ['latin] *nm, adj* latino.
latitude ['latitjuːd] *n* latitudine *f*.
latrine [lə'triːn] *n* latrina *f*.
latter ['latə] *adj* secondo, ultimo. **the latter** il secondo, questo.
lattice ['latis] *n* traliccio *m*, grata *f*.
laugh [laːf] *v* ridere. **laugh at** ridere per *or* di. *n* risata *f*; (*coll*) spasso *m*. **have a laugh** fare una risata. **laughable** *adj* ridicolo, risibile. **laughing stock** zimbello *m*. **laughter** *n* riso *m* (*pl* -a *f*), risata *f*.
launch[1] [loːntʃ] *v* varare; (*give a start*) lanciare; (*attack*) sferrare.
launch[2] [loːntʃ] *n* (*naut*) lancia *f*.
launder ['loːndə] *v* fare il bucato, lavare e stirare. **launderette** *n* lavanderia automatica *f*, lavanderia a gettoni *f*. **laundry** *n* (*place*) lavanderia *f*; (*clothes, etc.*) bucato *m*.
laurel ['lorəl] *n* alloro *m*, lauro *m*.
lava ['laːvə] *n* lava *f*.
lavatory ['lavətəri] *n* gabinetto *m*, ritirata *f*.
lavender ['lavində] *n* lavanda *f*.
lavish ['laviʃ] *adj* prodigo, generoso. *v* dispensare *or* spendere largamente.
law [loː] *n* legge *f*; (*profession*) diritto *m*; (*rule*) norma *f*, regola *f*. **law-abiding** *adj* ligio alla legge. **lawsuit** *n* causa *f*, processo *m*. **lawful** *adj* legittimo, lecito. **lawyer** *n* avvocato, -essa *m, f*.
lawn [loːn] *n* prato rasato *m*. **lawn-mower** *n* falciatrice *or* tosatrice per prati *f*.
lax [laks] *adj* rilassato; negligente.
laxative ['laksətiv] *nm, adj* lassativo.
***lay**[1] [lei] *v* posare, mettere; (*eggs*) deporre; (*table*) apparecchiare. **lay-by** *n* area *or* piazzola di sosta *or* parcheggio *f*. **lay down** posare per terra; stabilire. **lay off** (*workers*) sospendere. **lay on** disporre, installare. **layout** *n* disposizione *f*; (*sketch*) tracciato *m*, pianta *f*. **lay out** (*spread*) stendere; (*coll: spend*) sborsare. **be laid up** essere costretto di rimanere a letto.
lay[2] [lei] *adj* laico; non professionale. **layman** *n* laico, -a *m, f*; profano, -a *m, f*.
lay[3] [lei] *V* **lie**[1].
layer ['leiə] *n* strato *m*.
lazy ['leizi] *adj* pigro, indolente. **laziness** *n* pigrizia *f*.
***lead**[1] [liːd] *v* condurre; influenzare; (*bring*) portare; (*be at head of*) essere in testa di, essere al comando di; (*act as guide*) guidare; (*make go*) indurre. *n* direzione *f*, comando *m*; (*for dog*) guinzaglio *m*; (*theatre*) primo attore, prima attrice *m, f*. **be in the lead** (*sport*) essere in testa. **take the lead** (*sport*) passare in testa. **leader** *n* capo *m*, dirigente *m, f*; (*newspaper*) articolo di fondo *m*. **leadership** *n* direzione *f*, comando *m*. **leading** *adj* principale, primo.
lead[2] [led] *n* piombo *m*. **leaden** *adj* di piombo.
leaf [liːf] *n* (*plant*) foglia *f*; (*paper*) foglio *m*; (*table*) asse *f*. *v* **leaf through** sfogliare. **leaflet** *n* volantino *m*, manifestino *m*.
league [liːg] *n* lega *f*; classe *f*.
leak [liːk] *n* (*escape*) fuga *f*; (*crack*) fessura *f*; (*boat*) falla *f*; (*news*) trapelamento *m*. *v* perdere; (*boat*) far acqua; trapelare.
***lean**[1] [liːn] *v* appoggiare, inclinare, pendere. **lean against** appoggiarsi a. **lean out** sporgersi. **lean towards** tendere verso. **leaning** *n* inclinazione *f*, propensione *f*.
lean[2] [liːn] *adj* magro, scarno; (*poor*) povero.
leant [lent] *V* **lean**[1].
***leap** [liːp] *n* salto *m*, balzo *m*. **by leaps and bounds** a passi da gigante. *v* saltare, balzare. **leap-frog** *n* cavallina *f*. **leap year** anno bisestile *m*.
leapt [lept] *V* **leap**.
***learn** [ləːn] *v* imparare, studiare; (*become informed*) sentire, apprendere. **learned** *adj* dotto, erudito, colto. **learner** *n* (*beginner*) principiante *m, f*; allievo, -a *m, f*; apprendista *m, f*. **learning** *n* cultura *f*, erudizione *f*.
learnt [ləːnt] *V* **learn**.
lease [liːs] *n* affitto *m*, contratto d'affitto *m*. *v* affittare.
leash [liːʃ] *n* guinzaglio *m*.
least [liːst] *adj* minimo. *pron, adv* (il) meno. **at least** almeno. **not in the least** per nulla, affatto.
leather ['leðə] *n* cuoio *m*, pelle *f*. **leather goods** pelletteria *f sing*.
***leave**[1] [liːv] *v* lasciare; abbandonare; (*go out from*) uscire da; (*depart*) partire. **leave alone** lasciar stare, lasciare in pace.

leave home andar via. **leave out** omettere. **be left** rimanere. **be left over** avanzare.
leave[2] [liːv] *n* permesso *m*; (*holiday*) licenza *f*, congedo *m*.
lecherous ['letʃərəs] *adj* lussurioso, lascivo. **lecher** *n* libertino *m*. **lechery** *n* lascivia *f*.
lectern ['lektən] *n* leggio *m*.
lecture ['lektʃə] *n* lezione *f*, conferenza *f*; (*reprimand*) ramanzina *f*, sgridata *f*. *v* tenere una conferenza; dare un corso di lezioni; (*rebuke*) predicare, fare una paternale a. **lecturer** *n* conferenziere, -a *m*, *f*; (*university*) docente *m*, *f*.
led [led] *V* **lead**[1].
ledge [ledʒ] *n* (*window*) davanzale *m*; (*projecting part*) sporgenza *f*.
ledger ['ledʒə] *n* (libro) mastro *m*.
lee [liː] *n* (*shelter*) riparo *m*; (*naut*) sottovento *m*. **leeward** *adj*, *adv* sottovento.
leech [liːtʃ] *n* sanguisuga *f*.
leek [liːk] *n* porro *m*.
leer [liə] *v* guardare di sbieco. *n* sguardo sbieco *m*.
leeway ['liːwei] *n* (*naut*) deriva *f*. **make up leeway** recuperare lo svantaggio.
left[1] [left] *V* **leave**[1].
left[2] [left] *adj* sinistro. *n* sinistra *f*. **the Left** (*pol*) la Sinistra. *adv* a sinistra, verso sinistra, sulla sinistra. **left-hand** *adj* sinistro. **left-handed** *adj* mancino.
leg [leg] *n* gamba *f*; (*furniture*) piede *m*; (*lap*) tappa *f*; (*poultry*) coscia *f*; (*meat*) cosciotto *m*.
legacy ['legəsi] *n* lascito *m*, eredità *f*.
legal ['liːgəl] *adj* lecito, legittimo, legale. **legality** *n* legalità *f*. **legalize** *v* legalizzare, legittimare.
legend ['ledʒənd] *n* leggenda *f*. **legendary** *adj* leggendario.
Leghorn [ˌleg'hoːn] *n* Livorno *m*.
legible ['ledʒəbl] *adj* leggibile. **legibility** *n* leggibilità *f*.
legion ['liːdʒən] *n* legione *f*.
legislate ['ledʒisleit] *v* promulgare leggi. **legislation** *n* legislazione *f*.
legitimate [lə'dʒitimət] *adj* legittimo, lecito. *v* legittimare. **legitimacy** *n* legittimità *f*.
leisure ['leʒə] *n* agio *m*, tempo libero *m*. **leisurely** *adj* fatto con comodo.
lemon ['lemən] *n* limone *m*. *adj* color limone *invar*. **lemonade** *n* limonata *f*. **lemon juice** succo di limone *m*.
***lend** [lend] *v* prestare, dare in prestito.
length [leŋθ] *n* lunghezza *f*; (*time*) durata *f*; (*cloth*) taglio *m*. **at length** per disteso. **lengthen** *v* allungare. **lengthy** *adj* lungo.
lenient ['liːniənt] *adj* benigno, indulgente. **leniency** *n* indulgenza *f*.
lens [lenz] *n* lente *f*; (*camera*) obiettivo *m*.
lent [lent] *V* **lend**.
Lent [lent] *n* quaresima *f*.
lentil ['lentil] *n* lenticchia *f*.
Leo ['liːou] *n* Leone *m*.
leopard ['lepəd] *n* leopardo *m*.
leotard ['liːətaːd] *n* calzamaglia (*pl* calzemaglie) *f*.
leper ['lepə] *n* lebbroso, -a *m*, *f*. **leprosy** *n* lebbra *f*.
lesbian ['lezbiən] *n* lesbica *f*.
less [les] *adj* minore, meno. *nm*, *adv*, *prep* meno. **lessen** *v* diminuire. **lesser** *adj* minore, inferiore.
lesson ['lesn] *n* lezione *f*.
lest [lest] *conj* per paura che.
***let** [let] *v* lasciare, permettere; (*rent*) affittare. **let down** (*lower*) calare; (*hair*) sciogliere; (*disappoint*) deludere; (*dress*) allungare. **let in** fare entrare. **let know** far sapere. **let out** far uscire, liberare; (*dress*) allargare; (*secret*) lasciar sfuggire; (*emit*) fare.
lethal ['liːθəl] *adj* letale.
lethargy ['leθədʒi] *n* letargia *f*. **lethargic** *adj* letargico.
letter ['letə] *n* lettera *f*; (*character*) carattere *m*. **letter-box** *n* buca delle lettere *f*. **lettering** *n* iscrizione *f*.
lettuce ['letis] *n* lattuga *f*.
leukaemia [luː'kiːmiə] *n* leucemia *f*.
level ['levl] *n* livello *m*, piano *m*; (*height, position*) altezza *f*. *v* livellare, spianare. *adj* piano, uniforme; (*equal*) pari. **be level with** essere a livello di. **level crossing** passaggio a livello *m*. **level-headed** *adj* equilibrato.
lever ['liːvə] *n* leva *f*. **leverage** *n* leva *f*, stimolo *m*.
levy ['levi] *n* imposta *f*, contributo *m*. *v* imporre, esigere.
lewd [luːd] *adj* lascivo, osceno.
liable ['laiəbl] *adj* responsabile. **liable to** soggetto a, passibile di. **liability** *n* obbligo *m*, responsabilità *f*; (*comm*) passività *f*, deficit *m invar*.

liaison [liː'eizon] *n* legame *m*; (*sexual*) relazione amorosa *f*.
liar ['laiə] *n* bugiardo, -a *m*, *f*.
libel ['laibəl] *n* diffamazione *f*, calunnia *f*. *v* diffamare, calunniare. **libellous** *adj* diffamatorio, calunnioso.
liberal ['libərəl] *adj* liberale, generoso. *n* liberale *m*, *f*. **liberalism** *n* liberalismo *m*.
liberate ['libəreit] *v* liberare, mettere in libertà. **liberation** *n* liberazione *f*.
liberty ['libəti] *n* libertà *f*.
Libra ['liːbrə] *n* Libra *f*.
library ['laibrəri] *n* biblioteca *f*. **librarian** *n* bibliotecario, -a *m*, *f*.
libretto [li'bretou] *n* libretto *m*.
lice [lais] *V* **louse**.
licence ['laisəns] *n* licenza *f*, permesso *m*; (*driving*) patente (di guida) *f*; (*arms*) porto d'armi *m*. **license** *v* autorizzare. **licensee** *n* gestore autorizzato *m*, concessionario *m*.
lichen ['laikən] *n* lichene *m*.
lick [lik] *v* leccare. *n* leccata *f*.
lid [lid] *n* coperchio *m*.
***lie**[1] [lai] *v* giacere, stare sdraiato. **lie down** coricarsi, sdraiarsi. **lie in** (*stay in bed*) restare a letto; (*consist of*) consistere di. **lie with** spettare a.
lie[2] [lai] *n* (*untruth*) bugia *f*, menzogna *f*. *v* mentire, dire una bugia.
lieu [luː] *n* **in lieu of** invece di.
lieutenant [ləf'tenənt] *n* tenente *m*.
life [laif] *n* vita *f*. **lifeless** *adj* esanime.
lifebelt ['laifbelt] *n* salvagente *m*.
lifeboat ['laifbout] *n* scialuppa di salvataggio *f*.
life insurance *n* assicurazione sulla vita *f*.
life-jacket *n* cintura di salvataggio *f*.
lifeline ['laiflain] *n* linea di communicazione vitale *f*.
lifelong ['laifloŋ] *adj* di tutta la vita.
lifetime ['laiftaim] *n* vita *f*, durata della vita *f*.
lift [lift] *n* ascensore *m*; (*coll*: *ride*) autostop *m*. *v* sollevàre, alzare.
***light**[1] [lait] *n* luce *f*, lume *m*; illuminazione *f*. **switch on/off the light** accendere/spegnere la luce. *adj* chiaro. **light bulb** ampolla *f*. **lighthouse** *n* faro *m*. **light-year** *n* anno luce *m*. *v* accendere. **lighten** *v* rischiarare, illuminare. **lighter** *n* (*for cigarette*) accendino *m*. **lighting** *n* illuminazione *f*.
light[2] [lait] *adj* leggero. **light-headed** *adj* frivolo; (*giddy*) preso da vertigini. **light-hearted** *adj* gaio. **lighten** *v* alleggerire, alleviare. **lightness** *n* leggerezza *f*.
***light**[3] [lait] *v* **light upon** imbattersi in.
lightning ['laitniŋ] *n* fulmine *m*, lampo *m*. **lightning conductor** *n* parafulmine *m*.
like[1] [laik] *adj* simile, uguale. *prep* come. **be** *or* **look like** rassomigliare a. **liken** *v* paragonare. **likeness** *n* somiglianza *f*; (*portrait*) ritratto *m*. **likewise** *adv* parimenti, altrettanto.
like[2] [laik] *v* gradire; (*want*) volere. **I like . . .** mi piace . . . . **likeable** *adj* simpatico. **liking** *n* simpatia *f*, gusto *m*. **have a liking for** trovar simpatico *or* gradevole.
likely ['laikli] *adj* probabile, verosimile. *adv* probabilmente. **likelihood** *n* probabilità *f*.
lilac ['lailək] *nm*, *adj* lilla *invar*.
lily ['lili] *n* giglio *m*. **lily-of-the-valley** *n* mughetto *m*.
limb [lim] *n* arto *m*, membro *m* (*pl* -a *f*).
limbo ['limbou] *n* limbo *m*.
lime[1] [laim] *n* calce *f*. **limestone** *n* calcare *m*.
lime[2] [laim] *n* (*fruit*) limetta *f*; (*linden*) tiglio *m*.
limelight ['laimˌlait] *n* luci della ribalta *f pl*. **be in the limelight** essere alla ribalta.
limit ['limit] *n* limite *m*, ambito *m*. *v* limitare. **limitation** *n* limitazione *f*. **limitless** *adj* illimitato.
limousine ['liməˌziːn] *n* berlina *f*, limousine *f invar*.
limp[1] [limp] *v* zoppicare. *n* zoppicamento *m*.
limp[2] [limp] *adj* floscio; (*weak*) debole.
limpet ['limpit] *n* patella *f*.
line [lain] *n* linea *f*; (*row*) fila *f*; (*string*) corda *f*; (*wrinkle*) ruga *f*; (*of letters*) riga *f*. *v* rigare; (*clothes*) foderare; (*border*) fiancheggiare. **line up** allineare. **linear** *adj* lineare.
linen ['linin] *n* lino *m*; (*sheets, etc.*) biancheria *f*. *adj* di lino.
liner ['lainə] *n* (*naut*) transatlantico *m*; (*aero*) aereo di linea *m*.
linger ['liŋgə] *v* indugiare, soffermarsi. **lingering** *adj* protratto.
lingerie ['lɑ̃ʒəriː] *n* biancheria per signora *f*.
linguist ['liŋgwist] *n* linguista *m*, *f*; poliglotta *m*, *f*. **linguistic** *adj* linguistico. **linguistics** *n* linguistica *f*.

lining ['lainiŋ] *n* (*clothes*) fodera *f*; rivestimento interno *m*.
link [liŋk] *n* (*of chain*) anello *m*; (*bond*) legame *m*; (*mech*) collegamento *m*. *v* collegare, congiungere.
linoleum [li'nouliəm] *n* linoleum *m invar*.
linseed ['lin,siːd] *n* semi di lino *m pl*. **linseed oil** olio di semi di lino *m*.
lint [lint] *n* filaccia (di lino) *f*.
lion ['laiən] *n* leone *m*. **lioness** *n* leonessa *f*.
lip [lip] *n* labbro *m* (*pl* -a *f*). **lip-read** *v* capire dal movimento delle labbra. **lipstick** *n* rossetto *m*.
liqueur [li'kjuə] *n* liquore *m*.
liquid ['likwid] *nm*, *adj* liquido. **liquidate** *v* liquidare; eliminare. **liquidation** *n* liquidazione *f*.
liquor ['likə] *n* bevanda alcoolica *f*.
liquorice ['likəris] *n* liquirizia *f*.
lisp [lisp] *v* essere *or* parlar bleso. *n* blesità *f*.
list[1] [list] *n* lista *f*, elenco *m*. *v* elencare, registrare.
list[2] [list] *v* (*naut*) sbandare. *n* sbandamento *m*.
listen ['lisn] *v* ascoltare; (*heed*) badare. **listener** *n* ascoltatore, -trice *m*, *f*.
listless ['listlis] *adj* languido, svogliato.
lit [lit] *V* **light**.
litany ['litəni] *n* litania *f*.
literal ['litərəl] *adj* letterale. **literally** *adv* alla lettera, letteralmente.
literary ['litərəri] *adj* (*writing*) letterario; (*people*) letterato.
literate ['litərət] *adj* che sa leggere e scrivere. **literacy** *n* il saper leggere e scrivere *m*.
literature ['litrətʃə] *n* letteratura *f*.
litigation [liti'geiʃən] *n* lite *f*, causa *f*. **litigate** *v* essere in causa.
litre ['liːtə] *n* litro *m*.
litter ['litə] *n* rifiuti *m pl*, immondizia *f*; (*zool*) figliata *f*; (*bed, etc.*) lettiga *f*. *v* sparpagliare, lasciare in disordine.
little ['litl] *adj* piccolo, piccino; (*not much*) un po' di, poco; (*short*) breve. *nm*, *adv* poco. **little by little** a poco a poco.
liturgy ['litədʒi] *n* liturgia *f*.
live[1] [liv] *v* vivere; (*reside*) abitare, stare. **live by** *or* **on** vivere di. **live down** far dimenticare. **live up to** mettere in pratica, giustificare.
live[2] [laiv] *adj* vivo; (*broadcast*) dal vivo, in ripresa diretta; (*coal, etc.*) ardente; (*wire*) sotto tensione.
livelihood ['laivlihud] *n* vita *f*.
lively ['laivli] *adj* vivace, animato. **liveliness** *n* vivacità *f*.
liven ['laivn] *v* **liven up** animare.
liver ['livə] *n* fegato *m*.
livestock ['laivstok] *n* bestiame *m*.
livid ['livid] *adj* livido.
living ['liviŋ] *adj* vivente, vivo. *n* vita *f*. **living room** stanza di soggiorno *f*.
lizard ['lizəd] *n* lucertola *f*.
load [loud] *n* carico (*pl* -chi) *m*; (*weight*) peso *m*; (*quantity carried*) portata *f*; (*elec*) carica *f*. *v* caricare. **loaded** *adj* caricato, carico; (*question*) insidioso; (*slang*) ricco.
loaf[1] [louf] *n* pane *m*.
loaf[2] [louf] *v* oziare, girellare, stare con le mani in mano. **loafer** *n* bighellone, -a *m*, *f*; fannullone, -a *m*, *f*.
loan [loun] *n* prestito *m*. *v* prestare, dare in prestito.
loathe [louð] *v* aborrire, detestare. **loathing** *n* disgusto *m*. **loathsome** *adj* disgustoso.
lob [lob] (*sport*) *n* pallonetto *m*. *v* fare un pallonetto.
lobby ['lobi] *n* atrio *m*, anticamera *f*; (*theatre*) ridotto *m*. *v* influenzare con manovre di anticamera.
lobe [loub] *n* (*anat*) lobo *m*.
lobster ['lobstə] *n* aragosta *f*.
local ['loukəl] *adj* locale, del luogo. **locality** *n* località *f*. **localize** *v* circoscrivere, delimitare.
locate [lə'keit] *v* individuare; determinare la posizione di; situare. **location** *n* posizione *f*, sito *m*; (*cinema*) set *m invar*.
lock[1] [lok] *n* serratura *f*; (*canal*) conca *f*. **locksmith** *n* magnano *m*. **lock, stock, and barrel** barca e barattini. **under lock and key** sotto chiave. *v* serrare, chiudere a chiave; (*mech*) bloccare. **lock away** mettere al sicuro. **lock in** rinchiudere. **lock out** chiudere fuori; (*workers*) fare una serrata. **lock up** chiudere a chiave, mettere sotto chiave.
lock[2] [lok] *n* (*of hair*) ciocca *f*, ricciolo *m*.
locker ['lokə] *n* armadietto *m*.
locket ['lokit] *n* medaglione *m*.
locomotive [,loukə'moutiv] *n* locomotiva *f*.
locust ['loukəst] *n* cavalletta *f*.
lodge [lodʒ] *n* capanna *f*; (*porter's*) portineria *f*. *v* alloggiare; (*put in place, deposit*) deporre, collocare; (*report*)

presentare. **lodge a complaint** sporgere querela. **lodger** *n* pensionante *m, f.* **lodging** *n* alloggio *m.*
loft [loft] *n* solaio *m,* soffitta *f.* **lofty** *adj* alto; (*style*) nobile.
log [log] *n* ceppo *m,* tronco *m.* **logbook** *n* registro *m;* (*naut*) giornale di bordo *m;* (*mot*) libretto di circolazione *m. v* registrare.
logarithm ['logəriðəm] *n* logaritmo *m.*
loggerheads ['logəhedz] *n* **be at loggerheads** prendersi per i capelli, essere ai ferri corti.
logic ['lodʒik] *n* logica *f.* **logical** *adj* logico.
loin [loin] *n* (*cookery*) lombata *f.* **gird up one's loins** apprestarsi.
loiter ['loitə] *v* bighellonare, passare oziando.
lollipop ['loli,pop] *n* lecca lecca *m invar.*
London ['lʌndən] *n* Londra *f.*
lonely ['lounli] *adj* solitario, solo. **loneliness** *n* solitudine *f.*
long[1] [loŋ] *adj* lungo. *adv* a lungo. **as long as** finquanto. **long-distance** *adj* a lunga distanza; (*phone*) interurbano. **long-playing record** disco microsolco *m.* **long-range** *adj* (*distance*) a lunga portata; (*time*) a lunga scadenza. **long-sighted** *adj* presbite; (*having foresight*) previdente. **long-standing** *adj* di vecchia data. **long-wave** *adj* (*radio*) a onde lunghe. **long-winded** *adj* prolisso.
long[2] [loŋ] *v* bramare, aver gran desiderio (di). **longing** *n* brama *f,* desiderio ardente *m.*
longevity [lon'dʒevəti] *n* longevità *f.*
longitude ['londʒitjuːd] *n* longitudine *f.*
loo [luː] *n* (*coll*) gabinetto *m.*
look [luk] *n* sguardo *m,* occhiata *f;* (*appearance*) aspetto *m;* espressione *f. v* guardare; (*appear, seem*) sembrare, parere. **look after** (*care for*) occuparsi di, badare a. **look at** guardare, considerare. **look down on** guardare con disprezzo. **look for** cercare. **look forward to** aspettare con impazienza. **look out** guardar fuori, affacciarsi; (*be on guard*) stare attento. **look over** ripassare, riesaminare.
loom[1] [luːm] *v* apparire (indistintamente), intravedere; (*be imminent*) incombere.
loom[2] [luːm] *n* telaio *m.*
loop [luːp] *n* cappio *m,* laccio *m,* anello *m. v* fare un cappio *or* laccio, allacciare.
loophole ['luːphoul] *n* scappatoia *f.*
loose [luːs] *adj* sciolto, libero; (*tooth*) caduco. **come** *or* **get loose** allentarsi. **let loose** liberare. **loose-fitting** *adj* ampio. **loose-leaf** *adj* a fogli staccati. **loosely** *adv* scioltamente; in senso lato. **loosen** *v* sciogliere, allentare.
loot [luːt] *n* bottino *m. v* far man bassa, saccheggiare. **looting** *n* saccheggio *m.*
lop [lop] *v* potare. **lop off** mozzare.
lopsided [,lop'saidid] *adj* sbilenco, asimmetrico.
lord [loːd] *n* signore *m;* (*English title*) lord *m invar.* **lordship** *n* signoria *f.*
lorry ['lori] *n* autocarro *m,* camion *m invar.* **lorry-driver** *n* camionista *m.*
***lose** [luːz] *v* perdere, smarrire; (*clock*) ritardare. **lose interest** non interessarsi più. **lose one's temper** arrabbiarsi.
loss [los] *n* perdita *f,* danno *m.* **be at a loss** non sapere cosa fare, essere disorientato.
lost [lost] *V* **lose.** *adj* perso, smarrito. **lost cause** causa persa *f.* **lost property** oggetti smarriti *m pl.*
lot [lot] *n* (*destiny*) sorte *f;* (*of land*) lotto *m;* (*method of decision*) sorteggio *m;* (*comm*) partita *f;* (*coll: large amount*) grande quantità *f.* **a lot of** molto. **lots of** tanti. **the whole lot** tutto quanto. **what a lot of** quanto.
lotion ['louʃən] *n* lozione *f.*
lottery ['lotəri] *n* lotteria *f.*
lotus ['loutəs] *n* loto *m.*
loud [laud] *adj* forte, alto; (*gaudy*) vistoso. *adv* forte. **loud-mouthed** *adj* sguaiato. **loudspeaker** *n* altoparlante *m.* **loudness** *n* forza *f,* altezza di voce *f.*
lounge [laundʒ] *n* salotto *m;* sala di ritrovo *f. v* oziare, dondolarsi.
louse [laus] *n, pl* **lice** pidocchio *m.* **lousy** *adj* pidocchioso; (*slang: bad*) schifoso.
love [lʌv] *n* amore *m;* (*tennis*) zero *m.* **fall in love (with)** innamorarsi (di). **love affair** relazione amorosa *f.* **make love (to)** fare all'amore (con). **with love** (*in letter*) affettuosamente. *v* amare, voler bene a. **lovable** *adj* amabile, simpatico. **lovely** *adj* bello, grazioso, incantevole. **lover** *n* amante *m, f;* (*enthusiast*) appassionato, -a *m, f.* **loving** *adj* affettuoso.
low [lou] *adj* basso; (*coll*) depresso; volgare. *adv* basso, in basso. **lowbrow** *adj* incolto, popolare. **low-lying** *adj* situato in pianura. **low-necked** *adj* scollato. **lowly** *adj* umile, dimesso.

lower ['louə] *adj* più basso, inferiore. *v* abbassare, ridurre; (*flag*) ammainare; degradare.
loyal ['loiəl] *adj* fedele, devoto, leale. **loyalty** *n* fedeltà *f*, devozione *f*, lealtà *f*.
lozenge ['lozindʒ] *n* pastiglia *f*, pasticca *f*.
lubricate ['luːbrikeit] *v* lubrificare. **lubricant** *nm*, *adj* lubrificante. **lubrication** *n* lubrificazione *f*.
lucid ['luːsid] *adj* (*easily understood*) chiaro; (*clear*) limpido; (*bright*) lucido.
luck [lʌk] *n* fortuna *f*; (*chance*) sorte *f*. **bad luck** sfortuna *f*. **be in/out of luck** essere fortunato/sfortunato. **good luck** buona fortuna *f*. **lucky** *adj* fortunato.
lucrative ['luːkrətiv] *adj* lucroso, redditizio.
ludicrous ['luːdikrəs] *adj* ridicolo, irrisorio.
lug [lʌg] *v* tirare, trascinare.
luggage ['lʌgidʒ] *n* bagaglio *m*. **hand luggage** bagaglio a mano *m*. **left luggage** deposito bagagli *m*. **luggage rack** *n* (*rail*) rete portabagagli *f*.
lukewarm ['luːkwoːm] *adj* tiepido.
lull [lʌl] *n* momento di calma *m*; (*truce*) tregua *f*. *v* (*put to sleep*) far addormentare; calmare.
lumbago [lʌm'beigou] *n* lombaggine *f*.
lumber[1] ['lʌmbə] *n* legname *m*; (*useless articles*) cianfrusaglie *f pl*. *v* (*encumber*) ingombrare, accatastare. **lumberjack** *n* boscaiolo *m*.
lumber[2] ['lʌmbə] *v* (*move clumsily*) muoversi pesantemente *or* goffamente.
luminous ['luːminəs] *adj* luminoso.
lump [lʌmp] *n* massa *f*; (*swelling*) gonfiore *m*. **lump sum** somma globale *f*. **lump together** mettere insieme. **lumpy** *adj* grumoso.
lunacy ['luːnəsi] *n* pazzia *f*.
lunar ['luːnə] *adj* lunare.
lunatic ['lunətik] *n*, *adj* pazzo, -a, matto, -a. **lunatic asylum** manicomio *m*.
lunch [lʌntʃ] *n* colazione *f*, pranzo *m*. *v* far colazione, pranzare.
lung [lʌŋ] *n* polmone *m*.
lunge [lʌndʒ] *v* scagliarsi. *n* rapido movimento in avanti *m*.
lurch[1] [ləːtʃ] *v* barcollare, sbandare. *n* barcollamento *m*, sbandamento *m*.
lurch[2] [ləːtʃ] *n* **leave in the lurch** piantare in asso.
lure [luə] *n* (*bait*) esca *f*; (*fascination*) fascino *m*. *v* adescare, attirare, affascinare.
lurid ['luərid] *adj* raccapricciante.
lurk [ləːk] *v* (*be in hiding*) nascondersi; (*lie in wait*) stare in agguato.
luscious ['lʌʃəs] *adj* succulento.
lush [lʌʃ] *adj* lussureggiante.
lust [lʌst] *n* brama *f*; (*sexual*) libidine *f*; concupiscenza *f*. *v* **lust after** aver brama *or* sete di.
lustre ['lʌstə] *n* splendore *m*.
lute [luːt] *n* liuto *m*.
Luxembourg ['lʌksəm,bəːg] *n* Lussemburgo *m*.
luxury ['lʌkʃəri] *n* lusso *m*. **luxuriant** *adj* lussureggiante, rigoglioso. **luxurious** *adj* lussuoso, di lusso.
lynch [lintʃ] *v* linciare.
lynx [links] *n* lince *f*.
lyre [laiə] *n* lira *f*.
lyrical ['lirikəl] *adj* lirico.
lyrics ['liriks] *pl n* parole (di una canzone) *f pl*.

M

mac [mak] *n* (*coll*) impermeabile *m*.
macabre [mə'kaːbr] *adj* macabro.
macaroni [makə'rouni] *n* maccheroni *m pl*.
mace[1] [meis] *n* (*club*) mazza *f*.
mace[2] [meis] *n* (*spice*) macis *f invar*.
machine [mə'ʃiːn] *n* macchina *f*. **machine-gun** *n* mitragliatrice *f*. **machine tool** macchina utensile *f*. *v* lavorare a macchina. **machinery** *n* macchinario *m*; meccanismo *m*; (*system*) organizzazione *f*. **machinist** *n* macchinista *m*, *f*.
mackerel ['makrəl] *n* sgombro *m*.
mackintosh ['makin,toʃ] *n* impermeabile *m*.
mad [mad] *adj* matto, pazzo; furioso. **drive mad** far impazzire. **go mad** impazzire. **madden** *v* far impazzire. **madness** *n* pazzia *f*.
madam ['madəm] *n* signora *f*.
made [meid] *V* **make**.
magazine [,magə'ziːn] *n* (*publication*) rivista *f*, periodico *m*; (*phot*) magazzino *m*; (*rifle*) caricatore *m*.
maggot ['magət] *n* larva *f*.
magic ['madʒik] *adj* magico. *n* magia *f*, incanto *m*. **magician** *n* mago *m*, stregone *m*; (*conjurer*) illusionista *m*.

magistrate ['madʒistreit] *n* magistrato *m*, pretore *m*. **magistrature** *n* magistratura *f*, pretura *f*.
magnanimous [mag'nanimәs] *adj* magnanimo. **magnanimity** *n* magnanimità *f*.
magnate ['magneit] *n* magnate *m*.
magnet ['magnәt] *n* magnete *m*, calamita *f*. **magnetic** *adj* magnetico. **magnetism** *n* magnetismo *m*. **magnetize** *v* magnetizzare.
magnificent [mag'nifisnt] *adj* magnifico, splendido. **magnificence** *n* magnificenza *f*.
magnify ['magnifai] *v* magnificare, ingrandire. **magnifying glass** lente d'ingrandimento *f*. **magnification** *n* ingrandimento *m*.
magnitude ['magnitjuːd] *n* grandezza *f*.
magnolia [mag'noulіә] *n* magnolia *f*.
magpie ['magpai] *n* gazza *f*.
mahogany [mә'hogәni] *n* mogano *m*.
maid [meid] *n* domestica *f*, donna di servizio *f*. **old maid** vecchia zitella *f*.
maiden ['meidәn] *n* fanciulla *f*. *adj* primo; (*journey*) inaugurale. **maiden lady** signorina *f*. **maiden name** nome da ragazza *m*.
mail[1] [meil] *n* posta *f*. **mail order** vendita per catalogo *f*. *v* imbucare, mandare per posta.
mail[2] [meil] *n* (*armour*) maglia di ferro *f*. **mailed fist** pugno di ferro *m*.
maim [meim] *v* mutilare, storpiare.
main [mein] *adj* principale, essenziale. **mainland** *n* terra ferma *f*. **mainspring** *n* (*of watch*) molla principale *f*; (*impelling cause*) movente principale *f*. **mainstay** *n* (*chief support*) sostegno *m*, braccio destro *m*. **mainstream** *n* tendenza dominante *f*. *n* (*gas, water, etc.*) conduttura principale *f*. **in the main** nel complesso, in genere. **mainly** *adv* sopratutto; in genere.
maintain [mein'tein] *v* mantenere; (*support*) sostenere; (*assert*) affermare. **maintenance** *n* mantenimento *m*; (*machinery, etc.*) manutenzione *f*; (*alimony*) alimenti *m pl*.
maisonette [meizә'net] *n* casetta *f*.
maize [meiz] *n* mais *m invar*, granturco *m invar*.
majesty ['madʒәsti] *n* maestà *f*. **majestic** *adj* maestoso.
major ['meidʒә] *nm, adj* maggiore. **majority** *n* maggioranza *f*; (*age*) maggiore età *f*.
***make** [meik] *v* fare; produrre. **make believe** dare da intendere, far finta di. **make-believe** *n* finzione *f*, illusione *f*. **make do** arrangiarsi. **make out** preparare; decifrare; (*understand*) capire. **make up** costituire, costruire; inventare; compensare; (*cosmetics*) truccare. **make-up** *n* trucco *m*, truccatura *f*; composizione *f*; costituzione *f*. **maker** *n* creatore, -trice *m, f*; fabbricante *m, f*.
makeshift ['meikʃift] *adj* di fortuna, improvvisato. *n* espediente *m*.
maladjusted [malә'dʒʌstid] *adj* disadattato.
malaise [ma'leiz] *n* malessere *m*.
malaria [mә'leәriә] *n* malaria *f*.
male [meil] *n* maschio *m*. *adj* maschio, maschile.
malevolent [mә'levәlәnt] *adj* malevolo. **malevolence** *n* malevolenza *f*.
malfunction [mal'fʌŋkʃәn] *n* funzionamento difettoso *m*.
malice ['malis] *n* malizia *f*, malignità *f*. **with malice aforethought** con premeditazione maliziosa. **malicious** *adj* malizioso, maligno.
malignant [mә'lignәnt] *adj* maligno. **malignancy** *n* malignità *f*.
malinger [mә'liŋgә] *v* darsi malato, scansar fatiche. **malingerer** *n* scansafatiche *m, f invar*.
mallet ['malit] *n* maglio *m*, martello (di legno) *m*. **malleable** *adj* malleabile.
malnutrition [malnju'triʃәn] *n* malnutrizione *f*.
malt [moːlt] *n* malto *m*.
Malta ['moːltә] *n* Malta *f*. **Maltese** *n*(*m*+*f*), *adj* maltese.
maltreat [mal'triːt] *v* maltrattare. **maltreatment** *n* maltrattamento *m*.
mammal ['mamәl] *n* mammifero *m*.
mammoth ['mamәθ] *n* mammut *m*. *adj* enorme, mastodontico.
man [man] *n*, *pl* **men** uomo (*pl* uomini) *m*. *v* equipaggiare, presidiare. **manly** *adj* virile.
manage ['manidʒ] *v* dirigere, amministrare; (*cope*) farcela. **manage to** riuscire a, fare in modo da. **manage without** fare a meno di. **manageable** *adj* (*people*) trattabile, docile; (*things*) maneggevole. **management** *n* amministrazione *f*, direzione *f*. **manager** *n* direttore *m*. **manageress** *n* direttrice *f*. **managing director** consigliere delegato *m*.

mandarin ['mandərin] *n* mandarino *m*.
mandate ['mandeit] *n* mandato *m*. **mandatory** *adj* mandatario.
mandolin ['mandəlin] *n* mandolino *m*.
mane [mein] *n* criniera *f*.
mange [meindʒ] *n* rogna *f*. **mangy** *adj* rognoso.
mangle[1] ['maŋgl] *v* (*disfigure*) deformare, mutilare.
mangle[2] ['maŋgl] *n* (*wringer*) mangano *m*. *v* manganare.
manhandle [man'handl] *v* manovrare a mano; (*treat harshly*) malmenare.
manhole ['manhoul] *n* botola *f*. **manhole cover** tombino *m*.
mania ['meiniə] *n* mania *f*. **maniac** *n* maniaco, -a *m*, *f*. **maniacal** *adj* maniaco.
manicure ['manikjuə] *n* manicure *f invar*.
manifest ['manifest] *adj* evidente, palese. *v* manifestare, dimostrare. *n* (*comm*) manifesto (di bordo) *m*, nota di carico *f*.
manifesto [mani'festou] *n* manifesto *m*, proclama *m*.
manifold ['manifould] *adj* molteplice, vario. *n* (*tech*) collettore *m*.
manipulate [mə'nipjuleit] *v* maneggiare. **manipulation** *n* maneggio *m*. **manipulative** *adj* manipolatore.
mankind [ˌman'kaind] *n* umanità *f*, genere umano *m*.
man-made [ˌman'meid] *adj* artificiale, sintetico.
manner ['manə] *n* modo *m*, maniera *f*; stile *m*; sorta *f*, specie *f*. **manners** *pl n* maniere *f pl*, educazione *f sing*. **mannerism** *n* affettazione *f*, manierismo *m*.
manoeuvre [mə'nuːvə] *n* manovra *f*. *v* manovrare, maneggiare.
manor ['manə] *n* castello *m*, maniero *m*.
manpower ['manˌpauə] *n* manodopera *f*; forze di lavoro *f pl*; capacità lavorativa *f*.
mansion ['manʃən] *n* palazzo *m*, casa signorile *f*.
mantelpiece ['mantlpiːs] *n* mensola (del caminetto) *f*.
manual ['manjuəl] *nm*, *adj* manuale. **manually** *adv* a mano.
manufacture [manju'faktʃə] *n* manifattura *f*, fabbricazione *f*, confezione *f*. *v* fabbricare. **manufacturer** *n* fabbricante *m*.
manure [mə'njuə] *n* concime *f*, fertilizzante *m*.
manuscript ['manjuskript] *nm*, *adj* manoscritto.
many ['meni] *adj*, *pron* molti, -e. **as many** altrettanti, -e. **how many** quanti, -e. **so many** tanti, -e. **too many** troppi, -e.
map [map] *n* mappa *f*, carta geografica *f*; (*of town*) pianta *f*. **off the map** remoto. *v* **map out** tracciare.
maple ['meipl] *n* acero *m*.
mar [maː] *v* guastare, rovinare.
marathon ['marəθən] *n* maratona *f*.
marble ['maːbl] *n* marmo *m*; (*glass ball*) bilia *f*. *adj* di marmo, marmoreo.
march [maːtʃ] *n* marcia *f*. *v* marciare. **march-past** *n* sfilata *f*.
March [maːtʃ] *n* marzo *m*.
marchioness [ˌmaːʃə'nes] *n* marchesa *f*.
mare [meə] *n* cavalla *f*.
margarine [ˌmaːdʒə'riːn] *n* margarina *f*.
margin ['maːdʒin] *n* margine *m*. **marginal** *adj* marginale.
marguerite [ˌmaːgə'riːt] *n* margherita *f*.
marigold ['marigould] *n* calendola *f*.
marijuana [mari'waːnə] *n* marijuana *f invar*, canapa indiana *f*.
marina [mə'riːnə] *n* porticciuolo *m*.
marinade [ˌmari'neid] *n* marinata *f*. *v* marinare.
marine [mə'riːn] *adj* marino, marittimo. *n* (*fleet*) marina *f*; (*soldier*) soldato di marina *m*.
marital ['maritl] *adj* coniugale.
maritime ['maritaim] *adj* marittimo.
marjoram ['maːdʒərəm] *n* maggiorana *f*.
mark[1] [maːk] *n* segno *m*; (*brand*) marchio *m*; (*rating*) voto *m*; (*trace*) traccia *f*. **marksman** *n* tiratore scelto *m*. *v* segnare; notare; osservare; (*correct*, *grade*) dare i voti a. **mark off** delimitare. **mark out** tracciare. **marking** *n* marchio *m*. **markings** *pl n* segni caratteristici *m pl*.
mark[2] [maːk] *n* (*money*) marco *m*.
market ['maːkit] *n* mercato *m*. **market garden** orto *m*. **market research** ricerca di mercato *f*. *v* mettere in vendita. **marketing** *n* marketing *m invar*.
marmalade ['maːməleid] *n* marmellata *f*.
maroon[1] [mə'ruːn] *nm*, *adj* (*colour*) marrone rossastro.
maroon[2] [mə'ruːn] *v* abbandonare.
marquee [maː'kiː] *n* grande tenda *f*; padiglione *m*.
marquess ['maːkwis] *n* marchese *m*.
marriage ['maridʒ] *n* matrimonio *m*. **marriage licence** dispensa di matrimonio *f*.

marrow ['marou] *n* zucca *f*.
marry ['mari] *v* sposare. **married** *adj* sposato. **get married** sposarsi.
Mars [maːz] *n* Marte *m*. **Martian** *n*, *adj* marziano, -a.
marsh [maːʃ] *n* palude *f*. **marshy** *adj* paludoso.
marshal ['maːʃəl] *v* disporre; (*mil*) schierare. *n* maresciallo *m*.
martial ['maːʃəl] *adj* marziale.
martin ['maːtin] *n* balestruccio *m*.
martyr ['maːtə] *n* martire *m*, *f*. *v* martirizzare. **martyrdom** *n* martirio *m*.
marvel ['maːvəl] *n* meraviglia *f*. *v* meravigliarsi. **marvel at** stupirsi di, ammirare.
marvellous ['maːvələs] *adj* meraviglioso.
marzipan [maːzi'pan] *n* marzapane *m*.
mascara [ma'skaːrə] *n* mascara *m invar*.
mascot ['maskət] *n* portafortuna *m invar*, mascotte *f*.
masculine ['maskjulin] *adj* maschile, virile. **masculinity** *n* mascolinità *f*, virilità *f*.
mash [maʃ] *v* ridurre in polpa, schiacciare; (*cookery*) fare un purè di. *n* (*cookery*) passata *f*, purè *m*.
mask [maːsk] *n* maschera *f*. *v* mascherare; (*hide*) nascondere.
masochist ['masəkist] *n* masochista *m*, *f*. *adj* masochistico. **masochism** *n* masochismo *m*.
mason ['meisn] *n* muratore *m*; (*freemason*) massone *m*. **masonic** *adj* massonico. **masonry** *n* muratura *f*.
masquerade [maskə'reid] *n* mascherata *f*. *v* **masquerade as** mascherarsi da, farsi passare per.
mass[1] [mas] *n* massa *f*, (*bulk*) mole *f*; (*great number*) gran numero *m*; (*large amount*) grande quantità *f*. **masses** *pl n* (*coll*) mucchio *m sing*. **mass meeting** adunata popolare *f*. **mass-produced** *adj* prodotto in serie. **mass-production** *n* produzione in serie *or* massa *f*.
mass[2] [mas] *n* (*rel*) messa *f*.
massacre ['masəkə] *n* massacro *m*, strage *f*. *v* massacrare, far strage di.
massage ['masaːʒ] *n* massaggio *m*. *v* massaggiare. **masseur** *n* massaggiatore *m*. **masseuse** *n* massaggiatrice *f*.
massive ['masiv] *adj* massiccio, solido.
mast [maːst] *n* albeio *m*.
mastectomy [ma'stektəmi] *n* mastectomia *f*.
master ['maːstə] *n* padrone *m*, signore *m*; (*of ship*) capitano *m*; (*school*) professore *m*. **masterpiece** *n* capolavoro *m*. *v* dominare, impadronirsi di; (*learn*) conoscere a perfezione. **masterly** *adj* magistrale.
masturbate ['mastəbeit] *v* masturbarsi. **masturbation** *n* masturbazione *f*.
mat [mat] *n* (*covering*) tappeto *m*; (*for floor*) stuoia *f*; (*at door*) zerbino *m*; (*on table*) sottopiatto *m*.
match[1] [matʃ] *n* (*light*) fiammifero *m*. **matchbox** *n* scatola da fiammiferi *f*.
match[2] [matʃ] *v* (*clothes, colours, etc.*) andare bene insieme; corrispondere; (*oppose*) opporre; (*equal*) uguagliare. *n* (*equal*) uguale *m*, *f*, pari *m*, *f*; (*contest, partner*) partita *f*. **matchmaker** *n* sensale di matrimoni. **meet one's match** trovare un degno avversario.
mate [meit] *n* compagno, -a *m*, *f*; (*help*) aiuto *m*, assistente *m*, *f*; (*naut*) secondo *m*.
material [mə'tiəriəl] *n* (*substance*) sostanza *f*, materia *f*; materiale *m*; (*fabric*) stoffa *f*. *adj* materiale, essenziale. **materialize** *v* realizzarsi, prender corpo.
maternal [mə'təːnl] *adj* materno. **maternity** *n* maternità *f*.
mathematics [maθə'matiks] *n* matematica *f*. **mathematical** *adj* matematico. **mathematician** *n* matematico, -a *m*, *f*.
matinee ['matinei] *n* rappresentazione diurna *f*.
matins ['matinz] *n* mattutino *m*.
matriarch ['meitriaːk] *n* matrona *f*. **matriarchal** *adj* matriarcale.
matrimony ['matriməni] *n* matrimonio *m*. **matrimonial** *adj* matrimoniale.
matrix ['meitriks] *n* matrice *f*.
matron ['meitrən] *n* (*hospital*) capoinfermiera *f*; (*institution*) direttrice *f*.
matt [mat] *adj* matto, opaco.
matter ['matə] *v* importare. *n* materia *f*; (*thing, affair*) cosa *f*, affare *m*; (*of book, etc.*) argomento *m*, questione *f*. **as a matter of fact** in realtà, fatto sta che. **matter-of-fact** *adj* pratico. **what's the matter?** cosa c'è?
mattress ['matris] *n* materasso *m*.
mature [mə'tjuə] *v* maturare; (*become due*) scadere. **maturity** *n* maturità *f*.
maudlin ['moːdlin] *adj* lamentevole, querulo.

maul [mo:l] *v* dilaniare.
mausoleum [mo:sə'liəm] *n* mausoleo *m*.
mauve [mouv] *adj* (color) malva *invar*.
maxim ['maksim] *n* massima *f*.
maximum ['maksiməm] *nm*, *adj* massimo.
***may** [mei] *v* potere. **maybe** può darsi, forse.
May [mei] *n* maggio *m*.
mayonnaise [ˌmeiə'neiz] *n* maionese *f*.
mayor [meə] *n* sindaco *m*.
maze [meiz] *n* labirinto *m*.
me [mi:] *pron* mi; (*after prep*) me. **it's me** sono io.
meadow ['medou] *n* prato *m*.
meagre ['mi:gə] *adj* scarso.
meal[1] [mi:l] *n* (*food*) pasto *m*.
meal[2] [mi:l] *n* (*grain*) farina *f*.
***mean**[1] [mi:n] *v* significare, voler dire; intendere; destinare.
mean[2] [mi:n] *adj* gretto; (*miserly*) avaro; (*shabby*) meschino; (*low*) basso. **meanness** *n* grettezza *f*; avarizia *f*.
mean[3] [mi:n] *n* (*average*) media *f*. *adj* medio.
meander [mi'andə] *v* divagare.
meaning ['mi:niŋ] *n* significato *m*, senso *m*. *adj* significativo.
means [mi:nz] *n* mezzi *m pl*. **by means of** per mezzo di. **by no means** niente affatto. **by some means or other** in qualche modo.
meant [ment] *V* **mean**[1].
meanwhile ['mi:nwail] *adv also* **in the meantime** nel frattempo, intanto.
measles ['mi:zlz] *n* morbillo *m*. **German measles** *n* rosolio *f*, rubeola *f*. **measly** *adj* (*wretched*) miserabile.
measure ['meʒə] *n* misura *f*; (*action*) provvedimento *m*. **made to measure** fatto su misura. *v* misurare; (*estimate*) valutare. **measurement** *n* misura *f*. **measurements** *pl n* dimensioni *f pl*.
meat [mi:t] *n* carne *f*. **meaty** *adj* sostanzioso.
mechanic [mi'kanik] *n* meccanico *m*. **mechanical** *adj* meccanico. **mechanism** *n* meccanismo *m*. **mechanized** *adj* meccanizzato.
medal ['medl] *n* medaglia *f*.
meddle ['medl] *v* immischiarsi, intromettersi. **meddler** *n* ficcanaso *m invar*.
media ['mi:diə] *pl n* mezzi di comunicazione *m pl*.
median ['mi:diən] *adj* mediano. *n* mediana *f*.
mediate ['mi:dieit] *v* fare da mediatore *or* intermediario. **mediation** *n* mediazione *f*. **mediator** *n* mediatore, -trice *m*, *f*.
medical ['medikəl] *adj* medico. *n* (*examination*) esame medico *m*. **medication** *n* medicazione *f*. **medicinal** *adj* medicinale. **medicine** *n* (*science*) medicina *f*; (*substance*) medicinale *m*, farmaco *m*.
medieval [medi'i:vəl] *adj* medievale.
mediocre [mi:di'oukə] *adj* mediocre. **mediocrity** *n* mediocrità *f*.
meditate ['mediteit] *v* meditare. **meditation** *n* meditazione *f*.
Mediterranean [ˌmeditə'reiniən] *n* Mediterraneo *m*. *adj* mediterraneo.
medium ['mi:diəm] *n* (*spiritualist*) medium *m*, *f invar*; (*biology*) brodo (di coltura) *m*; (*agency*) mezzo *m*. **happy medium** giusto mezzo *m*. *adj* medio.
medley ['medli] *n* miscuglio *m*, pasticcio *m*.
meek [mi:k] *adj* mansueto, mite. **meekness** *n* mansuetudine *f*.
***meet** [mi:t] *v* incontrare; (*by arrangement*) trovare; (*gather*) riunirsi. **meeting** *n* incontro *m*; riunione *f*.
megaphone ['megəfoun] *n* megafono *m*.
melancholy ['melənkəli] *n* malinconia *f*. *adj also* **melancholic** malinconico.
mellow ['melou] *adj* maturo; (*wine*) amabile; (*soft*) morbido. *v* maturare; (*person*) intenerirsi.
melodrama ['melədra:mə] *n* melodramma *m*. **melodramatic** *adj* melodrammatico.
melody ['melədi] *n* melodia *f*. **melodious** *adj* melodioso.
melon ['melən] *n* melone *m*.
melt [melt] *v* fondere, sciogliere; (*feeling*) intenerire. **melt down** fondere. **melting point** punto di fusione *m*. **melting pot** crogiuolo *m*.
member ['membə] *n* membro *m*; (*of society, club, etc.*) socio, -a *m*, *f*; (*of parliament*) deputato, -a *m*, *f*. **membership** *n* (*number*) numero dei soci *m*; (*condition*) l'essere socio *m*.
membrane ['membrein] *n* membrana *f*.
memento [mə'mentou] *n* ricordo *m*.
memo ['memou] *n* appunto *m*.
memoirs ['memwa:z] *pl n* memorie *f pl*.
memorandum [memə'randəm] *n* appunto *m*, promemoria *m invar*; (*document*) memorandum *m invar*.

memorial [mi'mɔːriəl] *n* monumento *m*. *adj* commemorativo.
memory ['meməri] *n* (*faculty*) memoria *f*; (*recollection*) ricordo *m*. **memorable** *adj* memorabile. **memorize** *v* imparare a memoria.
men [men] *V* **man**.
menace ['menis] *n* minaccia *f*. *v* minacciare. **menacing** *adj* minaccioso.
menagerie [mi'nadʒəri] *n* serraglio *m*.
mend [mend] *v* riparare, aggiustare; (*get better*) migliorare. **mend one's ways** ravvedersi. *n* **be on the mend** stare rimettendosi. **mending** *n* rammendo *m*.
menial ['miːniəl] *adj* servile, umile.
meningitis [ˌmenin'dʒaitis] *n* meningite *f*.
menopause ['menəpoːz] *n* menopausa *f*.
menstrual ['menstruəl] *adj* mestruale. **menstruate** *v* mestruare. **menstruation** *n* mestruazione *f*.
mental ['mentl] *adj* mentale; (*home, hospital*) psichiatrico. **mentality** *n* mentalità *f*.
menthol ['menθəl] *n* mentolo *m*.
mention ['menʃən] *v* accennare a, parlare di, citare. **don't mention it!** prego! *n* menzione *f*, cenno *m*; citazione *f*.
menu ['menjuː] *n* menu *m invar*, lista dei cibi *f*.
mercantile ['məːkənˌtail] *adj* mercantile.
mercenary ['məːsinəri] *nm, adj* mercenario.
merchandise ['məːtʃəndaiz] *n* merce *f*.
merchant ['məːtʃənt] *n* commerciante *m, f*. **merchant navy** marina mercantile *f*.
mercury ['məːkjuri] *n* mercurio *m*.
mercy ['məːsi] *n* pietà *f*, carità *f*. **at the mercy of** alla mercè di. **merciful** *adj* pietoso, caritatevole.
mere [miə] *adj* puro, mero.
merge [məːdʒ] *v* fondere, amalgamare. **merger** *n* fusione *f*.
meridian [mə'ridiən] *n* meridiano *m*.
meringue [mə'raŋ] *n* meringa *f*.
merit ['merit] *n* merito *m*, valore *m*. *v* meritare.
mermaid ['məːmeid] *n* sirena *f*.
merry ['meri] *adj* allegro; (*coll*) brillo. **merry-go-round** *n* carosello *m*. **merry-making** *n* festa *f*.
mesh [meʃ] *n* maglia *f*; (*net*) rete *f*. **in mesh** ingranato.
mesmerize ['mezməraiz] *v* ipnotizzare; affascinare.
mess [mes] *n* confusione *f*, pasticcio *m*; (*eating place*) mensa *f*. **be in a mess** (*of things*) essere in disordine; (*of people*) trovarsi nei guai. **make a mess of** rovinare. *v* **mess about** perdersi in cose inutili; (*inconvenience*) disturbare. **mess up** rovinare. **messy** *adj* confuso, disordinato; (*dirty*) sporco.
message ['mesidʒ] *n* messaggio *m*. **messenger** *n* messaggero *m*; (*errand boy*) fattorino *m*.
met [met] *V* **meet**.
metabolism [mi'tabəlizm] *n* metabolismo *m*. **metabolic** *adj* metabolico.
metal ['metl] *n* metallo *m*. **metallic** *adj* metallico. **metallurgy** *n* metallurgia *f*.
metamorphosis [metə'moːfəsis] *n* metamorfosi *f invar*.
metaphor ['metəfə] *n* metafora *f*. **metaphoric(al)** *adj* metaforico.
metaphysics [ˌmetə'fiziks] *n* metafisica *f*. **metaphysical** *adj* metafisico.
meteor ['miːtiə] *n* meteora *f*. **meteoric** *adj* meteorico; rapidissimo.
meteorology [ˌmiːtiə'rolədʒi] *n* meteorologia *f*. **meteorological** *adj* meteorologico. **meteorologist** *n* meteorologo, -a *m, f*.
meter ['miːtə] *n* contatore *m*; (*parking*) parchimetro *m*. *v* misurare.
methane ['miːθein] *n* metano *m*.
method ['meθəd] *n* metodo *m*, modo *m*. **methodical** *adj* metodico, sistematico.
methylated spirits ['meθileitid] *n* alcool denaturato *m*.
meticulous [mi'tikjuləs] *adj* meticoloso.
metre ['miːtə] *n* metro *m*. **metric** *adj* metrico.
metronome ['metrənoum] *n* metronomo *m*.
metropolis [mə'tropəlis] *n* metropoli *f*. **metropolitan** *adj* metropolitano.
mettle ['metl] *n* **put someone on his mettle** mettere qualcuno alla prova.
mews [mjuːz] *n* vicolo *m*.
miaow [mi'au] *v* miagolare.
mice [mais] *V* **mouse**.
microbe ['maikroub] *n* microbo *m*.
microfilm ['maikrəˌfilm] *n* microfilm *m invar*.
microphone ['maikrəfoun] *n* microfono *m*.
microscope ['maikrəskoup] *n* microscopio *m*. **microscopic** *adj* microscopico. **microscopy** *n* microscopia *f*.

mid [mid] *adj* **in mid** ... a metà ..., in mezzo a ..., in pieno .... **midday** *n* mezzogiorno *m*. **midnight** *n* mezzanotte *f*. **mid-ocean** *n* alto mare *m*. **midsummer** *n* mezza estate *f*. **midway** *adv* a metà strada.

middle ['midl] *n* mezzo *m*, centro *m*. *adj* medio. **middle-aged** *adj* di mezza età. **Middle Ages** Medio Evo *m sing*. **middle-class** *adj* borghese. **middle man** *n* intermediario *m*.

midge [midʒ] *n* zanzara *f*.

midget ['midʒit] *n* nano *m*.

midst [midst] *n* mezzo *m*, centro *m*. **in the midst of** nel mezzo di, in mezzo a, fra.

midwife ['midwaif] *n* levatrice *f*. **midwifery** *n* ostetricia *f*.

might[1] [mait] *V* **may**.

might[2] [mait] *n* (*power*) forza *f*, potenza *f*.

mighty ['maiti] *adj* forte, potente. *adv* (*coll*) estremamente.

migraine ['miːgrein] *n* emicrania *f*.

migrate [mai'greit] *v* migrare. **migrant** *n*, *adj* migratore, -trice. **migration** *n* migrazione *f*. **migratory** *adj* migratorio.

Milan [mi'lan] *n* Milano *f*. **Milanese** *n*(*m*+*f*), *adj* milanese.

mild [maild] *adj* mite. **mildness** *n* mitezza *f*.

mildew ['mildjuː] *n* muffa *f*. **mildewy** *adj* ammuffito.

mile [mail] *n* miglio *m* (*pl* -a *f*). **mileage** *n* distanza percorsa in miglia *f*, chilometraggio *m*. **mileometer** *n* contachilometri *m invar*.

militant ['militənt] *n*(*m*+*f*), *adj* militante, attivista.

military ['militəri] *adj* militare. **militarism** *n* militarismo *m*. **militate** *v* militare. **militia** *n* milizia *f*.

milk [milk] *n* latte *m*. **milkman** *n* lattaio *m*. *v* mungere; (*exploit*) sfruttare.

mill [mil] *n* (*flour*) mulino *m*; (*textiles*) stabilimento *m*; (*tech*) fresa *f*; (*coffee*) macinino *m*. **millstone** *n* macina *f*; (*burden*) macigno *m*. *v* macinare; (*metal*) laminare; (*crowd*) circolare. **milling** *n* (*corn*) macinatura *f*; (*metal*) laminatura *f*; (*tech*) fresatura *f*; (*coins*) zigrinatura *f*.

millennium [mi'leniəm] *n* millennio *m*.

millet ['milit] *n* miglio *m*.

milligram ['mili,gram] *n* milligrammo *m*.

millilitre ['mili,liːtə] *n* millilitro *m*.

millimetre ['mili,miːtə] *n* millimetro *m*.

milliner ['milinə] *n* modista *f*.

million ['miljən] *n* milione *m*. **millionaire** *n* milionario, -a *m*, *f*. **millionth** *nm*, *adj* milionesimo.

mime [maim] *n* (*art*) mimica *f*; (*artist*) mimo, -a *m*, *f*. *v* mimare.

mimic ['mimik] *v* contraffare; (*ape*) scimmiottare. *n* imitatore, -trice *m*, *f*; contraffattore, -trice *m*, *f*. **mimicry** *n* mimica *f*; (*zool*) mimetismo *m*.

mimosa [mi'mouzə] *n* mimosa *f*.

minaret [minə'ret] *n* minareto *m*.

mince [mins] *v* tritare, tagliuzzare. **not mince one's words** parlare apertamente. *n* (*meat*) carne tritata *f*. **make mincemeat of** (*coll*) demolire. **mincer** *n* tritatutto *m invar*.

mind [maind] *n* mente *f*, intelletto *m*, spirito *m*; (*reason*) ragione *f*; (*opinion*) parere *m*. **bear in mind** tenere a mente. **make up one's mind** decidersi. **peace of mind** serenità *f*. **piece of one's mind** (*reprimand*) rimprovero *m*. **speak one's mind** parlar chiaro. **state of mind** stato d'animo *m*. *v* badare a, occuparsi di; (*watch out*) far attenzione. **do you mind if ...?** ti dispiace se ...? **never mind!** non importa! **mindful** *adj* attento. **mindless** *adj* (*heedless*) sbadato; (*senseless*) insensato.

mine[1] [main] *pron* il mio, la mia; (*pl*) i miei, le mie.

mine[2] [main] *n* miniera *f*; (*explosive*) mina *f*. *v* (*dig*) scavare; (*extract*) estrarre; (*mil*) minare. **mine-detector** *n* rilevatore di mine *m*. **minefield** *n* campo minato *m*. **minesweeper** *n* dragamine *m invar*. **miner** *n* minatore *m*.

mineral ['minərəl] *nm*, *adj* minerale.

mingle ['miŋgl] *v* mescolare, mischiarsi.

miniature ['minitʃə] *n* miniatura *f*. *adj* in miniatura.

minim ['minim] *n* (*music*) minima *f*.

minimum ['miniməm] *n* minimo *m*. **minimal** *adj* minimo. **minimize** *v* minimizzare.

mining ['mainiŋ] *n* estrazione *f*, scavo *m*; (*mil*) posa di mine *f*. *adj* minerario.

minister ['ministə] *n* (*pol*) ministro, -a *m*, *f*; (*rel*) sacerdote *m*; (*diplomat*) incaricato, -a *m*, *f*. *v* **minister to** soccorrere. **minister to the needs of** provvedere ai bisogni di. **ministerial** *adj* ministeriale. **ministry** *n* ministero *m*; (*clergy*) clero *m*.

mink [miŋk] *n* visone *m*.

minor ['mainə] *adj* minore, più piccolo, meno importante. *n* minorenne *m, f.* **minority** *n* minoranza *f*; (*age*) minorità *f*, età minore *f.*
minstrel ['minstrəl] *n* menestrello *m*, cantante *m.*
mint[1] [mint] *n* (*bot*) menta *f.*
mint[2] [mint] *n* zecca *f.* **be in mint condition** essere nuovo di zecca. **have a mint of money** avere un mucchio di soldi. *v* coniare.
minuet [minju'et] *n* minuetto *m.*
minus ['mainəs] *prep* meno.
minute[1] ['minit] *n* minuto *m*; momento *m.* **minutes** *pl n* (*of meeting*) verbale *m sing.* *v* (*record*) prendere nota; (*enter in minutes*) mettere agli atti.
minute[2] [mai'njuːt] *adj* minuto; (*detailed*) minuzioso.
minx [miŋks] *n* (*coll*) civetta *f.*
miracle ['mirəkl] *n* miracolo *m.* **miraculous** *adj* miracoloso.
mirage ['miraːʒ] *n* miraggio *m.*
mirror ['mirə] *n* specchio *m.* *v* riflettere, rispecchiare.
mirth [məːθ] *n* ilarità *f*, allegria *f.*
misadventure [misəd'ventʃə] *n* infortunio *m*, disavventura *f.*
misanthropist [miz'anθrəpist] *n* misantropo, -a *m, f.* **misanthropic** *adj* misantropico. **misanthropy** *n* misantropia *f.*
misapprehension [misapri'henʃən] *n* equivoco *m*, malinteso *m.* **misapprehend** *v* fraintendere.
misbehave [misbi'heiv] *v* comportarsi male. **misbehaviour** *n* cattiva condotta *f.*
miscalculate [mis'kalkjuleit] *v* calcolar male. **miscalculation** *n* calcolo errato *m.*
miscarriage [mis'karidʒ] *n* (*med*) aborto *m.* **miscarry** *v* abortire.
miscellaneous [misə'leiniəs] *adj* miscellaneo.
mischance [mis'tʃaːns] *n* sventura *f.*
mischief ['mistʃif] *n* (*harm*) danno *m*; (*of child, etc.*) fastidi *m pl*; (*teasing*) malizia *f.* **be up to mischief** combinare un brutto tiro. **make mischief** creare discordia. **mischief-maker** *n* attaccabrighe *m invar.* **mischievous** *adj* malizioso; (*of child*) birichino.
misconception [miskən'sepʃən] *n* malinteso *m.*
misconduct [mis'kondʌkt] *n* cattiva condotta *f.*
misdeed [mis'diːd] *n* misfatto *m*, delitto *m.*
misdemeanour [misdi'miːnə] *n* (*misbehaviour*) cattiva condotta *f*; (*crime*) delitto *m.*
miser ['maizə] *n* avaro, -a *m, f.* **miserly** *adj* avaro.
miserable ['mizərəbl] *adj* (*unhappy*) infelice, triste; (*pitiful*) pietoso; (*painful*) penoso; depresso.
misery ['mizəri] *n* miseria *f*; sofferenze *f pl.*
misfire [mis'faiə] *v* fare cilecca *or* fiasco.
misfit ['misfit] *n* (*person*) spostato, -a *m, f.*
misfortune [mis'foːtʃən] *n* sfortuna *f*, disgrazia *f.*
misgiving [mis'giviŋ] *n* dubbio *m.*
misguided [mis'gaidid] *adj* fuori posto, sviato.
mishap ['mishap] *n* disgrazia *f*, contrattempo *m.*
misjudge [mis'dʒʌdʒ] *v* farsi un'idea sbagliata di, giudicare male.
***mislay** [mis'lei] *v* smarrire.
***mislead** [mis'liːd] *v* ingannare. **misleading** *adj* ingannevole.
misnomer [mis'noumə] *n* termine improprio *m.*
misplace [mis'pleis] *v* mettere fuori posto.
misprint ['misprint] *n* errore tipografico *m.*
miss[1] [mis] *n* colpo mancato *m.* *v* mancare (a); (*not catch*) perdere; (*skip*) saltare; (*not find*) non trovare; (*regret absence of*) sentire la mancanza di. **miss out** omettere. **be missing** mancare.
miss[2] [mis] *n* signorina *f.*
missile ['misail] *n* missile *m.*
mission ['miʃən] *n* missione *f.* **missionary** *n, adj* missionario, -a.
mist [mist] *n* caligine *f*, foschia *f.* *v* offuscare. **misty** *adj* caliginoso, fosco.
***mistake** [mi'steik] *n* errore *m*, sbaglio *m.* **by mistake** per errore. **make a mistake** sbagliare, fare un errore. *v* (*confuse*) confondere, scambiare. **mistaken** *adj* sbagliato, falso.
mistletoe ['misltou] *n* vischio *m.*
mistress ['mistris] *n* padrona *f*; (*school*) insegnante *f*; (*lover*) amante *f.*
mistrust [mis'trʌst] *v* diffidare di, non aver fiducia in. *n* diffidenza *f*, sfiducia *f.* **mistrustful** *adj* diffidente.
***misunderstand** [misʌndə'stand] *v*

fraintendere, capir male. **misunderstanding** *n* malinteso *m*, equivoco *m*. **misunderstood** *adj* incompreso.
misuse [mis'juːs; *v* mis'juːz] *n* abuso *m*; uso incorretto *m*. *v* abusare; (*ill-treat*) maltrattare; (*use badly*) adoperare male.
mitigate ['mitigeit] *v* mitigare; (*law*) attenuare. **mitigation** *n* (*law*) attenuante *f*.
mitre ['maitə] *n* (*rel*) mitra *f*; (*carpentry*) ugnatura *f*. *v* ugnare.
mitten ['mitn] *n* mezzo quanto *m*, muffola *f*.
mix [miks] *v* mescolare, mischiare; combinare. **mix up** confondere. **mix-up** *n* confusione *f*. **mixed** *adj* misto. **mixer** *n* (*tech*) agitatore *m*. **be a good mixer** essere socievole. **mixture** *n* miscela *f*; miscuglio *m*.
moan [moun] *n* (*complaint*) lamento *m*; (*groan*) gemito *m*. *v* lamentarsi; gemere.
moat [mout] *n* fosso *m*, fossato *m*.
mob [mob] *n* folla *f*, marmaglia *f*, plebaglia *f*. *v* molestare, assalire.
mobile ['moubail] *adj* mobile. **mobility** *n* mobilità *f*. **mobilization** *n* mobilitazione *f*. **mobilize** *v* mobilitare.
moccasin ['mokəsin] *n* mocassino *m*.
mock [mok] *v* deridere, canzonare. *adj* finto, falso. **mockery** *n* presa in giro *f*, derisione *f*. **mocking** *adj* beffardo. **mocking-bird** *n* mimo *m*.
mode [moud] *n* modo *m*, maniera *f*.
model ['modl] *n* modello *m*; (*art*) modello, -a *m*, *f*; (*fashion*) indossatore, -trice *m*, *f*. *adj* modello, esemplare. *v* modellare, fare l'indossatore.
moderate ['modərət; *v* 'modəreit] *adj* misurato, moderato; (*price*) modico. *v* moderare. **moderation** *n* misura *f*, moderazione *f*. **in moderation** moderatamente.
modern ['modən] *adj* moderno. **modernization** *n* rimodernamento *m*. **modernize** *v* rimodernare.
modest ['modist] *adj* modesto. **modesty** *n* modestia *f*.
modify ['modifai] *v* modificare. **modification** *n* modifica *f*.
modulate ['modjuleit] *v* modulare. **modulation** *n* modulazione *f*.
module ['modjuːl] *n* modulo *m*.
mohair ['mouheə] *n* mohair *m invar*.
moist [moist] *adj* umido. **moisten** *v* inumidire; (*surface*) umettare. **moisture** *n* umidità *f*. **moisturize** *v* umidificare.
molar ['moulə] *nm*, *adj* molare.
molasses [mə'lasiz] *n* melassa *f*.
mold (*US*) *V* **mould**.
mole[1] [moul] *n* (*on skin*) neo *m*.
mole[2] [moul] *n* (*zool*) talpa *f*.
molecule ['molikjuːl] *n* molecola *f*. **molecular** *adj* molecolare.
molest [mə'lest] *v* molestare.
mollify ['molifai] *v* placare.
mollusc ['moləsk] *n* mollusco *m*.
mollycoddle ['molikodl] *v* coccolare.
molt (*US*) *V* **moult**.
molten ['moultən] *adj* fuso.
moment ['moumənt] *n* momento *m*, istante *m*. **at the moment** attualmente. **momentary** *adj* momentaneo. **momentous** *adj* grave, importante. **momentum** *n* impeto *m*, slancio *m*.
Monaco ['monəˌkou] *n* Monaco *f*.
monarch ['monək] *n* monarca *m*, *f*. **monarchist** *n*, *adj* monarchico, -a. **monarchy** *n* monarchia *f*.
monastery ['monəstəri] *n* monastero *m*. **monastic** *adj* monastico.
Monday ['mʌndi] *n* lunedì *m*.
money ['mʌni] *n* denaro *m*, soldi *m pl*. **money-box** *n* salvadanaio *m*. **money-lender** *n* usuraio *m*. **money order** vaglia *m invar*. **monetary** *adj* monetario.
mongol ['moŋgəl] *adj* mongolo; (*med*) mongoloide. **Mongolia** *n* Mongolia *f*.
mongrel ['mʌŋgrəl] *nm*, *adj* bastardo.
monitor ['monitə] *n* (*radio*) ascoltatore *m*; (*tech*) monitor *m invar*. *v* (*radio*) ascoltare; controllare. **monitoring service** servizio d'ascolto *m*.
monk [mʌŋk] *n* monaco *m*, frate *m*.
monkey ['mʌŋki] *n* scimmia *f*.
monogamy [mə'nogəmi] *n* monogamia *f*. **monogamous** *adj* monogamo.
monogram ['monəgram] *n* monogramma *m*.
monograph ['monəgraːf] *n* monografia *f*.
monolithic [ˌmonə'liθik] *adj* monolitico.
monologue ['monəlog] *n* monologo (*pl* -ghi) *m*.
monopolize [mə'nopəlaiz] *v* monopolizzare. **monopoly** *n* monopolio *m*.
monosyllable ['monəsiləbl] *n* monosillabo *m*. **monosyllabic** *adj* monosillabico, monosillabo.
monotony [mə'notəni] *n* monotonia *f*. **monotone** *n* tono uniforme *m*. **monotonous** *adj* monotono.

monsoon [mon'suːn] *n* monsone *m*.
monster ['monstə] *n* mostro *m*. **monstrosity** *n* mostruosità *f*. **monstrous** *adj* mostruoso.
month [mʌnθ] *n* mese *m*.
monthly ['mʌnθli] *n* (*periodical*) rivista mensile *f*. *adj* mensile. *adv* al mese, mensilmente.
monument ['monjumənt] *n* monumento *m*. **monumental** *adj* monumentale.
mood[1] [muːd] *n* umore *m*, stato d'animo *m*. **feel in the mood to** sentirsi disposto a, aver voglia di. **moodiness** *n* malumore *m*; volubilità *f*. **moody** *adj* capriccioso; (*sulky*) di malumore.
mood[2] [muːd] *n* (*gramm*) modo *m*.
moon [muːn] *n* luna *f*. **moonlight** *n* chiaro di luna *m*.
moor[1] [muə] *n* brughiera *f*. **moorhen** *n* gallinella d'acqua *f*.
moor[2] [muə] *v* ormeggiare, ancorare. **mooring** *n* ormeggio *m*, ancoraggio *m*.
moose [muːs] *n* alce *m*.
moot [muːt] *adj* discutibile.
mop [mop] *n* scopa di cotone per lavaggio *f*; (*of hair*) zazzera *f*. *v* **mop one's brow** asciugarsi la fronte. **mop up** asciugare; rastrellare.
mope [moup] *v* fare il broncio, immusonirsi.
moped ['mouped] *n* ciclomotore *m*.
moral ['morəl] *nf*, *adj* morale. **morals** *pl n* morale *f sing*. **morale** *n* morale *m*. **moralist** *n* moralista *m*, *f*. **morality** *n* moralità *f*, buon costume *m*.
morbid ['moːbid] *adj* morboso, patologico.
more [moː] *adv* più, di più; (*again*) ancora. *nm*, *adj* più. **more and more** sempre più. **more than** più di *or* che.
moreover [moː'rouvə] *adv* inoltre, per di più.
morgue [moːg] *n* obitorio *m*.
morning ['moːniŋ] *n* mattina *m*, mattinata *f*. **this morning** stamane. **tomorrow morning** domattina. *adj* del mattino, mattutino.
moron ['moːron] *n* deficiente *m*, *f*. **moronic** *adj* deficiente, scemo.
morose [mə'rous] *adj* scontroso.
morphine ['moːfiːn] *n* morfina *f*.
Morse code [moːs] *n* alfabeto Morse *m*.
morsel ['moːsəl] *n* boccone *m*.
mortal ['moːtl] *n*(*m*+*f*), *adj* mortale. **mortality** *n* mortalità *f*.
mortar ['moːtə] *n* (*vessel*, *arms*) mortaio *m*; (*building*) malta *f*.
mortgage ['moːgidʒ] *n* ipoteca *f*. *v* ipotecare, impegnare.
mortify ['moːtifai] *v* mortificare. **mortification** *n* mortificazione *f*.
mortuary ['moːtʃuəri] *n* camera ardente *or* mortuaria *f*.
mosaic [mə'zeiik] *n* mosaico *m*.
Moscow ['moskou] *n* Mosca *f*.
mosque [mosk] *n* moschea *f*.
mosquito [mə'skiːtou] *n* zanzara *f*.
moss [mos] *n* muschio *m*, musco *m*. **mossy** *adj* muscoso.
most [moust] *adj* (*majority*) la maggior parte di, il più di; (*greatest*) il più grande, il maggiore. *n* il più *m*; (*greatest part*) la maggior parte *f*; (*majority*) la maggioranza *f*, *i più m pl*. *adv* il più; (*very*) molto, assai.
motel [mou'tel] *n* motel *m invar*, autostello *m*.
moth [moθ] *n* lepidottero *m*. **clothes moth** tarma *f*. **mothball** *n* pallina antitarmica *f*.
mother ['mʌðə] *n* madre *f*; (*coll*) mamma *f*. *v* aver cura di come una madre. **mother-in-law** *n* suocera *f*. **mother-of-pearl** *n* madreperla *f*. **mother tongue** madrelingua *f*. **motherly** *adj* materno.
motion ['mouʃən] *n* moto *m*, movimento *m*; (*proposal*) mozione *f*; (*law*) istanza *f*. **go through the motions** far finta. **set in motion** avviare, mettere in moto. *v* accennare a, far cenno a. **motionless** *adj* immobile.
motivate ['moutiveit] *v* motivare, spingere. **motivation** *n* spinta *f*, stimolo *m*.
motive ['moutiv] *n* motivo *m*, ragione *f*.
motor ['moutə] *nm*, *adj* motore. **motorboat** *n* motoscafo *m*. **motor car** automobile *f*, macchina *f*. **motorcycle** *n* motocicletta *f*. **motorcyclist** *n* motociclista *m*, *f*. **motorway** *n* autostrada *f*. *v* andare in macchina. **motoring** *n* automobilismo *m*. **motorist** *n* automobilista *m*, *f*. **motorize** *v* motorizzare.
mottled ['motld] *adj* chiazzato.
motto ['motou] *n* motto *m*, massima *f*.
mould[1] *or US* **mold** [mould] *n* stampo *m*, forma *f*. *v* formare, foggiare, modellare.
mould[2] *or US* **mold** [mould] *n* muffa *f*. **mouldy** *adj* ammuffito. **go mouldy** ammuffire.

moult *or US* **molt** [moult] *v* mutare, fare la muta.
mound [maund] *n* tumulo *m*; (*heap*) mucchio *m*.
mount[1] [maunt] *v* montare. *n* (*setting*) montatura *f*.
mount[2] [maunt] *n* monte *m*.
mountain ['mauntən] *n* montagna *f*. **mountaineer** *n* alpinista *m, f*. **mountaineering** *n* alpinismo *m*. **mountainous** *adj* montuoso, alpestre.
mourn [moːn] *v* rimpiangere, essere in lutto per. **mourning** *n* lutto *m*, cordoglio *m*. **mournful** *adj* triste; lugubre.
mouse [maus] *n*, *pl* **mice** topo *m*. **mousetrap** *n* trappola (per topi) *f*. **mousy** *adj* (*colour*) grigio topo; timido.
mousse [muːs] *n* mousse *f*, spuma *f*.
moustache [mə'staːʃ] *n* baffi *m pl*.
mouth [mauθ] *n* bocca *f*; (*of river*) foce *f*. **mouth organ** armonica *f*. **mouthpiece** *n* (*spokesman*) portavoce *m invar*; (*of pipe*) bocchino *m*. *v* declamare. **mouthful** *n* boccone *m*.
move [muːv] *v* muovere, spostare; (*house*) traslocare; (*arouse feelings*) commuovere; (*propose*) proporre. **move away** *or* **off** allontanare; (*depart*) partire. **move back** indietreggiare; (*return*) tornare. **move forward** avanzare. **move in** occupare. **move out** uscire, sgombrare. **move up** (*raise*) salire; (*get closer*) avvicinarsi. *n* mossa *f*, passo *m*; (*house*) trasloco *m*. **movable** *adj* movibile. **movement** *n* movimento *m*; (*sign*) cenno *m*; (*tech*) meccanismo *m*. **moving** *adj* commovente; (*in motion*) in moto.
movie ['muːvi] *n* (*US*) film *m invar*.
***mow** [mou] *v* falciare.
mown [moun] *V* **mow**.
Mr ['mistə] *n* signor *m*.
Mrs ['misiz] *n* signora *f*.
much [mʌtʃ] *pron, adj* molto. *adv* molto, assai. **as much as** (tanto) quanto. **how much** quanto. **so much** tanto. **too much** troppo.
muck [mʌk] *n* letame *m*; (*coll: filth*) porcheria *f*. *v* **muck about** (*coll*) bighellonare. **muck up** (*coll*) rovinare.
mucus ['mjuːkəs] *n* muco *m*. **mucous membrane** mucosa *f*.
mud [mʌd] *n* fango *m*. **mudguard** *n* parafango *m*. **mudslinger** *n* maldicente *m, f*. **muddy** *adj* fangoso, inzaccherato.
muddle ['mʌdl] *n* confusione *f*, pasticcio *m*. *v* **muddle through** arrabattarsi. **muddle up** confondere. **muddler** *n* confusionario, -a *m, f*.
muff [mʌf] *n* manicotto *m*. *v* mancare, sbagliare.
muffle ['mʌfl] *v* smorzare, attutire.
mug [mʌg] *n* (*cup*) tazza *f*; (*coll: face*) muso *m*, ceffo *m*; (*slang: fool*) gonzo *m*. *v* assalire.
mulberry ['mʌlbəri] *n* (*fruit*) mora di gelso *f*; (*tree*) gelso *m*.
mule[1] [mjuːl] *n* (*zool*) mulo *m*. **mulish** *adj* (*stubborn*) duro.
mule[2] [mjuːl] *n* (*slipper*) ciabatta *f*, pianella *f*.
mullet ['mʌlit] *n* (*grey*) muggine *m*; (*red*) triglia *f*.
multicoloured [ˌmʌlti'kʌləd] *adj* multicolore.
multimillionaire [ˌmʌltimiljə'neə] *n* multimilionario, -a *m, f*.
multiple ['mʌltipl] *adj* multiplo, molteplice. *n* multiplo *m*.
multiply ['mʌltiplai] *v* moltiplicare. **multiplication** *n* moltiplicazione *f*. **multiplicity** *n* varietà *f*.
multiracial [ˌmʌlti'reiʃəl] *adj* multirazziale.
multitude ['mʌltitjuːd] *n* moltitudine *f*, massa *f*.
mum [mʌm] *adj* **keep mum** star zitto.
mumble ['mʌmbl] *v* borbottare.
mummy[1] ['mʌmi] *n* (*corpse*) mummia *f*. **mummify** *v* mummificare.
mummy[2] ['mʌmi] *n* (*coll: mother*) mamma *f*, mammina *f*.
mumps [mʌmps] *n* orecchioni *m pl*.
munch [mʌntʃ] *v* sgranocchiare.
mundane [mʌn'dein] *adj* mondano.
municipal [mju'nisipəl] *adj* municipale. **municipality** *n* comune *m*.
mural ['mjuərəl] *n* pittura murale *f*.
murder ['məːdə] *n* assassinio *m*. *v* assassinare, ammazzare; (*coll*) massacrare. **murderer** *n* assassino *m*. **murderess** *n* assassina *f*. **murderous** *adj* micidiale.
murmur ['məːmə] *n* mormorio *m*. *v* mormorare.
muscle ['mʌsl] *n* muscolo *m*.
muse[1] [mjuːz] *n* musa *f*.
muse[2] [mjuːz] *v* meditare, riflettere.
museum [mju'ziəm] *n* museo *m*.
mushroom ['mʌʃrum] *n* fungo *m*. *v* (*gather*) raccogliere funghi; (*spread*) dilagare, svilupparsi rapidamente.

music ['mjuːzik] *n* musica *f*. **musician** *n* musicista *m*, *f*.

musical ['mjuːzikl] *adj* musicale; (*gifted*) dotato per la musica. *n* musical *m invar*.

musk [mʌsk] *n* (*zool*) muschio *m*.

musket ['mʌskit] *n* moschetto *m*.

Muslim ['mʌzlim] *n*, *adj* musulmano, -a.

muslin ['mʌzlin] *n* mussola *f*.

mussel ['mʌsl] *n* mitilo *m*, cozza *f*.

***must**[1] [mʌst] *v* dovere. *n* (*coll*) cosa essenziale *f*.

must[2] [mʌst] *n* (*wine*) mosto *m*.

mustard ['mʌstəd] *n* senape *f*, mostarda *f*.

muster ['mʌstə] *v* radunare. **muster up courage** farsi coraggio. *n* **pass muster** essere accettabile.

mute [mjuːt] *adj* muto, taciturno. *n* muto, -a *m*, *f*; (*music*) sordina *f*.

mutilate ['mjuːtileit] *n* mutilare, mozzare. **mutilation** *n* mutilazione *f*.

mutiny ['mjuːtini] *n* ammutinamento *m*, ribellione *f*. *v* ammutinarsi, ribellarsi. **mutinous** *adj* ammutinato, ribelle.

mutter ['mʌtə] *v* brontolare, borbottare.

mutton ['mʌtn] *n* carne ovina *f*, castrato *m*. **dead as mutton** morto stecchito.

mutual ['mju:tʃuəl] *adj* mutuo, reciproco; comune.

muzzle ['mʌzl] *n* (*gun*) imboccatura *f*; (*animal*) muso *m*; (*device*) museruola *f*. *v* mettere la museruola a; (*silence*) far tacere.

my [mai] *adj* (il) mio, (la) mia; (*pl*) (i) miei, (le) mie.

myself [mai'self] *pron* io stesso; (*after prep*) me stesso; (*reflexive*) mi.

myopia [mai'oupiə] *n* miopia *f*. **myopic** *adj* miope.

mystery ['mistəri] *n* mistero *m*, segretò *m*. **mysterious** *adj* misterioso, strano.

mystic ['mistik] *n* mistico, -a *m*, *f*. **mystical** *adj* mistico, misterioso. **mysticism** *n* misticismo *m*, mistica *f*.

mystify ['mistifai] *v* mistificare, disorientare.

mystique [mi'stiːk] *n* mistica *f*.

myth [miθ] *n* mito *m*. **mythical** *adj* mitico. **mythological** *adj* mitologico. **mythology** *n* mitologia *f*.

N

nag[1] [nag] *v* rimbrottare, brontolare. **nagging** *adj* bisbetico.

nag[2] [nag] *n* ronzino *m*.

nail [neil] *n* (*anat*) unghia *f*; (*metal*) chiodo *m*. **nail-brush** *n* spazzolino per le unghie *m*. **nail-file** *n* lima per le unghie *f*. **nail polish** smalto per le unghie *m*. **nail-scissors** *pl n* forbici per le unghie *f pl*.

naive [nai'iːv] *adj* ingenuo. **naivety** *n* ingenuità *f*.

naked ['neikid] *adj* nudo, scoperto. **strip naked** spogliare. **nakedness** *n* nudità *f*.

name [neim] *v* chiamare. *n* nome *m*. **go by the name of** chiamarsi. **my name is . . .** mi chiamo . . . . **namesake** *n* omonimo *m*. **nameless** *adj* anonimo. **namely** *adv* cioè.

nanny ['nani] *n* bambinaia *f*.

nap[1] [nap] *n* (*doze*) pisolino *m*. *v* fare *or* schiacciare un pisolino.

nap[2] [nap] *n* (*cloth*) pelo *m*.

nape [neip] *n* nuca *f*.

napkin ['napkin] *n* tovagliolo *m*.

nappy ['napi] *n* pannolino *m*.

narcotic [naː'kotic] *nm*, *adj* narcotico.

narrate [nə'reit] *v* narrare, raccontare. **narration** *n* racconto *m*. **narrative** *n* narrativa *f*. **narrator** *n* narratore, -trice *m*, *f*.

narrow ['narou] *adj* stretto; limitato; (*person, mind, etc.*) ristretto. **narrow-gauge** *adj* (*railway*) a scartamento ridotto. **narrow-minded** *adj* gretto, di mente ristretta. *v* restringere, limitare. **narrowly** *adv* per un pelo, a stento.

nasal ['neizəl] *adj* nasale.

nasturtium [nə'stəːʃəm] *n* nasturzio *m*.

nasty ['naːsti] *adj* (*filthy*) disgustoso; (*offensive*) ripugnante; (*unpleasant*) cattivo, sgradevole. **nastiness** *n* cattiveria *f*.

nation ['neiʃən] *n* nazione *f*. **national** *adj* nazionale. **national insurance** assicurazione sociale *f*. **nationalism** *n* nazionalismo *m*. **nationalist** *n*(*m*+*f*), *adj* nazionalista. **nationality** *n* nazionalità *f*. **nationalization** *n* nazionalizzazione *f*. **nationalize** *v* nazionalizzare.

native ['neitiv] *n*, *adj* (*original inhabitant*) indigeno, -a; (*of town, etc.*) nativo, -a, oriundo, -a.

nativity [nə'tivəti] *n* natività *f*.

natural ['natʃərəl] *adj* naturale; normale;

istintivo. **naturalization** *n* naturalizzazione *f.* **naturalize** *v* naturalizzare.

nature ['neitʃə] *n* natura *f*; (*condition*) indole *f*; disposizione *f.*

naught [nɔːt] *n* nulla *m.* **come to naught** ridurre a zero.

naughty ['nɔːti] *adj* cattivo; (*mischievous*) birichino; indecente, spinto.

nausea ['nɔːziə] *n* nausea *f*; fastidio *m.* **nauseous** *adj* nauseabondo, disgustoso.

nautical ['nɔːtikəl] *adj* nautico.

naval ['neivəl] *adj* navale, marittimo.

nave[1] [neiv] *n* (*of church*) navata *f.*

nave[2] [neiv] *n* (*hub*) mozzo *m.*

navel ['neivəl] *n* ombelico *m.*

navigate ['navigeit] *v* navigare, pilotare. **navigable** *adj* navigabile. **navigation** *n* navigazione *f.* **navigator** *n* navigatore *m*; (*officer*) ufficiale di rotta *m.*

navy ['neivi] *n* marina militare *f.* **navy blue** *adj* blu marino.

near [niə] *adj* vicino. *prep* vicino a, accanto a. *adv* vicino. *v* avvicinare. **near at hand** a portata di mano. **near-sighted** *adj* miope. **nearby** *adj, adv, prep* vicino (a). **nearly** *adv* quasi.

neat [niːt] *adj* (*orderly*) ordinato, accurato; elegante; (*undiluted*) liscio. **neatness** *n* ordine *m*; eleganza *f.*

nebulous ['nebjuləs] *adj* vago, nebuloso.

necessary ['nesisəri] *adj* necessario, indispensabile. **necessity** *n* necessità *f*, bisogno *m.*

neck [nek] *n* (*anat*) collo *m*; (*of dress*) scollatura *f.* **have a stiff neck** avere il torcicollo. **neck and neck** testa a testa. **necklace** *n* collana *f.* **necktie** *n* cravatta *f.*

nectar ['nektə] *n* nettare *m.* **nectarine** *n* pesca noce *f.*

née [nei] *adj* nata.

need [niːd] *n* bisogno *m*, necessità *f*; (*poverty*) miseria *f.* **if need be** caso mai, se c'è bisogno. *v* aver bisogno di; (*require*) richiedere. **needed** *adj* necessario. **needless** *adj* inutile, superfluo. **needy** *adj* indigente, bisognoso.

needle ['niːdl] *n* ago *m*; (*knitting*) ferro *m*; (*gramophone*) puntina *f.* **needlework** *n* (*sewing*) cucitura *f*; (*embroidery*) ricamo *m.* *v* (*coll*) punzecchiare.

negative ['negətiv] *adj* negativo. *n* negativa *f.* **answer in the negative** rispondere di no.

neglect [ni'glekt] *n* negligenza *f*, trascuratezza *f.* *v* trascurare. **neglect to** mancare di. **negligent** *adj* negligente. **negligible** *adj* trascurabile.

negligée ['negliʒei] *n* negligé *m invar*, vestaglia *f.*

negotiate [ni'gouʃieit] *v* trattare, negoziare; (*obstacle, etc.*) superare. **negotiable** *adj* negoziabile. **negotiation** *n* trattativa *f*, negoziato *m.*

Negro ['niːgrou] *nm, adj* negro. **Negress** *n* negra *f.*

neigh [nei] *v* nitrire. *n* nitrito *m.*

neighbour ['neibə] *n* vicino, -a *m, f.* **next-door neighbour** vicino di casa *m.* **neighbourhood** *n* vicinanza *f*, paraggi *m pl.* **neighbouring** *adj* adiacente, vicino. **neighbourly** *adj* socievole, da buon vicino.

neither ['naiðə] *adj* nè l'uno nè l'altro. *adv* **neither ... nor ...** nè ... nè .... *pron* nessuno, nè l'uno nè l'altro.

neon ['niːon] *n* neon *m.*

nephew ['nefjuː] *n* nipote *m.*

nepotism ['nepətizəm] *n* nepotismo *m.*

nerve [nəːv] *n* nervo *m*; coraggio *m*; (*coll: cheek*) sfacciataggine *f*, faccia tosta *f.* **get on the nerves of** dare sui nervi a. **nerve-racking** *adj* snervante. **nervous** *adj* nervoso; apprensivo. **get nervous** inquietarsi. **nervous breakdown** esaurimento nervoso *m.*

nest [nest] *n* nido *m.* **nest egg** gruzzolo *m.* *v* annidarsi.

nestle ['nesl] *v* annidarsi, accoccolarsi.

net[1] [net] *n* rete *f.* **network** *n* rete *f.* *v* (*enclose*) cintare con reti; (*catch*) prendere con reti; (*ball*) mandare in rete. **netting** *n* reticolato *m.*

net[2] [net] *adj* netto.

Netherlands ['neðələndz] *pl n* Paesi Bassi *m pl.*

nettle ['netl] *n* ortica *f.* **nettle-rash** *n* orticaria *f.* *v* irritare.

neurosis [nju'rousis] *n* nevrosi *f.* **neurotic** *n, adj* nevrotico, -a.

neuter ['njuːtə] *adj* neutro. *v* castrare.

neutral ['njuːtrəl] *adj* neutrale; (*tech*) neutro. *n* neutrale *m, f.* **neutrality** *n* neutralità *f.* **neutralize** *v* neutralizzare. **neutron** *n* neutrone *m.*

never ['nevə] *adv* (non ...) mai. **never-ending** *adj* interminabile.

nevertheless [nevəðə'les] *adv, conj* ciononostante, tuttavia.

new [njuː] *adj* nuovo. **new-born** *adj* neonato. **newcomer** *n* nuovo venuto, nuova venuta *m, f.*

news [njuːz] *n* novità *f pl,* notizie *f pl,* informazioni *f pl.* **news agency** agenzia d'informazioni *f.* **newsagent** *n* giornalaio *m.* **news bulletin** notiziario *m;* (*radio*) giornale radio *m.* **news item** notizia *f.* **newspaper** *n* giornale *m.* **newsprint** *n* carta da giornale *f.* **newsreel** *n* cinegiornale *m.*

newt [njuːt] *n* tritone *m.*

New Year *n* Anno nuovo *m.* **Happy New Year!** Buon Anno! **New Year's Day** il Capodanno *m.* **New Zealand** *n* Nuova Zelanda *f.* **New Zealander** neozelandese *m, f.*

next [nekst] *adj* prossimo; (*nearest*) più vicino; (*following*) successivo, seguente. *adv* (*after*) dopo, poi; (*later*) in seguito. **next-of-kin** *n* parente prossimo *m, f.*

nib [nib] *n* pennino *m.*

nibble ['nibl] *n* (*morsel*) bocconcino *m.* *v* rosicchiare.

nice [nais] *adj* bello; piacevole, simpatico; (*subtle*) sottile; delicato; (*refined*) elegante, fine. **nicely** *adv* proprio bene. **nicety** *n* esattezza *f.* **niceties** *pl n* finezze *f pl,* sfumature *f pl.*

niche [nitʃ] *n* nicchia *f.*

nick [nik] *v* intaccare; (*slang: steal*) arraffare; (*slang: catch*) acchiappare. *n* tacca *f.* **in the nick of time** all'ultimo momento.

nickel ['nikl] *n* nichel *m;* (*US: coin*) nichelino *m.*

nickname ['nikneim] *n* nomignolo *m,* soprannome *m.* *v* soprannominare.

nicotine ['nikətiːn] *n* nicotina *f.*

niece [niːs] *n* nipote *f.*

niggling ['nigliŋ] *adj* insignificante.

night [nait] *n* notte *f;* (*evening*) sera *f.* **have a good/bad night** dormir bene/male. **night-club** *n* night *m invar.* **nightdress** *n* camicia da notte *f.* **nightfall** *n* tramonto *m.* **nightmare** *n* incubo *m.* **nightmarish** *adj* opprimente, spaventoso. **stay the night** pernottare.

nightingale ['naitiŋ,geil] *n* usignolo *m.*

nightly ['naitli] *adj* notturno; (*every night*) di tutte le sere. *adv* ogni notte *or* sera.

nil [nil] *n* nulla *m,* niente *m,* zero *m.*

nimble ['nimbl] *adj* agile, svelto. **nimbleness** *n* agilità *f.*

nine [nain] *nm, adj* nove. **ninepins** *n* birilli *m pl.* **ninth** *nm, adj* nono.

nineteen [nain'tiːn] *nm, adj* diciannove. **nineteenth** *nm, adj* diciannovesimo.

ninety ['nainti] *nm, adj* novanta. **ninetieth** *nm, adj* novantesimo.

nip[1] [nip] *v* pizzicare; (*bite*) morsicare. **nip in** intromettersi, entrare lestamente. **nip in the bud** stroncare sul nascere. **nip out** fare un salto. *n* (*frost*) gelo *m;* (*bite*) morso *m.* **nippy** *adj* (*speedy*) svelto; (*cold*) frizzante.

nip[2] [nip] *n* (*drop*) bicchierino *m,* sorso *m.*

nipple ['nipl] *n* capezzolo *m;* (*tech*) rubinetto *m.*

nit [nit] *n* lendine *m;* (*coll*) stupido, -a *m, f.*

nitrogen ['naitrədʒən] *n* azoto *m.*

no [nou] *adj* nessuno, neppure uno; (*forbidden*) vietato. *adv* no; (*with comparative*) non. *n* no *m invar.*

noble ['noubl] *n*(*m+f*), *adj* nobile. **nobility** *n* nobiltà *f.*

nobody ['noubodi] *pron* nessuno. *n* zero *m,* sconosciuto, -a *m, f.*

nocturnal [nok'təːnəl] *adj* notturno.

nod [nod] *n* cenno col capo *m.* *v* fare un cenno col capo; (*doze*) sonnecchiare; (*assent*) annuire; (*greet*) salutare. **nodding acquaintance** conoscenza superficiale *f.*

noise [noiz] *n* rumore *m;* (*loud*) baccano *m.* **background noise** rumori di fondo *m pl.* **big noise** (*coll*) pezzo grosso *m.* **noiseless** *adj* silenzioso. **noisy** *adj* rumoroso, chiassoso.

nomad ['noumad] *n*(*m+f*), *adj* nomade.

nominal ['nominl] *adj* nominale; simbolico.

nominate ['nomineit] *v* nominare; (*propose*) proporre. **nomination** *n* nomina *f.*

nominative ['nominətiv] *nm, adj* nominativo.

nonchalant ['nonʃələnt] *adj* indifferente, noncurante. **nonchalance** *n* indifferenza *f,* noncuranza *f.*

nonconformist [nonkən'foːmist] *n*(*m+f*), *adj* dissidente, anti-conformista.

nondescript ['nondiskript] *adj* inclassificabile, qualunque.

none [nʌn] *pron* nessuno, nulla, niente. *adv* affatto, punto. **none other than** nientedimeno che.

nonentity [non'entəti] *n* nullità *f*, zero *m*.
nonetheless [ˌnʌnðə'les] *adv* ciononostante, tuttavia.
nonsense ['nonsəns] *n* nonsenso *m*, assurdo *m*; (*coll*) sciocchezze *f pl*. **nonsensical** *adj* assurdo, sciocco. **talk nonsense** dire sciocchezze.
non-stop [non'stop] *adj* continuo, ininterrotto.
noodles ['nuːdlz] *pl n* tagliatelle *f pl*, taglierini *m pl*.
nook [nuk] *n* cantuccio *m*, angolo *m*.
noon [nuːn] *n* mezzogiorno *m*.
no-one ['nouwʌn] *pron* nessuno.
noose [nuːs] *n* nodo scorsoio *m*, laccio *m*.
nor [noː] *conj* nè, neppure, nemmeno.
norm [noːm] *n* norma *f*, modello *m*. **normal** *adj* normale, regolare. **normally** *adv* di solito.
north [noːθ] *n* nord *m*, settentrione *m*. *adj also* **northern** del nord, settentrionale. **northerly** *adj* di nordo; da nordo; a nordo. **north-east** *n* nordest *m*. **north-eastern** del nordest. **north-west** *n* nordovest *m*. **north-western** del nordovest.
Norway ['noːwei] *n* Norvegia *f*. **Norwegian** *n(m+f)*, *adj* norvegese.
nose [nouz] *n* naso *m*; (*of animal, aeroplane, etc.*) muso *m*. *v* fiutare. **nose around** esplorare. **nosy** *adj* (*coll*) curioso.
nostalgia [no'staldʒə] *n* nostalgia *f*, rimpianto *m*. **nostalgic** *adj* nostalgico.
nostril ['nostrəl] *n* narice *f*.
not [not] *adv* non. **not at all** niente affatto. **not even** neppure, neanche.
notable ['noutəbl] *adj* notevole, degno di nota.
notary ['noutəri] *n* notaio *m*.
notch [notʃ] *n* tacca *f*, intaglio *m*. *v* intaccare.
note [nout] *n* nota *f*, appunto *m*, commento *m*; (*money*) biglietto *m*. **note-book** *n* taccuino *m*. **notepaper** *n* carta da lettere *or* scrivere. **noteworthy** *adj* degno di nota, notevole. **take note of** prendere atto di. **take notes** prendere appunti. **notation** *n* notazione *f*. *v* notare; osservare. **noted** *adj* noto, rinomato.
nothing ['nʌθiŋ] *n* niente *m*, zero *m*. *adv* per nulla, niente (affatto). **next to nothing** quasi nulla. **nothing but** null'altro che. **nothing less than** semplicemente.
notice ['noutis] *n* avviso *m*, annuncio *m*; (*advance warning*) preavviso *m*; (*criticism*) recensione *f*. **give notice** (*dismiss*) licenziare. **notice-board** *n* tabellone *m*. **take notice of** fare attenzione a. *v* notare, rilevare. **noticeable** *adj* apparente, percettibile.
notify ['noutifai] *v* notificare, avvertire. **notification** *n* notifica *f*.
notion ['nouʃən] *n* nozione *f*, idea *f*.
notorious [nou'toːriəs] *adj* notorio, famigerato. **notoriety** *n* notorietà *f*.
notwithstanding [notwið'standiŋ] *prep* nonostante, malgrado. *adv* ciononostante, con tutto ciò.
nougat ['nuːgaː] *n* torrone *m*.
nought [noːt] *n* zero *m*.
noun [naun] *n* nome *m*, sostantivo *m*.
nourish ['nʌriʃ] *v* nutrire, alimentare. **nourishing** *adj* nutriente. **nourishment** *n* cibo *m*, alimento *m*.
novel[1] ['novəl] *n* romanzo *m*. **novelist** *n* romanziere, -a *m*, *f*.
novel[2] ['novəl] *adj* nuovo, originale; (*unusual*) insolito. **novelty** *n* novità *f*.
November [nə'vembə] *n* novembre *m*.
novice ['novis] *n* novizio, -a *m*, *f*.
now [nau] *adv* ora, adesso. **from now on** d'ora in poi. **just now** or ora. **nowadays** *adv* oggigiorno, al giorno d'oggi. **now and again** ogni tanto, di quando in quando. **until now** finora.
nowhere ['nouweə] *adv* in nessun luogo.
noxious ['nokʃəs] *adj* nocivo, malefico.
nozzle ['nozl] *n* (*spout*) becco *m*; (*tech*) ugello *m*.
nuance ['njuːãs] *n* sfumatura *f*.
nuclear ['njuːkliə] *adj* nucleare.
nucleus ['njuːkliəs] *n* nucleo *m*.
nude ['njuːd] *n*, *adj* nudo, -a. **nudism** *n* nudismo *m*. **nudist** *n* nudista *m*, *f*. **nudity** *n* nudità *f*.
nudge [nʌdʒ] *n* colpetto *m*. *v* dare un colpetto a.
nugget ['nʌgit] *n* pepita *f*.
nuisance ['njuːsns] *n* fastidio *m*, seccatura *f*; (*law*) infrazione *f*. **make a nuisance of oneself** seccare tutti.
null [nʌl] *adj* nullo. **null and void** senza validità legale.
numb [nʌm] *adj* intorpidito; (*stunned*) intontito. *v* intorpidire, paralizzare. **numbness** *n* torpore *m*.
number ['nʌmbə] *n* numero *m*; (*numeral*) cifra *f*; quantità *f*. **number plate** targa *f*. *v*

numerare, contare. **numberless** *adj* innumerevole.
numeral ['njuːmərəl] *n* cifra *f*.
numerical [njuː'merikl] *adj* numerico.
numerous ['njuːmərəs] *adj* numeroso.
nun [nʌn] *n* monaca *f*, suora *f*. **become a nun** prendere il velo. **nunnery** *n* convento *m*.
nurse [nəːs] *v* curare, fare l'infermiere; (*suckle*) allattare; (*hope, grievance, etc.*) nutrire, covare. *n* infermiere, -a *m, f*; (*children's*) balia *f*, bambinaia *f*. **nursing** *n* professione d'infermiere *f*. **nursing home** casa di cura *f*, clinica *f*.
nursery ['nəːsəri] *n* (*children's*) camera dei bambini *f*; (*plants, etc.*) vivaio *m*, serra *f*. **day nursery** asilo infantile *m*. **nursery rhyme** filastrocca *f*. **nursery school** giardino d'infanzia *m*.
nurture ['nəːtʃə] *v* (*feed*) nutrire; (*rear*) allevare. *n* nutrimento *m*; allevamento *m*.
nut [nʌt] *n* noce *f*; (*tech*) dado *m*; (*coll: head*) zucca *f*. **be nuts** (*coll*) essere matto. **in a nutshell** in poche parole. **nutcrackers** *pl n* schiaccianoci *m invar*. **nutmeg** *n* noce moscata *f*. **nut-tree** *n* noce *m*.
nutrient ['njuːtriənt] *adj* nutriente. *n* nutrimento *m*.
nutrition [nju'triʃən] *n* alimentazione *f*. **nutritious** *adj* nutriente.
nuzzle ['nʌzl] *v* accucciolarsi, rannicchiarsi.
nylon ['nailon] *n* nailon *m*.
nymph [nimf] *n* ninfa *f*. **nymphomaniac** *n* ninfomane *f*.

O

oak [ouk] *n* quercia *f*.
oar [oː] *n* remo *m*.
oasis [ou'eisis] *n, pl* **-ses** oasi *f invar*.
oath [ouθ] *n* (*promise*) giuramento *m*; (*profanity*) bestemmia *f*.
oats [outs] *pl n* avena *f sing*. **oatmeal** *n* farina d'avena *f*.
obedient [ə'biːdiənt] *adj* ubbidiente, obbediente. **obedience** *n* ubbidienza *f*, obbedienza *f*.
obese [ə'biːs] *adj* obeso. **obesity** *n* obesità *f*.
obey [ə'bei] *v* ubbidire, obbedire.
obituary [ə'bitjuəri] *n* necrologia *f*.
object ['obʒikt; *v* əb'ʒekt] *n* oggetto *m*; (*aim*) scopo *m*. *v* obiettare, protestare. **objection** *n* obiezione *f*, protesta *f*. **have no objection to** aver nulla in contrario a. **objectionable** *adj* offensivo, sgradevole, riprensibile. **objective** *nm, adj* obiettivo.
oblige [ə'blaidʒ] *v* costringere, obbligare; fare un favore a. **be obliged to** (*have to*) dovere; (*be grateful to*) essere riconoscente a. **obligation** *n* (*law*) obbligazione *f*; (*binding promise*) obbligo (*pl* -ghi) *m*; (*duty*) dovere *m*. **obligatory** *adj* obbligatorio. **obliging** *adj* cortese, accomodante.
oblique [ə'bliːk] *adj* obliquo; indiretto.
obliterate [ə'blitəreit] *v* obliterare, cancellare; (*destroy*) distruggere. **obliteration** *n* distruzione *f*.
oblivion [ə'bliviən] *n* oblio *m*. **oblivious** *adj* dimentico (*m pl* -chi).
oblong ['obloŋ] *adj* bislungo.
obnoxious [əb'nokʃəs] *adj* odioso, offensivo.
oboe ['oubou] *n* oboe *m*. **oboist** *n* oboista *m, f*.
obscene [əb'siːn] *adj* osceno. **obscenity** *n* oscenità *f*.
obscure [əb'skjuə] *adj* (*not clear*) ambiguo, oscuro; (*inconspicuous*) vago. *v* offuscare, velare. **obscurity** *n* oscurità *f*.
observe [əb'zəːv] *v* (*see*) osservare; notare, rilevare; (*rel*) praticare. **observance** *n* osservanza *f*. **observant** *adj* osservante. **observation** *n* osservazione *f*, attenzione *f*. **keep under observation** tenere in osservazione. **observatory** *n* osservatorio *m*. **observer** *n* osservatore, -trice *m, f*.
obsess [əb'ses] *v* ossessionare. **obsession** *n* ossessione *f*.
obsolescent [obsə'lesnt] *adj* che sta cadendo in disuso.
obsolete ['obsəliːt] *adj* caduto in disuso; antiquato.
obstacle ['obstəkl] *n* ostaçolo *m*.
obstetrics [ob'stetriks] *n* ostetricia *f*. **obstetrician** *n* ostetrico, -a *m, f*.
obstinate ['obstinət] *adj* ostinato. **obstinacy** *n* ostinatezza *f*.
obstreperous [əb'strepərəs] *adj* ribelle.
obstruct [əb'strʌkt] *v* impacciare, ostacolare. **obstruction** *n* impaccio *m*, ostacolo *m*.
obtain [əb'tein] *v* ottenere, procurare. **obtainable** *adj* ottenibile, raggiungibile.

obtrusive [əb'truːsiv] *adj* importuno; invadente. **obtrusion** *n* invadenza *f*.
obtuse [əb'tjuːs] *adj* ottuso.
obverse ['obvəːs] *n* faccia *f*, diritto *m*; (*counterpart*) inverso *m*.
obvious ['obviəs] *adj* ovvio, evidente.
occasion [ə'keiʒən] *v* causare. *n* (*time*) occasione *f*, volta *f*; (*cause*) motivo *m*, ragione *f*. **rise to the occasion** mostrarsi all'altezza. **occasional** *adj* saltuario, sporadico. **occasionally** *adv* ogni tanto.
occult ['okʌlt] *adj* occulto. *n* forze occulte *f pl*.
occupy ['okjupai] *v* occupare. **occupant** *or* **occupier** *n* occupante *m*, *f*. **occupation** *n* occupazione *f*; (*trade*) mestiere *m*, professione *f*. **occupational** *adj* del lavoro, professionale.
occur [ə'kəː] *v* succedere, capitare; (*come to mind*) venire in mente. **occurrence** *n* avvenimento *m*, caso *m*.
ocean ['ouʃən] *n* oceano *m*.
ochre ['oukə] *n* ocra *f*. *adj* (color) ocra.
o'clock [ə'klok] *adv* **one o'clock** l'una. **two/three/etc. o'clock** le due/tre/etc.
octagon ['oktəgən] *n* ottagono *m*. **octagonal** *adj* ottagonale.
octane ['oktein] *n* ottano *m*.
octave ['oktiv] *n* ottava *f*.
October [ok'toubə] *n* ottobre *m*.
octopus ['oktəpəs] *n* polpo *m*.
oculist ['okjulist] *n* oculista *m*, *f*.
odd [od] *adj* (*not even*) dispari; (*not paired*) scompagnato; (*strange*) strano, bizzarro; casuale; (*approximately*) circa. **oddity** *n* stranezza *f*; (*person*) eccentrico, -a *m*, *f*. **oddments** *pl n* rimasugli *m pl*, scampoli *m pl*.
odds [odz] *pl n* probabilità *f pl*, differenza *f sing*; (*betting*) posta *f sing*. **be at odds with** essere in disaccordo con. **lay odds** scommettere. **odds and ends** cosette varie *f pl*, rimasugli *m pl*.
ode [oud] *n* ode *f*.
odious ['oudiəs] *adj* odioso.
odour ['oudə] *n* odore *m*. **odourless** *adj* inodoro.
oesophagus [iː'sofəgəs] *n* esofago *m*.
of [ov] *prep* di.
off [of] *adv* via, distante. *prep* lontano da, fuori (di). *adj* (*holiday*) libero; (*food*) marcio, non buono. **be off** (*cancelled*) non aver luogo.
offal ['ofəl] *n* frattaglie *f pl*.
offend [ə'fend] *v* offendere. **offence** *n* offesa *f*; (*law*) infrazione alla legge *f*. **take offence** offendersi. **offender** *n* colpevole *m*, *f*; trasgreditore, -trice *m*, *f*.
offensive [ə'fensiv] *adj* offensivo; (*disagreeable*) sgradevole; insolente. *n* offensiva *f*.
offer ['ofə] *v* offrire, presentare, dare. *n* offerta *f*, proposta *f*.
offhand [of'hand] *adj* noncurante. *adv* all'improvviso.
office ['ofis] *n* (*place*) ufficio *m*; (*post, function*) carica *f*. **head office** *n* sede (centrale) *f*. **officer** *n* funzionario, -a *m*, *f*; (*mil, etc.*) ufficiale *m*.
official [ə'fiʃəl] *adj* ufficiale. *n* funzionario, -a *m*, *f*.
officious [ə'fiʃəs] *adj* inframmettente, invadente.
offing ['ofiŋ] *n* **in the offing** in vista.
off-load [of'loud] *v* scaricare.
off-peak [of'piːk] *adj* non di punta.
off-putting ['of,putiŋ] *adj* sconcertante, che lascia perplesso.
off-season [of'siːzn] *adj* fuori stagione.
offset [of'set; *n* 'ofset] *v* compensare, controbilanciare. *n* (*print*) offset *m invar*.
offshoot ['offuːt] *n* ramo *m*.
offshore ['offoː] *adv* al largo. *adj* di terra.
offside [of'said] *adv*, *adj* fuori gioco.
offspring ['ofspriŋ] *n* prole *f*; frutto *m*.
offstage ['ofsteidʒ] *adv*, *adj* fuori scena.
often ['ofn] *adv* spesso, sovente, molte volte. **how often** quante volte. **too often** troppe volte.
ogre ['ougə] *n* orco *m*.
oil [oil] *n* olio *m*; petrolio *m*; gasolio *m*. **oilfield** *n* giacimento petrolifero *m*. **oil-fired** *adj* a gasolio *or* nafta. **oil-painting** *n* pittura a olio *f*. **oilskin** *n* tela impermeabile *f*. **oil-well** *n* pozzo petrolifero *m*. *v* ungere, lubrificare. **oily** *adj* oleoso, untuoso.
ointment ['ointmənt] *n* unguento *m*.
old [ould] *adj* vecchio, antico (*m pl* -chi); (*not new*) usato. **old age** vecchiaia *f*. **old-fashioned** *adj* fuori moda. **old man** vecchio *m*. **old people** vecchi *m pl*. **old woman** vecchia *f*. **oldish** *adj* vecchiotto.
olive ['oliv] *n* oliva *f*. **olive green** *adj* verde oliva. **olive grove** oliveto *m*. **olive oil** olio d'oliva *m*. **olive-tree** *n* olivo *m*.
Olympic [ə'limpik] *adj* olimpico. **Olympic Games** olimpiadi *f pl*.

omelette ['omlit] *n* frittata *f*.
omen ['oumən] *n* presagio *m*, segno *m*.
ominous ['ominəs] *adj* sinistro, minaccioso.
omit [ou'mit] *v* omettere, tralasciare. **omission** *n* omissione *f*.
omnipotent [om'nipətənt] *adj* onnipotente. **omnipotence** *n* onnipotenza *f*.
on [on] *prep* su, sopra; a. *adv* su. *adj* (*gas, elec, etc.*) acceso; (*tap*) aperto.
once [wʌns] *adv* una volta. **all at once** ad un tratto. **at once** subito.
one [wʌn] *n, adj* uno, -a. *pron* uno; (*impersonal*) si. **oneself** *pron* sè (stesso); (*reflexive*) si. **one by one** a uno a uno. **one-sided** *adj* unilaterale; parziale; ineguale. **one-way street** senso unico *m*. **the one** quello, -a. **which one?** quale?
onion ['ʌnjən] *n* cipolla *f*.
onlooker ['onlukə] *n* spettatore, -trice *m, f*.
only ['ounli] *adj* solo, unico. *conj* ma. *adv* solo, soltanto. **only just** appena.
onset ['onset] *n* inizio *m*.
onshore ['onʃoː] *adv* a terra.
onslaught ['onsloːt] *n* attacco *m*, assalto *m*.
onus ['ounəs] *n* onere *m*, obbligo (*pl* -ghi) *m*.
onward ['onwəd] *adj* che progredisce *or* avanza. **onwards** *adv* (in) avanti.
onyx ['oniks] *n* onice *m*.
ooze [uːz] *v* colare, trasudare.
opal ['oupəl] *n* opale *m*.
opaque [ə'paik] *adj* opaco (*m pl* -chi). **opacity** *n* opacità *f*.
open ['oupən] *v* aprire; iniziare; inaugurare. **open wide** spalancare. *nm, adj* aperto. **lay oneself open to** esporsi a. **open-handed** *adj* generoso. **open-hearted** *adj* sincero. **open-minded** *adj* spregiudicato, libero da preconcetti. **open-mouthed** *adj, adv* a bocca aperta.
opening ['oupəniŋ] *adj* introduttivo, inaugurale. *n* apertura *f*; inaugurazione *f*.
opera ['opərə] *n* opera *f*. **opera glasses** binocoli da teatro *m pl*. **opera house** teatro dell'opera *m*. **opera singer** cantante lirico, -a *m, f*. **operetta** *n* operetta *f*.
operate ['opəreit] *v* operare. **operation** *n* operazione *f*; (*activity*) attività *f*; (*surgical*) intervento (chirurgico) *m*. **come into operation** entrare in vigore. **operative** *adj* operativo; attivo; (*surgical*) operatorio. **operator** *n* operatore, -trice *m, f*; (*phone*) telefonista *m, f*.
ophthalmic [of'θalmik] *adj* oftalmico.
opinion [ə'pinjən] *n* opinione *f*, parere *m*, giudizio *m*. **in the opinion of** secondo. **opinionated** *adj* dogmatico, intransigente.
opium ['oupiəm] *n* oppio *m*.
opponent [ə'pounənt] *n* avversario, -a *m, f*.
opportune [opə'tjuːn] *adj* opportuno, giusto.
opportunity [opə'tjuːnəti] *n* occasione *f*.
oppose [ə'pouz] *v* opporre, combattere; contrastare. **opposed** *adj* opposto, contrario. **opposition** *n* opposizione *f*.
opposite ['opəzit] *nm, adj* opposto, contrario. *prep* di fronte a, dirimpetto a.
oppress [ə'pres] *v* opprimere. **oppression** *n* oppressione *f*. **oppressive** *adj* oppressivo, opprimente. **oppressor** *n* oppressore *m*.
opt [opt] *v* optare. **opt out** decidere di non partecipare.
optical ['optikl] *adj* ottico. **optician** *n* ottico *m*. **optics** *n* ottica *f*.
optimism ['optimizəm] *n* ottimismo *m*. **optimist** *n* ottimista *m, f*. **optimistic** *adj* ottimistico.
optimum ['optiməm] *n* optimum *m*, meglio *m*. *adj* migliore.
option ['opʃən] *n* opzione *f*, scelta *f*. **optional** *adj* facoltativo.
opulent ['opjulənt] *adj* opulento. **opulence** *n* opulenza *f*.
or [oː] *conj* o, oppure. **either ... or ...** o ... o .... **or else** altrimenti.
oracle ['orəkl] *n* oracolo *m*.
oral ['oːrəl] *adj* orale.
orange ['orindʒ] *n* (*fruit*) arancia *f*; (*tree, colour*) arancio *m*. *adj* (*colour*) arancio, arancione. **orange juice** succo d'arancio *m*; (*drink*) spremuta d'arancio *f*. **orange squash** aranciata *f*.
orator ['orətə] *n* oratore, -trice *m, f*. **oration** *n* orazione *f*.
orbit ['oːbit] *n* orbita *f*.
orchard ['oːtʃəd] *n* frutteto *m*.
orchestra ['oːkəstrə] *n* orchestra *f*. **orchestral** *adj* orchestrale. **orchestrate** *v* orchestrare. **orchestration** *n* orchestrazione *f*.
orchid ['oːkid] *n* orchidea *f*.
ordain [oː'dein] *v* ordinare.
ordeal [oː'diːl] *n* dura prova *f*, travaglio *m*.

order ['oːdə] *n* ordine *m*; comando *m*; classe *f*, grado *m*; (*commission*) ordinazione *f*. **in order that** affinché, perché. **in order to** per, allo scopo di. **out of order** guasto. *v* ordinare. **order about** mandar qua e là.
orderly ['oːdəli] *adj* ordinato, regolare. *n* attendente *m*, inserviente *m*.
ordinal ['oːdinl] *adj* ordinale.
ordinary ['oːdənəri] *nm, adj* ordinario, solito, comune.
ore [oː] *n* minerale *m*.
oregano [ori'gaːnou] *n* origano *m*.
organ ['oːgən] *n* organo *m*. **organ-pipe** *n* canna d'organo *f*. **organic** *adj* organico. **organist** *n* organista *m, f*.
organism ['oːgənizəm] *n* organismo *m*.
organize ['oːgənaiz] *v* organizzare. **organization** *n* organizzazione *f*. **organizer** *n* organizzatore, -trice *m, f*.
orgasm ['oːgazəm] *n* orgasmo *m*.
orgy ['oːdʒi] *n* orgia *f*.
orient ['oːriənt] *n* oriente *m*. *v* orientare. **oriental** *adj* orientale.
orientate ['oːriənteit] *v* orientare. **orientation** *n* orientamento *m*.
origin ['oridʒin] *n* origine *f*. **originate** *v* originare. **originate from** derivare *or* provenire da. **originator** *n* creatore, -trice *m, f*; originatore, -trice *m, f*.
original [ə'ridʒinl] *adj* originale; (*authentic, primitive*) originario. *n* originale *m*. **originality** *n* originalità *f*. **originally** *adv* in origine.
ornament ['oːnəmənt] *n* ornamento *m*; (*music*) abbellimento *m*; (*object, fitting*) suppellittile *f*. *v* abbellire. **ornamentation** *n* abbellimento *m*.
ornate [oː'neit] *adj* ornato.
ornithology [oːni'θolədʒi] *n* ornitologia *f*. **ornithologist** *n* ornitologo, -a *m, f*.
orphan ['oːfən] *n* orfano, -a *m, f*. *v* rendere orfano. **be orphaned** rimanere orfano. **orphanage** *n* orfanotrofio *m*.
orthodox ['oːθədoks] *adj* ortodosso. **orthodoxy** *n* ortodossia *f*.
orthopaedic [oːθə'piːdik] *adj* ortopedico. **orthopaedics** *n* ortopedia *f*. **orthopaedist** *n* ortopedico, -a *m, f*.
oscillate ['osileit] *v* (far) oscillare; (*fluctuate*) vacillare. **oscillation** *n* oscillazione *f*.
ostensible [o'stensəbl] *adj* ostensibile.
ostentatious [osten'teiʃəs] *adj* ostentato, ostentoso.
osteopath ['ostiəpaθ] *n* osteologo, -a *m, f*.
ostracize ['ostrəsaiz] *v* osteggiare, mettere al bando.
ostrich ['ostritʃ] *n* struzzo *m*.
other ['ʌðə] *adj* altro, diverso. **on the other hand** d'altra parte. **other people** gli altri. *pron* altro. **each other** l'un l'altro.
otherwise ['ʌðəwaiz] *adv* altrimenti.
otter ['otə] *n* lontra *f*.
***ought** [oːt] *v* dovere.
our [auə] *adj* (il) nostro, (la) nostra; (*pl*) (i) nostri, (le) nostre.
ours [auəz] *pron* il nostro, la nostra; (*pl*) i nostri, le nostre.
ourselves [auə'selvz] *pron* noi (stessi); (*reflexive*) ci.
oust [aust] *v* espellere, soppiantare.
out [aut] *adj* (*not alight*) spetto. *adv* via, fuori; (*to the end*) alla fine. **feel out of it** sentirsi a disagio. **out of** (*without*) senza. **out of action** fuori servizio, guasto. **out of date** antiquato; (*ticket, etc.*) scaduto. **out of doors** all'aperto. **out of place** inopportuno. **out of pocket** in perdita. **out of print** esaurito, fuori stampa. **out of tune** stonato. **out of work** disoccupato.
outboard ['autboːd] *adj* fuoribordo.
outbreak ['autbreik] *n* scoppio *m*; (*riot*) sommossa; eruzione *f*; epidemia *f*.
outbuilding ['autbiːldiŋ] *n* edificio annesso *m*, dipendenza *f*.
outburst ['autbəːst] *n* scoppio *m*; (*invective*) tirata *f*.
outcast ['autkaːst] *n, adj* proscritto, -a, reietto, -a.
outcome ['autkʌm] *n* esito *m*, risultato *m*.
outcry ['autkrai] *n* grido *m*, scalpore *m*.
***outdo** [aut'duː] *v* sorpassare.
outdoor ['autdoː] *adj* all'aperto.
outer ['autə] *adj* esterno, esteriore.
outfit ['autfit] *n* corredo *m*, equipaggiamento *m*; (*coll*) compagnia *f*.
outgoing ['autgouiŋ] *adj* uscente, in partenza; (*person*) estroverso, espansivo. **outgoings** *pl n* spese *f pl*.
***outgrow** [aut'grou] *v* (*grow taller than*) sorpassare in altezza; (*clothes*) diventare troppo grande per.
outhouse ['authaus] *n* fabbricato annesso *m*.
outing ['autiŋ] *n* gita *f*, scampagnata *f*.
outlandish [aut'landiʃ] *adj* esotico.
outlast [aut'laːst] *v* durare più a lungo di, sopravvivere a.

outlaw ['autlɔː] *n* fuorilegge *m, f invar.* *v* mettere al bando, proscrivere.
outlay ['autlei] *n* spesa *f*, dispendio *m*.
outlet ['autlit] *n* sfogo *m*, sbocco *m*.
outline ['autlain] *v* delineare; (*draft*) abbozzare. *n* contorno *m*; (*general sketch*) abbozzo *m*. **outlines** *pl n* elementi *m pl*.
outlive [aut'liv] *v* sopravvivere a.
outlook ['autluk] *n* (*view*) veduta *f*; (*future prospect*) prospettiva *f*; (*mental view*) modo di vedere *m*, vedute *f pl*.
outlying ['autlaiiŋ] *adj* periferico, lontano.
outnumber [aut'nʌmbə] *v* superare in numero.
outpatient ['autpeiʃənt] *n* paziente esterno *or* ambulatoriale *m, f*.
outpost ['autpoust] *n* avamposto *m*.
output ['autput] *n* produzione *f*; (*yield*) rendimento *m*.
outrage ['autreidʒ] *n* oltraggio *m*. *v* oltraggiare.
outrageous [aut'reidʒəs] *adj* (*disgraceful*) vergognoso; offensivo; (*excessive*) esagerato.
outright ['autrait; *adv* aut'rait] *adj* completo, categorico. *adv* (*at once*) subito; (*entirely*) completamente; (*openly*) apertamente.
outset ['autset] *n* **at the outset** al principio.
outside [aut'said; *adj* 'autsaid] *adj* esterno, esteriore; (*extraneous*) estraneo. *adv* fuori, all'aperto. *prep* fuori di; (*except*) all'infuori di. *n* esterno *m*. **at the outside** (*coll*) tutt'al più. **outsider** *n* estraneo *m*; (*sport*) outsider *m invar.*
outsize ['autsaiz] *adj* di taglia forte, fuori misura.
outskirts ['autskəːtz] *pl n* dintorni *m pl*, periferia *f sing*.
outspoken [aut'spoukən] *adj* franco, esplicito, schietto.
outstanding [aut'standiŋ] *adj* (*striking*) eminente, notevole; (*unpaid*) in sospeso, arretrato.
outstrip [aut'strip] *v* distanziare.
outward ['autwəd] *adj* esterno, esteriore, superficiale; (*journey*) d'andata. **outwardly** *adv* in apparenza.
outweigh [aut'wei] *v* superare in importanza.
outwit [aut'wit] *v* superare in astuzia.
oval ['ouvəl] *nm, adj* ovale.
ovary ['ouvəri] *n* ovaia *f*.
ovation [ou'veiʃən] *n* ovazione *f*.
oven ['ʌvn] *n* forno *m*.
over ['ouvə] *adv* oltre, al di sopra; (*in excess*) in più; (*finished*) finito. *prep* su, sopra; (*across*) al di là di; (*more than*) più di. **over here** qui, da questa parte. **over there** là, laggiù.
overall ['ouvərɔːl] *adj* globale, completo. *n* (*workman's*) tuta *f*; (*scientist's*) camice *m*; (*woman's*) grembiulone *m*. *adv* in complesso.
overbalance [ouvə'baləns] *v* sbilanciare, perdere l'equilibrio.
overbearing [ouvə'beəriŋ] *adj* prepotente, altezzoso.
overboard ['ouvəbɔːd] *adv* in mare *or* acqua.
overcast [ouvə'kaːst] *adj* coperto, nuvoloso.
overcharge [ouvə'tʃaːdʒ] *v* far pagare troppo.
overcoat ['ouvəkout] *n* cappotto *m*, soprabito *m*.
***overcome** [ouvə'kʌm] *v* superare. *adj* sopraffatto, commosso.
overcrowded [ouvə'kraudid] *adj* sovraffollato. **overcrowding** *n* sovraffollamento *m*.
***overdo** [ouvə'duː] *v* esagerare; (*overcook*) stracuocere.
overdose ['ouvədous] *n* dose eccessiva *f*.
overdraft ['ouvədraːft] *n* scoperto (di conto) *m*.
***overdraw** [ouvə'drɔː] *v* andare allo scoperto.
overdrive ['ouvədraiv] *n* marcia sovramoltiplicata *f*.
overdue [ouvə'djuː] *adj* in ritardo, tardivo; (*bill*) scaduto.
overestimate [ouvə'estimeit] *v* sopravvalutare.
overexpose [ouvəik'spouz] *v* sovraesporre. **overexposure** *n* sovraesposizione *f*.
overflow [ouvə'flou; *n* 'ouvəflou] *v* (*flood*) inondare; (*river*) straripare; (*vessel*) traboccare. *n* (*outlet*) troppopieno *m*. **overflow pipe** scarico del troppopieno *m*.
overgrown [ouvə'groun] *adj* ricoperto di vegetazione.
***overhang** [ouvə'haŋ; *n* 'ouvəhaŋ] *v* sporgere sopra; (*impend*) incombere su, minacciare. *n* aggetto *m*; (*mountaineering*) strapiombo *m*.

overhaul [ouvə'hoːl] *v* (*investigate*) esaminare; (*repair*) ripassare, riparare. *n* esame minuzioso *m*.
overhead [ouvə'hed] *adv* in alto, di sopra. *adj* di sopra, aereo. **overheads** *pl n* spese generali *f pl*.
***overhear** [ouvə'hiə] *v* udire per caso; (*eavesdrop*) origliare.
overheat [ouvə'hiːt] *v* surriscaldare.
overjoyed [ouvə'dʒoid] *adj* felicissimo, colmo di gioia.
overland [ouvə'land] *adj, adv* per terra.
overlap [ouvə'lap] *v* sovrapporre, accavallare; coincidere *or* corrispondere in parte con.
***overlay** ['ouvəlei; *v* ouvə'lei] *n* copertura *f*. *v* ricoprire; incrostare.
overleaf [ouvə'liːf] *adv* **see overleaf** vedi retro.
overload [ouvə'loud; *n* 'ouvəloud] *v* sovraccaricare. *n* sovraccarico *m*.
overlook [ouvə'luk] *v* (*miss*) lasciarsi sfuggire, non rilevare; condonare; (*ignore*) non tener conto di, trascurare; (*house, etc.*) dare su.
overnight [ouvə'nait] *adv* di notte; (*suddenly*) d'un tratto. **stay overnight** pernottare.
overpower [ouvə'pauə] *v* sopraffare, dominare. **overpowering** *adj* irresistibile.
overrate [ouvə'reit] *v* sopravvalutare.
overreach [ouvə'riːtʃ] *v* **overreach oneself** sopravvalutare le proprie forze.
overriding [ouvə'raidiŋ] *adj* di primaria importanza.
overrule [ouvə'ruːl] *v* (*decision*) annullare; (*plea*) respingere.
***overrun** [ouvə'rʌn] *v* invadere, infestare.
overseas [ouvə'siːz] *adv* oltremare. *adj* d'oltremare, straniero.
overseer [ouvə'siə] *n* ispettore, -trice *m, f*, sorvegliante *m, f*.
overshadow [ouvə'ʃadou] *v* oscurare; (*render insignificant*) eclissare.
***overshoot** [ouvə'ʃuːt] *v* (*miss*) fallire; (*go beyond*) oltrepassare. **overshoot the mark** passare il segno. **overshoot the runway** atterrare lungo.
oversight ['ouvəsait] *n* svista *f*, inavvertenza *f*.
***oversleep** [ouvə'sliːp] *v* dormire troppo a lungo, dormire oltre all'ora stabilita.
overspill ['ouvəspil] *n* sovrappiù *m*.
overt [ou'vəːt] *adj* manifesto, palese.
***overtake** [ouvə'teik] *v* sorpassare.
***overthrow** [ouvə'θrou; *n* 'ouvəθrou] *v* rovesciare, sconfiggere. *n* rovesciamento *m*.
overtime ['ouvətaim] *n* ore straordinarie *f pl*.
overtone ['ouvətoun] *n* (*implication*) sfumatura *f*.
overture ['ouvətjuə] *n* (*music*) ouverture *f*, preludio *m*; (*proposal*) proposta *f*; (*political*) apertura *f*.
overturn [ouvə'təːn] *v* rovesciare, capovolgere.
overweight [ouvə'weit] *adj* **be overweight** pesare troppo.
overwhelm [ouvə'welm] *v* (*defeat*) sopraffare; (*crush*) schiacciare; (*with kindness, etc.*) colmare. **overwhelmingly** *adv* in modo schiacciante.
overwork [ouvə'wəːk] *v* (far) lavorar troppo. *n* eccesso di lavoro *m*.
overwrought [ouvə'roːt] *adj* teso, turbato, agitato.
ovulate ['ovjuleit] *v* ovulare. **ovulation** *n* ovulazione *f*.
owe [ou] *v* dovere. **owing** *adj* dovuto. **owing to** dovuto a, grazie a.
owl [aul] *n* gufo *m*, civetta *f*.
own [oun] *adj* proprio. **get one's own back** rendere pan per focaccia. **on one's own** da solo. *v* possedere; (*recognize*) riconoscere; confessare. **owner** *n* proprietario, -a *m, f*. **ownership** *n* proprietà *f*, possesso *m*.
ox [oks] *n, pl* **oxen** bue (*pl* buoi) *m*. **oxtail** *n* coda di bue *f*.
oxygen ['oksidʒən] *n* ossigeno *m*.
oyster ['oistə] *n* ostrica *f*.
ozone ['ouzoun] *n* ozono *m*.

P

pace [peis] *n* passo *m*; (*speed*) velocità *f*. **keep pace with** (*walking*) camminare di pari passo con; (*keep up to date*) tenersi al corrente di. *v* **pace off** misurare a passi. **pace up and down** andare su e giù.
Pacific [pə'sifik] *nm, adj* pacifico.
pacifism ['pasifizəm] *n* pacifismo *m*. **pacifist** *n* pacifista *m, f*.
pacify ['pasifai] *v* pacificare.
pack [pak] *n* (*parcel, package*) pacco *m*; (*of goods*) imballo *m*; (*rucksack*) zaino *m*; (*cards*) mazzo *m*; (*thieves*) banda *f*;

(*hounds*) muta *f*. **pack of lies** tessuto di bugie *m*. *v* imballare; (*suitcases*) fare (le valige); (*cram*) pigiare. **packed** *adj* (*full*) pieno zeppo. **packing** *n* confezione *f*, imballaggio *m*; (*tech*) guarnizione *f*. **do one's packing** fare le valige, fare i bagagli.

package ['pakidʒ] *n* pacco *m*. *adj* (*deal, etc.*) comprensivo.

packet ['pakit] *n* pacchetto *m*.

pact [pakt] *n* patto *m*.

pad[1] [pad] *n* (*cushion*) cuscinetto *m*, tampone *m*; (*notepaper*) taccuino *m*; (*paw*) zampa *f*. *v* imbottire. **pad out** (*speech, essay, etc.*) infarcire. **padding** *n* imbottitura *f*; infarcimento *m*.

pad[2] [pad] *v* camminare a passo felpato.

paddle[1] ['padl] *n* (*of boat*) pagaia *f*; (*tech*) spatola *f*; (*zool*) pinna *f*. **paddle-boat** *n* piroscafo a ruote *m*. *v* remare piano.

paddle[2] ['padl] *v* sguazzare (nell'acqua). **paddling pool** piscina per bambini *f*.

paddock ['padək] *n* recinto *m*; (*racing*) paddock *m invar*.

paddy-field ['padifiːld] *n* risaia *f*.

padlock ['padlok] *n* lucchetto *m*. *v* chiudere col lucchetto.

paediatric [piːdi'atrik] *adj* pediatrico. **paediatrician** *n* pediatra *m, f*. **paediatrics** *n* pediatria *f*.

pagan ['peigən] *n, adj* pagano, -a.

page[1] [peidʒ] *n* (*book*) pagina *f*.

page[2] [peidʒ] *n also* **page-boy** paggio *m*; (*hotel*) piccolo *m*. *v* (*coll*) chiamare.

pageant ['padʒənt] *n* corteo storico *m*. **pageantry** *n* fasto *m*.

paid [peid] *V* **pay**.

pain [pein] *n* dolore *m*, sofferenza *f*. **be at pains to** sforzarsi di. **on pain of** sotto pena di. **painkiller** *n* analgesico *m*. **painstaking** *adj* laborioso. *v* addolorare, far male a. **painful** *adj* doloroso. **painless** *adj* indolore.

paint [peint] *v* dipingere, pitturare; (*decorate*) verniciare. *n* colore *m*, vernice *f*. **paint-box** *n* scatola di colori *f*. **paintbrush** *n* pennello *m*. **painter** *n* pittore, -trice *m, f*; decoratore *m*. **painting** *n* guadro *m*, pittura *f*.

pair [peə] *n* paio *m* (*pl* -a *f*), coppia *f*. *v* accoppiare.

pal [pal] *n* (*coll*) compagno, -a *m, f*.

palace ['paləs] *n* palazzo *m*. **palatial** *adj* sontuoso.

palate ['palit] *n* palato *m*. **palatable** *adj* saporito.

pale[1] [peil] *adj* pallido. *v* impallidire. **paleness** *n* pallore *m*.

pale[2] [peil] *n* (*stake*) palo *m*. **beyond the pale** *adj* (*coll*) impossibile.

palette ['palit] *n* tavolozza *f*. **palette knife** spatola *f*.

pall[1] [poːl] *v* smettere *or* cessare di interessare; (*weary*) stancare.

pall[2] [poːl] *n* drappo funebre *m*.

palm[1] [paːm] *n* (*of hand*) palmo *m*. *v* **palm off** affibbiare. **palmist** *n* chiromante *m, f*. **palmistry** *n* chiromanzia *f*.

palm[2] [paːm] *n* (*tree*) palma *f*. **Palm Sunday** Domenica delle Palme *f*.

palpitation [ˌpalpi'teiʃən] *n* palpitazione *f*.

pamper ['pampə] *v* viziare.

pamphlet ['pamflit] *n* opuscolo *m*; (*polemical*) libello *m*.

pan [pan] *n* pentola *f*, casseruola *f*, padella *f*. **pancake** *n* fritella *f*. **Pancake Tuesday** martedì grasso *m*.

pancreas ['paŋkriəs] *n* pancreas *m invar*. **pancreatic** *adj* pancreatico.

panda ['pandə] *n* panda *m invar*.

pander ['pandə] *v* **pander to** favorire, andare incontro a.

pane [pein] *n* vetro *m*.

panel ['panl] *n* pannello *m*; (*jury*) lista *f*; (*instruments*) cruscotto *m*. **panelling** *n* rivestimento a pannelli *m*.

pang [paŋ] *n* dolore acuto *m*, spasimo *m*.

panic ['panik] *n* panico *m*, allarme *m*. **panic-stricken** *adj* colto dal panico. *v* essere in preda al panico. **panicky** *adj* apprensivo.

panorama [ˌpanə'raːmə] *n* panorama *m*.

pansy ['panzi] *n* (*flower*) viola del pensiero *f*; (*coll: homosexual*) finocchio *m*.

pant [pant] *v* anelare, sbuffare.

panther ['panθə] *n* pantera *f*.

pantomime ['pantəmaim] *n* pantomina *f*; (*Christmas*) spettacolo di Natale *m*.

pantry ['pantri] *n* dispensa *f*.

pants [pants] *pl n* mutande *f pl*.

papal ['peipl] *adj* papale. **papacy** *n* papato *m*.

paper ['peipə] *n* carta *f*; documento *m*; (*treatise*) discorso *m*; (*news*) giornale *m*. **paperback** *n* edizione economica *f*. **paper-clip** *n* fermaglio *m*, agrafe *f*. **paper-mill** *n* cartiera *f*. **paperweight** *n* fermacarte *m invar*. **paperwork** *n* lavoro

d'ufficio *m*; documenti *m pl*. *v* tappezzare.
paprika ['paprikə] *n* paprica *f*.
par [paː] *n* **above/below par** sopra/sotto la pari. **feel below par** sentirsi (un po') giù. **on a par with** alla pari con.
parable ['parəbl] *n* parabola *f*.
parabola [pə'rabələ] *n* parabola *f*.
parachute ['parəʃuːt] *n* paracadute *m invar*. *v* scendere col paracadute. **parachutist** *n* paracadutista *m, f*.
parade [pə'reid] *n* (*display*) sfoggio *m*; (*mil*) sfilata *f*; (*sea-front*) lungomare *m*. *v* ostentare, sfoggiare; sfilare.
paradise ['parədais] *n* paradiso *m*.
paradox ['parədoks] *n* paradosso *m*. **paradoxical** *adj* paradossale.
paraffin ['parəfin] *n* paraffina liquida *f*; (*oil*) cherosene *m*, petrolio da illuminazione *m*.
paragraph ['parəgraːf] *n* paragrafo *m*; (*news item*) trafiletto *m*.
parallel ['parəlel] *adj* parallelo. **parallel line** parallela *f*. *n* parallelo *m*; (*comparison*) paragone *m*.
paralyse ['parəlaiz] *v* paralizzare. **paralysis** *n*, *pl* **-ses** paralisi *f*. **paralytic** *n*, *adj* paralitico, -a.
parameter [pə'ramitə] *n* parametro *m*.
paramilitary [ˌparə'militəri] *adj* paramilitare.
paramount ['parəmaunt] *adj* sommo, supremo.
paranoia [ˌparə'noiə] *n* paranoia *f*. **paranoiac** *or* **paranoid** *n*, *adj* paranoico, -a.
parapet ['parəpit] *n* parapetto *m*.
paraphernalia [ˌparəfə'neiliə] *n* oggetti vari *m pl*, cianfrusaglie *f pl*.
paraphrase ['parəfreiz] *n* parafrasi *f*. *v* parafrasare.
paraplegic [ˌparə'pliːdʒik] *n*, *adj* paraplegico, -a. **paraplegia** *n* paraplegia *f*.
parasite ['parəsait] *n* parassita *m, f*. **parasitic** *adj* parassita, parassitico.
parasol ['parəsol] *n* parasole *m*.
paratrooper ['parəˌtruːpə] *n* (soldato) paracadutista *m*.
parcel ['paːsəl] *n* pacco *m*, pacchetto *m*. **by parcel post** a mezzo pacco postale. **part and parcel of** parte integrale di. v **parcel up** impacchettare.
parched [paːtʃt] *adj* riarso. **be parched with thirst** morire dalla sete.
parchment ['paːtʃmənt] *n* pergamena *f*, cartapecora *f*. **parchment paper** carta pergamenata *f*.
pardon ['paːdn] *n* perdono *m*; (*law*) grazia *f*; (*for minor fault*) scusa *f*. **I beg your pardon** mi scusi. *v* scusare; perdonare; graziare. *interj* prego? **pardonable** *adj* perdonabile.
pare [peə] *v* sbucciare, pelare. **pare down** ridurre.
parent ['peərənt] *n* padre, madre *m, f*. **parents** *pl n* genitori *m pl*. **parental** *adj* dei genitori. **parenthood** *n* l'essere genitori *m*.
parenthesis [pə'renθəsis] *n*, *pl* **-ses** parentesi *f*.
pariah [pə'raiə] *n* paria *m invar*.
Paris ['paris] *n* Parigi *f*. **Parisian** *n*, *adj* parigino, -a.
parish ['pariʃ] *n* parrocchia *f*; (*civil*) comune *m*. **parish priest** parroco (*pl* -chi) *m*. **parishioner** *n* parrocchiano, -a *m, f*.
parity ['pariti] *n* parità *f*.
park [paːk] *n* parco *m*. *v* parcheggiare, posteggiare. **parking** *n* posteggio *m*, parcheggio *m*. **parking meter** parchimetro *m*.
parliament ['paːləmənt] *n* parlamento *m*. **member of parliament** deputato *m*. **parliamentary** *adj* parlamentare.
parlour ['paːlə] *n* salotto *m*. **parlour game** gioco di società *m*.
Parmesan [ˌpaːmi'zan] *n* (*cheese*) (formaggio) parmigiano *m*, grana *m invar*.
parochial [pə'roukiəl] *adj* provinciale.
parody ['parədi] *n* parodia *f*. *v* parodiare.
parole [pə'roul] *v* rilasciare sulla parola. *n* rilascio sulla parola *m*.
paroxysm ['parəksizəm] *n* parossismo *m*, accesso *m*.
parrot ['parət] *n* pappagallo *m*.
parsley ['paːsli] *n* prezzemolo *m*.
parsnip ['paːsnip] *n* pastinaca *f*.
parson ['paːsn] *n* prete *m*, parroco *m*. **parsonage** *n* casa parrocchiale *f*, presbiterio *m*.
part [paːt] *n* parte *f*; (*theatre*) ruolo *m*; (*district*) quartiere *f*. **part-time** *adv*, *adj* a mezzo tempo. **spare part** pezzo di ricambio *m*. **take part** prender parte. *v* separare, spartire; (*hair*) dividere. **part with** rinunciare a. **parting** *n* separazione *f*, addio *m*; (*hair*) divisa dei capelli *f*, riga *f*.
***partake** [paːteik] *v* **partake of** consumare.

partial ['paːʃəl] *adj* parziale. **be partial to** avere un debole per. **partiality** *n* preferenza *f*. **partially** *adv* in parte.
participate [paː'tisipeit] *v* partecipare. **participant** *n* partecipante *m, f*. **participation** *n* partecipazione *f*.
participle ['paːtisipl] *n* participio *m*.
particle ['paːtikl] *n* particella *f*.
particular [pə'tikjulə] *adj* particolare, speciale; (*exacting*) esigente. *n* particolare *m*, dettaglio *m*. **particularly** *adv* in particolare, specie.
partisan [paːti'zan] *n, adj* partigiano, -a.
partition [paː'tiʃən] *n* spartizione *f*; (*of room*) tramezzo *m*. *v* spartire; tramezzare.
partly ['paːtli] *adv* in parte.
partner ['paːtnə] *n* (*comm*) socio *m*; compagno, -a *m, f*, partner (*pl* -s) *m, f*. *v* far da compagno a, associarsi a. **partnership** *n* società *f*, associazione *f*.
partridge ['paːtridʒ] *n* pernice *f*.
party ['paːti] *n* (*group*) compagnia *f*, gruppo *m*; (*entertainment*) festa *f*, trattenimento *m*; (*pol*) partito *m*; (*law*) parte *f*. **third party** terzi *m pl*.
pass [paːs] *n* (*mountain*) passo *m*, valico (*pl* -chi) *m*; (*permit*) permesso *m*; (*mil*) libera uscita *f*; (*school*) promozione *f*; (*sport*) allungo *m*. *v* passare, superare; promuovere; allungare. **pass by** (*disregard*) non curarsi di; (*in front of*) passare davanti a. **pass off** far passare (per). **pass on** trasmettere; (*die*) morire. **pass out** (*faint*) svenire.
passage ['pasidʒ] *n* passaggio *m*; (*in book*) brano *m*.
passenger ['pasindʒə] *n* viaggiatore, -trice *m, f*. **passenger train** treno viaggiatori *m*.
passer-by [ˌpaːsə'bai] *n* passante *m, f*.
passing ['paːsiŋ] *adj* passeggero, transitorio; casuale. **in passing** di passaggio *or* sfuggita; (*by the way*) tra parentesi.
passion ['paʃən] *n* passione *f*, entusiasmo *m*. **passionate** *adj* appassionato, ardente.
passive ['pasiv] *nm, adj* passivo. **passivity** *n* passività *f*.
Passover ['paːsouvə] *n* Pasqua degli ebrei *f*.
passport ['paːspoːt] *n* passaporto *m*.
password ['paːswəːd] *n* parola d'ordine *f*.
past [paːst] *prep* al di là di, oltre; (*after*) dopo. **five past six** le sei e cinque. *adj* passato, scorso; (*former*) ex. *adv* davanti, oltre. *n* passato *m*.
pasta ['pastə] *n* pasta *f*, pastasciutta *f*.
paste [peist] *n* pasta *f*; (*adhesive*) colla *f*. *v* incollare.
pastel ['pastəl] *n* pastello *m*.
pasteurize ['pastʃəraiz] *v* pastorizzare. **pasteurization** *n* pastorizzazione *f*.
pastime ['paːstaim] *n* passatempo *m*.
pastoral ['paːstərəl] *adj* pastorale.
pastry ['peistri] *n* pasta *f*. **pastry-cook** *n* pasticciere, -a *m, f*.
pasture ['paːstʃə] *n* pascolo *m*, pastura *f*. *v* pascolare.
pasty[1] ['peisti] *adj* pallido; (*consistency*) pastoso.
pasty[2] ['pasti] *n* (*pie*) pasticcio *m*.
pat[1] [pat] *adj* pronto, apposito. *adv* (*aptly*) a proposito; (*exactly*) precisamente.
pat[2] [pat] *n* (*light blow*) colpetto *m*; (*of butter*) pezzetto *m*. *v* dare un colpetto a.
patch [patʃ] *n* (*material*) pezza *f*, toppa *f*; (*land*) pezzo *m*. **go through a bad patch** attraversare un momento brutto. *v* rattoppare. **patch up** rattoppare, accomodare; (*quarrel*) comporre. **patchy** *adj* rattoppato; (*not uniform*) irregolare.
pâté ['patei] *n* pasticcio *m*, pâté *m invar*.
patent ['peitənt] *adj* manifesto, ovvio. **patent leather** pelle verniciata *f*. **patent medicine** specialità medicinale *f*. *n* brevetto *m*. *v* brevettare.
paternal [pə'təːnl] *adj* paterno. **paternity** *n* paternità *f*.
path [paːθ] *n* sentiero *m*; (*course, way*) via *f*, strada *f*.
pathetic [pə'θetik] *adj* patetico, commovente.
pathology [pə'θolədʒi] *n* anatomia patologica *f*. **pathological** *adj* patologico. **pathologist** *n* anatomo patologo, anatoma patologa *m, f*.
patient ['peiʃənt] *adj* paziente. *n* paziente *m, f*, malato, -a *m, f*. **be patient** pazientare, aver pazienza. **patience** *n* pazienza *f*.
patio ['patiou] *n* patio *m invar*.
patriarchal ['peitriaːkəl] *adj* patriarcale. **patriarch** *n* patriarca *m*.
patriot ['patriət] *n* patriota *m, f*. **patriotic** *adj* patriottico. **patriotism** *n* patriottismo *m*.
patrol [pə'troul] *n* pattuglia *f*. *v* andare in pattuglia, ispezionare.
patron ['peitrən] *n* patrono *m*, protettore *m*; (*customer*) cliente abituale *m, f*,

avventore, -a *m*, *f*. **patronage** *n* protezione *f*, auspici *m pl*. **patronize** *v* favorire, proteggere; frequentare. **patronizing** *adj* condiscendente.

patter[1] ['patə] *v* (*sound*) picchiettare. *n* picchiettio *m*.

patter[2] ['patə] *n* (*speech*) cicalata *f*, ciancia *f*. *v* cicalare, cianciare.

pattern ['patən] *n* modello *m*, tipo *m*; disegno *m*. *v* modellare.

paunch [poːntʃ] *n* pancia *f*. **paunchy** *adj* panciuto.

pauper ['poːpə] *n* povero, -a *m*, *f*; mendicante *m*, *f*. **pauperize** *v* impoverire.

pause [poːz] *n* pausa *f*; esitazione *f*. *v* fare una pausa; esitare.

pave [peiv] *v* pavimentare. **pave the way** preparare il terreno. **pavement** *n* marciapiede *m*. **paving stone** lastra da selciato *f*.

pavilion [pə'viljən] *n* padiglione *m*.

paw [poː] *n* zampa *f*. *v* (*ground*) scalpitare; (*handle*) palpeggiare.

pawn[1] [poːn] *n* (*deposit*) pegno *m*. **pawnbroker** *n* prestatore su pegno *m*. **pawnshop** *n* monte di pietà *m*. *v* pignorare, dare in pegno.

pawn[2] [poːn] *n* (*chess*) pedina *f*.

***pay** [pei] *n* paga *f*, stipendio *m*. **in the pay of** al servizio di. **pay-roll** *n* organico *m*. *v* pagare; (*settle*) saldare; (*profit*) rendere; (*attention, etc.*) fare. **pay back** rimborsare, restituire. **pay in** versare. **pay off** liquidare. **payable** *adj* pagabile. **payee** *n* beneficiario, -a *m*, *f*. **payment** *n* pagamento *m*, versamento *m*.

pea [piː] *n* pisello *m*.

peace [piːs] *n* pace *f*; tranquillità *f*. **breach of the peace** violazione dell'ordine pubblico *f*. **peace-loving** *adj* pacifico. **peace offering** dono propiziatorio *m*. **peace-time** *n* tempo di pace *m*. **peaceful** *adj* pacifico.

peach [piːtʃ] *n* (*fruit*) pesca *f*; (*tree*) pesco *m*.

peacock ['piːkok] *n* pavone *m*. **peacock blue** *nm*, *adj*. blu pavone. **peahen** *n* pavona *f*.

peak [piːk] *n* cima *f*, vetta *f*; (*highest point*) massimo *m*; (*on cap*) visiera *f*. **peak hours** ore di punta *f pl*. **peak load** carico massimo *m*. *v* raggiungere il massimo.

peal [piːl] *n* (*bells*) scampanio *m*; (*thunder, laughter*) scoppio *m*, scroscio *m*. *v* scampanare; (*thunder*) rimbombare.

peanut ['piːnʌt] *n* arachide *f*.

pear [peə] *n* (*fruit*) pera *f*; (*tree*) pero *m*.

pearl [pəːl] *n* perla *f*. **pearly** *adj* (*like pearl*) perlaceo; (*adorned with pearls*) perlato.

peasant ['peznt] *n* contadino, -a *m*, *f*.

peat [piːt] *n* torba *f*.

pebble ['pebl] *n* ciottolo *m*. **pebbly** *adj* ciottoloso.

peck [pek] *v* beccare; (*food*) mangiucchiare; (*kiss*) dare un bacetto a, baciucchiare. *n* beccata *f*; baciucchio *m*.

peckish ['pekiʃ] *adj* **feel peckish** sentirsi vuoto *or* affamato.

peculiar [pi'kjuːljə] *adj* strano, particolare. **peculiarity** *n* particolarità *f*, stranezza *f*.

pedal ['pedl] *n* pedale *m*. *v* pedalare.

pedantic [pi'dantik] *adj* pedante. **pedant** *n* pedante *m*, *f*. **pedantry** *n* pedanteria *f*.

peddle ['pedl] *v* spacciare.

pedestal ['pedistl] *n* piedistallo *m*.

pedestrian [pi'destriən] *adj* pedonale; (*commonplace*) pedestre. *n* pedone *m*. **pedestrian precinct** zona pedonale *f*.

pedigree ['pedigriː] *n* genealogia *f*; (*of animals*) pedigree *m invar*. *adj* di razza.

pedlar ['pedlə] *n* (*salesman*) venditore ambulante *m*.

peel [piːl] *n* buccia *f*. *v* sbucciare; (*paint, skin*) staccarsi. **peeler** *n* sbucciatore *m*. **peelings** *pl n* bucce *f pl*.

peep [piːp] *n* occhiata (furtiva) *f*, sguardo furtivo *m*. *v* dare un'occhiatina, spiare. **peep-hole** *n* spiraglio *m*. **peep out** mostrarsi appena.

peer[1] [piə] *v* **peer at** scrutare, guardare da presso.

peer[2] [piə] *n* pari *m*. **peerage** *n* nobiltà *f*.

peevish ['piːviʃ] *adj* permaloso, scontroso.

peg [peg] *n* piolo *m*; (*violin, etc.*) bischero *m*; (*washing*) molletta *f*. **off the peg** *adj* pronto. *v* (*prices*) stabilire. **peg out** (*coll*: *die*) crepare.

pejorative [pə'dʒorətiv] *adj* peggiorativo.

Peking [piː'kiŋ] *n* Pechino *f*. **Pekingese** *n* (*dog*) (cane) pechinese *m*.

pelican ['pelikən] *n* pellicano *m*.

pellet ['pelit] *n* pallottola *f*, pallina *f*; (*pill*) pillola *f*.

pelmet ['pelmit] *n* mantovana *f*.

pelt[1] [pelt] *v* scagliare; (*rain*) piovere

dirottamente, diluviare. *n* **at full pelt** a piena velocità.
pelt² [pelt] *n* pelliccia *f*.
pelvis ['pelvis] *n* pelvi *f*, bacino *m*. **pelvic** *adj* pelvico.
pen¹ [pen] *n* (*for writing*) penna *f*. *v* scrivere.
pen² [pen] *n* recinto *m*; (*for sheep*) ovile *m*; (*for pigs*) porcile *m*. *v* **pen in** rinchiudere.
penal ['piːnl] *adj* penale. **penalize** *v* punire. **penalty** *n* pena *f*; (*fine*) multa *f*. **penalty kick** (*sport*) calcio di rigore *m*.
penance ['penəns] *n* penitenza *f*.
pencil ['pensl] *n* matita *f*. **pencil-sharpener** *n* temperamatite *m invar*.
pendant ['pendənt] *n* ciondolo *m*.
pending ['pendiŋ] *adj* in sospeso. *prep* in attesa di.
pendulum ['pendjuləm] *n* pendolo *m*. **pendulum clock** orologio a pendolo *m*.
penetrate ['penitreit] *v* penetrate. **penetration** *n* penetrazione *f*.
pen-friend *n* amico, -a per corrispondenza *m*, *f*.
penguin ['peŋgwin] *n* pinguino *m*.
penicillin [peni'silin] *n* penicillina *f*.
peninsula [pə'ninsjulə] *n* penisola *f*. **peninsular** *adj* peninsulare.
penis ['piːnis] *n* pene *m*.
penitent ['penitənt] *n*(*m*+*f*), *adj* penitente. **penitence** *n* penitenza *f*, pentimento *m*. **penitentiary** *n* (*prison*) penitenziario *m*; (*church dignitary*) penitenziere *m*.
penknife ['pennaif] *n* temperino *m*.
pen-name *n* pseudonimo *m*.
pennant ['penənt] *n* pennello *m*.
penniless ['peniləs] *adj* al verde, senza un soldo.
pension ['penʃən] *n* pensione *f*. *v* **pension off** mettere a riposo, mettere in pensione. **pensioner** *n* pensionato, -a *m*, *f*.
pensive ['pensiv] *adj* pensoso, pensieroso, preoccupato.
pentagon ['pentəgən] *n* pentagono *m*. **pentagonal** *adj* pentagonale.
penthouse ['penthaus] *n* attico *m*.
pent-up [ˌpent'ʌp] *adj* represso.
penultimate [pi'nʌltimit] *adj* penultimo.
people ['piːpl] *n* popolo *m*, nazione *f*. *pl n* gente *f sing*; (*coll*: *family*) i suoi *m pl*. *v* popolare.
pepper ['pepə] *n* pepe *m*. **peppercorn** *n* grano di pepe *m*. **pepper-mill** *n* macinapepe *m invar*. **peppermint** *n* (*herb*) menta piperita *f*; (*sweet*) mentina *f*. **pepper-pot** *n* pepaiola *f*. *v* (*season*) pepare; (*dot*) cospargere; (*hit*) tempestare.
per [pəː] *prep* a. **as per** secondo. **per cent** percento. **percentage** *n* percentuale *f*.
perceive [pə'siːv] *v* rilevare, scorgere, accorgersi di.
perceptible [pə'septibl] *adj* percettibile; visibile. **perceptibility** *n* percettibilità *f*; visibilità *f*.
perception [pə'sepʃən] *n* percezione *f*. **perceptive** *adj* percettivo, sensibile.
perch¹ [pəːtʃ] *n* posatoio *m*. *v* posarsi.
perch² [pəːtʃ] *n* (*fish*) pesce persico *m*.
percolate ['pəːkəleit] *v* filtrare. **percolator** *n* percolatore *m*.
percussion [pə'kʌʃən] *n* percussione *f*.
perennial [pə'reniəl] *adj* perenne; perpetuo. *v* pianta perenne *f*.
perfect ['pəːfikt; *v* pə'fekt] *adj* perfetto, ideale; (*real*) vero. *v* perfezionare. **perfection** *n* perfezione *f*.
perforate ['pəːfəreit] *v* perforare. **perforation** *n* perforazione *f*.
perform [pə'foːm] *v* eseguire, compire; (*music, theatre*) recitare. **performance** *n* esecuzione *f*; recita *f*; (*show*) spettacolo *m*. **performer** *n* artista *m*, *f*.
perfume ['pəːfjuːm] *n* profumo *m*. *v* profumare. **perfumery** *n* profumeria *f*.
perfunctory [pə'fʌŋktəri] *adj* fatto alla buona, meccanico, indifferente.
perhaps [pə'haps] *adv* forse, magari.
peril ['peril] *n* rischio *m*. **perilous** *adj* rischioso, pericoloso.
perimeter [pə'rimitə] *n* perimetro *m*.
period ['piəriəd] *n* periodo *m*; (*full stop*) punto fermo *m*; (*med*) mestruazione *f*. *adj* antico (*m pl* -chi), storico. **periodic** *adj* periodico. **periodical** *nm*, *adj* periodico.
peripheral [pə'rifərəl] *adj* periferico. **periphery** *n* periferia *f*.
periscope ['periskoup] *n* periscopio *m*.
perish ['periʃ] *v* perire; (*food, etc.*) guastarsi, deperire. **perishable** *adj* deperibile.
perjure ['pəːdʒə] *v* spergiurare. **perjurer** *n* spergiuro, -a *m*, *f*. **perjury** *n* spergiuro *m*, giuramento falso *m*.
perk [pəːk] *v* **perk up** rianimarsi, ravvivarsi. **perky** *adj* vispo.
perm [pəːm] *n* permanente *f*. **have a perm** farsi fare la permanente.

permanent ['pəːmənənt] *adj* permanente.
permeate ['pəːmieit] *v* permeare.
permit ['pəːmit; *v* pə'mit] *n* permesso *m*, licenza *f*. *v* permettere. **permissible** *adj* permissibile. **permission** *n* permesso *m*. **permissive** *adj* permissivo.
permutation [pəːmju'teiʃən] *n* permutazione *f*.
pernicious [pə'niʃəs] *adj* pernicioso.
pernickety [pə'nikəti] *adj* pignolo.
perpendicular [,pəːpen'dikjulə] *nf*, *adj* perpendicolare.
perpetrate ['pəːpitreit] *v* commettere. **perpetration** *n* perpetrazione *f*. **perpetrator** *n* perpetratore, -trice *m*, *f*.
perpetual [pə'petʃuəl] *adj* perpetuo.
perpetuate [pə'petʃueit] *v* perpetuare. **perpetuation** *n* perpetuazione *f*. **in perpetuity** in perpetuo.
perplex [pə'pleks] *v* confondere, rendere perplesso. **perplexed** *adj* perplesso, confuso. **perplexing** *adj* imbarazzante. **perplexity** *n* perplessità *f*, imbarazzo *m*.
persecute ['pəːsikjuːt] *v* perseguitare. **persecution** *n* persecuzione *f*.
persevere [,pəːsi'viə] *v* perseverare. **perseverance** *n* perseveranza *f*, assiduità *f*. **persevering** *adj* perseverante, assiduo.
persist [pə'sist] *v* persistere, ostinarsi, perseverare. **persistence** *n* perseveranza *f*, persistenza *f*, ostinazione *f*. **persistent** *adj* ostinato, persistente.
person ['pəːsn] *n* persona *f*, individuo *m*. **personage** *n* personaggio *m*. **personal** *adj* personale; (*disparaging*) offensivo, di carattere personale. **personality** *n* personalità *f*; carattere *m*; celebrità *f*.
personify [pə'sonifai] *v* personificare. **personification** *n* personificazione *f*.
personnel [pəːsə'nel] *n* personale *m*, impiegati *m pl*.
perspective [pə'spektiv] *n* prospettiva *f*.
perspire [pə'spaiə] *v* sudare. **perspiration** *n* sudore *m*.
persuade [pə'sweid] *v* persuadere. **persuasion** *n* persuasione *f*. **persuasive** *adj* persuasivo.
pert [pəːt] *adj* (*lively*) vispo; impudente, insolente.
pertain [pə'tein] *v* **pertain to** riguardare, appartenere a. **pertinent** *adj* pertinente, a proposito. **pertinence** *n* pertinenza *f*.
perturb [pə'təːb] *v* turbare, sconcertare.
peruse [pə'ruːz] *v* leggere attentamente.
pervade [pə'veid] *v* pervadere. **pervasive** *adj* penetrante.
perverse [pə'vəːs] *adj* perverso. **perversity** *n* perversità *f*.
pervert ['pəːvəːt; *v* pə'vəːt] *n* pervertito, -a *m*, *f*. *v* pervertire. **perversion** *n* perversione *f*, pervertimento *m*.
pessimism ['pesimizəm] *n* pessimismo *m*. **pessimist** *n* pessimista *m*, *f*. **pessimistic** *adj* pessimista, pessimistico.
pest [pest] *n* animale *or* parassita nocivo *m*; (*coll*: *nuisance*) seccatore *m*. **pest control** disinfestazione *f*. **pesticide** *n* pesticida *m*.
pester ['pestə] *v* seccare.
pet [pet] *n* animale favorito *m*; (*favourite*) cocco, -a *m*, *f*. *adj* prediletto. **pet aversion** avversione spiccata *f*. **pet name** nomignolo *m*. *v* coccolare. **petting** *n* (*slang*) carezze amorose *f pl*.
petal ['petl] *n* petalo *m*.
petition [pə'tiʃən] *n* petizione *f*, supplica *f*. *v* presentare una petizione *or* supplica.
petrify ['petrifai] *v* pietrificare, paralizzare. **petrified** *adj* allibito, pietrificato.
petrol ['petrəl] *n* benzina *f*. **petrol-tank** *n* serbatoio *m*.
petroleum [pə'trouliəm] *n* petrolio *m*.
petticoat ['petikout] *n* sottana *f*.
petty ['peti] *adj* insignificante; (*mean*) meschino. **petty cash** piccola cassa *f*, fondo per le piccole spese *m*. **petty officer** capo *m*. **pettiness** *n* piccolezza *f*, meschinità *f*.
petulant ['petjulənt] *adj* scontroso, irritabile. **petulance** *n* scontrosità *f*, irritabilità *f*.
pew [pjuː] *n* banco (di chiesa) *m*.
pewter ['pjuːtə] *n* peltro *m*.
phantom ['fantəm] *n* fantasma *m*.
pharmacy ['faːməsi] *n* farmacia *f*. **pharmaceutical** *adj* farmaceutico. **pharmacist** *n* farmacista *m*, *f*.
pharynx ['fariŋks] *n* faringe *f*.
phase [feiz] *n* fase *f*.
pheasant ['feznt] *n* fagiano *m*.
phenomenon [fə'nomənən] *n*, *pl* **-ena** fenomeno *m*. **phenomenal** *adj* fenomenale.
phial ['faiəl] *n* fiala *f*.
philanthropy [fi'lanθrəpi] *n* filantropia *f*. **philanthropic** *adj* filantropico. **philanthropist** *n* filantropo, -a *m*, *f*.
philately [fi'latəli] *n* filatelia *f*. **philatelist** *n* filatelico, -a *m*, *f*.

philosophy [fi'losəfi] *n* filosofia *f*. **philosopher** *n* filosofo, -a *m*, *f*. **philosophical** *adj* filosofico.

phlegm [flem] *n* (*mucus*) muco *m*; (*sluggishness*) flemma *f*.

phlegmatic [fleg'matik] *adj* flemmatico.

phobia ['foubiə] *n* fobia *f*.

phone [foun] *n* (*coll*) telefono *m*. *v* telefonare (a).

phonetic [fə'netik] *adj* fonetico. **phonetics** *n* fonetica *f*.

phoney ['founi] (*coll*) *adj* falso, fasullo. *n* ipocrita *m*, *f*; impostore *m*.

phosphate ['fosfeit] *n* fosfato *m*.

phosphorescence [fosfə'resəns] *n* fosforescenza *f*. **phosphorescent** *adj* fosforescente.

phosphorus ['fosfərəs] *n* fosforo *m*.

photo ['foutou] *n* (*coll*) foto *f*.

photocopy ['foutou,kopi] *n* fotocopia *f*. *v* fotocopiare.

photogenic [,foutou'dʒenik] *adj* fotogenico.

photograph ['foutəgraːf] *n* fotografia *f*. *v* fotografare. **photographer** *n* fotografo *m*. **photographic** *adj* fotografico. **photography** *n* fotografia *f*.

phrase [freiz] *n* frase *f*, modo di dire *m*. *v* esprimere, formulare.

physical ['fizikəl] *adj* fisico.

physician [fi'ziʃən] *n* medico *m*.

physics ['fiziks] *n* fisica *f*. **physicist** *n* fisico, -a *m*, *f*.

physiology [,fizi'olədʒi] *n* fisiologia *f*. **physiological** *adj* fisiologico. **physiologist** *n* fisiologo, -a *m*, *f*.

physiotherapy [,fiziou'θerəpi] *n* fisioterapia *f*. **physiotherapist** *n* fisioterapista *m*, *f*.

physique [fi'ziːk] *n* fisico *m*.

piano [pi'anou] *n* pianoforte *m*. **pianist** *n* pianista *m*, *f*.

pick[1] [pik] *v* (*choose*) scegliere; (*pluck*) cogliere. **pick out** scegliere. **pickpocket** *n* borsaiolo *m*. **pick up** raccogliere; (*recover*) star meglio; (*passenger*) far salire; (*learn*) imparare. **pick-up** *n* pick-up *m*. *n* (*choice*) scelta *f*; (*best*) fior fiore *m*.

pick[2] [pik] *n* piccone *m*.

picket ['pikit] *n* picchetto *m*. *v* picchettare.

pickle ['pikl] *v* marinare; (*in vinegar*) mettere sott'aceto. *n* (*coll*: *predicament*) pasticcio *m*. **pickles** *pl n* sottaceti *m pl*. **pickled** *adj* sottaceto.

picnic ['piknik] *n* picnic *m invar*, colazione all'aperto *f*.

pictorial [pik'toːriəl] *adj* illustrato.

picture ['piktʃə] *v* immaginare, figurare. *n* (*painting*) quadro *m*; foto *f*; (*image*) immagine *f*; film *m*. **be in the picture** essere informato. **pictures** *n* (*coll*) cinema *m*. **put in the picture** mettere al corrente.

picturesque [piktʃə'resk] *adj* pittoresco.

pidgin ['pidʒən] *n* linguaggio bastardo *or* maccheronico *m*.

pie [pai] *n* pasticcio *m*; (*sweet*) crostata *f*.

piece [piːs] *n* pezzo *m*. **piecemeal** *adv* gradualmente, un po' alla volta. **piecework** *n* lavoro a cottimo *m*. *v* rappezzare. **piece together** aggiustare, mettere assieme.

Piedmont ['piːdmənt] *n* Piemonte *m*.

pier [piə] *n* molo *m*, banchina *f*.

pierce [piəs] *v* forare, penetrare. **piercing** *adj* acuto, penetrante; (*wind*) pungente.

piety ['paiəti] *n* devozione religiosa *f*.

pig [pig] *n* maiale *m*, porco (*pl* -ci) *m*. **pig-headed** *adj* ostinato, testardo. **pig-headedness** *n* testardaggine *f*. **pig-iron** *n* ghisa *f*. **piglet** *n* porcellino *m*. **pigskin** *adj* cinghiale. **pigsty** *n* porcile *m*. **pigtail** *n* codino *m*.

pigeon ['pidʒən] *n* piccione *m*. **carrier pigeon** piccione viaggiatore *m*. **clay pigeon** piattello *m*.

pigeon-hole *n* casella *f*. *v* incasellare.

pigment ['pigmənt] *n* pigmento *m*.

pike [paik] *n* (*fish*) luccio *m*.

pilchard ['piltʃəd] *n* sardina *f*, sarda *f*.

pile[1] [pail] *n* (*heap*) mucchio *m*; (*building*) fabbricato *m*. *v* accumulare. **pile on** (*coll*) esagerare. **pile up** accatastare.

pile[2] [pail] *n* (*post*) palo *m*. **pile-driver** *n* battipalo *m*.

pile[3] [pail] *n* (*of carpet, etc.*) pelo *m*.

piles [pailz] *pl n* (*med*) emorroidi *f pl*.

pilfer ['pilfə] *v* rubacchiare. **pilferer** *n* ladruncolo *m*.

pilgrim ['pilgrim] *n* pellegrino *m*. **pilgrimage** *n* pellegrinaggio *m*.

pill [pil] *n* pillola *f*. **pillbox** *n* scatoletta per pillole *f*; (*mil*) casamatta *f*.

pillage ['pilidʒ] *n* saccheggio *m*. *v* saccheggiare.

pillar ['pilə] *n* pilastro *m*, colonna *f*. **pillar-box** *n* buca delle lettere *f*.
pillion ['piljən] *n* sella posteriore *f*, sedile posteriore *m*. **ride pillion** viaggiare sul sedile posteriore.
pillow ['pilou] *n* guanciale *m*. **pillowslip** *n* federa *f*.
pilot ['pailət] *n* pilota *m*, *f*. *v* pilotare.
pimento [pi'mentou] *n* (*allspice*) pimento *m*; (*capsicum*) peperone *m*.
pimp [pimp] *n* ruffiano *m*.
pimple ['pimpl] *n* pustoletta *f*, foruncolo *m*.
pin [pin] *n* spillo *m*; (*brooch*) spilla *f*. **pincushion** *n* portaspilli *m invar*. **pinpoint** *v* determinare con precisione. **pinprick** *n* (*annoyance*) seccatura *f*. *v* puntare. **pin down** inchiodare. **pin-up** *n* (*girl*) ragazza da copertina *f*, pin-up *f invar*.
pinafore ['pinəfoː] *n* grembiulino *m*.
pincers ['pinsəz] *pl n* pinza *f sing*, tenaglia *f sing*.
pinch [pintʃ] *v* pizzicare; (*hurt*) far male a; (*coll*: *steal*) rubare; (*coll*: *catch*) acchiappare. *n* (*nip*) pizzicotto *m*; (*small quantity*) pizzico (*pl* -chi) *m*. **at a pinch** caso mai.
pine[1] [pain] *n* (*tree*) pino *m*. **pine-cone** *n* pigna *f*.
pine[2] [pain] *v* languire. **pine for** desiderare ardentemente.
pineapple ['painapl] *n* ananas *m*.
pinion[1] ['pinjən] *n* (*tech*) pignone *m*.
pinion[2] ['pinjən] *v* (*shackle*) legare.
pink [piŋk] *adj* rosa *invar*. *n* (*colour*) rosa *m invar*; (*flower*) garofano *m*. **in the pink of condition** in ottima forma.
pinnacle ['pinəkl] *n* cima *f*, colmo *m*; (*arch*) pinnacolo *m*.
pioneer [ˌpaiə'niə] *n* pioniere, -a *m*, *f*. *v* aprire la strada a.
pious ['paiəs] *adj* pio, devoto.
pip[1] [pip] *n* (*seed*) seme *m*, granello *m*.
pip[2] [pip] *n* (*phone*) segnale acustico *m*.
pipe [paip] *n* tubo *m*, condotto *m*; (*for smoking*) pipa *f*. **pipe-cleaner** *n* nettapipe *m invar*. **pipedream** *n* illusione *f*. **pipeline** *n* oleodotto *m*; linea di comunicazione *f*. *v* **pipe down!** sta zitto! **pipe up** farsi sentire. **piping** *n* (*sewing*) cordonetto *m*. **piping hot** caldo bollente.
piquant ['piːkənt] *adj* piccante, mordace.
pique [piːk] *n* dispetto *m*. *v* **feel piqued** risentirsi.
pirate ['paiərət] *n* pirata *m*. **pirate radio** radiopirata *m*. *v* (*radio*) servirsi abusivamente di; (*book*) plagiare. **piracy** *n* pirateria *f*.
pirouette [piru'et] *n* piroetta *f*. *v* piroettare.
Pisces ['paisiːz] *n* Pesci *m pl*.
piss [pis] (*vulgar*) *n* piscia *f*. *v* pisciare. **pissed** *adj* sbronzo.
pistachio [pi'staːʃiou] *n* pistacchio *m*.
pistol ['pistl] *n* pistola *f*.
piston ['pistən] *n* pistone *m*.
pit [pit] *n* fossa *f*; (*theatre*) platea *f*; (*scar*) buttero *m*. *v* **pit against** opporre.
pitch[1] [pitʃ] *n* lancio *m*; (*degree*) grado *m*; (*music*) tono *m*, registro *m*; (*sport*) campo *m*, terreno *m*. *v* lanciare; (*tent*) piantare; (*fix*) fissare; (*ship*) beccheggiare. **pitchfork** *n* forcone *m*.
pitch[2] [pitʃ] *n* pece *f*. **pitch-dark** *adj* buio pesto.
pitfall ['pitfoːl] *n* trappola *f*, tranello *m*.
pith [piθ] *n* midollo *m*. **pithy** *adj* succinto.
pittance ['pitəns] *n* somma irrisoria *f*.
pituitary [pi'tjuːitəri] *n* ipofisi *f*, glandola pituitaria *f*.
pity ['piti] *n* pietà *f*, compassione *f*; (*shame*) peccato *m*. **what a pity!** che peccato! *v* avere pietà di, compatire. **pitiful** *adj* (*wretched*) pietoso; (*contemptible*) miserabile. **pitiless** *adj* spietato.
pivot ['pivət] *n* perno *m*, fulcro *m*. *v* imperniare.
placard ['plakaːd] *n* cartellone *m*.
placate [plə'keit] *v* placare, conciliare.
place [pleis] *n* luogo *m*, posto *m*. **out of place** inopportuno. **put in one's place** umiliare. **take place** aver luogo, accadere. *v* mettere, posare, porre; (*order*) piazzare.
placenta [plə'sentə] *n* placenta *f*.
placid ['plasid] *adj* placido.
plagiarize ['pleidʒəraiz] *v* plagiare. **plagiarism** *n* plagio *m*. **plagiarist** *n* plagiario, -a *m*, *f*.
plague [pleig] *n* (*disease*) peste *f*; (*calamity*) piaga *f*. *v* tormentare, affliggere.
plaice [pleis] *n* passera di mare *f*.
plaid [plad] *n* plaid *m invar*.
plain [plein] *adj* chiaro; (*simple*) semplice; (*frank*) schietto; (*not patterned*) a tinta unita; (*unattractive*) brutto. **in plain clothes** in borghese. **plain cooking** cucina semplice *or* casalinga *f*. *n* pianura *f*.

plaintiff ['pleintif] *n* querelante *m, f*; attore, -trice *m, f*.

plaintive ['pleintiv] *adj* querulo, lamentoso.

plait [plat] *n* (*braid*) treccia *f*; (*pleat*) piega *f*. *v* intrecciare; piegare.

plan [plan] *n* piano *m*, progetto *m*; intenzione *f*; (*drawing*) disegno *m*; (*map*) pianta *f*. *v* progettare; intendere; (*econ*) pianificare.

plane[1] [plein] *n* (*flat surface*) piano *m*, livello *m*; (*coll*) aereo *m*. *adj* piano.

plane[2] [plein] *n* (*tool*) pialla *f*. *v* piallare.

plane[3] [plein] *n* (*tree*) platano *m*.

planet ['planit] *n* pianeta *m*. **planetarium** *n* planetario *m*. **planetary** *adj* planetario.

plank [plaŋk] *n* asse *f*, tavola *f*.

plankton ['plaŋktən] *n* plancton *m invar*.

plant [plaːnt] *n* (*bot*) pianta *f*; (*manufacturing*) impianto *m*, stabilimento *m*. *v* piantare. **plantation** *n* piantagione *f*.

plaque [plaːk] *n* placca *f*.

plasma ['plazmə] *n* plasma *m*.

plaster ['plaːstə] *n* intonaco *m*; (*med*) impiastro *m*; (*for wound*) cerotto *m*. **plaster of Paris** gesso *m*. *v* intonacare; impiastrare; ingessare.

plastic ['plastik] *adj* plastico. *n* plastica *f*.

plate [pleit] *n* (*dish*) piatto *m*; (*of metal*) lamiera *f*, lastra *f*; (*denture*) dentiera *f*; (*metallic ware*) argenteria *f*; (*in book*) tavola *f*, illustrazione *f*. **plate-glass** *n* cristallo *m*. *v* galvanizzare; (*silver*) argentare.

plateau ['platou] *n* altipiano *m*.

platform ['platfoːm] *n* piattaforma *f*; (*rail*) binario *m*.

platinum ['platinəm] *n* platino *m*.

platonic [plə'tonik] *adj* platonico.

platoon [plə'tuːn] *n* plotone *m*.

plausible ['ploːzəbl] *adj* ammissibile, credibile.

play [plei] *v* giocare; (*musical instrument*) suonare; (*act*) recitare. **play down** minimizzare. **play fair** comportarsi lealmente. **play truant** marinare la scuola. *n* gioco *m*, divertimento *m*; (*theatre*) spettacolo *m*. **playboy** *n* playboy *m*, buontempone *m*. **playground** *n* cortile di scuola *m*. **playmate** *n* compagno, -a di gioco *m, f*. **play-pen** *n* recinto per bambini *m*, box *m invar*. **play-school** *n* asilo *m*. **playwright** *n* commediografo, -a *m, f*; drammaturgo, -a *m, f*. **player** *n* giocatore, -trice *m, f*; (*music*) suonatore, -trice *m, f*; (*theatre*) attore, -trice *m, f*. **playful** *adj* scherzoso, giocoso. **playing card** carta da gioco *f*. **playing field** campo sportivo *m*.

plea [pliː] *n* difesa *f*, supplica *f*; (*excuse*) scusa *f*.

plead [pliːd] *v* implorare; perorare. **plead guilty/innocent** dichiararsi colpevole/innocente. **plead with** intercedere presso. **pleading** *n* perorazione *f*.

please [pliːz] *v* piacere (a), contentare, soddisfare. **please oneself** fare il proprio comodo. *adv* per favore, per cortesia. **pleased** *adj* contento, lieto, soddisfatto. **pleasing** *adj* piacevole, gradevole. **pleasure** *n* piacere *m*, favore *m*.

pleat [pliːt] *n* piega *f*. *v* pieghettare.

pledge [pledʒ] *n* promessa solenne *f*; (*undertaking*) impegno *m*. *v* impegnare, garantire; promettere solennemente.

plenty ['plenti] *n* abbondanza *f*. **in plenty** in abbondanza. **plenty of** abbastanza. **plentiful** *adj* abbondante.

pleurisy ['pluərisi] *n* pleurite *f*.

pliable ['plaiəbl] *adj* flessibile. **pliability** *n* flessibilità *f*.

pliers ['plaiəz] *pl n* pinza *f sing*, tenaglia *f sing*.

plight [plait] *n* stato *m*.

plimsoll ['plimsəl] *n* scarpa da tennis *f*.

plod [plod] *v* **plod along** tirare avanti. **plodder** *n* sgobbone, -a *m, f*.

plonk [ploŋk] *n* (*coll*) vino comune *m*.

plot[1] [plot] *n* (*story*) trama *f*, intreccio *m*; (*secret plan*) congiura *f*, complotto *m*. *v* tramare, complottare; (*trace*) tracciare. **plotter** *n* cospiratore, -trice *m, f*.

plot[2] [plot] *n* (*land*) lotto *or* pezzo di terreno *m*.

plough [plau] *n* aratro *m*. *v* arare; (*coll: fail exam*) trombare. **plough back** riinvestire. **plough through** (*book, etc.*) leggere con fatica.

pluck [plʌk] *v* cogliere; (*feathers*) spennare; (*tug at*) strappare. **pluck up courage** farsi coraggio. *n* (*courage*) fegato *m*. **be plucky** aver fegato.

plug [plʌg] *n* tappo *m*; (*elec*) spina *f*; (*mot*) candela *f*. *v* tappare.

plum [plʌm] *n* (*fruit*) prugna *f*, susina *f*; (*tree*) prugno *m*, susino *m*. *adj* (*colour*) prugna.

plumage ['pluːmidʒ] *n* piumaggio *m*.

plumb [plʌm] *adj* verticale. *adv* a piombo; (*absolutely*) proprio. *n* piombo

m, scandaglio *m*. *v* sondare; (*naut*) scandagliare. **plumber** *n* idraulico *m*.
plume [pluːm] *n* penna *f*, piuma *f*; (*on helmet*) pennacchio *m*.
plummet ['plʌmit] *v* piombare.
plump[1] [plʌmp] *adj* (*fat*) grassoccio, paffuto.
plump[2] [plʌmp] *v* **plump for** scegliere.
plunder ['plʌndə] *n* bottino *m*. *v* spogliare, depredare.
plunge [plʌndʒ] *n* tuffo *m*. *v* tuffare; immergere; (*rush*) lanciarsi. **plunger** *n* (*tech*) stantuffo *m*.
pluperfect [pluː'pəfikt] *n* trapassato remoto *m*.
plural ['pluərəl] *nm*, *adj* plurale. **in the plural** al plurale.
plus [plʌs] *adj* addizionale. *prep* più.
plush [plʌʃ] *n* felpa *f*. *adj* lussuoso.
plutocrat ['pluːtəkrat] *n* plutocrate *m*, *f*.
ply[1] [plai] *v* (*travel*) viaggiare regolarmente; (*trade*) esercitare.
ply[2] [plai] *n* (*layer*) strato *m*; (*wool*) filo *m*. **plywood** *n* legno compensato *m*.
pneumatic [nju'matik] *adj* pneumatico.
pneumonia [nju'mouniə] *n* polmonite *f*.
poach[1] [poutʃ] *v* (*game*) cacciare di frodo; (*fish*) pescare di frodo; (*encroach on*) usurpare. **poacher** *n* bracconiere *m*.
poach[2] [poutʃ] *v* (*cookery*) lessare. **poached egg** uovo affogato *m*, uovo in camicia *m*.
pocket ['pokit] *n* tasca *f*, taschino *m*; (*billiards*) buca *f*. **be out of pocket** rimetterci. *v* intascare. *adj* tascabile. **pocket-book** *n* taccuino *m*. **pocket-knife** *n* temperino *m*. **pocket-money** *n* soldi per le piccole spese *m pl*.
pod [pod] *n* baccello *m*.
podgy ['podʒi] *adj* grassotto, paffuto.
poem ['pouim] *n* poesia *f*.
poet ['pouit] *n* poeta *m*. **poetess** *n* poetessa *f*. **poetic** *adj* poetico. **poetry** *n* poesia *f*.
poignant ['poinjənt] *adj* intenso, vivo, commovente.
point [point] *n* punto *m*; (*sharp end*) punta *f*; (*elec*) presa *f*. **be on the point of** stare per. **make a point of** insistere su. **point-blank** *adv* a bruciapelo; (*coll*) di punto in bianco. *v* indicare, additare; (*aim*) puntare; (*brickwork*) affilettare. **pointed** *adj* acuto. **pointer** *n* (*hint*) indicazione *f*; (*dog*) pointer *m*. **pointing** *n* affilettatura *f*. **pointless** *adj* inutile.
poise [poiz] *n* equilibrio *m*, compostezza *f*, portamento *m*. *v* equilibrare, essere in equilibrio.
poison ['poizən] *n* veleno *m*. *v* avvelenare. **poisonous** *adj* velenoso.
poke [pouk] *n* spinta *f*, gomitata *f*. *v* (*stick into*) ficcare; (*thrust*) cacciare; (*fire*) attizzare. **poke about** frugare. **poke fun at** beffarsi di. **poker** *n* attizzatoio *m*. **poky** *adj* meschino, piccolo.
poker ['poukə] *n* (*cards*) poker *m*. **poker-faced** *adj* impassibile.
Poland ['poulənd] *n* Polonia *f*. **Pole** *n* polacco, -a *m*, *f*. **Polish** *nm*, *adj* polacco.
polar ['poulə] *adj* polare. **polar bear** orso bianco *m*. **polarize** *v* polarizzare. **polarity** *n* polarità *f*.
pole[1] [poul] *n* (*post*) palo *m*, asta *f*. **pole-vault** *n* salto all'asta *m*.
pole[2] [poul] *n* (*geog*) polo *m*.
police [pə'liːs] *n* polizia *f*. **policeman** *n* carabiniere *m*, poliziotto *m*, vigile *m*. **police station** questura *f*. *v* mantenere l'ordine, sorvegliare, vigilare.
policy[1] ['poləsi] *n* politica *f*, linea di condotta *f*.
policy[2] ['poləsi] *n* (*insurance*) polizza *f*.
polio ['pouliou] *n* poliomielite *f*.
polish ['poliʃ] *n* (*for shoes, etc.*) lucido *m*; (*for nails*) smalto *m*; raffinatezza *f*. *v* lucidare, lustrare. **polish off** (*dispose of quickly*) sbrigare; liquidare. **polish up** ripassare.
polite [pə'lait] *adj* cortese, garbato. **politeness** *n* cortesia *f*, garbo *m*.
politics ['politiks] *n* politica *f*. **politic** *adj* espediente. **political** *adj* politico. **politician** *n* uomo politico *m*.
polka ['polkə] *n* polca *f*.
poll [poul] *n* elezione *f*; (*casting of votes*) votazione *f*; (*votes cast*) voti *m pl*. **opinion poll** sondaggio d'opinioni *m*. *v* ottenere voti. **polling booth** cabina elettorale *f*.
pollen ['polən] *n* polline *m*. **pollinate** *v* impollinare. **pollination** *n* impollinazione *f*.
pollute [pə'luːt] *v* inquinare. **pollution** *n* inquinamento *m*.
polo ['poulou] *n* polo *m*. **polo-neck** *n* collo ciclista *m*. **polo-neck sweater** ciclista *f*.
polygamy [pə'ligəmi] *n* poligamia *f*. **polygamist** *n* poligamo *m*. **polygamous** *adj* poligamo.

polygon ['poligən] *n* poligono *m*. **polygonal** *adj* poligonale.
polytechnic [,poli'teknik] *n* politecnico *m*.
polythene ['poliθiːn] *n* politene *m*.
pomegranate ['pomigranit] *n* melagrana *f*.
pomp [pomp] *n* pompa *f*, sfarzo *m*. **pompous** *adj* pomposo, ampolloso.
pond [pond] *n* stagno *m*.
ponder ['pondə] *v* ponderare; valutare. **ponderous** *adj* ponderoso, pesante.
pontiff ['pontif] *n* pontefice *m*, papa *m*. **pontifical** *adj* pontificio. **pontificate** *v* pontificare.
pontoon [pon'tuːn] *n* pontone *m*; (*cards*) ventuno *m*.
pony ['pouni] *n* pony *m*.
poodle ['puːdl] *n* cane barbone *m*.
poof [puːf] *n* (*derog*) finocchio *m*.
pool[1] [puːl] *n* (*pond*) stagno *m*; (*puddle*) pozzanghera *f*; (*swimming*) piscina *f*.
pool[2] [puːl] *v* mettere in comune. *n* fondo comune *m*; (*football*) totocalcio *m*.
poor [puə] *adj* povero; mediocre; (*meagre*) magro; (*not good*) cattivo.
poorly ['puəli] *adj* malaticcio. *adv* male. **feel poorly** non sentirsi troppo bene.
pop[1] [pop] *v* schioccare, saltare. **pop in** fare una breve visita. **pop out** saltar fuori. **pop up** apparire. *n* schiocco *m*; (*drink*) bibita gassata *f*.
pop[2] [pop] *adj* popolare. **pop-art** *n* pop-art *f*. **pop music** musica pop *f*.
pope [poup] *n* papa *m*.
poplar ['poplə] *n* pioppo *m*.
poppy ['popi] *n* papavero *m*.
popular ['popjulə] *adj* popolare; (*favourite*) ben visto. **popularity** *n* popolarità *f*. **popularize** *v* divulgare.
population [,popju'leiʃən] *n* popolazione *f*. **populate** *v* popolare.
porcelain ['poːslin] *n* porcellana *f*.
porch [poːtʃ] *n* portico *m*.
porcupine ['poːkjupain] *n* porcospino *m*.
pore[1] [poː] *n* (*opening*) poro *m*.
pore[2] [poː] *v* **pore over** meditare su, essere assorto in.
pork [poːk] *n* carne suina *f*, carne di maiale *f*.
pornography [poː'nogrəfi] *n* pornografia *f*. **pornographic** *adj* pornografico.
porous ['poːrəs] *adj* poroso.
porpoise ['poːpəs] *n* focena *f*.
porridge ['poridʒ] *n* pappa di fiocchi d'avena *f*.
port[1] [poːt] *n* (*harbour*) porto *m*.
port[2] [poːt] *n* (*naut*: *left*) sinistra *f*, babordo *m*.
port[3] [poːt] *n* (*wine*) porto *m invar*.
portable ['poːtəbl] *adj* portatile.
portent ['poːtent] *n* (*omen*) presagio *m*; (*marvel*) portento *m*. **portentous** *adj* prodigioso, portentoso; grave.
porter ['poːtə] *n* (*janitor*) portinaio, -a *m*, *f*; (*carrier*) facchino *m*.
portfolio [poːt'fouliou] *n* (*pol*) portafoglio *m*; (*case*) cartella *f*.
porthole ['poːthoul] *n* oblò *m*.
portion ['poːʃən] *n* porzione *f*. *v* ripartire.
portrait ['poːtrət] *n* ritratto *m*. **portrait-painter** *n* ritrattista *m*, *f*.
portray [poː'trei] *v* rappresentare.
Portugal ['poːtjugl] *n* Portogallo *m*. **Portuguese** *n*(*m*+*f*), *adj* portoghese.
pose [pouz] *n* posa *f*; (*posture*) atteggiamento *m*. *v* posare, atteggiarsi (a); (*propound*) porre.
posh [poʃ] *adj* elegante.
position [pə'ziʃən] *n* posizione *f*, situazione *f*; (*employment*) posto *m*. *v* collocare, piazzare.
positive ['pozətiv] *adj* positivo; (*certain*) sicuro. *n* (*phot*) positiva *f*; (*gramm*) positivo *m*.
possess [pə'zes] *v* possedere, avere. **possessed** *adj* ossesso, frenetico. **possession** *n* possesso *m*. **possessions** *pl n* (*goods*) beni personali *m pl*. **possessive** *nm*, *adj* possessivo. **possessor** *n* possessore *m*, posseditrice *f*.
possible ['posəbl] *adj* possibile. **possibility** *n* possibilità *f*. **possibly** *adv* (*perhaps*) forse, può darsi; (*if possible*) possibilmente.
post[1] [poust] *n* (*pole*) palo *m*. *v* affiggere.
post[2] [poust] *n* (*job*) posto *m*. *v* collocare.
post[3] [poust] *n* (*mail*) posta *f*. **post-box** *n* buca da lettere *f*. **postcard** *n* cartolina *f*. **postman** *n* postino *m*. **postmark** *n* timbro postale *m*. **postmarked** *adj* timbrato. **post office** posta *f*, ufficio postale *m*. **post office box** casella postale *f*. *v* imbucare; (*book-keeping*) registrare. **keep posted** tenere al corrente. **postage** *n* tariffa postale *f*. **postage stamp** francobollo *m*. **postal** *adj* postale. **postal order** vaglia postale *m invar*.
poste restante [poust'restɑ̃t] *adv* fermo posta.

poster ['poustə] *n* cartellone *m*, manifesto *m*, avviso pubblicitario *m*

posterior [po'stiəriə] *adj* posteriore.

posterity [po'sterəti] *n* posterità *f*.

postgraduate [poust'gradjuit] *adj* di perfezionamento *or* specializzazione. *n* laureato, -a che continua gli studi universitari *m, f*.

posthumous ['postjuməs] *adj* postumo.

post-mortem [poust'moːtəm] *n* autopsia *f*.

postpone [pous'poun] *v* posporre, rinviare. **postponement** *n* rinvio *m*.

postscript ['pousskript] *n* poscritto *m*.

postulate ['postjuleit; *n* 'postjulət] *v* postulare. *n* postulato *m*.

posture ['postʃə] *n* posizione *f*; (*attitude*) atteggiamento *m*. *v* assumere una posa.

pot [pot] *n* vaso *m*; (*pan*) pentola *f*; (*container*) recipiente *m*. *v* (*plant*) piantare in vaso; (*billiards*) mandare in buca. **pot-belly** *n* pancione *m*. **pot-bellied** *adj* panciuto. **take pot luck** mangiare alla buona.

potassium [pə'tasjəm] *n* potassio *m*. **potash** *n* potassa *f*.

potato [pə'teitou] *n* patata *f*.

potent ['poutənt] *adj* potente, forte. **potency** *n* potenza *f*.

potential [pə'tenʃəl] *adj, nm* potenziale.

pot-hole ['pothoul] *n* (*cave*) spelonca *f*; (*in road*) buca *f*. **pot-holer** *n* speleologo, -a *m, f*. **pot-holing** *n* speleologia *f*.

potion ['pouʃən] *n* pozione *f*.

potter[1] ['potə] *v* **potter about** lavoricchiare.

potter[2] ['potə] *n* ceramista *m, f*, vasaio, -a *m, f*.

pottery ['potəri] *n* (*ware*) ceramica *f*; (*workshop*) laboratorio di ceramiche *m*.

potty[1] ['poti] *adj* (*coll*) matto.

potty[2] ['poti] *n* (*coll*) vaso da notte *m*, pitale *m*.

pouch [pautʃ] *n* borsa *f*, tasca *f*, sacchetto *m*.

poultice ['poultis] *n* cataplasma *m*.

poultry ['poultri] *n* pollame *m*. **poulterer** *n* pollivendolo, -a *m, f*.

pounce [pauns] *n* sbalzo *m*. *v* balzare. **pounce on** piombare su, saltare addosso a.

pound[1] [paund] *v* (*hit*) pestare, battere. *n* colpo *m*.

pound[2] [paund] *n* (*weight*) libbra *f*; (*sterling*) lira sterlina *f*.

pound[3] [paund] *n* (*enclosure*) recinto *m*.

pour [poː] *v* versare, riversarsi; (*rain*) scrosciare.

pout [paut] *v* fare il broncio. *n* broncio *m*.

poverty ['povəti] *n* povertà *f*, miseria *f*. **poverty-stricken** *adj* bisognoso, indigente.

powder ['paudə] *n* polvere *f*; (*cosmetic*) cipria *f*. **powder compact** portacipria *m invar*. **powder puff** piumino per la cipria *m*. *v* polverizzare, incipriare. **powdery** *adj* polveroso.

power ['pauə] *n* potere *m*; (*pol, phys, etc.*) potenza *f*; (*tech*) energia *f*, forza *f*. **powers** *pl n* facoltà *f pl*. **power station** centrale elettrica *f*. **powerful** *adj* potente. **powerless** *adj* impotente, incapace.

practicable ['praktikəbl] *adj* fattibile.

practical ['praktikəl] *adj* pratico. **for practical purposes** in pratica. **practical joke** beffa *f*. **practically** *adv* in effetto, quasi.

practice ['praktis] *n* pratica *f*; esercizio *m*; clientela *f*; (*sport*) allenamento *m*. **normal practice** regola *f*. **out of practice** fuori esercizio.

practise ['praktis] *v* praticare, esercitare; (*music*) esercitarsi; (*sport*) allenarsi. **practised** *adj* esperto, pratico. **practising** *adj* (*rel*) praticante.

practitioner [prak'tiʃənə] *n* **general practitioner** medico generico *m*.

pragmatic [prag'matik] *adj* prammatico; (*officious*) inframmettente; dogmatico. **pragmatism** *n* pragmatismo *m*; dogmatismo *m*.

Prague [praːg] *n* Praga *f*.

prairie ['preəri] *n* prateria *f*.

praise [preiz] *n* lode *f*, elogio *m*. *v* lodare, elogiare. **praiseworthy** *adj* lodevole.

pram [pram] *n* carrozzella *f*.

prance [praːns] *v* pavoneggiarsi; (*child*) saltellare; (*horse*) impennarsi.

prank [praŋk] *n* burla *f*, tiro *m*. **play a prank on** fare un tiro a.

prattle ['pratl] *v* cianciare, ciarlare.

prawn [proːn] *n* gambero *m*, palemone *m*.

pray [prei] *v* pregare. **prayer** *n* preghiera *f*. **prayer-book** *n* libro di preghiere *m*; (*missal*) messale *m*.

preach [priːtʃ] *v* predicare. **preach a sermon** fare una predica. **preacher** *n* predicatore *m*.

preamble [priː'ambl] *n* preambolo *m*.

prearrange [priːə'reindʒ] *v* predisporre.

precarious [pri'keəriəs] *adj* precario, incerto.
precaution [pri'koːʃən] *n* precauzione *f*.
precede [pri'siːd] *v* precedere. **precedence** *n* precedenza *f*. **precedent** *n* precedente *m*.
precinct ['priːsiŋkt] *n* (*area*) zona *f*; ambito *m*.
precious ['preʃəs] *adj* prezioso.
precipice ['presipis] *n* precipizio *m*.
precipitate [pri'sipiteit; *adj* pri'sipitət] *v* precipitare; (*hurry up*) affrettare. *n* precipitato *m*. *adj* precipitoso.
précis ['preisi] *n* sunto *m*.
precise [pri'sais] *adj* preciso, esatto; (*strict*) puntiglioso. **precision** *n* precisione *f*, esattezza *f*.
preclude [pri'kluːd] *v* precludere.
precocious [pri'kouʃəs] *adj* precoce. **precociousness** *n* precocità *f*.
preconceive [ˌpriːkən'siːv] *v* avere preconcetti su. **preconception** *n* preconcetto *m*.
precursor [ˌpriː'kəːsə] *n* precursore *m*.
predatory ['predətəri] *adj* predatore, rapace.
predecessor ['priːdisesə] *n* predecessore *m*.
predestine [pri'destin] *v* predestinare. **predestination** *n* predestinazione *f*.
predicament [pri'dikəmənt] *n* situazione imbarazzante *f*, pasticcio *m*.
predicate ['predikət] *n* predicato *m*.
predict [pri'dikt] *v* predire, pronosticare. **predictable** *adj* prevedibile. **prediction** *n* predizione *f*.
predispose [priːdi'spouz] *v* predisporre. **predisposition** *n* predisposizione *f*.
predominate [pri'domineit] *v* predominare, prevalere. **predominance** *n* predominio *m*, ascendente *m*.
pre-eminent [priː'eminənt] *adj* preminente, per eccellenza. **pre-eminence** *n* preminenza *f*.
preen [priːn] *v* **preen oneself** (*bird*) lisciarsi le penne; (*person*) agghindarsi.
prefabricate [priː'fabrikeit] *v* prefabbricare. **prefab** *n* (*coll*) casa prefabbricata *f*.
preface ['prefis] *n* prefazione *f*. *v* premettere.
prefect ['priːfekt] *n* prefetto *m*; (*school*) capoclasse *m*.
prefer [pri'fəː] *v* preferire. **preferable** *adj* preferibile. **preference** *n* preferenza *f*. **preference shares** azioni privilegiate *f pl*. **preferential** *adj* preferenziale, di favore.
prefix ['priːfiks] *n* prefisso *m*. *v* prefiggere.
pregnant ['pregnənt] *adj* incinta; (*animal*) gravida. **pregnancy** *n* gravidanza *f*.
prehistoric [ˌpriːhi'storik] *adj* preistorico. **prehistory** *n* preistoria *f*.
prejudice ['predʒədis] *n* pregiudizio *m*, prevenzione *f*. **have a prejudice against** esser prevenuto contro. *v* pregiudicare, compromettere. **prejudiced** *adj* prevenuto.
preliminary [pri'liminəri] *nm*, *adj* preliminare.
prelude ['preljuːd] *n* preludio *m*.
premarital [priː'maritl] *adj* prematrimoniale.
premature [premə'tʃuə] *adj* prematuro.
premeditate [priː'mediteit] *v* premeditare. **premeditation** *n* premeditazione *f*.
premier ['premiə] *adj* primo, primario. *n* primo ministro *m*.
première ['premieə] *n* prima (rappresentazione) *f*.
premise ['premis] *n* premessa *f*. **premises** *n* locali *m pl*. **off the premises** fuori. **on the premises** sul posto.
premium ['priːmiəm] *n* premio *m*; (*finance*) aggio *m*. **at a premium** (*econ*) sopra la pari.
premonition [ˌpremə'niʃən] *n* premonizione *f*.
preoccupied [priː'okjupaid] *adj* preoccupato. **preoccupation** *n* preoccupazione *f*.
prepare [pri'peə] *v* preparare. **preparation** *n* preparazione *f*. **preparatory** *adj* preparatorio.
preposition [ˌprepə'ziʃən] *n* preposizione *f*.
preposterous [pri'postərəs] *adj* assurdo.
prerequisite [priː'rekwizit] *n* requisito (principale) *m*.
prerogative [pri'rogətiv] *n* prerogativa *f*.
prescribe [pri'skraib] *v* prescrivere. **prescription** *n* prescrizione *f*; (*med*) ricetta medica *f*.
presence ['prezns] *n* presenza *f*; (*appearance*) aspetto *m*.
present[1] ['preznt] *adj* presente, attuale. *n* (*time*) presente *m*. **at present** attualmente. **for the present** per ora. **presently** *adv* quanto prima.
present[2] [pri'zent; *n* 'preznt] *v* presentare, offrire. *n* (*gift*) regalo *m*. **presentable** *adj* presentabile. **presentation** *n* presentazione *f*.

preserve [pri'zəːv] *v* conservare, preservare; (*appearances*) salvare. *n* (*food*) conserva *f*; (*reserve*) riserva *f*. **preservation** *n* preservazione *f*. **preservative** *nm*, *adj* preservativo.

preside [pri'zaid] *v* **preside over** presiedere a.

president ['prezidənt] *n* presidente *m*. **presidency** *n* presidenza *f*. **presidential** *adj* presidenziale.

press [pres] *v* premere; (*squeeze*) comprimere, schiacciare; far pressione su; insistere su; (*iron*) stirare. **press-button** *n* pulsante *m*. **press-stud** *n* bottone automatico *m*. *n* (*newspapers*) stampa *f*; (*printing*) macchina da stampa *f*; (*publishing house*) casa editrice *f*; (*tech*) torchio *m*. **press cutting** ritaglio (di giornale) *m*. **pressing** *adj* urgente.

pressure ['preʃə] *n* pressione *m*. **pressure-cooker** *n* pentola a pressione *f*. **pressurize** *v* pressurizzare; (*force*) far pressione su.

prestige [pre'stiːʒ] *n* prestigio *m*.

presume [pri'zjuːm] *v* presumere, supporre. **presumption** *n* presunzione *f*, supposizione *f*; arroganza *f*. **presumptuous** *adj* presuntuoso. **presumptive** *adj* presunto.

pretend [pri'tend] *v* pretendere; (*feign*) fingere, far finta. **pretence** *n* pretesa *f*; (*pretext*) pretesto *m*. **pretension** *n* pretensione *f*. **pretentious** *adj* pretenzioso, pieno di pretese.

pretext ['priːtekst] *n* pretesto *m*.

pretty ['priti] *adj* carino, simpatico. *adv* (*quite*) piuttosto, abbastanza; (*moderately*) quasi.

prevail [pri'veil] *v* prevalere. **prevail upon** persuadere, indurre. **prevalent** *adj* prevalente.

prevent [pri'vent] *v* impedire. **prevention** *n* prevenzione *f*; (*med*) profilassi *f*.

preview ['priːvjuː] *n* anteprima *f*.

previous ['priːviəs] *adj* precedente, anteriore. **previously** *adv* prima.

prey [prei] *n* preda *f*. **be/fall a prey to** essere/cadere in preda a. *v* **prey on** predare; (*fear, etc.*) rodere.

price [prais] *n* prezzo *m*. **price-list** *n* listino dei prezzi *m*. *v* valutare, fare il prezzo di. **priceless** *adj* impagabile; (*very amusing*) divertentissimo.

prick [prik] *v* pungere, punzecchiare. **prick up one's ears** drizzare le orecchie. *n* puntura *f*.

prickle ['prikl] *n* spina *f*. **prickly** *adj* spinoso; (*sensitive*) difficile. **prickly pear** fico d'India *m*.

pride [praid] *n* orgoglio *m*, amor proprio *m*; (*best part*) fiore *m*. *v* **pride oneself on** essere orgoglioso di.

priest [priːst] *n* prete *m*, sacerdote *m*. **priesthood** *n* sacerdozio *m*.

prig [prig] *n* borioso, -a *m, f*. **priggish** *adj* borioso.

prim [prim] *adj* affettato, compassato; (*formal*) cerimonioso.

primary ['praiməri] *adj* primario, fondamentale, primo. **primary school** scuola elementare *f*.

primate ['praimət] *n* primate *m*. **primacy** *n* primato *m*.

prime [praim] *adj* primo; di prima qualità. *n* fiore *m*, primavera *f*. *v* (*arms*) innescare; (*paint*) mesticare; (*information*) mettere al corrente; (*pump*) adescare. **primer** *n* (*book*) testo elementare *m*; (*paint*) mestica *f*.

primitive ['primitiv] *adj* primitivo.

primrose ['primrouz] *n* primula *f*.

primus stove ['praiməs] *n* fornello a petrolio *m*.

prince [prins] *n* principe *m*. **princess** *n* principessa *f*.

principal ['prinsəpəl] *adj* principale, primo. *n* (*of business*) principale *m, f*; (*of school*) direttore, -trice *m, f*; (*comm*) capitale *m*.

principle ['prinsəpəl] *n* principio *m*.

print [print] *v* stampare, imprimere; (*handwriting*) scrivere a stampatello. *n* stampa *f*; impressione *f*; (*phot*) copia *f*. **out of print** esaurito. **printer** *n* tipografo *m*. **printing** *n* tipografia *f*; (*edition*) tiratura *f*.

prior[1] ['praiə] *adj* precedente, anteriore. **prior to** prima di. **priority** *n* precedenza *f*.

prior[2] ['praiə] *n* priore *m*. **prioress** *n* priora *f*. **priory** *n* convento *m*, monastero *m*.

prise [praiz] *v* far leva su. **prise open** forzare.

prism ['prizm] *n* prismo *m*.

prison ['prizn] *n* prigione *f*. **prisoner** *n* prigioniero, -a *m, f*. **take prisoner** far prigioniero.

private ['praivət] *adj* privato, personale. *n* soldato semplice *m*. **privacy** *n* intimità *f*.

privet ['privət] *n* ligustro *m*.
privilege ['privəlidʒ] *n* privilegio *m*.
privy ['privi] *adj* privato. **be privy to** essere a conoscenza di.
prize [praiz] *n* (*reward*) premio *m*. **prize-fighter** *n* pugile *m*. **prize-giving** *n* distribuzione dei premi *f*. **prizewinner** *n* vincitore, -trice *m*, *f*. *v* apprezzare, valutare.
probable ['probəbl] *adj* probabile. **probability** *n* probabilità *f*.
probation [prə'beiʃən] *n* (*law*) libertà condizionata *f*; (*for job, etc.*) periodo di prova *m*. **probationary** *adj* di prova.
probe [proub] *v* esplorare, sondare. *n* (*investigation*) sondaggio *m*, inchiesta *f*; (*instrument*) sonda *f*.
problem ['probləm] *n* problema *m*. **problematic** *adj* problematico.
proceed [prə'siːd] *v* procedere, proseguire. **proceeds** *pl n* ricavo *m sing*, incasso *m sing*. **procedure** *n* procedura *f*; (*proceeding*) procedimento *m*.
process ['prouses] *n* processo *m*, andamento *m*; (*procedure*) procedimento *m*. *v* trattare, trasformare. **processed cheese** formaggio fuso *m*.
procession [prə'seʃən] *n* processione *f*, sfilata *f*.
proclaim [prə'kleim] *v* proclamare. **proclamation** *n* proclama *m*.
procrastinate [prə'krastineit] *v* procrastinare.
procreate ['proukrieit] *v* procreare. **procreation** *n* procreazione *f*.
procure [prə'kjuə] *v* procurare. **procurement** *n* approvvigionamento *m*.
prod [prod] *v* (*incite*) sollecitare; (*push*) spingere.
prodigy ['prodidʒi] *n* prodigio *m*.
produce [prə'djuːs; *n* 'prodjuːs] *v* produrre; (*pull out*) tirar fuori; (*theatre*) mettere in scena. *n* prodotti *or* generi agricoli *m pl*. **producer** *n* produttore, -trice *m*, *f*; (*theatre, etc.*) regista *m*, *f*. **product** *n* prodotto *m*, frutto *m*. **production** *n* produzione *f*; messa in scena *f*. **productive** *adj* produttivo; fertile. **productivity** *n* produttività *f*.
profane [prə'fein] *adj* profano. **profanity** *n* profanità *f*; (*language*) bestemmia *f*.
profess [prə'fes] *v* professare, manifestare; (*practise*) esercitare; (*imply*) pretendere di. **professed** *adj* (*avowed*) dichiarato. **profession** *n* professione *f*; dichiarazione *f*.
professional [prə'feʃənl] *n* professionista *m*, *f*. *adj* professionale. **professionalism** *n* professionismo *m*.
professor [prə'fesə] *n* professore, -essa *m*, *f*.
proficient [prə'fiʃənt] *adj* competente, provetto. **proficiency** *n* perizia *f*, competenza *f*.
profile ['proufail] *n* profilo *m*.
profit ['profit] *n* profitto *m*, guadagno *m*. *v* (*be of benefit to*) giovare a, essere utile a. **profit from** approfittare di, trarre profitto da. **profitable** *adj* vantaggioso; lucroso.
profound [prə'faund] *adj* profondo.
profuse [prə'fjuːs] *adj* abbondante, prodigo. **apologize profusely** profondersi in scuse. **profusion** *n* abbondanza *f*.
prognosis [prog'nousis] *n* prognosi *f*.
programme ['prougram] *n* programma *m*. *v* programmare.
progress ['prougres] *v* progredire, avanzare. *n* progresso *m*, andamento *m*. **progression** *n* progressione *f*. **progressive** *adj* progressivo.
prohibit [prə'hibit] *v* proibire, vietare. **prohibition** *n* proibizione *f*, divieto *m*; (*of alcohol*) proibizionismo *m*.
project ['prodʒekt; *v* prə'dʒekt] *n* progetto *m*, disegno *m*. *v* (*plan*) progettare; (*math, screen*) proiettare; (*protrude*) sporgere. **projectile** *n* proiettile *m*. **projection** *n* proiezione *f*; sporgenza *f*. **projector** *n* proiettore *m*.
proletariat [proulə'teəriət] *n* proletariato *m*. **proletarian** *n*, *adj* proletario, -a.
proliferate [prə'lifəreit] *v* proliferare.
prolific [prə'lifik] *adj* prolifico.
prologue ['proulog] *n* prologo (*pl* -ghi) *m*.
prolong [prə'loŋ] *v* prolungare.
promenade [promə'naːd] *v* fare una passeggiata. *n* passeggiata *f*; (*sea-front*) lungomare *m*.
prominent ['prominənt] *adj* prominente; eminente, importante. **prominence** *n* prominenza; eminenza *f*. **give prominence to** dar risalto a.
promiscuous [prə'miskjuəs] *adj* indiscriminato. **promiscuity** *n* promiscuità *f*.
promise ['promis] *v* promettere, assicurare. *n* promessa *f*, assicurazione *f*. **promising** *adj* che promette bene.

promontory ['promәntәri] *n* promontorio *m.*
promote [prә'mout] *v* promuovere; (*comm*) lanciare. **promotion** *n* promozione *f*; lancio *m.*
prompt [prompt] *adj* pronto, sollecito. *v* ispirare, suggerire.
prone [proun] *adv* bocconi. **be prone to** essere disposto *or* propenso a.
prong [proŋ] *n* rebbio *m.* *v* infilzare.
pronoun ['prounaun] *n* pronome *m.*
pronounce [prә'nauns] *v* pronunciare; dichiarare. **pronounced** *adj* pronunciato, spiccato. **pronouncement** *n* dichiarazione *f.* **pronunciation** *n* pronuncia *f.*
proof [pruːf] *n* prova *f*; (*printing*) bozza *f.* *adj* impenetrabile, resistente (a). *v* impermeabilizzare.
prop[1] [prop] *n* appoggio *m*, sostegno *m*; (*building*) puntello *m.* *v* **prop up** sorreggere, appoggiare; puntellare.
prop[2] [prop] *n* (*coll*) oggetto teatrale *m.*
propaganda [propә'gandә] *n* propaganda *f.*
propagate ['propәgeit] *v* propagare. **propagation** *n* propagazione *f.*
propel [prә'pel] *v* spingere avanti, azionare. **propellant** *n* propellente *m.* **propeller** *n* elica *f.*
proper ['propә] *adj* proprio; (*right*) particolare; (*good*) buono. **properly** *adv* come si deve; correttamente; (*well*) bene.
property ['propәti] *n* proprietà *f*; possesso *m*, beni *m pl.*
prophecy ['profәsi] *n* profezia *f.* **prophesy** *v* fare il profeta, predire.
prophet ['profit] *n* profeta *m.* **prophetess** *n* profetessa *f.* **prophetic** *adj* profetico.
propitious [prә'piʃәs] *adj* propizio, favorevole.
proportion [prә'poːʃәn] *n* proporzione *f.* **out of proportion** sproporzionato, smisurato. **proportional** *adj* proporzionale.
propose [prә'pouz] *v* proporre, intendere; fare una proposta di matrimonio. **proposal** *n* proposta *f*; offerta di matrimonio *f.* **proposition** *n* proposta *f*; (*gramm*) proposizione *f.*
proprietor [prә'praiәtә] *n* proprietario *m*, padrone *m.* **proprietress** *n* proprietaria *f*, padrona *f.*
propriety [prә'praiәti] *n* decoro *m*, decenza *f.*
propulsion [prә'pʌlʃәn] *n* propulsione *f.*
prose [prouz] *n* prosa *f.* **prosaic** *adj* prosaico, banale.
prosecute ['prosikjuːt] *v* citare in giudizio, processare. **prosecution** *n* processo *m.* **prosecutor** *n* procuratore *m*, pubblico ministero *m.*
prospect ['prospekt; *v* prә'spekt] *n* prospettiva *f*, aspettativa *f*; (*view*) prospetto *m.* *v* esplorare. **prospective** *adj* futuro.
prospectus [prә'spektәs] *n* prospetto *m.*
prosper ['prospә] *v* prosperare. **prosperity** *n* prosperità *f.* **prosperous** *adj* prospero, benestante.
prostitute ['prostitjuːt] *v* prostituire. *n* prostituta *f*, puttana *f.* **prostitution** *n* prostituzione *f.*
prostrate [pro'streit; *adj* 'prostreit] *v* prostrare, prosternare. *adj* abbattuto.
protagonist [prou'tagәnist] *n* protagonista *m, f.*
protect [prә'tekt] *v* proteggere. **protection** *n* protezione *f.* **protective** *adj* protettivo. **protector** *n* protettore, -trice *m, f.* **protectorate** *n* protettorato *m.*
protégé ['protәʒei] *n* protetto, -a *m, f.*
protein ['proutiːn] *n* proteina *f.*
protest [prә'test; *n* 'proutest] *v* protestare. *n* protesta *f*; (*comm*) protesto *m*; (*pol*) contestazione. **under protest** protestando.
Protestant ['protistәnt] *n*(*m*+*f*), *adj* protestante. **Protestantism** *n* protestantesimo *m.*
protocol ['proutәkol] *n* protocollo *m.*
proton ['prouton] *n* protone *m.*
protoplasm ['proutәplazәm] *n* protoplasma *m.*
prototype ['proutәtaip] *n* prototipo *m.*
protract [prә'trakt] *v* protrarre, prolungare.
protractor [prә'traktә] *n* goniometro *m.*
protrude [prә'truːd] *v* sporgere.
proud [praud] *adj* orgoglioso, fiero.
prove [pruːv] *v* dimostrare, confermare.
proverb ['provәːb] *n* proverbio *m.*
provide [prә'vaid] *v* provvedere, fornire. **provide against** premunirsi contro. **provided that** purchè. **providence** *n* provvidenza *f.*
province ['provins] *n* provincia *f.* **provincial** *adj* provinciale.
provision [prә'viʒәn] *n* provvedimento *m.* **provisions** *pl n* viveri *m pl*, provviste *f pl.* **provisional** *adj* provvisorio.
proviso [prә'vaizou] *n* stipulazione *f*, condizione *f.*

provoke [prə'vouk] *v* provocare, irritare. **provocation** *n* provocazione *f*. **provocative** *adj* provocativo.
prow [prau] *n* prua *f*, prora *f*.
prowess ['prauis] *n* (*ability*) bravura *f*;. (*bravery*) prodezza *f*, valore *m*.
prowl [praul] *v* girare furtivamente, vagare.
proximity [prok'simǝti] *n* prossimità *f*.
proxy ['proksi] *n* (*agency*, *authorization*) procura *f*; (*person*) procuratore, -trice *m*, *f*.
prude [pruːd] *n* persona che affetta pudore, puritano, -a *m*, *f*. **prudish** *adj* che affetta pudore, puritano.
prudent ['pruːdənt] *adj* prudente, cauto. **prudence** *n* prudenza *f*, avvedutezza *f*.
prune[1] [pruːn] *v* sfrondare; (*tree*) potare.
prune[2] [pruːn] *n* prugna secca *f*.
pry [prai] *v* curiosare, ficcare il naso (in).
psalm [saːm] *n* salmo *m*.
pseudonym ['sjuːdənim] *n* pseudonimo *m*.
psychedelic [ˌsaikə'delik] *adj* psichedelico.
psychiatry [sai'kaiətri] *n* psichiatria *f*. **psychiatric** *adj* psichiatrico. **psychiatrist** *n* psichiatra *m*, *f*.
psychic ['saikik] *adj* psichico.
psychoanalysis [ˌsaikouə'naləsis] *n* psicanalisi *f*. **psychoanalyse** *v* psicanalizzare. **psychoanalyst** *n* psicanalista *m*, *f*. **psychoanalytic** *adj* psicanalitico.
psychology [sai'kolədʒi] *n* psicologia *f*. **psychological** *adj* psicologico. **psychologist** *n* psicologo, -a *m*, *f*.
psychopath ['saikəpaθ] *n* psicopatico, -a *m*, *f*.
psychosis [sai'kousis] *n* psicosi *f*. **psychotic** *n*, *adj* psicotico, -a.
psychosomatic [ˌsaikəsə'matik] *adj* psicosomatico.
psychotherapy [ˌsaikə'θerəpi] *n* psicoterapia *f*. **psychotherapist** *n* psicoterapista *m*, *f*.
pub [pʌb] *n* bar *m invar*.
puberty ['pjuːbəti] *n* pubertà *f*.
pubic ['pjuːbik] *adj* pubico.
public ['pʌblik] *nm*, *adj* pubblico. **public holiday** festa civile *f*. **public library** biblioteca comunale *f*. **public school** collegio privato *m*. **public-spirited** *adj* dotato di senso civico. **publican** proprietario del bar *m*, oste *m*.
publication [ˌpʌbli'keiʃən] *n* pubblicazione *f*.
publicity [pʌb'lisəti] *n* pubblicità *f*. **publicist** *n* pubblicista *m*, *f*.
publicize ['pʌblisaiz] *v* divulgare; (*advertise*) fare la pubblicità a.
publish ['pʌbliʃ] *v* pubblicare. **publisher** *n* (*person*) editore *m*; (*firm*) casa editrice *f*.
pucker ['pʌkə] *v* corrugare, raggrinzare.
pudding ['pudiŋ] *n* budino *m*, dolce *m*.
puddle ['pʌdl] *n* pozzanghera *f*.
puerile ['pjuərail] *adj* puerile.
puff [pʌf] *n* (*of wind*) soffio *m*; (*of smoke*) buffata *f*; (*of breath*) alito *m*; (*powder*) piumino *m*; (*pipe*, *cigarette*) boccata *f*. **puff pastry** pasta sfoglia *f*. *v* sbuffare.
pull [pul] *n* tirata *f*, strappo *m*; (*influence*) ascendente *m*. *v* tirare; (*haul*) trascinare. **pull back** tirare indietro, trattenere. **pull down** tirar giù; demolire. **pull in** (*train*) entrare in stazione. **pull oneself together** riprendere animo. **pull up** tirar su; (*plant*, *etc.*) strappare; (*stop*) fermarsi.
pulley ['puli] *n* puleggia *f*.
pullover ['pulˌouvə] *n* pullover *m invar*.
pulp [pʌlp] *n* polpa *f*. *v* ridurre in polpa.
pulpit ['pulpit] *n* pulpito *m*.
pulsate [pʌl'seit] *v* palpitare, pulsare. **pulsation** *n* pulsazione *f*.
pulse[1] [pʌls] *n* (*beat*) polso *m*; (*elec*) impulso *m*; vitalità *f*. *v* pulsare.
pulse[2] [pʌls] *n* (*vegetables*) legumi *m pl*.
pulverize ['pʌlvəraiz] *v* polverizzare.
pump [pʌmp] *n* pompa *f*. **petrol pump** distributore di benzina *m*. *v* pompare; (*bullets*) scaricare.
pumpkin ['pʌmpkin] *n* zucca *f*.
pun [pʌn] *n* gioco di parole *m*. *v* fare giochi di parole.
punch[1] [pʌntʃ] *v* (*hit*) picchiare, dare un pugno *or* cazzotto a. *n* pugno *m*; (*coll*) cazzotto *m*; (*energy*) forza *f*. **punch-drunk** *adj* stordito.
punch[2] [pʌntʃ] *n* (*drink*) ponce *m*.
punch[3] [pʌntʃ] *n* (*tool*) punzone *m*. *v* (*tickets*) forare; (*tech*) punzonare; (*stamp*) timbrare.
punctual ['pʌŋktʃuəl] *adj* puntuale. **punctuality** *n* puntualità *f*.
punctuate ['pʌŋktʃueit] *v* interrompere ripetutamente; (*sentence*) mettere la punteggiatura. **punctuation** *n* punteggiatura *f*.
puncture ['pʌŋktʃə] *n* puntura *f*; (*tyre*) foratura *f*. **have a puncture** avere una gomma a terra. *v* forare, bucare.

pungent ['pʌndʒənt] *adj* pungente, aspro; caustico.
punish ['pʌniʃ] *v* punire, castigare. **punishment** *n* punizione *f*, castigo (*pl* -ghi) *m*. **punitive** *adj* punitivo.
punt[1] [pʌnt] *n* (*boat*) barchino *m*.
punt[2] [pʌnt] *v* (*bet*) puntare. **punter** *n* giocatore d'azzardo *m*, scommettitore *m*.
puny ['pjuːni] *adj* sparuto, debole.
pupil[1] ['pjuːpl] *n* (*school*) allievo, -a *m, f*, alunno, -a *m, f*.
pupil[2] ['pjuːpl] *n* (*anat*) pupilla *f*.
puppet ['pʌpit] *n* burattino *m*.
puppy ['pʌpi] *n* cagnolino *m*.
purchase ['pəːtʃəs] *v* acquistare, comprare. *n* acquisto *m*; (*tech*) presa *f*. **purchaser** *n* compratore, -trice *m, f*.
pure ['pjuə] *adj* puro. **purify** *v* purificare, depurare. **purity** *n* purezza *f*.
purée ['pjuərei] *n* puré *m*.
purgatory ['pəːgətəri] *n* purgatorio *m*.
purge [pəːdʒ] *v* (*purify*) purgare; (*pol*) epurare. *n* purga *f*, epurazione *f*.
puritan ['pjuəritən] *n, adj* puritano, -a. **puritanism** *n* puritanesimo *m*.
purl [pəːl] *v* (*knitting*) lavorare a punto rovescio; (*edge*) smerlare. *n* punto rovescio *m*; punto smerlo *m*.
purple ['pəːpl] *n* porpora *f*. *adj* purpureo; (*of face*) paonazzo.
purpose ['pəːpəs] *n* scopo *m*, proposito *m*. **on purpose** apposta.
purr [pəː] *n* fusa *f pl*. *v* far le fusa.
purse [pəːs] *n* borsa *f*; (*for money*) borsellino *m*. *v* contrarre.
purser ['pəːsə] *n* commissario di bordo *m*.
pursue [pə'sjuː] *v* (*seek to attain*) perseguire; (*follow closely*) perseguitare; (*continue*) seguire, proseguire. **pursuit** *n* (*quest*) ricerca *f*; (*chase*) inseguimento *m*; (*activity*) impiego (*pl* -ghi) *m*.
pus [pʌs] *n* pus *m*, materia *f*.
push [puʃ] *n* spinta *f*; (*effort*) sforzo *m*, energia *f*; iniziativa *f*. **push-chair** *n* carozzina *f*. *v* spingere; (*urge*) spronare; (*product*) lanciare. **push away** allontanare. **push back** respingere. **push-over** *n* vittima facile *f*. **pushing** *adj* energico, aggressivo.
***put** [put] *v* mettere, porre; (*question*) rivolgere; (*idea*) esprimere. **put about** (*rumour*) diffondere. **put across** (*explain*) spiegare. **put aside** *or* **by** mettere da parte, risparmiare. **put down** (*suppress*) sopprimere; (*land*) atterrare; (*ascribe*) attribuire. **put forward** proporre, nominare. **put off** rinviare; (*get rid of*) sbarazzarsi di; (*cause to dislike*) ripugnare. **put out** (*extinguish*) spegnere; (*inconvenience*) disturbare. **put up** (*lodge*) offrire alloggio a; (*stay*) prendere allogio; (*raise*) alzare; (*notice, etc.*) affiggere. **put up with** sopportare.
putrid ['pjuːtrid] *adj* putrido.
putt [pʌt] *v* colpire leggermente, fare il putting. *n* colpo leggero *m*, putting *m invar*.
putty ['pʌti] *n* stucco *m*. *v* stuccare.
puzzle ['pʌzl] *n* indovinello *m*; enigma *m*. *v* confondere, rendere perplesso. **puzzled** *adj* perplesso.
pygmy ['pigmi] *n, adj* pigmeo, -a.
pyjamas [pə'dʒaːməz] *pl n* pigiama *m sing*.
pylon ['pailən] *n* pilone *m*.
pyramid ['pirəmid] *n* piramide *f*.
python ['paiθən] *n* pitone *m*.

Q

quack[1] [kwak] *v* (*duck*) schiamazzare.
quack[2] [kwak] *n* (*med*) ciarlatano *m*, medicastro *m*.
quadrangle ['kwodraŋgl] *n* (*math*) quadrangolo *m*; (*arch*) corte quadrangolare *f*.
quadrant ['kwodrənt] *n* quadrante *m*.
quadrilateral [kwodrə'latərəl] *nm, adj* quadrilatero.
quadruped ['kwodruped] *n* quadrupede *m*.
quadruple [kwod'ruːpl] *adj* quadruplo.
quagmire ['kwagmaiə] *n* pantano *m*.
quail[1] [kweil] *n* (*bird*) quaglia *f*.
quail[2] [kweil] *v* aver paura, sgomentarsi.
quaint [kweint] *adj* interessante *or* pittoresco in un modo insolito.
quake [kweik] *v* tremare; (*person*) fremere. *n* (*coll*: *earthquake*) terremoto *m*.
Quaker ['kweikə] *n* quacchero, -a *m, f*.
qualify ['kwolifai] *v* qualificare; (*define*) precisare. **qualification** *n* qualifica *f*; (*limitation*) riserva *f*. **qualified** *adj* qualificato, idoneo; (*limited*) condizionato.
quality ['kwoləti] *n* qualità *f*.

qualm [kwaːm] *n* scrupolo *m*, apprensione *f*.
quandary ['kwondəri] *n* situazione difficile *f*, imbarazzo *m*.
quantify ['kwontifai] *v* quantificare.
quantity ['kwontəti] *n* quantità *f*.
quantum ['kwontəm] *n* quanto *m*.
quarantine ['kworəntiːn] *n* quarantena *f*. *v* mettere in quarantena.
quarrel ['kworəl] *n* lite *f*, bisticcio *m*. **pick a quarrel** attaccar briga. *v* litigare, bisticciare. **quarrelsome** *adj* litigioso.
quarry[1] ['kwori] *n* (*prey*) preda *f*.
quarry[2] ['kwori] *n* (*mining*) cava *f*. *v* scavare.
quarter ['kwoːtə] *n* quarto *m*; (*three months*) trimestre *m*; (*district*, *mercy*) quartiere *m*. **at close quarters** da vicino. **quarters** *pl n* (*mil*) accantonamento *m sing*. *v* dividere in quattro; (*mil*) acquartierare. **quarterly** *nm*, *adj* trimestrale.
quartet [kwoː'tet] *n* quartetto *m*.
quartz [kwoːts] *n* quarzo *m*.
quash [kwoʃ] *v* sopprimere; (*law*) annullare, cassare.
quaver ['kweivə] *n* (*music*) croma *f*; (*shaky voice*) tremolio *m*. *v* tremolare.
quay [kiː] *n* banchina *f*.
queasy ['kwiːzi] *adj* che sente nausea.
queen [kwiːn] *n* regina *f*.
queer [kwiə] *adj* strambo, bizzarro. **feel queer** sentirsi male. *n* (*coll*: *homosexual*) finocchio *m*.
quell [kwel] *v* reprimere, sopprimere.
quench [kwentʃ] *v* spegnere. **quench one's thirst** dissetarsi.
query ['kwiəri] *n* domanda *f*, quesito *m*. *v* chiedersi; (*raise doubt*) mettere in dubbio.
quest [kwest] *n* ricerca *f*.
question ['kwestʃən] *n* questione *f*, domanda *f*; (*gramm*) interrogazione *f*; problema *m*. **question mark** punto interrogativo *m*. *v* interrogare; (*query*) mettere in dubbio.
queue [kjuː] *n* coda *f*. *v* fare la coda, mettersi in coda.
quibble ['kwibl] *n* cavillo *m*. *v* cavillare.
quick [kwik] *adj* rapido, veloce; (*lively*) vivace. **quicksand** *n* sabbia mobile *f*. **quicksilver** *n* argento vivo *m*. **quick-tempered** *adj* impulsivo. **quick-witted** *adj* sveglio. *adv* presto. *n* **cut to the quick** toccare sul vivo. **quicken** *v* affrettare, accelerare.
quid [kwid] *n* (*coll*) sterlina *f*.
quiet ['kwaiət] *adj* tranquillo, quieto. **keep quiet** tacere, star zitto. *n* quiete *f*, tranquillità *f*, silenzio *m*. **on the quiet** di nascosto. **quieten** *v* calmare, acquietare.
quill [kwil] *n* penna *f*.
quilt [kwilt] *v* trapuntare. *n* trapunta *f*; (*duvet*) piumino *m*.
quince [kwins] *n* cotogna *f*.
quinine [kwi'niːn] *n* chinino *m*.
quinsy ['kwinzi] *n* angina *f*.
quintet [kwin'tet] *n* quintetto *m*.
quirk [kwəːk] *n* ticchio *m*, vezzo *m*.
***quit** [kwit] *v* lasciare, abbandonare; (*depart*) partire.
quite [kwait] *adv* perfettamente, bene, affatto, proprio; (*somewhat*) abbastanza.
quits [kwits] *adj* pari. **call it quits** far pari e patta. **double or quits** lascia o raddoppia.
quiver[1] ['kwivə] *v* fremere; (*voice*) tremolare. *n* fremito *m*; tremolio *m*.
quiver[2] ['kwivə] *n* (*arrows*) faretra *f*.
quiz [kwiz] *n* quiz *m invar*. *v* interrogare. **quizzical** *adj* (*odd*) curioso; (*ridiculing*) beffardo.
quota ['kwoutə] *n* quota *f*, rata *f*; (*trade*) contingente *m*.
quote [kwout] *v* citare; (*price*) quotare. **quotation** *n* citazione *f*. **quotation marks** virgolette *f pl*.
quotient ['kwouʃnt] *n* quoziente *m*.

R

rabbi ['rabai] *n* rabbino *m*.
rabbit ['rabit] *m* coniglio *m*.
rabble ['rabl] *n* plebaglia *f*.
rabies ['reibiːz] *n* rabbia *f*. **rabid** *adj* (*med*) idrofobo; furioso; fanatico.
race[1] [reis] *n* (*sport*) corsa *f*, gara *f*. **racecourse** *n* ippodromo *m*. **racehorse** *n* cavallo da corsa *m*. **race-track** *n* pista *f*. *v* correre; (*compete*) gareggiare con. **racing** *adj* da corsa. **racy** *adj* vivace, piccante.
race[2] [reis] *n* razza *f*. **racial** *adj* razziale. **racialism** *or* **racism** *n* razzismo *m*. **racialist** *or* **racist** *n*(*m*+*f*), *adj* razzista.
rack[1] [rak] *n* rastrelliera *f*; (*for plates*) scolapiatti *m invar*; (*tech*) cremagliera *f*;

(*for luggage*) rete *f*. *v* **rack one's brains** scervellarsi, lambiccarsi il cervello.
rack² [rak] *n* **go to rack and ruin** andare in malora.
racket¹ ['rakit] *n* (*bat*) racchetta *f*.
racket² ['rakit] *n* (*noise*) baccano *m*, chiasso *m*; (*dishonest scheme*) truffa *f*.
radar ['reidaː] *n* radar *m*.
radial ['reidiəl] *adj* radiale.
radiant ['reidiənt] *adj* raggiante; splendido; (*joyful*) esultante; (*phys, tech*) radiante. **radiance** *n* splendore *m*.
radiate ['reidieit] *v* irradiare, raggiare. **radiation** *n* irradiazione *f*; (*phys*) radiazione *f*. **radiator** *n* (*car*) radiatore *m*; (*central heating*) termosifone *m*.
radical ['radikəl] *n*(*m*+*f*), *adj* radicale.
radio ['reidiou] *nf invar*, *adj* radio.
radioactive [reidiou'aktiv] *adj* radioattivo. **radioactivity** *n* radioattività *f*.
radiography [reidi'ogrəfi] *n* radiografia *f*.
radiology [reidi'olədʒi] *n* radiologia *f*. **radiologist** *n* radiologo, -a *m*, *f*.
radish ['radiʃ] *n* ravanello *m*.
radium ['reidiəm] *n* radio *m*.
radius ['reidiəs] *n* raggio *m*.
raffia ['rafiə] *n* rafia *f*.
raffle ['rafl] *n* riffa *f*.
raft [raːft] *n* zattera *f*.
rafter ['raːftə] *n* trave *f*.
rag¹ [rag] *n* (*cloth*) straccio *m*, cencio *m*; (*derog: newspaper*) giornalaccio *m*. **ragged** *adj* lacero, cencioso.
rag² [rag] (*coll*) *v* prendere in giro. *n* baldoria *f*.
rage [reidʒ] *n* rabbia *f*, collera *f*; (*enthusiasm*) passione *f*, moda *f*. **be in a rage** essere furioso *or* arrabbiato. **fly into a rage** infuriarsi. *v* montare su tutte le furie, infuriarsi; (*storm, etc.*) imperversare. **rage against** inveire contro. **raging** *adj* furioso, violento.
raid [reid] *n* incursione *f*, razzia *f*. *v* fare un'incursione in, razziare, invadere. **raider** *n* razziatore *m*.
rail [reil] *n* (*bar*) sbarra *f*; (*barrier*) ringhiera *f*; (*handrail*) corrimano *m invar*; (*for train*) rotaia *f*, binario *m*. **by rail** col treno. **go off the rails** perdere le staffe. **railway** *n* ferrovia *f*.
railings ['reiliŋz] *pl n* cancellata *f sing*, inferriata *f sing*.
rain [rein] *n* pioggia *f*. **rainbow** *n* arcobaleno *m*. **raincoat** *n* impermeabile *m*. **raindrop** *n* goccia di pioggia *f*. *v* piovere. **rain cats and dogs** piovere a catinelle. **rainy** *adj* piovoso.
raise [reiz] *v* (*lift up*) alzare; (*rear*) allevare; (*bring up*) sollevare; (*increase*) aumentare; (*cause*) suscitare.
raisin ['reizən] *n* uva secca *f*.
rake [reik] *n* (*tool*) rastrello *m*. *v* rastrellare. **rake up the past** rivangare il passato.
rally ['rali] *n* (*meeting*) raduno *m*; (*mot*) rally *m invar*; (*recovery*) ricupero di forze *m*, ripresa *f*; (*tennis, etc.*) scambio di colpi *m*. *v* radunare; riprendersi.
ram [ram] *n* montone *m*. *v* ficcare; (*of ships*) speronare.
ramble ['rambl] *n* gita *f*, giro *m*. *v* vagare, girovagare; (*speech*) divagare; (*mind*) delirare. **rambling** *adj* (*unconnected*) sconnesso, sconclusionato. **rambling rose** rosa rampicante *f*.
ramp [ramp] *n* rampa *f*.
rampage [ram'peidʒ] *n* **go on the rampage** andare su tutte le furie.
rampant ['rampənt] *adj* (*unchecked*) sfrenato; (*heraldry*) rampante.
rampart ['rampaːt] *n* bastione *m*.
ramshackle ['ramʃakl] *adj* cadente.
ran [ran] *V* **run**.
ranch [raːntʃ] *n* fattoria (per l'allevamento di bestiame) *f*, ranch *m invar*.
rancid ['ransid] *adj* rancido.
rancour ['raŋkə] *n* amarezza *f*, rancore *m*.
random ['randəm] *adj* casuale, fortuito. *n* **at random** a casaccio.
randy ['randi] *adj* lascivo.
rang [raŋ] *V* **ring²**.
range [reindʒ] *n* (*assortment*) gamma *f*; (*mountains*) catena *f*; (*scope*) portata *f*; (*for shooting*) campo di tiro *m*; (*of voice*) estensione *f*; (*stove*) fornello *m*. **out of range** fuori tiro. **range-finder** *n* telemetro *m*. **within range** a portata; (*of gun*) a tiro. *v* (*arrange*) disporre; (*set in order*) schierare; (*between limits*) estendersi, variare.
rank¹ [raŋk] *n* (*class*) grado *m*; (*row*) fila *f*. **ranks** *pl n* truppe *f pl*. *v* (*arrange*) schierare; classificare; considerare.
rank² [raŋk] *adj* (*excessive*) rigoglioso; (*utter*) assoluto; (*smell*) puzzolente.
rankle ['raŋkl] *v* bruciare; (*cause bitterness*) amareggiare.
ransack ['ransak] *v* mettere sossopra, rovistare.

ransom ['ransəm] *n* riscatto *m.* *v* riscattare.
rap [rap] *v* picchiare, colpire. **rap over the knuckles** rimproverare. *n* colpetto *m.* **take the rap** accollarsi il biasimo.
rape [reip] *n* stupro *m*, violenza carnale *f*; (*abduction*) rapimento *m.* *v* violentare, stuprare; rapire.
rapid ['rapid] *adj* rapido, veloce. **rapidity** *n* rapidità *f.*
rapier ['reipiə] *n* spada *f*, stocco *m.*
rapture ['raptʃə] *n* estasi *f.* **rapturous** *adj* estatico.
rare[1] ['reə] *adj* (*scarce*) raro. **rarity** *n* rarità *f.*
rare[2] ['reə] *adj* (*meat*) al sangue.
rascal ['raːskəl] *n* briccone *m*, mascalzone *m.*
rash[1] [raʃ] *adj* avventato, sconsiderato. **rashness** *n* avventatezza *f*, imprudenza *f.*
rash[2] [raʃ] *n* (*med*) eruzione *f.*
rasher ['raʃə] *n* fetta (di prosciutto) *f.*
raspberry ['raːzbəri] *n* lampone *m.* **blow a raspberry** (*coll*) fare una pernacchia.
rat [rat] *n* ratto *m*; (*coll*: *traitor*) traditore *m.* **smell a rat** (*coll*) avere dei sospetti.
rate [reit] *n* (*charge*) tasso *m*; (*speed*) velocità *f*, passo *m*; (*degree*) grado *m.* **at any rate** comunque. **at this rate** così, a questo passo. **ratepayer** *n* contribuente *m, f.* **rates** *pl n* imposta *f sing.* *v* stimare, valutare, considerare.
rather ['raːðə] *adv* piuttosto, anzi. *interj* certo! altro che! **I would rather . . .** preferirei . . . .
ratify ['ratifai] *v* ratificare. **ratification** *n* ratifica *f.*
ratio ['reiʃiou] *n* rapporto *m*, proporzione *f.*
ration ['raʃən] *n* razione *f.* **rations** *pl n* viveri *m pl.* *v* razionare.
rational ['raʃənl] *adj* razionale.
rattle ['ratl] *v* sbatacchiare; (*disconcert*) sconcertare. *n* sbatacchio *m*; (*toy, instrument*) raganella *f*; (*in throat*) rantolo *m.*
raucous ['roːkəs] *adj* rauco.
ravage ['ravidʒ] *v* devastare. *n* devastazione *f.*
rave [reiv] *v* delirare. **rave about** andar pazzo di.
raven ['reivən] *n* corvo *m.*
ravenous ['ravənəs] *adj* vorace. **be ravenous** avere una fame da lupo.
ravine [rə'viːn] *n* burrone *m.*
ravish ['raviʃ] *v* (*delight*) incantare; (*rape*) violentare. **ravishing** *adj* incantevole.
raw [roː] *adj* (*not cooked*) crudo; (*not refined*) greggio; (*untrained*) inesperto. **raw material** materia prima *f.* **touch on the raw** toccare sul vivo.
ray[1] [rei] *n* raggio *m.*
ray[2] [rei] *n* (*fish*) razza *f.*
rayon ['reion] *n* raion *m.*
razor ['reizə] *n* rasoio *m.* **razor blade** lametta *f.*
reach [riːtʃ] *n* portata *f*; (*continuous stretch*) tratto *m.* **out of reach** fuori mano. **within reach** a portata di mano. *v* (*get to*) raggiungere; (*hand*) porgere.
react [ri'akt] *v* reagire. **reaction** *n* reazione *f.* **reactionary** *n, adj* reazionario, -a. **reactor** *n* reattore *m.*
***read** [riːd] *v* leggere; studiare. **well-read** *adj* istruito. **readable** *adj* leggibile. **reader** *n* lettore, -trice *m, f.* **readership** *n* lettori *m pl.* **reading** *n* lettura *f*; interpretazione *f.*
readjust [riːə'dʒʌst] *v* raggiustare.
ready ['redi] *adj* pronto, preparato; (*willing*) disposto. **get ready** preparare, prepararsi. **ready-made** *adj* confezionato. **ready money** contanti *m pl.*
real [riəl] *adj* reale, effettivo, genuino. **real estate** beni immobili *m pl.* **realism** *n* realismo *m.* **realist** *n* realista *m, f.* **realistic** *adj* realistico. **reality** *n* realtà *f.*
realize ['riəlaiz] *v* realizzare. **realization** *n* realizzazione *f.*
really ['riəli] *adv* effettivamente; (*before adj*) proprio. *interj* davvero.
realm [relm] *n* dominio *m*; (*special field*) campo *m.*
reap [riːp] *v* mietere; (*profit, etc.*) raccogliere.
reappear [riːə'piə] *v* riapparire. **reappearance** *n* ricomparsa *f.*
rear[1] [riə] *n* (*back*) dietro *m*, parte posteriore *f*; (*mil*) retroguardia *f.* **at the rear of** dietro a. **rear-view mirror** retrovisore *m.* **stay in the rear** restare per ultimo. *adj* posteriore.
rear[2] [riə] *v* (*raise*) allevare; (*horse, etc.*) impennarsi; (*elevate*) innalzare.
rearm [riː'aːm] *v* riarmare. **rearmament** *n* riarmo *m.*
rearrange [riːə'reindʒ] *v* riordinare. **rearrangement** *n* riordinamento *m.*

reason ['riːzn] *n* ragione *f*, causa *f*; (*judgment*) ragionevolezza *f*. **it stands to reason** è evidente. *v* ragionare. **reasonable** *adj* ragionevole, giusto. **reasoning** *n* modo di ragionare *m*.
reassure [riə'ʃuə] *v* rassicurare. **reassurance** *n* rassicurazione *f*.
rebate ['riːbeit] *n* sconto *m*.
rebel ['rebl] *v* ribellarsi. *n* ribelle *m*, *f*. **rebellion** *n* ribellione *f*. **rebellious** *adj* ribelle.
rebound [ri'baund; *n* 'riːbaund] *v* rimbalzare. *n* rimbalzo *m*.
rebuff [ri'bʌf] *v* respingere, rifiutare. *n* scacco *m*, rifiuto *m*.
***rebuild** [riː'bild] *v* ricostruire. **rebuilding** *n* ricostruzione *f*.
rebuke [ri'bjuːk] *n* rimprovero *m*. *v* rimproverare.
recall [ri'koːl] *v* richiamare; (*remember*) rievocare, ricordare. *n* richiamo *m*, memoria *f*. **past recall** irrevocabile.
recap ['riːkap] (*coll*) *v* ricapitolare. *n* ricapitolazione *f*.
recede [ri'siːd] *v* recedere, inclinarsi all'indietro.
receipt [rə'siːt] *v* quietanzare. *n* ricevuta *f*. **receipts** *pl n* incasso *m sing*, entrate *f pl*.
receive [rə'siːv] *v* ricevere; (*sustain*) sostenere, riportare; (*stolen goods*) ricettare. **receiver** *n* ricettatore, -trice *m*, *f*; (*bankruptcy*) curatore fallimentare *m*; (*phone*) ricevitore *m*.
recent ['riːsnt] *adv* recente. **recently** *adv* di recente, poco fa.
receptacle [rə'septəkl] *n* recipiente *m*; (*bot*) ricettacolo *m*.
reception [rə'sepʃən] *n* ricevimento *m*; (*radio*) ricezione *f*. **receptionist** *n* segretaria *f*, receptionist *f invar*. **receptive** *adj* ricettivo.
recess [ri'ses] *n* nicchia *f*; pausa *f*; (*holiday*) vacanza *f*. **recesses** *pl n* (*of mind, etc.*) recessi *m pl*.
recession [rə'seʃən] *n* recessione *f*.
recharge [riː'tʃaːdʒ] *v* ricaricare.
recipe ['resəpi] *n* ricetta *f*.
recipient [rə'sipiənt] *n* destinatario, -a *m*, *f*. *adj* ricevente.
reciprocate [rə'siprəkeit] *v* contraccambiare, reciprocare; (*tech*) alternarsi. **reciprocal** *adj* reciproco. **reciprocity** *n* reciprocità *f*.
recite [rə'sait] *v* recitare. **recital** *n* (*narrative*) racconto *m*; (*entertainment*) recital *m invar*. **recitation** *n* recitazione *f*.
reckless ['rekləs] *adj* imprudente, avventato. **recklessness** *n* avventatezza *f*.
reckon ['rekən] *v* contare; (*consider*) giudicare. **reckon on** contare su. **reckon with** prendere in considerazione. **reckoning** *n* (*bill*) resa dei conti *f*.
reclaim [ri'kleim] *v* redimere; (*land*) bonificare; (*material*) ricuperare. **reclamation** *n* bonifica *f*.
recline [rə'klain] *v* appoggiarsi.
recluse [rə'kluːs] *n* eremita *m*.
recognize ['rekəgnaiz] *v* riconoscere. **recognition** *n* riconoscimento *m*. **recognizable** *adj* riconoscibile.
recoil [rə'koil] *v* rinculare. **recoil from** rifuggire da. *n* rinculo *m*.
recollect [rekə'lekt] *v* rammentarsi di. **recollection** *n* memoria *f*, ricordo *m*.
recommence [riːkə'mens] *v* ricominciare.
recommend [rekə'mend] *v* raccomandare, consigliare. **recommendation** *n* raccomandazione *f*.
recompense ['rekəmpens] *v* compensare, risarcire. *n* indennizzo *m*, risarcimento *m*.
reconcile ['rekənsail] *v* mettere d'accordo, riconciliare. **reconcile oneself to** rassegnarsi a. **reconciliation** *n* rappacificazione *f*.
reconnoitre [rekə'noitə] *v* fare un sopralluogo; (*mil*) fare una ricognizione. **reconnaissance** *n* esplorazione *f*, sopralluogo (*pl* -ghi) *m*; (*mil*) ricognizione *f*.
reconstruct [riːkən'strʌkt] *v* ricostruire. **reconstruction** *n* ricostruzione *f*.
record [rə'koːd; *n* 'rekoːd] *v* registrare; notare; (*as document*) mettere a verbale. *n* nota *f*. registro *m*; (*court report*) verbale *m*; (*sport*) record *m invar*; disco *m*; (*dossier*) stato di servizio *m*. **keep a record of** prendere nota di. **off the record** ufficiosamente. **record-player** *n* giradischi *m invar*. **recorder** *n* (*music*) flautino *m*. **recording** *n* registrazione *f*.
recount [ri'kaunt] *v* riferire, raccontare.
recoup [ri'kuːp] *v* rifarsi di, compensare.
recourse [rə'koːs] *n* **have recourse to** ricorrere a. **without recourse** senza rivalsa.
recover [rə'kʌvə] *v* (*get back*) riprendere, ricuperare; (*regain health*) rimettersi.

recovery *n* ricupero *m*; (*health*) guarigione *f*.
recreation [rekri'eiʃən] *n* ricreazione *f*, passatempo *m*, svago *m*.
recrimination [rəkrimi'neiʃən] *n* recriminazione *f*.
recruit [rə'kruːt] *n* recluta *f*. *v* arruolare. **recruitment** *n* reclutamento *m*.
rectangle ['rektaŋgl] *n* rettangolo *m*. **rectangular** *adj* rettangolare.
rectify ['rektifai] *v* rettificare; (*elec*) raddrizzare.
rectum ['rektəm] *n* retto *m*.
recuperate [rə'kjuːpəreit] *v* ricuperare; (*get well again*) rimettersi. **recuperation** *n* ricupero *m*.
recur [ri'kəː] *v* ricorrere, ritornare. **recurrence** *n* ricorrenza *f*; (*of illness*) ricaduta *f*. **recurrent** *adj* ricorrente.
red [red] *adj* rosso. **go red** (*person*) arrossire; (*thing*) diventar rosso. **redcurrant** *n* ribes *m invar*. **red-handed** *adj* in flagrante. **red herring** diversivo *m*. **red-hot** *adj* rovente. **Red Indian** *n* pellerossa (*pl* pellirosse) *m*, *f*. *n* **in the red** scoperto. **reddish** *adj* rossastro.
redeem [rə'diːm] *v* redimere, estinguere, svincolare. **redeeming feature** particolare che salva *m*. **redeemable** *adj* redimibile. **redemption** *n* redenzione *f*; salvezza *f*; liberazione *f*.
redress [rə'dres] *n* riparazione *f*, soddisfazione *f*. *v* soddisfare, correggere.
reduce [rə'djuːs] *v* ridurre. **reduced** *adj* ridotto. **reduction** *n* riduzione *f*.
redundant [rə'dʌndənt] *adj* superfluo. **make redundant** (*employee*) mettere in cassa d'integrazione.
reed [riːd] *n* canna *f*; (*of musical instrument*) linguetta *f*.
reef [riːf] *n* scogliera *f*.
reek [riːk] *v* puzzare. *n* puzzo *m*.
reel[1] [riːl] *n* rocchetto *m*; (*fishing*) mulinello *m*; (*film*) rotolo *m*. *v* arrotolare. **reel off** rifilare.
reel[2] [riːl] *v* (*sway*) barcollare; (*of head*) girare.
refectory [rə'fektəri] *n* refettorio *m*.
refer [rə'fəː] *v* (*report, ascribe*) riferire; (*consult*) ricorrere, rivolgersi; (*send back*) rimandare. **referring to** con riferimento a. **reference** *n* riferimento *m*; (*testimonial*) referenza *f*, attestato *m*.
referee [refə'riː] *n* arbitro *m*. *v* arbitrare.
referendum [refə'rendəm] *n* referendum *m*.
refill ['riːfil] *n* refill *m invar*, pezzo di ricambio *m*.
refine [rə'fain] *v* raffinare. **refined** *adj* raffinato, squisito. **refinement** *n* (*tech*) raffinazione *f*; (*manners*) raffinatezza *f*. **refinery** *n* raffineria *f*.
reflation [rə'fleiʃn] *n* reflazione *f*.
reflect [rə'flekt] *v* riflettere; (*manifest*) rispecchiare. **reflection** *n* riflessione *f*. **on reflection** a pensarci su. **reflector** *n* riflettore *m*; (*of vehicle*) catarifrangente *m*.
reflex ['riːfleks] *nm*, *adj* riflesso. **reflexive** *adj* riflessivo.
reform [rə'foːm] *n* riforma *f*. *v* riformare, correggere. **reformation** *n* riforma *f*. **reformatory** *n* riformatorio *m*. **reformer** *n* riformatore, -trice *m*, *f*.
refract [rə'frakt] *v* rifrangere. **refraction** *n* rifrazione *f*.
refractory [rə'fraktəri] *adj* refrattario; (*stubborn*) ostinato.
refrain[1] [rə'frein] *v* astenersi, trattenersi.
refrain[2] [rə'frein] *n* ritornello *m*, ripresa *f*.
refresh [rə'freʃ] *v* rinfrescare, ristorare. **refresher course** corso di aggiornamento *m*. **refreshments** *pl n* rinfreschi *m pl*.
refrigerator [rə'fridʒəreitə] *n* frigorifero *m*.
refuel [riː'fjuːəl] *v* rifornirsi di carburante.
refuge ['refjuːdʒ] *n* rifugio *m*. **take refuge** rifugiarsi. **refugee** *n* profugo, -a *m*, *f*.
refund [ri'fʌnd; *n* 'riːfʌnd] *v* rimborsare. *n* rimborso *m*.
refuse[1] [rə'fjuːz] *v* rifiutare, dire di no; (*deny*) negare, respingere; (*prohibit*) vietare. **refusal** *n* rifiuto *m*; (*option*) diritto di opzione *m*.
refuse[2] ['refjuːs] *n* rifiuti *m pl*, immondizia *f*.
refute [ri'fjuːt] *v* confutare.
regain [ri'gein] *v* riacquistare, riprendere. **regain consciousness** riprendere i sensi, rianimarsi.
regal ['riːgəl] *adj* regale.
regard [rə'gaːd] *v* (*consider*) stimare; (*concern*) riguardare. *n* riguardo *m*; rispetto *m*; considerazione *f*; deferenza *f*. **with regard to** riguardo a, per quanto riguarda. **regardless of** senza badare *or* riguardo a.
regatta [rə'gatə] *n* regata *f*.
regent ['riːdʒənt] *n* reggente *m*. **regency** *n* reggenza *f*.

regime [rei'ʒiːm] *n* regime *m*.

regiment ['redʒimənt] *n* reggimento *m*. *v* irreggimentare. **regimental** *adj* reggimentale. **regimentation** *n* irreggimentazione *f*.

region ['riːdʒən] *n* regione *f*, zona *f*. **regional** *adj* regionale.

register ['redʒistə] *n* registro *m*; (*voting*) lista elettorale *f*; (*professional*) albo *m*. *v* registrare; (*show*) indicare; (*enter formally*) iscriversi. **registered letter** (lettera) raccomandata *f*. **registered office** sede legale *f*. **registrar** *n* segretario *m*; ufficiale di stato civile *m*. **registration** *n* registrazione *f*; iscrizione *f*. **registry office** ufficio di stato civile *m*.

regress [ri'gres] *v* regredire. **regression** *n* regressione *f*. **regressive** *adj* regressivo.

regret [rə'gret] *n* dispiacere *m*, rammarico *m*. **regrets** *pl n* (*sorrow*) rimorsi *m pl*; (*excuses*) scuse *f pl*. *v* rimpiangere, rammicarsi di. **regretful** *adj* spiacente. **regrettable** *adj* spiacevole.

regular ['regjulə] *adj* regolare. **regularity** *n* regolarità *f*.

regulate ['regjuleit] *v* regolare. **regulation** *n* regolamento *m*; (*rule*) regola *f*.

rehabilitate [riːhə'biliteit] *v* riabilitare. **rehabilitation** *n* riabilitazione *f*.

rehearse [rə'həːs] *v* (*theatre*) provare; (*enumerate*) ripetere, recitare. **rehearsal** *n* prova *f*. **dress rehearsal** prova generale *f*.

reign [rein] *n* regno *m*. *v* regnare; prevalere.

reimburse [riːim'bəːs] *v* rimborsare. **reimbursement** *n* rimborso *m*.

rein [rein] *n* redine *f*, briglia *f*. **give free rein to** dare libero sfogo a. *v* **rein in** frenare.

reincarnation [riːinkaː'neiʃən] *n* reincarnazione *f*.

reindeer ['reindiə] *n* renna *f*.

reinforce [riːin'foːs] *v* rinforzare. **reinforced concrete** cemento armato *m*. **reinforcement** *n* rinforzo *m*.

reinstate [ˌriːin'steit] *v* reintegrare. **reinstatement** *n* reintegrazione *f*.

reinvest [riːin'vest] *v* rinvestire.

reissue [riː'iʃuː] *n* nuova emissione *f*, ristampa *f*. *v* emettere di nuovo, ristampare.

reject [rə'dʒekt; *n* 'riːdʒekt] *v* rifiutare, respingere; (*discard*) scartare. *n* scarto *m*. **rejection** *n* rifiuto *m*.

rejoice [rə'dʒois] *v* rallegrarsi, gioire. **rejoicing** *n* allegrezza *f*, allegria *f*.

rejoin [rə'dʃoin] *v* (*join again*) ricongiungere; (*come back to*) tornare a; (*answer*) rispondere; (*law*) replicare. **rejoinder** *n* risposta *f*, replica *f*.

rejuvenate [rə'dʒuːvəneit] *v* ringiovanire. **rejuvenation** *n* ringiovanimento *m*.

relapse [rə'laps] *v* ricadere; (*med*) riammalarsi. *n* ricaduta *f*.

relate [rə'leit] *v* (*tell*) narrare; (*refer*) riferire, riguardare; (*be connected*) aver rapporto. **related** *adj* associato, congiunto; (*family*) parente.

relation [rə'leiʃn] *n* (*family*) parente *m*, *f*; (*connection*) rapporto *m*; (*narration*) racconto *m*. **relationship** *n* parentela *f*, rapporto *m*.

relative ['relətiv] *adj* relativo. **relative to** (*concerning*) riguardante. *n* parente *m*, *f*. **relativity** *n* relatività *f*.

relax [rə'laks] *v* rilassare, allentare; (*rest*) riposarsi. **relaxation** *n* distensione *f*, riposo *m*; (*entertainment*) svago *m*.

relay ['riːlei; *v* ri'lei] *n* (*shift*) turno *m*; (*elec*) relè *m invar*, soccorritore *m*; (*radio*) trasmissione *f*. **relay race** (corsa a) staffetta *f*. *v* trasmettere.

release [rə'liːs] *v* liberare, rimettere in libertà; (*launch*) lanciare; (*let go*) mollare; (*publication*) mettere in circolazione. *n* liberazione *f*; lancio *m*; (*press*) comunicato stampa *m*.

relent [rə'lent] *v* placarsi, cedere. **relentless** *adj* inesorabile, spietato.

relevant ['reləvənt] *adj* pertinente, a proposito. **relevance** *n* pertinenza *f*.

reliable [ri'laiəbl] *adj* fidato; sicuro; (*information*) attendibile. **reliability** *n* sicurezza *f*; (*person*) fidatezza *f*; attendibilità *f*.

relic ['relik] *n* reliquia *f*.

relief [rə'liːf] *n* (*alleviation*) sollievo *m*; (*help*) soccorso *m*; (*prominence*) rilievo *m*. **relief map** *n* plastico *m*, levata topografica *f*.

relieve [rə'liːv] *v* alleviare; (*help*) soccorrere. **feel relieved** sentirsi sollevato.

religion [rə'lidʒən] *n* religione *f*. **religious** *adj* religioso, devoto.

relinquish [rə'liŋkwiʃ] *v* abbandonare, rinunziare a.

relish ['reliʃ] *v* apprezzare, godere. *n* piacere *m*, godimento *m*.

reluctant [rəˈlʌktənt] *adj* restio, riluttante. **reluctance** *n* riluttanza *f*. **reluctantly** *adv* di malavoglia, a malincuore.
rely [rəˈlai] *v* contare, fare assegnamento, fidarsi (di).
remain [rəˈmein] *v* rimanere, restare. **remainder** *n* resto *m*, avanzo *m*. **remains** *pl n* resti *m pl*; (*mortal*) spoglie *f pl*.
remand [rəˈmaːnd] *v* rinviare. *n* rinvio *m*.
remark [rəˈmaːk] *n* nota *f*, osservazione *f*, commento *m*. *v* notare, osservare. **remarkable** *adj* notevole.
remarry [riːˈmari] *v* risposarsi.
remedy [ˈremədi] *n* rimedio *m*. *v* rimediare, correggere; (*heal*) curare. **remedial** *adj* (*school*) correttivo; (*law*) riparatore.
remember [riˈmembə] *v* ricordare, ricordarsi (di), rammentare. **remembrance** *n* memoria *f*, ricordo *m*.
remind [rəˈmaind] *v* ricordare, rammentare, richiamare alla mente. **reminder** *n* promemoria *m invar*, ricordo *m*.
reminiscence [reməˈnisens] *n* reminiscenza *f*. **reminiscent of** che rammenta.
remiss [rəˈmis] *adj* negligente, disattento.
remit [rəˈmit] *v* (*transmit*) rimettere; (*abate*) mitigare; (*send back*) rinviare; perdonare. **remittance** *n* rimessa *f*.
remnant [ˈremnənt] *n* scampolo *m*, resto *m*.
remorse [rəˈmoːs] *n* rimorso *m*. **remorseful** *adj* preso *or* tormentato dal rimorso. **remorseless** *adj* spietato.
remote [rəˈmout] *adj* remoto, lontano; (*faint*) pallido. **remote control** telecomando *m*.
remove [rəˈmuːv] *v* (*take off*) togliere; (*do away with*) eliminare; (*withdraw*) ritirare; (*move house*) traslocare. **removal** *n* (*house*) trasloco *m*; (*med*) ablazione *f*; (*act of removing*) rimozione *f*.
remunerate [rəˈmjuːnəreit] *v* ricompensare. **remuneration** *n* ricompensa *f*, rimunerazione *f*. **remunerative** *adj* rimunerativo.
renaissance [rəˈneisəns] *n* rinascimento *m*.
rename [riːˈneim] *v* rinominare.
render [ˈrendə] *v* rendere; rappresentare; (*give back*) restituire; (*cookery*) struggere, (*building*) incalcinare.
rendezvous [ˈrondivuː] *n* appuntamento *m*, convegno *m*.
renegade [ˈrenigeid] *n*, *adj* rinnegato, -a.
renew [rəˈnjuː] *v* rinnovare. **renewal** *n* rinnovamento *m*.
renounce [riˈnauns] *v* rinunciare a, ripudiare. **renouncement** *or* **renunciation** *n* rinunzia *f*.
renovate [ˈrenəveit] *v* rinnovare, ripristinare; (*buildings*) restaurare. **renovation** *n* ripristinamento *m*; restauro *m*.
renown [rəˈnaun] *n* fama *f*. **renowned** *adj* rinomato, famoso, celebre.
rent[1] [rent] *v* affittare; (*take, occupy*) prendere in affitto; (*let out*) dare in affitto. *n* affitto *m*.
rent[2] [rent] *n* (*tear*) strappo *m*, rottura *f*.
reopen [riːˈoupən] *v* riaprire. **reopening** *n* riapertura *f*.
reorganize [riːˈoːgənaiz] *v* riorganizzare. **reorganization** *n* riorganizzazione *f*.
rep[1] [rep] *n* (*coll*) teatro stabile, compagnia stabile *f*.
rep[2] [rep] *n* (*coll*) rappresentante *m*, *f*.
repair [riˈpeə] *v* riparare, aggiustare. *n* riparazione *f*. **beyond repair** irreparabile. **in good/bad repair** in buono/cattivo stato. **repairer** *n* riparatore, -trice *m*, *f*.
repartee [reparˈtiː] *n* battuta di spirito *f*.
repatriate [riːˈpatrieit] *v* rimpatriare. **repatriation** *n* rimpatrio *m*.
***repay** [riˈpei] *v* ripagare; (*refund*) rimborsare. **repayment** *n* rimborso *m*; ricompensa *f*.
repeal [rəˈpiːl] *v* revocare, annullare. *n* revoca *f*, annullamento *m*.
repeat [rəˈpiːt] *v* ripetere; (*food*) tornare a gola. *n* ripetizione *f*; (*music*) ripresa *f*.
repel [rəˈpel] *v* respingere. **repellent** *adj* repellente.
repent [rəˈpent] *v* pentirsi. **repentance** *n* penitenza *f*; (*regret*) pentimento *m*.
repercussion [riːpəˈkʌʃən] *n* ripercussione *f*.
repertoire [ˈrepətwaː] *n* repertorio *m*.
repertory [ˈrepətəri] *n* teatro stabile *m*. **repertory company** compagnia stabile *f*.
repetition [repəˈtiʃn] *n* ripetizione *f*. **repetitive** *adj* che si ripete.
replace [rəˈpleis] *v* rimpiazzare; (*put back*) rimettere a posto; sostituire. **replaceable** *adj* sostituibile. **replacement** *n* sostituzione *f*.
replay [ˈriːplei; *v* riːˈplei] *n* rivincita *f*. *v* fare la rivincita.
replenish [rəˈpleniʃ] *v* rifornire. **replenishment** *n* rifornimento *m*.

replica ['replikə] *n* facsimile *m invar*, copia *f*.
reply [rə'plai] *n* risposta *f*. *v* rispondere.
report [rə'poːt] *n* rapporto *m*, relazione *f*; (*school*) pagella *f*; (*rumour*) voce *f*; (*noise*) scoppio *m*. *v* (*relate*) riferire, fare un rapporto; denunciare; presentarsi. **reporter** *n* cronista *m*, *f*; reporter *m invar*.
repose [rə'pouz] *n* riposo *m*. *v* riposarsi.
reprehensible [repri'hensəbl] *adj* biasimevole, riprensibile.
represent [reprə'zent] *v* rappresentare; (*depict*) raffigurare. **representation** *n* rappresentazione *f*.
representative [reprə'zentətiv] *adj* rappresentativo, caratteristico. *m* rappresentante *m*, *f*; (*pol*) deputato, -a *m*, *f*.
repress [rə'pres] *v* reprimere. **repressed** *adj* represso. **repression** *n* repressione *f*. **repressive** *adj* repressivo.
reprieve [rə'priːv] *v* graziare. *n* grazia *f*.
reprimand ['reprimaːnd] *v* rimproverare, sgridare. *n* rimprovero *m*, predica *f*.
reprint [riː'print; *n* 'riːprint] *v* ristampare. *n* ristampa *f*.
reprisal [rə'praizəl] *n* rappresaglia *f*.
reproach [rə'proutʃ] *v* rimproverare, biasimare. *n* rimprovero *m*, biasimo *m*.
reproduce [riːprə'djuːs] *v* riprodurre. **reproduction** *n* riproduzione *f*. **reproductive** *adj* riproduttivo.
reprove [rə'pruːv] *v* rimproverare, sgridare. **reproof** *n* rimprovero *m*.
reptile ['reptail] *n* rettile *m*.
republic [rə'pʌblik] *n* repubblica *f*. **republican** *n*, *adj* repubblicano, -a.
repudiate [rə'pjuːdieit] *v* ripudiare; (*disown*) disconoscere; (*reject*) respingere. **repudiation** *n* ripudio *m*.
repugnant [rə'pʌgnənt] *adj* ripugnante. **repugnance** *n* ripugnanza *f*.
repulsion [rə'pʌlʃn] *n* ripulsione *f*, ripugnanza *f*. **repulsive** *adj* ributtante, schifoso.
repute [rə'pjuːt] *v* reputare, stimare. *n also* **reputation** reputazione *f*, fama *f*. **reputable** *adj* rispettabile, stimabile, onorevole. **reputedly** *adv* presumibilmente.
request [ri'kwest] *n* richiesta *f*, domanda *f*. *v* richiedere, domandare, sollecitare.
requiem ['rekwiəm] *n* requiem *m invar*.
require [rə'kwaiə] *v* richiedere; (*demand*) esigere, pretendere; rendere necessario. **requirement** *n* esigenza *f*, bisogno *m*.
requisite ['rekwizit] *adj* necessario, indispensabile. *n* requisito *m*.
requisition [ˌrekwi'ziʃən] *v* requisire. *n* (*mil*) requisizione *f*, ordine *m*.
re-route [riː'ruːt] *v* deviare.
resale [riː'seil] *n* rivendita *f*.
rescue ['reskjuː] *n* salvataggio *m*, soccorso *m*. *v* liberare; soccorrere. **rescuer** *n* liberatore, -trice *m*, *f*; soccorritore, -trice *m*, *f*.
research [ri'səːtʃ] *n* ricerca *f*, indagine *f*. *v* fare *or* compiere ricerche, indagare. **researcher** *n* ricercatore, -trice *m*, *f*.
resemble [rə'zembl] *v* somigliare, rassomigliare. **resemblance** *n* somiglianza *f*, rassomiglianza *f*.
resent [ri'zent] *v* risentirsi di, offendersi *or* sdegnarsi per. **resentful** *adj* offeso, sdegnoso. **resentment** *n* risentimento *m*, sdegno *m*, rancore *m*.
reserve [rə'zəːv] *v* riservare. *n* riserva *f*; (*manner*) riserbo *m*; (*circumspection*) riservatezza *f*. **reservation** *n* riserva *f*; (*booking*) prenotazione *f*.
reservoir ['rezəvwaː] *n* cisterna *f*, serbatoio *m*; (*artificial lake*) lago artificiale *m*, bacino di riserva *m*.
reside [rə'zaid] *v* dimorare, risiedere. **residence** *n* residenza *f*, dimora *f*. **residence permit** permesso di soggiorno *m*. **resident** *n*(*m*+*f*), *adj* residente. **residential** *adj* residenziale.
residue ['rezidjuː] *n* residuo *m*. **residual** *adj* residuo, rimanente.
resign [rə'zain] *v* dimettersi, rassegnare le dimissioni; (*surrender*) rinunciare a. **resign oneself to** rassegnarsi a. **resignation** *n* dimissioni *f pl*, rassegnazione *f*. **resigned** *adj* rassegnato.
resilient [rə'ziliənt] *adj* flessibile. **be resilient** (*person*) aver capacità di ricupero. **resilience** *n* flessibilità *f*, resilienza *f*; capacità di ricupero *f*.
resin ['rezin] *n* resina *f*. **resinous** *adj* resinoso.
resist [rə'zist] *v* resistere (a). **resistance** *n* resistenza *f*. **resistant** *adj* resistente.
***resit** [riː'sit] *v* ripetere.
resolute ['rezəluːt] *adj* deciso, risoluto. **resolution** *n* risoluzione *f*; (*determination*) risolutezza *f*; decisione *f*.
resolve [rə'zolv] *v* risolvere; decidere; (*clear up*) chiarire. *n* decisione *f*.

resonant ['rezənənt] *adj* risonante. **resonance** *n* risonanza *f.*

resort [rə'zoːt] *v* **resort** to ricorrere a. *n* (*recourse*) ricorso *m*; (*expedient*) risorsa *f*; (*holiday, etc.*) luogo di soggiorno *m*, stazione di villeggiatura *f.*

resound [rə'zaund] *v* risonare, echeggiare.

resource [rə'zoːs] *n* risorsa *f.* **resourceful** *adj* pieno di risorse, ingegnoso.

respect [rə'spekt] *v* rispettare, aver riguardo per. *n* rispetto *m*; (*esteem*) stima *f*, riguardo *m*; (*detail*) aspetto *m*. **pay one's respects to** rendere omaggio a. **with due respect** coi debiti riguardi. **with respect to** riguardo a, quanto a. **respectable** *adj* rispettabile; onesto; considerevole. **respectful** *adj* rispettoso. **respectively** *adv* rispettivamente.

respiration [respə'reiʃn] *n* respirazione *f.* **respirator** *n* (*med*) respiratore *m*; (*gas mask*) maschera antigas *f.* **respiratory** *adj* respiratorio.

respite ['respait] *n* tregua *f*, proroga *f.*

respond [rə'spond] *v* rispondere; reagire. **respondent** *n* (*law*) imputato, -a *m, f.* **response** *n* risposta *f*; reazione *f*; (*church*) responsorio *m*. **responsive** *adj* sensibile.

responsible [rə'sponsəbl] *adj* responsabile. **responsibility** *n* responsabilità *f.*

rest[1] [rest] *v* riposarsi; (*place*) posare; (*stay*) stare, fermarsi. *n* riposo; (*support*) appoggio *m*. **restful** *adj* riposante, tranguillo. **restive** *adj* restio. **restless** *adj* inquieto, irrequieto.

rest[2] [rest] *n* resto *m*.

restaurant ['restront] *n* ristorante *m*, trattoria *f.* **restaurant car** vagone ristorante *m*.

restore [rə'stoː] *v* ristabilire; (*building, etc.*) restaurare. **restoration** *n* ristabilimento *m*; restauro *m*; (*history*) restaurazione *f.*

restrain [rə'strein] *v* trattenere, reprimere, frenare. **restraint** *n* freno *m*, ritegno *m*; limitazione *f.*

restrict [rə'strikt] *v* restringere, limitare. **restriction** *n* restrizione *f*, limitazione *f.* **restrictive** *adj* restrittivo.

result [rə'zʌlt] *n* risultato *m*, esito *m*. *v* risultare, derivare. **resultant** *adj* risultante.

resume [rə'zjuːm] *v* riprendere; riassumere. **resumption** *n* ripresa *f.*

résumé ['reizumei] *n* riassunto *m*.

resurgence [ri'səːdʒəns] *n* risurrezione *f*, rinascita *f.*

resurrect [rezə'rekt] *v* risuscitare. **resurrection** *n* risurrezione *f.*

resuscitate [rə'sʌsəteit] *v* risuscitare.

retail ['riːteil] *n* vendita al dettaglio *or* minuto *f. v* (*sell*) vendere al dettaglio *or* minuto; (*tell*) raccontare, dettagliare. *adv, adj* al dettaglio *or* minuto. **retailer** *n* dettagliante *m*.

retain [rə'tein] *v* ritenere, mantenere. **retainer** (*law*) caparra *f.*

retaliate [rə'talieit] *v* contraccambiare, rendere la pariglia. **retaliation** *n* contraccambio *m*, rappresaglia *f.*

retard [rə'taːd] *v* ritardare, ostacolare. **retarded** *adj* tardivo.

retch [retʃ] *v* aver conati di vomito.

reticent ['retisənt] *adj* reticente, riservato, taciturno. **reticence** *n* reticenza *f*, riservatezza *f*, taciturnità *f.*

retina ['retinə] *n* retina *f.*

retinue ['retinjuː] *n* seguito *m*.

retire [rə'taiə] *v* ritirarsi; (*go to bed*) andare a letto; (*give up work*) andare in pensione. **retired** *adj* in pensione, a riposo; (*withdrawn*) ritirato, appartato. **retirement** *n* ritirata *f*; riposo *m*.

retort[1] [rə'toːt] *v* ribattere, rimbeccare. *n* (*reply*) ritorsione *f*, rimbecco *m*.

retort[2] [rə'toːt] *n* (*chem*) storta *f.*

retrace [ri'treis] *v* (*follow up*) rintracciare; (*go back over*) ripercorrere; risalire alle origini di.

retract [rə'trakt] *v* (*withdraw*) ritirare, far rientrare; (*disown*) disdire.

retreat [rə'triːt] *n* ritiro *m*; rifugio *m*, asilo *m*; (*mil*) ritirata *f. v* ritirarsi, indietreggiare.

retrieve [rə'triːv] *v* ricuperare; riparare; rimediare. **retrieval** *n* ricupero *m*. **retriever** *n* (*dog*) cane da riporto *m*.

retrograde ['retrəgreid] *adj* retrogrado.

retrospect ['retrəspekt] *n* **in retrospect** guardando indietro. **retrospective** *adj* retrospettivo.

return [rə'təːn] *v* tornare, ritornare; (*put back*) rimettere; (*reciprocate*) contraccambiare; (*give back*) restituire; (*send back*) rinviare. *n* ritorno *m*; restituzione *f*; rinvio *m*; (*profit*) utile *m*; (*report*) relazione *f*, rapporto *m*; (*statement*) rendiconto *m*. **by return of post** a giro di posta. **in return for** in cambio di. **return**

match rivincita *f*. **return ticket** biglietto di andata e ritorno *m*.
reunite [riːju'nait] *v* riunire. **reunion** *n* riunione *f*.
rev [rev] *v* (*mot*) imballare. *n* giro *m*. **rev counter** contagiri *m invar*.
reveal [rə'viːl] *v* rivelare, manifestare. **revelation** *n* rivelazione *f*.
revel ['revl] *v* (*take pleasure*) trovar diletto; (*make merry*) far baldoria. *n also* **revelry** baldoria *f*.
revenge [rə'vendʒ] *n* vendetta *f*. *v* vendicare.
revenue ['revinjuː] *n* (*income*) rendita *f*; (*yield*) reddito *m*; (*of state*) erario *m*; (*department*) fisco *m*.
reverberate [rə'vəːbəreit] *v* (*sound*) risonare, riecheggiare; (*heat, light*) riverberare. **reverberation** *n* riverberazione *f*.
reverence ['revərəns] *n* riverenza *f*, venerazione *f*. **reverend** *nm, adj* reverendo. **reverent** *adj* riverente. **reverential** *adj* reverenziale.
reverse [rə'vəːs] *v* rovesciare; (*inside out*) rivoltare; (*mot*) far marcia indietro. **reverse the charges** addebitare al destinatario. *adj* contrario, rovescio, inverso. *n* contrario *m*, rovescio *m*, inverso *m*; (*mot*) retromarcia *f*. **reversal** *n* rovesciamento *m*; (*law*) revoca *f*. **reversible** *adj* reversibile; (*law*) revocabile; (*fabric*) a due diritti.
revert [rə'vəːt] *v* ritornare.
review [rə'vjuː] *n* (*survey*) rassegna *f*, esame *m*; critica *f*, recensione *f*; (*mil, periodical*) rivista *f*. *v* riesaminare; fare la critica di; passare in rivista. **reviewer** *n* critico *m*.
revise [rə'vaiz] *v* rivedere, correggere. **revision** *n* revisione *f*.
revive [rə'vaiv] *v* rianimare, risvegliare; (*restore to use*) ripristinare. **revival** *n* risveglio *m*; ripristino *m*; (*theatre*) ripresa *f*.
revoke [rə'vouk] *v* revocare.
revolt [rə'voult] *v* ribellarsi; (*feel disgust*) provare orrore; (*cause disgust*) disgustare. **revolting** *adj* rivoltante, disgustoso; (*rebellious*) ribelle.
revolution [revə'luːʃən] *n* rivoluzione *f*; (*turn*) giro *m*. **revolutionary** *n, adj* revoluzionario, -a.
revolve [rə'volv] *v* (*turn*) girare; (*depend*) basarsi (su), dipendere (da). **revolver** *n* rivoltella *f*. **revolving** *adj* (*door*) girevole; (*credit*) rotativo.
revue [rə'vjuː] *n* rivista *f*.
revulsion [rə'vʌlʃən] *n* ripugnanza *f*, disgusto *m*; (*med*) revulsione *f*.
reward [rə'woːd] *n* ricompensa *f*, compenso *m*. *v* ricompensare, rimunerare. **rewarding** *adj* rimunerativo.
rhetoric ['retərik] *n* retorica *f*. **rhetorical** *adj* retorico.
rheumatism ['ruːmətizəm] *n* reumatismo *m*. **rheumatic** *adj* reumatico.
Rhine [rain] *n* Reno *m*.
rhinoceros [rai'nosərəs] *n* rinoceronte *m*.
rhododendron [roudə'dendrən] *n* rododendro *m*.
rhombus ['rombəs] *n* rombo *m*.
rhubarb ['ruːbaːb] *n* rabarbaro *m*.
rhyme [raim] *n* rima *f*. *v* rimare, far rima.
rhythm ['riðəm] *n* ritmo *m*. **rhythmic** *adj* ritmico.
rib [rib] *n* costola *f*. **ribbed** *adj* a coste, scanalato.
ribbon ['ribən] *n* nastro *m*. **torn to ribbons** ridotto a brandelli.
rice [rais] *n* riso *m*.
rich [ritʃ] *adj* ricco; (*full*) pieno, abbondante; (*food*) pesante; (*colour*) intenso. **riches** *pl n* ricchezza *f sing*. **richness** *n* ricchezza *f*.
rickety ['rikəti] *adj* traballante, instabile; (*med*) rachitico.
***rid** [rid] *v* liberare, sbarazzare. **get rid of** sbarazzarsi di. **good riddance!** che liberazione!
ridden ['ridn] *V* **ride**.
riddle[1] ['ridl] *n* indovinello *m*, enigma *m*. **speak in riddles** parlare per enigmi.
riddle[2] ['ridl] *v* crivellare.
***ride** [raid] *n* (*on horseback*) passeggiata a cavallo *f*; (*on bicycle*) passeggiata in bicicletta *f*; (*in vehicle*) corsa *f*, giro *m*. **take for a ride** (*make fun of*) prendere in giro; (*deceive*) imbrogliare. *v* cavalcare, andare a cavallo. **rider** *n* (*horse*) cavallerizzo, -a *m, f*; ciclista *m, f*; motociclista *m, f*; (*additional clause*) clausola aggiunta *f*, codicillo *m*. **riding school** maneggio *m*.
ridge [ridʒ] *n* (*geog*) cresta *f*; (*raised strip*) costa *f*; (*roof*) colmo *m*; (*meteorology*) espansione di alta pressione *f*. *v* corrugare, incresparsi.
ridicule ['ridikjuːl] *v* mettere in ridicolo, canzonare. *n* ridicolo *m*. **be an object of**

ridicule esser posto in ridicolo. **ridiculous** *adj* ridicolo, assurdo.
rife [raif] *adj* diffuso, corrente.
rifle[1] ['raifl] *n* fucile *m*. **rifle-range** *n* poligono di tiro *m*.
rifle[2] ['raifl] *v* svaligiare. **rifle through** rovistare *or* frugare in.
rift [rift] *n* crepa *f*, spacco *m*; (*in relations*) disaccordo *m*, screzio *m*; (*geol*) falda *f*.
rig [rig] *n* (*naut*) attrezzatura *f*; (*industry*) impianto *m*; (*fraudulent dealing*) broglio *m*, manipolazione *f*. *v* attrezzare; (*equip*) montare; manipolare, manovrare.
right [rait] *adj* corretto, giusto; (*geom*) retto; (*not left*) destro. **be right** aver ragione. **right-angled** *adj* ad angolo retto. **right-hand man** braccio destro *m*. **right wing** (*pol*) destra *f*. **right-winger** *n* persona di destra *f*. *n* bene *m*, giusto *m*; (*law*) diritto *m*; (*not left*) destra *f*. **right of way** (*vehicles*) precedenza *f*; (*law*) servità di passaggio *f*; (*path*) passaggio pubblico *m*. *adv* bene; (*exactly*) proprio; direttamente; completamente; (*direction*) a destra. **right away** subito. *v* (*restore to position*) raddrizzare; (*correct*) aggiustare, accomodare, metere a posto; (*redress*) riparare. **rightful** *adj* legittimo. **rightly** *adv* giustamente.
righteous ['raitʃəs] *adj* retto, giusto. **righteousness** *n* rettitudine *f*.
rigid ['ridʒid] *adj* rigido, inflessibile, rigoroso. **rigidity** *n* rigidezza *f*; (*stiffness*) rigidità *f*.
rigmarole ['rigməroul] *n* (*long procedure*) trafila *f*; (*nonsense*) filastrocca *f*.
rigour ['rigə] *n* rigore *m*. **rigorous** *adj* rigoroso, rigido.
rim [rim] *n* orlo *m*, bordo *m*; (*of wheel*) cerchio *m*; (*of spectacles*) montatura *f*.
rind [raind] *n* (*fruit*) buccia *f*, scorza *f*; (*cheese*) crosta *f*.
ring[1] [riŋ] *n* anello *m*; (*enclosure*) recinto *m*, pista *f*; (*boxing*) quadrato *m*, ring *m invar*. *v* cingere, circondare. **ringlet** *n* (*curl*) ricciolo *m*.
***ring**[2] [riŋ] *n* (*sound*) suono *m*, squillo *m*; (*inherent quality*) tono *m*; (*coll*) telefonata *f*, colpo di telefono *m*. *v* suonare; (*echo*) risonare, echeggiare; telefonare (a).
rink [riŋk] *n* pista di pattinaggio *f*.
rinse [rins] *v* sciacquare, risciacquare. *n* risciacquatura *f*; (*hair*) cachet *m*.
riot ['raiət] *n* rivolta *f*, sommossa *f*; (*uproar*) baccano *m*, fracasso *m*; (*profusion*) orgia *f*. **riot squad** squadra mobile *or* volante *f*. *v* insorgere, far baccano. **riotous** *adj* tumultuoso; (*noisy*) chiassoso, clamoroso; dissoluto.
rip [rip] *n* strappo *m*, squarcio *m*. *v* strappare, squarciare. **let rip** (*give vent to*) dare libero sfogo a.
ripe [raip] *adj* maturo. **ripen** *v* (far) maturare. **ripeness** *n* maturità *f*. **ripening** *n* maturazione *f*.
ripple ['ripl] *n* increspamento *m*, crespa *f*; (*sound*) mormorio *m*. *v* increspare, mormorare.
***rise** [raiz] *v* sorgere; (*get up*) alzarsi, levarsi; (*increase*) aumentare, salire; (*swell*) gonfiarsi; (*rebel*) insorgere. *n* salita *f*; aumento *m*. **give rise to** causare.
risen ['rizn] *V* **rise**.
risk [risk] *v* rischiare, arrischiare, correre il rischio di. *n* rischio *m*. **at the risk of** a rischio di. **risky** *adj* rischioso.
rissole ['risoul] *n* polpetta *f*, crocchetta *f*.
rite [rait] *n* rito *m*.
ritual ['ritʃuəl] *nm*, *adj* rituale.
rival ['raivəl] *n*(*m*+*f*), *adj* rivale. *v* rivaleggiare, competere. **rivalry** *n* rivalità *f*.
river ['rivə] *n* fiume *m*.
rivet ['rivit] *n* rivetto *m*. *v* rivettare. **riveting** *adj* affascinante.
road [roud] *n* strada *f*, via *f*. **road-block** *n* posto di blocco *m*. **road sign** cartello stradale *m*. **road-works** *pl n* lavori stradali *m pl*. **roadworthy** *adj* atto a prendere la strada.
roam [roum] *v* vagare, errare.
roar [roː] *v* (*wild beast*) ruggire, urlare; (*sea*) muggire. **roar with laughter** scoppiare dalle risa. *n* ruggito *m*, urlo *m*; muggito *m*; (*thunder*) rombo *m*; (*laughter*) scroscio *m*.
roast [roust] *v* arrostire; (*coffee*) tostare. *n* arrosto *m*.
rob [rob] *v* derubare, rapinare; (*plunder*) svaligiare. **robber** *n* ladro *m*, rapinatore *m*. **robbery** *n* rapina *f*. **armed robbery** rapina a mano armata *f*.
robe [roub] *n* abito lungo *m*, toga *f*.
robin ['robin] *n* pettirosso *m*.
robot ['roubot] *n* automa *m*.
robust [rə'bʌst] *adj* robusto.
rock[1] [rok] *n* (*stone*) roccia *f*, scoglio *m*; (*support*) rocca *f*. **on the rocks** (*coll*: *without money*) al verde; (*coll*: *with ice*) con

ghiaccio. **rock-bottom** *adj* bassissimo. **rock-crystal** *n* cristallo di rocca *m*. **rock-salt** *n* salgemma *m*. **rocky** *adj* roccioso.
rock² [rok] *v* dondolare, oscillare; (*baby*) cullare. **off one's rocker** (*coll*) matto. **rocking-chair** *n* sedia a dondolo *f*. **rocking-horse** *n* cavallo a dondolo *m*.
rocket ['rokit] *n* razzo *m*; (*reprimand*) cicchetto *m*. *v* (*increase sharply*) andare alle stelle.
rod [rod] *n* bastone *m*, stecca *f*; (*fishing*) canna (da pesca) *f*; (*piston*) biella *f*.
rode [roud] *V* **ride.**
rodent ['roudənt] *nm*, *adj* roditore.
roe¹ [rou] *n* (*deer*) capriolo *m*.
roe² [rou] *n* (*hard*) uova di pesce *f pl*; (*soft*) latte di pesce *m*.
rogue [roug] *n* (*dishonest person*) mariolo *m*; (*rascal*) briccone *m*, furfante *m*. **roguery** *n* bricconeria *f*. **roguish** *adj* bricconesco; (*mischievous*) furbo.
role [roul] *n* ruolo *m*, funzione *f*.
roll [roul] *v* rullare; (*wave*) ondeggiare; (*rotate*) roteare; (*ship*) rollare. **be rolling in money** guazzare nel denaro. **roll out** (*pastry*) spianare. **roll up** arrotolare. *n* rotolo *m*; (*bread*) panino *m*. **roll-call** *n* appello *m*. **roller** *n* cilindro *m*, rullo *m*. **roller-skate** *n* schettino *m*, pattino a rotelle *m*. **rolling-pin** *n* matterello *m*.
romance [rou'mans] *n* romanzo (cavalleresco) *m*; (*medieval tale*) romanza *f*; (*love affair*) idillio *m*, avventura amorosa *f*. **romantic** *adj* romantico; (*fanciful*) romanzesco.
Romania [ruː'meinjə] *n* Romania *f*. **Romanian** *n*, *adj* romeno, -a.
Rome [roum] *n* Roma *f*. **Roman** *n*, *adj* romano, -a. **Roman Catholic** *adj* cattolico (romano).
romp [romp] *v* giocare rumorosamente, ruzzare. **romp home** (*win easily*) vincere facilmente. **romp through** (*exam*) superare con facilità. *n* trambusto *m*; (*coll*) cagnara *f*.
roof [ruːf] *n*, *pl* **-s** tetto *m*. **hit the roof** (*coll*) andare su tutte le furie. **roof of the mouth** palato *m*.
rook [ruk] *n* (*bird*) corvo *m*; (*chess*) torre *f*; (*swindler*) truffatore, -trice *m*, *f*. *v* barare, truffare.
room [ruːm] *n* stanza *f*, sala *f*, camera *f*; (*space*) posto *m*, spazio *m*; opportunità *f*. **room temperature** temperatura ambiente *f*. *v* alloggiare. **roomy** *adj* spazioso, vasto.
roost [ruːst] *n* (*building*) pollaio *m*; (*pole*) posatoio *m*. **rule the roost** fare il gallo del pollaio. *v* appollaiarsi.
root¹ [ruːt] *n* radice *f*; (*cause*) fondo *m*. **root and branch** radicalmente. **root cause** causa prima *f*. **take root** mettere radice. *v* piantare, abbarbicare; (*become fixed*) mettere radici, radicare.
root² [ruːt] *v* grufolare; (*search*) frugacchiare. **root for** (*slang*) sostenere. **root out** scovare.
rope [roup] *n* corda *f*, fune *f*. **know the ropes** esser pratico, saperla lunga. **learn the ropes** familiarizzarsi.
rosary ['rouzəri] *n* rosario *m*.
rose¹ [rouz] *V* **rise.**
rose² [rouz] *n* rosa *f*. **rose-bush** *n* rosa *f*, rosaio *m*. **rosy** *adj* roseo.
rosé ['rouzei] *n* rosato *m*.
rosemary ['rouzməri] *n* rosmarino *m*.
rosette [rou'zet] *n* coccarda *f*, rosetta *f*.
roster ['rostə] *n* turno di servizio *m*; (*mil*) ruolino *m*.
rostrum ['rostrəm] *n* tribuna *f*, piattaforma *f*.
rot [rot] *v* putrefare, marcire; (*teeth, wood*) cariare. *n* putrefazione *f*; (*rotten matter*) marciume *m*; (*coll*: *nonsense*) sciocchezze *f pl*; declino *m*. **rotten** *adj* marcio; (*coll*: *annoying*) seccante.
rota ['routə] *n* turno (di servizio) *m*, lista *f*.
rotate [rou'teit] *v* rotare; (*crops*) avvicendare. **rotary** *adj* (*motion*) rotatorio; (*tech*) rotativo. **rotation** *n* rotazione *f*; avvicendamento *m*.
rouge [ruːʒ] *n* belletto *m*, rossetto *m*.
rough [rʌf] *adj* (*coarse*) ruvido; (*person*) rozzo; (*ground*) malagevole, irregolare; violento; (*sea, weather*) agitato, tempestoso; approssimativo; (*unrefined*) greggio. **rough-and-ready** *adj* improvvisato. **rough-and-tumble** *n* zuffa *f*, mischia *f*. *v* **rough it** vivere primitivamente. **rough out** abbozzare. **roughen** *v* irruvidire. **roughness** *n* ruvidezza *f*.
roulette [ruː'let] *n* roulette *f*.
round [raund] *adj* tondo, rotondo; circolare; sferico. *prep* tutto intorno a. *n* tondo *m*, cerchio *m*; (*tour*) giro *m*; (*game*) partita *f*; (*boxing*) ripresa *f*; (*ammunition*) scarica *f*; (*applause*) salva *f*. *adv* in giro. **all year round** tutto l'anno. **show round** fare da guida a. *v* **round off**

completare. **round up** (*number*) arrotondare.

roundabout ['raundəbaut] *n* anello stradale *m*. *adj* indiretto, obliquo.

rouse [rauz] *v* destare. **rousing** *adj* stimolante.

route [ruːt] *n* strada *f*, rotta *f*. **en route** per strada.

routine [ruː'tiːn] *n* uso *m*, abitudine *f*.

rove [rouv] *v* errare, vagabondare.

row[1] [rou] *n* fila *f*.

row[2] [rou] *v* remare. *n* remata *f*. **rowing boat** barca a remi *f*.

row[3] [rau] *n* (*quarrel*) rissa *f*, lite *f*; (*noise*) chiasso *m*, baccano *m*. *v* litigarsi.

rowdy ['raudi] *adj* chiassoso, turbolento. *n* attaccabrighe *m*, *f invar*.

royal ['roiəl] *adj* reale, regio, regale. **royalist** *n*(*m*+*f*), *adj* realista. **royalties** *pl n* diritti d'autore *m pl*. **royalty** *n* (*people*) reali *m pl*; (*status*) regalità *f*, dignità di re *f*.

rub [rʌb] *v* fregare, strofinare. **rub down** (*clean*) pulire fregando; (*dry*) asciugare fregando. **rub out** cancellare. **rub shoulders** venire in contatto.

rubber ['rʌbə] *n* gomma *f*, caucciù *m*.

rubbish ['rʌbiʃ] *n* (*waste*) immondizia *f*; (*derog*) robaccia *f*; (*nonsense*) sciocchezze *f pl*. **rubbish bin** pattumiera *f*.

rubble ['rʌbl] *n* frantumi *m pl*, macerie *f pl*.

ruby ['ruːbi] *n* rubino *m*. *adj* (color) rubino *or* vermiglio.

rucksack ['rʌksak] *n* sacco da montagna *m*, zaino *m*.

rudder ['rʌdə] *n* timone *m*.

rude [ruːd] *adj* (*discourteous*) scortese; (*unmannerly*) rozzo, grossolano; (*sturdy*) robusto. **rudeness** *n* scortesia *f*; grossolanità *f*; robustezza *f*.

rudiment ['ruːdimənt] *n* rudimento *m*.

rueful ['ruːfəl] *adj* triste, lamentevole.

ruff [rʌf] *n* gorgiera *f*.

ruffian ['rʌfiən] *n* ruffiano *m*, farabutto *m*.

ruffle ['rʌfl] *v* arruffare, increspare.

rug [rʌg] *n* tappeto *m*; (*travelling*) coperta da viaggio *f*; (*bedside*) scendiletto *m*.

rugby ['rʌgbi] *n* rugby *m invar*, palla ovale *f*.

rugged ['rʌgid] *adj* irregolare; rude.

ruin ['ruːin] *n* rovina *f*. *v* rovinare. **ruinous** *adj* rovinoso.

rule [ruːl] *n* regola *f*, norma *f*; (*ruler*) regolo *m*. **as a rule** di regola *or* solito. *v* regolare, dirigere; decidere, (*mark with lines*) rigare. **rule out** escludere. **ruler** *n* sovrano *m*, governatore *m*; (*school*) regolo *m*. **ruling** *n* direttiva *f*, decisione *f*.

rum [rʌm] *n* rum *m*.

rumble ['rʌmbl] *v* rimbombare, brontolare; (*stomach*) gorgogliare; (*coll*: *detect*) scoprire. *n* brontolio *m*, gorgoglio *m*.

rummage ['rʌmidʒ] *v* frugare, rovistare.

rummy ['rʌmi] *n* ramino *m*.

rumour ['ruːmə] *n* diceria *f*, voce *f*. *v* far correre voce.

rump [rʌmp] *n* groppa *f*, culatta *f*. **rump steak** bistecca *f*.

***run** [rʌn] *n* corsa *f*; (*outing*) gita *f*; serie *f invar*; durata *f*. **in the long run** a lungo andare. **on the run** in fuga. *v* correre; (*flow*) scorrere; funzionare; (*colour*) spandere; (*stockings*) smagliare; (*manage*) dirigere. **run away** *or* **off** fuggire. **runaway** *n*, *adj* fuggiasco, -a. **run down** (*slow*) rallentarsi; (*car, etc.*) investire; (*disparage*) parlar male di; (*find*) trovare. **run in** rodare. **run into** (*encounter*) incontrare per caso, imbattersi; (*collide with*) urtare; (*amount to*) raggiungere. **run out** (*supplies, etc.*) esaurirsi. **run over** (*car, etc.*) investire; (*overflow*) traboccare; (*rehearse*) ripassare. **runway** *n* pista di decollo *or* atterraggio *f*. **runner** *n* corridore *m*; (*messenger*) fattorino *m*; (*carpet*) passatoia *f*; (*plant*) pollone *m*. **runner bean** fagiolo (rampicante) *m*. **runner-up** *n* secondo arrivato, seconda arrivata *m*, *f*.

rung[1] [rʌŋ] *n* piolo *m*.

rung[2] [rʌŋ] *V* **ring**[2].

running ['rʌniŋ] *n* corsa *f*; funzionamento *m*; (*competition*) gara *f*. **be in the running** aver possibilità di vincere. **make the running** fare l'andatura. *adj* funzionante; regolare; consecutivo.

rupture ['rʌptʃə] *n* rottura *f*; (*med*) ernia *f*. *v* rompere.

rural ['ruərəl] *adj* campestre, rurale.

rush[1] [rʌʃ] *v* precipitarsi, avventarsi; (*convey with haste*) precipitare, spostare in fretta. *n* corsa precipitosa *f*; (*intense activity*) trambusto *m*; (*haste*) fretta e furia *f*; (*sudden coming*) accesso *m*. **rush hour** ora di punta *f*.

rush[2] [rʌʃ] *n* (*plant*) giunco *m*.

rusk [rʌsk] *n* biscotto (non dolce) *m*.

Russia ['rʌʃə] *n* Russia *f.* **Russian** *n, adj* russo, -a.
rust [rʌst] *n* ruggine *f.* **rustproof** *adj* inossidabile. *v* arrugginirsi. **rusty** *adj* arrugginito, rugginoso; (*out of practice*) fuori d'esercizio.
rustic ['rʌstik] *adj* rustico.
rustle ['rʌsl] *n* fruscio *m. v* frusciare, stormire.
rut [rʌt] *n* solco *m,* carreggiata *f;* (*fixed habit*) abitudine fissa *f.*
ruthless ['ruːθlis] *adj* spietato, implacabile.
rye [rai] *n* segala *f.*

S

sabbatical [sə'batikəl] *adj* sabbatico.
sable ['seibl] *n* zibellino *m. adj* di zibellino.
sabotage ['sabətaːʒ] *n* sabotaggio *m. v* sabotare. **saboteur** *n* sabotatore, -trice *m, f.*
sabre ['seibə] *n* sciabola *f.* **sabre-rattling** *n* minaccia di guerra *f,* bravata *f.*
saccharin ['sakərin] *n* saccarina *f.*
sachet ['saʃei] *n* sacchetto profumato *m.*
sack [sak] *n* sacco *m;* (*coll; dismissal*) licenziamento *m.* **get the sack** (*coll*) essere mandato a spasso. *v* (*coll*) mandare a spasso.
sacrament ['sakrəmənt] *n* sacramento *m.* **sacramental** *adj* sacramentale.
sacred ['seikrid] *adj* sacro, sacrosanto.
sacrifice ['sakrifais] *n* sacrificio *m;* (*comm*) perdita *f. v* sacrificare; (*comm*) vendere sottocosto.
sacrilege ['sakrəlidʒ] *n* sacrilegio *m.* **sacrilegious** *adj* sacrilego (*m pl* -ghi).
sad [sad] *adj* triste. **sadden** *v* rattristare. **sadness** *n* tristezza *f.*
saddle ['sadl] *n* sella *f. v* sellare.
sadism ['seidizəm] *n* sadismo *m.* **sadist** *n* sadico, -a *m, f.* **sadistic** *adj* sadico.
safe [seif] *adj* sicuro; (*unharmed*) salvo; innocuo. **safe and sound** sano e salvo. **safe-conduct** *n* salvacondotto *m.* **safeguard** *v* salvaguardare; proteggere. **safe keeping** custodia *f. n* cassaforte *f.* **safety** *n* sicurezza *f,* salvezza *f.* **safety-belt** *n* cintura di sicurezza *f.* **safety-catch** *n* sicura *f.* **safety-pin** *n* spillo di sicurezza *m.*
saffron ['safrən] *n* zafferano *m.*
sag [sag] *v* incurvarsi, piegarsi.
saga ['saːgə] *n* saga *f.*
sage[1] [seidʒ] *n, adj* saggio, -a. **sagacious** *adj* sagace, avveduto.
sage[2] [seidʒ] *n* (*herb*) salvia *f.*
Sagittarius [sadʒi'teəriəs] *n* Sagittario *m.*
sago ['seigou] *n* sagù *m.*
said [sed] *V* **say.**
sail [seil] *v* navigare; (*leave*) salpare. *n* vela *f.* **sailcloth** *n* tela olona *f.* **sailing** *n* vela *f,* sport della vela *m.* **sailing boat** barca a vela *f.* **sailor** *n* marinaio *m.*
saint [seint] *n* santo, -a *m, f. adj* santo. **saintly** *adj* santo, pio.
sake [seik] *n* beneficio *m,* interesse *m,* bene *m.* **for God's sake** per l'amor di Dio. **for the sake of** (*in order to*) tanto per. **for your own sake** per il tuo bene.
salad ['saləd] *n* insalata *f.*
salami [sə'laːmi] *n* salame *m.*
salary ['saləri] *n* stipendio *m.*
sale [seil] *n* vendita *f;* (*clearance*) liquidazione *f,* saldo *m.* **for** *or* **on sale** in vendita. **salesgirl** *n* commessa *f.* **salesman** *n* commesso *m.* **travelling salesman** commesso viaggiatore *m.*
saline ['seilain] *adj* salino. **salinity** *n* salinità *f.*
saliva [sə'laivə] *n* saliva *f.* **salivary** *adj* salivare. **salivate** *v* salivare.
sallow ['salou] *adj* giallastro, olivastro.
salmon ['samən] *n* salmone *m.*
salon ['salon] *n* salone *m.*
saloon [sə'luːn] *n* salone *m;* (*ship*) ritrovo per passeggeri *m.* **saloon car** berlina *f.*
salt [soːlt] *n* sale *m.* **salt-cellar** *n* saliera *f. adj also* **salty** salato, piccante. *v* salare.
salubrious [sə'luːbriəs] *adj* salubre.
salute [sə'luːt] *n* saluto *m. v* salutare.
salvage ['salvidʒ] *n* salvataggio *m,* ricupero *m. v* salvare, ricuperare.
salvation [sal'veiʃən] *n* salvezza *f;* (*theology*) salvazione *f.*
same [seim] *adj* stesso, medesimo; (*unchanged*) immutato. *pron* lo stesso, il medesimo. **all the same** (*nevertheless*) malgrado tutto. **at the same time** nello stesso tempo; (*notwithstanding*) con tutto ciò, ciononostante. **the same to you!** altrettanto! **sameness** *n* somiglianza *f,* uniformità *f,* monotonia *f.*
sample ['saːmpl] *n* campione *m;* (*specimen*) saggio *m. v* campionare; (*test*) assaggiare. **sampling** *n* campionatura *f.*

sanatorium [sanə'tɔːriəm] *n* sanatorio *m*.
sanctify ['saŋktifai] *v* santificare, consacrare.
sanctimonious [saŋkti'mouniəs] *adj* santocchio, santerello.
sanction ['saŋkʃən] *n* sanzione *f*. *v* sanzionare, sancire.
sanctity ['saŋktəti] *n* santità *f*.
sanctuary ['saŋktʃuəri] *n* santuario *m*; (*refuge*) asilo *m*, rifugio *m*.
sand [sand] *n* sabbia *f*. *v* (*sprinkle*) insabbiare; (*smooth*) smerigliare. **sand-blast** *v* pulire con un getto di sabbia. **sandpaper** *n* carta vetrata *f*. **sandy** *adj* (*consistency*) sabbioso; (*colour*) biondo rossiccio.
sandal ['sandl] *n* sandalo *m*.
sandwich ['sanwidʒ] *n* sandwich *m invar*, panino imbottito *m*. *v* inserire.
sane [sein] *adj* equilibrato, sano di mente. **sanity** *n* sanità di mente *f*, equilibrio *m*.
sang [saŋ] *V* **sing**.
sanitary ['sanitəri] *adj* igienico, sanitario. **sanitary towel** *n* pannolino igienico *m*.
sank [saŋk] *V* **sink**.
sap¹ [sap] *n* (*plant*) linfa *f*.
sap² [sap] *v* (*undermine*) minare, indebolire.
sapphire ['safaiə] *n* zaffiro *m*. *adj* zaffirino.
sarcasm ['saːkazəm] *n* sarcasmo *m*. **sarcastic** *adj* sarcastico.
sardine [saː'diːn] *n* sardina *f*.
Sardinia [saː'dinjə] *n* Sardegna *f*. **Sardinian** *n*, *adj* sardo, -a.
sardonic [saː'donik] *adj* sardonico.
sash¹ [saʃ] *n* (*scarf*) sciarpa *f*.
sash² [saʃ] *n* (*frame*) telaio *m*. **sash-cord** *n* corda del contrappeso *f*. **sash-window** *n* finestra alla ghigliottina *f*.
sat [sat] *V* **sit**.
satchel ['satʃəl] *n* cartella *f*.
satellite ['satəlait] *nm*, *adj* satellite. **satellite town** città satellite *f*.
satin ['satin] *nm*, *adj* raso.
satire ['sataiə] *n* satira *f*. **satirical** *adj* satirico. **satirist** *n* satirista *m*, *f*.
satisfy ['satisfai] *v* soddisfare. **satisfaction** *n* soddisfazione *f*. **satisfactory** *adj* soddisfacente.
saturate ['satʃəreit] *v* saturare. **saturated** *adj* saturo. **saturation** *n* saturazione *f*.
Saturday ['satədi] *n* sabato *m*.
sauce [sɔːs] *n* salsa *f*; (*coll*) impertinenza *f*. **saucy** *adj* impertinente, sfacciato. **sauciness** *n* impertinenza *f*, sfacciataggine *f*.
saucepan ['sɔːspən] *n* casseruola *f*, pentola *f*.
saucer ['sɔːsə] *n* piattino *m*, sottocoppa *f*.
sauerkraut ['sauəkraut] *n* sarcrauti *m pl*.
sauna [sɔːnə] *n* sauna *f*.
saunter [sɔːntə] *v* girovagare, andare a passeggio, girare. *n* giro *m*.
sausage ['sosidʒ] *n* salsiccia *f*, salame *m*.
savage ['savidʒ] *adj* selvaggio; feroce, crudele. *v* assalire, ferire. **savagery** *n* selvatichezza *f*; ferocia *f*, crudeltà *f*.
save¹ [seiv] *v* salvare; (*keep*) conservare; (*put aside*) risparmiare. **saver** *n* risparmiatore, -trice *m*, *f*. **saving** *n* economia *f*. **savings** *pl n* risparmi *m pl*.
save² [seiv] *prep* (*except*) salvo, eccetto.
saviour ['seivjə] *n* liberatore, -trice *m*, *f*; (*rel*) redentore *m*.
savoury ['seivəri] *adj* (*appetizing*) saporito, gustoso; (*piquant*) piccante. *n* piatto appetitoso *m*.
***saw**¹ [sɔː] *n* sega *f*. **sawdust** *n* segatura *f*. **sawmill** *n* segheria *f*. *v* segare.
saw² [sɔː] *V* **see**¹.
sawn [sɔːn] *V* **saw**¹.
saxophone ['saksəfoun] *n* sassofono *m*.
***say** [sei] *v* dire; (*declare*) dichiarare, affermare. **I say!** senti! guarda un po'! **(let's) say** (*as an estimate*) mettiamo, facciamo. *n* **have no say** non aver voce. **have one's say** dire la sua. **saying** *n* massima *f*, motto *m*, proverbio *m*.
scab [skab] *n* crosta *f*; (*biol*) scabbia *f*, rogna *f*; (*derog*: *non-striker*) crumiro, -a *m*, *f*. **scabby** *adj* rognoso, scabbioso.
scaffold ['skafəld] *n* (*execution*) patibolo *m*. **scaffolding** *n* impalcatura *f*, ponteggio *m*; (*theatre*) palco *m*.
scald [skoːld] *n* scottatura *f*. *v* scottare.
scale¹ [skeil] *n* (*thin plate*) lamina *f*; (*of fish, etc.*) scaglia *f*, squama *f*; tartaro *m*; incrostazione *f*. *v* squamare; incrostare. **scaly** *adj* squamoso.
scale² [skeil] *n* (*music, math, etc.*) scala *f*. **to scale** in proporzione. *v* (*climb*) scalare; (*climb over*) scavalcare. **scale down** ridurre proporzionalemente.
scales [skeilz] *pl n* bilancia *f sing*. **tip the scales** dare il crollo alla bilancia.
scallop ['skaləp] *n* (*zool*) pettine *m*; (*shell*) conchiglia *f*; (*edging*) dentellatura *f*.
scalp [skalp] *n* scalpo *m*. *v* scalpare.
scalpel ['skalpəl] *n* scalpello *m*.

scampi ['skampi] *pl n* scampi *m pl.*
scan [skan] *v* scrutare; (*radar, etc.*) analizzare, sondare; (*poetry*) scandire; (*glance at*) dare una scorsa a. **scanner** *n* analizzatore *m*, dispositivo di esplorazione *m.*
scandal ['skandl] *n* scandalo *m*; (*gossip*) maldicenza *f*, diceria *f.* **scandalmonger** *n* maldicente *m, f.* **scandalize** *v* scandalizzare. **scandalous** *adj* scandaloso.
scanty ['skanti] *adj also* **scant** scarso, insufficiente. **scantily dressed** vestito succintamente.
scapegoat ['skeipgout] *n* capro espiatorio *m.*
scar [skaː] *n* cicatrice *f*, sfregio *m. v* (*mark*) sfregiare; (*heal*) cicatrizzare. **scarred** *adj* sfregiato.
scarce [skeəs] *adj* scarso, raro. **scarcely** *adv* appena. **scarcity** *n* scarsezza *f.*
scare [skeə] *n* paura *f*, panico *m. v* impaurire, spaventare. **be scared** avere paura. **be scared stiff** avere una paura matta. **scarecrow** *n* spauracchio *m.* **scaremonger** *n* allarmista *m, f.*
scarf [skaːf] *n* sciarpa *f*; (*square*) foulard *m invar.*
scarlet ['skaːlit] *adj* scarlatto. **scarlet fever** scarlattina *f.* **scarlet runner** fagiolo di Spagna *m.*
scathing ['skeiðiŋ] *adj* sprezzante, sdegnoso.
scatter ['skatə] *v* spargere, disperdere, diffondere. **scatterbrained** *adj* scervellato, distratto.
scavenge ['skavindʒ] *v* (*streets*) spazzare; (*zool*) nutrirsi di cadaveri. **scavenger** *n* (*street cleaner*) spazzino *m*; (*zool*) animale necrofago *m.*
scene [siːn] *n* scena *f*, spettacolo *m.* **scenario** *n* scenario *m.*
scenery ['siːnəri] *n* (*landscape*) paesaggio *m*, veduta *f*; (*theatre*) scenario *m.*
scent [sent] *n* profumo *m*, odore *m*; (*track*) pista *f.* **throw off the scent** far perdere la traccia. *v* (*detect*) fiutare; (*perfume*) profumare.
sceptic ['skeptik] *n* scettico, -a *m, f.* **sceptical** *adj* scettico. **scepticism** *n* scetticismo *m.*
sceptre ['septə] *n* scettro *m.*
schedule ['ʃedjuːl] *n* programma *m*; (*timetable*) orario *m*; lista *f*, specchietto *m.* **according to schedule** secondo il previsto *or* programma. *v* programmare; (*list*) elencare.
scheme [skiːm] *n* schema *m*, progetto *m*, piano *m*; intrigo (*pl* -ghi) *m*, trama *f. v* progettare; tramare. **schematic** *adj* schematico.
schizophrenia [ˌskitsə'friːniə] *n* schizofrenia *f.* **schizophrenic** *n, adj* schizofrenico, -a.
scholar ['skolə] *n* persona erudita *f*, studioso, -a *m, f*; studente, -essa *m, f.* **scholarly** *adj* erudito, dotto. **scholarship** *n* erudizione *f*; studio *m*; (*award*) borsa di studio *f.*
scholastic [skə'lastik] *adj* scolastico.
school[1] [skuːl] *n* scuola *f.* **schoolboy** *n* scolaro *m.* **schoolfellow** *n* compagno, -a di scuola *m, f.* **schoolgirl** *n* scolara *f.* **schoolmaster** *n* maestro *m*; insegnante *m.* **schoolmistress** *n* maestra *f*, insegnante *f. v* istruire, ammaestrare.
school[2] [skuːl] *n* (*of fish*) banco *m*, frotta *f.*
schooner ['skuːnə] *n* goletta *f.*
sciatica [sai'atikə] *n* sciatica *f.* **sciatic** *adj* sciatico.
science ['saiəns] *n* scienza *f.* **science fiction** fantascienza *f.* **scientific** *adj* scientifico. **scientist** *n* scienziato, -a *m, f.*
scissors ['sizəz] *pl n* forbici *f pl.*
scoff[1] [skof] *v* (*mock*) beffare, schernire. *n* beffa *f.*
scoff[2] [skof] *v* (*coll: eat*) pappare.
scold [skould] *v* sgridare, rimproverare. **scolding** *n* sgridata *f*, lavata di capo *f.*
scone [skon] *n* focaccia *f.*
scoop [skuːp] *n* (*kitchen*) mestolo *m*; (*dredge*) benna *f*; (*coll*) colpo *m. v* scavare. **scoop out** scodellare. **scoop up** raccogliere, tirar su.
scooter ['skuːtə] *n* motoretta *f*, scooter *m invar*; (*child's*) monopattino *m.*
scope [skoup] *n* (*extent*) portata *f*; opportunità *f*; possibilità *f*; (*space for activity*) campo libero *m.*
scorch [skoːtʃ] *n* scottatura *f. v* abbruciacchiare. **scorcher** *n* (*coll*) giornata caldissima *f.*
score [skoː] *n* (*sport*) punteggio *m*; (*account*) conto *m*; (*debt*) debito *m*; (*ground*) causa *f*; (*music*) partitura *f.* **scoreboard** *n* tabellone *m. v* (*sport*) segnare; (*points*) notare; marcare; (*notches*) intaccare; orchestrare. **score off** aver la meglio su.

scorn [skoːn] *n* disprezzo *m*, sdegno *m*. *v* sdegnare, sprezzare. **scornful** *adj* sdegnoso, sprezzante.
Scorpio ['skoːpiou] *n* Scorpione *m*.
scorpion ['skoːpiən] *n* scorpione *m*.
scotch [skotʃ] *v* sopprimere.
Scotland ['skotlənd] *n* Scozia *f*. **Scot** *n* scozzese *m, f*. **Scotch** *n* (*whisky*) scotch *m invar*, whisky scozzese *m*. **Scottish** *or* **Scots** *adj* scozzese.
scoundrel ['skaundrəl] *n* furfante *m*, mascalzone *m*.
scour[1] [skauə] *v* (*clean*) pulire sfregando; (*rub*) fregare, forbire.
scour[2] [skauə] *v* (*search*) perlustrare.
scout [skaut] *v* esplorare, perlustrare. *n* (*mil*) vedetta *f*; (*boy*) giovane esploratore *m*; osservatore *m*.
scowl [skaul] *n* cipiglio *m*, guardataccia *f*. *v* accigliarsi.
scramble ['skrambl] *v* (*move hastily*) sgambettare; (*climb*) arrampicarsi; (*struggle*) azzuffarsi, battagliare; (*radio, etc.*) disturbare. **scrambled eggs** uova strapazzate *f pl*. *n* confusione *f*, parapiglia *f*; (*struggle*) lotta *f*.
scrap [skrap] *n* (*small piece*) pezzetto *m*, frammento *m*; (*metal*) rottame *m*. **scrapbook** *n* album *m invar*. **scraps** *pl n* rifiuti *m pl*; (*leftovers*) avanzi *m pl*, rimasugli *m pl*. *v* scartare, mettere fuori servizio. **scrappy** *adj* frammentario.
scrape [skreip] *v* raschiare, grattare. **scrape through** cavarsela; (*exam*) passare per il buco della serratura. **scrape together** racimolare, raccogliere. *n* (*embarrassing situation*) impaccio *m*.
scratch [skratʃ] *v* graffiare, grattare; cancellare; (*withdraw*) ritirarsi. *n* graffiatura *f*. **from scratch** da zero. **up to scratch** all'altezza della situazione.
scrawl [skroːl] *n* scarabocchio *m*. *v* scarabocchiare.
scream [skriːm] *v* strillare. *n* strillo *m*; (*coll*: *funny person*) spasso *m*.
screech [skriːtʃ] *v* stridere, cigolare. *n* strido *m* (*pl* -a *f*).
screen [skriːn] *n* paravento *m*; (*shelter*) riparo *m*; (*film, etc.*) schermo *m*. *v* (*hide*) nascondere; (*protect*) proteggere; (*check*) vagliare; (*cinema*) proiettare.
screw [skruː] *n* vite *f*. **screwdriver** *n* cacciavite *m invar*. *v* avvitare. **screw up one's courage** farsi coraggio.
scribble ['skribl] *n* sgorbio *m*. *v* scribacchiare. **scribbler** *n* scribacchino, -a *m, f*.
script [skript] *n* (*handwriting*) scrittura *f*; manuscritto *m*; (*theatre*) copione *m*.
Scripture ['skriptʃə] *n* Sacra Scrittura *f*, Bibbia *f*.
scroll [skroul] *n* (*roll*) rotolo *m*; (*ornament*) voluta *f*.
scrounge [skraundʒ] (*coll*) *v* scroccare. **scrounger** *n* scroccone, -a *m, f*.
scrub[1] [skrʌb] *v* lavare *or* pulire fregando forte. **scrubbing brush** spazzola dura *f*, spazzolone per lavare *m*.
scrub[2] [skrʌb] *n* (*bush*) macchia *f*.
scruffy ['skrʌfi] *adj* trasandato.
scruple ['skruːpl] *n* scrupolo *m*. **scrupulous** *adj* scrupoloso.
scrutiny ['skruːtəni] *n* esame accurato *m*. **scrutinize** *v* esaminare accuratamente.
scuffle ['skʌfl] *n* tafferuglio *m*. *v* azzuffarsi.
scullery ['skʌləri] *n* retrocucina *f*.
sculpt [skʌlpt] *v* scolpire. **sculptor** *n* scultore *m*. **sculptress** *n* scultrice *f*. **sculptural** *adj* scultorio. **sculpture** *n* scultura *f*.
scum [skʌm] *n* (*on liquids*) schiuma *f*; (*on metals*) scoria *f*; (*worthless people*) feccia *f*.
scurf [skəːf] *n* forfora *f*. **scurfy** *adj* forforoso.
scurrilous ['skʌriləs] *adj* scurrile.
scurvy ['skəːvi] *n* scorbuto *m*.
scuttle[1] ['skʌtl] *n* (*for coal*) secchio da carbone *m*.
scuttle[2] ['skʌtl] *v* (*run*) scorrazzare.
scuttle[3] ['skʌtl] *v* (*sink*) affondare.
scythe [saið] *n* falce *f*. *v* falciare.
sea [siː] *n* mare *m*. **at sea** in mare; perplesso. **by sea** per mare. **put out to sea** prendere il largo.
sea bed *n* fondo del mare *m*.
seafaring ['siːˌfeəriŋ] *adj* navigatore, -trice; marinaro. **seafarer** *n* navigatore *m*.
seafood ['siːfuːd] *n* frutti di mare *m pl*.
sea front *n* marina *f*.
seagoing ['siːgouiŋ] *adj* d'alto mare.
sea-gull *n* gabbiano *m*.
sea-horse *n* cavalluccio marino *m*.
seal[1] [siːl] *n* (*stamp*) sigillo *m*; chiusura *f*. *v* sigillare; (*close*) chiudere. **sealing wax** ceralacca *f*.
seal[2] [siːl] *n* (*animal*) foca *f*. **sealskin** *n* pelle di foca *f*.

sea-level *n* livello del mare *m*.
sea-lion *n* leone marino *m*.
seam [siːm] *n* cucitura *f*, giuntura *f*; (*geol*) vena *f*. *v* cucire.
seaman ['siːmən] *n* marinaio *m*.
search [səːtʃ] *v* frugare, rovistare. *n* (*act*) ricerca *f*; esame minuto *m*; (*for something hidden*) perquisizione *f*. **searchlight** *n* proiettore *m*. **search-party** *n* squadra di ricerca *f*. **search-warrant** *n* mandato di perquisizione *m*. **searching** *adj* (*careful*) minuzioso; (*observing*) indagatore, -trice *m*, *f*.
seashore ['siːʃoː] *n* spiaggia *f*, costa *f*.
seasick ['siːsik] *adj* **be seasick** avere il mal di mare. **seasickness** *n* mal di mare *m*.
seaside ['siːsaid] *n* **at** *or* **to the seaside** al mare.
season ['siːzn] *n* stagione *f*. **season ticket** abbonamento *m*. *v* (*wood*) stagionare; (*spice*) condire. **seasonable** *adj* (*timely*) opportuno. **seasoning** *n* condimento *m*.
seat [siːt] *n* sedile *m*; (*chair*) sedia *f*; (*place*) posto *m*; (*coll: behind*) sedere *m*; (*location*) sede *f*. **take a seat** accomodarsi. *v* (*cause to sit*) far sedere; (*provide with seat*) provvedere di posti (a sedere).
seaweed ['siːwiːd] *n* alga *f*.
seaworthy ['siːwəːði] *adj* atto a tenere il mare.
secluded [si'kluːdid] *adj* isolato, appartato. **seclusion** *n* isolamento *m*.
second ['sekənd] *n* secondo *m*; (*day*) due *m*; (*gear*) seconda *f*. *adj* secondo. **on second thoughts** ripensandoci bene. **second-hand** *adj* di seconda mano. **second-rate** *adj* mediocre. **second sight** chiaroveggenza *f*.
secondary ['sekəndəri] *adj* secondario.
secret ['siːkrit] *nm*, *adj* segreto. **top secret** *adj* riservatissimo. **secrecy** *n* segretezza *f*. **secretive** *adj* riservato, reticente.
secretary ['sekrətəri] *n* segretario, -a *m*, *f*. **secretarial** *adj* segretariale. **secretariat** *n* segreteria *f*, segretariato *m*.
secrete [si'kriːt] *v* (*biol*) secernere; (*conceal*) celare. **secretion** *n* secrezione *f*.
sect [sekt] *n* setta *f*. **sectarian** *adj* settario.
section ['sekʃən] *n* sezione *f*, parte *f*.
sector ['sektə] *n* settore *m*.
secular ['sekjulə] *adj* secolare; profano; laico.
secure [si'kjuə] *adj* sicuro; solido. *v* mettere al sicuro, assicurare; garantire; procurarsi. **security** *n* sicurezza *f*, garanzia *f*. **securities** *pl n* titoli *m pl*, obbligazioni *f pl*.
sedate [si'deit] *adj* pacato, posato. *v* calmare, tranquillizzare. **sedative** *n* sedativo *m*; calmante *m*.
sediment ['sedimənt] *n* sedimento *m*. **sedimentation** *n* sedimentazione *f*.
seduce [si'djuːs] *v* sedurre. **seducer** *n* seduttore, -trice *m*, *f*. **seduction** *n* seduzione *f*. **seductive** *adj* seducente.
***see**[1] [siː] *v* vedere. **see about** *or* **to** occuparsi di. **see home** accompagnare a casa. **see through** penetrare.
see[2] [siː] *n* (*bishop's*) diocesi *f*. **Holy See** Santa Sede *f*.
seed [siːd] *n* seme *m*; (*collective*) semenza *f*. **go to seed** (*bot*) sementire; (*decay*) scadere, declinare. *v* seminare. **seedling** *n* germoglio *m*, semenzale *m*. **seedy** *adj* (*shabby*) malconcio; indisposto.
***seek** [siːk] *v* cercare.
seem [siːm] *v* sembrare, parere. **seeming** *adj* apparente.
seen [siːn] *V* **see**[1].
seep [siːp] *v* infiltrare.
seesaw ['siːsoː] *n* altalena (a bilico) *f*. *adj* oscillante. *v* altalenare.
seethe [siːð] *v* bollire; (*be agitated*) fremere. **seethe with rage** fremere di rabbia.
segment ['segmənt] *n* segmento *m*, sezione *f*.
segregate ['segrigeit] *v* segregare. **segregation** *n* segregazione *f*.
seize [siːz] *v* (*grasp*) afferrare; (*by force*) impadronirsi di; confiscare. **seize up** grippare, ingranarsi. **seizure** *n* confisca *f*; conquista *f*; (*med*) attacco *m*.
seldom ['seldəm] *adv* raramente, di rado.
select [sə'lekt] *adj* scelto, distinto. *v* scegliere. **selection** *n* selezione *f*, scelta *f*. **selective** *adj* selettivo. **selectivity** *n* selettività *f*.
self [self] *n* io *m*, persona *f*.
self-assured *adj* sicuro di sè. **self-assurance** sicurezza di sè *f*.
self-centred *adj* egocentrico, egoista.
self-confident *adj* sicuro di sè. **self-confidence** *n* fiducia in sè.
self-conscious *adj* impacciato. **self-consciousness** *n* impaccio *m*.
self-contained *adj* (*not shared*) indipendente; (*uncommunicative*) riservato; (*self-sufficient*) autosufficiente.

self-critical *adj* autocritico. **self-criticism** *n* autocritica *f*.
self-defence *n* autodifesa *f*; (*law*) legittima difesa *f*.
self-discipline *n* autodisciplina *f*.
self-employed *adj* **be self-employed** lavorare in proprio.
self-evident *adj* manifesto, palese.
self-explanatory *adj* ovvio.
self-expression *n* espressione della propria personalità *f*.
self-government *n* autonomia *f*.
self-interest *n* interesse personale *m*.
selfish ['selfiʃ] *adj* egoista, egoistico. **selfishness** *n* egoismo *m*.
selfless ['selflis] *adj* altruista, altruistico. **selflessness** *n* altruismo *m*.
self-pity *n* autocommiserazione *f*.
self-portrait *n* autoritratto *m*.
self-possessed *adj* composto, padrone di sè.
self-preservation *n* conservazione *f*.
self-propelled *adj* che si muove per forza propria.
self-respect *n* amor proprio *m*. **self-respecting** *adj* dignitoso.
self-restraint *n* autocontrollo *m*.
self-righteous *adj* compiaciuto di sè stesso. **self-righteousness** *n* autocompiacimento *m*.
self-sacrifice *n* abnegazione *f*.
selfsame ['selfseim] *adj* identico, proprio lo stesso.
self-satisfied *adj* contento di sè. **self-satisfaction** *n* autocompiacimento *m*.
self-service *n* self-service *m invar*.
self-styled *adj* sedicente.
self-sufficient *adj* autosufficiente. **self-sufficiency** *n* autosufficienza *f*.
self-willed *adj* ostinato; (*wilful*) caparbio.
***sell** [sel] *v* vendere. **seller** *n* venditore, -trice *m*, *f*.
sellotape ® ['seləteip] *n* scotch ® *m invar*, nastro autoadesivo *m*.
semantic [sə'mantik] *adj* semantico. **semantics** *n* semantica *f*.
semaphore ['seməfoː] *n* semaforo *m*.
semen ['siːmən] *n* sperma *m*.
semibreve ['semibriːv] *n* semibreve *f*.
semicircle ['semisəːkl] *n* semicerchio *m*. **semicircular** *adj* semicircolare.
semicolon [ˌsemi'koulən] *n* punto e virgola *m*.
semifinal [semi'fainl] *n* semifinale *f*. **semifinalist** *n* semifinalista *m*, *f*.
seminar ['seminaː] *n* seminario *m*.
seminary ['seminəri] *n* seminario *m*.
semi-precious *adj* semiprezioso.
semiquaver ['semikweivə] *n* semicroma *f*.
semitone ['semitoun] *n* semitono *m*.
semolina [ˌsemə'liːnə] *n* semolino *m*.
senate ['senit] *n* senato *m*. **senator** *n* senatore *m*.
***send** [send] *v* mandare; (*dispatch*) spedire; trasmettere. **send for** (*person*) mandare a chiamare; (*thing*) mandare a prendere. **send in** sottoporre. **send on** (*readdress*) inoltrare. **sender** *n* mittente *m*, *f*.
senile ['siːnail] *adj* senile. **senility** *n* (*old age*) senilità *f*; (*mental infirmity*) senilismo *m*.
senior ['siːnjə] *adj* più anziano, maggiore. *n* anziano, -a *m*, *f*; superiore, -a *m*, *f*. **seniority** *n* anzianità *f*.
sensation [sen'seiʃən] *n* sensazione *f*. **cause a sensation** far sensazione *or* colpo. **sensational** *adj* sensazionale, che fa colpo.
sense [sens] *n* senso *m*. **take leave of one's senses** perder la ragione. **talk sense** parlare sensatamente. *v* intuire, capire.
sensible ['sensəbl] *adj* sensato, ragionevole; (*appreciable*) sensibile. **sensibility** *n* sensibilità *f*.
sensitive ['sensitiv] *adj* sensibile; delicato; (*physiology*) sensitivo. **sensitivity** *n* sensibilità *f*; suscettibilità *f*; delicatezza *f*.
sensual ['sensjuəl] *adj* sensuale. **sensuality** *n* sensualità *f*.
sensuous ['sensjuəs] *adj* gradevole ai sensi, voluttuoso.
sent [sent] *V* **send**.
sentence ['sentəns] *n* (*gramm*) frase *f*; (*law*) condanna *f*, pena *f*. **pass sentence** pronunciare (una) sentenza. *v* condannare.
sentiment ['sentimənt] *n* sentimento *m*. **sentimental** *adj* sentimentale. **sentimentality** *n* sentimentalità *f*.
sentry ['sentri] *n* sentinella *f*. **stand sentry** fare la guardia.
separate ['sepərət; *v* 'sepəreit] *adj* separato; distinto; indipendente. *v* separare. **separation** *n* separazione *f*.
September [sep'tembə] *n* settembre *m*.
septic ['septik] *adj* settico. **septicaemia** *n* setticemia *f*.

sequel ['siːkwəl] *n* seguito *m*; conseguenza *f*.
sequence ['siːkwəns] *n* successione *f*; (*math, cards*) sequenza *f*. **in sequence** in ordine successivo.
sequin ['siːkwin] *n* lustrino *m*.
serenade [serə'neid] *n* serenata *f*. *v* fare una serenata a.
serene [sə'riːn] *adj* sereno. **serenity** *n* serenità *f*.
sergeant ['saːdʒənt] *n* (*mil*) sergente *m*; (*police*) brigadiere *m*.
serial ['siəriəl] *n* (*novel*) romanzo a puntate *m*; (*play*) commedia a puntate *f*. *adj* (*in instalments*) a puntate; (*tech*) di *or* in serie. **serialize** *v* pubblicare *or* trasmettere a puntate.
series ['siəriːz] *n* serie *f*.
serious ['siəriəs] *adj* serio, grave. **are you serious?** dice sul serio? **seriousness** *n* serietà *f*.
sermon ['səːmən] *n* predica *f*.
serpent ['səːpənt] *n* serpente *m*. **serpentine** *adj* serpentino; (*winding*) serpeggiante.
serum ['siərəm] *n* siero *m*.
servant ['səːvənt] *n* domestico, -a *m, f*; servo, -a *m, f*.
serve [səːv] *v* servire. **it serves you right!** ti sta bene! te lo sei meritato!
service ['səːvis] *n* servizio *m*; (*disposal*) disposizione *f*; (*rel*) ufficio divino *m*. **of service** d'aiuto, utile. **service area/station** area/stazione di servizio *f*. *v* provvedere alla manutenzione di, controllare. **serviceable** *adj* pratico, funzionale.
serviette [ˌsəːvi'et] *n* tovagliolo *m*.
servile ['səːvail] *adj* servile. **servility** *n* servilità *f*.
session ['seʃən] *n* seduta *f*, sessione *f*.
***set** [set] *adj* fisso; (*ready*) pronto; prescritto; deciso; preparato; (*prearranged*) stabilito. *n* serie *f*, assortimento *m*; (*theatre, etc.*) set *m invar*, scenario *m*; (*tennis*) set *m invar*, partita *f*. *v* (*place*) mettere, posare; (*fix*) fissare; (*solidify*) indurirsi, rapprendersi; (*sun*) tramontare; (*jewel*) incastonare; (*hair*) mettere in piega; (*bones*) mettere a posto. **set about** (*begin to*) accingersi a; (*attempt*) cercare di; (*coll*) attaccare. **set aside** *or* **by** mettere da parte. **set back** (*hinder*) impedire; (*delay*) ritardare. **setback** *n* regresso *m*, contrattempo *m*. **set free** liberare. **set off** far esplodere; (*depart*) mettersi in viaggio; (*intensify*) mettere in risalto; compensare. **set out** partire. **set up** (*erect*) erigere; (*establish*) stabilire, metter su; (*prepare*) allestire. **setting** *n* (*environment*) ambiente *m*; (*jewel*) montatura *f*; (*theatre*) scenario *m*, messa in scena *f*; (*music*) messa in musica *f*; (*sun*) tramonto *m*.
settee [se'tiː] *n* canapè *m*, sofà *m*.
settle ['setl] *v* fissare, determinare; (*pay*) regolare, saldare; (*compose*) sistemare; decidere. **settle down** stabilizzarsi; (*live*) stabilirsi. **settlement** *n* decisione *f*; saldo *m*; colonia *f*. **settler** *n* colonizzatore, -trice *m, f*.
seven ['sevn] *nm, adj* sette. **seventh** *nm, adj* settimo.
seventeen [sevn'tiːn] *nm, adj* diciassette. **seventeenth** *adj* diciassettesimo.
seventy ['sevnti] *nm, adj* settanta. **seventieth** *adj* settantesimo.
sever ['sevə] *v* staccare.
several ['sevrəl] *pron* parecchi, diversi. *adj* parecchi, diversi; separato; (*own*) proprio.
severe [sə'viə] *adj* severo; grave; (*weather*) rigido; (*pain, etc.*) violento, vivo. **severity** *n* severità *f*, rigore *m*; violenza *f*.
***sew** [sou] *v* cucire. **sewing** n cucito *m*. **sewing machine** macchina da cucire *f*.
sewage ['sjuidʒ] *n* acque di scolo *or* scarico *f pl*.
sewer ['sjuə] *n* fogna *f*. **sewerage** *n* fognatura *f*.
sewn [soun] *V* **sew**.
sex [seks] *n* sesso *m*. **sexual** *adj* sessuale. **sexuality** *n* sessualità *f*.
sextet [seks'tet] *n* sestetto *m*.
shabby ['ʃabi] *adj* (*of poor appearance*) malconcio, trasandato; (*badly worn*) logoro, frusto; (*contemptible*) meschino.
shack [ʃak] *n* baracca *f*.
shade [ʃeid] *n* ombra *f*; (*colour*) tinta *f*; (*lamp*) paralume *m*. *v* ombreggiare; (*protect*) proteggere (dalla luce); (*drawing*) sfumare. **shading** *n* sfumatura *f*.
shadow ['ʃadou] *n* ombra *f*. *v* ombreggiare; (*follow*) pedinare. **shady** *adj* ombreggiato; (*dubious*) disonesto, losco.
shaft [ʃaːft] *n* (*pole*) asta *f*; (*passageway*) condotto *m*; (*handle*) manico *m*; (*light*) fascio *m*; (*sarcasm*) frecciata *f*.
shaggy ['ʃagi] *adj* peloso, irsuto.

***shake** [ʃeik] *n* scossa *f*. **no great shakes** di poco conto. *v* scuotere; agitare; (*tremble*) tremare; (*disturb*) fremere. **shake hands** stringere la mano. **shake off** liberarsi da. **shake-up** *n* riorganizzazione *f*. **shaky** *adj* tremolante; (*insecure*) malsicuro; precario.

shaken ['ʃeikn] *V* **shake**.

shall [ʃal] *aux translated by future tense.*

shallot [ʃə'lot] *n* scalogno *m*.

shallow ['ʃalou] *adj* poco profondo, basso, superficiale. **shallows** *pl n* bassofondo (*pl* bassifondi) *m sing*.

sham [ʃam] *adj* finto, falso. *n* finzione *f*, inganno *m*. *v* fingere, simulare.

shambles ['ʃamblz] *n* macello *m*.

shame [ʃeim] *v* svergognare. *n* vergogna *f*. **bring shame on** recar onta a, disonorare. **shamefaced** *adj* timido, vergognoso. **what a shame!** che peccato! **shameful** *adj* vergognoso. **shameless** *adj* svergognato, spudorato; (*brazen*) sfacciato. **shamelessness** *n* spudoratezza *f*, sfacciataggine *f*.

shampoo [ʃam'puː] *n* shampoo *m invar*. *v* **shampoo one's hair** lavarsi i capelli.

shamrock ['ʃamrok] *n* trifoglio d'Irlanda *m*.

shanty[1] ['ʃanti] *n* (*hut*) capanna *f*. **shanty town** baraccopoli *f*, bidonville (*pl* -s) *f*.

shanty[2] ['ʃanti] *n* (*song*) canzone marinaresca *f*.

shape [ʃeip] *n* forma *f*; condizione *f*. **take shape** concretizzarsi, prender forma. *v* formare, dar forma a; modellare; adattare. **shapeless** *adj* informe, confuso. **shapely** *adj* ben fatto, bello.

share [ʃeə] *n* porzione *f*, parte *f*; (*comm*) azione *f*. **shareholder** *n* azionista *m*, *f*. *v* dividere; (*jointly*) condividere. **share in** prender parte a. **share out** distribuire.

shark [ʃaːk] *n* pescecane (*pl* pescicani) *m*.

sharp [ʃaːp] *adj* (*cutting*) tagliente; (*not blunt*) aguzzo; brusco; (*distinct*) netto; (*flavour*) aspro, piccante; acuto; (*alert*) sveglio; (*biting*) mordace; (*shrewd*) scaltro. *adv* bruscamente; (*punctually*) in punto. *n* (*music*) diesis *m*. **sharpen** *v* affilare; (*pencil*) far la punta a; rendere più acuto.

shatter ['ʃatə] *v* (*break into fragments*) frantumare; (*destroy*) rovinare. **shattering** *adj* (*coll*) schiacciante.

shave [ʃeiv] *n* rasatura *f*. **have a close shave** cavarsela per un pelo. *v* farsi la barba; (*cut closely*) radere, rasare. **shaving brush/soap** pennello/sapone da barba *m*. **shaving cream** crema da barba *f*.

shawl [ʃoːl] *n* scialle *m*.

she [ʃiː] *pron* ella, lei. **she who** colei che.

sheaf [ʃiːf] *n* fascio *m*; (*cereals*) covone *m*.

***shear** [ʃiə] *v* tosare; (*tech*) spezzarsi; (*deprive*) privare. **shears** *pl n* cesoie *f pl*.

sheath [ʃiːθ] *n* guaina *f*. **sheathe** *v* rivestire; (*sword*) ringuainare.

***shed**[1] [ʃed] *v* (*let fall*) versare; (*lose*) perdere. **shed light on** far luce su.

shed[2] [ʃed] *n* capannone *m*; (*outhouse*) capanna *f*, rimessa *f*.

sheen [ʃiːn] *n* lucentezza *f*.

sheep [ʃiːp] *n* pecora *f*. **sheep-dog** *n* (cane da) pastore *m*. **sheepish** *adj* timido.

sheer[1] [ʃiə] *adj* (*mere*) mero; assoluto; (*steep*) a piombo; trasparente.

sheer[2] [ʃiə] *v* cambiar rotta.

sheet [ʃiːt] *n* (*bedding*) lenzuolo *m* (*pl* -a *f*); (*paper*) foglio *m*; (*iron, etc.*) lamiera *f*; (*glass*) lastra *f*. **sheet lightning** lampeggio *m*.

shelf [ʃelf] *n* (*support*) mensola *f*, ripiano *m*; (*ledge*) sporgenza *f*; (*rock*) scogliera *f*. **set of shelves** scaffale *m*.

shell [ʃel] *n* (*of egg, etc.*) guscio *m*; (*of fish*) conchiglia *f*; (*mil*) proiettile *m*; (*hollow casing*) involucro *m*. **shellfish** *n* crostaceo *m*, mollusco *m*; (*pl: as food*) frutti di mare *m pl*. **shell-shock** *n* psicosi traumatica da guerra *f*. *v* (*mil*) bombardare; (*eggs, etc.*) sgusciare; (*peas*) sgranare.

shelter ['ʃeltə] *n* riparo *m*, rifugio *m*; protezione *f*. **take shelter** ripararsi, rifugiarsi. *v* proteggere, dare asilo a.

shelve [ʃelv] *v* (*put aside*) mettere da parte; (*postpone*) rimandare, archiviare.

shepherd ['ʃepəd] *n* pastore *m*. **shepherdess** *n* pastora *f*.

sheriff ['ʃerif] *n* sceriffo *m*.

sherry ['ʃeri] *n* sherry *m invar*.

shield [ʃiːld] *n* schermo *m*; (*armour*) scudo *m*. *v* proteggere.

shift [ʃift] *v* spostare, trasferire; (*free oneself from*) liberarsi da. **shift for oneself** fare da sè. *n* turno *m*; (*change*) cambiamento *m*; (*artifice*) espediente *m*. **shifting** *adj* instabile, mutevole; (*sands*) mobile. **shifty** *adj* malizioso.

shimmer ['ʃimə] *v* luccicare. *n* luccichio *m*.

shin [ʃin] *n* stinco *m*.
***shine** [ʃain] *n* splendore *m*. *v* brillare, risplendere; (*polish*) lustrare.
shingle ['ʃiŋgl] *n* (*roof*) lastra di copertura *f*; (*stone*) ciottolo *m*; (*extent of pebbles*) ghiaia *f*.
shingles ['ʃiŋglz] *n* erpete *m*; (*coll*) fuoco di Sant'Antonio *m*.
ship [ʃip] *n* nave *f*. **shipowner** *n* armatore *m*. **shipshape** *adv* in ordine perfetto. **shipwreck** *n* naufragio *m*. **be shipwrecked** naufragare. **shipyard** *n* cantiere navale *m*. *v* spedire. **shipper** *n* spedizioniere *m*.
shirk [ʃəːk] *v* evitare, scansare. **shirker** *n* scansafatiche *m*, *f invar*.
shirt [ʃəːt] *n* camicia *f*.
shit [ʃit] (*vulgar*) *n* merda *f*. *v* cacare.
shiver ['ʃivə] *v* tremare, rabbrividire. *n* brivido *m*, tremito *m*. **have the shivers** (*cold*) avere i brividi; (*fear*) avere la tremarella.
shoal [ʃoul] *n* frotta *f*; (*fish*) banco *m*.
shock[1] [ʃok] *n* colpo *m*; (*encounter*) scontro *m*; (*elec*) scossa *f*; (*med*) shock *m invar*; impressione *f*. **shock absorber** ammortizzatore *m*. *v* colpire; disgustare; impressionare; dare una scossa a. **shocking** *adj* terribile; ripugnante, disgustoso.
shock[2] [ʃok] *n* (*hair*) chioma *f*.
shod [ʃod] *V* **shoe**.
shoddy ['ʃodi] *adj* scadente.
***shoe** [ʃuː] *n* scarpa *f*. **shoe-lace** *n* laccio delle scarpe *m*. **shoemaker** *n* calzolaio *m*. *v* (*horse*) ferrare.
shone [ʃon] *V* **shine**.
shook [ʃuk] *V* **shake**.
***shoot** [ʃuːt] *v* tirare, sparare; (*hit*) ferire; (*kill*) uccidere; (*film*) girare; (*bot*) germogliare. *n* (*plant*) rampollo *m*, germoglio *m*; (spedizione di) caccia *f*. **shooting** *n* tiro *m*, caccia *f*; (*firing*) sparatoria *f*. **shooting pain** dolore lancinante *m*. **shooting star** stella filante *f*.
shop [ʃop] *n* negozio *m*, bottega *f*; (*in factory, etc.*) officina *f*. **shopkeeper** *n* negoziante *m*, *f*. **shoplifter** *n* taccheggiatore, -trice *m*, *f*. **shoplifting** *n* taccheggio *m*. **shop-soiled** *adj* sciupato. **shop-window** *n* vetrina *f*. **shut up shop** chiudere bottega. **talk shop** parlare d'affari. *v* fare gli acquisti, fare la spesa. **shopper** *n* acquirente *m*, *f*. **shopping** *n* acquisti *m pl*. **go shopping** fare la spesa. **shopping bag** borsa per la spesa *f*.
shore[1] [ʃoː] *n* sponda *f*, riva *f*. **on shore** a terra.
shore[2] [ʃoː] *v* **shore up** puntellare.
shorn [ʃoːn] *V* **shear**.
short [ʃoːt] *adj* (*not long*) corto; breve; (*not tall*) basso; brusco. *adv* bruscamente; (*suddenly*) di botto. **in short** in breve. **nothing short of** addirittura. **run short** scarseggiare. **to cut a long story short** a farla breve. *n* (*film*) short *m invar*, cortometraggio *m*. **shortage** *n* mancanza *f*, carenza *f*. **shorten** *v* accorciare, abbreviare. **shortly** *adv* presto.
shortbread ['ʃoːtbred] *n* biscotto di pasta frolla *m*.
short-circuit *n* corto circuito *m*. *v* mettere in corto circuito.
shortcoming ['ʃoːtkʌmiŋ] *n* difetto *m*.
short cut *n* scorciatoia *f*.
shorthand ['ʃoːthand] *n* stenografia *f*. **shorthand typist** *n* stenodattilografo, -a *m*, *f*.
short list *n* rosa dei candidati *f*. *v* mettere nella rosa dei candidati.
short-lived *adj* di poca durata.
shorts [ʃoːts] *pl n* shorts *m pl*; calzoncini corti *m pl*.
short-sighted *adj* miope; (*lacking foresight*) imprevidente. **short-sightedness** *n* miopia *f*; imprevidenza *f*.
short story *n* novella *f*.
short-tempered *adj* irascibile.
short-term *adj* a breve scadenza.
short-wave *adj* a onde corte.
shot[1] [ʃot] *V* **shoot**.
shot[2] [ʃot] *n* sparo *m*, colpo *m*; (*pellet*) pallottola *f*; (*pellets*) pallini di piombo *m pl*; (*person*) tiratore *m*; (*phot*) istantanea *f*; (*film*) ripresa *f*. **off like a shot** via come un bolide. **shotgun** *n* fucile da caccia *m*.
should[1] [ʃud] *aux translated by conditional tense.*
should[2] [ʃud] *aux translated by conditional tense of* dovere.
shoulder ['ʃouldə] *n* spalla *f*; (*road*) banchina *f*. **give the cold shoulder** trattare con freddezza. **shoulder-blade** *n* scapola *f*. **shoulder-strap** *n* spallina *f*. *v* caricarsi sulle spalle; (*assume as burden*) addossarsi.
shout [ʃaut] *v* gridare, urlare. *n* grido *m* (*pl* -a *f*), urlo *m* (*pl* -a *f*). **shout at** sgridare, alzar la voce con. **shout down** far tacere a forza di grida.

shove [ʃʌv] *n* spinta *f*. *v* spingere.
shovel ['ʃʌvl] *v* spalare. *n* pala *f*. **shovelful** *n* palata *f*.
***show** [ʃou] *n* (*display*) mostra *f*, esposizione *f*; (*theatre*) spettacolo *m*; apparenza *f*; ostentazione *f*. **give the show away** rivelare tutto. **run the show** essere in controllo. **show business** mondo dello spettacolo *m*. **show-case** *n* vetrina *f*. **show-down** *n* (*final reckoning*) resa dei conti *f*. **showman** *n* (*theatre*) impresario *m*; showman *m invar*. **show-room** *n* sala d'esposizione *f*. *v* mostrare, manifestare, indicare, dimostrare. **show off** ostentare, darsi delle arie. **show up** (*reveal*) svelare; (*display*) far risaltare; (*appear*) presentarsi.
shower ['ʃauə] *n* (*bath*) doccia *f*; (*rain*) acquazzone *m*; (*blows*) grandine *f*. **have a shower** fare la doccia. *v* **shower with** tempestare di, inondare di.
shown [ʃoun] *V* **show**.
shrank [ʃraŋk] *V* **shrink**.
shred [ʃred] *n* (*piece torn off*) brandello *m*; (*bit, scrap*) briciolo *m*. *v* fare a brandelli *or* pezzetti.
shrew [ʃruː] *n* (*woman*) bisbetica *f*; (*zool*) toporagno *m*.
shrewd [ʃruːd] *adj* accorto, scaltro. **shrewdness** *n* accortezza *f*, scaltrezza *f*.
shriek [ʃriːk] *v* strillare. *n* strillo *m*.
shrill [ʃril] *adj* stridulo, acuto.
shrimp [ʃrimp] *n* gamberetto *m*.
shrine [ʃrain] *n* santuario *m*, reliquario *m*, tempio *m*.
***shrink** [ʃriŋk] *v* (*become tight*) restringersi; (*withdraw*) ritirarsi; (*become less*) ridursi. **shrink from** rifuggire da. **shrinkage** *n* restringimento *m*.
shrivel ['ʃrivl] *v* raggrinzirsi.
shroud [ʃraud] *n* lenzuolo funebre *m*; (*mist*) velo *m*. *v* avvolgere.
Shrove Tuesday [ʃrouv] *n* martedì grasso *m*.
shrub [ʃrʌb] *n* arbusto *m*.
shrug [ʃrʌg] *v* scrollare (le spalle). **shrug off** (*minimize*) prendere alla leggera; (*shake off*) scrollarsi di dosso. *n* scrollata (di spalle) *f*.
shrunk [ʃrʌŋk] *V* **shrink**.
shudder ['ʃʌdə] *n* brivido *m*, tremito *m*. *v* rabbrividire.
shuffle ['ʃʌfl] *v* mettere in disordine; rimaneggiare; (*cards*) mescolare; (*feet*) strascicare.
shun [ʃʌn] *v* scansare, sfuggire (a).
shunt [ʃʌnt] *v* (*rail*) smistare; (*get rid of*) mettere da parte; (*elec*) shuntare. *n* (*rail*) scambio *m*; (*elec*) shunt *m invar*.
***shut** [ʃʌt] *adj* chiuso. *v* chiudere. **shut down** (*work*) sospendere l'attività. **shut off** bloccare, sottrarsi a. **shut out** non lasciar entrare. **shut up** star zitto.
shutter ['ʃʌtə] *n* (*window*) persiana *f*; (*phot*) otturatore *m*.
shuttle ['ʃʌtl] *n* spola *f*, navetta *f*. **shuttlecock** *n* volano *m*. **shuttle service** servizio di spola *m*, servizio pendolare *m*.
shy [ʃai] *adj* timido, schivo. *v* (*horse*) scartare. **shy from** rifuggire da; (*shun*) schivare. **shyness** *n* timidezza *f*, diffidenza *f*.
sick [sik] *adj* malato; (*fed up*) stanco, stufo. **be sick** essere malato, star male; vomitare. **feel sick** sentirsi male, avere la nausea. **make sick** (*infuriate*) mandare in bestia; disgustare; far vomitare. **sick-bay** *n* infermeria *f*. *n* vomito *m*. **sicken** *v* ammalarsi. **sickening** *adj* nauseabondo, disgustante. **sickness** *n* malattia *f*.
sickle ['sikl] *n* falce *f*.
side [said] *n* lato *m*, fianco *m*; (*lake, etc.*) riva *f*; (*in battle, quarrel, etc.*) partito *m*, parte *f*. **on the other side** d'altra parte. **sideboard** *n* credenza *f*. **side-issue** *n* questione secondaria *f*. **sidelight** *n* (*mot*) luce di posizione *f*. **sidelong** *adj* di traverso, furtivo. **sidestep** *v* schivare. **side-street** *n* via laterale *f*. **sidetrack** *v* distrarre. **sideways** *adv* lateralmente; obliquamente. *v* **side with** essere dalla parte di. **siding** *n* binario di raccordo *m*.
sidle ['saidl] *v* andare a sghembo. **sidle up to** accostarsi furtivamente a.
siege [siːdʒ] *n* assedio *m*. **lay siege** assediare. **raise the siege** togliere l'assedio.
sieve [siv] *n* setaccio *m*. *v* setacciare.
sift [sift] *v* setacciare; (*examine*) vagliare.
sigh [sai] *v* sospirare. *n* sospiro *m*.
sight [sait] *n* vista *f*; (*coll*) spettacolo *m*; (*tech*) mirino *m*. **catch sight of** intravedere. **know by sight** conoscere di vista. **lose sight of** perdere di vista. **sights** *pl n* luoghi d'interesse *m pl*. **sightseeing** *n* turismo *m*.
sign [sain] *n* segno *m*, cenno *m*; (*inscription*) insegna *f*, segnale *m*; (*trace*) traccia *f*. **signpost** *n* indicatore *m*. *v* firmare,

ratificare. **sign off** ritirarsi. **sign on** (*employ*) assumere; (*commit oneself*) impegnarsi.

signal ['signəl] *n* segnale *m*. *v* segnalare.

signature ['signətʃə] *n* firma *f*. **signatory** *n* firmatario, -a *m*, *f*.

signify ['signifai] *v* significare; (*mean*) voler dire; (*be of consequence*) importare. **significance** *n* importanza *f*; (*meaning*) significato *m*. **significant** *adj* significativo, espressivo.

silence ['sailəns] *n* silenzio *m*. *v* ridurre al silenzio, far tacere; (*put to rest*) porre fine a. **silencer** *n* silenziatore *m*.

silent ['sailənt] *adj* silenzioso; tacito; muto. **keep silent** tacere, rimaner zitto.

silhouette [silu'et] *n* silhouette (*pl* -s) *f*.

silk [silk] *n* seta *f*. **silkworm** *n* baco da seta *m*. **silken** *adj* di seta. **silky** *adj* di seta; (*lustrous*) lucido; (*smooth*) morbido.

sill [sil] *n* (*window*) davanzale *m*.

silly ['sili] *adj* sciocco. **silliness** *n* sciocchezza *f*.

silt [silt] *n* limo *m*. *v* **silt up** insabbiarsi.

silver ['silvə] *n* argento *m*; (*cutlery, etc.*) argenteria *f*. *adj* d'argento, argenteo. *v* argentare.

similar ['similə] *adj* simile. **similarity** *n* somiglianza *f*.

simile ['siməli] *n* (*figure of speech*) similitudine *f*; (*example*) paragone *m*.

simmer ['simə] *v* sobbollire.

simple ['simpl] *adj* semplice. **simpleton** *n* sempliciotto, -a *m*, *f*. **simplicity** *n* semplicità *f*. **simplification** *n* semplificazione *f*. **simplify** *v* semplificare.

simulate ['simjuleit] *v* simulare, fingere. **simulation** *n* simulazione *f*, finzione *f*.

simultaneous [ˌsiməl'teinjəs] *adj* simultaneo.

sin [sin] *n* peccato *m*. *v* peccare. **sinful** *adj* peccaminoso. **sinner** *n* peccatore, -trice *m*, *f*.

since [sins] *adv* (*from then*) da allora; (*subsequently*) poi; (*ago*) fa. *prep* da. *conj* (*period*) da quando; dacchè; (*because*) poichè.

sincere [sin'siə] *adj* sincero. **sincerity** *n* sincerità *f*.

sinew ['sinjuː] *n* tendine *m*; (*force*) nerbo *m*.

***sing** [siŋ] *v* cantare. **singer** *n* cantante *m*, *f*. **singing** *n* canto *m*.

singe [sindʒ] *v* strinare; (*scorch*) bruciacchiare.

single ['siŋgl] *adj* (*one only*) singolo, solo; (*unmarried*) celibe. **single-breasted** *adj* a un petto. **single file** fila indiana *f*. **single-handed** *adj* (*unaided*) solo, senza aiuto. **single-minded** *adj* deciso, fermo, tenace. **single mindedness** *n* fermezza *f*, tenacia *f*. **single ticket** biglietto di andata solo *m*. *n* singolo *m*. *v* **single out** scegliere.

singular ['siŋgjulə] *nm*, *adj* singolare.

sinister ['sinistə] *adj* (*ominous*) di cattivo augurio.

***sink** [siŋk] *n* lavandino *m*. *v* (*submerge, go under*) affondare; (*go down*) calare, abbassarsi.

sinuous ['sinjuəs] *adj* tortuoso.

sinus ['sainəs] *n* seno *m*; (*nasal*) seno paranasale *m*. **sinusitis** *n* sinusite *f*.

sip [sip] *n* sorso *m*. *v* sorseggiare, bere a piccoli sorsi.

siphon ['saifən] *n* sifone *m*. *v* travasare con un sifone.

sir [səː] *n* signore *m*.

siren ['saiərən] *n* sirena *f*.

sirloin ['səːloin] *n* lombata *f*.

sister ['sistə] *n* sorella *f*; (*nursing*) infermiera capo sala *f*; (*rel*) suora *f*. **sister-in-law** *n* cognata *f*.

***sit** [sit] *v* sedere; posare; (*garment*) cadere; (*exam*) dare; (*be convened*) essere in seduta. **sit down** sedersi, mettersi a sedere. **sit on the fence** non prendere partito. **sit tight** non lasciarsi smuovere. **sitting** *n* seduta *f*. **sitting room** salotto *m*.

site [sait] *n* posizione *f*; (*building*) cantiere edile *m*. *v* situare.

situation [sitju'eiʃən] *n* situazione *f*; (*post*) posizione *f*. **situated** *adj* situato.

six [siks] *nm*, *adj* sei. **sixth** *nm*, *adj* sesto.

sixteen [siks'tiːn] *nm*, *adj* sedici. **sixteenth** *nm*, *adj* sedicesimo.

sixty ['siksti] *nm*, *adj* sessanta. **sixtieth** *nm*, *adj* sessantesimo.

size[1] [saiz] *n* dimensione *f*, grandezza *f*; (*garments*) misura *f*, taglia *f*. *v* **size up** valutare. **sizeable** *adj* notevole.

size[2] [saiz] *n* (*glue*) bozzima *f*. *v* imbozzimare.

sizzle ['sizl] *v* sfriggere. *n* sfrigolio *m*.

skate[1] [skeit] *v* pattinare. *n* pattino. **skater** *n* pattinatore, -trice *m*, *f*. **skating** *m* pattinaggio *m*.

skate[2] [skeit] *n* (*fish*) razza *f*.

skeleton ['skelitn] *n* scheletro *m*.

sketch [sketʃ] *n* abbozzo *m*; (*theatre*) bozzetto *m*. *v* abbozzare; delineare. **sketchbook** *n* albo di *or* per schizzi *m*. **sketchy** *adj* impreciso, superficiale.
skewer ['skjuə] *n* spiedo *m*.
ski [skiː] *n* sci *m*. **ski-lift** *n* sciovia *f*. *v* sciare. **skier** *n* sciatore, -trice *m, f*. **skiing** *n* sci *m*.
skid [skid] *v* slittare; (*car*) sbandare; (*plane*) derapare. *n* slittamento *m*; sbandamento *m*.
skill [skil] *n* abilità *f*, destrezza *f*. **skilful** *adj* abile, esperto. **skilled** *adj* abile, esperto; (*worker*) specializzato.
skim [skim] *v* (*milk*) scremare; (*glide over*) rasentare. **skim over** sfiorare; (*reading*) sfogliare.
skimp [skimp] *v* (*food, expense, etc.*) lesinare, risparmiare; (*person*) tenere a stecchetto; (*scrimp*) fare economia. **skimpy** *adj* (*scanty*) scarso; (*mean*) tirchio.
skin [skin] *n* pelle *f*; (*fruit*) buccia *f*, scorza *f*; (*film*) pellicola *f*; (*colouring*) carnagione *f*. **by the skin of one's teeth** per il rotto della cuffia. **skin-deep** *adj* superficiale. **skin-diving** *n* pesca subacquea *f*. **skinflint** *n* spilorcio *m*. **skin-graft** *n* innesto epidermico *m*. *v* sbucciare; (*animals*) scorticare. **skinny** *adj* magro, ossuto.
skip [skip] *v* saltare; (*leap*) balzellare. *n* balzo *m*.
skipper ['skipə] *n* capitano *m*.
skirmish ['skəːmiʃ] *n* scaramuccia *f*. *v* scontrarsi.
skirt [skəːt] *n* gonna *f*, sottana *f*. *v* costeggiare; (*edge*) orlare. **skirting board** zoccolo *m*.
skittle ['skitl] *n* birillo *m*.
skull [skʌl] *n* cranio *m*, teschio *m*. **skullcap** *n* calotta *f*, papalina *f*.
skunk [skʌŋk] *n* moffetta *f*; (*coll*) farabutto *m*.
sky [skai] *n* cielo *m*. **blow sky-high** far saltare per aria. **sky-blue** *adj* celeste. **skylark** *n* allodola *f*. **skylight** *n* lucernario *m*. **skyline** *n* profilo *m*, orizzonte *m*. **skyscraper** *n* grattacielo *m*.
slab [slab] *n* piastra *f*; (*thick piece*) fetta *f*.
slack [slak] *adj* (*loose*) lento; (*inactive*) fiacco; (*negligent*) indolente. *n* (*rope*) imbando *m*; (*comm*) attività ridotta *f*. *v* (*neglect duty*) trascurare. **slacken** *v* rallentare.
slacks [slaks] *pl n* calzoni sportivi *m pl*.
slag [slag] *n* scoria *f*.
slalom ['slaːləm] *n* slalom *m*.
slam [slam] *v* sbattere. *n* (*bridge*) slam *m invar*.
slander ['slaːndə] *n* diffamazione *f*. *v* diffamare. **slanderer** *n* diffamatore, -trice *m, f*. **slanderous** *adj* diffamatorio.
slang [slaŋ] *n* gergo *m*. *v* vituperare. **slanging match** battibecco *m*.
slant [slaːnt] *v* inclinare, inclinarsi; (*news*) presentare in modo tendenzioso. *n* (*slope*) inclinazione *f*; (*point of view*) punto di vista *m*; (*bias*) tendenza *f*.
slap [slap] *n* schiaffo *m*; (*rebuke*) rabbuffo *m*. **slap in the face** insulto *m*, umiliazione *f*. **slap on the back** felicitazione *f*. *v* schiaffeggiare. **slap-bang** *adv* (*right*) in pieno; (*suddenly*) di colpo. **slapdash** *adj* fatto a casaccio, abborracciato. **slap-happy** *adj* incosciente.
slash [slaʃ] *v* tagliare, squarciare. *n* taglio *m*.
slat [slat] *n* stecca *f*, assicella *f*.
slate [sleit] *n* lavagna *f*; (*geol*) ardesia *f*. **have a clean slate** aver la fedina pulita. **wipe the slate clean** ricominciare dimenticando il passato.
slaughter [sloːtə] *n* macello *m*; (*massacre*) strage *f*. *v* macellare, far strage di. **slaughterhouse** *n* macello *m*.
slave [sleiv] *n* schiavo, -a *m, f*. **slave-driver** *n* negriero, -a *m, f*. **slave labour** lavori forzati *m pl*. *v* sgobbare.
sledge [sledʒ] *n* slitta *f*.
sledgehammer ['sledʒˌhamə] *n* mazza *f*. **sledgehammer blow** mazzata *f*.
sleek [sliːk] *adj* (*glossy*) lucido; (*smooth*) liscio; (*soft*) morbido; (*unctuous*) mellifluo.
***sleep** [sliːp] *n* sonno *m*. **go to sleep** addormentarsi, prendere sonno. **have a good sleep** fare una bella dormita. *v* dormire; (*accommodate*) alloggiare. **sleep on** dormirci su. **sleeper** *n* dormiente *m, f*; (*timber beam*) traversina *f*; (*on train*) vagone letto *m*. **be a heavy/light sleeper** avere il sonno pesante/leggero. **sleeping bag** sacco a pelo *m*. **sleeping partner** (*econ*) socio accomandante *m*. **sleeping pill** sonnifero *m*. **sleepless** *adj* insonne. **sleepy** *adj* sonnolento.
sleet [sliːt] *n* nevischio *m*.

sleeve [sliːv] *n* manica *f*; (*tech*) manicotto *m*; (*record*) copertina *f*. **up one's sleeve** di riserva.
sleigh [slei] *n* slitta *f*. *v* andare in slitta.
slender ['slendə] *adj* snello; (*small*) esiguo, scarso.
slept [slept] *V* **sleep.**
slice [slais] *n* fetta *f*; parte *f*, porzione *f*; (*spatula*) paletta *f*. *v* affettare, tagliare a fette; (*sport*) tagliare.
slick [slik] *adj* (*sleek*) lucido; (*coll: smooth*) untuoso; (*coll: shrewd*) spigliato, scaltro.
slid [slid] *V* **slide.**
***slide** [slaid] *n* (*inclined plane*) scivolo *m*; (*microscope*) vetrino *m*; (*phot*) diapositiva *f*; (*hair*) fibbia *f*; (*act of sliding*) scivolata *f*. **slide-rule** *n* regolo calcolatore *m*. *v* scivolare. **let slide** lasciar correre. **sliding scale** scala mobile *f*.
slight [slait] *adj* leggero; (*frail*) esile. *n* affronto *m*, dispetto *m*, mancanza di rispetto *f*. *v* mancare di rispetto, ignorare.
slim [slim] *adj* magro, snello; (*poor*) povero; (*scant*) minimo. *v* dimagrare. **slimming** *adj* dimagrante.
slime [slaim] *n* melma *f*; (*secretion*) bava *f*. **slimy** *adj* melmoso; bavoso; (*servile*) untuoso.
***sling** [sliŋ] *n* (*weapon*) fionda *f*; (*bandage*) benda *f*, fascia *f*; (*rifle*) cinghia *f*; (*hoist*) braca *f*. **have one's arm in a sling** portare un braccio al collo. *v* (*throw*) lanciare, gettare; (*suspend*) sospendere.
***slink** [sliŋk] *v* sgattaiolare.
slip [slip] *n* errore *m*, svista *f*; (*garment*) sottana *f*; (*skid*) scivolata *f*; (*plant*) rampollo *m*; (*of paper*) pezzetto *m*. **slip of the tongue** lapsus linguae *m invar*. *v* scivolare. **let slip** lasciar scappare. **slip away** andarsene. **slip-knot** *n* nodo scorsoio *m*. **slip-road** *n* raccordo *m*. **slip up** fare uno sbaglio, prendere una papera.
slipper ['slipə] *n* pantofola *f*, ciabatta *f*.
slippery ['slipəri] *adj* scivoloso.
***slit** [slit] *n* taglio *m*, fessura *f*. *v* tagliare, squarciare.
slither ['sliðə] *v* scivolare.
slobber ['slobə] *v* sbavare.
sloe [slou] *n* (*fruit*) prugnola *f*; (*tree*) prugnolo *m*.
slog [slog] *v* (*walk*) avanzare a fatica; (*toil*) faticare. *n* camminata dura *f*; faticata *f*.
slogan ['slougən] *n* motto *m*, slogan *m invar*.
slop [slop] *v* versare; (*spill over*) traboccare. **slops** *pl n* (*food*) pappa *f sing*; (*dirty water*) lavatura *f sing*.
slope [sloup] *n* pendio *m*. *v* inclinarsi, pendere. **sloping** *adj* inclinato, obliquo.
sloppy ['slopi] *adj* (*wet*) bagnato; (*careless*) abborracciato; (*untidy*) scatto; sentimentale.
slot [slot] *n* fessura *f*, apertura *f*. **slot-machine** *n* (*vending*) apparecchio a gettoni *m*; (*gambling*) slot-machine *m invar*. *v* **slot into** incanalare.
slouch [slautʃ] *v* (*walk*) camminare dinoccolato; (*droop*) languire. *n* andatura dinoccolata *f*.
slovenly ['slʌvnli] *adj* sciatto, trascurato.
slow [slou] *adj* lento; (*late*) tardo; (*clock*) indietro *invar*. *adv* piano, adagio. *v* **slow down** rallentare.
slug [slʌg] *n* lumaca *f*.
sluggish ['slʌgiʃ] *adj* lento, inerte.
sluice [sluːs] *n* chiusa *f*. *v* (*flush*) lavare abbondantemente.
slum [slʌm] *n* quartiere povero *or* basso *m*; (*tumbledown house*) tugurio *m*, catapecchia *f*.
slumber ['slʌmbə] *v* sonnecchiare. *n* (*heavy*) dormita *f*; (*light*) dormiveglia *m invar*.
slump [slʌmp] *n* crollo *m*, caduta *f*. *v* cadere, crollare.
slung [slʌŋ] *V* **sling.**
slunk [slʌŋk] *V* **slink.**
slur [sləː] *v* (*speech*) biascicare; (*disparage*) denigrare; (*music*) legare. **slur over** passar sopra a. *n* affronto *m*; (*blot*) macchia *f*.
slush [slʌʃ] *n* melma *f*. **slushy** *adj* melmoso.
slut [slʌt] *n* (*immoral*) sgualdrina *f*; (*slovenly*) sciattona *f*.
sly [slai] *adj* astuto, scaltro. **on the sly** in sordina.
smack[1] [smak] *n* (*hit*) schiaffo *m*; (*sound*) schiocco *m*; (*kiss*) bacione *m*. **smack in the eye** (*snub*) rabbuffo *m*; (*disappointment*) delusione *f*. *v* schiaffeggiare, schioccare. **smack one's lips** leccarsi i baffi.
smack[2] [smak] *n* sapore *m*. *v* **smack of** (*taste*) sapere di; (*suggest*) ricordare.
small [smoːl] *adj* piccolo; (*low*) basso; (*humble*) umile; insignificante. **small change** spiccioli *m pl*. **small fry** persone

di poco conto *f pl.* **small-minded** *adj* gretto. **smallpox** *n* vaiolo *m.* **small talk** chiacchera *f,* cicaleccio *m.*
smart [smaːt] *adj* (*sharp*) acuto; intelligente; (*shrewd*) sveglio; elegante; brillante. *v* bruciare, sentire un vivo dolore. **smarten** *v* abbellire, ravvivarsi.
smash [smaʃ] *n* (*collision*) scontro *m;* (*ruin*) rovina *f,* disastro *m;* (*tennis*) smash *m invar.* **smash-and-grab raid** (*coll*) spaccata *f.* *v* (*shatter*) fracassare; (*destroy*) annientare. **smashing** *adj* (*coll*) magnifico.
smear [smiə] *v* (*grease*) ungere; (*daub*) spalmare; (*soil*) macchiare; (*defame*) calunniare. *n* macchia *f;* (*slur*) calunnia *f.*
***smell** [smel] *n* odore *m,* profumo *m;* (*faculty*) odorato *m.* *v* sentire l'odore di; (*perceive*) fiutare; (*stink*) puzzare. **smell a rat** fiutare un imbroglio. **smell of** aver odore di.
smelt [smelt] *V* **smell.**
smile [smail] *n* sorriso *m.* *v* sorridere.
smirk [sməːk] *n* sorriso compiaciuto *m.* *v* sorridere con aria compiaciuta.
smock [smok] *n* camiciotto *m;* (*artists'*) blusa *f.* **smocking** *n* nido d'ape *m,* punto smock *m.*
smog [smog] *n* smog *m invar.*
smoke [smouk] *n* fumo *m.* **smoke-screen** *n* cortina di fumo *f.* **smoke-stack** *n* fumaiolo *m.* *v* fumare; (*cure*) affumicare. **smokeless** *adj* senza fumo. **smoker** *n* (*person*) fumatore, -trice *m, f;* (*compartment*) scompartimento per fumatori *m.* **smoky** *adj* fumoso, che sa di fumo.
smooth [smuːð] *adj* (*not rough*) liscio; (*unruffled*) calmo; (*not harsh*) gradevole. *v* lisciare, spianare, facilitare.
smother ['smʌðə] *v* soffocare, sopprimere.
smoulder ['smouldə] *v* covare (sotto la cenere).
smudge [smʌdʒ] *n* sgorbio *m.* *v* sgorbiare.
smug [smʌg] *adj* soddisfatto di sè.
smuggle ['smʌgl] *v* **smuggle in/out** far entrare/uscire di contrabbando. **smuggler** *n* contrabbandiere, -a *m, f.* **smuggling** *n* contrabbando *m.*
snack [snak] *n* (*light meal*) spuntino *m.*
snag [snag] *n* (*impediment*) intoppo *m.* *v* (*stocking*) smagliare.
snail [sneil] *n* chiocciola *f,* lumaca *f.*
snake [sneik] *n* serpente *m.*
snap [snap] *v* (*noise*) schioccare; (*break suddenly*) spezzarsi; (*phot*) scattare. **snap out of it** riprendersi. **snap up** non lasciarsi sfuggire. *n* schiocco *m;* rottura improvvisa *f;* (*sudden bite*) morsicata *f;* (*phot*) istantanea *f;* (*short spell*) ondata *f.* **snapdragon** *n* bocca di leone *f.* *adj* istantaneo. **snappy** *adj* irritabile; (*lively*) vivace.
snare [sneə] *n* laccio *m,* lacciolo *m.* *v* prendere al laccio; accalappiare.
snarl[1] [snaːl] *v* (*growl*) ringhiare. *n* ringhio *m.*
snarl[2] [snaːl] *n* (*tangle*) groviglio *m.* *v* aggrovigliare.
snatch [snatʃ] *v* ghermire, agguantare. *n* strappo *m;* (*scrap*) frammento *m.*
sneak [sniːk] *v* muoversi furtivamente; (*coll: steal*) squagliarsela; (*slang: tell tales*) spifferare. *n* (*coll*) spifferone, -a *m, f;* (*despicable person*) vigliacco, -a *m, f.*
sneakers *pl n* scarpe da tennis *or* ginnastica *f pl.*
sneer [sniə] *n* (*derisory*) ghigno *m;* (*contemptuous*) sogghigno *m.* *v* ghignare; sogghignare. **sneer at** canzonare, burlarsi di.
sneeze [sniːz] *n* starnuto *m.* *v* starnutire. **sneeze at** (*coll*) sprezzare.
sniff [snif] *n* annusare, fiutare; aspirare col naso. *n* annusata *f,* fiuto *m.*
snigger ['snigə] *v* ridere sotto i baffi, ridacchiare. *n* ghigno *m.*
snip [snip] *v* tagliuzzare; (*cut off*) spuntare. *n* (*piece*) ritaglio *m;* (*bargain*) occasione *f.*
snipe [snaip] *n* (*bird*) beccaccino *m.* *v* sparare di sorpresa. **sniper** *n* tiratore scelto che spara di soppiatto *m.*
snivel ['snivl] *v* moccicare; (*whine*) frignare. **sniveller** *n* moccioso, -a *m, f;* frignone, -a *m, f.*
snob [snob] *n* snob *m, f invar.*
snoop [snuːp] *v* curiosare.
snooty ['snuːti] *adj* (*coll*) sdegnoso, altezzoso.
snooze [snuːz] *v* sonnecchiare. *n* pisolino *m.*
snore [snoː] *v* russare, ronfare.
snorkel ['snoːkəl] *n* respiratore a tubo *m.*
snort [snoːt] *n* sbuffata *f.* *v* sbuffare.
snout [snaut] *n* muso *m;* (*pig*) grugno *m;* (*nozzle*) becco *m.*
snow [snou] *n* neve *f.* **snowball** *n* palla di neve *f.* **snowbound** *adj* bloccato dalla neve. **snow-drift** *n* cumulo *or* banco di neve *m.* **snowdrop** *n* bucaneve *m invar.*

snowfall *n* nevicata *f*. **snowflake** *n* fiocco di neve *m*. **snowman** *n* pupazzo di neve *m*. **snow-plough** *n* spazzaneve *m invar*. **snowstorm** *n* tormenta *f*. *v* nevicare. **snowy** *adj* nevoso; (*colour*) niveo, candido.

snub [snʌb] *n* rabbuffo *m*, affronto *m*. *v* trattare con disprezzo. **snub-nosed** *adj* camuso.

snuff[1] [snʌf] *v* fiutare, aspirare. *n* tabacco da fiuto *m*. **snuffbox** *n* tabacchiera *f*.

snuff[2] [snʌf] *v* **snuff it** (*coll*: *die*) crepare. **snuff out** spegnere.

snug [snʌg] *adj* (*comfortable*) comodo; (*cosy*) intimo; (*close-fitting*) aderente.

snuggle ['snʌgl] *v* rannicchiarsi; (*cuddle*) coccolare.

so [sou] *adv* cosi, tanto; (*to that extent*) talmente. *conj* perciò, quindi. **and so on** eccetera. **if so** in tal caso. **in so far as** per quanto. **so-called** *adj* cosiddetto. **so far** finora. **so long as** finché. **so much** tanto. **so-so** *adv* discretamente, cosi cosi. **so to speak** per cosi dire.

soak [souk] *v* inzuppare, imbevere. **be soaked through** essere bagnato fradicio. **soak in** penetrare. **soak up** assorbire.

soap [soup] *n* sapone *m*. **soap-dish** *n* portasapone *m invar*. **soap flakes/powder** sapone in scaglie/polvere *m*. **soap-suds** *n* saponata *f sing*. *v* insaponare. **soapy** *adj* (*covered with soap*) insaponato; (*like soap*) saponoso.

soar [soː] *v* librarsi; (*rise*) salire.

sob [sob] *n* singhiozzo *m*. *v* singhiozzare.

sober ['soubə] *adj* sobrio, calmo. *v* **sober down** calmarsi. **sober up** smaltire una sbornia. **sobriety** *n* moderatezza *f*, serietà *f*.

soccer ['sokə] *n* calcio *m*, football *m invar*.

sociable ['souʃəbl] *adj* socievole. **sociability** *n* socievolezza *f*.

social ['souʃəl] *adj* (*of a community*) sociale; (*disposition*) socievole; (*of polite society*) mondano. **social security** previdenza sociale *f*. **social worker** assistente sociale *m*. **socialism** *n* socialismo *m*. **socialist** *n*(*m*+*f*), *adj* socialista.

society [sə'saiəti] *n* società *f*, compagnia *f*.

sociology [sousi'olədʒi] *n* sociologia *f*. **sociological** *adj* sociologico. **sociologist** *n* sociologo, -a.

sock[1] [sok] *n* (*short*) calzino *m*; (*long*) calza *f*.

sock[2] [sok] (*slang*) *n* colpo *m*. *v* picchiare; (*punch*) prendere a pugni.

socket ['sokit] *n* cavità *f*; (*eye*) orbita *f*, occhiaia *f*; (*elec*) presa *f*.

soda ['soudə] *n* (*water*) seltz *m invar*; (*sodium carbonate*) soda *f*; soda caustica *f*.

sodden ['sodn] *adj* fradicio.

sofa ['soufə] *n* sofà *m invar*.

soft [soft] *adj* (*not hard*) molle; (*not rough*) morbido, soffice; (*pleasant*) mite, dolce; (*soothing*) tenero; (*water*) dolce. *adv* piano. **soften** *v* ammorbidire, intenerirsi. **softly** *adv* pian piano, adagio, dolcemente.

soggy ['sogi] *adj* fradicio, inzuppato.

soil[1] [soil] *n* suolo *m*, terra *f*.

soil[2] [soil] *v* sporcare, insudiciare.

solar ['soulə] *adj* solare.

sold [sould] *V* **sell**.

solder ['soldə] *n* saldatura *f*. *v* saldare. **soldering iron** saldatore *m*.

soldier ['souldʒə] *n* soldato *m*. *v* **soldier on** tirare avanti.

sole[1] [soul] *adj* solo, unico.

sole[2] [soul] *n* (*foot*) pianta *f*; (*shoe, tech*) suola *f*.

sole[3] [soul] *n* (*fish*) sogliola *f*.

solemn ['soləm] *adj* solenne, serio.

solicitor [sə'lisitə] *n* avvocato, -essa *m, f*.

solicitous [sə'lisitəs] *adj* premuroso.

solid ['solid] *adj* solido, sodo, compatto; (*sound*) serio. *n* (corpo) solido *m*. **solidarity** *n* solidarietà *f*. **solidity** *n* solidità *f*; serietà *f*.

solitary ['solitəri] *adj* solitario, solo, isolato. **solitary confinement** *n* reclusione *or* segregazione cellulare *f*.

solitude ['solitjuːd] *n* solitudine *f*, isolamento *m*.

solo ['soulou] *n* assolo *m*. *adj* solo, solitario. **soloist** *n* solista *m, f*.

solstice ['solstis] *n* solstizio *m*.

soluble ['soljubl] *adj* solubile.

solution [sə'luːʃən] *n* soluzione *f*.

solve [solv] *v* risolvere. **solvent** *nm, adj* solvente. **solvency** *n* solvenza *f*.

sombre ['sombə] *adj* tetro, fosco.

some [sʌm] *adj* del, della; (*pl*) dei, delle; qualche; (*certain*) alcuni. *pron* alcuni, -e; (*before verb*) ne. **somebody** *or* **someone** *pron* qualcuno. **somebody else** qualcun altro. **some day** un bel giorno. **somehow**

adv in qualche modo, in un modo o in un altro. **some ... some ...** gli uni ... gli altri .... **something** *pron* qualcosa. **something else** qualcos'altro. **sometime** *adv* un giorno o l'altro, presto o tardi. **sometimes** *adv* qualche volta; (*now and then*) di tanto in tanto. **somewhat** *adv* piuttosto. **somewhere** *adv* in qualche parte. **somewhere else** altrove.

somersault ['sʌməsoːlt] *n* capriola *f*, salto mortale *m*. *v* fare una capriola, fare un salto mortale.

son [sʌn] *n* figlio *m*. **son-in-law** *n* genero *m*.

sonata [sə'naːtə] *n* sonata *f*.

song [soŋ] *n* canzone *f*; (*act of singing*) canto *m*. **for a song** per una sciocchezza.

sonic ['sonik] *adj* sonico. **sonic bang** *or* **boom** boato sonico *m*.

sonnet ['sonit] *n* sonetto *m*.

soon [suːn] *adv* presto, tra poco. **as soon as** appena. **how soon?** fra quanto tempo? **soon after** subito dopo. **too soon** in anticipo. **very soon** tra breve, quanto prima. **no sooner said than done** detto fatto. **sooner or later** presto o tardi, prima o poi.

soot [sut] *n* fuliggine *f*. **sooty** *adj* fuligginoso.

soothe [suːð] *v* calmare, mitigare.

sophisticated [sə'fistikeitid] *adj* raffinato, sofisticato.

sopping ['sopiŋ] *adj* fradicio.

soprano [sə'praːnou] *n* soprano *m*, *f*.

sordid ['soːdid] *adj* sordido.

sore [soː] *adj* doloroso. **sore throat** mal di gola *m*. *n* piaga *f*, ulcera *f*.

sorrow ['sorou] *n* dolore *m*, dispiacere *m*; (*cause of regret*) rincrescimento *m*. **sorrowful** *adj* triste, addolorato; (*distressing*) penoso.

sorry ['sori] *adj* dolente, spiacente, triste; (*wretched*) meschino, miserabile. **feel sorry for** compatire. **I'm sorry** mi dispiace *or* rincresce. *interj* pardon! scusi! scusate!

sort [soːt] *n* sorta *f*, specie *f invar*. **a good sort** una brava persona *f*. **out of sorts** giù di giri. *v* classificare, raggruppare. **sort out** smistare; (*choose*) scegliere.

soufflé ['suːflei] *n* soufflé *m invar*.

sought [soːt] *V* **seek**.

soul [soul] *n* anima *f*, spirito *m*.

sound[1] [saund] *n* suono *m*; (*noise*) rumore *m*. **sound effect** effetto sonoro *m*. **soundproof** *adj* fonoassorbente, impenetrabile al suono. **sound-track** *n* colonna sonora *f*. *v* suonare; (*seem*) sembrare.

sound[2] [saund] *adj* (*not damaged*) sano; valido, legittimo; (*sleep, etc.*) profondo.

sound[3] [saund] *n* (*med*) sonda *f*. *v* sondare; (*naut*) scandagliare.

soup [suːp] *n* minestra *f*; (*broth*) brodo *m*; (*with bread*) zuppa *f*. **be in the soup** trovarsi nei pasticci. **soup-ladle** *n* cucchiaione *m*. **soup-plate** *n* fondina *f*.

sour [sauə] *adj* acido; (*tart, harsh*) acerbo, agro.

source [soːs] *n* sorgente *f*, origine *f*.

south [sauθ] *n* sud *m*; (*of country*) meridione *m*. *adj also* **southern, southerly** del sud; meridionale. *adv* (*direction*) verso sud; (*location*) al sud; (*origin*) dal sud. **south-east** *n* sudest *m*. **South Pole** polo sud *m*. **south-west** *n* sudovest *m*. **southernmost** *adj* il più a sud.

souvenir [suːvə'niə] *n* ricordo *m*.

sovereign ['sovrin] *n*, *adj* sovrano, -a. **sovereignty** *n* sovranità *f*.

***sow**[1] [sou] *v* seminare; disseminare.

sow[2] [sau] *n* scrofa *f*.

sown [soun] *V* **sow**[1].

soya ['soiə] *n* soia *f*.

spa [spaː] *n* terme *f pl*, stazione termale *f*.

space [speis] *n* spazio *m*. *v* scaglionare; (*printing*) spaziare. **spaceman** *n* astronauta *m*. **spaceship** *n* astronave *f*. **spacious** *adj* ampio, spazioso.

spade [speid] *n* badile *m*, vanga *f*. **call a spade a spade** dire pane al pane.

spades [speidz] *pl n* (*cards*) picche *f pl*.

Spain [spein] *n* Spagna *f*. **Spaniard** *n* spagnolo, -a *m*, *f*. **Spanish** *nm*, *adj* spagnolo.

span [span] *n* (*hand*) spanna *f*; (*bridge*) arco *m*; (*extent*) portata *f*; (*time*) durata *f*. *v* stendersi attraverso.

spaniel ['spanjəl] *n* spaniel *m invar*.

spank [spaŋk] *v* sculacciare.

spanner ['spanə] *n* chiave *f*; (*adjustable*) chiave inglese *f*.

spare [speə] *adj* di riserva *or* scorta; (*surplus*) in più, disponibile; frugale; (*lean*) magro. **spare part** pezzo di ricambio *m*. **spare room** camera in più *f*. **spare time** tempo disponibile *m*. **spare wheel** ruota di scorta *f*. *v* (*not harm*) risparmiare; (*do without*) fare a meno di. **spare no**

expense non badare a spese. **sparing** *adj* parco, sobrio, limitato.

spark [spaːk] *n* scintilla *f*; (*gleam*) barlume *m*. *v* emettere scintille, scintillare; (*elec*) accendere. **sparking-plug** *n* candela (d'accensione) *f*.

sparkle ['spaːkl] *n* scintilla *f*, splendore *m*. *v* scintillare, brillare, risplendere. **sparkling** *adj* brillante; (*wine*) spumante.

sparrow ['sparou] *n* passero *m*.

sparse [spaːs] *adj* rado, scarso. **sparsely** *adv* poco.

spasm ['spazəm] *n* accesso *m*; (*muscular*) spasmo *m*. **spasmodic** *adj* spasmodico.

spastic ['spastik] *n*, *adj* spastico, -a.

spat [spat] *V* **spit**[1].

spate [speit] *n* piena *f*.

spatial ['speiʃl] *adj* spaziale.

spatula ['spatjulə] *n* spatola *f*.

spawn [spoːn] *n* (*zool*) uova *f pl*; (*brood*) progenie *f*. *v* deporre uova; (*give rise to*) generare, produrre (in abbondanza); (*derog*) figliare.

***speak** [spiːk] *v* parlare. **so to speak** per così dire. **speaking of** a proposito di. **speak out** parlare apertamente. **speak up** (*loudly*) parlare ad alta voce, parlare più forte. **speak up for** parlare a favore di. **strictly speaking** per essere precisi. **speaker** *n* oratore *m*; (*pol*) presidente *m*; (*hi-fi*) cassa acustica.

spear [spiə] *n* lancia *f*. *v* trafiggere.

special ['speʃəl] *adj* speciale, particolare; straordinario. **specialist** *n* specialista *m*, *f*. **speciality** *n* specialità *f*. **specialization** *n* specializzazione *f*. **specialize** *v* specializzare.

species ['spiːʃiːz] *n* specie *f invar*, genere *m*.

specify ['spesifai] *v* specificare, precisare. **specific** *adj* specifico, preciso. **specification** *n* specificazione *f*; (*detailed description*) specifica *f*.

specimen ['spesimin] *n* esemplare *m*, modello *m*; (*for test*) campione *m*.

speck [spek] *n* (*spot*) macchia *f*; (*particle*) granello *m*. **speckle** *n* macchia *f*, chiazza *f*. **speckled** *adj* chiazzato.

spectacle ['spektəkl] *n* spettacolo *m*. **spectacles** *pl n* occhiali *m pl*. **spectacled** *adj* occhialuto.

spectator [spek'teitə] *n* spettatore, -trice *m*, *f*.

spectrum ['spektrəm] *n* spettro *m*.

speculate ['spekjuleit] *v* speculare, meditare. **speculation** *n* speculazione *f*. **speculative** *adj* speculativo. **speculator** *n* speculatore, -trice *m*, *f*.

sped [sped] *V* **speed**.

speech [spiːtʃ] *n* (*faculty*) parola *f*; discorso *m*. **speechless** *adj* muto, senza parole.

***speed** [spiːd] *n* velocità *f*. **at full speed** a tutta corsa, a velocità massima. **speedboat** *n* fuoribordo *m*. **speed limit** limite di velocità *m*. **speedometer** *n* tachimetro *m*. *v* andare in fretta. **speed up** accelerare. **speedy** *adj* veloce; (*ready*) pronto.

***spell**[1] [spel] *v* (*read*) compitare, sillabare; (*write*) scrivere; significare. **spelling** *n* ortografia *f*.

spell[2] [spel] *n* (*magic*) incanto *m*, incantesimo *m*; fascino *m*. **cast a spell** incantare. **spellbind** *v* affascinare.

spell[3] [spel] *n* periodo *m*; (*work*) turno *m*; (*bout*) attacco *m*.

spelt [spelt] *V* **spell**[1].

***spend** [spend] *v* spendere; (*employ*) impiegare, dedicare; (*time*) trascorrere, passare; (*consume*) esaurire. **spendthrift** *n*, *adj* prodigo, -a.

spent [spent] *V* **spend**.

sperm [spəːm] *n* sperma *m*.

spew [spjuː] *n* vomito *m*. *v* vomitare.

sphere [sfiə] *n* sfera *f*. **spherical** *adj* sferico.

spice [spais] *n* (*cookery*) spezie *f invar*; (*flavour*) gusto *m*, sapore *m*. *v* condire (con spezie); dar gusto *or* interesse a. **spicy** *adj* piccante, aromatico; salace.

spider ['spaidə] *n* ragno *m*. **spider's web** ragnatela *f*.

spike [spaik] *n* punta *f*, chiodo *m*. *v* inchiodare; (*frustrate*) rendere inservibile.

***spill** [spil] *v* spandere, versare. **spill over** traboccare.

spilt [spilt] *V* **spill**.

***spin** [spin] *v* (*thread*) filare; (*rotate*) (far) girare. **spin-drier** *n* centrifuga *f*, idroestrattore *m*. **spin-dry** *v* asciugare con la centrifuga. **spin out** prolungare. **spin a yarn** raccontare una frottola. *n* rotazione *f*; (*phys*) spin *m invar*; (*short trip*) giro *m*.

spinach ['spinidʒ] *n* spinaci *m pl*.

spindle ['spindl] *n* fuso *m*. **spindly** *adj* esile, affusolato.

spine [spain] *n* (*anat*) spina dorsale *f*; (*book*) dorso *m*. **spinal** *adj* spinale,

vertebrale. **spine-chilling** *adj* agghiacciante. **spineless** *adj* smidollato, debole.
spinster ['spinstə] *n* nubile *f*; (*coll*) zitella *f*.
spiral ['spaiərəl] *n* spirale *f*. *adj* a spirale. **spiral staircase** scala a chiocciola *f*.
spire ['spaiə] *n* guglia *f*.
spirit ['spirit] *n* spirito *m*; (*drink*) superalcolico *m*. **be in high spirits** avere il morale alto; essere allegro. **spirit-level** *n* livella a bolla d'aria *f*. **that's the spirit!** così va bene! **spirited** *adj* vivace, vigoroso. **spiritless** *adj* (*without vigour*) fiacco; (*not lively*) abbattuto. **spiritual** *adj* spirituale. **spiritualism** *n* spiritismo *m*; (*philos*) spiritualismo *m*. **spiritualist** *n* spiritista *m*, *f*.
***spit**[1] [spit] *v* sputare; (*rain*) piovigginare; (*cat*) soffiare. **the spitting image of . . .** . . . nato e sputato. *n also* **spittle** sputo *m*, saliva *f*.
spit[2] [spit] *n* (*skewer*) spiedo *m*; (*land*) lingua di terra *f*. *v* (*skewer*) infilzare.
spite [spait] *n* dispetto *m*. **in spite of** nonostante, malgrado. *v* far dispetto a; (*annoy*) indispettire. **spiteful** *adj* dispettoso, maligno.
splash [splaʃ] *v* (*spatter*) spruzzare; (*mark with colour*) macchiare, chiazzare. *n* spruzzata *f*; (*sound*) tonfo *m*; (*liquid splashed*) spruzzo *m*; (*patch*) macchia *f*; (*showy display*) sfoggio *m*.
spleen [spliːn] *n* (*med*) milza *f*; (*peevishness*) malumore *m*. **vent one's spleen on** sfogarsi su.
splendid ['splendid] *adj* splendido, stupendo. **splendour** *n* splendore *m*.
splice [splais] *v* (*rope*) impiombare; (*tape*) giuntare. *n* impiombatura *f*; giuntura *f*.
splint [splint] *n* stecca *f*.
splinter ['splintə] *n* scheggia *f*. *v* frantumarsi.
***split** [split] *v* (*cleave*) spaccare; dividere, separare. **split hairs** cavillare. **split on** (*coll*) denunciare. **split up** dividersi, suddividere. *n* fenditura *f*; (*into fractions*) scissione *f*; separazione *f*. *adj* spaccato.
splutter ['splʌtə] *v* (*spit*) sputacchiare; (*talk confusedly*) farfugliare; (*splash*) spruzzare; (*engine*) scoppiettare.
***spoil** [spoil] *v* rovinare, sciupare; (*indulge*) viziare. **be spoiling for** aver una gran voglia di. **spoil-sport** *n* guastafeste *m*, *f invar*. **spoils** *pl n* spoglie *f pl*.
spoilt [spoilt] *V* **spoil**.
spoke[1] [spouk] *V* **speak**.
spoke[2] [spouk] *n* raggio *m*; (*rung*) piolo *m*. **put a spoke in someone's wheel** mettere un bastone fra le ruote a qualcuno.
spoken ['spoukn] *V* **speak**.
spokesman ['spouksmən] *n* portavoce *m*, *f invar*.
sponge [spʌndʒ] *n* spugna *f*. **sponge-cake** *n* pan di Spagna *m*. **throw in the sponge** gettare la spugna. *v* lavare con la spugna; (*coll*: *cadge*) scroccare. **sponger** *n* scroccone, -a *m*, *f*. **spongy** *adj* spugnoso.
sponsor ['sponsə] *n* garante *m*, *f*; (*TV*, *etc*.) finanziatore, -trice *m*, *f*. *v* essere garante di; rendersi responsabile di; finanziare; (*lend support*) patrocinare. **sponsorship** *n* garanzia *f*; finanziamento *m*.
spontaneous [spon'teinjəs] *adj* spontaneo. **spontaneity** *n* spontaneità *f*.
spool [spuːl] *n* rocchetto *m*.
spoon [spuːn] *n* cucchiaio *m*. **spoonfeed** *v* scodellare la pappa a. **spoonful** *n* cucchiaiata *f*.
sporadic [spə'radik] *adj* isolato.
sport [spoːt] *n* sport *m invar*; (*jesting*) scherzo *m*. **be a sport!** sii bravo! **sportsman** *n* sportivo *m*. **sportsmanship** *n* abilità sportiva *f*; spirito sportivo *m*. **sportswoman** *n* sportiva *f*. *v* (*display*) sfoggiare. **sporting** *adj* sportivo. **sporting chance** possibilità di successo *f*.
spot [spot] *n* (*mark*) macchia *f*, puntino *m*; (*pimple*) piccolo foruncolo *m*; (*place*) posto *m*, località *f*. **on the spot** sul posto. **spot check** controllo saltuario *m*. **spotlight** *n* riflettore *m*. *v* macchiare, punteggiare; (*see*) riconoscere, scoprire, osservare. **spotless** *adj* immacolato. **spotter** *n* osservatore, -trice *m*, *f*.
spouse [spaus] *n* sposo, -a *m*, *f*, coniuge *m*, *f*.
spout [spaut] *n* becco *m*, beccuccio *m*; (*chute*) scivolo *m*; (*jet*) getto *m*. **up the spout** (*lost*) perduto; (*in a bad way*) ridotto male. *v* (*discharge*) scaricare, gettare; (*gush out*) scaturire; (*coll*; *talk*) declamare.
sprain [sprein] *v* (*strain*) storcere; (*wrench*) slogare. *n* storta *f*; slogatura *f*.
sprang [spraŋ] *V* **spring**.
sprawl [sproːl] *v* stendersi lungo disteso; (*spread out*) estendersi. **send sprawling** mandare a gambe all'aria.

spray[1] [sprei] *n* (*appliance*) spray *m invar*, atomizzatore *m*; (*hail*) raffica *f*. *v* spruzzare, atomizzare; (*scatter*) spargere.
spray[2] [sprei] *n* (*branch*) frasca *f*.
***spread** [spred] *v* (*lay out*) stendere; (*distribute*) spargere; (*disseminate*) diffondere; (*apply layer*) spalmare. *n* estensione *f*, diffusione *f*; (*cover*) coperta *f*; (*coll*: *feast*) banchetto *m*.
spree [spriː] *n* baldoria *f*.
sprig [sprig] *n* ramoscello *m*.
sprightly ['spraitli] *adj* vivace.
***spring** [spriŋ] *v* (*rise suddenly*) saltare, balzare; (*move rapidly*) scattare. **spring a leak** aprire una falla. **spring from** derivare *or* provenire da. **spring up** (*arise*) nascere; (*originate*) sorgere; (*jump up*) balzare; (*come forth*) spuntare. *n* (*beginning*) origine *f*; (*source of water*) sorgente *f*; (*season*) primavera *f*; (*coil*) molla *f*. *adj* primaverile, giovane. **spring-board** *n* trampolino *m*. **spring onion** cipollina *f*.
sprinkle ['spriŋkl] *v* spargere, cospargere; (*liquid*) spruzzare. **sprinkler** *n* (*watering can*) annaffiatoio *m*; (*fire*) nebulizzatore (antincendio) *m*. **sprinkling** *n* (*of knowledge*) infarinatura *f*.
sprint [sprint] *n* (*sport*) sprint *m invar*; volata *f*. *v* correre di volata, scattare. **sprinter** *n* sprinter *m, f invar*, velocista *m, f*.
sprout [spraut] *v* germogliare. *n* germoglio *m*. **Brussels sprouts** cavolini di Bruxelles *m pl*.
spruce [spruːs] *n* abete *m*.
sprung [sprʌŋ] *V* **spring**.
spun [spʌn] *V* **spin**.
spur [spəː] *n* sprone *m*. **on the spur of the moment** lì per lì. *v* **spur on** incitare.
spurious ['spjuəriəs] *adj* falso, spurio.
spurn [spəːn] *v* sdegnare; rifiutare.
spurt [spəːt] *n* (*gush*) getto improvviso *m*, zampillo *m*; (*burst*) scatto *m*; (*effort*) sforzo *m*. *v* zampillare.
spy [spai] *n* spia *f*. *v* spiare, fare la spia. **spying** *n* spionaggio *m*.
squabble ['skwobl] *v* litigare, bisticciarsi. *n* alterco *m*, bisticcio *m*, lite *f*.
squad [skwod] *n* squadra *f*.
squadron ['skwodrən] *n* squadriglia *f*.
squalid ['skwolid] *adj* squallido.
squall [skwoːl] *n* raffica *f*.
squander ['skwondə] *v* sprecare, sperperare. **squanderer** *n* sprecone, -a *m, f*.
square [skweə] *n* quadrato *m*; (*street*) piazza *f*; (*instrument*) squadra *f*. *adj* quadro; (*math*) quadrato; (*corner*) ad angolo retto; perpendicolare; (*settled*) saldato; (*straightforward*) diretto, netto. **square meal** pasto sostanzioso *m*. *v* (*math*) quadrare; (*accounts*) saldare; (*regulate*) mettere a punto; (*coll*: *bribe*) corrompere. **square up to** affrontare.
squash [skwoʃ] *v* schiacciare, spremere; (*suppress*) sopprimere; ridurre al silenzio, umiliare. *n* (*drink*) spremuta *f*; (*sport*) squash *m invar*; (*crowd*) ressa *f*.
squat [skwot] *v* rannicchiarsi, accovacciarsi; (*occupy illegally*) occupare abusivamente. *adj* tarchiato, tozzo.
squawk [skwoːk] *v* schiamazzare. *n* schiamazzo *m*.
squeak [skwiːk] *v* stridere, cigolare. *n* strido *m*, cigolio *m*. **have a narrow squeak** scamparla bella.
squeal [skwiːl] *v* strillare; (*coll*: *complain*) protestare. *n* strillo *m*.
squeamish ['skwiːmiʃ] *adj* schizzinoso, schifiltoso.
squeeze [skwiːz] *v* (*press*) spremere; (*force*) pigiare; (*embrace*) stringere; (*press together*) comprimere. *n* stretta *f*; (*crowd*) calca *f*; (*comm*) restrizioni *f pl*.
squid [skwid] *n* calamaro *m*, seppia *f*.
squiggle ['skwigl] *n* sgorbio *m*. *v* sgorbiare.
squint [skwint] *v* (*be cross-eyed*) essere guercio *or* strabico; (*glance sideways*) guardare di traverso. *n* sguardo torto *m*, strabismo *m*. **squint-eyed** *adj* guercio, strabico.
squire ['skwaiə] *n* gentiluomo *m*, proprietario di terre *m*.
squirm [skwəːm] *v* (*wriggle*) dimenarsi, contorcersi; (*feel embarrassed*) essere sulle spine.
squirrel ['skwirəl] *n* scoiattolo *m*.
squirt [skwəːt] *v* schizzare. *n* (*jet*) schizzo *m*; (*syringe*) schizzetto *m*; (*derog*) ometto *m*, tizio *m*.
stab [stab] *v* pugnalare, accoltellare. **stab in the back** pugnalare alle spalle. *n* pugnalata *f*, coltellata *f*; (*try*) tentativo *m*. **have a stab at** tentare di.
stabilize ['steibilaiz] *v* stabilizzare. **stabilization** *n* stabilizzazione *f*. **stabilizer** *n* stabilizzatore *m*.

stable[1] ['steibl] *n* stalla *f*; (*racing*) scuderia *f*.

stable[2] ['steibl] *adj* stabile; (*firm*) saldo; permanente. **stability** *n* stabilità *f*, fermezza *f*.

staccato [stə'kaːtou] *adj* staccato.

stack [stak] *n* (*heap*) catasta *f*, mucchio *m*; (*chimney*) fumaiolo *m*. *v* accatastare, ammucchiare.

stadium ['steidiəm] *n* stadio *m*.

staff [staːf] *n* (*stick*) bastone *m*; (*flag-pole*) asta *f*; (*personnel*) personale *m*; (*mil*) stato maggiore *m*. *v* fornire di personale, impiegare.

stag [stag] *n* cervo *m*. **stag-beetle** *n* cervo volante *m*.

stage [steidʒ] *n* (*phase*) fase *f*; (*lap*) tappa *f*; periodo *m*, momento *m*; teatro *m*; (*platform*) palcoscenico *m*. **at this stage** a questo punto. **go on the stage** fare l'attore. **stage-coach** *n* diligenza *f*. **stage-craft** *n* scenotecnica *f*. **stage fright** timor panico *m*. **stage-manager** *n* direttore di scena *m*. *v* rappresentare, mettere in scena. **staging** *n* messa in scena *f*.

stagger ['stagə] *v* barcollare; (*shock*) colpire, impressionare; (*arrange*) scaglionare. **staggering** *adj* sconcertante.

stagnant ['stagnənt] *adj* stagnante, inattivo. **stagnate** *v* ristagnare. **stagnation** *n* ristagno *m*.

staid [steid] *adj* posato, serio.

stain [stein] *n* macchia *f*; tinta *f*, colore *m*. **stain remover** smacchiatore *m*. *v* macchiare; colorire. **stainless steel** acciaio inossidabile *m*.

stair [steə] *n* (*step*) scalino *m*, gradino *m*. **staircase** *n* scala *f*. **stairs** *pl n* scale *f pl*.

stake[1] [steik] *n* (*post*) palo *m*; (*execution*) rogo *m*. *v* (*support*) palare. **stake out** cintare. **stake out a claim** reclamare.

stake[2] [steik] *n* (*bet*) posta *f*, scommessa *f*. **at stake** in gioco. *v* mettere in gioco, scommettere. **stake one's life** scommettere l'osso del collo.

stale [steil] *adj* vecchio, stantio; (*bread*) raffermo.

stalemate ['steilmeːit] *n* stallo *m*; (*deadlock*) punto morto *m*. **reach stalemate** giungere a una posizione di stallo.

stalk[1] [stoːk] *n* stelo *m*, gambo *m*.

stalk[2] [stoːk] *v* (*follow*) inseguire furtivamente; (*stride haughtily*) camminare impettito.

stall[1] [stoːl] *n* banco *m*, chiosco *m*; (*newspapers*) edicola *f*; (*theatre*) poltrona di platea *f*. **stalls** *pl n* (*theatre*) platea *f sing*. *v* (*engine*) imballare; (*aeroplane*) picchiare; (*stop*) fermarsi.

stall[2] [stoːl] *v* (*delay*) tirar per le lunghe; (*act evasively*) cercar pretesti.

stallion ['staljən] *n* stallone *m*.

stamina ['staminə] *n* vigore *m*, capacità di resistenza *f*.

stammer ['stamə] *v* balbettare. *n* balbuzie *f*. **stammerer** *n* balbuziente *m*, *f*.

stamp [stamp] *v* marcare, imprimere; (*envelope*) affrancare; (*print on*) timbrare; (*documents*) bollare; (*with foot*) pestare. **stamp out** domare, annientare. *n* (*impression*) impronta *f*; marchio *m*; (*document*) bollo *m*; (*postage*) francobollo *m*; (*implement*) stampiglia *f*; (*rubber*) timbro *m*. **stamp-collector** *n* filatelico, -a *m*, *f*.

stampede [stam'piːd] *n* fuga precipitosa *f*. *v* fuggire in disordine.

***stand** [stand] *n* posizione *f*; (*platform*) tribuna *f*; (*exhibition*) stand *m invar*; (*music, etc.*) leggio *m*. *v* stare, essere; (*be upright*) stare in piedi; (*remain*) restare; (*tolerate*) sopportare, tollerare. **stand by** (*wait*) rimanere in attesa; (*help*) aiutare; (*remain faithful*) restar fedele a. **stand-by** *n* riserva *f*, scorta *f*. **stand for** significare; (*support*) sostenere. **stand-in** *n* controfigura *f*. **stand-offish** *adj* riservato. **stand out** (*project*) spiccare; (*be conspicuous*) risaltare. **standstill** *n* arresto *m*, fermata *f*. **come to a standstill** fermarsi. **stand up** alzarsi. **stand up for** prender la parte di. **stand up to** resistere a.

standard ['standəd] *n* standard *m invar*, modello *m*, campione *m*; (*level*) livello *m*; (*flag*) stendardo *m*, bandiera *f*. *adj* standard *invar*, normale. **standard lamp** torciera *f*, piantana *f*.

standing ['standiŋ] *n* posizione *f*, reputazione *f*; (*period*) durata *f*. *adj* fermo, fisso; permanente; abituale; (*upright*) in piedi. **leave standing** abbandonare sul posto.

stank [staŋk] *V* **stink**.

stanza ['stanzə] *n* strofa *f*.

staple[1] [steipl] *n* graffa *f*; (*stationery*) punto metallico *m*. *v* graffare; cucire (con punti metallici). **stapler** *n* cucitrice *f*.

staple[2] [steipl] *n* prodotto principale *m*; (*textile*) fiocco *m*. *adj* principale, base *invar*.

star [staɪ] *n* stella *f*; (*actor*) divo, -a *m, f*. **starfish** *n* stella di mare *f*. *adj* principale. *v* (*cinema, etc.*) primeggiare. **starry** *adj* stellato. **starry-eyed** *adj* (*coll*) ingenuo.

starboard ['staɪbəd] *n* dritta *f*.

starch [staɪtʃ] *n* amido *m*, fecola *f*. *v* inamidare. **starchy** *adj* (*food*) ricco d'amido; (*manner*) rigido.

stare [steə] *v* fissare; (*gaze fixedly*) sgranare gli occhi. **stare in the face** (*be obvious*) saltare agli occhi, essere ovvio. *n* sguardo fisso *m*.

stark [staɪk] *adj* rigido; (*bleak*) brullo. **stark mad** matto da legare. **stark naked** completamente nudo, nudo nato.

starling ['staɪliŋ] *n* storno *m*, stornello *m*.

start [staɪt] *n* (*beginning*) inizio *m*; (*point of departure*) partenza *f*; (*sudden movement*) soprassalto *m*; (*lead*) vantaggio *m*. **by fits and starts** a sbalzi. *v* iniziare, cominciare; partire; (*jump*) sussultare; (*set in motion*) mettere in moto. **to start with** per cominciare. **starter** *n* starter *m invar*, motorino d'avviamento *m*.

startle ['staɪtl] *v* (far) trasalire, sbigottire. **startling** *adj* sorprendente.

starve [staɪv] *v* affamare; (*to death*) (far) morire di fame; (*be very hungry*) soffrire la fame. **starve of** (far) soffrire per mancanza di. **starvation** *n* fame *f*.

state [steit] *n* stato *m*; pompa *f*; (*coll*) ansietà *f*. **statesman** *n* uomo di stato *m*. *adj* statale; solenne. *v* dichiarare, affermare; specificare; indicare. **stateless** *adj* apolide. **stately** *adj* solenne, maestoso. **statement** *n* affermazione *f*, dichiarazione *f*; (*bank, etc.*) estratto conto *m*.

static ['statik] *adj* fisso, statico. **statics** *n* statica *f*.

station ['steiʃən] *n* stazione *f*; (*headquarters*) sede *f*; (*rank*) condizione sociale *f*. **station-master** *n* capostazione (*pl* capistazione) *m*. **station-wagon** *n* (*US*) giardinetta *f*. *v* appostare, collocare.

stationary ['steiʃənəri] *adj* fermo; costante, fisso.

stationer ['steiʃənə] *n* cartolaio, -a *m, f*. **stationer's** *n* cartoleria *f*. **stationery** *n* oggetti di cancelleria *m pl*.

statistics [stə'tistiks] *n* statistica *f*. **statistical** *adj* statistico. **statistician** *n* statistico, -a *m, f*.

statue ['statjuː] *n* statua *f*.

stature ['statʃə] *n* statura *f*.

status ['steitəs] *n* posizione sociale *f*, rango *m*, prestigio *m*.

statute ['statjuɪt] *n* decreto *m*, legge *f*.

staunch [stoɪntʃ] *adj* fedele, leale. *v* stagnare.

stay [stei] *n* soggiorno *m*; arresto *m*; (*law*) sospensione *f*. *v* (*remain*) restare, rimanere; (*on holiday, etc.*) soggiornare; (*at hotel*) alloggiare (in); (*stop*) sostare; sospendere. **stay in** non uscire, restare a casa. **stay on** trattenersi. **stay out** rimaner fuori, non rientrare.

steadfast ['stedfaɪst] *adj* risoluto, saldo.

steady ['stedi] *adj* fermo, stabile; (*responsible*) serio; regolare; costante. *v* reggersi, tener fermo; calmare.

steak [steik] *n* (*meat*) bistecca *f*; (*fish*) trancia *f*.

***steal** [stiɪl] *v* rubare. **steal away** andarsene di nascosto. **steal a march on** prevenire.

stealthy ['stelθi] *adj* clandestino. **stealthily** *adv* di nascosto *or* soppiatto.

steam [stiɪm] *n* vapore *m*; (*coll*: *energy*) carica *f*. **let off steam** (*coll*) sfogarsi. *v* emettere vapore; (*cook*) cucinare a vapore. **steam up** appannarsi. **steamer** *n* (*boat*) piroscafo *m*; (*cookery*) pentola a vapore *f*. **steamy** *adj* pieno di vapore.

steam-roller *n* rullo compressore *m*; (*coll*) forza irresistibile *f*. *v* sopraffare.

steel [stiɪl] *n* acciaio *m*. *v* indurire. **steely** *adj* d'acciaio, inflessibile.

steep[1] [stiɪp] *adj* (*sheer*) ripido; (*coll*: *unreasonable*) eccessivo.

steep[2] [stiɪp] *v* (*soak*) inzuppare; (*tech*) macerare.

steeple ['stiɪpl] *n* (*spire*) guglia *f*; (*tower*) campanile *m*.

steer[1] [stiə] *n* (*ox*) manzo *m*.

steer[2] [stiə] *v* guidare, dirigere. **steer clear of** evitare. **steering-wheel** *n* volante *m*.

stem[1] [stem] *n* (*stalk*) gambo *m*; (*of pipe*) cannello; (*branch*) ramo *m*; (*of word*) radice *f*. *v* **stem from** derivare da.

stem[2] [stem] *v* contenere, arginare.

stench [stentʃ] *n* puzzo *m*.

stencil ['stensl] *n* (*device*) stampino *m*; (*duplicating machine*) ciclostile *m*. *v* stampinare; ciclostilare.

step [step] *n* passo *m*; (*stair*) gradino *m*; (*measure*) provvedimento *m*. **out of step** non conforme. **step by step** un poco alla volta, per gradi. **step-ladder** *n* scala a libretto *f*, scaleo *m*. **watch one's step**

stare attenti. *v* fare un passo; (*walk*) camminare. **step down** scendere; (*retire*) ritirarsi. **step in** entrare; intervenire. **step up** salire; aumentare; accelerare.
stepbrother ['stepbrʌðə] *n* fratellastro *m*.
stepdaughter ['stepdoːtə] *n* figliastra *f*.
stepfather ['stepfaːðə] *n* patrigno *m*.
stepmother ['stepmʌðə] *n* matrigna *f*.
stepsister ['stepsistə] *n* sorellastra *f*.
stepson ['stepsʌn] *n* figliastro *m*.
stereo ['steriou] *adj* stereo. **stereophonic** *adj* stereofonico.
stereotype ['steriətaip] *n* cliché *m*; (*tech*) stereotipia *f*. **stereotyped** *adj* (*trite*) stereotipato; (*tech*) stereotipo.
sterile ['sterail] *adj* sterile. **sterility** *n* sterilità *f*. **sterilization** *n* sterilizzazione *f*. **sterilize** *v* sterilizzare.
sterling ['stəːliŋ] *n* sterlina *f*. *adj* genuino.
stern[1] [stəːn] *adj* (*harsh*) severo; (*strict*) rigoroso.
stern[2] [stəːn] *n* (*ship*) poppa *f*.
stethoscope ['steθəskoup] *n* stetoscopio *m*.
stew [stjuː] *n* spezzatino *m*, stufato *m*. **be in a stew** essere preoccupato *or* turbato. *v* cuocere (a fuoco lento).
steward ['stjuəd] *n* amministratore, -trice *m*, *f*; (*ship*) cameriere di bordo *m*, steward *m invar*. **stewardess** *n* stewardess *f invar*, assistente di volo *f*. **stewardship** *n* gestione *f*; (*office*) carica di amministratore *f*.
stick[1] [stik] *n* (*wood*) bastone *m*; (*celery, etc.*) gambo *m*; (*small rod*) bastoncino *m*. **be in a cleft stick** non sapere che pesci pigliare.
***stick**[2] [stik] *v* attaccare, appiccicare; (*stab*) ficcare; (*remain*) rimanere. **stick it out** tener duro. **stick out** (*be conspicuous*) saltare agli occhi; (*put out*) tirar fuori. **stick to** (*not digress*) attenersi a, non divagare da; (*remain loyal*) restar fedele a. **stick up for** difendere, battersi per. **sticky** *adj* attaccaticcio; adesivo; (*weather*) pesante; (*coll*; *difficult*) complesso.
stickler ['stiklə] *n* pignolo, -a *m*, *f*. **stickler for ...** persona ligia a ... .
stiff [stif] *adj* rigido; (*hard to move, difficult*) duro; (*formal*) freddo. *adv* (*coll*) a morte. **stiffen** *v* irrigidire. **stiffness** *n* rigidezza *f*; durezza *f*.
stifle ['staifl] *v* soffocare.
stigma ['stigmə] *n* segno *m*, marchio *m*; (*disgrace*) stigma *m*.
stile [stail] *n* scaletta *f*.
still[1] [stil] *adj* (*quiet*) tranquillo; (*motionless*) immobile. *adv* ancora, tuttora. **stillborn** *adj* nato morto. *n* silenzio *m*; (*phot*) posa *f*. *v* calmare. **stillness** *n* silenzio *m*, tranquillità *f*.
still[2] [stil] *n* distilleria *f*; (*retort*) storta *f*.
stilt [stilt] *n* trampolo *m*; (*building*) palafitta *f*. **stilted** *adj* artificiale; (*pompous*) ampolloso.
stimulus ['stimjuləs] *n pl* **-li** stimolo *m*. **stimulant** *nm*, *adj* stimolante. **stimulate** *v* stimolare. **stimulation** *n* stimolo *m*.
***sting** [stiŋ] *v* (*wound*) pungere; (*incite*) spronare; (*coll*: *cheat*) truffare. *n* puntura *f*; (*pang*) morso *m*; (*incitement*) sprone *m*.
stingy ['stindʒi] *adj* tirchio, spilorcio. **stinginess** *n* tirchieria *f*, spilorceria *f*.
***stink** [stiŋk] *n* puzzo *m*. *v* puzzare. **stinking** *adj* puzzolente, fetente.
stint [stint] *n* dovere *m*, periodo di lavoro *m*. *v* risparmiare, fare economia.
stipulate ['stipjuleit] *v* pattuire, convenire. **stipulation** *n* patto *m*, condizione *f*, convenzione *f*.
stir [stəː] *v* mescolare, agitare; (*budge*) muoversi. **stir up** eccitare, incitare. *n* (*excitement*) scalpore *m*; confusione *f*. **stirring** *adj* (*touching*) commovente; eccitante.
stirrup ['stirəp] *n* staffa *f*.
stitch [stitʃ] *n* (*sewing*) punto *m*; (*knitting*) maglia *f*. *v* cucire; (*sew on*) attaccare; (*med*) suturare.
stoat [stout] *n* ermellino *m*.
stock [stok] *n* (*goods*) provvista *f*, stock *m invar*, riserva *f*; (*standing*) credito *m*; famiglia *f*; (*cookery*) brodo *m*. **stockbroker** *n* agente di cambio *m*. **stock exchange** borsa valori *f*. **stockholder** *n* azionista *m*, *f*. **stockpile** *v* far scorta di. **stocks and shares** titoli *m pl*. **stocktaking** *n* inventario *m*. *v* (*supply*) fornire, rifornire; tenere in magazzino.
stocking ['stokiŋ] *n* calza *f*.
stocky ['stoki] *adj* tarchiato, tozzo.
stodge [stodʒ] (*coll*) *n* (*food*) cibo pesante *m*; (*dull matter*) mattone *m*. **stodgy** *adj* pesante; (*tedious*) noioso.
stoical ['stouikl] *adj* stoico. **stoic** *n* stoico, -a *m*, *f*.
stoke [stouk] *v* alimentare. **stoke up** rimpinzarsi. **stoker** *n* fuochista *m*.

stole[1] [stoul] *V* **steal.**
stole[2] [stoul] *n* stola *f.*
stolen ['stoulən] *V* **steal.**
stomach ['stʌmək] *n* stomaco *m.* **stomach-ache** *n* mal di stomaco *m.* *v* (*tolerate*) sopportare.
stone [stoun] *n* pietra *f*; (*pebble*) sasso *m*; (*fruit*) nocciolo *m*; (*med*) calcolo *m.* **a stone's throw from** a due passi da. **stone-deaf** *adj* sordo come una campana. **stonemason** *n* muratore *m.* **stoneware** *n* gres *m invar.* *v* prendere a sassate; (*fruit*) snocciolare.
stood [stud] *V* **stand.**
stool [stuːl] *n* sgabello *m.* **stool-pigeon** *n* spia *f.*
stoop [stuːp] *v* curvare, chinarsi; (*condescend*) abbassarsi. *n* **walk with a stoop** camminar curvo.
stop [stop] *n* (*halt*) sosta *f*, fermata *f*; (*punctuation*) punto *m*; (*organ*) registro *m.* *v* finire, smettere; (*halt*) fermare; (*prevent*) impedire; (*withhold*) trattenere; (*block*) turare. **stop-press** *n* ultimissime *f pl.* **stop-watch** *n* cronometro a scatto *m.* **stoppage** *n* fermata *f*, arresto *m*; sospensione *f*; (*med*) blocco *m.* **stopper** *n* (*bung*) tappo *m.*
store [stoː] *n* (*supply*) provvista *f*, riserva *f*; (*shop*) bottega *f*; (*warehouse*) magazzino *m.* **storekeeper** *n* magazziniere *m.* *v* fare provviste di; conservare; accumulare; mettere in magazzino. **storage** *n* immagazzinamento *m*; (*comm*) magazzinaggio *m.*
storey ['stoːri] *n* piano *m.*
stork [stoːk] *n* cicogna *f.*
storm [stoːm] *n* tempesta *f*; (*thunder*) temporale *m.* *v* (*rage*) infuriarsi; (*rush*) precipitarsi; (*mil*) prendere d'assalto. **stormy** *adj* burrascoso.
story ['stoːri] *n* storia *f*, racconto *m*; (*news*) fatto di cronaca *m.*
stout [staut] *adj* (*fat*) grasso; intrepido; robusto.
stove [stouv] *n* stufa *f*; (*cooker*) cucina *f.*
stow [stou] *v* stivare; (*fill*) riempire (di). **stow away** mettere da parte; (*on boat, etc.*) imbarcarsi clandestinamente. **stowaway** *n* passeggero clandestino *m.* **stowage** *n* stivaggio *m.*
straddle ['stradl] *v* stare a cavalcioni, cavalcare.
straggle ['stragl] *v* disperdersi; (*lag behind*) rimanere indietro. **straggler** *n* ritardatario, -a *m, f.*
straight [streit] *adj* diritto; (*open*) franco, aperto. *adv* diritto, in linea retta; (*directly*) direttamente. **straight away** subito. **straightforward** *adj* franco, aperto; onesto; semplice. **straighten** *v* raddrizzare; (*order*) assettare.
strain[1] [strein] *v* filtrare, passare; (*force*) sforzare; (*sprain*) storcere. *n* sforzo *m*, tensione *f*; (*med*) storta *f*; (*tune*) melodia *f.* **strained** *adj* forzato; filtrato. **strainer** *n* filtro *m*, colino *m.*
strain[2] [strein] *n* (*race*) stirpe *f*, famiglia *f.*
strait [streit] *n* (*geog*) stretto *m.* **straits** *pl n* difficoltà *f pl.* *adj* **strait-laced** *adj* rigoroso, puritano.
strand[1] [strand] *n* (*hair*) ciocca *f*; (*rope*) fune *f.*
strand[2] [strand] *n* (*shore*) spiaggia *f*, sponda *f.* *v* arenare, incagliarsi.
strange [streindʒ] *adj* strano, misterioso; (*unaccountable*) inspiegabile. **stranger** *n* sconosciuto, -a *m, f*; estraneo, -a *m, f*; (*foreigner*) straniero, -a *m, f.*
strangle ['straŋgl] *v* strangolare. **strangulation** *n* strangolamento *m.*
strap [strap] *n* cinghia *f*; (*on garment*) spallina *f*; (*watch*) cinturino *m.* *v* **strap up** assicurare con cinghia; (*med*) fissare con cerotto. **strapping** *adj* robusto.
strategy ['stratədʒi] *n* strategia *f.* **strategic** *adj* strategico.
stratum ['straːtəm] *n*, *pl* **-ta** strato *m.*
straw [stroː] *n* paglia *f*; (*drinking*) cannuccia *f.*
strawberry ['stroːbəri] *n* fragola *f.*
stray [strei] *v* (*lose one's way*) smarrirsi; (*roam*) vagare. **stray from** deviare *or* allontanarsi da. *adj* (*animal*) randagio; (*lost*) smarrito; (*occasional*) isolato.
streak [striːk] *n* (*mark*) riga *f*, striscia *f*; (*vein*) vena *f*; (*lightning*) lampo *m.* *v* striare; venare; (*rush*) filare.
stream [striːm] *n* corso d'acqua *m*; (*brook*) ruscello *m*; corrente *f.* **streamline** *v* sveltire. **streamlined** *adj* aerodinamico, sveltito. *v* grondare, riversarsi. **streaming cold** forte raffreddore *m.*
street [striːt] *n* strada *f*, via *f.* **street-cleaner** *n* spazzino *m.* **street-light** *n* lampione *m.* **the man in the street** l'uomo qualunque *m.*
strength [streŋθ] *n* forza *f*; intensità *f*;

validità *f*; (*mil*) effettivo *m*. **strengthen** *v* rinforzare; (*give weight to*) convalidare.

strenuous ['strenjuəs] *adj* energico, fervente; (*activity*) arduo, duro.

stress [stres] *n* tensione *f*; pressione *f*, spinta *f*; (*emphasis*) rilievo *m*; accento *m*; (*med*) stress *m invar*. *v* mettere in rilievo, sottolineare; accentare; sottoporre a tensione.

stretch [stretʃ] *v* (*pull*) tirare; (*extend*) stendere; (*reach*) estendersi. **stretch one's legs** sgranchirsi le gambe. **stretch out** allungare, sdraiarsi. *n* (*expanse*) tratto *m*; (*time*) periodo *m*. **stretcher** *n* barella *f*, lettiga *f*.

stricken ['strikən] *adj* colpito.

strict [strikt] *adj* severo, rigoroso; esatto; (*absolute*) stretto.

***stride** [straid] *v* camminare a grandi passi. *n* passo *m*. **take in one's stride** (*do easily*) superare con facilità; (*adjust to*) prendersela con calma.

strife [straif] *n* lotta *f*, conflitto *m*.

***strike** [straik] *v* colpire; (*deal a blow*) battere; (*match*) accendere; (*oil*) scoprire; (*not work*) scioperare. **strike home** colpire nel segno. **strike off** radiare. **strike up** (*enter upon*) stringere. *n* sciopero *m*; (*discovery*) scoperta *f*. **striking** *adj* sorprendente, impressionante.

***string** [striŋ] *n* spago *m*, corda *f*; (*series*) fila *f*. **pull strings** manovrare, raccomandare. **strings** *pl n* (*music*) strumenti a corda *m pl*. *v* (*music*) incordare; (*racket*) mettere le corde a; (*beads*) infilare.

stringent ['strindʒənt] *adj* rigoroso, severo.

strip¹ [strip] *v* spogliare, denudare; (*car, etc.*) smontare; (*paint*) togliere. **strip of** privare di. **strip-tease** *n* spogliarello *m*.

strip² [strip] *n* striscia *f*, nastro *m*; (*comic*) fumetto *m*.

stripe [straip] *n* riga *f*, striscia *f*; (*mil*) gallone *m*. **striped** *adj* a righe *or* strisce.

***strive** [straiv] *v* (*try hard*) sforzarsi, adoperarsi; (*struggle*) lottare.

striven ['strivn] *V* **strive**.

strode [stroud] *V* **stride**.

stroke¹ [strouk] *n* colpo *m*; (*mark*) sbarra *f*; (*swimming*) bracciata *f*; (*med*) colpo apoplettico *m*; (*clock*) tocco *m*; (*tech*) corsa *f*. **stroke of genius** lampo di genio *m*. **stroke of lightning** fulmine *m*.

stroke² [strouk] *v* accarezzare, lisciare.

stroll [stroul] *n* passeggiatina *f*. **go for a stroll** andare a far quattro passi. *v* girovagare.

strong [stroŋ] *adj* forte, robusto, resistente. **stronghold** *n* roccaforte *f*. **strong language** parole grosse *f pl*. **strong-minded** *adj* risoluto. **strong point** forte *m*.

strove [strouv] *V* **strive**.

struck [strʌk] *V* **strike**.

structure ['strʌktʃə] *n* struttura *f*. **structural** *adj* strutturale.

struggle ['strʌgl] *n* (*fight*) lotta *f*; (*effort*) sforzo *m*. *v* lottare; sforzarsi.

strum [strʌm] *v* strimpellare.

strung [strʌŋ] *V* **string**.

strut¹ [strʌt] *v* (*prance*) camminare impettito.

strut² [strʌt] *n* (*support*) puntone *m*.

stub [stʌb] *n* (*cigarette, pencil, etc.*) mozzicone *m*; (*cheque*) matrice *f*; (*tree*) ceppo *m*. *v* urtare. **stub out** spegnere.

stubble ['stʌbl] *n* stoppia *f*; (*beard*) barba ispida *f*. **stubbly** *adj* pieno di stoppie; ispido.

stubborn ['stʌbən] *adj* ostinato, testardo. **stubbornness** *n* ostinatezza *f*, testardaggine *f*.

stuck [stʌk] *V* **stick²**.

stud¹ [stʌd] *n* (*ornament*) borchia *f*; (*nail*) ribattino *m*; (*button*) bottoncino *m*. *v* guarnire di borchie; (*jewel*) tempestare.

stud² [stʌd] *n* scuderia *f*. **stud-horse** *n* stallone *m*.

student ['stjuːdənt] *n* (*pupil*) studente, -essa *m, f*; (*scholar*) studioso, -a *m, f*.

studio ['stjuːdiou] *n* studio *m*.

study ['stʌdi] *n* studio *m*. *v* studiare; esaminare attentamente. **studied** *adj* studiato, premeditato. **studious** *adj* studioso, attento, premuroso.

stuff [stʌf] *n* roba *f*; (*substance*) sostanza *f*; (*fabric*) tessuto *m*. **know one's stuff** sapere il fatto proprio. *v* (*cookery*) farcire; (*animal*) imbalsamare; (*fill*) imbottire. **stuffing** *n* imbottitura *f*; (*cookery*) ripieno *m*. **stuffy** *adj* soffocante; (*tedious*) noioso; (*blocked up*) intasato; (*prim*) rigido, conservatore.

stumble [stʌmbl] *v* inciampare, fare un passo falso; (*speech*) impaperarsi. **stumbling block** ostacolo *m*.

stump [stʌmp] *n* (*tree*) ceppo *m*; (*limb*) moncone *m*.

stun [stʌn] *v* stordire; (*astound*) sbalordire. **stunning** *adj* sbalorditivo, stupefacente.
stung [stʌŋ] *V* **sting.**
stunk [stʌŋk] *V* **stink.**
stunt[1] [stʌnt] *v* arrestare la crescita di.
stunt[2] [stʌnt] *n* bravata *f*; acrobazia *f*; trovata pubblicitaria *f*.
stupid ['stjuːpid] *adj* stupido, sciocco. **stupidity** *n* stupidità *f*.
stupor ['stjuːpə] *n* stupore *m*, torpore *m*.
sturdy ['stəːdi] *adj* vigoroso, robusto. **sturdiness** *n* vigoria *f*.
sturgeon ['stəːdʒən] *n* storione *m*.
stutter ['stʌtə] *n* balbuzie *f*. *v* balbettare. **stutterer** *n* balbuziente *m, f*.
sty [stai] *n* porcile *m*.
stye [stai] *n* orzaiolo *m*.
style [stail] *n* stile *m*. **stylish** *adj* elegante. **stylist** *n* stilista *m, f*.
stylus ['stailəs] *n* puntina *f*.
suave [swaːv] *adj* cortese, affabile.
subconscious [sʌb'konʃəs] *nm, adj* subcosciente.
subcontract [sʌbkən'trakt] *n* subappalto *m*. *v* dare in subappalto.
subdivision [ˌsʌbdi'viʒən] *n* suddivisione *f*. **subdivide** *v* suddividere.
subdue [səb'djuː] *v* (*conquer*) soggiogare; (*repress*) reprimere; (*reduce intensity*) attenuare. **subdued** *adj* inibito; intimidito; attenuato.
subject ['sʌbdʒikt; *v* səb'dʒekt] *n* soggetto *m*, argomento *m*; (*study*) materia *f*; (*pol*) suddito, -a *m, f*. *adj* **subject to** soggetto a. *v* (*bring under control*) sottomettere; (*expose*) esporre, sottoporre. **subjective** *adj* soggettivo. **subjectivity** *n* soggettività *f*.
subjunctive [səb'dʒʌŋktiv] *nm, adj* congiuntivo.
***sublet** [ˌsʌb'let] *v* subaffittare.
sublimate ['sʌblimeit] *v* sublimare. *n* sublimato *m*. **sublimation** *n* sublimazione *f*.
sublime [sə'blaim] *adj* sublime.
submarine ['sʌbməriːn] *n* sottomarino *m*.
submerge [səb'məːdʒ] *v* sommergere. **submersion** *n* sommersione *f*.
submit [səb'mit] *v* (*yield*) sottomettersi, rassegnarsi; deferire; (*present*) sottoporre. **submission** *n* sottomissione *f*, rassegnazione *f*; (*theory*) tesi *f*.
subnormal [sʌb'noːməl] *adj* subnormale.
subordinate [sə'boːdinət] *adj* subordinato, inferiore. *n* subalterno *m*. *v* subordinare. **subordination** *n* subordinazione *f*.
subscribe [səb'skraib] *v* sottoscrivere, aderire; (*newspapers, etc.*) abbonarsi. **subscriber** *n* abbonato, -a *m, f*. **subscription** *n* abbonamento *m*; (*dues*) quota *f*; (*fund raised*) sottoscrizione *f*.
subsequent ['sʌbsikwənt] *adj* successivo, susseguente.
subservient [səb'səːviənt] *adj* subordinato; (*servile*) umile.
subside [səb'said] *v* decrescere, diminuire; (*give way*) cedere, avvallare; (*abate*) quietarsi. **subsidence** *n* avvallamento *m*.
subsidiary [səb'sidiəri] *adj* sussidiario; (*comm*) consociato.
subsidize ['sʌbsidaiz] *v* sovvenzionare. **subsidy** *n* sovvenzione *f*.
subsist [səb'sist] *v* sostentarsi. **subsistence** *n* sostentamento *m*. **subsistence money** acconto paga *m*, trasferta *f*.
substance ['sʌbstəns] *n* sostanza *f*, materia *f*; realtà *f*; (*wealth*) beni *m pl*. **substantial** *adj* sostanziale; (*meal*) sostanzioso; (*considerable*) notevole.
substitute ['sʌbstitjuːt] *n* (*person*) sostituto, -a *m, f*; (*thing*) surrogato *m*. *v* sostituire, rimpiazzare. **substitution** *n* sostituzione *f*.
subterfuge ['sʌbtəfjuːdʒ] *n* sotterfugio *m*.
subterranean [sʌbtə'reiniən] *adj* sotterraneo.
subtitle ['sʌbtaitl] *n* sottotitolo *m*.
subtle ['sʌtl] *adj* sottile, delicato; astuto, ingegnoso. **subtlety** *n* sottigliezza *f*, finezza *f*; astuzia *f*.
subtract [səb'trakt] *v* dedurre, sottrarre. **subtraction** *n* sottrazione *f*.
suburb ['sʌbəːb] *n* sobborgo *m*. **suburban** *adj* suburbano.
subvert [səb'vəːt] *v* sovvertire. **subversion** *n* sovversione *f*. **subversive** *n, adj* sovversivo, -a.
subway ['sʌbwei] *n* sottopassaggio *m*; (*US*) metropolitana *f*.
succeed [sək'siːd] *v* riuscire; (*be successful*) aver successo; (*follow*) succedere. **success** *n* successo *m*, buona riuscita *f*. **successful** *adj* (*person*) che ha successo; vittorioso; prospero, arrivato; (*thing*) riuscito. **succession** *n* successione *f*. **successive** *adj* successivo. **successor** *n* successore *m*.
succinct [sək'siŋkt] *adj* succinto.

succulent ['sʌkjulənt] *adj* succulento.
succumb [sə'kʌm] *v* soccombere.
such [sʌtʃ] *adj* tale; (*like*) del genere, simile. *adv* così. **such and such** tale dei tali. **such as** come. **such as it is** così com'è.
suck [sʌk] *v* succhiare; (*breast*) poppare. **suck up** assorbire; (*slang*) fare il leccapiedi.
sucker ['sʌkə] *n* (*plant*) pollone *m*; (*device*) ventosa *f*; (*slang*: *fool*) gonzo *m*.
suckle ['sʌkl] *v* allattare.
suction ['sʌkʃən] *n* aspirazione *f*. **suction pump** pompa aspirante *f*.
sudden ['sʌdən] *adj* improvviso, subitaneo. **all of a sudden** ad un tratto, all'improvviso.
suds [sʌdz] *pl n* saponata *f sing*.
sue [suː] *v* (*law*) citare, chiamare in giudizio, querelare. **sue for peace** chiedere *or* sollecitare la pace.
suede [sweid] *nm*, *adj* scamosciato.
suet ['suːit] *n* grasso di rognone *m*.
suffer ['sʌfə] *v* soffrire, patire; tollerare; (*undergo*) subire. **on sufferance** per tacita tolleranza. **suffering** *n* sofferenza *f*, dolore *m*.
sufficient [sə'fiʃənt] *adj* sufficiente. **sufficiency** *n* sufficienza *f*.
suffix ['sʌfiks] *n* suffisso *m*.
suffocate ['sʌfəkeit] *v* soffocare. **suffocation** *n* soffocazione *f*.
sugar ['ʃugə] *n* zucchero *m*. **sugar-beet** *n* barbabietola (da zucchero) *f*. **sugar-cane** *n* canna da zucchero *f*. **sugary** *adj* zuccherino, mellifluo.
suggest [sə'dʒest] *v* suggerire; proporre. **suggestible** *adj* suggestionabile. **suggestion** *n* suggerimento *m*; proposta *f*; (*psych*) suggestione *f*.
suicide ['suːisaid] *n* (*deed*) suicidio *m*; (*person*) suicida *m*, *f*. **commit suicide** suicidarsi. **suicidal** *adj* suicida.
suit [suːt] *n* (*garment*) abito *m*; (*law*) causa *f*; (*cards*) seme *m*, colore *m*; (*request*) preghiera *f*. **follow suit** seguire l'esempio; (*cards*) rispondere a colore. **suitcase** *n* valigia *f*. *v* accontentare, convenire a, soddisfare. **suit yourself!** fa come ti pare! **suitable** *adj* adatto; conveniente, opportuno. **suitability** *n* convenienza *f*.
suite [swiːt] *n* (*music*) suite *f invar*; (*retinue*) seguito *m*; (*furniture*) mobilia *f invar*; (*rooms*) fuga di stanze *f*.
sulk [sʌlk] *v* tenere il broncio. **sulky** *adj* imbronciato.
sullen ['sʌlən] *adj* accigliato, imbronciato.
sulphur ['sʌlfə] *n* zolfo *m*.
sultan ['sʌltən] *n* sultano *m*.
sultana [sʌl'taːnə] *n* uva sultanina *f*.
sultry ['sʌltri] *adj* afoso; (*person*) eccitante.
sum [sʌm] *n* somma *f*, addizione *f*; (*amount*) importo *m*, totale *m*. **do sums** far calcoli. *v* **sum up** riassumere. **summing-up** *n* riassunto *m*, riepilogo (*pl* -ghi) *m*.
summarize ['sʌməraiz] *v* riassumere. **summary** *nm*, *adj* sommario.
summer ['sʌmə] *n* estate *f*. *adj* d'estate, estivo.
summit ['sʌmit] *n* cima *f*, vertice *m*.
summon ['sʌmən] *v* convocare; (*law*) citare, chiamare in giudizio. **summon up courage** farsi coraggio.
summons ['sʌmənz] *v* citare in giudizio. *n* citazione *f*. **answer a summons** presentarsi in giudizio.
sumptuous ['sʌmptʃuəs] *adj* sontuoso.
sun [sʌn] *n* sole *m*. *v* **sun oneself** prendere il sole. **sunny** *adj* soleggiato; (*cheerful*) allegro.
sunbathe ['sʌnbeið] *v* fare i bagni di sole. **sunbathing** *n* bagni di sole *m pl*.
sunburn ['sʌnbəːn] *n* (*pain*) scottatura solare *f*, eritema solare *m*; (*tan*) abbronzatura *f*. **sunburnt** *adj* scottato dal sole; abbronzato.
Sunday ['sʌndi] *n* domenica *f*.
sundial ['sʌndaiəl] *n* meridiana *f*.
sundry ['sʌndri] *adj* diversi, parecchi. **all and sundry** tutti quanti.
sunflower ['sʌnˌflauə] *n* girasole *m*.
sung [sʌŋ] *V* **sing**.
sun-glasses ['sʌnglaːsiz] *pl n* occhiali da sole *m pl*.
sunk [sʌŋk] *V* **sink**.
sunlight ['sʌnlait] *n* luce del sole *f*.
sunrise ['sʌnraiz] *n* alba *f*.
sunset ['sʌnset] *n* tramonto *m*.
sunshine ['sʌnʃain] *n* sole *m*; (*good weather*) bel tempo *m*. **sunshine roof** tetto scorrevole *m*.
sunstroke ['sʌnstrouk] *n* colpo di sole *m*; insolazione *f*.
sun-tan ['sʌntan] *n* abbronzatura *f*.
super ['suːpə] *adj* (*coll*) magnifico.
superannuation [ˌsuːpəranju'eiʃən] *n*

(*retirement*) collocamento a riposo *m*; (*pension*) vitalizio *m*.

superb [suː'pəːb] *adj* superbo, magnifico.

supercilious [ˌsuːpə'siliəs] *adj* altero, borioso.

superficial [ˌsuːpə'fiʃəl] *adj* superficiale.

superfluous [su'pəːfluəs] *adj* superfluo.

superhuman [suːpə'hjuːmən] *adj* sovrumano.

superimpose [ˌsuːpərim'pouz] *v* sovraporre.

superintendent [ˌsuːpərin'tendənt] *n* soprintendente *m*; (*police*) commissario *m*.

superior [suːpiəriə] *adj* superiore. *n* superiore, -a *m*, *f*. **superiority** *n* superiorità *f*.

superlative [suː'pəːlətiv] *nm*, *adj* superlativo.

supermarket ['suːpəˌmaːkit] *n* supermercato *m*.

supernatural [ˌsuːpə'natʃərəl] *nm*, *adj* soprannaturale.

supersede [ˌsuːpə'siːd] *v* rimpiazzare, sostituire.

supersonic [ˌsuːpə'sonik] *adj* supersonico.

superstition [suːpə'stiʃən] *n* superstizione *f*. **superstitious** *adj* superstizioso.

supervise ['suːpəvaiz] *v* sorvegliare, soprintendere. **supervision** *n* sorveglianza *f*, soprintendenza *f*. **supervisor** *n* soprintendente *m*, *f*, sorvegliante *m*, *f*, ispettore, -trice *m*, *f*.

supper ['sʌpə] *n* cena *f*. **have supper** cenare.

supple ['sʌpl] *adj* flessibile; agile. **suppleness** *n* flessibilità *f*; agilità *f*.

supplement ['sʌpləmənt] *n* supplemento *m*, aggiunta *f*. *v* completare, integrare. **supplementary** *adj* supplementare.

supply [sə'plai] *n* provvista *f*, rifornimento *m*; (*econ*) offerta *f*. *v* provvedere, fornire. **supplier** *n* fornitore *m*.

support [sə'poːt] *n* appoggio *m*, sostegno *m*. **means of support** mezzi di sostentamento *m pl*. *v* reggere, sostenere; (*keep*) mantenere; (*tolerate*) sopportare.

suppose [sə'pouz] *v* supporre; (*think*) ritenere, pensare. **supposed** *adj* presunto. **be supposed to** dovere. **supposedly** *adv* per supposizione. **supposing** *conj* supponiamo che. **supposition** *n* supposizione *f*.

suppository [sə'pozitri] *n* supposta *f*.

suppress [sə'pres] *v* sopprimere; (*check*) soffocare; (*hide*) nascondere.

supreme [su'priːm] *adj* supremo, massimo. **supremacy** *n* supremazia *f*.

surcharge ['səːtʃaːdʒ] *n* soprattassa *f*.

sure [ʃuə] *adj* certo, sicuro. **make sure** assicurarsi.

surety ['ʃuərəti] *n* certezza *f*; garanzia *f*. **stand surety for** farsi garante per.

surf [səːf] *n* frangente *m*, risacca *f*. **surfing** *n* surfing *m invar*, sport dell'acquaplano *m*.

surface ['səːfis] *n* superficie *f*, faccia *f*. *adj* superficiale, esterno. *v* venire a galla, affiorare.

surfeit ['səːfit] *n* eccesso *m*.

surge [səːdʒ] *n* ondata *f*, riflusso *m*. *v* fluttuare, rifluire.

surgeon ['səːdʒən] *n* chirurgo *m*. **surgery** *n* (*subject*) chirurgia *f*; (*consulting room*) gabinetto medico *m*, infermeria *f*. **surgical** *adj* chirurgico.

surly ['səːli] *adj* scontroso.

surmount [sə'maunt] *v* superare.

surname ['səːneim] *n* cognome *m*.

surpass [sə'paːs] *v* sorpassare, superare.

surplus ['səːpləs] *n* eccesso *m*, avanzo *m*, residuato *m*.

surprise [sə'praiz] *n* sorpresa *f*; (*astonishment*) stupore *m*, meraviglia *f*. **take by surprise** (*amaze*) stupire; (*come upon unawares*) cogliere all'improvviso. *adj* (*unexpected*) inaspettato. *v* sorprendere; cogliere all'improvviso; stupire.

surrealism [sə'riəlizəm] *n* surrealismo *m*.

surrealist *n*(*m*+*f*), *adj* surrealista.

surrender [sə'rendə] *v* cedere; (*mil*) arrendersi. *n* resa *f*.

surreptitious [ˌsʌrəp'tiʃəs] *adj* furtivo, clandestino.

surround [sə'raund] *v* circondare; (*encircle*) accerchiare. *n* bordura *f*. **surrounding** *adj* circostante. **surroundings** *pl n* dintorni *m pl*; (*environment*) ambiente *m sing*.

survey ['səːvei; *v* sə'vei] *n* quadro generale *m*; (*official examination*) perizia *f*; rapporto *m*; valutazione *f*; (*of land*) agrimensura *f*; (*geog*) rilievo topografico *m*; (*poll*) sondaggio *m*. *v* contemplare; esaminare, fare una perizia di; prendere i rilievi di. **surveyor** *n* ispettore, -trice *m*, *f*; (*land*) agrimensore *m*; (*house*) geometra *m*, *f*; (*geog*) topografo, -a *m*, *f*.

survive [sə'vaiv] *v* sopravvivere. **survival** *n* sopravvivenza *f*. **survivor** *n* superstite *m*, *f*.
susceptible [sə'septəbl] *adj* suscettibile; predisposto. **susceptibility** *n* suscettibilità *f*; predisposizione *f*.
suspect [sə'spekt; *n*, *adj* 'sʌspekt] *v* sospettare; (*surmise*) dubitare. *n* persona sospetta *f*. *adj* sospetto.
suspend [sə'spend] *v* sospendere. **suspense** *n* incertezza *f*, apprensione *f*. **in suspense** in sospeso. **suspension** *n* sospensione *f*. **suspension bridge** ponte sospeso *m*.
suspicion [sə'spiʃən] *n* sospetto *m*, dubbio *m*. **suspicious** *adj* (*distrustful*) sospettoso, diffidente; (*questionable*) sospetto.
sustain [sə'stein] *v* sostenere; (*injury, etc.*) subire.
swab [swob] *n* tampone *m*; (*sample*) prelievo *m*.
swagger ['swagə] *v* (*strut*) pavoneggiarsi; (*boast*) boriarsi, grandeggiare. *n* boria *f*, andatura spavalda *f*.
swallow[1] ['swolou] *v* inghiottire, ingoiare; (*coll*: *believe*) bere; (*suppress*) reprimere. *n* gorgata *f*.
swallow[2] ['swolou] *n* (*bird*) rondine *f*.
swam [swam] *V* **swim**.
swamp [swomp] *n* palude *f*. *v* (*flood*) inondare, allagare; (*overwhelm*) travolgere.
swan [swon] *n* cigno *m*.
swank [swaŋk] (*coll*) *v* darsi delle arie. *n* boria *f*.
swap *or* **swop** [swop] *n* scambio *m*. *v* scambiare.
swarm [swoːm] *n* (*bees*) sciame *m*; (*crowd*) folla *f*. *v* sciamare; (*throng*) accalcarsi; (*teem*) brulicare.
swarthy ['swoːði] *adj* di carnagione scura.
swat [swot] *v* schiacciare.
sway [swei] *v* oscillare, vacillare; inclinare; influenzare. *n* oscillazione *f*. **hold sway over** esercitare potere su.
***swear** [sweə] *v* (*declare solemnly*) giurare; (*curse*) bestemmiare. **swear by** giurare su. **swear in** far prestare giuramento, insediare. **swear-word** *n*. bestemmia *f*.
sweat [swet] *v* sudare. *n* sudore *m*. **sweat-shirt** *n* argentina *f*. **sweater** *n* maglione *m*.
swede [swiːd] *n* ravizzone *m*.
Sweden ['swiːdn] *n* Svezia *f*. **Swede** *n* svedese *m*, *f*. **Swedish** *nm*, *adj* svedese.
***sweep** [swiːp] *v* spazzare; (*view*) percorrere. **sweep aside** scartare. **sweep the board** far piazza pulita. **sweep** *n* spazzata *f*; curva *f*; (*chimney*) spazzacamino *m*. **sweeping** *adj* radicale, di lunga portata. **sweeping statement** asserzione gratuita *f*.
sweet [swiːt] *adj* dolce; fresco; (*smell*) profumato; (*sound*) armonioso; (*temper*) amabile, carino. *n* caramella *f*; (*dessert*) dolce *m*. **sweet-and-sour** *adj* agrodolce. **sweetbread** *n* animella *f*. **sweetheart** *n* amoroso, -a *m*, *f*. **sweet pea** pisello odoroso *m*. **sweeten** *v* addolcire; alleviare. **sweetener** *n* dolcificante *m*; (*bribe*) bustarella *f*. **sweetness** *n* dolcezza *f*; (*taste*) sapore dolce *m*.
***swell** [swel] *v* aumentare, gonfiarsi. *n* (*sea*) ondata *f*. **swelling** *n* gonfiore *m*, tumore *m*, tumefazione *f*.
swelter ['sweltə] *v* soffocare *or* morire dal caldo. **sweltering** *adj* soffocante.
swept [swept] *V* **sweep**.
swerve [swəːv] *v* (*change direction abruptly*) scartare; deviare, scostarsi. *n* scarto *m*; deviazione *f*.
swift [swift] *adj* lesto; (*prompt*) pronto. *n* rondone *m*.
swig [swig] *v* tracannare. *n* sorso *m*.
swill [swil] *v* (*swig*) tracannare; (*rinse*) risciacquare. *n* (*rubbish*) rifiuti *m pl*; (*slops*) intruglio *m*; (*for pigs*) broda (per maiali) *f*.
***swim** [swim] *v* nuotare. *n* nuotata *f*. **go for a swim** andare a nuotare. **in the swim** attivo. **swimmer** *n* nuotatore, -trice *m*, *f*. **swimming** *n* nuoto *m*. **swimming costume** costume da bagno *m*. **swimming pool** *or* **baths** piscina *f*. **swimming trunks** calzoncini da bagno *m pl*.
swindle ['swindl] *v* truffare, imbrogliare. *n* truffa *f*. **swindler** *n* truffatore, -trice *m*, *f*, imbroglione, -a *m*, *f*.
swine [swain] *n* maiale *m*, porco (*pl* -ci) *m*.
***swing** [swiŋ] *v* dondolare, oscillare; (*club, etc.*) vibrare; influenzare. **swing open** spalancarsi. **swing round** voltarsi di scatto. *n* oscillazione *f*, ritmo *m*; (*in playground*) altalena *f*. **in full swing** in piena attività. **swing-door** *n* porta a due battenti *f*.
swipe [swaip] (*coll*) *n* botta *f*. *v* dare una botta (a); (*steal*) fregare.

swirl [swəːl] *v* turbinare. *n* turbine *m*.
swish [swiʃ] *v* (*sound*) sibilare; (*move*) brandire; (*rustle*) frusciare. *n* (*whip*) sferza *f*; (*sound*) sibilo *m*.
Swiss [swis] *n*, *adj* svizzero, -a.
switch [switʃ] *n* (*elec*) interruttore *m*; (*whip*) sferza *f*; (*change*) svolta *f*, cambiamento *m*. **switchback** *n* montagne russe *f pl*. **switchboard** *n* tavolo di controllo *m*; (*phone*) centralino *m*. *v* spostare, scambiare. **switch off** spegnere. **switch on** accendere. **switch over** commutare.
Switzerland ['switsələnd] *n* Svizzera *f*.
swivel ['swivl] *n* perno *m*. **swivel chair** sedia girevole *f*. *v* girare, rotare.
swollen ['swoulən] *V* **swell**. *adj* gonfio.
swoop [swuːp] *v* piombare, avventarsi. *n* calata improvvisa *f*. **at one fell swoop** d'un sol colpo.
swop *V* **swap**.
sword [soːd] *n* spada *f*. **cross swords** (*fight*) battersi; (*argue*) venire alle mani. **swordfish** *n* pesce spada *m*.
swore [swoː] *V* **swear**.
sworn [swoːn] *V* **swear**.
swot [swot] (*coll*) *v* sgobbare. *n* secchione, -a *m*, *f*.
swum [swʌm] *V* **swim**.
swung [swʌŋ] *V* **swing**.
sycamore ['sikəmoː] *n* sicomoro *m*.
syllable ['siləbl] *n* sillaba *f*.
syllabus ['siləbəs] *n* programma *m*, prospetto *m*.
symbol ['simbl] *n* simbolo *m*. **symbolic** *adj* simbolico. **symbolism** *n* simbolismo *m*. **symbolize** *v* simboleggiare.
symmetry ['simitri] *n* simmetria *f*. **symmetrical** *adj* simmetrico.
sympathy ['simpəθi] *n* simpatia *f*, comprensione *f*; compassione *f*. **sympathetic** *adj* simpatico, simpatizzante; compassionevole. **sympathetic to** favorevole a, ben disposto verso. **sympathize** *v* simpatizzare; essere d'accordo; compatire. **sympathizer** *n* simpatizzante *m*, *f*.
symphony ['simfəni] *n* sinfonia *f*. **symphony orchestra** orchestra sinfonica *f*. **symphonic** *adj* sinfonico.
symposium [sim'pouziəm] *n* simposio *m*.
symptom ['simptəm] *n* sintomo *m*. **symptomatic** *adj* sintomatico.
synagogue ['sinəgog] *n* sinagoga *f*.
synchromesh ['siŋkroumeʃ] *n* sincronizzatore *m*.
synchronize ['siŋkrənaiz] *v* sincronizzare.
syndicate ['sindikit] *n* sindacato *m*.
syndrome ['sindroum] *n* sindrome *f*.
synod ['sinəd] *n* sinodo *m*.
synonym ['sinənim] *n* sinonimo *m*. **synonymous** *adj* sinonimo.
synopsis [si'nopsis] *n*, *pl* **-ses** sinossi *f*; (*film*, *etc*.) sinopsi *f*. **synoptic** *adj* sinottico.
syntax ['sintaks] *n* sintassi *f*. **syntactic** *adj* sintattico.
synthesis ['sinθisis] *n*, *pl* **-ses** sintesi *f*. **synthesize** *v* sintetizzare. **synthetic** *adj* sintetico.
syphilis ['sifilis] *n* sifilide *f*.
syringe [si'rindʒ] *n* siringa *f*. *v* siringare; (*inject*) iniettare.
syrup ['sirəp] *n* sciroppo *m*; (*golden*) melassa *f*. **syrupy** *adj* sciropposo.
system ['sistəm] *n* sistema *m*. **systematic** *adj* sistematico.

T

tab [tab] *n* cartellino *m*, etichetta *f*. **keep tabs on** tener d'occhio.
tabby ['tabi] *n* (gatto) soriano *or* tigrato *m*.
table ['teibl] *n* tavola *f*; (*with modifier*) tavolo *m*; (*multiplication*) tavola pitagorica *f*; (*synopsis*) tabella *f*. **lay/clear the table** apparecchiare/sparecchiare la tavola. **table-cloth** *n* tovaglia *f*. **table-mat** *n* sottopiatto *m*. **table-napkin** *n* tovagliolo *m*. **tablespoon** *n* cucchiaio da tavola *m*; (*spoonful*) cucchiaiata *f*. **table tennis** tennis da tavolo *m*. **turn the tables** rovesciare le posizioni. *v* intavolare.
table d'hôte [taːblə'dout] *adj* a prezzo fisso.
tablet ['tablit] *n* tavoletta *f*; (*med*) pastiglia *f*.
taboo [ta'buː] *nm*, *adj* tabù.
tabulate ['tabjuleit] *v* presentare in forma sinottica.
tacit ['tasit] *adj* tacito.
tack [tak] *n* (*pin*) puntina *f*; (*naut*) bordata *f*; (*stitch*) punto lungo *m*. **get down to brass tacks** venire ai fatti. *v* (*sewing*) imbastire; (*sailing*) bordeggiare. **tack on** aggiungere. **tacking** *n* imbastitura *f*. **tacky** *adj* appiccicaticcio, appiccicoso.

tackle ['takl] *n* attrezzatura *f*; (*fishing*) arnesi da pesca *m pl*; (*hoisting*) paranco *m*; (*football*) carica *f*; (*rugby*) placcaggio *m*. *v* venire alle prese con, affrontare; caricare; placcare.

tact [takt] *n* tatto *m*, riguardo *m*. **tactful** *adj* riguardoso, diplomatico. **tactless** *adj* mancante di riguardo, senza tatto.

tactics ['taktiks] *pl n* tattica *f sing*. **tactical** *adj* tattico. **tactician** *n* tattico, -a *m, f*.

tadpole ['tadpoul] *n* girino *m*.

taffeta ['tafitə] *n* taffettà *m*.

tag [tag] *n* (*stub*) talloncino *m*; (*label*) etichetta *f*, cartellino *m*; (*refrain*) ritornello *m*; (*saying*) locuzione *f*. *v* **tag along** seguire. **tag on** aggiungere.

tail [teil] *n* coda *f*. **tail-board** *n* ribalta *f*. **tail-end** *n* finalino *m*. **tail-light** *n* fanalino *m*. **tails** *pl n* (*dress*) frac *m invar*; (*coin*) croce *f sing*.

tailor ['teilə] *n* sarto, -a *m, f*. **tailoring** *n* mestiere del sarto *m*.

taint [teint] *n* tara *f*, traccia di marcio *f*. *v* (*spoil*) guastare, contaminare. **tainted** *adj* tarato.

***take** [teik] *v* prendere; (*carry, convey*) portare; (*require*) volerci; (*bath, walk, etc.*) fare. **take after** assomigliare a. **take back** riportare. **take care** badare, far attenzione. **take care of** curarsi di. **take down** tirar giù; (*dictation*) prender nota di. **take in** (*visitors*) dare alloggio a; (*reduce*) stringere; (*understand*) comprendere; (*deceive*) ingannare. **take off** (*remove*) togliere; (*aero*) decollare; (*mimic*) parodiare. **take-off** *n* decollo *m*; caricatura *f*. **take on** assumere; (*fight*) affrontare. **take out** tirar fuori; accompagnare. **take over** (*assume control*) rilevare. **take-over** *n* rilievo *m*. **take place** accadere, aver luogo. **take to** affezionarsi a; (*addict*) darsi a.

taken ['teikn] *V* **take**.

talcum powder ['talkəm] *n* talco in polvere *m*; borotalco *m*.

tale [teil] *n* storia *f*, racconto *m*; (*gossip*) diceria *f*.

talent ['talənt] *n* talento *m*; (*gift*) dote *f*; (*aptitude*) attitudine *f*. **talented** *adj* dotato.

talk [toːk] *n* discorso *m*, conversazione *f*; (*lecture*) conferenza *f*; (*chat*) chiacchierata *f*. *v* parlare; conversare; chiacchierare. **talk about** parlare di. **talk nonsense** dire sciocchezze. **talk over** discutere. **talk round** persuadere. **talk sense** dire cose sensate. **talkative** *adj* loquace.

tall [toːl] *adj* alto. **tallboy** *n* canterano *m*. **tall order** impresa difficile *f*. **tall story** storia inverosimile *f*, frottola *f*.

tally ['tali] *n* (*score*) punteggio *m*; (*account*) conto *m*; (*label*) etichetta *f*, scontrino *m*. *v* corrispondere; coincidere (con).

talon ['talən] *n* artiglio *m*.

tambourine [tambə'riːn] *n* tamburello *m*.

tame [teim] *adj* docile, domestico. *v* addomesticare, domare.

tamper ['tampə] *v* **tamper with** alterare, falsificare; (*meddle*) ingerirsi in; (*bribe*) subornare.

tampon ['tampon] *n* tampone *m*.

tan [tan] *v* (*leather*) conciare; (*sun*) abbronzare. *n* (*colour*) castano *m*; abbronzatura *f*. *adj* castano.

tandem ['tandəm] *n* tandem *m invar*. **in tandem** in tandem.

tangent ['tandʒənt] *n* tangente *f*. **fly off at a tangent** pigliare un dirizzone.

tangerine [tandʒə'riːn] *n* mandarino *m*.

tangible ['tandʒəbl] *adj* tangibile.

tangle ['taŋgl] *n* groviglio *m*, confusione *f*. *v* ingarbugliare, imbrogliare. **tangle with** (*fight*) lottare con *or* contro.

tank [taŋk] *n* serbatoio *m*; (*pool*) vasca *f*; (*mil*) carro armato *m*. **tanker** *n* (*ship*) nave cisterna *f*; (*lorry*) autocisterna *f*.

tankard ['taŋkəd] *n* boccale *m*.

tantalize ['tantəlaiz] *v* tormentare.

tantamount ['tantəmaunt] *adj* **be tantamount to** equivalere a, essere come.

tantrum ['tantrəm] *n* accesso d'ira *m*, bizza *f*. **have tantrums** fare le bizze.

tap[1] [tap] *v* (*strike*) picchiare, dare un colpetto a; (*knock*) bussare. *n* colpetto *m*.

tap[2] [tap] *n* rubinetto *m*; (*on cask*) spina *f*, cannella *f*. **on tap** (*beer*) alla spina; (*ready*) a disposizione, pronto. *v* (*draw off*) spillare; (*phone*) intercettare; utilizzare.

tape [teip] *n* nastro *m*. **red tape** burocrazia *f*. **tape-measure** *n* metro *m*. **tape-recorder** *n* registratore a nastro *m*. *v* (*tie*) allacciare; (*record*) registrare.

taper ['teipə] *v* affusolare, assottigliarsi. **taper off** finire a punta. *n* cerino *m*, candela sottile *f*. **tapering** *adj* affusolato, a punta.

tapestry ['tapəstri] *n* arazzo *m*, tappezzeria *f*.
tapioca [tapi'oukə] *n* tapioca *f*.
tar [taː] *n* catrame *m*. *v* incatramare.
tarantula [tə'rantjulə] *n* tarantola *f*.
target ['taːgit] *n* bersaglio *m*, obiettivo *m*.
tariff ['tarif] *n* tariffa *f*.
tarmac ['taːmak] *n* macadam al catrame; (*runway*) pista *f*.
tarnish ['taːniʃ] *v* annerire, offuscare; (*stain*) macchiare. *n* annerimento *m*; macchia *f*.
tarpaulin [taː'poːlin] *n* copertone *m*.
tarragon ['tarəgən] *n* dragoncello *m*.
tart[1] [taːt] *adj* aspro, agro. **tartness** *n* asprezza *f*.
tart[2] [taːt] *n* torta *f*, crostata *f*; (*slang*) puttana *f*.
tartan ['taːtən] *n* tartan *m invar*, tessuto scozzese *m*.
tartar ['taːtə] *n* tartaro *m*. **cream of tartar** cremor di tartaro *m*.
task [taːsk] *n* compito *m*, dovere *m*. **take to task** rimproverare.
tassel ['tasəl] *n* nappa *f*, nappina *f*.
taste [teist] *n* gusto *m*, sapore *m*; (*liking*) amore *m*, apprezzamento *m*; (*small sample*) assaggio *m*. *v* assaggiare, gustare. **taste of** sapere di. **tasteful** *adj* squisito, di buon gusto. **tasteless** *adj* insipido; di cattivo gusto. **tasty** *adj* saporito, appetitoso.
tattered ['tatəd] *adj* stracciato, a brandelli.
tattoo[1] [tə'tuː] *n* tatuaggio *m*. *v* tatuare.
tattoo[2] [tə'tuː] *n* (*mil*) ritirata *f*.
taught [toːt] *V* **teach**.
taunt [toːnt] *v* rinfacciare, schernire. *n* derisione *f*, scherno *m*.
Taurus ['toːrəs] *n* Toro *m*.
taut [toːt] *adj* teso.
tavern ['tavən] *n* osteria *f*, trattoria *f*, taverna *f*.
tawdry ['toːdri] *adj* vistoso, volgare.
tax [taks] *n* tassa *f*, imposta *f*. **tax-collector** *n* esattore fiscale *m*. **tax evasion** evasione fiscale *f*. **taxpayer** *n* contribuente *m*, *f*. *v* tassare, imporre una tassa su; (*make demands*) mettere alla prova. **taxation** *n* tassazione *f*, tasse *f pl*.
taxi ['taksi] *n* tassì *m*. **taxi-driver** *n* tassista *m*, *f*. **taxi rank** posteggio (per tassì) *m*. *v* (*aero*) rullare.
tea [tiː] *n* tè *m*. **teacup** *n* tazza da tè *f*. **teapot** *n* teiera *f*. **teaspoon** *n* cucchiaino *m*. **tea-towel** *n* canovaccio *m*.

***teach** [tiːtʃ] *v* insegnare. **teacher** *n* insegnante *m*, *f*; (*primary school*) maestro, -a *m*, *f*; (*secondary school, university*) professore, -essa *m*, *f*. **teaching** *n* insegnamento *m*. **teachings** *pl n* dottrina *f sing*, precetti *m pl*.
teak [tiːk] *n* tek *m*.
team [tiːm] *n* squadra *f*; (*animals*) tiro *m*. **teamwork** *n* affiatamento *m*. *v* **team up with** mettersi insieme a, collaborare con.
***tear**[1] [teə] *n* strappo *m*. *v* strappare. **be torn between** dibattersi tra. **tear off** strappar via; (*run*) scappar via. **tear up** stracciare. **tearing** *adj* impetuoso, terribile.
tear[2] [tiə] *n* lacrima *f*. **burst into tears** scoppiare in lacrime. **in tears** sciolto in lacrime. **tear-gas** *n* gas lacrimogeno *m*. **tearful** *adj* lacrimoso.
tease [tiːz] *v* stuzzicare, canzonare; irritare.
teat [tiːt] *n* (*nipple*) capezzolo *m*; (*rubber*) tettarella *f*.
technical ['teknikəl] *adj* tecnico. **technicality** *n* tecnicismo *m*. **technician** *n* tecnico, -a *m*, *f*. **technique** *n* tecnica *f*. **technological** *adj* tecnologico. **technologist** *n* tecnologo, -a *m*, *f*. **technology** *n* tecnologia *f*.
teddy bear ['tedi͵beə] *n* orsacchiotto *m*.
tedious ['tiːdiəs] *adj* noioso. **tedium** *n* noia *f*.
tee [tiː] *n* tee *m invar*. *v* **tee off** cominciare (dal tee). **tee up** preparare, collocare sul tee.
teem [tiːm] *v* (*rain*) grondare. **teem with** formicolare *or* brulicare di.
teenage ['tiːneidʒ] *adj* adolescente. **teenager** *n* adolescente *m*, *f*.
teeth [tiːθ] *V* **tooth**.
teethe [tiːð] *v* mettere i denti. **teething** *n* dentizione *f*. **teething-ring** *n* dentaruolo *m*. **teething troubles** difficoltà iniziali *f pl*.
teetotal [tiː'toutl] *adj* astemio. **teetotaller** *n* astemio, -a *m*, *f*.
telecommunications [͵telikəmjuːni'keiʃənz] *pl n* telecomunicazioni *f pl*.
telegram ['teligram] *n* telegramma *m*.
telegraph ['teligraːf] *n* telegrafo *m*. *v* telegrafare. **telegraphic** *adj* telegrafico.
telepathy [tə'lepəθi] *n* telepatia *f*. **telepathic** *adj* telepatico.

telephone ['telifoun] *n* telefono *m*. *v* telefonare. **telephone box** cabina telefonica *f*. **telephone call** telefonata *f*, colpo di telefono *m*. **telephone exchange** centralino *m*. **telephone operator** telefonista *m, f*.
teleprinter ['teliprintə] *n* telescrivente *m*.
telescope ['teliskoup] *n* telescopio *m*. *v* incastrare, far scorrere l'uno nell'altro; (*shorten*) condensare. **telescopic** *adj* telescopico.
television ['teliviʒən] *n* televisione *f*. **television screen** video *m*. **television set** televisore *m*. **televise** *v* teletrasmettere, trasmettere per televisione.
telex ['teleks] *n* telex *m*. *v* trasmettere per telex.
***tell** [tel] *v* dire, raccontare; distinguere. **tell off** (*scold*) sgridare. **telling-off** *n* ramanzina *f*, sgridata *f*. **telling** *adj* efficace, indicativo.
temper ['tempə] *n* (*mood*) umore *m*, disposizione *f*; (*metal*) tempra *f*. **keep one's temper** contenersi, rimaner calmo. **lose one's temper** arrabbiarsi, andare in collera. *v* moderare, temperare; (*metal*) temprare.
temperament ['tempərəmənt] *n* temperamento *m*, indole *f*. **temperamental** *adj* capriccioso.
temperate ['tempərət] *adj* temperato.
temperature ['temprətʃə] *n* temperatura *f*. **have a temperature** (*med*) avere la febbre.
tempestuous [tem'pestjuəs] *adj* tempestoso, burrascoso.
temple[1] ['templ] *n* (*rel*) tempio *m*.
temple[2] ['templ] *n* (*anat*) tempia *f*.
tempo ['tempou] *n* tempo *m*; ritmo *m*, andamento *m*.
temporary ['tempərəri] *adj* temporaneo.
tempt [tempt] *v* tentare. **temptation** *n* tentazione *f*. **tempter** *n* tentatore *m*. **tempting** *adj* allettante, seducente; (*food*) appetitoso. **temptress** *n* tentatrice *f*.
ten [ten] *nm, adj* dieci. **tenth** *nm, adj* decimo.
tenable [tenəbl] *adj* sostenibile, tenibile.
tenacious [tə'neiʃəs] *adj* tenace, ostinato; (*persistent*) accanito. **tenacity** *n* tenacia *f*, ostinazione *f*; accanimento *m*.
tenant ['tenənt] *n* inquilino, -a *m, f*. **tenancy** *n* affitto *m*.
tend[1] [tend] *v* (*be inclined*) tendere. **tendency** *n* tendenza *f*, inclinazione *f*. **tendentious** *adj* tendenzioso.
tend[2] [tend] *v* (*care for*) curare, assistere, soccorrere.
tender[1] ['tendə] *adj* tenero, delicato; (*affectionate*) affettuoso; (*sensitive*) sensibile. **tenderness** *n* tenerezza *f*; affettuosità *f*.
tender[2] ['tendə] *n* offerta *f*; (*comm*) preventivo *m*, appalto *m*. *v* offrire; appaltare, preventivare. **tender one's resignation** dare *or* rassegnare le dimissioni.
tendon ['tendən] *n* tendine *m*.
tendril ['tendril] *n* viticcio *m*.
tenement ['tenəmənt] *n* casamento *m*, casa popolare *f*.
tennis ['tenis] *n* tennis *m*. **tennis-ball/racket** *n* palla/racchetta da tennis *f*. **tennis-court** *n* campo da tennis *m*. **tennis player** giocatore, -trice di tennis *m, f*.
tenor ['tenə] *n* tenore *m*.
tense[1] [tens] *adj* teso, rigido. **tension** *n* tensione *f*; (*mech*) trazione *f*.
tense[2] [tens] *n* tempo *m*.
tent [tent] *n* tenda *f*.
tentacle ['tentəkl] *n* tentacolo *m*.
tentative ['tentətiv] *adj* di prova, sperimentale; (*hesitant*) titubante.
tenterhooks ['tentəhuks] *pl n* **on tenterhooks** sulle spine.
tenuous ['tenjuəs] *adj* tenue.
tenure ['tenjə] *n* tenuta *f*, possesso *m*, esercizio *m*.
tepid ['tepid] *adj* tiepido.
term [təːm] *n* termine *m*; durata *f*; (*school*) trimestre *m*. **come to terms with** venire a patti con. **terms** *pl n* tariffa *f sing*; condizioni *f pl*; (*footing*) relazioni *f pl*.
terminal ['təːminəl] *n* (*elec*) terminale *m*; (*aero*) terminal *m invar*. *adj* finale, estremo.
terminate ['təːmineit] *v* terminare, porre termine a. **termination** *n* (*act*) terminazione *f*; (*end*) termine *m*, conclusione *f*.
terminology [təːmi'nolədʒi] *n* terminologia *f*.
terminus ['təːminəs] *n* stazione di testa *f*, capolinea (*pl* capilinea) *m*.
terrace ['terəs] *n* terrazzo *m*; (*row of houses*) fila di case *f*.
terrain [tə'rein] *n* terreno *m*.
terrestrial [tə'restriəl] *adj* terrestre.
terrible ['terəbl] *adj* terribile, spaventoso.
terrier ['teriə] *n* terrier *m invar*.

terrific [tə'rifik] *adj* (*coll*) tremendo, fantastico.
terrify ['terifai] *v* atterrire. **be terrified** avere una paura matta. **terrifying** *adj* spaventoso.
territory ['teritəri] *n* territorio *m*. **territorial** *adj* territoriale.
terror ['terə] *n* terrore *m*. **terror-stricken** *adj* terrorizzato, atterrito. **terrorism** *n* terrorismo *m*. **terrorist** *n* terrorista *m, f*. **terrorize** *v* terrorizzare.
test [test] *n* prova *f*; esame *m*; analisi *f*; (*psych*) test *m invar*; (*industry*) collaudo *m*. **test-tube** *n* provetta *f*. *v* provare; esaminare; analizzare; collaudare.
testament ['testəmənt] *n* testamento *m*.
testicle ['testikl] *n* testicolo *m*.
testify ['testifai] *v* testimoniare, attestare.
testimonial [testi'mouniəl] *n* benservito *m*, attestato di buona condotta *m*.
testimony ['testiməni] *n* testimonianza *f*, deposizione *f*; (*proof*) prova *f*.
tetanus ['tetənəs] *n* tetano *m*.
tether ['teðə] *v* impastoiare. *n* pastoia *f*. **be at the end of one's tether** non poterne più, essere agli sgoccioli.
text [tekst] *n* testo *m*. **textbook** *n* libro di testo *m*. **textual** *adj* testuale.
textile ['tekstail] *nm*, *adj* tessile.
texture ['tekstjuə] *n* struttura *f*; (*surface*) grana *f*.
Thames [temz] *n* Tamigi *m*.
than [ðən] *conj* di, che.
thank [θaŋk] *v* ringraziare. **thank you** grazie. **thanks** *pl n* grazie *f pl*. **thanks to** grazie a. **thankful** *adj* riconoscente, grato.
that [ðat] *adj*, *pron* quel(lo), quella. **that is** cioè. **that's all!** ecco tutto! *adv* talmente. *conj* che.
thatch [θatʃ] *n* (copertura di) paglia *f*. *v* coprire di paglia.
thaw [θoː] *n* disgelo *m*. *v* disgelare.
the [ðə] *art* il *or* lo, la; (*pl*) i *or* gli, le.
theatre ['θiətə] *n* teatro *m*; (*hospital*) sala operatoria *f*. **theatrical** *adj* teatrale.
theft [θeft] *n* furto *m*.
their [ðeə] *adj* (il) loro, (la) loro; (*pl*) (i) loro, (le) loro.
theirs [ðeəz] *pron* il loro, la loro; (*pl*) i loro, le loro.
them [ðem] *pron* (*before verb*) li, le; (*after verb or prep*) loro. **both of them** tutti e due. **none of them** nessuno di loro.
theme [θiːm] *n* tema *m*. **theme song** sigla (musicale) *f*. **thematic** *adj* tematico.
themselves [ðəm'selvz] *pron* loro stessi, -e; (*reflexive*) si; (*after prep*) sè stessi, -e.
then [ðen] *adv* (*at that time*) allora; (*next in time*) poi, dopo. **by then** a quel punto. **now and then** di tanto in tanto. *conj* dunque, allora. *adj* di allora.
theology [θi'olədʒi] *n* teologia *f*. **theologian** *n* teologo *m*. **theological** *adj* teologico.
theorem ['θiərəm] *n* teorema *m*.
theory ['θiəri] *n* teoria *f*. **theoretical** *adj* teorico.
therapy ['θerəpi] *n* terapia *f*. **therapeutic** *adj* terapeutico. **therapist** *n* terapista *m, f*.
there [ðeə] *adv* lì, là; (*to that place*) ci, vi. **thereabouts** *adv* da quelle parti, all'incirca. **thereafter** *adv* quindi, in seguito. **there are** ci sono. **thereby** *adv* così, in tal modo. **therefore** *adv* dunque, perciò, quindi. **there is** c'è; (*calling attention*) ecco. **there it is!** eccolo! **thereupon** *adv* quindi, subito dopo.
thermal ['θəːməl] *adj* termico; (*waters*) termale.
thermodynamics [θəːmoudai'namiks] *n* termodinamica *f*.
thermometer [θə'momitə] *n* termometro *m*.
thermonuclear [θəːmou'njukliə] *adj* termonucleare.
thermos ® ['θəːməs] *n* thermos ® *m invar*.
thermostat ['θəːməstat] *n* termostato *m*.
these [ðiːz] *pron*, *adj* questi, -e.
thesis ['θiːsis] *n*, *pl* **-ses** tesi *f*.
they [ðei] *pron* essi, -e, loro.
thick [θik] *adj* spesso; (*hair*) folto; (*fog*) fitto; stupido. **thick as thieves** amici per la pelle. **thickset** *adj* (*heavily built*) tarchiato; (*dense*) folto, fitto. **thick-skinned** *adj* insensibile. **through thick and thin** nella buona e nella cattiva sorte. **thicken** *v* addensare, ispessire, infittire. **thickness** *n* spessore *m*; (*layer*) strato *m*.
thief [θiːf] *n* ladro, -a *m, f*. **thieve** *v* rubare. **thieving** *n* ruberia *f*, il rubare *m*.
thigh [θai] *n* coscia *f*.
thimble ['θimbl] *n* ditale *m*.
thin [θin] *adj* sottile, fine; (*lean*) magro; (*not dense*) rado, sparso; (*weak*) debole. *v* diradare; (*lose weight*) dimagrare; (*dilute*) allungare. **thinner** *n* diluente *m*.
thing [θiŋ] *n* cosa *f*, oggetto *m*. **for one thing . . . for another . . .** anzitutto . . . e poi . . . . **things** *pl n* (*implements, possessions etc.*) roba *f sing*, cose *f pl*.

***think** [θiŋk] *v* pensare; (*believe*) credere, ritenere; (*imagine*) figurarsi. **thinker** *n* pensatore, -trice *m, f.*

thinking ['θiŋkiŋ] *adj* pensante, ragionevole. *n* pensiero *m*, il ragionare *m*. **to my way of thinking** a mio avviso.

third [θəːd] *nm, adj* terzo. **third party** terzi *m pl.*

thirst [θəːst] *n* sete *f. v* aver sete. **thirst for** *or* **after** bramare. **thirsty** *adj* assetato. **be thirsty** aver sete.

thirteen [θəːˈtiːn] *nm, adj* tredici. **thirteenth** *nm, adj* tredicesimo.

thirty ['θəːti] *nm, adj* trenta. **thirtieth** *nm, adj* trentesimo.

this [ðis] *pron, adj* questo, -a.

thistle ['θisl] *n* cardo *m.*

thorn [θoːn] *n* spina *f*; (*shrub*) spino *m*. **thorny** *adj* spinoso.

thorough ['θʌrə] *adj* accurato; profondo; radicale; diligente. **thoroughly** *adv* a fondo.

thoroughbred ['θʌrəbred] *n* purosangue *m. adj* di razzo, di puro sangue.

thoroughfare ['θʌrəfeə] *n* via *f*, passaggio *m.*

those [ðouz] *pron, adj* quei *or* quegli, quelle.

though [ðou] *conj* (*in spite of*) sebbene, benchè; (*yet, still*) tuttavia, pure. **as though** come se. **even though** anche se. **it looks as though** sembra che.

thought [θoːt] *V* **think**. *n* pensiero *m*; idea *f*. **on second thoughts** ripensandoci (su). **thoughtful** *adj* (*reflective*) pensoso; (*thought out*) profondo; (*considerate*) premuroso, sollecito; (*careful*) attento, prudente. **thoughtless** *adj* (*careless*) imprudente; (*heedless*) sbadato; (*unthinking*) avventato; (*inconsiderate*) irrispettoso.

thousand ['θauzənd] *adj* mille. *n* mille *m invar*, migliaio (*pl* -a) *m*. **thousandth** *nm, adj* millesimo.

thrash [θraʃ] *v* battere, bastonare. **thrash out** discutere a fondo. **thrashing** *n* (*defeat*) batosta *f*; (*beating*) botte *f pl.*

thread [θred] *n* filo *m*; (*screw*) filetto *m*, passo *m*. *v* infilare; filettare. **threadbare** *adj* logoro.

threat [θret] *n* minaccia *f*. **threaten** *v* minacciare. **threatening** *adj* minaccioso; (*letter*) minatorio.

three [θriː] *nm, adj* tre. **three-cornered** *adj* triangolare, a tre punte. **three-dimensional** *adj* tridimensionale. **three-ply** *adj* (*wood*) a tre strati; (*wool*) a tre capi. **three-quarter** *adj* a tre quarti. **three-speed** *adj* a tre marce.

thresh [θreʃ] *v* (*corn, etc.*) trebbiare; battere. **threshing** *n* trebbiatura *f.*

threshold ['θreʃould] *n* soglia *f.*

threw [θruː] *V* **throw.**

thrift [θrift] *n* frugalità *f*, economia *f*. **thrifty** *adj* frugale, parsimonioso. **be thrifty** fare economia.

thrill [θril] *n* brivido *m*, fremito *m*; (*excitement*) emozione *f*. *v* far rabbrividire; emozionare; entusiasmare. **be thrilled with** essere entusiasta di. **thriller** *n* (*book, film*) giallo *m*. **thrilling** *adj* emozionante, eccitante.

thrive [θraiv] *v* fiorire, riuscire. **thrive on** approfittare di. **thriving** *adj* prospero, fiorente.

throat [θrout] *n* gola *f*. **have a sore throat** aver mal di gola. **throaty** *adj* gutturale.

throb [θrob] *v* battere, palpitare. *n* battito *m*, palpito *m*. **throbbing** *adj* palpitante, pulsante.

throes [θrouz] *pl n* **in the throes of** alle prese con.

thrombosis [θromˈbousis] *n* trombosi *f.*

throne [θroun] *n* trono *m.*

throng [θroŋ] *n* folla *f*, calca *f*. *v* affollarsi, stiparsi.

throttle ['θrotl] *v* strozzare; (*suppress*) soffocare; (*mot*) regolare. *n* (*valve*) valvola a farfalla *f.*

through [θruː] *adj* diretto, di transito; finito. *adv* da una parte all'altra; (*to the end*) fino alla fine. *prep* da, per; (*place*) attraverso; (*time*) durante; (*by means of*) tramite, per mezzo di; (*past*) al di là di. **get through** (*phone*) ottenere la comunicazione; (*finish*) sbrigare. **throughout** *adv* completamente; (*time*) durante; (*always*) sempre.

***throw** [θrou] *n* lancio *m*, tiro *m*. *v* lanciare, gettare; (*coll*: *confuse*) lasciare perplesso, sconcertare. **throw away** buttar via. **throwaway** *adj* (*casual*) spigliato; (*remark*) lasciato cadere; (*to be discarded*) da buttar via. **throw in** buttar dentro; (*sport*) rimettere in gioco; (*include*) comprendere. **throw out** buttar fuori, mettere alla porta; (*put forward*) dare. **throw up** lanciare in aria; (*be sick*) rigettare.

thrown [θroun] *V* **throw.**
thrush[1] [θrʌʃ] *n* (*bird*) tordo *m.*
thrush[2] [θrʌʃ] *n* (*med*) mughetto *m.*
***thrust** [θrʌst] *n* spinta *f,* botta *f;* (*mil*) attacco *m.* *v* spingere, ficcare, lanciarsi. **thrust oneself on** imporsi a.
thud [θʌd] *n* tonfo *m.*
thug [θʌg] *n* delinquente *m.*
thumb [θʌm] *n* pollice *m.* **thumbmark** *n* impronta digitale *f.* *v* **thumb a lift** fare l'autostop.
thump [θʌmp] *n* tonfo *m.* *v* picchiare, battere.
thunder ['θʌndə] *n* tuono *m.* **thunderbolt** *n* fulmine *m.* **thunderstorm** *n* temporale *m.* **thunderstruck** *adj* sbalordito. *v* tuonare. **thundering** *adj* (*coll*) enorme. **thundery** *adj* temporalesco; (*menacing*) minaccioso.
Thursday ['θəːzdi] *n* giovedì *m.*
thus [ðʌs] *adv* così.
thwart [θwoːt] *v* frustrare.
thyme [taim] *n* timo *m.*
thyroid ['θairoid] *n* tiroide *f.*
tiara [ti'aːrə] *n* diadema *m.*
tick[1] [tik] *n* (*sound*) tictac *m invar,* ticchettio *m;* (*mark*) contrassegno *m,* visto *m;* (*moment*) attimo *m.* *v* ticchettare, fare tictac; contrassegnare, vistare. **tick off** (*coll: scold*) sgridare. **ticking-off** *n* (*coll*) lavata di capo *f.* **tick over** (*engine*) girare in folle.
tick[2] [tik] *n* (*insect*) zecca *f,* acaro *m.*
ticket ['tikit] *n* biglietto *m;* (*label, counterfoil*) scontrino *m.* **ticket collector** bigliettario, -a *m, f.* **ticket office** biglietteria *f.*
tickle ['tikl] *v* solleticare; (*make itch*) fare il solletico; (*gratify*) lusingare; (*amuse*) divertire. *n* irritazione *f;* (*itch*) prurito *m.* **ticklish** *adj* (*person*) che sente il solletico; (*tricky*) delicato, scabroso.
tide [taid] *n* marea *f;* corrente *f.* **tidemark** *n* battigia *f.* *v* **tide over** superare.
tidy ['taidi] *adj* ordinato; (*neat*) ben curato *or* tenuto; (*coll: considerable*) bello. *v* mettere in ordine. **tidy up** far pulizia. **tidiness** *n* ordine *m.*
tie [tai] *v* legare; (*join*) attaccare; (*lace up*) allacciare; (*sport*) pareggiare. **tie down** limitare, obbligare. **tie up** (*property, capital etc.*) vincolare. *n* legame *m;* (*neck*) cravatta *f;* (*bond*) vincolo *m;* pareggio *m;* (*music*) legatura *f.*
tier [tiə] *n* (*row*) fila *f;* (*rank*) gradino *m;* (*layer*) strato *m.*
tiger ['taigə] *n* tigre *f.*
tight [tait] *adj* stretto; (*fitting closely*) aderente; (*taut*) teso; (*coll: drunk*) brillo; (*coll: mean*) tirchio. **in a tight corner** con le spalle al muro. *adv* **hold tight** stringere, tenersi fermo. **sit tight** non muoversi. **tighten** *v* stringere, serrare. **tights** *pl n* collant *m invar.*
tile [tail] *n* (*roof*) tegola *f;* (*floor, wall*) piastrella *f,* mattonella *f.* *v* coprire con tegole *or* piastrelle.
till[1] [til] *V* **until.**
till[2] [til] *n* cassa *f.*
till[3] [til] *v* coltivare; (*plough*) arare.
tiller ['tilə] *n* (*rudder*) barra del timone *f.*
tilt [tilt] *v* inclinare. *n* inclinazione *f.* **at full tilt** di gran carriera, a tutta velocità.
timber ['timbə] *n* legname *m;* (*beam*) trave *f.* **timbered** *adj* costruito in legno, coperto di legno; (*wooded*) alberato.
time [taim] *n* tempo *m,* periodo *m;* (*occasion*) volta *f;* (*clock*) ora *f;* epoca *f.* **for a long time** (*past*) da molto tempo; (*future*) per molto tempo. **for the time being** per ora. **from time to time** ogni tanto, di quando in quando. **have a good time** divertirsi. **in time** a tempo; (*eventually*) alla fine. **one at a time** uno alla volta. **on time** in orario. **take one's time** fare con comodo. **time bomb** bomba a orologeria *f.* **timekeeper** *n* (*sport*) cronometrista *m;* (*overseer*) controllore *m.* **time-signal** *n* segnale orario *m.* **timetable** *n* orario *m.* *v* misurare il tempo; (*sport*) cronometrare; (*choose moment*) scegliere il momento. **timeless** *adj* eterno, permanente. **timely** *adj* opportuno, tempestivo.
timid ['timid] *adj* timido. **timidity** *n* timidezza *f.*
tin [tin] *n* (*metal*) stagno *m;* (*can*) latta *f,* scatola *f.* **tin-opener** *n* apriscatole *m invar.* *v* inscatolare; stagnare. **tinny** *adj* (*sound*) metallico.
tinge [tindʒ] *n* sfumatura *f,* tocco *m.* *v* **tinged with** misto a.
tingle ['tiŋgl] *v* formicolare. *n* formicolio *m,* prurito *m.*
tinker ['tiŋkə] *v* (*repair*) rabberciare, rattoppare; (*busy oneself*) affaccendarsi.
tinkle ['tiŋkl] *v* (far) tintinnare, squillare. *n* tintinnio *m,* squillo *m.*
tinsel ['tinsəl] *n* orpello *m.*
tint [tint] *n* tono *m,* tinta *f.* *v* colorire.

tiny ['taini] *adj* piccino, minuto.

tip[1] [tip] *n* (*end*) punta *f*, estremità *f*; (*summit*) cima *f*. **tiptoe** *v* camminare in punta di piedi. **on tiptoe** in punta di piedi.

tip[2] [tip] *v* (*topple*) rovesciare; (*dump*) scaricare. *n* luogo di scarico *m*.

tip[3] [tip] *n* (*money*) mancia *f*; (*hint*) consiglio *m*; informazione riservata *f*. *v* dare la mancia. **tip off** avvertire, prevenire.

tipsy ['tipsi] *adj* (*coll*) brillo. **get tipsy** ubriacarsi leggermente.

tire[1] ['taiə] *v* stancarsi, stancare; (*get fed up*) stufarsi. **tired** *adj* stanco; (*fed up*) stufo. **tireless** *adj* infaticabile; (*unceasing*) indefesso. **tiresome** *adj* noioso, seccante. **tiring** *adj* faticoso.

tire[2] (*US*) *V* **tyre**.

tissue ['tiʃuː] *n* tessuto *m*; (*handkerchief*) fazzoletto di carta *m*. **tissue paper** carta velina *f*.

tit [tit] *n* (*bird*) cincia *f*.

title ['taitl] *n* titolo *m*; (*law*) diritto *m*. **title-page** *n* frontespizio *m*. **title-role** *n* parte principale *f*. *v* intitolare.

to [tu] *prep* a, in; (*in order to*) per; (*towards*) verso; da. *adv* **to and fro** avanti e indietro. **to-do** *n* (*coll*) trambusto *m*.

toad [toud] *n* rospo *m*. **toadstool** *n* fungo *m*.

toast [toust] *n* (*bread*) toast *m invar*; (*speech, drink*) brindisi *m*. **drink a toast to** bere alla salute di. *v* tostare. **toaster** *n* tostapane *m invar*.

tobacco [tə'bakou] *n* tobacco *m*. **tobacconist** *n* tabaccaio, -a *m, f*.

toboggan [tə'bogən] *n* toboga *m invar*. *v* andare in toboga.

today [tə'dei] *adv* oggi; (*nowadays*) oggigiorno. **a week/fortnight today** oggi a otto/quindici. *n* oggi *m*.

toddler ['todlə] *n* bambino, -a *m, f*, piccino, -a *m, f*. **toddle** *v* sgambettare.

toe [tou] *n* dito del piede *m*; (*shoe*) punta *f*. **tread on someone's toes** pestare i piedi a qualcuno.

toffee ['tofi] *n* caramella mou *f*.

together [tə'geðə] *adv* insieme, assieme. **together with** insieme con, assieme a.

toil [toil] *n* fatica *f*. *v* faticare.

toilet ['toilit] *n* (*lavatory*) gabinetto *m*; (*dressing, etc.*) toilette (*pl* -s) *f*, toletta *f*. **toilet-paper** *n* carta igienica *f*. **toilet water** acqua da toletta *f*.

token ['toukən] *n* segno *m*, simbolo *m*; (*gift*) omaggio *m*; (*coin*) gettone *m*.

Tokyo ['toukiou] *n* Tokio *f*.

told [tould] *V* **tell**.

tolerate ['toləreit] *v* tollerare, sopportare. **tolerable** *adj* tollerabile. **tolerance** *n* tolleranza *f*. **tolerant** *adj* tollerante.

toll[1] [toul] *n* pedaggio *m*; (*duty*) dazio *m*.

toll[2] [toul] *n* (*bell*) rintocco *m*. *v* rintoccare.

tomato [tə'maːtou] *n* pomodoro *m*. **tomato juice/paste** succo/estratto di pomodoro *m*. **tomato sauce** salsa di pomodoro *f*.

tomb [tuːm] *n* tomba *f*. **tombstone** *n* pietra tombale *f*.

tomorrow [tə'morou] *nm, adv* domani. **the day after tomorrow** dopodomani. **tomorrow morning** domattina. **tomorrow week** domani a otto.

ton [tʌn] *n* tonnellata *f*. **tonnage** *n* tonnellaggio *m*.

tone [toun] *n* tono *m*. *v* armonizzare. **tone down** attenuare, smorzare. **tonality** *n* tonalità *f*.

tongs [toŋz] *pl n* pinza *f sing*; (*fire*) molle *f pl*.

tongue [tʌŋ] *n* lingua *f*. **hold one's tongue** star zitto, tacere. **tongue-tied** *adj* ammutolito; (*speech defect*) scilinguato.

tonic ['tonik] *n* ricostituente *m*; (*water*) acqua brillante *f*; (*music*) tonica *f*. *adj* tonico.

tonight [tə'nait] *adj* (*evening*) stasera; (*night*) stanotte.

tonsil ['tonsil] *n* tonsilla *f*. **tonsillitis** *n* tonsillite *f*.

too [tuː] *adv* (*also*) anche, pure; (*moreover*) inoltre; (*more than enough*) troppo. **too many** troppi. **too much** troppo.

took [tuk] *V* **take**.

tool [tuːl] *n* attrezzo *m*, arnese *m*; strumento *m*. **tool-shed** *n* ripostiglio per attrezzi *m*. **tools of the trade** ferri del mestiere *m pl*. *v* lavorare.

tooth [tuːθ] *n*, *pl* **teeth** dente *m*. **have a sweet tooth** essere ghiotto di dolci. **have a tooth out** farsi cavare un dente. **in the teeth of** (*in defiance of*) a dispetto di; (*in the presence of*) in cospetto di. **toothache** *n* mal di denti *m*. **tooth-brush** *n* spazzolino da denti *m*. **toothpaste** *n* dentifricio *m*. **toothpick** *n* stuzzicadenti *m*. **toothless** *adj* sdentato.

top[1] [top] *n* (*highest point*) cima *f*, vertice *m*; (*leading position*) testa *f*, capo *m*; (*lid*) coperchio *m*. **at the top of one's voice** a voce altissima; (*shouting*) a squarciagola. **from top to toe** da capo a piedi. **on top of** (*upon*) sopra, su; (*at the head of*) in testa a; (*following*) dopo, in seguito a. *adj* (*uppermost*) superiore, ultimo; (*greatest*) più alto; (*foremost*) principale. **at top speed** a velocità massima. **top-heavy** *adj* sovraccarico (*m pl* -chi); (*unbalanced*) sbilanciato. **topsoil** *n* terriccio *m*. *v* sorpassare, superare; (*be above*) sovrastare a; (*prune*) scapezzare. **top up** *v* riempire. **topless** *adj* (*dress*) a petto scoperto. **topmost** *adj* il più alto.

top[2] [top] *n* (*toy*) trottola *f*.

topaz ['toupaz] *n* topazio *m*.

topic ['topik] *n* argomento *m*. **topical** *adj* di attualità.

topography [tə'pogrəfi] *n* topografia *f*.

topple ['topl] *v* (far) cadere *or* crollare.

topsy-turvy [topsi'təːvi] *adv* sottosopra.

torch [toːtʃ] *n* fiaccola *f*; (*electric*) lampadina tascabile *f*, torcia elettrica *f*.

tore [toː] *V* **tear**[1].

torment ['toːment; *v* toː'ment] *n* supplizio *m*, tortura *f*. *v* tormentare, angosciare.

torn [toːn] *V* **tear**[1].

tornado [toː'neidou] *n* tornado *m*, turbine *m*.

torpedo [toː'piːdou] *n* siluro *m*, torpedine *f*. *v* silurare. **torpedo-boat** *n* torpediniera *f*.

torrent ['torənt] *n* torrente *m*. **torrential** *adj* torrenziale.

torso ['toːsou] *n* torso *m*.

tortoise ['toːtəs] *n* tartaruga *f*. **tortoise-shell** *nf*, *adj* tartaruga.

tortuous ['toːtʃuəs] *adj* tortuoso.

torture ['toːtʃə] *n* tortura *f*. *v* torturare.

Tory ['toːri] *n*, *adj* (*coll*) conservatore, -trice.

toss [tos] *v* (*throw*) lanciare; (*pitch*) sballottare; (*move restlessly*) agitarsi. **toss aside** buttar via. **toss back** rilanciare. **toss up** (*coin*) far testa o croce; tirare a sorte. **toss-up** *n* questione di fortuna *f*. *n* **toss of the head** scrollata del capo *f*.

tot[1] [tot] *n* (*child*) bimbo, -a *m*, *f*, piccino, -a *m*, *f*; (*drink*) bicchierino *m*.

tot[2] [tot] *v* **tot up** sommare, fare la somma di.

total ['toutəl] *n* totale *m*, ammontare *m*. *adj* totale, globale. *v* (*add up*) fare la somma di; (*add up to*) ammontare a.

totter ['totə] *v* barcollare, vacillare. **tottering** *adj* barcollante; (*shaky*) malsicuro.

touch [tʌtʃ] *n* (*sense*) tatto *m*; contatto *m*; (*music, painting*) tocco *m*; (*hint*) accenno *m*; (*med*) attacco leggero *m*. **touchstone** *n* pietra di paragone *f*, criterio *m*. *v*. toccare; (*lightly*) sfiorare; (*handle*) maneggiare, tastare; (*move*) commuovere. **touch-and-go** *adj* rischioso. **touch down** (*plane*) atterrare. **touch up** ritoccare, ripassare. **touch wood!** tocca ferro! **touched** *adj* commosso. **touching** *adj* commovente; adiacente. **touchy** *adj* permaloso.

tough [tʌf] *adj* (*hard*) duro; (*hardy*) tenace; robusto; resistente; difficile. *n* teppista *m*. **toughen** *v* indurire, rinforzare. **toughness** *n* robustezza *f*; durezza *f*; resistenza *f*.

toupee ['tuːpei] *n* toupet *m invar*, parrucca *f*.

tour [tuə] *n* giro *m*, viaggio *m*; (*theatre, sport*) tournée (*pl* -s) *f*. *v* viaggiare, fare un giro; fare una tournée. **tourism** *n* turismo *m*. **tourist** *n* turista *m*, *f*.

tournament ['tuənəmənt] *n* torneo *m*.

tow[1] [tou] *n* (*hemp*) stoppa *f*.

tow[2] [tou] *v* rimorchiare. *n* **in tow** a rimorchio. **tow-rope** *n* rimorchio *m*. **tow-path** *n* alzaia *f*.

towards [tə'woːdz] *prep* verso, incontro a.

towel ['tauəl] *n* asciugamano *m*. *v* asciugarsi. **towelling** *n* spugna *f*.

tower ['tauə] *n* torre *f*. *v* elevarsi. **tower above** dominare. **towering** *adj* dominante; (*very great*) smisurato; violento.

town [taun] *n* città *f*; (*smaller*) cittadina *f*. **go to town** andare in città; (*do thoroughly*) mettercela tutta. **town clerk** segretario comunale *m*. **town hall** municipio *m*. **town planner** urbanista *m*, *f*. **town planning** urbanistica *f*.

toxic ['toksik] *adj* tossico. **toxicity** *n* tossicità *f*.

toy [toi] *n* giocattolo *m*. *v* (*play*) giocherellare; (*trifle*) dilettarsi.

trace [treis] *n* traccia *f*. *v* (*indicate, sketch*) tracciare; (*follow, discover*) rintracciare. **traceable** *adj* rintracciabile.

track [trak] *n* (*footpath*) sentiero *m*; (*mark, trace*) traccia *f*, orma *f*; (*sport*) pista *f*; (*set course*) percorso *m*; (*record*) banda *f*. **keep track of** seguire. **off the**

beaten track fuori mano. **on the right track** sulla strada buona. *v* inseguire. **track down** scovare.

tract[1] [trakt] *n* (*region*) zona *f*; (*anat*) apparato *m*.

tract[2] [trakt] *n* (*treatise*) trattato *m*; (*pamphlet*) manifesto *m*.

tractor ['traktə] *n* trattore *m*.

trade [treid] *n* (*work*) mestiere *m*; commercio *m*, traffico *m*; (*business*) affari *m pl*. **trademark** *n* marchio depositato *m*. **tradesman** *n* fornitore *m*, esercente *m*, negoziante *m*. **trade union** sindacato *m*. **trade unionist** sindacalista *m*, *f*. *v* fare affari, commerciare. **trade on** approfittare di. **trader** *n* commerciante *m*, *f*.

trading ['treidiŋ] *n* commercio *m*. *adj* commerciale.

tradition [trə'diʃən] *n* tradizione *f*. **traditional** *adj* tradizionale.

traffic ['trafik] *n* traffico *m*. **traffic jam** intasamento *or* ingorgo (del traffico) *m*. **traffic-light** *n* semaforo *m*. *v* trafficare.

tragedy ['tradʒədi] *n* tragedia *f*. **tragic** *adj* tragico.

trail [treil] *n* traccia *f*, pista *f*. *v* (*follow*) inseguire; (*drag*) trascinare. **trailer** *n* rimorchio *m*.

train [trein] *n* (*rail*) treno *m*; (*dress*) strascico *m*; (*following*) seguito *m*; serie *f*. **train of events** svolgimento *m*. *v* (*teach*) istruire; (*impart skill*) addestrare, ammaestrare; (*sport*) allenare. **trainee** *n* allievo, -a *m*, *f*; (*apprentice*) apprendista *m*, *f*. **trainer** *n* allenatore, -trice *m*, *f*. **training** *n* addestramento *m*; allenamento *m*.

trait [treit] *n* caratteristica *f*.

traitor ['treitə] *n* traditore *m*. **traitress** *n* traditrice *f*. **turn traitor** passare al nemico.

tram [tram] *n* tram *m invar*.

tramp [tramp] *n* (*person*) vagabondo *m*; (*walk*) passeggiata *f*; (*sound*) calpestio *m*. *v* vagabondare, percorrere a piedi.

trample ['trampl] *v* calpestare. **trample on** pestare.

trampoline ['trampəliːn] *n* trampolino *m*.

trance [traːns] *n* trance *f invar*; (*daze*) stupore *m*.

tranquil ['traŋkwil] *adj* sereno, calmo. **tranquillity** *n* serenità *f*, calma *f*. **tranquillizer** *n* tranquillante *m*, sedativo *m*.

transact [tran'zakt] *v* **transact business** trattare, entrare in trattative. **transaction** *n* affare *m*, trattativa *f*.

transcend [tran'send] *v* trascendere, superare. **transcendental** *adj* trascendentale.

transcribe [tran'skraib] *v* trascrivere. **transcript** *or* **transcription** *n* trascrizione *f*.

transept ['transept] *n* transetto *m*.

transfer ['transfəː; *v* trans'fəː] *n* trasferimento *m*; (*design*) decalcomania *f*. *v* trasferire; (*drawing*) riportare. **transferable** *adj* trasferibile.

transform [trans'foːm] *v* trasformare. **transformation** *n* trasformazione *f*, mutamento *m*; (*phys*) conversione *f*. **transformer** *n* trasformatore *m*.

transfuse [trans'fjuːz] *v* trasfondere. **transfusion** *n* trasfusione *f*.

transgress [trans'gres] *v* trasgredire. **transgression** *n* trasgressione *f*, infrazione *f*.

transient ['tranziənt] *adj* transitorio, passeggero; (*phys*) transiente.

transistor [tran'zistə] *n* transistor *m invar*, transistore *m*. **transistorize** *v* transistorizzare.

transit ['transit] *n* passaggio *m*, transito *m*. **in transit** durante il trasporto, in transito. *adj* di passaggio *or* transito.

transition [tran'ziʃən] *n* transizione *f*; (*music*) modulazione *f*.

transitive ['transitiv] *adj* transitivo.

translate [trans'leit] *v* tradurre. **translation** *n* traduzione *f*. **translator** *n* traduttore, -trice *m*, *f*.

translucent [trans'luːsnt] *adj* semitrasparente, traslucido.

transmit [tranz'mit] *v* trasmettere. **transmission** *n* trasmissione *f*. **transmitter** *n* (*radio set*) trasmettitore *m*; (*station*) trasmittente *f*.

transparent [trans'peərənt] *adj* trasparente. **transparency** *n* trasparenza *f*; (*phot*) diapositiva *f*.

transplant [trans'plaːnt; *n* 'transplaːnt] *v* trapiantare. *n* trapianto *m*.

transport ['transpoːt; *v* trans'poːt] *n* trasporto *m*. *v* trasportare. **transportation** *n* trasporto *m*.

transpose [trans'pouz] *v* trasporre. **transposition** *n* trasposizione *f*.

transverse ['tranzvəːs] *adj* traverso, trasversale.

trap [trap] *n* trappola *f*; (*trick*) tranello

m; (*vehicle*) carrozzetta *f*. **trapdoor** *n* trabocchetto *m*. *v* prendere in trappola.
trapeze [trə'piːz] *n* trapezio *m*.
trash [traʃ] *n* (*rubbish*) robaccia *f*; rifiuti *m pl*; (*nonsense*) sciocchezze *f pl*. **trashy** *adj* di nessun valore.
trauma ['troːmə] *n* trauma *m*. **traumatic** *adj* traumatico.
travel ['travl] *n* viaggiare *m*, viaggi *m pl*. **travel agency** agenzia di viaggi *f*. *v* viaggiare. **traveller** *n* viaggiatore, -trice *m, f*. **traveller's cheque** assegno turistico *m*.
travesty ['travəsti] *n* travestimento *m*, parodia *f*.
trawl [troːl] *n* strascico (*pl* -chi) *m*. *v* pescare con strascico. **trawler** *n* peschereccio *m*.
tray [trei] *n* vassoio *m*.
treachery ['tretʃəri] *n* tradimento *m*, perfidia *f*. **treacherous** *adj* traditore, -trice, perfido; (*unreliable*) falso; (*dangerous*) pericoloso.
treacle ['triːkl] *n* melassa *f*.
***tread** [tred] *v* (*trample*) calcare, calpestare; (*walk*) camminare. *n* passo *m*; (*stair*) gradino *m*; (*tyre*) battistrada *m invar*.
treason ['triːzn] *n* tradimento *m*.
treasure ['treʒə] *n* tesoro *m*. *v* (*cherish*) aver caro; (*prize*) apprezzare; (*retain carefully*) tener caro. **treasurer** *n* tesoriere, -a *m, f*. **treasury** *n* tesoreria *f*. **Treasury** *n* Ministero del Tesoro *m*.
treat [triːt] *v* trattare; (*med*) curare. *n* piacere *m*. **treatment** *n* trattamento *m*.
treatise ['triːtiz] *n* trattato *m*, dissertazione *f*.
treaty ['triːti] *n* trattato *m*.
treble ['trebl] *adj* triplo, triplice; di soprano. *n* soprano. *v* triplicare. *adv* tre volte tanto.
tree [triː] *n* albero *m*.
trek [trek] *v* viaggiare (scomodamente). *n* viaggio (scomodo) *m*, migrazione *f*.
trellis ['trelis] *n* pergolato *m*, graticcio *m*.
tremble ['trembl] *v* tremare; (*be agitated*) fremere. *n* tremito *m*; fremito *m*.
tremendous [trə'mendəs] *adj* enorme; (*coll*) straordinario.
tremor ['tremə] *n* tremore *m*.
trench [trentʃ] *n* (*ditch*) fosso *m*; (*mil*) trincea *f*. **trenchant** *adj* tagliente, caustico.
trend [trend] *n* tendenza *f*; direzione *f*; (*fashion*) moda *f*. **trendy** *adj* di moda.
trespass ['trespəs] *v* trasgredire; (*rel*) peccare. *n* trasgressione *f*; peccato *m*.
trestle ['tresl] *n* trespolo *m*.
trial ['traiəl] *n* (*law*) processo *m*; (*test*) esame *m*, prova *f*; esperimento *m*; (*trouble*) disperazione *f*, dolore *m*. **by trial and error** (a) tentoni.
triangle ['traiaŋgl] *n* triangolo *m*. **triangular** *adj* triangolare.
tribe [traib] *n* tribù *f*. **tribal** *adj* tribale. **tribesman** *n* membro di tribù *m*.
tribunal [trai'bjuːnl] *n* tribunale *m*.
tributary ['tribjutəri] *nm*, *adj* tributario.
tribute ['tribjuːt] *n* tributo *m*, omaggio *m*. **pay tribute to** rendere omaggio a.
trick [trik] *n* espediente *m*; (*prank*) tiro *m*; (*artifice*) trucco *m*; (*cards*) bazza *f*. **confidence trick** truffa all'americana *f*. **do the trick** ottenere l'effetto voluto. *v* ingannare, abbindolare. **trickery** *n* inganno *m*. **tricky** *adj* (*crafty*) furbo; complicato, delicato.
trickle ['trikl] *v* gocciolare. *n* gocciolio *m*; flusso irregolare *m*. **trickle of water** filo d'acqua *m*.
tricycle ['traisikl] *n* triciclo *m*.
trifle ['traifl] *n* sciocchezza *f*, inezia *f*; (*food*) zuppa inglese *f*. **a trifle** (*a little*) un po', alquanto. *v* scherzare. **trifling** *adj* insignificante.
trigger ['trigə] *n* grilletto *m*. *v* **trigger off** far scattare.
trigonometry [trigə'nomətri] *n* trigonometria *f*.
trill [tril] *n* trillo *m*. *v* trillare; (*continuous*) trilleggiare.
trilogy ['trilədʒi] *n* trilogia *f*.
trim [trim] *adj* ordinato, ben messo *or* tenuto, assettato. *n* assetto *m*; (*ornament*) guarnizione *f*. *v* (*neaten*) assettare; guarnire; (*hair*) spuntare. **trimmings** *pl n* guarnizioni *f pl*.
trinket ['triŋkit] *n* gingillo *m*.
trio ['triːou] *n* trio *m*.
trip [trip] *n* (*excursion*) gita *f*; (*journey*) viaggio *m*; (*stumble*) passo falso *m*. *v* (*step lightly*) saltellare; (*stumble*) inciampare. **trip up** far cadere, fare lo sgambetto, inciampare. **tripper** *n* escursionista *m, f*.
tripe [traip] *n* trippa *f*.
triple ['tripl] *adj* triplo, triplice. *v* triplicare. **triplet** *n* trigemino, -a *m, f*.

tripod ['traipod] *n* cavalletto *m*, treppiede *m*.
trite [trait] *adj* banale, comune.
triumph ['traiʌmf] *n* trionfo *m*. *v* trionfare, esultare. **triumphant** *adj* trionfante.
trivial ['triviəl] *adj* insignificante, banale. **triviality** *n* affare di nessuna importanza *m*.
trod [trod] *V* **tread.**
trodden ['trodn] *V* **tread.**
trolley ['troli] *n* carrello *m*.
trombone [trom'boun] *n* trombone *m*.
troop [truːp] *n* banda *f*, gruppo *m*; (*mil*) truppa *f*. *v* **troop along** sfilare. **troop in/out** entrare/uscire in gruppo.
trophy ['troufi] *n* trofeo *m*.
tropic ['tropik] *n* tropico *m*. **tropical** *adj* tropicale.
trot [trot] *v* trottare. *n* trotto *m*, trottata *f*. **on the trot** (*coll*) di seguito. **trotter** *n* (*horse*) trottatore *m*; (*pig's foot*) zampa *f*.
trouble ['trʌbl] *n* disturbo *m*; difficoltà *f*; (*unpleasantness*) dispiacere *m*; preoccupazione *f*; (*annoyance*) fastidio *m*. **make trouble** creare guai. **the trouble is** il guaio è. **troublemaker** *n* sobillatore, -trice *m, f*. *v* disturbare, dare fastidio. **troubled** *adj* turbato, preoccupato, agitato. **troublesome** *adj* noioso, fastidioso.
trough [trof] *n* trogolo *m*; (*drinking*) abbeveratoio *m*.
trousers ['trauzəz] *pl n* calzoni *m pl*, pantaloni *m pl*.
trout [traut] *n* trota *f*.
trowel ['trauəl] *n* (*plastering*) cazzuola *f*; (*gardening*) vanghetto *m*.
truant ['truːənt] *n* **play truant** marinare la scuola; (*shirk duty*) batter la fiacca.
truce [truːs] *n* tregua *f*.
truck [trʌk] *n* carro *m*, vagone *m*.
trudge [trʌdʒ] *v* trascinarsi, camminare a stento.
true [truː] *adj* vero; corretto; genuino; (*mech*) centrato. **come true** avverarsi. **hold true for** valere per.
truffle ['trʌfl] *n* tartufo *m*.
trump [trʌmp] *n* briscola *f*; (*bridge*) atout *m invar*. **trump card** (*coll*) forte *m*. *v* (*cards*) tagliare; (*beat*) battere. **trump up** fabbricare.
trumpet ['trʌmpit] *n* tromba *f*. **blow one's own trumpet** vantare i propri meriti. *v* (*proclaim loudly*) strombazzare; (*elephant*) barrire.
truncheon ['trʌntʃən] *n* manganello *m*, bastone *m*.
trunk [trʌŋk] *n* tronco *m*; (*chest*) baule *m*; torso *m*; (*elephant*) proboscide *f*. **trunk call** telefonata interurbana *f*. **trunk road** strada maestra *or* statale *f*. **trunks** *pl n* calzoncini *m pl*.
truss [trʌs] *v* legare. *n* (*framework*) travatura *f*; (*bundle*) fastello; (*med*) cinto erniario *m*.
trust [trʌst] *n* fiducia *f*; (*hope*) fede *f*; (*law*) fedecommesso *m*; (*comm*) trust *m invar*. **trustworthy** *adj* degno di fiducia, fidato. *v* fidarsi di, aver fiducia in; (*hope*) augurarsi. **trustee** *n* fidecommissario *m*; curatore, -trice *m, f*. **trusty** *adj* fedele, leale.
truth [truːθ] *n* verità *f*, vero *m*. **truthful** *adj* veritiero, sincero.
try [trai] *v* tentare; (*test*) provare; (*law*) giudicare, processare; (*taste*) assaggiare. **try on** provare. *n* tentativo *m*; (*rugby*) meta *f*. **trying** *adj* difficile; (*distressing*) penoso; (*irritating*) seccante.
tsar [zaː] *n* zar *m invar*.
T-shirt ['tiːʃəːt] *n* maglietta *f*.
tub [tʌb] *n* tino *m*; (*bath*) vasca *f*. **tubby** *adj* grassoccio.
tuba ['tjuːbə] *n* tuba *f*.
tube [tjuːb] *n* tubo *m*; (*for toothpaste, etc.*) tubetto *m*; (*rail*) metropolitana *f*. **inner tube** *n* camera d'aria *f*. **tubing** *n* tubo *m*. **tubular** *adj* tubolare.
tuber ['tjuːbə] *n* tubero *m*.
tuberculosis [tjubəːkju'lousis] *n* tubercolosi *f*.
tuck [tʌk] *n* piega *f*, rimbocco *m*. **tuckshop** *n* spaccio di dolciumi *m*. *v* (*thrust into*) stipare; (*needlework*) rimboccare. **tuck in** ripiegare; (*coll*: *eat*) pappare, farsi una mangiata. **tuck up in bed** mettere a letto, coricare.
Tuesday ['tjuːzdi] *n* martedì *m*.
tuft [tʌft] *n* ciuffo *m*, fiocco *m*.
tug [tʌg] *v* (*pull*) tirare, dare uno strappo a; (*drag*) trascinare. *n* strappo *m*; (*boat*) rimorchiatore *m*.
tuition [tju'iʃən] *n* insegnamento *m*, istruzione *f*.
tulip ['tjuːlip] *n* tulipano *m*.
tumble ['tʌmbl] *v* cascare, ruzzolare; (*somersault*) fare un capitombolo. **tumble down** crollare. *n* caduta *f*, capitombolo *m*. **tumbler** *n* (*glass*) bicchiere *m*.

tummy ['tʌmi] (*coll*) *n* pancia *f*. **tummy-ache** *n* mal di pancia *m*.
tumour ['tjuːmə] *n* tumore *m*.
tumult ['tjuːmʌlt] *n* tumulto *m*. **tumultuous** *adj* tumultuoso.
tuna ['tjuːnə] *n also* **tunny** tonno *m*.
tune [tjuːn] *n* motivo *m*; melodia *f*, aria *f*. **call the tune** essere in comando. **in tune** in tono, intonato. **out of tune** fuori tono, stonato. **sing out of tune** stonare. **to the tune of** alla bellezza di. *v* accordare; (*radio*) sintonizzare. **tuner** *n* sintonizzatore *m*.
tunic ['tjuːnik] *n* tunica *f*.
tunnel ['tʌnl] *n* tunnel *m invar*, traforo *m*. *v* traforare.
tunny ['tʌni] *V* **tuna**.
turban ['təːbən] *n* turbante *m*.
turbid ['təːbid] *adj* torbido.
turbine ['təːbain] *n* turbina *f*.
turbot ['təːbət] *n* rombo *m*.
turbulent ['təːbjulənt] *adj* turbolento. **turbulence** *n* turbolenza *f*.
tureen [tə'riːn] *n* zuppiera *f*.
turf [təːf] *n* zolla erbosa *f*; (*sod*) piota *f*; (*peat*) torba *f*; (*horse-racing*) ippica *f*. *v* piotare. **turf out** (*coll*) buttar fuori.
turkey ['təːki] *n* tacchino *m*.
Turkey ['təːki] *n* Turchia *f*. **Turk** *n* turco, -a *m*, *f*. **Turkish** *nm*, *adj* turco.
turmeric ['təːmərik] *n* curcuma *f*.
turmoil ['təːmoil] *n* scompiglio *m*, confusione *f*.
turn [təːn] *v* girare, voltare; (*change*) cambiare; (*change direction*) svoltare. **turn against** alienare, ribellarsi a. **turn away** voltarsi da parte, guardar via; (*refuse admission*) mandar via. **turncoat** *n* rinnegato, -a *m*, *f*. **turn down** (*fold*) risvoltare; (*lower*) abbassare; (*reject*) rifiutare. **turn into** far diventare, convertire in. **turn off** (*stop flow*) chiudere; (*switch off*) spegnere; (*change direction*) voltare. **turn on** (*start flow*) aprire; (*switch on*) accendere; (*coll*) eccitare; (*attack*) aggredire. **turn out** (*switch off*) spegnere; produrre; (*send away*) cacciar via; (*empty*) vuotare; risultare; (*clothe*) vestire. **turn over** rovesciare. **turnover** *n* (*comm*) giro d'affari *m*; (*cookery*) pasticcio *m*. **turnstile** *n* tornello *m*. **turntable** *n* (*records*) giradischi *m invar*; (*rail*) piattaforma girevole *f*. **turn up** (*arrive*) capitare; (*come to light*) ricomparire; (*increase intensity*) alzare; (*occur*) succedere. *n* giro *m*, rivoluzione *f*; (*change of direction*) svolta *f*; (*in rota, game, etc.*) turno *m*. **turning** *n* curva *f*, svolta *f*. **turning point** momento critico *or* decisivo *m*.
turnip ['təːnip] *n* rapa *f*.
turpentine ['təːpəntain] *n* trementina *f*; (*oil*) essenza di trementina *f*.
turquoise ['təːkwoiz] *n* (*stone*) turchese *f*; (*colour*) turchese *m*. *adj* turchese.
turret ['tʌrit] *n* torretta *f*.
turtle ['təːtl] *n* testuggine *f*, tartaruga *f*. **turn turtle** cappottare, capovolgersi. **turtle-dove** *n* tortora *f*.
Tuscany ['tʌskəni] *n* Toscana *f*. **Tuscan** *n*, *adj* toscano, -a.
tusk [tʌsk] *n* zanna *f*.
tussle ['tʌsl] *n* zuffa *f*. *v* venire alle mani, azzuffarsi.
tutor ['tjuːtə] *n* insegnante (privato) *m*; (*coach*) ripetitore, -trice *m*, *f*. **tutorial** *n* periodo di istruzione (privata) *m*.
tuxedo [tʌk'siːdou] *n* smoking *m invar*.
tweed [twiːd] *n* tweed *m invar*, tessuto di lana scozzese *m*.
tweezers ['twiːzəz] *pl n* pinzette *f pl*.
twelve [twelv] *nm*, *adj* dodici. **twelfth** *nm*, *adj* dodicesimo.
twenty ['twenti] *nm*, *adj* venti. **twentieth** *nm*, *adj* ventesimo.
twice [twais] *adv* due volte; (*doubly*) il doppio.
twiddle ['twidl] *v* (far) girare. **twiddle one's thumbs** tener le mani in mano.
twig [twig] *n* ramoscello *m*.
twilight ['twailait] *n* crepuscolo *m*, penombra *f*.
twin [twin] *n*, *adj* gemello, -a. **twin beds** letti gemelli *m pl*.
twine [twain] *n* spago *m*, corda *f*. *v* attorcigliare.
twinge [twindʒ] *n* spasimo *m*.
twinkle ['twiŋkl] *v* scintillare, luccicare; (*wink*) ammiccare, strizzare l'occhio. *n* luccichio *m*; strizzata d'occhio *f*.
twirl [twəːl] *v* girare rapidamente, piroettare.
twist [twist] *v* torcere, intrecciare; (*sprain*) slogarsi; alterare. *n* movimento rotatorio *m*; (*curve*) svolta *f*; (*thread*) filo ritorto *m*. **twister** *n* (*cheat*) imbroglione, -a *m*, *f*.
twit [twit] *n* (*coll*) scemo, -a *m*, *f*.
twitch [twitʃ] *v* (*jerk*) strappare, dare uno strattone; (*body*) storcere. *n* contorsione *f*, spasimo *m*. **twitching** *adj* convulsivo.

twitter ['twitə] *v* cinguettare. *n* cinguettio *m*.

two [tuː] *nm, adj* due. **in twos** due a due. **two-faced** *adj* falso. **two-piece** *n* (*garment*) duepezzi *m invar*. **two-seater** *adj* a due posti. **two-way** *adj* a doppio senso; (*elec*) bipolare.

tycoon [tai'kuːn] *n* magnate *m*.

type [taip] *n* tipo *m*, genere *m*; (*print*) carattere *m*. **typescript** *n* dattiloscritto *m*. **typesetter** *n* compositore *m*. **typewriter** *n* macchina da scrivere *f*. **typewritten** *adj* scritto a macchina, dattiloscritto. *v* dattilografare. **typical** *adj* tipico, caratteristico. **typify** *v* servire da esempio, simbolizzare. **typist** *n* dattilografo, -a *m, f*.

typhoid ['taifoid] *n* tifo *m*.

typhoon [tai'fuːn] *n* tifone *m*.

typographical [ˌtaipə'grafikl] *adj* tipografico.

tyrant ['tairənt] *n* tiranno *m*. **tyrannical** *adj* tirannico. **tyranny** *n* tirannia *f*.

tyre *or US* **tire** ['taiə] *n* gomma *f*, copertone *m*.

U

ubiquitous [ju'bikwitəs] *adj* onnipresente.

udder ['ʌdə] *n* mammella *f*.

ugly ['ʌgli] *adj* (*not pretty*) brutto; (*not agreeable*) antipatico, sgradevole; (*vicious*) vile. **ugliness** *n* bruttezza *f*.

ulcer ['ʌlsə] *n* ulcera *f*.

ulterior [ʌl'tiəriə] *adj* ulteriore. **ulterior motive** secondo fine *m*.

ultimate ['ʌltimət] *adj* finale, definitivo, assoluto. **ultimately** *adv* alla fine. **ultimatum** *n* ultimatum *m invar*.

ultraviolet [ʌltrə'vaiələt] *adj* ultravioletto.

umbilical [ʌm'bilikəl] *adj* ombilicale.

umbrella [ʌm'brelə] *n* ombrello *m*.

umpire ['ʌmpaiə] *n* arbitro *m*. *v* arbitrare.

umpteen [ʌmp'tiːn] (*coll*) *adj* innumerevole. **umpteenth** *adj* ennesimo.

unable [ʌn'eibl] *adj* incapace. **be unable to** non potere.

unacceptable [ʌnək'septəbl] *adj* inaccettabile.

unaccompanied [ʌnə'kumpənid] *adj* solo, non accompagnato.

unaccountable [ʌnə'kauntəbl] *adj* inspiegabile.

unaccustomed [ʌnə'kʌstəmd] *adj* (*not used to*) poco abituato; (*unusual*) insolito.

unadulterated [ʌnə'dʌltəreitid) *adj* sincero.

unanimous [ju'nanimәs] *adj* unanime.

unapproachable [ʌnə'proutʃəbl] *adj* inaccessibile.

unarmed [ʌn'aːmd] *adj* disarmato.

unashamed [ʌnə'ʃeimd] *adj* svergognato, senza vergogna.

unattainable [ʌnə'teinəbl] *adj* irraggiungibile.

unattractive [ʌnə'traktiv] *adj* poco attraente, antipatico.

unauthorized [ʌn'oːθəraizd] *adj* non autorizzato, illecito.

unavoidable [ʌnə'voidəbl] *adj* inevitabile.

unaware [ʌnə'weə] *adj* ignaro. **be unaware of** ignorare. **unawares** *adv* di sorpresa.

unbalanced [ʌn'balənst] *adj* squilibrato.

unbearable [ʌn'beərəbl] *adj* insopportabile.

unbelievable [ʌnbi'liːvəbl] *adj* incredibile.

***unbend** [ʌn'bend] *v* raddrizzare. **unbending** *adj* rigido, inflessibile.

unbiased [ʌn'baiəst] *adj* imparziale.

unbreakable [ʌn'breikəbl] *adj* infrangibile.

unbridled [ʌn'braidld] *adj* sfrenato.

unbroken [ʌn'broukn] *adj* intatto; ininterrotto; (*not beaten*) imbattuto.

unbutton [ʌn'butn] *v* sbottonare.

uncalled-for [ʌn'koːldfoː] *adj* immeritato, gratuito.

uncanny [ʌn'kani] *adj* strano, misterioso.

uncertain [ʌn'səːtn] *adj* incerto, dubbio. **uncertainty** *n* incertezza *f*.

unchanged [ʌn'tʃeindʒd] *adj* immutato, invariato.

uncharitable [ʌn'tʃaritəbl] *adj* aspro, crudele.

uncivilized [ʌn'sivilaizd] *adj* barbaro.

uncle ['ʌŋkl] *n* zio *m*.

uncomfortable [ʌn'kʌmfətəbl] *adj* scomodo. **feel uncomfortable** sentirsi a disagio.

uncommon [ʌn'komən] *adj* poco comune, insolito.

uncompromising [ʌn'komprəmaiziŋ] *adj* intrattabile, intransigente.

unconditional [ʌnkən'diʃənl] *adj* incondizionale, senza riserve, categorico.

unconscious [ʌn'konʃəs] *adj* (*unaware*) inconscio, inconsapevole; (*med*) privo di coscienza. *n* inconscio *m*. **become unconscious** svenire, perdere conoscenza. **be unconscious of** essere ignaro di, non accorgersi di. **unconsciously** *adv* senza rendersene conto.
uncontrollable [ʌnkən'trouləbl] *adj* incontrollabile, irreprimibile.
unconventional [ʌnkən'venʃənl] *adj* anticonformista; non convenzionale.
unconvincing [ʌnkən'vinsiŋ] *adj* poco convincente. **unconvinced** *adj* non convinto, poco persuaso.
uncooked [ʌn'kukt] *adj* crudo, non cotto.
uncouth [ʌn'kuːθ] *adj* rozzo, grossolano.
uncover [ʌn'kʌvə] *v* scoprire, rivelare, esporre.
uncut [ʌn'kʌt] *adj* non tagliato, integro.
undecided [ʌndi'saidid] *adj* indeciso, irresoluto.
undeniable [ʌndi'naiəbl] *adj* innegabile, incontestabile.
under ['ʌndə] *adv*, *prep* sotto, al di sotto (di). **be under the weather** sentirsi poco bene. **under age** minorenne. **under lock and key** sottochiave. **under one's breath** sottovoce. **under the circumstances** in queste circostanze.
undercharge [ʌndə'tʃaːdʒ] *v* far pagare meno del dovuto, non far pagare abbastanza.
underclothes ['ʌndəklouðz] *pl n* biancheria intima *f sing*.
undercoat ['ʌndəkout] *n* (*paint*) prima mano *f*.
undercover [ʌndə'kʌvə] *adj* segreto.
***undercut** [ʌndə'kʌt] *v* (*comm*) offrire a un prezzo inferiore a.
underdeveloped [ʌndədi'veləpt] *adj* sottosviluppato.
underdog ['ʌndədog] *n* vittima *f*, persona che ha la peggio *f*.
underdone [ʌndə'dʌn] *adj* (*meat*) al sangue.
underestimate [ʌndə'estimeit] *v* sottovalutare.
underexpose [ʌndərik'spouz] *v* sottoesporre.
underfoot [ʌndə'fut] *adv* sotto i piedi.
***undergo** [ʌndə'gou] *v* subire, supportare.
undergraduate [ʌndə'gradjuət] *n* studente universitario, studentessa universitaria *m*, *f*.
underground ['ʌndəgraund; *adv* ʌndə'graund] *adj* sotterraneo; (*secret*) segreto; clandestino. **underground passage** sottopassaggio *m*. *adv* sottoterra. *n* resistenza *f*; (*railway*) metropolitana *f*.
undergrowth ['ʌndəgrouθ] *n* boscaglia *f*, macchia *f*.
underhand [ʌndə'hand] *adj* clandestino; (*dubious*) losco.
***underlie** [ʌndə'lai] *v* sottostare a; essere alla base di.
underline [ʌndə'lain] *v* sottolineare.
undermine [ʌndə'main] *v* minare, insidiare.
underneath [ʌndə'niːθ] *adv*, *prep* sotto, al di sotto (di).
undernourished [ʌndə'nʌriʃt] *adj* malnutrito.
underpants ['ʌndəpants] *pl n* mutande *f pl*.
underpass ['ʌndəpaːs] *n* sottopassaggio *m*.
underprivileged [ʌndə'privilidʒd] *adj* non privilegiato, derelitto.
underrate [ʌndə'reit] *v* sottovalutare.
understaffed [ʌndə'staːft] *adj* a corto di personale *or* manodopera.
***understand** [ʌndə'stand] *v* capire, comprendere; (*realize*) rendersi conto; (*believe*) credere. **understandable** *adj* comprensibile.
understanding [ʌndə'standiŋ] *n* comprensione *f*; (*knowledge*) conoscenza *f*; (*agreement*) accordo *m*. **on the understanding that** a condizione *or* premesso che. *adj* comprensivo, indulgente.
understate [ʌndə'steit] *v* minimizzare, attenuare. **understatement** *n* atto del minimizzare *m*.
understudy ['ʌndəstʌdi] *v* sostituire. *n* sostituto, -a *m*, *f*, attore, -trice supplente *m*, *f*.
***undertake** [ʌndə'teik] *v* intraprendere; (*accept obligation*) impegnarsi; (*warrant*) garantire. **undertaker** *n* imprenditore di pompe funebri *m*, becchino *m*. **undertaking** *n* impresa *f*; (*pledge*) impegno *m*, promessa *f*.
undertone ['ʌndətoun] *n* fondo *m*, senso occulto *m*. **in an undertone** a basso voce.
underwear ['ʌndəweə] *n* biancheria *or* maglieria intima *f*.
underwater ['ʌndəwoːtə; *adv* ʌndə'woːtə] *adj* subacqueo. *adv* sott'acqua.
underweight [ʌndə'weit] *adj* di peso insufficiente.

underworld ['ʌndəwəːld] *n* (*myth*) inferno *m*; (*crime*) malavita *f*.

***underwrite** [ʌndə'rait] *v* sottoscrivere; (*support*) sostenere; (*finance*) garantire; (*insurance*) riassicurare. **underwriter** *n* riassicuratore *m*, garante di una emissione *m*.

undesirable [ʌndi'zaiərəbl] *adj* indesiderabile, sgradito.

undignified [ʌn'dignifaid] *adj* poco dignitoso.

***undo** [ʌn'duː] *v* disfare, sciogliere, annullare; rovinare. **leave undone** tralasciare di fare. **undoing** *n* rovina *f*.

undoubted [ʌn'dautid] *adj* indubbio, incontestato, certo.

undress [ʌn'dres] *v* svestire, spogliarsi.

undue [ʌn'djuː] *adj* indebito, eccessivo.

undulate ['ʌndjuleit] *v* ondeggiare.

unearth [ʌn'əːθ] *v* scoprire, dissotterrare. **unearthly** *adj* (*ghostly*) spettrale; (*coll*) assurdo.

uneasy [ʌn'iːzi] *adj* turbato, imbarrazzato, a disagio.

uneducated [ʌn'edjukeitid] *adj* ignorante, senza coltura.

unemployed [ʌnem'ploid] *adj* disoccupato. **the unemployed** i disoccupati *m pl*. **unemployment** *n* disoccupazione *f*.

unending [ʌn'endiŋ] *adj* interminabile, che non finisce più.

unequal [ʌn'iːkwəl] *dj* disuguale; (*unevenly matched*) impari. **unequal to** non all'altezza di. **unequalled** *adj* senza pari.

uneven [ʌn'iːvn] *adj* (*not level*) irregolare; ineguale; (*odd*) dispari.

unexpected [ʌneks'pektid] *adj* inatteso.

unfailing [ʌn'feiliŋ] *adj* infallibile, immancabile.

unfair [ʌn'feə] *adj* ingiusto; (*dishonest*) sleale; (*sport*) non sportivo. **unfairness** *n* ingiustizia *f*; slealtà *f*.

unfaithful [ʌn'feiθfəl] *adj* infedele, disonesto; inesatto. **unfaithfulness** *n* infedeltà *f*.

unfamiliar [ʌnfə'miljə] *adj* (*not conversant*) poco familiare *or* pratico; (*not well-known*) poco conosciuto *or* noto.

unfasten [ʌn'faːsn] *v* slegare, sciogliere, disfare.

unfavourable [ʌn'feivərəbl] *adj* sfavorevole.

unfit [ʌn'fit] *adj* (*unsuitable*) inadatto, non idoneo; (*unable*) inabile; (*unwell*) indisposto.

unfold [ʌn'fould] *v* (*open out*) schiudere; (*develop*) sviluppare; (*reveal*) rivelare.

unforeseen [ʌnfoː'siːn] *adj* imprevisto. **unforeseeable** *adj* imprevedibile.

unfortunate [ʌn'foːtʃənət] *adj* sfortunato, disgraziato; (*unsuitable, unhappy*) infelice. **unfortunately** *adv* purtroppo.

unfriendly [ʌn'frendli] *adj* freddo; ostile.

unfurnished [ʌn'fəːniʃd] *adj* non ammobiliato.

ungrateful [ʌn'greitfəl] *adj* ingrato.

unguarded [ʌn'gaːdid] *adj* incustodito, indifeso; imprudente, indiscreto.

unhappy [ʌn'hapi] *adj* infelice, triste; inopportuno; (*infelicitous*) poco felice. **unhappily** *adv* sfortunatamente. **unhappiness** *n* infelicità *f*, tristezza *f*.

unhealthy [ʌn'helθi] *adj* malsano; (*morbid*) morboso.

unhurried [ʌn'hʌrid] *adj* calmo, senza fretta.

unhurt [ʌn'həːt] *adj* incolume.

unicorn ['juːnikoːn] *n* unicorno *m*.

uniform ['juːnifoːm] *adj* uniforme, costante. *n* uniforme *f*, divisa *f*. **uniformity** *n* uniformità *f*.

unify ['juːnifai] *v* unificare. **unification** *n* unificazione *f*.

unilateral [juːni'latərəl] *adj* unilaterale.

unimaginable [ʌni'madʒinəbl] *adj* inconcepibile. **unimaginative** *adj* poco immaginativo.

unimpaired [ʌnim'peəd] *adj* intatto, in pieno vigore.

uninhabited [ʌnin'habitid] *adj* disabitato, deserto. **uninhabitable** *adj* inabitabile.

unintentional [ʌnin'tenʃənl] *adj* involontario.

uninterested [ʌn'intristid] *adj* disinteressato. **uninteresting** *adj* poco interessante, noioso.

union ['juːnjən] *n* unione *f*, unificazione *f*; associazione *f*; (*trade*) sindacato *f*; (*tech*) collegamento *m*.

unique [juː'niːk] *adj* unico, solo.

unison ['juːnisn] *n* unisono *m*. **in unison** all'unisono.

unit ['juːnit] *n* unità *f*; (*whole*) insieme *m*.

unite [juː'nait] *v* unire, combinare, congiungere. **united** *adj* unito. **United Kingdom** Regno Unito *m*. **United Nations** Nazioni Unite *f pl*. **United States of America** Stati Uniti d'America *m pl*.

unity ['juːniti] *n* unità *f.*
universe ('juːnivəːs] *n* universo *m.* **universal** *adj* universale.
university [juːni'vəːsəti] *n* università *f. adj* universitario.
unjust [ʌn'dʒʌst] *adj* ingiusto.
unkempt [ʌn'kempt] *adj* spettinato; (*untidy*) sciatto.
unkind [ʌn'kaind] *adj* poco gentile; crudele.
unknown [ʌn'noun] *adj* sconosciuto, ignoto. *n* ignoto *m*; (*math*) incognita *f.* **unknown to** all'insaputa di.
unlawful [ʌn'loːfəl] *adj* illegale; illecito.
unless [ʌn'les] *conj* a meno che non, se non.
unlike [ʌn'laik] *adj* dissimile *or* diverso (da). **be unlike** non rassomigliarsi. **not unlike** assai simile a. *prep* a differenza di, all'inverso di.
unlikely [ʌn'laikli] *adj* improbabile, inverosimile.
unload [ʌn'loud] *v* scaricare, liberarsi di.
unlock [ʌn'lok] *v* aprire.
unlucky [ʌn'lʌki] *adj* sfortunato, disgraziato.
unmarried [ʌn'marid] *adj* non sposato; (*bachelor*) celibe; (*spinster*) nubile. **unmarried mother** ragazza madre *f.*
unmistakable [ʌnmi'steikəbl] *adj* inequivocabile, manifesto.
unnatural [ʌn'natʃərəl] *adj* contro natura; (*lacking natural feelings*) snaturato, disumano; anormale; forzato.
unnecessary [ʌn'nesəsəri] *adj* inutile, non necessario.
unnoticed [ʌn'noutist] *adj* inavvertito.
unobtainable [ʌnəb'teinəbl] *adj* irreperibile.
unoccupied [ʌn'okjupaid] *adj* libero, vacante, vuoto.
unofficial [ʌnə'fiʃəl] *adj* ufficioso.
unopposed [ʌnə'pouzd] *adj* incontrastato.
unpack [ʌn'pak] *v* (*case*) disfare (le valige); (*contents*) disimballare.
unpaid [ʌn'peid] *adj* non retribuito *or* rimunerato; (*debt, etc.*) non saldato *or* pagato.
unpardonable [ʌn'paːdnəbl] *adj* imperdonabile.
unpleasant (ʌn'pleznt] *adj* spiacevole, sgradevole, antipatico. **unpleasantness** *n* spiacevolezza *f*; (*disagreement*) dissenso *m.*
unpopular [ʌn'popjulə] *adj* impopolare. **be unpopular with** esser malvisto da.
unprecedented [ʌn'presidentid] *adj* inaudito, senza precedenti.
unpredictable [ʌnprə'diktəbl] *adj* imprevedibile.
unqualified [ʌn'kwolifaid] *adj* non qualificato; senza diploma; categorico, assoluto.
unquestionable [ʌn'kwestʃənəbl] *adj* indiscutibile, fuori questione. **unquestioned** *adj* indiscusso, incontestato.
unravel [ʌn'ravəl] *v* sciogliere, sbrogliare; (*clear*) chiarire.
unreadable [ʌn'riːdəbl] *adj* illeggibile; (*tedious*) noioso.
unreal [ʌn'riəl] *adj* irreale.
unreasonable [ʌn'riːzənəbl] *adj* irragionevole.
unrecognizable [ʌnˌrekəg'naizəbl] *adj* irriconoscibile.
unrelenting [ʌnri'lentiŋ] *adj* inesorabile; (*dogged*) accanito.
unreliable [ʌnri'laiəbl] *adj* da non fidarsene; (*news*) inattendibile.
unrepetant [ʌnri'pentənt] *adj* impenitente.
unrest [ʌn'rest] *n* agitazione *f*, fermento *m.*
unripe [ʌn'raip] *adj* immaturo, acerbo.
unruly [ʌn'ruːli] *adj* indisciplinato, turbolento.
unsafe [ʌn'seif] *adj* malsicuro, pericoloso.
unsatisfactory [ʌnsatis'faktəri] *adj* poco soddisfacente, che lascia desiderare.
unsavoury [ʌn'seivəri] *adj* sgradevole; (*coll*) disgustoso, poco pulito.
unscrew [ʌn'skruː] *v* svitare.
unscrupulous [ʌn'skruːpjuləs] *adj* senza scrupoli.
unselfish [ʌn'selfiʃ] *adj* altruistico.
unsettle [ʌn'setl] *v* turbare; disturbare; sconcertare. **unsettled** *adj* (*weather*) variabile; (*account*) non saldato; (*not fixed*) non sistemato; (*uncertain*) incerto.
unsightly [ʌn'saitli] *adj* brutto, spiacevole a vedersi.
unskilled [ʌn'skild] *adj* inesperto, non qualificato. **unskilled worker** *n* manovale *m.*
unsociable [ʌn'souʃəbl] *adj* poco socievole, scontroso.
unsound [ʌn'saund] *adj* imperfetto, difettoso; erroneo; (*ill-founded*) poco profondo.

unspeakable [ʌn'spiːkəbl] *adj* indicibile, inesprimibile; (*very bad*) inqualificabile.
unstable [ʌn'steibl] *adj* instabile.
unsteady [ʌn'stedi] *adj* malfermo, instabile; incostante; (*wavering*) traballante, barcollante.
unsuccessful [ʌnsək'sesfəl] *adj* non *or* mal riuscito, sfortunato, fallito.
unsuitable [ʌn'suːtəbl] *adj* inadatto; inopportuno; sconveniente. **unsuited** *adj* non idoneo, disadatto, sconvenevole.
unsure [ʌn'ʃuə] *adj* malsicuro, incerto.
untangle [ʌn'taŋgl] *v* districare.
unthinkable [ʌn'θiŋkəbl] *adj* inconcepibile, assurdo.
untidy [ʌn'taidi] *adj* disordinato, trascurato. **untidiness** *n* disordine *m*. trascuratezza *f*.
untie [ʌn'tai] *v* sciogliere, slegare.
until [ən'til] *prep* fino a; (*before*) prima di. *conj* finchè, fino a quando; fino al momento in cui.
untimely [ʌn'taimli] *adj* inopportuno, intempestivo, prematuro.
untoward [ʌntə'woːd] *adj* disgraziato.
untrue [ʌn'truː] *adj* non vero, falso, erroneo; infedele; inesatto.
unusual [ʌn'juːʒuəl] *adj* insolito, straordinario, eccezionale.
unwanted [ʌn'wontid] *adj* indesiderato, superfluo.
unwelcome [ʌn'welkəm] *adj* (*person*) malaccolto; (*news, etc.*) sgradito, spiacevole.
unwell [ʌn'wel] *adj* indisposto, ammalato.
unwieldy [ʌn'wiːldi] *adj* ingombrante.
unwilling [ʌn'wiliŋ] *adj* restio, riluttante; (*given reluctantly*) dato controvoglia.
***unwind** [ʌn'waind] *v* dipanare; (*relax*) rilassarsi.
unwise [ʌn'waiz] *adj* imprudente, insensato.
unwittingly [ʌn'witiŋli] *adv* senza saperlo, per inavvertenza.
unworthy [ʌn'wəːði] *adj* indegno. **unworthy of** che non merita.
unwrap [ʌn'rap] *v* disfare.
up [ʌp] *adv* su; (*erect*) in piedi; (*out of bed*) alzato. **be up against** essere alle prese con. **be up to** (*capable of*) essere all'altezza di; (*mischief*) tramare. **up here** quassù. **up there** lassù. **up to** fino a. **what's up?** cosa succede? *prep* su, su per. *n* **ups and downs** alti e bassi *m pl*.
upbringing ['ʌpbriŋiŋ] *n* educazione *f*.
update [ʌp'deit] *v* aggiornare.
upheaval [ʌp'hiːvl] *n* commozione *f*, sconvolgimento *m*.
uphill [ʌp'hil] *adv* in salita, in su. *adj* in salita, ascendente; difficile.
***uphold** [ʌp'hould] *v* sostenere, appoggiare.
upholster [ʌp'houlstə] *v* tappezzare. **upholsterer** *n* tappezziere *m*. **upholstery** *n* tappezzeria *f*.
upkeep ['ʌpkiːp] *n* mantenimento *m*, manutenzione *f*.
uplift [ʌp'lift] *v* edificare, incoraggiare. *n* edificazione *f*, incoraggiamento *m*.
upon [ə'pon] *prep* su, sopra.
upper ['ʌpə] *adj* superiore, più alto. **get the upper hand** prevalere. *n* tomaia *f*. **be on one's uppers** essere alle strette. **uppermost** *adj* il più alto.
upright ['ʌprait] *adj* verticale, in piedi; (*righteous*) retto, onesto.
uprising ['ʌpraiziŋ] *n* insurrezione *f*.
uproar ['ʌproː] *n* tumulto, fracasso. **uproarious** *adj* tumultuoso, chiassoso. **uproariously funny** da crepar dal ridere.
uproot [ʌp'ruːt] *v* sradicare.
***upset** [ʌp'set; *n* 'ʌpset] *v* sconvolgere, disturbare; (*knock over*) rovesciare. *adj* sconvolto, turbato; rovesciato. *n* disturbo *m*, contrattempo *m*. **upsetting** *adj* turbante, preoccupante.
upshot ['ʌpʃot] *n* conclusione *f*, effetto *m*.
upside down [ʌpsai'daun] *adv*, *adj* sottosopra, in disordine.
upstairs [ʌp'steəz] *adv* di sopra, al piano superiore.
upstream [ʌp'striːm] *adv* a monte, controcorrente.
uptight ['ʌptait] *adj* (*coll*) nervoso.
up-to-date [ʌptə'deit] *adj* aggiornato, di moda.
upward ['ʌpwəd] *adj* in salita, rivolto in alto. **upwards** *adv* in su, in alto; (*more*) più.
uranium [ju'reiniəm] *n* uranio *m*.
urban ['əːbən] *adj* urbano.
urchin ['əːtʃin] *n* monello, -a *m, f*.
urge [əːdʒ] *n* sprone *m*, impulso *m*. *v* esortare, spingere; insistere.
urgent ['əːdʒənt] *adj* urgente. **urgency** *n* urgenza *f*.
urine ['juːrin] *n* orina *f*. **urinal** *n* orinatoio *m*. **urinary** *adj* urinario. **urinate** *v* orinare.

urn ['əːn] *n* urna *f.*
us [ʌs] *pron* ci, ce; (*after prep*) noi.
usage ['juːzidʒ] *n* uso *m*, usanza *f.*
use [juːs; *v* juːz] *n* uso *m*, impiego (*pl* -ghi) *m*; utilità *f.* **it's no use!** è inutile! **what's the use?** a cosa serve? *v* usare, impiegare, adoperare. **use up** consumare. **used** *adj* (*car*) d'occasione. **be used to** essere abituato a. **useful** *adj* utile. **useless** *adj* inutile.
usher ['ʌʃə] *n* usciere *m.* *v* **usher in** far entrare, introdurre. **usherette** *n* maschera *f.*
usual ['juːzuəl] *adj* solito, usuale. **as usual** come di solito. **usually** *adv* di solito, generalmente.
usurp [ju'zəːp] *v* usurpare.
utensil [ju'tensl] *n* utensile *m*, arnese *m.*
uterus ['juːtərəs] *n* utero *m.*
utility [ju'tiləti] *n* utilità *f*, vantaggio *m*; servizio pubblico *m.* **utilize** *v* utilizzare.
utmost ['ʌtmoust] *adj* massimo, supremo. *n* massimo *m*, possibile *m.* **do one's utmost** fare del proprio meglio.
utter[1] ['ʌtə] *v* (*say*) pronunciare, emettere.
utter[2] ['ʌtə] *adj* (*absolute*) completo, assoluto.
U-turn ['juːtəːn] *n* cambio di direzione *m.*

V

vacant ['veikənt] *adj* libero, vuoto; vacuo. **vacancy** *n* (*job*) posto libero *m*; (*room*) camera libera *f.* **vacate** *v* lasciar libero, sgomberare.
vaccine ['vaksiːn] *n* vaccino *m.* **vaccinate** *v* vaccinare. **vaccination** *n* vaccinazione *f.*
vacillate ['vasileit] *v* vacillare.
vacuum ['vakjum] *n* vuoto *m.* **vacuum cleaner** *n* aspirapolvere *m invar.* **vacuum flask** *n* thermos *m invar.*
vagina [və'dʒainə] *n* vagina *f.* **vaginal** *adj* vaginale.
vagrant ['veigrənt] *n, adj* vagabondo, -a. **vagrancy** *n* vagabondaggio *m.*
vague [veig] *adj* vago.
vain [vein] *adj* (*worthless*) vano, inutile; (*conceited*) vanitoso. **in vain** invano.
valiant ['valiənt] *adj* valoroso.
valid ['valid] *adj* (*ticket, etc.*) valevole; (*sound*) valido. **validity** *n* validità *f.*
valley ['vali] *n* valle *f.*
value ['valjuː] *n* valore *m.* *v* valutare, stimare; dare importanza a. **valuable** *adj* prezioso, di valore. **valuables** *pl n* valori *m pl*, oggetti di valore *m pl.*
valve [valv] *n* valvola *f.*
vampire ['vampaiə] *n* vampiro *m.*
van[1] [van] *n* (*vehicle*) furgone *m*, camion *f.*
van[2] [van] *n* (*forefront*) avanguardia *f.*
vandal ['vandl] *n* vandalo *m.* **vandalism** *n* vandalismo *m.*
vanilla [və'nilə] *n* vaniglia *f.*
vanish ['vaniʃ] *v* sparire.
vanity ['vanəti] *n* vanità *f.*
vapour ['veipə] *n* vapore *m.* **vaporize** *v* vaporizzare.
variance ['veəriəns] *n* variazione *f.* **at variance** in disaccordo.
varicose veins ['varikous] *pl n* vene varicose *f pl.*
variety [və'raiəti] *n* varietà *f*, diversità *f.*
various ['veəriəs] *adj* vario, diverso.
varnish ['vaːniʃ] *n* vernice *f*, lacca *f.* *v* verniciare, laccare.
vary ['veəri] *v* variare; modificare; differire. **variant** *n* variante *f.* **variation** *n* variazione *f.* **varied** *adj* vario, svariato.
vase [vaːz] *n* vaso *m.*
vasectomy [və'sektəmi] *n* vasectomia *f.*
vast [vaːst] *adj* vasto, immenso.
vat [vat] *n* tino *m.*
Vatican ['vatikən] *n* Vaticano *m.* **Vatican City** la Città del Vaticano *f.*
vault[1] [voːlt] *n* volta *f*; (*cellar*) cantina *f*; (*safe*) camera di sicurezza *f.*
vault[2] [voːlt] *v* saltare, volteggiare. *n* salto *m.*
veal [viːl] *n* vitello *m.*
veer [viə] *v* virare, cambiar direzione.
vegetable ['vedʒtəbl] *n* ortaggio *m*, verdura *f.* *adj* vegetale; (*food*) di verdura. **vegetarian** *n, adj* vegetariano, -a. **vegetate** *v* vegetare. **vegetation** *n* vegetazione *f.*
vehement ['viːəmənt] *adj* violento, impetuoso.
vehicle ['viəkl] *n* veicolo *m*; (*means*) mezzo *m.*
veil [veil] *n* velo *m.* *v* velare; (*hide*) nascondere.
vein [vein] *n* vena *f*; (*leaf, marking*) venatura *f.*
velocity [və'losəti] *n* velocità *f.*
velvet ['velvit] *n* velluto *m.* **velvety** *adj* vellutato.

vending machine ['vendiŋ] *n* distributore automatico *m*.
veneer [və'niə] *n* piallaccio *m*; (*superficial layer*) vernice *f*.
venerate ['venəreit] *v* venerare. **venerable** *adj* venerabile.
venereal disease [və'niəriəl] *n* malattia venerea *f*.
Venetian blind [və'niːʃən] *n* veneziana *f*.
vengeance ['vendʒəns] *n* vendetta *f*. **with a vengeance** (*unexpectedly*) in modo insospettato; (*with violence*) violentemente.
Venice ['venis] *n* Venezia *f*.
venison ['venisn] *n* cacciagione *f*.
venom ['venəm] *n* veleno *m*; (*spite*) malignità *f*, cattiveria *f*. **venomous** *adj* velenoso; maligno, cattivo.
vent [vent] *n* (*outlet*) apertura *f*, sbocco *m*. **give vent to** sfogare. *v* esprimere, sfogare.
ventilate ['ventileit] *v* ventilare. **ventilation** *n* ventilazione *f*.
venture ['ventʃə] *n* impresa (rischiosa) *f*, avventura *f*. *v* azzardare, arrischiare.
venue ['venjuː] *n* sede *f*; (*place*) posto *m*.
verb [vəːb] *n* verbo *m*. **verbal** *adj* verbale. **verbatim** *adj* parola per parola.
verdict ['vəːdikt] *n* verdetto *m*, giudizio *m*.
verge [vəːdʒ] *n* orlo *m*, limite *m*. **on the verge of** sul punto di. *v* **verge on** tendere a, avvicinarsi a.
verify ['verifai] *v* verificare, confermare. **verification** *n* verifica *f*.
vermin ['vəːmin] *pl n* animali nocivi *m pl*, parassiti *m pl*; (*scum*) feccia *f sing*.
vermouth ['vəːməθ] *n* vermut *m invar*.
vernacular [və'nakjulə] *adj* indigeno, dialettale; volgare. *n* **in the vernacular** in volgare.
versatile ['vəːsətail] *adj* versatile, eclettico.
verse [vəːs] *n* verso *m*; (*poem*) poesia *f*. **in verse** in versi.
version ['vəːʃən] *n* versione *f*.
versus ['vəːsəs] *prep* contro.
vertebra ['vəːtibrə] *n*, *pl* **-brae** vertebra *f*. **vertebral** *adj* vertebrale. **vertebrate** *nm*, *adj* vertebrato.
vertical ['vəːtikl] *nf*, *adj* verticale.
vertigo ['vəːtigou] *n* vertigini *f pl*.
very ['veri] *adv* molto, assai. **the very next day** proprio il giorno dopo. *adj* proprio; esatto; (*same*) stesso; (*mere*) solo.
vessel ['vesl] *n* (*container*) recipiente *m*, vaso *m*; (*ship*) nave *f*, bastimento *m*.
vest [vest] *n* maglia *f*, maglietta *f*. *v* conferire, assegnare.
vestige ['vestidʒ] *n* vestigio *m*, traccia *f*.
vestry ['vestri] *n* sagrestia *f*.
vet [vet] (*coll*) *v* controllare, esaminare. *n* veterinario, -a *m*, *f*.
veteran ['vetərən] *n* veterano *m*; (*mil*) reduce *m*.
veterinary ['vetərinəri] *adj* veterinario. **veterinary surgeon** *n* veterinario, -a *m*, *f*.
veto ['viːtou] *n* veto *m*.
vex [veks] *v* vessare, irritare. **vexed question** argomento dibattuto *m*.
via [vaiə] *prep* per, attraverso, tramite.
viable ['vaiəbl] *adj* vitale, capace a vivere; (*workable*) praticabile, possibile; (*road*) transitabile. **viability** *n* praticabilità *f*; (*biol*) vitalità *f*.
viaduct ['vaiədʌkt] *n* viadotto *m*.
vibrate [vai'breit] *v* (far) vibrare. **vibration** *n* vibrazione *f*.
vicar ['vikə] *n* parroco *m*, vicario *m*. **vicarage** *n* parrocchia *f*.
vicarious [vi'keəriəs] *adj* vicario.
vice[1] [vais] *n* (*evil*) vizio *m*; (*fault*) difetto *m*.
vice[2] [vais] *n* (*tool*) morsa *f*.
vice-chancellor [vais'tʃaːnsələ] *n* (*university*) rettore *m*.
vice-president [vais'prezidənt] *n* vice-presidente *m*.
vice versa [vaisi'vəːsə] *adv* viceversa.
vicinity [vi'sinəti] *n* vicinanza *f*, prossimità *f*; (*neighbourhood*) vicinanze *f pl*, dintorni *m pl*.
vicious ['viʃəs] *adj* (*bad*) cattivo; (*crude*) crudele, maligno. **vicious circle** circolo vizioso *m*.
victim ['viktim] *n* vittima *f*. **fall victim to** essere preda a. **victimize** *v* perseguitare *or* punire ingiustamente; sacrificare.
victory ['viktəri] *n* vittoria *f*. **victorious** *adj* vittorioso.
video-tape ['vidiouteip] *n* video-cassetta *f*.
vie [vai] *v* gareggiare.
Vienna [vi'enə] *n* Vienna *f*.
view [vjuː] *n* vista *f*; (*scene*, *opinion*) veduta *f*. **in view of** in vista di; (*considering*) dato; (*on account of*) grazie a, a causa di. **on view** esposto. **viewfinder** *n* mirino *m*. **viewpoint** *n* punto di vista *m*. **with a view to** allo scopo di. *v* vedere;

osservare; ispezionare. **viewer** *n* spettatore, -trice *m, f*; telespettatore, -trice *m, f.*
vigil ['vidʒil] *n* veglia *f*, vigilia *f.* **vigilant** *adj* vigile.
vigour ['vigə] *n* vigore *m.* **vigorous** *adj* vigoroso; robusto.
vile [vail] *adj* vile, spregevole.
villa ['vilə] *n* villa *f.*
village ['vilidʒ] *n* villaggio *m*, paese *m.*
villain ['vilən] *n* farabutto *m*, villano *m.*
vindicate ['vindikeit] *v* rivendicare, giustificare; (*exonerate*) discolpare. **vindication** *n* rivendicazione *f*, giustificazione *f*; discolpa *f.*
vindictive [vin'diktiv] *adj* vendicativo, malevolo.
vine [vain] *n* vite *f.* **vineyard** *n* vigna *f.*
vinegar ['vinigə] *n* aceto *m.*
vintage ['vintidʒ] *n* vendemmia *f*; (*year*) annata *f.* *adj* (*wine*) pregiato; (*car*) d'epoca.
vinyl ['vainil] *adj* vinilico.
viola [vi'oulə] *n* viola *f.*
violate ['vaiəleit] *v* violare, trasgredire. **violation** *n* violazione *f*, trasgressione *f.*
violence ['vaiələns] *n* violenza *f.* **violent** *adj* violento.
violet ['vaiəlit] *n* (*colour*) (color) viola *m*, violetto *m*; (*flower*) viola *f*, violetta *f.* *adj* viola *invar*, violetto.
violin [vaiə'lin] *n* violino *m.* **violinist** *n* violinista *m, f.*
viper ['vaipə] *n* vipera *f.*
virgin ['vəːdʒin] *nf, adj* vergine. **virginity** *n* verginità *f.*
Virgo ['vəːgou] *n* Vergine *f.*
virile ['virail] *adj* virile. **virility** *n* virilità *f.*
virtual ['vəːtʃuəl] *adj* effettivo, in pratica.
virtue ['vəːtʃuː] *n* virtù *f*; (*admirable quality*) pregio *m.* **by virtue of** in virtù di, grazie a. **virtuoso** *n* virtuoso, -a *m, f.* **virtuous** *adj* virtuoso.
virulent ['virələnt] *adj* virulento. **virulence** *n* virulenza *f.*
virus ['vaiərəs] *n* virus *m invar.* **viral** *adj* virale.
visa ['viːzə] *n* visto *m.*
viscount ['vaikaunt] *n* visconte *m.* **viscountess** *n* viscontessa *f.*
viscous ['viskəs] *adj* viscoso. **viscosity** *n* viscosità *f.*
visible ['vizəbl] *adj* visibile; (*obvious*) evidente. **visibility** *n* visibilità *f.*
vision ['viʒən] *n* visione *f*; (*wisdom*) sagacia *f.* **visionary** *n, adj* visionario, -a.
visit ['vizit] *n* visita *f.* *v* visitare; (*person*) fare una visita a, andare a trovare; (*place*) andare a vedere; (*doctor*) consultare. **visitor** *n* visitatore, -trice *m, f*; (*guest*) ospite *m, f.*
visor ['vaizə] *n* visiera *f.*
visual ['viʒuəl] *adj* visivo, visuale. **visualize** *v* immaginare, concepire.
vital ['vaitl] *adj* vitale, essenziale; capitale. **vitality** *n* vitalità *f.*
vitamin ['vitəmin] *n* vitamina *f.*
vivacious [vi'veiʃəs] *adj* vivace, animato. **vivacity** *n* vivacità *f.*
vivid ['vivid] *adj* vivido, vivace.
vixen ['viksn] *n* volpe femmina *f.*
vocabulary [və'kabjuləri] *n* vocabolario *m.*
vocal ['voukəl] *adj* vocale; orale.
vocation [vou'keiʃən] *n* vocazione *f*; professione *f*; (*role*) funzione *f.* **vocational** *adj* vocazionale, professionale.
vociferous [və'sifərəs] *adj* rumoroso, chiassoso.
vodka ['vodkə] *n* vodka *f.*
voice [vois] *n* voce *f.* *v* esprimere, formulare, manifestare.
void [void] *nm, adj* vuoto. *v* vuotare; (*law*) annullare.
volatile ['volətail] *adj* (*chem*) volatile; capriccioso; (*unpredictable*) imprevedibile; esplosivo.
volcano [vol'keinou] *n* vulcano *m.* **volcanic** *adj* vulcanico.
volley ['voli] *n* raffica *f*, scarica *f*; (*tennis*) volata *f.* **volleyball** *n* pallavolo *f.*
volt [voult] *n* volt *m invar.* **voltage** *n* tensione *f*, voltaggio *m.*
volume ['voljum] *n* volume *m.* **voluminous** *adj* voluminoso.
volunteer [volən'tiə] *n* volontario, -a *m, f.* *v* offrirsi volontariamente; (*mil*) arruolarsi volontario; (*offer*) dare *or* offrire spontaneamente. **voluntary** *adj* volontario.
voluptuous [və'lʌptʃuəs] *adj* voluttuoso, sensuale.
vomit ['vomit] *v* vomitare. *n* vomito *m.*
voodoo ['vuːduː] *n* vodù *m.*
voracious [və'reiʃəs] *adj* vorace, insaziabile. **voracity** *n* voracità *f.*
vote [vout] *n* voto *m*, diritto di voto *m*, suffragio *m.* *v* votare, dare il proprio

voto; (*agree generally*) convenire. **voter** *n* elettore, -trice *m, f.*
vouch [vautʃ] *v* **vouch for** garantire, attestare. **vouchsafe** *v* degnarsi di dare, concedere.
voucher ['vautʃə] *n* buono *m*, tagliando *m.*
vow [vau] *n* voto *m*, giuramento *m. v* giurare; fare voto di.
vowel ['vauəl] *n* vocale *f.*
voyage ['voiidʒ] *n* viaggio *m*, escursione *f*; (*crossing*) traversata *f. v* viaggiare; attraversare.
vulgar ['vʌlgə] *adj* volgare. **vulgarity** *n* volgarità *f.* **vulgarize** *v* divulgare, volgarizzare; (*debase*) degradare.
vulnerable ['vʌlnərəbl] *adj* vulnerabile.
vulture ['vʌltʃə] *n* avvoltoio *m.*

W

wad [wod] *n* tampone *m*; pacchetto *m*; (*roll*) rotolo *m.* **wadding** *n* (*padding*) imbottitura *f.*
waddle ['wodl] *v* camminare dondolandosi. *n* andatura dondolante *f.*
wade [weid] *v* guadare, avanzare con fatica. **wader** *n* (*bird*) trampoliere *m.*
wafer ['weifə] *n* cialda *f*, wafer *m invar*; (*church*) ostia *f.*
waft [woft] *v* diffondere. *n* zaffata *f.*
wag [wag] *v* agitare, scuotere; (*tail*) dimenare. **set tongues wagging** suscitare pettegolezzi.
wage [weidʒ] *n* salario *m*, paga *f. v* **wage war** muover guerra.
wager ['weidʒə] *n* scommessa *f. v* scommettere.
wagon ['wagən] *n* vagone *m*, carrozza *f.* **be on the wagon** (*coll*) essere astemio.
waif [weif] *n* senzatetto *m invar*; (*foundling*) trovatello, -a *m, f.*
wail [weil] *n* gemito *m*, lamento *m. v* gemere, emettere un lamento.
waist [weist] *n* vita *f.* **waistcoat** *n* gilè *m.* **waistline** *n* misura *or* circonferenza della vita *f.*
wait [weit] *v* aspettare, attendere; servire, sostare. *n* attesa *f*; sosta *f.* **lie in wait** stare in agguato. **waiter** *n* cameriere *m.* **waiting-room** *n* sala d'aspetto *f.* **waitress** *n* cameriera *f.*
waive [weiv] *v* rinunciare. **waiver** *n* rinuncia *f*; (*document*) atto di rinuncia *m.*
***wake**[1] [weik] *v also* **wake up** svegliare, svegliarsi. *n* veglia *f.*
wake[2] [weik] *n* scia *f.* **in the wake of** subito dopo, nella scia di.
Wales [weilz] *n* Galles *m.*
walk [woːk] *v* camminare; (*go on foot*) andare a piedi. **walk in** entrare. **walk out on** piantare. **walkover** *n* vittoria incontestata *or* facile *f. n* cammino *m*, passeggiata *f*; (*gait*) passo *m.* **walker** *n* camminatore, -trice *m, f*; (*sport*) podista *m, f.*
wall [woːl] *n* muro *m*; (*internal*) parete *f.* **wallpaper** *n* carta da parati *f.*
wallet ['wolit] *n* portafoglio *m.*
wallop ['woləp] (*coll*) *v* (*thrash*) battere, picchiare. *n* (*blow*) colpo violento *m.*
wallow ['wolou] *v* sguazzare.
walnut ['woːlnʌt] *n* (*tree*) noce *m*; (*fruit*) noce *f.*
walrus ['woːlrəs] *n* tricheco *m.* **walrus moustache** baffi spioventi *m pl.*
waltz [woːlts] *n* valzer *m invar. v* ballare il valzer. **waltz through** (*coll*) superare facilmente.
wand [wond] *n* bacchetta *f.*
wander ['wondə] *v* vagare, girare; (*stray*) allontanarsi, delirare.
wane [wein] *v* calare, declinare. *n* declino *m*; (*moon*) calare *m.*
wangle ['waŋgl] (*coll*) *n* trucco *m*, intrigo (*pl* -ghi) *m. v* procurare con astuzia.
want [wont] *v* volere, desiderare, aver voglia di; (*lack*) mancare di; (*ought*) dovere. *n* (*need*) bisogno *m*, esigenza *f*; (*deficiency*) mancanza *f.* **wanted** *adj* (*asked for*) richiesto; (*police*) ricercato; (*advertisement*) cercasi.
wanton ['wontən] *adj* deliberato, gratuito, sfrenato. *n* libertino *m*, sgualdrina *f.*
war [woː] *n* guerra *f.* **warfare** *n* guerra *f.* **warmonger** *n* guerrafondaio *m.* **wartime** *n* tempo di guerra *m. v* far guerra, combattere.
warble ['woːbl] *n* trillo *m. v* trillare. **warbler** *n* uccello canoro *m.*
ward [woːd] *n* (*district*) distretto *m*; (*hospital*) corsia *f*, padiglione *m*; (*law*) pupillo, -a *m, f. v* **ward off** parare, scansare.
warden ['woːdn] *n* guardiano, -a *m, f*, custode *m, f.*
warder ['woːdə] *n* carceriere, -a *m, f.*

wardrobe ['wɔːdroub] *n* guardaroba *m invar*; (*cupboard*) armadio *m*.
warehouse ['weəhaus] *n* magazzino *m*.
warm [wɔːm] *adj* caldo; cordiale, caloroso; (*lively*) animato; (*enthusiastic*) ardente. **be warm** aver caldo. **get warm** scaldarsi. *v* riscaldare. **warmth** *n* caldo *m*; calore *m*; animazione *f*; ardore *m*.
warn [wɔːn] *v* mettere in guardia, ammonire; (*notify*) avvertire, preavvisare. **warning** *n* ammonimento *m*; preavviso *m*; allarme *m*.
warp [wɔːp] *v* deformare. *n* ordito *m*.
warrant ['worənt] *n* autorizzazione *f*, diritto *m*; (*law*) mandato *m*. *v* autorizzare; giustificare; garantire. **warranty** *n* (*comm*) garanzia *f*.
warren ['worən] *n* (*rabbit*) garenna *f*.
warrior ['woriə] *n* guerriero *m*. **unknown warrior** *n* milite ignoto *m*.
Warsaw ['wɔːsɔː] *n* Varsavia *f*.
wart [wɔːt] *n* verruca *f*.
wary ['weəri] *adj* diffidente, cauto. **be wary of** diffidare di; guardarsi dal.
was [woz] *V* **be**.
wash [woʃ] *v* lavare. **wash away** portare via; (*obliterate*) cancellare. **wash-basin** *n* lavandino *m*. **wash-out** *n* (*slang*) fiasco *m*. **wash up** lavare i piatti. *n* lavata *f*; (*clothes, etc.*) bucato *m*; (*painting*) acquerello *m*, guazzo *m*. **have a wash** lavarsi. **washable** *adj* lavabile. **washing** *n* bucato *m*. **washing-machine** *n* lavatrice automatica *f*.
washer ['woʃə] *n* rondella *f*.
wasp [wosp] *n* vespa *f*.
waste [weist] *v* sprecare, sciupare. **waste away** deperire. *n* spreco *m*; (*rubbish*) immondizia *f*; (*scrap*) scarti *m pl*, cascami *m pl*; (*geog*) deserto *m*. **waste-paper basket** cestino da rifiuti *m*. **waste-pipe** *n* tubo di scarico *m*. **wasteful** *adj* dispendioso, sprecone.
watch [wotʃ] *v* guardare, osservare; (*as spectator*) assistere a; (*keep an eye on*) tener d'occhio. **watch out** stare attento. **watch over** sorvegliare. *n* (*time*) orologio *m*; osservazione *f*; guardia *f*, sorveglianza *f*. **keep watch** fare la guardia. **watch-dog** *n* cane da guardia *m*. **watchful** *adj* vigile.
water ['wɔːtə] *n* acqua *f*. *v* annaffiare, irrigare. **water down** diluire; moderare, attenuare. **watery** *adj* acquoso; (*colour*) scialbo.
water-closet *n* gabinetto *m*.
water-colour *n* acquerello *m*.
watercress ['wɔːtəkres] *n* crescione *m*.
waterfall ['wɔːtəfɔːl] *n* cascata *f*.
waterfront ['wɔːtəfrʌnt] *n* lungomare *m*; (*wharf*) zona portuale *f*.
watering-can *n* annaffiatoio *m*.
water-lily *n* ninfea *f*.
waterlogged ['wɔːtəlogd] *adj* saturo d'acqua; (*ground*) acquitrinoso.
water-melon *n* cocomero *m*.
water-mill *n* mulino ad acqua *m*.
water polo *n* pallanuoto *f*.
waterproof ['wɔːtəpruf] *nm*, *adj* impermeabile. *v* impermeabilizzare.
watershed ['wɔːtəʃed] *n* spartiacque *m invar*.
water-ski *n* sci nautico *m*. *v* fare dello sci nautico. **water-skiing** *n* sci nautico *m*.
watertight ['wɔːtətait] *adj* stagno; (*irrefutable*) inconfutabile.
water-way *n* corso navigabile *m*.
waterworks ['wɔːtəwəːks] *n* impianto idrico *m*. **turn on the waterworks** (*coll*) mettersi a piangere.
watt [wot] *n* watt *m invar*. **wattage** *n* wattaggio *m*.
wave [weiv] *n* onda *f*; (*surge*) ondata *f*; (*sign*) cenno *m*. **waveband** *n* gamma di lunghezze d'onda *f*. *v* sventolare, far segno con; (*hair*) ondulare. **wave aside** scartare. **wavy** *adj* (*hair*) ondulato; (*line*) ondeggiante.
waver ['weivə] *v* (*vacillate*) titubare, esitare.
wax[1] [waks] *n* cera *f*. *v* dar la cera a, lucidare.
wax[2] [waks] *v* (*increase*) crescere; (*become*) diventare.
way [wei] *n* (*manner*) modo *m*; (*respect*) rispetto *m*, particolare *m*; (*street*) strada *f*; passaggio *m*. **by the way** a proposito. **give way** cedere; (*traffic*) dare la precedenza. **in a way** in un certo modo. **make way for** fare largo a. **out of the way** (*place*) fuori strada; (*unusual*) fuori del comune. **way in** entrata *f*. **way out** uscita *f*.
***waylay** [wei'lei] *v* abbordare; (*ambush*) tendere un agguato a.
wayward ['weiwəd] *adj* capriccioso, ribelle.
we [wiː] *pron* noi.

weak [wiːk] *adj* debole. **weaken** *v* indebolire. **weakling** *n* persona debole *f*. **weakness** *n* debolezza *f*; (*inclination*) debole *m*.
wealth [welθ] *n* ricchezza *f*, abbondanza *f*. **wealthy** *adj* ricco.
wean [wiːn] *v* svezzare.
weapon ['wepən] *n* arma *f*.
***wear** [weə] *v* portare, indossare; (*deteriorate*) consumare; (*last*) durare. **wear off** passare, dissiparsi. **wear out** consumare, indebolire; (*tire*) stancare. *n* (*use*) uso *m*; (*clothing*) abiti *m pl*, abbigliamento *m*; (*deterioration*) usura *f*.
weary ['wiəri] *adj* stanco, stufo. *v* stancare, stufare.
weasel ['wiːzl] *n* donnola *f*.
weather ['weðə] *n* tempo *m*. **weather-beaten** *adj* segnato dalle intemperie. **weather forecast** bollettino meteorologico *m*. *v* (*expose*) esporre all'aria, stagionare; (*overcome*) superare.
***weave** [wiːv] *v* tessere; (*devise*) ordire. *n* armatura *f*. **weaver** *n* tessitore *m*. **weaving** *n* tessitura *f*.
web [web] *n* tessuto *m*; (*spider*) ragnatela *f*. **webbed foot** piede palmato *m*.
wedding ['wediŋ] *n* matrimonio *m*; (*ceremony*) nozze *f pl*. **wedding-dress** *n* abito nuziale *m*. **wedding-ring** *n* fede *f*.
wedge [wedʒ] *n* cuneo *m*. *v* incuneare, incastrare.
Wednesday ['wenzdi] *n* mercoledì *m*.
weed [wiːd] *n* erbaccia *f*, malerba *f*. **weed-killer** *n* erbicida *m*. *v* diserbare, sarchiare. **weedy** *adj* coperto di erbacce; (*person*) sparuto.
week [wiːk] *n* settimana *f*. **weekday** *n* giorno feriale *or* lavorativo *m*. **weekend** *n* fine settimana *f*, week-end *m invar*.
weekly ['wiːkli] *nm*, *adj* settimanale. *adv* ogni settimana.
***weep** [wiːp] *v* piangere. **weeping** *n* pianto *m*. **weeping willow** salice piangente *m*. **weepy** *adj* (*coll*) lacrimoso, sentimentale.
weigh [wei] *v* pesare; (*have importance*) valere. **weigh anchor** salpare. **weighbridge** *n* pesa a ponte *f*, pesa pubblica *f*. **weigh up** soppesare, valutare. **weight** *n* peso *m*. **carry weight** aver peso. **lose weight** dimagrire. **put on weight** ingrassare. **weighty** *adj* pesante; importante.
weird [wiəd] *adj* strano, misterioso.
welcome ['welkəm] *interj* benvenuto! **welcome home!** ben tornato! *n* benvenuto *m*, buona *or* cordiale accoglienza *f*. *adj* benvenuto, gradito. *v* accogliere; (*greet*) dare il benvenuto a; (*accept gladly*) gradire.
weld [weld] *v* saldare. *n* saldatura *f*.
welfare ['welfeə] *n* benessere *m*; assistenza sociale *f*. **welfare worker** *n* assistente sociale *m*, *f*.
well[1] [wel] *n* pozzo *m*; (*stairs*) tromba *f*.
well[2] [wel] *adv* bene. *interj* beh! allora! **as well** (*also*) anche.
well-behaved *adj* educato, beneducato.
well-being *n* benessere *m*, bene *m*.
well-bred *adj* educato, beneducato.
well-built *adj* ben costruito.
wellingtons ['weliŋtənz] *pl n* stivali impermeabili *m pl*, stivali di gomma *m pl*.
well-known *adj* ben noto.
well-meaning *adj* ben intenzionato. **well-meant** *adj* fatto a fin di bene.
well-off *adj* benestante, agiato.
well-paid *adj* ben pagato *or* retribuito.
well-read *adj* colto.
well-spoken *adj* che parla bene.
well-to-do *adj* benestante, abbiente.
well-worn *adj* logoro; (*hackneyed*) trito.
Welsh [welʃ] *n*(*m*+*f*), *adj* gallese.
went [went] *V* **go**.
wept [wept] *V* **weep**.
were [wəː] *V* **be**.
west [west] *n* ovest *m*, occidente *m*. *adv also* **westward**(s) verso ovest, in direzione ovest.
western ['westən] *adj* occidentale, dell'ovest. *n* (*film*) western *m*.
wet [wet] *adj* bagnato, umido; (*rainy*) piovoso; (*paint*, *ink*, *etc.*) fresco. **wet blanket** guastafeste *m*, *f invar*. **wet through** bagnato fradicio; (*person*) bagnato fino alle ossa. *v* bagnare.
whack [wak] (*coll*) *n* colpo *m*; (*part*) fetta *f*. *v* colpire. **be whacked** essere sfinito.
whale [weil] *n* balena *f*. **have a whale of a time** (*coll*) divertirsi un mondo. **whaling** *n* caccia alla balena *f*.
wharf [woːf] *n* banchina *f*, scalo *m*.
what [wot] *pron* (che) cosa; (*relative*) quello che. *adj* che, quale. **what a . . . !** che . . . ! **what for?** perché? **what is the matter?** cosa c'è? cosa succede?
whatever [wot'evə] *pron* qualsiasi *or* qualunque cosa. *adj* qualsiasi, qualunque. **none whatever** nessuno. **nothing whatever** assolutamente nulla.

wheat [wiːt] *n* grano *m*, frumento *m*.
wheel [wiːl] *n* ruota *f*; (*pottery*) tornio *m*; (*steering*) volante *m*. **wheelbarrow** *n* carretta *f*, carriola *f*. **wheelchair** *n* sedia a rotelle *f*. *v* (*make turn*) far rotare; (*push*) spingere.
wheeze [wiːz] *v* ansimare. *n* respiro affannoso *m*.
whelk [welk] *n* buccino *m*.
when [wen] *adv* quando. *conj* quando; (*after which*) appena; (*whereas*) mentre. **whenever** *adv* qualora, ogni volta che.
where [weə] *conj*, *adv* dove. **whereabouts** *adv* dove, da che parte. **whereas** *conj* mentre. **whereby** *conj*, *adv* onde, per cui. **whereupon** *conj* dopoché, dal momento che. **wherever** *conj* dovunque. **wherewithal** *n* necessario *m*.
whether ['weðə] *conj* se.
which [witʃ] *pron* quale; (*relative*) il quale, la quale; che. *adj* quale. **which way?** da che parte?
whichever [witʃ'evə] *adj* qualunque, qualsiasi. *pron* quello che; (*person*) chiunque.
whiff [wif] *n* buffata *f*, zaffata *f*.
while [wail] *conj* mentre. *n* momento *m*. **a long while ago** molto tempo fa.
whim [wim] *n* capriccio *m*.
whimper ['wimpə] *v* piagnucolare. *n* piagnucolio *m*.
whimsical ['wimzikl] *adj* bizzarro, eccentrico.
whine [wain] *v* gemere; (*complain*) uggiolare. *n* uggiolio *m*, gemito *m*.
whip [wip] *n* frusta *f*. **whip-round** (*coll*) colletta *f*. *v* frustare; (*cookery*) frullare. **whipped cream** panna montata *f*.
whippet ['wipit] *n* levriere inglese *m*.
whirl [wəːl] *n* turbine *m*, giro vertiginoso *m*. **whirlpool** *n* vortice *m*. **whirlwind** *n* turbine *m*, tromba d'aria *f*. *v* girare (rapidamente).
whisk [wisk] *v* (*dust*) spolverare; (*cookery*) frullare. *n* piumino *m*; frullino *m*.
whisker ['wiskə] *n* pelo *m*. **whiskers** *pl n* basette *f pl*; (*moustache*, *cat*) baffi *m pl*.
whisky ['wiski] *n* whisky *m invar*.
whisper ['wispə] *v* bisbigliare, mormorare. *n* bisbiglio *m*, mormorio *m*.
whist [wist] *n* whist *m invar*.
whistle ['wisl] *v* fischiare; (*tune*) fischiettare. *n* (*sound*) fischio *m*; (*instrument*) fischietto *m*.
white [wait] *n* bianco *m*. *adj* bianco. **whitebait** *pl n* bianchetti *m pl*. **whiten** *v* imbiancare.
whitewash ['waitwoʃ] *n* intonaco *m*; (*cover-up*) riabilitazione *f*. *v* imbiancare, intonacare; (*cover up*) scolpare.
whiting ['waitiŋ] *n* (*fish*) merlango *m*.
Whitsun ['witsn] *n* Pentecoste *f*.
whizz [wiz] *v* (*hum*) sibilare; (*move*) guizzare.
who [huː] *pron* chi; (*relative*) che, il quale, la quale. **whoever** *pron* chiunque.
whole [houl] *n* totale *m*, insieme *m*. **as a whole** nell'insieme. **on the whole** tutto considerato, in fin dei conti. *adj* intero, tutto; intatto. **wholehearted** *adj* generoso. **wholemeal** *adj* integrale. **wholesale** *adv* all'ingrosso. **wholesaler** *n* grossista *m*, *f*. **wholesome** *adj* sano.
whom [huːm] *pron* che; (*relative*) il quale, la quale; (*after prep*) cui.
whooping cough ['huːpiŋ] *n* pertosse *f*.
whore [hoː] *n* (*derog*) puttana *f*.
whose [huːz] *pron* di chi. *adj* di cui; (*relative*) il cui, la cui.
why [wai] *adv*, *conj* perché, per cui.
wick [wik] *n* stoppino *m*.
wicked ['wikid] *adj* cattivo, malvagio. **wickedness** *n* cattiveria *f*, malvagità *f*.
wicker ['wikə] *n* vimini *m pl*.
wicket ['wikit] *n* porta *f*, sportello *m*. **a sticky wicket** una situazione scabrosa.
wide [waid] *adj* largo; (*spacious*) ampio. *adv* lontano. **open wide** *v* spalancare. **wide apart** spaziati. **wide awake** completamente sveglio; (*alert*) vigilante. **wide open** spalancato. **widespread** *adj* esteso, diffuso. **widen** *v* estendere, allargare.
widow ['widou] *n* vedova *f*. **widower** *n* vedovo *m*.
width [widθ] *n* larghezza *f*; (*cloth*) altezza *f*.
wield [wiːld] *v* (*weapon*) brandire; (*power*) esercitare.
wife [waif] *n* moglie *f*.
wig [wig] *n* parrucca *f*.
wiggle ['wigl] *v* dimenare.
wild [waild] *adj* selvatico; (*animal*, *place*) selvaggio; (*unrestrained*) feroce. **spread like wildfire** divampare. **wild with anger** fuori di sè dalla rabbia. **wild with joy** folle di gioia.
wilderness ['wildənəs] *n* deserto *m*, solitudine *f*.
wilful ['wilfəl] *adj* intenzionale; premeditato; ostinato.

will[1] [wil] *aux translated by future tense.*
will[2] [wil] *n* volontà *f*; (*law*) testamento *m*. **against one's will** malvolentieri, controvoglia. **at will** a piacere.
willing ['wiliŋ] *adj* (*disposed*) disposto; (*ready*) pronto, volonteroso. **willingness** *n* prontezza *f*; buona volontà *f*.
willow ['wilou] *n* salice *m*.
wilt [wilt] *v* appassire.
***win** [win] *v* vincere. **win back** riguadagnare. *n* vittoria *f*; (*games*) vincita *f*. **winner** *n* vincitore *m*.
wince [wins] *v* trasalire. *n* sussulto *m*, trasalimento *m*.
winch [wintʃ] *n* argano *m*. *v* **winch up** sollevare con l'argano.
wind[1] [wind] *n* vento *m*; (*breath*) fiato *m*. **get wind of** aver sentore di, fiutare. *v* sfiatare. **windy** *adj* esposto al vento.
***wind**[2] [waind] *v* (*twist*) serpeggiare. **wind up** (*roll up*) avvolgere; concludere; (*end up*) andare a finire; (*clock*) caricare; (*business*) liquidare.
wind-cheater *n* giacca a vento *f*.
windfall ['windfoːl] *n* frutto fatto cadere dal vento *m*; fortuna inaspettata *f*.
windlass ['windləs] *n* verricello *m*.
windmill ['wind,mil] *n* mulino a vento *m*.
window ['windou] *n* finestra *f*; (*train*) finestrino *m*; (*car*) cristallo *m*; (*cashier's*) sportello *m*. **French window** *n* portafinestra *f*. **window-dressing** *n* mostra *f*; (*show*) bella mostra *f*, inganno *m*. **window-sill** *n* davanzale *m*.
windpipe ['windpaip] *n* trachea *f*.
windscreen ['windskriːn] *n* parabrezza *m invar*. **windscreen wiper** tergicristallo *m*.
windswept ['windswept] *adj* battuto dai venti.
wine [wain] *n* vino *m*. **wineglass** *n* bicchiere da vino *m*. **wine list** carta dei vini *f*.
wing [wiŋ] *n* ala *f*. **in the wings** (*theatre*) tra le quinte. **wingspan** *n* apertura alare *f*.
wink [wiŋk] *v* strizzare l'occhio, ammiccare. *n* (*signal*) cenno *m*; (*instant*) attimo *m*. **have forty winks** schiacciare un pisolino.
winkle ['wiŋkl] *n* chiocciola di mare *f*.
winter ['wintə] *n* inverno *m*. **wintry** *adj* invernale.
wipe [waip] *v* strofinare; (*dry*) asciugare. **wipe away** *or* **off** cancellare, allontanare. **wipe out** eliminare; (*debts, etc.*) liquidare; (*annihilate*) annientare. **wiper** *n* strofinaccio *m*; (*windscreen*) tergicristallo *m*.
wire [waiə] *n* filo *m*; telegramma *m*. **wireless** *n* radio *f invar*. *v* (*elec*) montare; (*fasten*) legare con filo metallico; telegrafare. **wiry** *adj* secco, nerboruto.
wisdom ['wizdəm] *n* saggezza *f*. **wisdom tooth** *n* dente del giudizio *m*.
wise [waiz] *adj* saggio. **wisecrack** *n* battuta *f*.
wish [wiʃ] *n* desiderio *m*, voglia *f*. **wishes** *pl n* auguri *m pl*. *v* desiderare, volere; (*greeting*) augurare. **wishful thinking** pio desiderio *m*.
wisp [wisp] *n* (*hair*) ciocca *f*; (*smoke*) filo *m*.
wistful ['wistfəl] *adj* pensoso, malinconico.
wit [wit] *n* spirito *m*; arguzia *f*, intelligenza *f*; (*person*) uomo di spirito *m*. **be at one's wits' end** non saper più cosa fare. **live by one's wits** vivere di espedienti.
witch [witʃ] *n* strega *f*. **witchcraft** *n* stregoneria *f*. **witch-doctor** *n* stregone *m*.
with [wið] *prep* con; (*together with*) insieme a; (*because of*) per, a causa di.
***withdraw** [wið'droː] *v* ritirare; (*cash*) prelevare. **withdrawal** *n* ritiro *m*; (*mil*) ritirata *f*; prelevamento *m*.
wither ['wiðə] *v* (*lose freshness*) appassire; atrofizzare; (*decay*) avvizzire.
***withhold** [wið'hould] *v* trattenere; (*hide*) nascondere.
within [wi'ðin] *adv* dentro. *prep* entro, in. **within reach** a portata.
without [wi'ðaut] *prep* senza. *adv* fuori. **do without** fare a meno (di).
***withstand** [wið'stand] *v* resistere a.
witness ['witnis] *n* (*evidence*) testimonianza *f*; (*person*) testimone *m, f*. *v* testimoniare, attestare.
witty ['witi] *adj* spiritoso, arguto.
wizard ['wizəd] *n* mago *m*.
wobble ['wobl] *v* vacillare, traballare.
woke [wouk] *V* **wake**[1].
woken ['woukn] *V* **wake**[1].
wolf [wulf] *n* lupo *m*. **cry wolf** gridare al lupo. *v* divorare.
woman ['wumən] *n, pl* **women** donna *f*. **old woman** *n* vecchia *f*. **young woman** giovane *f*. **womanly** *adj* femminile.
womb [wuːm] *n* utero *m*.

won [wʌn] *V* **win.**
wonder ['wʌndə] *n* meraviglia *f*; miracolo *m*. *v* meravigliarsi; (*ask oneself*) domandarsi. **wonderful** *adj* meraviglioso.
wood [wud] *n* (*material*) legno *m*; (*as fuel*) legna *f*; (*forest*) bosco *m*. **wooden** *adj* di legno; rigido. **woody** *adj* (*wooded*) boscoso; (*tough*) legnoso.
woodcock ['wudkok] *n* beccaccia *f*.
woodcut ['wudkʌt] *n* silografia *f*, incisione su legno *f*.
woodland ['wudlənd] *n* boscaglia *f*.
woodpecker ['wudpekə] *n* picchio *m*.
wood-pigeon *n* colombaccio *m*.
wood-wind *n* strumenti a fiato *m pl*.
woodwork ['wudwəːk] *n* (*carpentry*) lavoro in legno *m*, falegnameria *f*; (*wooden parts*) parti in legno *f pl*.
woodworm ['wudwəːm] *n* tarlo *m*.
wool [wul] *n* lana *f*. **dyed in the wool** *adj* radicato, convinto. **woollen** *adj* di lana; (*industry*) laniero. **woolly** *adj* di lana, lanoso; confuso.
word [wəːd] *n* parola *f*. **in other words** altrimenti detto. **word for word** alla lettera. *v* esprimere, redigere. **wording** *n* espressione *f*, formulazione *f*.
wore [woː] *V* **wear.**
work [wəːk] *n* lavoro *m*; (*toil*) fatica *f*; (*product*) opera *f*. **workman** *n* operaio *m*. **works** *n* (*factory*) fabbrica *f*, stabilimento *m*. **workshop** *n* officina *f*. *v* lavorare; (*machine, etc.*) (far) funzionare. **work out** risolvere; risultare. **worker** *n* lavoratore, -trice *m, f*, operaio, -a *m, f*. **working** *n* operazione *f*, funzionamento *m*. **working class** classe operaia *f*. **working order** buon ordine *m*.
world [wəːld] *n* mondo *m*. **world war** guerra mondiale *f*. **world-wide** *adj* mondiale, universale. **worldly** *adj* temporale; mondano.
worm [wəːm] *n* verme *m*. *v* insinuarsi.
worn [woːn] *V* **wear.**
worry ['wʌri] *n* preoccupazione *f*, ansia *f*. *v* preoccupare; molestare. **worrying** *adj* preoccupante.
worse [wəːs] *adj* peggio, peggiore. *nm, adv* peggio. **from bad to worse** di male in peggio. **get worse** peggiorare. **worsen** *v* peggiorare.
worship ['wəːʃip] *n* adorazione *f*, omaggio *m*; (*rel*) culto *m*, servizio religioso *m*. *v* adorare; andare a messa, andare in chiesa.
worst [wəːst] *adj* peggiore, il più brutto. *nm, adv* peggio.
worsted ['wustid] *nm, adj* pettinato.
worth [wəːθ] *adj* **be worth** valere. **be worthless** non valere nulla. **be worthwhile** valere la pena. *n* merito *m*, valore *m*. **worthy** *adj* degno.
would [wud] *aux translated by conditional or imperfect tense.*
wound[1] [wuːnd] *n* ferita *f*. *v* ferire; offendere. **wounded** *adj* ferito.
wound[2] [waund] *V* **wind**[2].
wove [wouv] *V* **weave.**
woven ['wouvn] *V* **weave.**
wrangle ['raŋgl] *v* litigare, disputare. *n* lite *f*, disputa *f*.
wrap [rap] *v* (*envelop*) avvolgere; (*cover*) coprire; (*parcel*) incartare. *n* (*shawl*) scialle *m*; (*dressing-gown*) vestaglia *f*. **wrapper** *n* involucro *m*; (*book*) copertina *f*.
wreath [riːθ] *n* ghirlanda *f*, corona *f*. **wreathe** *v* incoronare. **wreathed in smiles** raggiante.
wreck [rek] *n* (*ship*) naufragio *m*; (*ruin*) relitto *m*, rovina *f*. *v* rovinare; demolire; naufragare. **wreckage** *n* rottami *m pl*.
wren [ren] *n* scricciolo *m*.
wrench [rentʃ] *v* storcere. **wrench open** forzare. *n* (*movement*) strappo *m*; (*injury*) storta *f*; (*spanner*) chiave *f*.
wrestle ['resl] *v* lottare. **wrestling** *n* lotta *f*.
wretch [retʃ] *n* (*unfortunate*) disgraziato, -a *m, f*; (*despicable*) incosciente *m, f*. **wretched** *adj* disgraziato, miserabile; (*pitiful*) pietoso.
wriggle ['rigl] *v* dimenarsi.
***wring** [riŋ] *v* torcere. **wring out** strizzare. **wringer** *n* strizzatoio *m*. **wringing wet** fradicio.
wrinkle ['riŋkl] *n* crespa *f*; (*face*) ruga *f*. *v* increspare; corrugare.
wrist [rist] *n* polso *m*.
writ [rit] *n* mandato *m*.
***write** [rait] *v* scrivere. **write down** trascrivere, registrare. **write off** (*comm*) cancellare. **writer** *n* scrittore, -trice *m, f*. **writing** *n* calligrafia *f*. **writings** *pl n* scritti *m pl*.
writhe [raið] *v* contorcersi.
written ['ritn] *V* **write.**
wrong [roŋ] *adv* male. *adj* (*not moral*) peccato; (*incorrect*) sbagliato. **be wrong** (*person*) aver torto, sbagliarsi. *n* torto *m*; ingiustizia *f*; (*law*) violazione *f*. *v* far

torto a, maltrattare. **wrongful** *adj* ingiustificato.
wrote [rout] *V* **write**.
wrought iron [ˌroːt'aiən] *n* ferro battuto *m*.
wrung [rʌŋ] *V* **wring**.
wry [rai] *adj* ironico, perverso; (*askance*) di sbieco.

X

xenophobia [ˌzenə'foubiə] *n* xenofobia *f*. **xenophobic** *adj* xenofobo.
Xmas ['krisməs] *V* **Christmas**.
X-ray ['eksrei] *n* raggio X *m*; (*photo*) radiografia *f*. *v* radiografare.
xylophone ['zailəfoun] *n* xilofono *m*.

Y

yacht [jot] *n* panfilo *m*. **yachting** *n* velismo *m*.
yank [jaŋk] *v* (*coll*) dare uno strattone a, tirare con violenza.
yap [jap] *v* guaire. *n* guaito *m*.
yard [jaːd] *n* cortile *m*; (*site*) cantiere *m*; (*railway*) scalo merci *m*. **yardstick** *n* (*measure*) metro *m*; (*standard*) pietra di paragone *f*.
yarn [jaːn] *n* (*thread*) filo *m*, filato *m*; storia *f*.
yawn [joːn] *v* sbadigliare. *n* sbadiglio *m*.
year [jiə] *n* anno *m*, annata *f*. **year-book** *n* annuario *m*. **yearly** *adj* annuo, annuale.
yearn [jəːn] *v* languire. **yearn for** bramare, desiderare vivamente. **yearning** *n* vivo desiderio *m*, brama *f*.
yeast [jiːst] *n* lievito *m*.
yell [jel] *v* gridare, urlare. *n* grido *m*, urlo *m*.
yellow ['jelou] *adj* giallo; (*coll*: *cowardly*) vigliacco. *n* giallo *m*. *v* ingiallire. **yellowy** *adj* giallastro.
yelp [jelp] *v* (*dog*) uggiolare. **yelp with pain** gridare per il dolore. *n* uggiolio *m*; grido di dolore *m*.
yes [jes] *nm*, *adv* sì.
yesterday ['jestədi] *nm*, *adv* ieri.
yet [jət] *adv* ancora; (*already*) già. *conj* ma, tuttavia. **as yet** finora.
yew [juː] *n* tasso *m*.
yield [jiːld] *v* produrre; (*surrender*) cedere; (*profit*, *interest*, *etc*.) rendere, fruttare. *n* frutto *m*, prodotto *m*; (*tech*) resa *f*; (*finance*) reddito *m*; (*harvest*) raccolto *m*.
yoga ['jougə] *n* yoga *m*.
yoghurt ['yogət] *m* iogurt *m*.
yoke [jouk] *n* giogo *m*; (*dress*) carrè *m*.
yolk [jouk] *n* tuorlo *m*.
you [juː] *pron* (*subject*: *fam*) tu; (*subject*: *pl*) voi; (*subject*: *fml*) Lei; (*direct object*) ti, vi, la; (*indirect object*) ti *or* te, vi *or* ve, le; (*after prep*) te, voi, Lei. **if I were you** se fossi (in) te.
young [jʌŋ] *adj* giovane. **youngster** *n* (*child*) bambino, -a *m*, *f*; (*youth*) ragazzo, -a *m*, *f*.
your [joː] *adj* (*fam*) (il) tuo, (la) tua, (i) tuoi, (le) tue; (*pl*) (il) vostro, (la) vostra, (i) vostri, (le) vostre; (*fml*) (il) suo, (la) sua, (i) suoi, (le) sue.
yours [joːz] *pron* (*fam*) il tuo, la tua, i tuoi, le tue; (*pl*) il vostro, la vostra, i vostri, le vostre; (*fml*) il suo, la sua, i suoi, le sue.
yourself [jə'self] *pron* (*fam*) tu stesso; (*fml*) Lei stesso; (*reflexive*) ti, si; (*after prep*) te stesso, Lei stesso.
yourselves [jə'selvz] *pron* voi stessi; (*reflexive*) vi.
youth [juːθ] *n* gioventù *f*; (*boy*) giovane *m*.
Yugoslavia [juːgou'slaːvjə] *n* Iugoslavia *f*. **Yugoslav** *n*, *adj* iugoslavo, -a.

Z

zeal [ziːl] *n* zelo *m*. **zealous** *adj* zelante.
zebra ['zebrə] *n* zebra *f*. **zebra crossing** passaggio zebrato *m*.
zero ['ziərou] *n* zero *m*. *v* mettere a zero, azzerare.
zest [zest] *n* (*enjoyment*) gusto *m*, entusiasmo *m*; (*piquancy*) nota piccante *f*.
zigzag ['zigzag] *nm*, *adj* zigzag. *v* andare a zigzag, serpeggiare.
zinc [ziŋk] *n* zinco *m*.
zip [zip] *n* chiusura *or* cerniera lampo *f*. *v* **zip up** chiudere la (cerniera) lampo.
zodiac ['zoudiak] *n* zodiaco *m*.
zone [zoun] *n* zona *f*.

zoo [zuː] *n* giardino zoologico *m*, zoo *m invar*. **zoologist** *n* zoologo, -a *m, f*. **zoology** *n* zoologia *f*.

zoom [zuːm] *v* (*noise*) ronzare; (*aircraft*) salire in candela; (*film*) zumare. *n* ronzio *m*. **zoom lens** zoom *m invar*, obiettivo zoom *m*.

Italian–Inglese

A

a, ad [a, ad] *prep* to; (*stato in luogo*) at, in; (*prezzo, ora, età*) at. **a 10 metri da** 10 metres away from. **a due a due** two by two. **alle dozzina** by the dozen. **andare a casa** go home. **100 km all'ora** 100 km an hour.
abate [a'bate] *sm* abbot.
abbagliare [abba'ʎare] *v* dazzle.
abbaiare [abba'jare] *v* bark. **abbaiata** *sf* bark.
abbaino [abba'ino] *sm* attic, garret.
abbandonare [abbando'nare] *v* abandon, leave. **abbandonarsi a** (*darsi senza ritegno*) indulge in; give in to. **abbandono** *sm* neglect; desertion.
abbassare [abbas'sare] *v* lower, reduce. **abbasso** *avv* down. **abbasso . . . !** *inter* down with . . . !
abbastanza [abbas'tantsa] *avv* enough.
abbattere [ab'battere] *v* knock down, fell; (*uccidere*) kill; (*deprimere*) depress. **abbattersi** *v* become disheartened.
abbazia [abba'tsia] *sf* abbey.
abbellire [abbel'lire] *v* embellish, adorn.
abbiente [ab'bjɛnte] *agg* prosperous, well-to-do.
abbigliare [abbi'ʎare] *v* dress. **abbigliamento** *sm* clothes *pl*; (*modo*) dress.
abboccare [abbok'kare] *v* bite. **abboccato** *agg* (*vino*) medium sweet.
abbonarsi [abbo'narsi] *v* subscribe; take out a season ticket (for). **abbonamento** *sm* subscription; season ticket. **abbonato, -a** *sm, sf* subscriber; ticket-holder.
abbondare [abbon'dare] *v* be plentiful, abound. **abbondante** *agg* plentiful, abundant. **abbondanza** *sf* abundance, plenty.
abbordare [abbor'dare] *v* approach; (*introdurre*) broach.
abborracciare [abborrat'tʃare] *v* botch.
abbottonare [abbotto'nare] *v* button up.
abbozzare [abbot'tsare] *v* sketch, outline. **abbozzare un sorriso** give a faint smile. **abbozzo** *sm* sketch.
abbracciare [abbrat'tʃare] *v* embrace. **abbraccio** *sm* embrace, hug.
abbreviare [abbre'vjare] *v* abbreviate, shorten. **abbreviazione** *sf* abbreviation.
abbronzare [abbron'dzare] *v* tan. **abbronzatura** *sf* (sun-)tan.
abbrustolire [abbrusto'lire] *v* toast.
abbuono [ab'bwɔno] *sm* allowance; (*sport*) handicap.
abdicare [abdi'kare] *v* abdicate. **abdicazione** *sf* abdication.
aberrazione [aberra'tsjone] *sf* aberration.
abete [a'bete] *sm* fir(-tree). **abete rosso** spruce.
abietto [a'bjɛtto] *agg* abject. **abiezione** *sf* low spirits *pl*.
abile ['abile] *agg* clever, good (at); (*adatto*) suitable. **abilità** *sf* cleverness, skill; (*destrezza*) dexterity.
abilitare [abili'tare] *v* train; (*a una professione*) qualify. **abilitazione** *sf* qualification, diploma.
abisso [a'bisso] *sm* abyss.
abitare [abi'tare] *v* live. **abitante** *s*(*m*+*f*) inhabitant. **abitazione** *sf* home, dwelling.
abitato [abi'tato] *agg* inhabited. *sm* built-up area; (*villaggio*) hamlet.
abito ['abito] *sm* suit; dress; (*rel, abitudine*) habit. **abituale** *agg* customary, usual; habitual.
abituarsi [abitu'arsi] *v* **abituarsi a** get used to, become accustomed to.
abitudine [abi'tudine] *sf* habit, custom. **avere l'abitudine di** be in the habit of. **d'abitudine** as a rule.
abolire [abo'lire] *v* abolish. **abolizione** *sf* abolition.

abominevole [abomi'nevole] *agg* abominable.
aborigeno [abo'ridʒeno] *sm* aborigine. *agg* aboriginal.
aborrire [abor'rire] *v* abhor, loathe.
abortire [abor'tire] *v* miscarry; fail. **aborto** *sm* miscarriage. **aborto procurato** abortion.
abrasivo [abra'zivo] *sm, agg* abrasive. **abrasione** *sf* abrasion.
abside ['abside] *sf* apse.
abusare [abu'zare] *v* abuse. **abusivo** *agg* unauthorized, improper. **abuso** *sm* abuse.
accademia [akka'dɛmja] *sf* academy. **accademico** *sm, agg* academic.
***accadere** [akka'dere] *v* happen. **accaduto** *sm* occurrence.
accampare [akkam'pare] *v* camp; (*avanzare*) put forward. **accampamento** *sm* camp.
accanirsi [akka'nirsi] *v* rage; persist. **accanito** *agg* (*ostinato*) dogged, stubborn; (*spietato*) merciless; (*violento*) fierce.
accanto [ak'kanto] *avv* nearby; (*casa*) next door. **accanto a** next to, near to, beside.
accantonare [akkanto'nare] *v* set aside.
accaparrare [akkapar'rare] *v* corner.
accappatoio [akkappa'tojo] *sm* bathrobe.
accarezzare [akkaret'tsare] *v* caress, stroke.
accasciare [akka'ʃare] *v* crush. **accasciarsi** *v* collapse.
accattone [akkat'tone], **-a** *sm, sf* scrounger.
accavallare [akkaval'lare] *v* (*sovrapporre*) overlap; (*accumulare*) pile up; (*incrociare*) cross.
accecare [attʃe'kare] *v* blind; block up. **accecante** *agg* blinding.
***accedere** [at'tʃedere] *v* accede.
accelerare [attʃele'rare] *v* accelerate, speed up. **accelerato** *sm* local train. **acceleratore** *sm* accelerator. **accelerazione** *sf* acceleration.
***accendere** [at'tʃendere] *v* light; (*luce, radio*) switch on, turn on. **accendino** *sm* (*fam*) lighter.
accennare [attʃen'nare] *v* make a sign, nod; refer to, hint at, touch on. **accenno** *sm* indication, mention.
accensione [attʃen'sjone] *sf* ignition.
accento [at'tʃento] *sm* accent, stress; tone. **accentare** *v* accent.
accentrare [attʃen'trare] *v* centralize, concentrate.
accentuare [attʃentu'are] *v* stress; (*aumentare*) heighten.
accerchiare [attʃer'kjare] *v* encircle. **accerchiamento** *sm* encirclement.
accertare [attʃer'tare] *v* verify, ascertain; (*dir*) establish. **accertamento** *sm* verification; establishment.
acceso [at'tʃezo] *agg* alight, switched on; (*colore*) vivid; (*eccitato*) burning.
accessibile [attʃes'sibile] *agg* (*luogo*) accessible; (*persona*) approachable.
accesso [at'tʃɛsso] *sm* access; (*med*) attack, fit.
accessorio [attʃes'sɔrjo] *agg* complementary, secondary. *sm* accessory, fitting.
accetta [at'tʃetta] *sf* hatchet.
accettare [attʃet'tare] *v* accept; admit. **accettabile** *agg* acceptable. **accettazione** *sf* acceptance; (*sala*) reception. **bene accetto** welcome. **male accetto** unwelcome.
acchiappare [akkjap'pare] *v* catch, grab (hold of), seize.
acciaio [at'tʃajo] *sm* steel. **acciaieria** *sf* steelworks.
accidente [attʃi'dɛnte] *sm* accident, mishap. **mandare un accidente a** (*fam*) curse. **non capire un accidente** not understand a thing. **accidenti!** *inter* my goodness! (*ira*) damn it! **accidenti a lui!** blast him! **accidentale** *agg* accidental.
accigliarsi [attʃi'ʎarsi] *v* frown. **accigliato** *agg* frowning.
***accingersi** [at'tʃindʒersi] *v* **accingersi a** set about; be on the point of.
acciuffare [attʃuf'fare] *v* seize.
acciuga [at'tʃuga] *sf* anchovy.
acclamare [akkla'mare] *v* acclaim. **acclamazione** *sf* acclamation.
acclimatare [akklima'tare] *v* acclimatize.
***accludere** [ak'kludere] *v* enclose.
accoccolarsi [akkokko'larsi] *v* squat.
***accogliere** [ak'kɔʎʎere] *v* receive, accept, welcome; contain. **accoglienza** *sf* welcome, reception.
accomodare [akkomo'dare] *v* (*riparare*) mend, fix; (*mettere in ordine*) arrange, tidy; (*sistemare*) settle. **accomodarsi** *v* make oneself comfortable; take a seat; (*mettersi d'accordo*) agree. **accomodamento** *sm* agreement; compromise. **accomodante** *agg* accommodating.

accompagnare [akkompa'ɲare] *v* accompany. **accompagnatore, -trice** *sm, sf* escort; (*musica*) accompanist.
acconciare [akkon'tʃare] *v* prepare; arrange. **acconciarsi i capelli** do one's hair. **acconciatura** *sf* hair-style.
***accondiscendere** [akkondi'ʃendere] *v* comply (with); condescend.
acconsentire [akkonsen'tire] *v* consent; acquiesce.
accoppare [akkop'pare] *v* (*fam*) kill, slaughter.
accorciare [akkor'tʃare] *v* shorten.
accordare [akkor'dare] *v* (*uniformare*) match; harmonize; (*concedere*) grant; (*musica*) tune. **accordarsi** *v* agree.
accordo [ak'kɔrdo] *sm* agreement. **essere** *or* **andare d'accordo** agree. **d'accordo!** agreed!
***accorgersi** [ak'kɔrdʒersi] *v* notice. **accorgimento** *sm* expedient, stratagem.
***accorrere** [ak'korrere] *v* come running, rush.
accorto [ak'kɔrto] *agg* shrewd. **fare accorto** warn, caution. **stare accorto** be wary. **accortezza** *sf* shrewdness.
accostare [akkos'tare] *v* approach. **accosto** *avv* near.
accovacciarsi [akkovat'tʃarsi] *v* crouch, huddle.
accreditare [akkredi'tare] *v* accredit.
***accrescere** [ak'kreʃere] *v* increase.
accumulare [akkumu'lare] *v* accumulate, heap. **accumulatore** *sm* accumulator.
accurato [akku'rato] *agg* accurate, thorough. **accuratezza** *sf* thoroughness, care.
accusare [akku'zare] *v* accuse; (*notificare*) acknowledge. **accusa** *sf* accusation, charge.
acerbo [a'tʃɛrbo] *agg* (*immaturo*) unripe; (*aspro*) sour.
acero ['atʃero] *sm* maple.
aceto [a'tʃeto] *sm* vinegar.
acido ['atʃido] *sm* acid. *agg* acid, sour. **acidità** *sf* acidity.
acne ['akne] *sf* acne.
acqua ['akkwa] *sf* water. **acqua ossigenata** hydrogen peroxide. **acqua in bocca!** keep mum!
acquaforte [akkwa'fɔrte] *sf, pl* **acqueforti** etching.
acquaio [ak'kwajo] *sm* kitchen sink.
acquaragia [akkwa'radʒa] *sf* turpentine, turps.
acquario [ak'kwarjɔ] *sm* aquarium.
acquatico [ak'kwatiko] *agg* aquatic, water.
acquavite [akkwa'vite] *sf* rough brandy.
acquazzone [akkwat'tsone] *sm* shower.
acquedotto [akkwe'dotto] *sm* aqueduct.
acquerello [akkwe'rɛllo] *sm* water-colour.
acquistare [akkwis'tare] *v* buy; (*ottenere*) acquire; (*guadagnare*) gain. **acquistarsi fama di** gain the reputation of. **acquisto** *sm* purchase. **buon acquisto** bargain.
acquoso [ak'kwozo] *agg* watery; (*terreno*) marshy.
acre ['akre] *agg* acrid, sharp.
acrilico [a'kriliko] *agg* acrylic.
acrobata [a'krɔbata] *s(m+f)* acrobat. **acrobatico** *agg* acrobatic. **acrobazia** *sf* acrobatics *pl.*
aculeo [a'kuleo] *sm* sting.
acustica [a'kustika] *sf* acoustics *pl.* **acustico** *agg* acoustic. **apparecchio acustico** *sm* hearing-aid.
acuto [a'kuto] *agg* acute, intense; (*aguzzo*) pointed; (*perspicace*) shrewd. *sm* (*musica*) top note.
ad *V* **a.**
adagiarsi [ada'dʒarsi] *v* lie down.
adagio [a'dadʒo] *avv* slowly; gently. *sm* (*musica*) slow movement, adagio.
adattabile [adat'tabile] *agg* adaptable. **adattabilità** *sf* adaptability.
adattare [adat'tare] *v* adapt. **adattarsi** *v* adapt oneself, resign oneself. **adatto** *agg* suitable (for); (*qualificato*) suited (to).
addebitare [addebi'tare] *v* charge.
addensare [adden'sare] *v* thicken; (*raccogliere*) gather.
addestrare [addes'trare] *v* train. **addestramento** *sm* training.
addetto [ad'detto] *agg* employed (in); destined (for), intended (for); assigned. *sm* (*pol*) attaché.
addietro [ad'djɛtro] *avv* (*fa*) ago; (*prima*) before.
addio [ad'dio] *inter* goodbye, farewell. *sm* parting, farewell.
addirittura [addirit'tura] *avv* (*persino*) even; (*direttamente*) straight away; absolutely.
additare [addi'tare] *v* point at; (*mostrare*) point out, show.
additivo [addi'tivo] *sm* additive.
addizionare [additsjo'nare] *v* add up. **addizionale** *agg* additional. **addizione** *sf* addition.

addolcire [addol'tʃire] *v* sweeten; (*mitigare*) soften.
addolorare [addolo'rare] *v* distress.
addome [ad'dɔme] *sm* abdomen. **addominale** *agg* abdominal.
addomesticare [addomesti'kare] *v* tame.
addormentare [addormen'tare] *v* put to sleep. **addormentarsi** *v* fall asleep, go to sleep. **addormentato** *agg* sleeping; (*di mente*) dull; (*intorpidito*) numb.
addossare [addos'sare] *v* lean; (*mettere a carico*) saddle with. **addossarsi** *v* shoulder.
addosso [ad'dɔsso] *avv, prep* on. **d'addosso** off. **essere uno addosso all'altro** be crowded together.
***addurre** [ad'durre] *v* advance, put forward; produce.
adeguare [ade'gware] *v* adjust.
adempiere [a'dempjere] *v also* **adempire** carry out.
adenoidi [ade'nɔidi] *sf pl* adenoids *pl.*
aderire [ade'rire] *v* adhere, stick. **aderire a** comply with; accept; (*associarsi*) join. **aderente** *agg* close; (*abito*) close-fitting. **aderenza** *sf* adhesion. **aderenze** *sf pl* (*fam*) contacts *pl.*
adescare [ades'kare] *v* lure.
adesione [ade'zjone] *sf* adhesion; (*consenso*) assent; support. **adesivo** *sm, agg* adhesive.
adesso [a'dɛsso] *avv* now; nowadays; (*poco fa*) just (now); (*fra poco*) any minute (now). **per adesso** for the time being.
adiacente [adja'tʃɛnte] *agg* adjacent. **adiacente a** next to.
adibire [adi'bire] *v* turn (into).
adirarsi [adi'rarsi] *v* get angry.
adito ['adito] *sm* entry. **dare adito a** give rise to.
adocchiare [adok'kjare] *v* spot.
adolescente [adole'ʃɛnte] *agg* adolescent. *s*(*m*+*f*) adolescent, teenager. **adolescenza** *sf* adolescence.
adombrare [adom'brare] *v* shade; (*celare*) hide. **adombrarsi** *v* take umbrage; (*cavalli*) shy.
adoperare [adope'rare] *v* use. **adoperarsi** *v* do one's best.
adorare [ado'rare] *v* adore, worship. **adorabile** *agg* adorable. **adoratore, -trice** *sm, sf* admirer. **adorazione** *sf* worship.
adornare [ador'nare] *v* adorn, decorate. **adorno** *agg* adorned, decked out.
adottare [adot'tare] *v* adopt, foster. **adottivo** *agg* adoptive. **adozione** *sf* adoption.
adrenalina [adrena'lina] *sf* adrenaline.
adulazione [adula'tsjone] *sf* flattery. **adulare** *v* flatter. **adulatore, -trice** *sm, sf* flatterer.
adulterare [adulte'rare] *v* adulterate; (*corrompere*) debase.
adultero [a'dultero], **-a** *sm, sf* adulterer, -ess. *agg* adulterous. **adulterio** *sm* adultery.
adulto [a'dulto], **-a** *s, agg* adult, grown-up.
adunare [adu'nare] *v* assemble. **adunanza** *sf* assembly. **adunata** *sf* meeting, gathering; (*mil*) parade.
aerare [ae'rare] *v* air, ventilate. **aeratore** *sm* ventilator.
aereo [a'ɛreo] *agg* aerial, air. *sm* aeroplane.
aerodinamica [aerodi'namika] *sf* aerodynamics. **aerodinamico** *agg* streamlined.
aerodromo [ae'rɔdromo] *sm* aerodrome.
aerolinea [aero'linea] *sf* airline.
aeronautica [aero'nautika] *sf* aeronautics; aviation; (*mil*) air-force. **aeronautico** *agg* aeronautical.
aeroplano [aero'plano] *sm* aeroplane, aircraft. **aeroplano a reazione** jet. **aeroplano di bombardamento** bomber. **aeroplano di combattimento** fighter.
aeroporto [aero'pɔrto] *sm* airport.
aerosol [aero'sɔl] *sm invar* aerosol.
afa ['afa] *sf* oppressive heat.
affabile [af'fabile] *agg* affable. **affabilità** *sf* affability.
affaccendarsi [affattʃen'darsi] *v* busy oneself. **affaccendato** *agg* busy.
affacciarsi [affat'tʃarsi] *v* show oneself, appear.
affamato [affa'mato] *agg* starving; (*bramoso*) eager (for). **affamare** *v* reduce to starvation.
affannare [affan'nare] *v* worry. **affannarsi** *v* do one's utmost. **affanno** *sm* (*difficoltà di respiro*) breathlessness; anxiety, worry. **affannoso** *agg* difficult.
affare [af'fare] *sm* affair, business; (*questione*) matter; (*fam*) thing; (*acquisto vantaggioso*) bargain. **affari** *sm pl* (*comm*) business *sing.* **affarista** *s*(*m*+*f*) speculator.
affascinare [affaʃi'nare] *v* fascinate, charm.

affastellare [affastel'lare] *v* tie in bundles; (*ammucchiare*) pile up; (*frasi, ecc.*) string together.

affaticare [affati'kare] *v* tire, strain.

affatto [af'fatto] *avv* quite; (*con negazione*) at all.

affermare [affer'mare] *v* affirm; assert. **affermarsi** *v* be successful.

afferrare [affer'rare] *v* seize, grab, clutch at.

affettare[1] [affet'tare] *v* affect, pretend. **affettato** *agg* affected; mannered.

affettare[2] [affet'tare] *v* slice. **affettato** *sm* sliced salami *or* ham.

affetto[1] [af'fɛtto] *sm* affection, feeling. **affettuoso** *agg* affectionate, loving.

affetto[2] [af'fɛtto] *agg* affected (by); (*med*) suffering (from).

affezionarsi [affetsjo'narsi] *v* become fond (of). **affezionato** *agg* fond, devoted. **affezione** *sf* fondness, affection; (*med*) disorder.

affibbiare [affib'bjare] *v* saddle with.

affidare [affi'dare] *v* entrust. **affidare alla memoria** commit to memory. **affidamento** *sm* trust. **dare affidamento** inspire confidence. **fare affidamento su** rely on.

***affiggere** [af'fiddʒere] *v* affix; (*manifesto*) put up.

affilare [affi'lare] *v* sharpen.

affiliare [affi'ljare] *v* (*dir*) foster; (*iscrivere*) enrol.

affinché [affin'ke] *cong* so that, in order that.

affinità [affini'ta] *sf* affinity. **affine** *agg* related. **affini** *sm pl* in-laws *pl*.

affissione [affis'sjone] *sf* bill-posting.

affisso [af'fisso] *agg* exhibited. *sm* poster, bill.

affittare [affit'tare] *v* rent, lease; (*dare in affitto*) let. **affitto** *sm* (*prezzo*) rent; (*locazione*) lease.

***affliggere** [af'fliddʒere] *v* afflict. **affliggersi** *v* grieve, worry. **afflizione** *sf* affliction.

***affluire** [afflu'ire] *v* flow; (*gente*) flock. **affluente** *sm* (*geog*) tributary. **affluenza** *sf* flow; (*di gente*) influx. **afflusso** *sm* flow.

affogare [affo'gare] *v* drown. **uovo affogato** *sm* poached egg.

affollare [affol'lare] *v* crowd. **affollamento** *sm* (*atto*) crowding; (*folla*) crowd.

affondare [affon'dare] *v* sink.

affrancare [affran'kare] *v* stamp. **affrancatura** *sf* postage.

affranto [af'franto] *agg* distraught.

affresco [af'fresko] *sm* fresco.

affrettare [affret'tare] *v* hurry, speed up.

affrontare [affron'tare] *v* face. **affronto** *sm* affront.

affumicare [affumi'kare] *v* (*annerire*) blacken (with smoke); (*gastr*) smoke; (*snidare*) smoke out. **affumicato** *agg* smoked.

afoso [a'fozo] *agg* sultry.

Africa ['afrika] *sf* Africa. **africano, -a** *s, agg* African.

agenda [a'dʒɛnda] *sf* diary.

agente [a'dʒɛnte] *sm* agent. **agente delle tasse** tax inspector. **agente di polizia** police officer.

agenzia [adʒen'tsia] *sf* agency.

agevole [a'dʒevole] *agg* easy. **agevolare** *v* facilitate. **agevolazione** *sf* concession.

agganciare [aggan'tʃare] *v* fasten, hook up.

aggettivo [addʒet'tivo] *sm* adjective.

agghiacciare [aggjat'tʃare] *v* freeze. **far agghiacciare il sangue** make one's blood run cold.

aggiornare [addʒor'nare] *v* bring up to date; (*rinviare*) postpone. **aggiornato** *agg* up-to-date.

aggirarsi [addʒi'rarsi] *v* **aggirarsi su** (*approssimarsi*) be about *or* around.

aggiudicare [addʒudi'kare] *v* award.

***aggiungere** [ad'dʒundʒere] *v* add. **aggiungersi** *v* join. **aggiunta** *sf* addition. **aggiuntivo** *agg* additional. **aggiunto** *sm* assistant.

aggiustare [addʒus'tare] *v* repair, adjust; (*ordinare*) tidy, arrange.

aggrappare [aggrap'pare] *v* clutch. **aggrapparsi a** cling to.

aggravare [aggra'vare] *v* make worse. **aggravarsi** *v* deteriorate.

aggredire [aggre'dire] *v* attack.

aggregare [aggre'gare] *v* aggregate. **aggregato** *sm, agg* aggregate.

aggressione [aggres'sjone] *sf* aggression, attack. **aggressivo** *agg* aggressive. **aggressore** *sm* aggressor, assailant.

aggrottare [aggrot'tare] *v* **aggrottare le ciglia** frown, knit one's brows.

aggruppare [aggrup'pare] *v* group.

agguato [ag'gwato] *sm* ambush, trap. **stare in agguato** lie in wait.

agiato [a'dʒato] *agg* well-off. **agiatezza** *sf* prosperity.

agile ['adʒile] *agg* agile, nimble. **agilità** *sf* agility.
agio ['adʒo] *sm* comfort, ease; (*di tempo*) leisure; (*mec*) play. **sentire a proprio agio** feel at ease.
agire [a'dʒire] *v* act; (*comportarsi*) behave; (*dir*) take legal action.
agitare [adʒi'tare] *v* wave, shake; (*incitare*) stir. **agitato** *agg* agitated, disturbed. **agitatore, -trice** *sm, sf* agitator.
agli ['aʎi] *prep+art* **a gli**.
aglio ['aʎo] *sm* garlic.
agnello [a'ɲello] *sm* lamb.
agnostico [a'ɲostiko], **-a** *s, agg* agnostic.
ago ['ago] *sm* needle. **ago da calza** knitting-needle. **lavoro ad ago** *sm* needlework.
agonia [ago'nia] *sf* agony. **agonizzare** *v* agonize, suffer anguish.
agonismo [ago'nizmo] *sm* fighting spirit.
agopuntura [agopun'tura] *sf* acupuncture.
agosto [a'gosto] *sm* August.
agrario [a'grarjo] *sm* land-owner. *agg* agrarian, agricultural. **riforma agraria** *sf* land reform. **agraria** *sf* agricultural science.
agricoltore [agrikol'tore] *sm* farmer.
agrifoglio [agri'foʎʎo] *sm* holly.
agro ['agro] *agg* sour, sharp, tart.
agrumi [a'grumi] *sm pl* citrus fruit *pl*.
aguzzare [agut'tsare] *v* sharpen.
ahimé [ai'mɛ] *inter* alas!
ai ['ai] *prep+art* **a i**.
Aia ['aja] *sf* **L'Aia** The Hague.
airone [ai'rone] *sm* heron.
aiuola [a'jwɔla] *sf* flower-bed.
aiutare [aju'tare] *v* help. **aiuto** *sm* help, aid; assistant.
aizzare [ait'tsare] *v* incite, provoke.
al [al] *prep+art* **a il**.
ala ['ala] *sf* wing; (*di cappello*) brim. **apertura alare** *sf* wing-span.
alabastro [ala'bastro] *sm* alabaster.
alano [a'lano] *sm* Great Dane.
alba ['alba] *sf* dawn. **albeggiare** *v* dawn.
albatro ['albatro] *sm* albatross.
albergare [alber'gare] *v* give hospitality to; shelter, harbour.
albergo [al'bɛrgo] *sm* hotel. **albergatore** *sm* innkeeper. **alberghiero** *agg* hotel.
albero ['albero] *sm* tree; (*mar*) mast. **albero a camme** camshaft.
albicocca [albi'kɔkka] *sf* apricot. **albicocco** *sm* apricot tree.
albo ['albo] *sm* roll, register; (*tavola*) notice-board.
album ['album] *sm* album.
alcali ['alkali] *sm* alkali. **alcalino** *agg* alkaline.
alchimia [alki'mia] *sf* alchemy. **alchimista** *sm* alchemist.
alcool ['alkool] *sm* alcohol.
alco(o)lismo [alko(o)'lizmo] *sm* alcoholism. **alco(o)lici** *sm pl* alcoholic drinks *pl*, spirits *pl*. **alco(o)lico** *agg* alcoholic. **alco(o)lizzato, -a** *sm, sf* alcoholic.
alcunché [alkun'ke] *pron* something, anything.
alcuno [al'kuno] *agg* some, any, a few. *pron* anyone, anybody. **alcuni** *pron* some, a few.
alfabeto [alfa'bɛto] *sm* alphabet.
alfiere[1] [al'fjɛre] *sm* (*portabandiera*) standard-bearer; (*fig*) forerunner.
alfiere[2] [al'fjɛre] *sm* (*scacchi*) bishop.
alfine [al'fine] *avv* in the long run.
alga ['alga] *sf* alga.
algebra ['aldʒebra] *sf* algebra.
aliante [ali'ante] *sm* glider. **aliantista** *s(m+f)* glider-pilot.
alibi ['alibi] *sm* alibi.
alice [a'litʃe] *sf* anchovy.
alienare [alje'nare] *v* alienate. **alienato** *agg* alienated; (*pazzo*) insane. **alienazione** *sf* alienation; (*pazzia*) madness.
alieno [a'ljɛno] *agg* alien, foreign.
alimentare [alimen'tare] *agg* alimentary. *v* feed. **alimentari** *sm pl* foodstuffs *pl*. **alimentazione** *sf* feeding; (*tec*) feed. **alimenti** *sm pl* alimony *sing*. **alimento** *sm* food.
aliquota [a'likwota] *sf* quota, share.
aliscafo [alis'kafo] *sm* hydrofoil.
alito ['alito] *sm* breath.
all' [all] *prep+art* **a l'**.
alla ['alla] *prep+art* **a la**.
allacciare [allat'tʃare] *v* tie up, fasten; (*amicizia, relazioni*) establish; (*tec*) connect.
allagare [alla'gare] *v* flood. **allagamento** *sm* flooding.
allargare [allar'gare] *v* broaden; (*sport*) open up.
allarmare [allar'mare] *v* alarm. **allarme** *sm* alarm. **allarmista** *s(m+f)* scaremonger, alarmist. **allarmistico** *agg* alarmist.
alle ['alle] *prep+art* **a le**.
alleanza [alle'antsa] *sf* alliance. **alleare** *v* ally.

alleato [alle'ato], **-a** *agg* allied. *sm*, *sf* ally.
allegare[1] [alle'gare] *v* enclose.
allegare[2] [alle'gare] *v* advance, put forward.
alleggerire [alleddʒe'rire] *v* lighten; (*sofferenza*) ease.
allegoria [allego'ria] *sf* allegory. **allegorico** *agg* allegorical.
allegro [al'legro] *agg* cheerful, merry. *sm* (*musica*) fast movement, allegro. **allegria** *sf* gaiety, fun, cheerfulness.
allenare [alle'nare] *v* train, coach. **allenatore, -trice** *sm*, *sf* trainer, coach.
allentare [allen'tare] *v* loosen. **allentare il passo** slow down.
allergia [aller'dʒia] *sf* allergy. **allergico** *agg* allergic.
allestire [alles'tire] *v* prepare, get ready; (*teatro*) stage; (*arredare*) fit out, equip. **allestimento** *sm* preparation; staging; fitting out.
allettare [allet'tare] *v* entice, tempt. **alettante** *agg* enticing, tempting.
allevare [alle'vare] *v* (*bambini*) bring up; (*animali*) breed, keep; (*piante*) grow. **allevamento** *sm* bringing up; (*educazione*) upbringing; (*cavalli*) stud farm; (*cani*) kennels *pl*. **allevatore, -trice** *sm*, *sf* breeder.
alleviare [alle'vjare] *v* relieve, alleviate.
allibratore [allibra'tore] *sm* bookmaker.
allievo [al'ljɛvo], **-a** *sm*, *sf* pupil, student; (*apprendista*) trainee. **allievo ufficiale** (*mil*) cadet.
alligatore [alliga'tore] *sm* alligator.
allineare [alline'are] *v* line up; (*adeguare*) adjust. **allineamento** *sm* alignment, coming into line.
allo ['allo] *prep+art* **a lo**.
allocco [al'lɔkko] *sm* tawny owl.
allodola [al'lɔdola] *sf* lark.
alloggiare [allod'dʒare] *v* house, put up; (*mil*) billet; (*prendere alloggio*) stay, lodge. **alloggio** *sm* accommodation; lodgings *pl*.
allontanare [allonta'nare] *v* move away; (*tener lontano*) keep away; (*pericolo, ecc.*) avert; (*licenziare*) dismiss. **allontanarsi** *v* go away, leave. **allontanamento** *sm* removal.
allora [al'lora] *avv* then; in that case. **da allora** since then, from that time on. **fino allora** until then.
alloro [al'lɔro] *sm* laurel; (*gastr*) bay leaf.
alluce ['allutʃe] *sm* big toe.
allucinazione [allufina'tsjone] *sf* hallucination. **allucinare** *v* hallucinate; (*abbagliare*) dazzle.
***alludere** [al'ludere] *v* allude, hint (at).
alluminio [allu'minjo] *sm* aluminium.
allungare [allun'gare] *v* lengthen, stretch; (*diluire*) water down; pass. **allungare gli orecchi** strain one's ears. **allungare il muso** (*fam*) make a long face. **allungare la strada** go the long way round. **allungamento** *sm* extension, lengthening.
allusione [allu'zjone] *sf* allusion.
almeno [al'meno] *avv* at least; if only.
Alpi ['alpi] *sf pl* **le Alpi** the Alps *pl*. **alpino** *agg* alpine.
alpinismo [alpi'nizmo] *sm* mountaineering.
alquanto [al'kwanto] *pron, agg* some; a fair amount of. **alquanti** *pron, agg* several; a number of. *avv* somewhat, rather.
alt [alt] *sm, inter* stop.
altalena [alta'lena] *sf* (*sospesa*) swing; (*a bilico*) see-saw; (*fig*) ups and downs *pl*.
altare [al'tare] *sm* altar.
alterare [alte'rare] *v* alter, change; (*falsificare*) forge; (*svisare*) distort; (*turbare*) upset, make angry; (*andare a male*) go off, spoil. **alterazione** *sf* alteration; forgery; deterioration.
alternare [alter'nare] *v* alternate; (*agric*) rotate. **alternarsi** *v* take turns. **alternativa** *sf* alternative. **alternato** *agg* alternating. **alterno** *agg* alternating, alternate.
altero [al'tɛro] *agg* haughty.
altezza [al'tettsa] *sf* height; (*profondità*) depth; (*di tessuto*) width; (*quota*) altitude; nobility; (*titolo*) Highness. **essere all'altezza di** be equal to, be up to.
altitudine [alti'tudine] *sf* height, altitude.
alto ['alto] *agg* high; (*statura*) tall; (*tessuto*) wide; (*suono forte*) loud; (*suono acuto*) shrill; (*profondo*) deep; (*geog*) northern; (*nobile*) lofty; (*di grado elevato*) high-ranking. *avv* high. *sm* top, upper part. **alti e bassi** ups and downs *pl*.
altoforno [alto'forno] *sm, pl* **altiforni** blast furnace.
altoparlante [altopar'lante] *sm* loudspeaker.
altopiano [alto'pjano] *sm, pl* **altipiani** plateau.
altrettanto [altret'tanto] *pron, agg* as much *or* many (again); (*medesimo*) the same. **altrettanto ... quanto ...** as ... as .... *avv* as, as much.

altri ['altri] *pron* others *pl*, another (person), someone else.
altro ['altro] *agg* other; another; (*in più*) more; (*ulteriore*) further; (*prossimo*) next. *pron* other (one), another (one); (*persona*) somebody else. **cos'altro?** what else? **l'un l'altro** one another, each other. **l'uno e l'altro** both. **nè l'uno nè l'altro** neither. **nessun'altro** nobody else. **nient'altro** nothing else. **non altro che** nothing but. **più che altro** more than anything. **qualcos'altro** something else. **se non altro** at least. **senz'altro** certainly. **tra l'altro** among other things. **tutt'altro!** far from it!
altronde [al'tronde] *avv* **d'altronde** on the other hand, however.
altrove [al'trove] *avv* elsewhere.
altrui [al'trui] *agg invar* other people's, someone else's.
altruista [altru'ista] *s(m+f)* altruist, unselfish person. **altruismo** *sm* altruism, unselfishness. **altruistico** *agg* unselfish, altruistic.
alunno [a'lunno], **-a** *sm, sf* pupil.
alveare [alve'are] *sm* beehive.
alzaia [al'tsaja] *sf* tow-line; (*strada*) tow-path.
alzare [al'tsare] *v* raise, lift; (*raccogliere*) pick up; (*carte da gioco*) cut. **alzarsi** *v* get up, rise. **alzare le spalle** shrug one's shoulders.
amaca [a'maka] *sf* hammock.
almalgamare [amalga'mare] *v* amalgamate, combine. **amalgama** *sm* amalgam.
amante [a'mante] *s(m+f)* lover. *agg* fond (of), keen (on).
amare [a'mare] *v* love, like. **amato** *agg* beloved. **amatore** *sm* lover; (*conoscitore*) connoisseur.
amarena [ama'rεna] *sf* sour cherry, black cherry.
amaro [a'maro] *agg* bitter; (*doloroso*) painful. *sm* bitterness; (*bibita*) bitters *pl*. **amarezza** *sf* bitterness.
ambasciata [amba'ʃata] *sf* embassy; message. **ambasciatore, -trice** *sm, sf* ambassador, ambassadress.
ambedue [ambe'due] *pron, agg* both.
ambidestro [ambi'dεstro] *agg* ambidextrous.
ambientarsi [ambjen'tarsi] *v* accustom oneself, settle down. **ambiente** *sm* environment, milieu; atmosphere. **temperatura ambiente** *sf* room temperature.
ambiguo [am'biguo] *agg* ambiguous; (*equivoco*) dubious; (*fam*) shady. **ambiguità** *sf* ambiguity; duplicity.
ambito[1] ['ambito] *sm* limits *pl*; sphere.
ambito[2] [am'bito] *agg* longed-for, coveted. **ambire** *v* covet.
ambivalente [ambiva'lεnte] *agg* ambivalent.
ambizione [ambi'tsjone] *sf* ambition. **ambizioso** *agg* ambitious.
ambo ['ambo] *agg* both.
ambra ['ambra] *sf, agg* amber. **ambra grigia** ambergris.
ambulante [ambu'lante] *agg* wandering. **biblioteca ambulante** *sf* mobile library. **venditore ambulante** *sm* pedlar.
ambulanza [ambu'lantsa] *sf* ambulance; (*infermeria mobile*) field hospital.
ambulatorio [ambula'tɔrjo] *sm* outpatients' department, clinic.
ameba [a'mεba] *sf* amoeba.
ameno [a'mεno] *agg* agreeable; (*divertente*) entertaining.
America [a'mεrika] *sf* America. **americano, -a** *s, agg* American.
ametista [ame'tista] *sf* amethyst.
amianto [a'mjanto] *sm* asbestos.
amichevole [ami'kevole] *agg* friendly.
amico [a'miko], **-a** *sm, sf* friend. *agg* friendly. **amicizia** *sf* friendship.
amido ['amido] *sm* starch.
ammaccare [ammak'kare] *v* dent. **ammaccatura** *sf* dent.
ammaestrare [ammaes'trare] *v* teach, train. **ammaestramento** *sm* teaching, training.
ammalarsi [amma'larsi] *v* fall ill.
ammansire [amman'sire] *v* tame, subdue.
ammassare [ammas'sare] *v* amass.
ammazzare [ammat'tsare] *v* kill, murder.
ammenda [am'mεnda] *sf* (*dir*) fine. **fare ammenda di** make amends for.
***ammettere** [am'mettere] *v* admit; permit; suppose; take for granted. **ammesso che** given that.
ammezzato [ammed'dzato] *agg* mezzanine. *sm* mezzanine floor.
ammiccare [ammik'kare] *v* wink (at).
amministrare [amminis'trare] *v* administer, manage, run. **amministrativo** *agg* administrative. **amministratore, -trice** *sm, sf* director. **amministratore delegato** managing director. **amministrazione** *sf* administration, management. **consiglio d'amministrazione** *sm* board of directors.

ammiraglio [ammi'raʎo] *sm* admiral. **ammiragliato** *sm* admiralty.

ammirare [ammi'rare] *v* admire. **ammiratore, -trice** *sm, sf* admirer, fan. **ammirazione** *sf* admiration. **ammirevole** *agg* admirable.

ammissibile [ammis'sibile] *agg* admissible, acceptable.

ammissione [ammis'sjone] *sf* admission, admittance. **esame d'ammissione** *sm* entrance examination. **tassa d'ammissione** *sf* entrance fee.

ammobiliare [ammobi'ljare] *v* furnish.

ammollare[1] [ammol'lare] *v* soften; (*nell'acqua*) soak.

ammollare[2] [ammol'lare] *v* let go, slacken.

ammoniaca [ammo'niaka] *sf* ammonia.

ammonire [ammo'nire] *v* warn; reprimand. **ammonimento** *sm* warning; reproof.

ammontare [ammon'tare] *sm, v* amount.

ammorbidire [ammorbi'dire] *v* soften.

ammortire [ammor'tire] *v* deaden.

ammucchiare [ammuk'kjare] *v* pile up.

ammuffire [ammuf'fire] *v* go mouldy. **ammuffito** *agg* mouldy.

ammutinamento [ammutina'mento] *sm* mutiny.

amnistia [amnis'tia] *sf* amnesty.

amo ['amo] *sm* hook. **abboccare all'amo** swallow the bait.

amorale [amo'rale] *agg* amoral.

amore [a'more] *sm* love; (*persona graziosa*) darling. **amor proprio** self-respect. **per amore di** for the sake of. **amoroso** *agg* loving.

ampère [ã'pɛr] *sm invar* ampere, amp.

ampio ['ampjo] *agg* wide, spacious; (*abbondante*) full.

amplificare [amplifi'kare] *v* amplify, enlarge. **amplificatore** *sm* amplifier.

ampolloso [ampol'loso] *agg* pompous.

amputare [ampu'tare] *v* amputate. **amputazione** *sf* amputation.

anacronismo [anakro'nizmo] *sm* anachronism.

anagrafe [a'nagrafe] *sf* register office.

anagramma [ana'gramma] *sm* anagram.

analcolico [anal'kɔlico] *agg* non-alcoholic. *sm* soft drink.

anale [a'nale] *agg* anal.

analfabeta [analfa'bɛta] *agg, s(m+f)* illiterate. **analfabetismo** *sm* illiteracy.

analgesico [anal'dʒeziko] *agg, sm* analgesic.

analizzare [analid'dzare] *v* analyse. **analisi** *sf* analysis (*pl* -ses). **in ultima analisi** when all is said and done. **analista** *s(m+f)* analyst. **analitico** *agg* analytic.

analogo [a'nalogo] *agg, m pl* **-ghi** analogous. **analogia** *sf* analogy.

ananas ['ananas] *sm* pineapple.

anarchico [a'narkiko], **-a** *agg* anarchic(al). *sm, sf* anarchist. **anarchia** *sf* anarchy.

anatema [ana'tɛma] *sm* anathema.

anatomia [anato'mia] *sf* anatomy. **anatomia patologica** pathology. **anatomico** *agg* anatomical. **anatomista** *s(m+f)* anatomist.

anatra ['anatra] *sf* duck. **anatroccolo** *sm* duckling.

anca ['anka] *sf* hip.

anche ['anke] *cong* too, as well, also; (*inoltre*) besides; (*perfino*) even.

ancora[1] ['ankora] *sm* anchor. **ancoraggio** *sm* moorings *pl*. **ancorare** *v* anchor.

ancora[2] [an'kora] *avv* still; (*in frasi negative*) yet; (*di nuovo*) again; (*un altro*) another; (*persino*) even. **ancora un po'** a little more; (*tempo*) a little longer.

***andare** [an'dare] *v* go; (*funzionare*) work, run; (*calzare*) fit; (*essere adatto*) suit; (*dovere*) must be, have to be. **a lungo andare** in the long run. **andare a genio** be to one's liking. **andare a piedi** walk. **andare a spasso** go for a walk. **andare avanti** proceed, progress, go on. **andar bene** go well; fit; (*salute*) be well. **andare in bicicletta** cycle. **andare incontro a** go towards, go and meet. **andarsene** go away, leave.

andata [an'data] *sf* **biglietto d'andata** *sm* single ticket.

andirivieni [andiri'vjɛni] *sm* coming and going; (*risposta evasiva*) prevarication.

andito ['andito] *sm* passage.

aneddoto [a'nɛddoto] *sm* anecdote.

anelare [ane'lare] *v* pant; (*aspirare*) yearn (for). **anelante** *agg* panting, out of breath.

anello [a'nɛllo] *sm* ring. **anello matrimoniale/di fidanzamento** wedding/engagement ring.

anemia [ane'mia] *sf* anaemia. **anemico** *agg* anaemic.

anemone [a'nɛmone] *sm* anemone.

anestetico [anes'tɛtiko] *agg, sm* anaesthetic. **anestesia** *sf* anaesthesia. **anestetista** *s(m+f)* anaesthetist.

anfetamina [anfeta'mina] *sf* amphetamine.
anfibio [an'fibjo] *sm, agg* amphibian.
angariare [anga'rjare] *v* harass.
angelica [an'dʒɛlika] *sf* angelica.
angelo ['andʒelo] *sm* angel; (*pesce*) angelfish. **angelo custode** guardian angel. **angelico** *agg* angelic.
anglicano [angli'kano], **-a** *s, agg* Anglican. **anglicanesimo** *sm* Anglicanism.
angolo ['angolo] *sm* corner; (*geom, ecc.*) angle. **angolare** *agg* angular. **pietra angolare** *sf* cornerstone.
angoscia [an'gɔʃa] *sf* anxiety, anguish. **angosciare** *v* distress. **angoscioso** *agg* distressed; distressing.
anguilla [an'gwilla] *sf* eel.
anguria [an'gurja] *sf* water-melon.
anice ['anitʃe] *sm* aniseed.
anima ['anima] *sf* soul; (*parte centrale*) core; (*fervore*) heart; (*di arma da fuoco*) bore. **rodersi l'anima** torment oneself.
animale [ani'male] *sm* animal; (*persona*) brute. *agg* animal.
animare [ani'mare] *v* animate; stimulate. **animato** *agg* animate; (*vivace*) spirited. **disegno** *or* **cartone animato** *sm* cartoon. **essere animato da** be inspired by.
animo ['animo] *sm* mind; (*cuore, coraggio*) heart; (*carattere*) nature. **farsi animo** pluck up courage. **in fondo all'animo** at the back of one's mind. **mettersi l'animo in pace** resign oneself. **stato d'animo** *sm* mood.
animosità [animozi'ta] *sf* animosity, spite.
annacquare [annak'kware] *v* water down.
annaffiare [annaf'fjare] *v* water.
annali [an'nali] *sm pl* annals *pl*.
annata [an'nata] *sf* year; (*raccolto*) crop; (*di vino*) vintage; (*importo*) income.
annebbiare [anneb'bjare] *v* become foggy; (*fig*) dim, cloud.
annegare [anne'gare] *v* drown. **annegamento** *sm* drowning.
***annettere** [an'nɛttere] *v* (*pol*) annex; attach. **annesso** *sm* annexe, appendage.
annichilare [anniki'lare] *v* annihilate, destroy.
annientare [annjen'tare] *v* annihilate, destroy. **annientamento** *sm* (total) destruction.
anniversario [anniver'sarjo] *sm, agg* anniversary.
anno ['anno] *sm* year. **anno bisestile** leap-year. **anno luce** light-year.
annodare [anno'dare] *v* knot *or* tie (together).
annoiare [anno'jare] *v* bore.
annotare [anno'tare] *v* note, jot down; (*postillare*) annotate.
annoverare [annove'rare] *v* number; enumerate.
annuale [annu'ale] *agg* annual, yearly.
annuario [annu'arjo] *sm* yearbook.
annuire [annu'ire] *v* nod in agreement; (*acconsentire*) agree.
annullare [annul'lare] *v* cancel; (*matrimonio*) annul; (*legge*) repeal. **annullamento** *sm* cancellation; annulment; repeal.
annunciare [annun'tʃare] *v* announce; (*precorrere*) herald. **annunciatore, -trice** *sm, sf* announcer. **annuncio** *sm* announcement, notice; (*pubblicità*) advertisement.
Annunciazione [annuntʃa'tsjone] *sf* Annunciation.
annuo ['annuo] *agg* yearly, annual.
annusare [annu'zare] *v* sniff; (*intuire*) smell.
annuvolare [annuvo'lare] *v* cloud (over).
ano ['ano] *sm* anus.
anodo ['anodo] *sm* anode.
anomalia [anoma'lia] *sf* anomaly. **anomalo** *agg* anomalous.
anonimo [a'nɔnimo] *agg* anonymous. **società anonima** *sf* limited company.
anormale [anor'male] *agg* abnormal. **anormalità** *sf* abnormality.
ansare [an'sare] *v* puff, pant.
ansia ['ansja] *sf* anxiety; (*angoscia*) dread; (*desiderio*) longing. **ansioso** *agg* anxious; longing; (*impaziente*) restless.
antagonismo [antago'nizmo] *sm* antagonism. **antagonista** *s(m+f)* adversary.
antartico [an'tartiko] *agg* antarctic.
antenato [ante'nato] *sm* forefather, ancestor.
antenna [an'tenna] *sf* (*zool*) antenna; (*radio, TV*) aerial.
anteprima [ante'prima] *sf* preview.
anteriore [ante'rjore] *agg* (*nel tempo*) preceding, previous; (*nello spazio*) front, fore.
antiabbagliante [antiabba'ʎante] *agg* anti-dazzle. **fari antiabbaglianti** *sm pl* dipped headlights *pl*.

antiaereo [antia'εreo] *agg* anti-aircraft.
antibiotico [antibi'ɔtiko] *agg, sm* antibiotic.
anticamera [anti'kamera] *sf* lobby, waiting-room. **fare anticamera** be kept waiting. **far fare anticamera** keep waiting.
antichità [antiki'ta] *sf* antiquity; (*oggetto*) antique.
anticiclone [antitʃi'klone] *sm* anticyclone.
anticipare [antitʃi'pare] *v* anticipate; advance; pay in advance. **anticipato** *agg* advanced; (*prima del tempo*) in advance. **anticipazione** *sf* anticipation; (*soldi*) advance.
anticipo [an'titʃipo] *sm* advance, deposit. **in anticipo** early; (*orologio*) fast.
antico [an'tiko] *agg, m pl* **-chi** old; ancient; antique. **all'antica** *agg* old-fashioned.
anticoncezionale [antikontʃetsjo'nale] *agg, sm* contraceptive.
anticonformista [antikonfor'mista] *agg, s(m+f)* non-conformist.
anticongelante [antikondʒe'lante] *sm* anti-freeze.
anticorpo [anti'kɔrpo] *sm* antibody.
antidoto [an'tidoto] *sm* antidote.
antifecondativo [antifekonda'tivo] *sm, agg* contraceptive.
antifurto [anti'furto] *sm* burglar alarm.
antilope [an'tilope] *sf* antelope.
antincendio [antin'tʃendjo] *agg* **equipaggiamento antincendio** fire-fighting equipment.
antiorario [antio'rarjo] *agg* anti-clockwise.
antipasto [anti'pasto] *sm* hors d'oeuvre, starter.
antipatia [antipa'tia] *sf* dislike, antipathy. **prendere in antipatia** take a dislike to. **antipatico** *agg* disagreeable, unpleasant.
antiquario [anti'kwarjo] *sm* antique dealer. **antiquariato** *sm* antique trade; (*negozio*) antique shop.
antiquato [anti'kwato] *agg* (*fuori moda*) old-fashioned; (*disusato*) obsolete.
antisemita [antise'mita] *s(m+f)* anti-Semite. *agg* anti-Semitic. **antisemitismo** *sm* anti-Semitism.
antisettico [anti'sεttiko] *sm, agg* antiseptic.
antisociale [antiso'tʃale] *agg* antisocial.
antistaminico [antista'miniko] *sm* antihistamine.
antitesi [an'titezi] *sf* antithesis (*pl* -ses).
antologia [antolo'dʒia] *sf* anthology.
antro ['antro] *sm* cave.
antropologia [antropolo'dʒia] *sf* anthropology. **antropologico** *agg* anthropological. **antropologo, -a** *sm, sf* anthropologist.
anulare [anu'lare] *agg* annular, ring-shaped. *sm* ring-finger.
anzi ['antsi] *cong* on the contrary; (*invece*) as a matter of fact; (*o meglio*) or better, better still; (*di più*) indeed.
anziano [an'tsjano], **-a** *agg* elderly; aged; senior. *sm, sf* elderly person.
anziché [antsi'ke] *cong* (*piuttosto*) rather than; (*invece*) instead of.
anzitutto [antsi'tutto] *avv* above all, first of all.
apatia [apa'tia] *sf* apathy.
ape ['ape] *sf* bee.
aperitivo [aperi'tivo] *sm* aperitif.
aperto [a'pεrto] *agg* open; (*pronto*) quick. **all'aperto** in the open, outdoors.
apice ['apitʃe] *sm* apex, top.
apocrifo [a'pɔkrifo] *agg* apocryphal.
apolide [a'pɔlide] *agg* stateless.
apostolo [a'pɔstolo] *sm* apostle. **apostolico** *agg* apostolic.
apostrofo [a'pɔstrofo] *sm* apostrophe.
appagare [appa'gare] *v* satisfy.
appalto [ap'palto] *sm* contract.
appannare [appan'nare] *v* (*vista*) dim, blur; (*vetri*) mist up.
apparato [appa'rato] *sm* show, display; (*tec*) machinery; (*biol*) system, apparatus. **apparato scenico** set.
apparecchiare [apparek'kjare] *v* prepare. **apparecchiare la tavola** lay the table. **apparecchio** *sm* set; device, instrument, appliance; (*fam*) (aero)plane; (*fam*) (tele)phone.
apparenza [appa'rεntsa] *sf* appearance. **apparente** *agg* apparent. **apparentemente** *avv* apparently; (*a prima vista*) to all appearances.
***apparire** [appa'rire] *v* appear; (*sembrare*) look, seem. **appariscente** *agg* striking.
appartamento [apparta'mento] *sm* flat, apartment.
appartare [appar'tare] *v* put aside. **appartarsi** *v* withdraw. **appartato** *agg* secluded.
***appartenere** [apparte'nere] *v* belong.
appassionare [appassjo'nare] *v* move, arouse passion; arouse interest. **appassionarsi per** be very fond of.

appena [ap'pena] *avv* barely, hardly; (*soltanto*) only; (*solo un po'*) only just; (*da poco*) just (recently). *cong* **appena ... che ...** no sooner ... than ....
***appendere** [ap'pendere] *v* hang.
appendice [appen'ditʃe] *sm* appendix. **appendicite** *sf* appendicitis.
appetito [appe'tito] *sm* appetite. **aver appetito** have an appetite, be hungry. **appetitoso** *agg* appetizing; tempting.
appianare [appja'nare] *v* level; (*dissidio, ecc.*) smooth (over), settle.
appiccare [appik'kare] *v* (*appendere*) hang; (*cominciare*) set off. **appiccar fuoco a** set fire to.
appiccicare [appittʃi'kare] *v* stick. **appiccicaticcio** *agg* sticky.
appigionare [appidʒo'nare] *v* let.
appioppare [appjop'pare] *v* give; (*affibbiare*) saddle with.
appisolarsi [appizo'larsi] *v* doze.
applaudire [applau'dire] *v* applaud. **applauso** *sm* applause.
applicare [appli'kare] *v* apply. **applicazione** *sf* application; concentration; (*dir*) enforcement. **applique** *sf, pl* **-s** wall-bracket.
appoggiare [appod'dʒare] *v* lean; (*posare*) lay; (*fondare*) base; (*favorire*) support. **appoggio** *sm* support.
***apporre** [ap'porre] *v* affix, append.
apportare [appor'tare] *v* bring about, produce. **apporto** *sm* contribution.
apposito [ap'pɔzito] *agg* special; (*adatto*) suitable. **appositamente** *avv* suitably; (*apposta*) deliberately; (*espressamente*) specially.
apposta [ap'pɔsta] *avv* deliberately, on purpose, specially. *agg invar* special.
***apprendere** [ap'prendere] *v* learn. **apprendista** *s(m+f)* apprentice, learner. **apprendistato** *sm* apprenticeship.
apprensione [appren'sjone] *sm* apprehension, concern. **apprensivo** *agg* apprehensive, uneasy.
appresso [ap'presso] *avv* close by, at hand; (*con sè*) with one; (*in sequito*) later. *prep* close to; (*dietro*) close behind. *agg invar* following.
apprestare [appres'tare] *v* prepare; (*porgere*) bring.
apprezzare [appret'tsare] *v* appreciate. **apprezzamento** *sm* appreciation; (*giudizio*) opinion; (*osservazione*) remark.
approfittare [approfit'tare] *v* profit (by), take advantage (of).
approfondire [approfon'dire] *v* deepen; (*studiare*) probe, go into.
approntare [appron'tare] *v* get ready.
approssimativo [approssima'tivo] *agg* approximate, rough. **approssimare** *v* approximate. **approssimarsi (a)** approach. **approssimazione** *sf* approximation.
approvare [appro'vare] *v* approve (of). **approvazione** *sf* approval.
appuntamento [appunta'mento] *sm* appointment; (*fam*) date.
appunto[1] [ap'punto] *sm* note; (*osservazione*) remark. **muovere** *or* **fare un appunto a** blame, find fault with.
appunto[2] [ap'punto] *avv* precisely, just.
appurare [appu'rare] *v* verify.
aprile [a'prile] *sm* April.
***aprire** [a'prire] *v* open; (*luce, radio, ecc.*) switch on. **apribottiglie** *sm invar* bottle-opener. **apriscatole** *sm invar* tin-opener.
aquila ['akwila] *sf* eagle. **aquilone** *sm* kite.
Arabia [a'rabja] *sf* Arabia. **arabo, -a** *s, agg* Arab; *sm* (*lingua*) Arabic.
arachide [a'rakide] *sf* ground-nut, peanut.
aragosta [ara'gosta] *sf* lobster.
araldo [a'raldo] *sm* herald. **araldica** *sf* heraldry. **araldico** *agg* heraldic.
arancio [a'rantʃo] *sm* orange tree. *agg invar* (*colore*) orange. **arancia** *sf* orange. **arancione** *sm, agg invar* orange.
arare [a'rare] *v* plough. **aratro** *sm* plough.
arazzo [a'rattso] *sm* tapestry.
arbitrare [arbi'trare] *v* arbitrate; (*sport*) referee. **arbitro** *sm* referee, umpire.
arbitrio [ar'bitrjo] *sm* will. **arbitrario** *agg* arbitrary.
arbusto [ar'busto] *sm* bush.
arca ['arka] *sf* ark.
arcaico [ar'kaiko] *agg* archaic.
arcata [ar'kata] *sf* arcade; (*di ponte*) span; (*anat*) arch.
archeologia [arkeolo'dʒia] *sf* archaeology. **archeologico** *agg* archaeological. **archeologo, -a** *sm, sf* archaeologist.
archetipo [ar'ketipo] *sm* archetype. *agg* archetypal.
archetto [ar'ketto] *sm* bow.
architetto [arki'tetto] *sm* architect. **architettonico** *agg* architectural. **architettura** *sf* architecture.
archivio [ar'kivjo] *sm* archives *pl*; (*comm*) file. **archiviare** *v* (place on) file;

(*questione, ecc.*) pigeon-hole. **archivista** *s(m+f)* archivist; (*comm*) filing clerk.
arciduca [artʃi'duka] *sm* archduke.
arciere [ar'tʃɛre] *sm* archer.
arcigno [ar'tʃiɲo] *agg* sullen.
arcipelago [artʃi'pɛlago] *sm, pl* **-ghi** archipelago.
arcivescovo [artʃi'veskovo] *sm* archbishop. **arcivescovado** *sm* archbishop's palace; (*dignità*) archbishopric.
arco ['arko] *sm* bow; (*anat, arch*) arch; (*geom*) arc. **quartetto d'archi** *sm* string quartet. **strumenti ad arco** *sm pl* strings *pl*. **tiro all'arco** *sm* archery.
arcobaleno ['arkobaleno] *sm* rainbow.
arcuato [arku'ato] *agg* arched. **dalle gambe arcuate** bow-legged.
***ardere** ['ardere] *v* burn. **ardente** *agg* burning; (*colore*) fiery; (*appassionato*) ardent.
ardesia [ar'dɛzja] *sf* slate.
ardire [ar'dire] *v* dare. **ardito** *agg* bold, daring; risky. **ardore** *sm* (*calore*) heat; passion.
arduo ['arduo] *agg* arduous, laborious; (*ripido*) steep.
area ['area] *sf* area; (*terreno*) land, ground.
arena[1] [a'rɛna] *sf* arena.
arena[2] [a'rena] *sf* (*sabbia*) sand.
arenaria [are'narja] *sf* sandstone.
arenarsi [are'narsi] *v* run aground; (*fermarsi*) come to a standstill.
argano ['argano] *sm* winch; (*mar*) capstan.
argentina [ardʒen'tina] *sf* polo-neck sweater.
argento [ar'dʒɛnto] *sm* silver. **argento vivo** quicksilver. **argentare** *v* silver(-plate). **argentato** *agg* silver-plated; (*colore*) silver. **argenteria** *sf* silver, silverware.
argilla [ar'dʒilla] *sf* clay.
argine ['ardʒine] *sm* embankment; barrier. **arginare** *v* stem, check.
argomento [argo'mento] *sm* argument, reason; (*materia*) subject, topic. **argomentare** *v* discuss, argue.
arguto [ar'guto] *agg* (*spiritoso*) witty; shrewd. **arguzia** *sf* wit, humour; shrewdness.
aria ['arja] *sf* air; (*aspetto*) look; (*musica*) tune; (*opera*) aria. **all'aria aperta** in the open, out-of-doors. **corrente d'aria** *sf* draught. **darsi delle arie** put on airs.
arido ['arido] *agg* dry, arid.
arieggiare [arjed'dʒare] *v* air.
ariete [a'rjɛte] *sm* ram. **Ariete** *sm* Aries.
aringa [a'ringa] *sf* herring.
arioso [a'rjozo] *agg* airy.
aristocratico [aristo'kratiko], **-a** *sm, sf* aristocrat. *agg* aristocratic. **aristocrazia** *sf* aristocracy.
aritmetica [arit'mɛtika] *sf* arithmetic. **aritmetico** *agg* arithmetic(al).
armadio [ar'madjo] *sm* cupboard; (*per abiti*) wardrobe.
armare [ar'mare] *v* arm; (*mar*) rig up; reinforce. **armarsi** *v* take up arms; (*provvedersi*) arm oneself. **arma** *sf, pl* **-i** weapon, arms *pl*; (*mil*) force. **armamento** *sm* armament; (*tec*) equipment.
armata [ar'mata] *sf* army; (*flotta*) fleet.
armato [ar'mato] *agg* armed; equipped.
armatura [arma'tura] *sf* scaffolding; (*elett*) armature.
armonia [armo'nia] *sf* harmony. **in armonia con** in keeping with. **armonica** *sf* harmonics. **armonica a bocca** mouth-organ. **armonico** *agg* harmonic. **armonioso** *agg* melodious. **armonizzare** *v* harmonize; (*colori, ecc.*) match.
arnese [ar'neze] *sm* tool; gadget. **arnese da cucina** kitchen utensil. **bene/male in arnese** in good/poor shape.
arnia ['arnja] *sf* beehive.
aroma [a'rɔma] *sm* aroma; aromatic herb, spice. **aromatico** *agg* aromatic.
arpa ['arpa] *sf* harp. **arpeggio** *sm* arpeggio. **arpista** *s(m+f)* harpist.
arpione [ar'pjone] *sm* hook; (*arma*) harpoon; (*cardine*) hinge.
arrabbiarsi [arrab'bjarsi] *v* become angry *or* annoyed. **far arrabbiare** annoy, anger. **arrabbiato** *agg* angry; (*cane*) rabid; (*furioso*) enraged.
arraffare [arraf'fare] *v* snatch.
arrampicarsi [arrampi'karsi] *v* climb (up). **arrampicata** *sf* climbing, climb.
arrangiare [arran'dʒare] *v* (*aggiustare*) mend; improvise; (*fam*) fix; (*musica*) arrange. **arrangiarsi** *v* manage; come to an agreement.
arrecare [arre'kare] *v* cause, bring about.
arredare [arre'dare] *v* furnish. **arredamento** *sm* furnishing; (*mobilio*) furniture. **arredatore, -trice** *sm, sf* interior decorator; (*cinema*) set decorator.
***arrendersi** [ar'rɛndersi] *v* surrender, give oneself up. **arrendevole** *agg* yielding.

arrestare [arres'tare] *v* stop; (*dir*) arrest. **arresto** *sm* stop, stoppage; arrest. **arresto cardiaco** heart failure.
arretrato [arre'trato] *agg* behind; (*non fatto*) outstanding, overdue; (*non sviluppato*) backward; (*numero di rivista, ecc.*) back. **arretrati** *sm pl* arrears *pl*; (*di paga*) back-pay *sing*.
arricchire [arrik'kire] *v* enrich. **arricchirsi** become rich.
arricciare [arrit'tʃare] *v* curl. **arricciare il naso** pull a face. **arricciare il pelo** bristle.
arringa [ar'ringa] *sf* address.
arrischiare [arris'kjare] *v* risk, venture. **arrischiato** *agg* risky; (*imprudente*) rash.
arrivare [arri'vare] *v* arrive; succeed; (*capitare*) happen. **arrivare a** (*riuscire*) manage to; (*giungere*) reach, get to; (*essere ridotto a*) be reduced to. **arrivare fino a** reach, get as far as. **ben arrivato!** welcome! **arrivo** *sm* arrival.
arrivederci [arrive'dertʃi] *inter* goodbye! (*fam*) see you!
arrogante [arro'gante] *agg* arrogant. **arroganza** *sf* arrogance.
arrossire [arros'sire] *v* blush.
arrostire [arros'tire] *v* roast. **arrosto** *sm, agg invar* roast.
arrotare [arro'tare] *v* sharpen. **arrotino** *sm* knife-grinder.
arrotolare [arroto'lare] *v* roll up.
arrotondare [arroton'dare] *v* round off.
arroventato [arroven'tato] *agg* red-hot.
arruffare [arruf'fare] *v* ruffle; (*confondere*) muddle.
arrugginirsi [arruddʒi'nirsi] *v* rust. **arrugginito** *agg* rusty.
arruolare [arrwo'lare] *v* enlist.
arsenale [arse'nale] *sm* arsenal; (*mar*) (naval) dockyard.
arsenico [ar'sɛniko] *sm* arsenic.
arso ['arso] *agg* burnt, parched.
arte ['arte] *sf* art; (*attività*) craft; (*abilità*) skill; (*astuzia*) cunning. **ad arte** on purpose; (*con artifizio*) cunningly. **artefice** *sm* craftsman.
arteria [ar'tɛria] *sf* artery. **arteria di traffico** main road, thoroughfare.
artico ['artiko] *agg* arctic.
articolare [artiko'lare] *v* articulate; (*suddividere*) split up.
articolo [ar'tikolo] *sm* article. **articoli** *sm pl* goods *pl*. **articolo di cronaca** news item. **articolo di fondo** leading article, leader.
artificiale [artifi'tʃale] *agg* artificial.
artificio [arti'fitʃo] *sm* stratagem, device. **fuochi d'artificio** *sm pl* fireworks *pl*.
artigiano [arti'dʒano] *sm* craftsman. **artigianato** *sm* craftsmanship; (*prodotti*) handicraft; (*classe*) craftsmen *pl*.
artiglieria [artiʎe'ria] *sf* artillery.
artiglio [ar'tiʎo] *sm* claw, talon. **cadere negli artigli di** fall into the clutches of.
artista [ar'tista] *s(m+f)* artist. **artistico** artistic.
arto ['arto] *sm* limb.
artrite [ar'trite] *sf* arthritis.
asbesto [az'bɛsto] *sm* asbestos.
ascella [a'ʃɛlla] *sf* armpit.
***ascendere** [a'ʃendere] *v* rise.
ascensore [aʃen'sore] *sm* lift.
ascesa [a'ʃeza] *sf also* **ascensione** ascent, climb.
ascesso [a'ʃɛsso] *sm* abscess.
asceta [a'ʃɛta] *s(m+f)* ascetic. **ascetico** *agg* ascetic. **ascetismo** *sm* asceticism.
ascia ['aʃa] *sf* axe.
asciugare [aʃu'gare] *v* dry. **asciugamano** *sm* towel. **asciugatoio** *sm* bath towel. **carta asciugante** *sf* blotting-paper.
asciutto [a'ʃutto] *agg* dry. **essere all'asciutto** (*salvo*) be safe; (*al verde*) be broke. **pasta asciutta** *sf* pasta.
ascoltare [askol'tare] *v* listen (to); heed, pay attention (to); (*lezioni, messa, ecc.*) attend. **ascoltatore, -trice** *sm, sf* listener. **dare ascolto a** pay attention to.
asfalto [as'falto] *sm* asphalt. **asfaltare** *v* asphalt.
Asia ['azja] *sf* Asia. **asiatico** *sm, agg* Asian, Asiatic.
asilo [a'zilo] *sm* refuge, shelter; (*pol*) asylum. **asilo infantile** kindergarten, nursery school. **dare asilo a** shelter.
asino ['azino] *sm* ass, donkey. **asineria** *sf* stupidity. **asinino** *agg* asinine. **tosse asinina** *sf* whooping cough.
asma ['azma] *sm* asthma. **asmatico** *agg* asthmatic.
asola ['azola] *sf* buttonhole.
asparago [as'parago] *sm* asparagus.
aspettare [aspet'tare] *v* await, wait (for). **aspettare con desiderio** look forward to. **aspettare un bambino** be expecting a baby. **aspettativa** *sf* expectation; (*licenza*) leave of absence.
aspetto[1] [as'pɛtto] *sm* appearance, look. **sotto questo aspetto** from this point of view.

aspetto[2] [as'pɛtto] *sm* waiting. **sala d'aspetto** *sf* waiting-room.
aspirare [aspi'rare] *v* inhale, breathe in; (*desiderare*) aspire. **aspirapolvere** *sm invar* vacuum cleaner.
aspirina [aspi'rina] *sf* aspirin.
asportare [aspor'tare] *v* remove, take away.
aspro ['aspro] *agg* sour, tart; (*vino*) rough; (*suono*) harsh; (*clima*) raw; (*fig*) hard. **asprezza** *sf* sourness; harshness.
assaggiare [assad'dʒare] *v* taste, try. **assaggio** *sm* taste; (*campione*) sample.
assai [as'sai] *avv* very; (very) much; (*abbastanza*) enough.
assalire [assa'lire] *v* assail, attack.
assalto [as'salto] *sm* attack.
assassinare [assassi'nare] *v* murder. **assassinio** *sm* murder. **assassino, -a** *sm, sf* murderer, murderess.
asse[1] ['asse] *sm* axis; (*mec*) axle.
asse[2] ['asse] *sf* (*tavola*) board, plank. **asse da stiro** ironing-board.
assediare [asse'djare] *v* besiege. **assedio** *sm* siege. **stato d'assedio** *sm* state of emergency.
assegnare [asse'ɲare] *v* assign, allot. **assegnazione** *sf* allocation.
assegno [as'seɲo] *sm* cheque. **assegno circolare** banker's draft. **assegno in bianco** blank cheque. **assegno sbarrato** crossed cheque. **assegno turistico** traveller's cheque.
assemblea [assem'blɛa] *sf* assembly, meeting.
assenso [as'sɛnso] *sm* assent, agreement.
assente [as'sɛnte] *agg* absent. **assentarsi** *v* absent oneself, stay away. **assenteismo** *sm* absenteeism. **assenza** *sf* absence; (*mancanza*) lack.
assentire [assen'tire] *v* assent, approve.
asserire [asse'rire] *v* assert, affirm. **asserzione** *sf* assertion, statement.
assessore [asses'sore] *sm* (*dir*) assessor; (*comunale*) councillor.
assestare [asses'tare] *v* arrange, settle.
assetato [asse'tato] *agg* thirsty.
assettare [asset'tare] *v* tidy, put in order.
assicurare [assiku'rare] *v* assure; (*dir*) insure; (*rendere certo*) ensure; (*procurare*) secure; (*lettera*) register. **assicurarsi** *v* take out insurance. **assicuratore** *sm* underwriter. **assicurazione** *sf* insurance.
assiduo [as'siduo] *agg* assiduous.
assieme [as'sjɛme] *avv* together.
assieparsi [assje'parsi] *v* crowd (round).
assillare [assil'lare] *v* pester.
assimilare [assimi'lare] *v* assimilate. **assimilazione** *sf* assimilation.
Assise [as'size] *sf* **corte d'Assise** *sf* Assizes *pl*.
assistente [assis'tɛnte] *s*(*m*+*f*) assistant; (*universitario*) lecturer; (*di volo*) steward, stewardess. **assistente sociale** social worker. **assistenza** *sf* assistance; (*sociale*) welfare.
***assistere** [as'sistere] *v* (*aiutare*) assist, help; be present at; (*sport*) watch; (*lezione*) attend.
asso ['asso] *sm* ace; champion. **piantare in asso** leave in the lurch.
associare [asso'tʃare] *v* associate, join. **associarsi** *v* join; become a partner *or* member. **associazione** *sf* association, society; (*comm*) partnership.
assoggettare [assoddʒet'tare] *v* subject.
assoluto [asso'luto] *agg* absolute, complete.
***assolvere** [as'sɔlvere] *v* (*rel*) absolve; (*dir*) discharge, acquit. **assoluzione** *sf* absolution; discharge, acquittal. **assolvimento** *sm* fulfilment.
assomigliare [assomi'ʎare] *v* resemble.
assonnato [asson'nato] *agg* sleepy; (*torpido*) sluggish.
assopirsi [asso'pirsi] *v* nod off; calm *or* cool down.
assorbire [assor'bire] *v* absorb. **assorbente** *agg* absorbent. **assorbente (igienico)** *sm* sanitary towel. **carta assorbente** *sf* blotting-paper.
assordare [assor'dare] *v* deafen; (*attutire un suono*) deaden.
assortire [assor'tire] *v* sort out. **assortimento** *sm* assortment.
***assuefare** [assue'fare] *v* accustom.
***assumere** [as'sumere] *v* assume; (*personale*) take on, engage; (*procurarsi*) obtain.
assunzione [assun'tsjone] *sf* engagement; (*di un obbligo*) undertaking; (*elevazione*) ascent; (*filos*) assumption. **Assunzione** *sf* (*rel*) Assumption.
assurdo [as'surdo] *agg* absurd, preposterous. *sm* absurdity.
asta ['asta] *sf* pole; (*mec*) rod; (*scrittura*) stroke. **a mezz'asta** at half-mast. **vendita all'asta** *sf* auction.

astante [as'tante] *s(m+f)* bystander.
astemio [as'tɛmjo], **-a** *sm, sf* teetotaller. *agg* teetotal.
***astenersi** [aste'nersi] *v* abstain, refrain.
asterisco [aste'risko] *sm* asterisk.
astinenza [asti'nɛntsa] *sf* abstinence.
astio ['astjo] *sm* rancour, resentment. **portar astio** bear a grudge.
***astrarre** [as'trarre] *v* abstract. **astratto** *sm, agg* abstract. **astrazione** *sf* abstraction.
astro ['astro] *sm* star.
astrologia [astrolo'dʒia] *sf* astrology. **astrologico** *agg* astrological. **astrologo, -a** *sm, sf* astrologer.
astronauta [astro'nauta] *s(m+f)* astronaut.
astronomia [astrono'mia] *sf* astronomy. **astronomico** *agg* astronomic(al). **astronomo, -a** *sm, sf* astronomer.
astuccio [as'tuttʃo] *sm* case.
astuto [as'tuto] *agg* astute, shrewd. **astuzia** *sf* shrewdness, cunning; (*azione*) trick.
Atene [a'tɛne] *sf* Athens. **ateniese** *s(m+f)*, *agg* Athenian.
ateo ['ateo], **-a** *sm, sf* atheist. *agg* atheistic.
atlante [at'lante] *sm* atlas.
atlantico [at'lantiko] *agg* Atlantic.
atleta [at'lɛta] *s(m+f)* athlete. **atletica** *sf* athletics. **atletico** *agg* athletic.
atmosfera [atmos'fɛra] *sf* atmosphere. **atmosferico** *agg* atmospheric.
atomo ['atomo] *sm* atom. **atomico** *agg* atomic.
atrio ['atrjo] *sm* (entrance) hall, lobby.
atroce [a'trɔtʃe] *agg* dreadful, terrible; (*feroce*) cruel. **atrocità** *sf* atrocity.
attaccare [attak'kare] *v* attach, fasten; (*appendere*) hang (up); (*incollare*) stick (on); apply; pass on; (*assalire, corrodere*) attack; (*iniziare*) begin. **attaccabottoni** *s(m+f)* *invar* (*fam*) bore. **attaccabrighe** *s(m+f)* *invar* (*fam*) troublemaker. **attaccapanni** *sm* (*gruccia*) coat-hanger; (*mobilia*) coat-rack. **attaccar briga** *or* **lite** pick a quarrel. **attaccaticcio** *agg* sticky. **attacco** *sm* attack; (*inizio*) opening; (*giuntura*) joint, fastening; (*elett*) plug.
attecchire [attek'kire] *v* (*radicarsi*) take root; (*diffondersi*) catch on.
atteggiare [atted'dʒare] *v* assume. **atteggiarsi** *v* pose. **atteggiamento** *sm* attitude, expression.
***attendere** [at'tɛndere] *v* await, wait (for); (*dedicarsi*) devote oneself to, look after. **attendibile** *agg* reliable, trustworthy.
***attenersi** [atte'nersi] *v* **attenersi a** keep to.
attentato [atten'tato] *sm* attack; attempted murder *or* assassination.
attento [at'tɛnto] *agg* attentive, alert; careful. **stare attento** pay attention, mind. *inter* careful! mind! look out!
attenzione [atten'tsjone] *sf* attention, care. **fare attenzione a** pay attention to.
atterrare [atter'rare] *v* (*di aereo*) land; (*gettare a terra*) knock down. **atterraggio** *sm* landing.
attesa [at'teza] *sf* wait; (*aspettativa*) expectation.
attestare [attes'tare] *v* certify, attest. **attestato** *sm* certificate, testimonial.
attiguo [at'tiguo] *agg* adjoining.
attimo ['attimo] *sm* instant, moment.
attirare [atti'rare] *v* attract, draw.
attitudine[1] [atti'tudine] *sf* (*disposizione*) aptitude, bent.
attitudine[2] [atti'tudine] *sf* attitude.
attivare [atti'vare] *v* activate, bring into action.
attivo [at'tivo] *agg* active; (*diligente*) busy. **bilancio attivo** *sm* credit balance. *sm* asset.
attizzare [attit'tsare] *v* poke; (*fig*) stir up.
atto[1] ['atto] *agg* suitable, fit.
atto[2] ['atto] *sm* action, act; gesture; (*dir*) deed. **atto di accusa** indictment. **atto di citazione** summons. **atto di nascita/morte** birth/death certificate. **atto matrimoniale** marriage certificate. **dare atto** give notice. **in atto** in progress.
attonito [at'tɔnito] *agg* astonished.
attorcigliare [attortʃi'ʎare] *v* twist.
attore [at'tore] *sm* actor; (*dir*) plaintiff.
attorniare [attor'njare] *v* surround.
attorno [at'torno] *avv* round, around, about. **guardarsi attorno** look round; (*fig*) be wary. **qui attorno** hereabouts.
***attrarre** [at'trarre] *v* attract. **attrattiva** *sf* attraction, fascination. **attrazione** *sf* attraction.
attraversare [attraver'sare] *v* cross; go through. **attraversamento** *sm* crossing.
attrezzo [at'trettso] *sm* tool, appliance. **attrezzi** *sm pl* equipment *sing*; kitchen utensils *pl*; (*teatro*) props *pl*. **attrezzare** *v*

equip; furnish. **attrezzatura** *sf* equipment.
attribuire [attribu'ire] *v* ascribe, attribute; (*assegnare*) award. **attributo** *sm* attribute.
attrice [at'tritʃe] *sf* actress.
attrito [at'trito] *sm* friction.
attuale [attu'ale] *agg* present, current; (*valido*) topical; (*filos*) actual. **attualmente** *avv* at present.
attualità [attuali'ta] *sf* topicality. *sf pl* news *sing*, current events *pl*. **di attualità** topical; (*di moda*) fashionable. **tornare di attualità** come back into fashion.
attuare [attu'are] *v* carry out, put into effect. **attuarsi** *v* come true, be fulfilled.
attutire [attu'tire] *v* mitigate; (*suono*) muffle.
audace [au'datʃe] *agg* daring, bold; risky, rash. **audacia** *sf* boldness, daring.
audiovisivo [audjovi'zivo] *agg* audio-visual.
auditorio [audi'tɔrjo] *sm* auditorium, studio.
audizione [audi'tsjone] *sf* audition; (*dir*) hearing.
augurare [augu'rare] *v* wish. **augurarsi** *v* hope. **augurio** *sm* wish; (*presagio*) omen.
aula ['aula] *sf* classroom; (*università*) lecture theatre; courtroom.
aumentare [aumen'tare] *v* increase. **aumentare di peso** put on weight. **aumento** *sm* increase.
aureo ['aureo] *agg* golden.
aureola [au'rɛola] *sf* halo.
aurora [au'rora] *sf* dawn.
ausiliare [auzi'ljare] *sm*, *agg also* **ausiliario** auxiliary.
austero [aus'tɛro] *agg* austere.
Australia [aus'tralja] *sf* Australia. **australiano, -a** *s*, *agg* Australian.
Austria ['austrja] *sf* Austria. **austriaco, -a** *s*, *agg* Austrian.
autarchia [autar'kia] *sf* self-sufficiency. **autarchico** *agg* self-sufficient.
autentico [au'tɛntiko] *agg* authentic, genuine. **autenticare** *v* authenticate.
autista[1] [au'tista] *s(m+f)* driver. **autista di piazza** taxi-driver.
autista[2] [au'tista] *agg* autistic.
auto ['auto] *sf* (*fam*) car.
autobiografia [autobiogra'fia] *sf* autobiography. **autobiografico** *agg* autobiographical.
autoblinda [auto'blinda] *sf* armoured car.
autobus ['autobus] *sm* bus.
autocarro [auto'karro] *sm* lorry.
autocolonna [autoko'lonna] *sf* convoy.
autocontrollo [autokon'trɔllo] *sm* self-control.
autocratico [auto'kratiko] *agg* autocratic.
autodidatta [autodi'datta] *s(m+f)* self-taught person.
autofurgone [autofur'gone] *sm* van.
autolettiga [autolet'tiga] *sf* ambulance.
autolinea [auto'linea] *sf* bus route.
automa [au'tɔma] *sm* automaton, robot.
automatico [auto'matiko] *agg* automatic. **distributore automatico** slot-machine. **automatizzare** *v* automate.
automezzo [auto'mɛddzo] *sm* motor vehicle.
automobile [auto'mobile] *sf* car. **automobilismo** *sm* motoring. **automobilista** *s(m+f)* motorist. **automobilistico** *agg* motor.
autonomo [au'tɔnomo] *agg* autonomous. **autonomia** *sf* autonomy.
autopsia [autop'sia] *sf* post-mortem, autopsy.
autore [au'tore], **-trice** *sm*, *sf* author; artist.
autorevole [auto'revole] *agg* authoritative.
autorimessa [autori'messa] *sf* garage.
autorità [autori'ta] *sf* authority. **autoritario** *agg* authoritarian.
autoritratto [autori'tratto] *sm* self-portrait.
autorizzare [autorid'dzare] *v* authorize. **autorizzazione** *sf* authorization; permit.
autostop [autos'tɔp] *sm invar* hitch-hiking. **fare l'autostop** hitch-hike.
autostrada [autos'trada] *sf* motorway.
autosufficiente [autosuffi'tʃɛnte] *agg* self-sufficient.
autotreno [auto'trɛno] *sm* articulated lorry.
autoveicolo [autove'ikolo] *sm* motor vehicle.
autunno [au'tunno] *sm* autumn. **autunnale** *agg* autumnal.
avambraccio [avam'brattʃo] *sm* forearm.
avanguardia [avan'gwardja] *sf* forefront; (*mil*) vanguard; (*arte*) avant-garde.
avanti [a'vanti] *avv* forward, ahead; (*prima*) before. **andare avanti** go forward, proceed. **avanti a** before, in front of. **avanti e indietro** backwards and forwards, to and fro. **d'ora in avanti** from now on. **tirare avanti** (*fam*) scrape along,

get by. *inter* come in! (*andiamo*) come now!

avantieri [avan'tjɛri] *avv* the day before yesterday.

avanzare[1] [avan'tsare] *v* advance; (*presentare*) put forward. **avanzata** *sf* advance.

avanzare[2] [avan'tsare] *v* be owed; remain, be left over. **avanzo** *sm* remainder; (*cibo*) left-overs *pl*.

avaro [a'varo], **-a** *agg* mean. *sm, sf* miser. **avarizia** *sf* meanness, stinginess.

avena [a'vena] *sf* oats *pl*. **farina d'avena** *sf* oatmeal.

***avere** [a'vere] *v* have; get. **aver caldo/freddo** be hot/cold. **aver fame/sete** be hungry/thirsty. **aver fretta** be in a hurry. **aver paura/sonno** be afraid/sleepy. *sm* (*comm*) credit; belongings *pl*; property.

aviazione [avja'tsjone] *sf* aviation, flying; (*arma*) air-force. **aviatore, -trice** *sm, sf* aviator, pilot.

avido ['avido] *agg* avid, eager.

aviolinea [avjo'linea] *sf* airline.

avo ['avo] *sm* (*nonno*) grandfather; (*antenato*) forefather, ancestor. **avito** *agg* ancestral.

avocado [avo'kado] *sm* avocado.

avorio [a'vɔrjo] *sm* ivory.

avvampare [avvam'pare] *v* blaze, flare up.

avvantaggiare [avvantad'dʒare] *v* profit, benefit.

***avvedersi** [avve'dersi] *v* become aware.

avvelenare [avvele'nare] *v* poison. **avvelenamento** *sm* poisoning. **avvelenatore, -trice** *sm, sf* poisoner.

***avvenire** [avve'nire] *v* happen. *sm* future. **avvenimento** *sm* event, occurrence.

avventato [avven'tato] *agg* rash, reckless. **avventare** *v* hurl; (*azzardare*) venture.

avventore [avven'tore], **-a** *sm, sf* patron, regular customer.

avventurare [avventu'rare] *v* venture, risk. **avventura** *sf* adventure; (*amorosa*) love affair. **avventuriere** *sm* adventurer.

avverbio [av'verbio] *sm* adverb.

avversario [avver'sario], **-a** *sm, sf* adversary, opponent. *agg* opposing.

avversione [avver'sjone] *sf* dislike, aversion.

avversità [avversi'ta] *sf* adversity.

avverso [av'vɛrso] *agg* adverse; opposing.

avvertire [avver'tire] *v* (*osservare*) notice; (*percepire*) feel; (*ammonire*) warn; (*avvisare*) inform. **avvertenza** *sf* warning, notice; (*attenzione*) care; (*istruzioni*) directions *pl*.

avvezzare [avvet'tsare] *v* (*educare*) train; (*abituare*) accustom.

avviare [avvi'are] *v* start (up), set going; (*comm*) set up; direct. **scuola d'avviamento** *sf* training college, technical college. **avviato** *agg* under way; (*prospero*) thriving.

avvicinare [avvitʃi'nare] *v* approach; (*portar vicino*) bring near.

avvilire [avvi'lire] *v* disgrace; (*scoraggiare*) dishearten; humiliate. **avvilito** *agg* downhearted; demoralized.

avviluppare [avvilup'pare] *v* entangle; (*avvolgere*) wrap up.

avvincente [avvin'tʃɛnte] *agg* fascinating.

avvisare [avvi'zare] *v* let know, advise; (*ammonire*) warn. **avviso** *sm* notice, note; announcement; (*pubblicità*) advertisement; opinion. **avviso circolare** circular. **come d'avviso** as advised.

avvizzire [avvit'tsire] *v* wither.

avvocato [avvo'kato] *sm* lawyer, barrister, solicitor; advocate, champion. **avvocatura** *sf* legal profession.

***avvolgere** [av'vɔldʒere] *v* envelop, wrap up; (*arrotolare*) roll up, wind.

avvoltoio [avvol'tojo] *sm* vulture.

azalea [adza'lɛa] *sf* azalea.

azienda [a'dziɛnda] *sf* firm, business, company; (*impresa*) undertaking. **azienda agricola** farm. **aziendale** *agg* business.

azione [a'tsjone] *sf* action; (*atto*) deed; (*mec*) movement, motion; (*dir*) lawsuit; (*comm*) share. **azionista** *s*(*m+f*) shareholder.

azoto [a'dzɔto] *sm* nitrogen.

azzardare [addzar'dare] *v* risk, venture. **azzardarsi** *v* dare. **azzardato** *agg* risky, rash. **azzardo** *sm* risk.

azzuffarsi [addzuf'farsi] *v* brawl, come to blows.

azzurro [ad'dzurro] *agg, sm* (sky) blue.

B

babbo ['babbo] *sm* (*fam*) dad, daddy.
babbuino [babbu'ino] *sm* baboon.
babordo [ba'bordo] *sm* port.
bacca ['bakka] *sf* berry.
baccalà [bakka'la] *sm* dried salt cod.
baccano [bak'kano] *sm* row, din, uproar.
baccello [bat'tʃɛllo] *sm* pod.
bacchetta [bak'ketta] *sf* rod, stick; (*musica*) baton.
baciare [ba'tʃare] *v* kiss. **bacio** *sm* kiss.
bacino [ba'tʃino] *sm* basin; (*anat*) pelvis.
baco ['bako] *sm* larva; (*da seta*) silkworm.
bada ['bada] *sf* **tenere a bada** hold at bay.
badare [ba'dare] *v* **badare a** pay attention to, take care to. **badare di** be careful to. **senza badare a** regardless of.
badessa [ba'dessa] *sf* abbess.
badia [ba'dia] *sf* abbey.
badile [ba'dile] *sm* spade.
baffo ['baffo] *sm* **farsene un baffo** (*fam*) not care a damn. **baffi** *sm pl* moustache *sing*. **leccarsi i baffi** lick one's lips. **ridere sotto i baffi** laugh up one's sleeve.
bagaglio [ba'gaʎo] *sm* baggage. **bagagliaio** *sm* (*ferr*) luggage van; (*auto*) boot. **deposito bagagli** *sm* left luggage.
bagattella [bagat'tella] *sf* (*gioco*) bagatelle; (*inezia*) trifle.
bagliore [ba'ʎore] *sm* flash.
bagnare [ba'ɲare] *v* wet. **bagnato** *agg* wet.
bagnino [ba'ɲino] *sm* beach attendant, lifeguard.
bagno ['baɲo] *sm* bath; (*locale*) bathroom. **fare il bagno** take a bath. **bagnante** *s*(*m*+*f*) bather. **bagnomaria** *sm* bain-marie.
baia ['baja] *sf* (*geog*) bay.
baionetta [bajo'netta] *sf* bayonet.
balbettare [balbet'tare] *v* stammer.
balbuziente [balbut'tsjɛnte] *s*(*m*+*f*) stammerer.
balcone [bal'kone] *sm* balcony. **balconata** *sf* (*teatro, ecc.*) gallery.
baldacchino [baldak'kino] *sm* canopy; (*rel*) baldachin.
baldanza [bal'dantsa] *sf* self-confidence; audacity. **baldanzoso** *agg* self-confident; audacious.
baldoria [bal'dɔrja] *sf* merrymaking. **far baldoria** make merry.
balena [ba'lena] *sf* whale.
balenare [bale'nare] *v* flash (with lightning); (*apparire subitamente*) come in a flash. **baleno** *sm* flash.
balia[1] ['balja] *sf* nurse.
balia[2] [ba'lia] *sf* **in balia di** in the power of, at the mercy of.
balistica [ba'listika] *sf* ballistics. **balistico** *agg* ballistic.
balla ['balla] *sf* (*involto*) bale; (*frottola*) fib, lie.
ballare [bal'lare] *v* dance.
ballata [bal'lata] *sf* ballad.
ballerino [balle'rino], **-a** *sm, sf* ballet-dancer.
balletto [bal'letto] *sm* ballet.
ballo ['ballo] *sm* ball; dance. **essere in ballo** be at stake.
ballottaggio [ballottad'dʒo] *sm* ballot. **ballottare** *v* ballot.
balneare [balne'are] *agg* bathing.
balocco [ba'lɔkko] *sm* toy, plaything.
balordo [ba'lordo] *agg* senseless, absurd; (*tonto*) dull.
balsamo ['balsamo] *sm* balsam; (*lenimento*) balm.
balza ['baltsa] *sf* (*rupe*) cliff; (*frangia*) fringe.
balzare [bal'tsare] *v* bounce, leap.
bambagia [bam'badʒa] *sf* cotton wool. **tenere nella bambagia** pamper, spoil.
bambinaia [bambi'naja] *sf* (children's) nurse, nanny.
bambino [bam'bino], **-a** *sm, sf* child (*pl* -ren). **bambinata** *sf* childishness. **bambinesco** *adj* puerile.
bamboccio [bam'bɔttʃo] *sm* (*scioccone*) simpleton; (*fantoccio*) rag-doll; (*bambino*) bonny child.
bambola ['bambola] *sf* doll.
bambù [bam'bu] *sm* bamboo.
banale [ba'nale] *adj* banal.
banana [ba'nana] *sf* banana. **banano** *sm* banana tree.
banca ['banka] *sf* bank. **bancario** *agg* bank, banking. **banchiere** *sm* banker.
bancarella [banka'rɛlla] *sf* barrow, stall.
bancarotta [banka'rotta] *sf* bankruptcy.
banchetto [ban'ketto] *sm* banquet. **banchettare** *v* banquet, feast.
banchina [ban'kina] *sf* (*porto*) wharf, quay; (*stazione*) platform.
banco ['banko] *sm* bench; (*di vendita*) counter; (*banca*) bank. **bancogiro** *sm* giro. **banconota** *sf* banknote.
banda[1] ['banda] *sf* (*lato*) side.
banda[2] ['banda] *sf* (*striscia*) stripe; (*radio*) band. **banda sonora** sound-track.

banda[3] ['banda] *sf* group, band; (*delinquenti*) gang.
bandiera [ban'djɛra] *sf* flag, banner. **bandiera di comodo** flag of convenience. **banderuola** *sf* pennant; (*ventaruola*) weather-vane; (*girella*) fickle person.
bandire [ban'dire] *v* proclaim; (*esiliare*) banish. **bandito** *sm* bandit. **banditore** *sm* town-crier. **bando** *sm* proclamation; banishment.
bangio ['bandʒo] *sm invar* banjo.
bar [bar] *sm invar* bar, café.
bara ['bara] *sf* bier, coffin. **aver un piede nella bara** have one foot in the grave.
baracca [ba'rakka] *sf* hut. **mandare avanti la baracca** carry on. **piantare baracca e burattini** abandon everything. **baraccone** *sm* stall, stand.
baraonda [bara'onda] *sf* hubbub, confusion.
barare [ba'rare] *v* cheat. **baro** *sm* cheat.
barattare [barat'tare] *v* barter. **baratto** *sm* barter, exchange.
barattolo [ba'rattolo] *sm* jar, tin.
barba ['barba] *sf* beard. **che barba!** what a bore! **barbuto** *adj* bearded.
barbabietola [barba'bjɛtola] *sf* beetroot.
barbaro ['barbaro] *sm* barbarian. *adj* barbarous.
barbiere [bar'bjɛre] *sm* barber.
barbiturato [barbitu'rato] *sm* barbiturate.
barca ['barka] *sf* boat. **barca a remi** rowing-boat. **barca a vela** sailing-boat. **barca a motore** motor boat. **barcamenarsi** *v* manage.
barcollare [barkol'lare] *v* totter, stagger.
bardare [bar'dare] *v* harness.
barella [ba'rella] *sf* stretcher. **barelliere** *sm* stretcher-bearer.
barile [ba'rile] *sm* barrel, cask.
barista [ba'rista] *sm* barman. *sf* barmaid.
baritono [ba'ritono] *sm* baritone.
barlume [bar'lume] *sm* glimmer.
barocco [ba'rokko] *sm, agg* baroque.
barometro [ba'rɔmetro] *sm* barometer.
barone [ba'rone] *sm* baron; (*dell'industria*) tycoon. **baronessa** *sf* baroness.
barra ['barra] *sf* bar, rod.
barricare [barri'kare] *v* barricade. **barricata** *sf* barricade.
barriera [bar'rjɛra] *sf* barrier.
baruffa [ba'ruffa] *sf* brawl.
barzelletta [bardzel'letta] *sf* joke, funny story.
bascula ['baskula] *sf* weighing machine.
base ['baze] *sf* basis (*pl* -ses); (*tec*) base. **a base di** made up of. **in base a** on the basis of. **basamento** *sm* pedestal; foundation. **basare** *v* base, found.
basetta [ba'zetta] *sf* sideburn.
basilica [ba'zilika] *sf* basilica.
basilico [ba'ziliko] *sm* basil.
basso ['basso] *agg* low, low-lying; (*poco profondo*) shallow. *avv* low, low down. *sm* (*musica*) bass. **a basso ... !** down with ... !
bassofondo [basso'fondo] *sm* shallows *pl*. **bassifondi** *sm pl* (*quartieri*) slums *pl*; (*strati sociali*) underworld *sing*.
bassotto [bas'sɔtto] *sm* dachshund.
bastardo [bas'tardo], **-a** *s, agg* bastard; (*non di razza*) mongrel.
bastare [bas'tare] *v* suffice, be enough. **basta!** *inter* enough! (*silenzio*) quiet! **basta che** provided that.
bastimento [basti'mento] *sm* ship.
bastonare [basto'nare] *v* beat, cane. **bastonata** *sf* caning, beating.
bastone [bas'tone] *sm* stick, cane; golf-club. **bastone da passeggio** walking stick.
battaglia [bat'taʎa] *sf* battle; campaign. **cavallo di battaglia** hobby-horse.
battaglio [bat'taʎʎo] *sm* (*campana*) clapper; (*porta*) door-knocker.
battaglione [batta'ʎone] *sm* battalion.
battello [bat'tɛllo] *sm* boat.
battere ['battere] *v* beat. **battere a macchina** type. **battere le mani** clap (one's hands). **in un batter d'occhio** in a flash. **senza batter ciglio** without batting an eyelid.
batteria [batte'ria] *sf* battery; (*sport*) heat; (*insieme*) set.
batterio [bat'tɛrjo] *sm* bacterium (*pl* -a). **batteriologia** *sf* bacteriology. **batteriologo, -a** *sm, sf* bacteriologist.
battesimo [bat'tezimo] *sm* baptism, christening. **battesimale** *adj* baptismal. **battezzare** *v* baptize, christen.
battibecco [batti'bekko] *sm* quarrel.
batticuore [batti'kwɔre] *sm* **avere il batticuore** have palpitations. **far venire il batticuore** make anxious.
battimani [batti'mani] *sm* applause.
battistero [battis'tɛro] *sm* baptistry.
battito ['battito] *sm* beat, pulsation.
battitore [batti'tore] *sm* (*sport*) server, striker; (*caccia*) beater.

battuta [bat'tuta] *sf* (*colpo*) blow; (*spiritosaggine*) witty remark; (*musica*) beat; (*sport*) service.
batuffolo [ba'tuffolo] *sm* wad.
baule [ba'ule] *sm* trunk. **fare i bauli** (*fam*) go away.
bava ['bava] *sf* dribble.
bavaglino [bava'ʎino] *sm* bib.
bavaglio [ba'vaʎo] *sm* gag. **mettere il bavaglio a** gag.
bavero ['bavero] *sm* collar.
bazzicare [battsi'kare] *v* associate with; frequent.
beatitudine [beati'tudine] *sf* beatitude.
beato [be'ato] *agg* blessed. **beato te!** lucky you!
bebè [be'bɛ] *sm* baby.
beccaccia [bek'kattʃa] *sf* woodcock. **beccaccino** *sm* snipe.
beccare [bek'kare] *v* peck; (*fam*) catch, collar.
becchino [bek'kino] *sm* undertaker; gravedigger.
becco[1] ['bekko] *sm* beak; (*bruciatore*) burner.
becco[2] ['bekko] *sm* (*caprone*) goat; (*cornuto*) cuckold.
Befana [be'fana] *sf* Epiphany.
beffare [bef'fare] *v* mock. **beffarsi di** make fun of. **beffa** *sf* jest, practical joke.
begli ['beʎi] *V* **bello.**
bei ['bɛi] *V* **bello.**
bel ['bel] *V* **bello.**
belare [be'lare] *v* bleat.
Belgio ['bɛldʒo] *sm* Belgium. **belga** *s*(*m*+*f*), *agg*, *m pl* **-gi** Belgian.
belletto [bel'letto] *sm* make-up, rouge.
bellezza [bel'lettsa] *sf* beauty. **che bellezza!** how lovely!
bello ['bɛllo] *agg* beautiful; fine; fair. **il bello è che** the odd thing is (that). **nel bel mezzo** right in the middle. **oh bella!** you don't say! **questa à bella!** (*ironico*) that's a good one! **sul più bello** at the crucial moment.
belva ['belva] *sf* wild animal.
bemolle [be'mɔlle] *sm* (*musica*) flat.
benché [ben'ke] *cong* although.
bendare [ben'dare] *v* (*fasciare*) bandage; (*coprire gli occhi*) blindfold. **benda** *sf* bandage; blindfold.
bene ['bɛne] *avv* well. **star bene** feel well; (*abito*) suit. **va bene** all right. *sm* good; (*amore*) love; wealth, property. **beni di consumo** consumer goods *pl*. **voler bene a** be fond of. **benino** *avv* fairly well, reasonably.
***benedire** [bene'dire] *v* bless, consecrate. **benedetto** *agg* blessed. **benedetti voi!** lucky you!
beneducato [benedu'kato] *agg* well-mannered.
beneficenza [benefi'tʃɛntsa] *sf* charity.
beneficio [bene'fitʃo] *sm* profit; advantage. **benefico** *agg* beneficial.
benessere [be'nɛssere] *sm* well-being, welfare.
benestante [benes'tante] *agg* comfortably off, well-to-do. **benestare** *sm* well-being; (*autorizzazione*) consent.
benevolo [be'nɛvolo] *agg* kindly, well-disposed.
beninteso [benin'tezo] *avv* naturally, of course.
benvenuto [benve'nuto] *sm*, *agg* welcome. **dare il benvenuto a** welcome.
benzina [ben'dzina] *sf* petrol. **far benzina** fill up. **distributore di benzina** *sm* petrol station *or* pump.
***bere** ['bere] *v* drink.
bernoccolo [ber'nokkolo] *sm* bump; (*disposizione*) flair.
berretto [ber'retto] *sm* cap, hat.
bersaglio [ber'saʎʎo] *sm* target.
bestemmia [bes'temmja] *sf* swear-word, curse. **bestemmiare** *v* swear, curse.
bestia ['bestja] *sf* animal, beast; ignoramus. **bestiale** *agg* bestial, brutal; (*fam: intenso*) beastly.
bestiame [bes'tjame] *sm* livestock.
betoniera [beto'njɛra] *sf* cement-mixer.
bettola ['bettola] *sf* low dive.
betulla [be'tulla] *sf* birch.
bevanda [be'vanda] *sf* drink, beverage. **bevibile** *agg* drinkable.
biada ['bjada] *sf* fodder, forage.
biancheria [bjanke'ria] *sf* (*indumenti intimi*) underwear; (*da casa*) linen.
bianchetti [bjan'ketti] *sm pl* whitebait *pl*.
bianchetto [bjan'ketto] *sm* whitewash.
bianco ['bjanko] *agg* white; (*non scritto*) blank. **sm** white.
biancospino [bjanko'spino] *sm* hawthorn.
biascicare [bjaʃi'kare] *v* (*cibo*) munch; (*parole*) mumble.
biasimare [bjazi'mare] *v* blame. **biasimo** *sm* blame.
Bibbia ['bibbja] *sf* Bible. **biblico** *agg* biblical.

bibita ['bibita] *sf* (soft) drink, beverage.
bibliografia [bibljogra'fia] *sf* bibliography. **bibliografico** *agg* bibliographical. **bibliografo, -a** *sm, sf* bibliographer.
biblioteca [bibljo'tɛka] *sf* library. **bibliotecario, -a** *sm, sf* librarian.
bicchiere [bik'kjɛre] *sm* glass, tumbler.
bicicletta [bitʃi'kletta] *sf* bicycle. **andare in bicicletta** cycle.
bicipite [bi'tʃipite] *sm* biceps.
bidè [bi'dɛ] *sm* bidet.
bidone [bi'done] *sm* drum, can.
bieco ['bjɛko] *agg* **guardare con occhio bieco** look askance at.
biennale [bien'nale] *agg* biennial. *sf* biennial event.
bietta ['bjetta] *sf* wedge.
biforcarsi [bifor'karsi] *v* branch off, fork. **biforcazione** *sf* fork, junction.
bigamia [biga'mia] *sf* bigamy. **bigamo** *sm* bigamist.
bighellonare [bigello'nare] *v* idle; (*girellare*) saunter.
bigio ['bidʒo] *agg* grey; (*tempo*) dull.
bigliardo [bi'ʎardo] *sm* billiards.
biglietto [bi'ʎetto] *sm* ticket; note; card. **bigliettaio, -a** *sm, sf* conductor. **biglietteria** *sf* booking-office.
bigodino [bigo'dino] *sm* curler, roller.
bigotto [bi'gɔtto], **-a** *sm, sf* bigot. *agg* bigoted.
bilancia [bi'lantʃa] *sf* scales *pl*; (*comm*) balance. **Bilancia** *sf* Libra. **bilanciare** *v* balance; (*pesare*) weigh.
bilancio [bi'lantʃo] *sm* balance sheet; budget.
bile ['bile] *sf* bile.
bilico ['biliko] *sm* **in bilico** in the balance.
bilingue [bi'lingwe] *agg* bilingual.
bilione [bi'ljone] *sm* a thousand millions.
bimbo ['bimbo], **-a** *sm, sf* child (*pl* -ren).
bimensile [bimen'sile] *agg* fortnightly.
binario [bi'narjo] *agg* binary. *sm* rails *pl*, railway line.
binocolo [bi'nɔkolo] *sm* binoculars *pl*.
biochimico [bio'kimiko], **-a** *agg* biochemical. *sm, sf* biochemist. *sf* (*scienza*) biochemistry.
biografia [biogra'fia] *sf* biography. **biografico** *agg* biographical. **biografo, -a** *sm, sf* biographer.
biologia [biolo'dʒia] *sf* biology. **biologico** *agg* biological. **biologo, -a** *sm, sf* biologist.
biondo ['bjondo] *agg* blond, fair-haired.
birbante [bir'bante] *sm* rascal, knave.
birbone [bir'bone] *sm* rogue, scamp.
birichino [biri'kino], **-a** *sm, sf* imp, mischievous child. *agg* impish, cheeky. **birichinata** *sf* childish prank.
birillo [bi'rillo] *sm* skittle.
birra ['birra] *sf* beer. **birreria** *sf* public house.
bis [bis] *inter* encore! **dare il bis** give an encore.
bisaccia [bi'zattʃa] *sf* knapsack, saddlebag.
bisbetico [biz'bɛtiko] *agg* cantankerous, peevish.
bisbigliare [bizbi'ʎare] *v* whisper. **bisbiglio** *sm* whisper.
biscia ['biʃa] *sf* snake.
biscotto [bis'kɔtto] *sm* biscuit.
bisestile [bizes'tile] *agg* **anno bisestile** leap-year.
bisognare [bizo'ɲare] *v* be necessary. **bisogno** *sm* need, requirement. **aver bisogno di** need. **non c'è bisogno** there is no need. **bisognoso** *agg* needy.
bistecca [bis'tekka] *sf* steak.
bisticciare [bistit'tʃare] *v* quarrel. **bisticcio** *sm* quarrel.
bistrattare [bistrat'tare] *v* ill-treat.
bitorzolo [bi'tortsolo] *sf* pimple.
bivio ['bivjo] *sm* junction, fork.
bizzarro [bid'dzarro] *agg* strange, odd.
bizzeffe [bid'dzɛffe] *avv* **a bizzeffe** galore.
blandire [blan'dire] *v* caress, entice. **blandizie** *sf pl* flattery *sing*.
blando ['blando] *agg* bland, mellow.
blasfemo [blas'fɛmo] *agg* blasphemous.
blatta ['blatta] *sf* cockroach.
blesità [blezi'ta] *sf* lisp. **parlar bleso** lisp.
bloccare [blok'kare] *v* block, blockade. **blocco** *sm* block; (*massa*) lump; blockade; (*ostruzione*) blockage. **in blocco** in bulk.
blu [blu] *agg* blue. **bluastro** *agg* bluish.
blusa ['bluza] *sf* blouse.
boa[1] ['bɔa] *sm invar* (*zool*) boa.
boa[2] *sf* (*mar*) buoy.
boato [bo'ato] *sm* roar, rumble. **boato sonico** sonic bang.
bobina [bo'bina] *sf* bobbin, reel.
bocca ['bokka] *sf* mouth; (*apertura*) opening. **in bocca al lupo!** good luck!
boccale [bok'kale] *sm* tankard.
boccata [bok'kata] *sf* mouthful.

bocchino [bok'kino] *sm* mouthpiece; cigarette-holder.
boccia ['bɔttʃa] *sf* (*sport*) bowl; (*vaso*) decanter; (*bot*) bud.
bocciare [bot'tʃare] *v* (*dir*) repeal; (*esami*) fail.
boccio ['bɔttʃo] *sm also* **bocciolo** bud.
boccone [bok'kone] *sm* mouthful.
bocconi [bok'koni] *avv* prone, flat on one's face.
bofonchiare [bofon'kjare] *v* snort.
boia ['bɔja] *sm invar* executioner. **boiata** *sf* (*fam*) rubbish.
boicottare [boikot'tare] *v* boycott. **boicottaggio** *sm* boycott.
bolide ['bɔlide] *sm* fire-ball. **andare come un bolide** go like a bomb. **passare come un bolide** flash past.
bolla[1] ['bolla] *sf* bubble; (*med*) blister.
bolla[2] ['bolla] *sf* (*sigillo*) seal; (*papale*) bull; (*comm*) bill.
bollare [bol'lare] *v* seal, stamp.
bolletta [bol'letta] *sf* (*comm*) bill, receipt. **essere in bolletta** (*fam*) be broke. **bollettino** *sm* bulletin, list.
bollire [bol'lire] *v* boil. **bollente** *agg* boiling. **bollito** *sm* boiled meat. **bollitore** *sm* kettle.
bollo ['bollo] *sm* stamp, seal. **bollo di circolazione** tax disc.
bomba ['bomba] *sf* bomb.
bombardare [bombar'dare] *v* bomb, shell. **bombardamento** *sm* bombardment, shelling.
bombetta [bom'betta] *sf* bowler hat.
bombola ['bombola] *sf* gas cylinder.
bonario [bo'narjo] *agg* good-natured.
bontà [bon'ta] *sf* goodness.
borbottare [borbot'tare] *v* mutter; rumble.
bordello [bor'dɛllo] *sm* brothel; (*confusione*) uproar.
bordo ['bordo] *sm* (*mar*) side; (*orlo*) border, edge. **a bordo** on board. **giornale di bordo** *sm* (ship's) log. **virare di bordo** (*mar*) tack.
borghese [bor'geze] *agg* bourgeois, middle-class; civilian. *s*(*m*+*f*) middle-class person; civilian. **in borghese** in civilian *or* plain clothes. **borghesia** *sf* middle class, bourgeoisie.
borgo ['borgo] *sm* (*paesello*) hamlet; (*sobborgo*) suburb.
boria ['bɔrja] *sf* conceit, arrogance. **metter su boria** put on airs. **borioso** arrogant, conceited.
borotalco [boro'talko] *sm invar* talcum powder.
borsa[1] ['borsa] *sf* bag; (*della spesa*) shopping bag; (*per documenti*) brief-case; (*diplomatica*) attaché case; (*dell'acqua*) hot-water bottle. **borsa di studio** scholarship, grant. **borsaiolo** *sm* pickpocket. **borsetta** *sf* handbag. **borsista** *s*(*m*+*f*) scholarship-holder.
borsa[2] ['borsa] *sf* (*comm*) stock exchange. **borsa nera** black market. **borsista** *sm* stockbroker.
bosco ['bɔsko] *sm* wood, forest. **boscaglia** *sf* thicket. **boschereccio** *agg* woody. **boschetto** *sm* grove. **boscoso** *agg* wooded.
botanico [bo'taniko], **-a** *agg* botanical. *sm*, *sf* botanist. *sf* botany.
botta ['bɔtta] *sf* blow. **fare a botte** come to blows. **dare le botte a** spank, slap.
botte ['botte] *sf* cask, barrel.
bottega [bot'tega] *sf* shop; (*laboratorio*) workshop. **bottegaio, -a** *sm*, *sf* shopkeeper. **botteghino** *sm* small shop; (*teatro*) box-office.
bottiglia [bot'tiʎa] *sf* bottle.
bottone [bot'tone] *sm* button. **attaccare un bottone a** (*fam*) buttonhole. **bottoni gemelli** cuff-links *pl*.
bozza ['bɔttsa] *sf* draft, sketch; (*stampa*) galley proof. **bozzetto** *sm* sketch.
bozzolo ['bɔttsolo] *sm* cocoon.
braccetto [brat'tʃetto] *sm* **a braccetto** arm in arm.
braccialetto [brattʃa'letto] *sm* bracelet.
bracciante [brat'tʃante] *sm* labourer.
bracciata [brat'tʃata] *sf* armful.
braccio ['brattʃo] *sm*, *pl* **-a** *f in anat sense* arm. **prendere in braccio** take into one's arms. **bracciolo** *sm* (*sedia*) arm.
braciola [bra'tʃɔla] *sf* chop.
bramare [bra'mare] *v* yearn *or* long for. **brama** *sf* longing, strong desire.
branchia ['brankja] *sf* gill.
branco ['branko] *sm* flock, drove, herd.
brancolare [branko'lare] *v* grope.
branda ['branda] *sf* camp-bed.
brandello [bran'dɛllo] *sm* shred, tatter.
brandire [bran'dire] *v* brandish.
brano ['brano] *sm* (*pezzo*) shred, piece; (*frammento di opera*) passage, extract.
branzino [bran'dzino] *sm* sea bass.
brasare [bra'zare] *v* braise. **brasato** *sm* braised beef.

bravo ['bravo] *agg* good; capable; (*dabbene*) decent. *inter* well done! **bravura** *sf* skill.
breccia ['brettʃa] *sf* breach.
bretelle [bre'tɛlle] *sf pl* braces *pl.*
breve ['brɛve] *agg* brief, short. *sf* breve. **per farla breve** to cut a long story short. **tra breve** shortly. **brevità** *sf* brevity.
brevetto [bre'vetto] *sm* patent. **brevettare** *v* patent.
brezza ['brettsa] *sf* breeze.
bricco ['brikko] *sm* jug, pot.
briccone [brik'kone] *sm* knave, rascal. *agg* knavish, mischievous.
briciola ['britʃola] *sf* crumb. **briciolo** *sm* tiny piece, morsel.
bridge ['bridʒ] *sm invar* (*carte*) bridge.
briga ['briga] *sf* trouble. **attaccar briga** pick a quarrel. **darsi** *or* **prendersi la briga di** go to the trouble of.
brigadiere [briga'djɛre] *sm* sergeant-major; (*generale*) brigadier.
brigante [bri'gante] *sm* brigand, bandit.
brigata [bri'gata] *sf* company, group; (*mil*) brigade; (*uccelli*) flock.
briglia ['briʎa] *sf* bridle. **tenere in briglia** rein in, restrain.
brillare [bril'lare] *v* shine, sparkle, glitter. **brillante** *agg* sparkling, brilliant. **brillo** *agg* tipsy.
brina ['brina] *sf* rime, hoar-frost.
brindare [brin'dare] *v* **brindare a** drink to, toast.
brindello [brin'dɛllo] *sm* shred, tatter.
brindisi ['brindizi] *sm* toast. **fare un brindisi a** drink to, toast.
brio ['brio] *sm* liveliness, vivacity.
britannico [bri'tanniko], **-a** *agg* British. *sm, sf* Briton, British person.
brivido ['brivido] *sm* shudder, shiver. **aver dei brividi** shudder, shiver.
brocca ['brɔkka] *sf* jug, pitcher.
broccolo ['brɔkkolo] *sm* broccoli.
brodo ['brɔdo] *sm* broth, soup. **tutto fa brodo** it is all grist to the mill.
broglio ['brɔʎo] *sm* malpractice, racket.
bronchite [bron'kite] *sf* bronchitis.
broncio ['brontʃo] *sm* **tenere** *or* **portare il broncio** sulk.
brontolare [bronto'lare] *v* mutter, grumble. **brontolone, -a** *sm, sf* grumbler.
bronzo ['brondzo] *sm* bronze.
bruciapelo [brutʃa'pelo] *sm* **a bruciapelo** point-blank.
bruciare [bru'tʃare] *v* burn, scorch. **bruciare le tappe** hurry. **bruciatura** *sf* burn, scald. **bruciore** *sm* burning sensation, intense desire.
bruco ['bruko] *sm* larva, caterpillar.
brufolo ['brufolo] *sm* pimple.
brughiera [bru'gjɛra] *sf* heath, moor.
brulicare [bruli'kare] *v* swarm, crawl, teem. **brulichio** *sm* swarming, teeming.
brullo ['brullo] *agg* bleak; barren.
bruno ['bruno] *agg* brown; dark.
brusco ['brusko] *agg* sharp; brusque, harsh; (*improvviso*) sudden.
brusio [bru'zio] *sm* bustle, hum.
bruto ['bruto] *sm, agg* brute. **brutale** *agg* brutal.
brutto ['brutto] *agg* ugly, plain; (*non buono*) bad. **avere brutta cera** look poorly. **far brutta figura** cut a sorry figure, disgrace oneself. **il brutto è che** the worst is (that), the difficulty is (that).
buca ['buka] *sf* hole, pit. **buca delle lettere** *sf* letter-box. **bucare** *v* make a hole in; (*biglietto*) punch; (*gomma*) puncture. **bucatura** *sf* puncture.
bucaneve [buka'neve] *sm invar* snowdrop.
bucato [bu'kato] *sm* washing. **fare il bucato** do the washing.
buccia ['buttʃa] *sf* peel, skin, rind.
buco ['buko] *sm* hole. **buco nell'acqua** failure.
buddismo [bud'dizmo] *sm* Buddhism. **buddista** *s*(*m*+*f*), *agg* Buddhist.
budello [bu'dɛllo] *sm* gut.
budino [bu'dino] *sm* pudding.
bue ['bue] *sm, pl* **buoi** ox (*pl* -en); (*carne*) beef.
bufalo ['bufalo], **-a** *sm, sf* buffalo.
bufera [bu'fɛra] *sf* gale, blizzard.
buffè [buf'fɛ] *sm invar* (*credenza*) sideboard; (*gastr*) buffet.
buffo ['buffo] *agg* comic(al), amusing. *sm* (*teatro*) comic. **il buffo è che** the odd thing is (that).
bugia[1] [bu'dʒia] *sf* lie. **dire bugie** tell lies. **bugiardo, -a** *sm, sf* liar.
bugia[2] [bu'dʒia] *sf* candlestick.
buio ['bujo] *sm, agg* dark. **al buio** in the dark. **buio pesto** pitch-dark.
bulbo ['bulbo] *sm* bulb. **bulbo oculare** eyeball.
Bulgaria [bulga'ria] *sf* Bulgaria. **bulgaro, -a** *s, agg* Bulgarian.
bullone [bul'lone] *sm* bolt.

buono[1] ['bwɔno], **-a** *agg* good; kind; (*giusto*) right. **a buon conto** apropos. **a buon mercato** cheap(ly). **alla buona** simply. **buoncostume** *sm* good conduct. **buongustaio, -a** *sm, sf* gourmet. **buongusto** *sm* good taste. **buono a nulla** *sm, agg* good-for-nothing. **buonsenso** *sm* good sense. **con le buone o con le cattive** by hook or by crook. *sm, sf* good person.
buono[2] ['bwɔno] *sm* (*documento*) bond, coupon, voucher.
buonora [bwo'nora] *sf* **alla buonora!** at last! **di buonora** early.
burattino [burat'tino] *sm* puppet.
burbero ['burbero], **-a** *agg* grumpy, gruff. *sm, sf* grumpy person.
burlare [bur'lare] *v* make a fool of; (*scherzare*) joke. **burlarsi di** make fun of. **burla** *sf* joke, jest.
burocrate [bu'rɔkrate] *sm* bureaucrat. **burocratico** *agg* bureaucratic. **burocrazia** *sf* bureaucracy; (*fam*) red tape.
burrasca [bur'raska] *sf* blizzard, storm. **burrascoso** *agg* stormy.
burro ['burro] *sm* butter.
burrone [bur'rone] *sm* ravine.
bussare [bus'sare] *v* knock.
bussola ['bussola] *sf* compass.
busta ['busta] *sf* envelope.
bustarella [busta'rella] *sf* bribe.
busto ['busto] *sm* bust; (*indumento*) corset.
buttare [but'tare] throw. **buttar giù** (*cibo*) gulp down; (*scritto*) jot down; (*gastr*) put in boiling water.

C

cabina [ka'bina] *sf* (*aero, mar*) cabin; (*telefono, ecc.*) booth; (*ascensore*) cage.
cablogramma [kablo'gramma] *sm* cable.
cacao [ka'kao] *sm* cocoa.
cacare [ka'kare] *v* (*volg*) shit.
caccia[1] ['kattʃa] *sf* hunt, chase; (*ricerca*) pursuit, search. **a caccia di** in search of. **caccia grossa** big game. **dar la caccia** pursue.
caccia[2] ['kattʃa] *sm invar* (*aero*) fighter; (*mar*) destroyer.
cacciagione [kattʃa'dʒone] *sf* game.
cacciare [kat'tʃare] *v* hunt; (*espellere*) throw *or* drive out; (*introdurre*) thrust; (*mettere*) stick, put.
cacciavite [kattʃa'vite] *sm* screwdriver.
cachi ['kaki] *agg, sm* khaki.
cacio ['katʃo] *sm* cheese.
cactus ['kaktus] *sm* cactus.
cadauno [kada'uno] *agg, pron* each.
cadavere [ka'davere] *sm* corpse.
***cadere** [ka'dere] *v* fall; (*aero*) crash. **cader dalle nuvole** be dumbfounded. **lasciar cadere** drop. **caduta** *sf* fall; (*aero*) crash.
cadetto [ka'detto] *sm* younger son; (*mil*) cadet.
caffè [kaf'fɛ] *sm* coffee; (*locale*) café. **caffettiera** *sf* coffee-pot; (*macchina*) coffee-maker.
caffeina [kaffe'ina] *sf* caffeine.
cafone [ka'fone] *sm* (*fam*) lout.
cagionare [kadʒo'nare] *v* cause. **cagione** *sf* cause, reason. **a cagion di** on account of, owing to.
cagna ['kaɲa] *sf* bitch.
cagnara [ka'ɲara] *sf* (*fam*) row, uproar.
calabrone [kala'brone] *sm* hornet.
calamaio [kala'majo] *sm* inkstand, inkwell.
calamaro [kala'maro] *sm* squid.
calamita [kala'mita] *sf* magnet.
calamità [kalami'ta] *sf* calamity.
calare [ka'lare] *v* lower, let down; (*maglia*) decrease, cast off; (*scendere*) go down; (*abbassarsi*) drop. **calata** *sf* descent; (*banchina*) quay.
calcagno [kal'kaɲo] *sm* heel. **stare alle calcagna di** follow closely.
calcare[1] [kal'kare] *v* press (hard); (*disegno*) trace. **calco** *sm* (*impronta di rilievo*) cast; (*disegno*) tracing.
calcare[2] [kal'kare] *sm* limestone.
calce ['kaltʃe] *sf* lime.
calcestruzzo [kaltʃes'truttso] *sm* concrete.
calcio[1] ['kaltʃo] *sm* (*chim*) calcium.
calcio[2] ['kaltʃo] *sm* (*fucile*) (rifle) butt.
calcio[3] ['kaltʃo] *sm* kick; (*sport*) football. **calcio di rigore** penalty (kick). **dare un calcio** kick.
calcolare [kalko'lare] *v* calculate; consider. **calcolatore, -trice** *sm, sf* calculator, computer.
calcolo[1] ['kalkolo] *sm* calculation; (*congettura*) reckoning; (*mat*) calculus. **a calcoli fatti** all things considered.
calcolo[2] ['kalkolo] *sm* (*med*) calculus, stone.

caldaia [kal'daja] *sf* boiler.
caldo ['kaldo] *agg* warm; (*molto*) hot. *sm* warmth; heat. **aver** *or* **far caldo** be hot.
caleidoscopio [kaleido'skɔpjo] *sm* kaleidoscope.
calendario [kalen'darjo] *sm* calendar.
calibro ['kalibro] *sm* calibre; (*mec*) gauge; (*strumento*) callipers *pl*.
calice ['kalitʃe] *sm* goblet; (*rel*) chalice; (*bot*) calyx.
caligine [ka'lidʒine] *sf* fog.
calligrafia [kalligra'fia] *sf* handwriting.
callo ['kallo] *sm* corn. **callifugo** *sm, pl* **-ghi** corn-plaster.
calmare [kal'mare] *v* calm; ease. **calmarsi** *v* calm down. **calma** *sf* calm, tranquillity. **perdere la calma** lose one's temper. **prendersela con calma** take it easy. **calmante** *sm* sedative. **calmo** *agg* calm.
calore [ka'lore] *sm* heat; (*cordialità*) warmth.
caloria [kalo'ria] *sf* calorie.
calorifero [kalo'rifero] *sm* radiator.
caloroso [kalo'rozo] *agg* warm.
calpestare [kalpes'tare] *v* trample on.
calunnia [ka'lunnja] *sf* calumny; (*diffamazione orale*) slander; (*scritta*) libel. **calunniare** *v* slander; libel.
calvo ['kalvo] *agg* bald. **calvizie** *sf* baldness.
calza ['kaltsa] *sf* (*corta*) sock; (*lunga*) stocking. **fare la calza** knit. **ferro da calza** *sm* knitting-needle.
calzare [kal'tsare] *v* put on; (*portare*) wear; (*convenire*) fit. **calzatura** *sf* footwear.
calzolaio [kaltso'lajo] *sm* shoemaker. **calzoleria** *sf* shoe shop.
calzoni [kal'tsoni] *sm pl* trousers *pl*.
camaleonte [kamale'onte] *sm* chameleon.
cambiale [kam'bjale] *sf* bill of exchange.
cambiare [kam'bjare] *v* change. **cambiar casa** move. **tanto per cambiare** just for a change. **cambiamento** *sm* change.
cambio ['kambjo] *sm* change; (*econ*) exchange; (*auto*) transmission, gearbox.
camera ['kamera] *sf* room; (*da letto*) bedroom; (*assemblea, tec*) chamber. **camera d'aria** (*pneumatico*) inner tube. **musica da camera** *sf* chamber music.
camerata[1] [kame'rata] *sf* dormitory.
camerata[2] [kame'rata] *s(m+f)* comrade; (*fam*) mate.
cameriera [kame'rjɛra] *sf* (*albergo*) chamber-maid; (*ristorante*) waitress; (*domestica*) maid.
cameriere [kame'rjɛre] *sm* (*ristorante*) waiter; servant.
camicia [ka'mitʃa] *sf* shirt; (*da donna*) blouse; (*tec*) jacket. **camicia da notte** night-gown. **camicia di forza** strait-jacket. **camiciola** *sf* (*maglia*) vest; T-shirt.
camino [ka'mino] *sm* fireplace; chimney.
camion ['kamjon] *sm invar* lorry. **camioncino** *sm* van.
cammello [kam'mɛllo] *sm* camel.
camminare [kammi'nare] *v* walk; (*procedere*) go. **camminata** *sf* walk.
cammino [kam'mino] *sm* way; (*percorso*) journey; (*sentiero*) path. **mettersi in cammino** set out.
camorra [ka'mɔrra] *sf* racket. **camorrista** *s(m+f)* racketeer.
camoscio [ka'mɔʃo] *sm* chamois; (*pelle*) chamois leather.
campagna [kam'paɲa] *sf* country; (*paesaggio*) countryside; (*terreno*) land; (*villeggiatura*) holidays *pl*; (*mil, propaganda, ecc.*) campaign. **campagnolo** *agg* rural, country.
campana [kam'pana] *sf* bell; (*di lampada*) lampshade. **campanello** *sm* bell. **campanile** *sm* bell tower.
campare [kam'pare] *v* live.
campeggiare [kamped'dʒare] *v* camp. **campeggio** *sm* camping; (*terreno*) campsite.
campestre [kam'pɛstre] *agg* rural, country.
campione [kam'pjone] *sm* (*sport, difensore*) champion; (*piccola quantità*) sample; (*di tessuto*) pattern. **campionario** *sm* sample collection; pattern book. **campionessa** *sf* champion.
campo ['kampo] *sm* field. **campo di golf** golf-course. **campo di tennis** tennis court.
camposanto [kampo'santo] *sm* cemetery.
camuffamento [kamuffa'mento] *sm* disguise; (*mil*) camouflage. **camuffare** *v* disguise; camouflage.
camuso [ka'muzo] *agg* snub-nosed.
Canada ['kanada] *sm* Canada. **Canadese** *s(m+f)*, *agg* Canadian.
canaglia [ka'naʎa] *sf* scoundrel; (*marmaglia*) rabble.
canale [ka'nale] *sm* canal; (*radio, TV*) channel. **Canale della Manica** (English)

Channel. **canale di scarico** drain. **canale di scolo** gutter.
canapa ['kanapa] *sf* hemp.
canapè [kana'pɛ] *sm* (*mobile*) settee; (*tartina*) canapé.
canarino [kana'rino] *sm* canary. *agg* canary yellow.
cancellare [kantʃel'lare] *v* cancel, wipe out; (*con gomma*) rub out; (*con penna*) cross out.
cancelliere [kantʃel'ljɛre] *sm* chancellor. **cancelleria** *sf* chancellery, chancery; (*cartoleria*) stationery.
cancello [kan'tʃɛllo] *sm* gate. **cancellata** *sf* railings *pl*.
cancro [kan'kro] *sm* cancer. **Cancro** *sm* Cancer.
cancrena [kan'krɛna] *sf* gangrene.
candeggiare [kanded'dʒare] *v* bleach. **candeggina** *sf* bleach.
candela [kan'dela] *sf* candle; (*auto*) sparking-plug. **precipitare in candela** do a nose-dive. **candelabro** *sm* candlestick; (*a bracci*) candelabra.
candidato [kandi'dato], **-a** *sm, sf* candidate. **candidatura** *sf* candidature.
candido ['kandido] *agg* spotless, snow-white; (*sincero*) candid.
candito [kan'dito] *agg* candied, crystallized.
cane ['káne] *sm* dog. **cane bastardo** mongrel. **cane da guardia** watch-dog. **cane da salotto** lap-dog.
canestro [ka'nɛstro] *sm* basket.
canguro [kan'guro] *sm* kangaroo.
canicola [ka'nikola] *sm* heat-wave.
canile [ka'nile] *sm* kennel.
canino [ka'nino] *agg* canine.
canna ['kanna] *sf* cane; (*pianta*) reed; (*fucile*) barrel; (*bicicletta*) cross-bar; (*pesca*) rod; (*tubo, organo*) pipe. **cannello** *sm* tube; (*per saldare*) blowpipe.
cannella [kan'nɛlla] *sf* cinnamon.
cannibale [kan'nibale] *sm* cannibal.
cannocchiale [kannok'kjale] *sm* telescope.
cannone [kan'none] *sm* cannon. **cannonata** *sf* cannon shot. **è una cannonata!** (*fam*) it's terrific!
cannuccia [kan'nuttʃa] *sf* (*per bibite*) (drinking) straw; (*di pipa*) stem.
canoa [ka'nɔa] *sf* canoe.
canone ['kanone] *sm* canon; (*soldi dovuti*) fee; (*per affitto*) rent.
canonico [ka'nɔniko] *agg* canonical. **diritto canonico** *sm* canon law. **canonica** *sf* rectory.
canonizzare [kanonid'dzare] *v* canonize.
canottaggio [kanot'taddʒo] *sm* rowing. **canottiere** *sm* oarsman.
canottiera [kanot'tjɛra] *sf* T-shirt.
canotto [ka'nɔtto] *sm* rowing-boat; (*di salvataggio*) lifeboat.
canovaccio [kano'vattʃo] *sm* (*per stoviglie*) dishcloth; (*teatro*) plot.
cantare [kan'tare] *v* sing; (*del gallo*) crow; (*cinguettare*) chirp; (*fam: fare la spia*) squeal. **cantata** *sf* singsong; (*musica*) cantata. **canterellare** *or* **canticchiare** *v* hum.
cantiere [kan'tjɛre] *sm* yard; (*mar*) shipyard, dockyard.
cantilena [kanti'lɛna] *sf* singsong.
cantina [kan'tina] *sf* cellar.
canto[1] ['kanto] *sm* song; (*poesia*) lyric; (*liturgia*) chant. **canto popolare** folk-song.
canto[2] ['kanto] *sm* (*angolo*) corner; (*parte*) side. **da canto** aside. **d'altro canto** on the other hand. **da un canto** in a way.
cantone[1] [kan'tone] *sm* corner. **cantonata** *sf* (street-)corner; (*errore*) blunder. **prendere una cantonata** blunder.
cantone[2] [kan'tone] *sm* (*geog*) canton.
cantoniere [kanto'njɛre] *sm* (*ferr*) signalman.
canuto [ka'nuto] *agg* white-haired.
canzonare [kantso'nare] *v* make fun of, tease, mock. **canzonatore, -trice** *sm, sf* mocker. **canzonatura** *sf* mockery.
canzone [kan'tsone] *sf* song; (*discorso noioso*) old story. **canzonetta** *sf* pop song.
caos ['kaɔs] *sm* chaos. **caotico** *agg* chaotic.
capace [ka'patʃe] *agg* (*abile*) capable; (*in grado di*) able. **capacità** *sf* capacity; ability.
capanna [ka'panna] *sf* hut. **capannone** *sm* shed; (*aero*) hangar.
caparbio [ka'parbjo] *agg* stubborn.
caparra [ka'parra] *sf* deposit.
capello [ka'pello] *sm* hair. **capelli** *sm pl* hair *sing*. **averne fin sopra i capelli (di)** be heartily sick (of). **capelluto** *agg* hairy. **cuoio capelluto** *sm* scalp.
capezzale [kapet'tsale] *sm* **al capezzale** at the bedside.
capezzolo [ka'pettsolo] *sm* nipple.
capire [ka'pire] *v* understand; (*rendersi*

conto) realize. **farsi capire** make oneself understood. **si capisce** naturally.
capitale [kapi'tale] *sm* (*econ*) capital. *sf* capital (city). *agg* capital. fundamental; (*principale*) main. **capitalismo** *sm* capitalism. **capitalista** *s*(*m*+*f*), *agg* capitalist.
capitano [kapi'tano] *sm* captain.
capitare [kapi'tare] *v* (*giungere*) turn up; (*presentarsi*) arise, come up; (*accadere*) happen. **capitar bene** strike lucky. **dove capita** anywhere.
capitello [kapi'tɛllo] *sm* capital.
capitolo [ka'pitolo] *sm* chapter. **aver voce in capitolo** have a say in the matter.
capo ['kapo] *sm* head; (*pezzo*) item; (*geog*) cape. **da capo** again, from the beginning. **da capo a fondo** from top to bottom. **da un capo all'altro** from one end to the other. **in capo a** within. **per sommi capi** briefly, in short. **venire a capo di** get to the bottom of.
capobanda [kapo'banda] *sm invar* ringleader; (*musica*) bandmaster.
capodanno [kapo'danno] *sm* New Year's Day.
capofitto [kapo'fitto] *agg* **a capofitto** headlong; (*con massimo impegno*) wholeheartedly.
capogiro [kapo'dʒiro] *sm* giddiness, dizzy spell. **fare venire il capogiro a** make dizzy.
capolavoro [kapola'voro] *sm* masterpiece.
capolinea [kapo'linea] *sm*, *pl* **capilinea** terminus.
capoluogo [kapo'lwɔgo] *sm*, *pl* **-ghi** main town, capital.
capomastro [kapo'mastro] *sm* foreman.
capoofficina [kapoofi'tʃina] *sm*, *pl* **capiofficina** foreman.
caporale [kapo'rale] *sm* corporal.
caposala [kapo'sala] *s*(*m*+*f*), *pl* **capisala, caposala** (*fabbrica*) foreman; (*albergo*) head-waiter; (*ospedale*) ward sister.
capostazione [kaposta'tsjone] *sm*, *pl* **capistazione** station-master.
capotare [kapo'tare] *v* (*auto*) overturn; (*mar*) capsize.
capote [ka'pɔt] *sf*, *pl* **-s** (*auto*) hood.
capotreno [kapo'trɛno] *sm* guard.
***capovolgere** [kapo'vɔldʒere] *v* overturn; (*fig*) turn upside down, reverse; (*mar*) capsize. **capovolgimento** *sm* reversal.
cappa ['kappa] *sf* cloak; (*di camino*) hood.
cappella[1] [kap'pɛlla] *sf* chapel. **cappellano** *sm* chaplain.
cappella[2] [kap'pɛlla] *sf* (*di fungo*) cap.
cappello [kap'pɛllo] *sm* hat. **cappellaio** *sm* hatter.
cappero ['kappero] *sm* caper. **capperi!** *inter* gosh! good heavens!
cappotta [kap'pɔtta] *sf* (*auto*) hood.
cappotto [kap'pɔtto] *sm* coat; (*bridge*) slam.
cappuccino [kapput'tʃino] *sm* coffee with milk, cappuccino; (*rel*) Capuchin friar.
cappuccio [kap'puttʃo] *sm* hood; (*tec*) cap; (*rel*) cowl.
capra ['kapra] *sf* goat. **capretto** *sm* kid. **capro** *sm* he-goat. **capro espiatorio** scapegoat.
capriccio [ka'prittʃo] *sm* whim, fancy. **fare i capricci** have tantrums.
Capricorno [kapri'kɔrno] *sm* Capricorn.
caprifoglio [kapri'fɔʎʎo] *sm* honeysuckle.
capriola[1] [kapri'ɔla] *sf* somersault, jump.
capriola[2] [kapri'ɔla] *sf* (*zool*) roe deer. **capriolo** *sm* roebuck.
capsico [kap'siko] *sm* capsicum.
capsula ['kapsula] *sf* capsule; (*di dente*) crown.
carabiniere [karabi'njɛre] *sm* policeman, soldier in police corps.
caraffa [ka'raffa] *sf* carafe, jug.
caramella [kara'mɛlla] *sf* sweet. **caramellato** *agg* candied; (*zucchero*) caramelized.
carato [ka'rato] *sm* carat.
carattere [ka'rattere] *sm* (*indole*) nature; (*forza, lettera*) character; characteristic; (*teatro*) role; type. **caratteristica** *sf* characteristic, (distinctive) feature; (*tec*) specification. **caratteristico** *agg* typical, distinctive.
carboidrato [karboi'drato] *sm* carbohydrate.
carbonchio [kar'bonkjo] *sm* carbuncle; (*vet*) anthrax; (*agric*) blight.
carbone [kar'bone] *sm* coal. **carbone coke** coke. **carbone di legna** charcoal. **carboncino** *sm* (*disegno*) charcoal.
carbonio [kar'bɔnjo] *sm* carbon.
carburante [karbu'rante] *sm* fuel.
carburatore [karbura'tore] *sm* carburettor.
carcassa [kar'kassa] *sf* carcass; (*fam*) wreck.
carcere ['kartʃere] *sm* prison, jail. **carcerato, -a** *sm, sf* prisoner. **carceriere, -a** *sm, sf* jailer.

carciofo [kar'tʃɔfo] *sm* artichoke.

cardiaco [kar'diako] *agg* cardiac. **attacco cardiaco** *sm* heart attack. **cardiologo, -a** *sm, sf* heart specialist, cardiologist.

cardinale [kardi'nale] *sm, agg* cardinal.

cardine ['kardine] *sm* hinge; (*fig*) cornerstone.

cardo ['kardo] *sm* (*bot*) thistle.

carena [ka'rɛna] *sf* hull. **(bacino di) carenaggio** *sm* dry dock.

carestia [kares'tia] *sf* famine.

carezzare [karet'tsare] *v* stroke, caress. **carezza** *sf* caress. **fare le carezze a** pat, stroke.

cariarsi [ka'rjarsi] *v* decay.

carica ['karika] *sf* (*impiego*) position; (*ufficio pubblico*) office; (*mil, elett*) charge; (*sport*) tackle.

caricare [kari'kare] *v* load; (*riempire*) fill; (*mil, elett*) charge; (*sport*) tackle; (*orologio, molla*) wind up.

caricatura [karika'tura] *sf* caricature.

carico ['kariko] *sm, pl* **-chi** (*di nave*) cargo; (*peso*) burden; (*tec*) load. **a carico di** (*contro*) against; (*a spese di*) at the expense of, chargeable to. **testimone a carico** witness for the prosecution. *agg* loaded, filled (with), full (of).

carie ['karje] *sf* (*dentaria*) tooth decay; (*di legno, cereali, ecc.*) rot.

carino [ka'rino] *agg* lovely, charming.

carità [kari'ta] *sf* charity; (*misericordia*) compassion. **aver carità di** take pity on. **fare la carità** give alms. **per carita!** God forbid!

carlinga [kar'linga] *sf* fuselage.

carnagione [karna'dʒone] *sf* complexion, skin.

carne ['karne] *sf* flesh; (*alimento*) meat. **carne di manzo/maiale/vitello** beef/pork/veal. **carnale** *agg* carnal. **carnoso** *agg* fleshy.

carneficina [karnefi'tʃina] *sf* slaughter. **carnefice** *sm* executioner.

carnevale [karne'vale] *sm* carnival.

carnivoro [kar'nivoro], **-a** *sm, sf* carnivore. *agg* carnivorous.

caro ['karo] *agg* dear. **aver caro** hold dear. **pagar caro** pay a lot for; (*fig*) pay dearly for. **cari** *sm pl* loved ones *pl*.

carogna [ka'roɲa] *sf* carrion; (*fam*) bastard, sod.

carosello [karo'zɛllo] *sm* merry-go-round.

carota [ka'rɔta] *sf* carrot.

carovana [karo'vana] *sf* caravan; procession.

carpione [kar'pjone] *sm* **in carpione** soused.

carponi [kar'poni] *avv* on all fours.

carrabile [kar'rabile] *agg* **passo carrabile** *sm* passageway.

carreggiata [karred'dʒata] *sf* carriageway, track. **rimettersi in carreggiata** catch up. **uscire di carreggiata** go off the road; (*fig*) go astray.

carrello [kar'rɛllo] *sm* (*vagoncino*) trolley; (*mec*) (under-)carriage.

carretta [kar'retta] *sf* cart.

carriera [kar'rjɛra] *sf* career; (*velọcità*) full speed. **fare carriera** get on, make good.

carriola [karri'ɔla] *sf* wheelbarrow.

carro ['karro] *sm* (*a quattro ruote*) wagon; (*a due ruote*) cart. **carro armato** armoured vehicle, tank. **carro attrezzi** breakdown van. **carro funebre** hearse. **carro merci** goods wagon.

carrozza [kar'rɔttsa] *sf* coach. **carrozza letto** sleeping-car, sleeper. **in carrozza!** all aboard!

carrucola [kar'rukola] *sf* pulley.

carta ['karta] *sf* paper; (*geog*) map; (*da gioco, documento*) card; (*statuto*) charter. **carta asciugante** *or* **assorbente** blotting paper. **carta carbone** carbon paper. **carta da parati** wallpaper. **cartapecora** *sf* parchment. **cartapesta** *sf* papier mâché. **cartastraccia** *sf* waste paper.

cartella [kar'tɛlla] *sf* (*custodia per fogli*) folder; (*busta di pelle*) brief-case; (*per scolari*) satchel; (*scheda*) card, file.

cartellino [kartel'lino] *sm* tag.

cartellò [kar'tɛllo] *sm* (*insegna*) sign; (*indicatore*) signpost, road sign; (*avviso*) notice, poster. **cartellone** *sm* poster.

cartilagine [karti'ladʒine] *sf* cartilage.

cartolaio [karto'lajo], **-a** *sm, sf* stationer. **cartoleria** *sf* stationer's (shop).

cartolina [karto'lina] *sf* postcard.

cartone [kar'tone] *sm* cardboard; (*disegno*) cartoon. **cartoni animati** (*cinema*) cartoons *pl*. **cartoncino** *sm* card.

cartuccia [kar'tuffʃa] *sf* cartridge.

casa ['kaza] *sf* home; (*edificio, dinastia*) house; (*comm*) firm. **a casa** (*stato in luogo*) at home; (*moto a luogo*) home. **a casa del diavolo** off the beaten track. **cambiar casa** move house. **casa di cura** nursing home. **casa popolare** council house.

casalinga [kaza'linga] *sf* housewife. **casalinghi** *sm pl* household goods *pl.* **casalingo** *agg* domestic; (*semplice*) homely, plain.

cascame [kas'kame] *sm* waste.

cascare [kas'kare] *v* fall; (*capelli, denti*) fall out; (*muri, ecc.*) fall down. **cascata** *sf* fall; (*d'acqua*) waterfall; (*perle, ecc.*) cascade.

cascina [ka'ʃina] *sf* dairy farm; (*casa colonica*) farmhouse.

casco ['kasko] *sm* helmet; (*parrucchieri*) hair-drier.

caseggiato [kazed'dʒato] *sm* block of buildings.

casella [ka'zɛlla] *sf* (*riquadro*) square; (*scompartimento*) compartment. **casella postale** post-office box. **casellario** *sm* (*mobile*) filing cabinet; (*ufficio*) registry.

casello [ka'zɛllo] *sm* (*ferr*) signal-box; (*autostrada*) toll-booth.

caserma [ka'zɛrma] *sm* barracks *pl.*

casino [ka'zino] *sm* (*fam*: *confusione*) row, racket; (*postribolo*) brothel; (*casa signorile*) lodge.

casinò [kazi'nɔ] *sm* casino.

caso ['kazo] *sm* case; (*affare*) matter; (*combinazione, destino*) chance; possibility. **a caso** at random. **fare caso a** heed, attach importance to. **in caso** in case. **in caso diverso** *or* **contrario** otherwise. **in ogni caso** in any case, at any rate. **per caso** by chance. **poniamo il caso** let us suppose.

cassa ['kassa] *sf* case, box; (*istituzione*) fund; (*dove si paga*) cash desk. **cassa da morto** coffin. **cassa pronta** ready cash. **libro di cassa** cash-book.

casseruola [kasse'rwɔla] *sf* casserole, saucepan.

cassetta [kas'setta] *sf* box; (*teatro*) takings *pl.* **cassetto** *sm* drawer. **cassettone** *sm* chest of drawers.

cassiere [kas'sjɛre], **-a** *sm, sf* cashier.

casta ['kasta] *sf* caste.

castagno [kas'taɲo] *sm* chestnut tree; (*colore*) chestnut. *agg* chestnut. **castagna** *sf* chestnut. **castagnola** *sf* (*petardo*) cracker.

castello [kas'tɛllo] *sm* castle; (*impalcatura*) scaffolding. **castello di poppa** quarterdeck. **castello di prua** forecastle.

castigare [kasti'gare] *v* punish. **castigo** *sm, pl* **-ghi** punishment.

casto ['kasto] *agg* chaste. **castità** *sf* chastity.

castoro [kas'tɔro] *sm* beaver.

castrare [kas'trare] *v* castrate, geld. **castrato** *sm* (*carne*) lamb.

casuale [kazu'ale] *agg* fortuitous, accidental; (*dir*) contingent. **casualmente** *avv* by chance.

catacomba [kata'komba] *sf* catacomb.

catafascio [kata'faʃo] *sm* **andare a catafascio** go to rack and ruin.

catalizzatore [kataliddza'tore] *sm* catalyst. *agg* catalytic.

catalogo [ka'talogo] *sm, pl* **-ghi** catalogue, list. **catalogare** *v* catalogue, list.

catapulta [kata'pulta] *sf* catapult; (*missili*) launcher. **catapultare** *v* launch.

catarifrangente [katarifran'dʒɛnte] *sm* reflector.

catarro [ka'tarro] *sm* catarrh.

catasta [ka'tasta] *sf* pile.

catastrofe [ka'tastrofe] *sf* catastrophe. **catastrofico** *agg* catastrophic.

catechismo [kate'kizmo] *sm* catechism.

categoria [katego'ria] *sf* category, class. **categorico** *agg* categorical, absolute, explicit.

catena [ka'tena] *sf* chain. **catena di montaggio** assembly line. **catenaccio** *sm* bolt; (*fam*: *macchina vecchia*) old crock; (*sport*) defensive tactics *pl.*

cateratta [kate'ratta] *sf* cataract; (*chiusa*) floodgate.

catetere [kate'tɛre] *sm* catheter.

catino [ka'tino] *sm* basin. **piovere a catinelle** rain cats and dogs.

catodo ['katodo] *sm* cathode.

catrame [ka'trame] *sm* tar.

cattedra ['kattedra] *sf* (*tavola*) desk; (*ufficio di insegnante*) teaching post; (*carica universitaria*) chair.

cattedrale [katte'drale] *sf* cathedral.

cattivarsi [katti'varsi] *v* win, gain.

cattivo [kat'tivo] *agg* bad; (*in senso morale*) wicked; (*scortese*) nasty; (*capriccioso*) naughty. **cattiveria** *sf* wickedness, naughtiness; (*parole cattive*) spiteful remark.

cattolico [kat'tɔliko], **-a** *s, agg* Catholic. **Cattolicesimo** *sm* Catholicism.

catturare [kattu'rare] *v* capture, arrest. **cattura** *sf* capture, arrest.

caucciù [kaut'tʃu] *sm* rubber.

causa ['kauza] *sf* cause; (*dir*) lawsuit,

action. **a causa di** because of, on account of. **fare causa a** sue. **causale** *agg* causal.
causare [kau'zare] *v* cause, give rise to, bring about.
caustico ['kaustiko] *agg* caustic.
cauto ['kauto] *agg* cautious, careful.
cautela *sf* caution; (*precauzione*) care.
cauzione [kau'tsjone] *sf* (*caparra*) security, bail. **rilasciare su cauzione** release on bail. **cauzionare** *v* pay a deposit.
cava ['kava] *sf* quarry.
cavalcare [kaval'kare] *v* ride; (*ponte*) span. **cavalcata** *sf* ride. **cavalcavia** *sm invar* flyover. **a cavalcioni** astride.
cavaliere [kava'ljɛre] *sm* knight; (*chi cavalca*) rider.
cavalleria [kavalle'ria] *sf* (*mil*) cavalry; (*medievale, cortesia*) chivalry. **cavalleresco** *agg* chivalrous. **cavallerizza** *sf* horsewoman; (*maneggio*) riding school. **cavallerizzo** *sm* horseman; (*chi insegna*) riding master.
cavalletta [kaval'letta] *sf* grasshopper.
cavalletto [kaval'letto] *sm* (*sostegno*) trestle, stand; (*da pittore*) easel.
cavallo [ka'vallo] *sm* horse; (*scacchi*) knight. **a cavallo** on horseback. **a cavallo di** astride, straddling. **andare a cavallo** ride. **cavallo dei pantaloni** crotch. **cavalla** *sf* mare. **cavallina** *sf* filly. **correre la cavallina** sow one's wild oats.
cavare [ka'vare] *v* draw *or* pull out. **cavarsela** *v* get by, manage. **cavarsi** *v* (*togliersi*) take off. **cavatappi** *sm invar* corkscrew.
caverna [ka'vɛrna] *sf* cave. **cavernoso** *agg* cavernous, hollow.
cavia ['kavia] *sf* guinea pig.
caviale [ka'vjale] *sm* caviar.
caviglia [ka'viʎa] *sf* ankle.
cavillare [kavil'lare] *v* quibble.
cavo[1] ['kavo] *sm, agg* (*vuoto*) hollow.
cavo[2] ['kavo] *sm* cable.
cavolo ['kavolo] *sm* cabbage. **cavoli di Bruxelles** Brussels sprouts *pl*. **cavolfiore** *sm* cauliflower. **testa di cavolo** (*fam*) clot.
cazzo ['kattso] *sm* (*volg*) prick.
cazzotto [kat'tsɔtto] *sm* (*fam*) punch. **fare a cazzotti** fight.
ce [tʃe] *V* **ci**.
cece ['tʃetʃe] *sm* chick-pea.
cecità [tʃetʃi'ta] *sf* blindness.
Cecoslovacchia [tʃekozlo'vakkja] *sf* Czechoslovakia. **ceco(slovacco), -a** *s, agg* Czech(oslovak).
cedere ['tʃɛdere] *v* yield; (*trasferire*) hand over; (*piegarsi*) give way. **cedere il passo** make way. **cedere il posto** give up one's seat.
cedola ['tʃɛdola] *sf* (*scontrino*) coupon; (*di titolo*) dividend voucher.
cedro[1] ['tʃedro] *sm* (*agrume*) citron.
cedro[2] ['tʃedro] *sm* (*conifera*) cedar.
ceffone [tʃef'fone] *sm* slap (in the face).
celare [tʃe'lare] *v* conceal, hide.
celebrare [tʃele'brare] *v* celebrate.
celebre ['tʃɛlebre] *agg* famous. **celebrità** *sf* fame; (*persona*) celebrity.
celere ['tʃɛlere] *agg* rapid. *sf* flying squad.
celeste [tʃe'lɛste] *agg, sm* sky-blue.
celibe ['tʃɛlibe] *agg* single. *sm* bachelor.
cella ['tʃɛlla] *sf* cell. **cella frigorifera** cold storage.
cellula ['tʃɛllula] *sf* cell.
cellulosa [tʃellu'loza] *sf* cellulose.
cemento [tʃe'mento] *sm* cement. **cemento armato** reinforced concrete. **cementare** *v* cement.
cena ['tʃena] *sf* supper, dinner. **cenare** *v* have supper *or* dinner.
cencio ['tʃentʃo] *sm* rag; (*per stoviglie*) dishcloth; (*per spolverare*) duster. **cencioso** *agg* ragged, tattered.
cenere ['tʃenere] *sf* ash. **Ceneri** *sf pl* Ash Wednesday *sing*.
cenno ['tʃenno] *sm* sign, gesture; (*col capo*) nod; (*con gli occhi*) wink; (*con la mano*) wave; (*allusione*) mention.
censimento [tʃensi'mento] *sm* census.
censurare [tʃensu'rare] *v* (*biasimare*) censure; (*sottoporre a censura*) censor. **censura** *sf* censorship; (*riprovazione*) censure.
centenario [tʃente'narjo], **-a** *sm, sf* centenarian. *sm* (*ricorrenza*) centenary. *agg* hundred-year-old.
centesimo [tʃen'tɛzimo] *sm* hundredth; (*soldo*) cent. *agg* hundredth.
centigrado [tʃen'tigrado] *agg* centigrade.
centimetro [tʃen'timetro] *sm* centimetre; (*nastro per misurare*) tape-measure.
cento ['tʃɛnto] *agg, sm* hundred. **per cento** per cent. **centinaio** *sm, pl* **-a** *f* hundred; (*circa cento*) about a hundred. **a centinaia** by the hundred, in hundreds.
centrale [tʃen'trale] *agg* central, principal. *sf* (*deposito*) main depot; (*del telefono*) exchange; (*di energia*) power station; (*di amministrazione*) head office. **centralino** *sm* switchboard. **centralinista** *s(m+f)* switchboard operator.

centro ['tʃɛntro] *sm* centre; (*mezzo*) middle; (*luogo di soggiorno*) resort; (*fam: colpo centrato*) bull's-eye.
ceppo ['tʃeppo] *sm* (*razza*) stock; (*base di albero*) stump; (*pezzo di legno*) block; (*auto*) brake-block. **ceppi** *sm pl* fetters *pl*.
cera[1] ['tʃera] *sf* wax; (*per lucidare*) polish. **dare la cera** wax. **ceralacca** *sf* sealing-wax.
cera[2] ['tʃera] *sf* (*aspetto*) air, expression. **aver buona/brutta cera** look well/ill. **far buona cera a** welcome heartily.
ceramica [tʃe'ramika] *sf* (*oggetto*) piece of pottery; (*materiale*) earthenware; (*arte*) pottery. **ceramiche** *sf pl* pottery *sing*. **ceramista** *s*(*m*+*f*) potter.
cercare [tʃer'kare] *v* look for, search for; (*nei libri*) look up; (*tentare*) try; (*volere*) want. **cerca** *sf* search; (*questua*) begging.
cerchia ['tʃerkja] *sf* circle.
cerchio ['tʃerkjo] *sm* circle; (*giocattolo, di botte*) hoop. **fare cerchio intorno a** circle round.
cereale [tʃere'ale] *sm, agg* cereal.
cerebrale [tʃere'brale] *agg* cerebral.
cerimonia [tʃeri'mɔnja] *sf* ceremony. **far cerimonie** stand on ceremony. **senza cerimonie** without fuss. **cerimoniale** *sm, agg* ceremonial.
cerino [tʃe'rino] *sm* (*candela*) taper; (*fiammifero*) wax match.
cerniera [tʃer'njɛra] *sf* hinge; (*di borsetta*) clasp. **cerniera lampo** zip fastener.
cernita ['tʃɛrnita] *sf* choice.
cero ['tʃero] *sm* (church) candle.
cerotto [tʃe'rɔtto] *sm* plaster.
certezza [tʃer'tettsa] *sf* certainty.
certificare [tʃertifi'kare] *v* certify. **certificato** *sm* certificate.
certo ['tʃɛrto] *agg* certain. *avv* certainly. **dare** *or* **sapere per certo** know for a fact. **tenere per certo** have no doubts about.
certuni [tʃer'tuni] *pron* some (people).
cervello [tʃer'vɛllo] *sm* brain; (*intelligenza, cibo*) brains *pl*. **dare al cervello** go to one's head.
cervo ['tʃɛrvo] *sm* deer, stag. **cervo volante** (*insetto*) stag beetle; (*aquilone*) kite. **cerva** *sf* deer, doe, hind.
cesello [tʃe'zɛllo] *sm* (*strumento*) engraving tool, small chisel. **cesellare** *v* engrave, chisel; (*fare con cura*) polish.
cesoie [tʃe'zɔje] *sf pl* shears *pl*.
cespo ['tʃespo] *sm* (*di erbe*) tuft; (*di fiori*) cluster. **cespo di lattuga** head of lettuce.
cespuglio [tʃes'puʎo] *sm* shrub, bush.
cessare [tʃes'sare] *v* cease, stop. **cessate il fuoco** *sm* cease-fire. **cessazione** *sf* cessation; (*comm*) termination, stoppage.
cessione [tʃes'sjone] *sf* relinquishment; (*dir*) transfer, assignment.
cesso ['tʃɛsso] *sm* (*fam*) loo, lavatory.
cesta ['tʃesta] *sf* basket.
cestino [tʃes'tino] *sm* waste-paper basket; (*da lavoro*) work-basket. **cestino da viaggio** packed lunch. **cestinare** *v* throw away; (*scritti*) reject.
cesto ['tʃesto] *sm* basket.
ceto ['tʃɛto] *sm* class.
cetriolo [tʃetri'ɔlo] *sm* cucumber. **cetriolino** *sm* gherkin.
che[1] [ke] *pron* (*persone: soggetto*) who; (*persone: oggetto*) whom, that; (*cose*) which, that; (*quando*) when; (*dove*) where; (*interrogativo*) what; (*indefinito*) something. *inter* what! (*come*) how! *agg* (*quale*) what; (*numero limitato*) which. **non è un gran che** it's nothing much.
che[2] [ke] *cong* that; (*comparativa*) than; (*quando*) when; (*dopo*) after; (*eccettuativa*) but.
checché [ke'ke] *pron* whatever.
chi [ki] *pron* (*soggetto*) who; (*oggetto*) whom; (*colui che*) he who; (*colei che*) she who; (*coloro che*) those who; (*chiunque*) whoever. **chi . . . chi . . .** some . . . others . . . . **di chi** whose.
chiacchierare [kjakkje'rare] *v* chat. **chiacchiera** *sf* chat; (*discorso inutile*) idle talk. **far due** *or* **quattro chiacchiere** chat. **chiacchierata** *sf* chat.
chiacchierone [kjakkje'rone], **-a** *agg* talkative; (*pettegolo*) gossipy. *sm, sf* chatterbox, gossip.
chiamare [kja'mare] *v* call; (*far venire*) send for; (*al telefono*) ring (up). **chiamare in giudizio** sue. **chiamare sotto le armi** call up. **chiamata** *sf* call. **chiamata in giudizio** summons. **chiamata urbana/interurbana** local/trunk call.
chiarire [kja'rire] *v* clarify; (*spiegare*) explain.
chiaro ['kjaro] *agg* clear; (*luminoso*) bright; (*non scuro*) light. *sm* light. *avv* clearly, distinctly. **chiaro e tondo** blunt. **mettere in chiaro** clear up.
chiasso ['kjasso] *sm* noise, racket, row. **far chiasso** kick up a row. **chiassoso** *agg* rowdy, noisy; (*colore*) loud.

chiavare [kja'vare] *v* (*volg*) screw, fuck.
chiave ['kjave] *sf* key; (*tec*) spanner; (*segno musicale*) clef. **chiave apritutto** master key. **chiave inglese** adjustable spanner.
chiavistello [kjavis'tɛllo] *sm* bolt, latch.
chiazzare [kjat'tsare] *v* spot; (*con colori diversi*) mottle. **chiazza** *sf* spot; (*sulla pelle*) patch, blotch. **chiazzato** *agg* spotty; blotchy; mottled.
chicco ['kikko] *sm* grain; (*di caffè*) bean; (*d'uva*) grape; (*di grandine*) hailstone; (*del rosario*) bead.
***chiedere** ['kjɛdere] *v* ask; (*per avere*) ask for; (*di diritto*) demand; (*vivamente*) beg; (*richiedere*) require; (*prezzo*) charge. **chiedersi** *v* wonder.
chiesa ['kjɛza] *sf* church.
chiglia ['kiʎa] *sf* keel.
chilo ['kilo] *sm* kilo.
chilometro [ki'lɔmetro] *sm* kilometre.
chimera [ki'mɛra] *sf* chimera.
chimico ['kimiko] *agg* chemical. *sm* chemist. **chimica** *sf* (*scienza*) chemistry; (*persona*) chemist.
china[1] ['kina] *sf* slope; decline.
china[2] ['kina] *sf* **inchiostro di china** *sm* Indian ink.
chinare [ki'nare] *v* bend; (*occhi*) lower. **chinarsi** *v* stoop.
chincaglieria [kinkaʎe'ria] *sf* fancy goods *pl*.
chiocciare [kjot'tʃare] *v* cluck; (*covare*) brood. **chioccia** *sf* broody hen.
chiocciola ['kjɔttʃola] *sf* snail; (*anat*) cochlea. **scala a chiocciola** *sf* spiral staircase.
chiodo ['kjɔdo] *sm* nail; fixed idea; (*fam*) debt. **chiodato** *agg* nailed; (*scarpe*) hobnailed.
chioma ['kjɔma] *sf* hair.
chiosco ['kjɔsko] *sm* kiosk, stall.
chiostro ['kjɔstro] *sm* cloister.
chiromante [kiro'mante] *s*(*m*+*f*) fortune-teller. **chiromanzia** *sf* fortune-telling.
chirurgia [kirur'dʒia] *sf* surgery. **chirurgico** *agg* surgical. **chirurgo** *sm* surgeon.
chissà [kis'sa] *avv* who knows, goodness knows; (*forse*) perhaps.
chitarra [ki'tarra] *sf* guitar.
***chiudere** ['kjudere] *v* close, shut; (*a chiave*) lock (up); (*sbattendo*) slam; (*spegnere*) turn *or* switch off; (*tappare*) stop up; (*recingere*) enclose. **chiudere bottega** shut up shop. **chiuder dentro** shut in. **chiudere in attivo/perdita** show a profit/loss.
chiunque [ki'unkwe] *pron* whoever; (*qualunque persona*) anyone.
chiusa ['kjuza] *sf* (*parte finale*) close; (*recinto*) enclosure; (*sbarramento artificiale*) lock; (*diga*) dam.
chiuso ['kjuzo] *agg* closed, shut.
chiusura [kju'zura] *sf* (*termine*) end; (*serratura*) fastener; (*il chiudere*) closing, shut-down.
ci [tʃi], **ce** *pron* (to) us; (*riflessivo*) ourselves; (*reciproco*) each other; (*impersonale*) one; (*di ciò*) about it *or* that. **ci conto su** I'm counting on it. **ci penso io** I'll think about it. *avv* (*lì*) there; (*qui*) here.
ciabatta [tʃa'batta] *sf* slipper.
cialda ['tʃalda] *sf* waffle; (*cialdino*) wafer.
ciambella [tʃam'bɛlla] *sf* (*pasta*) doughnut; (*cuscino*) rubber ring; (*di salvataggio*) lifebuoy.
ciambellano [tʃambel'lano] *sm* chamberlain.
cianciare [tʃan'tʃare] *v* prattle away, talk idly.
cianfrusaglia [tʃanfru'zaʎa] *sf* knick-knack, junk.
cianuro [tʃa'nuro] *sm* cyanide.
ciao ['tʃao] *inter* (*incontrandosi*) hello! (*congedandosi*) cheerio! goodbye!
ciarlare [tʃar'lare] *v* chatter, chat. **ciarla** *sf* (*chiacchiera*) chat; (*pettegolezzo*) gossip.
ciarlatano [tʃarla'tano] *sm* charlatan.
ciascuno [tʃas'kuno] *agg* each; (*ogni*) every. *pron* each one; (*ognuno*) everyone.
cibare [tʃi'bare] *v* feed. **cibo** *sm* food.
cicala [tʃi'kala] *sf* cicada.
cicalino [tʃika'lino] *sm* buzzer.
cicatrice [tʃika'tritʃe] *sf* scar.
cicca ['tʃikka] *sf* (*mozzicone*) fag end. **non valere una cicca** be not worth a thing.
cicchetto [tʃik'ketto] *sm* (*bicchierino*) nip; (*rimprovero*) dressing-down.
cicerone [tʃitʃe'rone] *sm* (tourist) guide.
ciclamino [tʃikla'mino] *sm* cyclamen.
ciclismo [tʃi'klizmo] *sm* cycling. **ciclista** *s*(*m*+*f*) cyclist.
ciclo ['tʃiklo] *sm* cycle. **ciclico** *agg* cyclical.
ciclomotore [tʃiklomo'tore] *sm* moped.
ciclone [tʃi'klone] *sm* cyclone.

cicogna [tʃi'koɲa] *sf* stork.
cicoria [tʃi'kɔrja] *sf* chicory. **cicoria belga** endive.
cicuta [tʃi'kuta] *sf* hemlock.
cieco ['tʃɛko], **-a** *agg* blind. *sm*, *sf* blind person.
cielo ['tʃɛlo] *sm* sky; (*sede divina*) heaven. **a cielo aperto** in the open. **per amor del cielo!** for heaven's sake!
cifra ['tʃifra] *sf* figure, number; (*somma*) amount; (*codice segreto*) cipher.
ciglio ['tʃiʎo] *sm*, *pl* **-a** *f in anat sense* eyelash; (*bordo*) edge. **non batter ciglio** not bat an eyelid.
cigno ['tʃiɲo] *sm* swan.
cigolare [tʃigo'lare] *v* creak, squeak. **cigolio** *sm* creaking, squeaking.
cilecca [tʃi'lekka] *sf* **far cilecca** misfire.
ciliegia [tʃi'ljɛdʒa] *sf* cherry. **ciliegio** *sm* cherry tree.
cilindro [tʃi'lindro] *sm* cylinder; (*rullo*) roller; (*cappello*) top hat.
cima ['tʃima] *sf* top, summit. **da cima a fondo** from top to bottom. **cimare** *v* (*piante*) trim, clip; (*tessuti*) shear.
cimelio [tʃi'mɛljo] *sm* (*oggetto prezioso*) treasure; (*ricordo*) relic, memento.
cimice ['tʃimitʃe] *sf* bedbug.
ciminiera [tʃimi'njɛra] *sf* chimney.
cimitero [tʃimi'tɛro] *sm* cemetery.
cimurro [tʃi'murro] *sm* distemper.
Cina ['tʃina] *sf* China. **cinese** *agg*, *s*(*m*+*f*) Chinese.
cincia ['tʃintʃa] *sf* tit(mouse). **cinciallegra** *sf* (great) tit.
cincin [tʃin'tʃin] *inter* cheers!
cinema ['tʃinema] *sm invar* cinema. **cinematografico** *agg* film. **cinematografo** *sm* cinema.
cinetico [tʃi'nɛtiko] *agg* kinetic. **cinetica** *sf* kinetics.
***cingere** ['tʃindʒere] *v* surround, encircle. **cingere d'assedio** besiege.
cinghia ['tʃingja] *sf* belt.
cinghiale [tʃin'gjale] *sm* (wild) boar; (*pelle*) pigskin.
cinguettare [tʃingwet'tare] *v* twitter. **cinguettio** *sm* twittering.
cinico ['tʃiniko], **-a** *agg* cynical. *sm*, *sf* cynic. **cinismo** *sm* cynicism.
cinquanta [tʃin'kwanta] *sm*, *agg* fifty. **cinquantesimo** *sm*, *agg* fiftieth.
cinque ['tʃinkwe] *sm*, *agg* five.
cintura [tʃin'tura] *sf* belt; (*giro della vita*) waist. **cintura di sicurezza** safety-belt. **cinturino** *sm* strap.
ciò [tʃɔ] *pron* this, that. **ciò che** what. **ciò detto** having said this. **ciònondimeno** *or* **ciònonostante** nevertheless, just the same. **con ciò** therefore. **e con ciò?** so what?
cioccolata [tʃokko'lata] *sf* chocolate; (*bevanda*) (drinking) chocolate. **cioccolatino** *sm* (piece of) chocolate. **cioccolato** *sm* chocolate.
cioè [tʃo'ɛ] *avv* that is; (*o piuttosto*) or better.
ciondolo ['tʃondolo] *sm* pendant. **ciondolare** *v* dangle; (*bighellonare*) hang about.
ciotola ['tʃɔtola] *sf* bowl.
ciottolo ['tʃɔttolo] *sm* pebble.
cipiglio [tʃi'piʎo] *sm* frown.
cipolla [tʃi'polla] *sf* onion.
cipresso [tʃi'prɛsso] *sm* cypress.
cipria ['tʃiprja] *sf* powder.
Cipro ['tʃipro] *sm* Cyprus. **cipriota** *agg*, *s*(*m*+*f*) Cypriot.
circa ['tʃirka] *prep* (*riguardo a*) about, concerning. *avv* (*pressappoco*) about, approximately.
circo ['tʃirko] *sm* circus.
circolare[1] [tʃirko'lare] *sf*, *agg* circular. **assegno circolare** *sm* banker's draft.
circolare[2] [tʃirko'lare] *v* circulate. **circolatorio** *agg* circulatory. **circolazione** *sf* circulation.
circolo ['tʃirkolo] *sm* circle.
***circoncidere** [tʃirkon'tʃidere] *v* circumcise. **circoncisione** *sf* circumcision.
circondare [tʃirkon'dare] *v* surround.
circonferenza [tʃirkonfe'rɛntsa] *sf* circumference.
circonvallazione [tʃirkonvalla'tsjone] *sf* ring-road.
***circoscrivere** [tʃirkos'krivere] *v* circumscribe.
circostante [tʃirkos'tante] *agg* surrounding.
circostanza [tʃirkos'tantsa] *sf* circumstances *pl*; (*condizione particolare*) occurrence. **di circostanza** fitting.
circuito [tʃir'kuito] *sm* circuit; (*sport*) (race-)track.
cisterna [tʃis'tɛrna] *sf* cistern; (*serbatoio*) tank. **nave cisterna** *sf* tanker.
citare [tʃi'tare] *v* (*riportare parole*) quote; (*nominare*) cite; (*dir*: *convocare*) summon(s). **citazione** *sf* quotation; summons.

citofono [tʃi'tɔfono] *sm* (*fam*) intercom.
città [tʃit'ta] *sf* town, city. **cittadina** *sf* small town; (*persona*) citizen. **cittadinanza** *sf* citizenship, nationality; (*popolazione*) people. **cittadino** *sm* citizen.
ciuco ['tʃuko] *sm* donkey.
ciuffo ['tʃuffo] *sm* tuft.
ciurma ['tʃurma] *sf* crew; (*ciurmaglia*) riff-raff.
civetta [tʃi'vetta] *sf* (*uccello*) owl; (*donna*) flirt. **civettare** *v* flirt.
civico ['tʃiviko] *agg* civic.
civile [tʃi'vile] *agg* civil; (*non militare*) civilian; (*incivilito*) civilized. **civilizzare** *v* civilize. **civismo** *sm* public spirit.
civiltà [tʃivil'ta] *sf* civilization; (*cortesia*) good breeding.
clacson ['klakson] *sm invar* horn, hooter.
clamore [kla'more] *sm* clamour; (*fig*) outcry, sensation. **clamoroso** *agg* noisy, sensational.
clandestino [klandes'tino] *agg* clandestine.
clarinetto [klari'netto] *sm* clarinet.
classe ['klasse] *sf* class; (*scuola*) form.
classico ['klassiko] *agg* classic, classical; typical. *sm* classic.
classificare [klassifi'kare] *v* classify. **classificatore** *sm* file. **classificazione** *sf* classification.
classismo [klas'sizmo] *sm* class-consciousness. **classista** *agg* class-conscious.
clausola ['klauzola] *sf* clause.
claustrofobia [klaustrofo'bia] *sf* claustrophobia.
clavicembalo [klavi'tʃembalo] *sm* harpsichord.
clavicola [kla'vikola] *sf* collar-bone.
clemenza [kle'mɛntsa] *sf* clemency; (*tempo*) mildness. **clemente** *agg* mild, clement.
cleptomane [klep'tɔmane] *s*(*m*+*f*), *agg* kleptomaniac. **cleptomania** *sf* kleptomania.
clero ['klɛro] *sm* clergy. **clericale** *agg* clerical.
cliché [kli'ʃe] *sm* (*stampa*) block; (*luogo comune*) cliché.
cliente [kli'ɛnte] *s*(*m*+*f*) (*di negozio*) customer; (*di professionista*) client; (*di albergo*) guest. **cliente abituale** patron. **clientela** *sf* customers *pl*, clientele; (*di professionista*) practice.
clima ['klima] *sm* climate. **climatico** *agg* climatic.
clinica ['klinika] *sf* clinic. **clinico** *agg* clinical.
cloro ['klɔro] *sm* chlorine.
clorofilla [kloro'filla] *sf* chlorophyll.
cloroformio [kloro'fɔrmjo] *sm* chloroform.
cloruro [klo'ruro] *sm* chloride.
coabitare [koabi'tare] *v* cohabit.
coagulare [koagu'lare] *v* coagulate; (*latte*) curdle; (*sangue*) clot. **coagulazione** *sf* coagulation; curdling; clotting.
coalizione [koali'tsjone] *sf* coalition. **coalizzarsi** *v* unite.
coatto [ko'atto] *agg* compulsory.
cobalto [ko'balto] *sm* cobalt.
cobra ['kɔbra] *sm invar* cobra.
cocaina [koka'ina] *sf* cocaine. **cocainomane** *s*(*m*+*f*) cocaine addict.
coccarda [kok'karda] *sf* rosette.
cocchio ['kɔkkjo] *sm* carriage, coach. **cocchiere** *sm* coachman.
coccinella [kottʃi'nɛlla] *sf* ladybird.
coccio ['kɔttʃo] *sm* (*terracotta*) earthenware; (*rottame*) piece, crock.
cocciuto [kot'tʃuto] *agg* stubborn, pig-headed. **cocciutaggine** *sf* stubbornness, pig-headedness.
cocco[1] ['kɔkko], **-a** *sm*, *sf* (*fam*: *amore*) pet, darling.
cocco[2] ['kɔkko] *sm* coconut tree *or* palm. **noce di cocco** *sf* coconut.
coccodrillo [kokko'drillo] *sm* crocodile.
cocente [ko'tʃɛnte] *agg* burning, scorching.
cocomero [ko'kɔmero] *sm* water-melon.
cocuzzolo [ko'kuttsolo] *sm* tip.
coda ['koda] *sf* tail; (*fila*) queue; (*musica*) coda. **con la coda dell'occhio** out of the corner of one's eye. **fare la coda** queue (up).
codardo [ko'dardo] *agg* cowardly.
codeina [kode'ina] *sf* codeine.
codesto [ko'desto] *agg* that. *pron* that (one).
codice ['kɔditʃe] *sm* code. **codice della strada** highway code.
coefficiente [koeffi'tʃɛnte] *sm* coefficient; (*causa*) contributory factor.
coerente [koe'rɛnte] *agg* coherent; (*fig*) consistent.
coesistere [koe'zistere] *v* coexist. **coesistenza** *sf* coexistence.
coetaneo [koe'taneo], **-a** *s*, *agg* contemporary.

cofano ['kɔfano] *sm* (*auto*) bonnet; (*forziere*) chest.

***cogliere** ['kɔʎere] *v* (*staccare*) pick; (*sorprendere, capire*) catch; (*colpire*) hit. **cogliere la palla al balzo** seize the opportunity.

coglione [ko'ʎone] (*volg*) *sm* testicle; (*sciocco*) fool. **coglioneria** *sf* foolishness.

cognato [ko'ɲato] *sm* brother-in-law. **cognata** *sf* sister-in-law.

cognizione [koɲi'tsjone] *sf* knowledge; (*dir*) cognizance.

cognome [ko'ɲome] *sm* surname.

coi ['koi] *prep+art* **con i.**

***coincidere** [koin'tʃidere] *v* coincide. **coincidenza** *sf* coincidence; (*treno, ecc.*) connection.

***coinvolgere** [koin'vɔldʒere] *v* involve.

coito ['kɔito] *sm* coitus, sexual intercourse.

col [kol] *prep+art* **con il.**

colare [ko'lare] *v* (*filtrare*) sieve, strain; (*gocciolare*) drip, trickle; (*fondere*) melt, cast; (*a picco*) sink. **colabrodo** *or* **colapasta** *sm invar* strainer, colander. **colatoio** *sm* strainer. **colino** *sm* sieve.

colazione [kola'tsjone] *sf* (*del mattino*) breakfast; (*di mezzogiorno*) lunch. **far colazione** (have) breakfast; (have) lunch.

colei [ko'lɛi] *pron* (*soggetto*) she; (*oggetto*) her. **colei che** (she) who.

colera [ko'lɛra] *sm invar* cholera.

colesterolo [koleste'rɔlo] *sm* cholesterol.

coll' [koll] *prep+art* **con l'.**

colla ['kɔlla] *sf* glue, paste.

collaborare [kollabo'rare] *v* collaborate; (*giornale*) contribute. **collaboratore, -trice** *sm, sf* collaborator; contributor. **collaborazione** *sf* collaboration; contribution.

collana [kol'lana] *sf* necklace; (*raccolta*) collection.

collants [kɔl'lã] *sm pl* tights *pl.*

collare [kol'lare] *sm* collar.

collasso [kol'lasso] *sm* collapse. **collasso cardiaco** heart failure.

collaterale [kollate'rale] *agg* collateral.

collaudare [kollau'dare] *v* test. **collaudo** *sm* test.

colle[1] ['kɔlle] *sm* (*altura*) hill.

colle[2] ['kɔlle] *sm* (*valico*) pass.

collega [kol'lɛga] *s*(*m+f*), *m pl* **-ghi** colleague.

collegare [kolle'gare] *v* connect, link (up). **collegarsi** *v* (*telefono*) get through. **collegamento** *sm* connection, link; (*mil*) liaison.

collegio [kol'lɛdʒo] *sm* college; (*convitto*) boarding school; (*consiglio*) board. **collegio di difesa** counsel for the defence. **collegio elettorale** constituency.

collegiale [kolle'dʒale] *s*(*m+f*) boarder. *agg* (*collettivo*) corporate, collective; (*di collegio*) college, boarding-school.

collera ['kollera] *sf* anger, rage.

colletta [kol'lɛtta] *sf* collection.

collettivo [kollet'tivo] *agg* collective.

colletto [kol'lɛtto] *sm* collar.

collettore [kollet'tore] *sm* collector; (*tec*) manifold.

collezionare [kolletsjo'nare] *v* collect. **collezione** *sf* collection.

collina [kol'lina] *sf* hill.

collisione [kolli'zjone] *sf* collision.

collo[1] ['kɔllo] *sm* neck. **collo del piede** instep.

collo[2] ['kɔllo] *sm* (*pacco*) parcel, package; (*bagaglio*) item of luggage.

collocare [kollo'kare] *v* place. **collocare a riposo** retire, pension off. **collocamento** *sm* (*occupazione*) employment, job; (*il collocare*) placing, setting; (*vendita*) sale. **collocamento a riposo** retirement. **ufficio di collocamento** *sm* employment exchange.

colloide [kol'lɔide] *sm* colloid. *agg* colloidal.

colloquio [kol'lɔkwjo] *sm* conversation, talk; (*intervista*) interview; (*esame*) oral (examination).

colmare [kol'mare] *v* fill; (*fino all'orlo*) fill to the brim; (*coprire di*) shower. **colmo** *sm* top, summit; (*culmine*) height; (*situazione paradossale*) last straw, limit.

colombo [ko'lombo], **-a** *sm, sf* dove, pigeon. **colombaia** *sf* dovecote.

colonia [ko'lɔnja] *sf* colony; (*per bambini*) holiday camp; (*per lavoro*) settlement. **coloniale** *agg* colonial.

colonna [ko'lonna] *sf* column; (*sostegno*) pillar; (*fila*) line, queue. **colonna vertebrale** spinal column, backbone.

colonnello [kolon'nɛllo] *sm* colonel.

colore [ko'lore] *sm* colour; (*sostanza colorante*) paint, dye, tint; (*carte da gioco*) suit. **farne di tutti i colori** get up to all sorts of mischief. **colorante** *sm* dye. **colorare** *v* colour.

colorire [kolo'rire] *v* colour; (*arrossire*) blush.
colorito [kolo'rito] *sm* (*carnagione*) complexion; (*tinta*) colour(ing). *agg* colourful.
coloro [ko'loro] *pron* (*soggetto*) they; (*oggetto*) them. **coloro che** (those) who.
colossale [kolos'sale] *agg* colossal, tremendous. **colosso** *sm* (*statua*) colossus; (*uomo*) giant.
colpa ['kolpa] *sf* fault; (*colpevolezza*) guilt; (*peccato*) sin. **dare la colpa a** blame. **per colpa di** through, because of. **prendersi la colpa** take the blame.
colpevole [kol'pevole] *agg* (*persona*) guilty; (*azione*) culpable. *s*(*m*+*f*) culprit. **dichiararsi colpevole** plead guilty.
colpire [kol'pire] *v* hit, strike.
colpo ['kolpo] *sm* stroke, blow; (*arma da fuoco*) shot; (*impresa*) move, raid. **colpo d'aria** draught. **far colpo** impress, cause a stir, make a hit.
coltello [kol'tɛllo] *sm* knife. **coltellata** *sf* stab.
coltivare [kolti'vare] *v* cultivate; (*far crescere*) grow. **coltivatore** *sm* grower. **coltivazione** *sf* cultivation; growing.
colto[1] ['kolto] *agg* cultivated, cultured.
coltura [kol'tura] *sf* cultivation; (*allevamento*) breeding; (*med*) culture.
colui [ko'lui] *pron* (*soggetto*) he; (*oggetto*) him. **colui che** (he) who.
coma ['kɔma] *sm invar* coma. **comatoso** *agg* comatose.
comandare [koman'dare] *v* (*reggere comando*) be in command, command; (*chiedere*) order; (*mec*) control. **comandamento** *sm* commandment. **comandante** *sm* commander. **comando** *sm* command; (*sede*) headquarters; (*mec*) control, drive. **comando a distanza** remote control.
combaciare [komba'tʃare] *v* coincide.
combattere [kom'battere] *v* fight. **combattente** *sm* serviceman. **combattimento** *sm* fight. **combattivo** *agg* pugnacious. **combattuto** *agg* undecided, torn.
combinare [kombi'nare] *v* combine; (*mettere d'accordo*) agree; (*concludere*) arrange, bring off, achieve. **combinazione** *sf* combination; (*caso*) chance.
combustibile [kombus'tibile] *sm* fuel. *agg* combustible.
combustione [kombus'tjone] *sf* combustion.
come ['kome] *avv* as; (*somiglianza*) like; (*in qual modo*) how.
comedone [kome'done] *sm* blackhead.
cometa [ko'meta] *sf* comet.
comico ['kɔmiko], **-a** *sm*, *sf* comic, comedian. *agg* comic(al), funny; (*commedia*) dramatic.
comignolo [ko'miɲolo] *sm* chimney-pot.
cominciare [komin'tʃare] *v* begin, start. **a cominciare da** from.
comitato [komi'tato] *sm* committee.
comitiva [komi'tiva] *sf* party.
comizio [ko'mitsjo] *sm* meeting.
commedia [kom'mɛdja] *sf* play, comedy; (*finzione*) play-acting, sham; (*scena comica*) farce. **commediante** *s*(*m*+*f*) (*fam*) ham; (*ipocrita*) humbug. **commediografo** *sm* playwright.
commemorare [kommemo'rare] *v* commemorate. **commemorativo** *agg* memorial.
commentare [kommen'tare] *v* comment (on). **commentario** *sm* commentary. **commentatore, -trice** *sm*, *sf* commentator. **commento** *sm* comment; (*radio*) commentary.
commercio [kom'mɛrtʃo] *sm* trade, commerce. **commercio all'ingrosso/al minuto** wholesale/retail trade. **mettere in commercio** put on sale.
commesso [kom'messo], **-a** *sm*, *sf* (*di negozio*) (shop) assistant; (*d'ufficio*) clerk. **commesso viaggiatore** travelling salesman.
commestibile [kommes'tibile] *agg* edible. **commestibili** *sm pl* foodstuffs *pl*, provisions *pl*.
***commettere** [kom'mettere] *v* (*fare*) commit; (*mettere insieme*) fit together, join; (*ordinare*) commission.
commissariato [kommissa'rjato] *sm* (*polizia*) police station. **commissario** *sm* (*polizia*) police inspector; (*sovietico*) commissar; (*amministratore*) commissioner.
commissione [kommis'sjone] *sf* commission; (*incombenza*) errand; (*ordinazione*) order; (*comitato*) board. **fare delle commissioni** go shopping.
commosso [kom'mɔsso] *agg* moved, touched.
commozione [kommo'tsjone] *sf* deep feelings *pl*; (*med*) concussion.
***commuovere** [kom'mwɔvere] *v* move,

touch. **commovente** *agg* moving, touching.
commutare [kommu'tare] *v* commute.
comò [ko'mɔ] *sm* chest of drawers.
comodino [komo'dino] *sm* bedside table.
comodo ['kɔmodo] *sm* convenience. *agg* comfortable; (*opportuno*) convenient; (*utile*) useful, handy. **far comodo** be useful *or* handy; (*garbare*) please, suit. **fare con comodo** take one's time. **comodare** *v* suit. **comodità** *sf* comfort.
compagnia [kompa'ɲia] *sf* company.
compagno [kom'paɲo], **-a** *sm*, *sf* companion, mate, friend. **compagno d'armi** fellow-soldier. **compagno di prigionia/viaggio** fellow-prisoner/traveller. **compagno di scuola** classmate.
***comparire** [kompa'rire] *v* appear. **comparsa** *sf* appearance; (*film*) extra.
compartimento [komparti'mento] *sm* compartment.
compassione [kompas'sjone] *sf* pity. **far compassione** arouse pity. **per compassione** out of pity. **compassionevole** *agg* (*che fa compassione*) pitiful; (*che ha compassione*) compassionate.
compasso [kom'passo] *sm* compasses *pl*.
compatire [kompa'tire] *v* be sorry for. **compatibile** *agg* compatible; (*perdonabile*) excusable.
compatriota [kompatri'ɔta] *s*(*m*+*f*) compatriot.
compatto [kom'patto] *agg* compact, dense; (*fig*) united. **compattezza** *sf* compactness; unity.
compendio [kom'pɛndjo] *sm* (*riassunto*) summary; (*trattato*) outline. **compendioso** *agg* brief.
compensare [kompen'sare] *v* compensate; (*ricompensare*) reward. (**legno**) **compensato** *sm* plywood. **compensazione** *sf* compensation; (*econ*) clearing. **compenso** *sm* compensation; reward. **in compenso** in return, in exchange.
competente [kompe'tɛnte] *agg* competent, qualified; (*adeguato*) fair. **competenza** *sf* experience, authority; (*dir*) competence.
competere [kom'pɛtere] *v* (*spettare*) be due; (*gareggiare*) compete, rival. **competitivo** *agg* competitive.
***compiacere** [kompja'tʃere] *v* please. **compiacersi** *v* be pleased, rejoice; congratulate; (*degnarsi*) be good enough. **compiaciuto** *agg* pleased, satisfied.
***compiangere** [kom'pjandʒere] *v* pity; (*rimpiangere*) mourn. **compianto** *sm* grief.
compiere ['kompjere] *v* (*finire*) complete; (*adempiere*) carry out, fulfil. **compiere ... anni** be ... years old. **compimento** *sm* fulfilment.
compilare [kompi'lare] *v* compile, draw up.
compito ['kompito] *sm* task; (*dovere*) duty; (*scuola*) homework.
compleanno [komple'anno] *sm* birthday.
complementare [komplemen'tare] *agg* complementary; (*secondario*) subsidiary. **complemento** *sm* complement; (*gramm*) object.
complesso [kom'plɛsso] *agg* complex; complicated. *sm* (*insieme*) whole; (*industria*) combine, group; (*psic*) complex; (*musica*) ensemble, band. **in complesso** (*tutto sommato*) on the whole; (*in tutto*) in all, altogether. **nel complesso** as a whole.
completo [kom'plɛto] *agg* complete; (*pieno*) full (up); (*assoluto*) total. *sm* (*abito*) suit; (*di maglia*) twin set; (*in generale*) outfit. **al completo** (*pieno*) full up; (*esaurito*) sold out; (*tutti presenti*) in full force. **completare** *v* complete, finish.
complicare [kompli'kare] *v* complicate; (*aggravare*) worsen. **complicato** *agg* complicated, complex; (*intricato*) involved. **complicazione** *sf* complication.
complice ['komplitʃe] *s*(*m*+*f*) accomplice; (*dir*) accessory. **complice in adulterio** co-respondent. **essere complice in** be a party to. **complicità** *sf* complicity.
complimento [kompli'mento] *sm* compliment. **complimenti** *sm pl* (*cerimonie*) ceremony *sing*; (*ossequi*) regards *pl*; (*auguri*) congratulations *pl*. **far complimenti** stand on ceremony. **complimentare** *v* compliment.
complotto [kom'plɔtto] *sm* plot. **complottare** *v* plot.
componente [kompo'nɛnte] *agg* component. *s*(*m*+*f*) component, member.
***comporre** [kom'porre] *v* (*costituire*) make up; (*assestare*) tidy; (*mettere assieme*) assemble, put together; (*musica*) compose; (*atteggiare*) put on. **comporre una lite** settle a quarrel.
comportare [kompor'tare] *v* (*richiedere*) involve; (*portare con sè*) imply; (*consentire*) permit. **comportarsi** *v* behave. **comportamento** *sm* behaviour.

compositore [kompozi'tore], **-trice** *sm, sf* (*musica*) composer; type-setter.
composizione [kompozi'tsjone] *sf* composition.
composto [kom'posto] *sm* compound, mixture. *agg* (*decoroso*) dignified; (*assestato*) neat; (*costituito*) made up (of), consisting (of); (*mat*) compound. **compostezza** *sf* self-possession; decorum; neatness.
comprare [komp'rare] *v* buy; (*corrompere*) bribe. **comprare all'ingrosso** buy wholesale. **compratore, -trice** *sm, sf* buyer.
***comprendere** [kom'prɛndere] *v* include; (*capire*) understand. **comprensibile** *agg* understandable, intelligible. **comprensione** *sf* understanding. **comprensivo** *agg* (*che include*) inclusive, comprehensive; (*tollerante*) understanding. **compreso** *agg* inclusive; (*capito*) understood.
compressa [kom'prɛssa] *sf* tablet, pill; (*garza*) compress.
compressore [kompres'sore] *sm* compressor.
***comprimere** [kom'primere] *v* compress; (*reprimere*) suppress.
***compromettere** [kompro'mettere] *v* compromise. **compromesso** *sm* compromise. **compromettente** *agg* compromising.
comprovare [kompro'vare] *v* confirm.
compunto [kom'punto] *agg* contrite.
comune [ko'mune] *agg* common. *sm* commune, municipality; (*autorità*) town council. **avere in comune** share. **fuori del comune** uncommon, unusual.
comunicare [komuni'kare] *v* communicate, announce; (*malattia*) pass on; (*rel*) administer Communion. **comunicarsi** *v* spread; receive Communion. **comunicato** *sm* communiqué, bulletin. **comunicato stampa** press release.
comunione [komu'njone] *sf* community; (*rel*) (Holy) Communion.
comunismo [komu'nizmo] *sm* communism. **comunista** *s*(*m*+*f*), *agg* communist.
comunità [komuni'ta] *sf* community.
comunque [ko'munkwe] *avv* (*in ogni modo*) anyhow, at any rate. *cong* however, no matter how.
con [kon] *prep* with; (*mezzo*) with, by.
conca ['konka] *sf* basin; (*valle*) depression.
concavo [kon'kavo] *agg* concave.
***concedere** [kon'tʃɛdere] *v* grant, award; (*permettere*) allow.
concentrare [kontʃen'trare] *v* concentrate. **concentramento** *sm* concentration. **concentrato** *sm* concentrate.
concentrico [kon'tʃɛntriko] *agg* concentric.
concepire [kontʃe'pire] *v* conceive; (*capire*) understand; (*nutrire*) entertain, cherish. **concepibile** *agg* conceivable.
conceria [kontʃe'ria] *sf* tannery.
concernere [kon'tʃɛrnere] *v* concern, regard. **per quanto mi concerne** as far as I am concerned.
concerto [kon'tʃɛrto] *sm* concert.
concessione [kontʃes'sjone] *sf* concession.
concetto [kon'tʃɛtto] *sm* concept, notion, idea.
concezione [kontʃe'tsjone] *sf* conception; (*pensiero*) concept.
conchiglia [kon'kiʎa] *sf* shell.
conciare [kon'tʃare] *v* (*pelli*) tan; (*tabacco*) cure; (*ridurre male*) get into a mess; spoil. **conciare per le feste** (*fam*) give a thrashing.
conciliare [kontʃi'ljare] *v* reconcile.
concilio [kon'tʃiljo] *sm* council.
concime [kon'tʃime] *sm* manure; (*artificiale*) fertilizer.
conciso [kon'tʃizo] *agg* concise, to the point.
concittadino [kontʃitta'dino], **-a** *sm, sf* fellow-citizen.
conclave [kon'klave] *sm* conclave.
***concludere** [kon'kludere] *v* conclude; (*operare con profitto*) achieve. **conclusione** *sf* conclusion, result. **in conclusione** to sum up, in short. **conclusivo** *agg* final, conclusive; (*determinante*) decisive.
concordare [konkor'dare] *v* agree, fix. **concordato** *sm* agreement.
concorrente [konkor'rɛnte] *agg* concurrent; (*rivale*) competing. *s*(*m*+*f*) competitor; (*a un concorso*) candidate, applicant. **concorrenza** *sf* competition. **far concorrenza** compete (with).
***concorrere** [kon'korrere] *v* contribute; (*gareggiare*) compete (for); (*convergere*) come together.
concorso [kon'korso] *sm* (*affluire*) concourse, gathering; contribution; contest, competition; (*esame*) competitive examination.
concreto [kon'krɛto] *sm, agg* concrete. **concretare** *v* get done.

condannare [kondan'nare] *v* condemn; (*dichiarare colpevole*) sentence. **condanna** *sf* conviction, sentence. **condannato, -a** *sm, sf* condemned person.

condensazione [kondensa'tsjone] *sf* condensation. **condensare** *v* condense.

condire [kon'dire] *v* season; (*insalata*) dress. **condimento** *sm* seasoning, dressing.

***condividere** [kondi'videre] *v* share.

condizione [kondi'tsjone] *sf* condition. **condizioni** *sf pl* state *sing*; (*comm*) terms *pl*. **condizioni di vita** standard of living *sing*. **essere in condizione di** be able to. **mettere in condizione di** enable to. **condizionale** *sm, agg* conditional.

condoglianza [kondo'ʎantsa] *sf* condolence. **fare le condoglianze** express one's sympathy.

condonare [kondo'nare] *v* remit, condone. **condono** *sm* remission.

condotta [kon'dotta] *sm* (*comportamento*) conduct, behaviour; (*di un'azione, ecc.*) handling; (*tubazione*) piping.

***condurre** [kon'durre] *v* (*portare*) lead; (*accompagnare*) take; (*auto*) drive; (*dirigere*) manage, run; (*eseguire, fis*) conduct; (*ridurre*) reduce. **condursi** *v* behave.

conduttore [kondut'tore] *agg* conducting. *sm* (*fis*) conductor; (*conducente*) driver. **conduttura** *sf* (*tubazione*) piping; (*condotto*) pipe.

confederazione [konfedera'tsjone] *sf* federation.

conferenza [konfe'rentsa] *sf* (*congresso*) conference; (*discorso*) lecture. **conferenza stampa** press conference. **conferenziere, -a** *sm, sf* lecturer, speaker.

conferire [konfe'rire] *v* award, confer; (*dare*) give.

confermare [konfer'mare] *v* confirm. **conferma** *sf* confirmation.

confessare [konfes'sare] *v* confess. **confessione** *sf* confession. **confessore** *sm* confessor.

confetto [kon'fɛtto] *sm* sugared almond.

confettura [konfet'tura] *sf* preserve.

confezionare [konfetsjo'nare] *v* make up. **confezione** *sf* (*involucro*) wrapping; (*lavorazione*) manufacture. **confezioni** *sf pl* (*abiti pronti*) ready-made clothes *pl*.

confidare [konfi'dare] *v* trust, confide. **confidenza** *sf* confidence. **dar confidenza a** be familiar with. **prendersi la confidenza** take the liberty. **confidenziale** *agg* confidential.

confinare [konfi'nare] *v* border (on); (*relegare*) confine; (*pol*) intern, banish. **confine** *sm* border.

confiscare [konfis'kare] *v* seize, confiscate. **confisca** *sf* seizure, confiscation.

conflitto [kon'flitto] *sm* conflict.

***confondere** [kon'fondere] *v* confuse; (*scambiare*) mistake for; (*mettere in imbarrazzo*) embarrass. **confondersi** *v* become mixed up.

conformare [konfor'mare] *v* conform, adapt. **conforme a** *agg* in conformity with, true to. **conformista** *s(m+f)* conformist.

confortare [konfor'tare] *v* comfort, console. **confortevole** *agg* comforting; (*comodo*) comfortable. **conforto** *sm* comfort.

confrontare [konfron'tare] *v* compare; (*dir*) confront. **confronto** *sm* comparison; (*dir*) confrontation. **a confronto di** compared with. **senza confronto** far and away.

confusione [konfu'zjone] *sf* confusion; (*ressa*) bustle; (*chiasso*) din, turmoil. **confusione mentale** mental aberration. **confuso** *agg* confused, muddled; vague; (*turbato*) bewildered.

congedare [kondʒe'dare] *v* dismiss; (*mil*) discharge. **congedarsi** *v* say goodbye (to); take leave (of). **congedo** *sm* (*commiato*) leave; discharge.

congegno [kon'dʒeɲɲo] *sm* device, gadget. **congegnare** *v* plan, devise.

congelare [kondʒe'lare] *v* freeze. **congelatore** *sm* freezer.

congenito [kon'dʒɛnito] *agg* congenital.

congestionato [kondʒestjo'nato] *agg* congested; (*traffico*) blocked; (*viso*) flushed. **congestione** *sf* congestion; (*traffico*) jam.

***congiungere** [kon'dʒundʒere] *v* (*unire*) join; (*collegare*) connect, link (up). **congiuntivite** *sf* conjunctivitis. **congiuntivo** *sm* subjunctive. **congiuntura** *sf* (*punto di unione*) joint; (*circostanza*) juncture; economic situation. **congiunzione** *sf* conjunction.

congiura [kon'dʒura] *sf* plot, conspiracy. **congiurato, -a** *sm, sf* plotter, conspirator.

congratularsi [kongratu'larsi] *v* congratulate.

congregare [kongre'gare] *v* congregate, gather. **congrega** *sf* band. **congregazione** *sf* congregation.

congresso [kon'grɛsso] *sm* congress.

congruo ['kɔngruo] *agg* adequate, fair.

coniare [ko'njare] *v* coin. **conio** *sm* coining; (*impronta, qualità*) stamp; (*matrice*) minting die.

conico ['kɔniko] *agg* conical.

conifero [ko'nifero] *agg* coniferous. **conifera** *sf* conifer.

coniglio [ko'niʎo] *sm* rabbit.

coniugare [konju'gare] *v* conjugate.

coniuge ['kɔnjudʒe] *s(m+f)* spouse. **coniugale** *agg* conjugal.

***connettere** [kon'nɛttere] *v* connect, link; associate; (*ragionare*) think straight. **connessione** *sf* connection.

connotati [konno'tati] *sm pl* description *sing*, distinguishing features *pl*.

cono ['kɔno] *sm* cone.

***conoscere** [ko'nɔʃere] *v* know; (*fare la conoscenza*) meet. **conoscere di famà/vista** know by reputation/sight. **conoscente** *s(m+f)* acquaintance. **conoscenza** *sf* knowledge; (*conoscente*) acquaintance; (*coscienza*) consciousness, senses *pl*. **conoscitore, -trice** *sm, sf* expert, connoisseur. **conosciuto** *agg* (well-)known, renowned.

conquistare [konkwis'tare] *v* conquer; (*fig*) gain. **conquista** *sf* conquest. **conquistatore, -trice** *sm, sf* conqueror.

consacrare [konsa'krare] *v* consecrate, dedicate.

consanguineo [konsan'gwineo], **-a** *agg* related (by blood). *sm, sf* blood relation.

consapevole [konsa'pevole] *agg* aware, conscious. **consapevolezza** *sf* awareness, consciousness.

consecutivo [konseku'tivo] *agg* consecutive; (*seguente*) following.

consegnare [konse'ɲare] *v* deliver, hand over; (*mil*) confine to barracks. **consegna** *sf* delivery; (*merce ordinata*) consignment; (*custodia*) care; (*deposito*) (safe) custody; (*mil: ordine*) order; (*mil: punizione*) confinement.

conseguire [konse'gwire] *v* . (*ottenere*) obtain, get; (*raggiungere*) achieve; (*risultare*) follow, ensue. **conseguenza** *sf* consequence, result; (*malattia*) aftereffect. **di conseguenza** consequently, as a result.

consenso [kon'sɛnso] *sm* approval; (*accordo*) agreement; (*permesso*) consent.

consentire [konsen'tire] *v* (*essere d'accordo*) agree; (*accondiscendere*) consent; (*permettere*) allow. **consenziente** *agg* consenting.

conservare [konser'vare] *v* keep, preserve. **conserva** *sf* preserve. **mettere in conserva** preserve; (*in scatola*) tin; (*in bottiglia*) bottle. **conservatore, -trice** *s, agg* conservative. **conservazione** *sf* preservation.

considerare [konside'rare] *v* consider; (*guardare*) examine; (*stimare*) esteem, think highly of; (*tener conto*) bear in mind. **consideratezza** *sf* caution. **considerato** *agg* careful, wary. **considerazione** *sf* (*prudenza*) caution; (*risguardo*) consideration; (*stima*) esteem, regard. **considerevole** *agg* considerable.

consigliare [konsi'ʎare] *v* advise, recommend. **consigliere** *sm* counsellor. **consigliere comunale** town councillor. **consigliere delegato** managing director. **consiglio** *sm* advice; (*organo amministrativo*) board; (*ente pubblico*) council; (*colloquio*) meeting. **consiglio d'amministrazione** board of directors.

***consistere** [kon'sistere] *v* consist. **consistente** *agg* substantial; (*convincente*) sound. **consistenza** *sf* consistency; (*fondamento*) basis. **consistenza di cassa/magazzino** cash/stock in hand.

consolare [konso'lare] *v* console, comfort; (*rallegrare*) cheer (up). **consolazione** *sf* consolation, comfort; (*piacere*) delight.

console ['kɔnsole] *sm* consul. **consolare** *agg* consular. **consolato** *sm* consulate.

consolidare [konsoli'dare] *v* consolidate; (*rinforzare*) reinforce.

consonante [konso'nante] *sf* consonant.

consono ['kɔnsono] *agg* **consono a** in keeping with; in accordance with.

consorte [kon'sɔrte] *s(m+f), agg* consort.

consorzio [kon'sɔrtsjo] *sm* partnership; (*impresa commerciale, banca*) consortium, trust; (*imprese riunite*) syndicate, cooperative.

constare [kon'stare] *v* consist. **a quanto mi consta** to my knowledge, as far as I know.

constatare [konsta'tare] *v* (*notare*) see; (*accertare*) ascertain, verify; (*riconoscere*) recognize. **constatazione** *sf* verification; recognition.

consueto [konsu'ɛto] *agg* (*solito*) usual; (*abituato*) used. **come di consueto** as usual. **di consueto** usually. **consuetudine** *sf* habit, custom.

consulente [konsu'lɛnte] *s(m+f)*, *agg* consultant. **consulenza** *sf* advice. **consultare** *v* consult. **consultazione** *sf* consultation; (*biblioteca*) reference. **consultivo** *agg* consultative, advisory.

consumare[1] [konsu'mare] *v* consume, use up; (*logorare*) wear out; (*dissipare*) squander; (*mangiare*) eat. **consumazione** *sf* (*bibita*) drink; (*spuntino*) snack. **consumismo** *sm* consumer society. **consumo** *sm* consumption; (*spreco*) waste. **articoli di consumo** *sm pl* consumer goods *pl.*

consumare[2] [konsu'mare] *v* (*portare a compimento*) consummate. **consumazione** *sf* consummation.

consuntivo [konsun'tivo] *sm* balance sheet.

contabile [kon'tabile] *s(m+f)* bookkeeper; (*ragioniere*) accountant. **valore contabile** *sm* book value. **contabilità** *sf* bookkeeping; accountancy. **tenere la contabilità** keep the books.

contachilometri [kontaki'lɔmetri] *sm invar* mileometer; (*tachimetro*) speedometer.

contadino [konta'dino], **-a** *agg* (*della campagna*) rustic; (*dei contadini*) peasant. *sm, sf* peasant; (*agricoltore*) farmer.

contagioso [konta'dʒozo] *agg* contagious, catching. **contagiare** *v* infect, contaminate.

contagiri [konta'dʒiri] *sm invar* rev(olution) counter.

contaminare [kontami'nare] *v* contaminate.

contanti [kon'tanti] *sm pl* cash *sing*, ready money *sing.*

contare [kon'tare] *v* count; (*proporsi*) think. **contato** *agg* limited. **ho i giorni contati** my days are numbered. **ho i minuti contati** I have no time to waste. **contatore** *sm* meter.

contatto [kon'tatto] *sm* contact. **essere/mantenersi/mettersi in contatto** be/keep/get in touch.

conte ['konte] *sm* count. **contea** *sf* (*suddivisione amministrativa*) county; (*titolo, dominio di conti*) earldom. **contessa** *sf* countess.

conteggio [kon'teddʒo] *sm* count, counting. **conteggiare** *v* (*calcolare*) count; (*far pagare*) charge.

contegno [kon'teɲo] *sm* bearing, behaviour. **darsi** *or* **assumere un contegno** strike an attitude. **contegnoso** *agg* dignified, reserved.

contemplare [kontem'plare] *v* contemplate; consider, provide for. **contemplazione** *sf* contemplation.

contempo [kon'tempo] *sm* **nel contempo** in the meantime, meanwhile.

contemporaneo [kontempo'raneo], **-a** *sm, sf* contemporary. *agg* contemporary; simultaneous.

***contendere** [kon'tendere] *v* dispute; (*litigarsi*) quarrel (over); oppose. **contendente** *s(m+f)* competitor.

***contenere** [konte'nere] *v* contain, hold; (*trattenere*) hold back. **contenersi** *v* (*dominarsi*) restrain oneself; (*comportarsi*) act. **contenitore** *sm* container.

contentare [konten'tare] *v* (*appagare*) satisfy; (*far contento*) please. **contentarsi** *v* be satisfied. **contentezza** *sf* satisfaction, contentment; (*gioia*) joy. **contento** *agg* (*soddisfatto*) pleased, satisfied; (*felice*) happy; (*allegro*) cheerful.

contenuto [konte'nuto] *sm* (*recipiente*) contents *pl*; (*argomento*) content. *agg* reserved, restrained.

contestare [kontes'tare] *v* contest; (*dir*) charge (with); (*impugnare*) challenge. **contestazione** *sf* dispute; notification.

contiguo [kon'tiguo] *agg* neighbouring, adjoining.

continente [konti'nɛnte] *sm, agg* continent. **continentale** *agg* continental. **continenza** *sf* continence.

contingente [kontin'dʒɛnte] *sm* quota; (*mil*) contingent. **contingenza** *sf* circumstance; contingency. **indennità di contingenza** *sf* cost of living allowance.

continuare [kontinu'are] *v* continue, carry on; (*riprendere*) resume; (*insistere*) keep on. **continuazione** *sf* continuation. **continuità** *sf* continuity. **continuo** *agg* endless; (*costante*) continual; (*ininterrotto*) continuous.

conto ['kɔnto] *sm* account; (*somma da pagare*) bill; calculation. **a conti fatti** all things considered. **a (ogni) buon conto** in any case. **far conto che** *or* **di** suppose, imagine; (*proporsi*) intend. **fare conto su** rely on. **per conto di** on behalf of. **per**

conto mio as far as I'm concerned; (*da solo*) on my own. **tener conto di** make a note of; consider, take into account.

***contorcere** [kon'tɔrtʃere] *v* twist. **contorcersi** *v* writhe. **contorsione** *sf* contortion. **contorsionista** *s*(*m*+*f*) contortionist.

contorno [kon'torno] *sm* (*linea*) outline; (*gastr*) vegetables *pl*, side-dish; (*ornamento*) surround, border.

contrabbandare [kontrabban'dare] *v* smuggle. **contrabbando** *sm* contraband, smuggling. **merce di contrabbando** *sf* smuggled goods *pl*.

contrabbasso [kontrab'basso] *sm* double-bass.

contraccambiare [kontrakkam'bjare] *v* reciprocate. **in contraccambio di** in return for.

contraccolpo [kontrak'kolpo] *sm* counter-blow; (*fig*) repercussion.

***contraddire** [kontrad'dire] *v* contradict. **contraddizione** *sf* contradiction. **spirito di contraddizione** *sm* contrariness.

contraddittorio [kontraddit'tɔrjo] *agg* contradictory. *sm* (*dir*) cross-examination.

contraente [kontra'ɛnte] *agg* contracting.

contraereo [kontra'ɛreo] *agg* anti-aircraft.

***contraffare** [kontraf'fare] *v* imitate; (*falsificare*) forge, counterfeit. **contraffattore, -trice** *sm*, *sf* counterfeiter, forger; imitator. **contraffazione** *sf* forgery.

contralto [kon'tralto] *sm* contralto.. *agg* alto.

***contrapporre** [kontrap'porre] *v* oppose, contrast. **contrapposizione** *sf* opposition, contrast.

contrariare [kontra'rjare] *v* irritate, oppose.

contrario [kon'trarjo] *agg* opposite, contrary; (*avverso*) unfavourable. *sm* contrary, opposite. **al contrario** on the contrary. **al contrario di** unlike. **essere contrario a** be opposed to.

***contrarre** [kon'trarre] *v* contract.

contrassegnare [kontrasse'ɲare] *v* mark. **contrassegno** *sm* mark.

contrastare [kontras'tare] *v* (*ostacolare*) bar, oppose; (*essere in conflitto*) clash; dispute. **contrasto** *sm* contrast; conflict.

contrattaccare [kontrattak'kare] *v* counter-attack. **contrattacco** *sm* counter-attack.

contrattempo [kontrat'tɛmpo] *sm* hitch.

contratto [kon'tratto] *sm* contract. **contrattare** *v* negotiate; (*mercanteggiare*) haggle.

contravvenzione [kontravven'tsjone] *sf* (*violazione*) infringement; (*multa*) fine. **contravventore, -trice** *sm*, *sf* offender.

contrazione [kontra'tsjone] *sf* contraction.

contribuire [kontribu'ire] *v* contribute. **contribuente** *sm*, *sf* taxpayer. **contributo** *sm* contribution; (*dir*) tax.

contristare [kontris'tare] *v* sadden.

contrito [kon'trito] *agg* contrite.

contro ['kontro] *prep*, *avv* against.

controbattere [kontro'battere] *v* rebut.

controbilanciare [kontrobilan'tʃare] *v* counterbalance.

controfirmare [kontrofir'mare] *v* countersign. **controfirma** *sf* countersignature.

controllare [kontrol'lare] *v* control; (*esaminare*) check. **controllo** *sm* control; (*verifica*) check; inspection. **controllo delle nascite** birth-control. **controllore** *sm* inspector.

contromano [kontro'mano] *avv* in the opposite direction.

contromarcia [kontro'martʃa] *sf* reverse (gear).

contropelo [kontro'pelo] *avv* against the grain.

controproducente [kontroprodu'tʃɛnte] *agg* self-defeating, counter-productive.

controrrdine [kon'trordine] *sm* countermand. **dare un contrordine** countermand.

controsenso [kontro'sɛnso] *sm* nonsense, contradiction in terms.

controversia [kontro'vɛrsja] *sf* controversy. **controverso** *agg* controversial.

controvoglia [kontro'vɔʎa] *avv* unwillingly.

conturbare [kontur'bare] *v* perturb.

contusione [kontu'zjone] *sf* bruise. **contuso** *agg* bruised.

convalescenza [konvale'ʃɛntsa] *sf* convalescence. **convalescente** *s*(*m*+*f*), *agg* convalescent. **convalescenziario** *sm* convalescent home.

convalidare [konvali'dare] *v* confirm. **convalida** *or* **convalidazione** *sf* confirmation.

convegno [kon'veɲo] *sm* meeting, rendezvous. **darsi convegno** make a date; meet.

***convenire** [konve'nire] *v* (*venire insieme*) come together, meet; (*essere d'accordo*) agree; (*ammettere*) admit; (*essere vantaggioso*) suit, pay, be worth it. **conveniente**

agg (*vantaggioso*) favourable, reasonable; (*adatto, adeguato*) suitable. **convenienza** *sf* (*utilità*) convenience; (*decoro*) propriety; (*l'essere adatto*) suitability.
convento [kon'vɛnto] *sm* convent.
convenzione [konven'tsjone] *sf* (*patto*) agreement; (*uso*) custom, convention.
***convergere** [kon'verdʒere] *v* converge. **convergente** *agg* converging.
conversare [konver'sare] *v* converse. **conversazione** *sf* conversation, talk.
conversione [konver'sjone] *sf* conversion; (*trasformazione*) change, turn(ing).
convertire [konver'tire] *v* convert, turn. **convertibile** *agg* convertible. **convertito, -a** *sm, sf* convert.
convesso [kon'vɛsso] *agg* convex.
***convincere** [kon'vintʃere] *v* convince. **convincente** *agg* convincing. **convinto** *agg* (*persuaso*) convinced; (*dimostrato colpevole*) convicted; (*fedele*) staunch. **convinzione** *sf* conviction.
convitato [konvi'tato] *sm* guest.
convito [kon'vito] *sm* banquet.
convitto [kon'vitto] *sm* boarding-school.
convocare [konvo'kare] *v* convoke, convene; (*radunare*) call together, rally.
convoglio [kon'vɔʎo] *sm* convoy. **convoglio funebre** funeral procession. **convogliare** *v* (*scortare*) convoy; (*condurre, trasportare*) convey.
convulsione [konvul'sjone] *sf* convulsion. **convulsivo** *agg* convulsive. **convulso** *agg* convulsed.
cooperare [koope'rare] *v* cooperate, collaborate; contribute. **cooperativa** *sf* cooperative. **cooperazione** *sf* cooperation, collaboration.
coordinare [koordi'nare] *v* coordinate. **coordinata** *sf* coordinate.
coperchio [ko'pɛrkjo] *sm* lid, cover.
coperta [ko'pɛrta] *sf* (*drappo*) blanket; (*riparo*) cover. **copertina** *sf* (*quaderno*) cover; (*libro*) dust-jacket.
coperto[1] [ko'pɛrto] *agg* covered; (*riparato*) sheltered; (*chiuso*) closed; (*nuvoloso*) overcast; (*nascosto*) concealed. *sm* **al coperto** under cover. **mettersi al coperto** shelter.
coperto[2] [ko'pɛrto] *sm* (*a tavola*) place (-setting); (*prezzo*) cover charge.
copertone [koper'tone] *sm* (*pneumatico*) tyre; (*telone*) tarpaulin.
copia ['kɔpia] *sf* copy; (*fig*) image. **bella/brutta copia** fair/rough copy. **copiare** *v* copy. **carta copiativa** *sf* carbon paper. **matita copiativa** *sf* indelible pencil. **copiatura** *sf* copy; (*trascrizione*) copying.
copioso [ko'pjozo] *agg* copious.
coppa ['kɔppa] *sf* cup; (*auto*) sump.
coppia ['kɔppja] *sf* couple. **a coppie** in pairs, in twos.
***coprire** [ko'prire] *v* cover; (*nascondere*) hide. **coprire un rumore** drown a noise.
coraggio [ko'raddʒo] *sm* courage, bravery; (*sfacciataggine*) nerve; (*cuore*) heart. **farsi coraggio** pluck up courage. **perdere coraggio** lose heart. **coraggioso** *agg* courageous, brave; (*ardito*) bold.
corallo [ko'rallo] *sm* coral.
corazzare [korat'tsare] *v* armour. **corazza** *sf* armour. **corazzata** *sf* battleship.
corbelleria [korbelle'ria] *sf* (*detto*) nonsense; (*atto*) foolery.
corda ['kɔrda] *sf* cord; (*cordicella, musica*) string; (*fune*) rope; (*geom*) chord. **avere la corda al collo** have one's back to the wall. **essere giù di corda** feel low. **tagliar la corda** (*andarsene di soppiatto*) sneak off; (*fuggire*) cut and run.
cordiale [kor'djale] *agg* cordial, warm. **cordiali saluti** kind regards *pl*. **cordialità** *sf* friendliness.
cordoglio [kor'dɔʎo] *sm* grief. **esprimere il proprio cordoglio** offer one's condolences.
cordone [kor'done] *sm* cord; (*schieramento*) cordon.
coreografo [kore'ɔgrafo] *sm* choreographer. **coreografia** *sf* choreography.
coriandoli [ko'rjandoli] *sm pl* confetti *sing*.
coricare [kori'kare] *v* lay down; (*mettere a letto*) put to bed. **coricarsi** *v* lie down; go to bed.
cornacchia [kor'nakkja] *sf* crow.
cornamusa [korna'muza] *sf* bagpipes *pl*.
cornetto [kor'netto] *sm* (*musica*) cornet; (*telefono*) receiver.
cornice [kor'nitʃe] *sf* frame; (*ambiente*) setting; (*arch*) cornice.
corno ['kɔrno] *sm, pl* **-a** *f in zool sense* horn; (*ramificato*) antler; (*musica*) French horn. **corno da caccia** bugle. **corno inglese** cor anglais. **dire corna di** run down. **fare le corna** (*non essere fedele*) be unfaithful; (*gesto*) make a V-sign. **non capire un corno** not understand a thing. **non valere un corno** not be

worth a brass farthing. **cornuto** *agg* horned.

coro ['kɔro] *sm* choir; (*canto*) chorus. **in coro** in chorus, all together.

corpo ['kɔrpo] *sm* body; (*mil, ecc.*) corps. **a corpo morto** headlong, whole-heartedly. **corpo a corpo** hand to hand. **corporatura** *sf* build. **corporeo** *agg* bodily.

corporazione [korpora'tsjone] *sf* guild, association.

corpulento [korpu'lɛnto] *agg* stout.

corpuscolo [kor'puskolo] *sm* corpuscle.

corredo [kor'rɛdo] *sm* outfit; (*mil*) equipment. **corredare** *v* fit out, equip; (*fig*) furnish (with).

***correggere** [kor'reddʒere] *v* correct; (*bevanda*) lace.

corrente [kor'rɛnte] *agg* current; (*che scorre*) running; (*andante*) common or garden. **essere/tenere al corrente** be/keep informed *or* up-to-date. **mettere al corrente** acquaint, inform. *sf* current, stream; (*tendenza, moda*) trend. **corrente d'aria** draught.

***correre** ['korrere] *v* run; (*veicoli*) go; (*circolare*) circulate. **correre dietro a** run after.

corretto [kor'rɛtto] *agg* correct, right, exact. **correttezza** *sf* fairness; (*educazione*) propriety.

correzione [korre'tsjone] *sf* correction. **correzione di bozze** proof-reading.

corridoio [korri'dojo] *sm* passage, corridor.

corridore [korri'dore] *sm* runner; (*automobilista*) racing-driver; (*ciclista*) racing-cyclist. **cavallo corridore** *sm* racehorse.

corriera [kor'rjɛra] *sf* coach.

corriere [kor'rjɛre] *sm* messenger, courier; (*merci*) carrier; (*posta*) mail.

corrimano [korri'mano] *sm* handrail.

***corrispondere** [korris'pondere] *v* correspond; (*accordarsi*) agree; (*pagare*) pay; (*ricambiare*) reciprocate. **corrispondente** *s*(*m*+*f*) correspondent. **corrispondenza** *sf* correspondence; (*posta*) mail; (*conformità*) relation; (*somiglianza*) likeness.

corroborare [korrobo'rare] *v* corroborate; (*rinforzare*) strengthen.

***corrodere** [kor'rodere] *v* corrode. **corrosione** *sf* corrosion.

***corrompere** [kor'rompere] *v* corrupt; (*con denaro*) bribe; (*guastare*) spoil. **corrotto** *agg* corrupt.

corrucciarsi [korrut'tʃarsi] *v* be angered and upset (by).

corrugare [korru'gare] *v* crease, wrinkle. **corrugare la fronte** knit one's brow.

corruzione [korru'tsjone] *sf* corruption; (*con denaro*) bribery.

corsa ['korsa] *sf* (*gara*) race; (*azione*) racing; (*atletica*) running; (*percorso*) run. **andare di corsa** (be in a) hurry. **di gran corsa** in a great hurry, in great haste. **fare una corsa (da)** (*fam*) pop over *or* round (to).

corsia [kor'sia] *sf* (*teatro, ecc.*) gangway; (*ospedale*) ward; (*autostrada*) lane; (*tappeto*) runner.

corsivo [kor'sivo] *agg* italic. *sm* italics *pl.*

corso[1] ['korso] *sm* course; (*econ*) circulation; (*quotazione*) rate; (*strada principale*) high street. **in corso** in progress; (*in sospeso*) pending; (*corrente*) present.

corso[2] ['kɔrso], **-a** *s, agg* Corsican.

corte ['korte] *sf* court; (*cortile*) courtyard. **corte marziale** court-martial. **fare la corte (a)** (*ragazza*) court; (*lusingare*) play up (to). **corteggiare** *v* court. **corteggio** *sm* retinue.

corteccia [kor'tettʃa] *sf* (*albero*) bark; (*frutto*) rind; (*anat*) cortex.

corteo [kor'tɛo] *sm* procession.

cortese [kor'teze] *agg* polite, courteous; (*gentile*) kind. **cortesia** *sf* politeness, courtesy; kindness. **avere la cortesia di** be so kind as to. **per cortesia** (*per favore*) please, kindly; (*per ragioni di cortesia*) out of politeness.

cortile [kor'tile] *sm* courtyard; (*casa colonica*) farmyard. **animali da cortile** *sm pl* farmyard animals *pl.*

cortina [kor'tina] *sf* curtain. **cortina di ferro** iron curtain. **cortina di fumo** smoke-screen.

corto ['korto] *agg* short. **a farla corta** to come to the point. **essere a corto di** be short of.

corvo ['kɔrvo] *sm* (*imperiale*) raven; (*comune*) rook.

cosa ['kɔza] *pron* what. **a cosa serve?** what is it for? *sf* thing; (*qualcosa*) something; (*faccenda*) matter. **a cose fatte** after the event. **cosa da nulla** nothing. **cosa da poco** trifle. **gran cosa** much. **qualsiasi** *or* **qualunque cosa** anything. **tante cose** (*augurio*) best wishes *pl.*

coscia ['kɔʃa] *sf* thigh; (*gastr*) leg.
cosciente [ko'ʃɛnte] *agg* aware. **coscienza** *sf* conscience; (*conoscenza*) consciousness; (*impegno*) conscientiousness. **avere la coscienza pulita/sporca** have a clear/guilty conscience. **in coscienza** morally, honestly. **coscienzioso** *agg* conscientious.
coscrizione [koskri'tsjone] *sf* draft, conscription. **coscritto** *sm* conscript, recruit.
così [ko'zi] *avv* (*in questo modo*) like this *or* that; (*tanto*) so; (*con agg qualificante un sostantivo*) such. *cong* so. **così ... come ...** as ... as .... **così così** so-so.
cosiddetto *agg* so-called.
cosmetico [koz'metiko] *sm, agg* cosmetic. **cosmesi** *or* **cosmetica** *sf* beauty culture.
cosmo ['kɔzmo] *sm* cosmos. **cosmonauta** *s(m+f)* astronaut. **cosmonautica** *sf* astronautics.
cosmopolita [kozmo'pɔlita] *s(m+f), agg* cosmopolitan.
coso ['kozo] *sm* (*fam*) thingummy.
***cospargere** [kos'pardʒere] *v* strew.
cospicuo [kos'pikuo] *agg* conspicuous; (*grande*) considerable.
cospirare [kospi'rare] *v* plot.
costa ['kɔsta] *sf* coast, coastline; (*litorale*) shore; (*coltello, libro*) back; (*costola*) rib.
costà [kos'ta] *avv* (over) there.
costante [kos'tante] *agg* constant, firm; (*saldo*) steady. *sf* constant. **costanza** *sf* steadfastness, firmness.
costare [kos'tare] *v* cost. **costar caro** be expensive. **mi è costato caro** I have paid dearly for it.
costeggiare [kosted'dʒare] *v* skirt; (*costa*) follow the coast.
costei [kos'tɛi] *pron* this woman.
costellare [kostel'lare] *v* stud.
costellazione [kostella'tsjone] *sf* constellation.
costernare [koster'nare] *v* dismay.
costiero [kos'tjɛra] *agg* coastal.
costipato [kosti'pato] *agg* (*stitico*) constipated; (*fam*: *raffreddato*) having a bad cold.
costituire [kostitu'ire] *v* (*formare*) set up, form; (*dar luogo*) constitute; (*dichiarare*) appoint. **costituirsi** *v* (*presentarsi spontaneamente*) give oneself up. **costituirsi parte civile** take legal proceedings. **costituzione** *sf* constitution.
costo ['kɔsto] *sm* cost, price. **costoso** *agg* costly, dear.
costola ['kɔstola] *sf* rib.
costoro [kos'toro] *pron* these people.
***costringere** [kos'trindʒere] *v* force, compel.
***costruire** [kostru'ire] *v* build, construct. **costruzione** *sf* construction; (*edificio*) building.
costui [kos'tui] *pron* this man.
costume [kos'tume] *sm* (*usanza*) custom, use; (*condotta*) behaviour; (*indumento*) costume; (*abitudine personale*) habit. **il buon costume** morality.
costura [kos'tura] *sf* seam.
cotogna [ko'toɲa] *sf* quince.
cotoletta [koto'letta] *sf* cutlet.
cotone [ko'tone] *sm* cotton. **cotone idrofilo** cotton-wool. **cotoniero** *agg* cotton. **cotonificio** *sm* cotton mill.
cotta ['kɔtta] *sf* **prendere una cotta** (*fam*) fall in love.
cottimo ['kɔttimo] *sm* piece-work.
cotto ['kɔtto] *agg* cooked; (*carne*) done; (*in forno*) baked. **farne di cotte e di crude** be up to all sorts of tricks. **nè cotto nè crudo** neither one thing nor the other.
cottura [kot'tura] *sf* cooking; (*in forno*) baking.
covare [ko'vare] *v* hatch; (*fig*) brood over; (*sotto la cenere*) smoulder. **covata** *sf* brood.
covo ['kovo] *sm* lair, den.
cozza ['kɔttsa] *sf* mussel.
cozzare [kot'tsare] *v* collide *or* clash (with); (*con le corna*) butt. **cozzo** *sm* collision, clash; butt.
crampo ['krampo] *sm* cramp.
cranio ['kranjo] *sm* skull.
cratere [kra'tɛre] *sm* crater.
cravatta [kra'vatta] *sf* tie.
creanza [kre'antsa] *sf* (good) manners *pl*, breeding.
creare [kre'are] *v* create, give rise to; (*eleggere*) appoint. **creatore** *sm* maker, creator. **creatura** *sf* creature. **creazione** *sf* creation.
credenza[1] [kre'dɛntsa] *sf* belief (*pl* -s), opinion; (*fede*) faith; (*comm*) credit.
credenza[2] [kre'dɛntsa] *sf* (*mobile*) sideboard.
credere ['kredere] *v* believe; (*pensare*) think; (*aver fiducia*) trust. **credibile** *agg* credible, believable. **credibilità** *sf* credibility.

credito ['kredito] *sm* credit; (*stima*) esteem. **creditore** *sm* creditor.
credulo ['kredulo] *agg* credulous. **credulone, -a** *sm, sf* gullible person.
crema ['krema] *sf* cream. **cremoso** *agg* creamy.
cremare [kre'mare] *v* cremate. **crematorio** *sm* crematorium. **cremazione** *sf* cremation.
cremisi ['kremizi] *agg, sm* crimson.
cren ['kren] *sm* horse-radish.
crepare [kre'pare] *v* burst, crack; (*fam: morire*) die, kick the bucket. **crepacuore** *sm* heartbreak.
crepitare [krepi'tare] *v* crackle. **crepitio** *sm* crackle, crackling.
crepuscolo [kre'puskolo] *sm* twilight, dusk; decline.
***crescere** ['kreʃere] *v* grow; (*maturarsi*) grow up; (*aumentare*) rise; (*sovrabbondare*) be left over. **crescita** *sf* growth.
crescione [kre'ʃone] *sm* (*d'acqua*) water-cress; (*inglese*) mustard and cress.
cresima ['krezima] *sf* confirmation. **cresimare** *v* confirm.
crespa ['krespa] *sf* (*ruga*) wrinkle; (*stoffa*) crease; (*piccola ondulazione*) ripple.
crespo ['krespo] *agg* frizzy. *sm* crepe.
cresta ['kresta] *sf* crest.
creta ['kreta] *sf* clay.
cretino [kre'tino], **-a** *sm, sf* idiot, fool. *agg* idiotic, foolish. **cretineria** *sf* stupidity; (*discorso, azione*) foolish thing.
cricca ['krikka] *sf* clique, gang.
cricco ['krikko] *sm* jack.
criceto [kri'tʃeto] *sm* hamster.
criminale [krimi'nale] *agg, s(m+f)* criminal. **crimine** *sm* crime. **criminoso** *agg* criminal.
criniera [kri'njera] *sf* mane.
cripta ['kripta] *sf* crypt.
crisalide [kri'zalide] *sf* chrysalis.
crisantemo [krizan'temo] *sm* chrysanthemum.
crisi ['krizi] *sf* crisis (*pl* -ses); (*med*) fit, attack.
cristallizzare [kristallid'dzare] *v* crystallize.
cristallo [kris'tallo] *sm* crystal; (*vetro*) plate-glass, (window) pane. **cristallino** *agg* crystalline; pure, limpid.
cristiano [kris'tjano], **-a** *agg* Christian. *sm, sf* Christian; (*essere umano*) soul.
Cristo ['kristo] *sm* Christ. **non c'è cristo** (*possibilità*) there isn't a chance. **povero cristo** poor devil.
criterio [kri'terjo] *sm* criterion (*pl* -a), norm; sense.
critico ['kritiko] *agg* critical. *sm* critic. **critica** *sf* criticism; (*scritto*) review; (*persona*) critic. **criticare** *v* criticize; review; (*biasimare*) blame.
crivellare [krivel'lare] *v* riddle. **crivello** *sm* sieve.
croccante [krok'kante] *agg* crisp. *sm* (*dolce*) praline.
crocchia ['krɔkkja] *sf* bun, chignon.
crocchio ['krɔkkjo] *sm* cluster.
croce ['krotʃe] *sf* cross. **a occhio e croce** roughly. **croce uncinata** swastika. **crocevia** *sm invar* crossroads. **fare a testa e croce** toss a coin. **punto a croce** *sm* cross-stitch.
crociare [kro'tʃare] *v* cross.
crociata [kro'tʃata] *sf* crusade. **crociato** *sm* crusader.
crocicchio [kro'tʃikkjo] *sm* crossroads.
crociera [kro'tʃera] *sf* cruise.
***crocifiggere** [krotʃifid'dʒere] *v* crucify.
crocifisso [krotʃi'fisso] *sm* crucifix. *agg* crucified.
croco ['krɔko] *sm* crocus.
crogiolarsi [krodʒo'larsi] *v* bask. **crogiolo** *sm* crucible; (*fig*) melting-pot.
crollare [krol'lare] *v* (*cadere*) collapse, slump; (*spalle*) shrug. **crollo** *sm* collapse, slump.
croma ['krɔma] *sf* quaver.
cromo ['krɔmo] *sm* (*metallo*) chromium. **giallo cromo** chrome yellow. **cromatura** *sf* chromium-plating.
cromosoma [kromo'sɔma] *sm* chromosome.
cronaca ['krɔnaka] *sf* (*narrazione*) chronicle; (*radio, TV, stampa*) news, review.
cronico ['krɔniko] *agg* chronic. *sm* chronic invalid.
cronista [kro'nista] *s(m+f)* reporter.
cronologico [krono'lɔdʒiko] *agg* chronological.
cronometro [kro'nɔmetro] *sm* chronometer, stop-watch. **cronometrare** *v* time.
crosta ['krɔsta] *sf* crust; (*ferita*) scab. **crostata** *sf* tart.
crostacei [kros'tatʃei] *sm pl* crustaceans *pl*, shellfish *pl*.
crucciare [krut'tʃare] *v* distress, worry.
cruciale [kru'tʃale] *agg* crucial.

cruciverba [krutʃi'vɛrba] *sm invar* crossword.
crudele [kru'dɛle] *agg* cruel; (*duro, aspro*) harsh; (*doloroso*) bitter. **crudeltà** *sf* cruelty; (*asprezza*) harshness.
crudo ['krudo] *agg* raw; (*rigido*) harsh; (*brusco*) crude; (*volgare*) coarse.
crumiro [kru'miro], **-a** *sm, sf* blackleg.
cruna ['kruna] *sf* eye (of a needle).
crusca ['kruska] *sf* bran.
cruscotto [krus'kɔtto] *sm* instrument panel; (*auto*) dashboard.
cubo ['kubo] *sm* cube. **cubico** *agg* cubic. **cubismo** *sm* cubism.
cuccagna [kuk'kaɲa] *sf* (*abbondanza*) plenty; (*allegria*) fun.
cuccetta [kut'tʃetta] *sf* couchette.
cucchiaio [kuk'kjajo] *sm* spoon; (*contenuto*) spoonful; (*da tavola*) tablespoon. **cucchiaino** *sm* teaspoon.
cucciolo ['kuttʃolo] *sm* puppy.
cucina [ku'tʃina] *sf* (*luogo*) kitchen; (*atto del cucinare*) cooking; (*cibo*) food; (*apparecchio*) cooker. **cucina casalinga** home cooking. **cucinare** *v* cook.
cucire [ku'tʃire] *v* sew, stitch; (*con cucitrice*) staple. **cucirino** *sm* sewing thread. **cucito** *sm* sewing, needlework. **cucitrice** *sf* (*persona*) seamstress; (*apparecchio*) stapler. **cucitura** *sf* seam.
cuculo ['kukulo] *sm* cuckoo.
cuffia ['kuffja] *sf* cap; bonnet; (*telefono, radio*) earphones *pl*, headphones *pl*.
cugino [ku'dʒino], **-a** *sm, sf* cousin.
cui ['kui] *pron* (*persone*) whom; (*cose*) which. **il cui, la cui, ecc.** whose. **in cui** (*quando*) when; (*dove*) where.
culla ['kulla] *sf* cradle. **cullare** *v* rock, lull. **cullarsi** *v* (*illudersi*) delude oneself.
culmine ['kulmine] *sm* summit, height. **culminare** *v* culminate.
culo ['kulo] *sm* (*fam*) bottom; (*volg*) arse.
culto ['kulto] *sm* worship; (*religione*) cult.
cultura [kul'tura] *sf* culture, learning; cultivation. **culturale** *agg* cultural.
cumulo ['kumulo] *sm* pile, heap.
cuneo ['kuneo] *sm* wedge.
cunetta [ku'netta] *sf* gutter.
***cuocere** ['kwɔtʃere] *v* (*cucinare*) cook; (*al forno*) bake; (*a lesso*) boil; (*alla griglia*) grill; (*arrosto*) roast; (*in umido*) stew; (*ceramica, ecc.*) fire. **cuocere a fuoco lento** simmer. **cuoco, -a** *sm, sf* cook.
cuoio ['kwɔjo] *sm* leather; (*pelle*) hide. **cuoio capelluto** scalp. **cuoio scamosciato** chamois leather, suede.
cuore ['kwɔre] *sm* heart. **di cuore** heartily. **di tutto cuore** with all one's heart. **mettersi il cuore in pace** set one's mind at rest. **nel cuore di** at the height of; (*notte*) at dead of. **senza cuore** heartless.
cupido ['kupido] *agg* greedy. **cupidigia** *sf* greed.
cupo ['kupo] *agg* (*profondo, suono*) deep; (*privo di luce, colore*) dark.
cupola ['kupola] *sf* dome.
cura ['kura] *sf* care; (*med*) cure, treatment. **curare** *v* look after, take care of; cure, treat. **curarsi** *v* mind *or* care about. **curativo** *agg* curative.
curatore [kura'tore], **-trice** *sm, sf* guardian. **curatela** *sf* guardianship.
curioso [ku'rjozo] *agg* curious; (*strano*) odd. **curiosità** *sf* curiosity. **curiosare** *v* pry.
curvare [kur'vare] *v* bend. **curvare il capo** bow one's head. **curva** *sf* bend, curve. **curvatura** *sf* curvature, sweep. **curvo** *agg* curved, bent.
cuscino [ku'ʃino] *sm* cushion; (*guanciale*) pillow. **cuscinetto** *sm* (*a sfere*) ball-bearing; (*a rulli*) roller-bearing. **stato cuscinetto** *sm* buffer state.
custode [kus'tɔde] *s*(*m*+*f*) keeper, caretaker. **custodia** *sf* custody, care, safe keeping; (*astuccio*) case. **custodire** *v* keep; look after; (*sorvegliare*) guard.
cutaneo [ku'taneo] *agg* cutaneous, skin.

D

da [da] *prep* from; (*moto a luogo*) to; (*stato in luogo*) at; (*durata*) for; (*fin da*) since; (*causa*) of, from; (*segno distintivo*) with; (*come*) as, like. **da allora** since then. **da allora in poi** ever since. **da lontano** from afar. **da molto** for a long time. **da noi** at home; (*al mio paese*) in my country.
dabbasso [dab'basso] *avv* downstairs.
dabbene [dab'bene] *agg* decent, honest.
daccapo [dak'kapo] *avv* (*di nuovo*) again, once more; (*da principio*) from the beginning, all over again.
dacché [dak'ke] *cong* since.
dado ['dado] *sm* die (*pl* dice); (*gastr*) cube; (*mec*) nut.

daffare [daf'fare] *sm invar* work, business.
dagli[1] ['daʎi] *prep+art* **da gli.**
dagli[2] ['daʎi] *inter* (*forza*) go on! come on! (*noioso*) not again! pack it in!
dai ['dai] *prep+art* **da i.**
daino ['daino] *sm* (fallow) deer. **daina** *sf* doe. **pelle di daino** *sf* buckskin.
dal [dal] *prep+art* **da il.**
dalia ['dalja] *sf* dahlia.
dall' [dall] *prep+art* **da l'.**
dalla ['dalla] *prep+art* **da la.**
dalle ['dalle] *prep+art* **da le.**
dallo ['dallo] *prep+art* **da lo.**
daltonismo [dalto'nizmo] *sm* colour-blindness. **daltonico** *agg* colour-blind.
dama ['dama] *sf* lady, noblewoman; (*gioco*) draughts; (*carta*) queen.
damasco [da'masko] *sm* damask.
dancing ['da:nsiŋ] *sm invar* dance-hall.
Danimarca [dani'marka] *sf* Denmark. **danese** *sm, agg* Danish; *s*(*m+f*) Dane.
dannare [dan'nare] *v* damn. **dannato, -a** *s, agg* damned. **dannazione** *sf* damnation; (*tormento*) trial.
danneggiare [danned'dʒare] *v* (*guastare*) damage; (*nuocere*) injure, harm. **danno** *sm* damage; injury, harm; (*pregiudizio*) detriment. **danno doloso** wilful damage. **dannoso** *agg* harmful.
danzare [dan'tsare] *v* dance. **danza** *sf* dancing; (*ballo*) dance. **danzatore, -trice** *sm, sf* dancer.
dappertutto [dapper'tutto] *avv* everywhere, all over the place.
dappoco [dap'pɔko] *agg invar* worthless; (*inetto*) good-for-nothing.
dappresso [dap'presso] *avv* close to, close up.
dapprima [dap'prima] *avv* at first.
dardeggiare [darded'dʒare] *v* dart. **dardo** *sm* dart.
***dare** ['dare] *v* give; (*avere come risultato*) make, come to; (*esame*) take; apply; (*colpire*) hit; (*fruttare*) yield. **dare ai** *or* **sui nervi a qualcuno** get on someone's nerves. **dare alla luce** give birth to. **dar da fare a** keep busy. **dar fine a** put an end to. **dare nell'occhio** catch the eye. **dare per scontato** take for granted. **dar retta a** listen to. **dare su** look out on to; (*affacciare*) face. **darsi a** (*dedicarsi*) devote oneself to; (*applicarsi*) go in for.
darsena ['darsena] *sf* dock.
data ['data] *sf* date. **di fresca data** recent. **di vecchia data** of long standing. **in che data?** when? **datare** *v* date; (*risalire*) go back (to).
dato ['dato] *agg* given; (*in vista*) considering, in view of. **dato che** supposing that, as, since. *sm* data. **dato di fatto** fact. **datore di lavoro** *sm* employer.
dattero ['dattero] *sm* (*frutto*) date; (*albero*) date-palm.
dattilografo [datti'lɔgrafo], **-a** *sm, sf* typist. **dattilografare** *v* type.
davanti [da'vanti] *avv* in front. *sm, agg* front. **davanti a** in front of; (*dirimpetto*) facing; (*in presenza di*) before.
davanzale [davan'tsale] *sm* window-sill.
davvero [dav'vero] *avv* really. **dici davvero?** do you (really) mean it?
dazio ['datsjo] *sm* (*imposta*) duty; (*ufficio*) customs (office).
dea ['dɛa] *sf* goddess.
debito[1] ['debito] *agg* due.
debito[2] ['debito] *sm* debt; (*comm*) debit; (*dovere*) duty. **estinguere/fare un debito** settle/incur a debt. **sentirsi in debito** be indebted. **debitore** *sm* debtor.
debole ['debole] *agg* weak, feeble; (*luce, suono, speranza*) faint. *sm* (*persona*) weakling; (*punto*) weak point; (*inclinazione*) weakness, foible. **debolezza** *sf* weakness; (*difetto*) failing.
debuttare [debut'tare] *v* make one's debut. **debutto** *sm* debut.
decade ['dɛkade] *sf* ten days *pl.*
***decadere** [deka'dere] *v* decline. **decadere da** (*dir*) forfeit. **decadente** *agg* decadent. **decadenza** *sf* decline; (*dir*) forfeiture, lapse. **decaduto** *agg* impoverished; (*scaduto*) fallen into disuse.
decalcomania [dekalkoma'nia] *sf* transfer.
decano [de'kano] *sm* dean; (*diplomatico*) doyen.
decantare[1] [dekan'tare] *v* (*lodare*) sing the praises of.
decantare[2] [dekan'tare] *v* (*liquido*) decant.
decapitare [dekapi'tare] *v* behead.
deceduto [detʃe'duto] *agg* deceased.
decennio [de'tʃɛnnjo] *sm* decade.
decente [de'tʃɛnte] *agg* decent. **decenza** *sf* decency, propriety.
decentrare [detʃen'trare] *v* decentralize. **decentramento** *sm* decentralization.
decesso [de'tʃɛsso] *sm* death.
decibel [detʃi'bɛl] *sm invar* decibel.
***decidere** [de'tʃidere] *v* decide (on); (*risolvere, determinare*) settle. **decidersi**

make up one's mind; (*indursi*) bring oneself to.
deciduo [de'tʃiduo] *agg* deciduous.
decifrare [detʃi'frare] *v* decipher; (*fam*) make out.
decimale [detʃi'male] *agg*, *sm* decimal.
decimo ['dɛtʃimo] *sm*, *agg* tenth.
decina [de'tʃina] *sf* ten; (*circa dieci*) ten or so. **a decine** (*fig*) by the dozen.
decisione [detʃi'zjone] *sf* decision, resolution; (*dir*) ruling. **decisivo** *agg* decisive; (*prova*) conclusive; (*voto*) casting.
deciso [de'tʃizo] *agg* (*fermo*) decided, firm, resolute; (*definito*, *risolto*) settled, resolved; (*spiccato*) decided, marked. **decisamente** *avv* decidedly; definitely.
declamare [dekla'mare] *v* declaim; (*protestare*) rail.
declinare [dekli'nare] *v* decline. **declinazione** *sf* (*fis*) declination; (*gramm*) declension. **declino** *sm* decline.
declivio [de'klivjo] *sm* slope.
decollare [dekol'lare] *v* take off. **decollo** *sm* take-off.
***decomporsi** [dekom'porsi] *v* disintegrate, decompose. **decomposizione** *sf* disintegration, decomposition.
decorare [deko'rare] *v* decorate. **decorazione** *sf* decoration.
decoro [de'kɔro] *sm* dignity; (*orgoglio*) pride. **decoroso** *agg* proper.
decorrere [de'korrere] *v* elapse. **con decorrenza da ...** with effect from. **decorso** *sm* (*svolgimento*) course; (*periodo*) lapse.
decrepito [de'krɛpito] *agg* decrepit.
decrescente [dekre'ʃɛnte] *agg* decreasing, diminishing; (*luna*) on the wane.
decreto [de'kreto] *sm* decree, order. **decreto di citazione** writ; (*testimone*) subpoena. **decretare** *v* decree, order; (*concedere*) award.
dedalo ['dɛdalo] *sm* maze.
dedicare [dedi'kare] *v* dedicate, devote; consecrate; (*intitolare*) name after. **dedicarsi a** (*occuparsi di*) take up, go in for. **dedica** *sf* dedication.
dedito ['dɛdito] *agg* devoted; (*assorbito*) engrossed (in); (*vizio*) addicted.
***dedurre** [de'durre] *v* deduce; (*desumere*) infer; (*prendere*, *derivare*) take, draw; (*sottrarre*) deduct. **deduzione** *sf* deduction.
defalcare [defal'kare] *v* deduct.
deferire [defe'rire] *v* defer, refer. **deferire al tribunale** sue. **deferente** *agg* deferential.
deficiente [defi'tʃɛnte] *agg* deficient; insufficient; (*inferiore alla media*) backward; (*fam*) moronic. *s*(*m*+*f*) moron, half-wit. **deficienza** *sf* deficiency, lack; (*scarsità*) shortage; (*idiozia*) mental deficiency.
deficit ['dɛfitʃit] *sm invar* deficit. **bilancio deficitario** *sm* debit balance.
definire [defi'nire] *v* define; (*risolvere*) settle. **definitivo** *agg* definitive. **in definitiva** (*dopo tutto*) after all; to sum up; (*in fin dei conti*) all things considered. **definizione** *sf* definition; settlement.
deflazione [defla'tsjone] *sf* deflation. **deflazionare** *v* deflate. **deflazionistico** *agg* deflationary.
***deflettere** [de'flettere] *v* deviate. **deflessione** *sf* deflection; deviation.
deformare [defor'mare] *v* deform, distort; (*mec*) warp; (*senso*) twist. **deformazione** *sf* deformation, distortion; warping. **deforme** *agg* deformed, misshapen; (*viso*) disfigured.
defunto [de'funto], **-a** *s*, *agg* deceased.
degenerare [dedʒene'rare] *v* degenerate. **degenerato**, **-a** *s*, *agg* degenerate.
degente [de'dʒɛnte] *agg* bedridden. **degenza** *sf* (*a letto*) stay in bed; (*in ospedale*) stay in hospital.
degli ['deʎi] *prep*+*art* **di gli**.
degnare [de'ɲare] *v* deign; deem *or* consider worthy. **degnarsi di** condescend to. **degno** *agg* worthy, deserving. **degno di fiducia** trustworthy. **degno di lode** praiseworthy. **degno di nota** noteworthy.
degradare [degra'dare] *v* degrade. **degradazione** *sf* degradation.
degustare [degus'tare] *v* taste, sample.
dei[1] ['dei] *prep*+*art* **di i**.
dei[2] ['dei] *V* **dio**.
deificare [deifi'kare] *v* deify.
del [del] *prep*+*art* **di il**.
delatore [dela'tore], **-trice** *sm*, *sf* informer. **delazione** *sf* denouncement; (*fam*) tip-off.
delegare [dele'gare] *v* delegate. **delega** *sf* (*procura*) proxy; (*dir*) power of attorney. **delegato**, **-a** *sm*, *sf* delegate. **delegazione** *sf* delegation.
deleterio [dele'tɛrjo] *agg* harmful.
delfino [del'fino] *sm* dolphin.
deliberare [delibe'rare] *v* deliberate;

(*decidere*) resolve. **deliberato** *agg* determined, resolved. **deliberazione** *sf* deliberation, decision.
delicato [deli'kato] *agg* delicate; (*gusto*) refined. **delicatezza** *sf* delicacy; (*tatto*) tact; refinement.
delimitare [delimi'tare] *v* define, circumscribe. **delimitazione** *sf* demarcation.
delineare [deline'are] *v* sketch, outline. **delinearsi** *v* (*presentarsi*) appear, emerge; (*apparire*) loom up, take shape.
delinquente [delin'kwεnte] *s(m+f)* delinquent, criminal; (*mascalzone*) rascal. **delinquenza** *sf* criminality.
deliquio [de'likwio] *sm* **cadere in deliquio** faint. **essere in deliquio** be in a faint.
delirare [deli'rare] *v* be delirious; (*farneticare*) rave. **delirio** *sm* delirium; (*follia*) frenzy.
delitto [de'litto] *sm* crime; (*reato*) offence; (*grave*) felony; (*lieve*) misdemeanour. **delittuoso** *agg* criminal.
delizia [de'litsja] *sf* delight. **delizioso** *agg* delightful; (*sapore*) delicious.
dell' [dell] *prep+art* **di l'**.
della ['della] *prep+art* **di la**.
delle ['delle] *prep+art* **di le**.
dello ['dello] *prep+art* **di lo**.
delta ['delta] *sm invar* delta.
***deludere** [de'ludere] *v* disappoint; (*render vano*) frustrate.
delusione [delu'zjone] *sf* disappointment. **deluso** *agg* disappointed.
demente [de'mente] *agg* insane. *s(m+f)* lunatic. **demenza** *sf* madness, insanity; (*med*) dementia.
democratico [demo'kratiko], **-a** *sm, sf* democrat. *agg* democratic. **democrazia** *sf* democracy.
democristiano [demokris'tjano], **-a** *sm, sf* Christian Democrat. *agg* Christian Democratic.
demografia [demogra'fia] *sf* demography. **demografico** *agg* demographic.
demolire [demo'lire] *v* demolish. **demolizione** *sf* demolition.
demone ['dεmone] *sm* demon; (*potenza ispiratrice*) genius; passion. **demonico** *agg* demonic.
demonio [de'mɔnjo] *sm* devil. **brutto come il demonio** as ugly as sin. **demoniaco** *agg* demoniacal, devilish.
demoralizzare [demoralid'dzare] *v* demoralize. **demoralizzarsi** *v* lose heart.
denaro [de'naro] *sm* money; (*grossezza di filo*) denier. **denaro spicciolo** small change.
denigrare [deni'grare] *v* denigrate; (*fam*) run down. **denigratorio** *agg* disparaging. **denigrazione** *sf* denigration, disparagement.
denominatore [denomina'tore] *sm* denominator. **denominare** *v* name. **denominazione** *sf* naming; (*nome*) name.
denotare [deno'tare] *v* denote, show.
denso ['dεnso] *agg* dense, thick. **densità** *sf* density; (*spessore*) thickness.
dente ['dεnte] *sm* tooth (*pl* teeth); (*ruota*) cog; (*forchetta*) prong. **a denti stretti** tight-lipped. **avere il dente avvelenato contro** have it in for. **dente del giudizio** wisdom tooth. **dente di latte** milk-tooth. **dente finto** false tooth. **dente sporgente** buck-tooth. **mettere i denti** teethe, cut one's teeth. **restare a denti asciutti** go hungry; (*fig*) go away empty-handed. **dentario** *agg* dental. **dentato** *agg* toothed.
dentellare [dentel'lare] *v* indent, notch. **dentellatura** *sf* indentation.
dentice ['dεntitʃe] *sm* sea bream.
dentiera [den'tjεra] *sf* denture.
dentifricio [denti'fritʃo] *sm* toothpaste.
dentista [den'tista] *s(m+f)* dentist.
dentro ['dentro] *avv* in; (*all'interno*) inside. *prep* in, inside; (*in casa*) indoors. **andar dentro** (*fam*) go to jail.
denunziare [denun'tsjare] *v also* **denunciare** denounce; (*riferire*) report; (*dichiarare*) declare; (*disdire*) terminate; (*rendere palese*) show. **denunzia** *or* **denuncia** *sf* report; (*accusa*) charge; declaration; notice of termination.
deodorante [deodo'rante] *agg, sm* deodorant.
deperire [depe'rire] *v* (*piante*) wither; (*animali*) waste away; (*persone*) get run down; (*cibi*) perish. **deperibile** *agg* perishable.
depilatorio [depila'tɔrjo] *agg* depilatory. *sm* hair-remover.
depliant [depli'ã] *sm, pl* **-s** leaflet.
deplorare [deplo'rare] *v* (*compiangere*) lament, regret; (*biasimare*) deplore, regret. **deplorevole** *agg* deplorable.
***deporre** [de'porre] *v* put *or* set down, deposit, lay; (*testimoniare*) (bear) witness. **deporre in giudizio** give evidence. **deposizione** *sf* deposition, testimony.

deportare [depor'tare] *v* deport. **deportato, -a** *sm, sf* deportee. **deportazione** *sf* deportation.
deposito [de'pɔzito] *sm* deposit; (*magazzino*) warehouse, store. **deposito bagagli** left-luggage office. **depositare** *v* deposit. **depositario** *sm* trustee.
depravare [depra'vare] *v* deprave.
depredare [depre'dare] *v* plunder.
depresso [de'prɛsso] *agg* depressed. **depressione** *sf* depression. **depressivo** *agg* depressive, depressant.
deprezzare [depret'tsare] *v* depreciate. **deprezzamento** *sm* depreciation.
***deprimere** [de'primere] *v* depress. **deprimente** *agg* depressing.
depurare [depu'rare] *v* purify. **depuratore** *sm* purifier. **depurazione** *sf* purification.
deputare [depu'tare] *v* delegate. **deputato, -a** *sm, sf* deputy; delegate; Member of Parliament.
deragliare [dera'ʎare] *v* be derailed, go off the rails. **deragliamento** *sm* derailment.
derapare [dera'pare] *v* skid.
derelitto [dere'litto], **-a** *agg* forsaken. *sm, sf* down-and-out; (*trovatello*) foundling.
deretano [dere'tano] *sm* behind.
***deridere** [de'ridere] *v* laugh at, mock, deride. **derisione** *sf* derision, ridicule. **derisorio** *agg* derisory, laughable.
deriva [de'riva] *sf* **alla deriva** adrift. **andare alla deriva** drift.
derivare [deri'vare] *v* derive; (*conseguire*) follow, result; (*sviare*) divert. **derivata** *sf* (*mat*) derivative. **derivato** *sm* (*chim*) derivative; (*sottoprodotto*) by-product. **derivazione** *sf* derivation, origin. **collegare in derivazione** (*elett, radio*) shunt.
dermatite [derma'tite] *sf* dermatitis. **dermatologo, -a** *sm, sf* dermatologist.
derogare [dero'gare] *v* deviate (from), depart (from); (*non osservare*) not comply (with); (*dir*) waive. **deroga** *sf* departure. **in deroga a** notwithstanding; (*dir*) waiving. **derogabile** *agg* not binding.
derrate [der'rate] *sf pl* provisions *pl*; (*alimentari*) foodstuffs *pl*.
derubare [deru'bare] *v* rob.
***descrivere** [des'krivere] *v* describe. **descrittivo** *agg* descriptive. **non descrivibile** indescribable. **descrizione** *sf* description, account.
deserto [de'zɛrto] *sm* desert, wilderness. *agg* (*vuoto*) deserted; (*disabitato*) uninhabited.
desiderare [dezide'rare] *v* wish; (*volere*) want; (*bramare*) long for, desire. **lasciare a desiderare** leave to be desired. **desiderabile** *agg* desirable.
desiderio [dezi'dɛrjo] *sm* wish; (*brama, rimpianto*) longing, desire. **aver desiderio di** wish *or* want to. **pio desiderio** wishful thinking.
designare [dezi'ɲare] *v* designate; (*denominare*) call; (*nominare, stabilire*) appoint.
desinare [dezi'nare] *sm* lunch, dinner. *v* lunch, dine.
desinenza [dezi'nɛntsa] *sf* ending.
***desistere** [de'zistere] *v* desist. **desistere da** give up.
desolato [dezo'lato] *agg* (*afflitto*) distressed; (*deserto*) desolate; (*devastato*) desolated. **desolante** *agg* distressing. **desolazione** *sf* desolation; distress.
despota ['dɛspota] *sm* despot.
destare [des'tare] *v* awake, rouse; (*suscitare*) arouse, awaken. **destar meraviglia** cause wonder.
destinare [desti'nare] *v* destine; (*assegnare*) intend, assign; (*dedicare*) devote; (*riservare*) set aside; (*indirizzare*) address; decide. **destinatario, -a** *sm, sf* (*lettera*) addressee; (*merci*) consignee. **esser destinato a** (*decretato dalla sorte*) be bound *or* destined to; (*condannato*) be doomed to. **destinazione** *sf* destination. **destino** *sm* destiny, fate.
destituire [destitu'ire] *v* dismiss. **destituito** *agg* dismissed; (*privo*) devoid. **destituzione** *sf* dismissal.
desto ['desto] *agg* (*sveglio*) (wide-)awake; (*vivace*) lively.
destra ['dɛstra] *sf* (*lato*) right, right-hand side; (*mano*) right hand; (*pol*) right (wing). **a destra** on *or* to the right. **tenere la destra** keep (to the) right.
destro ['dɛstro] *agg* (*lato*) right(-hand); (*abile*) skilful, dextrous; (*accorto*) clever. **destrezza** *sf* ability, skill, dexterity. **destrorso** *agg* from left to right; (*in senso orario*) clockwise.
detenere [dete'nere] *v* hold; (*trattenere in prigione*) detain. **detenuto, -a** *sm, sf* detainee. **detenzione** *sf* detention. **detenzione abusiva** unlawful possession.
detergente [deter'dʒɛnte] *sm, agg* detergent.

deteriorare [deterjo'rare] *v* deteriorate. **deterioramento** *sm* deterioration.
determinare [determi'nare] *v* determine; (*causare*) bring about. **determinante** *agg* determining, decisive. **determinato** *agg* (*preciso*) definite, distinct; (*stabilito*) appointed; (*noto*) given; (*particolare*) special; (*deciso*) determined. **determinazione** *sf* determination.
deterrente [deter'rɛnte] *sm, agg* deterrent.
detersivo [deter'sivo] *sm, agg* detergent.
detestare [detes'tare] *v* detest, loathe. **detestabile** *agg* hateful, odious.
detonatore [detona'tore] *sm* detonator. **detonante** *sm, agg* explosive. **capsula detonante** *sf* percussion cap.
***detrarre** [det'rarre] *v* deduct, take away; (*nuocere a*) detract (from).
detrimento [detri'mento] *sm* detriment, prejudice.
detrito [de'trito] *sm* debris; (*geol*) detritus.
dettagliare [detta'ʎare] *v* (*particolareggiare*) detail; (*vendere al minuto*) retail. **dettagliante** *s*(*m*+*f*) retailer. **dettaglio** *sm* detail; retail.
dettare [det'tare] *v* dictate. **dettar legge** lay down the law. **dettato** *sm* dictation.
detto ['detto] *agg* (*già citato*) above-mentioned, aforesaid; (*chiamato*) known as, alias. **detto fatto** no sooner said than done. **detto fra noi** between you and me. *sm* saying.
deturpare [detur'pare] *v* disfigure, deface.
devastare [devas'tare] *v* ravage, devastate. **devastazione** *sf* devastation, destruction.
devastatore [devasta'tore] *agg* devastating, destructive. *sm* devastator, destroyer.
deviare [devi'are] *v* deviate; (*spostare in altra direzione*) divert. **deviazione** *sf* deviation; (*fis*) deflection; (*traffico*) diversion, detour.
devolvere [de'vɔlvere] *v* devolve, assign.
devoto [de'vɔto] *agg* (*rel*) devout; (*dedicato, affezionato*) devoted. **devozione** *sf* devotion; devoutness.
di [di] *prep* of; (*partitivo*) some, any; (*moto da luogo*) from; (*paragone*) than.
diabete [dia'bɛte] *sm* diabetes. **diabetico, -a** *s, agg* diabetic.
diacono [di'akono] *sm* deacon.
diadema [dia'dɛma] *sm* diadem, tiara.
diaframma [dia'framma] *sm* diaphragm; (*divisione*) partition.
diagnosi ['djaɲozi] *sf* diagnosis (*pl* -ses). **fare la diagnosi di** diagnose.
diagonale [djago'nale] *sf, agg* diagonal.
diagramma [dia'gramma] *sm* diagram; (*grafico*) chart, curve.
dialetto [dia'lɛtto] *sm* dialect. **dialettale** *agg* dialect.
dialogo ['djalogo] *sm, pl* **-ghi** dialogue; (*trattative*) negotiations *pl*; (*colloquio*) conversation, talk.
diamante [dia'mante] *sm* diamond.
diametro ['djametro] *sm* diameter. **diametrale** *agg* diametrical.
diamine ['djamine] *inter* heavens! **che diamine ... !** what on earth ... !
diapason [di'apazon] *sm* tuning fork; (*tono*) pitch; (*estensione di voce*) range.
diapositiva [diapozi'tiva] *sf* transparency, slide.
diario [di'arjo] *sm* diary, journal. **diario di bordo** log-book.
diarrea [diar'rɛa] *sf* diarrhoea.
diavolo ['djavolo] *sm* devil. **che diavolo ... !** what the devil ... ! **un buon diavolo** a good chap. **diavoleria** *sf* mischief. **diavoletto** *sm* imp; (*bigodino*) roller, curler.
dibattere [di'battere] *v* debate. **dibattersi** *v* struggle. **dibattimento** *sm* hearing. **dibattito** *sm* debate. **dibattuto** *agg* (*discusso*) controversial, vexed; (*tormentato*) troubled.
dicastero [dikas'tɛro] *sm* ministry.
dicembre [di'tʃɛmbre] *sm* December.
diceria [ditʃe'ria] *sf* rumour, gossip.
dichiarare [dikja'rare] *v* declare; (*gioco di carte*) bid. **dichiarazione** *sf* declaration; bid; (*attestazione*) statement; (*amore*) proposal. **dichiarazione dei redditi** tax return.
diciannove [ditʃan'nɔve] *agg, sm* nineteen. **diciannovesimo** *sm, agg* nineteenth.
diciassette [ditʃas'sɛtte] *agg, sm* seventeen. **diciassettesimo** *sm, agg* seventeenth.
diciotto [di'tʃɔtto] *agg, sm* eighteen. **diciottesimo** *sm, agg* eighteenth.
dicitura [ditʃi'tura] *sf* caption.
didascalia [didaska'lia] *sf* caption; (*cinema*) subtitle; (*teatro*) stage directions *pl*.
didattico [di'dattiko] *agg* didactic.
didentro [di'dɛntro] **al/dal didentro** on/from the inside.

didietro [di'djɛtro] *sm* behind.
dieci ['djɛtʃi] *sm, agg* ten.
diesis [di'ɛzis] *sm* (*musica*) sharp.
dieta ['djɛta] *sf* diet. **essere a dieta** be on a diet.
dietro ['djɛtro] *avv* behind. *prep* (*luogo*) behind; (*tempo*) after; (*su, in seguito a*) on. **dietro front** about turn.
difatti [di'fatti] *cong* in fact.
***difendere** [di'fɛndere] *v* defend.
difensiva [difen'siva] *sf* defensive. **difensivo** *agg* defensive.
difensore [difen'sore] *sm* defender. **avvocato difensore** *sm* counsel for the defence.
difesa [di'feza] *sf* defence. **difesa legittima** self-defence. **senza difesa** defenceless. **stare sulla difesa** be on the defensive.
difeso [di'fezo] *agg* (*riparato*) sheltered; (*fortificato*) defended, protected.
difetto [di'fɛtto] *sm* (*mancanza*) lack; (*imperfezione*) defect, fault. **difettare** *v also* **far difetto** lack; (*venir meno*) fail; (*essere difettoso*) be defective *or* faulty. **difettoso** *agg* defective, faulty.
diffamare [diffa'mare] *v* denigrate; (*a voce*) slander; (*per iscritto*) libel. **diffamatorio** *agg* defamatory; slanderous; libellous. **diffamatore, -trice** *sm, sf* libeller; slanderer.
differente [diffe'rente] *agg* different, unlike.
differenza [diffe'rentsa] *sf* difference. **a differenza di** unlike. **differenziale** *sm, agg* differential. **differenziare** *v* differentiate.
differire [diffe'rire] *v* (*rimandare*) defer; (*esser diverso*) differ, be different.
difficile [dif'fitʃile] *agg* difficult; (*improbabile*) unlikely; (*duro*) hard. *sm* difficulty. *s*(*m+f*) difficult person.
difficoltà [diffikol'ta] *sf* difficulty; (*ostacolo*) trouble. **difficoltoso** *agg* difficult.
diffidare [diffi'dare] *v* (*non fidarsi*) mistrust, be suspicious of; (*avvisare*) warn, caution. **diffida** *sf* warning, notice. **diffidente** *agg* suspicious. **diffidenza** *sf* suspicion.
***diffondere** [dif'fondere] *v* spread; (*luce, calore, ecc.*) diffuse; (*dilungarsi*) dwell; (*comm*) promote.
diffusione [diffu'zjone] *sf* spreading, diffusion; (*giornali*) circulation. **diffuso** *agg* widespread; diffused; widely circulated; (*prolisso*) long-winded.
diga ['diga] *sf* dam, barrier.
digerire [didʒe'rire] *v* digest; (*assimilare*) take in; (*tollerare*) stand, bear; (*credere*) swallow. **digeribile** *agg* digestible. **digestione** *sf* digestion. **digestivo** *sm, agg* digestive.
digitale [didʒi'tale] *agg* **impronta digitale** *sf* finger-print.
digiunare [didʒu'nare] *v also* **stare a digiuno** fast. **digiuno** *sm* fast. **a digiuno** on an empty stomach. **essere a digiuno di** (*fig*) be without.
dignità [diɲi'ta] *sf* dignity; (*ufficio*) (high) rank. *sf pl* dignitaries *pl*. **dignitoso** *agg* dignified.
digredire [digre'dire] *v* digress.
digressione [digres'sjone] *sf* digression.
digrignare [digri'ɲare] *v* **digrignare i denti** gnash one's teeth; (*animali*) bare the teeth.
dilagare [dila'gare] *v* flood, spread. **dilagamento** *sm* flooding.
dilaniare [dila'njare] *v* rend.
dilapidare [dilapi'dare] *v* squander.
dilatare [dila'tare] *v* dilate, open (wide). **dilatazione** *sf* dilation.
dilatorio [dila'tɔrjo] *agg* dilatory. **dilazione** *sf* delay, deferment.
dileguare [dile'gware] *v* dispel. **dileguarsi** *v* disappear, fade.
dilemma [di'lemma] *sm* dilemma.
dilettante [dilet'tante] *agg, s*(*m+f*) amateur. **dilettantesco** *agg* amateurish.
dilettare [dilet'tare] *v* delight; (*far divertire*) amuse. **dilettarsi** *v* delight in, enjoy.
diletto[1] [di'lɛtto] *sm* (*piacere*) delight, pleasure; (*godimento*) enjoyment.
diletto[2] [di'lɛtto] *agg* beloved; (*preferito*) favourite.
diligente [dili'dʒɛnte] *agg* (*che lavora*) industrious; (*accurato*) conscientious; painstaking.
diligenza[1] [dili'dʒɛntsa] *sf* industry, conscientiousness. **con diligenza** conscientiously.
diligenza[2] [dili'dʒɛntsa] *sf* (*carrozza*) stage-coach.
diluire [dilu'ire] *v* dilute; (*allungare con acqua*) water down; (*vernice, ecc.*) thin (down).
dilungarsi [dilun'garsi] *v* (*andar per le lunghe*) talk at length, dwell.
diluvio [di'luvjo] *sm* flood, deluge.

dimagrire [dima'grire] *v also* **dimagrare** lose weight; (*di proposito*) slim; (*far sembrare snello*) make look slimmer.
dimenare [dime'nare] *v* wave (about); (*coda*) wag. **dimenarsi** *v* fidget, toss about.
dimensione [dimen'sjone] *sf* dimension. **a due/tre dimensioni** two-/three-dimensional.
dimenticare [dimenti'kare] *v* forget; (*perdonare*) forget about; (*trascurare*) neglect. **dimenticarsi (di)** forget (about). **dimentico** *agg, m pl* **-chi** forgetful; (*noncurante*) oblivious.
dimestichezza [dimesti'kettsa] *sf* familiarity. **aver dimestichezza con** be familiar with.
dimettere [di'mettere] *v* discharge; (*licenziare*) dismiss. **dimettersi** *v* resign.
dimezzare [dimed'dzare] *v* halve.
diminuire [diminu'ire] *v* diminish, reduce; (*calare*) drop; (*lavoro a maglia*) cast off, decrease. **diminuire di peso** lose weight. **diminuire di prezzo** cost less. **diminuire di valore** fall in value, be worth less. **diminutivo** *agg* diminutive. **diminuzione** *sf* decrease; drop, cut, fall.
dimissione [dimis'sjone] *sf* resignation. **dare** *or* **rassegnare le dimissioni** resign. **dimissionario** *agg* outgoing.
dimorare [dimo'rare] *v* stay, live. **dimora** *sf* (*abitazione*) home, abode; (*soggiorno*) stay, residence.
dimostrare [dimos'trare] *v* demonstrate; (*manifestare*) show, display; prove. **dimostrabile** *agg* demonstrable. **dimostrante** *s*(*m*+*f*) demonstrator. **dimostrativo** *agg* demonstrative. **dimostratore, -trice** *sm, sf* demonstrator. **dimostrazione** *sf* demonstration; (*prova*) proof.
dinamica [di'namika] *sf* dynamics. **dinamico** *agg* dynamic, forceful.
dinamite [dina'mite] *sf* dynamite.
dinamo ['dinamo] *sf invar* dynamo.
dinanzi [di'nantsi] *avv* ahead, forward. *agg invar* (*dirimpetto*) facing; (*precedente*) previous. *prep* **dinanzi a** (*davanti a*) in front of; (*dirimpetto*) opposite; in the presence of, before.
dinastia [dinas'tia] *sf* dynasty. **dinastico** *agg* dynastic.
dinoccolato [dinokko'lato] *agg* shambling. **camminare dinoccolato** *v* slouch.
dinosauro [dino'sauro] *sm* dinosaur.
dintorno [din'torno] *avv* around, about.
dintorni *sm pl* outskirts *pl*, surroundings *pl*.
dio ['dio] *sm, pl* **dei** god. **come un dio** wonderfully, beautifully.
diocesi ['diɔtʃezi] *sf* diocese.
diodo ['diodo] *sm* diode.
dipanare [dipa'nare] *v* unravel.
dipartimento [diparti'mento] *sm* department, district.
dipendente [dipen'dɛnte] *s*(*m*+*f*) (*impiegato*) employee. *agg* dependent, subordinate. **dipendenza** *sf* dependence; (*edificio*) annexe; (*filiale*) branch. **essere alle dipendenze di** be in the employ of.
***dipendere** [di'pɛndere] *v* depend (on); (*derivare*) be due (to), be caused (by). **dipende!** that depends! **dipende da te!** it is up to you!
***dipingere** [di'pindʒere] *v* paint; (*rappresentare*) depict. **dipingersi** *v* (*truccarsi*) make up. **dipinto** *sm* painting.
diploma [di'plɔma] *sm* diploma, certificate, qualification. **diplomarsi** *v* obtain a certificate, qualify.
diplomatico [diplo'matiko], **-a** *agg* diplomatic. *sm, sf* diplomat. **diplomazia** *sf* diplomacy.
diporto [di'pɔrto] *sm* pleasure, pastime.
diradare [dira'dare] *v* thin; (*nebbia*) clear.
diramare [dira'mare] *v* issue, broadcast. **diramarsi** *v* branch out *or* off. **diramazione** *sf* branch; (*comunicato, ecc.*) broadcasting, circulation.
***dire** ['dire] *v* say; (*raccontare, ordinare*) tell; (*significare*) mean. **a chi lo dici!** don't I know! **aver da dire su** find fault with. **è tutto dire** which is saying a lot. **inutile dire** it goes without saying. *sm* speech, words *pl*. **a dire di tutti** by all accounts. **oltre ogni dire** beyond all description.
diretto [di'rɛtto] *agg* direct; (*inteso*) meant, destined; (*guidato*) conducted. *sm* (*ferr*) through train. **direttissimo** *sm* (*ferr*) express train. **direttiva** *sf* directive; (*condotta*) policy. **direttivo** *agg* (*che dirige*) guiding; (*proprio alla direzione*) managerial. **direttore** *sm* manager; (*scuola*) headmaster; (*giornale*) editor; (*orchestra*) conductor. **direttrice** *sf* manageress; headmistress.
direzione [dire'tsjone] *sf* direction; (*il dirigere*) management, administration; (*sede*) head office. **assumere la direzione**

take charge. **in che direzione?** which way?

***dirigere** [di'ridʒere] *v* direct; (*rivolgere*) address; (*guidare*) lead; (*amministrare*) manage; (*giornale*) edit; (*orchestra*) conduct. **dirigersi verso** go towards, head for. **dirigibile** *sm* airship.

dirimpetto [dirim'pɛtto] *agg invar, avv* opposite.

diritto[1] [di'ritto] *agg* (*non curvo*) straight; (*eretto, onesto*) upright; (*fam: astuto*) crafty; (*fam: accorto*) shrewd; (*destro*) right(-hand). *avv* straight. **andar diritto** go straight ahead *or* on. *sm* (*moneta*) obverse; (*lato buono*) good side; (*tennis*) forehand.

diritto[2] [di'ritto] *sm* (*legge*) law; (*pretesa*) right; (*tassa*) due, duty. **a buon diritto** with good cause. **diritti d'autore** copyright *sing*; (*compenso*) royalties *pl*. **diritto acquisito** vested interest.

diroccato [dirok'kato] *agg* dilapidated.

dirottare [dirot'tare] *v* divert; change course.

dirotto [di'rotto] *agg* (*pianto*) copious; (*pioggia*) pouring.

disabitato [dizabi'tato] *agg* uninhabited.

disabituare [dizabitu'are] *v* wean.

disaccordo [dizak'kɔrdo] *sm* disagreement; variance. **essere** *or* **trovarsi in disaccordo su** disagree on, be at variance over.

disadatto [diza'datto] *agg* ill-suited.

disadorno [diza'dorno] *agg* bare.

disagevole [diza'dʒevole] *agg* uncomfortable.

disagio [di'zadʒo] *sm* (*imbarazzo*) uneasiness; (*mancanza di comodità*) discomfort. **essere a disagio** be ill at ease. **sentirsi a disagio** feel uneasy. **disagiato** *agg* uncomfortable; (*duro*) hard.

disamorarsi [dizamo'rarsi] *v* become estranged (from), cease to care (for).

disapprovare [dizappro'vare] *v* disapprove. **disapprovazione** *sf* disapproval.

disappunto [dizap'punto] *sm* disappointment.

disarmare [dizar'mare] *v* disarm; (*smantellare*) dismantle; (*edificio*) remove the scaffolding from. **disarmo** *sm* disarmament.

disarmonia [dizarmo'nia] *sf* discord.

disastro [di'zastro] *sm* disaster; (*incidente*) crash; (*fam: insuccesso*) utter failure. **combinare un disastro** (*fam*) make a mess. **disastroso** *agg* disastrous.

disattento [dizat'tɛnto] *agg* inattentive; (*sbadato*) careless. **disattenzione** *sf* carelessness; (*errore*) slip. **per disattenzione** through an oversight.

disavanzo [diza'vantso] *sm* deficit.

disavventura [dizavven'tura] *sf* misfortune.

disbrigo [diz'brigo] *sm*, *pl* **-ghi** settlement, dispatch.

discapito [dis'kapito] *sm* **a discapito di** at the cost of, to the prejudice of.

***discendere** [di'ʃendere] *v* descend; (*andar giù*) go down; (*venir giù*) come down. **discendente** *s*(*m*+*f*) descendant. **discendenza** *sf* descent; (*collettivo*) offspring. **discensore** *sm* lift.

discepolo [di'ʃepolo] *sm* disciple.

discernere [di'ʃɛrnere] *v* discern; distinguish.

discesa [di'ʃesa] *sf* descent; (*declivio*) slope. **discesa in picchiata** nose-dive. **in discesa** downhill.

***dischiudere** [dis'kjudere] *v* open; (*svelare*) disclose.

***disciogliere** [di'ʃɔʎere] *v* dissolve; (*liquefare*) melt.

disciplinare [diʃipli'nare] *v* discipline, control. *agg* disciplinary. **disciplina** *sf* discipline. **disciplinato** *agg* (well-)disciplined, orderly.

disco ['disko] *sm* disc; (*grammofono*) record; (*sport*) discus; (*hockey*) puck; (*telefono*) dial. **disco rosso/verde** red/green light.

discolo ['diskolo] *agg* mischievous.

discolpare [diskol'pare] *v* clear. **discolpa** *sf* justification, defence.

***disconoscere** [disko'noʃere] *v* refuse to acknowledge.

discontinuo [diskon'tinuo] *agg* discontinuous; (*non regolare*) erratic.

discorde [dis'kɔrde] *agg also* **discordante** discordant; (*contrastante*) conflicting; (*stonante*) clashing. **discordare** *v* disagree; conflict; clash. **discordia** *sf* disagreement.

***discorrere** [dis'korrere] *v* talk. **discorrere del più e del meno** talk about this and that. **e via discorrendo** and so on.

discorso [dis'korso] *sm* conversation, talk; (*in pubblico, gramm*) speech. **cambiare discorso** change the subject. **senza tanti discorsi** quite frankly. **tenere**

un discorso make a speech, give an address.
discoteca [disko'tɛka] *sf* (*locale*) discotheque; record collection.
discreto [dis'kreto] *agg* fair, reasonable; (*non importuno*) tactful, discreet; (*separato*) discrete. **discretamente** *avv* moderately well. **discrezionale** *agg* discretionary. **discrezione** *sf* discretion, moderation, tact.
discriminazione [diskrimina'tsjone] *sf* discrimination. **discriminare** *v* discriminate; (*dir*) extenuate.
discussione [diskus'sjone] *sf* discussion, debate; (*litigio*) argument. **mettere in discussione** discuss, debate; (*in dubbio*) question.
discusso [dis'kusso] *agg* discussed, controversial.
***discutere** [dis'kutere] *v* discuss, debate; (*litigare*) argue. **discutibile** *agg* debatable, questionable.
disdegnare [dizde'ɲare] *v* disdain, scorn. **disdegno** *sm* disdain, scorn.
***disdire** [diz'dire] *v* (*annullare*) cancel; (*negare*) deny; (*ritrattare*) withdraw, take back; (*mentire*) refute. **disdetta** *sf* notice; (*sfortuna*) bad luck; cancellation.
disegnare [dize'ɲare] *v* draw; (*progettare*) design, sketch; (*delineare*) outline. **disegnatore** *sm* draughtsman. **disegno** *sm* drawing; (*schizzo*) sketch; (*progetto*) design, plan; (*abbozzo*) outline. **a disegni** patterned. **disegno animato** (*cinema*) cartoon. **disegno di legge** bill.
diseredare [dizere'dare] *v* disinherit. **diseredato, -a** *s, agg* destitute.
disertare [dizer'tare] *v* desert. **disertore** *sm* deserter. **diserzione** *sf* desertion.
***disfare** [dis'fare] *v* undo; (*smontare*) take to pieces; (*valigia*) unpack; (*sciogliere*) melt. **disfatta** *sf* defeat. **disfattismo** *sm* defeatism. **disfattista** *s*(*m*+*f*), *agg* defeatist.
disgelare [dizdʒe'lare] *v* thaw (out); (*frigorifero*) defrost. **disgelo** *sm* thaw.
***disgiungere** [diz'dʒundʒere] *v* detach, separate.
disgraziato [dizgra'tsjato], **-a** *agg* unfortunate, unlucky; (*infelice*) wretched. *sm, sf* (*sventurato*) wretch; (*sciagurato*) scoundrel. **disgrazia** *sf* misfortune; (*incidente*) accident, mishap; (*sfavore*) disgrace; (*sfortuna*) bad luck.
disgregare [dizgre'gare] *v* break up. **disgregazione** *sf* break-up.
disguido [diz'gwido] *sm* (*equivoco*) misunderstanding; (*errore nel recapito*) mistake in delivery.
disgustare [dizgus'tare] *v* disgust. **disgusto** *sm* disgust, revulsion, loathing. **disgustoso** *agg* disgusting, loathsome, revolting.
disidratare [dizidra'tare] *v* dehydrate.
***disilludere** [dizil'ludere] *v* disillusion, disenchant. **disillusione** *sf* disenchantment, disillusion.
disimpegnare [dizimpe'ɲare] *v* free, release; (*oggetto dato in pegno*) redeem; (*mil*) relieve. **disimpegnarsi** *v* (*cavarsela*) acquit oneself, manage. **disimpegno** *sm* (*adempimento*) fulfilment; (*politica*) disengagement.
disinfettare [dizinfet'tare] *v* disinfect. **disinfettante** *sm* disinfectant. **disinfezione** *sf* disinfection.
disintegrare [dizinte'grare] *v* disintegrate; (*fis*) split, decay.
disinteressarsi [dizinteres'sarsi] *v* take no interest (in). **disinteressato** *agg* disinterested; (*altruistico*) unselfish.
disinvolto [dizin'vɔlto] *agg* unconstrained, self-possessed; (*spigliato*) free and easy, casual; (*senza ritegno*) uninhibited. **disinvoltura** *sf* ease, casualness; self-possession.
disistima [dizis'tima] *sf* lack of esteem; (*disprezzo*) contempt.
dislivello [dizli'vɛllo] *sm* difference (in level); (*fig*) inequality.
dislocare [dizlo'kare] *v* displace; (*mil*) detach.
dismisura [dizmi'zura] *sf* **a dismisura** excessively.
disoccupato [dizokku'pato], **-a** *s, agg* unemployed. **disoccupazione** *sf* unemployment. **sussidio di disoccupazione** *sm* unemployment benefit; (*fam*) dole.
disonesto [dizo'nɛsto] *agg* dishonest; (*immorale*) dishonourable; (*impudico*) shameless. **disonestà** *sf* dishonesty dishonourable behaviour; shamelessnes
disonorare [dizono'rare] *v* dishonour, d grace. **disonore** *sm* dishonour, disgra **disonorevole** *agg* dishonourable, graceful, shameful.
disopra [di'sopra] *avv* above; (*al* ano *superiore*) upstairs. *agg invar* (*su iore*) upper; (*posto più in alto*) higer up;

upstairs. *sm invar* top, upper part. **al disopra di** (*più di*) more than; (*superiore a*) above all; (*più alto di*) above. **dal disopra** from above.

disordinare [dizordi'nare] *v* upset, turn upside down. **disordinato** *agg* untidy; confuso; (*sregolato*) disorderly. **disordine** *sm* disorder; (*confusione*) muddle.

disorientare [dizorjen'tare] *v* (*confondere*) confuse, bewilder. **disorientarsi** *v* lose one's bearings, become confused.

disossare [dizos'sare] *v* bone.

disotto [di'sotto] *avv* below, underneath; (*al piano inferiore*) downstairs. *agg invar* below; (*tra due*) lower; (*in fondo*) bottom; downstairs.

dispaccio [dis'pattʃo] *sm* dispatch.

disparato [dispa'rato] *agg* dissimilar, different.

dispari ['dispari] *agg* odd.

disparte [dis'parte] *avv* **in disparte** aside, to one side. **tenersi in disparte** keep at a distance.

dispensa [dis'pɛnsa] *sf* distribution; (*mobile*) cupboard; (*locale*) pantry, larder; (*fascicolo*) number, issue; (*esonero*) exemption. **a dispense** in instalments. **dispensa ecclesiastica** dispensation. **dispensa universitaria** lecture notes *pl*. **dispensare** *v* dispense. **dispensario** *sm* clinic.

disperare [dispe'rare] *v* despair. **disperato** *agg* desperate. **disperazione** *sf* despair.

***disperdere** [dis'pɛrdere] *v* disperse, scatter; dissipate; (*sprecare*) waste. **dispersione** *sf* dispersion; waste.

dispetto [dis'pɛtto] *sm* spite; (*irritazione*) annoyance. **a dispetto di** despite. **fare un dispetto** annoy. **per dispetto** out of spite. **dispettoso** *agg* spiteful, annoying.

***dispiacere** [dispja'tʃere] *v* displease. **mi dispiace ...** (*non mi piace*) I don't like ... ; (*sono spiacente*) I'm sorry .... **ti dispiace ... ?** do you mind ... ? *sm* (*rammarico*) regret; (*noia*) displeasure; (*fastidio*) trouble, worry.

disponibile [dispo'nibile] *agg* available; (*libero*) vacant. **posto disponibile** *sm* vacancy.

disponibilità [disponibili'ta] *sf* availability. *sf pl* assets *pl*.

***disporre** [dis'porre] *v* dispose; (*collocare in ordine, stabilire*) arrange; prepare; induce; order. **disporre di** have available, have at one's disposal; (*avere*) have. **disporsi** *v* prepare, get ready; (*in fila*) line up.

dispositivo [dispozi'tivo] *sm* device.

disposizione [dispozi'tsjone] *sf* arrangement, layout; (*stato d'animo*) disposition; (*inclinazione*) bent; (*norma*) provision; (*comando*) order. **a disposizione** available.

disposto [dis'posto] *agg* arranged, laid out; (*pronto*) ready, willing; (*stabilito*) laid down.

disprezzare [dispret'tsare] *v* despise, scorn. **disprezzo** *sm* scorn, contempt.

disputare [dispu'tare] *v* dispute; (*litigare*) argue; (*contendere*) fight (over), strive (for); (*incontro*) play; (*corsa*) run. **disputa** *sf* dispute; (*lite*) argument.

dissanguare [dissan'gware] *v* bleed.

dissecare [disse'kare] *v* dissect.

disseccare [dissek'kare] *v* dry up.

disseminare [dissemi'nare] *v* scatter; (*diffondere*) spread.

dissenteria [dissente'ria] *sf* dysentery.

dissentire [dissen'tire] *v* dissent, disagree.

disseppellire [disseppel'lire] *v* unearth; (*esumare*) exhume.

dissertazione [disserta'tsjone] *sf* dissertation.

dissestare [disses'tare] *v* upset, unbalance. **dissestato** *agg* ruined; (*strada*) in poor condition; (*bilancio*) adverse.

dissetarsi [disse'tarsi] *v* quench one's thirst. **dissetante** *agg* thirst-quenching.

dissidente [dissi'dɛnte] *s*(*m*+*f*), *agg* dissident; (*rel*) non-conformist.

dissidio [dis'sidjo] *sm* disagreement; (*lite*) quarrel.

dissimile [dis'simile] *agg* different, unlike.

dissimulare [dissimu'lare] *v* dissimulate; (*fingere*) pretend; (*nascondere*) hide.

dissipare [dissi'pare] *v* dissipate; (*sospetti, dubbi, ecc.*) dispel; (*sprecare*) squander.

dissociare [disso'tʃare] *v* dissociate. **dissociazione** *sf* dissociation.

dissoluto [disso'luto] *agg* dissolute.

dissoluzione [dissolu'tsjone] *sf* dissolution, break-up.

***dissolvere** [dis'sɔlvere] *v* dispel; (*sciogliere*) dissolve.

dissotterrare [dissotter'rare] *v* unearth; (*esumare*) exhume.

***dissuadere** [dissua'dere] *v* dissuade, deter.

distaccare [distak'kare] *v* detach; (*sport*:

lasciar dietro) leave behind. **distaccarsi** *v* (*spiccare*) stand out; (*allontanarsi*) withdraw. **distaccamento** *sm* (*mil*) detachment. **distacco** *sm* detachment; (*separazione*) parting, separation; (*sport*: *vantaggio*) lead.

distante [dis'tante] *agg* distant, remote, far. *avv* far, far off. **distanza** *sf* distance; (*tempo*) interval.

***distare** [dis'tare] *v* be far (from).

***distendere** [dis'tɛndere] *v* spread; (*allungare*) stretch; (*appendere*) hang (up); (*mettere giù*) lay; (*rilassare*) relax. **distendersi** *v* lie down, relax.

distensione [disten'sjone] *sf* stretching; relaxation; (*pol*) détente. **distensivo** *agg* relaxing.

distesa [dis'teza] *sf* expanse; (*fila*) row.

disteso [dis'tezo] *agg* (*teso*) stretched; (*coricato*) lying down; (*braccio*) outstretched; (*spiegato*) spread out; relaxed.

distillare [distil'lare] *v* distil. **distilleria** *sf* distillery.

***distinguere** [dis'tingwere] *v* distinguish, tell; (*contrassegnare*) mark; draw a distinction; (*riconoscere*) recognize. **distinguibile** *agg* distinguishable; recognizable.

distinta [dis'tinta] *sf* list. **distinta delle spese** statement of expenses.

distintivo [distin'tivo] *agg* distinctive; (*atto a distinguere*) distinguishing. *sm* badge.

distinto [dis'tinto] *agg* distinct, different, separate; (*scelto*, *raffinato*) distinguished. **ben distinto** precise. **distinti saluti** yours faithfully.

distinzione [distin'tsjone] *sf* distinction. **fare una distinzione** make a distinction, discriminate. **senza distinzione** (*senza merito*) undistinguished; (*senza criterio*) indiscriminately; (*in modo equo*) impartially.

***distogliere** [dis'tɔʎere] *v* divert, turn away.

distorsione [distor'sjone] *sf* distortion; (*med*) sprain.

***distrarre** [dis'trarre] *v* distract; (*divertire*) amuse. **distrarsi** *v* amuse oneself; (*essere disattento*) be inattentive. **distratto** *agg* inattentive; (*assente*) absent-minded; (*sbadato*) careless. **distrazione** *sf* (*svago*) distraction, relaxation; (*sbadatezza*) carelessness; absent-mindedness; lack of attention.

distretto [dis'tretto] *sm* district.

distribuire [distribu'ire] *v* distribute; (*disporre*) arrange; (*assegnare*) hand out; (*le carte*) deal; (*posta*) deliver. **distributore** *sm* (*di accensione*) distributor; (*di benzina*) petrol pump, service station. **distribuzione** *sf* distribution; (*fornitura*) supply; arrangement; delivery. **distribuzione dei premi** prize-giving. **distribuzione dei ruoli** (*cinema*) casting.

districare [distri'kare] *v* disentangle; (*fig*) sort out. **districarsi** *v* extricate oneself.

***distruggere** [dis'truddʒere] *v* destroy, ruin. **distruttivo** *agg* destructive. **distrutto** *agg* destroyed, ruined; (*fig*) broken. **distruzione** *sf* destruction, ruin.

disturbare [distur'bare] *v* disturb; (*molestare*, *seccare*) trouble, bother; (*recar fastidio*) inconvenience; (*radio*) jam. **disturbo** *sm* trouble; (*incomodo*) nuisance, inconvenience; (*indisposizione*) upset, disorder; (*radio*) jamming; atmospherics *pl*, interference. **recar disturbo** trouble, inconvenience.

disubbidire [dizubbi'dire] *v* disobey.

disuguale [dizu'gwale] *agg* unequal; (*non regolare*) irregular. **disuguaglianza** *sf* difference, disparity.

disunire [dizu'nire] *v* separate, divide.

disuso [di'zuzo] *sm* disuse. **andare** *or* **cadere in disuso** fall into disuse, become obsolete. **disusato** *agg* obsolete, out-of-date; (*fuori moda*) old-fashioned.

dito ['dito] *sm*, *pl* **-a** *f* finger. **dito anulare/indice/medio/mignolo** ring/index/middle/little finger. **dito del piede** toe. **ditale** *sm* (*cucire*) thimble; (*guanto*) finger-stall.

ditta ['ditta] *sf* firm, company.

dittatore [ditta'tore] *sm* dictator. **dittatorio** *agg* dictatorial. **dittatura** *sf* dictatorship.

dittico ['dittiko] *sm* diptych.

dittongo [dit'tɔngo] *sm* diphthong.

diurno [di'urno] *agg* day(-time). **spettacolo diurno** *sm* matinee.

diva ['diva] *sf* (film-)star.

divagare [diva'gare] *v* digress, wander; (*distrarre*) distract.

divampare [divam'pare] *v* flare up, blaze.

divano [di'vano] *sm* divan, settee, couch.

diventare [diven'tare] *v* *also* **divenire** become, turn *or* grow (into). **diventar matto** go mad. **diventar pallido/rosso** go *or* turn pale/red.

divergere [di'vɛrdʒere] *v* diverge; (*essere diverso*) differ. **divergenza** *sf* divergence; difference.
diversi [di'vɛrsi] *agg* several. *pron* (*parecchi*) several (people); (*alcuni*) some (people).
diversivo [diver'sivo] *agg* diverting; distracting. *sm* diversion; distraction.
diverso [di'vɛrso] *agg* different; distinct, separate; (*di genere diverso*) various; (*comm*) sundry. **in caso diverso** otherwise. **diversamente** *avv* differently; (*se no*) otherwise. **diversità** *sf* difference, diversity.
divertente [diver'tɛnte] *agg* amusing, enjoyable. **divertimento** *sm* entertainment, amusement. **buon divertimento!** enjoy yourself! have a good time!
divertire [diver'tire] *v* amuse; (*ricreare*) entertain. **divertirsi** *v* enjoy oneself.
dividendo [divi'dɛndo] *sm* dividend.
***dividere** [di'videre] *v* divide; (*condividere*) share. **dividersi** *v* separate, part, split (up).
divieto [di'vjɛto] *sm* prohibition. **divieto di sorpasso/sosta/transito** no overtaking/stopping/thoroughfare.
divinare [divi'nare] *v* divine; (*prevedere*) foretell.
divincolarsi [divinko'larsi] *v* wriggle.
divino [di'vino] *agg* sacred, holy; (*sublime*) divine, heavenly. **divinità** *sf* divinity.
divisa [di'viza] *sf* uniform; motto. **divisa estera** foreign currency.
divisibile [divi'zibile] *agg* divisible. **divisibilità** *sf* divisibility.
divisione [divi'zjone] *sf* division; (*reparto*) department.
diviso [di'vizo] *agg* divided, separated; (*condiviso*) shared. **divisore** *sm* divisor.
divisorio [divi'zɔrjo] *sm* partition. *agg* dividing.
divo ['divo] *sm* (film-)star.
divorare [divo'rare] *v* devour, eat up.
divorzio [di'vɔrtsjo] *sm* divorce. **divorziare** *v* divorce.
divulgare [divul'gare] *v* spread; (*rivelare*) divulge; (*rendere accessibile*) popularize. **divulgazione** *sf* spreading; (*notizie*) broadcasting; popularization.
dizionario [ditsjo'narjo] *sm* dictionary.
dizione [di'tsjone] *sf* diction.
doccia ['dottʃa] *sf* shower; (*grondaia*) gutter.
docente [do'tʃɛnte] *s*(*m*+*f*) lecturer, teacher.
docile ['dɔtʃile] *agg* docile, mild; (*materiale*) easily worked. **docilità** *sf* mildness, submissiveness; workability.
documento [doku'mento] *sm* document, paper. **documentare** *v* document. **documentario** *agg*, *sm* documentary. **documentazione** *sf* documentation; (*dir*) evidence.
dodici ['doditʃi] *agg*, *sm* twelve. **dodicesimo** *sm*, *agg* twelfth.
dogana [do'gana] *sf* customs. **doganale** *agg* customs. **doganiere** *sm* customs officer.
doge ['dɔdʒe] *sm* doge.
doglie ['dɔʎʎe] *sf pl* **doglie del parto** labour pains *pl*.
dogma ['dɔgma] *sm* dogma. **dogmatico** *agg* dogmatic.
dolce ['doltʃe] *agg* sweet; (*mite*) mild; (*morbido*) soft. *sm* sweet. **dolcezza** *sf* sweetness; mildness; softness.
***dolere** [do'lere] *v* (*far male*) ache, hurt. **mi duole di** *or* **che . . .** I regret that . . . , I'm sorry that . . . .
dollaro ['dɔllaro] *sm* dollar.
dolo ['dɔlo] *sm* (*dir*) malice; (*inganno*) fraud.
dolore [do'lore] *sm* pain; (*male fisico*) ache; (*sofferenza morale*) sorrow; (*rincrescimento*) regret. **doloroso** *agg* painful; sorrowful.
domanda [do'manda] *sf* question; (*richiesta*) request; (*scritta*) application; (*econ*) demand; (*dir*) petition. **domandare** *v* (*per sapere*) ask; (*per avere*) ask for; (*esigere*) demand. **domandarsi** *v* wonder.
domani [do'mani] *avv* tomorrow. **a domani!** see you tomorrow! **domani a otto** tomorrow week. **domani l'altro** the day after tomorrow. *sm* tomorrow; future. **un domani** one day.
domare [do'mare] *v* tame; (*sedare*) put down; (*spegnere*) put out; (*frenare*) curb. **domatore** *sm* tamer.
domattina [domat'tina] *avv* tomorrow morning.
domenica [do'menika] *sf* Sunday.
domestico [do'mɛstiko] *agg* domestic; (*della casa*) household, home. **apparecchio domestico** household appliance. *sm* servant. **domestica** *sf* maid. **domestichezza** *sf* familiarity.

domiciliarsi [domitʃi'ljarsi] *v* settle.
domicilio [domi'tʃiljo] *sm* domicile, home.
dominare [domi'nare] *v* dominate; (*predominare*) prevail; (*frenare*) control; (*aver potestà*) rule. **dominio** *sm* domination; rule; (*territorio*) domain; (*proprietà*) possession. **pubblico dominio** (*proprietà*) common property; (*noto a tutti*) common knowledge.
domino ['dɔmino] *sm* (*gioco*) dominoes.
donare [do'nare] *v* give, present; (*star bene*) suit, become. **donatore, -trice** *sm, sf* donor. **donazione** *sf* donation, gift.
donde ['donde] *avv* (*da dove*) whence, from where; (*di che*) with which.
dondolare [dondo'lare] *v* swing, rock. **cavallo a dondolo** *sm* rocking-horse. **sedia a dondolo** *sf* rocking-chair.
donna ['dɔnna] *sf* woman (*pl* women); (*domestica*) maid, servant; (*giochi*) queen. **donnaiolo** *sm* philanderer. **donnesco** *agg* feminine.
donnola ['donnola] *sf* weasel.
dono ['dono] *sm* gift.
dopo ['dopo] *avv* after; (*poi*) then, afterwards; (*più tardi*) later (on); (*prossimo*) next. **a dopo!** see you later! **dopobarba** *agg, sm invar* after-shave. **dopo che** since. **dopo di che** whereupon. **dopodomani** *sm, avv* the day after tomorrow. **dopotutto** *avv* after all. **molto tempo dopo** long after.
dopopranzo [dopo'prantso] *avv* after lunch. *sm* afternoon.
doppiare[1] [dop'pjare] *v* (*cinema*) dub. **doppiaggio** *sm* dubbing.
doppiare[2] [dop'pjare] *v* double; (*sport*) lap.
doppio ['doppjo] *agg* double; (*insincero*) two-faced; (*duplice*) dual, twofold. **a doppio petto** double-breasted. **fare il doppio gioco** double-cross. *sm* double, twice as much *or* many. **doppione** *sm* duplicate.
dorare [do'rare] *v* gild; (*gastr*) coat with egg. **doratura** *sf* gilding, gold-plating.
dormicchiare [dormik'kjare] *v* doze, snooze.
dormire [dor'mire] *v* sleep; (*esser fermo*) lie dormant. **dormita** *sf* good sleep.
dormitorio [dormi'tɔrjo] *sm* dormitory.
dormiveglia [dormi'veʎa] *sm* **essere nel dormiveglia** be half-asleep.
dorso ['dorso] *sm* back; (*nuoto*) backstroke.
dose ['dɔze] *sf* dose; quantity. **dose eccessiva** overdose. **rincarare la dose** (*fam*) pile it on. **dosaggio** *sm* dosage.
dosso ['dɔsso] *sm* back. **togliersi un peso di dosso** take a weight off one's mind.
dotare [do'tare] *v* endow, provide. **dotato** *agg* gifted; endowed *or* provided (with); (*munito*) equipped (with). **dotazione** *sf* equipment; (*rendita*) endowment. **dote** *sf* (*matrimonio*) dowry; (*donazione*) endowment; (*qualità*) gift.
dotto[1] ['dɔtto] *agg* scholarly, learned. *sm* scholar.
dotto[2] ['dotto] *sm* (*condotto*) duct.
dottore [dot'tore], **-essa** *sm, sf* doctor.
dottrina [dot'trina] *sf* (*cultura*) learning; (*teoria, insieme di principi*) doctrine.
dove ['dove] *avv* where. *cong* (*se*) if; (*mentre*) whereas. **fin dove** as far as.
***dovere** [do'vere] *v* must, have to; (*esser lecito*) may; (*essere inevitabile*) be bound to; (*esser causato da*) be due to; (*al condizionale*) should, ought to. **come si deve** properly; (*persona*) proper, decent. *sm* duty. **doveroso** *agg* right and proper; (*obbligato*) (duty-)bound. **dovuto** *agg, sm* due.
dovunque [do'vunkwe] *avv* (*dappertutto*) everywhere; (*in qualsiasi luogo*) anywhere. *cong* wherever.
dozzina [dod'dzina] *sf* dozen. **a dozzine** by the dozen. **da dozzina** cheap, poor.
dragare [dra'gare] *v* dredge; (*mine*) sweep. **draga** *sf* dredge, dredger. **dragamine** *sm invar* minesweeper.
drago ['drago] *sm* dragon; (*aquilone*) kite. **dragone** *sm* dragon; (*mil*) dragoon.
dramma ['dramma] *sm* play; tragedy. **drammatico** *agg* dramatic; (*esagerato*) theatrical. **drammatizzare** *v* dramatize. **drammaturgo** *sm* playwright, dramatist.
drappello [drap'pɛllo] *sm* squad, band.
drappo ['drappo] *sm* cloth; (*funebre*) pall. **drappeggiare** *v* drape.
drastico ['drastiko] *agg* drastic.
drenare [dre'nare] *v* drain. **drenaggio** *sm* drainage.
dritta ['dritta] *sf* (*mano*) right (hand); (*parte*) right(-hand side); (*mar*) starboard.
dritto ['dritto] *agg* (*fam*) astute. *sm* (*non rovescio*) right side; (*fam*) crafty person, fast worker.
drizzare [drit'tsare] *v* (*raddrizzare*)

straighten; (*erigere*) erect. **drizzare le orecchie** prick up one's ears.
droga ['drɔga] *sf* drug; (*sostanza aromatica*) spice. **drogare** *v* drug, dope; spice. **drogarsi** *v* take drugs.
droghiere [dro'gjɛre], **-a** *sm, sf* grocer. **drogheria** *sf* grocer's shop. **articoli di drogheria** *sm pl* groceries *pl.*
dromedario [drome'darjo] *sm* dromedary.
dualismo [dua'lizmo] *sm* dualism.
dubbio ['dubbjo] *sm* doubt. **essere in dubbio** be in doubt, be uncertain. **mettere in dubbio** doubt, call in question. **senza dubbio** no doubt, doubtless. *agg also* **dubbioso** doubtful, uncertain; (*ambiguo*) dubious.
dubitare [dubi'tare] *v* doubt; (*essere in dubbio*) be in doubt; (*diffidare*) distrust. **non dubitare!** don't worry!
duca ['duka] *sm* duke.
duce ['dutʃe] *sm* leader.
duchessa [du'kessa] *sf* duchess.
due ['due] *sm, agg* two. **a due a due** two by two, in twos. **duepezzi** *sm invar* two-piece. **due punti** colon. **due volte** twice. **due volte tanto** twice as much *or* many. **nessuno dei due** neither of them. **tutti e due** both of them.
duello [du'ɛllo] *sm* duel. **duellare** *v* duel. **duellista** *or* **duellante** *sm* duellist.
duetto [du'etto] *sm* duet.
duna ['duna] *sf* dune.
dunque ['dunkwe] *cong* (*nel discorso*) well, now then; (*perciò*) so, therefore, hence; (*rafforzativo*) then. *sm* **trovarsi al dunque** come to the crunch. **venire al dunque** come to the point.
duo ['duo] *sm invar* duo.
duodeno [duo'dɛno] *sm* duodenum. **duodenale** *agg* duodenal.
duomo ['dwɔmo] *sm* cathedral.
duplex ['dupleks] *sm invar* (*telefono*) party-line.
duplicare [dupli'kare] *v* duplicate. **duplicato** *agg, sm* duplicate. **duplicatore** *sm* duplicator, copier. **duplice** *agg* double.
durare [du'rare] *v* last; (*cibo*) keep; (*abiti*) wear; (*sopportare*) endure.
durata [du'rata] *sf* length (of time), duration. **di breve durata** short(-lived), not lasting. **di lunga durata** lasting. **durata di una carica** term of office. **durevole** *agg* lasting.
duro ['duro] *agg* hard, tough. **aver la pelle dura** be thick-skinned. **aver la testa dura** be stubborn. **tener duro** hold out. **durezza** *sf* hardness. **durone** *sm* callus.
duttile ['duttile] *agg* ductile.

E

e [e], **ed** *cong* and; (*invece*) and then. **e ... e ...** both ... and .... **tutti e due** both (of them). **tutti e tre** all three (of them).
ebano ['ɛbano] *sm* ebony. **d'ebano** (*colore*) jet-black. **ebanista** *sm* cabinet-maker.
ebbene [eb'bɛne] *cong* well (then).
ebbro ['ɛbbro] *agg* intoxicated, drunk. **ebbrezza** *sf* intoxication; (*fig*) rapture, elation.
ebdomadario [ebdoma'darjo] *agg, sm* weekly.
ebete ['ɛbete] *agg* dull-witted.
ebollizione [ebolli'tsjone] *sf* boiling. **punto di ebollizione** *sm* boiling point.
ebraico [e'braiko] *agg* Jewish, Hebrew. *sm* (*lingua*) Hebrew.
ebreo [e'brɛo], **-a** *sm, sf* Jew. *agg* Jewish.
eccedere [et'tʃɛdere] *v* exceed; surpass. **eccedere i limiti** go too far.
***eccellere** [et'tʃɛllere] *v* excel, be outstanding. **eccellente** *agg* excellent. **eccellenza** *sf* excellence; (*titolo*) Excellency. **per eccellenza** par excellence.
eccentrico [et'tʃɛntriko] *agg, sm* eccentric. **eccentricità** *sf* eccentricity.
eccepibile [ettʃe'pibile] *agg* objectionable. **eccepire** *v* take exception (to), object (to).
eccesso [et'tʃɛsso] *sm* excess. **all'eccesso** excessively, to a fault. **eccesso di velocità** speeding. **eccessivo** *agg* excessive, exaggerated.
eccetera [et'tʃɛtera] etcetera, and so forth *or* on.
eccetto [et'tʃɛtto] *prep* except. **eccetto che** (*tranne che*) except for, but for; (*a meno che*) unless.
eccettuare [ettʃettu'are] *v* except, leave out.
eccezione [ettʃe'tsjone] *sf* exception. **ad eccezione di** except for. **eccezionale** *agg* exceptional.
eccidio [et'tʃidjo] *sm* slaughter.
eccitare [ettʃi'tare] *v* excite, stimulate; (*provocare*) stir up, rouse. **eccitamento** *sm*

excitement; (*stimolo*) incitement. **eccitante** *sm* stimulant. **eccitazione** *sf* excitement.
ecclesiastico [ekkle'zjastiko] *agg* clerical, ecclesiastic(al). *sm* clergyman.
ecco ['ɛkko] *avv* this *or* that is; (*qui*) here is; (*lì*) there is. **ecco fatto** that is that. **ecco tutto** that is all.
eccome [ek'kome] *avv*, *inter* and how, certainly.
echeggiare [eked'dʒare] *v* echo; (*risonare*) resound.
eclettico [e'klɛttiko] *agg* eclectic.
eclissare [eklis'sare] *v* eclipse. **eclisse** *or* **eclissi** *sf* eclipse.
eco ['ɛko] *s*(*m*+*f*), *pl* **-i** *m* echo. **echi di cronaca** gossip (column) *sing*. **far eco a** echo.
ecologia [ekolo'dʒia] *sf* ecology. **ecologico** *agg* ecological. **ecologo, -a** *sm*, *sf* ecologist.
economia [ekono'mia] *sf* economy; (*risparmio*) thrift, saving; (*scienza*) economics. **fare economie** economize, save. **economico** *agg* economic; (*a bassa spesa*) economical, cheap.
economizzare [ekonomid'dzare] *v* economize, save.
economo [e'kɔnomo] *sm* steward, supply officer.
ed [ed] *V* **e**.
edera ['edera] *sf* ivy.
edibile [e'dibile] *agg* edible.
edicola [e'dikola] *sf* bookstall.
edificare [edifi'kare] *v* (*erigere*) construct; (*stimolare al bene*) edify. **edificante** *agg* edifying. **edificio** *sm* building; (*fig*) structure.
edile [e'dile] *agg* building. *sm* builder. **edilizia** *sf* building trade. **edilizio** *agg* building.
Edimburgo [edim'burgo] *sf* Edinburgh.
editore [edi'tore], **-trice** *sm*, *sf* publisher. *agg* publishing. **edito** *agg* published.
editto [e'ditto] *sm* edict.
edizione [edi'tsjone] *sf* edition; (*tiratura*) issue.
educare [edu'kare] *v* educate; (*ammaestrare*) train. **educativo** *agg* educational. **educato** *agg* (*cortese*) polite. **bene/male educato** well-/ill-mannered. **educazione** *sf* education, upbringing; training; (*comportamento*) manners *pl*, breeding.
effeminato [effemi'nato] *agg* effeminate. **effeminatezza** *sf* effeminacy.
effervescente [efferve'ʃɛnte] *agg* effervescent, sparkling.
effetto [ef'fɛtto] *sm* effect; (*conseguenza*) result; impression; (*comm*) bill. **aver effetto** take effect. **dare effetto a** carry out. **fare effetto** work. **fare l'effetto di** give the impression of.
effettuare [effettu'are] *v* effect, bring about; (*realizzare*) carry out; (*fare*) make. **effettuabile** *agg* feasible. **effettuazione** *sf* execution.
efficace [effi'katʃe] *agg* effective, efficient. **efficacia** *sf* efficacy, effectiveness; force.
efficiente [effi'tʃɛnte] *agg* efficient. **efficienza** *sf* efficiency, effectiveness; (*mec*) working order.
effigie [ef'fidʒe] *sf* effigy; image.
effimero [ef'fimero] *agg* ephemeral.
effluente [efflu'ɛnte] *sm* effluent, sewage. **efflusso** *sm* outflow.
egida ['ɛdʒida] *sf* aegis.
Egitto [e'dʒitto] *sm* Egypt. **egiziano, -a** *s*, *agg* Egyptian. **egizio, -a** *s*, *agg* (ancient) Egyptian.
egli ['eʎi] *pron* he.
egocentrico [ego'tʃɛntriko] *agg* egocentric, self-centred.
egoista [ego'ista] *s*(*m*+*f*) egoist, selfish person. **egoistico** *agg* egoistic(al), selfish.
egotista [ego'tista] *s*(*m*+*f*) egotist, boaster. **egotistico** *agg* egotistic(al).
egregio [e'grɛdʒo] *agg* distinguished; (*in lettere*) dear.
eguale [e'gwale] *V* **uguale**.
egualitario [egwali'tarjo], **-a** *s*, *agg* egalitarian.
eiettore [ejet'tore] *sm* ejector. **sedile eiettore** *sm* ejector seat.
elaborare [elabo'rare] *v* elaborate, devise; (*dati*) process. **elaborato** *agg* elaborate. **elaboratore** *sm* (*elettronico*) computer; (*dati*) processor. **elaborazione** *sf* preparation, formulation; (*dati*) processing.
elargire [elar'dʒire] *v* lavish.
elastico [e'lastiko] *agg* elastic; (*molleggiante*) springy; (*fig*) flexible; (*agile*) nimble. *sm* elastic; (*anello*) elastic band; (*materasso*) spring.
elefante [ele'fante] *sm* elephant. **elefantesco** *agg* elephantine.
elegante [ele'gante] *agg* elegant; (*vestito*) smart; (*fine*) graceful; (*ingegnoso*) neat. **eleganza** *sf* elegance; smartness, stylishness.

***eleggere** [e'lɛddʒere] *v* elect, nominate. **eleggibile** *agg* eligible. **eleggibilità** *sf* eligibility.
elegia [ele'dʒia] *sf* elegy. **elegiaco** *agg* elegiac.
elemento [ele'mento] *sm* element; (*individuo*) fellow, individual. **elementare** *agg* elementary; (*naturale*) elemental.
elemosina [ele'mɔzina] *sf* alms, charity. **chiedere l'elemosina** beg. **fare l'elemosina** give alms.
elenco [e'lɛnko] *sm* list; (*telefonico*) directory; (*iscritti*) register. **elencare** *v* list; enumerate.
eletto [e'lɛtto] *agg* chosen; (*scelto*) select; (*nominato*) elected.
elettorale [eletto'rale] *agg* electoral, election. **collegio elettorale** *sm* constituency. **propaganda elettorale** *sf* electioneering. **scheda/urna elettorale** *sf* ballot-paper/box. **elettorato** *sm* electorate; (*diritto di eleggere*) franchise.
elettore [elet'tore], **-trice** *sm, sf* elector, voter; (*di collegio elettorale*) constituent.
elettrico [e'lɛttriko] *agg* electric(al). **elettricista** *sm* electrician. **elettricità** *sf* electricity.
elettrificare [elettrifi'kare] *v* electrify. **elettrificazione** *sf* electrification.
elettrizzare [elettrid'dzare] *v* electrify; (*fig*) thrill.
elettrodo [e'lɛttrodo] *sm* electrode.
elettrodomestico [elettrodo'mɛstiko] *sm* electric appliance.
elettrodotto [elettro'dotto] *sm* power line, mains.
elettrolisi [elet'trɔlizi] *sf* electrolysis. **elettrolitico** *agg* electrolytic.
elettrone [elet'trone] *sm* electron. **elettronica** *sf* electronics. **elettronico** *agg* electronic.
elettrotecnico [elettro'tɛkniko] *sm* electrical engineer.
elevare [ele'vare] *v* raise. **elevato** *agg* high; (*fig*) lofty. **elevazione** *sf* elevation; (*atto di alzare*) raising.
elezione [ele'tsjone] *sf* election. **elezioni politiche** general election *sing*.
elica ['ɛlika] *sf* propeller. **elicottero** *sm* helicopter.
eliminare [elimi'nare] *v* eliminate; (*escludere*) rule out. **eliminatoria** *sf* (*sport*) qualifying round. **eliminazione** *sf* elimination; exclusion.
elio ['ɛljo] *sm* helium.
ella ['ella] *pron* she; (*formula di cortesia*) you.
ellisse [el'lisse] *sf* ellipse. **ellittico** *agg* elliptical.
elmetto [el'metto] *sm also* **elmo** helmet.
elogio [e'lɔdʒo] *sm* praise. **elogiare** *v* praise.
eloquente [elo'kwɛnte] *agg* eloquent; (*significativo*) meaningful. **eloquenza** *sf* eloquence.
elsa ['elsa] *sf* hilt.
***eludere** [e'ludere] *v* elude, dodge, evade.
emaciato [ema'tʃato] *agg* emaciated.
emanare [ema'nare] *v* emanate; (*diffondere*) give off, send out; (*promulgare*) issue. **emanazione** *sf* emanation; promulgation.
emancipare [emantʃi'pare] *v* emancipate. **emancipazione** *sf* emancipation.
embargo [em'bargo] *sm* embargo.
emblema [em'blɛma] *sm* emblem; symbol, model. **emblematico** *agg* emblematic, symbolic.
embolia [embo'lia] *sf* embolism. **embolo** *sm* embolus.
embrione [embri'one] *sm* embryo. **embrionale** *agg* embryonic.
emendare [emen'dare] *v* amend. **emendamento** *sm* amendment.
emergenza [emer'dʒɛntsa] *sf* emergency.
***emergere** [e'mɛrdʒere] *v* emerge; (*distinguersi*) stand out; (*apparire*) appear.
***emettere** [e'mettere] *v* emit, give out; (*ordine, azioni*) issue; (*giudizio*) deliver; (*grido*) utter.
emicrania [emi'krania] *sf* migraine.
emigrare [emi'grare] *v* emigrate; (*animali*) migrate. **emigrante** *s*(*m*+*f*) emigrant. **emigrato, -a** *sm, sf* emigrant; (*pol*) exile. **emigrazione** *sf* emigration, migration; (*econ*) flight.
eminente [emi'nɛnte] *agg* eminent, distinguished; (*elevato*) high. **eminenza** *sf* eminence.
emisfero [emis'fɛro] *sm* hemisphere. **emisferico** *agg* hemispheric(al).
emissario[1] [emis'sarjo] *sm* (*mandatario*) emissary.
emissario[2] [emis'sarjo] *sm* (*canale, ecc.*) outlet.
emissione [emis'sjone] *sf* emission; (*econ*) issue. **emittente** *agg* issuing; (*radio*) transmitting.

emolliente [emol'ljɛnte] *sm, agg* emollient.
emorragia [emorra'dʒia] *sf* haemorrhage, bleeding.
emorroidi [emor'rɔidi] *sf pl* piles *pl.*
emotivo [emo'tivo] *agg* emotional; (*impressionabile*) excitable; (*che provoca emozione*) emotive, thrilling.
emozione [emo'tsjone] *sf* emotion; excitement. **emozionante** *agg* exciting. **emozionare** *v* excite; (*commuovere*) move.
empio ['empjo] *agg* impious; (*crudele*) cruel.
empire [em'pire] *v* fill.
empirico [em'piriko] *agg* empirical.
emporio [em'pɔrjo] *sm* store.
emù [e'mu] *sm* emu.
emulare [emu'lare] *v* emulate. **emulazione** *sf* rivalry; (*dir*) nuisance.
emulsione [emul'sjone] *sf* emulsion.
enciclopedia [entʃiklope'dia] *sf* encyclopaedia. **enciclopedico** *agg* encyclopaedic.
encomio [en'kɔmjo] *sm* praise. **encomiabile** *agg* praiseworthy.
endemico [en'dɛmiko] *agg* endemic.
energia [ener'dʒia] *sf* energy. **energetico** *sm, agg* tonic. **energico** *agg* energetic; (*forte*) forceful, strong.
enfasi ['ɛnfazi] *sf* emphasis (*pl* -ses). **enfatico** *agg* emphatic.
enfiare [en'fjare] *v* swell, inflate.
enigma [e'nigma] *sm* puzzle, riddle; (*mistero, persona misteriosa*) enigma, mystery. **enigmatico** *agg* puzzling; mysterious.
ennesimo [en'nɛzimo] *agg* nth; (*fam*) umpteenth.
enorme [e'norme] *agg* enormous, huge. **enormità** *sf* (*causa di indignazione*) enormity; (*errore*) blunder.
ente ['ɛnte] *sm* (*filos*) being; (*azienda*) undertaking, concern; authority; (*istituzione*) body.
enteroclisi [entero'klizi] *sm* enema.
entità [enti'ta] *sf* entity; importance; (*consistenza*) extent.
entrambi [en'trambi] *agg, pron* both.
entrare [en'trare] *v* enter; (*andar dentro*) go in(to); (*con difficoltà*) get in(to); (*venir dentro*) come in(to); (*associarsi*) join. **entrare in ballo** come into play. **entrare in vigore** come into effect.
entrata [en'trata] *sf* entrance, entry; (*accesso*) admission. **entrate** *sf pl* (*redditi*) income *sing*, earnings *pl*; (*incassi*) receipts *pl*; (*di enti pubblici*) revenue *sing*.
entro ['entro] *prep* within; (*ora/data precisata*) by. **entro oggi** before the day is out.
entusiasmo [entu'zjazmo] *sm* enthusiasm. **entusiasmare** *v* thrill, excite. **entusiasta** *s(m+f)* enthusiast. **entusiastico** *agg* enthusiastic.
enumerare [enume'rare] *v* list. **enumerazione** *sf* listing; list.
enunciare [enun'tʃare] *v* enunciate; (*esprimere*) express; formulate.
enzima [en'dzima] *sm* enzyme.
epatite [epa'tite] *sf* hepatitis.
epico ['ɛpiko] *agg* epic, heroic. **epica** *sf* epic poetry.
epidemia [epide'mia] *sf* epidemic. **epidemico** *agg* epidemic.
Epifania [epifa'nia] *sf* Epiphany; (*festa*) Twelfth Night.
epigramma [epi'gramma] *sm* epigram. **epigrammatico** *agg* epigrammatic.
epilessia [epiles'sia] *sf* epilepsy. **epilettico, -a** *s, agg* epileptic.
epilogo [e'pilogo] *sm, pl* **-ghi** epilogue; (*fig*) end, conclusion.
episodio [epi'zɔdjo] *sm* episode. **episodico** *agg* episodic; (*frammentario*) bitty; (*accidentale*) incidental; isolated.
epistola [e'pistola] *sf* epistle. **epistolare** *agg* epistolary.
epitaffio [epi'taffjo] *sm* epitaph.
epiteto [e'piteto] *sm* epithet.
epoca ['ɛpoka] *sf* period; (*tempo*) time. **a quell'epoca** at that time. **che fa epoca** epoch-making. **da quell'epoca** from that time on, since then.
eppure [ep'pure] *cong* and yet.
epurare [epu'rare] *v* purge. **epurazione** *sf* purging; purge.
equanime [e'kwanime] *agg* (*imparziale*) fair; (*sereno*) even-tempered. **equanimità** *sf* fairness, equanimity.
equatore [ekwa'tore] *sm* equator. **equatoriale** *agg* equatorial.
equazione [ekwa'tsjone] *sf* equation.
equestre [e'kwɛstre] *agg* equestrian.
equilibrare [ekwili'brare] *v* balance. **equilibrio** *sm* balance, equilibrium; moderation, common sense; (*padronanza di sè*) poise. **perdere l'equilibrio** lose one's balance. **tenere in equilibrio** balance. **tenersi in equilibrio** keep one's balance. **equilibrista** *s(m+f)* acrobat.

equinozio [ekwi'nɔtsjo] *sm* equinox.
equipaggiare [ekwipad'dʒare] *v* (*fornire*) equip; (*nave*) man. **equipaggiamento** *sm* kit. **equipaggio** *sm* crew.
equiparare [ekwipa'rare] *v* level.
equitazione [ekwita'tsjone] *sf* (horse-)riding.
***equivalere** [ekwiva'lere] *v* be equivalent, correspond. **equivalente** *sm, agg* equivalent.
equivoco [e'kwivoko] *sm* (*errore*) mistake; (*malinteso*) misunderstanding. **a scanso di equivoci** to avoid misunderstandings. *agg* ambiguous; (*di dubbia moralità*) questionable, shady. **non equivoco** unambiguous, straightforward.
equo ['ɛkwo] *agg* fair.
era ['ɛra] *sf* era, age.
erario [e'rarjo] *sm* Treasury. **erariale** *agg* fiscal.
erba ['ɛrba] *sf* grass; (*gastr*) herb. **in erba** green; (*fig*) budding. **erbaceo** *agg* herbaceous.
erbaccia [er'battʃa] *sf* weed.
erbicida [erbi'tʃida] *sm* herbicide, weedkiller.
erbivendolo [erbi'vendolo], **-a** *sm, sf* greengrocer.
erbivoro [er'bivoro] *sm* herbivore. *agg* herbivorous.
erede [e'rɛde] *s(m+f)* heir, heiress. **erede apparente** heir presumptive. **erede universale** sole heir.
eredità [eredi'ta] *sf* inheritance, heritage. **ereditare** *v* inherit. **ereditario** *agg* inherited, hereditary. **principe ereditario** *sm* crown prince. **ereditiera** *sf* heiress.
eremita [ere'mita] *sm* hermit. **eremitaggio** *sm* hermitage.
eretico [e'rɛtiko], **-a** *sm, sf* heretic. *agg* heretical. **eresia** *sf* heresy; (*fam*: *sproposito*) rubbish.
eretto [e'rɛtto] *agg* erect, upright. **erettile** *agg* erectile.
erezione [ere'tsjone] *sf* erection.
ergastolo [er'gastolo] *sm* life imprisonment *or* sentence.
erica ['ɛrika] *sf* heather.
***erigere** [e'ridʒere] *v* raise, erect; (*fondare, considerare*) set up.
ermellino [ermel'lino] *sm* ermine; (*bruno*) stoat.
ermetico [er'mɛtiko] *agg* (*aria*) air-tight; (*acqua*) water-tight; obscure.
ernia ['ɛrnja] *sf* hernia, rupture.
***erodere** [e'rodere] *v* erode.
eroe [e'rɔe] *sm* hero. **eroico** *agg* heroic. **eroina** *sf* heroine. **eroismo** *sm* heroism; (*atto*) heroic deed.
erogare [ero'gare] *v* distribute, deliver; (*in donazione*) donate. **erogazione** *sf* distribution, delivery; donation.
eroina [ero'ina] *sf* (*stupefacente*) heroin.
erosione [ero'zjone] *sf* erosion.
erotico [e'rɔtiko] *agg* erotic. **erotismo** *sm* eroticism.
erpete ['ɛrpete] *sm* herpes.
erpice ['erpitʃe] *sm* harrow.
errare [er'rare] *v* (*andare senza meta*) roam, wander; (*sbagliare*) err, be mistaken. **erratico** *agg* erratic. **errato** *agg* incorrect. **se non vado errato** if I am not mistaken.
erroneo [er'rɔneo] *agg* erroneous, wrong.
errore [er'rore] *sm* mistake, error. **errore giudiziario** miscarriage of justice. **per errore** by mistake, in error.
erudito [eru'dito] *agg* erudite, learned. **erudizione** *sf* learning.
eruttare [erut'tare] *v* (*ruttare*) belch; (*vulcano*) erupt; (*fig*) spew out. **eruzione** *sf* eruption.
esacerbare [ezatʃer'bare] *v* exacerbate.
esagerare [ezadʒe'rare] *v* exaggerate; (*caricare*) overdo. **esagerazione** *sf* exaggeration.
esagono [e'zagono] *sm* hexagon. **esagonale** *agg* hexagonal.
esalare [eza'lare] *v* exhale, give off. **esalazione** *sf* exhalation.
esaltare [ezal'tare] *v* exalt; (*lodare*) extol; (*entusiasmare*) thrill, stir. **esaltato, -a** *sm, sf* fanatic, hot-head.
esame [e'zame] *sm* examination, test; (*controllo*) inspection, check. **dare un esame** take an examination. **prendere in esame** consider, take into consideration.
esaminare [ezami'nare] *v* examine, test, check.
esanime [e'zanime] *agg* lifeless.
esasperare [ezaspe'rare] *v* (*irritare*) exasperate; (*inasprire*) sharpen, increase. **esasperazione** *sf* exasperation; sharpening, increase.
esatto [e'zatto] *agg* exact; correct; accurate; punctual. *avv* (*in punto*) exactly. **esattezza** *sf* exactness; accuracy, precision.

esattore [ezat'tore] *sm* (*tassa*) collector. **esattoria** *sf* tax office.

esaudire [ezau'dire] *v* grant.

esaurire [ezau'rire] *v* exhaust, use up; (*vendere completamente*) sell out; (*condurre a termine*) complete. **esaurirsi** *v* (*debilitarsi*) wear oneself out.

esca ['eska] *sf* bait; (*fig*) lure; (*per accendere*) tinder. **dar esca a** fan, stir up.

escandescenza [eskande'ʃɛntsa] *sf* **dare in escandescenze** flare up; (*fam*) fly off the handle.

eschimese [eski'meze] *s*(*m*+*f*), *agg* Eskimo.

esclamare [eskla'mare] *v* exclaim, cry out. **punto esclamativo** *sm* exclamation mark. **esclamazione** *sf* exclamation.

***escludere** [es'kludere] *v* exclude. **esclusione** *sf* exclusion. **ad esclusione di** except.

esclusivo [esklu'zivo] *agg* exclusive. **esclusiva** *sf* (*comm*) exclusive *or* sole right; (*rappresentenza*) sole agency. **escluso** *agg* excluded, impossible; (*eccettuato*) except; (*non compreso*) exclusive of, not including.

escogitare [eskodʒi'tare] *v* devise, think up.

escursione [eskur'sjone] *v* excursion, trip; (*a macchina*) drive; (*a piedi*) hike. **escursionista** *s*(*m*+*f*) tripper; hiker.

esecutivo [ezeku'tivo] *sm*, *agg* executive.

esecutore [ezeku'tore], **-trice** *sm*, *sf* (*dir*) executor; (*musica*) performer; (*carnefice*) executioner.

esecuzione [ezeku'tsjone] *sf* execution, performance.

eseguire [eze'gwire] *v* carry out; (*musica, teatro*) perform; (*dir*) execute.

esempio [e'zɛmpjo] *sm* example; model. **ad** *or* **per esempio** for instance. **dare l'esempio** set an example.

esemplare [ezem'plare] *agg* exemplary. *sm* example, model; (*tipico*) specimen. **esemplificare** *v* exemplify, illustrate.

esentare [ezen'tare] *v* exempt. **esentarsi da** get out of. **esente** *agg* exempt, free. **esenzione** *sf* exemption.

esequie [e'zɛkwje] *sf pl* (*cerimonie*) funeral rites *pl*; funeral *sing*.

esercente [ezer'tʃɛnte] *s*(*m*+*f*) retailer; (*negoziante*) shopkeeper. **esercire** *v* manage, run.

esercitare [ezertʃi'tare] *v* practise; (*usare*) exercise. **esercitazione** *sf* practice; exercise; (*mil*) drill. **esercizio** *sm* exercise; (*attività*) practice; (*azienda*) concern.

esibire [ezi'bire] *v* exhibit. **esibirsi** *v* (*dar spettacolo*) perform; (*mettersi in mostra*) show off. **esibizione** *sf* exhibition, show, display. **esibizionismo** *sm* exhibitionism. **esibizionista** *s*(*m*+*f*) exhibitionist.

***esigere** [e'zidʒere] *v* require, need, demand. **esigente** *agg* exacting. **esigenza** *sf* requirement; (*necessità*) need; (*pretesa*) demand. **esiguo** *agg* meagre.

esilarante [ezila'rante] *agg* exhilarating.

esile ['ɛzile] *agg* slender; (*debole*) feeble.

esiliare [ezi'ljare] *v* exile. **esiliarsi** *v* go into exile. **esiliato, -a** *sm*, *sf* exile. **esilio** *sm* exile.

***esimere** [e'zimere] *v* exempt, free.

esimio [e'zimjo] *agg* distinguished, outstanding.

esistenzialismo [ezistentsja'lizmo] *sm* existentialism. **esistenzialista** *s*(*m*+*f*), *agg* existentialist.

esistere [e'zistere] *v* exist, be. **esistente** *agg* existing. **esistenza** *sf* existence. **esistenza di cassa/magazzino** (*comm*) cash/stock in hand.

esitare [ezi'tare] *v* hesitate. **esitazione** *sf* hesitation.

esito ['ɛzito] *sm* outcome; (*dramma*) denouement. **buon esito** success.

esodo ['ɛzɔdo] *sm* exodus.

esofago [e'zɔfago] *sm* oesophagus; gullet.

esonerare [ezone'rare] *v* exempt. **esonero** *sm* exemption.

esorbitante [ezorbi'tante] *agg* exorbitant.

esorcizzare [ezortʃid'dzare] *v* exorcise. **esorcismo** *sm* exorcism.

esordire [ezor'dire] *v* start out; (*artista*) make one's debut. **esordio** *sm* start, debut.

esortare [ezor'tare] *v* urge. **esortazione** *sf* exhortation, encouragement.

esoso [e'zɔzo] *agg* (*avido*) greedy; exorbitant; odious.

esoterico [ezo'tɛriko] *agg* esoteric.

esotico [e'zɔtiko] *agg* exotic.

***espandere** [es'pandere] *v* expand, extend. **espandersi** *v* spread. **espansione** *sf* expansion; (*effusione d'affetto*) effusiveness. **espansivo** *agg* effusive; (*forza*) expansive.

espatriare [espa'trjare] *v* emigrate. **espatrio** *sm* expatriation.

espediente [espe'djɛnte] *sm* expedient, device; (*soluzione*) way out. **vivere di espedienti** live on one's wits.
***espellere** [es'pɛllere] *v* expel.
esperienza [espe'rjɛntsa] *sf* experience; experiment; (*conoscenza*) familiarity. **fare esperienza di** experience. **senza esperienza** inexperienced.
esperimento [esperi'mento] *sm* experiment; (*tentativo*) trial, test.
esperto [es'pɛrto], **-a** *sm, sf* expert, authority. *agg* expert (in); (*abile*) skilful (at); experienced (in).
espiare [espi'are] *v* expiate, atone. **capro espiatorio** *sm* scapegoat.
espletare [esple'tare] *v* accomplish.
esplicito [es'plitʃito] *agg* explicit. **esplicativo** *agg* explanatory.
***esplodere** [es'plɔdere] *v* explode. **far esplodere** explode, blow up.
esplorare [esplo'rare] *v* explore; (*investigare*) probe. **esploratore, -trice** *sm, sf* explorer; (*mil*) scout. **giovani esploratori** Boy Scouts *pl*. **esplorazione** *sf* exploration; (*mil*) reconnaissance.
esplosione [esplo'zjone] *sf* explosion.
esplosivo [esplo'zivo] *sm, agg* explosive.
esponente [espo'nɛnte] *sm* exponent; representative. **esponenziale** *agg* exponential.
***esporre** [es'porre] *v* expose; (*arrischiare*) risk; (*spiegare*) expound; (*mostrare*) exhibit, display.
esportare [espor'tare] *v* export. **esportatore, -trice** *sm, sf* exporter. **esportazione** *sf* export.
esposizione [espozi'tsjone] *sf* exhibition, show; (*spiegazione*) explanation; (*posizione, foto*) exposure.
esposto [es'posto] *agg* exhibited, displayed; exposed. *sm* statement.
espressione [espres'sjone] *sf* expression. **espressivo** *agg* expressive, eloquent.
espresso [es'prɛsso] *agg* express; (*manifestato*) expressed; (*dichiarato*) avowed, declared. **piatto espresso** *sm* specially prepared dish. *sm* (*lettera*) express letter; (*caffè*) espresso; (*ferr*) express train.
***esprimere** [es'primere] *v* express.
espulsione [espul'sjone] *sf* expulsion.
essa ['essa] *pron* (*persona*: *soggetto*) she; (*persona*: *oggetto*) her; (*cosa, animale*) it.
esse ['esse] *pron* (*soggetto*) they; (*oggetto*) them.
essenza [es'sɛntsa] *sf* essence. **essenziale** *agg* essential.
***essere** ['ɛssere] *v* be; (*ausiliare con forma attiva*) have. *sm* being; (*fam*) person, creature; (*condizione*) existence.
essi ['essi] *pron* (*soggetto*) they; (*oggetto*) them.
essiccare [essik'kare] *v* dry. **essiccatoio** *sm* dryer.
esso ['esso] *pron* (*persona*: *soggetto*) he; (*persona*: *oggetto*) him; (*cosa, animale*) it.
est [est] *sm* east. **dell'est** east, eastern.
estasi ['ɛstazi] *sf* ecstasy. **estatico** *agg* ecstatic.
estate [es'tate] *sf* summer. **estate di San Martino** Indian summer.
***estendere** [es'tɛndere] *v* extend, stretch; (*ampliare*) broaden. **estendersi** *v* (*stendersi*) stretch; (*diffondersi*) spread.
estensione [esten'sjone] *sf* extension; (*dimensione*) extent; (*distesa*) expanse; (*fig, musica*) range; (*significato*) wider sense.
estenuare [estenu'are] *v* exhaust. **estenuante** *agg* exhausting, wearing.
esteriore [este'rjore] *agg* outer, exterior, external. *sm* (*parte esterna*) outside; (*apparenze*) appearances *pl*.
esterno [es'tɛrno] *agg* external, outer, exterior. *sm* outside; (*scolaro*) day-boy; (*film*) exterior.
estero ['ɛstero] *agg* foreign. *sm* foreign countries *pl*. **all'estero** abroad.
esterrefatto [esterre'fatto] *agg* (*atterrito*) aghast, horrified; (*sbigottito*) amazed.
esteso [es'tezo] *agg* large, wide-ranging; (*fig*) thorough. **per esteso** in full.
estetica [es'tɛtika] *sf* aesthetics. **estetico** *agg* aesthetic.
estetista [este'tista] *s(m+f)* beauty specialist, beautician.
***estinguere** [es'tingwere] *v* put out; (*far svanire*) extinguish; (*econ*) wipe out; (*debito*) pay off; (*sete*) quench. **estinguersi** *v* die out. **estinto** *agg* extinguished; (*scomparso*) extinct. **estinzione** *sf* extinction; (*sete*) quenching; (*econ*) discharge.
estirpare [estir'pare] *v* eradicate.
estivo [es'tivo] *agg* summer.
***estorcere** [es'tɔrtʃere] *v* extort. **estorsione** *sf* extortion.
estradare [estra'dare] *v* extradite. **estradizione** *sf* extradition.

estraneo [es'traneo] *agg* extraneous, unrelated (to), unconnected (with); (*alieno*) foreign. **essere estraneo a** have no part in. **mantenersi estraneo a** have nothing to do with, keep clear of. *sm* stranger; unauthorized person. **estraniare** *v* estrange.
***estrarre** [es'trarre] *v* extract, draw (out); (*miniera*) mine; (*cava*) quarry. **estratto** *sm* extract; (*compendio*) abstract; (*stralcio*) excerpt. **estrazione** *sf* extraction.
estremo [es'trεmo] *agg* extreme; (*ultimo*) final; (*grandissimo*) utmost. *sm* extreme; (*colmo*) height; (*estremità*) end, tip. **estremi** *sm pl* particulars *pl*; (*dir*) essential elements *pl*. **estremismo** *sm* extremism. **estremista** *s*(*m*+*f*) extremist.
estro ['εstro] *sm* (*ghiribizzo*) whim, fancy; (*impulso*) inspiration; (*venereo*) heat. **estroso** *agg* whimsical, capricious; inspired.
estrogeno [es'trɔdʒeno] *sm* oestrogen.
estroverso [estro'vεrso], **-a** *sm, sf* extrovert. *agg* extroverted.
estuario [estu'arjo] *sm* estuary.
esuberante [ezube'rante] *agg* exuberant. **esuberanza** *sf* exuberance.
esule ['εzule] *s*(*m*+*f*) exile. **esulare** *v* lie outside, be beyond.
esultare [ezul'tare] *v* rejoice. **esultante** *agg* exultant.
esumare [ezu'mare] *v* exhume; (*fig*) unearth.
età [e'ta] *v* age. **all'età di dieci anni** at (the age of) ten. **età della ragione** age of discretion.
etere ['εtere] *sm* ether.
eterno [e'tεrno] *agg* eternal, everlasting; (*lunghissimo*) interminable. **eternità** *sm* eternity; (*molto tempo*) ages *pl*.
eterodosso [etero'dɔsso] *agg* heterodox.
eterogeneo [etero'dʒεneo] *agg* heterogeneous.
etica ['εtika] *sf* ethics. **etico** *agg* ethical.
etichetta[1] [eti'ketta] *sf* (*cartellino*) label.
etichetta[2] [eti'ketta] *sf* (*regole*) etiquette.
etimologia [etimolo'dʒia] *sf* etymology. **etimologico** *agg* etymological.
etnico ['εtniko] *agg* ethnic.
ettaro ['εttaro] *sm* hectare.
etto ['εtto] *sm* hundred grams.
eucalipto [euka'lipto] *sm* eucalyptus.
eufemismo [eufe'mizmo] *sm* euphemism. **eufemistico** *agg* euphemistic.
eunuco [eu'nuko] *sm, pl* **-chi** eunuch.
Europa [eu'rɔpa] *sf* Europe. **europeo, -a** *s, agg* European.
eutanasia [eutana'zia] *sf* euthanasia.
evacuare [evaku'are] *v* evacuate.
***evadere** [e'vadere] *v* escape (from); (*sbrigare*) dispatch; (*fattura*) settle; (*ordini*) execute; (*fisco*) avoid.
evanescente [evane'ʃεnte] *agg* (*suono*) fading; (*fugace*) fleeting; (*crema*) vanishing.
evangelista [evandʒe'lista] *sm* evangelist. **evangelico** *agg* evangelical.
evaporare [evapo'rare] *v* evaporate. **evaporatore** *sm* humidifier. **evaporazione** *sf* evaporation.
evasione [eva'zjone] *sf* escape; (*fisco*) evasion; (*comm*) execution.
evasivo [eva'zivo] agg evasive.
evaso [e'vazo], **-a** *agg* escaped; (*comm*) dispatched, dealt with. *sm, sf* fugitive, escaped convict.
evento [e'vεnto] *sm* event; (*eventualità*) eventuality. **in ogni evento** in any case, at all events.
eventuale [eventu'ale] *agg* possible, any. **eventualità** *sf* eventuality. **nell'eventualità di** *or* **che** in the event of. **eventualmente** *cong* if, in case.
evidente [evi'dente] *agg* obvious, manifest, clear; (*irrefutabile*) unmistakable. **evidenza** *sf* (*chiarezza*) clarity, obviousness. **mettere in evidenza** stress, emphasize. **mettersi in evidenza** make oneself conspicuous, draw attention to oneself. **tenere un'evidenza** (*comm*) keep pending.
evitare [evi'tare] *v* avoid; (*non arrecare*) spare, save.
evo ['εvo] *sm* **Medio Evo** Middle Ages *pl*.
evocare [evo'kare] *v* evoke.
evoluzione [evolu'tsjone] *sf* evolution. **evoluto** *agg* evolved, fully developed; advanced, progressive.
evviva [ev'viva] *inter* hurrah! **evviva . . . !** long live . . . !
extra ['εkstra] *agg invar* (*qualità*) first-rate; (*fuori del previsto*) additional. *sm invar* extra.

F

fa [fa] *avv* ago.
fabbisogno [fabbi'zoɲo] *sm* requirements *pl.*
fabbrica ['fabbrika] *sf* factory; (*officina*) works; (*edificio*) building. **fabbricante** *sm* manufacturer. **fabbricare** *v* manufacture, produce; (*costruire*) build; (*inventare*) make up. **fabbricato** *sm* building. **fabbricazione** *sf* manufacture, production.
fabbro ['fabbro] *sm* (*ferraio*) (black)smith.
faccenda [fat'tʃɛnda] *sf* matter; (*caso, circostanza*) business. **faccende domestiche** housework *sing.*
facchino [fak'kino] *sm* porter. **facchinaggio** *sm* porterage. **facchinata** *sf* (*lavoro*) drudgery.
faccia ['fattʃa] *sf* face; (*lato*) side. **avere una bella/brutta faccia** look well/unwell. **di faccia** opposite. **faccia tosta** (*fam*) cheek, nerve. **in faccia a** opposite. **facciata** *sf* front; (*pagina*) side.
facezia [fa'tʃɛtsja] *sf* pleasantry; (*detto spiritoso*) witticism. **faceto** *agg* facetious, witty.
facile ['fatʃile] *agg* easy; (*incline*) easily moved, prone. **facilità** *sf* ease, facility; (*l'esser facile*) easiness; (*capacità*) aptitude. **con facilità** with ease, readily; (*lingua*) fluently.
facilitare [fatʃili'tare] *v* facilitate; (*aiutare*) help. **facilitazione** *sf* facilitation, making easy. **facilitazioni di pagamento** easy terms *pl.*
facoltà [fakol'ta] *sf* faculty; (*potere*) power. **facoltativo** *agg* optional. **facoltoso** *agg* wealthy.
faggio ['faddʒo] *sm* beech.
fagiano [fa'dʒano] *sm* pheasant.
fagiolo [fa'dʒɔlo] *sm* bean. **andare a fagiolo** (*fam*) suit. **fagiolino** *sm* French bean.
fagotto [fa'gɔtto] *sm* bundle; (*musica*) bassoon. **far fagotto** pack up.
falcata [fal'kata] *sf* step.
falce ['faltʃe] *sf* sickle; (*manico lungo*) scythe.
falciare [fal'tʃare] *v* mow; (*fig*) mow down. **falciatrice** *sf* mower.
falco ['falko] *sm* hawk. **falcone** *sm* falcon; (*tec*) derrick.
falda ['falda] *sf* (*strato*) layer, sheet; (*di pendio*) foot; (*di cappello*) brim; (*di vestito*) skirt; (*di marsina*) tail.
falegname [fale'ɲame] *sm* joiner, carpenter. **falegnameria** *sf* (*arte*) joinery, carpentry; (*bottega*) joiner's shop.
falena [fa'lɛna] *sf* moth; (*cenere*) ash; (*persona fatua*) flighty person.
falla ['falla] *sf* leak. **aprire/chiudere una falla** spring/stop a leak.
fallace [fal'latʃe] *agg* fallacious.
fallire [fal'lire] *v* fail; (*non colpire*) miss; (*dir, comm*) go bankrupt. **fallimento** *sm* failure; bankruptcy.
fallito [fal'lito], **-a** *agg* unsuccessful. *sm, sf* bankrupt; (*fig*) failure.
fallo[1] ['fallo] *sm* (*errore*) fault; (*sport*) foul. **cogliere in fallo** find out. **essere in fallo** be at fault. **senza fallo** without fail, certainly.
fallo[2] ['fallo] *sm* (*membro virile*) phallus.
falò [fa'lo] *sm* bonfire.
falsare [fal'sare] *v* falsify; (*alterare*) distort. **falsario** *sm* (*documenti*) forger; (*monete*) counterfeiter.
falsariga [falsa'riga] *sf* (*modello*) pattern; (*norma*) lines *pl.*
falsificare [falsifi'kare] *v* falsify; (*arte*) fake. **falsificazione** *sf* falsification, faking; forgery, fake.
falso ['falso] *agg* false; (*falsificato*) counterfeit, faked, forged; (*fam*) bogus. *sm* (*non vero*) falsehood; (*reato*) forgery. **giurare il falso** commit perjury.
fama ['fama] *sf* fame, reputation.
fame ['fame] *sf* hunger; (*carestia*) famine. **aver fame** be hungry. **aver fame di** (*fig*) hunger for. **aver una fame da lupo** be ravenous. **fare la fame** go hungry. **morir di fame** starve to death; (*fig*) be starving.
famelico [fa'mɛliko] *agg* ravenous.
famigerato [famidʒe'rato] *agg* notorious.
famiglia [fa'miʎa] *sf* family. **in famiglia** at home.
familiare [fami'ljare] *agg* domestic; (*consueto, intimo*) familiar; (*semplice*) informal. *s(m+f)* (*parente*) relative. **familiarità** *sf* familiarity. **familiarizzarsi** *v* familiarize oneself.
famoso [fa'moso] *agg* famous, well-known; memorable.
fanale [fa'nale] *sm* lamp; (*auto*) light. **fanale anteriore** headlight. **fanale di coda** tail-light.
fanatico [fa'natiko], **-a** *agg* fanatical; (*fam: entusiasta*) wild (about). *sm, sf* fanatic; (*tifoso*) fan. **fanatismo** *sm* fanaticism.
fanciullo [fan'tʃullo], **-a** *sm, sf* child (*pl* -ren). **fanciullaggine** *sf* childish behaviour. **fanciullesco** *agg* childish, puerile;

(*innocente*) child-like. **fanciullezza** *sf* childhood.

fandonia [fan'dɔnja] *sf* nonsense.

fanfara [fan'fara] *sf* (brass-)band; (*composizione*) fanfare. **fanfaronata** *sf* boasting. **fanfarone, -a** *sm, sf* boaster.

fango ['fango] *sm* mud. **fare i fanghi** take mud-baths. **fangoso** *agg* muddy.

fannullone [fannul'lone], **-a** *sm, sf* idler, loafer.

fantascienza [fanta'ʃɛntsa] *sf* science fiction.

fantasia [fanta'zia] *sf* fantasy; (*capriccio*) fancy; imagination. *agg* (*moda*) fancy, patterned.

fantasma [fan'tazma] *sm* ghost, phantom.

fantasticare [fantasti'kare] *v* daydream, dream up. **fantastico** *agg* fantastic; (*non reale*) fanciful, strange.

fante ['fante] *sm* (*mil*) infantryman; (*carte*) knave, jack. **fanteria** *sf* infantry.

fantino *sm* jockey.

fantoccio [fan'tɔttʃo] *sm* puppet.

farabutto [fara'butto] *sm* rascal, rogue.

faraona [fara'ona] *sf* guinea-fowl.

farcire [far'tʃire] *v* stuff.

fardello [far'dello] *sm* burden.

***fare** ['fare] *v* (*agire*) do; (*produrre*) make; (*essere*) be; (*avere*) have; (*un mestiere, ecc.*) go in for, practise; (*comportarsi*) play; (*orologio*) say. **farcela** *v* (*riuscire*) manage; (*resistere*) be able to go on. **far attenzione** pay attention. **far bene** do good. **far bene a** be good for. **far chiamare** send for. **far entrare** let in. **fare il pieno** (*auto*) fill up. **far male** (*dolere*) hurt, ache; (*nuocere*) be bad for; (*agire male*) do the wrong thing. **far notare** point out. **fare per** be about to. **far vedere** show. **farsi** *v* (*diventare*) become, grow into; (*convertirsi*) turn into; (*tempo*) get.

farfalla [far'falla] *sf* butterfly; (*falena*) moth. **nuoto a farfalla** *sm* butterfly stroke.

farina [fa'rina] *sf* flour. **farina gialla** maize meal. **farina integrale** wholemeal. **farinaceo** *agg* floury, starchy. **farinoso** *agg* floury, mealy; (*neve*) powdery.

faringe [fa'rindʒe] *sf* pharynx. **faringite** *sf* pharyngitis.

farmacia [farma'tʃia] *sf* (*negozio*) chemist's (shop); (*scienza*) pharmacy. **farmacista** *s*(*m*+*f*) chemist. **farmaco** *sm* medicine.

farneticare [farneti'kare] *v* rave.

faro ['faro] *sm* lighthouse; (*lume, fig*) beacon; (*auto*) headlight.

farragine [far'radʒine] *sf* muddle, jumble.

farsa ['farsa] *sf* farce.

fascia ['faʃa] *sf* band; (*benda*) bandage; (*uniforme*) sash; (*postale*) wrapper; (*zona*) strip.

fasciare [fa'ʃare] *v* wrap; (*bambini*) swaddle; (*ferita*) dress, bandage.

fascicolo [fa'ʃikolo] *sm* (*opuscolo*) pamphlet, booklet; (*numero*) issue.

fascino ['faʃino] *sm* charm, fascination.

fascio ['faʃo] *sm* bundle, bunch.

fascismo [fa'ʃizmo] *sm* fascism. **fascista** *s*(*m*+*f*), *agg* fascist.

fase ['faze] *sf* phase; (*auto*) stroke.

fastidio [fas'tidjo] *sm* trouble; (*avversione*) dislike; (*cosa fastidiosa*) bother, inconvenience. **dar fastidio** trouble; (*molestare*) annoy, bother. **darsi fastidio** put oneself out. **fastidioso** *agg* troublesome, annoying.

fasto ['fasto] *sm* pomp.

fasullo [fa'zullo] *agg* (*fam*) bogus, phoney.

fata ['fata] *sf* fairy.

fatale [fa'tale] *agg* inevitable; (*funesto*) fatal; (*decisivo*) fateful; irresistible.

fatica [fa'tika] *sf* (*sforzo*) effort, labour; (*stanchezza, tec*) fatigue. **a fatica** with difficulty. **costar fatica** require an effort. **durare fatica** find it difficult. **reggere alla fatica** stand the strain. **faticare** *v* labour; (*stentare*) have difficulty. **faticoso** *agg* tiring.

fatta ['fatta] *sf* kind.

fattezze [fat'tettse] *sf pl* features *pl*.

fattibile [fat'tibile] *agg* feasible.

fatto[1] ['fatto] *agg* made, done. **a conti fatti** all things considered. **detto fatto** no sooner said than done. **fatto a macchina/mano** machine-/hand-made. **fatto su misura** tailor-made.

fatto[2] ['fatto] *sm* fact; (*avvenimento*) event; (*azione*) deed; (*affare*) business. **cogliere sul fatto** catch in the act. **dire il fatto suo** have one's say. **fatto compiuto** fait accompli. **fatto sta** the fact remains. **in fatto di** regarding.

fattore [fat'tore] *sm* factor; (*capo di fattoria*) steward.

fattoria [fatto'ria] *sf* farm, estate.

fattorino [fatto'rino] *sm* messenger; (*di negozio*) errand-boy; (*di autobus*) conductor.
fattura [fat'tura] *sf* (*confezione*) making; (*lavorazione*) construction, workmanship; (*conto*) bill; (*comm*) invoice. **fatturare** *v* (*comm*) invoice; (*manipolare*) doctor. **fatturato** *sm* turnover.
fatuo ['fatuo] *agg* foolish, fatuous.
fauci ['fautʃi] *sf pl* jaws *pl*; (*fig*) clutches *pl*.
fauna ['fauna] *sf* fauna.
fausto ['fausto] *agg* propitious.
fautore [fau'tore], **-trice** *sm, sf* supporter.
fava ['fava] *sf* broad bean.
favilla [fa'villa] *sf* spark. **far faville** sparkle, shine.
favo ['favo] *sm* honeycomb.
favola ['favola] *sf* fable, story. **favoloso** *agg* fabulous.
favore [fa'vore] *sm* favour; (*appoggio*) support. **di favore** (*biglietto*) complimentary; (*prezzo*) special. **per favore** please.
favoreggiare [favored'dʒare] *v* favour; (*dir*) aid and abet.
favorevole [favo'revole] *agg* favourable, in favour.
favorire [favo'rire] *v* favour; (*sostenere*) support; (*promuovere*) promote, foster. **favorito, -a** *s, agg* favourite. **favoritismo** *sm* favouritism.
fazione [fa'tsjone] *sf* faction, party. **fazioso** *agg* subversive.
fazzoletto [fattso'letto] *sm* handkerchief; (*da testa*) headsquare.
febbraio [feb'brajo] *sm* February.
febbre ['fɛbbre] *sf* temperature, fever; (*fam*: *sulle labbra*) cold sore; (*brama*) lust, passion. **febbre da fieno** hay fever. **febbricitante** *agg* feverish.
feccia ['fɛttʃa] *sf* dregs *pl*.
feci ['fɛtʃi] *sf pl* faeces *pl*.
fecola ['fɛkola] *sf* starch.
fecondare [fekon'dare] *v* fertilize. **fecondazione** *sf* fertilization. **fecondazione artificiale** artificial insemination. **fecondità** *sf* fertility. **fecondo** *agg* fertile; prolific, fruitful.
fede ['fede] *sf* faith; (*fiducia*) confidence, trust; (*anello*) wedding ring; (*attestazione*) proof.
fedele [fe'dele] *agg* faithful, true. *s*(*m*+*f*) believer; (*seguace*) follower. **fedeltà** *sf* faithfulness, fidelity.
federa ['fɛdera] *sf* pillow-case.
federale [fede'rale] *agg* federal.
federazione [federa'tsjone] *sf* federation, association.
fedina [fe'dina] *sf* police *or* criminal record.
fedine [fe'dine] *sf pl* side-whiskers *pl*.
fegato ['fegato] *sm* liver; (*coraggio*) guts *pl*. **mangiarsi il fegato** eat one's heart out.
felce ['feltʃe] *sf* fern; (*comune*) bracken.
felice [fe'litʃe] *agg* happy; (*fortunato*) lucky. **felicità** *sf* happiness, bliss. **felicitarsi con** congratulate. **felicitazioni** *sf pl* congratulations *pl*.
felino [fe'lino] *agg* feline.
felpa ['felpa] *sf* plush.
feltro ['feltro] *sm* felt.
femmina ['femmina] *sf* female; (*figlia*) daughter. *agg* female. **femminismo** *sm* feminism, women's movement. **femminista** *s*(*m*+*f*), *agg* feminist.
femminile [femmi'nile] *agg* female; (*da donna*) feminine, womanly; (*gramm*) feminine. **scuola femminile** *sf* girls' school. *sm* feminine (gender). **femminilità** *sf* femininity.
femore ['fɛmore] *sm* femur.
***fendere** ['fɛndere] *v* split, pierce; (*solcare*) plough (through). **fenditura** *sf* cleft; (*fessura*) crack.
fenicottero [feni'kɔttero] *sm* flamingo.
fenomeno [fe'nɔmeno] *sm* phenomenon (*pl* -a); (*prodigio*) marvel. **fenomenale** *agg* phenomenal; (*eccezionale*) extraordinary, remarkable.
feretro ['fɛretro] *sm* coffin.
ferie ['fɛrje] *sf pl* holidays *pl*. **giorno feriale** *sm* weekday.
ferire [fe'rire] *v* wound, injure, hurt. **ferita** *sf* wound, injury; (*persona*) casualty. **ferito** *sm* casualty.
fermacarte [ferma'karte] *sm invar* (*a molla*) paper-clip; (*pesante*) paperweight.
fermaglio [fer'maʎo] *sm* clasp, clip.
fermare [fer'mare] *v* stop; (*arrestare*) check; (*fissare*) secure, fasten; (*prenotare*) book. **fermarsi** stop; (*rimanere*) stay. **fermata** *sf* stop; (*tappa*) stay; (*veicoli*) halt. **fermata facoltativa** request stop.
fermentare [fermen'tare] *v* ferment. **fermentazione** *sf* fermentation. **fermento** *sm* ferment; (*fig*) unrest.
fermo ['fermo] *agg* still; (*non in moto*) stationary; (*saldo*) firm, steady. **restar fermo** stand still; (*fig*) hold good. *sm*

(*mec*) catch, fastener, lock; (*dir*) detention; (*sospensione*) stop.

feroce [fe'rotʃe] *agg* wild; (*crudele*) savage, ferocious; (*fig*) fierce. **ferocia** *sf* cruelty, ferocity.

ferragosto [ferra'gosto] *sm* mid-August holiday.

ferramenta [ferra'menta] *sf pl* ironmongery *sing*.

ferreo ['fɛrreo] *agg* iron.

ferro ['fɛrro] *sf* iron. **essere ai ferri corti** be at loggerheads. **ferro battuto** wrought iron. **ferro da calza** knitting needle. **ferro di cavallo** horseshoe. **tocca ferro!** touch wood!

ferrovia [ferro'via] *sf* railway. **ferroviario** *agg* rail(way), train. **ferroviere** *sm* railwayman.

fertile ['fɛrtile] *agg* fertile, fruitful. **fertilità** *sf* fertility, fruitfulness. **fertilizzante** *sm* fertilizer. **fertilizzare** *v* fertilize.

fervore [fer'vore] *sm* fervour. **fervente** *agg* fervent. **fervido** *agg* ardent; (*caloroso*) heartfelt; (*vivace*) lively.

fesso ['fesso] (*volg*) *agg*, *sm* idiot, fool. **fesseria** *sf* (*azione*) foolishness; (*parole*) nonsense; (*inezia*) trifle.

fessura [fes'sura] *sf* crack, slit; (*gettone, moneta*) slot.

festa ['festa] *sf* holiday; (*compleanno*) birthday; (*onomastico*) saint's day; (*festeggiamento*) celebration; (*ricevimento*) party. **far festa** (*non lavorare*) take a holiday, take time off; (*smettere il lavoro*) stop work; (*divertirsi*) make merry. **far festa a** give a warm welcome (to).

festeggiare [fested'dʒare] *v* celebrate; (*far festa*) give a hearty welcome (to). **festeggiamenti** *sm pl* festivities *pl*. **festeggiamento** *sm* celebration.

festività [festivi'ta] *sf* festivity, holiday. **festivo** *agg* (*della domenica*) Sunday; (*non-feriale*) holiday.

festone [fes'tone] *sm* festoon; (*ricamo*) scallop.

fetente [fe'tɛnte] *sm* (*volg*) stinker, scoundrel. *agg also* **fetido** stinking, foul. **fetore** *sm* stench.

feticcio [fe'tittʃo] *sm* fetish.

feto ['fɛto] *sm* foetus.

fetta ['fetta] *sf* slice. **tagliare a fette** slice, cut into slices. **fettuccia** *sf* (*nastro*) tape, ribbon. **fettuccine** *sf pl* noodles *pl*.

feudale [feu'dale] *agg* feudal. **feudalesimo** *sm* feudalism. **feudo** *sm* feud; (*proprietà terriera*) lands *pl*; (*fig*) domain.

fiaba ['fjaba] *sf* story, (fairy) tale.

fiacca ['fjakka] *sf* (*stanchezza*) weariness; (*pigrizia*) laziness; (*svogliatezza*) listlessness. **battere la fiacca** (*fam*: *stare in ozio*) kick one's heels; (*agire svogliatamente*) be sluggish. **fiaccare** *v* (*indebolire*) weaken; (*spossare*) wear out; (*spezzare*) break. **fiacco** *agg* (*debole*) weak; (*stanco*) exhausted, weary.

fiaccola ['fjakkola] *sf* torch. **alla luce di fiaccole** by torchlight.

fiala ['fjala] *sf* phial, medicine bottle.

fiamma ['fjamma] *sf* flame; (*improvvisa, irregolare*) flare; (*molto viva*) blaze. **in fiamme** on fire. **nuovo fiammante** brand-new. **fiammata** *sf* blaze, flare.

fiammeggiare [fjammed'dʒare] *v* blaze, flame.

fiammifero [fjam'mifero] *sm* match.

fiammingo [fjam'mingo] *agg* Flemish.

fiancheggiare [fjanked'dʒare] *v* flank; (*sostenere*) help.

fianco ['fjanko] *sm* side; (*mil*) flank. **di fianco a** (*vicino*) next to, by; (*lungo*) alongside.

fiasco ['fjasko] *sm* flask, (straw-covered) bottle; (*insuccesso*) flop. **far fiasco** flop.

fiatare [fja'tare] *v* breathe. **fiato** *sm* breath. **fiati** *sm pl* woodwind *pl*. **senza fiato** out of breath. **strumenti a fiato** *sm pl* wind instruments *pl*. **tutto d'un fiato** in one go.

fibbia ['fibbja] *sf* buckle.

fibra ['fibra] *sf* fibre; (*fig*) constitution.

ficcare [fik'kare] *v* poke, stick; (*fam*: *mettere*) put. **ficcanaso** *sm* busybody.

fico ['fiko] *sm* fig. **fico d'India** prickly pear. **non m'importa un fico (secco)** (*fam*) I couldn't care less. **non valere un fico** be worthless.

fidanzarsi [fidan'tsarsi] *v* get engaged. **fidanzamento** *sm* engagement. **fidanzato, -a** *sm, sf* fiancé, -e.

fidarsi [fi'darsi] *v* (*aver fiducia*) rely (on), trust; (*osare*) trust oneself, dare.

fido ['fido] *sm* (*econ*) credit.

fiducia [fi'dutʃa] *sf* trust, confidence. **aver fiducia in** trust. **di fiducia** (*fidato*) reliable, trustworthy; responsible. **fiduciario** *sm* (official) representative; (*dir*) trustee. **fiducioso** *agg* trusting.

fiele ['fjɛle] *sm* bile; (*fig*) ill-will.

fieno ['fjɛno] *sm* hay.
fiera ['fjɛra] *sf* fair; (*mostra*) exhibition; (*di beneficienza*) bazaar.
fiero ['fjɛro] *agg* (*orgoglioso*) proud; (*audace*) bold, spirited; (*feroce, violento*) fierce; (*austero*) severe. **fierezza** *sf* pride; boldness.
fifa ['fifa] (*fam*) *sf* fear. **aver fifa** be afraid. **fifone, -a** *sm, sf* coward.
figliastro [fi'ʎastro] *sm* stepson. **figliastra** *sf* stepdaughter.
figlio ['fiʎo] *sm* son; (*fig*: *frutto*) result, product. **figli** *sm pl* children *pl*. **figlia** *sf* daughter; (*comm*) counterfoil. **figliare** *v* give birth. **figliata** *sf* litter.
figlioccio [fi'ʎottʃo] *sm* godson. **figlioccia** *sf* goddaughter.
figliolo [fi'ʎɔlo] *sm* (*figlio*) son; (*ragazzo*) boy, young man; (*fam*) chap. **figliola** *sf* (*figlia*) daughter; (*ragazza*) girl. **figliolanza** *sf* offspring.
figura [fi'gura] *sf* figure; (*aspetto*) shape; (*illustrazione*) picture; (*tavola*) plate. **far bella figura** show up to advantage; make a good impression; (*riuscir bene*) do well. **far brutta figura** cut a sorry figure, disgrace oneself.
figurare [figu'rare] *v* represent, portray; (*simboleggiare*) stand for; (*mostrare*) pretend; (*risultare*) appear; (*far figura*) look smart. **figurarsi** *v* imagine. **figurati!** *inter* (*altro che*) of course! you bet! **figurina** *sf* figurine; (*cartoncino*) card. **figurino** *sm* fashion-plate; (*giornale*) fashion magazine. **figuro** *sm* shady character.
fila ['fila] *sf* row, line; (*coda*) queue; (*serie*) string. **di fila** (*di seguito*) in succession, in a row; (*senza interruzione*) on end, non-stop. **in fila indiana** in single file. **mettere in fila** line up. **mettersi in fila** queue up.
filantropo [fi'lantropo], **-a** *sm, sf* philanthropist. **filantropico** *agg* philanthropic.
filare [fi'lare] *v* spin; (*cavo, catena*) pay out; (*correre*) run, speed along.
filarmonico [filar'mɔniko] *agg* philharmonic.
filastrocca [filas'trɔkka] *sf* (*per bambini*) nursery rhyme; (*storia lunga*) tedious list, rigmarole.
filatelia [filate'lia] *sf* stamp-collecting, philately. **filatelico** *agg* stamp. **filatelista** *s*(*m*+*f*) stamp collector.
filatura [fila'tura] *sf* (*industria*) spinning; (*filanda*) spinning mill.
filetto [fi'letto] *sm* (*gastr*) fillet; border; (*filo sottile, mec*) thread; (*tipografia*) rule.
filettare *v* (*ornare*) decorate; (*bordare*) edge; (*mec*) thread. **filettatura** *sf* edging, braid; threading.
filiale [fi'ljale] *sf* branch. *agg* filial.
filibustiere [filibus'tjɛre] *sm* pirate; (*imbroglione*) rogue.
filigrana [fili'grana] *sf* filigree; (*carta*) watermark.
film [film] *sm invar* film. **filmare** *v* film.
filo ['filo] *sm* thread; (*filato*) yarn; (*metallico*) wire; (*coltello*) edge; (*elettrico*) flex. **filo d'erba** blade of grass. **filo spinato** barbed wire. **lana a due/tre fili** *sf* two-/three-ply wool. **perdere il filo** (*discorso*) lose track; (*taglio*) become blunt. **per filo e per segno** in detail.
filodrammatico [filodram'matiko], **-a** *sm, sf* amateur actor, amateur actress. *agg* amateur theatrical.
filologo [fi'lologo], **-a** *sm, sf* philologist. **filologia** *sf* philology. **filologico** *agg* philological.
filone [fi'lone] *sm* seam, vein; (*pane*) French loaf; (*fig*) current, line.
filosofia [filozo'fia] *sf* philosophy. **filosofico** *agg* philosophical. **filosofo, -a** *sm, sf* philosopher.
filtrare [fil'trare] *v* filter. **filtro** *sm* filter; (*colino*) strainer.
filza ['filtsa] *sf* string.
finale [fi'nale] *agg* final; (*ultimo*) last. *sf* (*sport*) final; (*gramm*) ending. *sm* (*musica*) finale. **finalista** *s*(*m*+*f*) finalist. **finalità** *sf* (*scopo*) purpose, aim; (*filosofia*) finality.
finanza [fi'nantsa] *sf* finance; (*fam*: *risorse economiche*) finances *pl*. **finanze** *sf pl* (*entrate dello Stato*) public revenue *sing*. **guardia di finanza** *sf* customs officer.
finanziare [finan'tsjare] *v* finance. **finanziamento** *sm* financing; (*fondi*) funds *pl*. **finanziario** *agg* financial. **finanziatore, -trice** *sm, sf* backer. **finanziera** *sf* frock-coat.
finché [fin'ke] *cong* (*per tutto il tempo che*) as long as; (*fino a quando*) until, till.
fine[1] ['fine] *sf* end; (*libro, film, ecc.*) ending. *sm* end; (*scopo*) aim; (*esito*) conclusion. **alla fine** (*luogo*) at the end; (*tempo*) in the end; (*finalmente*) at last. **in fin dei conti** when all is said and done, in the end. **secondo fine** ulterior motive, hidden purpose. **senza fine** endless.

fine² ['fine] *agg* fine; (*signorile*) refined; (*acuto*) sharp; (*penetrante*) subtle. **finezza** *sf* fineness; (*raffinatezza*) finesse, polish; (*minuzie*) nicety.

fine-settimana [finesetti'mana] *s(m+f) invar* weekend.

finestra [fi'nɛstra] *sf* window.

***fingere** ['findʒere] *v* pretend. **fingersi** *v* pretend to be.

finire [fi'nire] *v* finish; (*smettere*) stop; (*terminare, sboccare*) end; (*capitare*) end up. **andare a finire** (*capitare*) get to; (*concludersi*) turn out, end up. **finimondo** *sm* pandemonium. **finissaggio** *sm* finish. **finitura** *sf* finishing off; finishing touches *pl*.

Finlandia [fin'landja] *sf* Finland. **finlandese** *sm, agg* Finnish; *s(m+f)* (*abitante*) Finn.

fino¹ ['fino] *agg* fine, delicate; (*acuto*) subtle.

fino² ['fino] *avv* (*persino*) even. **fino a** (*tempo*) until, up to; (*luogo*) as far as. **fino a che punto?** how far? **fin da** (*passato*) since, as far back as; (*presente, futuro*) (as) from. **fin dove?** how far? **fino in fondo** right down, to the (very) end.

finocchio [fi'nɔkkjo] *sm* (*bot*) fennel; (*volg*) queer, gay.

finora [fi'nora] *avv* up to now, so far.

finta ['finta] *sf* pretence, sham; (*sport*) feint. **far finta di** pretend.

finto ['finto] *agg* false; (*simulato*) bogus; (*non reale*) mock; artificial. **fintapelle** *sf* imitation leather.

finzione [fin'tsjone] *sf* pretence; (*falsità*) falsehood; (*illusione*) fiction.

fio ['fio] *sm* **pagare il fio** pay the price.

fioccare [fjok'kare] *v* (*neve*) fall; (*fig*) come down thick and fast.

fiocco ['fjɔkko] *sm* flake; (*batuffolo*) flock; (*fibra tessile*) staple; (*nastro*) bow. **coi fiocchi** first-class, magnificent. **fiocchi d'avena** oatflakes *pl*. **fiocco di neve** snowflake.

fioco ['fjɔko] *agg* faint; (*luce*) dim.

fionda ['fjonda] *sf* catapult, sling.

fiordo ['fjɔrdo] *sm* fjord.

fiore ['fjore] *sm* flower; (*di albero*) blossom; (*meglio*) cream; (*carte da gioco*) club. **a fiori** floral. **fior di quattrini** pots of money *pl*. **in fiore** in bloom, in blossom. **fiorente** *agg* (*di fiore*) flowering; (*fig*) thriving, flourishing.

fiorentino [fjoren'tino], **-a** *s, agg* Florentine.

fioretto [fjo'retto] *sm* (*sport*) foil; (*musica, discorso*) embellishment.

fiorire [fjo'rire] *v* flower, bloom, blossom. **fioritura** *sf* flowering, blossoming; (*fiori*) bloom, blossom.

Firenze [fi'rɛntse] *sf* Florence.

firma ['firma] *sf* signature. **firmare** *v* sign. **firmatario** *sm* signatory.

fisarmonica [fizar'mɔnika] *sf* accordion.

fiscale [fis'kale] *agg* fiscal, tax. **fisco** *sm* treasury, tax authorities *pl*.

fischiare [fis'kjare] *v* whistle; (*disapprovare*) boo, hiss. **fischiata** *sf* booing, hissing. **fischiettare** *v* whistle (softly). **fischietto** *sm* whistle. **fischio** *sm* whistle, boo, hiss.

fisica ['fizika] *sf* physics; (*scienziata*) physicist.

fisico ['fiziko] *agg* physical. *sm* (*corpo*) body; (*costituzione*) make-up; (*scienziato*) physicist.

fisima ['fizima] *sf* whim, fancy.

fisiologia [fizjolo'dʒia] *sf* physiology. **fisiologico** *agg* physiological. **fisiologo, -a** *sm, sf* physiologist.

fisionomia [fizjono'mia] *sf* expression.

fisioterapia [fizjotera'pia] *sf* physiotherapy. **fisioterapista** *s(m+f)* physiotherapist.

fissare [fis'sare] *v* fix; (*attaccare*) fasten; (*guardare fissamente*) stare (at), gaze (at); (*prenotare*) book. **fissarsi di** be set on. **fissazione** *sf* fixation.

fissato [fis'sato] *agg* obsessed. *sm* (*fam*) fanatic, maniac. **essere fissato** have a bee in one's bonnet.

fissione [fis'sjone] *sf* fission.

fitta ['fitta] *sf* (*dolore*) twinge, sharp pain.

fittizio [fit'titsjo] *agg* fictitious.

fitto¹ ['fitto] *agg* thick, dense; (*conficcato*) stuck, driven in; (*tessuto, ecc.*) close. *sm* thick, middle. **a capo fitto** headlong. **buio fitto** pitch dark.

fitto² ['fitto] *sm* (*affitto*) rent.

fiume ['fjume] *sm* river; (*fig*) flood, stream. **fiumana** *sf* torrent.

fiutare [fju'tare] *v* smell; (*annusare rumorosamente*) sniff; (*intuire*) scent. **fiutare un inganno** (*fam*) smell a rat. **fiuto** *sm* scent, nose. **al fiuto** straight off, instinctively. **aver fiuto di** get wind of.

flaccido ['flattʃido] *agg* flabby, limp.

flacone [fla'kone] *sm* small bottle.

flagellare [fladʒel'lare] *v* flagellate, whip. **flagello** *sm* scourge, whip.
flagrante [fla'grante] *agg* flagrant. **cogliere in flagrante** catch in the act, catch red-handed.
flanella [fla'nɛlla] *sf* flannel.
flauto ['flauto] *sm* flute. **flauto dolce** recorder. **flautista** *s(m+f)* flautist.
flebile ['flɛbile] *agg* (*debole*) faint, feeble; (*lamentevole*) mournful, melancholy.
flemma ['flɛmma] *sf* coolness, imperturbability. **flemmatico** *agg* cool, self-possessed, phlegmatic.
flessibile [fles'sibile] *agg* flexible, pliable; versatile. **flessibilità** *sf* flexibility, pliability; versatility. **flessione** *sf* bending; (*diminuzione graduale*) drop, fall; (*ginnastica*) bend.
flessuoso [flessu'ozo] *agg* supple, lithe. **flessuosità** *sf* suppleness.
***flettere** ['flɛttere] *v* bend, bow; (*membra*) flex.
flipper ['flipper] *sm invar* pin-table.
flirt [flɜːt] *sm invar* (*amore superficiale*) flirtation; (*persona*) boy-friend, girl-friend. **flirtare** *v* flirt.
flora ['flɔra] *sf* flora.
florido ['flɔrido] *agg* (*prospero*) flourishing, thriving; (*colorito*) ruddy, glowing with health.
floscio ['flɔʃo] *agg* floppy, limp.
flotta ['flɔtta] *sf* fleet. **flottiglia** *sf* flotilla.
fluido ['fluido] *sm, agg* fluid. **fluidità** *sf* fluidity; (*scorrevolezza*) fluency; instability.
fluire [flu'ire] *v* flow.
fluorescente [fluore'ʃɛnte] *agg* fluorescent. **fluorescenza** *sf* fluorescence.
fluoro ['fluɔro] *sm* fluorine.
flusso ['flusso] *sm* flow, stream. **flusso e riflusso** ebb and flow. **flusso di sangue dal naso** nosebleed.
fluttuare [fluttu'are] *v* fluctuate.
fobia [fo'bia] *sf* phobia; (*fam*) (pet) aversion.
foca ['fɔka] *sf* seal.
focaccia [fo'kattʃa] *sf* bun. **rendere pan per focaccia** give as good as one gets.
focale [fo'kale] *agg* focal.
foce ['fotʃe] *sf* mouth, outlet.
focena [fo'tʃɛna] *sf* porpoise.
focolaio [foko'lajo] *sm* (*med*) focus; (*centro di diffusione*) hotbed, breeding ground.
focolare [foko'lare] *sm* hearth; (*fig*) fireside, home.
focoso [fo'kozo] *agg* fiery; (*ardente*) burning.
fodera ['fɔdera] *sf* lining; (*rivestimento*) cover. **foderare** *v* line; cover. **fodero** *sm* sheath.
foga ['foga] *sf* rush; (*ardore*) heat.
foggia ['fɔddʒa] *sf* fashion; (*forma*) shape. **foggiare** *v* shape, form, fashion.
foglia ['fɔʎʎa] *sf* leaf. **mettere le foglie** come into leaf. **fogliame** *sm* foliage.
foglio ['fɔʎʎo] *sm* sheet; (*giornale*) paper; (*banconota*) note. **foglio di via** travel-warrant. **foglio volante** leaflet.
fogna ['foɲa] *sf* sewer. **fognatura** *sf* sewerage.
foia ['fɔja] *sf* heat. **essere in foia** be on heat.
folata [fo'lata] *sf* gust.
folclore [fol'klɔre] *sm* folklore. **folcloristico** *agg* folk.
folgorare [folgo'rare] *v* flash; (*inveire*) rail; (*colpire con fulmine*) strike with lightning. **folgorare con lo sguardo** wither with a glance.
folla ['fɔlla] *sf* crowd; (*gran quantità*) host.
folle ['fɔlle] *agg* crazy; (*pazzo*) mad; (*sciocco*) foolish; (*auto*) neutral. **andare in folle** coast. **folletto** *sm* imp. **follia** *sf* madness, folly.
follicolo [fol'likolo] *sm* follicle.
folto ['folto] *sm, agg* thick.
fomentare [fomen'tare] *v* encourage; (*eccitare*) rouse. **fomento** *sm* (*impacco caldo*) poultice; (*sprone*) spur.
fonda ['fonda] *sf* anchorage.
fondamento [fonda'mento] *sm, pl* **-a** *f in literal sense* foundation. **fondamentale** *agg* fundamental, basic.
fondare [fon'dare] *v* found; (*istituire*) establish; base. **fondarsi su** be based on; (*fare assegnamento*) rely on. **fondatore, -trice** *sm, sf* founder. **fondazione** *sf* foundation, establishment.
***fondere** ['fondere] *v* melt, fuse; (*in una forma*) cast, mould; (*unire*) blend, merge.
fonderia [fonde'ria] *sf* foundry.
fondiario [fon'djarjo] *agg* land. **proprietà fondiaria** *sf* real estate.
fondina[1] [fon'dina] *sf* (*di pistola*) holster.
fondina[2] [fon'dina] *sf* (*piatto*) soup plate.
fondista [fon'dista] *s(m+f)* (*sport*) long

distance runner; (*giornalista*) leader writer.

fondo ['fondo] *agg* deep. *sm* bottom; (*feccia*) dregs *pl*; (*caffè*) grounds *pl*; (*estremità*) end; (*sfondo*) background; (*pittura*) primer; (*denaro*) fund; (*terreno*) estate. **a fondo** (*profondamente*) thoroughly; (*con tutte le forze*) wholeheartedly. **andare a fondo** sink. **andare a fondo di** get to the bottom of. **articolo di fondo** *sm* leading article. **dar fondo a** (*consumare*) use up. **fino in fondo** to the end. **fondo (di) cassa/magazzino** cash/stock in hand. **fondo stradale** road surface. **in fondo** (*sotto*) at *or* to the bottom; (*dietro*) at *or* to the back; (*in conclusione*) after all. **mandare a fondo** sink.

fonetica [fo'nɛtika] *sf* phonetics. **fonetico** *agg* phonetic.

fontana [fon'tana] *sf* fountain.

fonte ['fonte] *sf* spring; (*fig*) source. *sm* (*battesimale*) font.

foraggiare [forad'dʒare] *v* forage. **foraggio** *sm* forage.

forare [fo'rare] *v* perforate; (*gomma*) puncture; (*al trapano*) bore. **foratura** *sf* perforation; puncture.

forbici ['fɔrbitʃi] *sf pl* scissors *pl*; (*da siepe, cesoie*) shears *pl*; (*da potatura*) secateurs *pl*. **forbicina** *sf* earwig.

forbire [for'bire] *v* clean; (*fig*) polish.

forca ['forka] *sf* pitchfork; (*patibolo*) gallows. **va alla** *or* **sulla forca!** (*fam*) get stuffed! **forcella** *sf* fork; (*volatili*) wishbone.

forchetta [for'ketta] *sf* fork. **una buona forchetta** a hearty eater. **forchettata** *sf* forkful.

forcina [for'tʃina] *sf* hairpin.

forcipe ['fɔrtʃipe] *sm* forceps *pl*.

forense [fo'rɛnse] *agg* forensic.

foresta [fo'rɛsta] *sf* forest.

forestiero [fores'tjɛro], **-a** *agg* foreign. *sm, sf* foreigner.

forfait[1] [for'fɛ] *sm invar* (*contratto*) flat rate. **a forfait** all-in.

forfait[2] [for'fɛ] *sm invar* (*sport*) withdrawal. **dichiarare forfait** scratch.

forfora ['forfora] *sf* dandruff.

forma ['forma] *sf* form, shape; (*stampo*) mould; (*del calzolaio*) last. **a forma di X** X-shaped.

formaggio [for'maddʒo] *sm* cheese.

formale [for'male] *agg* formal. **formalità** *sf* formality.

formare [for'mare] *v* form; (*modellare*) shape; (*costituire*) make up; (*numero telefonico*) dial. **formarsi un'idea** get an idea. **formato** *sm* format, size. **formazione** *sf* formation; (*addestramento*) training.

formica [for'mika] *sf* ant. **formicaio** *sm* antheap; (*fig*) teeming crowd.

formicolare [formiko'lare] *v* swarm; (*provare sensazione*) tingle. **formicolio** *sm* swarming; (*sensazione*) pins and needles.

formidabile [formi'dabile] *agg* remarkable; (*molto forte*) powerful, formidable.

formula ['fɔrmula] *sf* formula (*pl* -ae).

formulare [formu'lare] *v* formulate; (*avanzare*) put forward; (*esprimere*) express. **formulario** *sm* (*modulo*) form.

fornace [for'natʃe] *sf* kiln, furnace.

fornaio [for'najo], **-a** *sm, sf* baker.

fornire [for'nire] *v* supply, furnish. **ben fornito** well-stocked. **fornitore** *sm* supplier. **fornitura** *sf* supply.

forno ['forno] *sm* oven. **fornello** *sm* cooker.

foro[1] ['foro] *sm* (*buco*) hole.

foro[2] ['fɔro] *sm* (*tribunale*) (law-)court; (*gli avvocati*) the bar; (*Roma*) forum.

forse ['forse] *avv* perhaps, maybe; (*circa*) about. **in forse** in doubt.

forsennato [forsen'nato] *agg* crazy, mad.

forte ['fɔrte] *agg* strong; (*grande*) large; (*bravo*) good; (*suono*) loud; (*intenso*) heavy. *avv* (*con forza*) hard; (*assai*) very much; (*velocemente*) fast; (*a voce alta*) loud. *sm* (*specialità*) strong point; (*persona*) powerful person; (*mil*) fort.

fortezza [for'tettsa] *sf* (*mil*) fortress; (*forza morale*) strength.

fortificare [fortifi'kare] *v* strengthen, fortify. **fortificazione** *sf* fortification.

fortuito [for'tuito] *agg* fortuitous, chance.

fortuna [for'tuna] *sf* fortune; (*buona sorte*) luck; success. **di fortuna** (*improvvisato*) makeshift; emergency. **fortuna che** fortunately. **fortunato** *agg* fortunate, lucky.

foruncolo [fo'runkolo] *sm* boil.

forza ['fɔrtsa] *sf* strength; (*potere, potenza*) power; (*fis, mil*) force. **a forza di** through, by dint of. **a tutta forza** with all one's strength. **bella forza!** there's nothing to it! **farsi forza** (*coraggio*) pluck up courage. **forza maggiore** force majeure, circumstances beyond one's control. **per forza** necessarily; (*controvoglia*) unwillingly. **per forza di cose** of necessity.

forzare [for'tsare] *v* force. **forzato** *sm* convict.
foschia [fos'kia] *sf* haze, mist.
fosco ['fɔsko] *agg* (*scuro*) dark; (*tetro*) gloomy.
fosfato [fos'fato] *sm* phosphate.
fosforescente [fosfore'ʃɛnte] *agg* phosphorescent. **fosforo** *sm* phosphorus.
fossa ['fɔssa] *sf* pit, hole; (*cimitero*) grave. **fossato** *sm* ditch; (*mil*) moat. **fossetta** *sf* dimple.
fossile ['fɔssile] *sm*, *agg* fossil.
fosso ['fɔsso] *sm* ditch. **saltare il fosso** (*fig*) take the plunge.
foto ['fɔto] *sf invar* (*fam*) snap, photo.
fotocopia [foto'kɔpja] *sf* photocopy.
fotogenico [foto'dʒɛniko] *agg* photogenic.
fotografare [fotogra'fare] *v* photograph. **fotografia** *sf* (*tecnica*) photography; (*copia*) photograph. **fotografico** *agg* photographic. **apparecchio fotografico** *sm* camera. **fotografo, -a** *sm*, *sf* photographer.
fottere ['fottere] (*volg*) *v* fuck. **fottuto** *agg* (*spacciato*) ruined, buggered.
fra [fra] *prep* (*fra due*) between; (*fra più di due*) among(st); (*entro*) in, within; (*partitivo*) of. **detto fra (di) noi** between ourselves. **fra l'altro** among other things; (*inoltre*) besides. **fra tutti** (*tutti insieme*) altogether, in all.
frac [frak] *sm invar* (*fam*) tails *pl*.
fracassare [frakas'sare] *v* smash. **fracassarsi** *v* break. **fracasso** *sm* (*chiasso*) racket, din, row; (*scalpore*) uproar.
fradicio ['fraditʃo] *agg* (*inzuppato*) sopping (wet), wet through; (*guasto*) rotten. **ubriaco fradicio** dead drunk.
fragile ['fradʒile] *agg* fragile; (*delicato*) frail.
fragola ['fragola] *sf* strawberry.
fragore [fra'gore] *sm* din. **fragoroso** *agg* roaring, resounding.
fragrante [fra'grante] *agg* fragrant.
***fraintendere** [frain'tendere] *v* misunderstand, misconstrue.
frammassone [frammas'sone] *sm* freemason. **frammassoneria** *sf* freemasonry.
frammento [fram'mento] *sm* fragment; (*scheggia*) splinter. **frammentario** *agg* fragmentary.
***frammettersi** [fram'mettersi] *v* (*interporsi*) come between; (*immischiarsi*) meddle.
frammezzo [fram'mɛddzo] *avv* **frammezzo a** in the midst of.
frana ['frana] *sf* landslide. **franare** *v* slide down; (*crollare*) cave in.
francamente [franka'mente] *avv* frankly.
franchezza [fran'kettsa] *sf* frankness.
franchigia [fran'kidʒa] *sf* exemption. **in franchigia** (*posta*) post-free; (*tassa*) tax-free.
Francia ['frantʃa] *sf* France. **francese** *sm*, *agg* French; *s*(*m+f*) French person.
franco[1] ['franko] *agg* (*schietto*) frank, open; (*disinvolto*) (self-)confident; (*libero*) free (of), exempt (from). **in porto franco** (*comm*) carriage paid.
franco[2] ['franko] *sm* (*moneta*) franc.
francobollo [franko'bollo] *sm* (postage) stamp.
***frangersi** ['frandʒersi] *v* break. **frangente** *sm* (*ondata*) breaker; (*crisi*) spot, predicament.
frangia ['frandʒa] *sf* fringe.
frantumare [frantu'mare] *v* crush. **in frantumi** in *or* to pieces.
***frapporre** [frap'porre] *v* interpose.
frase ['fraze] *sf* phrase; (*periodo*) sentence. **frase fatta** stock phrase.
frassino ['frassino] *sm* ash.
frastagliare [frasta'ʎare] *v* indent.
frastornato [frastor'nato] *agg* dizzy.
frastuono [fras'twɔno] *sm* din, uproar.
frate ['frate] *sm* friar.
fratello [fra'tɛllo] *sm* brother. **fratellanza** *sf* brotherhood. **fratellastro** *sm* stepbrother.
fraterno [fra'tɛrno] *agg* brotherly, fraternal. **fraternizzare** *v* fraternize.
frattaglie [frat'taʎe] *sf pl* offal *sing*; (*di pollame*) giblets *pl*.
frattanto [frat'tanto] *avv also* **nel frattempo** meanwhile, in the meantime.
frattura [frat'tura] *sf* fracture; (*fig*) break. **fratturare** *v* fracture, break.
frazione [fra'tsjone] *sf* fraction; (*borgata*) hamlet. **frazionare** *v* split up.
freccia ['frettʃa] *sf* arrow; (*auto*) indicator. **frecciata** *sf* shaft.
freddo ['freddo] *agg* cold; (*fig*) cool, chilly. *sm* cold. **aver freddo** be cold, feel cold. **fa freddo** it is cold. **fa un freddo cane** it is bitterly cold. **morir di freddo** be dying of cold. **soffrire il freddo** feel the cold.
freddura [fred'dura] *sf* pun.

fregare [fre'gare] *v* rub; (*per lucidare*) polish; (*per lavare*) scrub; (*fam*: *rubare*) pinch, swipe; (*volg*: *imbrogliare*) cheat. **fregata** *sf* rub(bing). **fregatura** *sf* (*volg*: *imbroglio*) swindle; (*fam*: *contrattempo*) wash-out, flop.
fregio ['fredʒo] *sm* ornament; (*arch*) frieze. **fregiare** *v* decorate.
fremere ['frɛmere] *v* quiver.
fremito ['frɛmito] *sm* quiver; (*di emozione*) thrill; (*brivido*) shudder.
frenare [fre'nare] *v* brake; (*fig*) restrain, control, check.
frenesia [frene'zia] *sf* frenzy. **frenetico** *agg* frenzied, raving.
freno ['freno] *sm* brake; (*fig*) check, restraint; (*cavallo*) bit. **allentare il freno** (*fig*) slacken the reins. **mordere il freno** champ at the bit. **stringere i freni** (*fig*) clamp down.
frequentare [frekwen'tare] *v* frequent, go to often; (*scuola, ecc.*) attend; (*persone*) mix with. **frequentatore, -trice** *sm, sf* regular. **frequente** *agg* frequent. **frequenza** *sf* frequency. **con frequenza** frequently.
fresa ['frɛza] *sf also* **fresatrice** cutter, milling machine.
fresco ['fresko] *agg* fresh; (*leggermente freddo*) cool. *sm* cool(ness); freshness; (*pittura*) fresco. **al fresco** in the cool; (*prigione*) in the cooler. **star fresco** (*nei guai*) be in a mess; (*sbagliarsi*) kid oneself.
fretta ['fretta] *sf* hurry. **aver fretta** be in a hurry. **far fretta a** hurry. **fatto in fretta** rushed, hurried. **frettoloso** *agg* rushed, hasty.
***friggere** ['friddʒere] *v* fry; (*scoppiettare bollendo*) sizzle.
frigido ['fridʒido] *agg* cold, frigid. **frigidità** *sf* coldness, frigidity.
frigorifero [frigo'rifero] *sm* refrigerator. **frigo** *sm invar* (*fam*) fridge.
fringuello [frin'gwello] *sm* chaffinch.
frittata [frit'tata] *sf* omelette. **frittella** *sf* pancake.
fritto ['fritto] *agg* fried. *sm* fried food. **star fritto** (*fam*) be in trouble, be in for it. **frittura** *sf* (*vivanda*) fried food; (*atto del friggere*) frying.
frivolo ['frivolo] *agg* frivolous. **frivolezze** *sf* frivolity, trifle.
frizione [fri'tsjone] *sf* (*massaggio*) rubdown; (*auto*) clutch; (*attrito*) friction.
frizzare [frit'tsare] *v* tingle; (*bevande*) sparkle; (*metallo rovente*) hiss.
frodare [fro'dare] *v* defraud. **frode** *sf* fraud. **frodo** *sm* smuggling. **cacciare** *or* **pescare di frodo** poach. **cacciatore** *or* **pescatore di frodo** *sm* poacher.
frollare [frol'lare] *v* ripen. **frollo** *agg* ripe; (*carne*) tender; (*selvaggina*) high; (*pasta*) short.
fronda ['fronda] *sf* (leafy) branch; (*fig*) embellishment.
fronte ['fronte] *sf* (*testa*) forehead; (*faccia*) face; (*parte anteriore*) front; (*arch*) façade. *sm* (*mil*) front. **a fronte** (*in faccia*) facing. **di fronte** (*dirimpetto*) opposite; (*da davanti*) from the front. **far fronte a** face.
fronteggiare [fronted'dʒare] *v* face, stand up to.
frontespizio [frontes'pitsjo] *sm* title-page.
frontiera [fron'tjera] *sf* frontier, border.
fronzoli ['frondzoli] *sm pl* frills *pl*.
frotta ['frɔtta] *sf* flock, swarm.
frottola ['frɔttola] *sf* fib.
frugale [fru'gale] *agg* frugal.
frugare [fru'gare] *v* rummage, go through; (*perquisire*) search.
frullare [frul'lare] *v* whisk; (*fig*) whirl. **frullino** *sm* whisk.
frumento [fru'mento] *sm* wheat.
frusciare [fru'ʃare] *v* rustle.
frustare [frus'tare] *v* whip. **frusta** *sf* whip. **frustata** *sf* lash.
frustrazione [frustra'tsjone] *sf* frustration. **frustrare** *v* frustrate, thwart.
frutta ['frutta] *sf* fruit. **frutta cotta** stewed fruit. **fruttare** *v* bear fruit; yield; (*rendere*) bring in; (*procurare*) earn.
frutteto [frut'teto] *sm* orchard.
fruttifero [frut'tifero] *agg* fruitful; (*redditizio*) profitable.
fruttivendolo [frutti'vendolo], **-a** *sm, sf* fruiterer, greengrocer.
frutto ['frutto] *sm* fruit; (*interesse*) yield; (*rendita*) income; profit. **frutti di mare** seafood *sing*.
fu [fu] *agg invar* late, deceased.
fucilare [futʃi'lare] *v* shoot. **fucilata** *sf* shot. **fucilazione** *sf* execution. **fucile** *sm* rifle; (*da caccia*) shotgun.
fucina [fu'tʃina] *sf* forge.
fuco[1] ['fuko] *sm* (*ape*) drone.
fuco[2] ['fuko] *sm* (*alga*) fucus.
fucsia ['fuksja] *sf* fuchsia.

fuga ['fuga] *sf* escape; (*musica*) fugue; (*serie*) suite. **mettere in fuga** put to flight. **prendere la fuga** take flight, flee, escape. **fugace** *agg* transient.

fuggire [fud'dʒire] *v* flee, escape, run away. **fuggiasco** *sm, agg* fugitive; (*profugo*) refugee.

fulcro ['fulkro] *sm* fulcrum; (*fig*) heart.

fuliggine [fu'liddʒine] *sf* soot. **fuligginoso** *agg* sooty.

fulminare [fulmi'nare] *v* (*dal fulmine*) strike (by lightning); (*dalla corrente*) electrocute; (*con uno sguardo*) wither; (*allibire*) dumbfound. **fulmine** *sm* lightning, thunderbolt. **un fulmine a ciel sereno** a bolt from the blue.

fumaiolo [fuma'jɔlo] *sm* (*casa*) chimney-pot; (*nave*) funnel, smoke-stack.

fumare [fu'mare] *v* smoke; (*emettere vapore*) steam. **fumata** *sf* smoke. **fumatore, -trice** *sm, sf* smoker.

fumetto [fu'metto] *sm* comic-strip. **fumettista** *s*(*m*+*f*) comic-strip writer.

fumo ['fumo] *sm* smoke. **andare in fumo** go up in smoke.

funambolo [fu'nambolo], **-a** *sm, sf* tight-rope walker.

fune ['fune] *sf* rope, cable; (*per bucato*) washing line.

funebre ['funebre] *agg* funeral; (*lugubre*) funereal.

funerale [fune'rale] *sm* funeral. **funereo** *agg* funereal.

funesto [fu'nɛsto] *agg* fatal; (*doloroso*) distressing.

fungo ['fungo] *sm* mushroom; (*non mangereccio*) toadstool; (*bot*) fungus (*pl* -gi).

funicolare [funiko'lare] *sf* funicular railway.

funivia [funi'via] *sf* cable-car.

funzionare [funtsjo'nare] *v* function, work. **funzionale** *agg* functional, practical. **funzionamento** *sm* operation, working.

funzionario [funtsjo'narjo] *sm* official; (*impiegato statale*) civil servant.

funzione [fun'tsjone] *sf* function; (*carica*) office; (*compito*) duty. **entrare in funzione** come into operation. **essere in funzione di . . .** act as . . . .

fuochista [fwo'kista] *sm* stoker.

fuoco ['fwɔko] *sm* fire; (*fis, mat, foto*) focus. **appiccare** *or* **dare fuoco a** set fire to. **a prova di fuoco** fireproof. **fuoco di Sant'Antonio** (*med*) shingles. **mettere a fuoco** (*foto*) focus. **prendere fuoco** catch fire.

fuorché [fwor'ke] *prep, cong* except.

fuori ['fwɔri] *avv* out; (*all'esterno*) outside. *prep also* **fuori di** *or* **da** out of. **esser fuori di sè** be beside oneself. **fuoribordo** *sm* (*motore*) outboard motor; (*barca*) motor boat. **fuori strada** (*veicoli*) off the road; (*fig*) on the wrong track. **mettere fuori combattimento** (*sport*) knock out; (*fig*) put out of the running.

furbo ['furbo] *agg* cunning, crafty. **furbacchione** *sm* cunning fellow. **furberia** *sf* cunning.

furetto [fu'retto] *sm* ferret.

furfante [fur'fante] *sm* rascal.

furgone [fur'gone] *sm* (delivery) van. **furgoncino** *sm* small (delivery) van.

furia ['furja] *sf* (*collera*) rage, fury; (*fretta*) rush, haste. **a furia di . . .** by dint of . . . .

furibondo [furi'bondo] *agg* furious.

furioso [fu'rjozo] *agg* violent, furious.

furore [fu'rore] *sm* fury, rage.

furtivo [fur'tivo] *agg* furtive, stealthy.

furto ['furto] *sm* theft. **furto con scasso** burglary. **piccolo furto** petty theft, petty larceny.

fusa ['fuza] *sf pl* **fare le fusa** purr.

fuscello [fu'ʃɛllo] *sm* twig.

fusibile [fu'zibile] *agg* fusible. *sm* (*elett*) fuse.

fusione [fu'zjone] *sf* fusion; (*colata*) casting; (*scioglimento*) melting; (*fig*) merging; (*comm*) merger.

fuso[1] ['fuzo] *agg* (*liquefatto*) melted, molten; (*colato*) cast.

fuso[2] ['fuzo] *sm* spindle; (*ancora*) shank. **diritto come un fuso** (*eretto*) straight as a ramrod; (*difilato*) like a shot. **fuso orario** time zone.

fusoliera [fuzo'ljɛra] *sf* fuselage.

fustagno [fus'taɲo] *sm* fustian; (*a coste*) corduroy.

fustella [fus'tɛlla] *sf* (*tec*) die.

fustigare [fusti'gare] *v* flog; (*fig*) lash out at.

fusto ['fusto] *sm* trunk; (*ossatura*) frame; (*barile*) barrel, cask; (*recipiente di metallo*) drum.

futile ['futile] *agg* futile; (*meschino*) petty.

futuro [fu'turo] *agg, sm* future.

G

gabbare [gab'bare] *v* cheat.
gabbia ['gabbja] *sf* cage. **gabbia degli imputati** dock.
gabbiano [gab'bjano] *sm* seagull.
gabinetto [gabi'netto] *sm* study, office; (*di medico*) surgery; (*WC*) toilet, lavatory; (*pol*) cabinet; (*di scienze*) laboratory.
gaffe ['gaf] *sf*, *pl* **-s** blunder. **fare una gaffe** (*fam*) put one's foot in it.
gagà [ga'ga] *sm* (*fam*) dandy.
gagliardo [ga'ʎardo] *agg* vigorous; (*robusto*) strapping; (*coraggioso*) brave. **gagliardetto** *sm* pennant, flag.
gaio ['gajo] *agg* cheerful.
gala ['gala] *sf* (*ricevimento*) feast. *sm* (*mar*) flags *pl*. *sf* (*stoffa*) frill; (*cravatta*) bow-tie.
galantuomo [galan'twɔmo] *sm* (true) gentleman, man of honour. **galante** *agg* gallant, courteous.
galassia [ga'lassja] *sf* galaxy.
galateo [gala'tɛo] *sm* etiquette, good manners *pl*.
galea [ga'lɛa] *sf* galley.
galeotto [gale'ɔtto] *sm* (*carcerato*) convict; (*furfante*) scoundrel; (*vogatore forzato*) galley slave.
galera [ga'lɛra] *sf* prison.
galla ['galla] *sf* **stare** *or* **rimanere a galla** float, keep afloat. **tenersi a galla** keep afloat; (*fig*) keep one's head above water. **venire a galla** come to the surface; (*fig*) come to light, emerge.
galleggiare [galled'dʒare] *v* float. **galleggiante** *agg* floating. *sm* float; (*tec*) ballcock.
galleria [galle'ria] *sf* gallery; (*traforo*) tunnel; (*passaggio sotterraneo*) subway; (*cinema, ecc.*) circle, balcony.
Galles ['galles] *sm* Wales. **gallese** *sm*, *agg* Welsh; *s*(*m*+*f*) Welsh person.
gallo ['gallo] *sm* cock. **galletto** *sm* cockerel; (*tec*) wing-nut. **gallina** *sf* hen.
gallone[1] [gal'lone] *sm* (*misura*) gallon.
gallone[2] [gal'lone] *sm* braid; (*mil*) stripe.
galoppare [galop'pare] *v* gallop. **galoppata** *sf* gallop; (*lavora faticoso*) hard work. **galoppo** *sm* gallop.
galvanizzare [galvanid'dzare] *v* galvanize.
gamba ['gamba] *sf* leg. **andare a gambe all'aria** fall flat on one's back; (*fallire*) fail. **a tre gambe** three-legged. **darsela a gambe** take to one's heels. **gambe storte** bandy *or* bow legs *pl*. **in gamba** (*valente*) smart. *inter* take care!
gambero ['gambero] *sm* (*di acqua dolce*) crayfish; (*gamberetto*) shrimp; (*gamberone*) prawn. **rosso come un gambero** as red as a lobster.
gambo ['gambo] *sm* (*pianta*) stem, stalk; (*tec*) shank.
gamma ['gamma] *sf* range; (*lunghezza d'onda*) wave-band.
ganascia [ga'naʃa] *sf* jaw; (*freno*) brake-shoe.
gancio ['gantʃo] *sm* hook.
ganghero ['gangero] *sm* hinge. **essere fuori dai gangheri** be beside oneself. **uscire dai gangheri** lose one's head.
gara ['gara] *sf* competition; (*corsa*) race; (*comm*) tender.
garage [ga'raʒ] *sm*, *pl* **-s** garage.
garantire [garan'tire] *v* guarantee; (*rendersi garante*) vouch for; (*assicurare*) assure. **essere garante per** *or* **di** vouch for. **rendersi garante per** (*dir*) stand bail for.
garanzia [garan'tsia] *sf* guarantee.
garbare [gar'bare] *v* please, suit. **garbato** *agg* polite, well-mannered. **garbo** *sm* (*maniera*) good manners *pl*, politeness; (*gentilezza*) charm.
garbuglio [gar'buʎo] *sm* muddle.
gareggiare [gared'dʒare] *v* compete.
gargarismo [garga'rizmo] *sm* gargle. **fare i gargarismi** gargle.
garitta [ga'ritta] *sf* cabin; (*mil*) sentry-box.
garofano [ga'rɔfano] *sm* carnation. **chiodo di garofano** *sm* clove.
garrire [gar'rire] *v* twitter. **garrito** *sm* twitter.
garrulo ['garrulo] *agg* (*uccello*) twittering; (*persona loquace*) garrulous.
garza ['gardza] *sf* gauze.
garzone [gar'dzone] *sm* boy, mate.
gas ['gas] *sm* gas. **a gas** gas. **gas asfissiante/esilarante** poison/laughing gas. **gassoso** *agg* gaseous.
gasolio [ga'zɔljo] *sm* fuel oil, diesel fuel.
gassosa [gas'soza] *sf* fizzy drink, lemonade.
gastrico ['gastriko] *agg* gastric.

gastronomia [gastrono'mia] *sf* gastronomy, cooking. **gastronomico** *agg* gastronomic(al). **gastronomo** *sm* (*buongustaio*) gourmet.
gattabuia [gatta'buja] *sf* (*fam*) clink.
gatto ['gatto] *sm* cat. **gatta** *sf* she-cat. **comprare una gatta nel sacco** buy a pig in a poke. **gatta ci cova!** I smell a rat! **una gatta da pelare** a tricky job to do. **gattino** *sm* kitten; (*bot*) catkin.
gazza ['gaddza] *sf* magpie.
gazzarra [gad'dzarra] *sf* uproar, row.
gazzella [gad'dzɛlla] *sf* gazelle.
gazzetta [gad'dzetta] *sf* gazette.
gelare [dʒe'lare] *v* freeze. **gelata** *sf* (hard) frost.
gelatina [dʒela'tina] *sf* gelatine.
gelato [dʒe'lato] *agg* frozen. *sm* ice-cream. **gelataio** *sm* ice-cream vendor. **gelateria** *sf* ice-cream shop *or* parlour.
gelido ['dʒɛlido] *agg* icy.
gelo ['dʒɛlo] *sm* frost; intense cold; (*sensazione*) chill.
gelone [dʒe'lone] *sm* chilblain.
gelosia¹ [dʒelo'zia] *sf* jealousy; (*cura attenta*) great care.
gelosia² [dʒelo'zia] *sf* (*finestra*) blind.
geloso [dʒe'lozo] *agg* jealous.
gelso ['dʒɛlso] *sm* (*mora*) mulberry; (*albero*) mulberry-tree.
gelsomino [dʒelso'mino] *sm* jasmine.
gemello [dʒe'mɛllo] *sm, agg* twin. **gemelli** *sm pl* (*di polsino*) cuff-links *pl*. **Gemelli** *sm pl* Gemini *sing*.
gemere ['dʒɛmere] *v* groan; (*colare*) drip, ooze; (*tubare*) coo. **gemito** *sm* groan.
gemma ['dʒɛmma] *sf* gem; (*bot*) bud.
gene ['dʒɛne] *sm* gene.
genealogia [dʒenealo'dʒia] *sf* (*scienza*) genealogy; (*stirpe*) pedigree. **albero genealogico** *sm* family tree.
generale [dʒene'rale] *sm, agg* general. **in generale** in general; (*di solito*) as a rule.
generalizzare [dʒeneralid'dzare] *v* generalize. **generalizzazione** *sf* generalization.
generare [dʒene'rare] *v* generate, produce. **generazione** *sf* generation.
genere ['dʒɛnere] *sm* kind, type; (*tipo di merce*) product, article; (*stile*) genre; (*gramm*) gender. **d'ogni genere** of all kinds. **il genere umano** mankind. **nel suo genere** in his way.
generico [dʒe'nɛriko] *agg* generic; general.
genero ['dʒɛnero] *sm* son-in-law.
generoso [dʒene'rozo] *agg* generous; (*vino*) full-bodied; (*cavallo*) thoroughbred.
genetica [dʒe'nɛtika] *sf* genetics. **genetico** *agg* genetic. **genetista** *s(m+f)* geneticist.
gengiva [dʒen'dʒiva] *sf* gum. **gengivite** *sf* gingivitis.
geniale [dʒe'njale] *agg* ingenious, clever. **genialità** *sf* brilliance.
genio¹ ['dʒɛnjo] *sm* genius; (*disposizione*) talent, gift; (*inclinazione*) taste. **andare a genio** be to one's liking, suit.
genio² ['dʒɛnjo] *sm* (*mil*) engineers *pl*.
genitali [dʒeni'tali] *sm pl* genitals *pl*.
genitore [dʒeni'tore] *sm* parent.
gennaio [dʒen'najo] *sm* January.
Genova ['dʒɛnova] *sf* Genoa. **genovese** *agg, s(m+f)* Genoese.
gente ['dʒɛnte] *sf* people *pl*.
gentile [dʒen'tile] *agg* kind; (*cortese*) polite; delicate. **gentilezza** *sf* kindness; politeness; (*atto gentile*) favour. **gentiluomo** *sm* (*nobile*) nobleman; (*persona retta*) gentleman.
genuino [dʒenu'ino] *agg* genuine, natural; authentic. **genuinità** *sf* authenticity, naturalness, spontaneity.
genziana [dʒen'tsjana] *sf* gentian.
geografia [dʒeogra'fia] *sf* geography. **geografico** *agg* geographical. **atlante geografico** *sm* atlas. **carta geografica** *sf* map. **geografo, -a** *sm, sf* geographer.
geologia [dʒeolo'dʒia] *sf* geology. **geologico** *agg* geological. **geologo, -a** *sm, sf* geologist.
geometra [dʒe'ɔmetra] *s(m+f)* surveyor.
geometria [dʒeome'tria] *sf* geometry. **geometrico** *agg* geometrical.
geranio [dʒe'ranjo] *sm* geranium.
gerarchia [dʒerar'kia] *sf* hierarchy. **gerarca** *sm* (*rel*) hierarch; (*capo*) leader. **gerarchico** *agg* hierarchical. **per via gerarchica** through official channels.
gerente [dʒe'rɛnte] *sm* manager.
gergo ['dʒɛrgo] *sm* slang, jargon.
geriatria [dʒerja'tria] *sf* geriatrics. **geriatrico** *agg* geriatric.
Germania [dʒer'manja] *sf* Germany. **germanico** *agg* German.
germe ['dʒɛrme] *sm* germ. **germinare** *v* germinate.
germogliare [dʒermo'ʎare] *v* bud, sprout; (*fig*) germinate. **germoglio** *sm* shoot; (*origine*) germ.

gesso ['dʒesso] *sm* (*minerale*) gypsum; (*da disegno*) chalk; (*a pronta presa*) plaster (of Paris); (*opera*) plaster cast.
gesta ['dʒɛsta] *sf pl* (noble) deeds *pl*, feats *pl*.
gesticolare [dʒestiko'lare] *v* gesticulate.
gestire [dʒes'tire] *v* manage, run. **gestione** *sf* management.
gesto ['dʒɛsto] *sm* gesture; (*azione*) deed; (*del capo*) nod; (*della mano*) wave.
Gesù [dʒe'zu] *sm* Jesus.
gesuita [dʒezu'ita] *sm* Jesuit. **gesuitico** *agg* Jesuitical.
gettare [dʒet'tare] *v* throw; (*emettere*) let out; (*tec*) cast. **gettare i soldi dalla finestra** throw money down the drain. **gettare le fondamenta** lay the foundations. **gettar luce su . . .** cast light on . . . . **gettata** *sf* cast; (*di reti*) casting.
getto ['dʒɛtto] *sm* (*lancio*) throw; (*di liquido o gas*) jet; (*metallo, ecc.*) casting.
gettone [dʒet'tone] *sm* counter, token.
ghermire [ger'mire] *v* clutch, grab.
ghetto ['getto] *sm* ghetto.
ghiacciaia [gjat'tʃaja] *sf* ice-box.
ghiacciaio [gjat'tʃajo] *sm* glacier.
ghiacciare [gjat'tʃare] *v* freeze. **ghiacciata** *sf* drink with crushed ice.
ghiaccio ['gjattʃo] *sm* ice. **di ghiaccio** (*freddissimo*) ice-cold, frozen; (*fig*) icy. **ghiacciolo** *sm* icicle; (*gelato*) ice lolly.
ghiaia ['gjaja] *sf* gravel.
ghianda ['gjanda] *sf* acorn.
ghiandaia [gjan'daja] *sf* jay.
ghiandola ['gjandola] *sf* gland. **ghiandolare** *agg* glandular.
ghigliottina [giʎot'tina] *sf* guillotine. **ghigliottinare** *v* guillotine.
ghignare [gi'ɲare] *v* sneer. **ghigno** *sm* sneer, smirk.
ghiotto ['gjotto] *agg* greedy; (*appetitoso*) inviting. **ghiottone, -a** *sm, sf* glutton, greedy person. **ghiottoneria** *sf* (*golosità*) gluttony; (*cibo ghiotto*) titbit.
ghiribizzo [giri'bittso] *sm* fancy, whim.
ghirigoro [giri'gɔro] *sm* flourish.
ghirlanda [gir'landa] *sf* garland, wreath.
ghiro ['giro] *sm* dormouse. **dormire come un ghiro** sleep like a log.
ghisa ['giza] *sf* cast iron.
già ['dʒa] *avv* already; (*un tempo*) once; (*ex*) formerly.
giacca ['dʒakka] *sf* coat; (*giacchetta*) jacket.
giacché [dʒak'ke] *cong* as, since.
giacchetta [dʒak'ketta] *sf* jacket.
***giacere** [dʒa'tʃere] *v* lie; (*in sospeso*) be in abeyance. **mettersi a giacere** lie down. **giacenza** *sf* abeyance; (*merce*) (unsold) stock; (*econ*) deposit. **giacimento** *sm* deposit.
giacinto [dʒa'tʃinto] *sm* hyacinth.
giada ['dʒada] *sf* jade.
giaggiolo [dʒad'dʒɔlo] *sm* iris.
giaguaro [dʒa'gwaro] *sm* jaguar.
giallo ['dʒallo] *agg* yellow. *sm* (*colore*) yellow; (*libro, film*) thriller. **giallo d'uovo** (egg) yolk. **giallastro** *agg* yellowish, sallow. **giallognolo** *agg* pale yellow, yellowish.
giammai [dʒam'mai] *avv* never. **se giammai** if ever.
Giappone [dʒap'pone] *sm* Japan. **giapponese** *s(m+f), agg* Japanese.
giardinetta [dʒardi'netta] *sf* estate car.
giardino [dʒar'dino] *sm* garden. **giardino d'infanzia** kindergarten, nursery school. **giardino zoologico** zoo. **giardinaggio** *sm* gardening. **giardiniere, -a** *sm, sf* gardener.
giarrettiera [dʒarret'tjera] *sf* suspender, garter.
giavellotto [dʒavel'lɔtto] *sm* javelin.
Gibilterra [dʒibil'terra] *sf* Gibraltar.
gigante [dʒi'gante] *sm, agg* giant. **gigantesco** *agg* gigantic, huge.
gigione [dʒi'dʒone] *sm* ham (actor). **fare il gigione** ham.
giglio ['dʒiʎo] *sm* lily.
gilè [dʒi'lɛ] *sm* waistcoat.
ginecologo [dʒine'kɔlogo], **-a** *sm, sf* gynaecologist. **ginecologia** *sm* gynaecology. **ginecologico** *agg* gynaecological.
ginepro [dʒi'nepro] *sm* juniper.
ginestra [dʒi'nɛstra] *sf* broom. **ginestrone** *sm* furze, gorse.
Ginevra [dʒi'nevra] *sf* Geneva.
gingillarsi [dʒindʒil'larsi] *v* (*divertirsi*) amuse oneself; (*perder tempo*) hang about.
ginnasio [dʒin'nazjo] *sm* secondary school.
ginnastica [dʒin'nastika] *sf* (*sport*) gymnastics; (*esercizi*) physical exercises *pl*.
ginocchio [dʒi'nokkjo] *sm pl* **-a** *f* knee. **ginocchioni** *avv also* **in ginocchio** on one's knees.
giocare [dʒo'kare] *v* play; (*in borsa*) gamble (on the Stock Exchange); (*scommettere*) bet. **giocata** *sf* (*partita*) game;

(*puntata*) stake, bet. **giocatore, -trice** *sm, sf* player; (*d'azzardo*) gambler.
giocattolo [dʒo'kattolo] *sm* toy.
giocherellare [dʒokerel'lare] *v* toy.
giochetto [dʒo'ketto] *sm* (*passatempo*) pastime; (*tranello*) trick; (*lavoro facile*) child's play.
gioco ['dʒɔko] *sm* (*divertimento, tec*) play; (*con regole, partita*) game; (*vizio*) gambling; (*combinazione di carte*) hand; (*posta*) stake; (*beffa*) trick. **entrare in gioco** come into play. **fare il doppio gioco** double-cross. **mettere in gioco** (*far agire*) bring into action; (*rischiare*) stake.
giocoliere [dʒoko'ljɛre] *sm* juggler.
giocondo [dʒo'kondo] *agg* cheerful, merry.
giogo ['dʒogo] *sm* yoke; (*valico*) pass; (*cima allungata*) ridge.
gioia[1] ['dʒɔja] *sf* joy, delight.
gioia[2] ['dʒɔja] *sf* (*gemma*) jewel.
gioire [dʒo'ire] *v* rejoice. **gioioso** *agg* joyful.
giornalaio [dʒorna'lajo], **-a** *sm, sf* newsagent.
giornale [dʒor'nale] *sm* (*quotidiano*) newspaper; (*registro*) journal; diary. **giornale di bordo** log(-book). **giornale radio** news (bulletin).
giornaliero [dʒorna'ljɛro] *agg* daily.
giornalismo [dʒorna'lizmo] *sm* journalism. **giornalista** *s(m+f)* journalist.
giornata [dʒor'nata] *sf* day. **a giornata** by the day. **di giornata** (*fresco*) fresh; (*di turno*) on duty. **donna a giornata** daily (woman). **vivere alla giornata** live from day to day.
giorno ['dʒorno] *sm* day. **a giorni** (*tra breve*) soon; (*a intervalli*) sometimes. **al giorno** a day. **al giorno d'oggi** nowadays. **che giorno è?** (*data*) what is the date? (*della settimana*) what day (of the week) is it? **da un giorno all'altro** (*improvvisamente*) suddenly; (*tra poco*) any day now. **di giorno** by day. **giorno festivo** holiday. **giorno libero** day off. **punto a giorno** *sm* hem-stitch. **un giorno o l'altro** one of these days.
giostra ['dʒɔstra] *sf* (*fiera*) merry-go-round; (*torneo*) tournament.
giovane ['dʒovane] *agg* young; (*giovanile*) youthful; (*non stagionato*) new. *sm* (*giovanotto*) young man, youth. *sf* young woman, girl. **giovanile** *agg* youthful, juvenile.
giovare [dʒo'vare] *v* help, do good.
giovedì [dʒove'di] *sm* Thursday.
giovenca [dʒo'vɛnka] *sf* heifer.
gioventù [dʒoven'tu] *sf* youth; (*i giovani*) young people *pl*.
giovevole [dʒo'vevole] *agg* useful.
gioviale [dʒo'vjale] *agg* genial, jolly.
giovinezza [dʒovi'nettsa] *sf* (*gioventù*) youth; (*qualità*) youthfulness. **seconda giovinezza** second childhood.
giradischi [dʒira'diski] *sm invar* record player.
giradito [dʒira'dito] *sm* whitlow.
giraffa [dʒi'raffa] *sf* giraffe.
giramento [dʒira'mento] *sm* **giramento di capo** dizzy spell; (fit of) dizziness.
girandola [dʒi'randola] *sf* (*fuochi d'artificio*) Catherine wheel; (*giocattolo*) toy windmill; (*fig*) fickle person.
girare [dʒi'rare] *v* turn; (*scansare*) get round, avoid; (*percorrere viaggiando*) travel, tour; (*andare da un posto all'altro*) go around; (*comm*) endorse; (*cinema*) shoot, take; (*camminare senza meta*) wander about; circulate. **girare a vuoto** (*mec*) idle. **mi gira la testa** I feel dizzy *or* giddy.
girarrosto [dʒirar'rɔsto] *sm* spit.
girasole [dʒira'sole] *sm* sunflower.
girino [dʒi'rino] *sm* tadpole.
giro ['dʒiro] *sm* turn; (*pista*) lap; (*percorso*) round; (*viaggio*) tour; (*passeggiata a piedi*) stroll, walk; (*in macchina*) drive; (*in bicicletta, a cavallo*) ride; (*periodo*) course, space; circulation; (*mec*) revolution. **andare in giro** go round. **essere in giro** (*fuori*) be out; (*in qualche posto*) be somewhere. **giro collo** neck. **giro d'affari** turnover. **giro d'orizzonte** survey. **giro manica** armhole. **guardarsi in giro** look around. **prendere in giro** make fun of.
gironzolare [dʒirondzo'lare] *v* stroll, wander (about).
girovago [dʒi'rɔvago] *sm, pl* **-ghi** vagabond, tramp. *agg* wandering. **girovagare** *v* stroll, wander (about).
gita ['dʒita] *sf* excursion, trip. **fare una gita** make an excursion, go on a trip.
giù [dʒu] *avv* down; (*dabbasso*) downstairs. **andare su e giù** (*salire e scendere*) go up and down; (*avanti e indietro*) go to and fro. **giù di lì** thereabouts. **in giù** (*moto*) down; (*stato*) low; (*in meno*) and under. **su per giù** thereabouts.

giubba ['dʒubba] *sf* jacket; (*mil*) tunic. **giubbotto di salvataggio** *sm* life-jacket.
giubilare [dʒubi'lare] *v* rejoice.
giubileo [dʒubi'lɛo] *sm* jubilee.
giudaismo [dʒuda'izmo] *sm* Judaism.
giudicare [dʒudi'kare] *v* judge; (*ritenere*) consider. **a giudicare da** judging by. **passare in giudicato** be beyond recall, be final.
giudice ['dʒuditʃe] *sm* judge. **giudice istruttore** examining magistrate.
giudiziario [dʒudi'tsjarjo] *agg* judicial.
giudizio [dʒu'ditsjo] *sm* judgment; (*parere*) opinion; (*dir*) sentence, verdict; (*buon senso*) common sense. **aver giudizio** be sensible. **citare in giudizio** summon. **comparire in giudizio** appear before a court. **dente del giudizio** *sm* wisdom tooth. **far giudizio** behave oneself. **rinviare a giudizio** commit for trial. **giudizioso** *agg* sensible.
giugno ['dʒuɲo] *sm* June.
giulivo [dʒu'livo] *agg* merry.
giullare [dʒul'lare] *sm* (*cantastorie*) minstrel; (*buffone*) clown.
giunco ['dʒunko] *sm* rush.
***giungere** ['dʒundʒere] *v* arrive (at), reach; (*riuscire*) manage; (*arrivare al punto di*) go so far as. **mi è giunto** I have received. **mi giunge nuovo** it is news to me.
giungla ['dʒungla] *sf* jungle.
giunta[1] ['dʒunta] *sf* addition; (*peso*) makeweight; (*sartoria*) insert. **giuntare** *v* (*unire*) join; (*cucire*) sew together; (*cinema, nastro*) splice.
giunta[2] ['dʒunta] *sf* (*comitato*) council; (*mil*) junta.
giunto ['dʒunto] *sm* joint.
giuntura [dʒun'tura] *sf* joint; (*accoppiamento*) coupling.
giunzione [dʒun'tsjone] *sf* junction; (*giunto*) joint.
giurare [dʒu'rare] *v* swear. **giuramento** *sm* oath. **giuramento falso** (*spergiuro*) perjury. **mancare al giuramento** break an oath. **prestar giuramento** swear, take an oath.
giurato [dʒu'rato], **-a** *sm, sf* juror. *agg* sworn.
giuria [dʒu'ria] *sf* jury.
giuridico [dʒu'ridiko] *agg* legal.
giurisdizione [dʒurizdi'tsjone] *sf* jurisdiction.
***giustapporre** [dʒustap'porre] *v* juxtapose. **giustapposizione** *sf* juxtaposition.
giustezza [dʒus'tettsa] *sf* correctness; (*esattezza*) precision.
giustificare [dʒustifi'kare] *v* justify. **giustificazione** *sf* justification; (*scusa*) excuse.
giustizia [dʒus'titsja] *sf* justice; (*equità*) fairness. **assicurare alla giustizia** bring to justice. **fare** *or* **rendere giustizia** do justice.
giusto ['dʒusto] *agg* just; (*equo*) fair; (*legittimo*) rightful; (*corretto*) right. *avv* (*proprio, appena*) just; (*esattamente*) correctly. *sm* (*persona*) righteous man.
glaciale [gla'tʃale] *agg* glacial; (*fig*) icy.
gladiolo [gla'diolo] *sm* gladiolus.
glassa ['glassa] *sf* icing. **glassare** *v* ice.
gli[1] [ʎi] *art* the.
gli[2] [ʎi] *pron* (*persona*) (to) him; (*cosa, animale*) (to) it.
glicerina [glitʃe'rina] *sf* glycerine.
glicine ['glitʃine] *sm* wisteria.
globo ['glɔbo] *sm* globe. **globo oculare** eyeball.
globulo ['glɔbulo] *sm* globule; (*med*) corpuscle. **globulare** *agg* globular.
gloria ['glɔrja] *sf* glory; (*vanto*) pride. **gloriarsi** *v* glory (in); (*vantarsi*) boast (of).
glorificare [glorifi'kare] *v* glorify.
glucosio [glu'kɔzjo] *sm* glucose.
gnomo ['ɲɔmo] *sm* gnome.
gnomone [ɲo'mone] *sm* sundial.
gobba ['gɔbba] *sf* hump.
gobbo ['gɔbbo], **-a** *sm, sf* hunchback. *agg* hunchbacked.
goccia ['gottʃa] *sf* drop. **goccia a goccia** drop by drop; (*fig*) little by little. **una goccia nel mare** a drop in the ocean. **gocciolare** *v* drip.
***godere** [go'dere] *v* enjoy; (*rallegrarsi*) rejoice. **godimento** *sm* enjoyment; (*piacere*) pleasure.
goffo ['gɔffo] *agg* awkward, clumsy. **goffaggine** *sf* awkwardness, clumsiness; (*atto*) clumsy action; (*parola*) blunder.
gol [gɔl] *sm invar* goal.
gola ['gola] *sf* throat; (*golosità*) greed, gluttony. **aver l'acqua alla gola** be in deep water. **far gola** tempt.
golf[1] [gɔlf] *sm invar* (*sport*) golf.
golf[2] [gɔlf] *sm invar* (*maglione*) sweater, jumper; (*con bottoni*) cardigan.
golfo ['golfo] *sm* gulf.
goliardo [go'ljardo] *sm* (university) student. **goliardico** *agg* university.

goloso [go'lozo] *agg* greedy. **golosità** *sf* greediness, gluttony.
golpe[1] ['golpe] *sf* smut, blight.
golpe[2] ['golpe] *sm* coup (d'état).
gomito ['gomito] *sm* elbow. **gomitata** *sf* dig with the elbow. **farsi avanti a (forza di) gomitate** elbow one's way forward.
gomitolo [go'mitolo] *sm* ball.
gomma ['gomma] *sf* rubber; (*colla*) gum; (*pneumatico*) tyre. **gommapiuma** *sf* foam rubber. **gommato** *agg* rubberized; gummed. **gommoso** *agg* rubbery.
gondola ['gondola] *sf* gondola. **gondoliere** *sm* gondolier.
gonfalone [gonfa'lone] *sm* banner, standard.
gonfiare [gon'fjare] *v* swell (up); (*riempire di gas, ecc.*) inflate, blow up; (*montare*) puff up; exaggerate. **gonfiatura** *sf* blowing up, swelling up; (*gonfiore*) swelling; exaggeration. **gonfio** *agg* swollen, inflated. **gonfiore** *sm* swelling.
gong ['gɔng] *sm invar* gong.
gonna ['gonna] *sf also* **gonnella** skirt.
gonorrea [gonor'rɛa] *sf* gonorrhea.
gonzo ['gondzo] *sm* simpleton.
gorgheggiare [gorged'dʒare] *v* trill, warble. **gorgheggio** *sm* trill, warble; (*di uccello*) warbling.
gorgo ['gorgo] *sm* whirlpool.
gorgogliare [gorgo'ʎare] *v* gurgle; (*intestino*) rumble. **gorgoglio** *sm* rumble; gurgle.
gorilla [go'rilla] *sm invar* gorilla.
gotico ['gɔtiko] *agg* Gothic.
gotta ['gotta] *sf* gout.
governante [gover'nante] *sf* (*incaricata della casa*) housekeeper; (*istitutrice*) governess.
governare [gover'nare] *v* govern; (*dirigere*) run; (*dominare*) rule; (*pilotare*) steer. **governativo** *agg* government, governmental. **governatore** *sm* governor. **governo** *sm* government; (*dominio*) rule; (*amministrazione*) management. **governo della casa** housekeeping.
gozzo ['goddzo] *sm* crop; (*med*) goitre. **averla nel** *or* **sul gozzo** be unable to swallow.
gozzovigliare [goddzovi'ʎare] *v* revel, go on a spree.
gracchiare [grak'kjare] *v* croak.
gracidare [gratʃi'dare] *v* croak.
gracile ['gratʃile] *agg* frail. **gracilità** *sf* frailty.
gradasso [gra'dasso] *sm* boaster, braggart. **fare il gradasso** boast, brag.
gradazione [grada'tsjone] *sf* gradation; (*sfumatura*) shade. **gradazione alcolica** alcoholic strength.
gradevole [gra'devole] *agg* agreeable.
gradiente [gra'djɛnte] *sm* gradient.
gradimento [gradi'mento] *sm* (*approvazione*) liking; (*piacere*) pleasure.
gradino [gra'dino] *sm* step. **gradinata** *sf* flight of steps.
gradire [gra'dire] *v* (*trovar piacevole*) find agreeable; (*accogliere con gioia*) welcome; (*accettare*) accept; (*nelle richieste*) like.
grado[1] ['grado] *sm* degree; (*mil, rango*) rank. **a gradi** step by step. **avanzare di grado** be promoted. **essere in grado di** be able to.
grado[2] ['grado] *sm* **di buon grado** willingly.
graduale [gradu'ale] *agg* gradual.
graduare [gradu'are] *v* graduate. **graduatoria** *sf* (*elenco*) list; (*ordine*) classification.
graffa ['graffa] *sf* bracket; (*fermaglio*) (paper-)clip.
graffiare [graf'fjare] *v* scratch. **graffiatura** *sf* scratch. **graffio** *sm* scratch.
grafico [gra'fico] *agg* graphic. *sm* (*diagramma*) chart, graph; (*persona*) graphic artist.
grafologo [gra'fɔlogo], **-a** *sm, sf* graphologist.
gramigna [gra'miɲa] *sf* couch-grass; (*malerba*) weed. **attaccarsi come la gramigna** cling like a leech.
grammatico [gram'matiko] *agg* grammatical. *sm* grammarian. **grammatica** *sm* grammar; (*persona*) grammarian.
grammo ['grammo] *sm* gram.
grammofono [gram'mɔfono] *sm* gramophone.
grana[1] ['grana] *sf* (*struttura*) grain. *sm* (*formaggio*) Parmesan (cheese).
grana[2] ['grana] *sf* (*seccatura*) nuisance. **piantare una grana** make trouble.
granaglie [gra'naʎe] *sf pl* cereals *pl.*
granaio [gra'najo] *sm* barn; (*zona produttrice di grano*) granary; (*locale sottotetto*) loft.
granata[1] [gra'nata] *sf* (*scopa*) broom.
granata[2] [gra'nata] *sf* (*mil*) grenade.
granata[3] [gra'nata] *sf* (*frutto*) pomegranate; (*pietra*) garnet.

Gran Bretagna [gran bre'taɲa] *sf* Great Britain.
grancassa [gran'kassa] *sf* (*musica*) bass drum. **batter la grancassa** blow one's own trumpet.
granchio ['grankjo] *sm* crab. **prendere un granchio** make a blunder.
grande ['grande] *agg* big; (*ampio, numeroso*) large; (*largo*) wide; (*fig*) great; (*adulto*) grown-up. **in grande** on a large scale. **in gran parte** largely. **non . . . un gran che** not . . . much.
grandeggiare [granded'dʒare] *v* (*emergere*) tower, stand out; (*darsi arie*) show off.
grandezza [gran'dettsa] *sf* (*dimensione, taglia*) size; (*altezza*) height; (*larghezza*) width; (*ampiezza*) breadth; (*fig*) greatness; (*mat, fis*) magnitude.
grandinare [grandi'nare] *v* hail. **grandine** *sf* hail. **chicco di grandine** *sm* hailstone.
grandioso [gran'djozo] *agg* grand.
granduca [gran'duka] *sm, pl* **-chi** grand duke. **granducato** *sm* grand duchy. **granduchessa** *sf* grand duchess.
granello [gra'nɛllo] *sm* grain; (*di frutta*) pip. **granello di pepe** peppercorn.
granita [gra'nita] *sf* crushed-ice drink.
granito [gra'nito] *sm* granite.
grano ['grano] *sm* (*granello*) grain; (*frumento*) wheat; (*cereale in genere*) corn, cereal.
granturco [gran'turko] *sm* maize.
granulo ['granulo] *sm* granule. **granulare** *agg* granular.
grappolo ['grappolo] *sm* bunch.
grasso ['grasso] *agg* fat; (*unto*) greasy, oily; (*che contiene grasso*) fatty. *sm* fat; (*sostanza untuosa*) grease. **grassoccio** *agg* plump.
grata ['grata] *sf* grating, grille. **gratella** *sf* grill.
graticcio [gra'tittʃo] *sm* trellis.
graticola [gra'tikola] *sf* grill.
gratifica [gra'tifika] *sf* bonus.
gratis ['gratis] *agg* free. *avv* for nothing, for love.
gratitudine [grati'tudine] *sf* gratitude.
grato ['grato] *agg* grateful, obliged; (*gradevole*) pleasant; (*gradito*) welcome.
grattacapo [gratta'kapo] *sm* worry, headache.
grattacielo [gratta'tʃɛlo] *sm* skyscraper.
grattare [grat'tare] *v* scratch; (*grattugiare*) grate; (*raschiare*) scrape; (*fam: rubare*) pinch.
grattugiare [grattu'dʒare] *v* grate. **grattugia** *sf* grater.
gratuito [gra'tuito] *agg* free; (*non retribuito*) unpaid; (*ingiustificato*) gratuitous; (*infondato*) unfounded.
gravare [gra'vare] *v* burden.
grave ['grave] *agg* (*serio*) grave; (*pesante*) heavy; (*malattia*) serious; (*perdita*) grievous. **gravità** *sf* gravity. **gravoso** *agg* hard, onerous.
gravido ['gravido] *agg* pregnant. **gravidanza** *sf* pregnancy.
grazia ['gratsja] *sf* grace; (*fascino*) charm; (*clemenza*) pardon; favour. **grazie** *sm pl, inter* thanks. **grazie a** thanks to.
Grecia ['grɛtʃa] *sf* Greece. **greco, -a** *s, agg, m pl* **-ci** Greek. **naso greco** *sm* Grecian nose.
gregge ['greddʒe] *sm* flock, herd.
greggio ['greddʒo] *agg* raw, crude.
grembiule [grem'bjule] *sm* apron; (*con petto*) pinafore; (*con maniche*) overall.
grembo ['grembo] *sm* lap.
gremire [gre'mire] *v* fill (up). **gremirsi** *v* get crowded.
gres ['grɛs] *sm* stoneware.
gretto ['gretto] *agg* mean; (*idea, animo*) narrow-minded. **grettezza** *sf* meanness; narrow-mindedness.
gridare [gri'dare] *v* shout; (*strillare*) yell, scream. **gridare aiuto** call for help. **grido** *sm, pl* **-a** *f* shout; cry; scream, yell. **di grido** (*noto*) famous; (*di moda*) fashionable. **l'ultimo grido** the latest fashion, the last word.
griffa ['griffa] *sf* claw.
grigio ['gridʒo] *agg* grey; (*fig*) drab. *sm* grey. **grigiastro** *agg* greyish. **grigiore** *sm* greyness; (*fig*) drabness. **grigioverde** *sm, agg* grey-green, khaki.
griglia ['griʎa] *sf* grill; (*saracinesca*) shutter; (*schermo*) grille; (*radio*) grid; (*focolare*) grate.
grilletto [gril'letto] *sm* trigger.
grillo ['grillo] *sm* cricket; (*capriccio*) whim. **gli è saltato il grillo di** he got it into his head to.
grimaldello [grimal'dɛllo] *sm* jemmy.
grinza ['grintsa] *sf* crease; (*ruga*) wrinkle. **non fare una grinza** (*calzare bene*) fit perfectly; (*filare bene*) be flawless.
gripparsi [grip'parsi] *v* (*auto*) seize up.

grondaia [gron'daja] *sf* gutter.
grondare [gron'dare] *v* drip; (*abbondantemente*) pour.
groppa ['grɔppa] *sf* back.
grossa ['grɔssa] *sf* (*comm*) gross. **dormire della grossa** sleep like a log.
grossezza [gros'settsa] *sf* (*volume*) bulk, size; (*spessore*) thickness.
grossista [gros'sista] *s*(*m*+*f*) wholesaler.
grosso ['grɔsso] *agg* large, big; (*spesso*) thick; (*non raffinato*) coarse; serious. **dirle grosse** tell fibs. **farne di grosse** cause all sorts of trouble. **grossolano** *agg* coarse, rough.
grotta ['grɔtta] *sf* cave; grotto.
grottesco [grot'tesko] *agg* grotesque.
groviera [gro'vjɛra] *s*(*m*+*f*) *also* **gruviera** (*formaggio*) gruyère.
groviglio [gro'viʎo] *sm* tangle; (*confusione*) mess.
gru [gru] *sf* crane.
gruccia ['gruttʃa] *sf* crutch; (*attaccapanni*) coat-hanger.
grugnire [gru'ɲire] *v* grunt. **grugnito** *sm* grunt.
grugno ['gruɲo] *sm* (*maiale*) snout; (*fam: muso*) mug.
grullo ['grullo] *agg* foolish.
grumo ['grumo] *sm* clot.
gruppo ['gruppo] *sm* group; (*mec*) unit.
gruviera [gru'vjɛra] *V* **groviera**.
gruzzolo ['gruttsolo] *sm* pile; (*risparmi*) nest-egg.
guadagnare [gwada'ɲare] *v* earn; (*ottenere*) gain; (*vincere*) win; (*raggiungere*) reach; (*risparmiare*) save.
guadagno [gwa'daɲo] *sm* (*retribuzione*) earnings *pl*; profit; advantage.
guado ['gwado] *sm* ford. **guadare** *v* wade.
guaina [gwa'ina] *sf* sheath.
guaio ['gwajo] *sm* trouble. **guai** *inter* woe betide you, us, etc.
guaire [gwa'ire] *v* whine, yelp. **guaito** *sm* whine, yelp.
guancia ['gwantʃa] *sf* cheek. **guanciale** *sm* pillow.
guanto ['gwanto] *sm* glove. **calzare come un guanto** fit like a glove. **gettare il guanto** throw down the gauntlet. **trattare coi guanti** treat with kid gloves.
guardaboschi [gwarda'bɔski] *sm* forester.
guardacaccia [gwarda'kattʃa] *sm invar* gamekeeper.
guardacoste [gwarda'kɔste] *sm invar* coastguard.
guardalinee [gwarda'linee] *sm invar* (*sport*) linesman.
guardamano [gwarda'mano] *sm invar* (*sciabola*) hilt; (*fucile*) guard; (*guanto*) protective glove.
guardare [gwar'dare] *v* look (at); (*affacciarsi*) look out; face; (*dare un'occhiata*) have a look; (*custodire*) look after, mind; (*stare a vedere*) watch; (*considerare*) view; (*cercare*) try to, be careful to. **andare a guardare** have a look. **Dio ne guardi!** God forbid! **guarda che roba!** just look at that! **guardar di sbieco** *or* **traverso** look askance (at). **guardare fisso** stare, gaze (at). **guarda un po'!** well, well!
guardaroba [gwarda'rɔba] *sm invar* (*luogo*) cloakroom; (*armadio*) wardrobe. **guardarobiera** *sf* cloakroom attendant.
guardarsi [gwar'darsi] *v* look at oneself. **guardarsi intorno** look around. **guardarsi da** (*fare attenzione a*) beware of; (*astenersi da*) refrain from. **me ne guardo bene!** heaven forbid!
guardata [gwar'data] *sf* look, glance.
guardavia [gwarda'via] *sm invar* guard-rail.
guardia ['gwardja] *sf* (*custodia*) watch, guard; (*turno*) duty; (*custode*) keeper, watchman; (*sentinella*) sentry; (*sport*) guard. **essere di guardia** be on duty; (*mil*) be on guard duty. **fare la guardia** (*sorvegliare*) guard, watch; (*badare*) watch over. **guardia di finanza** (*corpo*) Customs *pl*; (*singolo*) Customs officer. **mettere in guardia** warn. **guardiano** *sm* keeper, guardian.
guardingo [gwar'dingo] *agg* cautious, wary.
guarire [gwa'rire] *v* cure; (*rimettersi in salute*) recover; (*ferita*) heal. **guarigione** *sf* recovery; healing.
guarnigione [gwarni'dʒone] *sf* garrison.
guarnire [gwar'nire] *v* decorate; (*vestiario*) trim; (*gastr*) garnish; (*corredare*) equip; (*mil*) garrison. **guarnizione** *sf* decoration, trimming, garnish; (*tec*) packing; (*auto*) gasket.
guastafeste [gwasta'feste] *s*(*m*+*f*) *invar* spoilsport.
guastamestieri [gwastames'tieri] *s*(*m*+*f*) *invar* bungler; (*fam*) menace.
guastare [gwas'tare] *v* spoil; (*rovinare*) ruin, damage. **guastarsi** *v* (*cibi*) go bad; (*mec*) break down; (*tempo*) change for

the worse. **guasto** *agg* (*cibo*) bad, rotten; (*mec*) broken; (*salute, ecc.*) bad.

guazzabuglio [gwattsa'buʎo] *sm* hotchpotch, jumble.

guazzare [gwat'tsare] *v* splash about; (*fig*) wallow. **guazzo** *sm* pool; (*pittura*) gouache.

guercio ['gwertʃo] *agg* cross-eyed.

guerra ['gwɛrra] *sf* war; (*il guerreggiare*) warfare. **far guerra** wage war. **guerra mondiale** world war. **guerrafondaio** *sm, sf* warmonger.

guerreggiare [gwerred'dʒare] *v* fight.

guerresco [gwer'resko] *agg* (*bellicoso*) warlike; (*di guerra*) war.

guerriero [gwer'rjɛro] *agg* (*bellicoso*) warlike; (*combattivo*) aggressive. *sm* warrior.

guerriglia [gwer'riʎa] *sf* guerrilla warfare. **guerrigliero** *sm* guerrilla.

gufo ['gufo] *sm* owl.

guglia ['guʎa] *sf* (*arch*) spire; (*geog*) pinnacle.

guida ['gwida] *sf* guide; (*direzione, comando*) guidance, leadership; (*tappeto*) runner; (*elenco*) directory; (*auto*) drive, driving; (*comandi*) controls *pl*. **esame (di) guida** *sm* driving test. **guida a destra/sinistra** right-/left-hand drive. **scuola (di) guida** *sf* driving school.

guidare [gwi'dare] *v* guide; (*dirigere, comandare*) lead; (*auto*) drive; (*aero*) fly; (*nave*) steer; (*moto*) ride. **guidatore, -trice** *sm, sf* driver.

guinzaglio [gwin'tsaʎo] *sm* leash, lead. **mettere il guinzaglio** (*fig*) keep a tight rein (on). **tenere al guinzaglio** keep on a leash.

guisa ['gwiza] *sf* **a** *or* **in guisa di** in the manner of, like.

guizzare [gwit'tsare] *v* (*lampo*) flash; (*pesci*) dart; (*sfuggire*) wriggle; (*fiamma*) flicker. **guizzo** *sm* flash; dart; flicker.

guscio ['guʃo] *sm* shell; (*legumi*) pod.

gustare [gus'tare] *v* taste; (*trovar buono*) enjoy. **gusto** *sm* taste; (*piacere*) enjoyment. **con gusto** tastefully. **di gusto** heartily. **non aver gusto** be tasteless. **prenderci gusto** take a liking (to). **senza gusto** tasteless.

gutturale [guttu'rale] *agg* guttural.

H

hascisc [a'ʃiʃ] *sm* hashish.
hockey ['hɔki] *sm* hockey.

I

i [i] *art* the.
iattanza [jat'tantsa] *sf* arrogance.
ibernazione [iberna'tsjone] *sf* hibernation. **ibernare** *v* hibernate.
ibrido ['ibrido] *sm, agg* hybrid.
Iddio [id'dio] *sm* God.
idea [i'dɛa] *sf* idea; opinion; (*proposito*) intention. **cambiare idea** change one's mind. **dare l'idea** give the impression.
ideale [ide'ale] *sm, agg* ideal. **idealismo** *sm* idealism. **idealista** *s*(*m*+*f*) idealist. **idealistico** *agg* idealistic.
identico [i'dɛntiko] *agg* identical.
identificare [identifi'kare] *v* identify. **identificazione** *sf* identification.
identità [identi'ta] *sf* identity.
ideologia [ideolo'dʒia] *sf* ideology. **ideologico** *agg* ideological.
idillio [i'dilljo] *sm* idyll. **idillico** *agg* idyllic.
idioma [i'djɔma] *sm* language. **frase idiomatica** *sf* idiom.
idiota [i'kjɔta] *s*(*m*+*f*) idiot, fool. *agg* idiotic, stupid.
idiotismo [idjo'tizmo] *sm* (*lingua*) idiom; (*med*) idiocy.
idiozia [idjo'tsia] *sf* idiocy; stupidity.
idolo ['idolo] *sm* idol. **idoleggiare** *v* idolize.
idoneo [i'dɔneo] *agg* fit, suitable; (*capace*) able. **non idoneo** unfit, unsuitable. **idoneità** *sf* ability, suitability.
idrante [i'drante] *sm* hydrant. **idratante** *agg* (*crema*) moisturizing.
idraulico [i'drauliko] *agg* hydraulic. *sm* plumber. **idraulica** *sf* hydraulics.
idroelettrico [idroe'lettriko] *agg* hydroelectric.
idroestrattore [idroestrat'tore] *sm* spin-drier.
idrofilo [i'drɔfilo] *agg* **cotone idrofilo** *sm* cotton-wool.

idrofobia [i'drɔfobia] *sf* rabies, hydrophobia. **idrofobo** *agg* rabid, hydrophobic.
idrogeno [i'drɔdʒeno] *sm* hydrogen.
idrosci [idro'ʃi] *sm* water-skiing.
idrovolante [idrovo'lante] *sm* seaplane.
iena ['jɛna] *sf* hyena.
ieri ['jɛri] *avv*, *sm* yesterday. **ieri l'altro** the day before yesterday. **tutto ieri** all day yesterday.
iettatore [jetta'tore] *sm* jinx. **iettatura** *sf* bad luck; (*malocchio*) evil eye.
igiene [i'dʒɛne] *sf* hygiene. **igienico** *agg* hygienic; (*sano*) healthy. **assorbente igienico** *sm* sanitary towel. **carta igienica** *sf* toilet paper.
iglù [i'glu] *sm* igloo.
ignaro [i'ɲaro] *agg* unaware, ignorant.
ignobile [i'ɲɔbile] *agg* mean, base.
ignominia [iɲo'minja] *sf* disgrace.
ignorante [iɲo'rante] *agg* ignorant; (*non colto*) uneducated. *s*(*m*+*f*) ignoramus. **ignoranza** *sf* ignorance.
ignorare [iɲo'rare] *v* (*non sapere*) not know; (*trascurare, fingere di non conoscere*) ignore.
ignoto [i'ɲɔto] *agg* unknown. *sm* (*concetto*) unknown; (*persona*) unknown person.
ignudo [i'ɲudo] *agg* naked.
il [il] *art* the.
ilare ['ilare] *agg* cheerful. **ilarità** *sf* (*allegria*) cheerfulness; (*riso*) hilarity.
illecito [il'letʃito] *agg* illicit, unlawful.
illegale [ille'gale] *agg* illegal, unlawful. **illegalità** *sf* illegality.
illeggibile [illed'dʒibile] *agg* illegible; (*fig*) unreadable.
illegittimo [ille'dʒittimo] *agg* illegitimate. **illegittimità** *sf* illegitimacy.
illeso [il'lezo] *agg* unhurt.
illibato [illi'bato] *agg* pure, chaste.
illimitato [illimi'tato] *agg* unlimited, boundless.
illogico [il'lɔdʒiko] *agg* illogical, unsound. **illogicità** *sf* illogicality.
***illudere** [il'ludere] *v* deceive, fool. **illudersi** *v* delude oneself.
illuminare [illumi'nare] *v* light, illuminate; (*rischiarare*) light up; (*mostrare la verità*) enlighten; (*a giorno*) floodlight. **illuminazione** *sf* illumination, lighting. **illuminismo** *sm* Enlightenment.
illusione [illu'zjone] *sf* illusion; impression. **farsi (delle) illusioni** delude oneself; (*fam*) kid oneself. **non farsi (delle) illusioni** have no illusions. **illusionista** *s*(*m*+*f*) conjurer.
illusorio [illu'zɔrjo] *agg* illusory, vain.
illustrare [illus'trare] *v* illustrate; (*spiegare*) explain. **illustrativo** *agg* explanatory. **illustrato** *agg* illustrated. **illustratore, -trice** *sm*, *sf* illustrator. **illustrazione** *sf* illustration, explanation.
illustre [il'lustre] *agg* famous, illustrious. **illustre ignoto** *sm* nobody.
imbacuccare [imbakuk'kare] *v* wrap up.
imballare[1] [imbal'lare] *v* pack; (*involucro*) wrap; (*in scatole*) box; (*in casse*) crate. **imballaggio** *sm* packing; wrapping; boxing; crating.
imballare[2] [imbal'lare] *v* (*auto*) race.
imbalsamare [imbalsa'mare] *v* embalm. **imbalsamatore, -trice** *sm*, *sf* embalmer; (*di animali*) taxidermist.
imbambolato [imbambo'lato] *agg* bewildered.
imbandierare [imbandje'rare] *v* deck with flags.
imbandire [imban'dire] *v* prepare.
imbarazzare [imbarat'tsare] *v* embarrass; (*impedire*) hamper; (*ostacolare*) block, hinder. **imbarazzo** *sm* embarrassment; (*impaccio*) hindrance, trouble. **essere in imbarazzo** be in a difficult situation, be in a fix; (*scelta difficile*) be in a quandary. **mettere in imbarazzo** (*in situazione difficile*) put in a spot; (*a disagio*) make ill at ease.
imbarcare [imbar'kare] *v* take aboard. **imbarcarsi** *v* embark. **imbarcazione** *sf* craft, boat. **imbarco** *sm* embarkation; (*merci*) shipment.
imbastire [imbas'tire] *v* (*cucire*) tack; (*tracciare sommariamente*) draw up, outline.
imbattersi [im'battersi] *v* come across; (*fam*) bump into.
imbattibile [imbat'tibile] *agg* invincible, unbeatable.
imbavagliare [imbava'ʎare] *v* gag.
imbecille [imbe'tʃille] *agg* stupid, idiotic. *s*(*m*+*f*) fool, idiot; (*med*) imbecile.
imbellettare [imbellet'tare] *v* make up; (*fig*) embellish.
imbellire [imbel'lire] *v* beautify.
imbevuto [imbe'vuto] *agg* steeped (in), imbued (with).
imbiancare [imbjan'kare] *v* whiten; (*muri*)

whitewash; (*candeggiare*) bleach. **imbianchino** *sm* house-painter.
imbizzarrirsi [imbiddzar'rirsi] *v* get excited.
imboccare [imbok'kare] *v* (*cibo*) feed; (*suggerire*) prompt; enter; (*portare alla bocca*) put to one's mouth. **imboccatura** *sf* mouth; entrance; (*bocchino*) mouthpiece.
imbonire [imbo'nire] *v* entice, talk into buying. **imbonimento** *sm* (*discorso*) salestalk; (*elogio immeritato*) build-up.
imboscata [imbos'kata] *sf* ambush. **imboscato** *sm* shirker, (draft-)dodger.
imbottigliare [imbotti'ʎare] *v* bottle; (*mil*) blockade; (*traffico*) jam.
imbottire [imbot'tire] *v* stuff; (*sarto*) pad, wad. **coperta imbottita** *sf* quilt. **panino imbottito** *sm* sandwich. **imbottitura** *sf* stuffing; padding; wadding.
imbrattare [imbrat'tare] *v* soil, dirty.
imbrigliare [imbri'ʎare] *v* bridle.
imbroccare [imbrok'kare] *v* (*azzeccare*) get right.
imbrogliare [imbro'ʎare] *v* (*gabbare*) cheat; (*mettere in disordine*) mix up, muddle up; (*ingarbugliare*) tangle (up). **imbroglio** *sm* (*faccenda confusa*) muddle, mess; (*groviglio*) tangle; (*raggiro*) trick, swindle. **imbroglione, -a** *sm, sf* cheat, trickster, swindler.
imbronciarsi [imbron'tʃarsi] *v* sulk; (*cielo*) cloud over.
imbrunire [imbru'nire] *v* darken, get dark. *sm* nightfall.
imbruttire [imbrut'tire] *v* spoil.
imbucare [imbu'kare] *v* post.
imburrare [imbur'rare] *v* butter.
imbuto [im'buto] *sm* funnel.
imitare [imi'tare] *v* imitate. **imitazione** *sf* imitation.
immagazzinare [immagaddzi'nare] *v* store.
immaginare [immadʒi'nare] *v* imagine. **s'immagini!** (*tutt'altro*) not in the least! (*certamente*) by all means! **immaginario** *agg* imaginary. **immaginazione** *sf* imagination.
immagine [im'madʒine] *sf* image; (*figura, ritratto*) picture. **immagine reflessa** reflection.
immancabile [imman'kabile] *agg* unfailing, certain.
immangiabile [imman'dʒabile] *agg* inedible, uneatable.
immatricolarsi [immatriko'larsi] *v* register, enrol.
immaturo [imma'turo] *agg* unripe; (*fig*) immature; (*prematuro*) untimely.
immedesimarsi [immedezi'marsi] *v* identify oneself (with).
immediato [imme'djato] *agg* immediate. **immediatamente** *avv* immediately; directly; (*subito*) at once.
immemorabile [immemo'rabile] *agg* immemorial.
immemore [im'mɛmore] *agg* heedless, forgetful.
immenso [im'menso] *agg* huge, vast; enormous. **immensità** *sf* hugeness, immensity; (*gran numero*) mass, enormous number.
***immergere** [im'mɛrdʒere] *v* immerse; (*intingere*) dip; (*con forza, tuffare*) plunge; (*sottomarino*) submerge. **immersione** *sf* immersion; (*tuffo*) dive.
immeritato [immeri'tato] *agg* undeserved. **immeritevole** *agg* undeserving.
***immettere** [im'mettere] *v* admit, introduce.
immigrare [immi'grare] *v* immigrate. **immigrante** *s*(*m*+*f*), *agg* immigrant. **immigrato, -a** *s, agg* immigrant. **immigrazione** *sf* immigration.
imminente [immi'nɛnte] *agg* imminent. **imminenza** *sf* imminence.
immischiare [immis'kjare] *v* involve, mix up. **immischiarsi** *v* get involved, interfere.
immobile [im'mɔbile] *agg* (*che non si muove*) motionless, still; (*che non si può muovere*) immovable. **società immobiliare** *sf* building society. **immobilità** *sf* immobility, stillness. **beni immobili** *sm pl* real estate *sing*.
immobilizzare [immobilid'dzare] *v* immobilize; (*econ*) tie up.
immoderato [immode'rato] *agg* excessive. **immoderatezza** *sf* excessiveness; (*smoderatezza*) lack of moderation.
immodesto [immo'desto] *agg* conceited, immodest.
immolare [immo'lare] *v* sacrifice.
immondo [im'mondo] *agg* filthy. **immondezzaio** *sm* rubbish dump. **immondizia** *sf* (*sporcizia*) filth; (*spazzatura*) rubbish, garbage.
immorale [immo'rale] *agg* immoral.
immortale [immor'tale] *agg* immortal. **immortalare** *v* immortalize. **immortalità** *sf* immortality.

immune [im'mune] *agg* immune, free. **immunità** *sf* immunity. **immunizzare** *v* immunize.
immutabile [immu'tabile] *agg* immutable, unchangeable; (*costante*) unswerving. **immutabilità** *sf* immutability; firmness. **immutato** *agg* unchanged, unfailing.
impacchettare [impakket'tare] *v* parcel up, package.
impacciare [impat'tʃare] *v* hamper, hinder. **impaccio** *sm* obstacle, hindrance; (*situazione imbarazzante*) fix, predicament. **impacciato** *agg* awkward; (*imbarazzato*) ill at ease; (*goffo*) clumsy.
impadronirsi [impadro'nirsi] *v* **impadronirsi di** seize, take possession of; (*imparare a fondo*) master.
impagabile [impa'gabile] *agg* invaluable, priceless.
impalcatura [impalka'tura] *sf* (*struttura provvisoria*) scaffolding; (*struttura di sostegno*) framework; (*cervo*) antlers *pl*.
impallidire [impalli'dire] *v* turn pale; (*fig*) fade; (*offuscarsi*) grow dim.
impanare[1] [impa'nare] *v* (*mec*) thread.
impanare[2] [impa'nare] *v* (*gastr*) dip in breadcrumbs.
impannata [impan'nata] *sf* window-frame.
impantanarsi [impanta'narsi] *v* get bogged down.
imparare [impa'rare] *v* learn. **imparare a memoria** learn by heart.
impareggiabile [impared'dʒabile] *agg* incomparable.
impari ['impari] *agg invar* unequal.
impartire [impar'tire] *v* give, impart.
imparziale [impar'tsjale] *agg* impartial, unbiased; (*giusto*) fair.
impassibile [impas'sibile] *agg* impassive, unmoved.
impastare [impas'tare] *v* (*pane*) knead; (*lavorare*) mix; (*incollare*) paste. **impastatrice** *sf* mixer. **impasto** *sm* mixture.
impatto [im'patto] *sm* impact.
impaurire [impau'rire] *v* frighten.
impazietne [impa'tsjɛnte] *agg* impatient; (*desideroso*) anxious. **impazientirsi** *v* lose one's patience.
impazzare [impat'tsare] *v* be in full swing; (*gastr*) curdle. **all'impazzata** wildly.
impazzire [impat'tsire] *v* go mad. **far impazzire** drive mad.
impeccabile [impek'kabile] *agg* impeccable.
impedire [impe'dire] *v* prevent; (*sbarrare*) block; (*impacciare*) hinder. **impedimento** *sm* impediment; obstacle; (*l'impedire*) prevention.
impegnare [impe'ɲare] *v* (*dare in pegno*) pledge; (*tenere impegnato*) engage; (*obbligare*) bind; (*tenere occupato*) take up; (*prenotare*) book. **impegnarsi** *v* undertake, strive. **impegnativo** *agg* (*lavoro*) exacting, demanding; (*promessa*) binding. **impegnato** *agg* engaged; (*vincolato*) pledged; (*pol*) committed. **impegno** *sm* engagement; obligation; commitment; (*zelo*) eagerness, enthusiasm.
impenetrabile [impene'trabile] *agg* impenetrable, impervious.
impenitente [impeni'tɛnte] *agg* unrepentant. **scapolo impenitente** *sm* confirmed bachelor.
impennarsi [impen'narsi] *v* flare up; (*cavallo*) rear (up); (*aereo*) go into a climb.
impensabile [impen'sabile] *agg* unthinkable.
impensato [impen'sato] *agg* unforeseen.
impensierirsi [impensje'rirsi] *v* worry.
imperativo [impera'tivo] *sm*, *agg* imperative. **imperare** *v* rule.
imperatore [impera'tore] *sm* emperor. **imperatrice** *sf* empress.
impercettibile [impertʃet'tibile] *agg* imperceptible.
imperdonabile [imperdo'nabile] *agg* unforgivable.
imperfetto [imper'fetto] *agg* faulty, defective. *sm* imperfect (tense). **imperfezione** *sf* defect.
imperioso [impe'rjozo] *agg* imperious; (*ineluttabile*) pressing, impelling.
impermalirsi [imperma'lirsi] *v* take umbrage, take offence.
impermeabile [imperme'abile] *sm* raincoat. *agg* impervious; (*all'acqua*) waterproof; (*all'aria*) airtight. **impermeabilizzare** *v* waterproof.
imperniare [imper'njare] *v* hinge; (*fondare*) base.
impero [im'pɛro] *sm* (*territorio*) empire; (*autorità*) rule.
imperscrutabile [imperskru'tabile] *agg* inscrutable.
impersonale [imperso'nale] *agg* impersonal.

impersonare [imperso'nare] *v* (*simboleggiare*) personify; (*attore*) impersonate. **impersonarsi** *v* be the personification (of).
imperterrito [imper'tɛrrito] *agg* undaunted; unperturbed.
impertinente [imperti'nɛnte] *agg* impertinent, cheeky.
imperturbabile [impertur'babile] *agg* unruffled, imperturbable, calm. **imperturbato** *agg* unperturbed, unruffled.
impeto ['impeto] *sm* impetus, force; (*accesso*) outburst. **agire d'impeto** act on impulse.
impettito [impet'tito] *agg* stiff, erect. **camminare impettito** strut.
impetuoso [impe'twozo] *agg* impetuous.
impiallacciato [impjallat'tʃato] *agg* veneered. **impiallacciatura** *sf* veneer.
impiantare [impjan'tare] *v* set up; (*fondare*) establish; (*tec*) install. **impianto** *sm* plant, installation; (*fondazione*) establishment.
impiantito [impjan'tito] *sm* flooring.
impiastrare [impjas'trare] *v* smear. **impiastro** *sm* (*cataplasma*) poultice; (*persona uggiosa*) bore.
impiccare [impik'kare] *v* hang. **impiccato** *sm* hanged man.
impicciare [impit'tʃare] *v* be in the way, hamper. **impicciarsi** *v* meddle, interfere.
impiccio [im'pittʃo] *sm* (*ostacolo*) hindrance; (*guaio*) mess, trouble. **essere d'impiccio** *v* be in the way.
impiegare [impje'gare] *v* employ; spend. **impiegatizio** *agg* clerical. **impiegato, -a** *sm, sf* employee; (*funzionario*) official. **impiegati** *pl* (*collettivo*) staff *sing*, personnel *sing*.
impiego [im'pjɛgo] *sm, pl* **-ghi** use; (*denaro*) investment; (*posto, occupazione*) employment, job.
impietrito [impje'trito] *agg* petrified.
impigliarsi [impi'ʎarsi] *v* get entangled, get mixed up.
impiparsi [impi'parsi] *v* (*fam*) not care a damn.
implacabile [impla'kabile] *agg* implacable.
implicare [impli'kare] *v* (*coinvolgere*) involve; (*comportare*) imply, entail.
implicito [im'plitʃito] *agg* implicit.
implorare [implo'rare] *v* implore, entreat.
impolverare [impolve'rare] *v* cover with dust.
imponderabile [imponde'rabile] *agg* imponderable.
imponente [impo'nɛnte] *agg* imposing, impressive.
imponibile [impo'nibile] *agg* taxable. *sm* taxable income.
impopolare [impopo'lare] *agg* unpopular. **impopolarità** *sf* unpopularity.
***imporre** [im'porre] *v* impose; (*costringere*) oblige; (*ordinare*) order; (*comportare*) involve. **imporsi** *v* (*farsi valere*) assert oneself; (*incontrar favore*) go down well; (*rendersi necessario*) become necessary.
importante [impor'tante] *agg* important. *sm* important thing, main point. **importanza** *sf* importance. **di nessuna importanza** unimportant.
importare [impor'tare] *v* (*aver peso*) matter; (*comportare*) involve; (*introdurre dall'estero*) import. **non importa!** it doesn't matter! never mind! **non me ne importa niente!** (*fam*) I couldn't care less!
importazione [importa'tsjone] *sf* import; (*atto*) importation.
importo [im'pɔrto] *sm* amount.
importunare [importu'nare] *v* trouble, bother. **importuno** *agg* troublesome, tiresome, boring.
imposizione [impozi'tsjone] *sf* imposition.
impossessarsi [imposses'sarsi] *v* get hold of, seize.
impossibile [impos'sibile] *agg* impossible. **fare l'impossibile** do all one can. **impossibilità** *sf* impossibility.
imposta[1] [im'pɔsta] *sf* (*finestra*) shutter.
imposta[2] [im'pɔsta] *sf* (*econ*) tax, duty.
impostare[1] [impos'tare] *v* (*spedire*) post.
impostare[2] [impos'tare] *v* (*avviare*) get under way; (*questione, ecc.*) set out, state; (*nave*) lay down; (*voce*) pitch. **impostazione** *sf* approach.
impostore [impos'tore] *sm* imposter.
impotente [impo'tɛnte] *agg* powerless; (*med*) impotent. **impotenza** *sf* powerlessness; impotence.
impoverire [impove'rire] *v* impoverish. **impoverimento** *sm* impoverishment.
impraticabile [imprati'kabile] *agg* (*strada*) impassable; (*campo sportivo*) unfit for play.
impratichirsi [imprati'kirsi] *v* practise.

imprecare [impre'kare] *v* curse. **imprecazione** *sf* curse.
impreciso [impre'tʃizo] *agg* (*inesatto*) inaccurate; (*indeterminato*) imprecise, vague. **imprecisabile** *agg* indefinable. **imprecisione** *sf* inaccuracy; vagueness.
impregnare [impre'ɲare] *v* impregnate; (*fig*) imbue; (*inzuppare*) soak.
imprenditore [imprendi'tore] *sm* contractor; entrepreneur. **imprenditore di pompe funebri** undertaker. **imprenditore edile** building contractor. **piccolo imprenditore** tradesman.
impreparato [imprepa'rato] *agg* unprepared; (*lavoro*) untrained. **impreparazione** *sf* unpreparedness; lack of training.
impresa [im'preza] *sf* undertaking, enterprise; (*azienda*) concern, firm; (*azione*) deed; (*azione pericolosa*) exploit. **impresario** *sm* entrepreneur; (theatre) manager, impresario.
imprescindibile [impreʃin'dibile] *agg* that cannot be disregarded.
impressionare [impressjo'nare] *v* make an impression; (*spaventare*) frighten; (*turbare*) shock, upset; (*foto*) expose. **impressionarsi** *v* be upset, be shocked; be affected. **impressionabile** *agg* impressionable, easily affected; easily frightened. **impressionante** *agg* striking, impressive; frightening; upsetting.
impressione [impres'sjone] *sf* impression; sensation.
imprestare [impres'tare] *v* lend.
imprevidenza [imprevi'dentsa] *sf* lack of foresight. **imprevedibile** *agg* unforeseeable. **imprevidente** *agg* heedless.
imprevisto [impre'visto] *agg* unforeseen. **salvo imprevisti** if all goes well.
imprigionare [impridʒo'nare] *v* imprison.
***imprimere** [im'primere] *v* imprint, impress; (*dare*) impart; (*pittura*) prime.
improbabile [impro'babile] *agg* unlikely, improbable. **improbabilità** *sf* unlikelihood.
improduttivo [improdut'tivo] *agg* unproductive.
impronta [im'pronta] *sf* impression, mark, stamp. **impronta del piede** footprint. **impronta digitale** fingerprint. **improntare** *v* stamp. **all'improntо** at sight.
improprio [im'prɔprjo] *agg* (*inadatto*) inappropriate; (*inopportuno*) out of place; (*mat*) improper.
improrogabile [improro'gabile] *agg* **termine improrogabile** *sm* deadline.
improvvisare [improvvi'zare] *v* improvise. **improvvisamente** *avv* suddenly, all of a sudden. **improvvisata** *sf* surprise. **improvvisazione** *sf* improvisation.
imprudente [impru'dente] *agg* rash, imprudent. **imprudenza** *sf* imprudence. **commettere un'imprudenza** do something rash.
impudente [impu'dente] *agg* impudent.
impudico [impu'diko] *agg, m pl* **-chi** immodest.
impugnare[1] [impu'ɲare] *v* (*contestare*) challenge; (*dir*) contest.
impugnare[2] [impu'ɲare] *v* (*afferrare*) grasp. **impugnare le armi** take up arms. **impugnatura** *sf* handle; (*spada*) hilt; (*racchetta*) grip.
impulso [im'pulso] *sm* impulse. **dare impulso** boost. **impulsivo** *agg* impulsive.
impunemente [impune'mente] *avv* with impunity.
impunito [impu'nito] *agg* (*delitto*) unpunished.
impuntarsi [impun'tarsi] *v* refuse to budge, dig one's heels in.
impuro [im'puro] *agg* impure. **impurità** *sf* impurity.
imputare [impu'tare] *v* impute, attribute, ascribe; (*dir*) charge. **imputabile** *agg* attributable. **imputato, -a** *sm, sf* defendant, accused. **imputazione** *sf* charge.
imputridire [imputri'dire] *v* rot.
in [in] *prep* in; (*su, sopra*) on; (*moto a luogo*) to; (*dentro*) into; (*moto per luogo*) round, through; (*entro*) within; (*durante*) during.
inabile [in'abile] *agg* (*non capace*) unable, incapable; (*non idoneo*) unfit; (*per infortunio*) disabled; (*dir*) ineligible.
inabitabile [inabi'tabile] *agg* uninhabitable. **inabitato** *agg* uninhabited.
inaccessibile [inattʃes'sibile] *agg* inaccessible.
inaccettabile [inattʃet'tabile] *agg* unacceptable.
inadatto [ina'datto] *agg* unsuitable (for); (*incapace*) unfit (for).
inadeguato [inade'gwato] *agg* insufficient, inadequate.
inalare [ina'lare] *v* inhale.
inalienabile [inalje'nabile] *agg* inalienable.

inalterabile [inalte'rabile] *agg* unchangeable. **inalterato** *agg* unchanged.
inamidare [inami'dare] *v* starch.
inammissibile [innammis'sibile] *agg* inadmissible.
inanimato [inani'mato] *agg* inanimate, lifeless.
inappagabile [innappa'gabile] *agg* insatiable. **inappagato** *agg* unsatisfied.
inapplicabile [inappli'kabile] *agg* inapplicable.
inarcare [inar'kare] *v* arch, bend. **inarcare le sopracciglia** raise one's eyebrows.
inargentare [inardʒen'tare] *v* silver.
inaridire [inari'dire] *v* dry up.
inaspettato [inaspet'tato] *agg* unexpected.
inasprire [inas'prire] *v* exacerbate, make worse.
inattendibile [inatten'dibile] *agg* unreliable.
inatteso [inat'tezo] *agg* unexpected.
inattivo [inat'tivo] *agg* idle.
inattuabile [inat'twabile] *agg* impracticable.
inaudito [inau'dito] *agg* (*non udito prima*) unheard of; incredible, extraordinary.
inaugurare [inaugu'rare] *v* inaugurate, open. **inaugurazione** *sf* inauguration, opening.
inavveduto [inavve'duto] *agg* thoughtless, careless.
inavvertenza [inavver'tɛntsa] *sf* carelessness, oversight.
incagliarsi [inka'ʎarsi] *v* (*mar*) run aground; (*fig*) get stuck.
incalcolabile [inkalko'labile] *agg* incalculable.
incalzare [inkal'tsare] *v* follow closely; (*fig*) press.
incamminare [inkammi'nare] *v* start (off). **incamminarsi** *v* set off; (*avviarsi*) be on the way (to).
incanalare [inkana'lare] *v* channel.
incantare [inkan'tare] *v* enchant, charm. **incantarsi** *v* (*rimanere intontito*) be in a daze; (*mec*) jam, break down. **incantato** *agg* enchanted; (*intontito*) dazed, spellbound. **incantatore, -trice** *sm, sf* charmer. **incantesimo** *sm* charm, spell. **incantevole** *agg* charming, enchanting.
incanto[1] [in'kanto] *sm* spell, magic. **stare d'incanto** suit perfectly.
incanto[2] [in'kanto] *sm* (*vendita*) auction.
incapace [inka'patʃe] *agg* incapable.
incapacità *sf* inability; (*fisica*) disability; (*dir*) incapacity.
incappare [inkap'pare] *v* run into, come up against.
incarcerare [inkartʃe'rare] *v* imprison, jail.
incaricare [inkari'kare] *v* charge, entrust; order. **incaricarsi** *v* take charge. **incaricato, -a** *sm, sf* person in charge; (*università*) lecturer; (*funzionario*) official.
incarico [in'kariko] *sm, pl* **-chi** task, assignment, charge.
incarnare [inkar'nare] *v* embody; (*personaggio*) impersonate.
incartare [inkar'tare] *v* wrap (up).
incasellare [inkazel'lare] *v* pigeon-hole.
incassare [inkas'sare] *v* (*riscuotere*) collect, cash; (*sport*) take; (*inserire*) embed. **incasso** *sm* collection; (*entrata*) takings *pl*.
incastellatura [inkastella'tura] *sf* (*impalcatura*) scaffolding; (*mec*) casing.
incastonare [inkasto'nare] *v* set, mount. **incastonatura** *sf* setting, mounting.
incastrare [inkast'rare] *v* wedge, drive; (*imprigionare*) jam, sandwich; (*falegnameria*) mortise. **incastro** *sm* joint; (*cavità*) hollow, recess; mortise.
incatenare [inkate'nare] *v* chain; (*fig*) tie.
incatramare [inkatra'mare] *v* tar.
incauto [in'kauto] *agg* incautious.
incavare [inka'vare] *v* hollow out. **incavo** *sm* hollow; (*scanalatura*) groove.
incendiare [intʃen'djare] *v* set on fire; (*fig*) fire.
incendiario [intʃen'djarjo] *agg* incendiary. *sm* arsonist, fire-raiser.
incendio [in'tʃendjo] *sm* fire. **bocca d'incendio** *sf* (fire) hydrant. **incendio doloso** arson.
incenerire [intʃene'rire] *v* burn down; (*fig*) wither.
incenso [in'tʃɛnso] *sm* incense.
incensurabile [intʃensu'rabile] *agg* beyond reproach. **essere incensurato** have a clean record.
inceppare [intʃep'pare] *v* obstruct, hamper.
incertezza [intʃer'tettsa] *sf* uncertainty; (*dubbio*) doubt; (*indecisione*) hesitation.
incerto [in'tʃɛrto] *agg* uncertain; dubious; (*indeciso*) hesitant; (*malsicuro*) unsure. *sm* uncertainty.
incespicare [intʃespi'kare] *v* stumble, trip up.

incessante [intʃes'sante] *agg* ceaseless, constant.
incesto [in'tʃɛsto] *sm* incest. **incestuoso** *agg* incestuous.
incettare [intʃɛt'tare] *v also* **fare incetto di** corner, buy up. **incetta** *sf* cornering.
inchiesta [in'kjɛsta] *sf* inquiry, investigation; (*giornalismo*) report; (*scandalo*) probe.
inchinare [inki'nare] *v* bow, bend; (*abbassare*) lower. **inchinarsi** *v* bend down, bow; (*donna*) curtsey. **inchino** *sm* bow, curtsey.
inchiodare [inkjo'dare] *v* nail.
inchiostro [in'kjostro] *sm* ink. **inchiostro di china** Indian ink.
inciampare [intʃam'pare] *v* stumble (over), trip up. **inciampo** *sm* obstacle, stumbling block.
incidente [intʃi'dɛnte] *sm* (*episodio*) incident; (*infortunio*) accident; (*disputa*) argument.
incidenza [intʃi'dɛntsa] *sf* incidence.
***incidere**[1] [in'tʃidere] *v* cut (into); carve; (*intagliare*) engrave; (*ad acquaforte*) etch; (*registrare*) record; (*med*) incise, lance. **incisione** *sf* incision; cut; engraving; etching; recording. **incisivo** *agg* incisive. **per inciso** by the way, incidentally. **incisore** *sm* engraver.
***incidere**[2] [in'tʃidere] *v* **incidere su** affect.
incinta [in'tʃinta] *agg* pregnant.
incipriare [intʃi'prjare] *v* powder.
incitare [intʃi'tare] *v* incite. **incitamento** *sm* incitement, spur.
incivile [intʃi'vile] *agg* uncivilized; (*villano*) boorish, uncivil.
incivilire [intʃivi'lire] *v* civilize.
inclemente [inkle'mɛnte] *agg* harsh.
inclinare [inkli'nare] *v* incline; (*propendere*) tend, be inclined. **inclinazione** *sf* inclination; (*pendenza*) slope; (*disposizione d'animo*) leaning; (*simpatia*) liking; (*strada*) gradient. **incline** *agg* prone.
***includere** [in'kludere] *v* (*comprendere*) include; (*accludere*) enclose; (*implicare*) imply. **inclusione** *sf* inclusion. **incluso** *agg* included; (*comm*) inclusive.
incoerente [inkoe'rɛnte] *agg* incoherent; (*fig*) inconsistent.
incognita [in'kɔɲita] *sf* (*matematica*) unknown; (*fatto imprevedibile*) unknown factor, uncertainty; (*persona*) mystery, dark horse.
incognito [in'kɔɲito] *agg* unknown. *sm* incognito; (*ignoto*) unknown.
incollare [inkol'lare] *v* (*attaccare*) glue; (*spalmare*) paste.
incolore [inko'lore] *agg* colourless.
incolpare [inkol'pare] *v* blame.
incolto [in'kolto] *agg* (*non coltivato*) uncultivated; (*trascurato*) untidy; (*privo di coltura*) uncultured.
incolume [in'kɔlume] *agg* unharmed.
incombente [inkom'bɛnte] *agg* (*imminente*) impending; (*spettante*) incumbent.
incominciare [inkomin'tʃare] *v* begin, start. **(tanto) per cominciare** to begin with.
incomodo [in'kɔmodo] *agg* (*disagevole*) uncomfortable; (*inopportuno*) inconvenient. *sm* trouble, inconvenience. **il terzo incomodo** the odd man out. **incomodare** *v* inconvenience, trouble.
incomparabile [inkompa'rabile] *agg* incomparable.
incompatibile [inkompa'tibile] *agg* incompatible. **incompatibilità** *sf* incompatibility.
incompetente [inkompe'tɛnte] *agg* incompetent. *s(m+f)* incompetent person.
incompiuto [inkom'pjuto] *agg* unfinished.
incompleto [inkom'plɛto] *agg* incomplete.
incomprensibile [inkompren'sibile] *agg* incomprehensible. **incomprensibilità** *sf* incomprehensibility.
incompreso [inkom'prezo] *agg* misunderstood.
inconcepibile [inkontʃe'pibile] *agg* inconceivable.
inconciliabile [inkontʃi'ljabile] *agg* irreconcilable.
inconcludente [inkonklu'dɛnte] *agg* inconclusive.
incondizionato [inkonditsjo'nato] *agg* unconditional; (*pieno*) complete.
inconsapevole [inkonsa'pevole] *agg* unaware, unconscious.
inconscio [in'kɔnʃo] *agg* unconscious; (*persona*) unaware. *sm invar* unconscious.
inconsiderabile [inkonside'rabile] *agg* negligible. **inconsiderato** *agg* thoughtless. **inconsideratezza** *sf* thoughtlessness.
inconsistente [inkonsis'tɛnte] *agg* flimsy; (*infondato*) groundless.

inconsolabile [inkonso'labile] *agg* inconsolable.
inconsueto [inkonsu'ɛto] *agg* unusual.
incontenibile [inkonte'nibile] *agg* uncontrollable.
incontentabile [inkonten'tabile] *agg* hard to please, exacting.
incontrare [inkon'trare] *v* meet; (*esser popolare*) be a success. **incontrar favore** find favour. **incontrarsi per caso** run into.
incontrario [inkon'trarjo] *sm* **all'incontrario** (*a rovescio*) the wrong way round.
incontrastato [inkontras'tato] *agg* unopposed.
incontro[1] [in'kontro] *sm* meeting; (*partita*) match; (*gioco*) game; (*favore*) reception, success. **incontro alla pari** (*sport*) tie, draw.
incontro[2] [in'kontro] *avv* towards. **all'incontro** on the contrary. **andare incontro a** go towards, approach; (*fig*) meet halfway.
incontrollabile [inkontrol'labile] *agg* uncontrollable.
inconveniente [inkonve'njente] *sm* drawback, snag.
incoraggiare [inkorad'dʒare] *v* encourage.
incorniciare [inkorni'tʃare] *v* frame.
incoronare [inkoro'nare] *v* crown. **incoronazione** *sf* coronation.
incorporare [inkorpo'rare] *v* incorporate; annex.
incorreggibile [inkorred'dʒibile] *agg* incorrigible.
***incorrere** [in'korrere] *v* incur.
incorruttibile [inkorrut'tibile] *agg* incorruptible.
incosciente [inko'ʃɛnte] *agg* unconscious; (*sconsiderato*) irresponsible.
incredibile [inkre'dibile] *agg* incredible, unbelievable.
incredulo [in'krɛdulo] *agg* incredulous, disbelieving.
incremento [inkre'mento] *sm* (*aumento*) increase; (*sviluppo*) growth, expansion; (*mat*) increment. **incrementare** *v* increase; (*far prosperare*) promote.
increspare [inkres'pare] *v* (*acqua*) ripple; (*capelli*) curl. **increspare la fronte** frown.
incrinare [inkri'nare] *v* crack.
incrociare [inkro'tʃare] *v* cross. **incrociatore** *sm* cruiser. **incrocio** *sm* crossing; (*accoppiamento*) cross-breeding; (*frutto*) cross, hybrid.
incrostato [inkros'tato] *agg* encrusted.
incubatrice [inkuba'tritʃe] *sf* incubator. **incubazione** *sf* incubation.
incubo ['inkubo] *sm* nightmare.
incudine [in'kudine] *sf* anvil.
inculcare [inkul'kare] *v* inculcate.
incuneare [inkune'are] *v* wedge.
incurabile [inku'rabile] *agg* incurable.
incurante [inku'rante] *agg* heedless, unconcerned.
incuriosire [inkurjo'zire] *v* arouse curiosity.
incursione [inkur'sjone] *sf* incursion, raid. **incursione aerea** air-raid.
incustodito [inkusto'dito] *agg* unattended.
indagare [inda'gare] *v* investigate, inquire into. **indagine** *sf* inquiry, investigation; (*scientifica*) research; (*studio*) survey.
indebitamente [indebita'mente] *avv* unduly; (*ingiustamente*) unlawfully.
indebitarsi [indebi'tarsi] *v* run into debt. **indebitato** *agg* indebted.
indebolire [indebo'lire] *v* weaken. **indebolimento** *sm* weakening; (*debolezza*) weakness.
indecente [inde'tʃɛnte] *agg* indecent. **indecenza** *sf* indecency; (*vergogna*) disgrace.
indecifrabile [indetʃi'frabile] *agg* illegible.
indecisione [indetʃi'zjone] *sf* indecision.
indeciso [inde'tʃizo] *agg* undecided; (*non risolto, instabile*) unsettled.
indefesso [inde'fɛsso] *agg* tireless.
indefinibile [indefi'nibile] *agg* indefinable.
indefinito [indefi'nito] *agg* indefinite; (*non risolto*) unsettled.
indegno [in'deɲo] *agg* unworthy. **indegnità** *sf* base action.
indelicato [indeli'kato] *agg* tactless; indiscreet.
indemagliabile [indema'ʎabile] *agg* nonrun, ladder-proof.
indenne [in'dɛnne] *agg* unharmed, unscathed.
indennità [indenni'ta] *sf* (*risarcimento*) allowance; (*dir*) indemnity. **indennizzare** *v* compensate. **indennizzo** *sm* compensation.
inderogabile [indero'gabile] *agg* binding, irrevocable.
indescrivibile [indeskri'vibile] *agg* indescribable.

indesiderabile [indezide'rabile] *agg* undesirable.
indeterminabile [indetermi'nabile] *agg* indeterminate, imprecise.
indi ['indi] *avv* (*dopo*) then; (*da quel luogo*) from there. **indi a poco** soon after.
India ['indja] *sf* India. **indiano, -a** *s, agg* Indian.
indiavolato [indjavo'lato] *agg* (*molto agitato*) wild; (*eccessivo*) awful; (*indemoniato*) frenzied.
indicare [indi'kare] *v* indicate, show; (*significare*) mean. **indicativo** *agg* indicative. **indicato** *agg* indicated; (*adatto*) suitable.
indicatore [indika'tore] *sm* indicator; (*tec*) gauge; (*stradale*) signpost.
indicazione [indika'tsjone] *sf* indication; (*dato, notizia*) information; (*istruzione per l'uso*) direction.
indice ['inditʃe] *sm* index; (*dito*) index finger; (*tec*) pointer.
indietreggiare [indjetred'dʒare] *v* draw back, withdraw.
indietro [in'djɛtro] *avv* (*in arretrato*) in arrears; (*debole*) weak; (*moto*) back(wards).
indifeso [indi'fezo] *agg* undefended; (*fig*) defenceless.
indifferente [indiffe'rɛnte] *agg* indifferent; (*lo stesso*) all the same; (*che non interessa*) unimportant. **indifferenza** *sf* indifference, lack of interest.
indigeno [in'didʒeno] *sm, agg* native.
indigesto [indi'dʒɛsto] *agg* indigestible; (*non digerito*) undigested.
indignare [indi'ɲare] *v* fill with indignation.
indimenticabile [indimenti'kabile] *agg* unforgettable.
indipendente [indipen'dɛnte] *agg* independent. **indipendenza** *sf* independence.
***indire** [in'dire] *v* announce; (*radunare*) call.
indiretto [indi'rɛtto] *agg* indirect.
indirizzare [indirit'tsare] *v* address; (*rivolgere*) direct. **indirizzo** *sm* address; (*tendenza*) trend; direction.
indisciplinato [indiʃipli'nato] *agg* undisciplined.
indiscreto [indis'krɛto] *agg* indiscreet.
indiscusso [indis'kusso] *agg* beyond dispute, incontrovertible.
indispensabile [indispen'sabile] *agg* indispensable, essential.
indispettire [indispet'tire] *v* irritate.
indisposizione [indispozi'tsjone] *sf* indisposition, slight illness. **indisposto** *agg* indisposed, unwell.
indistinto [indis'tinto] *agg* indistinct. **indistinguibile** *agg* indistinguishable.
indivia [in'divia] *sf* endive.
individuale [individu'ale] *agg* individual.
individuare [individu'are] *v* (*determinare*) locate; (*riconoscere*) single out; (*scoprire*) discover, recognize.
individuo [indi'viduo] *sm* person; (*spreg*) fellow, character.
indivisibile [indivi'zibile] *agg* indivisible. **indiviso** *agg* undivided.
indizio [in'ditsjo] *sm* sign, indication; (*dir*) (circumstantial) evidence.
indole ['indole] *sf* nature, character.
indolenzire [indolen'tsire] *v* make sore, make ache. **indolenzito** *agg* sore, aching.
indomani [indo'mani] *sm* **l'indomani** the following day.
indossare [indos'sare] *v* (*mettersi indosso*) put on; (*portare*) wear. **indossatrice** *sf* model. **indosso** *avv* on.
indotto [in'dotto] *agg* induced.
indovinare [indovi'nare] *v* guess. **indovinato** *agg* (*riuscito*) successful; (*che sta bene*) becoming. **indovinello** *sm* puzzle, riddle. **indovino, -a** *sm, sf* fortune-teller.
indù [in'du] *s(m+f), agg* Hindu.
indubbio [in'dubbjo] *agg* certain, unmistakable.
indubitabile [indubi'tabile] *agg* unquestionable. **indubitato** *agg* certain, unquestioned.
indugiare [indu'dʒare] *v* delay; (*soffermarsi*) linger (over). **indugio** *sm* delay.
indulgente [indul'dʒɛnte] *agg* lenient. **indulgenza** *sf* indulgence.
indumento [indu'mento] *sm* garment.
indurire [indu'rire] *v* harden. **indurimento** *sm* hardening.
***indurre** [in'durre] *v* induce. **indurre in errore** mislead; (*fig*) lead astray. **indurre in tentazione** lead into temptation.
industria [in'dustrja] *sf* industry; (*attività industriale*) business.
industriale [indus'trjale] *agg* industrial. *sm* industrialist, manufacturer. **industrializzare** *v* industrialize. **industrializzazione** *sf* industrialization.

inebriare [inebri'are] *v* intoxicate.
inedito [in'ɛdito] *agg* unpublished.
ineducato [inedu'kato] *agg* ill-mannered.
ineguale [ine'gwale] *agg* unequal; (*non uniforme*) uneven.
ineluttabile [inelut'tabile] *agg* relentless; (*inevitabile*) unavoidable.
inerente [ine'rɛnte] *agg* (*riferentesi*) concerning; (*implicito*) inherent.
inerme [i'nɛrme] *agg* unarmed; (*senza difesa*) defenceless.
inerpicarsi [inerpi'karsi] *v* scramble up.
inerte [i'nɛrte] *agg* inert. **inerzia** *sf* sluggishness; (*fis*) inertia.
inesatto [ine'zatto] *agg* (*sbagliato*) wrong, incorrect; imprecise, inaccurate.
inesistente [inezis'tɛnte] *agg* non-existent.
inesorabile [inezo'rabile] *agg* inexorable.
inesperienza [inesper'jɛntsa] *sf* inexperience.
inesperto [ines'pɛrto] *agg* inexperienced.
inesplicabile [inespli'kabile] *agg* inexplicable.
inespressivo [inespres'sivo] *agg* expressionless.
inesprimibile [inespri'mibile] *agg* indescribable.
inetto [i'nɛtto] *agg* inept, inadequate; (*incapace*) unsuited (to), incapable (of).
inevaso [ine'vazo] *agg* outstanding.
inevitabile [inevi'tabile] *agg* unavoidable.
inezia [i'nɛtsja] *sf* trifle.
infagottare [infagot'tare] *v* bundle up, wrap up.
infallibile [infal'libile] *agg* infallible. **infallibilità** *sf* infallibility.
infame [in'fame] *agg* infamous, vile. **infamia** *sf* infamy, disgrace.
infangare [infan'gare] *v* muddy.
infante [in'fante] *s*(*m*+*f*) infant, newborn baby. **infantile** *agg* childlike; (*puerile*) childish, infantile. **asilo infantile** *sm* nursery school. **infanzia** *sf* infancy, childhood.
infarcire [infar'tʃire] *v* stuff.
infarinare [infari'nare] *v* (dip in) flour. **infarinatura** *sf* coating of flour; (*fig*) smattering.
infastidire [infasti'dire] *v* bother, trouble.
infaticabile [infati'kabile] *agg* tireless.
infatti [in'fatti] *cong* in fact, as a matter of fact, indeed.
infatuarsi [infatu'arsi] *v* become infatuated (with); fall (for).
infausto [in'fausto] *agg* inauspicious, unlucky.
infedele [infe'dele] *agg* unfaithful.
infelice [infe'litʃe] *agg* unhappy; (*inopportuno*) unfortunate; (*disgraziato*) wretched, unlucky; (*cattivo*) bad. *s*(*m*+*f*) unhappy person, wretch.
inferiore [infe'rjore] *agg* lower; (*di grado più basso*) inferior; (*numeri*) below, less than. **inferiorità** *sf* inferiority.
inferire [infe'rire] *v* (*arrecare*) inflict, cause; (*dedurre*) infer.
infermeria [inferme'ria] *sf* infirmary. **infermiere, -a** *sm, sf* nurse. **infermità** *sf* illness. **infermo** *sm, agg* invalid.
inferno [in'fɛrno] *sm* hell. **infernale** *agg* infernal, hellish.
inferriata [infer'rjata] *sf* grille.
infestare [infes'tare] *v* infest.
infettare [infet'tare] *v* infect; (*fig*) taint. **infettivo** *agg* infectious, catching. **infezione** *sf* infection.
infiacchire [infjak'kire] *v* weaken.
infiammare [infjam'mare] *v* set on fire; (*eccitare, med*) inflame. **infiammabile** *agg* inflammable. **infiammazione** *sf* inflammation.
infido [in'fido] *agg* untrustworthy.
infierire [infje'rire] *v* rage.
infilare [infi'lare] *v* thread, string; (*introdurre*) insert; (*imboccare*) turn into, take. **infilata** *sf* row, string.
infiltrarsi [infilt'rarsi] *v* infiltrate.
infimo ['infimo] *agg* (the) lowest.
infine [in'fine] *avv* in the end, finally.
infinito [infi'nito] *agg* infinite; (*interminabile*) endless; (*innumerevole*) countless. *sm* infinity; (*gramm*) infinitive. **infinità** *sf* infinity; (*gran numero*) large number, crowd.
infischiarsi [infis'kjarsi] *v* not give a damn.
infisso [in'fisso] *sm* frame.
inflazione [infla'tsjone] *sf* inflation.
inflessibile [infles'sibile] *agg* inflexible. **inflessione** *sf* inflection.
***infliggere** [in'fliddʒere] *v* inflict.
influenza [influ'ɛntsa] *sf* influence; (*med*) influenza, flu. **influenzare** *v* influence.
influire [influ'ire] *v* have an influence. **influire su** affect, influence. **influsso** *sm* influence.
infondato [infon'dato] *agg* groundless, unfounded.

***infondere** [in'fondere] *v* instil, inspire.
informare [infor'mare] *v* inform, tell; (*plasmare*) form, shape. **informarsi** *v* inquire, find out. **informazione** *sf* information.
informe [in'forme] *agg* shapeless.
informicolirsi [informiko'lirsi] *v* have pins and needles.
infortunio [infor'tunjo] *sm* accident.
infossato [infos'sato] *agg* hollow.
***inframmettersi** [infram'mettersi] *v* interfere.
***infrangere** [in'frandʒere] *v* break. **infrangibile** *agg* unbreakable.
infrazione [infra'tsjone] *sf* infringement, breach.
infreddarsi [infred'darsi] *v* catch a cold. **infreddatura** *sf* cold.
infrequente [infre'qwente] *agg* infrequent.
infuori [in'fwɔri] *avv* **all'infuori di** apart from, except.
infuriare [infu'rjare] *v* rage. **infuriarsi** *v* fly into a temper.
ingannare [ingan'nare] *v* deceive; (*truffare*) cheat; (*essere infedele*) be unfaithful. **inganno** *sm* deceit, deception, trick.
ingarbugliarsi [ingarbu'ʎarsi] *v* get entangled.
ingegnarsi [indʒe'ɲarsi] *v* get by, manage.
ingegnere [indʒe'ɲere] *sm* engineer. **ingegneria** *sf* engineering.
ingegno [in'dʒeɲo] *sm* genius, talent. **ingegnoso** *agg* ingenious, clever.
ingenuo [in'dʒɛnwo] *agg* ingenuous, naive. *sm* naive person. **fare l'ingenuo** feign innocence; pretend not to understand.
ingerirsi [indʒe'rirsi] *v* meddle, interfere.
ingessare [indʒes'sare] *v* put in plaster.
Inghilterra [ingil'terra] *sf* England.
inghiottire [ingjot'tire] *v* swallow.
inginocchiarsi [indʒinok'kjarsi] *v* kneel (down).
ingiuria [in'dʒurja] *sf* offence; insult; (*fig*) damage. **ingiuriare** *v* insult; (*oltraggiare*) offend. **ingiurioso** *agg* insulting, offensive.
ingiusto [in'dʒusto] *agg* unjust; unfair.
inglese [in'gleze] *sm* (*persona*) Englishman; (*lingua*) English. *sf* Englishwoman. *agg* English. **filare all'inglese** take French leave. **zuppa inglese** *sf* trifle.
ingoiare [ingo'jare] *v* gulp (down), swallow (down).
ingolfarsi [ingol'farsi] *v* (*auto*) flood; (*debiti*) be swamped.
ingombrare [ingomb'rare] *v* obstruct, get in the way.
ingombro [in'gombro] *agg* cluttered (with). *sm* obstruction; (*spazio*) space.
ingommare [ingom'mare] *v* stick.
ingordo [in'gordo] *agg* greedy. **ingordigia** *sf* greed.
ingorgarsi [ingor'garsi] *v* be blocked up. **ingorgo** *sm* obstruction; (traffic) jam.
ingranare [ingra'nare] *v* engage; (*fam*) get on. **ingranaggio** *sm* (*mec*) gear; (*fig*) works *pl*, mechanism.
ingrandire [ingran'dire] *v* enlarge, magnify. **ingrandimento** *sm* enlargement.
ingrassare [ingras'sare] *v* fatten, make fat; (*ungere*) grease. **ingrassarsi** *v* put on weight, get fat; (*arricchirsi*) profit.
ingrato [in'grato] *agg* ungrateful; (*sgradevole*) thankless. **ingratitudine** *sf* ingratitude.
ingrediente [ingre'djɛnte] *sm* ingredient.
ingresso [in'grɛsso] *sm* entrance; admission.
ingrossare [ingros'sare] *v* swell.
ingrosso [in'grɔsso] *avv* **all'ingrosso** wholesale.
ingualcibile [ingwal'tʃibile] *agg* crease-resistant.
inguaribile [ingwa'ribile] *agg* incurable.
inguine ['ingwine] *sm* groin.
inibire [ini'bire] *v* inhibit, forbid. **inibizione** *sf* inhibition.
iniettare [injet'tare] *v* inject. **iniezione** *sf* injection.
inimicizia [inimi'tʃitsja] *sf* enmity, hostility.
inimitabile [inimi'tabile] *agg* inimitable.
inimmaginabile [inimmadʒi'nabile] *agg* unimaginable.
inintelligibile [inintelli'dʒibile] *agg* unintelligible.
ininterrotto [ininter'rotto] *agg* uninterrupted, continuous.
iniziale [ini'tsjale] *agg* initial. *sf* initial (letter).
iniziare [ini'tsjare] *v* start, begin; (*avviare*) initiate. **iniziativa** *sf* initiative, enterprise. **inizio** *sm* beginning.
innaffiare [innaf'fjare] *v* water.
innalzare [innal'tsare] *v* raise.
innamorarsi [innamo'rarsi] *v* fall in love (with).

innanzi [in'nantsi] *prep* before. **innanzi tutto** first of all; (*sopratutto*) above all. *avv* (*prima*) before; (*avanti*) on, ahead. **d'ora innanzi** from now on, henceforth.
innato [in'nato] *agg* innate.
innegabile [inne'gabile] *agg* undeniable.
innestare [innes'tare] *v* (*piante*) graft; insert; (*med*) inoculate. **innestare una marcia** (*auto*) put into gear. **innesto** *sm* graft; (*auto*) clutch; (*med*) inoculation.
inno ['inno] *sm* hymn. **inno nazionale** national anthem.
innocente [inno'tʃɛnte] *agg* innocent. **dichiararsi innocente** (*dir*) plead not guilty. **innocenza** *sf* innocence.
innocuo [in'nɔkuo] *agg* innocuous, harmless.
innominabile [innomi'nabile] *agg* unmentionable.
innovare [inno'vare] *v* innovate. **innovatore, -trice** *sm, sf* innovator. **innovazione** *sf* innovation.
innumerevole [innume'revole] *agg* innumerable.
inoculare [inoku'lare] *v* inoculate.
inoffensivo [inoffen'sivo] *agg* inoffensive, harmless.
inoltrare [inol'trare] *v* send on, forward. **inoltrarsi** *v* advance.
inoltre [i'noltre] *avv* besides, furthermore.
inondare [inon'dare] *v* flood. **inondazione** *sf* flood.
inoperoso [inope'rozo] *agg* idle; (*econ*) unemployed.
inopportuno [inoppor'tuno] *agg* untimely; inopportune. **inopportunità** *sf* unsuitability; inappropriateness.
inorridire [inorri'dire] *v* horrify; be horrified.
inospitale [inospi'tale] *agg* inhospitable.
inosservato [inosser'vato] *agg* unobserved.
inossidabile [inossi'dabile] *agg* stainless.
inquadrare [inkwa'drare] *v* (*mettre in cornice*) frame; (*fig*) set; (*mil*) organize. **inquadratura** *sf* (*cine, TV*) shot.
inquietare [inkwje'tare] *v* worry. **inquietante** *agg* worrying. **inquieto** *agg* restless; (*preoccupato*) uneasy. **inquietudine** *sf* restlessness, worry.
inquilino [inkwi'lino], **-a** *sm, sf* tenant.
inquinare [inkwi'nare] *v* pollute. **inquinamento** *sm* pollution.
insabbiare [insab'biare] *v* (*pratica*) shelve.
insalata [insa'lata] *sf* salad; (*confusione*) muddle. **insalatiera** *sf* salad-bowl.
insalubre [insa'lubre] *agg* unhealthy.
insanabile [insa'nabile] *agg* incurable.
insanguinare [insangwi'nare] *v* stain with blood.
insaputa [insa'puta] *sf* **all'insaputa di** without the knowledge of.
insaziabile [insa'tsjabile] *agg* insatiable.
inscatolare [inskato'lare] *v* tin, can.
inscenare [inʃe'nare] *v* stage.
insegna [in'seɲa] *sf* (*emblema*) insignia *pl*; (*stemma*) coat of arms; motto; (*cartello*) sign.
insegnare [inse'ɲare] *v* teach. **insegnamento** *sm* teaching, education. **insegnante** *s*(*m*+*f*) teacher.
inseguire [inse'gwire] *v* pursue, chase. **inseguimento** *sm* pursuit, chase.
insensato [insen'sato] *agg* senseless, foolish.
insensibile [insen'sibile] *agg* (*leggerissimo*) imperceptible, very slight; (*indifferente*) insensitive, unfeeling.
inseparabile [insepa'rabile] *agg* inseparable.
inserire [inse'rire] *v* insert. **inserirsi** *v* introduce oneself, appear. **inserto** *sm* supplement. **inserzione** *sf* insertion; (*pubblicitaria*) advertisement.
inservibile [inser'vibile] *agg* useless.
inserviente [inser'vjɛnte] *s*(*m*+*f*) attendant.
insetto [in'sɛtto] *sm* insect. **insetticida** *sm* insecticide.
insicuro [insi'kuro] *agg* insecure.
insidia [in'sidja] *sf* snare, trap; (*pericolo*) danger. **insidioso** *agg* insidious.
insieme [in'sjɛme] *avv* together; (*allo stesso tempo*) at the same time. *sm* whole; (*abbigliamento*) outfit.
insigne [in'siɲe] *agg* notable, illustrious.
insignificante [insiɲifi'kante] *agg* insignificant, trivial.
insignire [insi'ɲire] *v* decorate, honour.
insincero [insin'tʃɛro] *agg* insincere.
insinuare [insinu'are] *v* insinuate, creep. **insinuazione** *sf* insinuation.
insipido [in'sipido] *agg* insipid, tasteless.
***insistere** [in'sistere] *v* insist (on). **insistente** *agg* insistent; (*incessante*) persistent, ceaseless. **insistenza** *sf* insistence.
insocievole [inso'tʃevole] *agg* unsociable.
insoddisfatto [insoddis'fatto] *agg* dissatisfied.

insofferente [insoffe'rente] *agg* intolerant, impatient.
insoffribile [insof'fribile] *agg* unbearable.
insolazione [insola'tsjone] *sf* sunstroke.
insolente [inso'lente] *agg* insolent. **insolenza** *sf* insolence.
insolito [in'sɔlito] *agg* unusual, strange.
insolubile [inso'lubile] *agg* insoluble.
insoluto *agg* unsolved; (*non pagato*) outstanding.
insomma [in'somma] *inter* well! now then! *avv* (*in conclusione*) in short, in other words.
insonnia [in'sonnja] *sf* insomnia, sleeplessness. **insonne** *agg* sleepless; (*fig*) indefatigable.
insopportabile [insoppor'tabile] *agg* unbearable, intolerable.
***insorgere** [in'sordʒere] *v* rebel, rise (up against); protest.
insormontabile [insormon'tabile] *agg* insurmountable.
insospettato [insospet'tato] *agg* unexpected, unsuspected.
insostenibile [insoste'nibile] *agg* (*non difensibile*) untenable; (*non sopportabile*) unbearable.
insostituibile [insostitu'ibile] *agg* irreplaceable.
insperato [inspe'rato] *agg* undreamt of, unexpected.
inspiegabile [inspje'gabile] *agg* inexplicable.
installare [instal'lare] *v* install, establish. **installarsi** *v* settle (down). **installazione** *sf* installation.
insù [in'su] *avv* up.
insubordinato [insubordi'nato] *agg* insubordinate.
insuccesso [insut'tʃɛsso] *sm* failure.
insudiciare [insudi'tʃare] *v* soil, dirty.
insufficiente [insuffi'tʃɛnte] *agg* insufficient, inadequate. **insufficienza** *sf* insufficiency; (*mancanza*) shortage.
insulina [insu'lina] *sf* insulin.
insultare [insul'tare] *v* insult. **insulto** *sm* insult, abuse; (*accesso*) fit.
insuperabile [insupe'rabile] *agg* insuperable, insurmountable; (*imbattibile*) unbeatable.
insurrezione [insurre'tsjone] *sf* insurrection.
insussistente [insussis'tɛnte] *agg* nonexistent, baseless.
intaccare [intak'kare] *v* attack; (*far tacche*) notch, nick; (*consumare*) eat into.
intagliare [inta'ʎare] *v* carve, cut.
intangibile [intan'dʒibile] *agg* intangible.
intanto [in'tanto] *avv* meanwhile, in the meantime; (*fam*: *invece*) but, whereas, while.
intasare [inta'zare] *v* clog, block. **intasamento** *sm* obstruction, blockage.
intascare [intas'kare] *v* pocket.
intatto [in'tatto] *agg* intact.
intavolare [intavo'lare] *v* (*iniziare*) begin.
integrale [integ'rale] *agg* complete, total. **calcolo integrale** *sm* integral calculus. **pane integrale** *sm* wholemeal bread.
integrare [integ'rare] *v* integrate.
integro ['integro] *agg* complete; (*onesto*) upright. **integrità** *sf* integrity.
intelletto [intel'lɛtto] *sm* intellect. **intellettuale** *s*(*m*+*f*), *agg* intellectual.
intelligente [intelli'dʒɛnte] *agg* intelligent. **intelligenza** *sf* intelligence. **intelligibile** *agg* intelligible.
intemperie [intem'pɛrje] *sf pl* bad weather *sing*.
intempestivo [intempes'tivo] *agg* untimely. **intempestività** *sf* untimeliness.
intendente [inten'dɛnte] *sm* superintendent, administrator. **intendenza** *sf* administration.
***intendere** [in'tɛndere] *v* (*udire*) hear; (*comprendere*) understand; (*aver intenzione*, *volere*) intend; (*significare*) mean. **intendersi** *v* (*andar d'accordo*) agree, get on; (*essere competente*) be knowledgeable (about). **s'intende** of course, it goes without saying.
intenditore [intendi'tore], **-trice** *sm*, *sf* connoisseur, good judge.
intenso [in'tɛnso] *agg* intense. **intensificare** *v* intensify. **intensità** *sf* intensity.
intento [in'tɛnto] *agg* busy. *sm* object, end.
intenzione [inten'tsjone] *sf* intention. **aver l'intenzione di** intend to. **bene/male intenzionato** *agg* well-/ill-disposed.
intercettare [intertʃet'tare] *v* intercept.
***interdire** [inter'dire] *v* (*proibire*) forbid; (*dir*) disqualify. **interdizione** *sf* ban, disqualification.
interessare [interes'sare] *v* interest; (*riguardare*) concern; (*stare a cuore*) matter. **interessarsi** *v* take an interest (in); (*prendersi cura*) look after, take care (of). **interessato** *agg* interested, concerned;

(*oppportunistico*) self-interested. **interesse** *sm* interest; (*tornaconto*) profit.
interferire [interfe'rire] *v* interfere. **interferenza** *sf* interference.
interiore [inte'rjore] *agg* inner, interior.
intermedio [inter'medjo] *agg* intermediate. **intermediario, -a** *s, agg* intermediary.
interminabile [intermi'nabile] *agg* endless, never-ending.
internare [inter'nare] *v* intern; (*med*) commit. **internamento** *sm* internment; commitment. **internato** *sm* (*convitto*) boarding school; (*scolaro*) boarder.
internazionale [internatsjo'nale] *agg* international.
interno [in'terno] *agg* inner, internal. *sm* inside, interior; (*telefono*) extension.
intero [in'tero] *sm, agg* whole. **per intero** in full.
interpellare [interpel'lare] *v* ask, consult.
interpretare [interpre'tare] *v* interpret, explain; (*teatro, ecc.*) play. **interpretazione** *sf* interpretation. **interprete** *s(m+f)* interpreter; (*teatro, ecc.*) actor, performer; (*cantante*) singer.
interrare [inter'rare] *v* inter, bury.
interrogare [interro'gare] *v* interrogate, question; examine, test; consult. **interrogatorio** *sm* examination; questioning. **interrogazione** *sf* interrogation; (*domanda*) question; (*dir*) questioning, examination.
***interrompere** [inter'rompere] *v* interrupt, break (off).
interruttore [interrut'tore] *sm* switch.
interruzione [interru'tsjone] *sf* interruption, break.
interurbano [interur'bano] *agg* **chiamata** *or* **telefonata interurbana** *sf* trunk-call.
intervallo [inter'vallo] *sm* interval, break.
***intervenire** [interve'nire] *v* intervene; (*assistere*) take part, attend; (*med*) operate. **intervento** *sm* intervention; operation.
intervista [inter'vista] *sf* interview. **intervistare** *v* interview. **intervistatore, -trice** *sm, sf* interviewer.
intesa [in'teza] *sf* agreement, understanding; (*pol*) entente. **inteso** *agg* (*volto a un fine*) intended, meant; (*compreso*) understood; (*convenuto*) agreed. **ben inteso** understood.
intestare [intes'tare] *v* head; (*mettere a nome di*) make out to. **intestatario, -a** *sm, sf* holder.
intestino [intes'tino] *sm* intestine.
intimare [inti'mare] *v* order; (*dichiarare*) declare.
intimidire [intimi'dire] *v* intimidate.
intimità [intimi'ta] *sf* intimacy; (*ambiente intimo, fig*) privacy.
intimo ['intimo] *agg* intimate; (*interno*) innermost. *sm* (*amico*) close friend; (*anima*) heart of hearts. **biancheria intima** *sf* underwear.
intimorire [intimo'rire] *v* intimidate, frighten.
***intingere** [in'tindʒere] *v* dip.
intingolo [in'tingolo] *sm* (*piatto*) stew; (*salsa*) sauce, gravy.
intirizzire [intirit'tsire] *v* grow numb. **intirizzito** *agg* numb.
intitolare [intito'lare] *v* entitle; dedicate.
intollerabile [intolle'rabile] *agg* intolerable, unbearable.
intollerante [intolle'rante] *agg* intolerant.
intonaco [in'tɔnako] *sm* plaster. **intonacare** *v* plaster, whitewash.
intonare [into'nare] *v* (*accordare*) tune, (*cominciare a cantare*) intone, strike up; (*armonizzare*) match.
intontire [inton'tire] *v* daze.
intorno [in'torno] *avv* around; (*circa*) about; (*argomento*) on, about.
intorpidire [intorpi'dire] *v* grow numb.
intossicante [intossi'kante] *agg* poisoning. **intossicazione** *sf* poisoning.
intraducibile [intradu'tʃibile] *agg* untranslatable.
intralciare [intral'tʃare] *v* hold up, hinder. **intralcio** *sm* hindrance, obstacle.
intransigente [intransi'dʒɛnte] *agg* intransigent.
intransitivo [intransi'tivo] *agg* intransitive.
***intraprendere** [intra'prɛndere] *v* undertake, take on, begin. **intraprendente** *agg* enterprising. **intraprendenza** *sf* enterprise, initiative.
intrattabile [intrat'tabile] *agg* intractable; (*fam*) impossible, difficult.
***intrattenere** [intratte'nere] *v* entertain. **intrattenersi** *v* linger; (*indugiare su*) dwell (on).
***intravedere** [intrave'dere] *v* catch a glimpse (of); (*intuire*) sense.
intreccio [in'trettʃo] *sm* plaiting; (*trama*) plot. **intrecciare** *v* intertwine; (*capelli*) braid.

intrepido [in'trɛpido] *agg* intrepid, brave.
intrigo [in'trigo] *sm, pl* **-ghi** plot, intrigue. **intrigare** *v* plot, intrigue.
intrinseco [in'trinseko] *agg* intrinsic.
intriso [in'trizo] *agg* soaked.
***introdurre** [intro'durre] *v* introduce; (*inserire*) insert; (*far entrare*) show in. **introdotto** *agg* (*conosciuto*) well-known, well-established; (*esperto*) well up in. **introduzione** *sf* introduction.
introito [in'trɔito] *sm* income; (*incasso*) takings *pl*.
***intromettersi** [intro'mettersi] *v* meddle, intervene.
intronare [intro'nare] *v* deafen.
introspettivo [introspet'tivo] *agg* introspective.
introvabile [intro'vabile] *agg* unobtainable, not to be found.
introverso [intro'vɛrso], **-a** *s, agg* introvert.
intrusione [intru'zjone] *sf* intrusion. **intruso, -a** *sm, sf* intruder.
intuitivo [intui'tivo] *agg* intuitive. **intuire** *v* sense. **intuito** *sm* intuition, instinct, insight.
inumano [inu'mano] *agg* inhuman.
inumidire [inumi'dire] *v* moisten.
inusitato [inuzi'tato] *agg* uncommon.
inutile [i'nutile] *agg* useless; (*non necessario*) unnecessary.
invadente [inva'dɛnte] *agg* intrusive. *s*(*m*+*f*) busybody.
***invadere** [in'vadere] *v* invade, flood.
invalido [in'valido], **-a** *agg* invalid; (*privo di valore*) null and void; (*mutilato*) disabled. *sm, sf* invalid; disabled person. **invalidare** *v* (*dir*) invalidate.
invano [in'vano] *avv* in vain. *agg* vain, useless.
invariabile [inva'rjabile] *agg* invariable, even. **invariato** *agg* unchanged.
invasione [inva'zjone] *sf* invasion.
invecchiare [invek'kjare] *v* age. **invecchiamento** *sm* ageing.
invece [in'vetʃe] *avv* instead (of); (*mentre*) whereas, while.
invendibile [inven'dibile] *agg* unsaleable. **invenduto** *agg* unsold.
inventare [inven'tare] *v* invent. **inventore** *sm* inventor. **invenzione** *sf* invention.
inventario [inven'tarjo] *sm* inventory.
inverno [in'vɛrno] *sm* winter. **invernale** *agg* winter, wintry.
inverosimile [invero'simile] *agg* unlikely.
inverso [in'vɛrso] *agg* contrary, opposite; (*mat*) inverse. *sm* contrary, opposite. **inversione** *sf* inversion; (*tec*) reversal.
invertebrato [inverte'brato] *sm, agg* invertebrate.
investigare [investi'gare] *v* investigate.
investire [inves'tire] *v* (*comm*) invest; (*scontrare*) collide, hit; (*scontrare persone*) hit, run down. **investimento** *sm* investment; collision, crash.
invetriata [invetri'ata] *sf* (*porta*) glass-door; (*finestra*) window.
invettiva [invet'tiva] *sf* invective.
inviare [invi'are] *v* dispatch, send (off). **inviato, -a** *sm, sf* (*diplomatico*) envoy; (*giornale*) correspondent. **invio** *sm* dispatch.
invidiare [invi'djare] *v* envy. **invidia** *sf* envy. **invidioso** *agg* envious.
invigorire [invigo'rire] *v* invigorate, strengthen.
invincibile [invin'tʃibile] *agg* invincible.
invisibile [invi'zibile] *agg* invisible.
invitare [invi'tare] *v* invite. **invitato, -a** *sm, sf* guest. **invito** *sm* invitation.
invocare [invo'kare] *v* invoke, call for.
invogliare [invo'ʎare] *v* tempt.
***involgere** [in'vɔldʒere] *v* wrap (up).
involontario [involon'tarjo] *agg* involuntary.
involtino [invol'tino] *sm* (*gastr*) roulade, olive.
involto [in'vɔlto] *sm* bundle, package.
involucro [in'vɔlukro] *sm* covering, wrapper.
invulnerabile [invulne'rabile] *agg* invulnerable.
inzaccherare [indzakke'rare] *v* spatter with mud.
inzuppare [indzup'pare] *v* soak.
io ['io] *pron* I. *sm* self.
iodio ['jɔdjo] *sm* iodine.
ione ['jone] *sm* ion.
iperbole [i'pɛrbole] *sf* hyperbole. **iperbolico** *agg* exaggerated; (*mat*) hyperbolic.
ipertensione [iperten'sjone] *sf* hypertension. **iperteso** *agg* hypertensive.
ipnosi [ip'nɔzi] *sf* hypnosis. **ipnotico** *agg* hypnotic. **ipnotismo** *sm* hypnotism.
ipnotizzare [ipnotid'dzare] *v* hypnotize. **ipnotizzatore, -trice** *sm, sf* hypnotist.
ipocondriaco [ipokon'driako], **-a** *s, agg* hypochondriac. **ipocondria** *sf* hypochondria.

ipocrita [i'pɔkrita] *s(m+f)* hypocrite. *agg* hypocritical. **ipocrisia** *sf* hypocrisy.
ipoteca [ipo'tɛka] *sf* mortgage. **ipotecare** *v* mortgage.
ipotenusa [ipote'nuza] *sf* hypotenuse.
ipotesi [i'pɔtezi] *sf* hypothesis (*pl* -ses). **nella migliore delle ipotesi** at best. **nella peggiore delle ipotesi** if the worst comes to the worst. **ipotetico** *agg* hypothetical.
ippica ['ippika] *sf* horse-racing. **ippico** *agg* horse.
ippocampo [ippo'kampo] *sm* sea-horse.
ippocastano [ippokas'tano] *sm* horse-chestnut.
ippodromo [ip'pɔdromo] *sm* racecourse.
ippopotamo [ippo'pɔtamo] *sm* hippopotamus.
ira ['ira] *sf* rage, anger. **irascibile** *agg* irascible.
iride ['iride] *sf* iris; (*arcobaleno*) rainbow.
Irlanda [ir'landa] *sf* Ireland. **irlandese** *sm, agg* Irish. **gli irlandesi** the Irish.
ironia [iro'nia] *sf* irony. **ironico** *agg* ironic(al).
irradiare [irra'djare] *v* radiate; (*fig*) irradiate.
irraggiungibile [irraddʒun'dʒibile] *agg* unattainable.
irragionevole [irradʒo'nevole] *agg* unreasonable.
irrazionale [irratsjo'nale] *agg* irrational.
irreale [irre'ale] *agg* unreal.
irregolare [irrego'lare] *agg* irregular. **irregolarità** *sf* irregularity.
irreperibile [irrepe'ribile] *agg* that cannot be found.
irrequieto [irre'kwjɛto] *agg* restless.
irresistibile [irrezis'tibile] *agg* irresistible.
irresoluto [irrezo'luto] *agg* wavering, undecided. **irresolutezza** *sf* indecision, wavering.
irresponsabile [irrespon'sabile] *agg* irresponsible. **irresponsabilità** *sf* irresponsibility.
irrigare [irri'gare] *v* irrigate. **irrigazione** *sf* irrigation.
irrigidire [irridʒi'dire] *v* stiffen. **irrigidimento** *sm* stiffening; (*fig*) obstinacy.
irrimediabile [irrime'djabile] *agg* irreparable.
irrisorio [irri'zɔrjo] *agg* derisory, ridiculous.
irritare [irri'tare] *v* irritate; (*dar fastidio*) annoy. **irritabile** *agg* irritable. **irritante** *agg* irritating; (*med*) irritant. **irritazione** *sf* irritation.
irriverenza [irrive'rɛntsa] *sf* disrespect.
***irrompere** [ir'rompere] *v* burst into; (*riversarsi*) pour into.
irsuto [ir'suto] *agg* shaggy, hairy.
irto ['irto] *agg* bristling (with).
***iscrivere** [is'krivere] *v* enrol, register; (*diventar socio*) join. **iscritto** *sm* member. **iscrizione** *sf* registration, enrolment; (*scritta*) inscription.
Islanda [is'landa] *sf* Iceland. **islandese** *sm, agg* Icelandic; *s(m+f)* Icelander.
isola ['izola] *sf* island.
isolare [izo'lare] *v* isolate; (*fis*) insulate. **isolamento** *sm* isolation; insulation.
ispettore [ispet'tore], **-trice** *sm, sf* inspector.
ispezionare [ispetsjo'nare] *v* inspect. **ispezione** *sf* inspection.
ispirare [ispi'rare] *v* inspire.
issare [is'sare] *v* hoist.
istamina [ista'mina] *sf* histamine.
istante [is'tante] *sm* instant, moment. **istantanea** *sf* snapshot. **istantaneo** *agg* instantaneous.
istanza [is'tantsa] *sf* (*domanda*) application, petition.
isterico [is'tɛriko] *agg* hysterical. **attacco isterico** *sm* hysterics *pl*. **isteria** *sf* hysteria.
istigare [isti'gare] *v* instigate.
istillare [istil'lare] *v* instil.
istinto [is'tinto] *sm* instinct.
istituire [istitu'ire] *v* institute, establish.
istituto [isti'tuto] *sm* institute; (*ente*) institution, organization. **istituzione** *sf* institution.
istrice ['istritʃe] *sm* porcupine; (*persona scontrosa*) touchy person.
***istruire** [istru'ire] *v* instruct, educate. **istruire un processo** (*dir*) prepare a case. **istruttore, -trice** *sm, sf* instructor, -tress, teacher. **giudice istruttore** *sm* examining magistrate. **istruttoria** *sf* (*dir*) examination. **istruttorio** *agg* preliminary. **istruzione** *sf* instruction, education, tuition.
Italia [i'talja] *sf* Italy. **italiano, -a** *s, agg* Italian.
itinerario [itine'rarjo] *sm* itinerary, route.
itterizia [itte'ritsja] *sf* jaundice.
Iugoslavia [jugo'slavja] *sf* Yugoslavia. **iugoslavo, -a** *s, agg* Yugoslav.
iuta ['juta] *sf* jute.

L

la[1] ['la] *art* the.
la[2] [la] *pron* (*cosa, animale*) it; (*persona*) her; (*formula di cortesia*) you.
là [la] *avv* there. **di là** (*nell'altra stanza*) in the other room; (*da quella parte*) that way. **in là** (*oltre*) further. **va là!** come off it!
labbro ['labbro] *sm, pl* **-a** *f in anat sense* lip; (*orlo*) brim.
labirinto [labi'rinto] *sm* labyrinth, maze.
laboratorio [labora'tɔrjo] *sm* laboratory; (*industria*) workshop.
laborioso [labo'rjozo] *agg* laborious.
laburista [labu'rista] *agg* Labour.
lacca ['lakka] *sf* lacquer.
laccio ['lattʃo] *sm* noose; (*trappola*) snare, trap; (*legame*) tie. **laccio da scarpe** shoe-lace.
lacerare [latʃe'rare] *v* lacerate, tear.
lacrima ['lakrima] *sf* tear.
lacrimogeno [lakri'mɔdʒeno] *agg* **gas lacrimogeno** *sm* tear-gas.
lacuna [la'kuna] *sf* gap.
ladro ['ladro] *sm* thief. **al ladro!** stop thief! **vestito come un ladro** dressed like a tramp.
laggiù [lad'dʒu] *avv* down there.
lagnarsi [la'ɲarsi] *v* complain. **lagna** *sf* bore.
lago ['lago] *sm* lake.
laico ['laiko] *agg* lay. *sm* layman.
lama[1] ['lama] *sf* blade. **lametta** *sf* razor-blade.
lama[2] ['lama] *sm invar* (*zool*) llama.
lambiccarsi [lambik'karsi] *v* **lambiccarsi il cervello** rack one's brains.
lambire [lam'bire] *v* lick, lap.
lamentare [lamen'tare] *v* lament. **lamentarsi (di)** complain (about). **lamentela** *sf* complaint. **lamentevole** *agg* pitiful. **lamento** *sm* lament. **lamentoso** *agg* plaintive.
lamiera [la'mjɛra] *sf* sheet.
lamina ['lamina] *sf* thin layer; (*metallo*) foil. **laminare** *v* (*riddure in lamine*) roll; (*coprire con lamine*) laminate. **laminato** *sm* laminate. **laminatoio** *sm* rolling-mill.
lampada ['lampada] *sf* lamp. **lampadario** *sm* chandelier. **lampadina** *sf* (light) bulb. **lampadina tascabile** torch.
lampeggiare [lamped'dʒare] *v* flash.
lampione [lam'pjone] *sm* lamp-post.
lampo ['lampo] *sm* flash; (*temporale*) lightning. **cerniera lampo** *sf* zip.
lampone [lam'pone] *sm* raspberry.
lampreda [lam'prɛda] *sf* lamprey.
lana ['lana] *sf* wool. **di lana** woollen. **industria laniera** *sf* wool industry. **lanificio** *sm* woollen mill.
lancetta [lan'tʃetta] *sf* hand.
lancia[1] ['lantʃa] *sf* (*arma*) lance.
lancia[2] ['lantʃa] *sf* (*barca*) launch. **lancia di salvataggio** lifeboat.
lanciare [lan'tʃare] *v* throw, fling; (*diffondere*) launch; (*bombe*) drop. **lanciafiamme** *sm invar* flame-thrower. **lanciamissili** *sm invar* rocket-launcher. **lanciare un grido** utter a cry. **lancio** *sm* throw, fling; launching.
languire [lan'gwire] *v* languish; (*diminuire di forza*) flag. **languido** *agg* languid.
lanterna [lan'tɛrna] *sf* lantern.
lanugine [la'nudʒine] *sf* down.
lapide ['lapide] *sf* (*sepolcrale*) tombstone; (*commemorativa*) memorial tablet.
lapis ['lapis] *sm* pencil.
lardo ['lardo] *sm* lard, dripping.
largo ['largo] *agg* wide, broad. **al largo di** away from, off. **far largo a** make room for. **larghezza** *sf* width, breadth; (*fig*) generosity.
larice ['laritʃe] *sm* larch.
laringe [la'rindʒe] *sf* larynx. **laringite** *sf* laryngitis.
larva ['larva] *sf* larva; (*spettro*) shadow.
lasciare [la'ʃare] *v* leave; (*permettere*) let. **lascito** *sm* legacy.
lascivo [la'ʃivo] *agg* lascivious.
laser ['lazer] *sm invar* laser.
lassativo [lassa'tivo] *sm, agg* laxative.
lasso ['lasso] *sm* (*periodo*) lapse. *agg* (*rilassato*) loose.
lassù [las'su] *avv* up there.
lastra ['lastra] *sf* plate; sheet.
lastricare [lastri'kare] *v* pave. **lastrico** *sm* pavement; (*miseria*) poverty.
latente [la'tɛnte] *agg* latent.
laterale [late'rale] *agg* lateral, side.
laterizi [late'ritsi] *sm pl* bricks *pl*, tiles *pl*.
latice ['latitʃe] *sm* latex.
latino [la'tino] *sm, agg* Latin.
latitante [lati'tante] *agg* fugitive. **rendersi latitante** abscond.
latitudine [lati'tudine] *sf* latitude.

lato[1] ['lato] *sm* side. **da un lato ... dall'altro ...** on the one hand ... on the other .... **d'altro lato** on the other hand.
lato[2] ['lato] *agg* **in senso lato** in a broad sense.
latrare [la'trare] *v* bark.
latrina [la'trina] *sf* latrine.
latta ['latta] *sf* (*lamiera*) tin, tinplate; (*recipiente*) tin, can.
lattaio [lat'tajo] *sm* milkman.
latte ['latte] *sm* milk. **latte magro** skimmed milk. **latteo** *agg* milky. **latteria** *sf* dairy. **lattiera** *sf* milk jug.
lattuga [lat'tuga] *sf* lettuce.
laurea ['laurea] *sf* degree. **laurearsi** *v* graduate. **laureato, -a** *sm, sf* graduate. **essere laureato in ...** have a degree in ....
lauro ['lauro] *sm* laurel.
lauto ['lauto] *agg* generous, sumptuous.
lava ['lava] *sf* lava.
lavabo [la'vabo] *sm* wash-basin.
lavaggio [la'vaddʒo] *sm* washing. **lavaggio a secco** dry-cleaning. **lavaggio del cervello** brain-washing.
lavagna [la'vaɲa] *sf* slate; (*scolastica*) blackboard.
lavanda[1] [la'vanda] *sf* (*bot*) lavender.
lavanda[2] [la'vanda] *sf* wash(ing).
lavandaia [lavan'daja] *sf* laundress, washer-woman.
lavanderia [lavande'ria] *sf* laundry; (*a gettoni*) launderette.
lavandino [lavan'dino] *sm* sink.
lavapiatti [lava'pjatti] *sm also* **lavastoviglie** *invar* dishwasher.
lavatrice [lava'tritʃe] *sf* washing machine.
lavare [la'vare] *v* wash. **lavare a secco** *v* dry-clean. **lavare il capo a** tell off. **lavarsi** *v* (have a) wash. **lavata di capo** *sf* telling-off. **lavatura** *sf* washing; (*acqua sporca*) dishwater.
lavativo [lava'tivo] *sm* (*fam*) bore, pain in the neck.
lavorare [lavo'rare] *v* work; (*con fatica*) labour; (*aziende, negozi, ecc.*) do business; (*il terreno*) till; (*teatro, ecc.*) act, play. **lavorativo** *agg* working. **lavorato** *agg* finished; (*metallo*) wrought; (*a macchina*) machined.
lavoratore [lavora'tore], **-trice** *sm, sf* worker. **lavoratore a cottimo** piece-worker.
lavorazione [lavora'tsjone] *sf* manufacture; (*fattura*) workmanship; work. **lavorazione in serie** mass-production.
lavoro [la'voro] *sm* work; (*occupazione*) job; (*teatro, ecc.*) play. **lavori di casa** *sm pl* housework *sing*. **lavoro a cottimo** *sm* piece-work. **lavoro straordinario** *sm* overtime.
lazzarone [laddza'rone] *sm* scoundrel.
le[1] [le] *art* the.
le[2] [le] *pron* (*persona*) (to) her; (*cosa, animale*) (to) it; (*formula di cortesia*) (to) you; (*pl*) them.
leale [le'ale] *agg* sincere; (*onesto*) fair. **lealtà** *sf* loyalty, fairness.
lebbroso [leb'brozo], **-a** *agg* leprous. *sm, sf* leper. **lebbra** *sf* leprosy.
leccare [lek'kare] *v* lick. **leccalecca** *sm invar* (*fam*) lollipop. **leccapiedi** *sm invar* (*fam*) bootlicker. **leccare i piedi a** lick the boots of. **leccornia** *sf* titbit, tasty morsel.
lecito ['letʃito] *agg* (*dir*) lawful; (*permesso*) allowed.
lega ['lega] *sf* league, alliance; (*metalli*) alloy.
legale [le'gale] *agg* legal; (*legittimo*) lawful. **medicina legale** *sf* forensic medicine. **numero legale** *sm* quorum. **ora legale** *sf* summer-time. **legalizzare** *v* legalize, certify.
legame [le'game] *sm* tie, bond; (*fig*) link; (*amoroso*) liaison.
legare [le'gare] *v* tie (up), bind; (*assicurare*) fasten. **matto da legare** crazy, mad as a hatter.
legato [le'gato] *agg* tied (up); (*libro*) bound; (*impacciato*) stiff. *sm* (*papale*) legate; (*testamento*) legacy.
legatura [lega'tura] *sf* binding.
legge ['leddʒe] *sf* law; (*votata dal parlamento*) act (of parliament); (*norma di condotta*) rule. **progetto di legge** *sm* bill. **proposta di legge** *sf* draft bill.
leggenda [led'dʒɛnda] *sf* legend; (*didascalia*) caption. **leggendario** *agg* legendary.
***leggere** ['leddʒere] *v* read.
leggero [led'dʒɛro] *agg* light; (*lieve*) slight. **leggerezza** *sf* lightness; (*frivolezza*) levity; (*sconsideratezza*) thoughtlessness.
leggiadro [led'dʒadro] *agg* graceful, lovely.
leggibile [led'dʒibile] *agg* readable, legible.
leggio [led'dʒio] *sm* music stand; (*chiesa*) lectern.

legione [le'dʒone] *sf* legion.
legislazione [ledʒizla'tsjone] *sf* legislation. **legislatore** *sm* legislator.
legittimo [le'dʒittimo] *agg* lawful; (*tale per legge*) legitimate; proper; justifiable.
legna ['leɲa] *sf invar* firewood. **mettere legna al fuoco** add fuel to the fire.
legname [le'ɲame] *sm* timber; (*in tronchi*) logs *pl*.
legnata [le'ɲata] *sf* blow. **un sacco di legnate** *sm* (*fam*) a good hiding.
legno ['leɲo] *sm* wood. **di legno** wooden, wood. **lavoro in legno** *sm* woodwork; (*edilizia*) timberwork. **legno compensato** plywood. **legno impiallacciato** veneer.
lei ['lɛi] *pron* (*soggetto*) she; (*oggetto*) her; (*formula di cortesia*) you.
lembo ['lembo] *sm* (*orlo*) edge, border; (*striscia*) strip.
lemme lemme ['lɛmme 'lɛmme] *avv* (*fam*) very leisurely.
lena ['lena] *sf* vigour. **lavorare di buona lena** (*fam*) put one's back into it.
lente ['lɛnte] *sf* lens. **lente a contatto** contact lens. **lente d'ingrandimento** magnifying glass. **lenti** *sf pl* glasses *pl*.
lenticchia [len'tikkja] *sf* lentil.
lentiggine [len'tiddʒine] *sf* freckle. **lentigginoso** *agg* freckled.
lento ['lɛnto] *agg* slow; (*allentato*) loose. **lento a capire** slow in the uptake.
lenza ['lɛntsa] *sf* (fishing-)line.
lenzuolo [len'tswɔlo] *sm*, *pl* **-a** *f when referring to a pair* sheet.
leone [le'one] *sm* lion. **leonessa** *sf* lioness.
leopardo [leo'pardo] *sm* leopard.
lepido ['lepido] *agg* witty.
lepre ['lepre] *sf* hare. **lepre in salmì** jugged hare. **labbro leporino** *sm* hare-lip.
lesbico ['lɛzbiko] *agg* lesbian. **lesbica** *sf* lesbian.
lesina ['lezina] *sf* awl; (*taccagneria*) (*fam*) meanness. **lesinare** *v* skimp.
lesione [le'zjone] *sf* injury; (*med*) lesion; (*danno*) damage. **parte lesa** *sf* injured party.
lessare [les'sare] *v* boil. **lesso** *sm* boiled meat.
lessico ['lɛssiko] *sm* lexicon; vocabulary.
lesto ['lɛsto] *agg* swift, quick. **lesto di lingua** glib. **lesto di mano** light-fingered. **lestofante** *sm* swindler.
letale [le'tale] *agg* lethal, deadly.
letame [le'tame] *sm* manure, dung; (*fig*) filth. **letamaio** *sm* dung-heap; (*luogo sudicio*) pigsty.
letargico [le'tardʒiko] *agg* lethargic. **letargo** *sm* (*zool*) hibernation; (*med, torpore*) lethargy.
letizia [le'titsja] *sf* joy, gladness.
lettera ['lettera] *sf* letter. **alla lettera** literally; verbatim. **lettera d'accompagnamento/raccomandata** covering/registered letter. **lettera di sollecitazione** reminder. **lettera maiuscola/minuscola** capital/small letter.
letterario [lette'rarjo] *agg* literary.
letteratura [lettera'tura] *sf* literature.
lettiga [let'tiga] *sf* litter; (*barella*) stretcher.
letto ['lɛtto] *sm* bed.
lettore [let'tore], **-trice** *sm, sf* reader; (*universitario*) modern language lecturer.
lettura [let'tura] *sf* reading.
leucemia [leutʃe'mia] *sf* leukaemia.
leva[1] ['lɛva] *sf* (*mec*) lever; (*fig*) incentive. **far leva** lever. **far leva su** exploit, play on.
leva[2] ['lɛva] *sf* call-up; conscripts *pl*.
levante [le'vante] *sm* east.
levare [le'vare] *v* (*alzare*) raise, lift; (*togliere*) take away *or* off; (*estrarre*) pull out. **levare di mezzo** get rid of, remove. **levarsi** *v* (*alzarsi*) rise; (*dal letto*) get up. **levarsi la fame** satisfy one's hunger. **levarsi la sete** quench one's thirst. **levata della posta** *sf* mail collection. **levata del sole** *sf* sunrise.
levatoio [leva'tojo] *agg* **ponte levatoio** *sm* drawbridge.
levatrice [leva'tritʃe] *sf* midwife.
levigare [levi'gare] *v* smooth; polish; (*pomiciare*) rub down; (*con carta vetrata*) sand down.
levriere [le'vrjɛre] *sm* greyhound.
lezione [le'tsjone] *sf* lesson; class; (*durata*) period; (*universitaria*) lecture.
lezioso [le'tsjozo] *agg* affected, mannered.
lezzo ['lettso] *sm* stench; (*sudiciume*) filth.
li [li] *pron* them.
lì [li] *avv* there. **giù di lì** thereabouts. **lì per lì** (*sul momento*) there and then; (*dapprima*) at first.
libbra ['libbra] *sf* pound.
libellula [li'bellula] *sf* dragonfly.
liberale [libe'rale] *s*(*m*+*f*), *agg* liberal.
liberare [libe'rare] *v* free, liberate; (*salvare*) save, rescue. **liberazione** *sf* liberation; release.

libero ['libero] *agg* free; (*sgombro*) clear; exempt. **aria libera** *sf* open air. **libero pensatore** *sm* freethinker. **tempo libero** *sm* time off.

libertà [liber'ta] *sf* freedom, liberty. **giorno di libertà** *sm* day off. **libertà condizionata** probation. **libertà provvisoria** bail. **mettere in libertà** set free.

Libra ['libra] *sf* Libra.

libraio [li'brajo] *sm* bookseller. **libreria** *sf* (*negozio*) bookshop; (*raccolta di libri*) library; (*casa editrice*) publishers *pl*.

libro ['libro] *sm* book. **a libro** hinged. **libro di cassa** cash register. **libro giallo** thriller. **libro mastro** ledger. **libro nero** blacklist.

licenza [li'tʃɛntsa] *sf* licence, permission; (*scuola*) leaving certificate.

licenziare [litʃen'tsjare] *v* dismiss. **licenziamento** *sm* dismissal.

liceo [li'tʃɛo] *sm* secondary school, high school.

lichene [li'kɛne] *sm* lichen.

lido ['lido] *sm* shore.

lieto ['ljɛto] *agg* glad, happy.

lieve ['ljɛve] *agg* slight, light.

lievito ['ljɛvito] *sm* yeast; (*fig*) ferment.

lignaggio [li'ɲaddʒo] *sm* lineage, pedigree.

ligustro [li'gustro] *sm* privet.

lilla ['lilla] *agg, sm invar* lilac.

lima ['lima] *sf* file. **limare** *v* file. **limatura** *sf* filing; (*polvere*) filings *pl*.

limitare [limi'tare] *v* limit, restrict. **limitazione** *sf* limitation, restraint.

limite ['limite] *sm* limit; (*confine*) boundary. **caso limite** *sm* borderline case. **limitrofo** *agg* bordering.

limo ['limo] *sm* mud, slime.

limone [li'mone] *sm* (*albero*) lemon-tree; (*frutto*) lemon. **limonata** *sf* lemonade.

limpido ['limpido] *agg* clear.

lince ['lintʃe] *sf* lynx.

linciare [lin'tʃare] *v* lynch. **linciaggio** *sm* lynching.

lindo ['lindo] *agg* clean, tidy.

linea ['linea] *sf* line; (*corpo umano*) figure. **lineetta** *sf* dash.

lineamenti [linea'menti] *sm pl* features *pl*; (*elementi essenziali*) outlines *pl*.

lineare [line'are] *agg* linear; coherent; (*di indirizzo stabile*) unswerving.

linfa ['linfa] *sf* lymph; (*bot*) sap.

lingua ['lingwa] *sf* tongue; (*linguaggio*) language. **linguaggio** *sm* language.

linguista *s(m+f)* linguist. **linguistico** *agg* linguistic.

lino ['lino] *sm* (*pianta*) flax; (*tessuto*) linen. **olio di lino** *sm* linseed oil.

liocorno [lio'kɔrno] *sm* unicorn.

liquefare [likwe'fare] *v* liquefy, melt. **liquefazione** *sf* liquefaction.

liquidare [likwi'dare] *v* liquidate; (*conti*) settle; (*merci*) sell off; (*sciogliere*) wind up. **liquidazione** *sf* liquidation, settlement; (*svendita*) clearance sale; winding-up; (*indennità*) leaving bonus. **liquidatore** *sm* receiver.

liquido ['likwido] *sm, agg* liquid, fluid.

liquirizia [likwi'ritsja] *sf* liquorice.

liquore [li'kwore] *sm* liqueur.

lira[1] ['lira] *sf* (*moneta*) lira. **lira sterlina** pound sterling.

lira[2] ['lira] *sf* (*musica*) lyre.

lirico ['liriko] *agg* lyrical; opera. **cantante lirico** *s(m+f)* opera singer. **dramma lirico** *sm* opera. **teatro lirico** *sm* opera house. **lirica** *sf* lyric poetry.

lisca ['liska] *sf* fish-bone.

lisciare [li'ʃare] *v* smooth. **liscio** *agg* smooth; (*bevanda*) neat. **andar liscio** go smoothly. **passarla liscia** get off scot-free.

liseuse [li'zøz] *sf, pl* -s bed-jacket.

liso ['lizo] *agg* worn.

lista ['lista] *sf* (*striscia*) strip; (*elenco*) list. **lista elettorale** electoral register. **listare** *v* border. **listino** *sm* list.

litania [lita'nia] *sf* litany.

lite ['lite] *sf* quarrel; (*dir*) (law)suit.

litigare [liti'gare] *v* quarrel. **litigio** *sm* quarrel, row. **litigioso** *agg* quarrelsome; (*dir*) contentious.

litorale [lito'rale] *agg* coastal. *sm* shore.

litro ['litro] *sm* litre.

liturgia [litur'dʒia] *sf* liturgy. **liturgico** *agg* liturgical.

liuto [li'uto] *sm* lute.

livellare [livel'lare] *v* level. **livella** *sf* level. **livellatore, -trice** *sm, sf* leveller.

livello [li'vello] *sm* level. **livello del mare** sea-level. **passaggio a livello** *sm* level crossing.

livido ['livido] *agg* livid. *sm* bruise.

Livorno [li'vorno] *sf* Leghorn.

livrea [li'vrɛa] *sf* livery.

lizza ['littsa] *sf* **entrare in lizza** compete.

lo[1] [lo] *art* the.

lo[2] [lo] *pron* (*persona*) him; (*cosa, animale*) it.

lobo ['lɔbo] *sm* lobe.
locale[1] [lo'kale] *agg* local.
locale[2] [lo'kale] *sm* room, spot. **locale notturno** night-club. **località** *sf* locality.
localizzare [lokalid'dzare] *v* (*individuare*) locate; (*circoscrivere*) localize.
locanda [lo'kanda] *sf* inn. **locandiere, -a** *sm, sf* innkeeper.
locatario [loka'tarjo] *sm* tenant.
locatore [loka'tore] *sm* landlord.
locazione [loka'tsjone] *sf* lease, tenancy.
locomotiva [lokomo'tiva] *sf* locomotive, engine.
lodare [lo'dare] *v* praise. **lode** *sf* praise. **lodevole** *agg* praiseworthy.
logaritmo [loga'ritmo] *sm* logarithm.
loggia ['loddʒa] *sf* loggia; (*massone*) lodge. **loggione** *sm* gallery.
logica ['lɔdʒika] *sf* logic. **logico** *agg* logical.
logistica [lo'dʒistika] *sf* logistics. **logistico** *agg* logistic(al).
logorare [logo'rare] *v* wear out. **logoramento** *sm* wear; (*mentale*) strain. **logorio** *sm* wear and tear. **logoro** *agg* worn out.
Londra ['londra] *sf* London. **londinese** *s(m+f)* Londoner.
longevo [lon'dʒɛvo] *agg* long-lived. **longevità** *sf* longevity.
longitudine [londʒi'tudine] *sf* longitude. **longitudinale** *agg* longitudinal.
lontano [lon'tano] *agg* far, far away; (*assente*) absent; distant; vague. *avv* far. **lontananza** *sf* distance.
lontra ['lontra] *sf* otter.
loquace [lo'kwatʃe] *agg* loquacious.
lordo ['lordo] *agg* (*peso*) gross; (*sporco*) filthy.
loro ['loro] *pron* (*soggetto*) they; (*oggetto*) them; (*formula di cortesia*) you; (*di essi*) theirs. *agg* their.
losco ['losko] *agg* sinister.
loto ['lɔto] *sm* lotus.
lotta ['lɔtta] *sf* struggle, fight; (*sport*) wrestling. **lottare** *v* struggle, fight; wrestle.
lotteria [lotte'ria] *sf* lottery.
lotto ['lɔtto] *sm* portion; (*comm*) lot; lottery.
lozione [lo'tsjone] *sf* lotion.
lubrificante [lubrifi'kante] *agg* lubricating. *sm* lubricant. **lubrificare** *v* lubricate. **lubrificazione** *sf* lubrication.
lucchetto [luk'ketto] *sm* padlock.
luccicare [luttʃi'kare] *v* shine, sparkle.
luccio ['luttʃo] *sm* pike.
lucciola ['luttʃola] *sf* firefly.
luce ['lutʃe] *sf* light.
lucernario [lutʃer'narjo] *sm* skylight.
lucertola [lu'tʃɛrtola] *sf* lizard.
lucidare [lutʃi'dare] *v* polish.
lucido ['lutʃido] *agg* shiny, glossy; (*fig*) lucid. *sm* polish.
luglio ['luʎo] *sm* July.
lugubre ['lugubre] *agg* lugubrious.
lui ['lui] *pron* (*soggetto*) he; (*oggetto*) him.
lumaca [lu'maka] *sf* snail; (*persona*) slowcoach.
lume ['lume] *sm* light; lamp. **far lume su** throw light on.
luminoso [lumi'nozo] *agg* bright, shining.
luna ['luna] *sf* moon. **avere la luna** be in a bad mood. **luna di miele** honeymoon. **luna-park** *sm invar* fun-fair. **lunare** *agg* lunar. **sbarcare il lunario** make ends meet.
lunedì [lune'di] *sm* Monday.
lungo[1] ['lungo] *agg* long; (*alto*) tall; (*lento*) slow; (*diluito*) weak. **alla lunga** in the long run. **a lungo** (for) long. **di gran lunga** by far. **lunghezza** *sf* length.
lungo[2] ['lungo] *prep* along. **lungomare** *sm* seashore.
luogo ['lwɔgo] *sm* place. **aver luogo** take place. **fuori luogo** out of place. **in luogo di** instead of. **luogotenente** *sm* lieutenant.
lupo ['lupo] *sm* wolf. **lupa** *sf* she-wolf.
luppolo ['luppolo] *sm* hop.
lurido ['lurido] *agg* filthy.
lusingare [luzin'gare] *v* flatter; (*illudere*) delude. **lusinga** *sf* flattery; delusion. **lusinghiero** *agg* flattering, alluring.
Lussemburgo [lussem'burgo] *sm* Luxembourg.
lusso ['lusso] sm luxury. **di lusso** luxury, de luxe. **lussuoso** *agg* luxurious.
lustrare [lus'trare] *v* polish. **lustrino** *sm* sequin. **lustro** *sm* polish, sheen; lustre.
lutto ['lutto] *sm* mourning; (*dolore*) grief.

M

ma [ma] *cong* but. **macché!** *inter* (*neanche per sogno*) of course not! not on your life! **ma davvero?** really? **ma no!** of course not! **ma sì!** of course!

macabro ['makabro] *agg* macabre.
maccheroni [makke'roni] *sm pl* macaroni *sing*.
macchia[1] ['makkja] *sf* spot; stain.
macchia[2] ['makkja] *sf* (*arbusti*) bush.
macchiare [mak'kjare] *v* stain. **caffè macchiato** *sm* coffee with a dash of milk.
macchietta [mak'kjetta] *sf* (*persona*) character.
macchina ['makkina] *sf* machine; (*automobile*) car. **macchina da scrivere** typewriter. **macchina fotografica** camera.
macchinare [makki'nare] *v* plot.
macchinario [makki'narjo] *sm* machinery.
macchinista [makki'nista] *s*(*m*+*f*) machinist; (*ferr*) engine driver.
macedonia [matʃe'dɔnja] *sf* fruit salad.
macellare [matʃel'lare] *v* slaughter. **macelleria** *sf* butcher's shop. **macellaio** *sm* butcher. **macello** *sm* slaughterhouse; (*fig*) shambles.
macerare [matʃe'rare] *v* soak; macerate.
macerie [ma'tʃɛrje] *sf pl* ruins *pl*.
macina ['matʃina] *sf* millstone, grindstone. **macinare** *v* grind. **macinino** *sm* (*da caffè*) coffee-mill; (*da pepe*) pepper-mill.
madido ['madido] *agg* soaking wet.
Madonna [ma'donna] *sf* **la Madonna** the Virgin Mary.
madornale [mador'nale] *agg* gross.
madre ['madre] *sf* mother; (*comm*) counterfoil. **madreperla** *sf* mother-of-pearl.
madrigale [madri'gale] *sm* madrigal.
maestà [mae'sta] *sf* majesty. **maestoso** *agg* majestic; imposing.
maestro [ma'ɛstro] *sm* master; teacher. *agg* principal, main. **colpo maestro** *sm* master-stroke. **maestra** *sf* mistress; teacher. **maestranze** *sf pl* work force *sing*.
mafia ['mafja] *sf* mafia. **mafioso, -a** *sm, sf* member of the Mafia.
magagna [ma'gaɲa] *sf* flaw, fault.
magari [ma'gari] *inter* most certainly! (*oh se . . .*) if only . . . . *avv* (*forse*) perhaps; (*perfino*) even.
magazzino [magad'dzino] *sm* store, warehouse. **magazzinaggio** *sm* warehousing. **magazziniere** *sm* warehouseman.
maggio ['maddʒo] *sm* May.
maggiorana [maddʒo'rana] *sf* marjoram.
maggioranza [maddʒo'rantsa] *sf* majority.
maggiore [mad'dʒore] *s*(*m*+*f*), *agg* major; (*più grande*) greater, larger; (*più vecchio*) older; (*di due fratelli*) elder; (*superlativo*) greatest, oldest, eldest. *sm* major. **andare per la maggiore** be a hit.
maggiorenne [maddʒo'rɛnne] *agg* of age. *s*(*m*+*f*) major.
maggiormente [maddʒor'mente] *avv* (all the) more; (*di più*) most.
magia [ma'dʒia] *sf* magic. **magico** *agg* magic(al).
magistero [madʒis'tɛro] *sm* teaching (profession). **scuola di magistero** *sf* college of education. **magistrale** *agg* (*di maestro*) magisterial; (*da maestro*) masterly.
magistrato [madʒis'trato] *sm* magistrate.
maglia ['maʎa] *sf* stitch; (*rete*) mesh; (*indumento intimo*) vest; T-shirt; (*maglione*) jersey. **fare la maglia** knit. **lavoro a maglia** *sm* knitting. **maglieria** *sf* knitwear. **maglione** *sm* jersey, pullover.
magnanimo [ma'ɲanimo] *agg* magnanimous.
magnete [ma'ɲɛte] *sm* (*auto*) magneto; (*calamita*) magnet. **magnetismo** *sm* magnetism.
magnetofono [maɲe'tɔfono] *sm* tape-recorder.
magnifico [ma'ɲifiko] *agg* magnificent, splendid. **magnificenza** *sf* magnificence.
magnolia [ma'ɲɔlja] *sf* magnolia.
mago ['mago] *sm* (*stregone*) sorcerer; (*illusionista*) magician.
magro ['magro] *agg* thin; (*fig*) meagre; (*povero di grasso*) lean. **magra** *sf* (*fiume*) low level; (*fig*) shortage.
mai ['mai] *avv* never, ever. **caso** *or* **se mai** in case, if ever. **come mai** how (on earth).
maiale [ma'jale] *sm* pig; (*carne*) pork.
maionese [majo'neze] *sf* mayonnaise.
mais ['mais] *sm* maize.
maiuscolo [ma'juskolo] *agg* capital. **maiuscola** *sf* capital (letter).
malaccorto [malak'kɔrto] *agg* ill-advised.
malafede [mala'fede] *sf* bad faith.
malandato [malan'dato] *agg* in bad condition.
malanno [ma'lanno] *sm* misfortune, trouble.
malapena [mala'pena] *sf* **a malapena** scarcely.
malaria [ma'larja] *sf* malaria.
malato [ma'lato], **-a** *agg* sick, ill. *sm, sf* sick person, patient. **malattia** *sf* illness, disease.
malavita [mala'vita] *sf* underworld.
malavoglia [mala'vɔʎa] *sf* reluctance.

malavveduto [malavve'duto] *agg* unwise.
malconcio [mal'kontʃo] *agg* shabby.
malcontento [malkon'tɛnto] *agg* dissatisfied. *sm* dissatisfaction.
maldestro [mal'dɛstro] *agg* awkward.
maldicente [maldi'tʃɛnte] *agg* slanderous.
male ['male] *avv* (*non bene*) badly; (*in modo non buono*) ill; (*in modo imperfetto*) not well; (*indisposto*) unwell. **sentirsi male** feel unwell *or* ill. *sm* evil; (*dolore*) pain. **andare a male** go bad. **di male in peggio** from bad to worse. **far male** hurt. **mal di denti** toothache. **mal di gola** sore throat. **mal di mare** sea-sickness. **mal di testa** headache.
***maledire** [male'dire] *v* curse, damn. **maledizione** *sf* curse.
maleducato [maledu'kato] *agg* ill-mannered, rude.
malefico [ma'lɛfiko] *agg* harmful.
malerba [ma'lɛrba] *sf* weed.
malessere [ma'lɛssere] *sm* malaise.
malevolo [ma'lɛvolo] *agg* hostile.
malfamato [malfa'mato] *agg* ill-famed.
malfatto [mal'fatto] *agg* badly made.
malfattore [malfat'tore] *sm* evil-doer.
malfermo [mal'fermo] *agg* unsteady.
malfido [mal'fido] *agg* unreliable.
malgrado [mal'grado] *prep* notwithstanding, in spite of.
malia [ma'lia] *sf* charm. **maliardo** *agg* bewitching.
maligno [ma'liɲo] *agg* spiteful; (*med*) malignant.
malinconia [malinko'nia] *sf* melancholy, gloom. **malinconico** *agg* gloomy, dismal.
malincuore [malin'kwɔre] *avv* **a malincuore** reluctantly, half-heartedly.
malinteso [malin'tezo] *agg* misunderstood, mistaken. *sm* misunderstanding.
malizia [ma'litsja] *sf* cunning, malice. **malizioso** *agg* malicious, cunning.
mallevadore [malleva'dore] *sm* guarantor, surety.
malmenare [malme'nare] *v* manhandle.
malnutrito [malnu'trito] *agg* undernourished.
malora [ma'lora] *sf* ruin. **andare in malora** (*fam*) go to the dogs. **va in malora!** (*al diavolo*) go to hell!
malsano [mal'sano] *agg* unhealthy.
malsicuro [malsi'kuro] *agg* unsafe.
malta ['malta] *sf* mortar.
maltempo [mal'tempo] *sm* bad weather.
malto ['malto] *sm* malt.
maltrattare [maltrat'tare] *v* ill-treat. **maltrattamento** *sm* ill-treatment.
malumore [malu'more] *sm* bad temper.
malva ['malva] *sm invar* (*colore*) mauve. *sf* (*bot*) mallow.
malvagio [mal'vadʒo] *agg* wicked.
malversare [malver'sare] *v* embezzle. **malversatore, -trice** *sm, sf* embezzler. **malversazione** *sf* embezzlement.
malvisto [mal'visto] *agg* unpopular.
malvivente [malvi'vɛnte] *sm* crook.
malvolentieri [malvolen'tjɛri] *avv* reluctantly.
mamma ['mamma] *sf* mother, mum(my). **mamma mia!** good gracious!
mammella [mam'mɛlla] *sf* breast.
mammifero [mam'mifero] *sm* mammal.
mammola ['mammola] *sf* violet.
manata [ma'nata] *sf* handful.
mancare [man'kare] *v* (*aver difetto*) lack; (*essere assente*) be missing; (*fallire, sentire la mancanza*) miss. **ci mancherebbe altro!** that would be the limit! **mancare alla parola** not keep one's word. **sentirsi mancare** feel faint.
mancia ['mantʃa] *sf* tip. **dar la mancia** tip.
mancino [man'tʃino], **-a** *sm, sf* left-hander. *agg* left-handed, left. **colpo mancino** *sm* underhand trick.
mandare [man'dare] *v* send. **mandare a fondo** sink. **mandare avanti** run. **mandar giù** (*cibo*) swallow. **mandar via** dismiss.
mandarino[1] [manda'rino] *sm* (*cinese*) mandarin.
mandarino[2] [manda'rino] *sm* (*albero*) mandarin tree; (*frutto*) mandarin, tangerine.
mandato [man'dato] *sm* commission; (*pol*) mandate; (*dir*) warrant.
mandibola [man'dibola] *sf* jaw.
mandolino [mando'lino] *sm* mandolin.
mandorla ['mandorla] *sf* almond. **mandorlo** *sm* almond-tree.
mandria ['mandrja] *sf* herd, flock.
mandrino [man'drino] *sm* (*tec*) spindle, mandrel.
maneggiare [maned'dʒare] *v* handle. **maneggio** *sm* handling; (*addestramento cavalli*) riding-school; (*intrigo*) plot.
manette [ma'nette] *sf pl* handcuffs *pl*.
mangano ['mangano] *sm* mangle.
mangereccio [mandʒe'rɛttʃo] *agg* edible.
mangiare [man'dʒare] *v* eat; (*corrodere*) eat into; (*dissipare*) squander; (*carte, scacchi, ecc.*) take. **dar da mangiare a**

feed. **far da mangiare** prepare a meal. **mangiare la foglia** smell a rat. **mangiarsi il fegato** fret. *sm* food.
mangiatoia [mandʒa'toja] *sf* manger.
mangime [man'dʒime] *sm* fodder.
maniaco [ma'niako], -a *agg* maniacal. *sm, sf* maniac. **mania** *sf* mania.
manica ['manika] *sf* sleeve. **senza maniche** sleeveless.
manichino [mani'kino] *sm* mannequin, (tailor's) dummy.
manico ['maniko] *sm* handle; (*violino, ecc.*) neck.
manicomio [mani'kɔmjo] *sm* lunatic asylum.
maniera [ma'njɛra] *sf* manner.
manifattura [manifat'tura] *sf* manufacture.
manifestare [manifes'tare] *v* show; express; (*pol*) demonstrate. **manifestazione** *sf* display, show; expression; demonstration.
manifesto[1] [mani'festo] *sm* poster, bill; (*pol*) manifesto. **manifestino** *sm* leaflet.
manifesto[2] [mani'festo] *agg* clear, manifest.
maniglia [ma'niʎa] *sf* handle.
manipolare [manipo'lare] *v* manipulate.
mano ['mano] *sf, pl* **-i** hand; (*strato*) coat. **alla mano** ready, to hand. **a portata di mano** within reach. **dar** *or* **stringere la mano a** shake hands with. **di prima/seconda mano** first-/second-hand. **far man bassa** make a clean sweep. **fuori mano** outlying, off the beaten track. **man mano che** as. **mettere le mani avanti** take precautions. **sotto mano** handy.
manodopera [mano'dɔpera] *sf invar* labour, workforce.
***manomettere** [mano'mettere] *v* tamper with, violate.
manopola [ma'nɔpola] *sf* (*manubrio*) hand-grip; (*guanto*) mitten; (*radio, ecc.*) *knob.*
manoscritto [mano'skritto] *sm* manuscript. *agg* handwritten.
manovale [mano'vale] *sm* labourer.
manovella [mano'vɛlla] *sf* handle, crank.
manovrare [manov'rare] *v* handle, manoeuvre. **manovra** *sf* manoeuvre.
mansione [man'sjone] *sf* function, duty.
mansueto [mansu'ɛto] *agg* gentle, meek.
mantello [man'tɛllo] *sm* coat, cloak.
***mantenere** [mante'nere] *v* maintain, keep. **mantenimento** *sm* maintenance.
mantice ['mantitʃe] *sm* bellows *pl.*
manto ['manto] *sm* cloak, mantle.
manuale [manu'ale] *agg, sm* manual.
manubrio [ma'nubrjo] *sm* handlebar.
manutenzione [manuten'tsjone] *sf* maintenance, upkeep; (*auto*) servicing.
manzo ['mandzo] *sm* (*animale*) steer; (*carne*) beef.
mappa ['mappa] *sf* map. **mappamondo** *sm* globe.
maratona [mara'tona] *sf* marathon.
marca ['marka] *sf* brand.
marcare [mar'kare] *v* mark; (*sport*) score; accentuate.
marchese [mar'keze] *sm* marquis. **marchesa** *sf* marchioness.
marchio ['markjo] *sm* mark; (*comm*) trade-mark. **marchio depositato** registered trade-mark.
marcia[1] ['martʃa] *sf* march; (*auto*) gear; (*sport*) walking. **fare marcia indietro** reverse; (*fig*) back out. **mettere in marcia** get going, set off.
marcia[2] ['martʃa] *sf* (*materia*) pus.
marciapiede [martʃa'pjɛde] *sm* pavement.
marciare [mar'tʃare] *v* march; (*sport*) walk; (*fam*: *funzionare*) work.
marcio ['martʃo] *agg* rotten; (*fig*) corrupt. *sm* rottenness; rotten part.
marcire [mar'tʃire] *v* rot, go bad. **marciume** *sm* rot.
marco[1] ['marko] *sm* mark.
mare ['mare] *sm* sea; (*grande quantità*) host. **alto mare** high sea. **essere in alto mare** (*fig*) be floundering, be at sea. **mare agitato** *or* **mosso** rough sea. **maretta** *sf* choppy sea.
marea [ma'rɛa] *sf* tide.
maresciallo [mare'ʃallo] *sm* (*sottufficiale*) sergeant major; (*ufficiale*) field-marshal.
margarina [marga'rina] *sf* margarine.
margherita [marge'rita] *sf* daisy.
margine ['mardʒine] *sm* edge, border; (*fig*) margin.
marina [ma'rina] *sf* navy. **marinaio** *sm* sailor.
marinare [mari'nare] *v* marinate. **marinare la scuola** play truant.
marionetta [marjo'netta] *sf* puppet.
maritare [mari'tare] *v* marry; (*mescolare*) mix. **maritarsi** *v* get married.
marito [ma'rito] *sm* husband.
marittimo [ma'rittimo] *agg* sea; maritime.

marmaglia [mar'maʎa] *sf* rabble.
marmellata [marmel'lata] *sf* jam; (*di agrumi*) marmalade.
marmo ['marmo] *sm* marble.
marra ['marra] *sf* hoe.
marrone [mar'rone] *sm* chestnut. *agg* brown.
marsupiale [marsu'pjale] *sm, agg* marsupial.
martedì [marte'di] *sm* Tuesday.
martellare [martel'lare] *v* hammer; (*fig*) pound. **martellata** *sf* hammer-blow; (*fig*) heavy blow. **martello** *sm* hammer; (*porta*) knocker; (*orologio*) striker.
martinetto [marti'netto] *sm* jack.
martin pescatore [mar'tin peska'tore] *sm* kingfisher.
martire ['martire] *s*(*m*+*f*) martyr. **martirio** *sm* martyrdom. **martoriare** *v* torture.
marxismo [mar'ksizmo] *sm* Marxism. **marxista** *s*(*m*+*f*), *agg* Marxist.
marzapane [martsa'pane] *sm* marzipan.
marziale [mar'tsjale] *agg* martial.
marzo ['martso] *sm* march.
mascalzone [maskal'tsone] *sm* rascal, scoundrel. **mascalzonata** *sf* nasty trick.
mascara [mas'kara] *sm* mascara.
mascella [ma'ʃɛlla] *sf* jaw.
maschera ['maskera] *sf* mask; (*travestimento*) disguise; (*cinema, teatro*) usherette. **mascherare** *v* mask; (*con costumi*) dress up; (*celare*) disguise; (*schermare*) screen; (*mimetizzare*) camouflage.
maschile [mas'kile] *agg* male; (*gramm*) masculine; (*per ragazzi*) boys'; (*per uomini*) men's.
maschio ['maskjo] *sm* male; (*ragazzo*) boy.
masochismo [mazo'kizmo] *sm* masochism. **masochista** *s*(*m*+*f*) masochist.
massa ['massa] *sf* mass; (*gran numero*) heap, lot; (*elett*) earth.
massacrare [massa'krare] *v* massacre. **massacro** *sm* massacre.
massaggiare [massad'dʒare] *v* massage. **massaggio** *sm* massage.
massaia [mas'saja] *sf* housewife.
masserizie [masse'ritsje] *sf pl* fixtures and fittings *pl*.
massiccio [mas'sittʃo] *agg* solid.
massima ['massima] *sf* maxim; (*norma*) rule. **di massima** general, informal. **in linea di massima** as a general rule, on the whole.
massimo ['massimo] *agg* greatest; (*estremo*) utmost; (*il più alto*) highest; (*il migliore*) best; (*fis*) maximum. *sm* maximum; (*tutto ciò che*) most; (*meglio*) best.
massone [mas'sone] *sm* freemason. **massoneria** *sf* freemasonry.
masticare [masti'kare] *v* chew; (*borbottare*) mutter. **gomma da masticare** *sf* chewing gum.
mastice ['mastitʃe] *sm* mastic; (*per vetri*) putty.
mastino [mas'tino] *sm* mastiff.
mastro ['mastro] *sm* ledger.
matassa [ma'tassa] *sf* skein, hank.
matematico [mate'matiko], **-a** *agg* mathematical. *sm, sf* mathematician. *sf* mathematics.
materasso [mate'rasso] *sm* mattress. **materassino (pneumatico)** *sm* air-bed.
materia [ma'tɛrja] *sf* matter; substance; (*argomento, disciplina*) subject; (*fam: marcia*) pus. **entrare in materia** broach a subject. **materia prima** raw material.
materiale [mate'rjale] *sm, agg* material. **materialismo** *sm* materialism. **materialista** *s*(*m*+*f*) materialist.
materno [ma'tɛrno] *agg* maternal, motherly. **scuola materna** *sf* nursery school. **maternità** *sf* motherhood; (*ospedale*) maternity hospital.
matita [ma'tita] *sf* pencil.
matriarcale [matriar'kale] *agg* matriarchal.
matrice [ma'tritʃe] *sf* matrix; (*modulo*) counterfoil.
matricola [ma'trikola] *sf* register; (*numero*) serial number; (*studente*) freshman. **matricolare** *v* register.
matrigna [ma'triɲa] *sf* stepmother.
matrimonio [matri'mɔnjo] *sm* marriage, matrimony; (*festa nuziale*) wedding. **matrimoniale** *agg* matrimonial. **letto matrimoniale** *sm* double bed.
matta ['matta] *sf* (*carte*) joker.
mattatoio [matta'tɔjo] *sm* slaughterhouse.
matterello [matte'rɛllo] *sm* rolling-pin.
mattina [mat'tina] *sf* morning. **mattinata** *sf* morning; (*teatro*) matinée. **mattiniero** *agg* early rising.
matto ['matto] *agg* mad. **andar matto per** be crazy about. **matto da legare** mad as a hatter. **scacco matto** checkmate.
mattone [mat'tone] *sm* brick; (*fam: noioso*) bore. **mattonella** *sf* tile; (*biliardo*) cushion.

mattutino [mattu'tino] *agg* morning.
maturare [matu'rare] *v* mature, ripen; (*med*) come to a head. **maturazione** *sf* ripening. **maturità** *sf* maturity. **esame di maturità** *sm* school-leaving examination, A level(s). **maturo** *agg* ripe; mature.
mausoleo [mauzo'lɛo] *sm* mausoleum.
mazza ['mattsa] *sf* club; (*martello*) sledgehammer. **mazzata** *sf* heavy blow.
mazzo ['mattso] *sm* bunch; (*carte*) pack. **fare il mazzo** shuffle the cards *or* pack.
me [me] *pron* me. *V* **mi.**
meccanico [mek'kaniko] *agg* mechanical. *sm* mechanic. **meccanica** *sf* mechanics. **meccanismo** *sm* mechanism, works. **meccanizzare** *v* mechanize. **meccanizzazione** *sf* mechanization.
meccanografico [mekkano'grafiko] *agg* data processing.
medaglia [me'daʎa] *sf* medal. **medaglione** *sm* medallion; (*gioiello*) locket.
medesimo [me'dezimo] *agg* same.
media ['mɛdja] *sf* mean, average; (*scuola*) secondary school. **fare la media di** average.
mediana [me'djana] *sf* median. **mediano** *agg* median, medial.
mediante [me'djante] *prep* through, by (means of).
mediatore [medja'tore], **-trice** *sm*, *sf* intermediary; (*comm*) broker. **mediazione** *sf* mediation; brokerage.
medicare [medi'kare] *v* treat; (*ferita*) dress. **medicina** *sf* medicine.
medicinale [meditʃi'nale] *agg* medicinal. *sm* medicine.
medico ['mɛdiko] *sm* doctor, physician. *agg* medical. **medico chirurgo** surgeon. **medico condotto** medical officer. **medico generico** general practitioner.
medievale [medje'vale] *agg* medieval.
medio ['mɛdjo] *agg* middle; average; (*scuola*) secondary. *sm* middle finger.
mediocre [me'djɔkre] *agg* mediocre, poor.
meditare [medi'tare] *v* meditate, ponder. **meditazione** *sf* meditation.
mediterraneo [mediter'raneo] *sm*, *agg* Mediterranean.
medium ['mɛdjum] *s*(*m*+*f*) *invar* medium.
medusa [me'duza] *sf* jelly-fish.
megafono [me'gafono] *sm* loudspeaker.
megera [me'dʒɛra] *sf* harridan.
meglio ['mɛʎo] *agg*, *avv* (*comparativo*) better; (*superlativo*) best. *sm* best. **alla meglio** as well as possible. **tanto meglio!** so much the better!
mela ['mela] *sf* apple. **mela cotogna** quince. **melo** *sm* apple-tree.
melagrana [mela'grana] *sf* pomegranate. **melograno** *sm* pomegranate tree.
melanzana [melan'dzana] *sf* aubergine, egg-plant.
melassa [me'lassa] *sf* treacle, molasses.
melma ['melma] *sf* slime.
melodia [melo'dia] *sf* melody. **melodico** *agg* melodious. **melodioso** *agg* melodious, sweet-sounding.
melodramma [melo'dramma] *sm* melodrama.
melone [me'lone] *sm* melon.
membrana [mem'brana] *sf* membrane; (*acustica*) diaphragm.
membro ['mɛmbro] *sm*, *pl* **-a** *f in collective sense* member; (*anat*) limb.
memoria [me'mɔrja] *sf* memory; (*oggetto ricordo*) souvenir; (*scritto*) memoir. **a memoria** by heart. **prendere memoria di** make a note of. **memoriale** *sm* memorial; petition; (*raccolta di documenti*) record. **memorizzare** *v* memorize.
menare [me'nare] *v* lead; (*portare*) take, bring; (*assestare*) strike. **a menadito** at one's fingertips.
mendicare [mendi'kare] *v* beg. **mendicante** *s*(*m*+*f*) beggar.
meno ['meno] *avv* (*comparativo*) less; (*superlativo*) least; (*mat*) minus. *agg invar* (*minore*) less; (*in minor numero*) fewer. *prep* (*eccetto*) but (for), except (for). **a meno che** unless. **fare a meno di** do without. **meno male!** thank goodness! **o meno** (*o no*) or not. **tanto meno** let alone. **venir meno** (*svenire*) faint; (*mancare*) fail. **venir meno alla parola** break one's word. *sm invar* (the) least. **i meno** *sm pl* (the) minority *sing.*
menomare [meno'mare] *v* diminish; (*danneggiare*) injure, disable. **menomato, -a** *s*, *agg* disabled.
menopausa [meno'pauza] *sf* menopause.
mensa ['mɛnsa] *sf* table; refectory; (*mil*) mess.
mensile [men'sile] *agg* monthly. *sm* (*giornale*) monthly; (*paga*) monthly pay.
mensola ['mɛnsola] *sf* bracket, shelf; (*caminetto*) mantelpiece.
menta ['menta] *sf* mint; (*peperina*) peppermint; (*romana*) spearmint.

mente ['mente] *sf* mind; intellect. **venire in mente** occur; come to mind. **mentale** *agg* mental. **mentalità** *sf* mentality.
mentire [men'tire] *v* lie. **mentito** *agg* false.
mento ['mento] *sm* chin.
mentre ['mentre] *cong* while, as; (*laddove*) whereas.
menu [mə'ny] *sm* menu.
menzionare [mentsjo'nare] *v* mention. **menzione** *sf* mention.
menzogna [men'dzoɲa] *sf* lie. **menzognero** *agg* lying, false.
meraviglia [mera'viʎa] *sf* wonder, marvel; (*stupore*) surprise. **a meraviglia** wonderfully. **meravigliare** *v* surprise, amaze. **meraviglioso** *agg* marvellous, wonderful.
mercante [mer'kante] *sm* merchant, trader. **mercanteggiare** *v* trade, deal; (*contrattare*) haggle, bargain. **mercantile** *agg* mercantile. **nave mercantile** *sf* merchant ship.
mercanzia [merkan'tsia] *sf* merchandise, goods *pl*.
mercato [mer'kato] *sm* market. **a buon mercato** cheap, inexpensive.
merce ['mertʃe] *sf* merchandise, goods *pl*; (*in magazzino*) stock.
mercenario [mertʃe'narjo] *agg*, *sm* mercenary.
merciaio [mer'tʃajo], **-a** *sm*, *sf* haberdasher. **merceria** *sf* haberdashery.
mercoledì [mercole'di] *sm* Wednesday.
mercurio [mer'kurjo] *sm* mercury.
merda ['merda] *sf* (*volg*) shit.
merenda [me'renda] *sf* (afternoon) snack, tea.
meridiano [meri'djano] *sf* (*geog*) meridian. *agg* (*di mezzogiorno*) midday. **meridiana** *sf* (*geog*) meridian line; (*orologio solare*) sundial.
meridionale [meridjo'nale] *agg* southern, south. *s*(*m*+*f*) southerner. **meridione** *sm* south.
meringa [me'ringa] *sf* meringue.
meritare [meri'tare] *v* deserve, merit. **meritevole** *agg* deserving, worthy.
merito ['merito] *sm* merit. **a pari merito** equal. **in merito a** regarding, as to, about. **per merito di** thanks to.
merletto [mer'letto] *sm* lace.
merlo ['merlo] *sm* blackbird; (*sempliciotto*) fool.
merluzzo [mer'luttso] *sm* cod; (*nasello*) hake.
mero ['mero] *agg* mere.
meschino [mes'kino] *agg* wretched, mean.
mescolare [mesko'lare] *v* mix; (*unire*) blend. **mescolatore, -trice** *sm*, *sf* mixer.
mese ['meze] *sm* month.
messa[1] ['messa] *sf* (*rel*) Mass. **messale** *sm* missal.
messa[2] ['messa] *sf* (*il mettere*) placing, putting.
messaggio [mes'saddʒo] *sm* message. **messaggero** *sm* messenger; (*fig*) herald.
messo ['messo] *sm* usher.
mestiere [mes'tjere] *sm* job, trade; (*manuale*) craft; profession. **di mestiere** by profession. **essere del mestiere** be an expert. **ferri del mestiere** *sm pl* tools of the trade *pl*.
mesto ['mesto] *agg* sad, mournful. **mestizia** *sf* sadness.
mestolo ['mestolo], **-a** *sm*, *sf* ladle, kitchen spoon.
mestruazione [mestrua'tsjone] *sf* menstruation; (*fam*) period. **mestruale** *agg* menstrual.
meta ['meta] *sf* goal, aim; destination; (*rugby*) try.
metà [me'ta] *sf* half; (*centro*) middle. **a metà strada** half-way. **fare a metà** halve; (*fam*) go halves.
metabolismo [metabo'lizmo] *sm* metabolism. **metabolico** *agg* metabolic.
metafisico [meta'fiziko], **-a** *agg* metaphysical. *sm*, *sf* metaphysician. *sf* metaphysics.
metafora [me'tafora] *sf* metaphor, figure of speech. **metaforico** *agg* metaphorical.
metallo [me'tallo] *sm* metal. **metallico** *agg* metallic. **metallurgia** *sf* metallurgy.
metamorfosi [meta'mɔrfozi] *sf* metamorphosis, transformation.
metano [me'tano] *sm* methane.
meteora [me'teɔra] *sf* meteor. **meteorico** *agg* meteoric.
meteorologia [meteorolo'dʒia] *sf* meteorology. **meteorologico** *agg* meteorological, weather. **bollettino meteorologico** *sm* weather report. **previsioni meteorologiche** *sf pl* weather forecast *sing*.
meticcio [me'tittʃo], **-a** *s*, *agg* half-caste.
meticoloso [metiko'lozo] *agg* meticulous.
metodista [meto'dista] *s*(*m*+*f*), *agg* methodist.
metodo ['metodo] *sm* method. **metodico** *agg* methodical.

metro ['metro] *sm* metre; (*per misurare*) rule; (*a nastro*) tape-measure. **metrico** *agg* (*misura*) metric; (*poesia*) metrical.
metropoli [me'trɔpoli] *sf* metropolis. **metropolitana** *sf* underground (railway).
***mettere** ['mettere] *v* put; place; lay (down); (*indossare*) put on, wear; (*supporre*) suppose. **mettersi sotto** get down to it.
mezzo [meddzo] *agg* half; (*medio*) middle. **mezzogiorno** *sm* noon, midday; (*geog*) south. *sm* half; (*centro*) middle; (*strumento*) means. **a** *or* **per mezzo di** by, through. **mezzi** *pl* means *pl*. *avv* half; (*quasi*) nearly. **andarci di mezzo** (*avere la peggio*) suffer for it; (*essere in gioco*) be at stake. **togliere di mezzo** get rid of.
mi [mi], **me** *pron* (to) me; (*riflessivo*) myself.
miagolare [mjago'lare] *v* mew, miaow. **miagolio** *sm* mewing.
mica[1] ['mika] *avv* (*fam*) at all.
mica[2] ['mika] *sf* mica.
miccia ['mittʃa] *sf* fuse.
microbo ['mikrobo] *sm* microbe.
microcosmo [mikro'kɔzmo] *sm* microcosm.
microfilm ['mikrofilm] *sm invar* microfilm.
microfono [mi'krɔfono] *sm* microphone; (*telefono*) mouthpiece.
microscopio [mikro'skɔpjo] *sm* microscope. **microscopico** *agg* microscopic.
microsolco [mikro'sɔlko] *sm* microgroove; (*disco a 33 giri*) LP; (*disco a 45 giri*) EP.
midollo [mi'dollo] *sm* marrow; (*bot*) pith. **bagnato fino al midollo** soaked to the skin. **fino al midollo** to the core. **midollo spinale** spinal cord.
miele ['mjɛle] *sm* honey.
mietere ['mjɛtere] *v* reap, harvest; (*uccidere*) mow down. **mietitore, -trice** *sm, sf* reaper, harvester. **mietitrebbiatrice** *sf* combine harvester. **mietitura** *sf* reaping, harvesting; (*periodo, messe*) harvest.
migliaio [mi'ʎajo] *sm, pl* **-a** *f* thousand; (*circa mille*) about a thousand.
miglio[1] ['miʎo] *sm, pl* **-a** *f* mile.
miglio[2] ['miʎo] *sm* (*bot*) millet.
migliore [mi'ʎore] *agg* (*comparativo*) better; (*superlativo*) best. *sm* best.
mignolo ['miɲolo] *sm* (*della mano*) little finger; (*del piede*) little toe.
migrare [mi'grare] *v* migrate. **migratorio** *agg* migratory. **migrazione** *sf* migration.
milione [mi'ljone] *sm* million. **milionesimo** *sm, agg* millionth.
militare [mili'tare] *agg* military. *sm* soldier. *v* militate. **militarismo** *sm* militarism. **militarista** *s(m+f), agg* militarist.
milite ['milite] *sm* soldier, warrior. **milizia** *sf* (*corpo armato*) militia.
millantare [millan'tare] *v* boast. **millantato credito** *sm* false pretences *pl*. **millantatore, -trice** *sm, sf* braggart, show-off. **millanteria** *sf* boasting.
mille ['mille] *agg, sm* thousand. **millennio** *sm* millennium. **millesimo** *agg, sm* thousandth.
milligrammo [milli'grammo] *sm* milligram.
millimetro [mil'limetro] *sm* millimetre.
mimetizzare [mimetid'dzare] *v* camouflage. **mimetizzazione** *sf* camouflage.
mimica ['mimika] *sf* mime. **mimico** *agg* mimic. **mimo** *sm* mime; (*uccello*) mocking-bird.
mina ['mina] *sf* mine; (*di matita*) lead. **minare** *v* mine; (*insidiare*) undermine. **minatore** *sm* miner.
minaccia [mi'nattʃa] *sf* threat. **minacciare** *v* threaten. **minaccioso** *agg* threatening.
minareto [mina'reto] *sm* minaret.
minerale [mine'rale] *agg, sm* mineral.
minerario [mine'rarjo] *agg* mining.
minestra [mi'nɛstra] *sf* soup.
mingherlino [minger'lino] *agg* skinny.
miniatura [minja'tura] *sf* miniature.
miniera [mi'njɛra] *sf* mine.
minimo ['minimo] *agg* (*il più piccolo*) least, smallest, slightest; (*più basso*) minimum; (*piccolissimo*) very small, very slight; (*molto basso*) very low. *sm* minimum; (*la minima cosa*) least.
ministero [mini'stɛro] *sm* (*pol*) ministry. **pubblico ministero** public prosecutor.
ministro [mi'nistro] *sm* minister.
minore [mi'nore] *s(m+f), agg* (*più piccolo*) less, smaller; (*più basso*) lower; (*più giovane*) younger; (*superlativo*) least, lowest, youngest; (*mat, musica*) minor. **minorità** *sf* minority.
minorenne [mino'rɛnne] *s(m+f)* minor. *agg* under age.
minuetto [minu'etto] *sm* minuet.
minuscolo [mi'nuskolo] *agg* small, diminutive. **minuscola** *sf* small letter.

minuta [mi'nuta] *sf* draft.
minuto[1] [mi'nuto] *agg* small, minute; detailed. **al minuto** retail. **vendere al minuto** retail.
minuto[2] [mi'nuto] *sm* (*primo*) minute. **minuto secondo** second. **spaccare il minuto** be dead on time.
mio ['mio], *m pl* **miei** *agg* my. *pron* mine.
miope ['miope] *agg* short-sighted. **miopia** *sf* short-sightedness.
mira ['mira] *sf* aim.
miracolo [mi'rakolo] *sm* miracle. **miracoloso** *agg* miraculous.
miraggio [mi'raddʒo] *sm* mirage.
mirare [mi'rare] *v* aim; (*prendere mira*) take aim. **mirino** *sm* sight; (*foto*) view-finder.
mirtillo [mir'tillo] *sm* bilberry. **mirtillo rosso** cranberry.
miscela [mi'ʃɛla] *sf* mixture; (*caffè, tè, tabacco*) blend. **miscelare** *v* mix, blend.
mischia ['miskja] *sf* fray.
mischiare [mis'kjare] *v* mix; (*carte*) shuffle.
miscuglio [mis'kuʎo] *sm* mixture.
miseria [mi'zɛrja] *sm* poverty; (*inezia*) pittance; squalor. **miserabile** *agg* miserable, wretched.
misericordia [mizeri'kɔrdja] *sf* mercy. **senza misericordia** merciless; (*spietato*) ruthless.
misero ['mizero] *agg* poor, wretched.
missile ['missile] *sm* missile.
missione [mis'sjone] *sf* mission. **missionario, -a** *s, agg* missionary.
mistero [mis'tɛro] *sm* mystery. **misterioso** *agg* mysterious.
mistico ['mistiko], **-a** *agg* mystical. *sm, sf* mystic. *sf* mysticism. **misticismo** *sm* mysticism.
misto ['misto] *agg* mixed.
misura [mi'zura] *sf* measure; (*taglia, dimensione*) size; (*atto e modo del misurare*) measurement; moderation. **fatto su misura** made to measure. **prendere delle misure** take steps.
misurare [mizu'rare] *v* measure; limit; (*indumenti*) try on. **misurato** *agg* measured, moderate.
mite ['mite] *agg* mild, moderate.
mito ['mito] *sm* myth. **mitico** *agg* mythical. **mitologia** *sf* mythology. **mitologico** *agg* mythological.
mitra[1] ['mitra] *sf* (*rel*) mitre.
mitra[2] ['mitra] *sm invar* tommy-gun.
mitragliatrice [mitraʎa'tritʃe] *sf* machine-gun. **mitragliamento** *sm* machine-gun fire; (*fig*) bombarding. **mitragliare** *v* machine-gun; (*fig*) bombard.
mittente [mit'tɛnte] *s*(*m*+*f*) sender.
mobile ['mɔbile] *agg* mobile, moving; movable. **squadra mobile** *sf* flying squad. *sm* piece of furniture. **mobili** *sm pl* furniture *sing*.
mobilia [mo'bilja] *sf* furnishings *pl*; (*mobili*) furniture.
mobiliare [mobi'ljare] *agg* movable. *v* furnish.
mobilitare [mobili'tare] *v* mobilize. **mobilitazione** *sf* mobilization.
mocassino [mokas'sino] *sm* moccasin.
moccolo ['mɔkkolo] *sm* candle-end. **reggere il moccolo** play gooseberry. **tirare dei moccoli** (*fam*) swear.
moda ['mɔda] *sf* fashion. **di** *or* **alla moda** in fashion, fashionable. **fuori moda** out of fashion. **passare di moda** go out of fashion.
modalità [modali'ta] *sf* procedure, formality.
modellare [model'lare] *v* model. **modella** *sf* model. **modello** *sm* model; (*disegno*) pattern.
moderare [mode'rare] *v* moderate, lower; control. **moderatore** *sm* moderator; (*TV, radio*) chairman. **moderazione** *sf* moderation, restraint.
moderno [mo'dɛrno] *agg* modern; (*al passo coi tempi*) up-to-date. **modernizzare** *v* modernize, bring up-to-date.
modestia [mo'dɛstja] *sf* modesty. **modesto** *agg* modest, unassuming; (*umile*) humble.
modificare [modifi'kare] *v* modify, alter. **modifica** *sf* alteration, modification.
modista [mo'dista] *sf* milliner.
modo ['mɔdo] *sm* manner, way; opportunity; (*gramm*) mood. **ad ogni modo** anyhow, in any case. **di modo che** (*affinchè*) so that; (*e così*) and so. **in modo da** so that. **in qualche modo** somehow. **modo di dire** expression, idiom. **modo di fare** manner. **per modo di dire** so to speak.
modulare [modu'lare] *v* modulate.
modulo ['mɔdulo] *sm* form; (*mat, tec*) modulus.
mogano ['mɔgano] *sm* mahogany.
mogio ['mɔdʒo] *agg* downhearted.

moglie ['moʎe] *sf* wife.
moina [mo'ina] *sf* **fare moine** coax.
molare [mo'lare] *v* grind. *agg* molar. **pietra molare** *sf* millstone. **mola** *sf* grinding wheel.
mole ['mɔle] *sf* pile, mass; (*grandezza*) size.
molecola [mo'lɛkola] *sf* molecule.
molesto [mo'lɛsto] *agg* troublesome, annoying. **molestare** *v* trouble, annoy. **molestia** *sf* annoyance, nuisance.
molla ['mɔlla] *sf* spring; (*stimolo*) mainspring. **molle** *sf pl* tongs *pl*. **mollare** *v* (*lasciar andare*) let go; (*allentare*) loosen, slacken. **molleggiato** *agg* sprung. **molletta** *sf* (*biancheria*) (clothes-)peg; (*capelli*) hair-pin.
molle ['mɔlle] *agg* soft; (*bagnato*) wet; (*debole*) weak. **mettere in molle** steep.
mollusco [mol'lusko] *sm* mollusc.
molo ['mɔlo] *sm* jetty; (*banchina*) wharf.
molteplice [mol'teplitʃe] *agg* manifold; varied.
moltiplicare [moltipli'kare] *v* multiply.
moltitudine [molti'tudine] *sm* multitude, host.
molto ['molto] *agg* a lot of, lots of, much; (*pl*) many; (*tempo*) long. *avv* much, a lot; (*con agg e avv positivi*) very. *pron.* a lot, much; (*pl*) many.
momento [mo'mento] *sm* moment. **a momenti** (*tra poco*) shortly; (*quasi*) almost. **al momento d'oggi** nowadays. **dal momento che** since.
monaca ['mɔnaka] *sf* nun. **monaco** *sm* monk.
Monaco ['mɔnako] *sf* (*principato*) Monaco; (*di Baviera*) Munich.
monarca [mo'narka] *sm* monarch, king. **monarchia** *sf* monarchy. **monarchico, -a** *sm, sf* monarchist.
monastero [monas'tɛro] *sm* monastery. **monastico** *agg* monastic.
monco ['monko] *agg* maimed. **essere monco di . . .** have . . . missing. **moncherino** *sm* stump.
mondezzaio [mondet'tsajo] *sm* rubbish heap; (*ambiente sudicio*) pigsty. **mondare** *v* (*sbucciare*) peel; (*togliere erbacce*) weed.
mondo ['mondo] *sm* world. **mandare all'altro mondo** (*fam*) send to hell. **mettere al mondo** give birth to. **vivere nel mondo della luna** have one's head in the clouds. **mondiale** *agg* world; (*diffuso*) world-wide.
monello [mo'nɛllo] *sm* urchin. **monelleria** *sf* prank.
moneta [mo'neta] *sf* coin; (*denaro*) money; (*spicciola*) (small) change. **monetario** *agg* monetary.
monito ['mɔnito] *sm* warning.
monocolore [monoko'lore] *agg* plain; (*pol*) one-party.
monocromo [mo'nɔkromo] *agg, sm* monochrome.
monogamo [mo'nɔgamo], **-a** *agg* monogamous. *sm, sf* monogamist. **monogamia** *sf* monogamy.
monolitico [mono'litiko] *agg* monolithic.
monologo [mo'nɔlogo] *sm, pl* **-ghi** monologue.
monopolio [mono'pɔljo] *sm* monopoly. **monopolizzare** *v* monopolize.
monoteismo [monote'izmo] *sm* monotheism.
monotono [mo'nɔtono] *agg* monotonous. **monotonia** *sf* monotony.
monsone [mon'sone] *sm* monsoon.
monta ['monta] *sf* (*accoppiamento*) mounting; (*luogo*) stud-farm; (*modo di cavalcare*) riding.
montacarichi [monta'kariki] *sm* goods lift.
montaggio [mon'taddʒo] *sm* assembly; (*cinema*) editing.
montagna [mon'taɲa] *sf* mountain. **montagne russe** switchback *sing*.
montare [mon'tare] *v* (*salire*) climb; (*tec*) assemble; (*incorniciare*) mount; (*film*) edit; (*macchina*) get in(to). **montare a cavallo** get on a horse; (*cavalcare*) ride. **montatura** *sf* assembly; (*occhiali*) frame; (*pubblicitaria*) stunt.
monte ['monte] *sm* mountain; (*davanti a nome*) Mount. **a monte** above, upstream. **andare a monte** fall through. **mandare a monte** upset; (*disdire*) cancel. **monte di pietà** pawnshop. **monte premi** jackpot. **montuoso** *agg* mountainous.
montone [mon'tone] *sm* ram; (*carne*) mutton.
monumento [monu'mento] *sm* monument. **monumentale** *agg* monumental.
mora ['mɔra] *sf* (*gelso*) mulberry; (*rovo*) blackberry.
morale [mo'rale] *agg* moral. *sf* (*dottrina*) ethics *pl*; morality, morals *pl*; (*insegnamento*) moral. *sm* morale. **essere su/giù**

di morale be cheerful/depressed. **moralizzare** *v* moralize.
morbido ['mɔrbido] *agg* soft.
morbillo [mor'billo] *sm* measles.
morbo ['mɔrbo] *sm* disease. **morboso** *agg* morbid; pathological.
***mordere** ['mɔrdere] *v* bite; (*afferrare*) grip. **mordere il freno** strain at the leash. **mordace** *agg* biting, caustic.
morfina [mor'fina] *sf* morphine.
morigerato [moridʒe'rato] *agg* sober, clean-living.
***morire** [mo'rire] *v* die. **avere una fame/sete da morire** be terribly hungry/thirsty.
mormorare [mormo'rare] *v* murmur. **mormorio** *sm* murmur.
moro[1] ['mɔro] *agg* dark; (*nero*) black; (*carnagione*) swarthy; (*capelli*) brown.
moro[2] ['mɔro] *sm* (*gelso*) mulberry.
morsa ['mɔrsa] *sf* vice. **morsetto** *sm* clamp; (*elett*) terminal.
morsicare [morsi'kare] *v* gnaw, bite. **morso** *sm* bite; (*fig*) sting; (*cavallo*) bit.
mortaio [mor'tajo] *sm* mortar.
mortale [mor'tale] *agg* mortal; (*implacabile*) deadly. **mortalità** *sf* mortality.
morte ['mɔrte] *sf* death.
morto ['mɔrto] *agg* dead. *sm* dead person; (*carte*) dummy. **fare il morto** float (on one's back).
mosaico [mo'zaiko] *sm* mosaic.
mosca ['moska] *sf* fly; (*barbetta*) goatee. **mosca cieca** blindman's buff. **moscerino** *sm* small fly.
Mosca ['moska] *sf* Moscow.
moscato[1] [mos'kato] *agg* muscat(el). **noce moscata** *sf* nutmeg.
moscato[2] [mos'kato] *agg* (*cavallo*) dappled.
moschea [mos'kɛa] *sf* mosque.
moschetto [mos'ketto] *sm* musket. **moschettiere** *sm* musketeer.
mossa ['mɔssa] *sf* movement; (*fig*) move.
mosso ['mɔsso] *agg* (*mare*) rough; (*capelli*) wavy.
mostarda [mos'tarda] *sf* mustard.
mostrare [mos'trare] *v* show. **mostra** *sf* show, exhibition; ostentation; (*campione*) sample. **mettere in mostra** display.
mostro ['mɔstro] *sm* monster. **mostruosità** *sf* monstrosity. **mostruoso** *agg* monstrous.
motivo [mo'tivo] *sm* ground, reason; (*disegno, musica*) motif. **motivare** *v* motivate. **motivazione** *sf* motivation.
moto[1] ['mɔto] *sm* motion; (*sommossa*) rebellion. **mettere in moto** set in motion, start (up).
moto[2] ['mɔto] *sf* (*fam*) motor-bike.
motocicletta [mototʃik'letta] *sf* motorcycle. **motociclista** *s*(*m*+*f*) motor-cyclist.
motore [mo'tore] *sm* engine. *agg* motor. **albero motore** *sm* crankshaft. **motorino d'avviamento** *sm* starter (motor).
motoscafo [moto'skafo] *sm* motor-boat.
motto ['mɔtto] *sm* motto; (*detto*) saying.
movimento [movi'mento] *sm* movement; activity. **movimentato** *agg* lively, busy.
mozione [mo'tsjone] *sf* motion.
mozzare [mot'tsare] *v* cut off; (*coda*) dock. **mozzare il fiato** take one's breath away.
mozzicone [mottsi'kone] *sm* butt.
mucca ['mukka] *sf* cow.
mucchio ['mukkjo] *sm* heap.
muco ['muko] *sm* mucus. **mucosa** *sf* mucous membrane.
muda ['muda] *sf* moulting.
muffa ['muffa] *sf* mould. **muffoso** *agg* mouldy.
muggire [mud'dʒire] *v also* **mugghiare** bellow; (*mare*) roar; (*vento*) howl.
mughetto [mu'getto] *sm* lily of the valley.
mugnaio [mu'ɲajo] *sm* miller.
mugolare [mugo'lare] *v* howl, whine.
mulattiera [mulat'tjɛra] *sf* (mule-)track.
mulino [mu'lino] *sm* mill; (*a vento*) windmill. **mulinello** *sm* whirlpool; (*pesca*) reel.
mulo ['mulo] *sm* mule.
multa ['multa] *sf* fine.
multicolore [multiko'lore] *agg* multicoloured.
multiplo ['multiplo] *agg, sm* multiple.
mummia ['mummja] *sf* mummy. **mummificare** *v* mummify.
***mungere** ['mundʒere] *v* milk.
municipio [muni'tʃipjo] *sm* (*comune*) municipality; (*sede*) town hall. **municipale** *agg* municipal.
munire [mu'nire] *v* supply; fortify.
munizione [muni'tsjone] *sf* munitions *pl*; (military) stores *pl*. **munizioni** *sf pl* ammunition *sing*.
***muovere** ['mwɔvere] *v* move.
muraglia [mu'raʎa] *sf* wall.
muratore [mura'tore] *sm* bricklayer.
muro ['muro] *sm* wall. **mura** *sf pl* city

walls *pl.* **parlare al muro** talk to a brick wall.
musa ['muza] *sf* muse.
muschio[1] ['muskjo] *sm* (*bot*) moss. **muscoso** *agg* mossy.
muschio[2] ['muskjo] *sm* (*odore*) musk.
muscolo ['muskolo] *sm* muscle.
museo [mu'zɛo] *sm* museum.
museruola [muze'rwɔla] *sf* muzzle.
musica ['muzika] *sf* music. **musicale** *agg* musical, music. **musicista** *s(m+f)* musician.
muso ['muzo] *sm* snout; (*spreg*) mug. **mettere il muso lungo** pull a long face.
mussolina [musso'lina] *sf* muslin.
mutande [mu'tande] *sf pl also* **mutandine** (*da donna*) panties *pl*; (*da uomo*) underpants *pl*; (*da bagno*) swimming trunks *pl*.
mutare [mu'tare] *v* change; (*fare la muta*) shed. **mutabile** *or* **mutevole** *agg* changeable; (*fig*) fickle. **mutamento** *sm* change. **mutazione** *sf* mutation.
mutilare [muti'lare] *v* maim, mutilate. **mutilato, -a** *sm, sf* disabled person.
muto ['muto], **-a** *agg* silent; (*affetto da mutismo*) dumb. *sm, sf* mute. **linguaggio dei muti** *sm* deaf-and-dumb language.
mutuo ['mutuo] *agg* mutual. *sm* loan. **mutuo ipotecario** mortgage. **mutua** *sf* insurance.

N

nafta ['nafta] *sf* fuel oil.
nailon ['nailon] *sm invar* nylon.
nanna ['nanna] *sf* **fare la nanna** (*fam*) sleep.
nano ['nano], **-a** *s, agg* dwarf.
Napoli ['napoli] *sf* Naples. **napoletano, -a** *s, agg* Neapolitan.
nappa ['nappa] *sf* tassel; (*fam*: *naso*) conk; (*pelle*) nappa.
narciso [nar'tʃizo] *sm* narcissus; (*giunchiglia*) daffodil.
narcotico [nar'kɔtiko] *agg, sm* narcotic. **narcosi** *sf* narcosis.
narice [na'ritʃe] *sf* nostril.
narrare [nar'rare] *v* tell. **narrativa** *sf* fiction. **narrazione** *sf* tale.
***nascere** ['naʃere] *v* be born; (*fig*) (a)rise, start (up). **far nascere** give rise to. **nascita** *sf* birth. **atto di nascita** *sm* birth certificate.
***nascondere** [nas'kondere] *v* hide. **nascondiglio** *sm* hide-out. **nascondino** *sm* hide-and-seek.
nascosto [nas'kosto] *agg* hidden.
nasello [na'zɛllo] *sm* hake.
naso ['nazo] *sm* nose. **cacciare** *or* **ficcare il naso (in)** poke one's nose (into).
nastro ['nastro] *sm* ribbon; (*tec*) tape. **nastro sonoro** sound-track. **nastro trasportatore** conveyor belt.
nasturzio [nas'turtsjo] *sm* nasturtium.
natale [na'tale] *agg* native. **Natale** *sm* Christmas. **natalizio** *agg* Christmas. **giorno natalizio** *sm* birthday.
natatoia [nata'toja] *sf* flipper, fin.
natica ['natika] *sf* buttock.
nativo [na'tivo] *agg* native.
nato ['nato] *agg* born. **appena nato** newborn. **... nato e sputato** the (spitting) image of .... **nato morto** stillborn.
natura [na'tura] *sf* nature. **naturale** *agg* natural. **naturalezza** *sf* spontaneity; simplicity. **naturalistico** *agg* naturalistic.
naturalizzare [naturalid'dzare] *v* naturalize. **naturalizzazione** *sf* naturalization.
naufragio [nau'fradʒo] *sm* shipwreck; (*fig*) wreck. **naufragare** *v* be shipwrecked; (*fig*) come to grief. **naufrago, -a** *sm, sf* survivor.
nausea ['nauzea] *sf* nausea. **dare la nausea a** make sick. **provar nausea** feel sick. **nauseante** *agg* nauseating, sickening. **nauseato** *agg* nauseated, sickened.
nautico ['nautiko] *agg* nautical. **sport nautici** *sm pl* water sports *pl*.
navata [na'vata] *sf* (*centrale*) nave; (*laterale*) aisle.
nave ['nave] *sf* ship. **nave cisterna** tanker. **nave di salvataggio** lifeboat. **nave traghetto** ferry. **navale** *agg* naval. **navalmeccanica** *sf* shipbuilding. **navalmeccanico** *sm* shipyard worker.
navetta [na'vetta] *sf* shuttle.
navigare [navi'gare] *v* sail, navigate. **navigatore** *sm* navigator. **navigazione** *sf* navigation.
nazionalizzare [natsjonalid'dzare] *v* nationalize. **nazionalizzazione** *sf* nationalization.
nazione [na'tsjone] *sf* nation. **nazionale** *agg* national; (*econ*) domestic. **nazionalismo** *sm* nationalism. **nazionalista** *s(m+f), agg* nationalist. **nazionalità** *sf* nationality.

nazismo [na'dzizmo] *sm* Nazism, National Socialism. **nazista** *s(m+f)*, *agg* Nazi.
ne [ne] *pron* of it *or* them, about it *or* them; (*partitivo*) some, any. *avv* from there.
nè [ne] *cong* neither, nor; (*con altra negazione*) either. **nè ... nè ...** neither ... nor ....
neanche [ne'anke] *avv*, *cong*, *also* **nemmeno**, **neppure** neither; either; (*rafforzativo*) not even.
nebbia ['nebbja] *sf* fog; (*foschia*) haze, mist. **nebbioso** *agg* foggy.
necessario [netʃes'sarjo] *agg* necessary, needed (for). *sm* necessary. **lo stretto necessario** the bare necessities *pl*.
necessità [netʃessi'ta] *sf* necessity, need. **di prima necessità** essential. **in caso di necessità** if necessary. **trovarsi nella necessità di** be obliged to.
negare [ne'gare] *v* deny. **negato** *agg* denied; (*senza disposizione*) hopeless (at). **negazione** *sf* denial, negation.
negativa [nega'tiva] *sf* negative. **negativo** *agg* negative.
negli ['neʎi] *prep+art* **in gli**.
negligente [negli'dʒente] *agg* negligent. **negligenza** *sf* negligence.
negoziare [nego'tsjare] *v* negotiate.
negozio [ne'gɔtsjo] *sm* shop; (*affare*) deal. **negoziante** *s(m+f)* shopkeeper; dealer; (*all'ingrosso*) wholesaler; (*al minuto*) retailer.
negro ['negro], **-a** *agg* Negro, black. *sm*, *sf* Negro, black person. **negriere** *sm* slaver; (*fig*) slave-driver.
nei ['nei] *prep+art* **in i**.
nel [nel] *prep+art* **in il**.
nell' [nell] *prep+art* **in l'**.
nella ['nella] *prep+art* **in la**.
nelle ['nelle] *prep+art* **in le**.
nello ['nello] *prep+art* **in lo**.
nemico [ne'miko], **-a** *agg* enemy, hostile; (*dannoso*) bad. *sm*, *sf* enemy.
nemmeno [nem'meno] *V* **neanche**.
neo ['nɛo] *sm* mole; (*posticcio*) beauty-spot.
neon ['nɛon] *sm* neon.
neonato [neo'nato], **-a** *agg* new-born. *sm*, *sf* new-born baby.
neozelandese [neodzelan'deze] *agg* New Zealand. *sm*, *sf* New Zealander.
nepotismo [nepo'tizmo] *sm* nepotism.
neppure [nep'pure] *V* **neanche**.
nerbo ['nɛrbo] *sm* whip; (*fig*) force.
nero ['nero] *agg*, *sm* black. **bestia nera** *sf* bugbear. **borsa nera** *sf* black market. **nerastro** *agg* blackish.
nervo ['nɛrvo] *sm* nerve; (*bot*) rib, vein; (*corda*) string. **avere i nervi** be on edge, be irritable. **dare ai** *or* **sui nervi a qualcuno** get on somebody's nerves. **nervoso** *agg* nervous; irritable; (*eccitabile*) highly strung. **esaurimento nervoso** *sm* nervous breakdown.
nesso ['nɛsso] *sm* connection.
nessuno [nes'suno] *agg* no. *pron* (*persone*) nobody, no-one; (*cose*) none; (*qualcuno*) anybody.
nettare [net'tare] *sm* nectar.
netto ['netto] *agg* clean; (*fig*) clear, sharp; (*peso*, *comm*) net. **nettezza** *sf* cleanliness; (*precisione*) clarity. **nettezza urbana** *sf* street-cleaning; refuse collection.
neutrale [neu'trale] *s(m+f)*, *agg* neutral. **neutralità** *sf* neutrality. **neutralizzare** *v* neutralize; (*fig*) counteract.
neutro ['nɛutro] *sm*, *agg* neutral; (*gramm*, *sesso*) neuter. **neutrone** *sm* neutron.
neve ['neve] *sf* snow. **cumulo di neve** *sm* snowdrift. **pupazzo di neve** *sm* snowman. **nevato** *or* **nevoso** *agg* snowy.
nevicare [nevi'kare] *v* snow. **nevicata** *sf* snowfall.
nevischio [ne'viskjo] *sm* sleet.
nevralgia [nevral'dʒia] *sf* neuralgia.
nevrosi [ne'vrɔzi] *sf* neurosis. **nevrotico, -a** *s*, *agg* neurotic.
nibbio ['nibbjo] *sm* kite.
nicchia ['nikkja] *sf* niche, recess.
nichel ['nikel] *sm* nickel. **nichelare** *v* nickel-plate. **nichelatura** *sf* nickel-plating.
nichilismo [niki'lizmo] *sm* nihilism. **nichilista** *s(m+f)* nihilist.
nicotina [niko'tina] *sf* nicotine.
nido ['nido] *sm* nest. **nido d'ape** honeycomb. **nido d'infanzia** crèche, day nursery. **nidiata** *sf* brood.
niente ['njɛnte] *pron* nothing; (*con altra negazione*) anything. *sm* nothing; (*cosa da poco*) slightest thing. **da niente** unimportant. **niente paura!** don't be afraid! **non fa niente** (*non importa*) it doesn't matter.
ninfa ['ninfa] *sf* nymph. **ninfomane** *sf*, *agg* nymphomaniac.
ninfea [nin'fɛa] *sf* water lily.
ninna-nanna [ninna'nanna] *sm* lullaby.

ninnolo ['ninnolo] *sm* (*balocco*) toy; (*gingillo*) knick-knack.
nipote [ni'pote] *sm* (*di nonni*) grandson; (*di zii*) nephew. *sf* (*di nonni*) granddaughter; (*di zii*) niece.
nitido ['nitido] *agg* neat; (*fig*) clear.
nitrire [ni'trire] *v* neigh. **nitrito** *sm* neigh.
no [nɔ] *avv* no. *sm* no; (*rifiuto*) refusal. **come no!** of course! and how! **se no** otherwise, or else. **uno sì e uno no** every other one.
nobile ['nɔbile] *agg* noble. *sm* nobleman. *sf* noblewoman. **nobiltà** *sf* nobility.
nocca ['nɔkka] *sf* knuckle; (*del cavallo*) fetlock.
nocciola [not'tʃɔla] *sf* hazel-nut. *agg, sm invar* (*colore*) hazel. **nocciolina (americana)** *sf* peanut. **nocciolo** *sm* (*pianta*) hazel.
nocciolo ['nottʃɔlo] *sm* (*bot*) stone, kernel; (*fig*) heart, point; (*tec*) core.
noce ['notʃe] *sm* (*albero*) walnut(-tree); (*legno*) walnut. *sf* (*frutto*) walnut. **noce di burro** pat of butter. **noce di cocco** coconut. **noce moscata** nutmeg. **nocepesca** *sf* nectarine.
nocivo [no'tʃivo] *agg* harmful.
nodo ['nɔdo] *sm* knot; (*incrocio*) junction; (*trama*) plot. **avere un nodo alla gola** have a lump in one's throat. **nodo scorsoio** slip-knot. **nodoso** *agg* knotty.
noi ['noi] *pron* (*soggetto*) we; (*oggetto*) us.
noia ['nɔja] *sf* (*tedio*) boredom; (*fastidio*) nuisance; (*fam*) bore. **avere delle noie con** have trouble with. **dare noia (a)** trouble, bother. **noioso** *agg* boring; (*fastidioso*) troublesome.
noleggiare [noled'dʒare] *v* hire, rent. **noleggio** *sm* hire; (*prezzo*) rental. **nolo** *sm* freight. **dare a nolo** hire (out). **prendere a nolo** hire, rent.
nomade ['nɔmade] *agg* nomadic. *s*(*m*+*f*) nomad.
nome ['nome] *sm* name; (*gramm*) noun. **a nome di** on behalf of. **conoscere di nome** know by name. **fare il nome di** mention; (*proporre*) propose. **nome di battaglia** pseudonym. **nomignolo** *sm* nickname.
nomina ['nɔmina] *sf* appointment. **nominare** *v* mention; name; (*eleggere*) appoint.
non [non] *avv* not. **non . . . affatto** not at all. **non . . . mai** never. **non . . . nessuno** nobody. **non . . . niente** *or* **nulla** nothing. **nonché** *cong* as well as.
noncurante [nonku'rante] *agg* heedless.
nondimeno [nondi'meno] *cong* nevertheless.
nonno ['nɔnno] *sm* grandfather; (*fam*) grand-dad. **nonna** *sf* grandmother; (*fam*) grandma, granny. **nonni** *sm pl* grandparents *pl*.
nono ['nɔno] *sm, agg* ninth.
nonostante [nonos'tante] *prep* notwithstanding, in spite of. *cong* (al)though.
nontiscordardimè [nontiskordardi'me] *sm* forget-me-not.
nord [nɔrd] *sm* north. **a nord** north. **del nord** north, northern. **nord-est** *sm* north-east. **nord-ovest** *sm* north-west.
norma ['nɔrma] *sf* rule, standard; (*istruzione*) direction; regulation. **a norma di legge** according to (the) law.
normale [nor'male] *agg* normal, regular; standard. *sf* perpendicular. **normalmente** *avv* as a rule.
Norvegia [nor'vedʒa] *sf* Norway. **norvegese** *s*(*m*+*f*), *agg* Norwegian.
nostalgia [nostal'dʒia] *sf* nostalgia; (*della casa*) homesickness. **aver nostalgia di** miss. **nostalgico** *agg* nostalgic, homesick.
nostro ['nɔstro] *agg* our. *pron* ours. **nostrano** *agg* local, home-grown.
nota ['nɔta] *sf* note; list.
notaio [no'tajo] *sm* notary.
notare [no'tare] *v* note; (*osservare*) notice. **far notare** point out.
notificare [notifi'kare] *v* notify; inform. **notificazione** *sf* notification; (*avviso*) notice.
notizia [no'titsja] *sf* news (item), information. **notiziario** *sm* news (bulletin).
noto ['nɔto] *agg* well-known, renowned. **render noto** make known.
notorio [no'tɔrjo] *agg* renowned; (*spreg*) notorious. **notorietà** *sf* renown.
notte ['nɔtte] *sf* night. **buona notte!** goodnight! **dare la buona notte** bid goodnight. **nottata** *sf* night.
notturno [not'turno] *agg* night, nocturnal. *sm* (*musica*) nocturne.
novanta [no'vanta] *sm, agg* ninety. **novantesimo** *sm, agg* ninetieth.
nove ['nɔve] *sm, agg* nine.
novella [no'vɛlla] *sf* short story. **novellista** *s*(*m*+*f*) short-story writer.
novello [no'vɛllo] *agg* new.
novembre [no'vɛmbre] *sm* November.
novità [novi'ta] *sf* novelty; (*notizie*) news.

novizio [no'vitsjo] *sm* beginner, novice.
nozione [no'tsjone] *sf* notion, idea.
nozze ['nɔttse] *sf pl* wedding *sing*. **viaggio di nozze** *sm* honeymoon.
nube ['nube] *sf* cloud. **nubifragio** *sm* cloudburst.
nubile ['nubile] *agg* unmarried, single.
nuca ['nuka] *sf* nape of the neck.
nucleo ['nukleo] *sm* nucleus. **nucleo familiare** family. **nucleare** *agg* nuclear.
nudo ['nudo] *agg* bare, naked. *sm* nude. **a piedi nudi** barefoot. **nudismo** *sm* nudism. **nudista** *s(m+f)* nudist. **nudità** *sf* nudity, nakedness.
nulla ['nulla] *pron* nothing; (*con altra negazione*) anything. *sm* nothing; (*cosa da poco*) slightest thing. **da nulla** unimportant. **non fa nulla!** (*non importa*) it doesn't matter!
nullo ['nullo] *agg* null. **dichiarar nullo** annul. **nullaosta** *sm invar* clearance. **nullità** *sf* cipher.
numero ['numero] *sm* number; (*segno*) numeral. **numero chiuso** quota. **numero legale** quorum.
numismatica [numiz'matika] *sf* numismatics. **numismatico, -a** *sm, sf* numismatist.
***nuocere** ['nwɔtʃere] *v* harm.
nuora ['nwɔra] *sf* daughter-in-law.
nuotare [nwo'tare] *v* swim. **nuotatore, -trice** *sm, sf* swimmer. **nuoto** *sm* swimming.
nuovo ['nwɔvo] *agg* new. **Nuova York** *sf* New York. **Nuova Zelanda** *sf* New Zealand.
nutrire [nu'trire] *v* feed, nourish. **nutrire affetto per** feel affection for. **nutriente** *agg* nourishing. **nutrimento** *sm* nourishment.
nuvola ['nuvola] *sf* cloud. **senza nuvole** cloudless. **nuvoloso** *agg* cloudy; (*cielo*) overcast.
nuziale [nu'tsjale] *agg* wedding.

O

o [o] *cong* or. **o . . . o . . .** either . . . or . . . . **o l'uno o l'altro** either.
oasi ['ɔazi] *sf* oasis (*pl* -ses).
***obbedire** [obbe'dire] *v* obey. **obbedienza** *sf* obedience.
obbligare *v* bind, force. **obbligarsi** *v* undertake. **obbligato** *agg* fixed, set; (*riconoscente*) obliged. **obbligatorio** *agg* compulsory. **obbligazione** *sf* (*dir*) obligation; (*comm*) bond, debenture. **obbligo** *sm, pl* **-ghi** duty, obligation. **essere d'obbligo** be compulsory *or* obligatory.
obbrobrio [ob'brɔbrjo] *sm* disgrace.
obeso [o'bɛzo] *agg* obese. **obesità** *sf* obesity.
obiettare [objet'tare] *v* object. **obiezione** *sf* objection.
obiettivo [objet'tivo] *sm* objective; (*scope*) aim; (*foto, ecc.*) lens. *agg* objective.
obitorio [obi'tɔrjo] *sm* morgue.
oblazione [obla'tsjone] *sf* offering.
oblio [o'blio] *sm* oblivion.
obliquo [o'blikwo] agg oblique.
oblò [o'blɔ] *sm* porthole.
oblungo [o'blungo] *agg* oblong.
oboe ['ɔboe] *sm* oboe.
oca ['ɔka] *sf* goose (*pl* geese); (*maschio*) gander.
occasionale [okkazjo'nale] *agg* (*fortuito*) chance; immediate; (*saltuario*) occasional.
occasione [okka'zjone] *sf* chance, opportunity; (*buon affare*) bargain; (*circostanza*) occasion.
occhiali [ok'kjali] *sm pl* glasses *pl*, spectacles *pl*. **occhiali da sole** sun-glasses *pl*. **occhialuto** *agg* bespectacled.
occhio ['ɔkkjo] *sm* eye; (*bot*) bud. **a occhi chiusi** blindly. **a occhio** by sight. **a occhio nudo** with the naked eye. **a quattr'occhi** in private. **costare un occhio della testa** cost the earth. **dare nell'occhio** catch the eye. **tenere d'occhio** keep an eye on.
occidente [ottʃi'dɛnte] *sm* west. **occidentale** *agg* west, western.
***occorrere** [ok'korrere] *v* be necessary. **all'occorrenza** in case of need.
occulto [ok'kulto] *agg* occult; (*nascosto*) hidden.
occupare [okku'pare] *v* occupy; (*far lavorare*) employ; (*tempo*) spend; (*carica*) hold; (*tener occupato*) keep busy. **occuparsi di** concern oneself with. **occupato** *agg* engaged; (*indaffarato*) busy. **occupazione** *sf* occupation.
oceano [o'tʃɛano] *sm* ocean.
ocra ['ɔkra] *sf* ochre.
oculare [oku'lare] *agg* **testimonio oculare** *sm* eye-witness.

oculista [oku'lista] *s(m+f)* oculist.
ode ['ɔde] *sf* ode.
odiare [o'djare] *v* hate, loathe. **odio** *sm* hatred, hate, loathing. **avere in odio** hate, detest. **odioso** *agg* hateful.
odierno [o'djɛrno] *agg* of today; modern.
odissea [odis'sɛa] *sf* odyssey.
odontoiatria [odontoja'tria] *sf* dentistry.
odorare [odo'rare] *v* smell. **odorato** *sm* sense of smell. **odore** *sm* smell, odour. **sentir un odore di** smell. **odoroso** *agg* sweet-smelling.
***offendere** [of'fɛndere] *v* offend; (ledere) injure, hurt. **offendere la legge** break the law. **offendersi** *v* take offence. **offensiva** *sf* offensive. **offensivo** *agg* offensive. **offensore** *sm* attacker; (*dir*) offender.
offerta [of'fɛrta] *sf* offer; (*comm*) bid; (*econ*) supply. **offerente** *s(m+f)* bidder.
offesa [of'feza] *sf* offence; insult; (*danno*) harm.
officina [offi'tʃina] *sf* works, workshop. **capo officina** *sm* (works) foreman.
***offrire** [of'frire] *v* offer; (*comm*) bid. **offrirsi** *v* offer; present oneself.
offuscare [offus'kare] *v* dim; (*foto, ecc.*) blur; (*fig*) obscure.
oggetto [od'dʒetto] *sm* object; (*argomento*) subject; (*cosa*) thing. **oggettività** *sf* objectivity. **oggettivo** *agg* objective.
oggi ['oddʒi] *avv, sm* today. **al giorno d'oggi** nowadays. **oggi a otto** a week today.
ogni ['oɲi] *agg* every, each. **ad** *or* **in ogni modo** in any case. **ogni tanto** every so often, now and then.
Ognissanti [oɲis'santi] *sm* All Saints' Day.
ognuno [o'ɲuno] *pron* everybody, everyone; (*ciascuno*) each.
ohimè [oi'mɛ] *inter* alas!
Olanda [o'landa] *sf* Holland. **olandese** *agg* Dutch. **gli olandesi** the Dutch.
oleodotto [oleo'dotto] *sm* (*oil*) pipeline.
oleoso [ole'ozo] *agg* oily.
olfatto [ol'fatto] *sm* sense of smell.
olimpiade [olim'piade] *sf* Olympic games *pl*. **olimpico** *agg* Olympian. **olimpionico** *agg* Olympic.
olio ['ɔljo] *sm* oil. **olio combustibile** (*gasolio*) fuel oil.
oliva [o'liva] *sf* olive. **oliveto** olive grove. **olivo** *sm* olive-tree.
olmo ['olmo] *sm* elm-tree.
olocausto [olo'kausto] *sm* holocaust, sacrifice.
oltraggiare [oltrad'dʒare] *v* outrage. **oltraggio** *sm* outrage. **oltraggio al pudore** indecent behaviour. **oltraggioso** *agg* outrageous.
oltranza [ol'trantsa] *sf* **ad oltranza** to the (bitter) end.
oltre ['oltre] *avv* (*luogo*) further, farther; (*tempo*) beyond. *prep* beyond; (*più di*) more than, over. **oltre a** besides, apart from.
oltremare [oltre'mare] *avv* overseas.
oltremodo [oltre'mɔdo] *avv* exceedingly.
oltrepassare [oltrepas'sare] *v* exceed; surpass.
omaggio [o'maddʒo] sm (*dono*) (complimentary) gift. **porgere omaggi a** pay respects to. **rendere omaggio a** pay homage to.
ombelico [ombe'liko] *sm, pl* **-chi** navel. **ombelicale** *agg* umbilical.
ombra ['ombra] *sf* shadow; (*opposto di luce*) shade. **ombretto** *sm* eye-shadow.
ombrello [om'brɛllo] *sm* umbrella.
omero ['ɔmero] *sm* humerus.
***omettere** [o'mettere] *v* omit, leave out.
omicida [omi'tʃida] *agg* murderous. *s(m+f)* murderer, murderess. **omicidio** *sm* homicide, murder. **omicidio colposo** manslaughter.
omissione [omis'sjone] *sf* omission.
omogeneo [omo'dʒɛneo] *agg* homogeneous. **omogeneità** *sf* homogeneity.
omologare [omolo'gare] *v* ratify.
omonimo [o'mɔnimo] *agg* homonymous. *nm* namesake; (*parola*) homonym.
omosessuale [omosessu'ale] *s(m+f)*, *agg* homosexual. **omosessualità** *sf* homosexuality.
oncia ['ontʃa] *sf* ounce.
onda ['onda] *sf* wave. **a onde** wavy. **ondata** *sf* wave, surge.
onde ['onde] *avv* whence. *cong* so that.
ondeggiare [onded'dʒare] *v* wave, sway, roll; (*fig*) waver.
ondulare [ondu'lare] *v* (*capelli*) wave. **ondulato** *agg* wavy; (*lastra, cartone*) corrugated.
onere ['ɔnere] *sm* burden. **oneroso** *agg* burdensome.
onesto [o'nɛsto] *agg* honest; (*prezzo*) fair. **onestà** *sf* honesty, integrity.
onice ['ɔnitʃe] *sm* onyx.

onnipotente [onnipo'tɛnte] *agg* omnipotent.
onnivoro [on'nivoro] *agg* omnivorous.
onomastico [ono'mastiko] sm saint's day.
onorare [ono'rare] *v* honour.
onorario [ono'rarjo] *agg* honorary. *sm* fee.
onore [o'nore] *sm* honour. **a onor del vero** to tell the truth. **fare onore a** honour; do credit *or* justice to. **farsi onore** distinguish oneself. **onorevole** *agg* honourable.
onorificenza [onorifi'tʃɛntsa] *sf* honour. **onorifico** *agg* honorary.
onta ['onta] *sf* shame.
ontano [on'tano] *sm* alder.
opaco [o'pako] *agg*, *m pl* **-chi** opaque, dull.
opale [o'pale] *sm* opal.
opera ['ɔpera] *sf* work; (*teatro*) opera; (*azione*) deed; institution. **mettere in opera** put into practice; instal. **per opera di** thanks to. **operetta** *sf* operetta, light opera. **operoso** *agg* active.
operaio [ope'rajo], **-a** *sm*, *sf* worker. *agg* working.
operare [ope'rare] *v* function, work; (*med*) operate. **farsi operare** have an operation. **operatore** *sm* (*cinema*) cameraman; (*di borsa*) stockbroker. **operatorio** *agg* operating. **operazione** *sf* operation.
opinione [opi'njone] *sf* opinion.
oppio ['ɔppjo] *sm* opium.
opponente [oppo'nɛnte] *agg* opposing. *s*(*m*+*f*) adversary.
***opporre** [op'porre] *v* oppose. **opporre resistenza** offer resistance. **opporsi a** set oneself against; object to.
opportuno [oppor'tuno] *agg* opportune. **opportunismo** *sm* opportunism. **opportunista** *s*(*m*+*f*) opportunist. **opportunità** *sf* opportunity.
opposizione [oppozi'tsjone] *sf* opposition.
opposto [op'posto] *agg*, *sm* opposite. **all'opposto** on the contrary.
oppressione [oppres'sjone] *sf* oppression. **oppresso** *agg* oppressed. **oppressore** *sm* oppressor.
***opprimere** [op'primere] *v* oppress, burden.
oppure [op'pure] *cong* or, or else.
opulento [opu'lɛnto] *agg* opulent.
opuscolo [o'puskolo] *sm* pamphlet, booklet.
ora[1] ['ora] *sf* hour; (*tempo*) time. **alla buon'ora!** at last! **all'ora** (*velocità*) per hour. **di buon'ora** early. **ora di punta** rush-hour. **ora legale** summer-time. **ora straordinaria** overtime.
ora[2] ['ora] *avv* (*adesso*) now; (*appena*) just. **d'ora in poi** from now on, henceforth. **or ora** just (now).
orale [o'rale] *agg* oral. *sm* (*esame*) viva.
orario [o'rarjo] *agg* (*all'ora*) per hour; time. **in senso orario** clockwise. **segnale orario** time-signal. *sm* (*ore*) hours *pl*; (*tabella*) timetable. **in orario** on time.
orazione [ora'tsjone] *sf* speech. **oratore** *sm* orator. **oratorio** *sm* (*chiesa*) oratory; (*musica*) oratorio.
orbene [or'bɛne] *avv* well (now).
orbita ['ɔrbita] *sf* orbit. **orbitare** *v* orbit.
orchestra [or'kɛstra] *sf* orchestra. **orchestrare** *v* orchestrate. **orchestrazione** *sf* orchestration.
orchidea [orki'dɛa] *sf* orchid.
orco ['ɔrko] *sm* ogre.
orda ['ɔrda] *sf* horde.
ordigno [or'diɲo] *sm* device.
ordinare [ordi'nare] *v* order; (*mettere in ordine*) tidy up; (*sistemare*) arrange; (*rel*) ordain. **ordinamento** *sm* order; arrangement; system. **ordinazione** *sf* order; (*rel*) ordination.
ordinario [ordi'narjo] *agg*, *sm* ordinary.
ordine ['ordine] *sm* order. **ordine del giorno** agenda.
ordire [or'dire] *v* (*tessile*) warp; (*fig*) hatch. **ordito** *sm* warp; (*fig*) plot.
orecchio [o'rekkjo] *sm* ear. **a orecchio** by ear. **a portato d'orecchio** within earshot. **orecchino** *sm* ear-ring. **orecchioni** *sm pl* mumps *sing*.
orefice [o'refitʃe] *sm* goldsmith, jeweller. **oreficeria** *sf* jewellery; (*negozio*) jeweller's (shop).
orfano ['ɔrfano], **-a** *s*, *agg* orphan. **orfanotrofio** *sm* orphanage.
organico [or'ganiko] *agg* organic. *sm* personnel. **organismo** *sm* organism; (*fig*) body.
organizzare [organid'dzare] *v* organize, arrange. **organizzazione** *sf* organization, body. **organizzatore, -trice** *sm*, *sf* organizer.
organo ['ɔrgano] *sm* organ. **organetto** *sm* barrel-organ.
orgasmo [or'gazmo] *sm* orgasm.
orgia ['ɔrdʒa] *sf* orgy.

orgoglio [or'goʎo] *sm* pride. **orgoglioso** *agg* proud.
orientare [orjen'tare] *v* orient(ate); direct. **orientarsi** *v* find one's bearings; tend. **orientamento** *sm* orientation; (*direzione*) trend. **senso d'orientamento** *sm* sense of direction.
oriente [o'rjɛnte] *sm* East. **orientale** *agg* oriental, eastern, east.
orifizio [ori'fitsjo] *sm* orifice, opening.
origano [o'rigano] *sm* oregano.
originare [oridʒi'nare] *v* (*avere origini*) originate; (*dare origini*) give rise to.
origine [o'ridʒine] *sf* origin; (*inizio*) beginning. **originale** *sm, agg* original; eccentric. **originalità** *sf* originality; eccentricity. **originario** *agg* native.
origliare [ori'ʎare] *v* eavesdrop.
orina [o'rina] *sf* urine. **orinare** *v* urinate. **orinatorio** *agg* urinary.
oriundo [o'rjundo] *agg* native.
orizzonte [orid'dzonte] *sm* horizon. **giro d'orizzonte** *sm* general survey. **orizzontale** *agg* horizontal. **orizzontarsi** *v* find one's bearings.
orlo ['orlo] *sm* edge; (*abisso*) brink; (*bicchiere*) rim; (*tessuto*) hem. **orlare** *v* hem; (*bordare*) trim.
orma ['orma] *sf* footprint; track.
ormai [or'mai] *avv* by now; (*passato*) by then.
ormeggiare [ormed'dʒare] *v* moor. **ormeggio** *sm* mooring.
ormone [or'mone] *sm* hormone.
ornare [or'nare] *v* adorn, decorate. **ornamentale** *agg* ornamental. **ornamento** *sm* ornament, decoration.
ornitologia [ornitolo'dʒia] *sf* ornithology. **ornitologo, -a** *sm, sf* ornithologist.
oro ['ɔro] *sm* gold. **d'oro** gold, golden.
orologio [oro'lɔdʒo] *sm* clock; (*da polso o tasca*) watch. **orologeria** *sf* clockwork; (*negozio*) watchmaker's (shop). **bomba ad orologeria** *sf* time-bomb. **orologiaio** *sm* watchmaker.
oroscopo [o'rɔskopo] *sm* horoscope.
orpello [or'pɛllo] *sm* tinsel.
orrendo [or'rɛndo] *agg* hideous, horrifying.
orribile [or'ribile] *agg* horrible, dreadful.
orrore [or'rore] *sm* horror, dread, loathing. **avere orrore di** loathe.
orso ['orso], **-a** *sm, sf* bear. **orsacchiotto** *sm* bear-cub; (*giocattolo*) teddy-bear.
ortica [or'tika] *sf* nettle. **orticaria** *sf* nettle-rash.
orto ['ɔrto] *sm* kitchen garden. **ortaggi** *sm pl* vegetables *pl*. **orticoltore** *sm* horticulturist. **orticoltura** *sf* horticulture. **ortolano** *sm* greengrocer.
ortodosso [orto'dɔsso] *agg* orthodox. **ortodossia** *sf* orthodoxy.
ortografia [ortogra'fia] *sf* spelling. **errore ortografico** *sm* spelling mistake.
ortopedia [ortope'dia] *sf* orthopaedics. **ortopedico** *agg* orthopaedic.
orzaiolo [ordza'jɔlo] *sm* stye.
orzo ['ɔrdzo] *sm* barley.
osare [o'zare] *v* dare; risk.
osceno [o'ʃɛno] *agg* obscene. **oscenità** *sf* obscenity.
oscillare [oʃil'lare] *v* swing, oscillate.
oscurare [osku'rare] *v* darken; (*fig*) obscure. **oscuramento** *sm* darkening; (*guerra*) black-out. **oscurità** *sf* dark; (*fig*) obscurity.
ospedale [ospe'dale] *sm* hospital. **ospedaliero** *agg* hospital.
ospitare [ospi'tare] *v* offer hospitality (to); (*albergare*) put up. **ospitale** *agg* hospitable.
ospite ['ɔspite] *s(m+f)* (*persona ospitata*) guest; (*oste*) host, hostess.
ospizio [os'pitsjo] *sm* hostel.
ossatura [ossa'tura] *sf* (*arch*) framework; (*anat*) bone structure.
ossequio [os'sɛkwjo] *sm* homage. **ossequi** *sm pl* (*saluti*) regards *pl*. **ossequioso** *agg* respectful.
osservare [osser'vare] *v* obscure; (*notare*) notice. **osservanza** *sf* observance. **osservatore, -trice** *sm, sf* observer. **osservatorio** *sm* observatory. **osservazione** *sf* observation; (*nota*) remark. **fare un'osservazione** comment; criticize.
ossessionare [ossessjo'nare] *v* haunt. **ossessionante** *agg* haunting. **ossessione** *sf* obsession. **ossesso** *agg* possessed.
ossia [os'sia] *cong* or rather, in other words.
ossigeno [os'sidʒeno] *sm* oxygen. **ossidare** *v* oxidize. **ossido** *sm* oxide.
osso ['ɔsso] *sm, pl* **-a** *f in collective sense* bone. **ossuto** *agg* bony.
ostacolare [ostako'lare] *v* hinder, obstruct. **ostacolo** *sm* obstacle, hindrance; (*atletica*) hurdle. **corsa a ostacolo** *sf* obstacle race; hurdling.

ostaggio [os'taddʒo] *sm* hostage.
oste ['ɔste] *sm* host, innkeeper.
ostello [os'tɛllo] *sm* refuge; (*per la gioventù*) (youth-)hostel.
ostentare [osten'tare] *v* show off. **ostentato** *agg* ostentatious.
osteria [oste'ria] *sf* inn.
ostetrico [os'tɛtriko] *sm* obstetrician. **ostetrica** *sf* obstetrician; (*levatrice*) midwife. **ostetricia** *sf* obstetrics; midwifery.
ostia ['ɔstja] *sf* (*rel*) host; (*cialda*) wafer.
ostile [os'tile] *agg* hostile. **ostilità** *sf* hostility.
ostinarsi [osti'narsi] *v* persist. **ostinatezza** *sf* obstinacy, stubbornness. **ostinato** *agg* obstinate, stubborn.
ostrica ['ɔstrika] *sf* oyster.
ostruire [ostru'ire] *v* obstruct, block. **ostruzione** *sf* obstruction.
otite [o'tite] *sf* otitis.
otorinolaringoiatra [otorinolaringo'jatra] *s(m+f)* ear, nose, and throat specialist.
ottagono [ot'tagono] *sm* octagon.
ottano [ot'tano] *sm* octane.
ottanta [ot'tanta] *sm, agg* eighty. **ottantesimo** *agg, sm* eightieth.
ottava [ot'tava] *sf* octave. **ottavo** *sm, agg* eighth.
***ottenere** [otte'nere] *v* obtain, get. **ottenibile** *agg* obtainable.
ottico ['ɔttiko] *agg* optic. *sm* optician. **ottica** *sf* (*persona*) optician; (*scienza*) optics.
ottimismo [otti'mizmo] *agg* optimistic.
ottimo ['ɔttimo] *agg* excellent, very good.
otto ['ɔtto] *agg, sm* eight.
ottobre [ot'tobre] *sm* October.
ottone [ot'tone] *sm* brass. **ottoni** *sm pl* (*musica*) brass *pl*.
otturare [ottu'rare] *v* plug; (*dente*) fill. **otturatore** *sm* (*foto*) shutter.
ottuso [ot'tuzo] *agg* dull; (*non tagliente*) blunt; (*angolo*) obtuse.
ovaia [o'vaja] *sf* ovary.
ovale [o'vale] *agg, sm* oval.
ovatta [o'vatta] *sf* wadding; (*cotone idrofilo*) cotton wool.
ovazione [ova'tsjone] *sf* ovation.
ovest ['ɔvest] *sm* west. **a ovest di** (to the) west of. **dell'ovest** west, western.
ovile [o'vile] *sm* sheepfold.
ovulo ['ɔvulo] *sm* ovum; (*bot*) ovule. **ovulazione** *sf* ovulation.
ovunque [o'vunkwe] *avv* everywhere. *cong* wherever.
ovvero [ov'vero] *cong* or (rather).
ovvio ['ɔvvjo] *agg* obvious.
oziare [o'tsjare] *v* loaf. **ozio** *sm* (*pigrizia*) idleness; (*tempo libero*) leisure, spare time. **ozioso** *agg* idle.

P

pacato [pa'kato] *agg* calm.
pacchia ['pakkja] *sf* godsend.
pacco ['pakko] *sm* parcel. **pacchetto** *sm* packet, small parcel.
pace ['patʃe] *sf* peace.
pacificare [patʃifi'kare] *v* pacify, appease; reconcile. **pacifico** *agg* peaceful; (*ovvio*) self-evident.
pacifismo [patʃi'fizmo] *sm* pacifism. **pacifista** *s(m+f)* pacifist.
padella [pa'dɛlla] *sf* frying pan.
padiglione [padi'ʎone] *sm* pavilion.
Padova ['padova] *sf* Padua.
padre ['padre] *sm* father. **padre adottivo** foster-father. **padrino** *sm* godfather.
padrone [pa'drone], **-a** *sm, sf* master, mistress; owner; (*fam*) boss. **padronale** *agg* private; (*non di servizio*) owner's. **padronanza** *sf* mastery. **padroneggiarsi** *v* control oneself.
paesaggio [pae'zaddʒo] *sm* landscape.
paese [pa'eze] *sm* country; village; (*città*) town. **paesano** *agg* rural, country.
paffuto [paf'futo] *agg* plump.
paga ['paga] *sf* pay, wages *pl*.
pagaia [pa'gaja] *sf* paddle.
pagano [pa'gano], **-a** *s, agg* pagan, heathen.
pagare [pa'gare] *v* pay. **pagamento** *sm* payment.
pagella [pa'dʒɛlla] *sf* school report.
paggio ['paddʒo] *sm* page(-boy).
pagina ['padʒina] *sf* page.
paglia ['paʎa] *sf* straw. **paglierìccio** *sm* palliasse. **paglietta** *sf* steel wool; (*cappello*) straw hat.
pagliaccio [pa'ʎattʃo] *sm* clown. **pagliacciata** *sf* buffoonery.
pagnotta [pa'ɲɔtta] *sf* loaf (of bread).
pago ['pago] *agg* contented (with).
pagoda [pa'gɔda] *sf* pagoda.
paio ['pajo] *sm, pl* **-a** *f* pair; (*due o circa due*) couple.

pala ['pala] *sf* shovel; (*di remo*) blade. **palata** *sf* shovel(ful). **soldi a palate** *sm pl* pots *or* bags of money *pl.*

palato [pa'lato] *sm* palate.

palazzo [pa'lattso] *sm* (*edificio*) building; (*appartamenti*) block of flats; (*casa di principe, ecc.*) palace. **palazzina** *sf* villa.

palco ['palko] *sm* platform, stand; (*teatro*) box. **palcoscenico** *sm* stage.

palese [pa'leze] *agg* obvious, clear. **palesare** *v* reveal.

palestra [pa'lɛstra] *sf* gymnasium.

paletto [pa'letto] *sm* bolt.

palio ['paljo] *sm* **mettere in palio** offer as a prize.

palla ['palla] *sf* ball. **pallacanestro** *sm* basketball. **pallanuoto** *sm* water polo.

palleggiare [palled'dʒare] *v* (*tennis*) knock up; (*calcio*) dribble. **palleggio** *sm* knock-up, dribbling.

pallido ['pallido] *agg* pale; (*fig*) faint.

pallino [pal'lino] *sm* (*bocce*) jack; (*fig*) craze. **a pallini** with polka dots.

pallone [pal'lone] *sm* ball; (*calcio*) football; (*aerostato*) balloon.

pallottola [pal'lɔttola] *sf* pellet; (*rivoltella*) bullet.

palma[1] ['palma] *sf* (*albero*) palm(-tree).

palma[2] ['palma] *sf* (*anat*) palm. **piede palmato** *sm* webbed foot.

palmo ['palmo] *sm* palm.

palo ['palo] *sm* pole; (*di porta*) post.

palombaro [palom'baro] *sm* diver.

palpare [pal'pare] *v* feel; pat. **palpabile** *agg* palpable.

palpebra ['palpebra] *sf* eyelid. **battere le palbebre** blink.

palpitare [palpi'tare] *v* throb.

paltò [pal'tɔ] *sm invar* overcoat.

palude [pa'lude] *sf* marsh, swamp. **terreno paludoso** *sm* marshland.

panca ['panka] *sf* bench. **panchetto** *sm* (foot)stool. **panchina** *sf* bench, garden seat. **pancone** *sm* work-bench.

pancetta [pan'tʃetta] *sf* bacon.

pancia ['pantʃa] *sf* belly; (*fam*) tummy. **mal di pancia** *sm* (*fam*) tummy-ache. **panciotto** *sm* waistcoat. **panciuto** *agg* (*persona*) pot-bellied; (*cosa*) bulging.

pancreas ['pankreas] *sm invar* pancreas.

panda ['panda] *sm invar* panda.

pandemonio [pande'mɔnjo] *sm* uproar.

pane ['pane] *sm* bread; (*forma*) loaf. **buono come il pane** as good as gold. **guadagnarsi il pane** earn one's living. **pan grattato** breadcrumbs *pl.* **pan tostato** toast. **panettiere** *sm* baker. **panificio** *sm* bakery.

panfilo ['panfilo] *sm* yacht.

panico ['paniko] *sm* panic.

paniere [pa'njɛre] *sm* basket.

panino [pa'nino] *sm* roll. **panino imbottito** sandwich.

panna[1] ['panna] *sf* cream. **panna montata** whipped cream.

panna[2] ['panna] *sf* (*mec*) breakdown.

pannello [pan'nɛllo] *sm* panel.

panno ['panno] *sm* cloth. **panni** *sm pl* (*vestiti*) clothes *pl.* **pannolino** *sm* nappy.

panorama [pano'rama] *sm* panorama, view.

pantaloni [panta'loni] *sm pl* trousers *pl*; (*corti*) shorts *pl.*

pantano [pan'tano] *sm* bog.

pantera [pan'tɛra] *sf* panther.

pantofola [pan'tɔfola] *sf* slipper.

pantomima [panto'mima] *sf* play-acting.

paonazzo [pao'nattso] *agg* purple.

papa ['papa] *sm* pope. **ogni morte di papa** once in a blue moon. **vivere come un papa** live like a lord. **papale** *agg* papal.

papà [pa'pa] *sm* (*fam*) dad(dy).

papavero [pa'pavero] *sm* poppy.

papera ['papera] *sf* slip, blunder. **prendere una papera** slip up.

papero ['papero], **-a** *sm*, *sf* gosling.

papiro [pa'piro] *sm* papyrus; (*fam*) paper.

pappa ['pappa] *sm* mush. **pappare** *v* gobble up.

pappagallo [pappa'gallo] *sm* parrot.

paprica ['paprika] *sf* paprika.

parabola [pa'rabola] *sf* (*storia*) parable; (*mat*) parabola.

parabrezza [para'brettsa] *sm invar* windscreen.

paracadute [paraka'dute] *sm invar* parachute. **paracadutista** *s*(*m*+*f*) parachutist; (*mil*) paratrooper.

paradiso [para'dizo] *sm* paradise, heaven.

paradosso [para'dɔsso] *sm* paradox. **paradossale** *agg* paradoxical.

parafango [para'fango] *sm* mudguard.

paraffina [paraf'fina] *sf* paraffin.

parafrasi [pa'rafrazi] *sf* paraphrase.

parafulmine [para'fulmine] *sm* lightning conductor.

parafuoco [para'fwɔko] *sm*, *pl* **-chi** fireguard, firescreen.

paragonare [parago'nare] *v* compare. **paragonabile** *agg* comparable. **paragone** *sm* comparison. **senza paragone** without equal.
paragrafo [pa'ragrafo] *sm* paragraph.
paralisi [pa'ralizi] *sf* paralysis (*pl* -ses). **paralitico, -a** *sm, sf* cripple. **paralizzare** *v* paralyse.
parallelo [paral'lɛlo] *agg, sm* parallel. **parallela** *sf* parallel (line). **parallelogrammo** *sm* parallelogram.
paralume [para'lume] *sm* lampshade.
paranoia [para'nɔja] *sf* paranoia. **paranoico** *agg* paranoid.
parapetto [para'pɛtto] *sm* parapet.
parare [pa'rare] *v* adorn; (*evitare*) ward off; (*sport*) save.
parasole [para'sole] *sm* sunshade.
parassita [paras'sita] *agg* parasitic. *s(m+f)* parasite.
parata[1] [pa'rata] *sf* (*sfilata*) parade.
parata[2] [pa'rata] *sf* (*scherma*) parry; (*calcio, ecc.*) save.
parato [pa'rato] *sm* **carta da parati** *sf* wallpaper.
paraurti [para'urti] *sm invar* bumper.
paravento [para'vɛnto] *sm* screen.
parcheggiare [parked'dʒare] *v* park. **parcheggio** *sm* parking; (*luogo*) car park.
parchimetro [par'kimetro] *sm* parking meter.
parco[1] ['parko] *sm* park; (*industriale*) depot; (*auto*) fleet.
parco[2] ['parko] *agg* frugal, moderate.
parecchio [pa'rekkjo] *agg* quite a lot of, several. **parecchio tempo** quite a long time. *pron* quite a lot, several. *avv* quite a lot.
pareggiare [pared'dʒare] *v* equal; (*sport*) draw; (*comm*) balance. **pareggio** *sm* balance; draw.
parente [pa'rɛnte] *s(m+f)* relative, relation. **parentela** *sf* relationship; (*parenti*) relations *pl*.
parentesi [pa'rɛntezi] *sf* bracket, parenthesis (*pl* -ses). **fra parentesi** incidentally.
***parere** [pa'rere] *v* seem, appear; (*suono*) sound; (*tatto*) feel. **faccio come mi pare** I do as I like. *sm* opinion.
parete [pa'rete] *sf* wall; (*monte*) face.
pari ['pari] *agg* equal, same; (*non dispari*) even; equivalent. **alla pari** (*in famiglia*) au pair. **essere pari** be quits; (*forze*) be equal *or* level. *s(m+f)* equal, peer.
Parigi [pa'ridʒi] *sf* Paris. **parigino, -a** *s, agg* Parisian.
parità [pari'ta] *sf* parity. **a parità di condizioni** all things being equal.
parlamento [parla'mento] *sm* parliament. **parlamentare** *agg* parliamentary.
parlare [par'lare] *v* speak, talk. **parlar chiaro** speak clearly; (*fig*) speak one's mind. *sm* talk; (*parlata*) way of speaking, dialect.
parmigiano [parmi'dʒano] *agg* Parmesan. *sm* Parmesan cheese.
parodia [paro'dia] *sf* parody.
parola [pa'rɔla] *sf* word. **parola d'ordine** password. **parole crociate** *sf pl* crossword *sing*.
parolacce [paro'lattʃe] *sf pl* bad language *sing*.
parrochia [par'rɔkkja] *sf* parish. **parroco** *sm, pl* **-chi** parish priest.
parrucca [par'rukka] *sf* wig.
parrucchiere [parruk'kjɛre] *sm* hairdresser.
parte ['parte] *sf* part; (*porzione*) share; (*lato*) side; (*dir*) party. **a parte** apart; extra. **dall'altra parte** on the other hand. **da parte** aside. **da parte mia** from me. **da queste parti** round here. **per parte mia** as far as I am concerned.
partecipare [partetʃi'pare] *v* participate, take part; (*condividere*) share; announce. **partecipazione** *sf* sharing; announcement; presence.
partenza [par'tɛntsa] *sf* departure; (*sport*) start.
participio [parti'tʃipjo] *sm* participle.
particolare [partiko'lare] *agg* particular, special. *sm* detail.
partigiano [parti'dʒano], **-a** *s, agg* partisan.
partire [par'tire] *v* leave; go away; start.
partita [par'tita] *sf* game; (*incontro*) match; (*contabilità*) entry; (*merci*) lot.
partito [par'tito] *sm* party; condition; decision. **mal partito** predicament. **per partito preso** having made up one's mind.
partitura [parti'tura] *sf* score.
parto ['parto] *sm* birth; (*umano*) childbirth; (*atto*) delivery. **partorire** *v* give birth (to).
parziale [par'tsjale] *agg* partial; (*predisposto*) biased.
pascere ['paʃere] *v* feed (on). **ben pasciuto** well-fed, plump.

pascolare [pasko'lare] *v* graze. **pascolo** *sm* pasture.
Pasqua ['paskwa] *sf* Easter. **Pasqua degli ebrei** Passover.
passabile [pas'sabile] *agg* fair.
passaggio [pas'saddʒo] *sm* passage; (*traversata*) crossing. **dare un passaggio** give a lift. **diritto di passaggio** *sm* right of way. **essere di passaggio** be on the way through. **vietato il passaggio** no thoroughfare.
passaporto [passa'pɔrto] *sm* passport.
passare [pas'sare] *v* pass; go past; (*gastr*) strain.
passatempo [passa'tɛmpo] *sm* pastime.
passato [pas'sato] *agg* past; (*scorso*) last. *sm* past.
passatoia [passa'toja] *sf* runner.
passeggero [passed'dʒɛro], **-a** *agg* passing, transient. *sm*, *sf* passenger.
passeggiare [passed'dʒare] *v* go for a walk *or* stroll. **passeggiata** *sf* walk, stroll; (*non a piedi*) ride.
passerella [passe'rɛlla] *sf* footbridge.
passero ['passero] *sm* sparrow.
passibile [pas'sibile] *agg* liable (to).
passione [pas'sjone] *sf* passion.
passivo [pas'sivo] *agg* passive; (*comm*) debit. *sm* (*gramm*) passive; (*comm*) liability.
passo ['passo] *sm* step; (*andatura*) pace; (*velocità*) rate; (*geog*) pass; (*di vite*) thread. **cedere il passo** give way. **fare due passi** go for a stroll. **sbarrare il passo** block the way. **segnare il passo** mark time.
pasta ['pasta] *sf* dough; (*minestra*) pasta; (*impasto*) paste; (*dolce*) pastry. **pasta frolla** shortcrust pastry. **pasta sfoglia** puff pastry.
pastello [pas'tɛllo] *sm* pastel.
pasticca [pas'tikka] *sf* lozenge.
pasticceria [pastittʃe'ria] *sf* (*negozio*) confectioner's (shop); (*pasticcini*) pastries *pl*. **pasticciere** *sm* confectioner.
pasticciare [pastit'tʃare] *v* bungle, mess up. **pasticcio** *sm* mess; (*gastr*) pie.
pastiglia [pas'tiʎa] *sf* tablet.
pasto ['pasto] *sm* meal. **vino da pasto** *sm* table wine.
pastore [pas'tore] *sm* shepherd; (*prete*) minister. **cane pastore** *sm* sheepdog. **pastorale** *agg* pastoral.
pastorizzare [pastorid'dzare] *v* pasteurize. **pastorizzazione** *sf* pasteurization.
pastoso [pas'tozo] *agg* mellow.
pastrano [pas'trano] *sm* overcoat.
pastura [pas'tura] *sf* pasture.
patata [pa'tata] *sf* potato.
patella [pa'tɛlla] *sf* (*anat*) knee-cap; (*zool*) limpet.
patente[1] [pa'tɛnte] *agg* patent.
patente[2] [pa'tɛnte] *sf* licence.
paterno [pa'tɛrno] *agg* paternal. **paternale** *sf* lecture. **paternità** *sf* paternity.
patetico [pa'tɛtiko] *agg* pathetic, moving.
patibolo [pa'tibolo] *sm* gallows.
patina ['patina] *sf* coat.
patire [pa'tire] *v* suffer. **patimento** *sm* suffering, pain. **patito** *sm* (*fam*) fan.
patologico [pato'lɔdʒiko] *agg* pathological.
patria ['patrja] *sf* country; home.
patrigno [pa'triɲo] *sm* stepfather.
patrimonio [patri'mɔnjo] *sm* estate; fortune. **patrimonio pubblico** public heritage.
patriota [patri'ɔta] *s*(*m*+*f*) patriot. **patriottico** *agg* patriotic. **patriottismo** *sm* patriotism.
patrocinio [patro'tʃinjo] *sm* defence. **patrocinare** *v* defend.
patrono [pa'trɔno] *sm* patron. **patronato** *sm* patronage; institution.
pattinare [patti'nare] *v* skate. **pattinaggio** *sm* skating. **pattino** *sm* skate; (*mec*) shoe.
patto ['patto] *sm* pact, agreement; condition, term. **pattuire** *v* agree.
pattuglia [pat'tuʎa] *sf* patrol.
pattumiera [pattu'mjɛra] *sf* dustbin.
paura [pa'ura] *sf* fear; (*spavento*) fright. **aver paura di** be afraid of, fear. **far paura** scare. **pauroso** *agg* (*che fa paura*) frightening; (*che ha paura*) timid, afraid.
pausa ['pauza] *sf* pause, interval.
pavimento [pavi'mento] *sm* floor.
pavone [pa'vone] *sm* peacock. **pavonessa** *sf* peahen.
pavoneggiarsi [pavoned'dʒarsi] *v* show off.
paziente [pa'tsjɛnte] *s*(*m*+*f*), *agg* patient. **pazientare** *v* wait patiently. **pazienza** *sf* patience.
pazzo ['pattso], **-a** *agg* crazy, insane. *sm*, *sf* lunatic. **pazzesco** *agg* mad; incredible. **pazzia** *sf* madness, folly.
peccare [pek'kare] *v* sin. **pecca** *sf* fault. **peccato** *sm* sin. **che peccato!** what a pity! **peccatore, -trice** *sm*, *sf* sinner.

pece ['petʃe] *sf* pitch.
pecora ['pɛkora] *sf* sheep; (*femmina*) ewe.
peculiare [peku'ljare] *agg* peculiar.
pedaggio [pe'daddʒo] *sm* toll.
pedale [pe'dale] *sm* pedal. **pedalare** *v* pedal.
pedana [pe'dana] *sf* platform; (*sport*) springboard.
pedante [pe'dante] *agg* pedantic. *s*(*m*+*f*) pedant.
pedata [pe'data] *sf* kick; (*orma*) footprint.
pedestre [pe'dɛstre] *agg* pedestrian.
pediatria [pedja'tria] *sf* paediatrics. **pediatra** *s*(*m*+*f*) paediatrician. **pediatrico** *agg* paediatric.
pedicure [pedi'kure] *sf* (*cura*) pedicure. *s*(*m*+*f*) *invar* chiropodist.
pedina [pe'dina] *sf* piece; (*scacchi*) pawn. **muovere una pedina** make a move; (*fig*) pull strings.
pedinare [pedi'nare] *v* shadow.
pedone [pe'done] *s*(*m*+*f*) pedestrian. **pedonale** *agg* pedestrian.
peggio ['pɛddʒo] *agg* (*comparativo*) worse; (*superlativo*) the worst. *sm* the worst. **alla peggio** if the worst comes to the worst.
peggiorare [peddʒo'rare] *v* (*stare*) get worse; (*rendere*) make worse. **peggioramento** *sm* worsening.
peggiore [ped'dʒore] *agg* (*comparativo*) worse; (*superlativo*) the worst. *s*(*m*+*f*) the worst.
pegno ['peɲo] *sm* pledge, pawn.
pelare [pe'lare] *v* peel, skin; (*fig*) fleece. **pelarsi** *v* (*fam*) go bald.
pelle ['pɛlle] *sf* skin; (*cuoio*) hide; (*frutta*) peel; (*carnagione*) complexion. **rimetterci la pelle** lose one's life.
pellegrino [pelle'grino] *sm* pilgrim. **pellegrinaggio** *sm* pilgrimage.
pellicano [pelli'kano] *sm* pelican.
pelliccia [pel'littʃa] *sf* fur; (*mantello*) fur coat. **pellicciaio** *sm* furrier.
pellicola [pel'likola] *sf* film; membrane.
pelo ['pelo] *sm* hair; (*pelame*) coat. **cercare il pelo nell'uovo** split hairs. **contro pelo** against the grain. **per un pelo** by a whisker.
peltro ['peltro] *sm* pewter.
peluria [pe'lurja] *sf* down.
pelvi ['pɛlvi] *sf* pelvis.
pena ['pena] *sf* (*dolore*) pain; (*disturbo*) trouble; punishment. **valere la pena** be worth it, be worthwhile.
penale [pe'nale] *agg* criminal, penal. *sf* fine.
penare [pe'nare] *v* find difficult, be hardly able to.
pendente [pen'dɛnte] *agg* hanging; (*dir, comm*) pending; (*torre*) leaning. *sm* pendant. **pendenza** *sf* slope, incline.
pendere ['pɛndere] *v* hang (down); incline, slope; (*dir*) be pending.
pendio [pen'dio] *sm* slope.
pendolare [pendo'lare] *v* swing. *s*(*m*+*f*) commuter. **pendolo** *sm* pendulum.
pene ['pɛne] *sm* penis.
penetrare [pene'trare] *v* penetrate, pierce. **penetrante** *agg* penetrating, piercing; acute. **penetrazione** *sf* penetration.
penicillina [penitʃil'lina] *sf* penicillin.
penisola [pe'nizola] *sf* peninsula.
penitente [peni'tɛnte] *s*(*m*+*f*), *agg* penitent. **penitenza** *sf* penance; (*gioco*) forfeit. **penitenziario** *sm* jail.
penna ['penna] *sf* feather; (*da scrivere*) pen. **penna a sfera** ball-point pen. **penna stilografica** fountain pen. **pennuto** *agg* feathered.
pennello [pen'nɛllo] *sm* brush.
penombra [pe'nombra] *sf* twilight.
penoso [pe'nozo] *agg* painful.
pensare [pen'sare] *v* think; intend. **pensarci** *v* think about it. **pensarci sopra** think it over. **pensatore, -trice** *sm, sf* thinker.
pensiero [pen'sjɛro] *sm* thought; (*mente, parere*) mind. **essere in pensiero** worry. **pensieroso** *agg* thoughtful; pensive.
pensile ['pɛnsile] *agg* hanging.
pensionare [pensjo'nare] *v* pension off. **pensionato** *sm* pensioner; (*collegio*) boarding-school. **pensione** *sf* pension. **essere in pensione** be retired. **mezza pensione** half board. **pensione completa** full board.
pentagono [pen'tagono] *sm* pentagon. **pentagonale** *agg* pentagonal.
Pentecoste [pente'kɔste] *sf* Whitsun.
pentirsi [pen'tirsi] *v* regret, be sorry for; (*rel*) repent. **pentimento** *sm* regret; repentance.
pentola ['pentola] *sf* pot.
penultimo [pe'nultimo] *agg* penultimate.
penzolare [pendzo'lare] *v* dangle. **penzoloni** *avv* dangling.
pepe ['pepe] *sm* pepper. **pepare** *v* pepper. **pepato** *agg* peppery, hot. **peperone** *sm*

capsicum; (*frutto*) pepper; (*peperoncino*) chili.

pepita [pe'pita] *sf* nugget.

per ['per] *prep* for; (*attraverso*) through; (*mat, entro, tramite*) by. **per caso** by chance. **per cento** per cent. **per di più** in addition. **per lo meno** at least. **per ora** for the present. **per terra** on the floor. **per volta** at a time. **stare per** be about to, be on the point of.

pera ['pera] *sf* pear. **pero** *sm* pear-tree.

perbacco [per'bakko] *inter* by Jove!

perbene [per'bɛne] *agg invar* respectable, nice. *avv* well, nicely.

percentuale [pertʃentu'ale] *agg* per cent. *sf* percentage.

percepire [pertʃe'pire] *v* notice, be aware (of); (*riscuotere*) receive. **percepibile** *agg* noticeable; (*comm*) due. **percettibile** *agg* perceptible. **percezione** *sf* perception.

perché [per'ke] *avv* why. *cong* because, as; (*affinché*) so that. *sm* reason.

perciò [per'tʃo] *cong* so, therefore.

***percorrere** [per'korrere] *v* cover.

percorso [per'korso] *sm* trip, run.

percossa [per'kɔssa] *sf* blow, impact.

***percuotere** [per'kwɔtere] *v* strike, hit.

percussione [perkus'sjone] *sf* percussion.

***perdere** ['pɛrdere] *v* lose; (*colare*) leak; (*sprecare*) waste. **lascia perdere!** skip it! **perdere di vista** lose sight of. **perdersi** *v* get lost. **perdita** *sf* loss; leak; waste.

perdonare [perdo'nare] *v* forgive. **perdono** *sm* forgiveness, pardon.

perenne [pe'rɛnne] *agg* perpetual.

perfetto [per'fɛtto] *agg* perfect.

perfezionare [perfetsjo'nare] *v* (*migliorare*) improve; make perfect. **perfezionarsi** *v* specialize. **perfezionamento** *sm* specialization. **perfezione** *sf* perfection. **perfezionista** *s(m+f)* perfectionist.

perfidia [per'fidja] *sf* treachery, wickedness. **perfido** *agg* treacherous, wicked.

perfino [per'fino] *avv* even.

perforare [perfo'rare] *v* pierce, perforate.

pergamena [perga'mɛna] *sf* parchment.

pericolo [pe'rikolo] *sm* danger; risk. **pericolante** *agg* unsafe. **pericoloso** *agg* dangerous; risky.

periferia [perife'ria] *sf* periphery; (*città*) suburbs *pl*. **periferico** *agg* suburban; peripheral.

perimetro [pe'rimetro] *sm* perimeter.

periodico [peri'ɔdiko] *agg* periodic. *sm* periodical.

periodo [pe'riodo] *sm* period.

peripezia [peripe'tsia] *sf* vicissitude.

perire [pe'rire] *v* perish, die.

periscopio [peri'skɔpjo] *sm* periscope.

perito [pe'rito], **-a** *s, agg* expert. **perizia** *sf* (*bravura*) skill, expertise; (*pratica*) experience; (*valutazione*) examination, expert opinion.

perla ['pɛrla] *sf* pearl.

perlomeno [perlo'meno] *avv* at least.

perlustrare [perlus'trare] *v* patrol; (*mil*) reconnoitre. **perlustrazione** *sf* patrol; reconnaissance.

permaloso [perma'lozo] *agg* touchy.

permanente [perma'nɛnte] *agg* permanent, lasting. *sf* (*fam*) perm. **permanenza** *sf* (*soggiorno*) stay. **in permanenza** permanently. **permanere** *v* remain.

permeare [perme'are] *v* permeate. **permeabile** *agg* permeable.

permesso [per'messo] *sm* permission; licence; (*congedo*) leave, pass. **(con) permesso?** may I? (*inter*) allow me!

***permettere** [per'mettere] *v* allow, permit.

pernice [per'nitʃe] *sf* partridge.

perno ['pɛrno] *sm* pivot, pin. **far perno su** hinge on.

pernottare [pernot'tare] *v* spend the night.

pero ['pero] *sm* pear-tree. **pera** *sf* pear.

però [pe'ro] *cong* but; (*tuttavia*) still, yet, however.

perossido [pe'rɔssido] *sm* peroxide.

perpendicolare [perpendiko'lare] *agg, sf* perpendicular.

perpetuo [per'pɛtuo] *agg* perpetual.

perplesso [per'plɛsso] *agg* puzzled; (*incerto*) undecided. **perplessità** *sf* perplexity; indecision.

perquisire [perkwi'zire] *v* search. **perquisizione** *sf* search.

perseguire [perse'gwire] *v* pursue. **perseguimento** *sm* pursuit.

perseguitare [persegwi'tare] *v* persecute. **persecuzione** *sf* persecution.

perseverare [perseve'rare] *v* persevere. **perseveranza** *sf* perseverance.

persiana [per'sjana] *sf* shutter, blind.

persiano [per'sjano] *agg* Persian.

persico ['pɛrsiko] *agg* Persian. **(pesce) persico** *sm* perch.

persino [per'sino] *avv* even.

***persistere** [per'sistere] *v* persist. **persistenza** *sf* persistence.
perso ['pɛrso] *agg* lost. **a tempo perso** in one's spare time.
persona [per'sona] *sf* person; (*qualcuno*) somebody. **di** *or* **in persona** in person, personally; (*personificato*) personified. **persona di servizio** domestic (help).
personaggio [perso'naddʒo] *sm* (*teatro, ecc.*) character; celebrity.
personale [perso'nale] *agg* personal. *sm* (*aspetto*) figure; (*dipendenti*) staff. *sf* (*mostra*) one-man show. **personale di direzione** management. **personale qualificato** skilled workers *pl*.
personalità [personali'ta] *sf* personality.
personificare [personifi'kare] *v* personify. **personificazione** *sf* personification.
perspicace [perspi'katʃe] *agg* keen, shrewd.
***persuadere** [persua'dere] *v* persuade; convince. **persuasione** *sf* persuasion; conviction. **persuasivo** *agg* convincing. **persuaso** *agg* convinced.
pertanto [per'tanto] *cong* thus, therefore, so.
pertica ['pɛrtika] *sf* pole.
pertinace [perti'natʃe] *agg* stubborn; (*deciso*) determined.
pertinente [perti'nɛnte] *agg* pertaining (to); (*domanda*) relevant.
pertosse [per'tosse] *sf* whooping cough.
***pervadere** [per'vadere] *v* pervade.
***pervenire** [perve'nire] *v* arrive (at).
pervertire [perver'tire] *v* corrupt, pervert. **perverso** *agg* perverse. **pervertito, -a** *sm, sf* pervert.
pesare [pe'zare] *v* weigh. **pesa** *sf* (*pesatura*) weighing; (*basculla*) weighbridge. **pesante** *agg* heavy; (*aria*) stuffy; (*duro*) rough. **peso** *sm* weight; (*onere*) burden.
pesca[1] ['pɛska] *sf* (*bot*) peach. **pesco** *sm* peach-tree.
pesca[2] ['peska] *sf* fishing; (*industria*) fishery; (*quantità*) catch. **pescare** *v* fish; (*trovare*) pick up, get hold of; (*acciuffare*) catch. **pescatore** *sm* fisherman; (*con lenza*) angler.
pesce ['peʃe] *sm* fish. **buttarsi a pesce su** make a dive for. **pesce d'aprile** April fool. **sano come un pesce** fit as a fiddle. **pescivendolo, -a** *sm, sf* fishmonger.
pessimismo [pessi'mizmo] *sm* pessimism. **pessimista** *s*(*m+f*) pessimist. **pessimistico** *agg* pessimistic.
pessimo ['pɛssimo] *agg* very bad; (*scadente, incapace*) very poor.
pestare [pes'tare] *v* crush; (*fam: picchiare*) give a (good) hiding. **pestare i piedi a qualcuno** tread on someone's toes. **pestello** *sm* pestle.
peste ['pɛste] *sf* plague; (*fig*) pest, curse.
pesto ['pesto] *agg* crushed. **essere buio pesto** be pitch dark.
petalo ['pɛtalo] *sm* petal.
petizione [peti'tsjone] *sf* petition.
petrolifero [petro'lifero] *agg* oil.
petrolio [pe'trɔljo] *sm* oil. **lampada a petrolio** *sf* paraffin lamp. **petroliera** *sf* (oil-)tanker.
pettegolo [pet'tegolo], **-a** *sm, sf* gossip. *agg* gossipy. **pettegolezzo** *sm* gossip.
pettinare [petti'nare] *v* comb. **pettinarsi** *v* comb one's hair. **pettinato** *sm* (*tessuto*) worsted. **pettinatura** *sf* combing; (*acconciatura*) hair-style. **pettine** *sm* comb.
petto ['pɛtto] *sm* breast; (*torace*) chest. **a doppio/un petto** double-/single-breasted.
petulante [petu'lante] *agg* pert.
pezza ['pɛttsa] *sf* rag; (*toppa*) patch; (*pannolino*) napkin. **pezza da piedi** doormat. **pezza di tessuto** roll of cloth. **pezzato** *agg* spotted. **pezzente** *s*(*m+f*) beggar.
pezzo ['pɛttso] *sm* piece; (*tempo*) period; (*giornale*) article. **pezzo di ricambio** spare part. **pezzo di terreno** plot of land. **pezzo grosso** (*fam*) VIP, big shot.
***piacere** [pja'tʃere] *v* please. **mi piace . . .** I like . . . . *sm* pleasure; favour. **a piacere** ad lib, freely. **far piacere a** please. **per piacere** please, if you please. **piacevole** *agg* pleasant.
piaga ['pjaga] *sf* sore; (*fig*) wound.
piagnucolare [pjaɲuko'lare] *v* whine, whimper. **piagnucolio** *sm* whining, whimpering. **piagnucolone, -a** *sm, sf* (*fam*) crybaby.
pialla ['pjalla] *sf* plane. **piallare** *v* plane.
pianella [pja'nɛlla] *sf* (*mattonella*) tile; (*pantofola*) mule, slipper.
pianerottolo [pjane'rɔttolo] *sm* landing.
pianeta [pja'neta] *sm* planet.
***piangere** ['pjandʒere] *v* weep, cry. **far piangere** *v* move to tears; (*ironico*) be pathetic.
pianificare [pjanifi'kare] *v* plan. **pianificatore, -trice** *sm, sf* planner. **pianificazione** *sf* planning.

pianista [pja'nista] *s(m+f)* pianist.
piano[1] ['pjano] *agg* flat, level; (*chiaro*) clear. *avv* (*adagio*) slow, slowly; (*con cautela*) carefully; (*a voce bassa*) softly. **pian piano** very slowly, very softly; (*poco alla volta*) little by little.
piano[2] ['pjano] *sm* plane, level; (*casa*) floor, storey; (*autobus*) deck. **primo piano** foreground. **secondo piano** background.
piano[3] ['pjano] *sm* (*progetto*) plan. **piano di studi** syllabus. **piano regolatore** town plan.
pianoforte [pjano'fɔrte] *sm* pianoforte; (*fam*) piano. **pianoforte a coda** grand piano.
pianta ['pjanta] *sf* (*bot*) plant; (*disegno*) plan; (*carta di città*) map. **di sana pianta** from scratch. **in pianta stabile** on the permanent staff. **pianta del piede** sole.
piantagione [pjanta'dʒone] *sf* plantation.
piantare [pjan'tare] *v* plant; (*conficcare*) drive; (*tenda*) pitch; (*abbandonare*) quit. **piantare grave** (*fam*) make trouble. **piantare in asso** leave in the lurch.
pianterreno [pjanter'reno] *sm* ground floor.
pianto ['pjanto] *sm* crying; tears *pl*.
pianura [pja'nura] *sf* plain.
piastra ['pjastra] *sf* plate. **piastrella** *sf* tile. **piastrellare** *v* tile.
piattaforma [pjatta'forma] *sf* platform. **piattaforma di lancio** launching pad. **piattaforma girevole** turntable.
piatto ['pjatto] *agg* flat. *sm* plate; (*portata*) dish, course; (*bilancia*) pan. **lavare i piatti** wash up.
piazza ['pjattsa] *sf* square; (*comm*) market; (*posto*) place; (*fam*: *calvizie*) bald patch. **a due piazze** (*letto*, *ecc*.) double. **a una piazza** single. **far piazza pulita** make a clean sweep. **scendere in piazza** demonstrate. **piazzaforte** *sf* stronghold. **piazzale** *sm* square. **piazzare** *v* place. **piazzista** *sm* salesman, commercial traveller.
picca ['pikka] *sf* pike. **picche** *sf pl* (*carte*) spades *pl*. **rispondere picche** turn down flat.
piccante [pik'kante] *agg* sharp, spicy; (*arguto*) spirited; (*licenzioso*) racy.
picchiare [pik'kjare] *v* hit, strike; (*colpire*) beat; (*bussare*) knock. **picchiata** *sf* (*aereo*) (nose-)dive.
picchio ['pikkjo] *sm* woodpecker.
piccino [pit'tʃino] *agg* tiny. *sm* child (*pl* -ren).
piccione [pit'tʃone] *sm* pigeon, dove. **piccionaia** *sf* dovecot; (*fam*: *teatro*) (the) gods.
picco ['pikko] *sm* peak. **a picco** sheer. **colare** *or* **mandare a picco** sink.
piccolo ['pikkolo], **-a** *agg* small, little. *sm, sf* little one, child (*pl* -ren). **da piccolo** as a child. **fin da piccolo** since childhood. **in piccolo** on a small scale. **piccolezza** *sf* (*inezia*) trifle.
piccone ['pikkone] *sm* pick-axe.
pidocchio [pi'dokkjo] *sm* louse (*pl* lice). **pidocchioso** *agg* lousy; (*fig*) mean.
piede ['pjɛde] *sm* foot (*pl* feet). **a piedi** on foot. **a piedi nudi** barefoot. **essere tra i piedi** be in the way. **fatto con i piedi** (*fam*) slipshod. **in piedi** standing. **togliersi dai piedi** get out of the way. **piedistallo** *sm* pedestal.
piega ['pjɛga] *sf* fold; crease; (*ornamento*) pleat. **messa in piega** *sf* set. **mettere in piega** *v* set. **prendere una brutta piega** take a turn for the worse.
piegare [pje'gare] *v* bend; (*foglio, tessuto*) fold.
pieghettare [pjeget'tare] *v* pleat.
pieghevole [pje'gevole] *agg* folding; flexible.
piena ['pjɛna] *sf* flood, spate; (*folla*) crowd.
pieno ['pjɛno] *agg* full. **in pieno** completely; exactly. (*nel mezzo*) in the middle of. **pieno zeppo** full up, chock full. **fare il pieno** (*auto*) fill up.
pietà [pje'ta] *sf* pity, compassion; (*devozione*) piety. **fare pietà** arouse pity. **pietoso** *agg* pitiful.
pietanza [pje'tantsa] *sf* dish, course.
pietra ['pjɛtra] *sf* stone. **pietra dura** semiprecious stone. **pietra di paragone** touchstone. **pietrina** *sf* flint.
piffero ['piffero] *sm* pipe; (*sonatore*) piper.
pigiama [pi'dʒama] *sm* pyjamas *pl*.
pigiare [pi'dʒare] *v* press, squeeze. **pigiatura** *sf* pressing.
pigione [pi'dʒone] *sf* rent.
pigliare [pi'ʎare] (*fam*) *V* **prendere**.
pigmento [pig'mento] *sm* pigment. **pigmentazione** *sf* pigmentation.
pigmeo [pig'mɛo] *sm* pygmy.
pigna ['piɲa] *sf* pine-cone.
pignatta [pi'ɲatta] *sf* pot.

pignolo [pi'ɲɔlo], **-a** *agg* fussy, pedantic. *sm*, *sf* pedant.
pigolare [pigo'lare] *v* peep, chirp. **pigolio** *sm* peeping, chirping.
pigro ['pigro], **-a** *agg* idle, lazy. *sm*, *sf* lazy person, loafer. **pigrizia** *sf* laziness, idleness.
pila ['pila] *sf* pile; (*elett*) battery.
pilastro [pi'lastro] *sm* pillar, column.
pillola ['pillola] *sf* pill.
pilone [pi'lone] *sm* pillar; (*ponte*) pier; (*elett*) pylon.
pilotare [pilo'tare] *v* pilot; (*auto*) drive. **pilota** *sm* pilot.
pinacoteca [pinako'tɛka] *sf* picture gallery.
pineta [pi'neta] *sf* pine forest.
pingue ['pingwe] *agg* fat.
pinguino [pin'gwino] *sm* penguin.
pinna ['pinna] *sf* fin.
pinnacolo [pin'nakolo] *sm* pinnacle.
pino ['pino] *sm* pine (tree). **pinolo** *sm* pine-seed.
pinza ['pintsa] *sf* pliers *pl*; (*zool*) pincer. **pinzetta** *sf* tweezers *pl*.
pio ['pio] *agg* pious.
pioggia ['pjoddʒa] *sf* rain. **pioggerella** *sf* *also* **pioggia fine** drizzle.
piolo [pi'ɔlo] *sm* peg; (*scala*) rung.
piombare[1] [pjom'bare] *v* hurtle, plunge; (*avventarsi*) pounce.
piombare[2] [pjom'bare] *v* (*otturare*) fill; (*sigillare*) seal (with lead). **piombo** *sm* lead; (*piombino*) plummet.
pioniere [pjo'njɛre], **-a** *sm*, *sf* pioneer.
pioppo ['pjoppo] *sm* poplar.
***piovere** ['pjɔvere] *v* rain; (*fig*) pour (in). **piovere a catinelle** rain cats and dogs. **piovigginare** *v* drizzle. **piovoso** *agg* rainy.
piovra ['pjɔvra] *sf* (giant) squid; (*persona*) blood-sucker.
pipa ['pipa] *sf* pipe.
pipistrello [pipi'strɛllo] *sm* bat.
pira ['pira] *sf* pyre.
piramide [pi'ramide] *sf* pyramid.
pirata [pi'rata] *sm* pirate. **pirata della strada** hit-and-run driver. **pirateria** *sf* piracy.
piroscafo [pi'rɔskafo] *sm* steamer; (*da carico*) freighter; (*di linea*) liner.
piscia ['piʃa] (*volg*) *sf* piss. **pisciare** *v* piss.
piscina [pi'ʃina] *sf* swimming pool.
pisello [pi'zɛllo] *sm* pea. **pisello odoroso** sweet pea.
pisolino [pizo'lino] *sm* **fare** *or* **schiacciare un pisolino** take a nap.
pista ['pista] *sf* track; (*aero*) runway.
pistola [pis'tɔla] *sf* pistol. **pistola a spruzzo** spray-gun. **pistolettata** *sf* pistol-shot.
pistone [pis'tone] *sm* piston.
pitocco [pi'tɔkko], **-a** *sm*, *sf* beggar; (*avaro*) miser.
pitone [pi'tone] *sm* python.
pittore [pit'tore] *sm* painter.
pittoresco [pitto'resko] *agg* picturesque.
pittura [pit'tura] *sf* painting; (*descrizione*) picture; (*vernice*) paint. **pitturare** *v* paint.
più [pju] *avv* (*comparativo*) more; (*superlativo*) most. **al più presto** as soon as possible. **il più** the majority. **il più possibile** as much as possible. **più volte** several times. **sempre più . . .** more and more . . . . **tanto più** especially. **tutt'al più** at most.
piuma ['pjuma] *sf* feather. **piumino** *sm* down; (*per cipria*) powder-puff; (*letto*) eiderdown, duvet.
piuttosto [pjut'tɔsto] *avv* rather.
piviere [pi'vjɛre] *sm* plover.
pizzicare [pittsi'kare] *v* pinch; (*pungere*) sting; (*musica*) pluck. **pizzico** *sm*, *pl* **-chi** pinch, dash. **pizzicore** *sm* itch. **pizzicotto** *sm* pinch.
pizzo ['pittso] *sm* (*merletto*) lace; (*barba*) goatee.
placare [pla'kare] *v* calm down, placate.
placca ['plakka] *sf* plate; (*ornamento*) plaque; (*med*) patch.
placenta [pla'tʃɛnta] *sf* placenta.
placido ['platʃido] *agg* placid.
plagiare [pla'dʒare] *v* plagiarize. **plagiario**, **-a** *sm*, *sf* plagiarist.
planare [pla'nare] *v* glide. **planata** *sf* glide.
plasmare [plaz'mare] *v* mould. **plasma** *sm* plasma.
plastica ['plastika] *sf* (*arte*) modelling; (*med*) plastic surgery; (*materia*) plastic. **plasticare** *v* model. **plastico** *agg* plastic.
platano ['platano] *sm* plane-tree.
platea [pla'tɛa] *sf* stalls *pl*.
platino ['platino] *sm* platinum.
platonico [pla'tɔniko] *agg* platonic.
plausibile [plau'zibile] *agg* plausible.
plebe ['plɛbe] *sf* plebs *pl*; (*plebaglia*) mob, riff-raff. **plebeo** *agg* plebeian; common.
plebiscito [plebi'ʃito] *sm* plebiscite.
pleurite [pleu'rite] *sf* pleurisy.
plico ['pliko] *sm* parcel.

plotone [plo'tone] *sm* platoon.
plumbeo ['plumbeo] *agg* leaden.
plurale [plu'rale] *agg, sm* plural.
plutocratico [pluto'kratiko] *agg* plutocratic. **plutocrate** *sm* plutocrat. **plutocrazia** *sf* plutocracy.
pneumatico [pneu'matiko] *sm* tyre. *agg* (*mec*) pneumatic; (*gonfiabile*) inflatable.
po' [po] *V* **poco.**
pochino [po'kino] *agg* not much *or* many. *avv, pron* very little *or* few. *sm* bit.
poco ['pɔko] *agg* little; (*tempo*) short. *avv* little, not very. *pron* little, not much. **a poco a poco** little by little. **da poco** unimportant. **fra poco** soon. **pochi** *pron, agg* few *pl.* **poco dopo** not long after. **poco fa** a short while ago. **poco male!** never mind! **un poco** *or* **po'** a little.
podere ['podere] *sm* estate.
podestà [podes'ta] *sm* mayor.
podio ['pɔdjo] *sm* platform.
podismo [po'dizmo] *sm* track events *pl*; (*corsa*) running. **podista** *s*(*m+f*) track athlete; runner.
poema [po'ɛma] *sm* poem.
poi ['pɔi] *avv* then; (*più tardi*) later. *sm* future. **da . . . in poi** from . . . onwards. **il senno di poi** *sm* hindsight.
poiché [pɔi'ke] *cong* as, since.
polacco [po'lakko], **-a** *agg* Polish. *sm, sf* Pole. *sm* (*lingua*) Polish.
polarizzare [polarid'dzare] *v* polarize. **polare** *agg* polar. **stella polare** *sf* pole star.
polca ['pɔlka] *sf* polka.
polemica [po'lɛmika] *sf* polemic; controversy. **polemico** *agg* contentious, polemical.
polenta [po'lɛnta] *sf* (*gastr*) maize porridge; (*fam: persona lenta*) slow-coach.
policlinico [poli'kliniko] *sm* hospital.
poligamo [po'ligamo], **-a** *agg* polygamous. *sm, sf* polygamist. **poligamia** *sf* polygamy.
poligono [po'ligono] *sm* polygon.
polimero [po'limero] *sm* polymer.
polistirolo [polisti'rɔlo] *sm* polystyrene.
politecnico [poli'tɛkniko] *sm* polytechnic.
politene [poli'tene] *sm* polythene.
politico [po'litiko] *agg* political. *sm* politician. **politica** *sf* politics; (*linea di condotta*) policy.
polizia [poli'tsia] *sf* police. **poliziesco** *agg* police. **romanzo** *or* **film poliziesco** *sm* thriller. **poliziotto** *sm* policeman.
polizza ['pɔlittsa] *sf* policy; (*ricevuta*) voucher.
pollame [pol'lame] *sm* poultry. **pollaio** *sm* chicken coop. **pollastra** *sf* pullet; (*fam*) lass, chick. **pollastro** cockerel; (*fam*) gullible person, mug.
pollice ['pɔllitʃe] *sm* thumb; (*del piede*) big toe.
polline ['pɔlline] *sm* pollen.
pollo ['pollo] *sm* chicken. **far ridere i polli** be ridiculous.
polmone [pol'mone] *sm* lung. **polmonare** *agg* pulmonary. **polmonite** *sf* pneumonia.
polo ['pɔlo] *sm* pole. **essere ai poli opposti** be poles apart.
Polonia [po'lɔnja] *sf* Poland.
polpa ['polpa] *sf* flesh; (*carne*) meat; (*fig*) substance. **polpetta** *sf* meatball. **polposo** *agg* fleshy.
polpaccio [pol'pattʃo] *sm* (*anat*) calf.
polso ['polso] *sm* wrist; (*med*) pulse; (*polsino*) cuff.
poltiglia [pol'tiʎa] *sf* mush; mixture.
poltrona [pol'trona] *sf* easy chair, armchair; (*teatro*) stall.
poltrone [pol'trone], **-a** *sm, sf* idler, loafer.
polvere ['pɔlvere] *sf* dust; powder. **polveriera** *sf* powder-keg. **polverizzare** *v* pulverize. **polveroso** *agg* dusty.
pomata [po'mata] *sf* ointment.
pomeriggio [pome'riddʒo] *sm* afternoon. **pomeridiano** *agg* afternoon.
pomice ['pɔmitʃe] *sm* pumice-stone.
pomo ['pomo] *sm* (*frutto*) apple; (*albero*) apple-tree.
pomodoro [pomo'dɔro] *sm* tomato.
pompa[1] ['pompa] *sf* pump. **pompa antincendio** fire-engine. **pompare** *v* pump (up).
pompa[2] ['pompa] *sf* pomp. **far pompa di** show off. **impresario di pompe funebri** *sm* undertaker. **pomposo** *agg* pompous.
pompelmo [pom'pɛlmo] *sm* grapefruit.
pompiere [pom'pjɛre] *sm* fireman.
ponderare [ponde'rare] *v* consider. **ponderato** *agg* careful. **ponderoso** *agg* ponderous.
ponente [po'nɛnte] *sm* west.
ponte ['ponte] *sm* bridge; (*impalcatura*) scaffolding. **ponte aereo** air-lift. **ponte radio** radio link. **ponte sospeso** suspension bridge.

pontefice [pon'tefitʃe] *sm* pontiff. **pontificare** *v* pontificate. **pontificio** *agg* papal.
pontile [pon'tile] *sm* pier; (*da sbarco*) landing stage.
popolare [popo'lare] *agg* popular; working-class; (*tradizionale*) folk. **casa popolare** *sf* council house. *v* populate. **popolarità** *sf* popularity. **popolarizzare** *v* popularize.
popolo ['pɔpolo] *sm* people; common people. **popolazione** *sf* population.
popone [po'pone] *sm* melon.
poppa[1] ['poppa] *sf* (*mar*) stern. **avere il vento in poppa** sail before the wind.
poppa[2] ['poppa] *sf* (*anat*) breast. **poppare** *v* suck.
porcellana [portʃel'lana] *sf* porcelain, china.
porco ['pɔrko] *sm, pl* **-ci** pig. *agg* (*volg*) bloody. **porcaio** *sm* pig-sty. **porcellino d'India** *sm* guinea-pig. **porcheria** *sf* muck, filth; (*cibo*) disgusting stuff; (*cosa malfatta*) rubbish. **porcospino** *sm* porcupine.
***porgere** ['pɔrdʒere] *v* give, hand. **porgere aiuto** offer help.
pornografia [pornogra'fia] *sf* pornography. **pornografico** *agg* pornographic.
poro ['pɔro] *sm* pore. **poroso** *agg* porous.
porpora ['porpora] *agg invar, sf* purple.
***porre** ['porre] *v* put; set, place. **porre in dubbio** question. **porre in evidenza** stress. **porre rimedio** set right.
porro ['pɔrro] *sm* leek.
porta ['pɔrta] *sf* door. **a porte chiuse** behind closed doors; (*dir*) in camera. **mettere alla porta** (*fig*) throw out. **porta di sicurezza** emergency exit.
portabagagli [portaba'gaʎi] *sm invar* luggage-rack; (*facchino*) porter.
portabile [por'tabile] *agg* portable.
portacenere [porta'tʃenere] *sm invar* ashtray.
portachiavi [porta'kjavi] *sm invar* key-ring.
portaerei [porta'ɛrei] *sf* aircraft-carrier.
portafinestra [portafi'nɛstra] *sf, pl* **portefinestre** French window.
portafoglio [porta'fɔʎʎo] *sm* wallet; (*borsa*) briefcase; (*pol*) portfolio.
portalettere [porta'lettere] *sm invar* postman.
portamonete [portamo'nete] *sm invar* purse.
portare [por'tare] *v* bring; (*prendere*) take; (*trasportare*) carry; (*indossare*) wear; (*addurre*) put forward. **essere portato** have a gift (for). **portatore** *sm* carrier; (*comm*) bearer.
portasapone [portasa'pone] *sm invar* soap-dish.
portasigarette [portasiga'rette] *sm invar* cigarette-case.
portaspilli [porta'spilli] *sm invar* pincushion.
portauovo [portauovo] *sm invar* egg-cup.
portavoce [porta'votʃe] *sm invar* spokesman, mouthpiece.
portento [por'tɛnto] *sm* portent; (*persona*) prodigy.
portico ['pɔrtiko] *sm* arcade; (*di casa*) porch.
portinaio [porti'najo], **-a** *sm, sf* doorkeeper; caretaker. **portineria** *sf* caretaker's lodge.
porto[1] ['pɔrto] *sm* port, harbour.
porto[2] ['pɔrto] *sm* (*comm*) carriage. **porto d'armi** gun licence.
porto[3] ['pɔrto] *sm* (*vino*) port.
Portogallo [porto'gallo] *sm* Portugal. **portoghese** *agg, s(m+f)* Portuguese; *sm* (*lingua*) Portuguese. **fare il portoghese** gate-crash.
portone [por'tone] *sm* front door.
porzione [por'tsjone] *sf* portion, share.
posa ['pɔza] *sf* (*atteggiamento*) pose; (*foto*) exposure.
posare [po'zare] *v* put *or* lay down; rest; (*ritratto*) pose.
poscritto [pos'kritto] *sm* postscript.
positivo [pozi'tivo] *agg* positive; affirmative; practical. **positiva** *sf* (*foto*) positive.
posizione [pozi'tsjone] *sf* position.
***posporre** [pos'porre] *v* postpone; (*mettere dopo*) place after. **posposizione** *sf* postponement.
***possedere** [posse'dere] *v* possess, own. **possedimento** *sm also* **possesso** possession. **possessore** *sm* owner.
possibile [pos'sibile] *agg* possible. **fare il possibile** do one's best. **possibilità** *sf* possibility; (*capacità*) means. **possibilmente** *avv* if possible.
posta[1] ['posta] *sf* post, mail; (*ufficio*) post office. **a giro di posta** by return of post. **mettersi alla posta (di)** be on the lookout (for). **posta aerea** air mail. **postale** *agg* postal.
posta[2] ['posta] *sf* (*gioco*) bet, stake.

post-bellico [post'bɛlliko] *agg* post-war.
posteggiare [posted'dʒare] *v* park. **posteggio** *sm* parking; (*spazio*) parking space.
posteriore [poste'rjore] *agg* back, rear; (*tempo*) later.
posterità [posteri'ta] *sf* posterity.
posticcio [pos'tittʃo] *agg* artificial. *sm* hairpiece.
posticipare [postitʃi'pare] *v* defer.
postino [pos'tino] *sm* postman.
posto ['posto] *sm* (*luogo*) place; (*spazio*) room; (*impiego*) position; (*da sedere*) seat. **essere a posto** be in order; (*star bene*) be well, be content. **mettere a posto** tidy up; repair. **sul posto** on the spot.
postumo ['pɔstumo] *agg* posthumous.
potabile [po'tabile] *agg* (*spreg*) drinkable. **acqua potabile** *sf* drinking water.
potare [po'tare] *v* prune.
potassio [po'tassjo] *sm* potassium. **potassa** *sf* potash.
potente [po'tɛnte] *agg* powerful; (*efficace*) potent; (*valido*) forceful. **potenza** *sf* power; (*forza*) strength; (*efficacia*) potency.
potenziale [poten'tsjale] *agg*, *sm* potential. **potenzialità** *sf* capacity.
potenziare [poten'tsjare] *v* strengthen, expand. **potenziamento** *sm* strengthening, expansion.
***potere**[1] [po'tere] *v* can, be able; (*possibilità, permesso*) may. **non poterne più** (*essere sfinito*) be exhausted; (*essere al limite della sopportazione*) be unable to stand it any longer. **può darsi** maybe.
potere[2] [po'tere] *sm* power.
povero ['pɔvero], **-a** *agg* poor. *sm*, *sf* poor person. **povero di** lacking in. **povertà** *sf* poverty; (*scarsità*) want, lack.
pozza ['pottsa] *sf* pool. **pozzanghera** *sf* puddle.
pozzo ['pottso] *sm* well; (*cavità*) shaft. **pozzo nero** cesspool.
pranzare [pran'tsare] *v* have dinner; (*a mezzogiorno*) have lunch. **pranzo** *sm* dinner; lunch. **dopo pranzo** (*nel pomeriggio*) in the afternoon. **sala da pranzo** *sf* dining room.
pratica ['pratika] *sf* practice; experience; (*incartamento*) file. **praticante** *s*(*m*+*f*) apprentice; (*rel*) churchgoer. **praticare** *v* practise; (*fare*) make; frequent; associate (with).
pratico ['pratiko] *agg* practical; (*esperto*) skilled; (*funzionale*) useful, handy. **all'atto pratico** in practice. **essere pratico di** be familiar with.
prato ['prato] *sm* meadow; (*giardino*) lawn. **pratolina** *sf* daisy.
preavvisare [preavvi'zare] *v also* **preavvertire** inform in advance; (*ammonire*) warn. **preavviso** *sm* (advance) notice; warning.
pre-bellico [pre'bɛlliko] *agg* pre-war.
precario [pre'karjo] *agg* precarious.
precauzione [prekau'tsjone] *sf* (*cautela*) caution, care; (*provvedimento*) precaution. **precauzionale** *agg* precautionary.
precedente [pretʃe'dɛnte] *agg* previous, preceding, former. *sm* (*dir*) precedent. **precedenti (penali)** *sm pl* (criminal) record *sing*. **precedentemente** *avv* before. **precedenza** *sf* priority. **in precedenza** previously.
precedere [pre'tʃɛdere] *v* precede.
precipitare [pretʃipi'tare] *v* hurl (down); (*affrettare*) hasten; (*chim*) precipitate; (*cadere*) crash; (*piombare*) plunge. **precipitoso** *agg* hurried; (*fig*) rash.
precipizio [pretʃi'pitsjo] *sm* precipice.
precisare [pretʃi'zare] *v* specify; (*fam*) spell out. **precisazione** *sf* clarification. **precisione** *sf* precision. **preciso** *agg* precise, exact; identical.
precoce [pre'kɔtʃe] *agg* precocious; premature, untimely.
preconcetto [prekon'tʃɛtto] *sm* preconceived idea, prejudice.
precursore [prekur'sore] *sm* forerunner.
preda ['preda] *sf* prey; (*bottino*) booty. **essere in preda a** be struck by. **in preda alle fiamme** in flames. **predare** *v* plunder.
predecessore [predetʃes'sore] *sm* predecessor.
predestinare [predesti'nare] *v* preordain.
predetto [pre'detto] *agg* aforesaid.
predica ['prɛdika] *sf* sermon; (*ramanzina*) telling-off. **predicare** *v* preach.
prediletto [predi'lɛtto], **-a** *s*, *agg* favourite.
***predire** [pre'dire] *v* predict, foretell.
***predisporre** [predis'porre] *v* arrange (in advance); predispose.
predominare [predomi'nare] *v* prevail. **predominio** *sm* sway.
prefabbricato [prefabbri'kato] *agg* prefabricated.
prefazione [prefa'tsjone] *sf* preface, foreword.
preferire [prefe'rire] *v* prefer. **preferenza** *sf* preference. **preferibile** *agg* preferable.

prefetto [pre'fɛtto] *sm* prefect. **prefettura** *sf* prefecture.

***prefiggere** [pre'fiddʒere] *v* fix (in advance); (*gramm*) prefix. **prefiggersi** *v* resolve.

prefisso [pre'fisso] *sm* (*gramm*) prefix; (*telefono*) (area) code.

pregare [pre'gare] *v* pray. **prego** *inter* (*per favore*) please! (*risposta*) don't mention it!

pregevole [pre'dʒɛvole] *agg* valuable.

preghiera [pre'gjɛra] *sf* prayer; (*domanda*) request.

pregiato [pre'dʒato] *agg* valued. **pregio** *sm* regard; merit. **di nessun pregio** worthless.

pregiudicare [predʒudi'kare] *v* prejudice; (*danneggiare*) harm. **pregiudicato** *sm* ex-convict.

pregiudizio [predʒu'ditsjo] *sm* prejudice, bias.

pregustare [pregus'tare] *v* look forward to.

preistorico [preis'tɔriko] *agg* prehistoric.

prelato [pre'lato] *sm* prelate.

prelevare [prele'vare] *v* withdraw.

prelibato [preli'bato] *agg* exquisite.

preliminare [prelimi'nare] *agg* preliminary. *sm* element.

preludio [pre'ludjo] *sm* prelude.

prematuro [prema'turo] *agg* premature.

premeditato [premedi'tato] *agg* premeditated.

premere ['prɛmere] *v* press. **mi preme (di) sapere** I am anxious to know.

premiare [pre'mjare] *v* award a prize to; (*ricompensare*) reward. **premio** *sm* prize; reward; (*comm*) premium.

preminente [premi'nente] *agg* pre-eminent.

premura [pre'mura] *sf* (*fretta*) haste; (*riguardo*) solicitude, attention. **fare premura a** hurry up. **farsi premura** take care. **premuroso** *agg* thoughtful, solicitous.

***prendere** ['prɛndere] *v* take; (*cogliere, subire, catturare*) catch; (*ricevere*) receive; (*ritirare*) pick up; (*occupare*) take up; (*assumere*) take on; (*ottenere*) get. **andare a prendere** fetch. **prendere alla lettera** take literally. **prendere per il naso** mock. **prendere qualcuno per il bavero** pull someone's leg. **prendere un granchio** (*fig*) make a blunder. **prendersela** *v* take it amiss; (*con qualcuno*) get angry with; (*a cuore*) take it to heart.

prenotare [preno'tare] *v* book, reserve. **prenotazione** *sf* booking, reservation.

preoccupare [preokku'pare] *v* worry. **preoccupazione** *sf* worry.

preparare [prepa'rare] *v* prepare; (*tavola*) lay; (*letto*) make. **preparare la strada** pave the way. **preparativo** *sm* arrangement. **preparazione** *sf* preparation.

preposizione [preposi'tsjone] *sf* preposition.

prepotente [prepo'tɛnte] *agg* overbearing. *s(m+f)* (*fam*) bully.

prerogativa [preroga'tiva] *sf* privilege.

presa ['preza] *sf* hold; (*stretta*) grasp; (*elett*) socket; (*carte*) trick; (*cattura*) capture. **cane da presa** *sm* retriever. **essere alle prese con** wrestle with. **far presa** set. **macchina da presa** *sf* cine-camera. **presa di posizione** taking sides. **presa in giro** leg-pull. **venire alle prese** come to grips.

presbite ['prɛzbite] *agg* long-sighted.

prescindere [pre'ʃindere] *v* **a prescindere da** apart from.

***prescrivere** [pre'skrivere] *v* prescribe. **prescrizione** *sf* ordinance. **prescrizione medica** doctor's orders *pl*; (*ricetta*) prescription.

presentare [prezen'tare] *v* present; (*far conoscere*) introduce; (*mostrare*) show; offer. **presentatore, -trice** *sm, sf* compere, question-master.

presente [pre'zɛnte] *agg* present; in the presence of; (*questo*) this. *sm* present. **i presenti** those present *pl*. **tener presente** keep in mind.

presentimento [presenti'mento] *sm* presentiment, foreboding.

presenza [pre'zentza] *sf* presence; appearance. **di presenza** personally. **fare atto di presenza** put in an appearance. **presenziare (a)** *v* attend.

preservare [prezer'vare] *v* preserve; protect. **preservativo** *sm* preservative; (*guaina profilattica*) condom. **preservazione** *sf* preservation.

preside ['prɛzide] *sm* headmaster; (*di facoltà*) dean. *sf* headmistress.

presidente [prezi'dɛnte] *sm* president; (*di assemblea*) chairman. **presidente della camera** (*pol*) speaker. **presidente del Consiglio** (*pol*) Prime Minister. **presidenza** *sf*

(*pol*) presidency; chairmanship. **assumere la presidenza** take the chair.
presidio [pre'zidjo] *sm* garrison; (*fig*) protection. **presidiare** *v* garrison; protect.
***presiedere** [pre'sjɛdere] *v* be in charge (of).
pressa ['prɛssa] *sf* press. **pressare** *v* press.
pressappoco [pressap'pɔko] *avv* about, roughly.
pressione [pres'sjone] *sf* pressure.
presso ['prɛsso] *prep* near; (*insieme a, fra*) with; (*accanto a*) by; (*indirizzo*) care of, c/o. *avv* nearby. **pressoché** *avv* almost.
prestabilire [prestabi'lire] *v* prearrange.
prestare [pres'tare] *v* lend. **prestare aiuto** help. **prestar fede** believe. **prestar giuramento** take an oath. **prestazione** *sf* (*rendimento*) performance. **prestazioni** *sf pl* services *pl*.
prestigio [pres'tidʒo] *sm* prestige. **gioco di prestigio** *sm* conjuring trick. **prestigiatore, -trice** *sm, sf* conjurer. **prestigioso** *agg* prestigious.
prestito ['prɛstito] *sm* loan. **dare in prestito** lend. **prendere in prestito** borrow.
presto ['prɛsto] *avv* (*tra poco*) soon; (*in fretta*) quickly; (*di buon'ora*) early. **si fa presto** (*facilmente*) it's easy.
***presumere** [pre'zumere] *v* imagine. **presunto** *agg* presumed; (*erede*) presumptive. **presuntuoso** *agg* presumptuous. **presunzione** *sf* presumption.
***presupporre** [presup'porre] *v* presuppose, assume; (*richiedere*) require. **presupposizione** *sf* assumption.
prete ['prɛte] *sm* priest.
***pretendere** [pre'tendere] *v* (*esigere, presumere*) expect; (*sostenere*) claim. **pretensioso** *agg* pretentious.
pretesa [pre'teza] *sf* claim; (*presunzione*) pretention. **aver poche/molte pretese** be easy/difficult to please.
pretesto [pre'testo] *sm* pretext; (*occasione*) opportunity.
prettamente [pretta'mente] *avv* typically.
***prevalere** [preva'lere] *v* prevail.
***prevedere** [preve'dere] *v* foresee; (*considerare*) provide for. **prevedibile** *agg* foreseeable.
***prevenire** [preve'nire] *v* (*precedere*) arrive before; (*fig*) anticipate; (*evitare*) avert; (*avvertire*) warn. **prevenuto** *agg* (*maldisposto*) biased.
preventivo [preven'tivo] *agg* precautionary; (*dir*) preventive. *sm* estimate. **preventivare** *v* estimate. **prevenzione** *sf* (*ostilità*) bias; (*provvedimento*) prevention.
previdente [previ'dɛnte] *agg* far-sighted, provident. **previdenza** *sf* foresight. **previdenza sociale** social security.
previo ['prɛvjo] *agg* prior.
previsione [previ'zjone] *sf* forecast; (*aspettativa*) anticipation; (*comm*) estimate. **previsto** *agg* foreseen; (*dir*) provided for. **meno/più del previsto** less/more than anticipated.
prezioso [pre'tsjozo] *agg* precious, valuable.
prezzemolo [pret'tsemolo] *sm* parsley.
prezzo ['prɛttso] *sm* price; (*tariffa*) rate; (*trasporto pubblico*) fare. **a buon prezzo** cheaply.
prigione [pri'dʒone] *sf* prison, jail. **prigionia** *sf* captivity. **prigioniero, -a** *sm, sf* prisoner.
prima ['prima] *avv* (*in anticipo*) first, in advance; (*precedentemente*) before; (*più presto*) earlier; (*una volta*) once; (*in primo luogo*) first. *sf* (*teatro*) première; (*auto*) first gear; (*treno*) first class.
primario [pri'marjo] *agg* primary. *sm* (*med*) consultant.
primato [pri'mato] *sm* supremacy; record.
primavera [prima'vɛra] *sf* spring. **primaverile** *agg* spring.
primitivo [primi'tivo] *agg* primitive; original.
primizia [pri'mitsja] *sf* early produce; (*notizia*) latest news.
primo ['primo] *agg* first; (*precedente*) former; (*principale*) main. **per primo** first.
primula ['primula] *sf* primrose.
principale [printʃi'pale] *agg* principal, main. *sm* principal; (*fam*) boss.
principe ['printʃipe] *sm* prince. **principato** *sm* principality. **principesco** *agg* princely. **principessa** *sf* princess.
principio [prin'tʃipjo] *sm* beginning; (*fondamento*) principle; origin. **da** *or* **in principio** at first. **per principio** on principle.
priorità [priori'ta] *sf* priority.
prisma ['prizma] *sm* prism.
privare [pri'vare] *v* deprive.
privato [pri'vato], **-a** *agg* private; personal. *sm, sf* private citizen. **privatista** *s(m+f)* (*scolaro*) private school pupil;

(*candidato*) external student. **privativa** *sf* monopoly. **privazione** *sf* privation, loss.
privilegio [privi'ledʒo] *sm* privilege. **privilegiato** *agg* privileged.
privo ['privo] *agg* devoid (of), without. **privo di denaro** penniless. **privo di sensi** (*svenuto*) unconscious.
probabile [pro'babile] *agg* probable, likely. **poco probabile** unlikely. **probabilità** *sf* probability, likelihood; (*possibilità*) chance.
problema ['problɛma] *sm* problem. **problematico** *agg* problematic; doubtful.
proboscide [pro'boʃide] *sf* trunk.
procedere [pro'tʃɛdere] *v* proceed; (*comportarsi*) behave. **procedimento** *sm* (*svolgimento*) course; (*tec*) process; (*dir*) proceedings *pl*.
processione [protʃes'sjone] *sf* procession.
processo [pro'tʃɛsso] *sm* process; (*dir*) trial, lawsuit. **essere sotto processo** be on trial. **processo verbale** minutes *pl*.
procinto [pro'tʃinto] *sm* **essere in procinto di** be on the point of, be about to.
proclamare [prokla'mare] *v* proclaim. **proclamazione** *sf* proclamation.
proclive [pro'klive] *agg* prone (to).
procreare [prokre'are] *v* procreate. **procreazione** *sf* procreation.
procurare [proku'rare] *v* get; (*dare, causare*) give. **procura** *sf* power of attorney. **per procura** by proxy. **procuratore** *sm* proxy; (*magistrato*) attorney; (*comm*) agent.
proda ['prɔda] *sf* bank.
prode ['prɔde] *agg* valiant.
prodigare [prodi'gare] *v* lavish. **prodigo** *agg, m pl* **-ghi** prodigal, lavish.
prodigio [pro'didʒo] *sm* prodigy. **prodigioso** *agg* wonderful, marvellous.
prodotto [pro'dotto] *sm* product; (*alimentare*) foodstuff; (*chimico*) chemical.
***produrre** [pro'durre] *v* produce; cause; (*mostrare*) show; (*fare*) make. **produrre un testimonio** call a witness. **produttivo** *agg* productive. **produttività** *sf* productivity. **produttore** *sm* producer. **produzione** *sf* production; (*fabbricazione*) manufacture; (*quantità*) output.
profanare [profa'nare] *v* desecrate; (*contaminare*) debase. **profano** *agg* profane; (*empio*) sacrilegious; (*inesperto*) ignorant.
***proferire** [profe'rire] *v* utter, pronounce.
professare [profes'sare] *v* profess. **professionale** *agg* professional; vocational; (*connesso alla professione*) occupational. **professione** *sf* profession; (*mestiere*) trade. **di professione** by profession. **professionista** *s*(*m*+*f*) professional (person).
professore [profes'sore], **-essa** *sm, sf* teacher. **professore titolare/incaricato** university professor/lecturer.
profeta [pro'fɛta] *sm* prophet. **profetico** *agg* prophetic. **profezia** *sf* prophecy.
proficuo [pro'fikuo] *agg* useful.
profilo [pro'filo] *sm* profile; (*contorno*) outline. **profilare** *v* outline; (*mec*) profile. **profilato** *sm* (*mec*) section.
profittare [profit'tare] *v* profit; (*approfittare*) take advantage; (*progredire*) make progress. **profittatore** *sm* profiteer. **profitto** *sm* profit; advantage. **trarre profitto** benefit.
profondo [pro'fondo] *agg* deep; (*radicato*) deep-rooted. *sm* depth. **profondare** *v* sink. **profondità** *sf* depth.
profugo ['prɔfugo], **-a** *sm, pl* **-ghi**, *sf* refugee.
profumare [profu'mare] *v* perfume. **profumato** *agg* perfumed; fragrant. **profumeria** *sf* perfumery. **profumo** *sm* fragrance, scent.
profusione [profu'zjone] *sf* profusion.
progettare [prodʒet'tare] *v* plan; (*tec*) design. **progettazione** *sf* planning. **progetto** *sm* project, plan. **progetto di legge** bill. **progetto di massima** preliminary plan.
prognosi ['prɔɲozi] *sf* prognosis.
programma [pro'gramma] *sm* programme; prospectus; (*scuola*) syllabus. **programmare** *v* programme. **programmatore, -trice** *sm, sf* programmer. **programmazione** *sf* programming.
progredire [progre'dire] *v* make progress, get on. **progressione** *sf* progression. **progressivo** *agg* progressive. **progresso** *sm* progress. **fare progressi** improve, make progress.
proibire [proi'bire] *v* forbid, prohibit. **proibito** *agg* forbidden. **proibizionismo** *sm* prohibition.
proiettare [projet'tare] *v* project; (*gettar fuori*) eject; (*cine*) screen. **proiettile** *sm* projectile; (*mil*) shell. **a prova di proiettile** bullet-proof. **proiettore** *sm* projector.
prole ['prɔle] *sf* offspring.
proletario [prole'tarjo], **-a** *s, agg* proletarian. **proletariato** *sm* proletariat.

prolifico [pro'lifiko] *agg* prolific.
prolisso [pro'lisso] *agg* long-winded.
prologo ['prɔlogo] *sm, pl* **-ghi** prologue.
prolungare [prolun'gare] *v* extend; (*tempo*) prolong; (*spazio*) lengthen. **prolungarsi** *v* (*dilungarsi*) dwell (on). **prolunga** *sf* extension. **prolungamento** *sm* extension.
promemoria [prome'mɔrja] *sm invar* memorandum.
***promettere** [pro'mettere] *v* promise. **promessa** *sf* promise. **promesso** *agg* promised. **promettente** *agg* promising.
prominente [promi'nente] *agg* prominent, jutting (out). **prominenza** *sf* prominence, projection.
promiscuo [pro'miskuo] *agg* mixed; (*scuola*) co-educational; (*relazioni*) promiscuous.
promontorio [promon'tɔrjo] *sm* headland.
promozione [promo'tsjone] *sf* promotion.
***promuovere** [pro'mwɔvere] *v* promote; provoke.
pronome [pro'nome] *sm* pronoun.
pronosticare [pronosti'kare] *v* forecast. **pronostico** *sm* forecast.
pronto ['pronto] *agg* ready; (*rapido*) prompt; (*vivace*) lively. *inter* (*telefono*) hello!
prontuario [prontu'arjo] *sm* handbook.
pronunciare [pronun'tʃare] *v* pronounce. **pronunciarsi a favore di** declare oneself in favour of. **pronuncia** *sf* pronunciation.
propaganda [propa'ganda] *sf* propaganda. **propagandista** *s*(*m*+*f*) propagandist.
propagare [propa'gare] *v* propagate.
propenso [pro'penso] *agg* inclined; favourable.
propizio [pro'pitsjo] *agg* propitious; favourable.
proponimento [proponi'mento] *sm* resolution.
***proporre** [pro'porre] *v* propose; intend; suggest.
proporzione [propor'tsjone] *sf* proportion; (*mat*) ratio. **in proporzione a** compared with. **proporzionale** *agg* proportional.
proposito [pro'pɔzito] *sm* purpose; intention; (*scopo*) aim; (*progetto*) plan. **a proposito** (*opportunamente*) at the right time; (*inter*) by the way; (*opportuno*) to the point. **a proposito di** with regard to. **cambiare proposito** change one's mind.
proposizione [propozi'tsjone] *sf* proposition; clause.
proposta [pro'posta] *sf* proposal.
proprietà [proprje'ta] *sf* property; (*precisione, decoro*) propriety; (*possesso*) ownership. **essere di proprietà di** belong to. **proprietà letteraria** copyright.
proprio ['prɔprjo] *agg* one's (own); (*mat, gramm*) proper, characteristic. *avv* exactly, just; (*veramente*) really.
propulsione [propul'sjone] *sf* propulsion.
prora ['prɔra] *sf* prow.
prorogare [proro'gare] *v* (*rinviare*) put off, adjourn; (*prolungare*) extend. **proroga** *sf* adjournment; extension.
***prorompere** [pro'rompere] *v* burst out.
prosa ['prɔza] *sf* prose; theatre. **prosaico** *agg* prosaic.
prosciugare [proʃu'gare] *v* drain.
prosciutto [pro'ʃutto] *sm* ham.
***proscrivere** [pro'skrivere] *v* proscribe.
proseguire [prose'gwire] *v* continue, go on. **proseguimento** *sm* continuation.
prosperare [prospe'rare] *v* prosper, thrive. **prosperità** *sf* prosperity. **prospero** *agg* prosperous, thriving.
prospettiva [prospet'tiva] *sf* (*tec*) perspective; (*previsione*) prospect, outlook. **prospettare** *v* (*esporre*) show; (*guardare*) look out (on). **prospettarsi** *v* (*essere in vista*) be in sight.
prospetto [pros'pɛtto] *sm* (*tabella*) list; (*pubblicità*) prospectus.
prossimo ['prɔssimo] *agg* near; (*seguente*) next; (*vicino nel passato, stretto*) close. **passato/trapassato prossimo** *sm* (*gramm*) present/past perfect. *sm* neighbour. **prossimità** *sf* proximity.
prostituire [prostitu'ire] *v* prostitute. **prostituta** *sf* prostitute. **prostituzione** *sf* prostitution.
protagonista [protago'nista] *s*(*m*+*f*) protagonist, chief character.
***proteggere** [pro'teddʒere] *v* protect, shelter; favour.
proteina [prote'ina] *sf* protein.
protesi ['prɔtezi] *sf* prosthesis.
protesta [pro'tɛsta] *sf* protest. **protestare** *v* protest; (*dichiarare*) declare. **protesto** *sm* protest.
protestante [protes'tante] *s*(*m*+*f*), *agg* Protestant.
protetto [pro'tɛtto], **-a** *agg* protected; favourite. *sm, sf* protégé; favourite. **protettorato** *sm* protectorate. **protettore** *sm*

protector, defender. **santo protettore** patron saint.

protezione [prote'tsjone] *sf* protection; (*mecenatismo*) patronage. **protezione antincendio** fireproofing.

protocollo [proto'kɔllo] *sm* protocol; register. **carta protocollo** *sf* foolscap (paper).

protone [pro'tone] *sm* proton.

prototipo [pro'tɔtipo] *sm* prototype.

***protrarre** [pro'trarre] *v* protract; (*prorogare*) put off.

prova ['prɔva] *sf* proof; evidence; (*esame, testimonianza*) test; (*cimento*) trial; (*tentativo*) try; (*sarto*) fitting; (*teatro*) rehearsal. **a prova di acqua** waterproof. **a prova di fuoco** fireproof. **dar buona prova di sè** give a good account of oneself. **reggere alla prova** stand the test.

provare [pro'vare] *v* try (out); (*collaudare*) test; (*spettacolo*) rehearse; (*assaggiare*) taste; (*dimostrare*) prove; (*mettere alla prova*) put to the test; (*abito, ecc.*) try on.

***provenire** [prove'nire] *v* come (from); (*fig*) spring (from), be caused (by). **provenienza** *sf* origin, source.

proverbio [pro'vɛrbjo] *sm* proverb, saying. **proverbiale** *agg* proverbial.

provetta [pro'vetta] *sf* test-tube.

provincia [pro'vintʃa] *sf* province. **di provincia** provincial.

provocare [provo'kare] *v* provoke, cause. **provocatorio** *agg* provocative. **provocazione** *sf* provocation.

***provvedere** [provve'dere] *v* make provision for, provide for; (*prendere provvedimenti*) take steps; (*badare a*) see to; (*procurare*) provide. **provvedimento** *sm* step, measure. **provveditore** *sm* administrator; (*agli studi*) education officer.

provvidenza [provvi'dentsa] *sf* providence; (*fam*) godsend. **provvidenziale** *agg* providential.

provvigione [provvi'dʒone] *sf* commission.

provvisorio [provvi'zɔrjo] *agg* provisional.

provvista [prov'vista] *sf* provisions *pl*, stock. **provvisto** *agg* supplied, provided.

prua ['prua] *sf* prow.

prudente [pru'dɛnte] *agg* prudent, careful, cautious. **prudenza** *sf* care, caution.

***prudere** ['prudere] *v* itch. **prurito** *sm* itch.

prugna ['pruɲa] *sf* plum; (*secca*) prune. **prugno** *sm* plum-tree.

pseudonimo [pseu'dɔnimo] *sm* pseudonym.

psicanalisi [psica'nalizi] *sf* psycho-analysis. **psicanalista** *s*(*m*+*f*) psycho-analyst. **psicanalitico** *agg* psycho-analytical.

psichiatra [psi'kjatra] *s*(*m*+*f*) psychiatrist. **psichiatria** *sf* psychiatry.

psichico ['psikiko] *agg* psychic.

psicologo [psi'kɔlogo], **-a** *sm, sf* psychologist. **psicologia** *sf* psychology. **psicologico** *agg* psychological.

psicopatico [psiko'patiko], **-a** *agg* psychopathic. *sm, sf* psychopath.

psicosi [psi'kɔzi] *sf* psychosis. **psicotico, -a** *s, agg* psychotic.

psicosomatico [psikoso'matiko] *agg* psychosomatic.

psicoterapia [psikotera'pia] *sf* psychotherapy. **psicoterapista** *s*(*m*+*f*) psychotherapist.

pubblicare [pubbli'kare] *v* publish. **pubblicazione** *sf* publication, issue. **pubblicista** *s*(*m*+*f*) (freelance) journalist.

pubblicità [pubblitʃi'ta] *sf* publicity; advertising. **fare pubblicità** advertise. **piccola pubblicità** classified advertisements *pl*. **pubblicitario** *agg* advertising, publicity.

pubblico ['pubbliko] *agg* public. *sm* public; (*teatro*) audience.

pubertà [puber'ta] *sf* puberty.

pudico [pu'diko] *agg, m pl* **-chi** modest; (*vergognoso*) bashful.

pudore [pu'dore] *sm* modesty; (*vergogna*) shame. **oltraggio al pudore** *sm* indecent behaviour. **senza pudore** shameless.

puerile [pue'rile] *agg* puerile.

pugilato [pudʒi'lato] *sm* boxing. **fare del pugilato** box. **pugile** *sm* boxer. **pugilistico** *agg* boxing.

pugnalare [puɲa'lare] *v* stab. **pugnalata** *sf* stab. **pugnale** *sm* dagger.

pugno ['puɲo] *sm* fist; (*colpo*) punch; (*piccola quantità*) fistful. **essere un pugno in un occhio** be an eyesore. **fare a pugni** fight; (*fig*) clash. **prendere a pugni** punch. **tenere in pugno** clutch; (*fig*) control.

pulce ['pultʃe] *sf* flea. **gioco della pulce** *sm* tiddly-winks.

pulcino [pul'tʃino] *sm* chick. **bagnato come un pulcino** wet through.

puledro [pu'ledro] *sm* colt. **puledra** *sf* filly.

puleggia [pu'leddʒa] *sf* pulley.

pulire [pu'lire] *v* clean; (*lavando*) wash; (*con strofinaccio, ecc.*) wipe (clean); (*con*

spazzola) brush; (*sfregando*) scour; (*lucidare*) polish. **pulirsi il naso** blow one's nose. **pulito** *agg* clean.
pulizia [puli'tsia] *sf* (*il pulire*) cleaning; (*l'essere pulito*) cleanliness. **far le pulizie** do the cleaning. **far pulizia** clean; (*sgombrare*) clear out.
pullman ['pullman] *sm invar* coach.
pullover [pul'lɔver] *sm invar* pullover.
pullulare [pullu'lare] *v* swarm.
pulpito ['pulpito] *sm* pulpit. **montare in pulpito** preach.
pulsare [pul'sare] *v* throb, beat. **pulsante** *sm* button; (*campanello*) buzzer.
***pungere** ['pundʒere] *v* sting; (*morsicare*) bite; (*con spillo*) prick. **pungente** *agg* pungent; (*fig*) sharp; (*ispido*) prickly. **pungiglione** *sm* sting. **pungolo** *sm* goad.
punire [pu'nire] *v* punish. **punibile** *agg* punishable. **punitivo** *agg* punitive. **punizione** *sf* punishment; (*sport*) penalty.
punta ['punta] *sf* point; (*estremità*) tip. **ora di punta** *sf* rush hour. **prendere di punta** clash (with).
puntare [pun'tare] *v* point, direct; (*scommettere*) bet.
puntata [pun'tata] *sf* (*scritto*) instalment, part.
punteggiare [punted'dʒare] *v* punctuate. **punteggiatura** *sf* punctuation.
punteggio [pun'teddʒo] *sm* score.
puntellare [puntel'lare] *v* prop up. **puntello** *sm* prop; (*fig*) support.
puntiglioso [punti'ʎozo] *agg* stubborn. **puntiglio** *sm* stubbornness.
puntina [pun'tina] *sf* (*da disegno*) drawing pin; (*grammofono*) stylus.
punto ['punto] *sm* point; (*segno*) dot; (*med, ricamo, maglia*) stitch. *avv* (*affatto*) at all. **di punto in bianco** point-blank. **due punti** colon. **in punto** (*tempo*) on the dot, sharp. **mettere a punto** put right; (*auto*) tune; (*fig*) clarify. **punto esclamativo/interrogativo** exclamation/question mark. **punto e virgola** semicolon. **punto fermo** full stop.
puntuale [puntu'ale] *agg* punctual, on time.
puntualizzare [puntualid'dzare] *v* define, precisely.
puntura [pun'tura] *sf* sting, bite; (*di spillo, ecc.*) prick; (*med*) injection, puncture; (*dolore*) stitch.
punzecchiare [pundzek'kjare] *v* sting, bite, prick; (*stuzzicare*) tease.
punzonare [puntso'nare] *v* punch. **punzonatrice** *sf* punch. **punzone** *sm* punch, die.
pupa ['pupa] *sf* (*fam*) baby; (*bambola*) doll. **pupattola** *sf* doll. **pupazzo** *sm* puppet. **pupo** (*fam*) baby, little boy.
pupilla [pu'pilla] *sf* pupil.
purché [pur'ke] *cong* provided that, as long as.
pure ['pure] *avv* also, too. *cong* even (though); (*tuttavia*) yet.
purè [pu're] *sm invar* purée. **purè di patate** mashed potatoes *pl*.
purgare [pur'gare] *v* purge; purify. **purga** *sf* purge; (*il purgare*) purging, cleansing; (*purgante*) laxative; (*gastr*) soaking.
purgatorio [purga'tɔrjo] *sm* purgatory.
purificare [purifi'kare] *v* purify.
puritano [puri'tano], **-a** *s, agg* puritan.
puro ['puro] *agg* pure. **purezza** *sf* purity. **purosangue** *agg, sm invar* throughbred.
purpureo [pur'pureo] *agg* purple.
purtroppo [pur'trɔppo] *avv* unfortunately.
pus [pus] *sm invar* pus.
***putrefare** [putre'fare] *v* putrefy, rot. **putrefatto** *or* **putrido** *agg* putrid, rotten.
puttana [put'tana] *sf* whore; (*fam*) tart.
puzzare [put'tsare] *v* stink, smell. **puzzo** *sm* stench, smell. **puzzolente** *agg* stinking.

Q

qua [kwa] *avv* here. **(al) di qua di** on this side of. **di qua** (*stato in luogo*) here; (*moto a luogo*) over here; (*da qui*) from here. **fin qua** (*spazio*) up to here; (*tempo*) so far. **per di qua** this way. **qua sopra/sotto/vicino** up/down/near here.
quacchero ['kwakkero], **-a** *sm, sf* Quaker.
quaderno [kwa'dɛrno] *sm* exercise-book.
quadrante [kwa'drante] *sm* (*mat, astron*) quadrant; (*orologio*) dial; (*solare*) sundial.
quadrato [kwa'drato] *agg* square; (*sensibile*) level-headed. *sm* square. **quadrare** *v* square; (*far senso*) make sense; (*garbare*) please.
quadretto [kwa'dretto] *sm* small square; (*fig*) scene. **a quadretti** check(ed), chequered.

quadrifoglio [kwadri'fɔʎʎo] *sm* four-leafed clover; (*autostrada*) clover-leaf.
quadro[1] ['kwadro] *agg* square.
quadro[2] ['kwadro] *sm* (*dipinto*) picture; (*ambito*) scope; (*tabella*) table. **quadri** *sm pl* (*carte*) diamonds *pl.* **a quadri** check(ed), chequered.
quadrupede [kwa'drupede] *agg, sm* quadruped.
quaggiù [kwad'dʒu] *avv* down here.
quaglia ['kwaʎa] *sf* quail.
qualche ['kwalke] *agg* some, any; (*alcuni*) a few. **in qualche luogo** somewhere. **in qualche modo** somehow. **qualcosa** *pron also* **qualche cosa** something, anything. **qualcuno** *pron* somebody, anybody.
quale ['kwale] *agg, pron* what; (*fra numero limitato*) which; (*come*) as. **tale e quale** just like. *inter* what! *avv* as.
qualificare [kwalifi'kare] *v* qualify. **qualifica** *sf* title; position; (*doti professionali*) qualification; (*giudizio*) report. **qualificativo** *agg* qualifying. **qualificato** *agg* skilled.
qualità [kwali'ta] *sf* quality; (*specie*) sort, kind. **qualitativo** *agg* qualitative.
qualora [kwa'lora] *cong* in case.
qualunque [kwa'lunkwe] *agg invar also* **qualsiasi** any; (*ogni*) every; (*non importa quale*) whatever, whichever. **l'uomo qualunque** the man in the street.
quando ['kwando] *avv* when. *cong* when; (*ogniqualvolta*) whenever; (*mentre*) whereas; (*giacché*) since. **da quando** (*dacché*) (ever) since; (*da quanto tempo*) since when. **di quando in quando** from time to time. **fino a quando** until; (*interrogativo*) until when; (*per quanto tempo*) how long.
quantità [kwanti'ta] *sf* quantity. **quantitativo** *sm* amount.
quanto ['kwanto] *agg* how much *or* many; (*esclamativo*) what (a lot of); (*relativo*) as much *or* many ... as. *pron* how much *or* many; as much *or* many; (*quello che*) what. *avv* how (much *or* many); (*tempo*) how long; (*distanza*) how far; (*come*) as; (*nella misura che*) as much as. **da quanto** (*tempo*) how long; (*per ciò che*) as far as. **per quanto** however; (*per ciò che*) as far as. **quanto a** as for. **quanto fa?** how much is it? **quanto mai** very much indeed. **quanto prima** soon. **quanto tempo** how long.
quaranta [kwa'ranta] *agg, sm* forty.
quarantena *sf* quarantine. **quarantesimo** *sm, agg* fortieth.
quaresima [kwa'rezima] *sf* Lent.
quarta ['kwarta] *sf* (*auto*) fourth *or* top gear; (*musica*) fourth. **partire in quarta** (*fam*) be off like a shot.
quartetto [kwar'tetto] *sm* quartet.
quartiere [kwar'tjɛre] *sm* district, quarter. **quartieri bassi** slums *pl.*
quarto ['kwarto] *agg* fourth. *sm* quarter. **sono le due e/meno un quarto** it is a quarter past/to two.
quarzo ['kwartso] *sm* quartz.
quasi ['kwazi] *avv* nearly, almost; (*con valore negativo*) hardly. *cong* (*come se*) as if.
quassù [kwas'su] *avv* up here.
quatto quatto ['kwatto 'kwatto] *avv* very quickly.
quattordici [kwat'tɔrditʃi] *agg, sm* fourteen. **quattordicesimo** *agg, sm* fourteenth.
quattrini [kwat'trini] *sm pl* money *sing*; (*fam*) cash *sing*. **quattrini a palate** loads of money *sing*. **senza quattrini** penniless.
quattro ['kwattro] *sm, agg* four. **dirne quattro a qualcuno** give someone a piece of one's mind. **far quattro passi** go for a stroll. **farsi in quattro** go out of one's way.
quegli ['kweʎi] *V* **quello**.
quei ['kwei] *V* **quello**.
quel [kwel] *V* **quello**.
quello ['kwello] *agg* that (*pl* those). *pron* that (one) (*pl* those); (*lo stesso*) the same. **di quello che** than. **quello che** the one who (*pl* those who); (*ciò che*) what.
quercia ['kwɛrtʃa] *sf* oak.
querela [kwe'rela] *sf* lawsuit, action. **presentare** *or* **sporgere querela** bring an action. **querelante** *s*(*m*+*f*) plaintiff.
questionario [kwestjo'narjo] *sm* questionnaire.
questione [kwes'tjone] *sf* question; (*affare*) matter; problem; (*disputa*) argument. **fare una questione** make an issue. **mettere in questione** question.
questo ['kwesto] *agg* this (*pl* these). *pron* this (one) (*pl* these). **con questo** (*con queste parole*) with these words; (*ciònonostante*) in spite of this.
questura [kwes'tura] *sf* police station. **questore** *sm* police inspector.
qui ['kwi] *avv* here. **di qui** from here; (*moto a luogo*) here; (*tempo*) from now

(on). **fin qui** up to here; (*tempo*) up to now.
quietanza [kwje'tantsa] *sf* receipt.
quietare [kwje'tare] *v* calm. **quiete** *sf* calm; (*assenza di moto*) rest.
quindi ['kwindi] *cong* so. *avv* afterwards.
quindici ['kwinditʃi] *agg, sm* fifteen. **quindici giorni** a fortnight. **quindicesimo** *agg, sm* fifteenth. **quindicinale** *sm* fortnightly.
quinta ['kwinta] *sf* (*teatro*) wing. **dietro le quinte** behind the scenes.
quintessenza [kwintes'sɛntsa] *sf* quintessence.
quintetto [kwin'tetto] *sm* quintet.
quinto ['kwinto] *sm, agg* fifth.
quota ['kwɔta] *sf* (*porzione*) share; (*altitudine*) height; (*livello*) level; (*econ*) quota. **quota zero** square one. **quotare** *v* appreciate; (*borsa*) quote. **quotazione** *sf* quotation.
quotidiano [kwoti'djano] *agg, sm* daily.
quoziente [kwo'tsjɛnte] *sm* quotient.

R

rabarbaro [ra'barbaro] *sm* rhubarb.
rabberciare [rabber'tʃare] *v* patch, mend; (*scritto*) re-hash.
rabbia ['rabbja] *sf* fury, rage; (*idrofobia*) rabies. **che rabbia!** how infuriating! **fare rabbia a** make angry. **rabbioso** *agg* furious; (*idrofobo*) rabid.
rabbino [rab'bino] *sm* rabbi. **rabbinico** *agg* rabbinical.
rabbonire [rabbo'nire] *v* calm down, soothe.
rabbrividire [rabbrivi'dire] *v* shiver; (*fig*) shudder.
rabbuffare [rabbuf'fare] *v* (*scompigliare*) ruffle; (*sgridare*) scold. **rabbuffo** *sm* telling-off, scolding.
rabbuiarsi [rabbu'jarsi] *v* darken.
raccapezzare [rakkapet'tsare] *v* scrape together. **raccapezzarsi** *v* make out.
raccapricciare [rakkaprit'tʃare] *v* be horrified. **raccapricciante** *agg* horrifying.
raccattare [rakkat'tare] *v* pick up, collect.
racchetta [rak'ketta] *sf* racket; (*ping-pong*) bat.
***raccogliere** [rak'kɔʎere] *v* pick; (*riprendere da terra*) pick up; (*riunire*) collect; (*fare il raccolto*) gather, harvest. **raccoglimento** *sm* attention. **raccoglitore** *sm* (*cartella*) binder.
raccolta [rak'kɔlta] *sf* collecting; collection; (*agric*) harvesting. **fare la raccolta (di)** collect.
raccolto [rak'kɔlto] *agg* (*concentrato nei pensieri*) deep in thought; (*rannicchiato*) crouching. *sm* harvest, crop.
raccomandare [rakkoman'dare] *v* recommend; (*esortare*) urge. **mi raccomando!** please do! **raccomandarsi a** rely on. **(lettera) raccomandata** *sf* registered letter. **raccomandato, -a** *sm, sf* protégé. **raccomandazione** *sf* recommendation.
raccomodare [rakkomo'dare] *v also* **racconciare** repair, mend.
raccontare [rakkon'tare] *v* tell. **racconto** *sm* story, tale; (*resoconto*) account.
raccorciare [rakkor'tʃare] *v* shorten.
raccordare [rakkor'dare] *v* connect. **raccordo** *sm* connection; (*strada, ecc.*) junction.
racimolare [ratʃimo'lare] *v* scrape together.
radar ['radar] *sm invar* radar.
raddolcire [raddol'tʃire] *v* sweeten; (*acqua*) soften.
raddoppiare [raddop'pjare] *v* double; (*fig*) redouble.
raddrizzare [raddrit'tsare] *v* straighten; (*elett*) rectify. **raddrizzatore** *sm* rectifier.
***radere** ['radere] *v* (*sbarbare*) shave; (*sfiorare*) graze. **radere al suolo** raze to the ground.
radiale [ra'djale] *agg* radial.
radiare [ra'djare] *v* expel; (*mil*) cashier; cancel. **radiare dall'albo** strike off the register.
radiatore [radja'tore] *sm* radiator.
radiazione[1] [radja'tsjone] *sf* (*fis*) radiation.
radiazione[2] [radja'tsjone] *sf* expulsion; cancellation.
radica ['radika] *sf* briar.
radicale [radi'kale] *agg* radical. *sm* (*chim*) radical; (*mat*) root.
radicare [radi'kare] *v* (take) root. **radicato** *agg* deep-rooted.
radicchio [ra'dikkjo] *sm* chicory.
radice [ra'ditʃe] *sf* root. **mettere radici** take root. **radice quadrata/cubica** square/cube root.
radio[1] ['radjo] *sm invar* radium.

radio[2] ['radjo] *sf invar* radio. **giornale radio** *sm* news (broadcast). **segnale radio** *sm* time signal.
radioattivo [radjoat'tivo] *agg* radioactive. **radioattività** *sf* radioactivity.
radiocontrollato [radjokontrol'lato] *agg* radio-controlled.
radiodiffusione [radjodiffu'zjone] *sf also* **radiotrasmissione** broadcast. **radiodiffuso** *agg* broadcast.
radiografare [radjogra'fare] *v* X-ray. **radiografia** *sf* (*immagine*) X-ray; (*procedimento*) radiography.
radiologo [ra'djɔlogo], **-a** *sm, pl* **-ghi**, *sf* radiologist.
rado ['rado] *agg* sparse. **di rado** rarely. **radura** *sf* clearing.
radunare [radu'nare] *v* gather. **radunarsi** *v* assemble. **radunata** *sf* assembly, meeting. **raduno** *sm* meeting.
rafano ['rafano] *sm* radish.
raffica ['raffika] *sf* (*vento*) gust; (*colpi*) volley.
raffigurare [raffigu'rare] *v* represent.
raffinare [raffi'nare] *v* refine. **raffinatezza** *sf* refinement. **raffinazione** *sf* refining. **raffineria** *sf* refinery.
rafforzare [raffor'tsare] *v* reinforce.
raffreddare [raffred'dare] *v* cool. **raffreddarsi** *v* (*diventar freddo*) cool down; (*fam: prendersi un raffreddore*) catch a cold. **raffreddamento** *sm* cooling (down *or* off). **raffreddore** *sm* cold.
raffrenare [raffre'nare] *v* restrain.
raffrontare [raffron'tare] *v* compare. **raffronto** *sm* comparison.
rafia ['rafia] *sf* raffia.
raganella [raga'nɛlla] *sf* rattle.
ragazza [ra'gattsa] *sf* girl; (*innamorata*) girl-friend. **da ragazza** as a girl. **nome da ragazza** *sm* maiden name. **ragazza madre** unmarried mother.
ragazzo [ra'gattso] *sm* boy, lad; (*fam*) fellow, chap; (*innamorato*) boy-friend. **da ragazzo** as a boy. **fin da ragazzo** since childhood.
raggiare [rad'dʒare] *v* radiate.
raggio ['raddʒo] *sm* ray; (*geom*) radius; (*ambito*) range; (*ruota*) spoke. **raggio d'azione** range; (*fig*) scope. **fare i raggi** X-ray.
raggirare [raddʒi'rare] *v* trick. **raggiro** *sm* trick.
***raggiungere** [rad'dʒundʒere] *v* reach; (*riunirsi*) join; (*allinearsi*) catch up (with); (*conseguire*) attain. **raggiungibile** *agg* within reach; attainable.
raggiustare [raddʒus'tare] *v* mend; (*fig*) set right.
raggomitolare [raggomito'lare] *v* roll up. **raggomitolarsi** *v* curl up.
raggrinzare [raggrin'tsare] *v also* **raggrinzire** wrinkle, crease.
raggrumare [raggru'mare] *v* clot.
raggruppare [raggrup'pare] *v* group (together). **raggrupparsi** *v* assemble. **raggruppamento** *sm* grouping; (*gruppo*) group; (*mil*) unit.
ragguagliare [raggwa'ʎare] *v* level; (*paragonare*) compare; inform; (*mat*) convert. **ragguaglio** *sm* comparison; information; (*resoconto*) report; conversion.
ragia ['radʒa] *sf* **acqua ragia** *sf* turpentine.
ragionare [radʒo'nare] *v* reason; discuss. **ragionamento** *sm* reasoning; discussion.
ragione [ra'dʒone] *sf* reason; (*diritto*) right; (*rapporto*) rate; (*spiegazione*) account; (*mat*) ratio. **a ragione** rightly. **a ragion veduta** after due consideration. **aver ragione** be right. **dar ragione a qualcuno** admit that someone is right. **rendersi ragione (di)** account (for).
ragioneria [radʒone'ria] *sf* accountancy. **ragionere, -a** *sm, sf* accountant.
ragionevole [radʒo'nevole] *agg* reasonable.
ragliare [ra'ʎare] *v* bray. **raglio** *sm* bray.
ragno ['raɲo] *sm* spider. **ragnatela** *sf* cobweb.
ragù [ra'gu] *sm* meat sauce.
raid ['reid] *sm invar* (*mil*) raid; (*sport*) rally.
raion ['rajon] *sm invar* rayon.
rallegrare [ralleg'rare] *v* cheer up. **rallegrarsi** *v* be delighted; congratulate. **rallegramenti** *sm pl* congratulations *pl*.
rallentare [rallen'tare] *v* slacken, slow down. **rallentamento** *sm* slackening, slowing down.
rame ['rame] *sm* copper. **ramaiolo** *sm* ladle.
ramengo [ra'mengo] *sm* **andare a ramengo** (*fam*) go to the dogs.
ramificare [ramifi'kare] *v* ramify. **ramificazione** *sf* ramification.
ramino [ra'mino] *sm* rummy.
rammaricarsi [rammari'karsi] *v* regret; (*lamentarsi*) complain. **rammarico** *sm, pl* **-chi** regret.

rammendare [rammen'dare] *v* darn. **rammendo** *sm* (*atto*) darning; (*parte rammendata*) darn.
rammentare [rammen'tare] *v* (*ricordare*) recall; (*richiamare alla memoria*) call to mind.
rammollire [rammol'lire] *v* soften. **rammollito** *agg* soft; (*rimbambito*) doddering.
ramo ['ramo] *sm* branch. **ramoscello** *sm* twig.
rampa ['rampa] *sf* ramp; (*scala*) flight. **rampante** *agg* rampant.
rampicante [rampi'kante] *agg* climbing. *sm* (*pianta*) creeper.
rampino [ram'pino] *sm* hook.
rampollo [ram'pɔllo] *sm* offspring; (*pianta*) shoot; (*acqua*) spring.
rampone [ram'pone] *sm* (*pesca*) harpoon; (*alpinismo*) crampon.
rana ['rana] *sf* frog; (*nuoto a rana*) breaststroke. **uomo rana** *sm* frogman.
rancido ['rantʃido] *agg* rancid.
rancio ['rantʃo] *sm* meal.
rancore [ran'kore] *sm* grudge.
randagio [ran'dadʒo] *agg* stray.
randello [ran'dɛllo] *sm* club.
rango ['rango] *sm* rank; (*posizione sociale*) standing.
rannicchiarsi [rannik'kjarsi] *v* crouch, huddle.
rannuvolarsi [rannuvo'larsi] *v* cloud over; (*fig*) darken.
ranocchio [ra'nokkjo] *sm* frog.
rantolare [ranto'lare] *v* wheeze.
ranuncolo [ra'nunkolo] *sm* buttercup.
rapa ['rapa] *sf* turnip.
rapace [ra'patʃe] *agg* rapacious. **uccello rapace** *sm* bird of prey.
rapare [ra'pare] *v* crop.
rapido ['rapido] *agg* quick, rapid. *sm* express (train).
rapina [ra'pina] *sf* robbery. **rapinare** *v* rob.
rapire [ra'pire] *v* (*rapinare*) rob; (*persone*) kidnap, abduct; (*estasiare*) enrapture. **rapimento** *sm* kidnapping; (*estasi*) rapture.
rappezzare [rappet'tsare] *v* patch.
rapporto [rap'porto] *sm* (*legame*) connection; relationship; (*resoconto*) report; (*mec, mat*) ratio.
***rapprendersi** [rap'prendersi] *v* coagulate; (*latte*) curdle.
rappresaglia [rappre'zaʎa] *sf* reprisal.
rappresentare [rappresen'tare] *v* represent; (*significare*) mean; (*teatro*) show. **rappresentante** *s*(*m*+*f*) representative, agent. **rappresentanza** *sf* agency. **rappresentativo** *agg* representative. **rappresentazione** *sf* representation; description; (*teatro, cine*) performance.
raro ['raro] *agg* rare; exceptional. **rarità** *sf* rarity.
rasare [ra'zare] *v* shave; (*erba, ecc.*) cut. **rasoio** *sm* razor.
raschiare [ras'kjare] *v* scrape; (*cancellare*) scratch out. **raschiatura** *sf* scratching; scratch. **raschietto** *sm* scraper.
rasentare [razen'tare] *v* go close (to); (*fig*) come close (to).
raso ['razo] *agg* (*liscio*) smooth; (*sbarbato*) shaved. *sm* (*tessuto*) satin.
raspa ['raspa] *sf* rasp. **raspare** *v* rasp.
rassegnare [rasse'ɲare] *v* **rassegnare le dimissioni** resign. **rassegnarsi** *v* resign oneself. **rassegna** *sf* review; inspection; (*resoconto*) survey.
rasserenarsi [rassere'narsi] *v* clear up; (*fig*) cheer up.
rassettare [rasset'tare] *v* tidy up; (*accomodare*) repair.
rassicurare [rassiku'rare] *v* reassure.
rassomigliare [rassomi'ʎare] *v* resemble. **rassomigliarsi** *v* look alike.
rastrello [ras'trɛllo] *sm* rake. **rastrellamento** *sm* (*polizia*) round-up. **rastrellare** *v* rake; (*fig*) comb. **rastrelliera** *sf* rack.
rata ['rata] *sf* instalment.
ratificare [ratifi'kare] *v* ratify. **ratifica** *sf* ratification.
ratto[1] ['ratto] *sm* (*zool*) rat.
ratto[2] ['ratto] *sm* (*rapimento*) rape.
rattoppare [rattop'pare] *v* patch. **rattoppo** *sm* (*toppa*) patch.
rattrappire [rattrap'pire] *v* make numb.
rattristare [rattris'tare] *v* sadden. **rattristarsi** *v* become sad, grieve.
rauco ['rauko] *agg* hoarse.
ravanello [rava'nello] *sm* radish.
***ravvedersi** [ravve'dersi] *v* mend one's ways.
ravviare [ravvi'are] *v* tidy (up).
ravvicinare [ravvitʃi'nare] *v* bring near; reconcile. **ravvicinamento** *sm* (*pol*) rapprochement.
ravvisare [ravvi'zare] *v* recognize.
ravvivare [ravvi'vare] *v* revive.
***ravvolgere** [rav'vɔldʒere] *v* wrap (up).

raziocinio [ratsjo'tʃinjo] *sm* reason; common sense.
razionale [ratsjo'nale] *agg* rational. **razionalizzare** *v* rationalize. **razionalizzazione** *sf* rationalization.
razionare [ratsjo'nare] *v* ration. **razionamento** *sm* rationing. **razione** *sf* ration.
razza[1] ['rattsa] *sf* race; (*specie*) kind; (*stirpe*) descent; (*animali*) breed. **di ogni razza** of all sorts. **di razza incrociata** crossbred. **di razza (pura)** (*animali*) pedigree, thoroughbred. **razziale** *agg* racial. **razzismo** *sm* racialism, racism. **razzista** *agg*, *s*(*m*+*f*) racist, racialist.
razza[2] ['rattsa] *sf* (*pesce*) ray, skate.
razzia [rat'tsia] *sf* raid.
razzo ['rattso] *sm* rocket.
re [re] *sm* king.
reagire [rea'dʒire] *v* react. **reagente** *sm* reagent.
reale[1] [re'ale] *agg* real. **realismo** *sm* realism. **realista** *s*(*m*+*f*) realist. **realistico** *agg* realistic. **realtà** *sf* reality. **in realtà** in (actual) fact.
reale[2] [re'ale] *agg* (*regale*) royal. **realista** *agg*, *s*(*m*+*f*) royalist.
realizzare [realid'dzare] *v* realize; (*effettuare*) put into effect; (*sport*) score. **realizzabile** *agg* feasible. **realizzazione** *sf* realization; (*teatro, ecc.*) production. **prezzo di realizzo** cost price.
reato [re'ato] *sm* offence; (*grave*) crime.
reattivo [reat'tivo] *agg* reactive. *sm* (*chim*) reagent; (*psic*) test.
reattore [reat'tore] *sm* reactor; (*aereo*) jet.
reazione [rea'tsjone] *sf* reaction. **motore a reazione** jet engine. **reazionario, -a** *s*, *agg* reactionary.
rebbio ['rebbjo] *sm* prong.
recapito [re'kapito] *sm* (*indirizzo*) address; (*consegna*) delivery. **recapitare** *v* deliver.
recare [re'kare] *v* (*portare*) bear; (*arrecare*) cause.
recensire [retʃen'sire] *v* review. **recensione** *sf* review. **recensore, -a** *sm*, *sf* reviewer.
recente [re'tʃɛnte] *agg* recent. **recentissime** *sf pl* latest news *sing*.
recessione [retʃes'sjone] *sf* recession.
recinto [re'tʃinto] *sm* enclosure; (*per animali*) pen. **recintare** *v* enclose.
recipiente [retʃi'pjɛnte] *sm* container.
reciproco [re'tʃiproko] *agg* reciprocal, mutual. **reciprocare** *v* reciprocate. **reciprocità** *sf* reciprocity.
recitare [retʃi'tare] *v* (*versi, ecc.*) recite; (*una parte*) play; (*sostenere un ruolo*) act; (*fingere*) put on an act. **recita** *sf* performance. **recital** *sm invar* recital. **recitazione** *sf* recitation.
reclamare [rekla'mare] *v* complain; (*richiedere*) demand; protest. **reclamo** *sm* complaint.
reclame [re'klam] *sf invar* advertisement. **fare (della) reclame** advertise.
reclusione [reklu'zjone] *sf* confinement; imprisonment.
reclutare [reklu'tare] *v* recruit. **recluta** *sf* recruit.
record ['rekord] *sm invar* record.
recriminare [rekrimi'nare] *v* recriminate.
redarguire [redargu'ire] *v* rebuke.
redattore [redat'tore], **-trice** *sm*, *sf* editor. **redazione** *sf* editorial staff; (*ufficio*) editor's office; (*atto del redigere*) editing, compiling.
reddito ['reddito] *sm* income; (*statale*) revenue; (*utile*) return. **imposta sul reddito** *sf* income tax. **reddito imponibile** taxable income.
redentore [reden'tore] *agg* redeeming. *sm* redeemer.
***redigere** [re'didʒere] *v* (*compilare*) draw up; (*scrivere*) write; (*giornale*) edit.
***redimere** [re'dimere] *v* redeem. **redimibile** *agg* redeemable.
redini ['redini] *sf pl* reins *pl*.
redivivo [redi'vivo] *agg* (*fig*) another.
reduce ['rɛdutʃe] *agg* returning. *sm* (*mil*) veteran; (*superstite*) survivor.
refe ['refe] *sm* thread.
referendum [refe'rɛndum] *sm invar* referendum.
referenza [refe'rɛntsa] *sf* reference.
refettorio [refet'tɔrjo] *sm* refectory.
refrattario [refrat'tarjo] *agg* refractory; (*fig*) unmoved (by).
refrigerare [refridʒe'rare] *v* refresh, cool.
regalare [rega'lare] *v* give (away). **regalo** *sm* gift, present.
regale [re'gale] *agg* regal.
regata [re'gata] *sf* regatta.
reggente [red'dʒɛnte] *sm* ruler. *agg* ruling.
***reggere** ['rɛddʒere] *v* (*sostenere*) hold; support; (*resistere*) stand; (*dirigere*) run; (*gramm*) govern; (*durare*) last. **reggere al confronto con** bear comparison with. **reggere alla prova** stand the test. **reggersi** *v* stand.

reggia ['rɛddʒa] *sf* royal palace.
reggimento [reddʒi'mento] *sm* regiment.
reggipetto [reddʒi'pɛtto] *sm* bra.
regia [re'dʒia] *sf* (*cinema*) direction; (*teatro*) production.
regime [re'dʒime] *sm* regime. **essere a regime** be on a diet. **regime di vita** way of life.
regina [re'dʒina] *sf* queen.
regio ['rɛdʒo] *agg* royal.
regione [re'dʒone] *sf* region. **regionale** *agg* regional.
regista [re'dʒista] *sf* (*cine*) director; (*teatro*, *TV*) producer.
registrare [redʒis'trare] *v* record; (*in registro*) register; (*mettere a punto*) adjust. **registratore** *sm* recorder; register. **registrazione** *sf* record; registration; adjustment; (*radio*, *TV*) recording. **registro** *sm* register. **cambiar registro** (*fam*) change one's tune.
regnare [re'ɲare] *v* rule, reign. **regno** *sm* (*territorio*) kingdom, realm; (*periodo*, *potere*) reign.
regola ['rɛgola] *sm* rule; norm. **di regola** normally. **in regola** in order. **per vostra regola** for your information. **regolamentare** *agg* prescribed. **regolamento** *sm* (*il regolare*) regulation; (*norme*) rules *pl*; (*comm*) settlement.
regolare [rego'lare] *v* regulate; (*mettere a punto*) adjust; (*comm*) settle. **regolarsi** *v* act; control oneself. *agg* regular. **regolarità** *sf* regularity. **regolarizzare** *v* regularize.
regolo ['rɛgolo] *sm* ruler; (*calcolatore*) slide-rule.
reincarnazione [reinkarna'tsjone] *sf* reincarnation.
reintegrare [reinte'grare] *v* reinstate. **reintegrazione** *sf* reinstatement.
relativo [rela'tivo] *agg* relative; concerning; (*corrispondente*) relevant. **relativamente a** regarding. **relatività** *sf* relativity.
relazione [rela'tsjone] *sf* relation(ship), connection; (*resoconto*) report. **essere in buone relazioni** be on good terms. **in relazione a** as regards. **mettere in relazione** relate.
relegare [rele'gare] *v* relegate.
religione [reli'dʒone] *sf* religion. **religiosa** *sf* nun. **religioso** *agg* religious.
reliquia [re'likwja] *sf* relic. **reliquiario** *sf* reliquary.
relitto [re'litto] *sm* wreck; (*rottame*) wreckage.
remare [re'mare] *v* row. **remata** *sf* stroke. **fare una remata** go for a row.
reminiscenza [remini'ʃɛntsa] *sf* recollection.
remissivo [remis'sivo] *agg* meek.
remoto [re'mɔto] *agg* remote.
***rendere** ['rɛndere] *v* return; (*fruttare*) bring in; (*far diventare*) make; be efficient. **render conto di** account for. **render l'idea** make oneself clear. **rendere omaggio** pay homage. **rendersi conto** (*spiegare*) explain; (*capire*) realize. **rendere un servizio** do a favour.
rendimento [rendi'mento] *sm* (*utile*) yield; (*resa*) output; (*fis*, *mec*) efficiency.
rendita ['rɛndita] *sf* income; (*econ*) revenue; (*reddito*) yield.
rene ['rɛne] *sm* kidney. **reni** *sf pl* (*fam*) back *sing*.
renna ['rɛnna] *sf* reindeer.
reparto [re'parto] *sm* department; (*mil*) unit. **capo reparto** departmental head; (*maestranza*) foreman; (*negozio*) supervisor.
repellente [repel'lɛnte] *agg* repellent; (*ripugnante*) repulsive.
repentaglio [repen'taʎo] *sm* **mettere a repentaglio** jeopardize.
reperibile [repe'ribile] *agg* to be found; (*disponibile*) available.
repertorio [reper'tɔrjo] *sm* repertoire; (*elenco*) list.
replica ['rɛplika] *sf* repetition; (*risposta*) reply; (*teatro*) performance; objection; copy. **replicare** *v* repeat; reply; perform again; object.
repressione [repres'sjone] *sf* repression. **represso** *agg* repressed.
***reprimere** [re'primere] *v* repress, control.
repubblica [re'pubblika] *sf* republic. **repubblicano** *agg* republican.
reputare [repu'tare] *v* consider. **reputazione** *sf* reputation.
requisire [rekwi'zire] *v* requisition. **requisito** *sm* requirement. **requisitoria** *sf* (*dir*) indictment; (*rimprovero*) reproof.
resa ['reza] *sf* (*l'arrendersi*) surrender; (*restituzione*) return; (*rendimento*) yield. **resa dei conti** statement (of accounts); (*fig*) reckoning.
***rescindere** [re'ʃindere] *v* rescind.

residente [rezi'dɛnte] *s(m+f)*, *agg* resident. **residenza** *sf* residence; (*permanenza*) stay.

residuo [re'ziduo] *agg* residual. *sm* residue; (*fig*) trace. **residuato** *sm* surplus.

resina ['rɛzina] *sf* resin.

resistere [re'zistere] *v* resist; (*sopportare*) bear; (*non essere danneggiato*) be resistant (to). **resistente** *agg* resistant, proof (against). **resistenza** *sf* resistance; (*capacità di resistere*) endurance.

resoconto [rezo'konto] *sm* report.

***respingere** [res'pindʒere] *v* push back, repel; (*rifiutare*) reject; (*bocciare*) fail. **respingente** *sm* buffer.

respirare [respi'rare] *v* breathe. **respiratore** *sm* respirator. **respiratorio** *agg* respiratory. **respirazione** *sf* respiration. **respiro** *sm* breath; (*fig*) breathing space. **sentirsi mancare il respiro** feel breathless.

responsabile [respon'sabile] *agg* responsible. *s(m+f)* person responsible. **responsabilità** *sf* responsibility. **prendersi la responsabilità** take the responsibility.

ressa ['rɛssa] *sf* crowd.

restare [res'tare] *v* remain; (*avanzare*) be left (over). **restarci male** (*delusi*) be disappointed; (*offesi*) be offended. **restare d'accordo** agree. **restante** *sm* remainder.

restaurare [restau'rare] *v* restore. **restauro** *sm* restoration; (*riparazione*) repair.

restio [res'tio] *agg* restive; (*bambini*) fractious.

restituire [restitu'ire] *v* return; (*fig*) restore. **restituzione** *sf* return.

resto ['rɛsto] *sm* remainder; (*di denaro*) change. **del resto** (*d'altronde*) on the other hand; (*inoltre*) besides.

***restringere** [res'trindʒere] *v* (*limitare*) restrict; (*ridurre di larghezza*) narrow; (*vestiario*) take in; (*tessuto*) shrink. **restringimento** *sm* shrinkage, narrowing. **restrizione** *sf* restriction.

rete ['rete] *sf* net; (*sistema, tec*) network; (*calcio*) goal; (*inganno*) trap. **rete metallica** wire netting.

reticente [reti'tʃɛnte] *agg* reticent.

reticolato [retiko'lato] *sm* (*disegno*) grid; (*graticcio*) grating. **reticolo** *sm* lattice, grating.

retina ['rɛtina] *sf* retina.

retorica [re'tɔrika] *sf* rhetoric. **retorico** *agg* rhetorical.

retribuire [retribu'ire] *v* reward. **retribuzione** *sf* reward; (*paga*) payment.

retro ['rɛtro] *sm* back.

retroattivo [retroat'tivo] *agg* retrospective.

***retrocedere** [retro'tʃɛdere] *v* recede; (*ritirarsi*) retreat; (*mil*) demote; (*sport*) move down.

retrodatare [retroda'tare] *v* back-date.

retrogrado [re'trɔgrado] *agg* retrograde; (*fig*) backward, reactionary.

retroguardia [retro'gwardja] *sf* rearguard.

retromarcia [retro'martʃa] *sf* reverse.

retroscena [retro'ʃɛna] *sm invar* backstage; (*fig*) background.

retrospettivo [retrospet'tivo] *agg* retrospective.

retrovisore [retrovi'zore] *sm* rear-view mirror.

retta[1] ['rɛtta] *sf* (*geom*) straight line.

retta[2] ['rɛtta] *sf* **dar retta a** listen to, pay attention to.

retta[3] [rɛtta] *sf* fee for board and lodging.

rettangolo [ret'tangolo] *sm* rectangle. **rettangolare** *agg* right-angled, rectangular.

rettificare [rettifi'kare] *v* rectify, correct; (*mec*) grind. **rettifica** *sf* rectification, correction; grinding.

rettile ['rɛttile] *sm* reptile.

rettilineo [retti'lineo] *agg* straight.

retto ['rɛtto] *agg* straight; (*leale*) upright, straightforward; correct; (*geom*) right.

rettore [ret'tore] *sm* rector.

reumatismo [reuma'tizmo] *sm* rheumatism. **reumatico** *agg* rheumatic.

reverendo [reve'rɛndo] *agg* reverend. *sm* (*fam*) priest.

reversibile [rever'sibile] *agg* reversible.

revisione [revi'zjone] *sf* revision; (*tec*) overhaul; (*dei conti*) audit; (*dir*) review. **revisore** *sm* auditor; (*di bozze*) proofreader.

revocare [revo'kare] *v* revoke.

riabbassare [riabbas'sare] *v* lower again.

riabbottonare [riabbotto'nare] *v* button up.

riabbracciare [riabbrat'tʃare] *v* embrace again.

riabilitare [riabili'tare] *v* rehabilitate. **riabilitazione** *sf* rehabilitation.

riaccompagnare [riakkompa'ɲare] *v* take back.

riacquistare [riakkwis'tare] *v* (*ricomprare*) buy back; (*ricuperare*) recover.

riaddormentarsi [riaddormen'tarsi] *v* fall asleep again.
riaffermare [riaffer'mare] *v* reaffirm.
riallacciare [riallat'tʃare] *v* re-tie; (*fig*) renew.
rialto [ri'alto] *sm* rise.
rialzare [rial'tsare] *v* raise (again). **rialzo** *sm* rise.
***riammettere** [riam'mettere] *v* re-admit. **riammissione** *sf* re-admission.
riammogliarsi [riammo'ʎarsi] *v* remarry.
rianimare [riani'mare] *v* revive; (*fig*) cheer (up).
***riapparire** [riappa'rire] *v* reappear.
***riaprire** [riap'rire] *v* reopen; (*riprendere*) resume. **riapertura** *sf* reopening; resumption.
riarmare [riar'mare] *v* rearm; (*nave*) refit; (*edificio*) reinforce. **riarmamento** *sf* rearmament.
riassestare [riasses'tare] *v* rearrange.
riassettare [riasset'tare] *v* tidy up.
riassicurare [riassiku'rare] *v* reassure; (*dir*) reinsure. **riassicurazione** *sf* reassurance; reinsurance.
***riassumere** [rias'sumere] *v* take on again; (*compendiare*) sum up; (*condensare*) summarize. **riassunto** *sm* summary. **riassunzione** *sf* re-employment; (*dir*) resumption.
riattaccare [riattak'kare] *v* (*con filo*) sew on again; (*con colla*) stick on again; (*riprendere*) resume.
riattivare [riatti'vare] *v* reactivate; put back into service; (*strada*) reopen.
***riavere** [ria'vere] *v* have again; (*ricuperare*) recover.
riavvicinare [riavvitʃi'nare] *v* approach again; (*fig*) reconcile. **riavvicinamento** *sm* (*pol*) rapprochement.
ribadire [riba'dire] *v* rivet; (*fig*) confirm.
ribaldo [ri'baldo] *sm* rogue.
ribaltare [ribal'tare] *v* turn over; (*mandar sottosopra*) overturn. **ribalta** *sf* (*asse*) flap; (*teatro*) proscenium; (*fig*) limelight. **tornare alla ribalta** (*questione*) come up again. **venire alla ribalta** come on to the scene. **ribaltabile** *agg* folding; (*tavolo*) drop-leaf; (*camion*) tip-up.
ribassare [ribas'sare] *v* reduce. **ribasso** *sm* reduction. **essere in ribasso** drop.
ribattere [ri'battere] *v* hit back; (*chiodo*) rivet; (*sport*) return; (*confutare*) refute; (*replicare*) answer back.
ribelle [ri'belle] *agg* rebellious. *s*(*m*+*f*) rebel. **ribellarsi** *v* revolt. **ribellione** *sf* rebellion.
ribes ['ribes] *sm* (red)currant. **ribes nero** blackcurrant.
riboccare [ribok'kare] *v* overflow.
ribollire [ribol'lire] *v* boil (again); ferment; (*fig*) seethe.
ribrezzo [ri'brettso] *sm* disgust. **far ribrezzo** disgust. **provar ribrezzo** be disgusted (by).
ributtare [ribut'tare] *v* throw again; (*buttar fuori*) throw out; vomit; (*rifiutare*) reject.
ricacciare [rikat'tʃare] *v* turn out (again); (*rimettere*) push back.
***ricadere** [rika'dere] *v* fall (back); (*pendere*) hang (down). **ricaduta** *sf* relapse.
ricalcare [rikal'kare] *v* (*disegno*) trace; (*fig*) follow faithfully. **ricalco** *sm* tracing.
ricamare [rika'mare] *v* embroider. **ricamo** *sm* embroidery.
ricambiare [rikam'bjare] *v* (*sostituire*) change; (*scambiare*) exchange; (*di nuovo*) change again. **di ricambio** spare.
ricapitolare [rikapito'lare] *v* sum up.
ricaricare [rikari'kare] *v* recharge; (*armi*) reload; (*orologio*) wind up again; (*pipa*) refill.
ricattare [rikat'tare] *v* blackmail. **ricattatore, -trice** *sm, sf* blackmailer. **ricatto** *sm* blackmail.
ricavare [rika'vare] *v* obtain, get; (*dedurre*) deduce. **ricavato** *or* **ricavo** *sm* proceeds *pl*.
ricchezza [rik'kettsa] *sf* wealth.
riccio[1] ['rittʃo] *agg* curly. *sm* curl; (*voluta*) scroll. **ricciolouto** *or* **ricciuto** *agg* curly.
riccio[2] ['rittʃo] *sm* (*zool*) hedgehog; (*castagna*) (chestnut) husk. **riccio di mare** sea-urchin.
ricco ['rikko], **-a** *agg* rich. *sm, sf* rich person.
ricerca [ri'tʃerka] *sf* search; (*scientifica*) research; (*indagine*) investigation. **ricercare** *v* search (for); investigate. **ricercato** *agg* (much-)wanted; in (great) demand; (*affettato*) precious; (*raffinato*) refined. **ricercatezza** *sf* affectation; refinement. **ricercatore, -trice** *sm, sf* (*persona*) research worker; (*apparecchio*) detector.
ricetta [ri'tʃetta] *sf* recipe.
ricettare [ritʃet'tare] *v* receive. **ricettatore** *sm* receiver (of stolen goods).

ricettivo [ritʃet'tivo] *agg* receptive. **ricettività** *sf* receptivity.

***ricevere** [ri'tʃevere] *v* receive; (*accogliere*) welcome. **ricevimento** *sm* reception; (*ricevuta*) receipt. **ricevitore** *sm* receiver; (*impiegato*) collector. **ricevuta** *sf* receipt. **ricezione** *sf* reception.

richiamare [rikja'mare] *v* call back; (*far tornare, ricordare*) recall; (*rimproverare*) rebuke. **richiamare in vita** revive. **richiamo** *sm* call; recall; rebuke. **far da richiamo** act as a decoy.

***richiedere** [ri'kjedere] *v* (*aver bisogno*) require; (*per sapere*) ask; (*per ottenere*) ask for. **richiesta** *sf* request; (*econ*) demand; (*burocratica*) application. **richiesto** *agg* in (great) demand; necessary.

ricino ['ritʃino] *sm* **olio di ricino** *sm* castor-oil.

ricominciare [rikomin'tʃare] *v* start again.

ricompensa [rikom'pɛnsa] *sf* reward. **ricompensare** *v* (*contraccambiare*) repay; (*premiare*) reward.

riconciliare [rikontʃi'ljare] *v* reconcile; (*procurare di nuovo*) win back. **riconciliarsi** *v* make it up.

ricondurre [rikon'durre] *v* take back; (*di nuovo*) take again.

***riconoscere** [riko'noʃere] *v* recognize; (*ammettere*) admit. **riconoscente** *agg* grateful. **riconoscenza** *sf* gratitude. **riconoscibile** *agg* recognizable. **riconoscimento** *sm* recognition; admission; identification.

riconquistare [rikonkwis'tare] *v* win back.

ricopiare [riko'pjare] *v* copy.

***ricoprire** [rikop'rire] *v* cover (again); (*occupare*) hold; (*rivestire*) coat; (*colmare*) smother.

ricordare [rikor'dare] *v* remember; (*richiamare alla memoria*) recall; (*far ricordare*) remind. **ricordo** *sm* recollection; (*oggetto*) souvenir. **ricordo di famiglia** heirloom. **ricordo d'infanzia** childhood memory. **ricordi** *sm pl* (*libro*) memoirs *pl*.

***ricorrere** [ri'korrere] *v* resort; (*dir*) appeal; (*ripetersi*) recur. **ricorso** *sm* resort, recourse; (*dir*) appeal.

ricostituente [rikostitu'ɛnte] *sm* tonic. **ricostituire** *v* reconstitute.

***ricostruire** [rikostru'ire] *v* rebuild; (*fig*) reconstruct. **ricostruzione** *sf* reconstruction.

ricotta [ri'kɔtta] *sf* cottage cheese.

ricoverare [rikove'rare] *v* take in; (*all'ospedale*) send to hospital. **ricoverato, -a** *sm, sf* (*ospedale*) patient; (*ospizio*) inmate. **ricovero** *sm* shelter; (*ospizio*) home; (*in ospedale*) admission to hospital.

ricrearsi [rikre'arsi] *v* amuse oneself. **ricreazione** *sf* recreation; (*scuola*) playtime; (*pausa*) break.

ricredersi [ri'kredersi] *v* change one's mind.

ricuperare [rikupe'rare] *v* recover; (*mar*) salvage. **ricupero** *sm* recovery; salvage.

ricurvo [ri'kurvo] *agg* bent.

ricusare [riku'zare] *v* decline.

***ridare** [ri'dare] *v* (*dare nuovamente*) give again; (*restituire*) give back.

***ridere** ['ridere] *v* laugh. **(cosa) da ridere** (*divertente*) funny; (*inezia*) of no importance. **far ridere** be funny; be ridiculous. *sm* laughter.

ridicolo [ri'dikolo] *agg* ridiculous. *sm* absurdity; (*derisione*) ridicule.

ridimensionare [ridimensjo'nare] *v* reorganize; (*ridurre*) cut down; (*fig*) reappraise.

***ridire** [ri'dire] *v* (*riferire*) tell; (*criticare*) find fault with; (*dire di nuovo*) repeat.

ridosso [ri'dɔsso] *sm* **a ridosso di** close to; (*dietro*) behind.

***ridurre** [ri'durre] *v* reduce; (*trasformare*) turn. **riduzione** *sf* reduction; cut; adaptation.

rielaborare [rielabo'rare] *v* work out again; modify.

***riempire** [riem'pire] *v* fill; (*compilare*) fill in; (*gastr*) stuff. **riempitivo** *sm* filler; (*fig*) stopgap.

rientrare [rien'trare] *v* (*tornare*) return; (*rincasare*) come *or* go home; (*far parte*) come within, form part of; (*entrare nuovamente*) re-enter. **rientro** *sm* return; re-entry; (*rientranza*) recess.

riepilogare [riepilo'gare] *v* summarize. **riepilogo** *sm, pl* **-ghi** recapitulation.

riesumare [riezu'mare] *v* exhume; (*fig*) unearth.

rievocare [rievo'kare] *v* recall; commemorate.

***rifare** [ri'fare] *v* make *or* do again; (*ricostruire*) rebuild; imitate.

riferire [rife'rire] *v* relate; report. **riferimento** *sm* reference. **punto di riferimento** *sm* landmark.

rifilare [rifi'lare] (*fam*) *v* palm off; (*dire d'un fiato*) reel off.
rifinire [rifi'nire] *v* (*dare l'ultima mano*) give the finishing touch; (*ritoccare*) touch up. **rifinitura** *sf* finishing touches *pl*; (*guarnizione*) fittings *pl*.
rifiutare [rifju'tare] *v* refuse; decline. **rifiuto** *sm* refusal; (*scarto*) refuse, rubbish.
riflessione [rifles'sjone] *sf* reflection; (*osservazione*) remark.
riflessivo [rifles'sivo] *agg* thoughtful; (*gramm*) relexive.
riflesso [ri'flɛsso] *sm* reflection; (*med*) reflex. **di riflesso** indirectly.
***riflettere** [ri'flɛttere] *v* reflect; (*pensarci su*) think (over *or* about). **riflettersi su** (*ripercuotersi*) affect. **riflettore** *sm* reflector; (*cinema, ecc.*) floodlight.
***rifondere** [ri'fondere] *v* recast; (*ricomporre*) recompose; (*risarcire*) refund.
riformare [rifor'mare] *v* reform; (*formare di nuovo*) re-form. **riforma** *sf* reform.
rifornire [rifor'nire] *v* supply (with). **rifornirsi di benzina** (*auto*) fill up. **rifornimento** *sm* supply.
rifuggire [rifud'dʒire] *v* escape (again); (*fig*) shrink (from).
rifugiarsi [rifu'dʒarsi] *v* (take) shelter. **rifugiato, -a** *sm, sf* refugee.
rifugio [ri'fudʒo] *sm* shelter. **rifugio antiaereo** air-raid shelter. **rifugio fiscale** tax-haven.
***rifulgere** [ri'fuldʒere] *v* glow.
riga ['riga] *sf* line; (*fila*) row; (*righello*) ruler. **a righe** striped. **riga a T** T-square. **rigare** *v* rule; (*tracciar strisce*) stripe; (*scalfire*) score.
rigaglie [ri'gaʎe] *sf pl* giblets *pl*.
rigettare [ridʒet'tare] *v* (*buttar fuori*) throw out; (*fig*) reject; vomit; (*gettare indietro*) throw back.
rigido ['ridʒido] *agg* rigid, stiff; (*freddo*) severe. **rigidezza** *or* **rigidità** *sf* rigidity; (*fig*) rigour, severity.
rigirare [ridʒi'rare] *v* turn round; (*fig*) twist round. **rigiro** *sm* twist. **giri e rigiri** *sm pl* twists and turns *pl*.
rigo ['rigo] *sm* line; (*musica*) stave.
rigoglioso [rigo'ʎozo] *agg* blooming.
rigonfio [ri'gonfjo] *agg* swollen.
rigore [ri'gore] *sm* rigour; (*calcio*) penalty (kick). **a rigor di logica** strictly speaking. **a rigore** in point of fact. **di rigore** compulsory. **rigoroso** *agg* rigorous.
rigovernare [rigover'nare] *v* (*i piatti*) wash up; (*animali*) tend.
riguardare [rigwar'dare] *v* regard. **riguardo** *sm* regard; (*cautela*) care; consideration. **di riguardo** of consequence. **riguardo a** regarding. **riguardo a me** as for me. **senza riguardo** inconsiderate. **riguardoso** *agg* thoughtful, respectful.
rilanciare [rilan'tʃare] *v* launch; (*asta, carte*) raise.
rilasciare [rila'ʃare] *v* (*liberare*) release; (*consegnare*) issue.
rilassare [rilas'sare] *v* relax; (*allentare*) slacken. **rilassamento** *sm* relaxation.
rilegare [rile'gare] *v* bind; (*incastonare*) set. **rilegatura** *sf* binding.
***rileggere** [ri'lɛddʒere] *v* re-read.
rilevare [rile'vare] *v* (*notare*) notice; (*comm*) take over; (*topografia*) survey.
rilievo [ri'ljɛvo] *sm* relief; importance; (*osservazione*) remark; survey. **mettere in rilievo** stress, emphasize.
riluttante [rilut'tante] *agg* reluctant.
rima ['rima] *sf* rhyme.
rimandare [riman'dare] *v* send back; (*posporre*) defer.
***rimanere** [rima'nere] *v* remain; (*essere*) be. **rimanere d'accordo** agree. **rimanere in dubbio** be left in doubt. **rimaner male** be put out; (*deluso*) be disappointed; (*offeso*) be hurt.
rimasugli [rima'zuʎi] *sm pl* left-overs *pl*.
rimbalzare [rimbal'tsare] *v* bounce; (*proiettile*) ricochet.
rimbambire [rimbam'bire] *v* become childish. **rimbambito** *agg* (*fam*) gaga.
rimbeccare [rimbek'kare] *v* retort. **di rimbecco** sharply.
rimboccare [rimbok'kare] *v* turn down. **rimboccarsi le maniche** roll up one's sleeves.
rimbombare [rimbom'bare] *v* resound.
rimborsare [rimbor'sare] *v* reimburse. **rimborso** *sm* refund.
rimediare [rime'djare] *v* remedy; (*fam: racimolare*) scrape together; (*accomodare*) patch; (*provvedere*) take care. **rimedio** *sm* remedy.
rimescolare [rimesko'lare] *v* stir; (*carte*) shuffle.
rimessa [ri'messa] *sf* (*deposito*) depot; garage; (*trasferimento*) remittance; (*perdita*) loss. **rimessa in gioco** (*calcio*) throw-in.

***rimettere** [ri'mettere] *v* put back; (*indossare*) put back on; (*spedire*) send; (*denaro*) remit. **rimetterci** *v* lose. **rimettersi** *v* (*riaversi*) recover; (*affidarsi*) trust.
rimodernare [rimoder'nare] *v* modernize.
rimontare [rimon'tare] *v* (*mettere insieme*) reassemble; (*sport*) catch up; (*risalire*) go up; (*a cavallo*) remount; (*auto*) get back in.
rimorchiare [rimor'kjare] *v* (have in) tow. **rimorchio** *sm* trailer. **cavo da rimorchio** *sm* tow-rope.
rimorso [ri'mɔrso] *sm* remorse. **rimorso di coscienza** pangs of conscience *pl.*
rimostrare [rimos'trare] *v* remonstrate.
rimpasto [rim'pasto] *sm* (*fig*) reshuffle.
rimpatriare [rimpa'trjare] *v* repatriate. **rimpatrio** *sm* repatriation.
***rimpiangere** [rim'pjandʒere] *v* regret. **rimpianto** *sm* regret.
rimpiattino [rimpjat'tino] *sm* hide-and-seek.
rimpiazzare [rimpjat'tsare] *v* replace.
rimpiccolire [rimpikko'lire] *v* make smaller.
rimpinzarsi [rimpin'tsarsi] *v* stuff oneself, gorge.
rimproverare [rimprove'rare] *v* reproach; (*sgridare*) scold; (*fam*) tell off; (*biasimare*) blame. **rimprovero** *sm* reproach; blame.
***rimuovere** [ri'mwɔvere] *v* remove; (*distogliere*) dissuade.
Rinascimento [rinaʃi'mento] *sm* Renaissance.
rinascita [ri'naʃita] *sf* rebirth; (*fig*) revival.
rincagnato [rinka'ɲato] *agg* **naso rincagnato** *sm* pug nose, snub nose.
rincalzare [rinkal'tsare] *v* (*sorreggere*) prop up; (*lenzuola*) tuck in.
rincarare [rinka'rare] *v* (*rendere più caro*) raise (the price of); (*essere più caro*) rise, become more expensive.
rincasare [rinka'zare] *v* return home.
***rinchiudere** [rin'kjudere] *v* shut in.
rinchiuso [rin'kjuzo] *agg* shut in; (*aria*) stale, fusty. *sm* enclosure. **saper di rinchiuso** smell fusty *or* musty.
***rincorrere** [rin'korrere] *v* run after, chase. **rincorsa** *sf* run-up.
***rincrescere** [rin'kreʃere] *v* cause regret *or* sorrow. **mi rincresce di . . .** I'm sorry to . . . . **ti rincresce . . . ?** do you mind . . . ? **rincrescimento** *sm* regret.
rinculare [rinku'lare] *v* recoil.
rinforzare [rinfor'tsare] *v* reinforce, strengthen. **rinforzo** *sm* reinforcement.
rinfrescare [rinfres'kare] *v* cool; (*pulire*) freshen up; (*memoria*) refresh; (*ravvivare*) brush up. **rinfrescata** *sf* cooling. **darsi una rinfrescata** freshen up. **rinfreschi** *sm pl* refreshments *pl.* **rinfresco** *sm* (*ricevimento*) party.
rinfusa [rin'fuza] *sf* **alla rinfusa** higgledy-piggledy.
ringhiare [rin'gjare] *v* growl, snarl.
ringhiera [rin'gjɛra] *sf* railing; (*delle scale*) banister.
ringiovanire [rindʒova'nire] *v* rejuvenate; (*nell'aspetto*) make look younger.
ringraziare [ringra'tsjare] *v* thank. **ringraziamento** *sm* thanks *pl.* **lettera di ringraziamento** *sf* thank-you letter.
rinnegare [rinne'gare] *v* deny. **rinnegato, -a** *s, agg* renegade.
rinnovare [rinno'vare] *v* renew. **rinnovamento** *sm* renewal; (*rimodernamento*) renovation. **rinnovazione** *sf* renewal; renovation.
rinoceronte [rinotʃe'ronte] *sm* rhinoceros.
rinomato [rino'mato] *agg* renowned. **rinomanza** *sf* renown.
rinsaldare [rinsal'dare] *v* consolidate; (*inamidare*) starch.
rintoccare [rintok'kare] *v* (*campana*) toll; (*orologio*) strike. **rintocco** *sm* toll; stroke.
rintracciare [rintrat'tʃare] *v* trace; track down.
rintronare [rintro'nare] *v* thunder; (*assordare*) deafen.
rintuzzare [rintut'tsare] *v* (*rendere ottuso*) blunt; (*respingere*) repel; (*ribattere*) refute; (*frenare*) check.
rinunciare [rinun'tʃare] *v* give up; (*fare a meno*) forgo; (*dir*) renounce; (*non voler fare*) refrain (from). **rinunce** *sf pl* (*privazioni*) hardship *sing.* **rinuncia** *sf* abandonment; renunciation.
***rinvenire**[1] [rinve'nire] *v* (*ritrovare*) recover.
***rinvenire**[2] [rinve'nire] *v* (*ritornare in sè*) come to; (*riprendere freschezza*) revive.
rinviare [rinvi'are] *v* (*mandare indietro*) send back; (*posporre*) put off; (*dir*) adjourn; (*indirizzare*) refer. **rinvio** *sm* postponement; adjournment; (*testo*) (cross-)reference.

rinvigorire [rinvigo'rire] *v* invigorate; (*ritornar vigoroso*) regain strength.
rione [ri'one] *sm* district. **rionale** *agg* local.
riordinare [riordi'nare] *v* rearrange; (*comm*) reorder.
riorganizzare [riorganid'dzare] *v* reorganize. **riorganizzazione** *sf* reorganization.
ripagare [ripa'gare] *v* pay back.
riparare [ripa'rare] *v* (*aggiustare*) repair; (*porre rimedio*) make up (for), redress; protect; (*esame*) repeat. **ripararsi** *v* take shelter. **riparazione** *sf* repair; redress.
riparo [ri'paro] *sm* shelter; (*protezione*) cover; (*mec*) guard. **mettersi al riparo (da)** shelter (from).
ripartire[1] [ripar'tire] *v* (*partire di nuovo*) leave *or* start (up) again.
ripartire[2] [ripar'tire] *v* (*dividere*) split up; distribute.
ripassare [ripas'sare] *v* (*tornare*) pass again; (*visitare*) call back; (*attraversare*) cross again; (*rivedere*) review; (*mec*) overhaul. **ripassata** *sf* (*pittura*) fresh coat of paint; revision, overhaul; (*stirata*) press.
ripensare [ripen'sare] *v* think (over); (*mutare pensiero*) reconsider. **ripensare a** (*tornare col pensiero*) recall.
ripentirsi [ripen'tirsi] *v* repent; (*cambiar pensiero*) have second thoughts.
***ripercuotersi** [riper'kwɔtersi] *v* (*suono*) reverberate; (*fig*) have an effect.
ripercussione [riperkus'sjone] *sf* repercussion.
ripetere [ri'petere] *v* repeat. **ripetizione** *sf* repetition; (*studio*) coaching.
ripiano [ri'pjano] *sm* terrace; (*scomparto*) shelf.
ripido ['ripido] *agg* steep.
ripiegare [ripje'gare] *v* fold again; (*fig*) make do. **di ripiego** makeshift.
ripieno [ri'pjɛno] *agg* filled, stuffed. *sm* filling, stuffing.
***riporre** [ri'porre] *v* put (back).
riportare [ripor'tare] *v* (*portare indietro*) bring back; (*ricondurre*) take again; (*riferire*) report; (*ricevere*) get; (*mat*) carry. **riporto** *sm* carrying forward; amount carried forward.
riposare [ripo'zare] *v* rest. **riposarsi** *v* take a rest. **riposo** *sm* rest. **andare a riposo** retire. **mettere a riposo** pension off. **senza riposo** without interruption.
ripostiglio [ripos'tiʎo] *sm* cubby-hole.
***riprendere** [ri'prɛndere] *v* take again; (*recuperare*) recover; (*ricominciare*) resume. **riprendersi (da)** get over.
ripresa [ri'preza] *sf* resumption; (*innovamento*) renewal; (*calcio*) second half; (*boxe*) round; (*auto*) acceleration; (*cine*) shot.
ripristinare [ripristi'nare] *v* restore. **ripristino** *sm* restoration.
***riprodurre** [ripro'durre] *v* reproduce. **riproduzione** *sf* reproduction.
riprova [ri'prɔva] *sf* fresh proof; confirmation. **riprovare** *v* blame; (*esame*) fail.
ripudiare [ripu'djare] *v* repudiate.
ripugnante [ripu'ɲante] *agg* repugnant. **ripugnare** *v* disgust.
ripulsione [ripul'sjone] *sf* repulsion.
risaia [ri'zaja] *sf* rice-field.
risalire [risa'lire] *v* (*andar su*) go up (again); (*nel tempo*) go back.
risaltare [risal'tare] *v* (*distinguersi*) stand out; (*sporgere*) project. **far risaltare** bring out. **risalto** *sm* emphasis; projection.
risanare [risa'nare] *v* heal; (*fig*) improve; (*bonificare*) reclaim.
risaputo [risa'puto] *agg* well-known.
risarcire [rizart'ʃire] *v* compensate. **risarcimento** *sm* compensation.
risata [ri'zata] *sf* laugh. **fare** *or* **farsi una bella risata** have a good laugh. **scoppiare in una risata** burst out laughing.
riscaldare [riskal'dare] *v* heat, warm up. **riscaldamento** *sm* heating; (*impianto*) heating system.
riscatto [ris'katto] *sm* ransom; (*econ*) redemption. **riscattare** *v* ransom; redeem.
rischiarare [riskja'rare] *v* illuminate.
rischiare [ris'kjare] *v* risk. **rischiare di** run the risk of. **rischio** *sm* risk. **rischioso** *agg* risky.
risciacquare [riʃa'kware] *v* rinse. **risciacquatura** *sf* (*atto*) rinsing; (*acqua*) dishwater. **risciacquo** *sm* mouthwash.
riscontrare [riskon'trare] *v* (*rilevare*) find; (*confrontare*) compare; (*controllare*) check. **riscontro** *sm* finding; comparison; check; (*lettera*) reply.
riscossa [ris'kɔssa] *sf* (*riconquista*) recovery; (*insurrezione*) revolt.
***riscuotere** [ris'kwɔtere] *v* (*ritirare denaro*) draw; (*riportare*) win, earn; (*scuotere*) shake.
risentire [risen'tire] *v* (*provare*) feel; (*mostrare*) show; (*udire di nuovo*) hear again; (*soffrire*) feel the effects of. **risentirsi** *v*

resent. **risentimento** *sm* resentment; consequence.
riserbo [ri'sɛrbo] *sm* reserve.
riserva [ri'sɛrva] *sf* (*provvista*) supply; (*scorta, sport*) reserve; (*dubbio*) reservation. **riservare** *v* reserve, keep; (*prenotare*) book; (*dimostrare*) show. **riservatezza** *sf* discretion; (*segretezza*) confidential nature; (*carattere*) reserve. **riservato** *agg* reserved; confidential.
risibile [ri'zibile] *agg* laughable.
risiedere [ri'sjɛdere] *v* reside.
risma ['rizma] *sf* (*carta*) ream; (*spreg*) kind.
riso[1] ['rizo] *sm* (*bot*) rice.
riso[2] ['rizo] *sm, pl* **-a** *f* laughter; (*risata*) laugh; ridicule.
risoluto [riso'luto] *agg* resolute. **risolutezza** *sf* decisiveness.
risoluzione [risolu'tsjone] *sf* resolution; (*mat*) solution; (*dir*) cancellation.
***risolvere** [ri'sɔlvere] *v* resolve; (*mat, indovinello*) solve; (*dir*) cancel; (*scomporre*) break down. **risolversi** *v* (*fig*) turn out; decide.
risonare [riso'nare] *v also* **risuonare** ring; (*echeggiare*) resound.
***risorgere** [ri'sɔrdʒere] *v* rise again. **far risorgere** revive. **risorgimento** *sm* revival.
risorsa [ri'sorsa] *sf* resource.
risparmiare [rispar'mjare] *v* spare; (*economizzare, mettere da parte*) save. **risparmiatore, -trice** *sm, sf* saver. **risparmio** *sm* saving; (*denaro*) savings *pl*. **fare risparmio (di)** save.
rispecchiare [rispek'kjare] *v* reflect.
rispettare [rispet'tare] *v* respect; (*mantenere*) keep.
rispettivo [rispet'tivo] *agg* respective.
rispetto [ris'pɛtto] *sm* respect. **rispetto a** (*in relazione a*) with respect to, as to; (*in confronto*) compared to. **rispettoso** *agg* respectful.
risplendere [ris'plɛndere] *v* shine.
***rispondere** [ris'pondere] *v* answer; (*rimbeccare*) answer back; (*obbedire*) respond; (*carte*) follow suit. **rispondere di no/sì** say no/yes. **rispondere male** give a wrong answer; (*sgarbatamente*) answer back. **rispondere picche** give a flat refusal.
risposta [ris'posta] *sf* answer, reply. **botta e risposta** tit for tat. **per tutta risposta** merely. **senza risposta** unanswered.
rissa ['rissa] *sf* brawl.
ristabilire [ristabi'lire] *v* restore.
ristagnare [rista'ɲare] *v* stagnate; (*fig*) come to a standstill; (*comm*) be slack. **ristagno** *sm* stagnation; (*econ*) slump.
ristampare [ristam'pare] *v* reprint. **ristampa** *sf* reprint.
ristorante [risto'rante] *sm* restaurant. **vagone ristorante** *sm* dining car.
ristorare [risto'rare] *v* restore. **ristorarsi** *v* refresh oneself. **ristoro** *sm* refreshment.
ristretto [ris'tretto] *agg* (*limitato*) restricted; (*angusto*) narrow; (*caffè*) very strong. **brodo ristretto** *sm* consommé.
risultare [rizul'tare] *v* appear; gather; (*conseguire*) ensue. **mi risulta che . . .** I gather that . . . .
risultato [rizul'tato] *sm* result.
risuonare [riswo'nare] *V* **risonare**.
risurrezione [rizurre'tsjone] *sf* resurrection.
risuscitare [risuʃi'tare] *v* revive; (*rel*) resurrect.
risvegliare [rizve'ʎare] *v* wake (up); (*fig*) awaken, revive.
ritaglio [ri'taʎo] *sm* cutting.
ritardare [ritar'dare] *v* be late; (*orologio*) be slow; (*differire*) delay. **ritardatario, -a** *sm, sf* latecomer. **ritardo** *sm* delay. **in ritardo** late.
ritegno [ri'teɲo] *sm* reserve; (*freno*) restraint.
***ritenere** [rite'nere] *v* think; consider; (*trattenere*) hold.
ritirare [riti'rare] *v* withdraw; (*ottenere in consegna*) collect. **ritirarsi** *v* withdraw; (*interrompere un'attività*) retire. **ritirata** *sf* retreat. **ritiro** *sm* withdrawal; (*il prendere*) collection; (*luogo appartato*) retreat.
ritmo ['ritmo] *sm* rhythm. **ritmico** *agg* rhythmic(al).
rito ['rito] *sm* rite; (*usanza*) custom. **di rito** customary.
ritoccare [ritok'kare] *v* touch up.
ritornare [ritor'nare] *v* return; (*andare indietro*) go back. **biglietto di andata e ritorno** return ticket. **di ritorno** back. **viaggio di andata e ritorno** round trip. **ritornello** *sm* refrain.
***ritrarre** [ri'trarre] *v* (*tirare indietro*) draw back; (*rappresentare*) portray.
ritratto [ri'tratto] *sm* portrait. **ritrattista** *s(m+f)* portrait-painter.

ritroso [ri'trozo] *agg* (*scontroso*) contrary; (*restio*) unwilling. **a ritroso** (*indietro*) backwards; (*controcorrente*) against the stream.
ritrovare [ritro'vare] *v* find (again); (*recuperare*) recover; (*incontrare*) meet again. **ritrovarsi** *v* meet (again); (*orientarsi*) get one's bearings; (*essere a proprio agio*) feel at ease. **ritrovato** *sm* invention; expedient. **ritrovo** *sm* meeting-place; club.
ritto ['ritto] *agg* upright.
rituale [ritu'ale] *agg*, *sm* ritual.
riunire [riu'nire] *v* gather; (*ricongiungere*) reunite; (*convocare*) call. **riunione** *sf* meeting.
***riuscire** [riu'ʃire] *v* succeed; (*andare a finire*) turn out; (*aver capacità*) be good (at). **mi riesce antipatico/simpatico** I dislike/like him. **riuscita** *sf* result; success.
riva ['riva] *sf* shore; (*fiume*) bank.
rivale [ri'vale] *s(m+f)*, *agg* rival. **rivalità** *sf* rivalry.
rivalutare [rivalu'tare] *v* (*econ*) revalue; (*fig*) reappraise. **rivalutazione** *sf* revaluation; reappraisal.
***rivedere** [rive'dere] *v* see again; (*incontrare*) meet again; (*ripassare*) go over. **rivedere i conti** audit (the accounts).
rivelare [rive'lare] *v* reveal. **rivelatore** *sm* (*tec*) detector. **rivelazione** *sf* revelation.
rivendere [ri'vendere] *v* resell; (*al dettaglio*) retail. **rivendita** *sf* resale; (*negozio*) shop.
rivendicare [rivendi'kare] *v* claim.
riverberare [riverbe'rare] *v* reverberate.
riverire [rive'rire] *v* revere; respect; (*salutare*) pay one's respects (to). **riverenza** *sf* reverence; respect; (*inchino*) bow; (*di donne*) curtsy.
rivestire [rives'tire] *v* cover; (*vernice*) coat; (*fodera*) line. **rivestire una carica** hold an office; (*conferirla*) confer an office. **rivestirsi** *v* dress again, change (clothes). **rivestimento** *sm* covering; coating; lining.
rivetto [ri'vetto] *sm* rivet.
riviera [ri'vjɛra] *sf* coastal region. **Riviera** *sf* Riviera.
rivincita [ri'vintʃita] *sf* return match. **prendersi la rivincita** take one's revenge.
rivista [ri'vista] *sf* review; (*periodico*) magazine; (*teatro*) revue.
***rivolgere** [ri'vɔldʒere] *v* turn. **rivolgersi** *v* (*indirizzare*) address; (*ricorrere*) turn to; (*per domandare, ecc.*) apply.
rivolta [ri'vɔlta] *sf* revolt; (*mar*, *mil*) mutiny.
rivoltare [rivol'tare] *v* turn; (*ripugnare*) revolt; (*insalata*) toss. **rivoltarsi** *v* (*ribellarsi*) revolt.
rivoltella [rivol'tella] *sf* revolver. **rivoltellata** *sf* shot.
rivoluzione [rivolu'tsjone] *sf* revolution. **rivoluzionario, -a** *s*, *agg* revolutionary.
rivulsione [rivul'sjone] *sf* revulsion.
rizzare [rit'tsare] *v* raise; erect. **far rizzare i capelli** make one's hair stand on end. **rizzare le orecchie** prick up one's ears.
roba ['rɔba] *sf* stuff, things *pl*. **bella roba!** that's a fine thing! **robaccia** *sf* rubbish.
robusto [ro'busto] *agg* sturdy; solid. **robustezza** *sf* sturdiness; (*fig*) vigour.
rocca[1] ['rɔkka] *sf* fortress. **cristallo di rocca** *sm* rock-crystal.
rocca[2] ['rɔkka] *sf* (*conocchia*) distaff; (*bobina*) reel. **rocchetto** *sm* reel; (*elett*) coil.
roccia ['rɔttʃa] *sf* rock; (*sport*) rock-climbing. **roccioso** *agg* rocky.
rodaggio [ro'daddʒo] *sm* running-in.
***rodere** ['rɔdere] *v* gnaw. **rodersi il fegato** (*fig*) be eaten up. **roditore** *sm* rodent.
rododendro [rodo'dɛndro] *sm* rhododendron.
rogna ['rɔɲa] *sf* (*animali*) mange; (*agric*) scab; (*fam*) pain in the neck. **rognoso** *agg* mangy; (*noioso*) boring.
rognone [ro'ɲone] *sm* kidney.
rogo ['rɔgo] *sm* stake; (*incendio*) fire.
Roma ['roma] *sf* Rome. **romano, -a** *s*, *agg* Roman. **fare alla romana** go Dutch.
Romania [roma'nia] *sf* Romania. **romeno, -a** *s*, *agg* Romanian.
romanico [ro'maniko] *agg* Romanesque.
romantico [ro'mantiko] *agg* romantic. **romanticismo** *sm* romanticism; sentimentalism.
romanza [ro'mandza] *sf* romance.
romanzo[1] [ro'mandzo] *sm* novel; (*storia inventata*) fiction. **romanzo a fumetti** comic strip. **romanzo d'appendice** serial story. **romanzo fiume** saga. **romanzesco** *agg* romantic; fantastic.
romanzo[2] [ro'mandzo] *agg* (*lingua*) Romance.
rombo[1] ['rɔmbo] *sm* (*geom*) rhombus; (*pesce*) turbot.

rombo[2] ['rombo] *sm* roar. **rombare** *v* roar.
***rompere** ['rompere] *v* break; (*spezzare*) break off. **rompere l'anima** (*volg*) pester. **rompicapo** *sm* (*fam*) headache; (*indovinello*) puzzle. **a rompicollo** at breakneck speed. **rompiscatole** *s*(*m*+*f*) (*fam*) pain in the neck.
ronda ['ronda] *sf* **fare la ronda** (*mil*) be on watch; (*polizia*) be on the beat.
rondella [ron'dɛlla] *sf* washer.
rondine ['rondine] *sf* swallow.
rondo[1] [ron'do] *sm* (*musica*) rondo.
rondo[2] [ron'do] *sm* (*incrocio*) roundabout.
rondone [ron'done] *sm* swift.
ronfare [ron'fare] *v* (*fam*) snore.
ronzare [ron'dzare] *v* buzz. **ronzio** *sm* buzz(ing).
ronzino [ron'dzino] *sm* nag.
rosa ['rɔza] *sf* rose. **all'acqua di rose** (*fam*) watered-down. *agg invar* pink. **veder tutto rosa** see everything through rose-coloured spectacles. **rosato** *agg* (*vino*) rosé. **roseo** *agg* rosy. **rosetta** *sf* (*coccarda*) rosette; (*mec*) washer.
rosario [ro'zarjo] *sm* rosary.
rosbif [rɔz'bif] *sm invar* roast beef.
rosicare [rozi'kare] *v also* **rosicchiare** nibble; (*rodere*) gnaw.
rosmarino [rozma'rino] *sm* rosemary.
rosolare [rozo'lare] *v* brown.
rosolia [rozo'lia] *sf* German measles.
rospo ['rɔspo] *sm* toad.
rossetto [ros'setto] *sm* lipstick; (*belletto*) rouge.
rosso ['rosso] *agg* red. *sm* red; (*l'essere rosso*) redness. **rosso d'uovo** egg-yolk. **rossastro** *or* **rossiccio** *agg* reddish. **rossore** *sm* blush.
rosticceria [rostittʃe'ria] *sf* rotisserie.
rostro ['rɔstro] *sm* rostrum.
rotaia [ro'taja] *sf* rail.
rotare [ro'tare] *v* rotate. **rotatorio** *agg* rotatory. **rotazione** *sf* rotation.
roteare [rote'are] *v* wheel; (*occhi*) roll.
rotella [ro'tɛlla] *sf* small wheel; (*mobili*) castor; (*ginocchio*) knee-cap. **gli manca una rotella** (*fam*) he has a screw loose. **pattino a rotelle** *sm* roller-skate.
rotolare [roto'lare] *v* roll. **rotolo** *sm* roll. **andare a rotoli** *or* **rotoloni** go to rack and ruin. **rotoloni** *avv* rolling (over and over).
rotondo [ro'tondo] *agg* round.
rotta[1] ['rotta] *sf* route. **cambiar rotta** change course.
rotta[2] ['rotta] *sf* (*disfatta*) rout; (*breccia*) breach. **a rotta di collo** at breakneck speed. **mettere in rotta** (put to) rout.
rotto ['rotto] *agg* broken. **per il rotto della cuffia** by the skin of one's teeth. **rottame** *sm* fragment. **rottami** *sm pl* scrap *sing*. **rottura** *sf* break; (*violazione*) breach; (*interruzione*) breakdown.
rovente [ro'vɛnte] *agg* red-hot.
rovere ['rɔvere] *sm* oak.
rovesciare [rove'ʃare] *v* upset; (*abbattere*) overthrow; (*gettare*) throw (back). **rovesciarsi** *v* overturn; (*barca, ecc.*) capsize; (*affluire*) pour. **rovescio** *sm* shower; (*retro*) back; (*danno*) setback; (*sport*) backhand. **andare a rovescio** go wrong. **a rovescio** the wrong way round; (*capovolto*) upside-down; (*col dentro fuori*) inside out.
rovinare [rovi'nare] *v* ruin. **rovina** *sf* ruin. **andare in rovina** collapse. **mandare in rovina** ruin. **rovinoso** *agg* ruinous.
rovistare [rovis'tare] *v* ransack.
rovo ['rɔvo] *sm* bramble.
rozzo ['roddzo] *agg* rough; (*fig*) coarse.
ruba ['ruba] *sf* **andare a ruba** sell like hot cakes.
rubacchiare [rubak'kjare] *v* pilfer.
rubare [ru'bare] *v* steal. **rubacuori** *s*(*m*+*f*) charmer. **rubare il tempo a qualcuno** take up someone's time. **ruberia** *sf* theft.
rubinetto [rubi'netto] *sm* tap. **rubinetto di chiusura** stopcock.
rubino [ru'bino] *sm* ruby.
rubrica [ru'brika] *sf* (*indirizzi*) address-book; (*telefonica*) directory; (*quaderno*) index-book; (*giornale*) feature.
rude ['rude] *agg* rough.
rudere ['rudere] *sm* ruin; (*persona*) wreck.
ruffiano [ruf'fjano] *sm* pimp; (*adulatore*) bootlicker.
ruga ['ruga] *sf* wrinkle. **rugoso** *agg* wrinkled.
ruggine ['ruddʒine] *sf* rust; (*astio*) ill-feeling. **rugginoso** *agg* rusty.
ruggire [rud'dʒire] *v* roar. **ruggito** *sm* roar.
rugiada [ru'dʒada] *sf* dew. **goccia di rugiada** *sf* dewdrop.
rullare [rul'lare] *v* roll; (*aereo*) taxi. **rullio** *sm* rolling. **rullo** *sm* roll; (*tec*) roller.
rum [rum] *sm* rum.
ruminare [rumi'nare] *v* ruminate.
rumore [ru'more] *sm* noise; (*diceria*) rumour; sensation. **rumoreggiare** *v* make a noise; rumble. **rumoroso** *agg* noisy.

ruolo ['rwɔlo] *sm* roll; (*teatro, funzione*) role. **insegnante non di ruolo** supply teacher. **personale di ruolo** permanent staff.
ruota ['rwɔta] *sf* wheel. **andare a ruota libera** free-wheel. **a ruota** circular. **far la ruota** (*pavoneggiarsi*) show off. **seguire a ruota** follow close behind.
rupe ['rupe] *sf* cliff.
rupia [ru'pia] *sf* rupee.
rurale [ru'rale] *agg* rural.
ruscello [ru'ʃɛllo] *sm* stream.
ruspa ['ruspa] *sf* bulldozer. **(pollo) ruspante** *sm* free-range chicken.
russare [rus'sare] *v* snore.
Russia ['russja] *sf* Russia. **russo, -a** *s, agg* Russian.
rustico ['rustiko] *agg* rustic; (*contadino*) rural; (*rozzo*) rough.
ruttare [rut'tare] *v* belch. **rutto** *sm* belch.
ruvido ['ruvido] *agg* rough. **ruvidezza** *sf* roughness.
ruzzare [rut'tsare] *v* romp.
ruzzolare [ruttso'lare] *v* tumble; (*rotolare*) roll (down). **ruzzolone** *sm* tumble. **fare un ruzzolone** (*fam*) come a cropper.

S

sabato ['sabato] *sm* Saturday. **il** *or* **di sabato** on Saturdays.
sabbia ['sabbja] *sf* sand. **sabbie mobili** quicksand *sing*. **sabbiare** *v* sand-blast. **sabbioso** *agg* sandy.
sabotaggio [sabo'taddʒo] *sm* sabotage. **sabotare** *v* sabotage. **sabotatore, -trice** *sm, sf* saboteur.
sacca ['sakka] *sf* bag; (*fig*) pocket.
saccarina [sakka'rina] *sf* saccharine.
saccente [sat'tʃɛnte] *s(m+f), agg* know-all.
saccheggiare [sakked'dʒare] *v* sack, loot. **saccheggiatore** *sm* plunderer, looter. **saccheggio** *sm* sacking, looting.
sacco ['sakko] *sm* sack. **cogliere con le mani nel sacco** catch red-handed. **sacco a pelo** sleeping-bag. **sacco da montagna** rucksack. **sacco postale** mail-bag. **un sacco di** lots of.
sacerdote [satʃer'dɔte] *sm* priest. **sacerdozio** *sm* priesthood.
sacramento [sakra'mento] *sm* sacrament.
sacrificare [sakrifi'kare] *v* sacrifice; (*rinunciare*) give up; (*non valorizzare*) waste. **sacrificio** *sm* sacrifice; (*di sè*) self-sacrifice.
sacrilegio [sakri'ledʒo] *sm* sacrilege; (*fig*) crime. **sacrilego** *agg, m pl* **-ghi** sacrilegious; criminal.
sacro ['sakro] *agg* sacred. *sm* (*osso*) sacrum. **sacrosanto** *agg* sacrosanct.
sadico ['sadiko], **-a** *agg* sadistic. *sm, sf* sadist. **sadismo** *sm* sadism.
saetta [sa'etta] *sf* flash (of lightning); (*mec*) bit; (*freccia*) arrow.
sagace [sa'gatʃe] *agg* sagacious. **sagacia** *sf* sagacity.
saggio[1] ['saddʒo], **-a** *agg* wise; (*sapiente*) sage. *sm, sf* sage. **saggezza** *sf* wisdom.
saggio[2] ['saddʒo] *sm* trial; (*metalli preziosi*) assay; (*prova*) proof; (*dimostrazione pubblica*) display; (*scritto critico*) essay. **saggiare** *v* test; assay. **saggiatura** *sf* assay; (*segno*) hallmark. **saggista** *s(m+f)* essayist.
Sagittario [sadʒit'tarjo] *sm* Sagittarius.
sagoma ['sagoma] *sf* outline; (*forma, modello*) pattern. **sagomare** *v* shape.
sagra ['sagra] *sf* feast.
sagrestano [sagres'tano] *sm* sacristan. **sagrestia** *sf* vestry.
sala ['sala] *sf* room, hall. **sala da pranzo** dining-room. **sala d'aspetto** waiting-room. **sala di lettura/macchine** reading-/engine-room. **sala operatoria** operating theatre.
salace [sa'latʃe] *agg* salacious.
salamandra [sala'mandra] *sf* salamander.
salame [sa'lame] *sm* salami; (*fig*) fool.
salamoia [sala'mɔja] *sf* brine. **mettere in salamoia** pickle.
salare [sa'lare] *v* salt. **salato** *agg* salty; (*conservato*) salted; (*caro*) dear.
salario [sa'larjo] *sm* pay; (*settimanale*) wages *pl*; (*mensile*) salary. **salariale** *agg* pay.
salassare [salas'sare] *v* bleed.
salda ['salda] *sf* size, sizing. **dare la salda a** size; (*inamidare*) starch.
saldare [sal'dare] *v* (*tec*) solder; (*autogeno*) weld; (*econ*) settle, pay. **saldatore** *sm* (*operaio*) solderer, welder; (*utensile*) soldering iron. **saldatrice** *sf* welder. **saldatura** *sf* welding; soldering.
saldo[1] ['saldo] *agg* solid; firm. **saldezza** *sf* solidity; firmness.

saldo[2] ['saldo] *sm* settlement; (*somma da pagare*) balance. **saldi** *sm pl* (*merce*) remnants *pl.*

sale ['sale] *sm* salt. **non aver sale in zucca** be stupid. **restar di sale** be dumbfounded. **salgemma** *sm* rock-salt. **salino** *agg* saline.

salice ['salitʃe] *sm* willow(-tree). **salice piangente** weeping willow.

saliente [sa'ljɛnte] *agg, sm* salient.

***salire** [sa'lire] *v* climb, go up; (*autobus, treno*) board, get on; (*auto*) get in; (*alzarsi, crescere*) rise. **far salire** send up. **saliscendi** *sm invar* (*chiusura*) latch; (*fig*) ups and downs *pl.* **salita** *sf* climb; entrance; (*tratto che sale*) slope. **in salita** uphill; (*che aumenta*) rising.

saliva [sa'liva] *sf* saliva. **salivale** *agg* salivary. **salivare** *v* salivate.

salma ['salma] *sf* corpse.

salmo ['salmo] *sm* psalm.

salmone [sal'mone] *sm* salmon.

salone [sa'lone] *sm* living-room; (*esposizione*) show; (*parrucchiere*) salon.

salotto [sa'lɔtto] *sm* drawing-room, lounge.

salpare [sal'pare] *v* weigh anchor.

salsa ['salsa] *sf* sauce; (*a base di carne*) gravy. **in tutte le salse** in all kinds of ways. **salsiera** *sf* sauce-boat; gravy-boat.

salsiccia [sal'sittʃa] *sf* sausage.

salso ['salso] *agg* salt(y). **salsedine** *sf* saltiness.

saltare [sal'tare] *v* jump; (*balzare*) leap; (*tralasciare*) skip; (*bottone, etc.*) come off; (*gastr*) sauté. **far saltare** destroy, blow up; (*serratura*) force; (*governo*) bring down. **saltare di palo in frasca** switch from one subject to another. **saltare (in aria)** (*esplodere*) blow up. **saltare in bestia** fly into a rage. **saltare in mente** cross one's mind, get into one's head.

saltellare [saltel'lare] *v also* **salterellare** skip *or* hop about.

saltimbanco [saltim'banko] *sm* acrobat; (*spreg*) charlatan.

salto ['salto] *sm* jump, leap; (*omissione*) gap. **in un salto** in a jiffy. **salto con l'asta** pole-vault. **salto in alto/lungo** high-/long-jump. **saltuario** *agg* intermittent, occasional.

salubre ['salubre] *agg* healthy.

salumeria [salume'ria] *sf* delicatessen. **salumi** *sm pl* cold meats *pl.* **salumiere, -a** *sm, sf* pork-butcher; grocer.

salutare [salu'tare] *v* greet; (*mil*) salute. **salutami tuo fratello** remember me to your brother. **saluto** *sm* greeting; salute. **cordiali/distinti saluti** yours sincerely/faithfully.

salute [sa'lute] *sf* health; (*benessere*) welfare. *inter* (*a chi starnutisce*) bless you! (*nei brindisi*) cheers!

salvare [sal'vare] *v* save; (*trarre in salvo*) rescue; protect. **salvacondotto** *sm* pass. **salvadanaio** *sm* money-box. **salvagente** *sm* (*ciambella*) lifebelt; (*giacca*) life-jacket; (*strada*) traffic island. **salvaguardare** *v* safeguard. **salvaguardia** *sf* safeguard. **salvataggio** *sm* rescue.

salve ['salve] *inter* hello! (*salute*) bless you!

salvia ['salvja] *sf* sage.

salvietta [sal'vjetta] *sf* (*tovagliolo*) napkin; (*asciugamano*) towel.

salvo ['salvo] *agg* safe. **mettere in salvo** save, put aside. *prep* except (for), bar(ring). **salvo che** except that; (*a meno che*) unless. **salvezza** *sf* salvation; (*sicurezza*) safety.

sambuco [sam'buko] *sm, pl* **-chi** elder.

sanare [sa'nare] *v* heal; (*porre rimedio*) rectify; (*bonificare*) reclaim. **sanatorio** *sm* sanatorium.

sancire [san'tʃire] *v* sanction; ratify.

sandalo[1] ['sandalo] *sm* sandal.

sandalo[2] ['sandalo] *sm* (*legno*) sandalwood.

sangue ['sangwe] *sm* blood. **al sangue** (*gastr*) rare. **a sangue caldo/freddo** warm-/cold-blooded. **farsi cattivo sangue** get worked up. **puro sangue** thoroughbred. **sangue freddo** sang-froid, composure. **sanguemisto** *sm* half-breed.

sanguigno [san'gwiɲo] *agg* blood; (*colore*) blood-red; (*costituzione*) sanguine.

sanguinare [sangwi'nare] *v* bleed. **sanguinario** *agg* bloodthirsty. **sanguinolento** *agg* bleeding; (*insanguinato*) bloody. **sanguinoso** *agg* bloody.

sanguisuga [sangwi'suga] *sf* leech.

sanità [sani'ta] *sf* health; (*salubrità*) wholesomeness. **sanità mentale** sanity. **sanitario** *agg* sanitary; (*di medicina*) medical.

sano ['sano] *agg* healthy; (*integro*) sound; (*salubre*) wholesome; (*di mente*) sane;

intact. **sano come un pesce** sound as a bell. **sano e salvo** safe and sound.
santo ['santo], **-a** *agg* holy; (*seguito da nome*) Saint; pious; sacred; (*rafforzativo*) blessed. *sm, sf* saint. **santerello, -a** *sm, sf* (*fam*) goody-goody. **santificare** *v* sanctify; (*venerare*) hallow; canonize. **santità** *sf* holiness; (*fig*) sanctity. **santuario** *sm* sanctuary.
sanzione [san'tsjone] *sf* sanction. **sanzionare** *v* sanction.
***sapere** [sa'pere] *v* know; (*essere capace, aver imparato*) can, know how (to); (*aver odore*) smell (of); (*aver sapore*) taste (of). **buono a sapersi** worth knowing. **far sapere a** let know, inform. **non ne voglio sapere** I don't want to have anything to do with it. **non si sa mai** you never can tell. **per quanto ne sappia** as far as I know. **saperla lunga** know a thing or two. **venire a sapere** learn, gather. *sm* knowledge, learning.
sapienza [sa'pjɛntsa] *sf* wisdom; learning. **sapiente** *agg* wise; learned. **sapientone, -a** *sm, sf* (*fam*) know-all.
sapone [sa'pone] *sm* soap. **sapone in polvere** soap-powder. **saponetta** *sf* bar of soap. **saponiera** *sf* soap-dish. **saponoso** *agg* soapy.
sapore [sa'pore] *sm* taste, flavour. **saporito** *agg* tasty; (*salato*) rather salty; (*arguto*) witty.
saracinesca [saratʃi'neska] *sf* roller-blind; (*di chiusa*) floodgate.
sarcasmo [sar'kazmo] *sm* sarcasm. **sarcastico** *agg* sarcastic.
sarchio ['sarkjɔ] *sm* hoe. **sarchiare** *v* hoe.
sarda ['sarda] *sf also* **sardina** pilchard, sardine.
Sardegna [sar'deɲa] *sf* Sardinia. **sardo, -a** *s, agg* Sardinian.
sardonico [sar'dɔniko] *agg* sardonic.
sarta ['sarta] *sf* dressmaker. **sarto** *sm* tailor. **sartoria** *sf* (*laboratorio*) dressmaker's *or* tailor's workshop; (*tecnica*) dressmaking, tailoring.
sasso ['sasso] *sm* stone; (*ciottolo*) pebble; (*roccia*) rock. **prendere a sassate** pelt with stones, stone. **sassoso** *agg* stony.
sassofono [sas'sɔfono] *sm* saxophone. **sassofonista** *s(m+f)* saxophonist.
Satana ['satana] *sm* Satan. **satanico** *agg* satanic.
satellite [sa'tɛllite] *agg, sm* satellite.
satirico [sa'tiriko] *agg* satirical. **satira** *sf* satire. **satireggiare** *v also* **mettere in satira** satirize.
satiro ['satiro] *sm* satyr.
satollo [sa'tollo] *agg* full up.
saturare [satu'rare] *v* saturate; (*fig*) cram. **saturazione** *sf* saturation. **saturo** *agg* saturated; crammed, full.
savio ['savjo] *agg* wise; prudent.
saziare [sa'tsjare] *v* satisfy; (*riempire presto*) be filling. **saziarsi** *v* have one's fill; (*stancarsi*) tire. **sazietà** *sf* surfeit. **a sazietà** more than enough. **mangiare a sazietà** eat *or* have one's fill. **sazio** *agg* satisfied; (*fam*) full up; (*stanco*) tired.
sbadato [zba'dato] *agg* careless, thoughtless. **sbadataggine** *sf* carelessness, thoughtlessness.
sbadigliare [zbadi'ʎare] *v* yawn. **sbadiglio** *sm* yawn.
sbafare [zba'fare] *v* (*scroccare*) scrounge; (*mangiare avidamente*) gobble up. **mangiare/vivere a sbafo** scrounge a meal/living.
sbagliare [zba'ʎare] *v* make a mistake; (*scambiare*) mistake. **sbagliare i calcoli** miscalculate; (*fig*) make a (big) mistake. **sbagliar il passo** stumble; (*mil*) be out of step. **sbagliar numero** get the wrong number. **sbagliar ortografia** spell incorrectly. **sbagliarsi sul conto di** be wrong about. **sbagliato** *agg* wrong, mistaken. **calcolo sbagliato** *sm* miscalculation. **pronuncia sbagliata** *sf* mispronunciation. **sbaglio** *sm* mistake.
sbalestrato [zbales'trato] *agg* unsettled; (*smarrito*) lost.
sballare [zbal'lare] *v* (*merce*) unpack. **sballato** *agg* wild.
sballottare [zballot'tare] *v* toss about. **sballottamento** *sm* tossing.
sbalordire [zbalor'dire] *v* astonish; (*turbare*) bewilder, shock. **sbalordimento** *sm* astonishment; shock, bewilderment. **sbalorditivo** *agg* amazing; (*incredibile*) staggering.
sbalzare[1] [zbal'tsare] *v* throw, fling. **sbalzo** *sm* jerk, jolt; (*fig*) jump. **a sbalzi** jerkily; (*fig*) by fits and starts.
sbalzare[2] [zbal'tsare] *v* (*metallo*) emboss. **lavoro a sbalzo** *sm* embossing.
sbandare [zban'dare] *v* (*auto*) skid; (*mar*) list; (*aero*) bank; (*disperdere*) break *or* split up. **sbandata** *sf* skid. **prendere una sbandata per** have a crush on. **sbandato** *agg* scattered; (*fig*) bewildered.

sbaragliare [zbara'ʎare] *v* (put to) rout. **andare** *or* **buttarsi allo sbaraglio** risk everything. **mettere allo sbaraglio** jeopardize.

sbarazzarsi [zbarat'tsarsi] *v* get rid of.

sbarbare [zbar'bare] *v* shave. **sbarbatello** *sm* novice.

sbarcare [zbar'kare] *v* land; (*merce*) unload. **sbarco** *sm* landing; unloading.

sbarra ['zbarra] *sf* bar, barrier; (*segno grafico*) stroke. **sbarramento** *sm* barrage; block(age). **sbarrare** *v* bar, block; (*porta*) bolt; (*assegno*) cross; (*occhi*) open wide.

sbatacchiare [zbatak'kjare] *v* slam; (*ali*) flap.

sbattere ['zbattere] *v* (*scaraventare*) fling; (*chiudere violentemente*) slam; (*urtare*) bash; (*ali*) flap; (*gastr*) whip, beat. **non saper dove sbattere la testa** not know which way to turn. **sbatter fuori** (*fam*) chuck out.

sbavare [zba'vare] *v* (*emettere bava*) dribble; (*colore, ecc.*) smudge. **sbavatura** *sf* dribble; smudge.

sberla ['zbɛrla] *sf* slap.

sbiadire [zbja'dire] *v* fade. **sbiadito** *agg* faded; (*fig*) dull.

sbiancare [zbjan'kare] *v* whiten.

sbianchire [zbian'kire] *v* whiten; (*gastr*) blanch.

sbieco ['zbjɛko] *agg* crooked. **guardar di sbieco** look askance at. **tagliar di sbieco** cut on the bias.

sbigottire [zbigot'tire] *v* astonish; (*turbare*) dismay. **sbigottimento** *sm* astonishment; dismay.

sbilancio [zbi'lantʃo] *sm* (*squilibrio*) lack of equilibrium; (*econ*) deficit. **sbilanciare** *v* unbalance.

sbilenco [zbi'lɛnko] *agg* crooked.

sbloccare [zblok'kare] *v* free, release; (*prezzi*) unfreeze.

sboccare [zbok'kare] *v* come out; (*condurre*) lead; (*fiume*) flow (into). **sbocco** *sm* outlet.

sbocciare [zbot'tʃare] *v* bloom, blossom.

sbollentare [zbollen'tare] *v* blanch.

sbornia [zbɔrnja] *sf* **postumi di una sbornia** *sm pl* hangover *sing*. **prendere una sbornia** get drunk.

sborsare [zbor'sare] *v* pay out, disburse. **sborso** *sm* disbursement.

sbottare [zbot'tare] *v* burst out.

sbottonare [zbotto'nare] *v* unbutton.

sbozzare [zbot'tsare] *v* sketch; (*fig*) outline.

sbracciarsi [zbrat'tʃarsi] *v* gesticulate; (*rimboccarsi le maniche*) roll up one's sleeves; (*fig*) do one's utmost. **sbracciato** *agg* (*abito*) sleeveless.

sbraitare [zbrai'tare] *v* yell; protest.

sbranare [zbra'nare] *v* tear to pieces.

sbrattare [zbrat'tare] *v* tidy up. **stanza di sbratto** *sf* lumber-room.

sbriciolare [zbritʃo'lare] *v* crumble.

sbrigare [zbri'gare] *v* get done, finish (off); (*risolvere*) settle. **sbrigarsi** *v* (*far presto*) hurry up; (*liberarsi*) get rid (of). **sbrigativo** *agg* quick; (*superficiale*) hasty.

sbrigliare [zbri'ʎare] *v* unbridle, give free rein (to). **sbrigliatezza** *sf* unruliness. **sbrigliato** *agg* unruly, wild.

sbrindellare [zbrindel'lare] *v* tear to shreds. **sbrindellato** *agg* in rags *or* tatters.

sbrodolare [zbrodo'lare] *v* (*insudiciare*) soil; (*fig*) spin out; (*fam*) waffle.

sbrogliare [sbro'ʎare] *v* disentangle. **sbrogliarsi** *v* extricate oneself.

sbronzo ['zbrondzo] *agg* drunk. **prendersi una sbronza** get drunk.

sbruffare [zbruf'fare] *v* spurt; (*fig*) brag.

sbucare [zbu'kare] *v* come out, emerge; (*fig*) spring up.

sbucciare [zbut'tʃare] *v* peel; (*escoriare*) scrape. **sbucciapatate** *sm invar* potato-peeler. **sbucciatura** *sf* scrape, graze.

sbudellare [zbudel'lare] *v* disembowel; (*gastr*) gut. **sbudellarsi dal ridere** split one's sides laughing.

sbuffare [zbuf'fare] *v* puff, pant; (*rabbia*) snort.

scabbia ['skabbia] *sf* scabies. **scabbiosa** *sf* (*bot*) scabious.

scabroso [ska'brozo] *agg also* **scabro** rough; (*problema*) thorny, knotty.

scacciare [skat'tʃare] *v* drive out *or* away; (*fig*) dispel; expel.

scacco ['skakko] *sm* (*quadretto*) check; (*figurina del gioco*) chessman. **scacchi** *sm pl* (*gioco*) chess *sing*. **scacco matto** checkmate. **subire uno scacco** suffer a setback. **scacchiera** *sf* chess-board; (*per dama*) draught-board.

***scadere** [ska'dere] *v* expire; (*perdere valore*) decline; (*econ*) fall due. **scadente** *agg* poor. **scadenza** *sf* expiry; (*effetti*) maturity. **a breve/lunga scadenza** short-/long-term. **scadimento** *sm* decline.

scafandro [ska'fandro] *sm* diving-suit; (*astronauta*) space-suit.
scaffale [skaf'fale] *sm* shelf. **scaffalatura** *sf* shelving.
scafo ['skafo] *sm* hull.
scagionare [skadʒo'nare] *v* exonerate.
scaglia ['skaʎa] *sf* scale; (*sapone*) flake. **scagliare** *v* flake.
scagliare [ska'ʎare] *v* (*lanciare*) fling, hurl.
scaglione [ska'ʎone] *sm* group; (*mil*) echelon. **scaglionare** *v* stagger; (*mil*) range. **scaglionamento** *sm* staggering.
scala ['skala] *sf* stairs *pl*, staircase; (*piano*) level; (*misura, rapporto*) scale; (*apparecchio*) ladder. **far le scale** climb the stairs; (*musica*) practise scales. **scala a chiocciola** spiral staircase. **scala di corda** rope-ladder. **scala portatile** steps *pl*, step-ladder. **scalinata** *sf* flight of stairs.
scalare [ska'lare] *v* scale. *agg* graduated; (*fis*) scalar. **scalata** *sf* climb. **scalatore, -trice** *sm, sf* climber.
scalcagnato [skalka'ɲato] *agg* shabby.
scaldare [skal'dare] *v* warm (up); (*a temperatura più elevata*) heat (up). **scaldabagno** *sm* water-heater.
scalfire [skal'fire] *v* scratch.
scalmanato [skalma'nato] *agg* flustered. *sm, sf* hothead. **scalmana** *sf* chill; (*fig*) craze.
scalo ['skalo] *sm* (*banchina*) pier; (*porto d'approdo*) port of call; (*aero*) stopover. **far scalo** (*mar*) call; (*aero*) land, stop. **scalo merci** (*mar*) wharf; (*ferr*) goods yard. **senza scalo** non-stop.
scalogna [ska'loɲa] *sf* bad luck. **scalognato** *agg* unlucky.
scaloppa [ska'lɔppa] *sf* cutlet. **scaloppina** *sf* escalope.
scalpello [skal'pɛllo] *sm* chisel; (*chirurgia*) scalpel. **scalpellare** *v* chisel; cut away.
scalpore [skal'pore] *sm* sensation.
scaltro ['skaltro] *agg* shrewd.
scalzo ['skaltso] *agg* barefoot.
scambiare [skam'bjare] *v* (*dare in cambio*) exchange; (*confondere*) mistake, mix up. **scambievole** *agg* mutual. **scambio** *sm* exchange; (*ferr*) points *pl*. **libero scambio** free trade.
scamosciato [skamo'ʃato] *agg* suede.
scampagnata [skampa'ɲata] *sf* outing.
scampanato [skampa'nato] *agg* flared.
scampare [skam'pare] *v* escape; (*evitare*) avoid. **Dio ce ne scampi!** God forbid! **scamparla bella** have a narrow escape. **scampato, -a** *sm, sf* (*superstite*) survivor. **scampo** *sm* way out.
scampo ['skampo] *sm* prawn.
scampolo ['skampolo] *sm* remnant.
scanalare [skana'lare] *v* groove; (*colonna*) flute. **scanalatura** *sf* groove; flute.
scandagliare [skanda'ʎare] *v* sound (out). **scandaglio** *sm* sounding.
scandalizzare [skandalid'dzare] *v* shock; (*dar scandalo*) scandalize. **scandalo** *sm* scandal. **scandaloso** *agg* scandalous.
scandire [skan'dire] *v* (*pronunciare*) articulate; (*versi*) scan.
scanno ['skanno] *sm* stall.
scansare [skan'sare] *v* dodge, shirk; (*spostare*) shift. **scansarsi** *v* get out of the way. **scansafatiche** *s(m+f) invar* loafer.
scapaccione [skapat'tʃone] *sm* slap.
scapestrato [skapes'trato], **-a** *agg* wild, unruly. *sm, sf* madcap, daredevil.
scapigliato [skapi'ʎato] *agg* dishevelled; (*fig*) reckless.
scapitare [skapi'tare] *sm* loss; (*danno*) injury. **a scapito di** to the detriment of.
scapola ['skapola] *sf* shoulder-blade.
scapolo ['skapolo] *agg* single. *sm* bachelor.
scappamento [skappa'mento] *sm* (*auto*) exhaust.
scappare [skap'pare] *v* run away; escape, flee. **devo scappare** (*ho fretta*) I must rush. **lasciarsi scappar di bocca** blurt out. **scappare di mente** slip one's mind. **scappatella** *sf* escapade. **scappatoia** *sf* way out; (*fig*) loophole.
scappellotto [skapel'lɔtto] *sm* smack. **passare a scappellotti** (*fam*) scrape through.
scarabocchio [skara'bɔkkjo] *sm* (*macchia*) blot; (*sgorbio*) scrawl; (*disegno*) doodle. **scarabocchiare** *v* scrawl; doodle.
scarafaggio [skara'faddʒo] *sm* cockroach.
scaramanzia [skaraman'tsia] *sf* spell. **per scaramanzia** for luck.
scaramuccia [skara'muttʃa] *sf* skirmish.
scaraventare [skaraven'tare] *v* hurl, fling.
scarcerare [skartʃe'rare] *v* release (from prison). **scarceramento** *sm* release.
scardinare [skardi'nare] *v* unhinge.
scaricare [skari'kare] *v* discharge; (*deporre un carico*) unload; (*sfogare*) vent; (*liquido*) empty; (*gas*) let out. **scaricare la colpa** shift the blame. **scarica** *sf* discharge; (*raffica*) volley. **scaricalasino** *sm invar* piggy-bank.

scarico ['skariko] *sm, pl* **-chi** discharge; unloading; (*di rifiuti*) dumping; (*i rifiuti stessi*) rubbish; (*deposito di rifiuti*) dump; (*auto*) exhaust. **a mio scarico** in my defence. **a scarico di coscienza** to clear one's conscience. *agg* (*vuoto*) empty; (*batteria*) flat.
scarlattina [skarlat'tina] *sf* scarlet fever.
scarlatto [skar'latto] *agg, sm* scarlet.
scarno ['skarno] *agg* skinny; (*spoglio*) bare; (*povero*) scanty.
scarpa ['skarpa] *sf* shoe. **scarpe da ginnastica** *or* **tennis** plimsolls *pl*. **scarpone** *sm* boot. **scarponi da calciatore/sci** football-/ski-boots *pl*.
scarso ['skarso] *agg* poor; (*manchevole*) lacking (in); (*insufficiente*) short. **un chilo scarso** just under a kilo. **scarseggiare** *v* be scarce; be short (of); (*fig*) lack (in). **scarsezza** *or* **scarsità** *sf* shortage; lack.
scartabellare [skartabel'lare] *v* skim *or* flip through.
scartare[1] [skar'tare] *v* (*togliere dalla carta*) unwrap; (*respingere*) discard, reject. **scarto** *sm* (*cosa scartata*) reject; (*alle carte*) discard. **merci di scarto** *sf pl* inferior goods *pl*, rejects *pl*.
scartare[2] [skar'tare] *v* (*spostarsi lateralmente*) swerve. **scarto** *sm* swerve, skid; difference.
scassare [skas'sare] *v* (*fam*: *guastare*) smash, bust; (*il terreno*) break up. **furto con scasso** *sm* burglary.
scassinare [skassi'nare] *v* force (open). **scassinatore, -trice** *sm, sf* burglar; (*di banche*) bank-robber.
scatenare [skate'nare] *v* unleash; cause. **scatenarsi** *v* break out.
scatola ['skatola] *sf* box; carton; (*di latta*) tin. **averne piene le scatole** (*fam*) be fed up to the back teeth (with). **cibo in scatola** *sm* tinned food. **rompere le scatole** (*fam*) be a nuisance. **scatolame** *sm* tinned goods *pl*.
scattare [skat'tare] *v* spring; (*rilasciarsi*) spring up; (*armi*) go off; (*aprirsi*) spring open; (*chiudersi*) snap shut. **far scattare** release. **scattare a vuoto** misfire. **scatto** *sm* release; (*rumore*) click; (*sport*) spurt; (*accesso*) outburst. **a scatti** jerkily. **di scatto** suddenly.
scaturire [skatu'rire] *v* gush; (*fig*) arise.
scavalcare [skaval'kare] *v* step *or* climb over; (*saltando*) jump over; (*sbalzare di sella*) throw; (*superare*) overtake.
scavare [ska'vare] *v* dig; mine; (*pozzo*) sink; (*trovare*) dig up; (*sartoria*) widen. **scavatore** *sm* digger. **scavatura** *sf* excavation. **scavo** *sm* excavation.
***scegliere** ['ʃeʎere] *v* choose. **c'è (molto) da scegliere** there is plenty to choose from. **c'è poco da scegliere** there is little choice.
scellerato [ʃelle'rato], **-a** *agg* wicked. *sm, sf* wicked person. **scelleratezza** *sf* wickedness; (*atto*) misdeed.
scelta ['ʃelta] *sf* choice, selection; quality. **a scelta** according to preference. **non aver possibilità di scelta** have no choice. **scelto** *agg* chosen, picked; (*eccellente*) choice.
scemare [ʃe'mare] *v* diminish.
scemo ['ʃemo], **-a** *agg* stupid, idiotic; (*sciocco*) foolish. *sm, sf* fool, idiot. **scemenza** *sf* (*azione*) idiocy, foolishness; (*parole*) nonsense.
scena ['ʃɛna] *sf* scene; (*palcoscenico*) stage. **mettere in scena** stage, produce. **scenario** *sm* (*teatro*) set; (*cinema*) scenario, script; (*fig*) setting. **scenata** *sf* scene, row. **sceneggiare** *v* adapt, dramatize. **sceneggiatura** *sf* script. **scenico** *agg* scenic.
***scendere** ['ʃendere] *v* (*andar giù*) go down; (*venir giù*) come down; (*autobus, treno*) get off; (*auto*) get out; (*calare*) drop; (*sostare*) stop. **scendere a un accordo** reach an agreement. **scendere dal letto** get up. **scendiletto** *sm invar* (*tappetino*) bedside rug; (*vestaglia*) dressing-gown.
sceriffo [ʃe'riffo] *sm* sheriff.
scervellarsi [ʃervel'larsi] *v* rack one's brains. **scervellato** *agg* hare-brained.
scettico ['ʃɛttiko], **-a** *agg* sceptical. *sm, sf* sceptic. **scetticismo** *sm* scepticism.
scettro ['ʃɛttro] *sm* sceptre.
scheda ['skɛda] *sf* card; (*di schedario*) index-card; (*elettorale*) ballot(-paper). **schedare** *v* catalogue; (*archiviare*) file. **schedario** *sm* file; (*mobile*) filing cabinet; (*elenco*) list. **schedina** *sf* coupon.
scheggia ['skeddʒa] *sf* splinter. **scheggiare** *v* splinter, chip.
scheletro ['skɛletro] *sm* skeleton; (*tec*) framework. **scheletrico** *agg* skeletal; (*fig*) bare.
schema ['skɛma] *sm* scheme; (*abbozzo*) outline; (*modello*) pattern. **schema di legge** bill. **schematico** *agg* schematic.

scherma ['skerma] *sf* fencing. **tirare di scherma** fence. **schermaglia** *sf* skirmish. **schermitore, -trice** *sm, sf* fencer.

schermo ['skermo] *sm* screen; (*difesa*) shield. **schermare** *v* screen, shield. **schermire** *v* protect.

schernire [sker'nire] *v* scorn, mock. **schernitore, -trice** *agg* scornful, mocking. **scherno** *sm* mockery, derision; (*oggetto di scherno*) laughing-stock.

scherzare [sker'tsare] *v* joke; (*prendere alla leggera*) trifle (with); (*giocare*) play. **c'è poco da scherzare** it is not a laughing matter. **scherzi!** *inter* you must be joking! **scherzo** *sm* joke; (*tiro*) trick; (*musica*) scherzo. **per scherzo** for fun, as a joke. **scherzoso** *agg* playful; (*giocoso*) jocular.

schettinare [sketti'nare] *v* roller-skate. **schettinaggio** *sm* roller-skating. **schettino** *sm* roller-skate.

schiacciare [skjat'tʃare] *v* (*spiaccicare*) squash; (*frantumare*) crush; (*noci*) crack. **schiacciare un pisolino** have a nap. **schiacciante** *agg* crushing. **schiaccianoci** *sm* nutcrackers *pl*. **schiacciasassi** *sm* steam-roller.

schiaffare [skjaf'fare] *v* (*fam*) chuck.

schiaffo ['skjaffo] *sm* slap. **schiaffeggiare** *v* slap.

schiamazzare [skjamat'tsare] *v* cackle; (*far baccano*) make a row. **schiamazzo** *sm* cackle; row.

schiantare [skjan'tare] *v* shatter, burst. **schianto** *sm* crash.

schiappa ['skjappa] *sf* (*fam*) washout.

schiarire [skja'rire] *v* clear (up). **schiarimento** *sm* clearing up; (*spiegazione*) explanation; information.

schiavo ['skjavo], **-a** *s, agg* slave. **schiavitù** *sf* slavery.

schiena ['skjɛna] *sf* back. **colpire alla schiena** stab in the back. **mal di schiena** *sm* backache. **schienale** *sm* back.

schiera ['skjɛra] *sf* band; (*moltitudine*) mass, crowd. **schieramento** *sm* formation; line-up. **schierare** *v* line up; (*mil*) deploy. **schierarsi contro** take sides against. **schierarsi dalla parte di** side with.

schietto ['skjetto] *agg* sincere; genuine; frank. **a dirla schietta** (to speak) frankly. **schiettezza** *sf* genuineness; frankness.

schifo ['skifo] *sm* disgust. **avere a schifo** loathe. **far schifo** *v* (*essere disgustoso*) be disgusting; (*disgustare*) (fill with) disgust. **schifare** *v* disgust. **schifezza** *sf* rubbish, muck. **schifiltoso** *agg* fussy; (*esigente*) fastidious. **schifoso** *agg* disgusting.

schioccare [skjok'kare] *v* crack; (*dita*) snap.

schioppo ['skjɔppo] *sm* gun; (*da caccia*) shotgun. **schioppettata** *sf* (gun)shot.

***schiudersi** ['skjudersi] *v* open (up).

schiuma ['skjuma] *sf* foam; (*birra*) froth; (*sapone*) lather; (*feccia*) scum. **aver la schiuma alla bocca** foam at the mouth. **schiumare** *v* skim. **schiumoso** *agg* foamy; frothy; lathery.

schivare [ski'vare] *v* avoid; (*fam*) dodge; (*boxe*) duck.

schizofrenia [skitsofre'nia] *sf* schizophrenia. **schizofrenico, -a** *s, agg* schizophrenic.

schizzare [skit'tsare] *v* (*zampillare*) spurt; (*spruzzare*) squirt; (*sporcare*) splash; (*disegnare*) sketch. **schizzar via** dash off. **schizzetto** *sm* spray; syringe; (*giocattolo*) water-pistol. **schizzo** *sm* spurt; squirt; splash; sketch.

schizzinoso [skittsi'nozo] *agg* fastidious; squeamish.

sci [ʃi] *sm* (*attrezzo*) ski; (*attività*) skiing. **fare dello sci** ski, go skiing. **sci nautico** water-ski; water-skiing. **sciare** *v* ski. **sciatore, -trice** *sm, sf* skier.

scia ['ʃia] *sf* wake; (*traccia*) trail. **seguire la scia di** follow in the footsteps of.

sciabola ['ʃabola] *sf* sabre.

sciacallo [ʃa'kallo] *sm* jackal.

sciacquare [ʃak'kware] *v* rinse (out). **sciacquata** *sf* rinse. **sciacquatura** *sf* (*azione*) rinsing; (*acqua*) dishwater. **sciacquo** *sm* rinsing; (*liquido*) mouthwash.

sciagura [ʃa'gura] *sf* disaster; (*incidente*) accident, crash. **sciagurato** *agg* (*sfortunato*) unlucky, wretched; (*malvagio*) wicked.

scialacquare [ʃalak'kware] *v* squander. **scialacquatore, -trice** *sm, sf* spendthrift.

scialbo ['ʃalbo] *agg* pale; faint; (*fig*) dull.

scialle ['ʃalle] *sm* shawl.

scialo ['ʃalo] *sm* waste.

sciame ['ʃame] *sm* swarm. **sciamare** *v* swarm.

sciancato [ʃan'kato] *agg* lame; (*sedia, ecc.*) shaky, rickety.

sciarada [ʃa'rada] *sf* charade.

sciarpa ['ʃarpa] *sf* scarf.
sciatica ['ʃatika] *sf* sciatica. **sciatico** *agg* sciatic.
sciatto ['ʃatto] *agg* slovenly; (*fam*) sloppy.
scientifico [ʃen'tifiko] *agg* scientific.
scienza ['ʃɛntsa] *sf* science. **scienziato, -a** *sm, sf* scientist; (*studioso*) scholar.
scimmia ['ʃimmja] *sf* monkey; (*senza coda*) ape. **brutto come una scimmia** as ugly as sin. **scimmiottare** *v also* **fare la scimmia a** ape.
scimpanzè [ʃimpan'tse] *sm* chimpanzee.
scimunito [ʃimu'nito], **-a** *agg* foolish. *sm, sf* fool.
***scindere** ['ʃindere] *v* separate; divide.
scintilla [ʃin'tilla] *sf* spark. **dare** *or* **emettere scintille** spark. **scintillare** *v* sparkle; (*lampeggiare*) flash.
sciocco ['ʃɔkko], **-a** *agg* foolish. *sm, sf* fool. **sciocchezza** *sf* foolish thing; (*cosa da niente*) trifle; (*l'essere sciocco*) foolishness. **dire sciocchezze** talk nonsense.
***sciogliere** ['ʃɔʎere] *v* (*fondere*) melt; dissolve; (*porre fine*) break up; (*disfare*) undo; (*allentare*) loosen; (*slegare*) untie; (*società*) wind up. **scioglimento** *sm* dissolution; breaking up; melting.
sciolto ['ʃɔlto] *agg* loose; (*agile*) nimble. **aver la lingua sciolta** have the gift of the gab. **versi sciolti** *sm pl* blank verse *sing*. **scioltezza** *sf* nimbleness; (*fig*) fluency.
scioperare [ʃope'rare] *v* (go on) strike. **scioperante** *s*(*m*+*f*) striker. **scioperato** *agg* lazy. **sciopero** *sm* strike. **entrare in sciopero** go on strike. **far sciopero** strike. **sciopero bianco/lampo** sit-down/wildcat strike.
sciorinare [ʃori'nare] *v* (*bucato*) hang out; (*fig*) show off; (*spreg*) dash off. **sciorinare bugie** tell a string of lies.
sciovinismo [ʃovi'nizmo] *sm* chauvinism. **sciovinista** *s*(*m*+*f*) chauvinist.
scipito ['ʃipito] *agg* insipid.
scippare [ʃip'pare] *v* snatch. **scippatore, -trice** *sm, sf* bag-snatcher.
scirocco [ʃi'rɔkko] *sm* sirocco.
sciroppo [ʃi'rɔppo] *sm* syrup. **sciroppato** *agg* in syrup. **sciropposo** *agg* syrupy.
scisma ['ʃizma] *sm* schism. **scismatico** *agg* schismatic.
scissione [ʃis'sjone] *sf* split. **scisso** *agg* split.
sciupare [ʃu'pare] *v* (*rovinare*) ruin, spoil; (*perdere*) waste. **sciuparsi** *v* (*salute*) ruin one's health; (*sgualcirsi*) get creased. **sciupato** *agg* ruined; wasted; (*di aspetto*) haggard. **sciupio** *sm* waste. **sciupone, -a** *sm, sf* wastrel.
scivolare [ʃivo'lare] *v* slide; (*sfuggire, sdrucciolare*) slip; (*aero*) glide. **scivolata** *sf* slide; glide. **scivolo** *sm* chute; (*mar*) slipway. **scivolone** *sm* slip; (*caduta*) tumble. **scivoloso** *agg* slippery.
sclerosi [skle'rɔzi] *sf* sclerosis. **sclerotico** *agg* sclerotic.
scoccare [skok'kare] *v* (*orologio*) strike; (*scagliare*) fling.
scocciare [skot'tʃare] *v* bother. **scocciarsi** *v* get bored. **scocciatore, -trice** *sm, sf* bore; (*fam*) pest. **scocciatura** *sf* bore.
scodella [sko'dɛlla] *sf* bowl. **scodellare** *v* serve; (*minestra*) ladle out; (*fig*) come out with.
scoglio ['skɔʎo] *sm* rock; (*fig*) stumbling block. **scogliera** *sf* cliff; (*a fior d'acqua*) reef. **scoglioso** *agg* rocky.
scoiattolo [sko'jattolo] *sm* squirrel.
scolare [sko'lare] *v* drain; (*gastr*) strain. **scolapiatti** *sm invar* draining-board. **scolo** *sm* drainage; (*condotto*) drain.
scolaro [sco'laro], **-a** *sm, sf* pupil; disciple. **scolastico** *agg* (*della scuola*) school; (*spreg*) bookish; (*filosofio*) scholastic.
scollato [skol'lato] *agg* low-necked.
scolorire [skolo'rire] *v also* **scolorare** discolour, fade. **scolorito** *agg* faded.
scolpire [skol'pire] *v* sculpt; (*incidere*) carve; (*fig*) impress.
scombinare [skombi'nare] *v* upset. **scombinato** *agg* (*mal combinato*) badly arranged; confused.
scombro ['skombro] *sm also* **sgombro** mackerel.
scombussolare [skombusso'lare] *v* upset; (*stordire*) stun.
***scommettere** [skom'mettere] *v* bet. **scommessa** *sf* bet. **scommettitore, -trice** *sm, sf* punter.
scomodare [skomo'dare] *v* trouble, inconvenience. **scomodità** *sf* discomfort; (*disagio*) inconvenience. **scomodo** *agg* (*non comodo*) uncomfortable; inconvenient.
scompaginare [skompadʒi'nare] *v* throw into disarray; (*fig*) upset.
***scomparire** [skompa'rire] *v* disappear; (*fig*) look insignificant.
scomparso [skom'parso], **-a** *agg* vanished. *sm, sf* deceased. *sf* disappearance.

scompartimento [skomparti'mento] *sm* compartment. **scomparto** *sm* compartment; (*parete*) partition.
scompigliare [skompi'ʎare] *v* upset; confuse; (*capelli*) ruffle. **scompiglio** *sm* confusion.
***scomporre** [skom'porre] *v* take apart; resolve; decompose; (*turbare*) perturb. **senza scomporsi** unperturbed. **scomposto** *agg* broken down; (*in disordine*) untidy; (*indecoroso*) unseemly.
scomunicare [skomuni'kare] *v* excommunicate. **scomunica** *sf* excommunication.
sconcertare [skontʃer'tare] *v* baffle. **sconcertato** *agg* bewildered.
sconcio ['skontʃo] *agg* indecent; obscene. *sm* disgrace. **sconcezza** *sf* obscenity. **dire sconcezze** use foul language. **sconciare** *v* spoil.
sconfessare [skonfes'sare] *v* repudiate.
***sconfiggere** [skon'fiddʒere] *v* defeat. **sconfitta** *sf* defeat. **sconfitto** *agg* defeated, beaten. **dichiararsi sconfitto** acknowledge defeat.
sconfortante [skonfor'tante] *agg* disheartening. **sconforto** *sm* discouragement; depression.
scongelare [skondʒe'lare] *v* defrost.
scongiurare [skondʒu'rare] *v* beseech; (*evitare*) avoid; (*rel*) exorcise. **scongiuro** *sm* exorcism.
***sconnettere** [skon'nɛttere] *v* disconnect. **sconnesso** *agg* (*fig*) disjointed.
sconosciuto [skono'ʃuto], **-a** *agg* unknown. *sm*, *sf* stranger.
sconquassare [skonkwas'sare] *v* smash; shake (up). **sconquassato** *agg* shattered.
sconsiderato [skonside'rato] *agg* thoughtless. **sconsideratezza** *sf* thoughtlessness.
sconsigliare [skonsi'ʎare] *v* advise against; dissuade.
sconsolato [skonso'lato] *agg* disconsolate.
scontare [skon'tare] *v* (*detrarre*) deduct; (*econ*) discount; (*debito*) pay off. **sconto** *sm* discount.
scontentare [skonten'tare] *v* dissatisfy; (*lasciare scontento*) disappoint. **scontentezza** *sf* dissatisfaction; disappointment. **scontento** *agg* displeased; disappointed.
scontrarsi [skon'trarsi] *v* meet; (*veicoli*) crash. **scontro** *sm* encounter; (*discussione*) argument; (*violento*) clash; crash.
scontrino [skon'trino] *sm* check.
scontroso [skon'trozo] *agg* surly. **scontrosità** *sf* surliness.
***sconvenire** [skonve'nire] *v* be unsuitable; (*non essere decoroso*) be unbecoming. **sconveniente** *agg* unfavourable; unbecoming.
***sconvolgere** [skon'vɔldʒere] *v* upset. **sconvolgimento** *sm* upset; confusion. **sconvolto** *agg* upset.
scopa ['skopa] *sf* broom. **scopare** *v* sweep; (*volg*) screw.
scoperchiare [skoper'kjare] *v* take the lid off.
scoperto [sko'pɛrto] *agg* uncovered; (*aperto*) open; (*nudo*) bare. *sm* open; (*conto*) overdraft. **allo scoperto** outdoors, in the open (air). **scoperta** *sf* discovery.
scopo ['skɔpo] *sm* purpose. **a** *or* **allo scopo di** in order to. **senza scopo** pointless.
scoppiare [skop'pjare] *v* burst; explode; (*manifestarsi*) break out. **scoppiettare** *v* crackle. **scoppio** *sm* explosion; outbreak; (*rumore*) bang.
***scoprire** [sko'prire] *v* (*fatti, cose nuove*) discover; (*togliere copertura*) uncover, bare; (*esporre*) expose; (*manifestare*) show. **scoprire le (proprie) carte** lay one's cards on the table.
scoraggiare [skorad'dʒare] *v* discourage, dishearten.
scorbuto [skor'buto] *sm* scurvy. **scorbutico** *agg* (*fig*) cantankerous.
scorciare [skor'tʃare] *v* shorten. **scorciatoia** *sf* short cut.
scordare [skor'dare] *v* *also* **scordarsi** forget.
scordato [skor'dato] *agg* (*musica*) out of tune.
scoreggia [sko'reddʒa] (*volg*) *sf* fart. **scoreggiare** *v* fart.
***scorgere** [skɔrdʒere] *v* notice.
scoria ['skɔrja] *sf* slag; (*fig*) dross.
scorno ['skɔrno] *sm* humiliation.
scorpione [skor'pjone] *sm* scorpion. **Scorpione** *sm* Scorpio.
scorrazzare [skorrat'tsare] *v* run about. **scorrazzata** *sf* trip.
***scorrere** ['skorrere] *v* (*liquido*) run, flow; (*tempo*) pass (by); (*scivolare*) glide; (*leggere in fretta*) run through. **scorrevole** *agg* flowing. **scorrevolezza** *sf* fluidity; (*fig*) fluency.
scorretto [skor'rɛtto] *agg* incorrect; (*sgarbato*) impolite; (*non leale*) unfair.

scorrettezza *sf* incorrectness, lack of manners; unfairness.
scorsa ['skɔrsa] *sf* glance.
scorso ['skɔrso] *agg* last. **l'anno scorso** last year.
scorsoio [skor'sɔjo] *agg* **nodo scorsoio** *sm* slip-knot.
scorta ['skɔrta] *sf* escort; (*provvista*) stock, supply; reserve. **di scorta** spare. **fare la scorta a** escort. **fare una scorta (di)** stock up (on). **sotto la scorta di** under the guidance of. **sulla scorta di** on the basis of. **scortare** *v* escort.
scortese [skor'teze] *agg* rude. **scortesia** *sf* rudeness.
scorticare [skorti'kare] *v* skin; (*escoriare*) graze.
scorza ['skɔrtsa] *sf* skin; (*corteccia*) bark.
scosceso [sko'ʃezo] *agg* steep.
scossa ['skɔssa] *sf* shock; (*scatto, sbalzo*) jerk; (*tremore*) shake. **a scosse** jerkily. **scosso** *agg* shaken.
scostare [skos'tare] *v* shift. **scostarsi** *v* move aside; (*deviare*) stray. **scostamento** *sm* shifting; (*mat*) deviation. **scostante** *agg* unpleasant.
scostumato [skostu'mato] *agg* dissolute, licentious. **scostumatezza** *sf* licentiousness.
scotennare [skoten'nare] *v* skin; (*di cuoio capelluto*) scalp.
scottare [skot'tare] *v* burn; (*con liquido bollente*) scald; (*causare bruciatura*) scorch; (*essere caldo*) be hot. **scottatura** *sf* burning; scalding; scorching; (*ustione*) burn, scald.
scovare [sko'vare] *v* (*stanare*) flush out; (*rintracciare*) track down; (*trovare*) find.
Scozia ['skɔtsja] *sf* Scotland. **scozzese** *agg* Scottish, Scotch; *s*(*m*+*f*) Scot.
screanzato [skrean'tsato] *agg* rude.
screditare [skredi'tare] *v* discredit.
scremare [skre'mare] *v* skim.
screpolare [skrepo'lare] *v* crack. **screpolatura** *sf* crack.
screziato [skre'tsjato] *agg* variegated.
scribacchiare [skribak'kjare] *v* scribble.
scricchiolare [skrikkjo'lare] *v* creak. **scricchiolio** *sm* creaking noise.
scricciolo ['skrittʃolo] *sm* wren.
scrigno ['skriɲo] *sm* casket.
scriminatura [skrimina'tura] *sf* parting.
scritta ['skritta] *sf* inscription; (*dir*) document.
scritto ['skritto] *agg* written. *sm* writing; letter; document. **scrittoio** *sm* (writing-) desk. **scrittore, -trice** *sm, sf* writer.
scrittura [skrit'tura] *sf* writing; (*contratto*) engagement; (*calligrafia*) handwriting. **(Sacra) Scrittura** (Holy) Scripture. **scritturare** *v* engage.
scrivania [skriva'nia] *sf* (writing-)desk.
***scrivere** ['skrivere] *v* write; (*compitando*) spell. **scrivere bene/male** (*calligrafia*) have a good/bad handwriting; (*stile*) write well/badly; (*compitare*) spell correctly/incorrectly.
scroccare [skrok'kare] *v* scrounge. **vivere a scrocco** scrounge a living. **scroccone, -a** *sm, sf* scrounger.
scrocco ['skrɔkko] *sm* **coltello a scrocco** *sm* clasp-knife. **serratura a scrocco** *sf* spring-lock, latch.
scrofa ['skrɔfa] *sf* sow.
scrollare [skrol'lare] *v* shake; (*spalle*) shrug.
scrosciare [skro'ʃare] *v* thunder; (*pioggia*) pelt down. **scroscio** *sm* (*pioggia*) downpour. **scroscio di applausi** thunderous applause. **scroscio di risa** roar of laughter.
scrostare [skros'tare] *v* scrape (off).
scroto ['skrɔto] *sm* scrotum.
scrupolo ['skrupolo] *sm* scruple, qualm. **avere** *or* **farsi scrupoli (di)** have qualms (about). **essere onesto fino allo scrupolo** be scrupulously honest. **senza scrupoli** unscrupulous. **scrupoloso** *agg* scrupulous, meticulous.
scrutare [skru'tare] *v* scan; (*indagare*) delve into. **scrutatore, -trice** *sm, sf* scrutineer. **scrutinare** *v* scrutinize. **scrutinio** *sm* scrutiny; (*elezioni*) poll.
scucire [sku'tʃire] *v* unstitch. **scucitura** *sf* rip.
scudo ['skudo] *sm* shield. **farsi scudo** shield oneself. **scuderia** *sf* (*ricovero*) stable; (*allevamento*) stud; (*auto*) racing team. **scudetto** *sm* (*calcio*) league championship.
scugnizzo [sku'ɲittso] *sm* urchin.
sculacciare [skulat'tʃare] *v* spank. **sculacciata** *sf* spanking.
scultore [skul'tore] *sm* sculptor. **scultrice** *sf* sculptress. **scultura** *sf* sculpture.
scuola ['skwɔla] *sf* school. **scuola dell'obbligo** compulsory schooling. **scuola guida** driving school. **scuola materna** nursery school. **scuola pubblica** state school.

***scuotere** ['skwɔtere] *v* shake; (*le spalle*) shrug. **scuotersi di dosso** shrug off.
scure ['skure] *sf* axe.
scuro ['skuro] *agg* dark. *sm* dark, darkness. **scuretto** *sm* (window-)shutter. **scurire** *v* darken.
scusa ['skuza] *sf* excuse; apology. **chiedere scusa a qualcuno** beg someone's pardon. **scusabile** *agg* excusable; justifiable. **scusante** *sf* excuse; justification. **scusare** *v* excuse; pardon. **scusarsi** *v* apologize; justify oneself. **mi scusi!** (I'm) sorry! I beg your pardon!
sdegnare [zde'ɲare] *v* (*disprezzare*) scorn; irritate. **sdegnato** *agg* indignant; irritated. **sdegno** *sm* indignation. **sdegnoso** *agg* disdainful.
sdoppiare [zdop'pjare] *v* split (in two). **sdoppiamento** *sm* split. **sdoppiamento della personalità** split personality.
sdraiarsi [zdra'jarsi] *v* (*stendersi*) stretch out; (*mettersi a giacere*) lie down. **sdraia** *sf also* **sedia a sdraio** deck-chair.
sdrucciolare [zdruttʃo'lare] *v* slip. **sdrucciolevole** *agg* slippery. **sdrucciolone** *sm* slip.
sdrucire [zdru'tʃire] *v* rip.
se[1] [se] *cong* if; whether; (*se solo*) if only. **come se** as though. **se non altro** if nothing else, at least.
se[2] [se] *V* **si**.
sè [se] *pron* one(self); (*lui*) him(self); (*lei*) her(self); (*cosa, animale*) it(self); (*loro*) them(selves). **da sè** on one's own. **di per sè** in itself. **fra sè e sè** to oneself. **va da sè** it goes without saying.
sebbene [seb'bɛne] *cong* (al)though.
seccare [sek'kare] *v* dry (up); (*importunare*) bother. **seccarsi** *v* (*diventar secco*) dry up; (*annoiarsi*) get bored; (*infastidirsi*) get annoyed. **secca** *sf* shallow; (*fig*) fix. **seccante** boring; annoying. **seccato** *agg* annoyed; (*fam*) fed up. **seccatore, -trice** *sm, sf* nuisance. **seccatura** *sf* nuisance. **secco** *agg* dry; (*essicato*) dried; (*fig*) sharp. **lavare a secco** dry-clean. **rimanere in secco** be left high and dry.
secchia ['sekkja] *sf* bucket. **secchio** *sm* pail; (*per carbone*) coal-scuttle. **secchione** *sm* (*fam: sgobbone*) swot.
***secernere** [se'tʃɛrnere] *v* secrete.
secessione [setʃes'sjone] *sf* secession.
secolo ['sɛkolo] *sm* century; (*periodo*) age. **al secolo** alias. **secolare** *agg* centuries old; (*laico*) secular.
secondino [sekon'dino] *sm* warder.
secondo[1] [se'kondo] *sm, agg* second. **in un secondo tempo** on a later occasion. **secondo fine** *sm* ulterior motive.
secondo[2] [se'kondo] *prep* according to; depending on. *inter* it depends!
secrezione [sekre'tsjone] *sf* secretion.
sedano ['sɛdano] *sm* celery. **sedano rapa** celeriac.
sedare [se'dare] *v* calm; (*reprimere*) quell. **sedativo** *agg, sm* sedative.
sede ['sɛde] *sf* seat; (*comm*) office; residence; (*seduta*) sitting. **in altra sede** (*luogo*) elsewhere; (*tempo*) some other time. **Santa Sede** Holy See. **sede centrale** headquarters. **sede legale** registered office.
***sedere** [se'dere] *v* sit (down). **dar da sedere** offer a seat. **sedersi** *v* sit down, take a seat. **tirarsi su a sedere** sit up. *sm* (*deretano*) bottom. **sedentario** *agg* sedentary.
sedia ['sɛdja] *sf* chair.
sedicente [sedi'tʃɛnte] *agg* so-called, would-be.
sedici ['seditʃi] *agg, sm* sixteen. **sedicesimo** *sm, agg* sixteenth.
sedile [se'dile] *sm* seat.
sedimento [sedi'mento] *sm* sediment. **sedimentazione** *sf* sedimentation.
sedizione [sedi'tsjone] *sf* sedition; rebellion. **sedizioso** *agg* seditious.
***sedurre** [se'durre] *v* seduce; (*attrarre*) entice. **seducente** *agg* alluring, tempting. **seduttore, -trice** *agg* seductive. **seduzione** *sf* seduction; temptation.
seduta [se'duta] *sf* session; (*pasto, posa*) sitting; (*riunione*) meeting. **seduta spiritica** seance. **seduta stante** forthwith.
sega ['sega] *sf* saw. **a sega** saw-toothed. **sega a catena** chain-saw. **sega da traforo** fretsaw. **segare** *v* saw. **segatrice** *sf* saw. **segatura** *sf* (*azione*) sawing; (*frammenti*) sawdust.
segale ['segale] *sf* rye.
seggio ['sɛddʒo] *sm* seat; (*carica*) chair. **seggiola** *sf* chair. **seggiolino** *sm* seat. **seggiolone** *sm* armchair; (*per bambini*) high chair.
seggiovia [seddʒo'via] *sf* chair-lift.
seghettare [seget'tare] *v* serrate.
segmento [seg'mento] *sm* segment. **segmentare** *v* divide up. **segmentazione** *sf* segmentation; (*fig*) breaking up.

segnalare [seɲa'lare] *v* signal; (*indicare*) point out; (*render noto*) report. **segnalato** *agg* announced, reported; (*straordinario*) outstanding. **segnalatore** *sm* (*persona*) signaller; indicator; alarm. **segnalazione** *sf* signalling; report; notification; (*nota informativa*) notice. **segnalazione stradale** road sign. **segnale** *sm* signal; (*cartello*) sign; (*telefono*) tone. **segnaletica** *sf* road signs *pl*.

segnalibro [seɲa'libro] *sm* bookmark.

segnapunti [seɲa'punti] *sm invar* (*tabellone*) score-board; (*libretto*) score-book.

segnare [se'ɲare] *v* mark; (*marchiare*) brand. **segnare i punti** keep the score. **segnare le ore** tell the time.

segno ['seɲo] *sm* sign; (*traccia*) mark. **come** *or* **in segno di** as a sign of, in token of. **essere segno che** mean. **tiro a segno** *sm* target practice.

sego ['sego] *sm* fallow.

segregare [segre'gare] *v* segregate, set apart. **segregazione** *sf* segregation; isolation. **segregazione cellulare** solitary confinement.

segretario [segre'tarjo], **-a** *sm*, *sf* secretary; (*chi redige verbali, ecc.*) clerk. **segretariato** *sm* secretariat. **segreteria** *sf* secretary's office; (*enti pubblici*) secretariat.

segreto [se'greto] *agg* secret. *sm* secret; (*intimità*) depth; (*segretezza*) secrecy. **in segreto** in secret; (*riservatamente*) confidentially. **nel segreto più assoluto** in utmost secrecy. **segreti del mestiere** tricks of the trade *pl*. **segreto di Pulcinella** open secret. **segreta** *sf* dungeon. **segretezza** *sf* secrecy.

seguace [se'gwatʃe] *s*(*m*+*f*) follower; disciple.

seguente [se'gwɛnte] *agg* following; (*futuro*) next.

segugio [se'gudʒo] *sm* bloodhound; (*fig*) sleuth.

seguire [se'gwire] *v* follow; (*frequentare*) attend. **segue a tergo** continued overleaf, PTO. **seguitare** *v* continue. **seguito** *sm* following; succession; favour; continuation; consequence. **di seguito** on end, non-stop. **in seguito** later (on). **in seguito a** as a result of, because of.

sei ['sɛi] *agg*, *sm* six.

selce ['seltʃe] *sf* flint; (*strada*) paving-stone. **selciato** *sm* paving.

selettivo [selet'tivo] *agg* selective. **selettività** *sf* selectivity. **selettore, -trice** *sm*, *sf* selector.

selezionare [seletsjo'nare] *v* select; grade. **selezionamento** *sm* selection. **selezione** *sf* selection; (*scelta*) choice. **selezione automatica** (*telefono*) automatic dialling, STD.

sella ['sɛlla] *sf* saddle. **sellare** *v* saddle.

seltz ['sɛlts] *sm invar* soda-water.

selva ['selva] *sf* forest. **selvoso** *agg* wooded.

selvaggio [sel'vaddʒo], **-a** *agg* wild; (*incivile*) savage. *sm*, *sf* savage. **selvaggina** *sf* game. **selvatico** *agg* wild; (*scontroso*) uncouth.

semaforo [se'maforo] *sm* traffic lights *pl*.

semantica [se'mantika] *sf* semantics. **semantico** *agg* semantic.

sembrare [sem'brare] *v* seem. **cosa te ne sembra?** what do you think of it?

seme ['seme] *sm* seed; (*di mele, pere, ecc.*) pip; (*carte da gioco*) suit. **sementa** *sf* (*operazione*) sowing; (*semente*) seed. **semente** *sf* seed. **semenza** *sf* seed; (*perle*) seed-pearls *pl*.

semestre [se'mɛstre] *sm* half-year. **semestrale** *agg* half-yearly.

semibreve [semi'brɛve] *sf* semibreve.

semicerchio [semi'tʃerkjo] *sm* semicircle.

semicircolare [semitʃirko'lare] *agg* semicircular.

semicroma [semi'krɔma] *sf* semiquaver.

semidio [semi'dio] *sm* demi-god.

semifinale [semifi'nale] *sf* semifinal. **semifinalista** *s*(*m*+*f*) semifinalist.

semiminima [semi'minima] *sf* crotchet.

seminare [semi'nare] *v* sow; (*fig*) scatter, strew. **semina** *sf* sowing. **seminale** *agg* seminal. **uscire dal seminato** digress.

seminario [semi'narjo] *sm* (*rel*) seminary; (*università*) seminar. **seminarista** *sm* seminarist.

seminterrato [seminter'rato] *sm* basement.

seminudo [semi'nudo] *agg* half-naked.

semita [se'mita] *s*(*m*+*f*) Semite. *agg also* **semitico** Semitic.

semitono [semi'tɔno] *sm* semitone.

semivivo [semi'vivo] *agg* half-dead.

semola ['semola] *sf* (*crusca*) bran. **semolino** *sm* semolina.

semovente [semo'vɛnte] *agg* self-propelled.

semplice ['semplitʃe] *agg* simple; (*di un solo elemento*) single; (*senza affettazione*) plain. **semplicemente** *avv* simply; (*soltanto*) only. **semplicione** *sm* simpleton. **semplicità** *sf* simplicity. **semplificare** *v* simplify; facilitate. **semplificazione** *sf* simplification.

sempre ['sɛmpre] *avv* always; (*ancora*) still. **da sempre** from the beginning. **per sempre** for ever. **sempre che** (*purché*) as long as, provided that; (*ammesso che*) supposing that. **sempre più** more and more. **sempreverde** *s*(*m*+*f*), *agg* evergreen. **una volta per sempre** once and for all.

senape ['sɛnape] *sf* mustard.

senato [se'nato] *sm* senate. **senatore** *sm* senator.

senile [se'nile] *agg* senile. **senilità** *sf* senility.

senno ['senno] *sm* wits *pl*; (*sensatezza*) (common) sense. **con senno** sensibly. **senno di poi** hindsight. **uscir di senno** go out of one's mind.

seno ['seno] *sm* bosom, breast; (*grembo*) womb; (*anat*) sinus; (*mat*) sine; (*geog*) inlet. **allattare al seno** breast-feed. **in seno a** (*nel mezzo di*) within; (*tra le braccia*) in the arms of.

sensale [sen'sale] *sm* broker.

sensato [sen'sato] *agg* sensible. **sensatezza** *sf* good sense.

sensazione [sensa'tsjone] *sf* feeling, sensation. **sensazionale** *agg* sensational.

sensibile [sen'sibile] *agg* (*che sente*) sensitive; (*notevole*) appreciable; perceptible; susceptible. **sensibilità** *sf* sensitivity. **sensibilizzare** *v* sensitize.

sensitivo [sensi'tivo] *agg* (*funzione*) sensory; (*sensibile*) sensitive. **sensitività** *sf* sensitivity.

senso ['sɛnso] *sm* sense; (*significato*) meaning; (*direzione, modo*) way. **a senso** in one's own words; (*tradurre*) freely. **far senso** (*ripugnare*) disgust. **in senso antiorario** anticlockwise. **in senso orario** clockwise. **non aver senso** not make sense; be pointless. **senso proibito** no entry. **senso unico** one-way. **sensorio** *agg* sensory. **sensuale** *agg* sensual; sensuous. **sensualità** *sf* sensuality; sensuousness.

sentenza [sen'tɛntsa] *sf* sentence, judgment; (*massima*) saying. **sputare sentenze** be sententious. **sentenziare** *v* pass judgment *or* sentence; rule; decree. **sentenzioso** *agg* sententious.

sentiero [sen'tjɛro] *sm* path.

sentimento [senti'mento] *sm* feeling; (*concetto*) sense. **sentimenti** *sm pl* (*modo di sentire*) sentiments *pl*.

sentinella [senti'nɛlla] *sf* sentry.

sentire [sen'tire] *v* feel; (*col gusto*) taste; (*con l'udito*) hear; (*con l'olfatto*) smell; (*dare ascolto*) listen to; (*aver notizia*) gather. **al mio modo di sentire** to my way of thinking. **sentirsela** *v* feel like. **sentirsi** *v* feel.

sentito [sen'tito] *agg* (*udito*) heard; sincere. **per sentito dire** by hearsay.

sentore [sen'tore] *sm* inkling.

senza ['sɛntsa] *prep* without. **rimanere senza** run out of. **senza contare** apart from; over and above. **senza dire** not to mention. **senza fallo** certainly. **senz'altro** definitely. **senza soldi** penniless. **senzatetto** *s*(*m*+*f*) *invar* homeless person.

separare [sepa'rare] *v* separate, divide. **separarsi** *v* part; (*coniugi*) separate. **separazione** *sf* separation, division; parting.

sepolcro [se'polkro] *sm* tomb. **sepolcrale** *agg* sepulchral.

sepolto [se'polto] *agg* buried. **sepoltura** *sf* burial.

***seppellire** [seppel'lire] *v* bury.

seppia ['seppja] *sf* (*zool*) cuttlefish. *agg, sm invar* (*colore*) sepia.

seppure [sep'pure] *cong* even though, even if.

sequela [se'kwɛla] *sf* succession.

sequestrare [sekwes'trare] *v* seize, confiscate; (*persona*) imprison unlawfully; (*rapire*) kidnap. **sequestro** *sm* seizure, confiscation; kidnapping; illegal confinement.

sera ['sera] *sf* evening, night. **buona sera!** (*di pomeriggio*) good afternoon! (*di sera*) good evening! **si fa sera** it is getting dark. **serale** *agg* evening, night. **serata** *sf* evening, night; (*ricevimento*) party; (*teatro*) performance.

serbare [ser'bare] *v* (*mantenere*) keep; (*metter da parte*) put aside. **serbare gratitudine verso** be grateful to. **serbatoio** *sm* tank; (*penna*) barrel; (*fucile, ecc.*) magazine.

serbo ['sɛrbo] *sm* **dare in serbo** put into

custody. **mettere in serbo** put by *or* aside. **tenere in serbo** keep in store.
serenata [sere'nata] *sf* serenade.
serenella [sere'nɛlla] *sf* lilac.
sereno [se'reno] *agg* calm, serene; (*cielo*) clear; (*senza preoccupazioni*) carefree; objective. *sm* clear sky; (*aperto*) open air. **serenità** *sf* serenity; objectivity.
sergente [ser'dʒɛnte] *sm* sergeant.
serico ['sɛriko] *agg* silk.
serie ['sɛrje] *sf invar* series; (*assortimento*) set; (*sport*) division. **fuori serie** (*auto*) custom-built. **modello di serie** *sm* production model. **prodotto in serie** mass-produced. **produzione in serie** *sf* mass-production.
serio ['sɛrjo] *agg* serious; (*degno di fiducia*) trustworthy; (*comm*) reputable. *sm* seriousness. **sul serio** (*seriamente*) seriously; (*davvero*) really. **serietà** *sf* seriousness; (*fidatezza*) reliability.
sermone [ser'mone] *sm* sermon; (*rimprovero*) lecture.
serpeggiare [serped'dʒare] *v* wind.
serpente [ser'pɛnte] *sm* snake, serpent. **serpente a sonagli** rattlesnake. **serpentino** *agg* snake-like.
serra ['sɛrra] *sf* greenhouse, hothouse.
serraglio [ser'raʎo] *sm* menagerie.
serrare [ser'rare] *v* close; (*a chiave*) lock; (*stringere*) tighten; (*denti, pugni*) clench. **serrare al cuore** embrace. **serramento** *sm* (*di finestra*) window-frame; (*di porta*) door-frame. **serrata** *sf* lock-out. **serrato** *agg* closed; (*fila*) serried; (*fig*) to the point.
serratura [serra'tura] *sf* lock. **buco della serratura** *sm* keyhole. **serratura a cilindro** Yale lock ®. **serratura a lucchetto** padlock. **serratura a scatto** latch.
servire [ser'vire] *v* serve; (*fam: occorrere*) be useful; (*carte da gioco*) deal. **a cosa serve?** what is the use? **cosa ti serve?** what do you need? **posso servirti?** can I help you? **servirsi** *v* use; make use; (*di cibo*) help oneself. **servile** *agg* servile; (*fig*) slavish. **servitore** *sm* servant. **servitù** *sf* (*schiavitù*) slavery; (*personale di servizio*) servants *pl*. **ridurre in servitù** enslave.
servizio [ser'vitsjo] *sm* service; (*lavoro*) work; favour; (*giornale*) report; (*turno*) duty. **a mezzo servizio** part-time. **donna di servizio** *sf* maid. **fare servizio** (*trasporto*) run; (*negozio*) be open. **fuori servizio** off duty; (*che non funziona*) out of order. **in servizio** on duty. **servizievole** *agg* obliging.
servo ['sɛrvo], **-a** *sm, sf* servant.
sesamo ['sɛzamo] *sm* sesame.
sessanta [ses'santa] *agg, sm* sixty. **sessantesimo** *agg, sm* sixtieth.
sessione [ses'sjone] *sf* session.
sesso ['sɛsso] *sm* sex. **sessuale** *agg* sexual. **sessualità** *sf* sexuality.
sestetto [ses'tetto] *sm* sextet.
sesto[1] ['sɛsto] *sm, agg* sixth.
sesto[2] ['sɛsto] *sm* order; (*di arco*) curve. **mettere in sesto** tidy up. **rimettersi in sesto** get back on one's feet again.
seta ['seta] *sf* silk.
setaccio [se'tattʃo] *sm* sieve. **setacciare** *v also* **passare al setaccio** sift, sieve.
sete ['sete] *sf* thirst. **aver sete** be thirsty. **mettere la seta a** make thirsty.
setola ['setola] *sf* bristle.
setta ['sɛtta] *sf* sect. *agg, sm* sectarian.
settanta [set'tanta] *agg, sm* seventy. **settantesimo** *agg, sm* seventieth.
sette ['sɛtte] *agg, sm* seven. **settimo** *agg, sm* seventh.
settembre [set'tɛmbre] *sm* September.
settentrione [setten'trjone] *sm* north. **settentrionale** *agg* northern, north.
settico ['sɛttiko] *agg* septic. **setticemia** *sf* blood-poisoning.
settimana [setti'mana] *sf* week; (*paga*) week's wages. **a metà settimana** mid-week. **a settimane** by the week; (*una si e una no*) every other week. **fine settimana** *sf* week-end. **settimanale** *agg, sm* weekly.
settore [set'tore] *sm* sector; (*campo*) field.
severo [se'vɛro] *agg* severe, strict; (*grave*) serious. **severità** *sf* severity.
seviziare [sevi'tsjare] *v* torture; (*violentare*) rape. **sevizie** *sf pl* torture *sing*.
sezione [se'tsjone] *sf* section; (*tribunale*) division; (*sezionamento*) dissection. **sezionare** *v* dissect; (*dividere in sezioni*) section.
sfaccendato [sfattʃen'dato], **-a** *agg* idle. *sm, sf* loafer.
sfaccettare [sfattʃet'tare] *v* cut.
sfacchinare [sfakki'nare] *v* slave. **sfacchinata** *sf* heavy work.
sfacciato [sfat'tʃato], **-a** *agg* impudent; (*svergognato*) shameless; (*vistoso*) gaudy. *sm, sf* impudent *or* shameless person.

sfacciataggine *sf* impudence; shamelessness.
sfacelo [sfa'tʃɛlo] *sm* ruin; (*disfacimento*) decay. **andare in sfacelo** break up; (*fam*) go to rack and ruin.
sfaldarsi [sfal'darsi] *v* flake; (*sbriciolarsi*) crumble. **sfaldatura** *sf* flaking; crumbling.
sfalsare [sfal'sare] *v* stagger.
sfamare [sfa'mare] *v* feed. **sfamarsi** *v* satisfy one's hunger.
sfarfallare [sfarfal'lare] *v* (*svolazzare*) flutter; (*esser volubile*) flit; (*auto*) wobble.
sfarzo ['sfartso] *sm* magnificence, pomp. **senza sfarzo** simply. **sfarzosità** *sf* sumptuousness; ostentation. **sfarzoso** *agg* sumptuous; ostentatious.
sfasciare [sfa'ʃare] *v* (*rompere*) smash.
sfatare [sfa'tare] *v* refute.
sfavillante [sfavil'lante] *agg* glittering, sparkling.
sfavore [sfa'vore] *sm* disfavour, discredit. **andare a sfavore di** go against. **sfavorevole** *agg* unfavourable; (*contrario*) adverse.
sfegatato [sfega'tato] *agg* passionate.
sfera ['sfɛra] *sf* sphere; (*ambiente*) circle; (*campo*) field. **cuscinetto a sfere** *sm* ball-bearing. **penna a sfera** *sf* ball-point pen. **sferico** *agg* spherical.
sferrare [sfer'rare] *v* (*attacco*) launch; (*pugno*) deal. **sferrare un calcio** kick.
sferza ['sfɛrtsa] *sf* whip. **sferzare** *v* whip; lash.
sfiatato [sfja'tato] *agg* breathless; (*strumento musicale*) cracked; (*fam*) hoarse.
sfibrare [sfi'brare] *v* (*indebolire*) weaken. **sfibrante** *agg* enervating. **sfibrato** *agg* exhausted.
sfida ['sfida] *sf* challenge. **sfidare** *v* challenge; (*invitare*) defy; (*fig*) brave.
sfiducia [sfi'dutʃa] *sf* distrust. **avere sfiducia di** distrust; lack confidence in. **sfiduciarsi** *v* lose confidence. **sfiduciato** *agg* distrustful; (*di sè stesso*) diffident; (*scoraggiato*) disheartened.
sfigurare [sfigu'rare] *v* disfigure; make a bad impression.
sfilacciare [sfilat'tʃare] *v* fray.
sfilare[1] [sfi'lare] *v* (*togliere di dosso*) take off; (*ago*) unthread.
sfilare[2] [sfi'lare] *v* parade. **sfilata** *sf* parade; (*lunga fila*) long row.
sfilza ['sfiltsa] *sf* string.
sfinge ['sfindʒe] *sf* sphinx.
sfinire [sfi'nire] *v* wear out. **sfinimento** *sm* exhaustion.
sfiorare [sfjo'rare] *v* skim (over); (*toccando*) graze, barely touch; (*successo, ecc.*) be on the verge of.
sfiorito [sfjo'rito] *agg* withered.
sfitto ['sfitto] *agg* vacant.
sfocato [sfo'kato] *agg* (*foto*) out of focus; (*fig*) hazy.
sfociare [sfo'tʃare] *v* flow (into); (*fig*) result. **sfocio** *sm* outlet.
sfogare [sfo'gare] *v* let out; (*fig*) give vent to. **sfogarsi** *v* (*sfogar l'ira*) give vent to one's anger; (*confidarsi*) pour out one's heart; (*bambino*) run wild. **sfogo** *sm* outlet; (*sollievo*) relief.
sfoggiare [sfod'dʒare] *v* show off. **sfoggio** *sm* display; ostentation.
sfogliare[1] [sfo'ʎare] *v* *also* **dare una sfogliata a** (*pagine*) leaf or skim through.
sfogliare[2] [sfo'ʎare] *v* (*levar le foglie*) strip (of leaves). **sfoglia** *sf* leaf; (*gastr*) puff pastry.
sfolgorare [sfolgo'rare] *v* blaze; (*occhi*) shine.
sfollare [sfol'lare] *v* disperse; evacuate. **sfollamento** *sm* evacuation. **sfollato, -a** *sm, sf* evacuee.
sfondare [sfon'dare] *v* break through; (*schiantare*) smash; (*logorare*) wear out. **sfondato** *agg* (*senza fondo*) bottomless; (*logoro*) worn out. **ricco sfondato** rolling in money. **sfondo** *sm* background, setting.
sformare [sfor'mare] *v* pull out of shape; (*estrarre dalla forma*) turn out. **sformato** *sm* (*gastr*) pie.
sfornito [sfor'nito] *agg* **sfornito di** lacking in, without.
sfortuna [sfor'tuna] *sf* bad luck; (*contrattempo*) misfortune. **sfortunato** *agg* unlucky; (*senza successo*) unfortunate.
sforzare [sfor'tsare] *v* force, strain. **sforzarsi di** try hard to. **sforzo** *sm* effort.
sfottere ['sfottere] *v* (*fam*) take the mickey (out of). **sfottimento** *sm* teasing, ridicule.
sfracellare [sfratʃel'lare] *v* shatter.
sfrangiato [sfran'dʒato] *agg* fringed.
sfrattare [sfrat'tare] *v* turn out, evict. **sfratto** *sm* eviction.
sfregare [sfre'gare] *v* rub; (*lucidando*) polish; (*lavando*) scrub. **sfregamento** *sm* rubbing; polishing; scrubbing.

sfrenare [sfre'nare] *v* let loose. **sfrenatezza** *sf* lack of restraint; wild behaviour. **sfrenato** *agg* unbridled; (*senza ritegno*) immoderate.

***sfriggere** ['sfriddʒere] *v also* **sfrigolare** sizzle.

sfrondare [sfron'dare] *v* prune.

sfrontato [sfron'tato] *agg* impudent, brazen; (*fam*) cheeky. **sfrontatezza** *sf* effrontery; (*fam*) cheek.

sfruttare [sfrut'tare] *v* exploit. **sfruttamento** *sm* exploitation; utilization. **sfruttatore, -trice** *sm, sf* exploiter.

sfuggire [sfud'dʒire] *v* shun; (*scappare*) escape from. **lasciarsi sfuggire** let slip; (*occasione*) let go by. **sfuggire di mano** slip out of one's hand. **sfuggire di mente** slip one's mind. **sfuggente** *agg* (*mento, fronte*) receding. **di sfuggita** fleetingly.

sfumare [sfu'mare] *v* (*svanire*) disappear; (*colori, suoni*) fade away, tone down. **sfumato** *agg* (*pittura*) shaded; (*fig*) vague. **sfumatura** *sf* nuance.

sfuriata [sfu'rjata] *sf* outburst; (*tempesta*) storm; (*rabbuffo*) telling-off.

sfuso ['sfuzo] *agg* (*sciolto*) loose; (*liquefatto*) melted.

sgabello [zga'bɛllo] *sm* stool.

sgabuzzino [zgabut'tsino] *sm* cubby-hole.

sgambettare [zgambet'tare] *v* (*camminare a piccoli passi*) toddle (along); (*fare lo sgambetto*) trip up.

sganciare [zgan'tʃare] *v* unhook; (*bombe*) release; (*fam: sborsare*) fork out.

sgangherato [zgange'rato] *agg* (*sfasciato*) rickety; (*sconnesso*) incoherent; (*esagerato*) boisterous.

sgarbato [zgar'bato] *agg* rude, discourteous. **sgarbatezza** *sf* rudeness, discourtesy.

sgarbugliare [zgarbu'ʎare] *v* disentangle.

sgargiante [zgar'dʒante] *agg* showy.

sgarrare [zgar'rare] *v* be *or* go wrong.

sgelare [zdʒe'lare] *v* thaw out; (*surgelati*) defrost.

sghembo ['zgembo] *agg* crooked. **di sghembo** askew.

sgherro ['zgɛrro] *sm* thug.

sghignazzare [zgiɲat'tsare] *v* laugh sarcastically, sneer; (*sguaiatamente*) guffaw. **sghignazzata** *sf* sarcastic laughter; guffaw.

sghiribizzo [zgiri'bittso] *sm* whim.

sgobbare [zgob'bare] (*fam*) *v* slave. **sgobbata** *sf* grind. **sgobbone, -a** *sm, sf* slogger; (*studente*) swot.

sgocciolare [zgottʃo'lare] *v* drip; (*vuotare*) drain. **sgocciolatura** *sf* dripping; (*macchie*) drips *pl*. **essere agli sgoccioli** be *or* have nearly finished.

sgolarsi [zgo'larsi] *v* shout oneself hoarse.

sgombrare [zgom'brare] *v also* **sgomberare** clear; (*vuotare*) empty; (*portar via*) clear away; evacuate; (*lasciar libero*) vacate.

sgombro[1] ['zgombro] *sm also* **sgombero** (*trasloco*) move; clearing (away); evacuation. *agg* clear; empty.

sgombro[2] ['zgombro] *V* **scombro**.

sgomentare [zgomen'tare] *v* dismay. **sgomento** *sm* dismay.

sgonfiare [zgon'fjare] *v* deflate; (*fam*) annoy. **sgonfiarsi** *v* go down; (*pneumatico*) go flat; (*fig*) be deflated. **sgonfio** *agg* deflated, flat.

sgorbia ['zgɔrbja] *sf* gouge.

sgorbio ['zgɔrbjo] *sm* (*macchia*) blot; (*scarabocchio*) scrawl.

sgorgare [zgor'gare] *v* gush (out); (*uscire*) spring.

sgradevole [zgra'devole] *agg* disagreeable, unpleasant. **sgradito** *agg* disagreeable; (*non gradito*) unwelcome.

sgrammaticato [zgrammati'kato] *agg* ungrammatical.

sgranare [zgra'nare] *v* shell; (*occhi*) open wide.

sgranchire [zgran'kire] *v* stretch.

sgravare [zgra'vare] *v* relieve; (*partorire*) give birth.

sgraziato [zgra'tsjato] *agg* ungainly, awkward.

sgretolare [zgreto'lare] *v* break up. **sgretolarsi** *v* crumble. **sgretolato** *agg* crumbling.

sgridare [zgri'dare] *v* scold; (*fam*) tell off. **sgridata** *sf* scolding; (*fam*) telling-off.

sguaiato [zgwa'jato] *agg* unseemly; vulgar; (*grossolano*) coarse. **sguaiataggine** *sf* vulgarity; coarseness.

sgualcire [zgwal'tʃire] *v* crease, crumple.

sgualdrina [zgwal'drina] *sf* (*spreg*) tart.

sguardo ['zgwardo] *sm* look; (*occhiata*) glance; (*fisso*) stare; (*prolungato*) gaze. **al primo sguardo** at first sight. **fissare lo sguardo su** stare at. **gettare uno sguardo su** glance at.

sguarnire [zgwar'nire] *v* strip.

sguattero ['zgwattero], **-a** *sm, sf* skivvy.

sguazzare [zgwat'tsare] *v* splash about; (*fig*) wallow.
sguinzagliare [zgwintsa'ʎare] *v* let loose.
sgusciare[1] [zgu'ʃare] *v* (*scivolare*) slip.
sgusciare[2] [zgu'ʃare] *v* shell; (*uova, noci*) crack.
shampoo [ʃam'pu] *sm invar* shampoo.
si [si] *pron* (*lui*) himself; (*lei*) herself; (*cosa, animale*) itself; (*loro*) themselves; (*reciproco*) each other; (*riflessivo*) oneself; (*indefinito*) one.
sì [si] *avv* yes. **credo di sì** I think so. **dire di sì** say yes. **far cenno di sì** nod. **spero di sì** I hope so. **un giorno sì e uno no** every other day.
sia ['sia] *cong* **sia ... sia ...** whether ... or ... ; (*entrambi*) both.
siamese [sia'meze] *agg*, *s*(*m*+*f*) Siamese.
sibilare [sibi'lare] *v* hiss. **sibilo** *sm* hiss.
sicario [si'karjo] *sm* hired assassin.
sicché [sik'ke] *cong* (*di modo che*) and so; (*e perciò*) so that.
siccità [sittʃi'ta] *sf* drought.
siccome [sik'kome] *cong* as, since.
Sicilia [si'tʃilja] *sf* Sicily. **siciliano, -a** *s*, *agg* Sicilian.
sicomoro [siko'mɔro] *sm* sycamore.
sicura [si'kura] *sf* safety catch.
sicurezza [siku'rettsa] *sf* safety; certainty; (*garanzia*) security; (*confidenza*) self-assurance. **di sicurezza** safety. **per maggior sicurezza** to be on the safe side. **pubblica sicurezza** police. **sicurezza sociale** social security; welfare.
sicuro [si'kuro] *agg* safe; (*tranquillo*) secure; certain, sure; (*fidato*) reliable; (*saldo*) steady. *sm* safety; safe place. **andar sul sicuro** take no chances. **dare per sicuro** be certain about. **di sicuro** certainly. **star sicuro** not worry.
sidro ['sidro] *sm* cider.
siepe ['sjɛpe] *sf* hedge.
siero ['sjɛro] *sm* serum.
siesta ['sjɛsta] *sf* siesta; (*fam*) nap. **fare la siesta** take a nap.
sifilide [si'filide] *sf* syphilis.
sifone [si'fone] *sm* siphon.
sigaretta [siga'retta] *sf* cigarette. **sigaro** *sm* cigar.
sigillare [sidʒil'lare] *v* seal. **sigillatura** *sf* sealing, seal. **sigillo** *sm* seal. **anello con sigillo** *sm* signet-ring.
sigla ['sigla] *sf* initials *pl*; (*auto*) registration number. **sigla musicale** signature tune. **siglare** *v* initial.
significare [siɲifi'kare] *v* mean; (*simboleggiare*) stand for. **significativo** *agg* meaningful, significant; important. **significato** *sm* meaning; importance.
signora [si'ɲora] *sf* lady; (*donna*) woman (*pl* women); (*cortesia*) madam; (*seguito dal cognome*) Mrs; (*padrona*) mistress; (*moglie*) wife. **fare la signora** live like a lady.
signore [si'ɲore] *sm* gentleman; (*uomo*) man (*pl* men); (*cortesia*) sir; (*seguito dal cognome*) Mr; (*padrone*) master.
signoreggiare [siɲored'dʒare] *v* rule.
signoria [siɲo'ria] *sf* domination.
signorile [siɲo'rile] *agg* elegant, high-class; (*uomo*) gentlemanly; (*donna*) ladylike. **signorilità** *sf* elegance; refinement.
signorina [siɲo'rina] *sf* young lady *or* woman; (*cortesia*) madam; (*seguito dal cognome*) Miss; (*non sposata*) unmarried woman. **nome da signorina** *sm* maiden name.
silenzio [si'lɛntsjo] *sm* silence. **far silenzio** be quiet. **silenziare** *v* muffle. **silenziatore** *sm* silencer. **silenzioso** *agg* silent, quiet.
silicio [si'litʃo] *sm* silicon. **silice** *sf* silica. **silicone** *sm* silicone. **silicosi** *sf* silicosis.
sillaba ['sillaba] *sf* syllable. **sillabare** *v* (*gramm*) syllabify; (*fig*) spell out. **sillabario** *sm* spelling book.
silo ['silo] *sm* silo.
silofono [si'lɔfono] *sm* xylophone.
silurare [silu'rare] *v* torpedo; (*far fallire*) wreck; (*destituire*) dismiss. **siluramento** *sm* torpedoing; wrecking; dismissal. **siluro** *sm* torpedo.
silvestre [sil'vɛstre] *agg* woody; (*selvaggio*) wild.
silvia ['silvja] *sf* (*bot*) wood anemone; (*zool*) warbler.
simbolo ['simbolo] *sm* symbol; (*rel*) creed. **simboleggiare** *v* symbolize. **simbolico** *agg* symbolic.
simile ['simile] *agg* like, similar; (*predicato*) alike; (*tale*) such. **similitudine** *sf* simile.
simmetria [simme'tria] *sf* symmetry. **simmetrico** *agg* symmetrical.
simpatia [simpa'tia] *sf* (*sentimento di attrazione*) liking; (*qualità*) likeableness; (*affinità*) sympathy. **avere** *or* **provare simpatia per** like, take to. **simpatico** *agg* nice, likeable; (*piacevole*) agreeable; (*anat*) sympathetic. **simpatizzare** *v* sympathize.

simposio [sim'pɔzjo] *sm* symposium.
simulare [simu'lare] *v* feign; (*imitare*) simulate. **simulacro** *sm* image; (*fig*) semblance. **simulazione** *sf* simulation.
simultaneo [simul'taneo] *agg* simultaneous. **simultaneità** *sf* simultaneity.
sinagoga [sina'gɔga] *sf* synagogue.
sincero [sin'tʃɛro] *agg* sincere, true; (*non artefatto*) genuine. **sincerità** *sf* sincerity.
sincopare [sinko'pare] *v* syncopate. **sincope** *sf* syncope; (*musica*) syncopation.
sincronizzare [sinkronid'dzare] *v* synchronize. **sincronizzatore** *sm* synchronizer. **sincronizzazione** *sf* synchronization.
sindacale [sinda'kale] *agg* (*di sindacato*) (trade) union. **sindacalismo** *sm* trade unionism. **sindacalista** *s(m+f)* trade unionist.
sindacare [sinda'kare] *v* check; (*contabilità*) audit; (*fig*) criticize.
sindacato [sinda'kato] *sm* (*operaio*) trade union; (*padronale, d'impresa*) consortium; (*finanziario*) syndicate.
sindaco ['sindako] *sm* mayor; (*comm*) auditor.
sindrome ['sindrome] *sf* syndrome.
sinfonia [sinfo'nia] *sf* symphony. **sinfonico** *agg* symphonic. **orchestra sinfonica** *sf* symphony orchestra.
singhiozzare [singjot'tsare] *v* (*avere il singhiozzo*) hiccup; (*piangere*) sob. **singhiozzo** *sm* sob; hiccup. **a singhiozzi** by fits and starts.
singolare [singo'lare] *agg* singular; (*strano*) strange. *sm* singular. **singolarità** *sf* singularity; strangeness.
singolo ['singolo] *agg* single, individual. *sm* (*persona*) individual; (*telefono*) private line; (*tennis*) singles; (*canottaggio*) skiff.
sinistra [si'nistra] *sf* left(-hand side); (*mano*) left hand. **a sinistra** on *or* to the left. **tenere la sinistra** keep to the left. **uomo di sinistra** *sm* left-winger.
sinistrare [sinis'trare] *v* damage. **sinistrato, -a** *sm, sf* victim. **zona sinistrata** *sf* disaster area.
sinistro [si'nistro] *agg* left; (*lato*) left-hand; (*fig*) sinister. *sm* accident; (*pugilato*) left.
sino ['sino] *cong* **sino a** (*tempo*) until; (*luogo*) as far as. *avv* (*persino*) even. **sinora** *avv* (*per ora*) so far; (*fino ad ora*) up to now.
sinossi [si'nɔssi] *sf* synopsis (*pl* -ses). **sinottico** *agg* synoptic.
sintassi [sin'tassi] *sf* syntax. **sintattico** *agg* syntactic(al).
sintesi ['sintezi] *sf* synthesis (*pl* -ses). **in sintesi** (*in poche parole*) in short; (*sommariamente*) summing up. **sintetico** *agg* synthetic; (*fig*) concise. **sintetizzare** *v* synthesize; (*riassumere*) summarize.
sintomo ['sintomo] *sm* symptom. **sintomatico** *agg* symptomatic.
sintonizzare [sintonid'dzare] *v* tune in.
sinuoso [sinu'ozo] *agg* sinuous, winding.
sinusite [sinu'zite] *sf* sinusitis.
sipario [si'parjo] *sm* curtain.
sirena [si'rɛna] *sf* siren; (*creatura*) mermaid.
siringa [si'ringa] *sf* syringe; (*bot*) lilac; catheter. **siringare** *v* syringe; catheterize.
sismico ['sizmiko] *agg* seismic. **sismografo** *sm* seismograph.
sistema [sis'tɛma] *sm* system; (*modo di fare*) way; method. **sistemare** *v* (*mettere a posto*) arrange; (put in) order; (*risolvere*) settle; organize; (*collocare*) place; install. **sistemarsi** *v* settle (down); (*lavoro*) get a job. **sistematico** *agg* systematic; methodical. **sistemazione** *sf* arrangement; (*composizione*) settlement; (*alloggio*) accommodation; (*lavoro*) job.
situare [situ'are] *v* place; (*collocare*) locate. **situazione** *sf* situation. **situazione di fatto** state of affairs.
slabbrare [zlab'brare] *v* (*vasellame*) chip; (*tessuto*) tear.
slacciare [zlat'tʃare] *v* undo, untie.
slanciare [zlan'tʃare] *v* hurl. **slanciato** *agg* slender, slim. **slancio** *sm* swing; (*di passione, ecc.*) burst. **di slancio** in a rush; (*fig*) on impulse.
slattare [zlat'tare] *v* wean.
slavato [zla'vato] *agg* washed out; (*fig*) dull.
sleale [zle'ale] *agg* disloyal; (*fatto senza lealtà*) unfair. **gioco sleale** *sm* foul play. **slealtà** *sf* disloyalty; unfairness.
slegare [zle'gare] *v* untie. **slegato** *agg* untied; (*non rilegato*) unbound; (*fig*) disjointed.
slip [zlip] *sm invar* (*mutande*) briefs *pl*; (*da bagno*) swimming trunks *pl*.
slitta ['zlitta] *sf* sleigh, sledge; (*tec*) slide. **slittare** *v* slip; (*ruote*) skid; (*scivolare*) slide.

slogan ['zlɔgan] *sm invar* slogan.
slogare [zlo'gare] *v* dislocate. **slogatura** *sf* dislocation.
sloggiare [zlod'dʒare] *v* dislodge.
smacchiare [zmak'kjare] *v* clean. **smacchiatore** *sm* stain-remover. **smacchiatura** *sf* cleaning.
smacco ['zmakko] *sm* defeat.
smagliante [zma'ʎante] *agg* dazzling.
smagliarsi [zma'ʎarsi] *v* (*calze*) ladder; (*pelle*) stretch.
smagrire [zma'grire] *v* slim.
smaltare [zmal'tare] *v* enamel; (*unghie*) paint; (*ceramica*) glaze. **smalto** *sm* enamel; glaze; (*per le unghie*) nail-varnish.
smaltire [zmal'tire] *v* digest; (*fig*) swallow; (*comm*) dispose of.
smanceroso [zmantʃe'rozo] *agg* affected; (*smorfioso*) mawkish. **smanceria** *sf* affectation.
smania ['zmanja] *sf* craving; (*agitazione*) frenzy. **aver la smania addosso** fidget. **smaniare** *v* (*essere agitato*) fret; (*essere furioso*) rave; (*desiderare*) crave (for).
smantellare [zmantel'lare] *v* dismantle; (*fig*) pull to pieces.
smargiassata [zmardʒas'sata] *sf* brag; bravado. **smargiasso, -a** *sm, sf* braggart. **fare lo smargiasso** brag.
smarrire [zmar'rire] *v* lose; (*non riuscire a trovare*) mislay. **smarrirsi** *v* (*persone*) lose one's way; (*cose*) be mislaid, go astray. **smarrimento** *sm* loss; (*svenimento*) fainting-fit; (*turbamento*) bewilderment.
smascherare [zmaske'rare] *v* unmask, reveal. **smascheramento** *sm* unmasking.
smembrare [zmem'brare] *v* dismember.
smemorato [zmemo'rato], **-a** *agg* forgetful; (*distratto*) absent-minded. *sm, sf* forgetful *or* absent-minded person. **smemorataggine** *sf* forgetfulness; (*dimenticanza*) lapse of memory. **smemoratezza** *sf* forgetfulness; absent-mindedness.
smentire [zmen'tire] *v* deny; (*ritrattare*) retract; (*dimostrare la falsità*) belie. **smentita** *sf* denial.
smeraldo [zme'raldo] *sm* emerald. *agg invar* (*colore*) emerald-green.
smerciare [zmer'tʃare] *v* sell. **smercio** *sf* sale.
smerigliare [zmeri'ʎare] *v* (*mec*) grind; (*vetro*) frost. **carta smerigliata** *sf* (*grossa*) emery paper; (*fine*) sandpaper. **vetro smerigliato** *sm* frosted glass. **smeriglio** *sm* emery.
smerlare [zmer'lare] *v* scallop. **smerlo** *sm* scallop.
***smettere** ['zmettere] *v* stop.
smidollato [zmidol'lato] *agg* spineless.
smilitarizzare [zmilitarid'dzare] *v* demilitarize. **smilitarizzazione** *sf* demilitarization.
smilzo ['zmiltso] *agg* lean.
sminuire [zminu'ire] *v* diminish; (*fig*) belittle.
sminuzzare [zminut'tsare] *v* break into small pieces; (*sbriciolare*) crumble.
smistare [zmis'tare] *v* sort (out); (*ferr*) shunt.
smisurato [zmizu'rato] *agg* boundless; enormous.
smobilitare [zmobili'tare] *v* demobilize. **smobilitazione** *sf* demobilization.
smoderato [zmode'rato] *agg also* **smodato** immoderate. **smoderatezza** *sf* lack of moderation; excess.
smoking ['zmɔkiŋ] *sm invar* dinner-jacket.
smontare [zmon'tare] *v* (*scomporre*) dismantle, take apart; (*totalmente*) strip; (*da veicoli*) get out *or* off. **smontaggio** *sm* dismantling; stripping.
smorfia ['zmɔrfja] *sf* wry face. **fare una smorfia** pull a face; (*di dolore*) wince with pain. **smorfioso** *agg* simpering.
smorto ['zmɔrto] *agg* pale, wan; (*fig*) colourless.
smorzare [zmor'tsare] *v* (*colori*) tone down; (*suoni*) muffle; (*luce*) dim; (*fig*) dampen. **smorzata** *sf* (*tennis*) drop-shot.
smunto ['zmunto] *agg* emaciated.
***smuovere** ['zmwɔvere] *v* shift; (*commuovere*) touch; dissuade.
smussare [zmus'sare] *v* smooth; (*angolo*) round off; (*fig*) soften. **smussarsi** *v* become blunt.
snaturare [znatu'rare] *v* distort. **snaturato** *agg* unnatural; degenerate.
snazionalizzare [znatsjonalid'dzare] *v* denationalize. **snazionalizzazione** *sf* denationalization.
snellire [znel'lire] *v* slim (down); simplify; speed up. **snellezza** *sf* slimness. **snello** *agg* slim; (*agile*) nimble; simple, easy.
snervare [zner'vare] *v* exhaust.
snidare [zni'dare] *v* drive out.
snob ['znɔb] *agg, s(m+f) invar* snob. **snobbare** *v* snub. **snobismo** *sm* snobbery.
snocciolare [znottʃo'lare] *v* stone; (*fam: spendere*) shell out; (*fam: spiattellare*) rattle off.

snodare [zno'dare] *v* unknot; (*articolare meglio*) loosen (up); (*piegare*) bend. **snodabile** *agg* (*tec*) articulated. **snodato** *agg* flexible, loose.

soave [so'ave] *agg* delicate, sweet. **soavità** *sf* sweetness, delicacy.

sobbalzare [sobbal'tsare] *v* jolt; (*trasalire*) jump. **di sobbalzo** with a start.

sobbarcarsi [sobbar'karsi] *v* undertake.

sobbollire [sobbol'lire] *v* simmer.

sobborgo [sob'borgo] *sm* suburb.

sobillare [sobil'lare] *v* incite, stir up. **sobillatore, -trice** *sm, sf* trouble-maker.

sobrio ['sɔbrjo] *agg* sober. **sobrietà** *sf* sobriety.

***socchiudere** [sok'kjudere] *v* half-close. **socchiuso** *agg* half-closed; (*porta*) ajar.

soccombere [sok'kombere] *v* succumb.

***soccorrere** [sok'korrere] *v* assist; come to the aid of; (*salvare*) rescue.

soccorritore [sokkorri'tore], **-trice** *agg* helping. *sm, sf* helper.

soccorso [sok'korso] *sm* help, assistance; rescue. **pronto soccorso** first aid; (*all'ospedale*) casualty ward. **soccorsi** *sm pl* (*rinforzi*) reinforcements *pl*; (*rifornimenti*) supplies *pl*.

socialdemocratico [sotʃaldemo'kratiko], **-a** *sm, sf* social democrat. **socialdemocrazia** *sf* social democracy.

sociale [so'tʃale] *agg* social; (*benessere*) welfare; (*comm*) relating to a firm, company. **assistente sociale** *s*(*m*+*f*) welfare officer, social worker. **assistenza sociale** *sf* welfare. **tessera sociale** *sf* membership card.

socialismo [sotʃa'lizmo] *sm* socialism. **socialista** *agg, s*(*m*+*f*) socialist.

società [sotʃe'ta] *sf* society; (*comm*) company, partnership; association. **gioco di società** *sm* parlour game. **mettersi in società** go into partnership. **società anonima** limited company. **società dei consumi** consumer society. **società per azioni** limited company.

socievole [so'tʃevole] *agg* social; (*persona*) sociable. **socievolezza** *sf* sociability.

socio ['sɔtʃo], **-a** *sm, sf* partner; member.

sociologia [sotʃolo'dʒia] *sf* sociology. **sociologico** *agg* sociological. **sociologo, -a** *sm, sf* sociologist.

soda ['sɔda] *sf* soda.

sodalizio [soda'litsjo] *sm* brotherhood; (*amicizia*) fellowship.

***soddisfare** [soddis'fare] *v* satisfy; (*appagare*) gratify; (*riparare*) make amends for. **soddisfacente** *agg* satisfactory; satisfying. **soddisfatto** *agg* satisfied; (*contento*) pleased. **soddisfazione** *sf* satisfaction. **bella satisfazione!** big deal!

sodio ['sɔdjo] *sm* sodium.

sodo ['sɔdo] *agg* firm; (*fig*) sound. **uovo sodo** *sm* hard-boiled egg. *avv* hard; (*profondamente*) soundly.

sofà [so'fa] *sf* sofa, settee.

sofferente [soffe'rɛnte] *agg* suffering. **sofferenza** *sf* suffering.

soffermarsi [soffer'marsi] *v* linger (over).

soffiare [sof'fjare] *v* blow; (*sbuffare*) puff; (*dama, scacchi*) huff. **soffiare di rabbia** fume (with rage). **soffio** *sm* puff; (*med*) murmur. **in un soffio** in a flash. **per un soffio** by a whisker.

soffice ['sɔffitʃe] *agg* soft.

soffietto [sof'fjetto] *sm* bellows *pl*; (*fam: articoletto*) plug. **a soffietto** folding. **lavorar di soffietto** (*fam*) tell tales.

soffitta [sof'fitta] *sf* attic.

soffitto [sof'fitto] *sm* ceiling.

soffocare [soffo'kare] *v* suffocate, choke; (*reprimere*) suppress, stifle. **soffocamento** *sm* suffocation.

***soffriggere** [sof'friddʒere] *v* brown.

***soffrire** [sof'frire] *v* suffer (from); (*sopportare*) bear, stand; (*consentire*) allow. **soffrire la fame** go hungry. **soffrir di (mal di) cuore** have heart trouble.

sofisma [so'fizma] *sm* sophistry. **sofisticare** *v* (*sottilizzare*) quibble; (*fam*) split hairs; (*adulterare*) doctor.

soggetto [sod'dʒɛtto] *sm* subject; (*argomento*) topic; person. **recitare a soggetto** improvise. *agg* subject, liable; (*sottomesso*) subjected; (*predisposto*) prone. **soggettivo** *agg* subjective. **soggezione** *sf* subjection; embarrassment; (*timore*) awe. **aver soggezione di** (*sentirsi imbarrazzato*) feel uneasy in the presence of; (*averne timore*) be overawed by. **ispirare soggezione a** make uneasy; overawe.

sogghignare [soggi'ɲare] *v* sneer.

***soggiacere** [soddʒa'tʃere] *v* be subjected; succumb.

soggiorno [sod'dʒorno] *sm* stay; (*luogo*) resort; (*stanza*) living room. **permesso di soggiorno** *sm* residence permit. **soggiornare** *v* stay.

***soggiungere** [sod'dʒundʒere] *v* add.

soglia ['sɔʎa] *sf* threshold.
sogliola ['sɔʎola] *sf* sole.
sognare [so'ɲare] *v* dream; (*ad occhi aperti*) daydream. **sognatore, -trice** *sm, sf* dreamer. **sogno** *sm* dream. **fare un sogno** have a dream. **neanche per sogno!** not likely!
soia ['sɔja] *sf* soya (bean).
solaio [so'lajo] *sm* (*soffitta*) loft; (*piano di edificio*) floor.
solare [so'lare] *agg* solar. **luce solare** *sf* sunlight.
solco ['solko] *sm* (*agric*) furrow; (*traccia*) track; (*lampo*) streak; (*disco*) groove.
soldato [sol'dato] *sm* soldier. **andare soldato** join up. **fare il soldato** be in the army.
soldo ['sɔldo] *sm* penny. **soldi** *sm pl* (*denaro*) money *sing*. **essere al soldo di** be in the pay of. **essere senza soldi** be penniless.
sole ['sole] *sm* sun. **al sole** in the sun. **chiaro come il sole** clear as daylight. **fare un bagno di sole** sunbathe. **occhiali da sole** *sm pl* sun-glasses *pl*. **soleggiato** *agg* sunny.
solenne [so'lɛnne] *agg* solemn; (*fig*) tremendous. **solennità** *sf* solemnity; (*festa*) holiday. **solennizzare** *v* solemnize.
***solere** [so'lere] *v* be in the habit of.
soletta [so'letta] *sf* sole; (*suola interna*) insole.
solfato [sol'fato] *sm* sulphate. **solforico** *agg* sulphuric. **solfuro** *sm* sulphide.
solidale [soli'dale] *agg* (*tec*) integral; (*d'accordo*) in agreement (with); (*dir*) joint. **solidarietà** *sf* solidarity.
solidificare [solidifi'kare] *v* harden. **solidificarsi** *v* set. **solidificazione** *sf* hardening; setting.
solido ['sɔlido] *agg* solid; stable; (*robusto, valido*) sound; (*colori*) fast. *sm* solid. **solidità** *sf* solidity; stability; soundness; fastness.
soliloquio [soli'lɔkwjo] *sm* soliloquy.
solista [so'lista] *s(m+f)* soloist.
solitario [soli'tarjo], **-a** *agg* solitary. *sm, sf* loner. *sm* (*brillante, gioco*) solitaire.
solito ['sɔlito], **-a** *agg* usual. *pron* same. *sm* (*abitudine*) habit; (*cosa*) usual. **come al solito** as usual. **di solito** usually, as a rule. **essere solito a fare** be used to doing.
solitudine [soli'tudine] *sf* solitude.
sollazzare [sollat'tsare] *v* amuse.
sollecitare [solletʃi'tare] *v* press for; (*affrettare*) speed up; (*mec*) stress; (*chiedere con insistenza*) solicit. **sollecitazione** *sf* solicitation, entreaty; (*mec*) stress. **lettera di sollecitazione** *sf* reminder.
sollecito [sol'letʃito] *agg* (*fatto con premura*) prompt; (*premuroso*) solicitous. **sollecitudine** *sm* (*prontezza*) dispatch; (*preoccupazione*) solicitude.
solleticare [solleti'kare] *v* tickle; (*fig*) arouse. **solletico** *sm* tickle. **fare il solletico** tickle. **sentire** *or* **soffrire il solletico** be ticklish.
sollevare [solle'vare] *v* raise; (*tirar su*) lift (up). **sollevarsi** *v* rise; (*riprendersi*) recover.
sollievo [sol'ljɛvo] *sm* relief.
solo ['solo] *agg* alone; by oneself; (*unico*) only, sole; (*semplice*) mere; (*musica*) unaccompanied. *avv* (*soltanto*) only; (*ma*) but. **da solo** alone, by oneself. **solo che** only. **solo soletto** quite alone. **una sola volta** once only. **un solo** just one, only one.
solstizio [sol'stitsjo] *sm* solstice.
soltanto [sol'tanto] *avv* only.
solubile [so'lubile] *agg* soluble. **solubilità** *sf* solubility. **soluzione** *sf* solution.
solvente [sol'vɛnte] *agg, sm* solvent. **solvibile** *agg* (*comm*) solvent. **solvibilità** *sm* (*comm*) solvency.
soma ['sɔma] *sf* burden.
somaro [so'maro] *sm* donkey.
somigliare [somi'ʎare] *v* resemble, be like. **somigliante** *agg* similar. **somiglianza** *sf* resemblance.
somma ['somma] *sf* sum. **fare la somma** add up. **tirare le somme** sum up. **sommare** *v* add *or* sum up. **tutto sommato** all things considered.
sommario [som'marjo] *agg* brief; (*dir*) summary. *sm* summary, outline.
***sommergere** [som'mɛrdʒere] *v* submerge. **sommergibile** *sm* submarine.
sommesso [som'messo] *agg* meek.
somministrare [somminis'trare] *v* administer.
sommità [sommi'ta] *sf* peak, summit.
sommo ['sommo] *agg* highest; (*fig*) supreme. *sm* peak.
sommossa [som'mɔssa] *sf* riot.
sommozzatore [sommottsa'tore] *sm* skindiver; (*mil*) frogman.

sonaglio [so'naʎo] *sm* bell. **serpente a sonagli** *sm* rattlesnake.

sonare [so'nare] *v also* **suonare** sound; (*campanello*) ring; (*musica*) play; (*orologio*) strike; (*fam*: *imbrogliare*) cheat. **sonata** *sf* (*musica*) sonata; (*fam*: *bastonatura*) caning; (*fam*: *fregatura*) swindle. **prendersi una sonata** be taken in. **sonato** *agg* (*compiuto*) past; (*rimbambito*) gaga.

sonda ['sonda] *sf* probe. **sondaggio** *sm* probing, sounding; (*indagine*) poll. **sondare** *v* sound, probe.

sonnambulo [son'nambulo], **-a** *sm*, *sf* sleep-walker.

sonnecchiare [sonnek'kjare] *v* doze.

sonnifero [son'nifero] *agg* soporific. *sm* sleeping pill.

sonno ['sonno] *sm* sleep; (*senso di torpore*) drowsiness. **aver sonno** be sleepy. **fare un bel sonno** have a good sleep. **sonnolento** *agg* sleepy, drowsy. **sonnolenza** *sf* drowsiness.

sonoro [so'nɔro] *agg* sound; (*che risona*) resonant; (*consonanti*) voiced. **sonorità** *sf* resonance; (*fis*) acoustics *pl*.

sontuoso [sontu'ozo] *agg* sumptuous. **sontuosità** *sf* sumptuousness.

soporifero [sopo'rifero] *agg*, *sm* soporific.

sopperire [soppe'rire] *v* provide for.

soppesare [soppe'zare] *v* weigh up.

soppiantare [soppjan'tare] *v* supplant.

soppiatto [sop'pjatto] *agg* **di soppiatto** stealthily. **entrare/uscire di soppiatto** steal in/away.

sopportare [soppor'tare] *v* (*reggere*) support; (*fig*) bear, stand. **sopportabile** *agg* bearable. **sopportazione** *sf* endurance.

***sopprimere** [sop'primere] *v* suppress; abolish. **soppressione** *sf* suppression; abolition.

sopra ['sopra] *prep* on, upon; (*senza contatto diretto*) over, above. **al di sopra di** above; (*oltre*) beyond. *avv* on; (*più in su*) above; (*al piano superiore*) upstairs. **come/vedi sopra** (*nei rinvii*) as/see above.

soprabito [so'prabito] *sm* overcoat.

sopracciglio [soprat'tʃiʎo] *sm* eyebrow.

sopraccitato [soprattʃi'tato] *agg* above-mentioned.

sopraccoperta [soprakko'pɛrta] *sf* (*letto*) counterpane; (*libro*) dust-jacket.

***sopraffare** [sopraf'fare] *v* overcome; dominate.

sopraffino [sopraf'fino] *agg* excellent; highly refined.

sopraggiungere [soprad'dʒundʒere] *v* turn up; (*accadere improvvisamente*) happen, arise.

sopralluogo [sopral'lwɔgo] *sm*, *pl* **-ghi** (on the spot) inspection; (*statistica*) poll.

sopralzo [so'praltso] *sm* extension.

soprammobile [sopram'mɔbile] *sm* knick-knack.

soprannaturale [soprannatu'rale] *agg*, *sm* supernatural.

soprannome [sopran'nome] *sm* nickname. **soprannominare** *v* call.

soprannumero [sopran'numero] *sm* excess.

soprano [so'prano], **-a** *sm*, *sf* soprano.

soprappensiero [soprappen'sjɛro] *avv* lost in thought.

soprappiù [soprap'pju] *sm* surplus; (*aggiunta*) addition. **di** *or* **per soprappiù** in addition, besides.

soprapprezzo [soprap'prɛttso] *sm* (*econ*) premium; (*maggiorazione*) increase in price.

soprassalto [sopras'salto] *sm* sudden start. **di soprassalto** suddenly.

soprassedere [soprasse'dere] *v* put off.

soprattassa [soprat'tassa] *sf* additional charge.

soprattutto [soprat'tutto] *avv* above all; (*per la maggior parte*) mainly.

sopravanzare [sopravan'tsare] *v* be left over.

sopravvalutare [sopravvalu'tare] *v* overrate. **sopravvalutazione** *sf* overestimate.

***sopravvenire** [sopravve'nire] *v* turn up; (*accadere d'improvviso*) happen, arise.

sopravvento [soprav'vɛnto] *agg*, *avv* windward. *sm* (*fig*) upper hand.

***sopravvivere** [soprav'vivere] *v* survive. **sopravvissuto, -a** *sm*, *sf* survivor. **sopravvivenza** *sf* survival.

soprelevare [soprele'vare] *v* raise.

***soprintendere** [soprin'tɛndere] *v* supervise; be in charge of. **soprintendente** *s*(*m*+*f*) superintendent. **soprintendenza** *sf* (*atto*) supervision; (*ufficio*) superintendence.

sopruso [so'pruzo] *sm* outrage.

soqquadro [sok'kwadro] *sm* **mettere a soqquadro** turn upside down.

sorbetto [sor'betto] *sm* sorbet, water ice.

sorbire [sor'bire] *v* sip. **sorbirsi** *v* (*sopportare*) put up with.
sorcio ['sortʃo] *sm* mouse (*pl* mice).
sordido ['sordido] *agg* sordid. **sordidezza** *sf* sordidness.
sordina [sor'dina] *sf* (*musica*) mute. **in sordina** (*fig*) on the quiet.
sordo ['sordo], **-a** *agg* deaf; (*smorzato*) dull; (*fig*) hidden. **sordo come una campana** deaf as a post. *sm, sf* deaf person. **fare il sordo** feign deafness. **sordità** *sf* deafness.
sordomuto [sordo'muto], **-a** *agg* deaf and dumb. *sm, sf* deaf-mute.
sorella [so'rella] *sf* sister. **sorellastra** *sf* step-sister, half-sister.
***sorgere** ['sordʒere] *v* rise; (*aver origine*) arise. **sorgente** *sf* source. **acqua sorgiva** *sf* spring water.
soriano [so'rjano] *sm, agg* tabby.
sormontare [sormon'tare] *v* surmount; (*stoffa*) overlap.
sornione [sor'njone] *agg* sly.
sorpassare [sorpas'sare] *v* (*oltrepassare*) overtake; (*eccedere*) exceed. **sorpassare in altezza/lunghezza** be higher/longer. **sorpassato** *agg* (*non più attuale*) out of date. **sorpasso** *sm* overtaking. **divieto di sorpasso** *sm* no overtaking.
***sorprendere** [sor'prɛndere] *v* surprise; (*cogliere all'improvviso*) catch. **sorprendente** *agg* surprising. **sorpresa** *sf* surprise.
***sorreggere** [sor'rɛddʒere] *v* hold up; sustain. **sorreggersi** *v* stand upright.
***sorridere** [sor'ridere] *v* smile; (*destar piacere*) appeal. **sorridente** *agg* smiling. **sorriso** *sm* smile.
sorso ['sorso] *sm* (*sorsata*) sip; (*d'un fiato*) gulp; (*piccola quantità*) drop. **sorseggiare** *v also* **bere a piccoli sorsi** sip.
sorta ['sɔrta] *sf* kind, sort. **di sorta** (*di nessun tipo*) whatever.
sorte ['sɔrte] *sf* fate; fortune; (*condizione propria*) lot. **sorteggiare** *v also* **tirare a sorte** draw lots. **sorteggio** *sm* draw.
sortilegio [sorti'lɛdʒo] *sm* spell.
sorvegliare [sorve'ʎare] *v* watch; (*sovrintendere*) oversee; (*vigilare*) keep an eye on. **sorvegliante** *s*(*m*+*f*) overseer; (*custode*) caretaker; (*guardiano*) watchman. **sorveglianza** *sf* surveillance, watch.
sorvolare [sorvo'lare] *v* fly over; (*fig*) skip.
sosia ['sɔzja] *sm invar* double.
***sospendere** [sos'pɛndere] *v* suspend; (*attaccare in alto*) hang; interrupt; (*seduta*) adjourn; defer. **sospendere il lavoro** stop work. **sospensione** *sf* suspension; interruption; (*cessazione*) stoppage. **sospeso** *agg* hanging; (*non definito*) outstanding. **col fiato sospeso** with bated breath. **in sospeso** in suspense; (*non risolto*) pending.
sospettare [sospet'tare] *v* suspect; (*diffidare*) distrust, be suspicious (of).
sospetto [sos'pɛtto] *agg* suspect, suspicious. **persona sospetta** *sf* suspect. *sm* suspicion. **sospettoso** *agg* distrustful.
***sospingere** [sos'pindʒere] *v* push; (*fig*) drive. **a ogni piè sospinto** at every step.
sospirare [sospi'rare] *v* sigh; (*aspettare con ansia*) long *or* yearn for. **sospiro** *sm* sigh.
sosta ['sɔsta] *sf* stop; pause; (*riposo*) rest; (*aspettare*) wait. **divieto di sosta** no waiting. **senza sosta** ceaselessly; without stopping. **sostare** *v* stop; pause; wait; rest.
sostantivo [sostan'tivo] *agg* substantive. *sm* noun.
sostanza [sos'tantsa] *sf* matter; (*parte utile*) substance; (*parte nutritiva*) nourishment; (*patrimonio*) property. **cibo di sostanza** nourishing food. **in sostanza** essentially. **sostanza alimentare** foodstuff. **sostanziale** *agg* substantial; essential. **sostanzioso** *agg* nourishing.
sostegno [sos'teɲo] *sm* support.
***sostenere** [soste'nere] *v* support; (*asserire*) maintain; (*tenere alto*) keep up; (*tollerare*) stand. **sostenere una carica** hold an office. **sostenere una parte** act a part. **sostenersi** *v* (*star su*) hold oneself up, stand up; (*fig*) hold water. **sostenibile** *agg* tenable.
sostenitore [sosteni'tore], **-trice** *agg* supporting. *sm, sf* supporter.
***sostentare** [sosten'tare] *v* support; maintain. **sostentamento** *sm* support; maintenance.
sostenuto [soste'nuto] *agg* (*contegnoso*) reserved; (*musica*) sostenuto. **sostenutezza** *sf* reserve.
sostituire [sostitu'ire] *v* substitute; (*rimpiazzare*) replace. **sostituto, -a** *sm, sf* deputy, substitute. **sostituzione** *sf* substitution; replacement.

sottaceto [sotta'tʃeto] *avv* **mettere sottaceto** pickle. **sottaceti** *sm pl* pickles *pl*.
sottalimentazione [sottalimenta'tsjone] *sf* undernourishment.
sottana [sot'tana] *sf* skirt; (*sottoveste*) slip, underskirt; (*rel*) cassock.
sottecchi [sot'tekki] *avv* **di sottecchi** stealthily.
sottentrare [sotten'trare] *v* replace.
sotterfugio [sotter'fudʒo] *sm* subterfuge.
sotterraneo [sotter'raneo] *agg* underground. *sm* basement. **sotterranea** *sf* underground (railway); (*fam*) tube.
sotterrare [sotter'rare] *v* bury. **sotterra** *avv* underground.
sottile [sot'tile] *agg* thin; fine; (*acuto*) sharp. **sottigliezza** *sf* thinness; sharpness; (*sofisticheria*) nicety.
sottinsù [sottin'su] *avv* **di sottinsù** from below.
***sottintendere** [sottin'tɛndere] *v* imply, infer; (*non esprimere*) leave out. **sottinteso** *agg* implied; (*chiaro da sè*) understood. *sm* allusion. **senza sottintesi** plainly.
sotto ['sotto] *prep* under; (*al di sotto di*) below, beneath; (*in cambio di*) on. *avv* underneath, below; (*al piano di sotto*) downstairs. **andar sotto le armi** join up. **metter sotto** (*investire*) run down. **mettersi sotto** get down to. **sotto la pioggia** in the rain. **sotto questo punto di vista** from this point of view. **sotto questo riguardo** in this respect. **sotto sotto** deep down.
sottobanco [sotto'banko] *avv* under the counter.
sottobicchiere [sottobik'kjɛre] *sm* mat, coaster.
sottobraccio [sotto'brattʃo] *avv* arm-in-arm. **prendere sottobraccio qualcuno** take someone's arm.
sottocchio [sot'tɔkkjo] *avv* **tenere sottocchio** keep an eye on.
sottocommissione [sottokommis'sjone] *sf* subcommittee; subcommission.
sottocoppa [sotto'kɔppa] *sm invar* mat; (*piattino*) saucer.
***sottoesporre** [sottoes'porre] *v* underexpose.
sottofondo [sotto'fondo] *sm* foundation; (*suono*) background noise. **musica in sottofondo** *sf* background music.
sottolineare [sottoline'are] *v* underline; (*fig*) stress.
sottomano [sotto'mano] *avv* (*a portata di mano*) within (easy) reach, on hand; (*di nascosto*) on the quiet; (*sport*) underhand.
***sottomettere** [sotto'mettere] *v* (*assoggettare*) subject; (*costringere a sottostare*) subdue; subordinate. **sottomettersi** *v* submit. **sottomesso** *agg* subdued; (*obbediente*) submissive.
sottopassaggio [sottopas'saddʒo] *sm* underpass.
***sottoporre** [sotto'porre] *v* (*presentare*) submit; (*costringere*) subject, expose. **sottoporsi a un'operazione** undergo an operation. **sottoposto, -a** *sm, sf* subordinate.
sottoprodotto [sottopro'dotto] *sm* by-product.
sottordine [sot'tordine] *sm* suborder. **in sottordine** of minor importance.
***sottoscrivere** [sotto'skrivere] *v* sign; (*fig*) support; (*econ*) underwrite, subscribe. **sottoscritto, -a** *sm, sf* undersigned; (*fam*) yours truly. **sottoscrizione** *sf* subscription.
sottosopra [sotto'sopra] *avv* upside down.
***sottostare** [sotto'stare] *v* be under; (*sottomettersi*) give in. **sottostante** *agg* (down) below.
sottosuolo [sotto'swɔlo] *sm* subsoil.
sottoterra [sotto'tɛrra] *avv* underground.
sottotitolo [sotto'titolo] *sm* subtitle.
sottovalutare [sottovalu'tare] *v* underestimate.
sottoveste [sotto'vɛste] *sf* slip.
sottovoce [sotto'votʃe] *avv* in a low voice, softly.
***sottrarre** [sot'trarre] *v* remove; (*mat*) subtract; (*salvare*) save (from). **sottrarsi a** escape; (*evitare*) avoid. **sottrazione** *sf* subtraction; removal.
sottufficiale [sottuffi'tʃale] *sm* non-commissioned officer; (*mar*) petty officer.
sovente [so'vɛnte] *avv also* **di sovente** frequently.
soverchio [so'verkjo] *agg* excessive. **soverchieria** *sf* bullying; (*sopruso*) outrage.
sovietico [so'vjɛtiko], **-a** *s, agg* Soviet.
sovrabbondante [sovrabbon'dante] *agg* plentiful; excessive. **sovrabbondanza** *sf* plenty; excess.
sovraccaricare [sovrakkari'kare] *v* overburden; (*tec*) overload. **sovraccarica** *sf* overcharge. **sovraccarico** *agg, m pl* **-chi** overloaded.

***sovr(a)esporre** [sovr(a)es'porre] *v* over-expose. **sovresposizione** *sf* over-exposure.
sovraffollato [sovraffol'lato] *agg* over-crowded.
sovrano [so'vrano], **-a** *agg* sovereign, supreme. *sm, sf* sovereign. **sovranità** *sf* sovereignty; (*fig*) supremacy.
sovrappopolato [sovrappopo'lato] *agg* overpopulated.
***sovrapporre** [sovrap'porre] *v* superimpose; (*fig*) set over; (*accavallare*) overlap.
sovrastante [sovra'stante] *agg* towering; (*imminente*) impending.
sovreccitare [sovrettʃi'tare] *v* over-excite. **sovreccitarsi** *v* become over-excited. **sovreccitazione** *sf* over-excitement.
sovrumano [sovru'mano] *agg* superhuman.
sovvenzione [sovven'tsjone] *sf* subsidy. **sovvenzionare** *v* subsidize.
sovversione [sovver'sjone] *sf* subversion. **sovversivo, -a** *s, agg* subversive. **sovvertire** *v* subvert.
sozzo ['sottso] *agg* filthy; (*fig*) loathsome. **sozzura** *sf* filth; loathsomeness.
spaccare ['spakkare] *v* (*fendere*) split; (*rompere*) break; (*legna*) chop. **spaccarsi** *v* split (open); break (up). **spaccare il minuto** be dead on time. **fare la spaccata** do the splits. **spacco** *sm* split; (*strappo*) tear; (*giacca*) vent.
spacciare ['spattʃare] *v* (*vendere*) sell off; (*mettere in circolazione*) peddle; (*dichiarar inguaribile*) give up. **spacciato** *agg* (*fam*: *rovinato*) done for. **spacciatore, -trice** *sm, sf* pedlar; (*di droghe*) pusher; (*di notizie false*) rumour-monger. **spaccio** *sm* sale; (*negozio*) shop; (*mil, fabbrica*) canteen.
spaccone [spak'kone] *sm* braggart. **fare lo spaccone** brag.
spada ['spada] *sf* sword; (*sport*) épée. **a spada tratta** vigorously. **pesce spada** *sm* sword-fish. **tirar di spada** fence. **spadaccino** *sm* swordsman. **spadista** *s*(*m*+*f*) fencer.
spadroneggiare [spadroned'dʒare] *v* be bossy.
spaesato [spae'zato] *agg* lost.
Spagna ['spaɲa] *sf* Spain. **spagnolo, -a** *agg, sm* Spanish; *sm, sf* (*abitante*) Spaniard.
spago ['spago] *sm* string, twine.
spalancare [spalan'kare] *v* open wide. **spalancare gli orecchi** prick up one's ears. **spalancato** *agg* wide open.
spalare [spa'lare] *v* shovel.
spalla ['spalla] *sf* shoulder; (*dorso*) back. **alle spalle di** (*stato*) behind; (*moto*) from behind. **aver le spalle grosse** be broad-shouldered. **aver sulle spalle** (*fig*) be responsible for. **alzar le spalle** shrug one's shoulders. **ridere alle spalle di qualcuno** laugh behind someone's back. **vivere alle spalle di** live off. **spallata** *sf* (*spinta*) push with the shoulder; (*alzata di spalle*) shrug. **spalletta** *sf* parapet.
spalmare [spal'mare] *v* spread.
spanare [spa'nare] *v* strip.
spanciare [span'tʃare] *v* bulge. **spanciarsi dalle risa** split one's sides laughing.
***spandere** ['spandere] *v* (*versare*) shed; (*involontariamente*) spill; (*stendere, divulgare*) spread.
spanna ['spanna] *sf* span.
spappolare [spappo'lare] *v* crush.
sparare [spa'rare] *v* fire; (*tirare*) shoot. **spararle grosse** (*fam*) shoot a line; tell tall stories. **sparata** *sf* volley. **sparo** *sm* shot.
sparecchiare [sparek'kjare] *v* clear (away).
spareggio [spa'reddʒo] *sm* (*sport*) decider.
***spargere** ['spardʒere] *v* scatter; (*versare*) shed; (*involontariamente*) spill; (*sale, pepe, ecc.*) sprinkle; (*diffondere*) spread.
***sparire** [spa'rire] *v* disappear. **far sparire (nascondere)** hide; (*fam*: *rubare*) pinch.
sparlare [spar'lare] *v* speak ill (of).
sparo ['sparo] *sm* shot.
sparpagliare [sparpa'ʎare] *v* scatter.
spartire [spar'tire] *v* divide; (*in parti*) share out; (*musica*) score. **spartiacque** *sm invar* watershed. **spartineve** *sm invar* snow-plough. **spartitraffico** *sm* traffic island. **spartito** *sm* score.
sparuto [spa'ruto] *agg* gaunt; (*esiguo*) scanty.
sparviere [spar'vjere] *sm* sparrow-hawk.
spasimare [spazi'mare] *v* suffer agonies; (*fig*) crave, long (for). **spasimo** *sm* pang; (*med*) spasm. **spasmodico** *agg* spasmodic.
spassarsela [spas'sarsela] *v* enjoy oneself.
spassionato [spassjo'nato] *agg* dispassionate.
spasso ['spasso] *sm* fun. **andare a spasso** go for a walk. **mandare a spasso** (*fam*: *licenziare*) sack; (*fam*: *liberarsene*) get rid of. **portare a spasso** take for a walk. **quel**

ragazzo è uno spasso! that boy is a scream! **spassoso** *agg* amusing.

spastico ['spastiko], **-a** *s, agg* spastic. **spasticità** *sf* spasticity.

spatola ['spatola] *sf* spatula; (*di pittore*) palette-knife; (*zool*) spoonbill.

spatriare [spatri'are] *v* expatriate.

spaurire [spau'rire] *v* scare. **spauracchio** *sm* scarecrow.

spavaldo [spa'valdo] *agg* defiant; (*baldanzoso*) bold; (*arrogante*) cocky. **spavalderia** *sf* defiance; boldness; cockiness.

spaventare [spaven'tare] *v* frighten, scare. **spaventarsi** *v* get frightened, get scared. **spaventapasseri** *sm* scarecrow. **spaventevole** *agg* terrifying. **spavento** *sm* fright. **fare spavento** frighten, scare. **prendersi uno spavento** have a fright. **spaventoso** *agg* frightful; (*terribile*) dreadful; (*enorme*) tremendous.

spazientirsi [spatsjen'tirsi] *v* lose one's patience.

spazio ['spatsjo] *sm* space; (*estensione limitata*) room; distance. **spaziale** *agg* space, spatial. **spaziare** *v* space; (*fig*) range. **spazioso** *agg* roomy.

spazzare [spat'tsare] *v* sweep; (*spazzar via*) sweep away. **spazzacamino** *sm* chimney-sweep. **spazzaneve** *sm invar* snowplough. **spazzatura** *sf* cleaning; sweeping; (*rifiuti*) rubbish. **spazzaturaio** *sm* dustman. **spazzino** *sm* road sweeper.

spazzola ['spattsola] *sf* brush. **capelli a spazzola** crew-cut. **spazzola per capelli** hairbrush. **spazzolare** *v* brush. **spazzolino da denti/unghie** *sm* tooth-/nail-brush. **spazzolone** (*per lavare*) scrubbing brush.

specchio ['spɛkkjo] *sm* mirror; model; (*prospetto*) table; summary. **specchio d'acqua** sheet of water. **specchio retrovisore** driving mirror. **specchiarsi** *v* (*guardarsi*) look at oneself in the mirror; (*riflettersi*) be reflected. **specchiato** *agg* (*fig*) exemplary. **specchiera** *sf* large mirror; (*toletta*) dressing-table. **specchietto** *sm* small mirror; (*tavola*) table, summary.

speciale [spe'tʃale] *agg* special; particular; (*fuori del solito*) peculiar. **specialista** *s(m+f)* specialist. **specialità** *sf* speciality; (*prodotto speciale*) specialty; (*farmaceutica*) proprietary medicine. **specializzarsi** *v* specialize. **specializzato** *agg* specialized; (*operaio*) skilled; (*medico*) specialist. **specializzazione** *sf* specialization.

specie ['spɛtʃe] *sf invar* kind, sort; (*bot, zool*) species; surprise. **mi fa specie** it surprises me. **sotto specie di** in the form of.

specificare [spetʃifi'kare] *v* specify. **specifica** *sf* detailed list. **specificazione** *sf* specification. **specifico** *agg* specific.

speculare [speku'lare] *v* speculate. **speculativo** *agg* speculative. **speculatore, -trice** *sm, sf* speculator; (*di borsa*) stockbroker. **speculazione** *sf* speculation.

spedalità [spedali'ta] *sf* hospitalization.

spedire [spe'dire] *v* send; post; (*inoltrare*) forward. **spedire all'altro mondo** (*fam*) bump off. **spedito** *agg* (*veloce*) quick; (*corrente*) fluent. **speditore, -trice** *sm, sf* sender; (*comm*) shipper. **spedizione** *sf* dispatch; (*trasporto*) shipment; (*cosa spedita*) consignment. **casa di spedizione** forwarding *or* shipping agents *pl.* **fare una spedizione** send a consignment. **spedizioniere** *sm* shipping *or* forwarding agent.

***spegnere** ['speɲere] *v* extinguish, put out; (*con interruttore*) switch *or* turn off; (*sete*) quench. **spegnersi** *v* go out; (*motore*) stall.

spelacchiato [spelak'kjato] *agg* (*con pochi peli*) mangy; (*logoro*) threadbare.

spellare [spel'lare] *v* skin; (*escoriare*) graze. **spellarsi** *v* peel. **spellatura** *sf* skinning; grazing; peeling.

spelonca [spe'lonka] *sf* hovel.

***spendere** ['spɛndere] *v* spend. **senza spender fatica** effortlessly. **spendere bene/male** use one's money wisely/unwisely. **spendereccio** *agg* extravagant.

spennacchiare [spennak'kjare] *v also* **spennare** pluck; (*fig*) fleece.

spensierato [spensje'rato] *agg* carefree. **spensierataggine** *sf* thoughtlessness; irresponsibility. **spensieratezza** *sf* lightheartedness.

spento ['spento] *agg* out, off; (*fig*) dull.

spenzolare [spendzo'lare] *v* dangle.

speranza [spe'rantsa] *sf* hope. **avere buone speranze** have high hopes. **avere una speranza** have a chance. **filo di speranza** *sm* glimmer of hope. **senza speranza** hopeless.

sperare [spe'rare] *v* hope; (*aspettarsi*) expect. **sperare (in) bene** hope for the best. **sperare in Dio** trust in God. **spero di no/si** I hope not/so.

***sperdersi** ['sperdersi] *v* get lost. **sperduto** *agg* lost; (*fuori mano*) out-of-the-way; (*solo*) lonely.

spergiurare [sperdʒu'rare] *v* commit perjury, perjure oneself. **spergiuro** *sm* perjury; (*persona*) perjurer.

spericolato [speriko'lato] *agg* reckless.

sperimentare [sperimen'tare] *v* experiment (with); (*mettere alla prova*) try out, test; (*farne esperienza*) experience. **sperimentale** *agg* experimental.

sperma ['sperma] *sm* sperm.

sperone [spe'rone] *sm* spur; (*mar*) ram. **sperone di cavaliere** larkspur. **speronare** *v* ram.

sperperare [sperpe'rare] *v* squander. **sperpero** *sm* waste.

sperticato [sperti'kato] *agg* (*fig*) excessive.

spesa ['speza] *sf* expenditure; (*costo*) expense; (*acquisto*) purchase; (*compra*) shopping. **a spese di** at the expense of. **con poca spesa** cheaply; (*fig*) easily. **conto spese** *sm* expense account. **far la spesa** go shopping. **non badare a spese** spare no expense. **senza spesa** free. **spese** *sf pl* cost *sing*, charges *pl*. **spese generali** overheads *pl*. **essere spesato** have one's expenses paid.

spesso ['spesso] *agg* thick. *avv* often, frequently. **spesse volte** very often, frequently. **spessore** *sm* thickness.

spettacolo [spet'takolo] *sm* show; (*rappresentazione*) performance; (*vista*) sight. **dare spettacolo di sè** make an exhibition of oneself. **spettacolo pomeridiano** matinée. **spettacoloso** *agg* spectacular.

spettare [spet'tare] *v* (*competere per dovere*) be up (to); (*appartenere per diritto*) be due (to); (*essere di pertinenza*) be the concern (of).

spettatore [spetta'tore], **-trice** *sm*, *sf* spectator; (*testimone*) witness. **spettatori** *sm pl* audience *sing*.

spettinare [spetti'nare] *v* ruffle the hair of. **spettinato** *agg* unkempt, dishevelled.

spettro ['spettro] *sm* ghost; (*fig*) spectrum.

spezie ['spetsje] *sf pl* spices *pl*.

spezzare [spet'tsare] *v* break; (*staccando*) break off; (*fare a pezzi*) break up; (*gastr*) cut up. **spezzatino** *sm* stew. **spezzettare** *v* chop (up). **spezzone incendiario** *sm* incendiary bomb.

spia ['spia] *sf* spy, informer; (*indizio*) sign; (*apertura*) spy-hole; (*tec*) warning light. **fare la spia** be a spy; (*polizia*) inform; (*riportare*) tell tales.

spiaccicare [spjattʃi'kare] *v* squash.

***spiacere** [spja'tʃere] *v* displease. **mi spiace . . .** I dislike . . . . **mi spiace di . . .** (*rammarico*) I'm sorry . . . . **se non ti spiace** if you don't mind. **spiacevole** *agg* unpleasant, disagreeable; (*increscioso*) regrettable.

spiaggia ['spjaddʒa] *sf* (sea-)shore, beach.

spianare [spja'nare] *v* level; (*render liscio*) smooth; (*radere al suolo*) flatten, raze (to the ground); (*fig*) iron out. **spianato** *agg* smooth. **spianatoia** *sf* pastry board. **spianatoio** *sm* rolling-pin. **a tutto spiano** flat out.

spiantare [spjan'tare] *v* uproot; (*rovinare*) ruin.

spiare [spi'are] *v* spy (on); (*aspettare*) look out for; explore.

spiazzo ['spjattso] *sm* open space; (*radura*) clearing.

spiccare [spik'kare] *v* pick; (*pronunciare distintamente*) spell out; (*dir*) issue; (*comm*) draw; (*risaltare*) stand out. **spiccare il volo** take off. **spiccato** *agg* distinct, marked; (*notevole*) striking. **spicco** *sm* prominence. **far spicco** catch the eye.

spicchio ['spikkjo] *sm* segment; (*aglio*) clove.

spicciare [spit'tʃare] *v* dispatch. **spicciarsi** *v* hurry up. **spicciativo** *agg* quick; (*brusco*) abrupt. **spiccio** *agg* swift. **alla spicciolata** in dribs and drabs. **spiccioli** *sm pl* (small) change *sing*. **spicciolo** *agg* small.

spiedo ['spjɛdo] *sm* spit. **spiedino** *sm* skewer.

spiegare [spje'gare] *v* (*distendere*) unfold; (*ali*) spread; (*vele*) unfurl; (*render chiaro*) explain. **spiegarsi** *v* (*capire*) understand; (*diventar comprensibile*) explain oneself, make oneself understood. **spieghiamoci!** let's get it straight! **spiegabile** *agg* explicable.

spiegazione [spjega'tsjone] *sf* explanation; (*ragione*) reason.

spiegazzare [spjegat'tsare] *v* crumple (up), crease.

spietato [spje'tato] *agg* (*senza pietà*) pitiless; (*accanito*) relentless.

spifferare [spiffe'rare] *v* blab, blurt out. **spiffero** *sm* (*fam*) draught.

spiga ['spiga] *sf* ear. **disegno a spiga** *sm* herringbone pattern.
spigliato [spi'ʎato] *agg* (free and) easy; (*padrone di sè*) self-possessed. **spigliatezza** *sf* ease.
spigola ['spigola] *sf* bass.
spigolare [spigo'lare] *v* glean. **spigolature** *sf pl* tit-bits *pl*.
spigolo ['spigolo] *sm* corner; edge.
spilla ['spilla] *sf* brooch. **spilla da cravatta** tie-pin.
spillare [spil'lare] *v* tap; (*attingere*) draw.
spillo ['spillo] *sm* pin. **spillo di sicurezza** safety-pin.
spilluzzicare [spilluttsi'kare] *v* nibble.
spilorcio [spi'lortʃo], **-a** *agg* stingy. *sm, sf* miser. **spilorceria** *sf* meanness.
spina ['spina] *sf* (*bot*) thorn; (*aculeo*) sting; (*riccio*) quill; (*elett*) plug. **birra alla spina** *sf* draught beer. **spina di pesce** fishbone. **spina dorsale** backbone. **star sulle spine** be on tenterhooks. **spinare** *v* bone. **spinato** *agg* (*pesce*) filleted; (*filo*) barbed.
spinacio [spi'natʃo] *sm* (*bot*) spinach. **spinaci** *sm pl* (*gastr*) spinach *sing*.
***spingere** ['spindʒere] *v* push, drive; (*stimolare*) urge; (*premere*) press.
spino ['spino] *sm* (*bot*) blackthorn, bramble. **spineto** *sm* bramble bush. **spinoso** *agg* prickly, thorny.
spinta ['spinta] *sf* push; pressure; (*aiuto*) (helping) hand; (*stimolo*) boost; (*fis*) thrust. **spinto** *agg* pushed; disposed; (*fam*) extremist. **spintone** *sm* hard push, shove; (*raccomandazione*) good word.
spionaggio [spio'naddʒo] *sm* espionage. **spione** *sm* (*fam*) tell-tale.
spiovente [spjo'vɛnte] *agg* (*baffi*) drooping; (*spalle*) stooping; (*tetto*) sloping.
spira ['spira] *sf* coil. **spirale** *agg, sf* spiral.
spiraglio [spi'raʎo] *sm* chink; (*di luce, speranza*) glimmer; (*aria*) breath (of air).
spirare[1] [spi'rare] *v* (*soffiare*) blow; (*emettere*) give off *or* out; (*emanare*) be given off *or* out.
spirare[2] [spi'rare] *v* (*morire*) expire.
spirito ['spirito] *sm* spirit; (*animo*) mind; sense of humour. **bello spirito** wit. **condizioni di spirito** *sm pl* mood *sing*. **con spirito** wittily. **pieno di spirito** (*vivace*) lively; (*arguto*) witty.
spiritosaggine [spirito'zaddʒine] *sf* witticism.
spiritoso [spiri'tozo], **-a** *agg* witty. *sm, sf* funny person.
spirituale [spiritu'ale] *agg* spiritual. **spiritualismo** *sm* spiritualism. **spiritualista** *s(m+f)* spiritualist.
spiumare [spju'mare] *v* pluck.
spizzicare [spittsi'kare] *v* nibble. **a spizzico** *or* **spizzichi** in dribs and drabs.
***splendere** ['splɛndere] *v* shine. **splendido** *agg* brilliant; (*meraviglioso*) splendid. **splendore** *sm* brilliance; splendour.
spodestare [spodes'tare] *v* (*cacciare*) oust; (*privare di beni*) dispossess.
spogliare [spo'ʎare] *v* strip; (*svestire*) undress; (*esaminare*) go through; sort out. **spogliarsi** *v* undress. **spogliarello** *sm* strip-tease. **spogliatoio** *sm* changing-room. **spoglie** *sf pl* (*bottino*) spoils *pl*; (*mortali*) (mortal) remains *pl*. **spoglio** *agg* (*nudo*) bare; (*privo*) devoid (of); (*libero*) free (from). **fare lo spoglio** (*corrispondenza*) sort out; (*dati*) extract; (*voti*) scrutinize.
spola ['spɔla] *sf* shuttle; (*macchina da cucire*) spool, bobbin. **far la spola** shuttle, ply. **spoletta** *sf* bobbin; (*tec, mil*) fuse.
spolmonarsi [spolmo'narsi] *v* shout oneself hoarse.
spolverare [spolve'rare] *v* dust. **spolverat(ur)a** *sf* dusting.
sponda ['sponda] *sf* (*mare, lago*) shore; (*fiume*) bank; (*bordo*) edge; (*biliardo*) cushion.
spontaneo [spon'taneo] *agg* spontaneous. **di mia spontanea volontà** of my own free will. **spontaneità** *sf* spontaneity.
spopolare [spopo'lare] *v* depopulate; (*vuotare*) empty; (*aver successo*) be a hit.
spora ['spɔra] *sf* spore.
sporadico [spo'radiko] *agg* sporadic.
sporco ['spɔrko] *agg* dirty; dishonest. **aver la coscienza sporca** have a guilty conscience. **sporcizia** *sf* dirt, filth; (*fam*) muck.
***sporgere** ['spɔrdʒere] *v* stick out, project, protrude. **sporgersi** *v* lean out. **sporgere querela contro** sue. **sporgente** *agg* jutting out; (*dente*) protruding; (*occhio*) bulging. **sporgenza** *sf* projection.
sport [spɔrt] *sm invar* sport. **fare per sport** do for fun.
sporta ['spɔrta] *sf* (*sacca*) shopping-bag; (*quantità*) bagful. **una sporta di legnate** a good hiding. **un sacco e una sporta** a lot.
sportello [spor'tɛllo] *sm* counter; (*per biglietti*) ticket office; (*porta*) door.

sportivo [spor'tivo] *agg* sports; (*interessato*) sporty, sporting; (*leale*) sportsmanlike, sporting. *sm* sportsman. **sportiva** *sf* sportswoman.

sposa ['spɔza] *sf* bride. **sposalizio** *sm* wedding. **sposare** *v* marry; (*fig*) wed. **sposarsi** *v* get married. **sposata** *sf* married woman. **sposato** *sm* married man. **sposino, -a** *sm, sf* newly-wed. **sposo** *sm* bridegroom.

spossare [spos'sare] *v* exhaust. **spossatezza** *sf* exhaustion; (*stanchezza*) weariness. **spossato** *agg* worn out, weary.

spossessare [sposses'sare] *v* dispossess.

spostare [spos'tare] *v* shift; (*rimuovere*) displace; (*turbare*) upset; transfer. **spostamento** *sm* shift; displacement; transfer.

spostato [spos'tato], **-a** *agg* (*fuori posto*) out of place; (*fig*) unsettled. *sm, sf* misfit.

spranga ['spranga] *sf* crossbar; (*chiavistello*) bolt. **sprangare** *v* bolt.

sprazzo ['sprattso] *sm* flash.

sprecare [spre'kare] *v* waste. **è tempo/fiato sprecato** it is a waste of breath/time. **spreco** *sm* waste. **sprecone, -a** *sm, sf* spendthrift.

spregevole [spre'dʒevole] *agg* despicable. **spregiare** *v* despise, spurn. **spregiativo** *agg* disparaging; (*gramm*) pejorative.

spregiudicato [spredʒudi'kato], **-a** *agg* (*senza pregiudizi*) open-minded; (*senza scrupoli*) unscrupulous. *sm, sf* unscrupulous person. **spregiudicatezza** *sf* open-mindedness; unscrupulousness.

spremere ['sprɛmere] *v* squeeze. **spremersi il cervello** rack one's brains. **spremilimoni** *sm* lemon squeezer. **spremuta** *sf* (*bevanda*) juice.

sprezzare [spret'tsare] *v* despise. **sprezzante** *agg* contemptuous. **sprezzo** *sm* scorn.

sprigionare [spridʒo'nare] *v* give off.

sprint [sprint] *sm invar* (*sport*) sprint; (*auto*) pick-up. *sf* sports car.

sprizzare [sprit'tsare] *v* (*acqua*) squirt; (*sangue*) spurt; (*fig*) burst with.

sprofondare [sprofon'dare] *v* collapse; (*affondare*) sink; (*lasciarsi sopraffare*) be overwhelmed (by). **sprofondarsi** *v* sink; (*fig*) immerse oneself. **sprofondamento** *sm* collapse. **sprofondato** *agg* (*fig*) immersed, engrossed.

spronare [spro'nare] *v* spur (on). **spronata** *sf* spur. **sprone** *sm* spur.

sproporzionato [sproportsjo'nato] *agg* out of proportion; disproportionate. **sproporzione** *sf* lack of proportion.

sproposito [spro'pɔzito] *sm* blunder; (*strafalcione*) howler. **a sproposito** (*inopportunamente*) at the wrong time; (*fuori luogo*) in the wrong place. **commettere uno sproposito** do something silly. **costare uno sproposito** cost the earth. **spropositato** *agg* excessive.

sprovvisto [sprov'visto] *agg also* **sprovveduto** short (of); (*privo*) lacking (in). **alla sprovvista** unawares.

spruzzare [sprut'tsare] *v* spray; (*senza intenderlo*) splash. **spruzzata** *sf* sprinkling. **spruzzatore** *sm* sprinkler; (*profumi*) atomizer. **spruzzo** *sm* spray; (*schizzo*) spurt; splash.

spudorato [spudo'rato] *agg* shameless. **spudoratezza** *sf* shamelessness.

spugna ['spuɲa] *sf* sponge; (*tessuto*) towelling; (*fam*) boozer. **bere come una spugna** drink like a fish. **spugnatura** *sf* sponging down. **spugnoso** *agg* spongy.

spuma ['spuma] *sf* froth. **spumante** *sm* sparkling wine. **spumare** *v* (*bevande gassate*) fizz; (*vino*) sparkle. **spumare dalla rabbia** (*fam*) foam at the mouth. **spumeggiare** *v* froth. **spumoso** *agg* frothy.

spuntare [spun'tare] *v* (*germogliare*) sprout; (*apparire improvvisamente*) emerge; (*sorgere*) rise; (*fig*) overcome; (*capelli, ecc.*) trim. **spuntato** *agg* (*matita*) blunt; (*vino*) sour.

spuntino [spun'tino] *sm* snack.

spunto ['spunto] *sm* cue; idea; (*sport*) spurt. **prendere lo spunto da** start (off) from.

spuntone [spun'tone] *sm* spike.

spurgare [spur'gare] *v* clear out. **spurgarsi** *v* clear one's throat.

spurio ['spurjo] *agg* spurious.

sputacchiare [sputak'kjare] *v* splutter. **sputacchiera** *sf* spitoon.

sputare [spu'tare] *v* spit. **sputa fuori!** spit it out! **sputar sentenze** lecture. **sputar veleno** speak spitefully. **sputo** *sm* spit(tle), saliva; (*espettorato*) sputum.

squadernare [skwader'nare] *v* leaf through.

squadra[1] ['skwadra] *sf* (*strumento*) square. **a squadra** at right angles. **fuori squadra** crooked; (*fuori posto*) out of place; (*disordinato*) disorderly. **squadrare** *v* square; (*fig*) eye.

squadra[2] ['skwadra] *sf* (*mil*) section, squad; (*aero*) squadron; (*gruppo*) gang; (*sport*) team. **squadra mobile** flying squad. **squadriglia** *sf* band; (*mar*, *aero*) squadron.
squadro ['skwadro] *sm* angel-fish.
squagliarsi [skwa'ʎarsi] *v* melt. **squagliarsela** *v* sneak off.
squalificare [skwalifi'kare] *v* disqualify. **squalifica** *sf* disqualification.
squallido ['skwallido] *agg* dismal; (*fig*) squalid. **squallore** *sm* dreariness, squalor.
squalo ['skwalo] *sm* dog-fish; (*pescecane*) shark.
squama ['skwama] *sf* scale. **squamare** *v* scale. **squamoso** *agg* scaly.
squarciare [skwar'tʃare] *v* tear (to pieces), rend. **a squarciagola** at the top of one's voice. **squarcio** *sm* (*stoffa*) tear; (*ferita*) gash; (*fig*) passage.
squartare [skwar'tare] *v* quarter. **squartatoio** *sm* cleaver.
squassare [skwas'sare] *v* shake violently.
squattrinato [skwattri'nato] *agg* penniless.
squilibrare [skwili'brare] *v* unbalance. **squilibrarsi** *v* lose one's balance. **squilibrato** *agg* (mentally) unbalanced. **squilibrio** *sm* lack of equilibrium; (*econ*) imbalance; disproportion; (*mentale*) derangement.
squillare [skwil'lare] *v* ring; (*tromba*) sound; (*voce*) be shrill. **squillo** *sm* ring; (*suono*) squeal; (*tromba*) sound. **ragazza squillo** *sf* call-girl.
squinternare [skwinter'nare] *v* take to pieces; (*fig*) upset.
squisito [skwi'zito] *agg* excellent; delicious; (*raffinato*) exquisite. **squisitezza** *sf* deliciousness; delicacy.
squittire [skwit'tire] *v* (*uccelli*) chirp; (*topi*) squeak.
sradicare [sradi'kare] *v* (*divellere*) uproot; (*fig*) root out, eradicate.
sregolato [srego'lato] *agg* (*smodato*) immoderate; (*scapestrato*) wild.
stabbio ['stabbjo] *sm* pen; (*porcile*) pigsty; (*letame*) dung.
stabile ['stabile] *agg* stable; (*che non oscilla*) steady; permanent; (*durevole*) lasting.
stabilimento [stabili'mento] *sm* establishment; (*fabbrica*) factory, works; (*edificio*) building.
stabilire [stabi'lire] *v* establish; decide. **stabilirsi** *v* settle. **stabilità** *sf* stability. **stabilito** *agg* (*istituito*) established; (*fissato*) fixed; (*convenuto*) agreed. **stabilizzare** *v* stabilize. **stabilizzarsi** *v* settle. **stabilizzazione** *sf* stabilization.
staccare [stak'kare] *v* (*togliere*) take off; (*separare*) detach; (*tagliando*) cut off; (*strappando*) pluck; (*sganciare*) unhook; (*risaltare*) stand out. **staccare il lavoro** (*fam*) knock off work. **staccarsi** *v* move away; (*venir via*) come off; separate. **staccato** *agg* detached; separate; (*musica*) staccato.
stadio ['stadjo] *sm* (*sport*) stadium; (*tec*, *fase*) stage.
staffa ['staffa] *sf* stirrup; (*mec*) bracket; (*calza*) heel. **perdere le staffe** (*fig*) lose one's temper. **staffetta** *sf* courier; (*sport*) relay(-race).
staffilare [staffi'lare] *v* lash; (*fig*) lash out (at). **staffilata** *sf* lash; (*fig*) lashing criticism. **staffile** *sm* stirrup-strap; (*sferza*) lash.
stagione [sta'dʒone] *sf* season; (*condizioni atmosferiche*) weather. **fuori stagione** out of season; (*fig*) untimely. **stagionale** *agg* seasonal. **stagionare** *v* season; (*invecchiare*) age; mature. **stagionatura** *sf* ageing; maturing; seasoning.
stagno[1] ['staɲo] *sm* (*metallo*) tin. **stagnare** *v* tin; (*saldare*) solder; (*chiudere*) seal. **stagnola** *sf* tin foil.
stagno[2] ['staɲo] *sm* (*bacino d'acqua*) pool. *agg* (*a tenuta d'acqua*) watertight. **stagnare** *v* stagnate; (*sangue*) stanch; (*fermare*) stop.
stalagmite [stalag'mite] *sf* stalagmite.
stalattite [stalat'tite] *sf* stalactite.
stalla ['stalla] *sf* stable; (*bovini*) cow-shed; (*fig*) pigsty. **stallaggio** *sm* stabling. **stallone** *sm* stallion.
stallo ['stallo] *sm* seat; (*scacchi*) stalemate. **andare in stallo** (*aero*) stall.
stamattina [stamat'tina] *avv also* **stamani** this morning.
stamberga [stam'bɛrga] *sf* hovel.
stambugio [stam'budʒo] *sm* cubby-hole.
stame ['stame] *sm* (*bot*) stamen; (*tessile*) fine yarn.
stamigna [sta'miɲa] *sf* bunting.
stampa ['stampa] *sf* printing; (*giornali*) press; (*immagine*, *foto*) print. **errore di stampa** *sm* misprint. **stampe** *sf pl* (*posta*) printed matter *sing*. **stampaggio** (*foto*) printing; (*metallo*) forging; (*plastici*) moulding. **stampare** *v* print; publish;

(*con pressa*) press; forge; mould. **stampatello** *sm* block letters *pl*. **stampato** *sm* printed matter; (*modulo*) form; (*disegno*) print. **stampatore, -trice** *sm, sf* printer.
stampella [stam'pɛlla] *sf* crutch.
stampiglia [stam'piʎa] *sf* stamp. **stampigliare** *v* stamp.
stampino [stam'pino] *sm* stencil; (*punzone*) punch.
stampo ['stampo] *sm* mould; (*matrice*) die; (*fig*) kind, sort.
stanare [sta'nare] *v* drive out.
stancare [stan'kare] *v* tire; (*annoiare*) bore. **stancarsi** *v* get tired, tire. **stanchezza** *sf* tiredness; (*fiacchezza*) fatigue. **stanco** *agg* tired; bored.
standard ['standard] *sm invar* standard. **standardizzare** *v* standardize. **standardizzazione** *sf* standardization.
stanga ['stanga] *sf* bar. **stangare** *v* (*colpire*) thrash; (*bocciare*) fail; (*scuola*) give a bad mark; (*far pagare troppo*) rob. **stangata** *sf* blow.
stanotte [sta'nɔtte] *avv* tonight.
stante ['stante] *agg* **a sè stante** apart. **seduta stante** straight away. *prep* (*a causa di*) on account of.
stantio [stan'tio] *agg* stale.
stantuffo [stan'tuffo] *sm* piston; (*di pressa idraulica*) plunger.
stanza ['stantsa] *sf* room; (*poesia*) stanza. **stanza da bagno** bathroom. **stanza da pranzo** dining-room.
stanziare [stan'tsjare] *v* allocate; deliberate.
stappare [stap'pare] *v* uncork.
***stare** ['stare] *v* stay, remain; (*abitare*) live; (*essere*) be; (*vestiario*) suit; (*spettare*) be up to. **come stai?** how are you? **lasciar stare** leave alone. **non poter stare senza** be unable to do without. **stare a dieta** be on a diet. **stare in guardia** be on one's guard. **stare per** be about to. **sto bene** I am well. **sto male** I am not well.
starna ['starna] *sf* partridge.
starnutire [starnu'tire] *v* sneeze. **starnuto** *sm* sneeze.
stasera [sta'sera] *avv* this evening.
stasi ['stazi] *sf* standstill.
statale [sta'tale] *agg* state. **strada statale** *sf* trunk road. *s*(*m*+*f*) civil servant.
statica ['statika] *sf* statics. **statico** *agg* static; (*senza movimento*) motionless.
statista [sta'tista] *sm* statesman.
statistica [sta'tistika] *sf* statistics. **statistico** *agg* statistical.
stato ['stato] *sm* state; condition; (*posizione sociale*) status. **colpo di stato** *sm* coup d'état. **Stati Uniti** *sm pl* United States *pl*. **stato d'animo** mood. **ufficio di stato civile** *sm* register office. **statunitense** *s*(*m*+*f*), *agg* American.
statua ['statua] *sf* statue. **statuario** *agg* statuary.
statura [sta'tura] *sf* (*altezza*) height; (*fig*) stature.
statuto [sta'tuto] *sm* statute; constitution. **statutario** statutory.
stavolta [sta'vɔlta] *avv* this time.
stazione [sta'tsjone] *sf* station; (*località di soggiorno*) resort. **stazionamento** *sm* parking. **stazionare** *v* stop; park. **stazionario** *agg* stationary.
stecca ['stekka] *sf* small stick; (*biliardo*) cue; (*persiane*) slat; (*sigarette*) carton; (*hockey*) stick. **steccare** *v* fence (in); (*sonare*) play a wrong note. **steccato** *sm* fence. **a stecchetto** (*senza soldi*) hard up; (*senza cibo*) on short rations. **stecchito** *agg* (*rinsecchito*) dried up; (*magrissimo*) skinny. **morto stecchito** stone dead. **stecco** *sm* dry twig. **steccone** *sm* post.
stella ['stella] *sf* star. **alle stelle** (*prezzi*) sky-high. **stella alpina** edelweiss. **stella cadente** *or* **filante** shooting star; (*di carta*) streamer. **stella di mare** starfish. **stellare** *agg* (*astron*) stellar; (*forma*) star-shaped; (*bot*) stellate. **stellato** *agg* starry; (*fig*) studded. **stelletta** (*mil*) star; (*fam*) pip.
stelo ['stɛlo] *sm* stem; (*fiore*) stalk; (*gambo di utensile*) shank.
stemma ['stɛmma] *sm* coat of arms.
stemp(e)rare [stemp(e)'rare] *v* dissolve.
stendardo [sten'dardo] *sm* standard.
***stendere** ['stɛndere] *v* (*allungare*) stretch (out); (*distendere*) spread (out); (*bucato*) hang out; (*contratto*) draw up. **stendersi** *v* stretch out.
stenodattilografia [stenodattilogra'fia] *sf* shorthand typing. **stenodattilografo, -a** *sm, sf* shorthand typist. **stenografare** *v* take down in shorthand. **stenografia** *sf* shorthand. **stenografo, -a** *sm, sf* stenographer.
stentare [sten'tare] *v* find it hard, have difficulty. **stentatezza** *sf* difficulty. **stentato** *agg* laboured; (*di crescita arrestata*) stunted; (*pieno di stenti*) hard.

stento *sm* hardship; difficulty. **a stento** barely.
steppa ['steppa] *sf* steppe.
sterco ['sterko] *sm* excrement; (*letame*) dung.
stereo ['stereo] *agg, sm* stereo.
stereofonico [stereo'fɔniko] *agg* stereophonic; (*fam*) stereo.
stereotipato [stereoti'pato] *agg* stereotyped; (*fisso*) frozen. **concezione stereotipata** *sf* stereotype.
sterile ['sterile] *agg* sterile; (*fig*) vain. **sterilire** *v* sterilize. **sterilità** *sf* sterility; (*fig*) uselessness. **sterilizzare** *v* sterilize. **sterilizzatore** *sm* sterilizer. **sterilizzazione** *sf* sterilization.
sterlina [ster'lina] *sf* pound (sterling).
sterminare [stermi'nare] *v* exterminate. **sterminato** *agg* boundless. **sterminio** *sm* extermination.
sterna ['sterna] *sf* tern.
sterno ['sterno] *sm* breastbone.
sterzo ['stertso] *sm* (*auto*) steering; (*bicicletta*) handlebars *pl*. **sterzare** *v* (*auto*) steer; (*fig*) swerve. **sterzata** *sf* steering; swerve. **fare una sterzata** make a sharp turn.
stesso ['stesso] *agg* same; (*proprio*) very; (*personificato*) itself; (*in persona*) personally; (*rafforzativo, riflessivo*) myself, yourself, etc.
stesura [ste'zura] *sf* drafting; draft.
stetoscopio [stetos'kɔpjo] *sm* stethoscope.
stia ['stia] *sf* chicken coop. **essere (pigiati) come in una stia** be cooped up.
stigma ['stigma] *sm* stigma. **stigmatizzare** *v* stigmatize.
stilare [sti'lare] *v* draw up.
stile ['stile] *sm* style; (*eleganza*) stylishness. **di stile** stylish. **in grande stile** in style. **stilista** *s*(*m*+*f*) stylist. **stilistico** *agg* stylistic. **stilizzare** *v* stylize.
stilla ['stilla] *sf* drop. **a stilla a stilla** drop by drop. **stillare** *v* (*trasudare*) ooze, exude; (*gocciolare*) drip. **stillarsi il cervello** rack one's brains. **stillicidio** *sm* constant trickle.
stilo ['stilo] *sm* (*per scrivere*) stylus; (*stadera*) beam. **stilografica** *sf* fountain-pen.
stima ['stima] *sf* (*buona opinione*) esteem, regard; (*giudizio*) estimation; (*valutazione*) estimate. **a mia stima** in my estimation. **aver stima di** hold in high esteem. **con (la massima) stima** (*in lettere*) yours faithfully.
stimare [sti'mare] *v* estimate; (*apprezzare*) value, esteem; consider. **stimatore, -trice** *sm, sf* (*perito*) valuer; (*ammiratore*) admirer.
stimolare [stimo'lare] *v* stimulate; (*fig*) arouse; (*appetito*) whet. **stimolante** *sm* stimulant. **stimolatore cardiaco** *sm* pacemaker. **stimolazione** *sf* (*med*) stimulation; (*fig*) arousal. **stimolo** *sm* stimulus (*pl* -li).
stinco ['stinko] *sm* shin. **stincata** *sf* blow on the shin.
***stingere** ['stindʒere] *v* (*macchiare*) run; (*sbiadire*) fade.
stipare [sti'pare] *v* pack, cram.
stipendio [sti'pendjo] *sm* salary. **stipendio arretrato** back pay.
stipite ['stipite] *sm* doorpost.
stipulare [stipu'lare] *v* stipulate. **stipulazione** *sf* stipulation.
stiracchiare [stirak'kjare] *v* stretch; (*lesinare*) skimp. **stiracchiare sul prezzo** haggle. **stiracchiamento** *sm* stretching; haggling. **stiracchiatura** *sf* distortion.
stirare [sti'rare] *v* (*col ferro*) iron, press. **stirarsi** *v* stretch. **stiro** *sm* ironing; pressing. **ferro da stiro** *sm* iron. **tavolo da stiro** *sm* ironing-board.
stirpe ['stirpe] *sf* (*origine*) descent, extraction; (*razza*) race; family; (*discendenti*) offspring.
stitico ['stitiko] *agg* constipated; (*fig*) stingy. **stitichezza** *sf* constipation.
stiva ['stiva] *sf* hold. **stivaggio** *sm* stowage.
stivale [sti'vale] *sm* boot. **lustrar gli stivali a** (*fig*) lick the boots of. **rompere gli stivali a** (*fig*) pester.
stivaletto [stiva'letto] *sm* bootee.
stizza ['stittsa] *sf* anger. **avere** *or* **provare stizza per** be angry about. **stizzire** *v* anger. **stizzirsi** *v* get angry. **stizzito** *agg* angry. **stizzoso** *agg* irritable.
stoccafisso [stokka'fisso] *sm* dried cod.
stoccata [stok'kata] *sf* stab; (*scherma*) thrust; (*battuta*) gibe. **stocco** *sm* rapier.
Stoccolma [stok'kolma] *sf* Stockholm.
stoffa ['stɔffa] *sf* fabric, material; (*dote*) makings *pl*. **ha della stoffa** he has what it takes.
stoico ['stɔiko], **-a** *agg* stoical. *sm, sf* stoic.
stoino [sto'ino] *sm* doormat.
stola ['stɔla] *sf* stole.

stolto ['stolto], **-a** *agg* foolish. *sm, sf* fool. **stoltezza** *sf* foolishness; (*azione*) foolish action; (*parole*) nonsense.
stomaco ['stɔmako] *sm* stomach; (*fam*) tummy; (*fam*: *coraggio*) guts. **mal di stomaco** *sm* stomach-ache. ... **mi sta** *or* **rimane sullo stomaco** I cannot stomach .... **stomacare** *v* nauseate. **stomachevole** *agg* revolting.
stonare [sto'nare] *v* (*cantare*) sing out of tune; (*sonare*) play out of tune; (*contrastare*) clash. **stonata** *sf* wrong note. **stonato** *agg* out of tune; clashing; (*turbato*) upset.
stoppa ['stoppa] *sf* tow. **stoppare** *v* (*otturare*) block; (*sport*) stop. **stoppaccio** *sm* wad. **stoppie** *sf pl* stubble *sing*. **stoppino** *sm* wick.
***storcere** ['stortʃere] *v* twist; (*piegare*) bend. **storcersi il naso** turn up one's nose. **storcersi la bocca** make a wry face. **storcersi per il dolore** writhe in pain. **storcimento** *sm* twisting; wrench.
stordire [stor'dire] *v* stun; (*rumore*) deafen. **stordimento** *sm* (*stato d'animo*) bewilderment. **stordito** *agg* stunned; bewildered; (*distratto*) scatter-brained.
storia ['stɔrja] *sf* history; (*racconto*) story, tale; (*frottola*) fib, lie; (*faccenda*) business. **la solita storia** the same old story. **libro di storia** history book. **storie** *sf pl* (*trambusto*) fuss *sing*. **storiella** *sf* little story; (*barzelletta*) joke; (*fandonia*) fib.
storico ['stɔriko], **-a** *agg* (*della storia*) historical; (*famoso*) historic. *sm, sf* historian.
storione [sto'rjone] *sm* sturgeon.
stormo ['stormo] *sm* (*uccelli*) flock; (*cani*) pack; (*persone*) crowd; (*fig*) mess. **sonare a stormo** sound the alarm.
stornare [stor'nare] *v* (*allontanare*) avert; dissuade; transfer; annul. **storno** *sm* transfer.
stornello [stor'nɛllo] *sm also* **storno** (*uccello*) starling.
storno ['storno] *agg* dapple-grey.
storpio ['stɔrpjo], **-a** *agg* crippled. *sm, sf* cripple. **storpiare** *v* cripple; mispronounce.
storto ['stɔrto] *agg* crooked; (*sbagliato*) wrong. **aver gli occhi storti** squint. **aver le gambe storte** be bandy-legged. **storta** *sf* twist, sprain; (*recipiente*) retort. **prendersi una storta alla caviglia** twist one's ankle.
stoviglie [sto'viʎe] *sf pl* crockery *sing*. **lavar le stoviglie** wash the dishes, wash up.
strabico ['strabiko] *agg* cross-eyed. **strabismo** *sm* squint. **essere affetto da strabismo** have a squint.
strabiliante [strabi'ʎante] *agg* amazing.
straboccare [strabok'kare] *v* overflow. **strabocchevole** *agg* excessive.
stracarico [stra'kariko] *agg, m pl* **-chi** overloaded; (*fig*) overburdened.
stracciare [strat'tʃare] *v* tear; (*facendo a pezzi*) tear up.
straccio ['strattʃo] *sm* rag. *agg* waste. **straccione, -a** *sm, sf* ragamuffin; beggar.
stracco ['strakko] (*fam*) *agg* worn out, done in. **stracco morto** dead beat.
stracotto [stra'kɔtto] *agg* overcooked. **cotto e stracotto** overdone. *sm* (*gastr*) stew, casserole.
strada ['strada] *sf* road, street; (*percorso*) way; (*itinerario*) route; (*cammino*) journey; (*varco*) path. **a mezza strada** halfway. **che strada fai?** which way are you going? **far strada a qualcuno** show someone the way. **farsi strada** (*aprirsi un passaggio*) clear a way for oneself; (*ottener successo*) do well for oneself. **fuori strada** off the road; (*fig*) on the wrong track. **lungo** *or* **per la strada** on the way. **strada facendo** on the way. **stradale** *agg* road. **codice stradale** *sm* highway code. **lavori stradali** *sm pl* roadworks *pl*.
strafalcione [strafal'tʃone] *sm* blunder.
***strafare** [stra'fare] *v* overdo it.
straforo [stra'foro] *sm* **di straforo** indirectly; (*di nascosto*) on the quiet; (*di sfuggita*) in passing.
strage ['stradʒe] *sf* slaughter; (*distruzione*) havoc; (*fam*) mass.
stragrande [stra'grande] *agg* huge. **stragrande maggioranza** *sf* great majority.
stralciare [stral'tʃare] *v* take out; (*dedurre*) deduct; (*mettere in liquidazione*) wind up. **stralcio** *sm* removal; extract; liquidation. **vendere a stralcio** sell off.
stralunare [stralu'nare] *v* roll one's eyes. **stralunato** *agg* (*fig*) distraught.
stramazzare [stramat'tsare] *v* fall to the ground.
strambo ['strambo] *agg* odd; eccentric. **stramberia** *sf* oddity; eccentricity.

strampalato [strampa'lato] *agg* weird.
strangolare [strango'lare] *v* strangle. **strangolarsi** *v* choke. **strangolamento** *sm* strangulation.
straniero [stra'njɛro], **-a** *agg* foreign. *sm, sf* foreigner; (*termine burocratico*) alien.
strano ['strano] *agg* strange, odd. *sm* strange *or* odd thing. **strano a dirsi** oddly enough. **stranezza** *sf* peculiarity; (*atteggiamento*) odd behaviour.
straordinario [straordi'narjo] *agg* extraordinary; (*insolito*) unusual; special. **lavoro straordinario** *sm* overtime. *sm* unusual thing; overtime.
strapagare [strapa'gare] *v* (*fam*) pay through the nose.
strapazzare [strapat'tsare] *v* wear out; (*trattar male*) ill-treat. **uova strapazzate** *sf pl* scrambled eggs *pl*. **strapazzata** *sf* (*sgridata*) dressing-down; (*faticata*) strain. **strapazzo** *sm* strain; ill-treatment. **vestiti da strapazzo** *sm pl* working clothes *pl*.
strapieno [stra'pjɛno] *agg* full up.
strapiombare [strapjom'bare] *v* overhang, jut out. **a strapiombo** sheer, overhanging.
strappare [strap'pare] *v* snatch; (*portar via*) pull off *or* out; (*rompendo*) tear (off *or* out); (*in più pezzi*) tear up. **strappata** *sf* tug. **strappo** *sm* pull, tug; (*strattone*) jerk; tear. **strappo muscolare** pulled *or* torn muscle.
straripare [strari'pare] *v* overflow. **straripamento** *sm* overflowing.
strascicare [straʃi'kare] *v* trail; (*con fatica*) drag; (*fig*) drag out; (*pronuncia*) drawl. **strascico** *sm, pl* **-chi** (*fig*) after-effect; (*vestito*) train.
strascinare [straʃi'nare] *v* drag along.
stratagemma [strata'dʒɛmma] *sm* stragem; (*fig*) trick.
strategia [strate'dʒia] *sf* strategy. **strategico** *agg* strategic. **stratego, -a** *sm, sf* strategist.
strato ['strato] *sm* layer; (*vernice*) coat; (*geol, classe*) stratum (*pl* -a). **stratificato** *agg* stratified.
strattone [strat'tone] *sm* pull, jerk. **a strattoni** jerkily.
stravagante [strava'gante] *agg* extravagant. **stravaganza** *sf* extravagance.
stravecchio [stra'vɛkkjo] *agg* very old.
***stravincere** [stra'vintʃere] *v* win hands down; (*battere*) beat hollow.
straviziare [stravi'tsjare] *v* over-indulge. **stravizio** *sm* over-indulgence.
***stravolgere** [stra'vɔldʒere] *v* twist; (*fig*) affect deeply. **stravolgere gli occhi** roll one's eyes. **stravolgimento** *sm* twisting; contortion. **stravolto** *agg* twisted; (*fig*) deeply upset.
straziare [stra'tsjare] *v* torture, torment. **straziare il cuore a qualcuno** break someone's heart. **cuore straziato** *sm* broken heart. **strazio** *sm* torment, agony. **far strazio di** (*fig*) play havoc with.
strega ['strega] *sf* witch. **stregare** *v* bewitch. **stregone** *sm* wizard; (*mago*) sorcerer; (*popoli primitivi*) witch-doctor. **stregoneria** *sf* witchcraft; sorcery. **fare stregonerie** cast spells.
stregua ['stregwa] *sf* **alla stregua di** in the same way as. **a questa stregua** at this rate.
stremato [stre'mato] *agg* exhausted.
stremo ['strɛmo] *sm* limit.
strenna ['strɛnna] *sf* gift.
strenuo ['strɛnuo] *agg* valiant; (*fig*) untiring.
strepitare [strepi'tare] *v* make a din; (*gridando*) shout. **strepito** *sm* clamour, uproar. **fare strepito** cause a stir. **strepitoso** *agg* noisy; (*fragoroso*) resounding; (*fig*) tremendous.
streptococco [strepto'kɔkko] *sm* streptococcus. **streptomicina** *sf* streptomycin.
stretta ['stretta] *sf* hold; (*abbraccio*) embrace; (*presa*) grip; critical point; (*situazione difficile*) predicament. **essere** *or* **trovarsi alle strette** be in a tight corner. **stretta alla gola** lump in the throat. **stretta di mano** handshake.
stretto ['stretto] *agg* narrow; (*vestiario*) tight; (*rigoroso*) strict; (*denti, pugni*) clenched. *sm* strait. **strettoia** *sf* (*strada*) narrowing of the road; (*fig*) tight spot.
striato [stri'ato] *agg* striped.
stricnina [strik'nina] *sf* strychnine.
stridere ['stridere] *v* (*strillare*) shriek, screech; (*insetti*) chirp; (*cigolare*) squeak; (*fig*) clash. **stridente** *agg* strident; clashing. **strido** *sm, pl* **-a** *f* shriek, screech; squeak; chirp.
strigliata [stri'ʎata] *sf* dressing-down.
strillare [stril'lare] *v* scream; (*parlare ad alta voce*) shout. **strillo** *sm* scream. **strillone** *sm* news-vendor.
striminzito [strimin'tsito] *agg* skimpy; (*magro*) skinny.

strimpellare [strimpel'lare] *v* strum.
strinare [stri'nare] *v* scorch.
stringa ['stringa] *sf* lace. **stringare** *v* lace (up); (*fig*) condense.
***stringere** ['strindʒere] *v* (*avvicinare*) squeeze *or* press (together); (*serrare*) clasp, clutch; (*vestiario*) pinch; (*concludere*) make; (*denti, pugni*) clench. **il tempo stringe** time is getting short. **stringere i tempi** speed things up; (*musica*) quicken the tempo. **stringere la cinghia** (*fig*) tighten one's belt. **stringere la mano a** shake hands with. **stringere un'amicizia** strike up a friendship. **stringi stringi** when all is said and done.
striscia ['striʃa] *sf* strip; (*riga larga*) stripe; (*traccia*) streak. **a strisce** striped. **strisce pedonali** *sf pl* zebra crossing *sing*. **strisciare** *v* creep, crawl; (*sfiorando*) slide; (*sfiorare*) graze. **strisciare i piedi** drag one's feet. **colpire di striscio** graze. **striscione** *sm* banner.
stritolare [stritõ'lare] *v* crush.
strizzare [strit'tsare] *v* wring out; (*spremere*) squeeze. **strizzar l'occhio** wink. **strizzata** *sf* squeeze; wink.
strofinare [strofi'nare] *v* rub. **strofinaccio** *sm* rag. **strofinata** *sf* quick rub. **strofinio** *sm* prolonged rubbing.
strombazzare [strombat'tsare] *v* shout from the roof-tops. **strombazzare i propri meriti** blow one's own trumpet.
strombettare [strombet'tare] *v* blare; (*auto*) blow the horn.
stroncare [stron'kare] *v* break off; (*tagliando*) cut off; (*fig*) cut short; (*criticare*) slate. **stroncatura** *sf* slating.
stronzo ['strontso] *sm* (*volg*) turd; (*fig*) idiot.
stropicciare [stropit'tʃare] *v* rub. **stropicciarsene** *v* (*fam*) not care a damn.
strozzare [strot'tsare] *v* strangle, choke; (*med*) strangulate. **strozzatura** *sf* narrowing; (*occlusione*) bottle-neck; strangling. **strozzino, -a** *sm, sf* usurer.
***struggere** ['struddʒere] *v* melt; (*fig*) eat up. **struggersi** *v* be consumed.
strumento [stru'mento] *sm* instrument; (*arnese*) tool. **strumento ad arco** stringed instrument. **strumento a fiato** woodwind instrument. **strumentale** *agg* instrumental. **strumentare** *v* orchestrate.
strusciare [stru'ʃare] *v* scrape.
strutto ['strutto] *sm* lard.
struttura [strut'tura] *sf* structure. **strutturale** *agg* structural. **strutturare** *v* structure. **strutturazione** *sf* organization.
struzzo ['struttso] *sm* ostrich. **fare lo struzzo** bury one's head in the sand.
stuccare[1] [stuk'kare] *v* plaster; (*decorare*) stucco. **stuccatore** *sm* plasterer; stucco-worker. **stucco** *sm* plaster; (*per finestre*) putty; (*arte*) stucco. **rimaner di stucco** be dumbfounded.
stuccare[2] [stuk'kare] *v* (*nauseare*) make sick; (*annoiare*) bore. **stucchevole** *agg* sickly; boring. **stucco** *agg* sick (of).
studente [stu'dente], **-essa** *sm, sf* student. **studentesco** *agg* (*di scuola*) school; university.
studiare [stu'djare] *v* study; (*cercar di trovare*) try and find. **studiare a memoria** learn by heart. **studiato** *agg* studied; affected.
studio ['studjo] *sm* study; (*progetto*) plan; (*di avvocato*) office; (*di medico*) surgery; (*di artista, fotografo, ecc.*) studio. **allo studio** under consideration. **fare gli studi** study.
studioso [stu'djozo], **-a** *agg* studious. *sm, sf* scholar.
stufa ['stufa] *sf* stove, heater. **stufare** *v* (*gastr*) stew; (*fam*: *annoiare*) bore. **stufarsi di** get sick and tired of. **stufato** *sm* stew. **stufo** *agg* fed up (with).
stuoia ['stwɔja] *sf* mat. **stuoino** *sm* door-mat.
stuolo ['stwɔlo] *sm* crowd.
***stupefare** [stupe'fare] *v* astound. **stupefacente** *sm* drug, narcotic. **stupefatto** *agg* astonished, amazed.
stupendo [stu'pendo] *agg* stupendous.
stupido ['stupido] *agg* stupid; (*sciocco*) foolish. **stupidaggine** *sf* stupidity; (*atto*) foolish thing; (*parole*) nonsense; (*inezia*) trifle. **dir stupidaggini** talk nonsense. **stupidità** *sf* stupidity.
stupire [stu'pire] *v* amaze, astonish. **stupirsi** *v* be amazed *or* astonished (at). **stupore** *sm* astonishment, amazement; (*med*) stupor.
stuprare [stu'prare] *v* rape. **stupro** *sm* rape.
sturare [stu'rare] *v* uncork. **sturabottiglie** *sm invar* corkscrew. **sturalavandini** *sm invar* plunger.

stuzzicare [stuttsi'kare] *v* prod; (*molestare*) annoy; (*punzecchiare*) tease; (*stimolare*) excite. **stuzzicadenti** *sm invar* toothpick. **stuzzicar l'appetito** whet the appetite. **stuzzicante** *agg* exciting; appetizing.

su [su] *prep* on; (*senza contatto*) over; (*più in alto di*) above; (*vicino*) by; (*verso*) towards; (*intorno a, circa*) about; (*oltre*) after. **dare su** look out over. **novanta volte su cento** (*fig*) nine times out of ten. *avv* (*in alto*) up; (*indosso*) on; (*al piano superiore*) upstairs. **avercela su con** (*fam*) be cross with. **in su** up; (*età, numero*) upwards. **su per giù** roughly. *inter* come on!

subacqueo [su'bakkweo] *agg* underwater.

subaffittare [subaffit'tare] *v* sublet. **dare in subaffitto** sublet.

subalterno [subal'tɛrno], **-a** *s*, *agg* subordinate.

subappaltare [subappal'tare] *v* subcontract. **subappalto** *sm* subcontract.

subbia ['subbja] *sf* chisel.

subbio ['subbjo] *sm* beam.

subbuglio [sub'buʎo] *sm* turmoil; confusion.

subconscio [sub'kɔnʃo] *sm*, *agg* subconscious.

subdolo ['subdolo] *agg* underhand.

subentrare [suben'trare] *v* take the place of; succeed.

subire [su'bire] *v* suffer; (*sottoporsi a*) undergo.

subissare [subis'sare] *v* (*fig*) overwhelm. **subisso** *sm* (*fam*) load; (*rovina*) ruin.

subito ['subito] *avv* at once, immediately. **subito prima** just before. **subitaneità** *sf* suddenness. **subitaneo** *agg* sudden.

sublimare [subli'mare] *v* sublimate. **sublimato** *sm* sublimate. **sublimazione** *sf* sublimation.

sublime [sub'lime] *agg*, *sm* sublime.

subnormale [subnor'male] *agg*, *sm* subnormal.

subodorare [subodo'rare] *v* **subodorare un inganno** smell a rat.

subordinare [subordi'nare] *v* subordinate. **subordinato, -a** *agg*, *s* subordinate. **subordinazione** *sf* subordination.

subornare [subor'nare] *v* suborn. **subornazione** *sf* subornation.

suburbano [subur'bano] *agg* suburban.

***succedere** [sut'tʃɛdere] *v* follow; succeed; (*capitare*) happen. **cosa sta succedendo?** what is happening? **cosa ti succede?** what is the matter with you? **sono cose che succedono** these things will happen.

successione [suttʃes'sjone] *sf* succession. **successione delle colture** crop rotation. **tasse di successione** *sf pl* death duties *pl*. **successivamente** *avv* subsequently. **successivo** *agg* (*seguente*) following; (*uno dopo l'altro*) consecutive. **successore** *sm* successor.

successo [sut'tʃɛsso] *sm* success. **aver cattivo successo** be unsuccessful. **aver successo** be successful.

succhiare [suk'kjare] *v* suck. **succhietto** *or* **succhiotto** *sm* dummy. **succhione** *sm* sucker.

succhiello [suk'kjɛllo] *sm* gimlet.

succinto [sut'tʃinto] *agg* scanty; (*fig*) succinct.

succitato [suttʃi'tato] *agg* above-mentioned.

succo ['sukko] *sm* juice; (*fig*) essence, gist. **succoso** *agg* juicy; (*fig*) meaty. **succulento** *agg* succulent, juicy; (*pasto*) tasty.

succube ['sukkube] *s*(*m*+*f*) slave.

succursale [sukkur'sale] *sf* branch.

sud [sud] *sm* south. **abitante del sud** *s*(*m*+*f*) southerner. **al sud** (*stato*) in the south; (*moto*) to the south. **del sud** south, southern. **Sudafrica** *sf* South Africa. **sudafricano, -a** *s*, *agg* South African. **Sudamerica** *sf* South America. **sudamericano, -a** *s*, *agg* South American.

sudare [su'dare] *v* sweat, perspire; (*lavorar molto*) toil. **sudar freddo** be in a cold sweat. **sudata** *sf* sweat. **sudaticcio** *agg* sweaty.

suddetto [sud'detto] *agg* above-mentioned.

suddito ['suddito], **-a** *sm*, *sf* subject.

***suddividere** [suddi'videre] *v* subdivide, divide. **suddivisione** *sf* division, subdivision.

sud-est [sud'ɛst] *sm* south-east. **del sud-est** south-east(ern).

sudicio ['suditʃo] *agg* dirty; (*molto sporco*) filthy. *sm invar* filth. **sudiciume** *sm* filth.

sudore [su'dore] *sm* sweat, perspiration.

sud-ovest [sud'ɔvest] *sm* south-west. **del sud-ovest** south-west(ern).

sufficiente [suffi'tʃɛnte] *agg* enough;

(*adeguato*) sufficient; presumptuous. **sufficiente a se stesso** self-sufficient. *sm* enough. **avere il sufficiente per vivere** have enough to live on. **sufficienza** *sf* sufficiency. **a sufficienza** more than enough.
suffisso [suf'fisso] *sm* suffix.
suffragio [suf'fradʒo] *sm* suffrage. **suffragetta** *sf* suffragette.
suffumicare [suffumi'kare] *v* fumigate. **suffumicazione** *sf* fumigation.
suga ['suga] *agg* **carta suga** *or* **sugante** *sf* blotting paper.
suggello [sud'dʒɛllo] *sm* seal. **suggellare** *v* seal.
suggerire [suddʒe'rire] *v* suggest; (*consigliare*) advise; (*richiamare*) bring to mind; (*teatro*) prompt. **suggerimento** *sm* suggestion; piece of advice. **suggeritore, -trice** *sm, sf* prompter.
suggestione [suddʒes'tjone] *sf* suggestion; impression; (*fascino*) charm. **suggestionabile** *agg* easily influenced, impressionable. **suggestionabilità** *sf* suggestibility. **suggestionare** *v* influence; (*persuadere*) induce. **suggestivo** *agg* suggestive; evocative. **domanda suggestiva** *sf* leading question.
sughero ['sugero] *sm* cork.
sugli ['suʎi] *prep+art* **su gli**.
sugna ['suɲa] *sf* pork fat.
sugo ['sugo] *sm* (*succo*) juice; (*salsa*) sauce; (*fig*) (main) point. **senza sugo** (*fig*) pointless. **sugoso** *agg* juicy; (*fig*) meaty.
sui ['sui] *prep+art* **su i**.
suicida [sui'tʃida] *agg* suicidal. *s(m+f)* suicide. **suicidarsi** *v* commit suicide. **suicidio** *sm* suicide.
suino [su'ino] *sm* pig, swine. *agg* pig. **carne suina** *sf* pork.
sul [sul] *prep+art* **su il**.
sulfureo [sul'fureo] *agg* sulphurous.
sull' [sull] *prep+art* **su l'**.
sulla ['sulla] *prep+art* **su la**.
sulle ['sulle] *prep+art* **su le**.
sullo ['sullo] *prep+art* **su lo**.
sultano [sul'tano] *sm* sultan. **(uva) sultanina** *sf* sultana.
sunto ['sunto] *sm* summary. **sunteggiare** *v also* **fare il sunto** sum up, summarize.
suo ['suo], *m pl* **suoi** *agg* (*uomo*) his; (*donna*) her; (*cosa, animale*) its; (*riflessivo*) one's. *pron* his; hers. **a ciascuno il suo** to each his own.
suocera ['swɔtʃera] *sf* mother-in-law; (*spreg*) battle-axe. **suocero** *sm* father-in-law.
suola ['swɔla] *sf* sole. **suolare** *v* (*mettere la suola*) sole.
suolo ['swɔlo] *sm* ground; (*terreno*) soil.
suonare [swo'nare] *V* **sonare**.
suono ['swɔno] *sm* sound; tone. **suono falso** discord; (*fig*) false ring.
suora ['swɔra] *sf* nun, sister.
super ['super] *agg* (*benzina*) four-star.
superare [supe'rare] *v* (*dimensione, quantità*) exceed; (*oltrepassare*) go beyond, surpass; (*di passaggio*) pass, overtake; (*sostenere*) get over *or* through. **superato** *agg* (*antiquato*) old-fashioned; (*non più valido*) obsolete.
superbo [su'pɛrbo] *agg* haughty; (*fiero*) proud; (*fig*) magnificent, superb. **superbia** *sf* haughtiness. **senza superbia** modestly.
supercongelato [superkondʒe'lato] *agg* deep-frozen.
superficie [super'fitʃe] *sf* surface; area. **alla superficie** on the surface. **superficiale** *agg* superficial; (*geom*) plane. **tensione superficiale** *sf* surface tension.
superfluo [su'pɛrfluo] *agg* (*eccessivo*) superfluous; (*inutile*) unnecessary. *sm* surplus.
superiore [supe'rjore] *agg* (*più in alto*) upper; (*maggiore*) higher; (*fig*) superior; (*di grado*) senior; advanced. **superiore alla media** above average. **superiorità** *sf* superiority.
superlativo [superla'tivo] *sm, agg* superlative.
supermercato [supermer'kato] *sm* supermarket.
supero ['supero] *sm* surplus.
supersonico [super'sɔniko] *agg* supersonic.
superstite [su'pɛrstite] *agg* surviving. *s(m+f)* survivor.
superstizione [supersti'tsjone] *sf* superstition. **superstizioso** *agg* superstitious.
superuomo [supe'rwɔmo] *sm* superman.
supervisione [supervi'zjone] *sf* supervision. **supervisore** *sm* supervisor.
supino [su'pino] *agg* supine. **giacere supino** lie on one's back.
suppellettili [suppel'lɛttili] *sf pl* furnishings *pl*; (*di casa*) household goods *pl*.
suppergiù [supper'dʒu] *avv* roughly, more or less.

supplemento [supple'mento] *sm* supplement; (*prezzo*) additional charge; (*biglietto*) excess fare. **supplementare** *agg* additional, extra; (*econ, mat*) supplementary.
supplicare [suppli'kare] *v* implore. **supplica** *sf* plea. **in atto di supplica** imploringly. **supplicante** *s*(*m*+*f*) supplicant. **supplichevole** *agg* imploring.
supplire [sup'plire] *v* make up for; (*fare le veci*) stand in for. **supplente** *s*(*m*+*f*) supply teacher.
supplizio [sup'plitsjo] *sm* torture; (*pena di morte*) capital punishment. **suppliziare** *v* torture.
***supporre** [sup'porre] *v* suppose; imagine. **supposizione** *sf* supposition. **supposto che** assuming that, supposing.
supporto [sup'pɔrto] *sm* support; (*mec*) bearing; (*sostegno*) stand.
supposta [sup'posta] *sf* suppository.
suppurare [suppu'rare] *v* fester. **suppurazione** *sf* festering.
supremo [su'prɛmo] *agg* supreme; (*massimo*) highest. **supremazia** *sf* supremacy.
surgelare [surdʒe'lare] *v* freeze. **surgelato** *sm* frozen food.
surreale [surre'ale] *agg* unreal. **surrealismo** *sm* surrealism. **surrealista** *s*(*m*+*f*), *agg* surrealist.
surriscaldare [surriskal'dare] *v* overheat. **surriscaldamento** *sm* overheating.
surrogare [surro'gare] *v* substitute. **surrogato** *sm, agg* substitute. **surrogazione** *sf* surrogation.
suscettibile [suʃet'tibile] *agg* capable (of), susceptible; (*facile a risentirsi*) touchy. **suscettibilità** *sf* susceptibility. **offendere la suscettibilità di qualcuno** hurt someone's feelings.
suscitare [suʃi'tare] *v* provoke, give rise to.
susina [su'zina] *sf* plum, damson. **susino** *sm* plum-tree, damson-tree.
susseguirsi [susse'gwirsi] *v* follow (each other). **susseguente** *agg* following, subsequent.
sussidiare [sussi'djare] *v* subsidize. **sussidiario** *agg* subsidiary. **sussidio** *sm* aid; (*di denaro*) subsidy.
sussistere [sus'sistere] *v* exist; (*esser fondato*) subsist. **sussistenza** *sf* subsistence; (*mil*) catering.
sussultare [sussul'tare] *v* (give a) start. **far sussultare** startle. **sussulto** *sm* start.
sussurrare [sussur'rare] *v* murmur; (*dire a bassa voce*) whisper. **sussurro** *sm* murmur; whisper.
sutura [su'tura] *sf* suture. **suturare** *v* suture.
suvvia [suv'via] *inter* come on!
svago ['zvago] *sm* diversion; (*divertimento*) amusement. **svagare** *v* distract. **svagarsi** *v* amuse oneself. **svagatezza** *sf* absent-mindedness. **svagato** *agg* absent-minded.
svaligiare [zvali'dʒare] *v* ransack. **svaligiatore, -trice** *sm, sf* burglar.
svalutare [zvalu'tare] *v* devalue. **svalutazione** *sf* devaluation.
svanire [zva'nire] *v* vanish; (*fig*) fade away; (*esaurirsi*) lose strength. **svanito** *agg* (*odore*) evaporated; (*mente*) feeble-minded.
svantaggio [zvan'taddʒo] *sm* disadvantage; (*pregiudizio*) drawback; (*danno*) detriment. **svantaggiato** *agg* handicapped. **svantaggioso** *agg* disadvantageous; detrimental.
svariare [zva'rjare] *v* vary; diversify. **svariato** *agg* various.
svasato [zva'zato] *v* flared. **svasatura** *sf* flare.
svastica ['zvastika] *sf* swastika.
svecchiare [zvek'kjare] *v* renew.
svedese [zve'deze] *agg* Swedish. *sm* (*lingua*) Swedish; (*fiammifero*) safety match. *s*(*m*+*f*) (*persona*) Swede.
svegliare [zve'ʎare] *v* wake up; (*fig*) arouse. **svegliarsi** *v* wake up. **sveglia** *sf* call; (*mil*) reveille; (*orologio*) alarm-clock. **sveglio** *agg* awake; (*fig*) quick (-witted).
svelare [zve'lare] *v* reveal.
svelto ['zvɛlto] *agg* quick; intelligent; (*slanciato*) slim. **svelto di mano** light-fingered. **sveltezza** *sf* quickness; (*rapidità*) speed; slimness. **sveltire** *v* quicken; (*render disinvolto*) smarten *or* liven up; make (more) slender.
svendere ['zvendere] *v* sell off. **svendita** *sf* sale.
***svenire** [zve'nire] *v* faint. **svenevole** *agg* mawkish. **svenimento** *sm* fainting fit.
sventare [zven'tare] *v* foil. **sventatezza** *sf* thoughtlessness. **sventato** *agg* thoughtless.
sventola ['zvɛntola] *sf* fan; (*pugilato*) hook; (*schiaffo*) slap. **sventolare** *v* flutter; (*arieggiare*) air.

sventrare [zven'trare] *v* rip open; (*animale*) disembowel; (*fig*) demolish. **sventramento** *sm* demolition.

sventura [zven'tura] *sf* misfortune; (*mala sorte*) bad luck. **per colmo di sventura** to crown it all. **per mia sventura** unluckily for me. **sventurato** *agg* unlucky.

svergognare [zvergo'ɲare] *v* (put to) shame. **svergognatezza** *sf* impudence. **svergognato, -a** *sm, sf* shameless *or* impudent person.

svernare [zver'nare] *v* winter.

sverza ['zvɛrtsa] *sf* splinter. **sverzare** *v* splinter.

svestire [zves'tire] *v* undress.

Svezia ['zvetsja] *sf* Sweden.

svezzare [zvet'tsare] *v* wean. **svezzamento** *sm* weaning.

sviare [zvi'are] *v* divert; (*fig*) lead astray. **sviare il discorso** change the subject. **sviamento** *sm* diversion. **sviato** *agg* misguided.

svignarsela [zvi'ɲarsela] *v* sneak away.

svigorire [zvigo'rire] *v* weaken.

sviluppo [zvi'luppo] *sm* development; (*crescita*) growth. **età dello sviluppo** *sf* puberty. **sviluppare** *v* develop; (*produrre*) generate; (*estendersi*) grow.

svincolare [zvinko'lare] *v* release; (*riscattare*) redeem. **svincolarsi** *v* free oneself (from). **svincolo** *sm* release; (*comm*) clearance; (*autostrada*) exit.

svisare [zvi'zare] *v* twist.

sviscerare [zviʃe'rare] *v* disembowel; (*fig*) exhaust. **sviscerarsi per** dote on. **sviscerato** *agg* passionate; (*spreg*) obsequious.

svista ['zvista] *sf* oversight.

svitare [zvi'tare] *v* unscrew. **svitato, -a** *sm, sf* (*fam*) nut.

Svizzera ['zvittsera] *sf* Switzerland. **svizzero, -a** *s, agg* Swiss.

svogliato [zvo'ʎato] *agg* listless; unenthusiastic; (*indolente*) slack. **svogliatezza** *sf* listlessness.

svolazzare [zvolat'tsare] *v* flutter. **svolazzo** *sm* flourish.

***svolgere** ['zvɔldʒere] *v* develop. **svolgersi** *v* proceed, go; (*distendersi*) unfold; (*voltarsi*) turn. **svolgimento** *sm* development. **svolta** *sf* turning; (*fig*) turning point; curve.

svuotare [zvwo'tare] *v* empty.

T

tabacco [ta'bakko] *sm* tobacco. **tabaccaio, -a** *sm, sf* tobacconist. **tabaccheria** *sf* tobacconist's (shop).

tabella [ta'bella] *sf* table; list. **tabellone** *sm* notice-board; (*per affissioni murali*) hoarding; (*sport*) score-board.

tabù [ta'bu] *agg, sm* taboo.

tabulatore [tabula'tore], **-trice** *sm, sf* tabulator.

tacca ['takka] *sf* nick; (*macchia*) blotch; (*qualità*) kind; (*difetto*) fault.

taccagno [tak'kaɲo] *agg* stingy. **taccagneria** *sf* stinginess.

taccheggiatore [takkeddʒa'tore], **-trice** *sm, sf* shop-lifter. **taccheggio** *sm* shop-lifting.

tacchino [tak'kino] *sm* turkey.

taccia ['tattʃa] *sf* (bad) reputation. **tacciare** *v* accuse.

tacco ['takko] *sm* heel. **battere i tacchi** click one's heels.

taccuino [takku'ino] *sm* note-book.

***tacere** [ta'tʃere] *v* be *or* keep quiet; (*fam*) shut up; (*non dir nulla*) say nothing. **far tacere** hush.

tachimetro [ta'kimetro] *sm* speedometer.

tacito ['tatʃito] *agg* tacit; (*silenzioso*) silent. **taciturno** *agg* taciturn.

tafano ['tafano] *sm* horsefly.

tafferuglio [taffe'ruʎo] *sm* brawl.

taglia ['taʎa] *sf* (*premio*) reward; (*statura*) size.

tagliando [ta'ʎando] *sm* coupon; (*scontrino*) voucher.

tagliare [ta'ʎare] *v* cut; (*staccare, interrompere*) cut off; (*trinciare*) carve; (*in più parti*) cut up; (*vino*) blend. **tagliaboschi** *sm invar* woodcutter. **tagliacarte** *sm invar* paper-knife. **tagliapietre** *sm invar* stonemason. **tagliare la testa al toro** settle a matter once and for all.

tagliente [ta'ʎente] *agg* cutting.

tagliere [ta'ʎere] *sm* chopping board.

taglio ['taʎo] *sm* cut; (*parte staccata*) piece; (*parte tagliente*) (cutting) edge; (*importo*) denomination.

tagliola [ta'ʎɔla] *sf* trap.

tagliuzzare [taʎut'tsare] *v* chop up; (*a strisce*) cut to shreds.

tailleur [ta'jœr] *sm* suit.

talco ['talko] *sm* talc.

tale ['tale] *agg* such; certain. **tal dei tali** so-and-so. **tale quale** exactly like. **tale . . . tale . . .** like . . . like . . . . **un (certo) tale** a certain person.

talento [ta'lento] *sm* talent.

talismano [taliz'mano] *sm* talisman, charm.

talloncino [tallon'tʃino] *sm* counterfoil.

tallone [tal'lone] *sm* heel. **tallonare** *v* shadow; (*sport*) mark.

talora [ta'lora] *avv* at times.

talpa ['talpa] *sf* mole.

taluni [ta'luni] *pron, agg* some.

talvolta [tal'vɔlta] *avv* sometimes.

tamburo [tam'buro] *sm* drum; (*sonatore*) drummer; (*mec*) barrel, drum. **tamburellare** *v* drum. **tamburello** *sm* tambourine.

Tamigi [ta'midʒi] *sm* Thames.

tamponare [tampo'nare] *v* plug; (*auto*) bump into. **tamponare una falla** stop a leak. **tampone** *sm* plug; tampon.

tana ['tana] *sf* den.

tanfo ['tanfo] *sm* musty smell.

tangente [tan'dʒɛnte] *sf* tangent. **tangenziale** *sf* (*strada*) ring road.

tangibile [tan'dʒibile] *agg* tangible.

tango ['tango] *sm* tango.

tanto ['tanto] *agg* (so) much *or* many; (*altrettanto*) as much *or* many; (*molto*) a lot (of). **tanto . . . quanto . . .** as much . . . as . . . . *pron* a lot; much *or* many. **tanti** *pron* (*persone*) so many (people). **tanto per** so much for. *avv* so (much); (*soltanto*) just. **da tanto** (*tempo*) for such a long time. **di tanto in tanto** from time to time. **ogni tanto** from time to time. **tanti auguri!** best wishes! congratulations! **tanto meglio** so much the better. **tanto più che** especially as.

tappa ['tappa] *sf* stage; (*sosta*) stop.

tappare [tap'pare] *v* shut; (*con tappo*) bung (up). **tapparsi il naso** hold one's nose. **tapparsi le orecchie** close one's ears.

tapparella [tappa'rɛlla] *sf* blind.

tappeto [tap'peto] *sm* carpet; (*piccolo*) rug; (*sport, tec*) mat. **mettere al tappeto** knock down.

tappezzare [tappet'tsare] *v* (*di carta*) paper; (*di legno*) panel; (*di stoffa*) cover, upholster. **tappezzeria** *sf* (*carta*) wallpaper; (*stoffa*) tapestry; (*legno*) panelling; (*mobili*) upholstery. **tappezziere** *sm* decorator; upholsterer.

tappo ['tappo] *sm* stopper, plug; (*sughero*) cork; (*a vite*) screw-cap.

tara ['tara] *sf* tare; defect. **tarato** *agg* (*tec*) calibrated; (*difettoso*) tainted.

tarantola [ta'rantola] *sf* tarantula.

tarchiato [tar'kjato] *agg* sturdy.

tardare [tar'dare] *v* be late. **tardi** *avv* late. **tardivo** *agg* late; retarded. **tardo** *agg* (*lento*) slow; (*tempo*) late; (*età*) ripe old.

targa ['targa] *sf* plate; (*auto*) number-plate. **targare** *v* (*auto*) register.

tariffa [ta'riffa] *sf* rate; (*trasporto pubblico*) fare; (*dogana*) tariff.

tarlo ['tarlo] *sm* woodworm. **tarlo del dubbio** gnawing doubt. **tarlato** *agg* worm-eaten.

tarma ['tarma] *sf* moth.

tarpare [tar'pare] *v* **tarpare le ali a** clip the wings of.

tartagliare [tarta'ʎare] *v* stammer.

tartaro ['tartaro] *sm* tartar.

tartaruga [tarta'ruga] *sf* tortoise.

tartassare [tartas'sare] *v* ill-treat.

tartina [tar'tina] *sf* canapé.

tartufo [tar'tufo] *sm* truffle.

tasca ['taska] *sf* pocket. **avere le tasche piene (di)** (*fam*) be sick and tired (of). **conoscere come le proprie tasche** know like the back of one's hand. **tascabile** *agg* pocket.

tassa ['tassa] *sf* tax; (*imposta*) duty; (*giudiziaria, scolastica*) fee. **tassametro** *sm* meter.

tassare [tas'sare] *v* tax. **tassare troppo** (*fig*) overtax. **tassabile** *agg* taxable; subject to duty. **tassativo** *agg* express; definite.

tassello [tas'sɛllo] *sm* dowel; (*prelievo*) wedge; (*indumento*) gusset.

tassì [tas'si] *sm* taxi. **tassista** *sm* taxi-driver.

tasso[1] ['tasso] *sm* (*zool*) badger.

tasso[2] ['tasso] *sm* (*bot*) yew(-tree).

tasso[3] ['tasso] *sm* (*rapporto*) rate.

tastare [tas'tare] *v* feel. **tastare il terreno** (*fig*) see how the land lies. **tastiera** *sf* keyboard. **tasto** *sm* key; (*argomento*) subject; (*tatto*) touch. **a tastoni** feeling one's way.

tattica ['tattika] *sf* tactics *pl.* **tattico** *agg* tactical.

tatto ['tatto] *sm* touch; (*fig*) tact. **con tatto** tactfully. **mancare di tatto** be tactless. **senza tatto** tactlessly.

tatuaggio [tatu'addʒo] *sm* tattoo. **tatuare** *v* tattoo.
tautologia [tautolo'dʒia] *sf* tautology. **tautologico** *agg* tautological.
taverna [ta'vɛrna] *sf* inn, pub.
tavola ['tavola] *sf* table; (*asse*) board. **tavola calda** snack-bar. **tavola da disegno/stiro** drawing/ironing board. **tavola di comando** console. **tavola nera** blackboard. **tavola reale** (*gioco*) backgammon.
tavolato [tavo'lato] *sm* (*pavimento*) flooring; (*assito*) partition; (*geog*) plateau.
tavolo ['tavolo] *sm* table; (*ufficio, studio*) desk.
tavolozza [tavo'lɔttsa] *sf* palette.
tazza ['tattsa] *sf* cup; (*gabinetto*) lavatory pan; (*fontana*) basin.
te [te] *pron* you. *V* **ti**.
tè [te] *sm* tea.
teatro [te'atro] *sm* theatre; (*attività professionale*) stage; (*complesso di opere*) plays *pl*. **teatro lirico** (*edificio*) opera house; (*genere*) opera. **teatrale** *agg* theatrical.
tecnica ['tɛknika] *sf* technique; technology.
tecnico ['tɛkniko], **-a** *agg* technical. *sm, sf* technician, engineer; expert. **tecnicismo** *sm* technicality.
tecnologia [teknolo'dʒia] *sf* technology. **tecnologico** *agg* technological.
tedesco [te'desko], **-a** *s, agg* German.
tedio ['tɛdjo] *sm* tediousness. **tedioso** *agg* tedious.
tegame [te'game] *sm* (frying-)pan. **uova al tegame** *sf pl* fried eggs *pl*.
teglia ['teʎa] *sf* baking tin.
tegola ['tegola] *sf* (roofing-)tile. **coprire di tegole** tile. **tetto di tegole** *sm* tiled roof.
tela ['tela] *sf* cloth; (*pittura*) canvas; (*teatro*) curtain. **tela cerata** oilcloth. **tela da lenzuola** sheeting. **tela di lino** linen.
telaio [te'lajo] *sm* loom; (*auto*) chassis; (*tec*) frame.
telecabina [teleka'bina] *sf* cable-car.
telecomando [teleko'mando] *sm* remote control. **telecomandare** *v* operate by remote control.
telecronaca [tele'krɔnaka] *sf* news bulletin. **telecronista** *s*(*m*+*f*) television commentator.
telefonare [telefo'nare] *v* telephone; (*fam*) phone. **telefonata** *sf* telephone call. **telefonata urbana/interurbana/con preavviso** local/trunk/personal call. **telefonico** *agg* telephone. **telefonista** *s*(*m*+*f*) telephonist. **telefono** *sm* telephone.
telegiornale [teledʒor'nale] *sm* television news.
telegrafare [telegra'fare] *v* telegraph. **telegrafico** *agg* telegraph; (*conciso*) telegraphic. **telegrafista** *s*(*m*+*f*) telegraph operator.
telegramma [tele'gramma] *sm* telegram.
telepatia [telepa'tia] *sf* telepathy. **telepatico** *agg* telepathic.
teleschermo [tele'skermo] *sm* television screen.
telescopio [tele'skɔpjo] *sm* telescope.
telespettatore [telespetta'tore], **-trice** *sm, sf* viewer.
teletrasmissione [teletrazmis'sjone] *sf* television programme.
televisione [televi'zjone] *sf* televison; (*fam*) TV. **televisore** *sm* television set.
telone [te'lone] *sm* tarpaulin.
tema ['tɛma] *sm* theme, subject; (*scolastico*) essay. **fuori tema** off the point.
temerario [teme'rarjo] *agg* reckless; (*avventato*) rash. **temerità** *sf* temerity.
temere [te'mere] *v* fear, be afraid. **non temere!** don't worry!
temperamento [tempera'mento] *sm* temperament.
temperare [tempe'rare] *v* temper; (*matita*) sharpen. **temperato** *agg* temperate. **temperino** *sm* pen-knife.
temperatura [tempera'tura] *sf* temperature.
tempesta [tem'pesta] *sf* storm. **tempestare** *v* storm; (*ornare*) stud; (*importunare*) bombard. **tempestoso** *agg* stormy.
tempestivo [tempes'tivo] *agg* timely. **tempestività** *sf* timeliness.
tempia ['tɛmpja] *sf* temple.
tempio ['tɛmpjo] *sm* temple.
tempista [tem'pista] *s*(*m*+*f*) opportunist.
tempo ['tɛmpo] *sm* time; (*atmosferico*) weather; (*gramm*) tense; (*musica*) tempo, movement. **a suo tempo** (*passato*) originally; (*futuro*) in due course; (*al momento giusto*) at the right time. **a tempo debito** in due course. **a tempo perso** in one's spare time. **da tempo** for some time. **in un primo tempo** at first. **tempo da cani** foul weather.
temporale[1] [tempo'rale] *agg* temporal.
temporale[2] [tempo'rale] *sm* (thunder)storm. **temporalesco** *agg* stormy.

temporaneo [tempo'raneo] *sm* temporary.
temporeggiare [tempored'dʒare] *v* mark time, temporize.
temprare [tem'prare] *v* temper. **tempra** *sf* (*tec*) tempering, temper; (*fig*) fibre; (*voce*) timbre.
tenace [te'natʃe] *agg* firm; (*fig*) tenacious. **tenacia** *sf* tenacity. **tenacità** *sf* tenacity, firmness.
tenaglie [te'naʎe] *sf pl* pincers *pl*; (*pinze*) pliers *pl*; (*molle*) tongs *pl*.
tenda ['tɛnda] *sf* (*drappo*) curtain; (*da campo*) tent; (*tendone da sole*) awning. **tenda alla veneziana** Venetian blind. **tendina** *sf* net curtain.
tendenza [ten'dentsa] *sf* tendency; (*attitudine*) bent; (*orientamento, econ*) trend. **tendenziale** *agg* potential. **tendenzioso** *agg* tendentious.
***tendere** ['tɛndere] *v* (*mettere in tensione*) stretch; (*porgere*) hold out; (*reti*) cast. **tendere a** (*mirare*) aim at; be inclined to; (*volgersi verso*) tend towards. **tendere un tranello** set a trap.
tendine ['tɛndine] *sm* tendon.
tenebre ['tɛnebre] *sf pl* darkness *sing*. **tenebroso** *agg* dark; (*fig*) mysterious.
tenente [te'nɛnte] *sm* lieutenant.
***tenere** [te'nere] *v* hold; (*mantenere, trattenere*) keep; (*seguire una direzione*) keep to. **tenerci a** attach great importance to. **tenere a** (*volere*) want. **tener d'occhio** keep an eye on. **tener presente** bear in mind.
tenero ['tɛnero] *agg* tender. **tenerezza** *sf* tenderness.
tenia ['tɛnja] *sf* tapeworm.
tennis ['tɛnnis] *sm* tennis. **tennista** *s*(*m+f*) tennis player.
tenore [te'nore] *sm* tenor; content. **a tenore di** in accordance with. **tenore di vita** living standard.
tensione [ten'sjone] *sf* tension.
tentacolo [ten'takolo] *sm* tentacle.
tentare [ten'tare] *v* (*cercare*) try; (*sperimentare*) try out; (*cercare di fare*) attempt; (*invogliare*) tempt. **tentativo** *sm* attempt. **tentatore** *sm* tempter. **tentatrice** *sf* temptress. **tentazione** *sf* temptation. **aver la tentazione (di)** be tempted (to).
tentennare [tenten'nare] *v* wobble; hesitate.
tentoni [ten'toni] *avv* **a tentoni** groping one's way.
tenue ['tɛnue] *agg* slender; (*debole*) faint; (*fig*) slight.
tenuta [te'nuta] *sf* (*divisa*) uniform; (*possedimento fondiario*) estate; capacity; (*auto*) road-holding; (*tec*) seal. **a tenuta d'acqua** water-tight. **a tenuta d'aria** air-tight.
teologia [teolo'dʒia] *sf* theology. **teologico** theological. **teologo, -a** *sm, sf* theologist.
teorema [teo'rɛma] *sm* theorem.
teoria [teo'ria] *sf* theory. **in teoria** theoretically.
teorico [te'ɔriko], **-a** *agg* theoretical. *sm, sf* theorist.
tepore [te'pore] *sm* warmth.
teppa ['teppa] *sf also* **teppaglia** rabble. **teppismo** *sm* hooliganism. **teppista** *s*(*m+f*) hooligan.
terapia [tera'pia] *sf* therapy. **terapeutico** *agg* therapeutic. **terapista** *s*(*m+f*) therapist.
tergicristallo [terdʒikris'tallo] *sm* windscreen-wiper.
tergiversare [terdʒiver'sare] *v* prevaricate.
tergo ['tɛrgo] *sm* **a tergo** (*di dietro*) behind. **vedi a tergo** (*nei rinvii*) please turn over, PTO.
terme ['tɛrme] *sf pl* (thermal) baths *pl*. **termale** *or* **termico** *agg* thermal.
terminare [termi'nare] *v* end. **terminazione** *sf* ending. **termine** *sm* term; limit; (*punto estremo*) end; (*comm*) expiry (date). **a breve/lungo termine** short-/long-term. **ai termini di legge** by law. **a rigor di termini** strictly speaking. **terminologia** *sf* terminology.
termodinamica [termodi'namika] *sf* thermodynamics.
termometro [ter'mɔmetro] *sm* thermometer.
termonucleare [termonukle'are] *agg* thermonuclear.
termos *V* **thermos.**
termosifone [termosi'fone] *sm* radiator.
termostato [ter'mɔstato] *sm* thermostat. **termostatico** *agg* thermostatic.
terra ['tɛrra] *sf* earth; (*estensione di terreno, paese*) land; (*suolo*) soil. **a terra** (*senza soldi*) broke; (*depresso*) in low spirits; (*gomma*) flat. **collegare** *or* **mettere a terra** (*elett*) earth. **raso terra** close to the ground.
terraglia [ter'raʎa] *sf* earthenware. **terraglie** *sf pl* (*vasellame*) crockery *sing*.

terrapieno [terra'pjɛno] *sm* embankment.
terrazza [ter'rattsa] *sf* terrace. **terrazzo** *sm* terrace; (*alpinismo*) ledge.
terremoto [terre'mɔto] *sm* earthquake. **terremotato, -a** *sm, sf* earthquake victim.
terreno[1] [ter'reno] *agg* earthly, worldly. **piano terreno** ground floor.
terreno[2] [ter'reno] *sm* land; (*suolo*) ground; (*podere*) plot (of land); (*fig*) field.
terreo ['tɛrreo] *agg* earthy; (*colorito*) deathly pale.
terrestre [ter'rɛstre] *agg* terrestrial.
terribile [ter'ribile] *agg* terrible.
territorio [terri'tɔrjo] *sm* territory. **territoriale** *agg* territorial.
terrore [ter'rore] *sm* terror. **aver terrore (di)** be terrified (of). **terrorismo** *sm* terrorism. **terrorista** *s(m+f)* terrorist. **terroristico** *agg* terrorist. **terrorizzare** *v* terrorize.
terzo ['tɛrtso] *agg, sm* third. **terzi** *sm pl* (*comm, dir*) third party *sing*. **terzina** *sf* triplet.
tesa ['teza] *sf* (*cappello*) brim; (*reti*) spreading.
teschio ['tɛskjo] *sm* skull.
tesi ['tɛzi] *sf* thesis (*pl* -ses).
teso ['tezo] *agg* taut; (*nervoso*) tense. **stare con le orecchie tese** prick up one's ears.
tesoro [te'zɔro] *sm* treasure; (*tesoreria, pol*) treasury. **far tesoro (di)** treasure. **tesoriere** *sm* treasurer.
tessera ['tɛssera] *sf* card; (*lasciapassare*) pass; (*ferr*) season-ticket. **tesseramento** *sm* rationing. **tesserare** *v* give a membership card; ration.
tessere ['tɛssere] *v* weave. **tessitura** *sf* weaving; (*stabilimento*) (weaving) mill; (*trama*) plot. **tessuto** *sm* fabric; (*bot, zool, fig*) tissue.
tessile ['tɛssile] *agg* textile. *sm* textile; (*operaio*) textile worker.
testa ['tɛsta] *sf* head. **a testa** (*ciascuno*) each, per head. **colpo di testa** *sm* (*sport*) header; (*fig*) whim. **essere in testa** be in the lead. **fare a testa e croce** toss up. **passare in testa** take the lead. **rompersi la testa** rack one's brains.
testamento [testa'mento] *sm* will; (*bibbia*) testament.
testardo [tes'tardo] *agg* stubborn. **testardaggine** *sf* stubbornness.
testata [tes'tata] *sf* (*intestazione*) heading; (*colpo di testa*) butt; (*auto*) cylinder head; (*parte anteriore*) head.
testicolo [tes'tikolo] *sm* testicle.
testimone [testi'mɔne] *s(m+f)* witness. **testimoniale** *sm* evidence. **testimonianza** *sf* testimony; (*prova*) evidence. **testimoniare** *v* testify; (*deporre in giudizio*) (bear) witness.
testo ['tɛsto] *sm* text; (*libro*) text-book. **far testo** be an authority. **testuale** *agg* exact.
testone [tes'tone] *sm* (*stupido*) blockhead; (*testardo*) pig-headed person.
testuggine [tes'tuddʒine] *sf* tortoise; (*di mare*) turtle.
tetano ['tɛtano] *sm* tetanus.
tetro ['tɛtro] *agg* gloomy.
tetta ['tetta] *sf* (*fam*) breast. **tettarella** *sf* dummy.
tetto ['tetto] *sm* roof (*pl* -s). **essere senza tetto** be homeless. **tettoia** *sf* roofing, canopy.
Tevere ['tevere] *sm* Tiber.
thermos ® *or* **termos** ['tɛrmos] *sm invar* thermos (flask) ®.
ti [ti], **te** *pron* (to) you; (*riflessivo*) yourself.
tiara ['tjara] *sf* tiara.
tic [tik] *sm invar* tic.
ticchettare [tikket'tare] *v* click; (*pioggia*) patter; (*orologio*) tick.
ticchio ['tikkjo] *sm* whim.
tictac [tik'tak] *sm* tick.
tiepido ['tjɛpido] *agg* lukewarm.
tifo ['tifo] *sm* (*med*) typhus; (*fam: sport*) fanaticism. **fare il tifo per** be a fan of. **(febbre) tifoide** *sf* typhoid (fever).
tifone [ti'fone] *sm* typhoon.
tifoso [ti'fozo], **-a** *sm, sf* fan.
tiglio ['tiʎo] *sm* lime(-tree); (*fibra*) bast.
tigna ['tiɲa] *sf* ringworm.
tignola [ti'ɲɔla] *sf* moth.
tigre ['tigre] *sf* tiger.
timbrare [tim'brare] *v* stamp; (*posta*) postmark. **timbro** *sm* stamp; postmark; (*suono*) timbre.
timido ['timido] *agg* shy; (*timoroso*) timid.
timo ['timo] *sm* (*bot*) thyme.
timone [ti'mone] *sm* rudder; (*fig*) helm. **timoniere** *sm* helmsman; (*canottaggio*) cox.
timore [ti'more] *sm* fear. **senza timore** fearless. **timoroso** *agg* fearful; (*preoccupato*) anxious.
timpano ['timpano] *sm* (*anat*) ear-drum;

(*musica*) kettle-drum. **timpani** *sm pl* timpani *pl*.
tinca ['tinka] *sf* tench.
***tingere** ['tindʒere] *v* dye; (*macchiare*) spot.
tino ['tino] *sm* tub, vat.
tinta ['tinta] *sf* colour; (*sfumatura*) shade. **tintarella** *sf* tan. **tinto** *agg* dyed; (*macchiato*) tinged. **tintore** *sm* dyer. **tintoria** *sf* cleaners. **tintura** *sf* dyeing; (*med*) tincture.
tipo ['tipo] *sm* type; (*genere*) sort, kind. **tipico** *agg* typical.
tipografia [tipogra'fia] *sf* typography; (*stamperia*) press. **tipografico** *agg* typographical. **tipografo, -a** *sm, sf* printer.
tiranneggiare [tiranned'dʒare] *v* tyrannize. **tirannia** *sf* tyranny. **tirannico** *agg* tyrannical. **tiranno** *sm* tyrant.
tirante [ti'rante] *sm* (connecting) rod; brace.
tirapiedi [tira'pjɛdi] *sm invar* hanger-on.
tirare [ti'rare] *v* pull, draw; (*lanciare*) throw; (*sparare*) shoot. **tirare avanti** keep going. **tirar fuori** pull out; (*estrarre*) take out. **tirare in lungo** draw out. **tirarsi indietro** draw back. **tirarsi su** draw oneself up; (*fam*) get back on one's feet. **tirata** *sf* pull; (*discorso*) tirade. **tiratura** *sf* printing; (*numero*) run.
tirchio ['tirkjo] *agg* stingy.
tiritera [tiri'tɛra] *sf* rigmarole.
tiro ['tiro] *sm* (*lancio*) throw; (*arma*) shot. **fuori tiro** out of range.
tirocinio [tiro'tʃinjo] *sm* apprenticeship.
tiroide [ti'rɔide] *sf* thyroid.
titolare [tito'lare] *agg* titular, regular. *s(m+f)* proprietor.
titolo ['titolo] *sm* title; (*comm*) share; (*obbligazione*) bond; (*filato*) count. **a titolo di** out of.
titubare [titu'bare] *v* hesitate.
tizio ['titsjo] *sm* fellow. **Tizio, Caio, e Sempronio** Tom, Dick, and Harry.
tizzo ['tittso] *sm* ember.
toboga [to'bɔga] *sm invar* toboggan.
toccare [tok'kare] *v* touch; (*riguardare*) concern. **tocca a me** it is my turn; (*spettare di diritto*) I am entitled; (*spettare di dovere*) it is up to me. **toccasana** *sm invar* panacea.
tocco[1] ['tokko] *sm* touch; (*campana*) stroke; (*l'una*) one o'clock.
tocco[2] ['tɔkko] *sm* (*pezzo*) hunk.
toga ['tɔga] *sf* toga.
***togliere** ['tɔʎere] *v* take away; (*indumenti*) take off. **ciò non toglie che** it does not alter the fact that. **togliere di mezzo** get out of the way. **togliersi** *v* (*levarsi*) take off; (*soddisfare*) satisfy.
toletta [to'letta] *sf also* **toilette** toilet; (*mobile*) dressing table; (*acconciatura*) toilette; (*abito*) outfit.
tollerare [tolle'rare] *v* tolerate, stand; (*permettere*) allow. **tollerabile** *agg* bearable. **tollerante** *agg* tolerant. **tolleranza** *sf* tolerance.
tomaia [to'maja] *sf* upper.
tomba ['tomba] *sf* tomb.
tombola[1] ['tombola] *sf* (*gioco*) tombola; bingo.
tombola[2] ['tombola] *sf* (*caduta*) fall.
tomo ['tɔmo] *sm* tome; (*tipo strano*) odd type.
tonaca ['tɔnaka] *sf* (*frati, monache*) habit; (*preti*) cassock.
tonalità [tonali'ta] *sf* tonality; (*colore*) shade.
tonare [to'nare] *v* thunder.
tonchio ['tonkjo] *sm* weevil.
tondo ['tondo] *agg* round. *sm* round plate; (*forma*) circle. **parlar chiaro e tondo** speak bluntly.
tonfo ['tonfo] *sm* thud; (*nell'acqua*) splash.
tonico ['tɔniko] *agg* tonic. **tonica** *sf* (*musica*) tonic.
tonnellata [tonnel'lata] *sf* ton. **tonnellaggio** *sm* tonnage.
tonno ['tonno] *sm* tuna, tunny.
tono ['tɔno] *sm* tone. **cambiar tono** change (one's) tune. **fuori tono** out of tune. **giù di tono** out of sorts. **in tono** in tune; (*fisicamente*) fit.
tonsilla [ton'silla] *sf* tonsil. **tonsillite** *sf* tonsillitis.
tonto ['tɔnto], **-a** *agg* silly. *sm, sf* fool.
topazio [to'patsjo] *sm* topaz.
topico ['tɔpiko] *agg* local; (*fig*) topical.
topo ['tɔpo] *sm* mouse (*pl* mice); (*campagnolo*) fieldmouse. **topo di biblioteca** bookworm.
topografia [topogra'fia] *sf* topography. **topografico** *agg* topographical.
toporagno [topo'raɲo] *sm* shrew.
toppa ['tɔppa] *sf* patch; (*serratura*) keyhole.
torace [to'ratʃe] *sm* chest.

torba ['tɔrba] *sf* peat.
torbido ['tɔrbido] *agg* turbid, muddy. **c'è del torbido** there's something fishy going on.
***torcere** ['tɔrtʃere] *v* twist; (*strizzare*) wring out. **torcere il collo a qualcuno** wring someone's neck. **torcere il naso** turn up one's nose. **torcersi il collo** crane one's neck. **torcicollo** *sm* crick in the neck.
torchio ['tɔrkjo] *sm* press. **torchiare** *v* press.
torcia ['tɔrtʃa] *sf* torch.
tordo ['tordo] *sm* thrush.
Torino [to'rino] *sf* Turin.
torma ['torma] *sf* herd; (*persone*) throng.
tormentare [tormen'tare] *v* torment. **tormento** *sm* torment; (*infastidire*) plague.
tornaconto [torna'konto] *sm* advantage.
tornante [tor'nante] *sm* hairpin bend.
tornare [tor'nare] *v* return; (*andare di nuovo*) go back; (*venire di nuovo*) come back; (*ricominciare*) start again. **ben tornato!** welcome back! **qualcosa non torna** something is not quite right.
torneo [tor'nɛo] *sm* tournament.
tornio ['tɔrnjo] *sm* lathe. **tornire** *v* turn. **tornitore** *sm* (*tec*) lathe operator; (*di legno*) wood turner.
toro ['tɔro] *sm* bull. **Toro** *sm* Taurus.
torpedine [tor'pɛdine] *sf* torpedo.
torpedone [torpe'done] *sm* coach.
torpido ['tɔrpido] *agg* sluggish. **torpore** *sm* sluggishness.
torre ['torre] *sf* tower; (*scacchi*) rook, castle. **torretta** *sf* turret.
torrefare [torre'fare] *v* roast. **torrefazione** *sf* roasting.
torrente [tor'rɛnte] *sm* torrent. **torrenziale** *agg* torrential.
torrido ['tɔrrido] *agg* torrid.
torrone [tor'rone] *sm* nougat.
torso ['torso] *sm* stalk; (*frutta*) core; (*anat*) torso. **a torso nudo** bare-chested.
torsolo ['torsolo] *sm* stalk; (*frutta*) core.
torta ['torta] *sf* cake; (*di frutta*) tart; (*pasticcio*) pie.
tortiglione [torti'ʎone] *sm* spiral. **a tortiglione** spiral.
torto[1] ['tɔrto] *sm* wrong; (*colpa*) fault. **a torta** wrongfully. **aver torto** be wrong. **dar torto a** prove wrong.
torto[2] ['tɔrto] *agg* twisted.
tortora ['tortora] *sf* turtle-dove.
tortuoso [tortu'ozo] *agg* tortuous.
torturare [tortu'rare] *v* torture. **tortura** *sf* torture.
torvo ['torvo] *agg* surly.
tosare [to'zare] *v* shear; (*cani*) clip; (*fig*) fleece. **tosatrice** *sf* (*capelli*) hair-clippers *pl*; (*erba*) lawn-mower. **tosatura** *sf* shearing; clipping.
Toscana [tos'kana] *sf* Tuscany. **toscano, -a** *s*, *agg* Tuscan.
tosse ['tosse] *sf* cough. **tossire** *v* cough.
tossico ['tossiko] *agg* poisonous. *sm* poison. **tossicità** *sf* toxicity. **tossicomane** *s*(*m*+*f*) drug addict. **tossicomania** *sf* drug addiction. **tossina** *sf* toxin.
tostare [tos'tare] *v* roast; (*pane*) toast. **tostapane** *sm invar* toaster.
tosto ['tɔsto] *agg* **faccia tosta** *sf* (*fam*) cheek.
totale [to'tale] *agg*, *sm* total. **totalità** *sf* entirety.
totalitario [totali'tarjo] *agg* (*pol*) totalitarian.
totano ['tɔtano] *sm* squid.
totocalcio [toto'kaltʃo] *sm* football pools *pl*.
tovaglia [to'vaʎa] *sf* table-cloth. **tovagliolo** *sm* napkin, serviette.
tozzo[1] ['tottso] *agg* squat; (*persone*) stocky.
tozzo[2] ['tottso] *sm* piece.
tra [tra] *prep* among(st); (*tra due*) between; (*nel mezzo*) in the midst of; (*tempo*) in. **tra breve** *or* **poco** soon. **tra l'altro** among other things; (*inoltre*) besides.
traballare [trabal'lare] *v* wobble; (*persone*, *fig*) totter.
traboccare [trabok'kare] *v* overflow. **trabocchetto** *sm* trap.
tracannare [trakan'nare] *v* gulp down.
traccia ['trattʃa] *sf* track, trail; (*orma*) footprint; (*indizio*) trace. **tracciare** *v* trace; (*abbozzare*) sketch (out); (*a grandi linee*) outline. **tracciato** *sm* layout.
trachea [tra'kɛa] *sf* windpipe.
tracolla [tra'kɔlla] *sf* shoulder-strap. **a tracolla** over one's shoulder. **borsetta a tracolla** *sf* shoulder-bag.
tradire [tra'dire] *v* betray; (*coniugi*) be unfaithful (to). **tradimento** *sm* treachery; (*dir*) treason. **a tradimento** by surprise. **traditore** *sm* traitor. **traditrice** *sf* traitress.
tradizione [tradi'tsjone] *sf* tradition. **tradizionale** *agg* traditional.

***tradurre** [tra'durre] *v* translate; (*condurre*) convey. **traduttore, -trice** *sm, sf* translator. **traduzione** *sf* translation.
trafelato [trafe'lato] *agg* out of breath.
trafficare [traffi'kare] *v* (*commerciare*) trade, deal; (*spreg*) traffic; (*darsi da fare*) busy oneself. **traffico** *sm* traffic.
***trafiggere** [tra'fiddʒere] *v* pierce.
trafila [tra'fila] *sf* (*operazione*) (lengthy) procedure. **trafilare** *v* draw. **trafiletto** *sm* paragraph.
traforare [trafo'rare] *v* bore, drill; (*legno*) cut with a fretsaw. **traforatrice** *sf* drill; (*sega*) fretsaw. **traforo** *sm* tunnel; fretsaw.
tragedia [tra'dʒɛdja] *sf* tragedy.
traghetto [tra'getto] *sm* ferry. **traghettare** *v* ferry (across).
tragico ['tradʒiko] *agg* tragic. *sm* tragedy; (*autore*) tragedian; (*attore*) tragic actor. **prendere sul tragico** dramatize.
tragitto [tra'dʒitto] *sm* journey; (*traversata*) crossing.
traguardo [tra'gwardo] *sm* finish; (*sport*) winning-post; (*fig*) goal.
traiettoria [trajet'tɔrja] *sf* trajectory; (*di volo*) flight-path.
trainare [trai'nare] *v* pull *or* haul along; (*rimorchiare*) tow. **traino** *sm* haulage; (*rimorchio*) trailer; (*con pattini*) sledge.
tralasciare [trala'ʃare] *v* leave out; interrupt; (*trascurare*) neglect.
tralcio ['traltʃo] *sm* shoot.
traliccio [tra'littʃo] *sm* (*tessuto*) ticking; (*struttura*) truss; (*graticcio*) trellis.
tram [tram] *sm invar* tram.
trama ['trama] *sf* (*tessile*) weft; (*fig*) plot. **tramare** *v* plot.
tramandare [traman'dare] *v* hand down.
trambusto [tram'busto] *sm* turmoil.
tramezzare [tramed'dzare] *v* interpose; (*dividere un locale*) partition (off). **tramezzo** *sm* partition.
tramite ['tramite] *sm* means *pl*; intermediary. *prep* (*per mezzo di*) through.
tramontana [tramon'tana] *sf* (*nord*) north; (*vento*) north wind.
tramontare [tramon'tare] *v* set; (*aver fine*) come to an end; (*dileguarsi*) wane. **tramonto** *sm* sunset; (*fig*) decline.
tramortire [tramor'tire] *v* stun.
trampolino [trampo'lino] *sm* springboard; (*piscina*) diving-board; (*palestra*) trampoline; (*sci*) ski-jump.
trampolo ['trampolo] *sm* stilt.
tramutare [tramu'tare] *v* transform.
trancia ['trantʃa] *sf* (*taglierina*) cutter; (*gastr*) slice.
tranello [tra'nɛllo] *sm* trap; (*fig*) catch.
trangugiare [trangu'dʒare] *v* gulp down; (*fig*) swallow.
tranne ['tranne] *prep* except *or* but (for).
tranquillo [tran'kwillo] *agg* quiet, calm. **stare tranquillo** keep quiet *or* calm; (*non turbarsi*) not worry. **tranquillità** *sf* calm. **tranquillante** *sm* tranquillizer.
transatlantico [transat'lantiko] *agg* transatlantic. *sm* ocean liner.
transazione [transa'tsjone] *sf* (*comm*) transaction; (*dir*) settlement.
transistor [tran'sistor] *sm invar* transistor.
transitivo [transi'tivo] *agg* transitive.
transito ['transito] *sm* transit. **transito interrotto** road closed. **transitabile** *agg* practicable. **transitorio** *agg* transitory; (*fis*) transient.
transizione [transi'tsjone] *sf* transition.
tranvai [tran'vaj] *sm* tram. **tranvia** *sf* tramway.
trapanare [trapa'nare] *v* drill. **trapanatrice** *sf* drill. **trapanatura** *sf* drilling. **trapano** *sm* drill.
trapassare [trapas'sare] *v* run through; pass. **trapassato** *sm* past perfect. **trapasso** *sm* passing; transition; (*dir*) transfer.
trapelare [trape'lare] *v* leak out.
trapezio [tra'pɛtsjo] *sm* (*geom*) trapezium; (*sport*) trapeze. **trapezista** *s*(*m*+*f*) trapeze artist.
trapiantare [trapjan'tare] *v* transplant. **trapianto** *sm* transplant; (*agric*) transplantation.
trappola ['trappola] *sf* trap, snare.
trapuntare [trapun'tare] *v* quilt; (*ricamare*) embroider. **trapunta** *sf* quilt.
***trarre** ['trarre] *v* draw. **trarre in inganno** deceive. **trarre in tentazione** lead into temptation.
trasalire [trasa'lire] *v* jump.
trasandato [trazan'dato] *agg* untidy.
***trascendere** [tra'ʃɛndere] *v* transcend.
trascinare [traʃi'nare] *v* drag; (*fig*) carry away.
***trascorrere** [tras'korrere] *v* spend; (*tempo*) pass.
***trascrivere** [tras'krivere] *v* transcribe. **trascrizione** *sf* transcription.
trascurare [trasku'rare] *v* neglect; (*omettere*) fail. **trascurato** *agg* neglected; (*noncurante*) careless; (*sciatto*) slovenly.

trasferire [trasfe'rire] *v* transfer. **trasferirsi** *v* (*traslocare*) move. **trasferibile** *agg* transferable. **trasferimento** *sm* transfer. **trasferta** *sf* (*sport*) away match; (*viaggio*) business trip; (*indennità*) travelling expenses *pl*.

trasformare [trasfor'mare] *v* transform; (*cambiare*) change. **trasformare in** turn into. **trasformatore** *sm* transformer. **trasformazione** *sf* transformation.

trasfusione [trasfu'zjone] *sf* (*med*) transfusion.

trasgredire [trazgre'dire] *v* disobey; (*legge*) infringe. **trasgressione** *sf* infringement.

traslocare [trazlo'kare] *v* move; (*impiegato*) transfer. **trasloco** *sm*, *pl* **-chi** move; transfer.

***trasmettere** [traz'mettere] *v* transmit; (*communicare*, *dir*) convey; (*radio*) broadcast. **trasmettitore** *sm* transmitter; (*malattia*) carrier. **trasmissione** *sf* transmission; broadcast. **trasmittente** *sf* transmitter.

trasmodato [trazmo'dato] *agg* excessive.

trasognato [traso'ɲato] *agg* dreamy.

trasparente [traspa'rɛnte] *agg* transparent. *sm* transparency. **trasparenza** *sf* transparency.

trasparire [traspa'rire] *v* show through; (*alla luce*) shine through; (*palesarsi*) appear.

traspirare [traspi'rare] *v* transpire.

trasportare [traspor'tare] *v* carry; (*trascinare*) transport, carry away. **trasportatore** *sm* carrier; (*tec*) conveyor. **trasporto** *sm* transport; (*comm*) carriage; (*inoltro*) forwarding; (*per nave*) shipping.

trastullare [trastul'lare] *v* amuse. **trastullo** *sm* amusement; (*fig*) plaything.

trasudare [trasu'dare] *v* ooze.

trasversale [trazver'sale] *agg* transverse.

trasvolare [trazvo'lare] *v* fly across; (*fig*) barely touch.

tratta ['tratta] *sf* (*comm*) draft; (*traffico illecito*) trade.

trattare [trat'tare] *v* treat, deal with, handle. **si tratta di . . .** it is about . . . , it is a question of . . . . **trattabile** *agg* negotiable; (*persona*) tractable. **trattamento** *sm* treatment. **trattativa** *sf* negotiation. **trattato** *sm* (*opera*) treatise; (*dir*) treaty.

tratteggiare [tratted'dʒare] *v* hatch; (*abbozzare*) outline.

***trattenere** [tratte'nere] *v* (*far rimanere*) keep (back); (*frenare*) restrain, hold back; (*detrarre*) withhold. **trattenersi** *v* (*restare*) stay; restrain oneself. **trattenimento** *sm* reception; (*spettacolo*) show.

tratto ['tratto] *agg* drawn. *sm* stroke; (*elemento caratteristico*) feature; (*frazione*) stretch; (*brano*) passage. **a tratti** at times. **di tratto in tratto** every now and then. **d'un tratto** all of a sudden.

trattore [trat'tore] *sm* tractor.

trattoria [tratto'ria] *sf* restaurant.

traudire [trau'dire] *v* mishear.

trauma ['trauma] *sm* trauma. **traumatico** *agg* traumatic.

travagliare [trava'ʎare] *v* torment. **travaglio** *sm* torment; (*angoscia*) distress. **travaglio di parto** labour.

travasare [trava'zare] *v* decant.

trave ['trave] *sf* beam; (*di tetto*) rafter; (*di soffitto*) joist. **fare una trave di ogni fuscello** make a mountain out of a molehill.

traversare [traver'sare] *v* cross; (*da parte a parte*) go through. **traversata** *sf* crossing. **traversina** *sf* sleeper.

traverso [tra'vɛrso] *agg* cross, transverse. *sm* breadth, width. **andare di traverso** (*cibo*) go down the wrong way. **a traverso** sideways on. **guardare di traverso** look askance at. **prendere di traverso** take the wrong way.

travestire [traves'tire] *v* disguise. **travestito, -a** *sm*, *sf* (*psic*) transvestite.

traviare [travi'are] *v* lead astray. **traviamento** *sm* straying; corruption.

travisare [travi'zare] *v* distort. **travisamento** *sm* distortion.

***travolgere** [tra'vɔldʒere] *v* sweep away; (*investire*) knock down; (*fig*) overwhelm. **travolgente** *agg* sweeping; overwhelming.

trazione [tra'tsjone] *sf* traction; (*auto*) drive.

tre [tre] *agg*, *sm* three.

trebbiare [treb'bjare] *v* thresh. **trebbia** *or* **trebbiatrice** *sf* threshing machine. **trebbiatura** *sf* threshing.

treccia ['trettʃa] *sf* braid, plait. **farsi le trecce** plait one's hair.

tredici ['treditʃi] *agg*, *sm* thirteen. **tredicesimo** *sm*, *agg* thirteenth.

tregua ['trɛgwa] *sf* truce; (*riposo*) rest. **senza tregua** unremitting; without respite; (*senza sosta*) non-stop.

tremare [tre'mare] *v* tremble; (*di freddo*) shiver; (*per emozioni*) shudder. **la tremarella** *sf* (*fam*) the shivers *pl*.

tremendo [tre'mɛndo] *agg* terrible, dreadful.
trementina [tremen'tina] *sf* turpentine.
tremito ['trɛmito] *sm* shaking, shudder(ing).
tremolare [tremo'lare] *v* quiver; (*stelle*) twinkle; (*luce*) flicker.
tremore [tre'more] *sm* tremor; (*agitazione*) trembling.
treno ['trɛno] *sm* train. **treno accelerato/diretto/direttissimo/rapido** slow/fast/through/express train. **treno di gomme/ruote** set of tyres/wheels.
trenta ['trenta] *sm, agg* thirty. **trentesimo** *sm, agg* thirtieth.
trepidare [trepi'dare] *v* be anxious.
trespolo ['trespolo] *sm* trestle; (*sgabello*) stool.
triangolo [tri'angolo] *sm* triangle. **triangolare** *agg* triangular.
tribolare [tribo'lare] *v* suffer; (*far soffrire*) torment. **vita tribolata** *sf* hard life.
tribordo [tri'bordo] *sm* starboard.
tribù [tri'bu] *sf* tribe. **membro di tribù** *sm* tribesman.
tribuna [tri'buna] *sf* platform; (*palco riservato*) gallery; (*campo sportivo*) stand; (*coperta*) grandstand.
tribunale [tribu'nale] *sm* court.
tributo [tri'buto] *sm* tribute. **tributare** *v* render. **tributario** *agg* (*tributi*) tax; (*fiume*) tributary.
tricheco [tri'keko] *sm* walrus.
triciclo [tri'tʃiklo] *sm* tricycle.
tricolore [triko'lore] *sm, agg* tricolour.
tric-trac ['tric'trac] *sm invar* backgammon.
tridimensionale [tridimensjo'nale] *agg* three-dimensional.
trifoglio [tri'fɔʎʎo] *sm* clover.
triglia ['triʎa] *sf* red mullet. **far l'occhio di triglia** (*fam*) make sheep's eyes.
trigonometria [trigonome'tria] *sf* trigonometry.
trillare [tril'lare] *v* trill. **trillo** *sm* trill.
trilogia [trilo'dʒia] *sf* trilogy.
trimestre [tri'mɛstre] *sm* quarter; (*scolastico*) term. **trimestrale** *agg* quarterly.
trina ['trina] *sf* lace.
trincare [trin'kare] *v* drink.
trincea [trin'tʃɛa] *sf* (*mil*) trench; (*ferr*) cutting. **trincerare** *v* entrench. **trinceramento** *sm* entrenchment.
trinciare [trin'tʃare] *v* cut up; (*pollo, ecc.*) carve; (*in strisce sottili*) shred. **trinciato** *sm* (*tabacco*) shag.
trinità [trini'ta] *sf* trinity.
trio ['trio] *sm* trio.
trionfare [trion'fare] *v* triumph. **trionfale** *agg* triumphal. **trionfante** *agg* triumphant. **trionfo** *sm* triumph; success.
triplice ['triplitʃe] *agg* threefold. **in triplice copia** in triplicate. **triplo** *agg* treble, triple; (*di tre parti*) threefold. **il triplo** *sm* three times as much.
tripode ['tripode] *sm* tripod.
trippa ['trippa] *sf* tripe.
tripudiare [tripu'djare] *v* rejoice. **tripudio** *sm* jubilation.
triste ['triste] *agg* sad. **tristezza** *sf* sadness.
tristo ['tristo] *agg* (*malvagio*) wicked; (*meschino*) mean.
tritare [tri'tare] *v* grind; (*carne*) mince. **carne tritata** *sf* mince. **tritacarne** *sm invar* mincer. **trito** *agg* chopped, ground, minced; (*fig*) trite.
trittico ['trittiko] *sm* triptych.
trivellare [trivel'lare] *v* drill, bore. **trivella** *sf* auger; (*succhiello*) gimlet; (*miniera*) drill. **trivellazione** *sf* drilling, boring.
triviale [tri'vjale] *agg* vulgar; (*banale*) trivial. **trivialità** *sf* vulgarity; triviality.
trofeo [tro'fɛo] *sm* trophy.
trogolo ['trɔgolo] *sm* trough.
troia ['trɔja] (*volg*) *sf* (*scrofa*) sow; (*prostituta*) whore. **troiaio** *sm* pigsty. **troiata** *sf* (*lavoro mal fatto*) awful mess; (*azione sudicia*) dirty trick.
tromba ['tromba] *sf* trumpet; (*mil*) bugle; (*auto*) horn; (*ascensore, scale*) well; (*anat*) tube. **tromba d'aria** tornado. **trombetta** *sm* trumpeter; (*trombettiere*) bugler. **trombone** *sm* trombone. **trombonista** *s*(*m*+*f*) trombonist.
trombosi [trom'bɔzi] *sf* thrombosis.
troncare [tron'kare] *v* cut off; (*spezzare, fig*) break off.
tronco[1] ['tronko] *agg* cut off, broken off; (*mat, parole*) truncated.
tronco[2] ['tronko] *sm* trunk; (*tratto*) section; (*arch*) shaft.
tronfio ['tronfjo] *agg* puffed up, pompous.
trono ['trɔno] *sm* throne.
tropico ['trɔpiko] *sm* tropic. **tropicale** *agg* tropical.
troppo ['trɔppo] *agg* too much; (*pl*) too many. *avv* too much; (*con agg e avv*) too.
trota ['trɔta] *sf* trout.

trottare [trot'tare] *v* trot. **trotto** *sm* trot; (*andatura svelta*) brisk pace. **andare al piccolo trotto** jog-trot. **rompere il trotto** break into a gallop. **trotterellare** *v* jog (along); (*bambini*) toddle (along).

trottola ['trɔttola] *sf* (spinning) top.

trovare [tro'vare] *v* find. **andare a trovare** go to see, call on. **trovare in fallo** catch red-handed. **trovarsi** *v* (*essere*) be; (*per caso*) happen to be; (*sentirsi*) get on; (*incontrarsi*) meet; (*pensare*) think. **trovata** *sf* good idea; expedient. **trovata pubblicitaria** publicity stunt. **trovatello, -a** *sm, sf* foundling.

truccare [truk'kare] *v* make up; (*falsificare*) doctor; (*auto*) soup up; (*sport*) fix. **truccarsi** *v* disguise oneself; (*imbellettarsi*) put make-up on. **truccatore, -trice** *sm, sf* make-up artist. **truccatura** *sf* (*teatro*) making-up; (*belletto, ecc.*) make-up. **trucco** *sm* make-up; (*inganno*) trick.

truce ['trutʃe] *agg* grim.

truciolo ['trutʃolo] *sm* (wood) chip, shaving.

truffare [truf'fare] *v* cheat, swindle; (*dir*) defraud. **truffa** *sf* swindle; (*dir*) fraud. **truffatore, -trice** *sm, sf* swindler, cheat.

truppa ['truppa] *sf* troop; (*fig*) horde.

tu [tu] *pron* you. **a tu per tu** face to face.

tuba ['tuba] *sf* (*musica*) tuba; (*cappello*) top-hat; (*anat*) tube.

tubare [tu'bare] *v* coo.

tubercolosi [tuberko'lɔzi] *sf* tuberculosis.

tubo ['tubo] *sm* pipe, tube; (*flessibile*) hose(-pipe); (*anat*) canal. **tubazione** *sf* piping. **tubetto** *sm* tube. **tubolare** *agg* tubular.

tuffare [tuf'fare] *v* plunge, dip. **tuffarsi** *v* plunge; (*fare un tuffo*) dive. **tuffo** *sm* dive.

tulipano [tuli'pano] *sm* tulip.

tumefatto [tume'fatto] *agg* swollen.

tumore [tu'more] *sm* tumour.

tumulto [tu'multo] *sm* uproar; (*sommossa*) riot. **tumultuoso** *agg* tumultuous; (*chiassoso*) rowdy.

tunica ['tunika] *sf* tunic.

tuo ['tuo], *m pl* **tuoi** *agg* your. *pron* yours.

tuono ['twɔno] *sm* thunder. **tuonare** *v* thunder.

tuorlo ['twɔrlo] *sm* yolk.

turare [tu'rare] *v* plug; (*con sughero*) cork. **turarsi il naso** hold one's nose. **turacciolo** *sm* stopper; (*di sughero*) cork; (*botte*) bung.

turba ['turba] *sf* mob.

turbante [tur'bante] *sm* turban.

turbare [tur'bare] *v* trouble; disturb; (*sconvolgere*) upset. **turbarsi** *v* get upset. **turbamento** *sm* disturbance, anxiety.

turbina [tur'bina] *sf* turbine.

turbine ['turbine] *sm* whirl; (*neve, sabbia*) storm; (*fig*) (seething) horde. **turbine di vento** whirlwind. **turbolento** *agg* turbulent; (*inquieto*) unruly.

turchese [tur'keze] *s*(*m*+*f*), *agg* turquoise.

Turchia [tur'kia] *sf* Turkey. **turco, -a** *sm, agg* Turkish; *sm, sf* (*persona*) Turk. **bestemmiare come un turco** swear like a trooper. **fumare come un turco** smoke like a chimney. **parlare (in) turco** (*fam*) talk double Dutch.

turchino [tur'kino] *agg, sm* deep blue.

turismo [tu'rizmo] *sm* tourism; (*culturale*) sight-seeing. **fare del turismo** tour, travel. **turista** *s*(*m*+*f*) tourist; sightseer.

turlupinare [turlupi'nare] *v* swindle; (*fam*) take in.

turno ['turno] *sm* (*volta*) turn; (*lavoro*) shift; (*mil*) guard. **essere di turno** be on duty. **fare a turno** take turns. **lavoro a turni** *sm* shift-work.

turpe ['turpe] *agg* foul. **turpiloquio** *sm* foul language.

tuta ['tuta] *sf* overalls *pl*; (*sport*) track-suit.

tutela [tu'tɛla] *sf* defence; (*dir*) guardianship, protection. **tutelare** *v* protect; (*salvaguardare*) safeguard.

tuttavia [tutta'via] *cong* nevertheless.

tutto ['tutto] *agg* all; (*intero*) the whole (of); (*pl*) every. *pron* everything; (*pl*) everybody *sing*. *avv* completely. **a tutta velocità** at full speed. **il tutto** the whole (thing), everything. **innanzi tutto** first of all. **in tutti i modi** anyhow. **noi tutti** all of us. **tutt'ad un tratto** all of a sudden. **tutt'altro** anything but. **tutti e due** both (of them). **tutti i giorni** every day. **una volta per tutte** once and for all.

tuttora [tut'tora] *avv* still.

U

ubbia [ub'bia] *sf* silly idea; prejudice.
ubbidire [ubbi'dire] *v* obey; (*essere ubbidiente*) be obedient; (*dar retta*) listen (to). **ubbidiente** *agg* obedient. **ubbidienza** *sf* obedience.
ubriacare [ubria'kare] *v* make drunk, intoxicate. **ubriacarsi** *v* get drunk. **ubriachezza** *sf* drunkenness. **ubriaco, -a** *s, agg, m pl* **-chi** drunk. **ubriaco fradicio** dead drunk.
uccello [ut'tʃɛllo] *sm* bird.
***uccidere** [ut'tʃidere] *v* kill; (*assassinare*) murder. **uccisione** *sf* killing; murder. **ucciso** *agg* killed; murdered. **uccisore** *sm* killer; murderer.
***udire** [u'dire] *v* hear. **udibile** *agg* audible. **udienza** *sf* hearing; (*formale*) audience. **uditivo** *agg* (*fis*) audible; (*med*) auditory. **udito** *sm* hearing. **uditore, -trice** *sm, sf* listener. **uditorio** *sm* audience.
uffa ['uffa] *inter* **uffa, che noia!** what a bore!
ufficiale [uffi'tʃale] *agg* official. *sm* officer. **ufficiale di stato civile** registrar.
ufficio [uf'fitʃo] *sm* office; (*dovere, compito*) duty. **d'ufficio** official; (*ufficialmente*) officially; (*in veste ufficiale*) ex officio. **ufficio di collocamento** employment exchange. **ufficioso** *agg* unofficial.
ufo ['ufo] *avv* **a ufo** for nothing. **mangiare a ufo** scrounge a meal.
uggia ['uddʒa] *sf* boredom. **avere in uggia** dislike. **prendere in uggia** take a dislike to. **uggioso** *agg* boring.
uggiolare [uddʒo'lare] *v* whine.
ugola ['ugola] *sf* (*anat*) uvula; (*fig*) voice.
uguagliare [ugwa'ʎare] *v* (*essere uguale*) equal; (*rendere uguale*) equalize, even out; (*livellare*) level. **uguaglianza** *sf* equality.
uguale [u'gwale] *agg also* **eguale** the same; uniform; (*mat*) equal. *sm* equal. **ugualmente** *avv* equally; uniformly; (*tuttavia*) just *or* all the same.
ulcera ['ultʃera] *sf* ulcer.
uliva [u'liva] *V* **oliva.**
ulteriore [ulte'rjore] *agg* further. **ulteriormente** *avv* further; (*più avanti*) farther on; (*in seguito*) subsequently.
ultimo ['ultimo], **-a** *agg* last; (*più recente*) latest; (*fondamentale*) ultimate. *sm, sf* last. **all'ultimo** at the end; (*in fine*) finally. **fino all'ultimo** to the very end. **ultimamente** *avv also* **negli ultimi tempi** lately.
ultimare *v* finish. **ultimatum** *sm invar* ultimatum. **ultimazione** *sf* completion.
ultrasensibile [ultrasen'sibile] *agg* hypersensitive.
ultrasonico [ultra'sɔniko] *agg* supersonic.
ultravioletto [ultravio'letto] *agg* ultraviolet.
ululare [ulu'lare] *v* howl. **ululato** *sm* howling; (*urlo*) howl.
umanesimo [uma'nezimo] *sm* humanism. **umanista** *s*(*m*+*f*) humanist. **umanistico** *agg* humanist.
umano [u'mano] *agg* human; (*compassionevole*) humane; (*comprensivo*) understanding. **umanità** *sf* humanity. **umanitario** *agg* humanitarian.
umettare [umet'tare] *v* moisten.
umido ['umido] *agg* damp; (*clima*) humid. *sm* dampness; humidity; (*gastr*) stew. **cucire in umido** stew. **umidità** *sf* dampness; humidity.
umile ['umile] *agg* humble. **umiltà** *sf* (*virtù, sentimento*) humility; (*qualità*) humbleness.
umiliare [umi'ljare] *v* humiliate, humble. **umiliazione** *sf* humiliation.
umore [u'more] *sm* (*disposizione*) mood; (*indole*) temperament; (*liquido*) humour. **essere di buon/cattivo umore** be in a good/bad mood; (*abitualmente*) be good-/bad-tempered. **umorismo** *sm* humour. **umorista** *s*(*m*+*f*) humorist. **umoristico** *agg* humorous; (*spiritoso*) witty.
un [un] *V* **uno.**
unanime [u'nanime] *agg* unanimous. **unanimità** *sf* unanimity. **all'unanimità** unanimously.
uncino [un'tʃino] *sm* hook. **uncinare** *v* hook. **croce uncinata** *sf* swastika. **uncinetto** *sm* crochet-hook. **lavorare all'uncinetto** crochet.
undici ['unditʃi] *agg, sm* eleven. **undicesimo** *sm, agg* eleventh.
***ungere** ['undʒere] *v* grease; (*rel*) anoint.
Ungheria [unge'ria] *sf* Hungary. **ungherese** *s*(*m*+*f*), *agg* Hungarian.
unghia ['ungja] *sf* nail; (*artiglio*) claw; (*minima distanza*) hair's breadth. **unghie** *sf pl* (*fig*) clutches *pl*. **unghiata** *sf* scratch; (*temperino*) indentation.
unguento [un'gwɛnto] *sm* ointment.
unico ['uniko] *agg* only; (*esclusivo*) sole; (*senza pari*) unique; (*enfatico*) one and only. **unicamente** *avv* only.

unicorno [uni'kɔrno] *sm* unicorn.

unificare [unifi'kare] *v* unify; (*fondere*) merge; standardize. **unificazione** *sf* union; merger; standardization.

uniforme [uni'forme] *sf*, *agg* uniform. **uniformare** *v* (*adattare*) bring into line (with); (*render piano*) level out; standardize. **uniformarsi** *v* comply (with); adapt (to). **uniformità** *sf* uniformity; (*di superficie*) evenness; (*accordo*) agreement.

unione [u'njone] *sf* union; (*concordia*) unity.

unire [u'nire] *v* join; (*fig*) unite. **unirsi** *v* join; (*insieme con altri*) join up with.

unità [uni'ta] *sf* unity; (*misura*, *mil*) unit. **unità di misura** measure.

unito [u'nito] *agg* united; (*tinta*) plain. **unitamente a** together with.

università [universi'ta] *sf* university. **universitario, -a** *sm*, *sf* university student.

universo [uni'vɛrso] *sm* universe. **universale** *agg* universal.

uno ['uno] *agg* one, a. *art* a, an. *pron* one; (*qualcuno*) someone. **fare un po' per uno** share equally. **nè l'uno nè l'altro** neither. **non me ne va bene una!** I can't get one thing right! **tutt'uno** the same thing. **uno a uno** one by one.

unto ['unto] *agg* (*cosparso di grasso*) greasy, oily; (*spalmato*) greased, oiled; (*sporco*) dirty. *sm* grease; (*gastr*) fat. **untuoso** *agg* greasy; (*fig*) unctuous.

uomo ['wɔmo] *sm*, *pl* **uomini** man (*pl* men). **l'uomo qualunque** the man in the street. **uomo d'affari** businessman. **uomo di fiducia** right-hand man. **uomo di spirito** wit.

uopo ['wɔpo] *sm* **all'uopo** (*a tale scopo*) for this purpose; (*al momento opportuno*) at the right moment. **essere d'uopo** be necessary.

uovo ['wɔvo] *sm*, *pl* **-a** *f* egg. **uovo al burro** *or* **tegame** fried egg. **uovo alla coque** boiled egg. **uovo in camicia** poached egg. **uovo sodo/strapazzato** hardboiled/scrambled egg.

uragano [ura'gano] *sm* hurricane; (*tempesta*) storm.

uranio [u'ranjo] *sm* uranium.

urbano [ur'bano] *agg* (*di città*) town, urban; (*cortese*) urbane. **nettezza urbana** refuse collection. **urbanistica** *sf* town-planning. **urbanista** *s*(*m*+*f*) town-planner.

urgente [ur'dʒɛnte] *agg* urgent. **urgenza** *sf* urgency. **aver urgenza di** need urgently. **chiamata d'urgenza** *sf* emergency call.

urgere ['urdʒere] *v* (*sollecitare*) urge; (*abbisognare*) be required urgently.

urina [u'rina] *sf* urine. **urinare** *v* urinate. **urinario** *agg* urinary.

urlare [ur'lare] *v* scream; (*animali*) howl; (*dire ad alta voce*) shout. **urlo** *sm*, *pl* **-a** *f* shout; howl; scream.

urna ['urna] *sf* urn. **andare alle urne** go to the polls.

urrà [ur'ra] *inter* hurrah!

urtare [ur'tare] *v* knock *or* bump (into); (*dare uno spintone*) jostle; (*fig*) annoy. **urtarsi** *v* (*scontrarsi*) clash; (*auto*) collide; (*fig*) get irritated. **urto** *sm* (*spinta*) push; (*scontro*) clash, collision.

usare [u'zare] *v* use; (*essere solito a*) be accustomed to; (*essere di moda*) be fashionable; (*servirsi di*) make use of; (*fig*) exercise. **usanza** *sf* custom; habit.

uscio ['uʃo] *sm* door. **mettere fuori dell'uscio** turn out (of the house). **uscio di casa** front door.

***uscire** [u'ʃire] *v* leave; (*andar fuori*) go out; (*venir fuori*) come out; (*scendere*) get off; (*sboccare*) lead. **uscir di mente** slip one's mind. **uscir di strada** go off the road. **uscire in macchina** go for a drive. **uscita** *sf* (*passaggio*) exit, way out; (*sbocco*) outlet; (*motto di spirito*) witty remark; (*spesa*) outlay; (*a carte*) lead. **essere in libera uscita** be off duty. **giorno di libera uscita** *sm* day off. **uscita di sicurezza** emergency exit.

usignolo [uzi'ɲɔlo] *sm* nightingale.

uso ['uzo] *sm* use; (*usanza*) custom; (*voga*) fashion. **c'è l'uso** it is customary. **uso e consumo** wear and tear. **usuale** *agg* usual; customary; common.

ustionare [ustjo'nare] *v* scald. **ustione** *sf* scald.

usufruire [uzufru'ire] *v* benefit (from).

usura[1] [u'zura] *sf* usury. **a usura** with interest. **usuraio, -a** *sm*, *sf* usurer.

usura[2] [u'zura] *sf* (*tec*) wear. **resistente all'usura** hard-wearing.

usurpare [uzur'pare] *v* usurp. **usurpatore, -trice** *sm*, *sf* usurper.

utensile [u'tɛnsile] *sm* tool, utensil. **macchina utensile** *sf* machine tool.

utente [u'tɛnte] *s*(*m*+*f*) user.

utero ['utero] *sm* womb.
utile ['utile] *agg* useful; (*persona di aiuto*) helpful. **in tempo utile** in good time. **tornar utile** come in handy. *sm* profit. **utili** *sm pl* (*reddito*) income *sing*. **utilità** *sf* usefulness, use; profit. **utilizzare** *v* utilize. **utilizzazione** *sf* utilization.
utopia [uto'pia] *sf* utopia.
uva ['uva] *sf* grapes *pl*. **acino d'uva** *sm* grape. **uva secca** *or* **passa** raisins *pl*. **uva spina** gooseberry.

V

vacanza [va'kantsa] *sf* holiday; (*l'essere vacante*) vacancy. **vacante** *agg* vacant.
vacca ['vakka] *sf* cow. **vaccata** *sf* (*volg*) rubbish. **vacchetta** *sf* (*cuoio*) cowhide.
vaccinare [vattʃi'nare] *v* vaccinate. **vaccinazione** *sf* vaccination. **vaccino** *sm* vaccine.
vacillare [vatʃil'lare] *v* totter; (*essere incerto*) waver.
vagabondo [vaga'bondo] **-a** *agg* roving. *sm*, *sf* vagrant; (*spreg*) loafer. **vagabondare** *v* wander (about).
vagare [va'gare] *v* stray.
vagina [va'dʒina] *sf* vagina.
vagire [va'dʒire] *v* wail. **vagito** *sm* wail(ing).
vaglia[1] ['vaʎa] *sm invar* money order. **vaglia postale** postal order.
vaglia[2] ['vaʎa] *sf* **di vaglia** of note.
vagliare [va'ʎare] *v* sift; (*argomenti, ecc.*) weigh (up). **vagliatura** *sf* sifting; (*esame attento*) careful consideration. **vaglio** *sm* sieve; close examination.
vago ['vago] *agg* vague. **vaghezza** *sf* vagueness.
vagone [va'gone] *sm* (*per passeggeri*) carriage; (*per merci*) wagon. **vagone letto/ristorante** sleeping-/dining-car.
vaiolo [va'jɔlo] *sm* smallpox.
valanga [va'langa] *sf* avalanche; (*fig*) shower.
valente [va'lɛnte] *agg* skilled, clever.
***valere** [va'lere] *v* (*aver valore*) be worth; (*aver merito*) be good; (*aver forza legale*) apply; (*esser regolare*) be valid; (*contare*) count; (*essere utile*) be of use; (*importare*) matter. **far valere** assert. **farsi valere** demand respect; (*imporsi*) assert oneself. **vale a dire** that is to say. **tanto vale** one might as well. **valere la pena** be worth it. **valere un occhio della testa** be worth a fortune.
valevole [va'levole] *agg* valid.
valicare [vali'kare] *v* cross. **valico** *sm*, *pl* **-chi** pass; crossing.
valido ['valido] *agg* valid; (*efficace*) effective; (*forte*) strong. **validità** *sf* validity.
valigia [va'lidʒa] *sf* suitcase. **far le valigie** pack. **valigeria** *sf* (*merce*) travel goods *pl*.
valle ['valle] *sf also* **vallata** valley. **a valle di** below. **scendere a valle** go downhill. **vallone** *sm* deep valley; (*depressione*) gorge.
valletto [val'letto] *sm* page; assistant.
valore [va'lore] *sm* value; (*pregio*) worth; validity; (*significato*) meaning; (*coraggio*) valour. **aver valore di** amount to. **carte valori** *sf pl* securities *pl*. **di valore** of value, valuable; (*professionista*) leading. **imposta di valore aggiunto (IVA)** valued added tax (VAT). **privo di valore** worthless; of no value. **valori** *sm pl* valuables *pl*.
valorizzare [valorid'dzare] *v* exploit; (*mettere in evidenza*) make the most of. **valorizzazione** *sf* exploitation.
valuta [va'luta] *sf* currency.
valutare [valu'tare] *v* value; (*calcolare*) estimate; (*tenere in considerazione*) rate; (*vagliare*) weigh. **valutazione** *sf* evaluation; estimation; (*calcolo approssimativo*) estimate.
valvola ['valvola] *sf* valve; (*elett*) fuse. **valvola di sicurezza** safety-valve.
valzer ['valtser] *sm invar* waltz.
vampa ['vampa] *sf* blaze; (*arrossamento*) flush. **vampata** *sf* blaze; (*fig*) burst; flush; (*al viso*) blush.
vampiro [vam'piro] *sm* vampire.
vandalo ['vandalo] *sm* vandal. **vandalismo** *sm* vandalism.
vaneggiare [vaned'dʒare] *v* rave.
vanesio [va'nɛzjo] *agg* fatuous, vain.
vangare [van'gare] *v* dig (over). **vanga** *sf* spade.
vangelo [van'dʒɛlo] *sm* gospel.
vaniglia [va'niʎa] *sf* vanilla.
vanità [vani'ta] *sf* vanity. **vanitoso** *agg* vain.
vano ['vano] *agg* vain. *sm* (*locale*) room; (*spazio*) space. **rendere vano** make useless. **riuscir vano** be unsuccessful.

vantaggio [van'taddʒo] *sm* advantage; (*sport*) lead, handicap; profit. **vantaggiare** *v* favour. **vantaggioso** *agg* advantageous.

vantare [van'tare] *v* boast (of). **vantarsi** *v* boast, brag. **vantatore, -trice** *sm, sf* boaster, braggart. **vanteria** *sf* boasting, bragging. **vanto** *sm* (*vanteria*) boasting, bragging; (*atto*) boast.

vanvera ['vanvera] *sf* **a vanvera** (*senza riflettere*) without thinking; (*a casaccio*) at random.

vapore [va'pore] *sm* steam; (*nave*) steamer. **a tutto vapore** full steam ahead. **vaporizzare** *v* vaporize. **vaporizzatore** *sm* vaporizer; (*profumi*) atomizer.

varare [va'rare] *v* launch. **varo** *sm* launch(ing).

varcare [var'kare] *v* cross; (*eccedere*) go beyond. **varco** *sm* opening. **aspettare al varco** lie in wait (for).

variare [va'rjare] *v* change; (*esser diverso*) vary. **(tanto) per variare** (just) for a change. **variare d'aspetto** look different. **variabile** *sf, agg* variable. **variabilità** *sf* variability. **variante** *sf* variant. **variato** *agg* varied. **variazione** *sf* variation.

varicella [vari'tʃɛlla] *sf* chicken-pox.

varicoso [vari'kozo] *agg* varicose.

varietà [varje'ta] *sf* variety. *sm* (*teatro*) variety.

vario ['varjo] *agg* (*variato*) varied; (*diverso*) various, different; (*non regolare*) variable. **variopinto** *agg* multicoloured. **vari** *pron pl* various people *pl*, several people *pl*.

vasca ['vaska] *sf* basin; (*da bagno*) bath-tub; (*tino*) vat; (*piscina*) (swimming-) pool. **fare una vasca** (*sport*) swim a length.

vascello [va'ʃɛllo] *sm* vessel, warship. **ufficiale di vascello** *sm* naval officer.

vasellame [vazel'lame] *sm* crockery; (*di metallo prezioso*) plate; (*di porcellana*) china; (*di vetro*) glassware.

vaso ['vazo] *sm* pot; (*per fiori recisi*) vase; (*anat*) vessel. **vaso da fiori** flower-pot. **vaso da notte** chamber-pot. **vasaio, -a** *sm, sf* potter.

vassoio [vas'sojo] *sm* tray; (*del muratore*) mortar-board.

vasto ['vasto] *agg* wide, vast. **vastità** *sf* vastness.

Vaticano [vati'kano] *sm* Vatican. **città del Vaticano** *sf* Vatican City.

vaticinio [vati'tʃinjo] *sm* prediction. **vaticinare** *v* predict.

ve [ve] *V* **vi**.

vecchio ['vekkjo] *agg* old. *sm* old man. **vecchia** *sf* old woman. **vecchiaia** *sf* old age. **vecchiotto** *agg* oldish, fairly old; (*fuori moda*) out-of-date.

vece ['vetʃe] *sf* **fare le veci di** take the place of. **in mia vece** in my place.

***vedere** [ve'dere] *v* see. **avere a che vedere con** have to do with. **dare a vedere** let it be understood. **far vedere** show. **non vederci più** (*fam*) be furious. **non veder l'ora di** look forward to. **stare a vedere** (*attendere*) see; (*guardare*) watch; (*scommettere*) bet. **vedere di buon occhio** approve (of). **vediamo un po'** let's see *sm*. **a mio vedere** in my opinion.

vedetta [ve'detta] *sf* look-out.

vedova ['vedova] *sf* widow. **vedovo** *sm* widower. **rimaner vedova** *or* **vedovo** be widowed. **vedovanza** *sf* widowhood.

veemente [vee'mɛnte] *agg* vehement.

vegetale [vedʒe'tale] *agg, sm* vegetable. **vegetariano, -a** *s, agg* vegetarian. **vegetativo** *agg* vegetative. **vegetazione** *sf* vegetation.

vegetare [vedʒe'tare] *v* vegetate. **vegeto** *agg* flourishing. **vivo e vegeto** alive and kicking.

vegliare [ve'ʎare] *v* (*vigilare*) watch; (*fare la veglia*) keep watch; (*star sveglio*) stay up. **veglia** *sf* watch, vigil; (*lo star desto*) wakefulness; (*festa*) party; (*funebre*) wake. **veglione** *sm* ball, party.

veicolo [ve'ikolo] *sm* vehicle; (*malattia*) carrier.

vela ['vela] *sf* sail; (*sport*) sailing. **a gonfie vele** booming. **barca a vela** *sf* sailing-boat. **volo a vela** *sm* gliding. **veleggiare** *v* sail; (*velivolo*) glide. **veliero** *sm* sailing-ship.

velare [ve'lare] *v* veil; cover; (*offuscare*) cloud, dim; (*suono*) muffle.

veleno [ve'leno] *sm* poison. **avere il veleno in corpo** (*fam*) have a chip on one's shoulder. **sputare veleno** (*fig*) vent one's spleen. **velenoso** *agg* poisonous; (*fig*) venomous.

velino [ve'lino] *agg* **carta velina** *sf* flimsy (paper). **velina** *sf* (*copia*) carbon copy.

velivolo [ve'livolo] *sm* aircraft; (*aliante*) glider.

velleità [vellei'ta] *sf* vain ambition.

vellicare [velli'kare] *v* titillate.
vello ['vɛllo] *sm* fleece.
velluto [vel'luto] *sm* velvet. **di velluto** velvet. **vellutato** *agg* velvety.
veloce [ve'lotʃe] *agg* quick, fast. **velocista** *s(m+f)* sprinter. **velocità** *sf* speed; (*fis*) velocity. **eccedere la velocità** (*auto*) speed.
velodromo [ve'lɔdromo] *sm* cycle-track.
veltro ['veltro] *sm* greyhound.
vena ['vena] *sf* vein; (*fig*) talent; inspiration. **essere in vena** be in the mood.
venale [ve'nale] *agg* saleable; (*spreg*) mercenary.
vendemmiare [vendem'mjare] *v* harvest (grapes). **vendemmia** *sf* grape harvest.
vendere ['vendere] *v* sell. **aver ... da vendere** have ... to spare; have plenty of .... **vendere a contanti** sell for cash. **vendere al dettaglio** *or* **minuto** retail. **vendere all'asta** auction. **vendere all'ingrosso** sell wholesale. **vendere fumo** bluff. **vendibile** *agg* saleable; (*messo in vendita*) for sale.
vendetta [ven'detta] *sf* revenge; (*castigo meritato*) vengeance.
vendicare [vendi'kare] *v* avenge. **vendicarsi** take revenge. **vendicativo** *agg* vindictive.
vendita ['vendita] *sf* sale. **vendita a rate** hire-purchase. **venditore, -trice** *sm, sf* vendor; (*negoziante*) shopkeeper.
venerare [vene'rare] *v* revere; (*rel*) worship. **venerabile** *agg* venerable. **venerazione** *sf* veneration.
venerdì [vener'di] *sm* Friday. **Venerdì Santo** Good Friday.
venereo [ve'nɛreo] *agg* venereal.
Venezia [ve'netsja] *sf* Venice. **veneziana** *sf* Venetian blind. **veneziano, -a** *s, agg* Venetian.
veniale [ve'njale] *agg* venial.
***venire** [ve'nire] *v* come; (*riuscire*) come out; (*essere*) be. **far venire** (*mandare a chiamare*) call, send for. **mi viene da ...** I feel like .... **venire alle mani** come to blows. **venire incontro** come towards; (*incontrare*) meet; (*fig*) meet halfway. **venir meno** (*mancare*) be lacking; (*svenire*) pass out.
ventaglio [ven'taʎo] *sm* fan.
venti ['venti] *agg, sm* twenty. **ventesimo** *agg, sm* twentieth.
ventilare [venti'lare] *v* air; (*agric*) winnow. **ventilato** *agg* airy, ventilated. **ventilazione** *sf* ventilation.
vento ['vɛnto] *sm* wind.
ventosa [ven'toza] *sf* sucker.
ventre ['vɛntre] *sm* stomach; abdomen; (*forma*) belly; (*grembo materno*) womb. **ventrale** *agg* ventral.
ventricolo [ven'trikolo] *sm* ventricle.
ventriloquo [ven'trilokwo], **-a** *sm, sf* ventriloquist.
ventura [ven'tura] *sf* fortune. **alla ventura** at random. **andare** *or* **mettersi alla ventura** trust to luck; take a chance. **soldato di ventura** *sm* mercenary.
venturo [ven'turo] *agg* next.
vera ['vera] *sf* wedding ring.
verace [ve'ratʃe] *agg* (*veritiero*) truthful; (*vero*) true, real. **veracità** *sf* truthfulness.
veranda [ve'randa] *sf* veranda.
verbale [ver'bale] *sm* record, minutes *pl*. **mettere a verbale** put on record. *agg* verbal.
verbo ['vɛrbo] *sm* verb; (*parola*) word. **verboso** *agg* verbose, long-winded.
verde ['verde] *agg* green. *sm* green; (*natura*) greenery; (*zona*) green belt. **essere** *or* **trovarsi al verde** be broke. **verdastro** *agg* greenish. **verdeggiare** *v* be verdant; (*diventar verde*) turn green.
verdetto [ver'detto] *sm* verdict.
verdura [ver'dura] *sf* greens *pl*, vegetables *pl*.
verga ['verga] *sf* rod. **verga magica** magic wand. **vergare** *v* line; (*scrivere*) write.
vergine ['verdʒine] *sf, agg* virgin. **Vergine** *sf* Virgo. **verginale** *agg* virginal. **verginità** *sf* virginity.
vergogna [ver'goɲa] *sf* shame; (*disonore*) disgrace. **fare vergogna** shame. *inter* shame on you! **vergognarsi** *v* be *or* feel ashamed (of); (*non osare*) be too shy (to). **vergognoso** *agg* shameful; shy.
verificare [verifi'kare] *v* check. **verificarsi** *v* (*avvenire*) occur; (*avverarsi*) come true. **verifica** *sf* control; verification; (*dei conti*) audit. **verificabile** *agg* verifiable. **verificazione** *sf* verification, check; audit.
verità [veri'ta] *sf* truth; (*giustezza*) truthfulness. **veritiero** *agg* truthful.
verme ['vɛrme] *sm* worm; (*larva di insetto*) maggot.
vermiglio [ver'miʎo] *agg, sm* vermilion.
vermut ['vɛrmut] *sm invar* vermouth.

verniciare [verni'tʃare] *v* paint; (*con vernice trasparente*) varnish; (*a smalto*) enamel. **vernice** *sf* varnish, lacquer; (*apparenza*) veneer; (*strato sottile*) film. **verniciata** *sf* coat of paint. **verniciatura** *sf* painting; varnishing.
vero ['vero] *agg* true; real. *sm* truth. **a onor del vero** to tell the truth. **di vero cuore** from the bottom of one's heart. **vero e proprio** out and out.
verosimile [vero'simile] *agg* likely. **aver del verosimile** be likely.
verricello [verri'tʃɛllo] *sm* winch.
verro ['vɛrro] *sm* boar.
verruca [ver'ruka] *sf* wart.
versare [ver'sare] *v* pour (out); (*rovesciare*) spill; (*spargere*) shed; (*pagare*) pay; (*trovarsi*) find oneself. **versamento** *sm* payment, deposit. **versante** *sm* side. **versato** *agg* paid (up); (*pratico*) skilled.
versatile [ver'satile] *agg* versatile. **versatilità** *sf* versatility.
versione [ver'sjone] *sf* version; (*traduzione*) translation.
verso[1] ['vɛrso] *prep* towards; (*circa*) about. **verso il basso** down(wards). **verso l'alto** up(wards).
verso[2] ['vɛrso] *sm* (*metrica*) verse; (*suono particolare*) sound; gesture; direction; (*modo*) means. **in verso antiorario** anticlockwise. **in verso orario** clockwise. **per un verso o per un altro** in one way or another.
vertebra ['vɛrtebra] *sf* vertebra (*pl* -brae). **vertebrato** *agg, sm* vertebrate.
vertenza [ver'tentsa] *sf* dispute; (*dir*) lawsuit.
verticale [verti'kale] *agg, sf* vertical.
vertice ['vɛrtitʃe] *sm* summit; (*mat*) vertex.
vertigini [ver'tidʒini] *sf pl* dizziness *sing*; (*attacco*) dizzy spell *sing*; (*med*) vertigo *sing*. **aver le vertigini** feel dizzy *or* giddy. **vertiginoso** *agg* dizzy.
vescica [ve'ʃika] *sf* bladder; (*bolla cutanea*) blister.
vescovo ['veskovo] *sm* bishop. **vescovado** *sm* (*dignità*) bishopric; (*territorio*) diocese; (*palazzo*) bishop's palace. **vescovile** *agg* episcopal.
vespa ['vɛspa] *sf* wasp. **vespaio** *sm* wasps' nest.
vestaglia [ves'taʎa] *sf* dressing-gown; (*vestaglietta*) housecoat.
veste ['vɛste] *sf* dress; (*rel*) vestment; (*fig*) capacity. **in veste di amico** as a friend. **in veste ufficiale** in an official capacity. **vestiario** *sm* wardrobe; (*indumenti*) clothes *pl*. **capo di vestiario** *sm* item of clothing.
vestibolo [ves'tibolo] *sm* vestibule, lobby.
vestigio [ves'tidʒo] *sm* trace.
vestire [ves'tire] *v* dress; (*indossare*) wear; (*detto di abiti*) fit. **vestirsi** *v* dress. **vestito** *sm* dress.
veterano [vete'rano], **-a** *s, agg* veteran.
veterinario [veteri'narjo] *agg* veterinary. *sm* veterinary surgeon, vet. **veterinaria** *sf* veterinary science.
veto ['vɛto] *sm invar* veto.
vetro ['vetro] *sm* glass; (*di finestra*) pane. **vetro smerigliato** frosted glass. **vetraio** *sm* glazier. **vetrata** *sf* (*porta*) glass door; (*finestra*) stained-glass window.
vetta ['vetta] *sf* top.
vettore [vet'tore] *sm* vector; (*comm*) carrier.
vettovaglie [vetto'vaʎe] *sf pl* provisions *pl*.
vettura [vet'tura] *sf* carriage; (*auto*) car. **biglietto di vettura** *sm* (*comm*) bill of lading.
vezzeggiare [veddzed'dʒare] *v* fondle.
vi [vi], **ve** *pron* (to) you; (*riflessivo*) yourselves; (*reciproco*) each other. *avv* (*qui*) here; (*lì*) there.
via[1] ['via] *sf* way; (*strada*) street; (*sentiero*) path. **in via di costruzione** under construction. **in via eccezionale** exceptionally. **per via aerea** by air. **per via di** (*a causa di*) because of. **via mare/terra** by sea/land.
via[2] ['via] *avv* away; (*suvvia*) come on. *sm invar* starting signal. **e così via** and so on. **va via!** go on! **via le mani!** hands off! **via via** gradually; (*a mano a mano*) as.
viabilità [viabili'ta] *sf* road conditions *pl*.
viadotto [via'dotto] *sm* viaduct.
viaggiare [viad'dʒare] *v* travel; (*veicoli*) run; (*essere trasportato*) be carried. **viaggiatore, -trice** *sm, sf* traveller; passenger. **piccione viaggiatore** *sm* carrier pigeon.
viaggio [vi'addʒo] *sm* journey, trip. **mettersi in viaggio** set out *or* off. **viaggio d'andata/di ritorno** outward/return journey. **viaggio d'andata e ritorno** round trip. **viaggio di nozze** honeymoon.
viale [vi'ale] *sm* avenue.
viandante [vian'dante] *s(m+f)* wayfarer.

viavai [via'vaj] *sm* coming and going.
vibrare [vib'rare] *v* vibrate; (*fig*) quiver; (*assestare*) hurl. **vibrare un colpo** deal a blow. **vibrazione** *sf* vibration; (*fremito*) quiver.
vicario [vi'karjo] *sm* vicar.
viceconsole [vitʃe'kɔnsole] *s*(*m*+*f*) vice-consul.
vicedirettore [vitʃediret'tore], **-trice** *sm, sf* assistant manager; (*scuola*) deputy head.
vicenda [vi'tʃɛnda] *sf* event; succession. **vicendevolmente** *avv also* **a vicenda** (*a turno*) in turns; (*scambievolmente*) each other, one another.
vicepresidente [vitʃeprezi'dɛnte], **-essa** *sm, sf* vice-president, vice-chairman.
viceversa [vitʃe'vɛrsa] *avv* vice versa; (*invece*) but.
vicinanza [vitʃi'nantsa] *sf* vicinity.
vicinato [vitʃi'nato] *sm* neighbourhood.
vicino [vi'tʃino], **-a** *agg* near; (*accanto*) next; (*confinante*) neighbouring; (*fig*) close. *avv* close (by); near (by); (*accanto a*) beside, by. **da vicino** at close quarters. *sm, sf* neighbour. **vicino di casa** next-door neighbour.
vicolo ['vikolo] *sm* alley.
video ['video] *sm invar* (television) screen.
vidimare [vidi'mare] *v* certify. **vidimazione** *sf* certification.
vietare [vje'tare] *v* prohibit; (*impedire*) prevent. **vietato** *agg* forbidden. **ingresso vietato** no admission. **sosta vietata** no parking.
vigente [vi'dʒɛnte] *agg* current; (*dir*) in force.
vigilare [vidʒi'lare] *v* watch (over); keep a watch (on). **vigilante** *agg* watchful. **vigilanza** *sf* vigilance; (*controllo*) supervision; (*urbana*) police.
vigile ['vidʒile] *agg* watchful. *sm* policeman. **vigile del fuoco** fireman.
vigilia [vi'dʒilja] *sf* eve; (*rel*) vigil. **vigilia di Natale/Capodanno** Christmas/New Year's Eve.
vigliacco [vi'ʎakko] *agg* cowardly. *sm, sf* coward. **vigliaccheria** *sf* cowardice; cowardly action.
vigna ['viɲa] *sf* vineyard.
vignetta [vi'ɲetta] *sf* sketch; (*umoristica*) cartoon.
vigore [vi'gore] *sm* force; (*forza vitale*) vigour. **entrare in vigore** (*dir*) come into force. **vigoria** *sf* energy.
vile ['vile] *agg* (*vigliacco*) cowardly; (*basso*) base, low. *s*(*m*+*f*) coward. **vilipendio** *sm* contempt.
villa ['villa] *sf* villa. **villa di campagna** country house.
villaggio [vil'laddʒo] *sm* village.
villano [vil'lano]. **-a** *agg* rude; (*rozzo*) uncouth; offensive. *sm, sf* lout, boor. **villania** *sf* rudeness.
villeggiare [villed'dʒare] *v* spend a holiday. **villeggiatura** *sf* holidays *pl*.
viltà [vil'ta] *sf* cowardice; cowardly action.
viluppo [vi'luppo] *sm* tangle.
vimini ['vimini] *sm pl* wicker *sing*. **di vimini** wicker. **lavoro in vimini** *sm* wickerwork.
***vincere** ['vintʃere] *v* win; (*battere*) beat; (*sopraffare*) overcome; (*sconfiggere*) defeat. **lasciarsi vincere (da)** yield (to). **vincita** *sf* win.
vincitore [vintʃi'tore], **-trice** *sm, sf* winner; (*di battaglia*) victor. *agg* winning, victorious.
vincolare [vinko'lare] *v* bind; (*comm*) tie up. **vincolo** *sm* tie.
vino ['vino] *sm* wine. **vino di mele** cider. **vinicolo** *agg* wine.
viola[1] [vi'ɔla] *sf* (*bot*) violet. *agg, sm invar* (*colore*) violet. **viola del pensiero** pansy. **violacciocca** *sf* stock; (*gialla*) wallflower. **violaceo** *agg* violet.
viola[2] [vi'ɔla] *sf* (*musica*) viola.
violare [vio'lare] *v* violate; (*una donna*) rape; (*domicilio*) break into. **violare l'ordine pubblico** cause a breach of the peace. **violazione** *sf* violation. **violazione carnale** rape. **violazione della pace** breach of the peace. **violazione di domicilio** house-breaking.
violentare [violen'tare] *v* force; (*una donna*) rape. **violentatore** *sm* rapist. **violento** *agg* violent. **violenza** *sf* violence.
violetta [vio'letta] *sf* violet. **violetto** *agg, sm invar* violet.
violino [vio'lino] *sm* violin. **violinista** *s*(*m*+*f*) violinist.
violoncello [violon'tʃɛllo] *sm* (violon)cello. **violoncellista** *s*(*m*+*f*) (violon)cellist.
viottolo [vi'ɔttolo] *sm* path.
vipera ['vipera] *sf* viper.
virale [vi'rale] *agg* viral.
virare [vi'rare] *v* (*alare*) haul (in); (*mutar*

direzione) veer, change course; (*aero*) turn.

virgola ['virgola] *sf* comma; (*mat*) point. **tra virgolette** in inverted commas.

virile [vi'rile] *agg* virile; masculine; (*fig*) manly. **virilità** *sf* virility.

virtù [vir'tu] *sf* virtue; faculty. **in virtù di** by virtue of, in accordance with. **virtuale** *agg* virtual.

virtuoso [virtu'ozo], **-a** *agg* virtuous. *sm, sf* virtuoso.

virulento [viru'lɛnto] *agg* virulent.

virus ['virus] *sm invar* virus.

viscere ['viʃere] *sm* internal organ. *sf pl* intestines *pl*; (*di animali*) entrails *pl*. **le viscere della terra** the bowels of the earth *pl*.

vischio ['viskjo] *sm* mistletoe; (*estratto*) bird-lime; (*fig*) snare. **viscido** *agg* slimy.

visconte [vis'konte] *sm* viscount.

viscoso [vis'kozo] *agg* viscous. **viscosa** *sf* viscose. **viscosità** *sf* viscosity.

visibile [vi'zibile] *agg* visible. **andare/mandare in visibilio** go/send into raptures. **visibilità** *sf* visibility.

visiera [vi'zjera] *sf* visor; (*berretto*) peak; (*scherma*) mask.

visione [vi'zjone] *sf* sight; (*apparizione*) vision; idea; (*cinema*) showing. **prendere in visione** inspect. **ricevere in visione** receive on approval. **visionario, -a** *sm, sf* visionary.

visita ['vizita] *sf* visit; (*persona*) visitor; (*esame*) examination. **visita domiciliare** domiciliary visit; (*perquisizione*) house search. **visitare** *v* visit; (*andare a trovare*) call on; (*med*) examine. **visitatore, -trice** *sm, sf* visitor.

visivo [vi'zivo] *agg* visual. **campo visivo** *sm* field of vision.

viso ['vizo] *sm* face. **a viso aperto** openly. **far buon viso a cattiva sorte** make the best of it. **fare il viso lungo** sulk.

visone [vi'zone] *sm* mink.

vispo ['vispo] *agg* lively; (*svelto*) brisk.

vista ['vista] *sf* sight; (*spettacolo*) view. **avere in vista** have in mind. **a vista** on sight. **a vista d'occhio** before one's very eyes. **conoscere di vista** know by sight. **perdere di vista** lose sight (of).

visto ['visto] *sm* visa. **visto di soggiorno** tourist visa.

vistoso [vis'tozo] *agg* showy; (*notevole*) considerable.

visuale [vizu'ale] *agg* visual. *sf* view; line of vision. **visualizzare** *v* visualize.

vita[1] ['vita] *sf* life; (*durata*) lifetime. **a vita** for life. **condanna a vita** *sf* life sentence. **essere in fin di vita** be at death's door. **guadagnarsi la vita** earn one's living.

vita[2] ['vita] *sf* (*corpo*) waist.

vitale [vi'tale] *agg* vital. **vitalità** *sf* vitality.

vitalizio [vita'litsjo] *agg* life(long). *sm* (*rendita*) annuity.

vitamina [vita'mina] *sf* vitamin.

vite[1] ['vite] *sf* (*bot*) vine. **viticcio** *sm* tendril. **viticoltura** *sf* viticulture.

vite[2] ['vite] *sf* (*mec*) screw. **cadere in vite** (*aero*) go into a spin.

vitello [vi'tɛllo] *sm* calf; (*gastr*) veal. **vitellone** *sm* bullock; (*fig*) loafer.

vitreo ['vitreo] *agg* glassy, vitreous.

vittima ['vittima] *sf* victim; (*chi subisce danni*) casualty. **essere vittima di un incidente** be involved in an accident. **fare la vittima** (*fig*) be a martyr.

vitto ['vitto] *sm* food; (*nutrimento giornaliero*) board. **vitto e alloggio** board and lodging.

vittoria [vit'tɔrja] *sf* victory; (*sport*) win. **vittorioso** *agg* victorious.

vituperare [vitupe'rare] *v* berate. **vituperio** *sm* insult; (*causa*) disgrace.

viva ['viva] *inter* hurrah! **viva . . . !** long live . . . !

vivacchiare [vivak'kjare] *v* manage.

vivace [vi'vatʒe] *agg* lively; (*intenso*) bright. **vivacità** *sf* liveliness; brightness.

vivaio [vi'vajo] *sm* nursery; (*pesci*) fish-pond.

vivanda [vi'vanda] *sf* food; (*piatto*) dish.

***vivere** ['vivere] *v* live; (*trascorrere*) spend. **avere di che vivere** have enough to live on. **lasciar vivere** leave in peace. **vivere alla giornata** live from hand to mouth. *sm* life; (*modo di vivere*) living.

viveri ['viveri] *sm pl* provisions *pl*.

vivido ['vivido] *agg* vivid.

vivisezione [vivise'tsjone] *sf* vivisection.

vivo ['vivo] *agg* living; (*vivace*) lively; (*intenso*) bright. **a viva forza** by force. **farsi vivo** show up; (*mettersi in contatto*) get in touch. *sm* living person; (*fig*) heart. **ferire nel vivo** wound to the quick.

viziare [vi'tsjare] *v* spoil; (*dir*) vitiate.

vizio ['vitsjo] *sm* vice; bad habit; defect; (*peccato*) sin. **vizio parziale (di mente)** diminished responsibility. **vizioso** *agg* depraved.

vizzo ['vittso] *agg* withered.

vocabolo [vo'kabolo] *sm* word. **vocabolario** *sm* vocabulary; dictionary.

vocale [vo'kale] *agg* vocal. *sf* vowel.

vocazione [voka'tsjone] *sf* vocation; (*inclinazione naturale*) leaning. **vocazionale** *agg* vocational.

voce ['votʃe] *sf* voice; expression; (*elemento di elenco*) heading; opinion. **a bassa voce** softly. **ad alta voce** out loud. **aver voce in capitolo** have a say in the matter. **corre voce** rumour has it. **dire a (viva) voce** tell personally. **sotto voce** in an undertone.

vociare [vo'tʃare] *v* bawl.

vociferare [votʃife'rare] *v* talk at the top of one's voice; (*fig*) rumour.

vodka ['vɔdka] *sf* vodka.

vogare [vo'gare] *v* row. **vogatore** *sm* oarsman.

voglia ['voʎa] *sf* wish; (*disposizione*) will; (*capriccio*) fancy; (*med*) birthmark. **avere una gran voglia di** be dying to. **aver voglia di (fare)** feel like (doing), want to (do). **di buona voglia** willingly. **di cattiva** *or* **mala voglia** unwillingly.

voi ['voi] *pron* you.

volano [vo'lano] *sm* (*mec*) flywheel; (*sport*) shuttlecock.

volare [vo'lare] *v* fly. **volar giù** hurtle down. **volata** *sf* (*sport*) sprint; (*corsa rapida*) dash. **di volata** in a rush. **fare una volata** make a dash.

volatile [vo'latile] *agg* volatile.

volentieri [volen'tjɛri] *avv* willingly; with pleasure. **fare volentieri** like doing.

***volere** [vo'lere] *v* want; (*desiderare*) wish; (*comando*) will; (*intendere*) mean; (*cortesia*) like. **l'hai voluto tu!** you've asked for it! **neanche a volere** not even if you try. **non vuol dire** (*non ha importanza*) it doesn't matter. **se Dio vuole** God willing. **senza volere** without meaning to. **volerci** *v* take. **voler bene a** (*aver affetto*) be fond of; (*amare*) love. **voler dire** mean.

volgare [vol'gare] *agg* vulgar; common. *sm* (*lingua*) vernacular. **volgarità** *sf* vulgarity. **volgarizzare** *v* popularize.

***volgere** ['vɔldʒere] *v* turn. **col volgere degli anni** with the passing of time. **volgere alla fina** near the end. **volgere la parola a** address.

volgo ['volgo] *sm* common people *pl*.

volo ['volo] *sm* flight. **cogliere al volo** seize. **volo a vela** gliding. **volo in picchiata** nose-dive.

volontà [volon'ta] *sf* will. **di mia spontanea** *or* **propria volontà** of my own free will.

volontario [volon'tarjo], **-a** voluntary. *sm, sf* volunteer. **volontario del sangue** blood donor. **volontariato** *sm* voluntary service.

volonteroso [volonte'rozo] *agg* willing.

volpe ['volpe] *sf* fox; (*femmina*) vixen.

volta[1] ['vɔlta] *sf* time; turn. **alla volta** at a time. **alla volta di** towards. **a volte** sometimes. **spesse volte** often. **una buona volta** once and for all. **una volta** once; (*nelle fiabe*) once upon a time.

volta[2] ['vɔlta] *sf* (*arch*) vault.

voltare [vol'tare] *v* turn. **voltagabbana** *s(m+f) invar* fickle person.

volto ['volto] *sm* face.

volubile [vo'lubile] *agg* fickle.

volume [vo'lume] *sm* volume; (*mole*) size. **voluminoso** *agg* voluminous; (*ingombrante*) bulky.

voluta [vo'luta] *sf* scroll.

voluttuoso [voluttu'ozo] *agg* voluptuous. **voluttà** *sf* voluptuousness.

vomitare [vomi'tare] *v* vomit, be sick. **aver voglia di vomitare** feel sick. **vomito** *sm* (*atto*) vomiting; (*materia*) vomit. **mi viene il vomito** I feel sick.

vongola ['vongola] *sf* clam.

vorace [vo'ratʃe] *agg* greedy.

voragine [vo'radʒine] *sf* chasm, gulf.

vortice ['vɔrtitʃe] *sm* vortex; (*gorgo*) whirlpool; (*fig*) whirl.

vostro ['vɔstro] *agg* your. *pron* yours.

votare [vo'tare] *v* vote; (*approvare*) pass; put to the vote; (*dedicare*) devote. **votazione** *sf* voting; (*scrutinio*) ballot; (*scuola*) marks *pl*. **voto** *sm* vote; (*promessa*) vow; (*scuola*) mark. **a pieni voti** with full marks. **pronunciare i voti** take one's vows.

vulcano [vul'kano] *sm* volcano. **vulcanico** *agg* volcanic; (*fig*) brilliant.

vulnerabile [vulne'rabile] *agg* vulnerable. **vulnerabilità** *sf* vulnerability.

vuotare [vwo'tare] *v* empty. **vuotare il sacco** (*fig*) spill the beans.

vuoto ['vwɔto] *agg* empty. *sm* void; (*fis*) vacuum; (*fig*) emptiness, gap. **andare a vuoto** fail. **a vuoto** in vain. **girare a vuoto** (*mec*) idle.

X

xenofobo [kse'nɔfobo], **-a** *agg* xenophobic. *sm, sf* xenophobe. **xenofobia** *sf* xenophobia.
xerocopiare [kseroko'pjare] *v* Xerox ®.
xilofono [ksi'lɔfono] *sm* xylophone.

Y

yoga ['jɔga] *sm invar* yoga.
yoghurt ['jɔgurt] *sm invar* yoghurt.

Z

zacchera ['dzakkera] *sf* splash (of mud).
zaffata [dzaf'fata] *sf* whiff; (*getto di liquido*) splash.
zafferano [dzaffe'rano] *sm* saffron.
zaffiro [dzaf'firo] *sm* sapphire.
zaino ['dzajno] *sm* kit-bag; (*alpinisti*) rucksack.
zampa ['dzampa] *sf* leg; (*con unghie*) paw; (*maiale*) trotter. **a quattro zampe** on all fours. **zampe di gallina** *sf pl* (*rughe*) crow's-feet *pl*; (*scrittura*) scrawl *sing*. **zampare** *v* paw (the ground). **aver lo zampino in** have a hand in. **mettere lo zampino** interfere.
zampillare [dzampil'lare] *v* spurt, gush. **zampillo** *sm* spurt.
zampogna [dzam'poɲa] *sf* bagpipes *pl*.
zangola ['dzangola] *sf* churn. **zangolare** *v* churn.
zanna ['dzanna] *sf* fang; (*di elefante, cinghiale*) tusk.
zanzara [dzan'dzara] *sf* mosquito. **zanzariera** *sf* mosquito-net.
zappare [dzap'pare] *v* hoe. **zappa** *sf* hoe.
zattera ['dzattera] *sf* raft.
zazzera ['dzaddzera] *sf* mop of hair.
zebra ['dzɛbra] *sf* zebra. **zebre** *sf pl* (*passaggio*) zebra crossing *sing*. **zebrato** *agg* striped.
zecca[1] ['dzekka] *sf* mint. **nuovo di zecca** brand-new. **zecchino** *sm* gold coin.
zecca[2] ['dzekka] *sf* (*zool*) tick.
zelo ['dzelo] *sm* zeal. **zelante** *agg* keen, zealous.
zenzero ['dzendzero] *sm* ginger.
zeppa ['dzeppa] *sf* wedge. **zeppare** *v* wedge.
zeppo ['dzeppo] *agg* (**pieno**) **zeppo** packed, cram-full.
zerbino [dzer'bino] *sm* (door-)mat.
zero ['dzɛro] *sm* nought; (*fig, mat*) zero; (*sport*) nil; (*tennis*) love.
zia ['dzia] *sf* aunt.
zibellino [dzibel'lino] *sm* sable.
zibetto [dzi'betto] *sm* civet.
zigzag [dzig'dzag] *sm* zigzag. **andare a zigzag** zigzag.
zimbello [dzim'bello] *sm* decoy; (*oggètto di scherno*) laughing-stock. **zimbellare** *v* lure.
zinco ['dzinko] *sm* zinc.
zingaro ['dzingaro], **-a** *s, agg* gipsy.
zio ['dzio] *sm* uncle.
zirlare [dzir'lare] *v* chirp.
zitella [dzi'tɛlla] *sf* spinster. **vecchia zitella** (*spreg*) old maid.
zittire [dzit'tire] *v* (*far tacere*) hush; (*disapprovazione*) hiss.
zitto ['dzitto] *agg* quiet. **star zitto** keep quiet; (*fam*) shut up.
zoccolo ['dzɔkkolo] *sm* clog; (*zool*) hoof; base; (*parete*) skirting-board.
zodiaco [dzo'diako] *sm* zodiac.
zolfo ['dzolfo] *sm* sulphur.
zolla ['dzolla] *sf* clod.
zona ['dzɔna] *sf* zone; area. **zona pedonale** pedestrian precinct. **zona verde** (*periferica*) green belt.
zonzo ['dzondzo] *avv* **andare a zonzo** wander about.
zoo [dzo] *sm invar* zoo.
zoologia [dzoolo'dʒia] *sf* zoology. **zoologico** *agg* zoological. **zoologo, -a** *sm, sf* zoologist.
zoppicare [dzoppi'kare] *v* limp; (*tavolo, ecc.*) be rickety; (*fig*) be shaky. **zoppo** *agg* lame; rickety; shaky.
zotico ['dzɔtiko], **-a** *agg* boorish. *sm, sf* boor.
zucca ['dzukka] *sf* pumpkin; (*fam: testa*) nut. **zuccone** *sm* (*fam*) blockhead.
zucchero ['dzukkero] *sm* sugar. **zucchero a velo** icing sugar. **zucchero semolato** castor sugar. **zuccherare** *v* sweeten.
zucchino [dzuk'kino], **-a** *sm, sf* courgette.
zuffa ['dzuffa] *sf* scuffle, brawl.
zuppa ['dzuppa] *sf* soup. **zuppa inglese** trifle. **zuppiera** *sf* tureen. **zuppo** *agg* drenched.